"Gedro and Rocco provide a much-needed volume for tomorrow's leaders in education, management, HR, and more. Special attention to the needs, rights, and contributions of workers and students at the intersections of sex, race, and gender will make this volume useful to anyone responsible for workplace environment, equity, and productivity for years to come."

Linda Heidenreich, *Washington State University*

THE ROUTLEDGE HANDBOOK OF LGBTQ IDENTITY IN ORGANIZATIONS AND SOCIETY

Sexuality, gender, gender identity, and gender expression are fluid constructs, and the ways in which identity development intersects with organizations and exists in society are complex. The book is comprised of a range of multi-disciplinary and globally inspired perspectives representing leading-edge scholarship by authors from over a dozen countries on a range of issues and contexts regarding LGBTQ identity and experience. It is intended for a wide readership: those who are in LGBTQ-related academic fields; those who want to broaden their coursework by offering supplemental readings that center the perspectives of LGBTQ identities; and those who want to acquire knowledge and education on the subject of LGBTQ identity. There are 36 chapters written by scholars in fields such as social work, law, queer studies, business, human resource management and development, entrepreneurship, criminal justice, economics, marketing, religion, architecture, sport, theater, psychology, human ecology, and adult education. The chapters can be read in sequence, and the book can also be used as a reference work for which educators, practitioners, and non-academics can identify and select particular chapters that inform areas of inquiry.

Julie A. Gedro is Dean of the School of Business, Undergraduate Studies, at Empire State University, where she is also a tenured Full Professor. Dr. Gedro's awards include the State University of New York (SUNY) Chancellor's Award for Excellence in Scholarship and Creative Activities; the Empire State College (now University) Altes Prize for Outstanding Community Service for her LGBTQ scholarship and activism; the Empire State College (now University) Susan H. Turben Award for Excellence in Scholarship; and the Academy of Human Resource Development (AHRD) Laura L. Bierema Award for Excellence in Critical Human Resource Development (HRD).

Tonette S. Rocco is a tenured Full Professor of Adult Education and Human Resource Development in the Department of Educational Policy Studies, Florida International University. She is Editor-in-Chief of *New Horizons in Adult Education and Human Resource Development* and serves on a dozen editorial boards. She is one of only 25 Houle Scholars from the United States, a member of the 2016 class of the International Adult and Continuing Education Hall of Fame, 2016 Outstanding HRD Scholar, and a recipient of more than 35 awards for scholarship, mentoring, and service. She has published 11 books and 300 articles, chapters, and papers.

ROUTLEDGE INTERNATIONAL HANDBOOKS

For more information about this series, please visit: www.routledge.com

THE ROUTLEDGE HANDBOOK OF LGBTQ IDENTITY IN ORGANIZATIONS AND SOCIETY

Edited by Julie A. Gedro and Tonette S. Rocco

Routledge
Taylor & Francis Group

NEW YORK AND LONDON

Cover image: ivanastar

First published 2024
by Routledge
605 Third Avenue, New York, NY 10158

and by Routledge
4 Park Square, Milton Park, Abingdon, Oxon, OX14 4RN

Routledge is an imprint of the Taylor & Francis Group, an informa business

Library of Congress Cataloging-in-Publication Data
Names: Gedro, Julie, 1962– editor. | Rocco, Tonette S., 1954– editor.
Title: The Routledge handbook of LGBTQ identity in organizations and society / edited by Julie A. Gedro and Tonette S. Rocco.
Description: New York, NY : Routledge, 2024. | Includes bibliographical references and index.
Identifiers: LCCN 2023055716 | ISBN 9780367651633 (hardback) | ISBN 9780367651640 (paperback) | ISBN 9781003128151 (ebook)
Subjects: LCSH: Gay people—Identity. | Identity (Psychology)
Classification: LCC HQ76.25 .R678 2024 | DDC 306.76—dc23/eng/20240309
LC record available at https://lccn.loc.gov/2023055716

ISBN: 978-0-367-65163-3 (hbk)
ISBN: 978-0-367-65164-0 (pbk)
ISBN: 978-1-003-12815-1 (ebk)

DOI: 10.4324/9781003128151

Typeset in Galliard
by Apex CoVantage, LLC

This book is dedicated to:

Nicholas Michael Lim born on September 4, 1952, and passed on July 17, 1993. He was a childhood friend whose life and death inspired my quest to understand the meaning of "queer."

Tonette S. Rocco

To all of my teachers: Thank you for my education.

Julie A. Gedro

CONTENTS

Contents

FIGURES

TABLES

CONTRIBUTORS

Joel Anderson, *Australian Catholic University and La Trobe University*

Tyler M. Argüello, *California State University*

Liana Bernard, *Portland State University*

Warren J. Blumenfeld, *University of Massachusetts Amherst*

Sarah Bonnemaison, *Dalhousie University*

Saul Carliner, *Concordia University*

Alan Chaffe, *University of Victoria*

Liyun Wendy Choo, *University of Auckland*

Lindsey Churchill, *University of Central Oklahoma*

Brenda Cossman, *University of Toronto*

Matthew J. Cull, *University of Edinburgh*

Charlene Désir, *Nova Southeastern University*

Nick Drydakis, *Anglia Ruskin University, UK*

Jessica N. Fish, *University of Maryland*

Jacqueline Gahagan, *Dalhousie University*

Julie A. Gedro, *Empire State University*

Benton Goff, *Southern Illinois University Carbondale*

Chloe Goldbach, *Southern Illinois University Carbondale*

André P. Grace, *University of Alberta*

Jeffrey R. Hankey, *York University*

Shawn H. E. Harmon, *Dalhousie University*

Geovanna N. Hernandez, *Florida International University*

Jordan D. X. Hinton, *La Trobe University*

Debaro Huyler, *Florida International University*

Satveer Kler, *Southern Illinois University Carbondale*

Douglas Knutson, *Oklahoma State University*

Hilary Landorf, *Florida International University*

Anne Namatsi Lutomia, *Purdue University*

Larry R. Martinez, *Portland State University*

Sage A. Mauldin, *University of Oklahoma*

Parker McDurmon, *Southern Illinois University Carbondale*

Ciarán McFadden, *University of Stirling*

Craig M. McGill, *Kansas State University*

Ariel G. Mekler, *Baruch College*

Robert C. Mizzi, *University of Manitoba*

Sunny L. Munn, *The Ohio State University*

Bolivar X. Nieto, *Florida International University*

Megan S. Paceley, *University of Connecticut*

Kelly L. Reddy-Best, *Iowa State University*

Renaud Redien-Collot, *Université de Reims-Champagne-Ardenne*

Kimoré Reid, *Life After Therapy, LLC*

Julian M. Rengers, *University of Groningen*

Tonette S. Rocco, *Florida International University*

Itxaso Rodríguez-Ordóñez, *California State University Long Beach*

Dorothy Owino Rombo, *State University of New York Oneonta*

Kevin J. Rose, *Purdue School of Engineering and Technology*

Gina R. Rosich, *University of Saint Joseph*

Kyle Ross, *NACADA: The Global Community for Academic Advising*

Nick Rumens, *Oxford Brookes Business School*

Katherine Schweighofer, *Dickinson College*

Yenisleidy Simon-Mengana, *Florida International University*

Contributors

Kathleen Trotta, *California Department of State Hospitals*

Catherine Wadley, *Florida International University*

Gerald Walton, *Lakehead University*

Iva Žegura, *University Psychiatric Hospital Vrapče*

FOREWORD

It's a delight to offer some personal reflections on the people addressed in this very important new book, *The Routledge Handbook of LGBTQ Identity in Organizations and Society*. This compendium provides us all with an excellent intersectional view of the many issues involved with this topic. In the 50 years I've been doing this work, I've learned that most people in the world want the opportunity to learn more about something they don't yet understand. On these issues, the positive response has been astounding.

When a Wall Street firm brought me to Singapore to train their executives on Lesbian, Gay, Bisexual, and Transgender Issues in the Workplace ("Queer" was not used then), I was told not to tell the person at Customs specifically why I was there. Otherwise, any mention of homosexuality would have me put on the next plane back to the United States. So, I said "diversity training."

I was also told not to expect the audience in Singapore to respond to me in the same expressive way audiences elsewhere reacted. They would show little emotion.

The day before I spoke, Ray, my husband now of 47 years, and I went to the nation's cultural museum so that I might better acquaint myself with Singaporean history. That night, we asked our tour guide to take us to a Gay bar. He drove us to what seemed like a four-story shopping center with escalators, locally called "The four floors of whore." Every space was occupied by a bar, and the only Gay bar was on the fourth floor. When we entered, each person presented themselves as beautiful women, and beautiful they were. We said to our guide, "Isn't there a bar where Gay men present as men?" Our former military, former bodyguard, and bouncer guide said, "Yes, but why would you want to go there?"

The room was packed with mostly Singaporean bankers the next morning for what would be the first such training on the issue ever given there or in Hong Kong, Sydney, Melbourne, Tokyo, or Mumbai, the next stops. I began by telling them of our evening adventure, and they all laughed knowingly of the building's name, and of us wanting to be with cis-gender Gay men.

I train everyone about LGBTQ+ issues by storytelling and have done so for 50 years. The most effective way of bridging the gap between collegiate and corporate policy and collegiate and corporate culture is through the heart, not the head. All true shifts in attitudes happen when we put faces on the issue and connect soul to soul.

That doesn't mean a business case isn't made for the training. I'd begin with, "In the war for talent, in order to attract and retain the best and brightest people we have to create a work environment in which people feel safe and valued." In the beginning of my public speaking, I had all of my hard facts typed neatly on a sheet of paper that is now in Cornell University's Human Sexuality Archive. I spoke about Evelyn Hooker's 1953 study comparing Gay and Straight men's emotional health, the American Psychiatric Association's 1969 removal of homosexuality from their list of disorders, the 1951 Clellan Ford and Frank Beach study of homosexual behavior in mammals, etc., but what secured the attention of thousands of college students from 1974 to 1985 was the story of how I grew up with a secret I was afraid to share with anyone for fear they wouldn't love me anymore. For many of them at the time, I was the first Gay person they ever met. What they wanted to know was, "How did your parents react?" "Is it a choice?" "Have you ever had sex with a woman?" "Would you take a pill that would make you Straight?"

In the corporate training I did globally from 1986 to the beginning of COVID-19 pandemic in 2019, I began, out of necessity, because of pushback by fundamentalist Christians, by saying, "I'm not here to change your personal values, but rather focus on professional behavior." And then, after explaining the differences between sexual orientation, sexual behavior, and sexual identity, as well as the differences between sex, gender identity, gender role, and gender expression, I'd say, "Here are the words that are considered welcoming and here are the words that are considered unwelcoming." But when the audience laughs and cries with you, which they have done with me in every country in which I was allowed to provide such training, is when the chasm is bridged.

That is what happened in Singapore. They laughed and cried with me and stood and clapped at the end because I was helping them better understand not just their colleagues but also their families. After my two-hour presentation, I stood for another hour with a dozen Singaporean women who wanted to know more about how to create a welcoming environment at home, how to help a Gay nephew come out, how to know if your child is Lesbian, Gay, Bisexual, or Transgender?

When I ascended the steps to the stage of the National Security Agency (NSA), where I spoke to a command performance, standing room only gathering of NSA, FBI, and CIA senior managers, I no longer had my fact sheet in my hand because I knew that information was less useful than telling my story. The world had changed with me from when I was fired by the Catholic Church and when I was hired by the NSA. After presenting all of the aforementioned information on the business case and the short talk on sexuality, I told them of my being an Irish Catholic middle child of 7 years who was the super-achiever of the family, senior class President in high school, university yearbook editor, and columnist and reporter for the Michigan Catholic newspaper. Not being out as a Gay man took a terrible toll on me, until I came to the point I didn't want to live anymore and drank a bottle of turpentine. As I had my stomach pumped, I promised myself that I would no longer live in fear to meet the expectations of others. I came out and was fired.

No parent in the audience wanted their child to grow up in a home in which they were afraid to come out to their folks. With every corporate audience, I gave them a homework assignment to go back to their offices and tell their colleagues that they had just come from a presentation on Lesbian, Gay, Bisexual, and Transgender issues in the workplace. "Say the words. Using the acronym allows you to avoid saying the words. When I came out I didn't tell my folks that I was LGBTQ. I said I was Gay."

> And when you go home tonight, I want you to sit at the dinner table and ask each member of the family about their day, and then I want you to say, "I was at a presentation on Lesbian, Gay, Bisexual, and Transgender issues".

The next day, I got an e-mail from one of the top people at the NSA who wrote:

> Brian, you changed my life. I did what you said to do at the dinner table, and two hours later my teenage daughter walked into the bedroom and said, "Dad, we need to talk. I'm a Lesbian." And then I said what you told us to say when someone comes out to us, I said, "Thank you, honey, for telling me." Well, then she burst into tears, and I burst into tears, and we hugged, and it never would have happened if I hadn't said the word "Lesbian".

On the long plane ride home from New York, where I had done two days of training for AT&T, back to Atlanta, where Ray was the openly Gay head of the Lehman Brothers office from 1991 to 1994, I sat next to a guy who, like me, preferred to talk rather than read. "Are you heading home?" he asked me. We quickly learned that he lived in the most conservative area of town, and I in the most liberal. "What do you do for work?" I asked him.
He replied:

> We'll, I'm probably best known for being an advocate for Christian values in the workplace. I've been featured in *Inc* and *Fortune* magazines, and actually got one of President Bush's "Thousand Point of Light" awards. But, how about you? What do you do for work?

"I do workshops and presentations for corporations on Lesbian, Gay, Bisexual, and Transgender issues in the workplace," I replied.
"What's their reasoning behind having you do that?" he asked quite surprised.

> Imagine that you're a Gay person and when you step into your office, you find an unsigned piece of paper on your desk that reads, "A man shall not lie with a man as with a woman. Such is an abomination. Leviticus 22." How much work would you get done that day?

"I wouldn't get any work done," he said. "I'd be wondering all day who put that in there."
"That's why they have me come in. It's not about challenging your personal moral views. It's about productivity, which results from people treating each other with professional respect."
"That makes sense. But is it really that bad where they have you train?"
I listed for him some of my clients, including the U.S. State Department and most the Fortune 50 companies, and then said:

> It's not as if people are walking into the men's room in corporate headquarters and seeing the word "Faggot" on the bathroom wall. But when people assume that there are no Gay or Transgender people around, they feel freer making comments. I quickly establish by raising of hands how many people know and care about someone who is Lesbian, Gay, Bisexual, or Transgender? For those without their hands up it's a wake-up call that their non-supportive comments have been overheard by the siblings, nephews and nieces of Gay people.

"What do you do in these workshops?" he asked.

> I make the business case, help them understand what behaviors are considered unprofessional, and what behaviors are considered welcoming, but the most powerful thing

I do is tell them my story. Many people say they know Gay or Transgender people, but they've never been given the opportunity to understand what it's like growing up in a home, a church, or a workplace where you're afraid to tell people who you are.

"I don't think I know any Gay people, and I've never taken the time to talk to someone firsthand about it. Will you tell me your story?" he asked.

Never passing up an opportunity to create an ally, I did. For the next couple of hours, I told him about growing up Catholic, wanting to be a priest, never thinking I would go to hell for my secret same-sex attractions but knowing I couldn't tell anyone. To make the point, I told him that when I graduated from a Catholic boy's prep school, the faculty unanimously voted for me to receive the Christian Leadership Award, and how eight years later, when I came out so publicly, my name was taken off the plaque. He winced. I told him that it's back up, but only after having been taken down twice. The guy who kept having a new nameplate made up was the straight track coach who had been two years ahead of me in school. I paraphrased Edmund Burke, "All that must happen for evil to triumph is for good people to sit by and do nothing."

He asked all the questions I had heard before, especially about my family and their response, and I answered them all with gratitude for his interest. As we were landing, he looked at me and said, "Brian, as sure as I'm sitting in this seat, I know God had you sit next to me, and I'll never think about this issue in the same way again. I wish my wife had been with us." He then pulled out a copy of a magazine in which he was featured, signed it, and gave it to me, as I pulled out a copy of my book, *Gay Issues in the Workplace* and signed it for him.

For as long as I've been writing and speaking about LGBTQ+ people and issues in columns, books, DVDs, and public trainings, I've known my role and of how different it needed to be from the approach taken by some others in my Rainbow Community. I have never had the option of being angry. We need to have the voices of angry people decrying the injustices we experience in our lives. Doing so during the AIDS epidemic was crucial to getting much-needed drugs released at a reasonable price. But, if I wrote and spoke with anger, I'd never have access to another corporate audience. After my first few corporate workshops, a man came up to me and said, "You know, you're the first diversity trainer who hasn't come in here and guilt tripped us."

I was once referred to as the "Mr. Rogers of the Gay Community." I speak from my heart. My hands are open and not in fists. As soon as you scare someone, the wall goes up and they're then unreachable.

Early in my unintended, unchartered career as an educator on Lesbian, Gay, Bisexual, Transgender, and Queer Issues, I was invited with other sexuality educators to participate in a daylong series of workshops for private school teachers. Each sexuality educator would present their workshop once in the morning and once in the afternoon. My morning workshop on Gay issues had maybe 20 people there. The afternoon session, however, was packed. When my friends and I were saying our "good-byes" to one another in the parking lot, a car approached us very quickly. When it stopped, out stepped a woman who headed right towards me.

"We need to talk," she said.

"Okay, how can I help?" I said as I led her to a more private space.

I objected to you being invited to speak today. I'm a conservative Christian and I oppose homosexuality. I refused to step foot in your presentation, because I didn't want to be seen as supporting you. But I stood outside the room this afternoon and listened. Brian, I know that you are speaking the truth from your heart. I heard it. But if I go home and tell my children that I've changed my mind about homosexuality, what happens to all of the other things I've told them I'm against? I seriously don't know what to do with you.

First, thank you for making the effort to come up here to talk. I want you to know that I hear you and I understand you. But I can't help you, other than to say you can contact me any time you'd like to talk. I'm now a card in the hand you've been dealt. You have to play your hand. You can't unhear what you heard today. You'll do the right thing. You have a good heart.

In the time that I've been focused on these issues, I've witnessed great change. I consider it a great privilege to have lived at this time and to have had the opportunities I've had to help change the world. We stand on the shoulders of others as those who follow will stand on ours. One group to whom we owe a great debt are the Suffragettes. When women challenged the gender roles to which they had been assigned, they opened the discussion to what does it mean to be male or female? Today we ask, "Are there only two sexes?" "Are Gay, Straight and Bi our only options?" "Is 'gender' a social construct?" "How many more letters will be added to the acronym?"

I was asked many years ago to address the question, "Are Gay people part of God's plan?" It's a great question, whether or not you believe in a higher power. Is homosexuality nature's intention, or are we freaks of nature? If LGBTQIANB2S+ people are freaks of nature, then the most we can hope for is to be accommodated. But, if we're an important part of the evolutionary process, our existence and contributions should be celebrated.

The McDonald's Corporation brought me in once to work with their LGBTQ Employee Resource Group. The ERG had gotten everything on its Wish List. "What's next?" they asked me. "What's next," I answered, "is you telling management what unique gifts we bring to the table."

The entire premise of "valuing diversity" in the corporate world is the belief that each different group brings unique perspectives and gifts to the table. It's been easy for us to tell the world about how we're discriminated against, but of far more interest today for Straight cis-gender people is "What do you have that we don't have?"

In response to the question, "Are Gay people part of God's plan," I replied that when I die, I imagine that God will ask me, "Brian, did you sing the song I taught you?"

Brian McNaught
"The godfather of gay diversity training."
The New York Times
www.brian-mcnaught.com

1

INTRODUCTION

Julie A. Gedro

Over the last 50 years, the complex tapestry of sexual minority issues has grown increasingly visible, adjudicated, researched, publicized, and contested in virtually every dimension of life, throughout the world. The assumption that societies, economies, political structures, cultural systems, and workplaces are or should be characterized by pervasive and tacit heteromasculinity is being challenged on multiple fronts. Gedro and Mizzi (2014, pp. 445–446, citing Anderson, 2009) observe that "heteromasculinity is a form of masculinity that suppresses women and sexual minorities [lesbian, gay, bisexual, transgender, and queer] . . . through the unmediated and unchallenged use of language, understandings, beliefs or practices that privilege heterosexual men." The normative expectation of heterosexuality as the overarching, immutable organizing framework for social, political, and organizational systems and structures is accompanied by the assumption that gender is a fixed and stable binary category. The complexity of LGBTQ issues is characterized by the interwoven nature of multiple facets: gender, gender identity, gender expression, and sexual orientation—and the multi-layered implications for those (who are mostly marginalized) people who are not identified as heteronormative and/or gender conforming.

A disruption of the assumptions of heteronormativity and gender as an immutable, naturally occurring phenomena requires intentional focus and interrogation of underlying historical, social, economic, psychological, political, and cultural contexts to create possibilities for re-configuring organizations through expanded mind sets. Much of organizational life is, as Butler (1999) observes, a "performance" in which the expectations for gender roles are acted out through various demonstrations of adherence to gender roles. Speech, dress, mannerisms, and even occupational choice are subject to regulatory expectations for heterosexuality and gender-conformance, whether overtly and consciously, or tacitly and subconsciously. These regulatory expectations demand interrogation, and this interrogation can be the focus of policymakers, practitioners, and scholars. Sexuality and gender and all their manifestations require overt and conscious consideration by policymakers, practitioners, and scholars. The variation of how these topics and how members of these different sub-populations are treated, protected, or persecuted, or wittingly or unwittingly marginalized, is dizzying in scope. This handbook serves as a comprehensive reference that interrogates aspects of being LGBTQ in societies, economies, political structures, cultural systems, and organizations in a way that provides a framework for understanding LGBTQ concerns. Given the interconnected nature of the world

DOI: 10.4324/9781003128151-1

today, it is necessary to examine LGBTQ issues through a global lens. Given the fact that different countries around the world have varying degrees of equal rights and stances on inclusion for LGBTQ people, some country-specific analyses offer insights into these variations. Given the fact that gender, gender identity, gender expression, and sexual orientation are necessarily political issues and that there exists a constellation of considerations related to law and policy, it is necessary to examine LGBTQ issues through lenses of law, political structures, and policy. Given the fact that culture is both a creation as well as a reflection of what it means to be human, including LGBTQ humans, it is necessary to examine cultural structures. Given the fact that gender, gender identity, gender expression, and sexual orientation each has their own sets of implications for daily life and human interaction, it is necessary to examine LGBTQ issues through social, psychological, and political research lenses. Finally, because the workplace is a microcosm of the broader global, social, and political environment, and because work and the workplace are modern constructs that frame our lives, it is necessary to examine LGBTQ issues in organizational contexts (Rocco et al., 2009).

The purpose of this handbook is to provide a reference work which offers theoretical, research, and practice perspectives on Lesbian, Gay, Bisexual, Transgender, Queer, and Questioning issues in global, national, social, political, cultural, psychological, and organizational contexts. The handbook offers valuable resources and insights for a variety of readers.

The handbook is intended to serve as a primary text, a reader, or a reference work for different types of readers. In order to articulate what we have in mind in terms of readership, and who we intend to serve, permit us to elaborate. Note that we describe the readership in no particular order, hierarchy, or privilege. Students of LGBTQ issues will be able to acquire a broad as well as deep understanding of issues related to sexuality and gender identity as they are situated in organizational and social contexts. This book may serve as a reference book, where undergraduate and graduate students have one resource that is replete with analyses and critiques from leading authors and researchers who examine multiple issues, all revolving around LGBTQ identity. Undergraduate students will likely be in upper-level courses, though we do not necessarily rule out any type of level of coursework or academic programming for which the book as a whole or specific chapters could be valuable.

Next, and in particular because the handbook was inspired by the dearth of single-volume works that compile multi-disciplinary and globally inspired perspectives on LGBTQ issues, we intend for this work to be valuable for faculty in multiple disciplines. Faculty in areas such as human resource development and management, marketing, communication, technology, consulting, and strategy will benefit from the chapters in Part VI, Organizational Contexts, though it is likely that all chapters in all sections could offer insights for these disciplines. Faculty in sociology, political science, education, psychology, social work, and law will find that the chapters that examine LGBTQ identity through these lenses will be able to enrich their courses by including readings that broaden the lens and consider sexuality and gender identity. Faculty in women's studies and sexual minority studies are arguably the more "obvious" readers for the handbook, and our intention is to offer this reader with its globalized authorship and its currency of interrogation of the issues.

In addition to a primary text or a reference resource for academic contexts, we offer this handbook as a useful resource for multiple types of practitioners including those who work in leadership and championship and influencer positions of diversity, equity, inclusion, and belonging initiatives. Career development professionals, particularly those who currently work with either LGBTQ clients or students, may find the handbook a comprehensive, contextually rich resource to enrich their work. Because of the non-linearity of the development of a sexual or gender-diverse identity, and because of the situationally dependent considerations for LGBTQ people as they navigate their careers (see Gedro, 2009 for some background on this), career development professionals will benefit from the broad acquisition of knowledge regarding different occupational fields as well as some environmental (writ broadly, not simply ecological) career considerations for their LGBTQ clients. Similarly, we hope that those who are in the mental health and wellness professions find the handbook useful in their counseling. We conceive of the range of content in this handbook to provide some depth and breadth of understanding of LGBTQ issues that affect day-to-day life, and also the life course considered in a longitudinal perspective. Lastly, and for many of the reasons noted heretofore, we hope the handbook is of interest and use for those in positions of leadership and executive coaching. We make no assumptions about the sexual orientation and gender identity of the readership, and this needs to be made clear, lest we demonstrate the same type of assumptions of heteronormativity that we problematize. In other words, readers likely (hopefully) represent a variety of identities themselves. We intend for the book to have broad appeal.

Organization of the Handbook

The sequencing of each part is intentional, because we have determined it to be optimal to present the large-scale matters, then national, followed by disciplinary, and then organizationally situated chapters. However, the handbook is not necessarily intended to be read in sequence. Rather, we expect that across the readership, there might be a need and an interest to focus on particular subject matter pertinent to different needs. Practitioners might read specific chapters to gain insights on client identity, needs, or context. Educators might select chapters for a particular course module.

There are six parts of the handbook, and within each part, there are chapters related to the subject area of that part. Because the subject of LGBTQ identity is a multi-level construct, we saw it as important to frame the handbook using as wide of an "angle" as possible. Therefore, Part I examines LGBTQ identity on a global scale, as a human rights matter. As Mizzi and Walton (Chapter 4) point out, it is insufficient for LGBTQ activists to operate from the self-referential positionality of self-service; instead, it is important particularly in 2023, for LGBTQ activists to embrace a larger-scale consideration of responsibility for advocating and working for social justice for all marginalized people, in all countries of the world. Part I is comprised of five chapters that present a global perspective on LGBTQ human rights (Landorf et al., Chapter 2), LGBTQ rights and the United Nations (Mekler, Chapter 3), queer leaders in transnational organizations (Mizzi, Chapter 4), "global" queer pedagogy (Mizzi & Walton, Chapter 5), and a world religion analysis of LGBTQ identity (Blumenfeld, Chapter 6).

Part II contains five chapters. The fundamental, organizing theme of this part is that each chapter focuses on a particular national context, which means that taken together, there is a composite perspective of LGBTQ human rights and social justice issues in specific geographic, national settings. Lutomia and Rombo (Chapter 7) present their work on contemporary legal and policy practices on LGBTQ activism in Kenya, as they trace the "othering" of LGBTQ communities from pre-colonial to colonial to present day. Cossman (Chapter 8) examines the history of LGBTQ rights in Canada, in which she suggests that even though Canada is arguably considered a model of LGBTQ rights, a more complicated analysis involves, among other considerations, how LGBTQ constitutional rights in Canada have both a liberal (in which LGBTQ rights are "enshrined in law") and a critical (in which there is a refusal to assimilate and reproduce heteronormative institutions such as marriage) lens. Žegura (Chapter 9) presents information regarding human rights and social justice in psychological practice working with LGBTQ people in Croatia. The context of LGBTQ issues in China is examined by Le and

Choo (Chapter 10), followed by an analysis of mental health supports for Black and Caribbean lesbian, bisexual, and transgender women (Désir and Reid, Chapter 11).

After the examination of national and societal contexts, Part III turns attention to *law, political structures, and policy* and is comprised of five chapters. This part provides readers with information on the intersections of LGBTQ identity and factors that shape or even dictate their lives. The historical context of employment law and employment rights (or perhaps better said, the lack of legal protections) for transgender and gender non-conforming people is examined (Rosich, Chapter 12). As a population at risk for family rejection, depression, mental illness, substance abuse, homelessness, and engagement in sex work, LGBTQ people have an arguably higher likelihood than those of the majoritarian population to have intersections with the criminal justice system (Trotta, Chapter 13). Because of the significance of work, and employment prospects and possibilities, as a determinant of income and as a factor in job satisfaction, there is a chapter that examines the economics of being LGBT (Drydakis, Chapter 14). Housing represents another dimension of life and quality of life for all people, including LGBTQ people, and Harmon and Gahagan (Chapter 15) interrogate the issue of LGBTQ housing policy in Canada, framing their analysis through a lens of intergenerational justice. Grace and Hankey (Chapter 16) present an example of a project (the CHEW project, which stands for community, health, empowerment, and wellness) which serves as a wraparound intervention for sexual and gender-minority youth who have faced trauma and neglect in terms of housing, health, and other vulnerabilities.

In Part IV, attention is turned to the *cultural structures* that influence and illuminate LGBTQ identity. There are seven chapters in this part that examine issues of language, geography, architecture, musical theater, dress and fashion, and brand cause marketing, sports, and religion. Knutson (Chapter 17) unpacks gender pronouns and identity terminology for transgender and non-binary people. Paceley and Fish (Chapter 18) evaluate the literature related to LGBTQ youth and geographic communities, and they make the argument that social contexts alter health and well-being for LGBTQ youth, more so than any inherent factor or set of factors for LGBTQ youth. The authors adopt and present a strength-based perspective for creating geographic contexts that equip LGBTQ youth to thrive, rather than to suffer from disproportionate risk for mental, physical, or emotional suffering. Related to geographic contexts is the subject of architecture. Chapter 19 (Bonnemaison) presents a historical review of queer architecture—buildings and space designed for and by queer people. "Queer architecture" includes public monuments, celebrations, exhibitions, and residences. In Chapter 20, McGill and Ross examine theater as a site for public pedagogy; they argue that queer people learn how to construct their identities (what it means to be queer) in large part through their observations in cultural spaces (such as theater). Their conceptual framework consists of three components: public pedagogy, queer theory and politic, and reception theory. Next in Chapter 21, Reddy-Best examines the role that dress and fashion play in the negotiation of LGBTQ identity. Reddy-Best argues that although the field of fashion studies has examined the ways that those in positions of power and privilege employ dress to communicate identity, less has been written about the intersections of LGBTQ, identity, and dress. Therefore, this chapter examines how LGBTQ employee's dress and fashion act as communication mechanisms for identity. Along similar lines as the physical, tangible construct of dress, Chapter 22 (Argüello) interrogates the commercialization of HIV through the "RED" brand, arguing that brand/cause marketing fosters the participation of those in first-world countries in neo-colonization of Africa through the consumption of brand cause marketing. Chapter 23 (Schweighofer) looks at the different ways that sports culture embraces or marginalizes LGBTQ athletes, and the movement from "strategic distancing" (which refers to the intentional editing of references to sexual minority and gender non-conformity status) to "strategic acceptance" (which refers to openness and inclusivity).

Part V focuses on *social, psychological, and research contexts.* It is comprised of four chapters that address issues of identity (Cull, Chapter 24), health and prejudice (Hinton, Chapter 25), conversion therapy in the United States (Mauldin & Churchill, Chapter 26), and research practices (Nieto, Hernandez, Rocco, & Munn, Chapter 27). Using an historical, contextualist lens, Cull's chapter provides an analysis of identity, arguing for the primacy and dependency of context for the meaning of identity. Cull's chapter traverses the historical underpinnings of contextualism and also provides a survey of contemporary scholarship. There is no complete understanding of a social identity (e.g., woman) without a contextual basis. In Chapter 25, Hinton critiques historical and contemporary models of LGBTQ identity development, focusing on social and environmental elements of identity development and argues that social prejudices impact LGBTQ identity which help us understand the foundations of health disparities for sexual minorities. Mauldin and Churchill's chapter follows (Chapter 26) and offers a comprehensive analysis of conversation therapy. It explains what conversation therapy is, how it harms those upon whom it is practiced (sexual and gender minorities), and it examines the legal landscape of conversation therapy in the United States and around the world. This chapter provides a "case study" in the form of a discussion of their grassroots activism to prohibit the practice of conversation therapy in the state of Oklahoma. This part concludes with a chapter that examines LGBTQ research (Nieto, Hernandez, Rocco, & Munn, Chapter 27). There are several questions that this chapter addresses regarding LGBTQ research. These questions include *how* dimensions of LGBTQ identity are examined in research; in other words, to what extent is LGBTQ identity visible and legitimized as a category of analysis (in the same way that identities such as race, age, gender, and ability are visible and legitimized)? To what extent are LGBTQ issues researched? This chapter hearkens back to the inspiration and motivations for the handbook itself: which is to say that LGBTQ identity is an area in which research and scholarship are emergent, yet comparatively under-explored and barely visible. Therefore, this part concludes with this "loop-closing" chapter on LGBTQ and research.

In Part VI, the handbook turns attention to *organizational contexts.* By "organizational contexts," we mean primarily (though not exclusively) work, career, and occupational contexts. LGBTQ identity is operationalized within the context of interactions with others, and interactions with others systematically and necessarily occur at workplaces and organizations. Intrapersonal relationships (as in the relationships that individuals have with themselves, posing and answering fundamental and existential questions such as "Who am I?") are crucial as well, because they represent one's internal experience of the world and of the world of work. Rumens' chapter (Chapter 28) begins this part, with a queer theory analysis of LGBTQ sexual and gender identities in the workplace. Rumens draws upon the Butlerian (1999) construct of identity as performative rather than essentialized and presents insights that dislodge the assumptions regarding sexual orientation, gender expression, and gender identity in the workplace. Martinez and Bernard (Chapter 29) then examine the construct of allyship in the workplace; LGBTQ people should not bear the challenges of disrupting heteronormative workplace environments on their own. Rather, it is through the comprehensive engagement of LGBTQ people and non-targeted employees (whom Rengers et al. describe as allies) to proactively create workplace environments that are inclusive for sexual minorities (and all employees for that matter).

Rengers (Chapter 30) provides insights regarding the challenges and the opportunities for LGBTQ expatriates. For LGBTQ employees who work in countries in which they are not citizens (expatriates), there can be concerns regarding safety, security, discrimination, and variations in terms of the extent to which their host country's laws or policies protect them. Rengers offers insights regarding the identity management concerns of LGBTQ people during the stages of expatriation and offers recommendations for employers to adopt formal policies and practices that can support their LGBTQ expatriate employees. Redien-Collot's chapter (Chapter 31) focuses on LGBTQ entrepreneurship. The preceding chapters in this part locate LGBTQ management within the system of the organization and employer; Redien-Collot's chapter connects to LGBTQ and identity but through the lens of entrepreneurship and therefore self-employment. This chapter explores the ways in which entrepreneurship provides a mechanism for emancipation by limiting the discrimination they experience in a workplace, and it also brings to light issues related to LGBTQ entrepreneurship as a means of reproducing a commercially heteronormative status quo.

Gedro's chapter (Chapter 32) considers the ways in which those who are LGBTQ people in recovery (from alcoholism and/or addiction) have a myriad of considerations when it comes to navigating their careers, both as sexual minorities and as people in recovery. Workplace contexts are pervaded by heteronormative assumptions, which means that LGBTQ people can have challenges with respect to their sexual minority identities in workplace contexts. Moreover, because there is a pervasive stigma regarding alcoholism, addiction, and recovery, LGBTQ people in recovery face a particularly complex set of considerations when it comes to navigating their workplaces and their careers. McFadden (Chapter 33) problematizes the historical emergence of the "employee resource group" (ERG) which were initially employee-created and led and have become increasingly part of organizational strategies to create and shape a "brand" around inclusion. McFadden uses a queer lens to interrogate the purpose and sponsorship of LGBTQ employee resource groups, questioning the effectiveness of such groups to actually achieve their intended purpose of creating inclusion for LGBTQ employees. Whose voices are heard and legitimized? Whose voices are silenced? These questions seem paradoxical with respect to ERGs, and yet the control over resources and the possible perception (or reality) of ERGs as an extension of a commercial, managerialist agenda disrupt their ability to empower LGBTQ employees. Rose (Chapter 34) examines the particular concerns of LGBTQ employees in dealing with dysfunctional leaders. Rose unpacks constructs of heteromasculinity, intersectionality, and power relationships in the organizational context and, after said analysis, offers some recommendations for disrupting dysfunctional leaders (which benefits all employees). Next, Carliner (Chapter 35) offers an analysis of bullying in the workplace, using a variety of ways of examining the subject including anecdotes and research.

In the concluding chapter (Chapter 36), we offer reflections on the current and future realities of LGBTQ communities and allies. We developed a list of questions and sent the questions to all authors who submitted chapter proposals and who were invited to submit a chapter because of the depth and breadth of academic and scholarly expertise. Who better to offer these reflections, than the authors and proposed authors of the chapters that comprise this volume?

Conclusion

Sexuality, gender, gender identity, and gender expression are fluid constructs, and the ways in which identity development intersects with organizations and exists in society are vastly complex. We have done our best to put a handbook together that represents as broad and as deep of a range of subjects as possible with the intention of creating a resource for academics, scholars, students, practitioners, activists, coaches, and any other readership interested in going deep. An image that comes to mind when thinking about the composition and organization of the handbook is that of a globe or an orb that slowly turns and the light refracts different rays, colors, and intensities that are ever changing. We envision this book a bit of a metaphorical travel guide that examines a range of dimensions of LGBTQ identity around the world and in myriad contexts. Although not inevitable, it is likely that this volume is the first of an ongoing series of handbooks on the subject, because of how dynamic the subject matter is and how the scholarship across the disciplines represented in the handbook is catching up (or keeping up?) with the changes. We hope this handbook is a generative, informative, thought-provoking guide. Perhaps we leave as many remaining questions as definitive answers.

References

Anderson, E. (2009). *Inclusive masculinity. The changing nature of masculinities.* Routledge.

Butler, J. (1999). *Gender trouble* (Rev. ed.). Routledge.

Gedro, J. (2009). LGBT career development. *Advances in Developing Human Resources, 11*(1), 54–66.

Gedro, J., & Mizzi, R. C. (2014). Feminist theory and queer theory: Implications for HRD theory and practice. *Advances in Developing Human Resources, 16*(4), 445–456.

Rocco, T. S., Gedro, J., & Kormanik, M. B. (Eds.). (2009). Sexual minority issues in HRD: Raising awareness [special issue]. *Advances in Developing Human Resources, 11*(1).

I
Global Context

2

A GLOBAL PERSPECTIVE ON LGBTQ RIGHTS AS HUMAN RIGHTS

Hilary Landorf, Catherine Wadley, and Yenisleidy Simon-Mengana

Non-governmental organizations (NGOs) working for the protection of human rights play a crucial role both in connecting advocacy for those rights with the communities they serve and in protecting individuals whose rights have been violated. They help define and promote international human rights norms, develop institutional mechanisms to ensure adherence to those norms, and monitor national and local human rights practices. There are many hundreds of NGOs throughout the world whose mission encompasses support of LGBTQ people and the protection of their human rights. They do this in various ways including lobbying the United Nations (UN) and states for changes in policies and laws, bringing test cases in legal systems, offering direct assistance to those whose rights have been violated or are in danger, assisting in developing legislation to protect or enact rights and collecting information and data so as to promote knowledge of and respect for the rights of LGBTQ people.

International NGOs advocating for LGBTQ people use a human rights framework as the basis of support and protection of LGBTQ people who may be discriminated against or denied their rights on the basis of their Sexual Orientation and Gender Identity (SOGI). Advocacy for the rights of LGBTQ people is often associated with identity politics, while human rights invoke universal rights as defined by the United Nations in the 1948 Universal Declaration of Human Rights (UDHR) and the 1966 International Covenant on Civil and Political Rights (ICCPR). Depending on the context of their research, advocacy, or support, these organizations have to navigate the commonalities and differences between identity politics and human rights in order to be effective in advocating for, protecting and preventing discrimination against, LGBTQ people.

In this chapter, we look at five distinct LGBTQ international organizations which we describe as transnational NGOs (Table 2.1). Each of these organizations ascribes to a human rights framework. We examine how each one uses a human rights framework to drive and inform their work, the methods they employ to navigate issues of identity and cultural context, and some of the advances they have facilitated in the rights of LGBTQ people throughout the world.

Background

Human Rights and International Law

The presentation in the UDHR of human rights as individual, inherent, inalienable, and universal is less than 100 years old. It is usually described as a Western construct rooted in Greek

 DOI: 10.4324/9781003128151-3

philosophy and the liberal Enlightenment, though this has been contested (Howard, 1995; Falk, 1992). The connection of human rights with advocacy for the rights of LGBTQ people is even more recent though there are also historical antecedents. There is no reference in any form to sexual orientation or gender in United Nations documents, including the 1948 UDHR, 1966 ICCPR, or in any UN treaties. Rather the arguments for freedoms of expression and protection of behaviors and practices for LGBTQ people based on SOGI (hereinafter referred to as LGBTQ rights) have become legitimized through the expansion of the application and support of human rights for various groups that have emerged in the 21st century, notably women, indigenous peoples, sexual minorities, and refugees. Consequently, social movements and activism have secured the recognition of human rights for LGBTQ people through resolutions, recommendations, international adjudications, and statements of international bodies along with the establishment of norms for behavior and passing of laws in many member states.

The growing institutional and public support for the human rights of the LGBTQ community as part of the larger mainstream human rights movements has led the UN to shift its stance on LGBTQ rights. In 2010, UN Secretary-General Ban Ki-moon publicly pledged support for ending discrimination of homosexuality saying, "where this is tension between cultural attitudes and universal human rights, universal human rights must come first" (Secretary-General, 2010). From the time of this statement, the UN has become increasingly and consistently supportive of LGBTQ rights, mostly through the Human Rights Council and the Office of the High Commissioner on Human Rights (OHCHR) at the UN. In its most recent document presenting the position of the UN on the core obligations of States towards LGBTI persons, in which the I stands for Intersex, the OHCHR states, "The legal obligations of States to safeguard the human rights of LGBTI people are well established in international human rights law on the basis of the Universal Declaration of Human Rights, international human rights treaties, and customary international law" (Born Free and Equal, 2019, p. 2).

Despite UN recognition and adoption of favorable laws in many countries, support and advocacy for LGBTQ rights remain contested and controversial topics in the human rights field. As recently as 2016, a significant number of UN member states voted against the appointment of an SOGI Independent Expert arguing that sexual orientation and gender identity are not universally recognized as human rights concepts and are not codified in international law (OutRight Action International, 2016b). Moreover, the UN generally has no ability to enforce human rights; the principal mechanism for implementing and protecting rights is through the State, so essentially rights only exist when individual countries or states within those countries support them through legislature, policy, and enforcement. As such, it is the national and regional governments and institutions that have the power to either reject and control the behavior of LGBTQ people or assert tolerance and diversity through legislation and judicial systems. Even if these countries are parties to international treaties on rights, there is no specific reference to LGBTQ rights in any of them, and there is little consequence legally for violation of these treaties.

Discrimination against LGBTQ people and denial of their rights based on SOGI largely occur in a domestic or local denial of these rights on the basis of their incompatibility with a national identity, culture, or morality. In most countries, there is a long-standing and continuing debate in which freedom of sexual expression is pitted against the prohibitions of many religious beliefs, traditions, and cultural values, even where there is legislation to protect LGBTQ rights. In many countries or states within those countries, same-sex activity is illegal and harshly penalized, and other seemingly liberal countries have not yet extended rights and protection for such things as gay marriage and adoption. Worldwide, people are still subject to persistent human rights violations because of their actual or perceived sexual orientation and gender identity. These human rights violations take many forms, from denials of the rights to life, free-dom from torture, and security of the person, to discrimination in accessing economic, social, and cultural rights such as health, housing, education, and the right to work.

It should be noted that many advocates concerned with LGBTQ rights in the United States and other countries in the global North have not chosen to frame their struggles in human rights terms but have based their campaigns on civil rights, conducting them through domestic courts, as for example the campaigns for gay marriage and the repeal of "Don't Ask, Don't Tell." As Mertus (2007) has observed, "human rights framings also may be viewed as unduly restric-tive and even detrimental when identity is the central organizing factor" (p. 1036).

Transnational Advocacy and NGOs

NGOs organized around support for LGBTQ rights and advocacy are important constitu-ents of a larger social movement network often described as a transnational advocacy network (TAN). A TAN is defined as a network "of activists, distinguishable largely by the centrality of principled ideas or values in motivating their formation" (Keck & Sikkink, 1999, p. 89). These activists operate beyond national boundaries and "engage in contentious political activities using diffusion of movements across borders and international mobilization" (Tarrow, 2005, p. 29). By using their international connections, groups and individuals are able to persuade, pressurize, and gain leverage over much more powerful organizations and governments trans-nationally. Examples of TANs are the movement to abolish slavery in the 1800s, the campaign for women's suffrage, and the current-day environmental movements. Because TANs rely on the support of a large membership in the movement to succeed transnationally, the various groups and institutions in a network must be able to articulate a global identity and "frame issues to make them comprehensible to target audiences, to attract attentions and encourage action and to fit with favourable institutional venues" (Keck & Sikkink, 1999, p. 90). In the 21st century, increased organizational capacities and the accelerated spread of new communications tech-nologies and social media have allowed social movement networks to expand geographically, intensify communication and cooperation, identify grievances, publicize their causes to a larger audience, and mobilize immediate support for action and protests (Seo et al., 2009).

The modern-day LGBTQ rights political network is a relatively new TAN that started with the coalescence of various groups in the 1990s "through international AIDS activism; activism around world conferences for women and human rights; and targeted efforts to persuade the main gatekeeper organizations for human rights—Amnesty International and Human Rights Watch—to include gays and lesbians in their campaigns" (Linde, 2018, p. 2). Adoption of LGBTQ claims as denial and discrimination of human rights by these major gatekeepers helped validate LGBTQ rights and include them in the human rights advocacy mainstream, giving LGBTQ organizations access to international organizations both directly and indirectly. Within the network, LGBTQ advocates continue to lobby the international community toward legal norms and protections for LGBTQ individuals within the existing human rights treaties. How-ever, they also seek to create new international law and norms specific to LGBTQ individuals and communities and promote new international human rights that are important to LGBTQ lives, including the right to sexuality (Mertus, 2009).

NGOs: Brokers and Gatekeepers

Key players in a TAN are NGOs, which serve as direct tools of the individuals and communities they support and in turn draw large support from the very community they seek to protect.

They initiate actions and pressure more powerful actors to take positions, introduce new ideas, provide information, and lobby for policy changes (Keck & Sikkink, 1998). A large body of research on the development of international human rights law and institutions has identified the crucial role played by nongovernmental agents in "defining international human rights norms, developing institutional mechanisms to ensure adherence to international norms, and monitoring national and local human rights practices" (Smith et al., 1998, p. 380).

Within the transnational LGBTQ network, there are now almost 1,800 NGOs throughout the world in almost every country, as well as communities and advocacy groups in those countries where formal LGBTQ organizations are banned. Included in these are a number of established international or transnational NGOs whose mission is specifically to promote, protect, and support the rights of people throughout the world who are discriminated against on the basis of SOGI (Thoreson, 2014). These transnational NGOs, five of which are discussed in this chapter, are based in the power centers of the Global North (London, New York, Washington DC, Geneva) and play an extremely important role in setting the advocacy agenda of the network. Because of their size, resources, influence, and global reach, they are instrumental in framing the underlying and emerging issues, strategizing and lobbying, creating policies, and creating an international profile for issues raised by other NGOs in the network. They can negotiate with major international bodies, take up a local domestic campaign, and use international influence to bring about changes in policies and practices in a country or community, and even help smaller organizations engage with the UN, as will be detailed in the Findings section. They are at the forefront of movement building particularly in the issue and norm-setting standards for gender equity and LGBTQ rights.

The transnational antecedents of these transnational LGBTQ organizations can be found in the Post Second World War homosexual rights movement in Europe which began to re-form though new national associations and convened as a transnational movement in 1951 with the International Committee for Sexual Equality (ICSE). The ICSE created a multinational network based on a universal concept of a gay identity and advocated for gay rights to the UN under the UDHR (Rupp, 2011).

Since then, a significant number of transnational organizations were formed to advocate for LGBTQ rights. For example, OutRight was founded in 1990 by the activist Julie Dorf as the first transnational LGBTQ organization specifically advocating for gay rights as human rights. Its original name was the International Gay and Lesbian Human Rights Commission (IGLHRC). ILGA, founded in 1978, adopted the UDHR as a platform in 1995. In addition, once major transnational Human Rights organizations—Amnesty International (founded in 1961) and Human Rights Watch (founded in 1978)—expanded their mandate to include LGBTQ rights, LGBTQ organizations had access to influential international bodies and governments through these gatekeeper organizations. By contextualizing demands within international human rights law (Mertus, 2007) as opposed to fighting for civil rights in domestic forums, and by using human rights as a unifying framework, these organizations became the backbone of the transnational advocacy network for LGBTQ rights as the movement assumed a transnational identity.

The organizations examined in this chapter (Table 2.1) play a crucial role as brokers and gatekeepers in the LGBTQ Transnational Advocacy Network. Brokers, according to Stovel and Shaw (2012), bridge a gap in social structure through their ability to help goods, information, opportunities, or knowledge flow across that gap. Brokers can work in many different capacities: as liaisons, itinerants, coordinators, gatekeepers, and representatives or any combinations of these, depending on the information flow, situation, purpose, and group orientation (Stovel & Shaw, 2012, p. 142).

Method

For this chapter, our population of interest consisted of LGBTQ organizations whose mission includes a global scope and international outreach, as well as advocacy for LGBTQ rights and protection of LGBTQ people on the basis of SOGI. We found eight organizations that met these criteria: OutRight, Open for Business, HRC Global, ILGA Global, All Out, Global Equity Fund, ARC International, and the Council for Global Equality. We contacted a senior administrator from each of the organizations via email, asking if they would be willing to participate in our study by engaging in a one-hour interview with us to talk about the role of their LGBTQ organization. Administrators from all of the organizations except ARC International and the Global Equity Fund responded to our invitation. After talking briefly with a senior administrator from HRC, we were informed that their policies prohibited them from holding an interview with us. We conducted interviews with a senior administrator from the five other LGBTQ organizations via Zoom. Everyone with whom we talked agreed on their names and responses to our questions being used for this chapter.

The Organizations

The five organizations we examined in this chapter are listed in chronological order in terms of their founding in Table 2.1.

Table 2.1 List of Organizations

Organization	Year Founded	Website	Description
International Lesbian Gay Bisexual Trans and Intersex Association (ILGA WORLD)	1978	https://ilga.org	Organization bringing together more than 1,600 LGBTQ groups from around the world represented in over 140 countries. Regularly petitions the UN and government and is accredited by the United Nations for NGO Economic and Social Council (ECOSOC) consultative status.
OutRight Action International (previously International Gay and Lesbian Human Rights Commission [IGLHRC])	1990	https://OutRightinternational.org	Works at the international, regional, and national levels to research, document, defend, and advance human rights for LGBTIQ people around the world. Action has a permanent presence to advocate at the United Nations Headquarters in New York.

(Continued)

Table 2.1 (Continued)

Organization	Year Founded	Website	Description
Council for Global Equality	2008	http://globalequality.org/	Coalition of prominent U.S.-based human rights and LGBTI advocacy organizations that together encourage a U.S. voice through the Congress, White House and State Department, and other organizations in support of human rights for LGBTI communities around the world.
All Out	2010	https://allout.org/en	Advocacy member organization focusing on changing policy through targeted campaigns reacting to crisis or opportunities and using social media and protests to publicize and mobilize.
Open for Business	2015	https://open-for-business.org/	Coalition of leading global businesses making an economic and business case for LGBTQ inclusion and creating advocates in local business communities.

Findings

All the five organizations included in this chapter are transnational advocacy organizations. Their work encompasses a global reach, inclusive of all people irrespective of borders, culture, or affiliation, with the common goal of creating a positive normative framework for human rights based on SOGI. Although their strategies and approaches differ, all of them seek to influence international and state organizations. In addition, they all provide resources to domestic and local organizations and act as information brokers in the transnational movement for LGBTQ rights.

Through an analysis of individual interviews and a review of documents and websites for each organization, four major themes emerged in relation to how the organizations used a human rights framework to support their work both individually, as part of a network and as part of a transnational movement. These are (1) complementarity of the organizations, (2) use of a human rights framework, (3) importance of global influence, and (4) importance of local or domestic voices in the movement. These findings will be discussed later.

Complementarity of the Organizations

The leaders we interviewed in all five LGBTQ organizations view their respective organization as part of a larger organic whole. Each leader has deep knowledge of the history, mission, goals, and strategies of the other organizations and the roles they each has played in the landscape of LGBTQ global advocacy and the transnational network in which they operate.

Julie Dorf exemplifies in her own work how well these organizations complement each other in their quest for global equality. Dorf founded OutRight International in 1990 and served as its Executive Director until 1999. During her tenure in the 1990s, she was part of a group that successfully advocated with Amnesty International, Human Rights Watch, the Lawyers Committee for Human Rights, and other NGOs to include LGBTQ issues in their mandates. In 2008, she created the Council on Global Equality. Dorf's knowledge of each organization's mission and goals and her awareness of how each fits into the overall transnational movement for LGBTQ rights were evident throughout her interview. For example, in response to the question, "How do you differentiate your organization's mission and goals from other organizations fighting for human and civil rights for LGBTQ people," Dorf said that the reason she started the Council on Global Equality was that LGBTQ groups would "have a consistent voice advocating for our communities in Washington in the foreign policy space. There were lots of groups doing pieces of that, but no one pulling it together with a consistent strategy and one voice" (J. Dorf, personal communication, January 5, 2021).

Matt Beard, Executive Director of All Out, expressed his knowledge of other organizations and their complementarity by talking about what All Out was NOT. "We are not high-level advocates; we don't do the work that, for example, Out Right does, being at the United Nations. We are not spending our days at the White House like the Council for Global Equality" (M. Beard, personal communication, October 20, 2020). Beard went on to describe the overall model of the organizations with a metaphor: "To bake a cake of human rights change, you need all of the ingredients. You need the flour, the butter, the sugar. If one of them is missing, the cake isn't really as delicious." He went to say, "We see ourselves as complementing our sister organizations in that space." Andre Plessis, Executive Director of ILGA World, also referred to other LGBTQ organizations that work in the global sphere as "sister organizations" (A. Plessis, personal communication, December 10, 2020).

Not only do the leaders we interviewed feel a sense of sisterhood among their global LGBTQ partner organizations, but they are also reflective of the sources of this sense of kinship and complementarity. One source can be found in their conception of global as both encompassing the entire world as well as universal. Matt Beard was clear in his conception of this dual definition of global: "Global means two things. One is global as in international reach and across the world. And global also means operating at the global level" (M. Beard, personal communication, October 30, 2020). Other sources of kinship can be found within their organization's mission statements which all include serving as a voice for human rights for LGBTQ people in general and advancing LGBTQ rights around the world. Because of the intersections in their missions, the organizations' leaders feel the need to keep abreast of their sister organizations' work.

There was also crossover in the organizations. Examples include the following: staff and board members of one organization serve as board members for another organization; Out-Right is a member of the Council for Global Equality and ILGA; Open for Business is also a member of ILGA and its advisory boards include OutRight staff; and All Out includes ILGA staff on its Advisory Board. Jon Miller, Chair and Founder of Open For Business, emphasized that they were particularly interested in collaboration, and before embarking on new programs, they consult with other organizations.

Use of the Human Rights Framework

Julie Dorf has a positive view of the human rights framework. She said the following:

> As a human rights practitioner who has used this framework for my entire career, human rights are a powerful set of tools and a powerful way to achieve greater justice. Are they the "be all end all"? No. Do they consider every single aspect of inequality?

No. Do they look at the history of colonialism and where this language came from? There are endless problems that one could poke holes at as a way of achieving social change. But the human rights set of tools and language is a very, very powerful one because it speaks to the vast majority of people. It resonates on a values level, in people's real lives, in laws and policies, and in the way our society has structured itself.

(J. Dorf, personal communication, January 5, 2021)

The five LGBTQ transnational organizations included in this chapter have all adopted a human rights framework in their advocacy work. The perspectives from which this framework are articulated and the ways in which it is used vary from one organization to another. These variances will be discussed later.

ILGA invokes the UDHR in its constitution. One of the organization's three aims and objectives is "To promote the universal respect for and observance of human rights and fundamental freedoms, including the elimination of all forms of discrimination and also including the realization of the specific provisions of the following international human rights instruments" (ILGA Constitution, 2016, C3.1.3). This sentence is followed by nine international human rights covenants. In a similar way, in its vision statement, OutRight references particular Articles of the UDHR: "A world where LGBTIQ people everywhere enjoy full human rights and fundamental freedoms (Article 2), exercise self-determination (Article 29), form strong communities (Article 28), and thrive personally and economically (Articles 21–27)" (OutRight Action International, n.d., About Us).

The Council for Global Equality includes human rights twice in defining itself on its website as "a coalition of prominent U.S.-based human rights and LGBTI advocacy organizations that together encourage a clear U.S. voice for the human rights of LGBTI communities around the world" (The Council for Global Equality, 2017). In its self-definition, All Out invokes human rights through fighting to deny their negation for all:

> All Out is a global movement for love and equality. We're mobilizing thousands of people to build a world where no person will have to sacrifice their family or freedom, safety or dignity, because of who they are or who they love.
>
> *(All Out, n.d.a)*

Finally, as a self-defined "action-oriented coalition" (Open For Business, n.d.a, About Us), per its mission statement, Open For Business articulates its approach to the achievement of human rights for LGBTQ people through building a consensus that "anti-LGBT policies run counter to the interests of business and economic development" (Open For Business, n.d.a, About Us).

Whether in their constitution, mission, vision, or self-definition, all five LGBTQ organizations covered in this chapter use human rights as the framework of their work. Some, like the ILGA and OutRight, invoke the UDHR directly, and others, such as Open For Business and All Out, refer more generally to the fight for the freedoms that the UDHR guarantees. Where the organizations differ is the ways in which they use human rights in their advocacy and actions. These range from putting the positive freedoms of human rights at the forefront of their work, to focusing on the benefits of human rights' non-discrimination. Context is key in the majority of the organization's actions, and the organizations tailor their use of human rights according to local needs.

Open for Business is the most obvious example of an organization that adapts the language it uses in its advocacy work to local needs. Jon Miller, Founder and Chair of the Board of Open for Business, described to us the organization's work in Kenya. As part of Open For Business' "local influencer" program, it has been working with local civil society organizations in-country.

18

Jon was careful to point out that local organizations invite Open for Business, to work with them, and that Open for Business takes its mandate from these local organizations. As Jon told us, ahead of a hearing in the high court on decriminalizing homosexuality in Kenya, Open for Business published a commissioned report in 2019 titled The Economic Case for LGBT + Inclusion in Kenya (Open for Business, 2019a). Jon told us that immediately after publishing this report, the public conversation changed, from a discussion about a clash of irreconcilable moral and cultural systems to one of economic costs and benefits. Although homosexuality in Kenya is not yet decriminalized, as he described it, "the phrase 'LGBT + discrimination costs the Kenyan economy Sh130 billion to Sh18 billion dollars a year' made headlines in pretty much all the Kenyan media" (J. Miller, personal communication, November 18, 2020). He went on to say that "this kind of work starts to unlock a conversation which then becomes the strategic advocacy in a more behind-the-scenes way, facilitated by the air cover of the headlines we can create by publishing this data." Open for Business found that local coalition partners and local companies that had been reluctant to come to roundtable discussions about LGBT+ inclusion joined these discussions after the report was published. Kenya has not yet decriminalized homosexuality, but the fact that the petitioners' case was heard, and that it was covered widely in the media, has inspired many local organizations in Kenya to continue their work for LGBTQ rights.

According to Matt Beard, since the inception of All Out in 2010, the human rights framework has been the macro-theory of change for the organization. This framework gives a codified set of principles with which the organization can run its campaigns and deliver its messaging. However, Beard is quick to point out that, in countries around the world where LGBTQ rights are not recognized, and particularly where they are criminalized, the human rights framework is rejected by the political mainstream, and if used, this can be counterproductive and create backlash (M. Beard, personal communication, October 30, 2020). In these countries, Beard says that All Out translates human rights principles into more "politically palatable values—like justice, freedom, equality, sometimes even love." As an example, in September 2020, in the midst of the COVID-19 pandemic, All Out launched a fundraising campaign in support of Casa Frida, a temporary shelter to support LGBTQ + youth. The focus of this campaign is not on LGBTQ rights as human rights but on equality for all. In just a few days, more than 150 All Out members donated more than US$2,000 to support Casa Frida.

On the other end of the spectrum, in All Out's recent campaign asking the European Union to take action against the "LGBT-free zones" established in Poland, they explicitly used the language of human rights. After presenting to the European Commission in person more than 340,000 signatures on a petition to take action against the "free zones," Beard gave an interview on Sky News in which he said that "over 400 LGBT Polish people have written to the European Union expressing their fear that their fundamental civil and political rights as EU citizens are now being violated" (All Out, n.d.b, Highlights). As proof of the power of global LGBTQ advocacy campaigns, on March 11, the European Parliament passed a resolution declaring the entire European Union an "LGBTIQ Freedom Zone" (European Parliament, 2021).

Jessica Stern, Executive Director of OutRight, was passionate in expressing the power of the human rights framework:

> When you are told that you a criminal by virtue of who you love or what your gender expression is, you are defined as outside the law. The human rights framework says that all people are entitled to rights, that rights are universal, that rights are indivisible, and that rights are given to you by virtue of your being human.
>
> *(J. Stern, personal communication, October 28, 2020)*

She went on to explain that the human rights framework was not the only one OutRight uses; however, not only because human rights as a framework is not equally respected everywhere in the world but also because, as she put it, "What do you do when aligning with the human rights framework makes you seem like the other? When human rights are too controversial or are associated with a Western or imperialistic agenda?" (J. Stern, personal communication, October 28, 2020). OutRight, like the other organizations discussed in this chapter, uses every strategy in its toolbox, depending on the local context, to move the needle in the fight for equality for LGBTQ people.

The Importance of Global Influence

All the organizations reaffirmed the importance of a global reach in their work and that advocacy for LGBTQ rights is no longer a purely domestic issue. In fact, for those people who live in countries that criminalize homosexuality or ban LGBTQ organizations, there is no justice on the domestic front, and often their only option is help from within the transnational movement. Consequently, these transnational organizations understand it is critical to have access to power and influence at the global level, a strong presence on the international stage, and an embracing global reach, if they are to make a difference globally for the LGBTQ community. A large part of their work and their role in the LGBTQ rights movement is in maintaining and growing that influence in various sectors that include international treaty bodies, states, human rights organizations, national groups, transnational corporations, and key influencers for human rights throughout the world. Access to high-level global bodies brings credibility, resources, and clout to these organizations and enables them to bring international attention for LGBTQ rights campaigns.

All the transnational LGBTQ organizations examined have a deep commitment to global change and a demonstrated record of success. While they utilize diverse approaches and tools to move LGBTQ issues forward, they understand that it is critically important to have "a seat at the table" in order to make real progress. For example, OutRight, ILGA, and Open for Business all emphasized the implications of having a strong presence within mechanisms of global influence such as the United Nations while the Council for Global Equality focuses on exerting pressure on the U.S. federal government.

Jessica Stern, OutRight's Executive Director, emphasized that "the UN controls vast budgets; it has the ability to authorize wars and sanctions and is also a way of conveying world opinion. . . . It is undeniable that it is a place of concentrated power and resources" (J. Stern, personal communication, October 28, 2020). Through its daily work at the UN, OutRight influences governments, establishes critical alliances, informs partners on the ground, lobbies to pass resolutions, and advances the representation of LGBTQ people and issues. Stern described their consultative status with the Economic and Social Council (ECOSOC) as a path to the front door of influence and power—it entitles them to sit in negotiations, observe what governments are saying about LGBTQ issues, deliver statements into the record, and it puts the UN and member states on notice that the LGBTQ community is present. Having a seat at the UN table has allowed OutRight to make significant advances for LGBTQ rights. For example, OutRight, together with 46 Filipino groups, submitted a report to the UN condemning the violence against LGBTQ groups in the Philippines. The report itself and the advocacy work that followed were instrumental in the passage of the Gender Fair Ordinance Act in the Philippines. This law includes non-discriminatory measures and represents a significant step forward in the direction of LGBTQ rights in the Philippines.

Similarly, capitalizing on its strategic presence at the UN, OutRight created the UN LGBTI Core Group composed of cross-regional member states, the European Union (as an observer), the Office of the High Commissioner for Human Rights, the Human Rights Watch, and Out-Right, to lobby jointly for protection against violence and discrimination based on sexual orientation and gender identity based on Human Rights. The work of this group contributed significantly to the creation of a UN independent expert position in 2016, a historic win for LGBTQ representation globally (OutRight Action International, 2016a). The OutRight network of influence extends to other regional human rights mechanisms, including the Organization of American States and the African Commission on Human and Peoples' Rights.

ILGA has built a significant international influence presence through its offices and the hundreds of NGOs that make up its membership. ILGA-Europe also has consultative status with the UN ECOSOC and maintains advocacy and outreach efforts at the UN Human Rights Council in Geneva. Moreover, through their work with the UN Special Procedures, ILGA-Europe draws attention to the most appalling violations of human rights and provides guidance in the drafting of solutions (ILGA, n.d.).

Although an influential presence at the UN and similar bodies can propel changes and move an organization's vision forward, international mechanisms are not the only avenues to exert strong influence. The Council for Global Equality, for example, recognizes the critical role of the UN, the Organization of American States, and the World Health Organization among others in the advancement of human rights and LGBTQ rights. However, its focus is on advocating to the U.S. government, especially the White House and Congress, ensuring that U.S. foreign policies consider the human rights and civil protection of LGBTQ persons (The Council for Global Equality, 2017). Because of the influential standing of its members, this translates into participation by their staff in congressional hearings, supporting congressional letters, providing evidence directly to the U.S. government of the positive impact of having inclusive foreign policies, and advising U.S. agencies and government personnel on policy documentation.

Open for Business also acknowledges the vital role of participating in these high-level spaces of influence and decision-making. Open for Business collaborated with the UN Office of the High Commissioner for Human Rights to produce a report titled "Channels of Influence" (Open For Business, 2019b) which advises companies on how to best operate in countries violating LGBTQ rights (J. Miller, personal communication, November 18, 2020). Open for Business engages a multitude of other highly influential global platforms including the World Economic Forum at Davos, the European Parliament, and even the Vatican where it argues the economic and business case for advancing LGBTQ rights.

Open For Business has a unique position for influence through the multinational corporations that make up its coalition membership. Its Global Influencer Program aims to create a collective and coherent global voice in support of LGBTQ inclusion as a business and economic development issue and demonstrate that there is a global business consensus that supporting LGBTQ rights is good for business. It uses its membership and connections with high-level businesses and executives globally and nationally to influence media and personally advocate with governments and media. When Open For Business campaigned in Kenya on the basis of the business case for LGBTQ inclusions, it used support of prominent business executives as well as using its connections to gain significant attention in the international press and the notice of internationally renowned businesspeople.

Although All Out is an activist people organization with a focus on campaigns, it is supported by an international advisory board of renowned civil rights organizers, online and offline campaigners, issue experts, policymakers and analysts, and human rights activists from around the world. They also run "pressure campaigns" which are directed at key decision-makers, corporations, and government bodies.

Local Voices Matter: An Inclusive Approach to Social Change

The recognition of local knowledge and the pursuit of collaboration at the local level emerged as a significant trend among the majority of the organizations included in this chapter. They acknowledged the importance of working with local partners on the ground to achieve long lasting meaningful change.

All Out's recognition of the role of local partners is foundational. Its training for young LGBTQ activists on digital rights, its crowdfunding campaigns, and its global petitions are all built on a model that is increasingly more accessible. Grounded on the belief that technology can be a powerful social change tool, All Out invests in training local partners on using that tool more effectively to support LGBTQ communities fight for freedom and equality. As Matt Beard, All Out's Executive Director, argues:

> We believe the fight for equality, and human rights, and dignity of LGBT+ people all around the world will be won and lost on one of these [mobile devices] as well as in the courts, and the streets; a small screen is going to be another place where those rights are won and lost.
>
> *(M. Beard, personal communication, October 30, 2020)*

An example of a successful collaboration with partners on the ground is All Out's response to the 2017 Chechnya crisis when gay men were incarcerated and tortured in detention centers. In partnership with the Russian LGBT Network, All Out not only set up an online petition to denounce this atrocity but also set up a crowdfunding campaign that received donations from 80 different countries. The funds were utilized to rescue victims of and support those targeted by the Chechen government (M. Beard, personal communication, October 30, 2020).

According to Jessica Stern, "OutRight has helped launched thousands of LGBT activists and organizations into deeper and more sophisticated advocacy for their communities," adding that LGBTQ activists working at a local level are the "best advocates for change in their own communities and better equipped to devise and implement solutions because they have lived experience and credibility" (personal communication, October 28, 2020). OutRight supports local advocacy efforts through training in topics such as human rights documentation, safety, accurate reporting as well as hands-on workshops on project management, digital advocacy, and financial administration. OutRight also plays a critical role in connecting local partners with global decision-makers. One way in which they do so is through "Outright Week of Advo-cacy" at the UN, which brings a global delegation of LGBTQ activists to have access to high-level officials, government representatives, international media, and other influencers at the UN headquarters in New York (OutRight International, n.d.).

One of Open for Business' major programmatic efforts is the Local Influencer Program described by Jon Miller as,

> "partnerships at the local level with local civil society organizations led by local people on the ground, fueled by locally commissioned data about the economic implications of discrimination on the ground in the countries that we are working in. And then we use that to unlock networks of advocates in the local business community"

(J. Miller, personal communication, November 18, 2020). Within the Local Influencer Program, there is a particular focus on four regions—Asia Pacific, East Africa, Eastern Europe, and the Carib-bean. The organization starts a local influencer program by doing research in that geographical area and connecting with local activists to produce reports on an LGBTQ issue with a particular focus on the economic and business effects resulting from LGBTQ discrimination. Examples include partnering with Virgin Atlantic to produce an innovative report on the impact that anti-LGBTQ policies and stigma has on the Caribbean tourism economy and working with Google and a foundation partner to construct a data-driven economic case for LGBTQ rights in Eastern Europe. By making an economic and business case for non-discrimination and decriminalization of activities based on SOGI, Open For Business can unlock new and powerful channels of advocacy which may not as easily as accessed as by starting with a human rights argument (Open For Business, n.d.b., Local).

In addition to their long-term programs, Open For Business also organizes collective action from coalition partners to support LGBTQ rights movements around the world. For example, they are working with two local organizations—Lawyers for LGBTQ and Allies Network (LLAN) and Marriage for All Japan—particularly by identifying additional multinational corporations to support Japan's movement for marriage equality. When Brunei implemented a penal code that criminalizes same-sex acts with death by stoning, Open For Business created a guidance note for coalition partners to communicate the situation to employees with clear suggested actions such as removing the Sultanate of Brunei's hotels from their supplier lists.

ILGA is a coalition of organizations from more than 150 countries representing many local communities which are described as the foundation of the organizations. ILGA is driven by local activists—and its board is democratically selected from local queer activists around the world (ILGA, n.d.). ILGA as an organization provides

> access outside their own community to the UN and to other (global and domestic) LGBTQ organizations . . . people are often so isolated in their national environments connecting internationally only with other human rights activists. We give them a global stage and people feel so much more united with others in the queer movement which is actually very global.
>
> *(A. Plessis, personal communication, December 10, 2020)*

ILGA provides resources and support to local groups through research, reports, and capacity-building trainings. It holds regular conferences and meetings for networking and information sharing and capacity building. Recently, ILGA World launched a toolkit to help members within each region on how to engage with the UN Treaty Bodies. Local organizations are also used to vet potential members in their regions and are in integral part of the membership approval process (ILGA, n.d.).

The Council for Global Equality does not operate directly in other countries, rather it relies on its coalition members for information and insight from their individual targeted constituencies—both domestically and globally—to bring to a shared advocacy effort for global protection of LGBTQ rights. The Council then uses leverage, diplomacy, and influence of the U.S. Government, U.S. agencies, U.S. embassies, and the State Department as well as multinational corporations to promote and effect just treatment of LGBTQ individuals in other countries throughout the world. In particular, it connects local LGBTQ groups with local offices and embassies (Council for Global Equality, 2017).

Implications for Policy and Practice

Based on the findings, where the LGBTQ organizations are situated today, and the literature on TANS, LGBTQ rights, and NGOs, we have identified two major implications for policy and practice which are outlined in the following.

Changing Laws and Opinion—Softly

Despite many years of engagement with multiple UN institutions by LGBTQ activists, very few states unequivocally protect and support the rights of LGBTQ people through domestic legislation and enforcement of that legislation. What has been more successful is a soft-law approach, one where NGOs create a climate of opinion supportive of LGBTQ people by working through the UN and other treaty bodies, debating issues in public forums, and constantly challenging and promoting a standard of state policy in relation to these rights. By issuing normative sexual rights statements grounded in international human rights, they provide standards that act as "both models and inducements" for behavior and legislation (Roseman, 2011, p. 338). A notable example of this is the 2006 Yogyakarta Principles (and the 2017 update) which address a broad range of international human rights standards and their application to SOGI issues.

Just as critical to setting the path for domestic legislation are the multiple, continuous, and public activities and programs by these LGBTQ organizations. These activities and programs contribute to a cascade of norms which create a supportive and normative environment for LGBTQ people both globally and locally. Norms are standards or patterns of appropriate or desirable social behavior. Where states have no domestic or local motivation for supporting LGBTQ rights, international and transnational influences become far more important than domestic pressures for adopting norms, and international norms set the standards for the appropriate behavior of states. "A combination of pressure for conformity, desire to enhance international legitimation, and the desire of state leaders to enhance their self-esteem facilitate norm cascades" (Finnemore & Sikkink, 1998, p. 895). Bob (2009) explains how non-governmental actors can create new norms of international law by framing "long-felt grievances as normative claims" and then introduce these new rights into the international agenda by convincing transnational NGOs to support them and put pressure states to accept them (p. 2).

Each of these five organizations in this chapter provide platforms, an international perspective, and a human rights framework for activities which contribute collectively and individually to this cascade of norms. Social media campaigns, leverage of corporate connections, international boycotts, collection and publication of data, public debates, and advising and lobbying foreign affairs departments are all examples of activities which seek to promote and reinforce positive norms in support of SOGI issues. However, in order to influence opinion, policy, and practice, these organizations need to work together in promoting a cohesive message and framework; it is the human rights framework that provides the overall consistency and effectiveness.

Boomerang Effect—Local to Global and Back Again

A key aspect of the work of the LGBTQ organizations in this chapter is their interaction with local groups and activists. In their seminal work on the function of transnational movements, Keck and Sikkink (1998) describe a key feature of a TAN as "the ability to call upon powerful actors to affect a situation, where weaker members of a network are unlikely to have influence" (p. 16). Keck and Sikkink describe this interaction as a "boomerang pattern of influence" and outline how it activates transnational activist networks. When an NGO or local group in one state cannot get traction for their cause, it throws a boomerang towards the TAN. The group's hope is that, by getting international allies to bring pressure on the government of their state, the boomerang will return, hitting its target with international pressure. This pressure can be applied from high-profile constituents of the TAN such as a multinational corporation, international allies of a regime, or a transnational citizens' mobilization on social media. Transnational NGOs such as the five LGBTQ organizations in this chapter play a pivotal role in taking up local causes and supporting campaigns. It is possible to see the boomerang effect in their activities and their roles as brokers, coordinators, and allies, as the boomerang "passes through" various other groups, media, and government departments before returning to make a difference at the place from which it was originally thrown.

The use of the boomerang metaphor can also illustrate challenges for the NGOs. Tarrow (2005) notes that the boomerang works best when thrown upwards (in terms of global hierarchies of power) rather than horizontally towards other similar groups which are not connected to the major power centers of the network (Tarrow, 2005, p. 158). Moreover, when the point of decision-making is further away, those in the locality most directly affected may have less opportunity for input. Also, NGOs that represent a coalition based on solidarity and human rights must be careful not to reproduce features of global power relationships. Perhaps the most challenging issue for these transnational NGOs is in choosing which boomerangs they catch and pass on.

The relationship with local groups is not just one way; transnational NGOs rely on local groups in many different ways. As global representatives of a transnational network, these NGOs have to be seen to support all LGBTQ people throughout the world, yet as Keck and Sikkink (1998) point out, "most international organizations cannot afford to maintain staff people in a variety of countries . . . forging links with local organizations allows groups to receive and monitor information from many countries at a low cost" (p. 22). Through interviews and evidence gathering, local activists are able to collect information that may not be otherwise available to international NGOs.

As we have seen with the work of the LGBTQ organizations in this chapter, discussions and implementation of those rights and protections have to be tailored to the local context and resonate with the local cultural framework in order for human rights to be accepted as they relate to SOGI. Local activists are essential as translators and advisors in helping spread and vernacularize these concepts as a strategy for providing human rights as a foundation for the protection of LGBTQ people.

Conclusion

For the LGBTQ transnational organizations in this chapter, connecting the identity politics of LGBTQ activism with mainstream human rights advocacy provides both challenges and advantages. There is still research and controversy around the globalization of sexual identity, and perceived dangers in a global solidarity of a gay identity being defined by the global North (Binnie, 2004; Silva & Ornat, 2013) or of human rights being an imposition of Western Imperialism over vulnerable states. However, the very existence of transnational organizations organized around advocacy for LGBTQ rights supports the idea of a universal gay identity, however defined, as opposed to individual and domestic cultures and beliefs about SOGI. And as we have seen, the transnational organizations are often the most essential to advocating and helping those most oppressed.

The LGBTQ organizations featured in this chapter are characterized by the persistence of their efforts to achieve LGBTQ equality globally and the contagious optimism with which they embrace this work. For several of them, the next few years are expected to bring additional opportunities to amplify their work. All Out, for instance, seeks to engage more supporters in the global South through meaningful opportunities including training for activists in Latin America and Africa. OutRight foresees an opportunity to continue pushing for the decriminalization of homosexuality and the enactment of legal gender-identity recognition. Open for Business seeks to continue shedding light on the role of the business angle in this advocacy movement and hopes to scale up its existing programs. Both ILGA and the Council for Global Equality agree that LGBTQ rights work can make additional strides, through the UN sustainable development framework and its 2030 agenda.

> I really believe that the global LGBTIQ movement is one of the fastest growing and most effective movements the world has ever seen and the amount of progress in the last 100 years, in the last 20 years, in the last 2 years is extraordinary. I believe that when you establish that progress is possible, that it inspires people.
>
> *(J. Stern, personal communication, October 28, 2020)*

While each organization's specific future plans are tied to their areas of expertise, they agree on an overarching long-term goal: to achieve LGBTQ equality, to ensure safety and dignity for all LGBTQ people, and to end all forms of discrimination against LGBTQ people. They truly see themselves in a journey towards progress in which the ultimate goal is that they will not be needed any longer.

References

All Out. (n.d.a). *What is all out.* https://allout.org/en/what-all-out

All Out. (n.d.b). *Highlights: Fighting against "LGBT-free zones" in Poland.* https://allout.org/en/highlights/fighting-against-lgbt-free-zones-poland

Binnie, J. (2004). *The globalization of sexuality.* SAGE. https://doi.org/10.4135/9781446218341

Bob, C. (2009). *The international struggle for new human rights.* University of Pennsylvania Press. www.jstor.org/stable/j.ctt3fhfth.3

Born Free and Equal. (2019). *United Nations OCHR* (2nd ed.). www.ohchr.org/Documents/Publications/Born_Free_and_Equal_WEB.pdf

The Council for Global Equality. (2017). www.globalequality.org/

European Parliament. (2021). *Parliament declares the European Union an "LGBTIQ Freedom Zone".* www.europarl.europa.eu/news/en/press-room/20210304IPR99219/parliament-declares-the-european-union-an-lgbtiq-freedom-zone

Falk, R. (1992). Cultural foundations for the international protection of human rights. In A. An-Na'im (Ed.), *Human rights in a cross cultural perspective: A quest for consensus.* University of Pennsylvania Press.

Finnemore, M., & Sikkink, K. (1998). International norms dynamics and political change. *International Organization, 52*(4), 887–917.

Howard, R. (1995). *Human rights and the search for the community.* Westview Press.

ILGA: Constitution. (2016). https://ilga.org/downloads/ILGA_Constitution_2016.pdf

ILGA: The International Lesbian, Gay, Bisexual, Trans and Intersex Association, ILGA. (n.d.). https://ilga.org

Keck, M. E., & Sikkink, K. (1998). *Activists beyond borders: Advocacy networks in international politics.* Cornell University Press.

Keck, M. E., & Sikkink, K. (1999). Transnational advocacy networks in international and regional politics. *International Social Science Journal, 51,* 89–101. https://doi.org/10.1111/1468-2451.00179

Linde, R. (2018). *Gatekeeper persuasion and issue adoption: Amnesty international and the transnational LGBTQ network.* Rhode Island College Faculty Publications. https://digitalcommons.ric.edu/facultypublications/406

Mertus, J. (2007). The rejection of human rights framings: The case of LGBT advocacy in the US. *Human Rights Quarterly, 29*(4), 1036–1064. www.jstor.org/stable/20072835

Mertus, J. (2009). Applying the gatekeeper model of human rights activism: The U.S.-based movement for LGBT rights. In C. Bob (Ed.), *The international struggle for new human rights.* University of Pennsylvania Press. www.jstor.org/stable/j.ctt3fhfth.6

Open For Business. (n.d.a). *About us.* http://Open-for-Business.org/About

Open For Business. (n.d.b). *Local influencer programs.* https://open-for-business.org/local-influencer-program

Open For Business (2019a). *Kenya.* http://Open-for-Business.org/Kenya-economic-case

Open For Business. (2019b). *Channels of influence.* https://open-for-business.org/reports

OutRight Action International. (n.d.). *About us.* https://outrightinternational.org/about-us

OutRight Action International. (2016a). *United Nations makes history on sexual orientation and gender identity.* https://outrightinternational.org/content/un-human-rights-council-establishes-independent-lgbt-expert

OutRight Action International. (2016b). *Equality prevails at UN general assembly; SOGI independent expert position protected.* https://outrightinternational.org/content/sogi-independent-expert-position-protected

Roseman, M. J., & Miller, A. M. (2011). Normalizing sex and its discontents: Establishing sexual rights in international law. *Harvard Journal of Law and Gender, 34,* 313–375. https://doi.org/10.1080/1 4754835.2017.1332518

Rupp, L. (2011). The persistence of transnational organizing: The case of the homophile movement. *The American Historical Review, 161*(4), 1014–1039.

Secretary-General Ban Ki-Moon, Pledges Support for Decriminalization of Homosexuality. (2010, December 21). *United Nations human rights office of the high commissioner.* www.ohchr.org/EN/NewsEvents/Pages/SGpledgessupportfordecriminalizationhomosexuality.aspx

Seo, H., Kim, J. Y., & Yang, S. (2009). Global activism and new media: A study of transnational NGOs' online public relations. *Public Relations Review, 35*(2), 123–126. https://doi.org/10.1016/j.pubrev.2009.02.002.

Silva, J. M., & Ornat, M. (2013). The globalization of sexuality: An interview with Jon Binnie. *Revista Latino-americana de Geografia e Genero, 4*(2), 195–200. https://doi.org/10.5212/Rlagg.v.4.i1.3048

Smith, J., Pagnucco, R., & Lopez, G. A. (1998). Globalizing human rights: The work of transnational human rights NGOs in the 1990s. *Human Rights Quarterly, 20*(2), 379–412. The Johns Hopkins University Press. www.jstor.org/stable/762770

Stovel, K., & Shaw, L. (2012). Brokerage. *Annual Review of Sociology, 38,* 139–158 https://doi.org/10.1146/annurev-soc-081309-150054

Tarrow, S. (2005). *The new transactional activism.* Cambridge.

Thoreson, R. (2014). *Transnational LGBT activism.* University of Minnesota Press.

The Yogyakarta Principles. https://yogyakartaprinciples.org/

3

WHY NOW?

LGBTI Rights and the United Nations

Ariel G. Mekler

In 1992, Douglas Sanders, an openly gay man, spoke on behalf of Human Rights Advocates and the International Lesbian and Gay Association (ILGA), addressing the 44th session of the United Nations (UN) Sub-Commission on the Prevention of Discrimination and Protection of Minorities (Kayal et al., 1993). The Sub-Commission was the main subsidiary body of the former UN Commission on Human Rights. In his address, Sanders proposed the appointment of a Special Rapporteur to study discrimination against gays and lesbians (Sanders, 1996). Another 25 years passed before the Human Rights Council appointed an Independent Expert on protection against violence and discrimination based on sexual orientation and gender identity, otherwise known as the Independent Expert on sexual orientation and gender identity (IE SOGI).

The appointment of the Independent Expert is one of a growing number of UN wide efforts committed to the fundamental rights of lesbian, gay, bisexual, transgender, and intersex (LGBTI) people. Since the passing of resolution 17/19 in 2011, the first UN Human Rights Council resolution on sexual orientation and gender identity (SOGI), numerous organizations across the UN system, from the Office of the High Commissioner of Human Rights (OHCHR) to the United Nations Development Programme (UNDP), have affirmed their commitment to the elimination of discrimination and violence based on SOGI (UN HRC, 2011). This affirmation is part of a larger normative change strategy I call LGBTI mainstreaming. I use the LGBTI acronym in the context of LGBTI mainstreaming as a place holder embodying a long history of sexual diversity and gender expansiveness. I do not include the Q, which represents queer, in the acronym because UN's wide work on sexual orientation and gender identity as of early 2022 regularly uses LGBTI when referring to identity-based categories. Like gender mainstreaming, which evaluates the impact of any UN action on women and men with the goal of achieving gender equality, LGBTI mainstreaming asserts an LGBTI perspective through human rights, international development, and peace and security sectors at the United Nations and is used to raise awareness of LGBTI inequality within research, implementation, and monitoring of programs, policy development, legislation, and resource allocation across the United Nations.

The purpose of this chapter is to examine why LGBTI mainstreaming has gained considerable traction at the UN since the passing of resolution 17/19 by the Human Rights Council in 2011 (UN HRC, 2011). I suggest that although the makeup of the Council presented a political opportunity for LGBTI human rights defenders to put their international rights

DOI: 10.4324/9781003128151-4

on UN agendas, the formation of international LGBTI rights and subsequent mainstreaming at the UN owes its success to transnational advocacy networks (TANs) who have advocated at the international level for decades on behalf of sexual orientation, gender identity, gender expression, and more recently sex characteristics on behalf of intersex people (SOGIESC). Transnational advocacy networks are made up of various actors, including, but not limited to, non-governmental organizations, international non-governmental organizations, intergovernmental organizations, governments, activist groups, independent experts, and civil society leaders. These actors operate in particular international, social, and political contexts and are bound together by a common discourse and shared values (Keck & Sikkink, 1998). Although transnational advocacy networks blur the boundaries between state relations, national citizens, and the international system, their presence can help to explain the variation and the extent to which states internalize human rights norms, namely by putting norm-violating states on the international agenda, empowering and legitimatizing the claims of domestic opposition groups against norm-violating governments, and challenging norm-violating governments by putting pressure on them from above (e.g., international organizations) and below (e.g., domestic advocacy groups). In short, transnational advocacy networks offer a platform for a multiplicity of voices to be heard on international and domestic policies (Keck & Sikkink 1998). The success of LGBTI mainstreaming, I argue, is in part due to transnational advocacy network actors' strategic use of identity-based categories, like LGBTI, and more neutral terminology, like sexual orientation, gender identity, gender expression, and sex characteristics.

This chapter is organized in two parts: first, the passing of resolution 17/19 is explored through the lens of political process theory to examine how the makeup of the Council presented a political opportunity for LGBTI human rights defenders to put their international rights on the UN human rights agenda (UN HRC, 2011). Political process theory, otherwise known as political opportunity theory, is useful to examine how external factors either improve or hinder social movement mobilization (McAdam, 1996; Tarrow, 1996; Tilly, 1978). Next, the formation of international LGBTI rights at the UN by LGBTI transnational advocacy networks is examined using the analytical framework of the three UNs (Weiss et al., 2017). The UN is a complex system that can be thought of as three different, yet interactive, parts—the First UN, that is, member states; the Second UN, that is, the Secretariat and UN career staff; and lastly, the Third UN, that is, civil society broadly defined—who work to cooperate across multiple issue areas (Weiss et al., 2017). The range of transnational advocacy networks working on the advancement of international LGBTI rights is immense. As such, the focus of this chapter is on transnational advocacy network actors who work, or have worked, directly on the formation of international LGBTI rights at the UN using the analytical framework of the three UNs. Narrowing the scope of the network to member states, the Secretariat and UN career staff, and civil society members involved in this process underscores the interactive and interdependent relationship between all three UNs while simultaneously demonstrating how the boundaries between movement and authority structure are blurred when it comes to the formation of international LGBTI rights. It also provides insight into how state and state-adjacent actors capitalize on political opportunities via reciprocal claim making across all three UNs.

Political Opportunity: Human Rights Council on Sexual Orientation and Gender Identity

Broadly defined, political opportunities represent, *"consistent—but not necessarily formal, permanent, or national—signals to social or political actors which either encourage or discourage them to use their internal resources to form social movements"* (Tarrow, 1996, p. 54 italicization in original). In short, political opportunities provide the possibility for action when exogenous factors to a movement, like a shift in institutional structure or a change in ideological outlook from those in power, enhance or inhibit mobilization (McAdam, 1996; Tarrow, 1983; Tilly, 1978). Political opportunity theory is "a staple in social movement inquiry" (McAdam, 1996, p. 22). Despite critiques among social movement scholars that the theory is imprecise, elusive, and runs the risk of being conceptually stretched too thin, the primarily state-centric theory is regularly organized around four main dimensions: (1) the opening of access to an institutionalized political system, (2) shifting elite alignments, (3) presence of influential allies, and (4) the repressive capacity of the state (McAdam, 1996). The relevance of these dimensions, however, becomes a question of political opportunities for whom and political opportunities for what (Meyer & Minkoff, 2004).

As a universal and formal intergovernmental organization (IGO), the United Nations constitutes and constructs the social world while simultaneously having the convening power and legitimacy to make universal claims in part because, given its universal membership, it has no competitor (Barnett & Finnemore, 2004; Rittberger et al., 2006; Weiss et al., 2017). Despite its ability to make universal claims, the UN cannot force member states to take a particular action, such as signing, or ratifying agreed upon treaties. At its core, the UN is comprised of six principal organs including the General Assembly, the Security Council, the Economic and Social Council, the Secretariat, the International Court of Justice, and the Trusteeship Council. Within these principal organs exist programs like the United Nations Development Programme, commissions such as the Commission on the Status of Women, and subsidiary bodies like the Human Rights Council. Formed in 2006, the Human Rights Council is the intergovernmental body responsible for the protection and promotion of international human rights. It consists of 47 member states elected by the UN General Assembly. Each state serves on the Council for a period of three years and cannot be re-elected after two consecutive terms (OHCHR, 2020).

On June 17, 2011, the Council adopted its first ever human rights resolution on SOGI: resolution 17/19 (UN HRC, 2011). Drafted by South Africa and presented to the Council by Brazil, the resolution called on the Office of the High Commissioner for Human Rights to conduct a study on SOGI documenting discriminatory laws and practices; acts of violence against individuals; and to suggest how international human rights law can be used to counter the violence and discrimination experienced. The passing of the resolution did two things. First, it recognized the violence and discrimination perpetrated against individuals because of their presumed or proclaimed sexual orientation or gender identity as a human rights violation worthy of international attention. Second, it linked LGBTI rights to the larger international human rights regime legitimizing the former within the later.

Resolution 17/19 is not the first time the international community recognized violence and discrimination based on SOGI. While the term "international community" evades consensus, for the purpose of this chapter, the term refers to the governments that make up the United Nations. Beginning in 2002 and 2012, the UN General Assembly included the protection of sexual orientation and gender identity, respectively, in its resolutions on extrajudicial, summary, or arbitrary execution (UN GA, 2003, 2012). These resolutions condemn the killing of individuals after being accused of a crime or by a government official without judicial process. Incorporating sexual orientation and gender identity into the resolutions on extrajudicial, summary, or arbitrary executions underscores the reality that homosexuality and gender nonconformity are criminalized in certain parts of the world, and those accused of such "crimes" are subject to this type of egregious violence. Being included in these resolutions sent a signal to the international community that sexual orientation and gender identity are a worthy protected class. What makes resolution 17/19 different from the General Assembly resolution on extrajudicial, summary, or arbitrary executions is the fact that it recognized violence and discrimination based on SOGI as distinct and in need of protection within the broader United Nations human rights regime. As such, the creation and passing of resolution 17/19 presented LGBTI human rights defenders a political opportunity to put their international rights on the UN human rights agenda (UN HRC, 2011).

When it comes to resolution 17/19, the makeup of the Council provided a larger pre-existing LGBTI transnational network the opportunity to include their international rights within the larger institutionalized UN human rights regime (UN HRC, 2011). States who voted in favor of the resolution signaled their capacity to be elite allies to actors across the network. As primary actors, member states hold the most decision-making power at the UN. This enables them to serve as allies across the network using their elite status to further advance international LGBTI rights across UN fora. States like Argentina and Brazil were in a unique position, given their historical support of international LGBTI rights at the UN (O'Flaherty & Fisher, 2008). Their previous support made them part of the pre-existing LGBTI transnational advocacy network while simultaneously serving as an elite ally to other actors in the network. This dual standing allowed them to advocate on behalf of the larger LGBTI transnational network while drawing on past experiences. Their positioning, along with the other states who voted in favor of the resolution, provided actors within the larger LGBTI transnational advocacy network direct access to the Human Rights Council's legal process by securing an entry point for mobilization within the Council's institutionalized system (see Aylward, 2020).

Resolution 17/19 passed with 23 in favor, 19 against, 3 abstaining, and 2 absent (UN HRC, 2011). When the resolution was brought to the floor, the Council included 12 new member states from the previous year; however, at the time of the vote, Libya's membership was suspended by the General Assembly because of the violent response by the Qadhafi regime to political protesters. Of the new remaining Council members, a majority voted in favor of resolution 17/19 signaling two things. The first was a diminished capacity to repress or obstruct the advancement of international LGBTI rights. The second was the fact that the new structural makeup of the Council brought with it an ideological shift among member states who held that the violence and discrimination experienced based on SOGI was in fact a grave human rights abuse worthy of the Council's attention (see Vance et al., 2018). At the same time, the divisive nature of the resolution signaled a strong divide between member states on the Council who voted in favor of the resolution and governments from Islamic and African countries who requested the withdrawal of the resolution (Jordaan, 2017).

Had the makeup of the Council been different, the resolution, most likely, would have been delayed, dropped, or rejected. The Council makeup was a necessary, but not fully sufficient, component for the adoption of the resolution. It was also a necessary, but not fully sufficient, component for the continued mobilization of international LGBTI rights and subsequent mainstreaming of SOGI at the UN. To better understand the success of the latter two processes, we must examine the work of an LGBTI transnational advocacy network at the United Nations to appreciate how the boundaries between movement and authority structure are blurred.

LGBTI Transnational Advocacy Networks

The following section provides a brief overview of an LGBTI transnational advocacy network using the First, Second, and Third UN framework to historicize the formation of international LGBTI rights across the UN. The subsequent mainstreaming process owes its success to those who have advocated at the international level for decades on behalf of sexual orientation, gender identity, gender expression, and more recently sex characteristics.

Member States: The First UN

The UN is an intergovernmental organization comprised of member states who assembled based on the norm of sovereignty. There are currently 193 member states, each bringing different values, ideologies, and capacities (Weiss et al., 2017). As mentioned earlier, the UN system is complex and best thought of as three separate, yet interactive, parts (Weiss et al., 2017). The First UN comprises all 193 member states (Weiss et al., 2017). Member states sign treaties, create policy, sponsor, and vote on resolutions, which, when passed, are considered formal decrees of the United Nations. Resolutions are not binding documents; however, they serve as guiding rules or recommendations agreed upon by governments and the issuing UN body. Member-state representatives govern primary and subsequent UN bodies, including the Human Rights Council (Weiss et al., 2017).

To date, only three resolutions on SOGI have been issued by the Human Rights Council. This is not to insinuate that the issue has been absent from member-state advocacy over the years. Attempts were made by Brazil in 2003 to bring a human rights and sexual orientation resolution before the former UN Commission on Human Rights. The resolution was deferred to 2004 and dropped in 2005 due to heavy objections from the Holy See, the foreign policy arm of the Vatican, and the Organization of Islamic Conferences (Beetham, 2014; Aylward, 2020). In 2005, New Zealand condemned the Commission for failing to address the 2003 resolution, delivering a joint statement on behalf of 32 states in support of the universality of human rights regardless of sexual orientation (O'Flaherty & Fisher, 2008). After the Commission was replaced by the Human Rights Council in 2006, Norway delivered a joint statement on behalf of 54 states requesting to discuss the issue of sexual orientation and gender identity, marking the first use of the term gender identity in a member-state UN statement (O'Flaherty & Fisher, 2008). In 2008, the topic of sexual orientation and gender identity was raised at the General Assembly by Argentina in a joint statement on behalf of 66 states calling on all member states to commit to the promotion and protection of human rights regardless of SOGI. In 2011, just months before resolution 17/19 was sponsored by South Africa, the Council received yet another joint statement presented by Colombia on behalf of 85 states once again condemning the violence and discrimination experienced based on SOGI (Joint Statement, 2011).

The aforementioned examples demonstrate two things. First, they show growing state support over the past decade for the protection of SOGI within the larger human rights regime. This growing support signaled to both states and INGOs an increase in political openness across the First UN in support of international LGBTI rights. This openness, in turn, afforded acting Council members the opportunity to reform Human Rights Council policy on SOGI when the 2011 resolution was brought to the floor. Having South Africa sponsor the resolution presented another essential political opportunity for the formation of international LGBTI rights. It offered an adjacent signaling to the international community that the violence and discrimination experienced based upon SOGI minority status was not simply a western issue but a matter affecting individuals from all corners of the world.

Unfortunately, member-state support does not automatically mean that the state has a decent record protecting individuals from targeted SOGI violence or discrimination. Black South African lesbians, transwomen, and gender non-conforming populations, for example, face disproportionate levels of gender- and sexual-based violence (GSBV), despite a clear prohibition of discrimination based on sexual orientation in the South African post-apartheid constitution (Action Aid, 2009). Similarly, Brazil's domestic legal framework ensures the protection of LGBTI persons; however, the country has one of the highest murder rates in the world of individuals based upon SOGI minority status (Mendes et al., 2020). While these two states have reaffirmed their commitment at the international level to the eradication of violence and discrimination based on sexual orientation or gender identity, their domestic reality is a stark reminder of the egregious types of violence perpetrated against individuals on account of their SOGI.

The second thing government statements and resolutions demonstrate is a clear use of language that avoids identity-based categories, such as gay, lesbian, bisexual, transgender, or intersex. Ironically, the growing inclusion of gender identity in member-state advocacy initiatives regularly treats gender identity or expression as something experienced by transgender people rather than something experienced by all people (Franke, 2012; Otto, 2015). Such oversights are important to keep in mind because the language agreed upon by member states sets a precedent throughout the international system and is implemented in future UN policies. It also plays a key role in the way states understand their international obligations. In 1993, for example, the General Assembly adopted resolution 47/237, designating May 15 as International Day of Families (UN GA, 1993). The simple act of pluralizing the word family demonstrates an acknowledgment by states that families exist in multiple forms. Debate over the ever-changing notion of what family means is ongoing and includes, but is not limited to, the protection of single-parent families, same-sex partnerships, and children born out of wedlock (Carmona, 2017). This example demonstrates how language adopted by states has the power to determine who is included or excluded from United Nations policy.

Given the authority member states have in the formation of LGBTI rights, the balance of representation is a tricky matter when considering the diverse range of global sexualities and gender expressions. Statements and resolutions that use neutral terminology like sexual orientation and gender identity indicate that member states are perhaps adept at averting the use of western negotiated identity-based categories, like LGBTI, in formal documents. However, even the use of supposedly neutral terminology perpetuates standardized assumptions that everyone has a distinct sexual orientation or specific gender identity (Waites, 2009). Such assumptions omit indigenous sexual identities, gender non-conforming, and asexual individuals from programing and policy initiatives (Cottet & Picq, 2019; Waites, 2009). At the same time, states resisting LGBTI identities are rendered inferior to western progressive values (Klapeer, 2017; Rahman, 2014). States opposing international LGBTI rights argue that the west is creating new rights and "impos[ing] those rights upon others" (Voss, 2017, p. 19). Paradoxically, both pro-LGBTI and anti-LGBTI governments believe their position on SOGI to be universal, viewing the other side as revisionist and controversial (Voss, 2017).

The divisive nature of international LGBTI rights has, and will continue, to be a widening gulf between member states. Although the "translation of western LGBT sexualities onto the rest of the world is usually implied," member states in support of international LGBTI rights are cognizant of how identity-based categories are perceived across the international community (Cottet & Picq, 2019, p. 2). By using more neutral language in formal documents, and linking fundamental rights of individuals regardless of SOGI, member states can focus their attention on the disproportionate levels of violence and discrimination experienced because of one's perceived or proclaimed SOGI. While this strategy leaves something to be desired, like specific representation of LGBTI individuals, member states are but one part of the larger LGBTI transnational advocacy network. The next section explores the role of Second UN actors in the formation of international LGBTI rights, including their strategic use of the LGBTI acronym.

The Secretariat and Career Staff: The Second UN

In addition to member states, the UN is comprised of a Secretariat and career staff. These actors represent the Second UN entity. As international civil servants, Second UN actors present new ideas and debate (in)formally with member states about contemporary global affairs (Weiss et al., 2009). The Second UN creates and interprets bureaucratic rules by developing both authority and autonomy through professional expertise. Staff members tackle problems, advocate for change, and carry the responsibility of implementation within the UN system (Barnett & Finnemore, 2004; Weiss et al., 2009). Long-serving staff members and, by extension, the UN departments, programs, or committees they work for, help serve, supplement, and assist states, operating as support to increase effectiveness of member states broaching common problems (Claude, 1956; Rittberger et al., 2006). When it comes to international LGBTI rights, the Office of the UN High Commissioner for Human Rights, a subsidiary department of the UN Secretariat, has taken the lead over the years working directly with member states and international non-governmental organizations.

Seizing the opportunity to mobilize after the 17/19 resolution passed, the OHCHR published a 60-page booklet in 2012, *Born Free and Equal*, for states to better understand their legal obligations to protect the human rights of LGBTI individuals. The following year, the OHCHR launched the Free and Equal Campaign aimed at promoting the equal rights of LGBTI people. Campaigns and publications are a way for the Second UN to raise awareness of a particular issue through educational means. Campaigns also function as an accountability politic allowing network members the opportunity to hold powerful actors outside the network accountable to previously agreed upon principles (Keck & Sikkink, 1998). Campaigns and publications also open political access to the UN, creating a political opportunity for different actors in the network to mobilize using the information provided. Second UN actors, by virtue of their position within the institution, add a degree of legitimacy to topics of international interest and are political actors working to shape political action (Barnett & Finnemore, 2004; Weiss et al., 2017).

As international civil servants, long-time staff at the OHCHR shape political action by underscoring the disproportionate violence and discrimination experienced based on SOGI through campaigns like Free and Equal. They also shape the formation of LGBTI rights through the application and use of identity-based categories. Unlike formal First UN statements and resolutions that use more neutral language, Second UN actors use identity-based categories such as lesbian, gay, bisexual, transgender, and more recently, intersex, to emphasize how these specific individuals experience oppression. These acts are important because they demonstrate how Second UN actors shape political action outside the realm of the state. By choosing to acknowledge that LGBTI people exist, that they are not sick, diseased, or deviant, Second UN actors normalize LGBTI persons through representation and visibility. While the passing of resolution 17/19 mitigated previous forms of institutional repression by directly making SOGI a relevant issue within the greater international human rights regime, the ability of OHCHR staff to shape political action stems from high-level officials, like the former High Commissioner for Human Rights, Navi Pillay, and former Secretary-General Ban Ki-moon, incorporating the fundamental rights of LGBTI people as part of their UN work (OHCHR Statement, 2008; OHCHR Report, 2011, 2015; Secretary-General Statement, 2011).

As a former legal scholar, Navi Pillay helped develop the equality clause in the post-apartheid South African Constitution, which prohibits discrimination on the grounds of sexual orientation. As the UN High Commissioner of Human Rights, she adamantly denounced human rights violations against LGBTI people. In 2010, she addressed the issue of violence and criminal sanctions based on SOGI at a side event during the 15th session of the Human Rights Council. She also read a written statement on behalf of Secretary-General Ban Ki-moon addressing the same topic (Secretary-General Statement, 2010). Like Navi Pillay, Secretary-General Ban Ki-moon, a career former diplomat and politician from South Korea, was an avid supporter of LGBTI rights. Early in his tenure as Secretary-General, he pledged his support for the decriminalization of homosexuality urging all states to protect the rights of LGBTI people (Secretary-General Statement, 2010). As high-level Secretariats, these actions signaled other LGBTI transnational advocacy network actors of their influential ally position. As allies, Navi Pillay and Ban Ki-moon acted as guarantors against state sponsored homo-transphobia providing the larger LGBTI transnational advocacy network opportunities to mobilize on behalf of LGBTI rights at the United Nations. This positioning fostered the formation of international LGBTI rights prior to resolution 17/19 by creating a new political openness within the institutional politics of the UN that centered the visibility of LGBTI people through the use of identity-based categories.

By using identity-based categories, Second UN actors are constituting and constructing the social world by formulating new ways of doing their own work in response to the changing world (Barnett & Finnemore, 2004). In his comparative study of European LGBT movements, Philip Ayoub (2016) keenly observes, "Visibility facilitates the construction of politically salient identity markers and can inspire marginalized people to create the networks of trust and solidarity that lead to mobilization" (p. 23). Through the use of identity-based categories, members of the Second UN help the formation of international LGBTI rights and subsequent mainstreaming by enabling a pathway for LGBTI individuals to reach beyond state boundaries. This type of pathway is vital for those existing within states that criminalizes individuals on account of their SOGI. Bypassing local government to create a direct connection with international forums like the OHCHR is what international relations scholars Margaret E. Keck and Kathryn Sikkink (1998) refer to as the boomerang pattern of influence. These international alliances in turn put pressure on a state to adhere to their international obligations from the outside.

Second UN actors such as Navi Pillay, Ban Ki-moon, and the countless international civil service staff who work within the Secretariat recognized the growing salience of identity-based categories and made a conscious decision to employ this language in their outward facing advocacy (see OHCHR, 2012). Second UN actors capitalized on their informal power relations within the UN to seize the opportunity and incorporate identity-based categories in their own work. Through this action, Second UN actors paved the way for other transnational advocacy network actors, whether member states or INGOs, to shift the formal institutional structure towards policy reform. UN bureaucracy ended up defining new international interests by serving as allies to the rest of the network and by establishing an entry point within the institutionalized political system of the UN. To ignore the workings of the Second UN is to assume that the formation of international LGBTI rights only comes into being when states deem it appropriate. As the aforementioned examples demonstrate, the formation of international LGBTI rights owes a great deal to members of the Second UN who have strategically used their independent diplomatic skills to bring the issue to the forefront of UN agendas.

Before discussing the Third UN, I want to briefly acknowledge that adjacent to developments in the UN proper, Second UN actors have addressed the rights of LGBTI individuals for decades. In 1990, the World Health Organization declassified homosexuality as a mental disease from the International Statistical Classification of Diseases (Sanders, 1996). With the formation of UNAIDS in 1996, Second UN actors emphasized the social and legal systematic discriminations experienced by gay men, bisexuals, and sex workers signifying an early acknowledgment of the human rights violations experienced on account of one's SOGI (UNAIDS, 1999, 2002). Mentioning sex workers is important in this context because of the disproportionate number of transgender women, in particular transgender women of color, who pursue sex work as a means of survival (Aylward, 2020). Although early UNAIDS documents failed to directly mention transgender sex workers, contemporary research clearly documents the disproportionate rate of infection among transgender individuals who have transactional sex (Aylaward, 2020; WHO, 2015).

As the aforementioned section demonstrates, Second UN actors have played a large role in the formation of international LGBTI rights and subsequent mainstreaming. Their actions reveal the complexity associated with the way state-adjacent actors blur the line between movement and authority structure. I now turn to the Third UN to explore how civil society, broadly defined, has participated in the formation of international LGBTI rights.

Civil Society: The Third UN

The Third UN entity is comprised of various individuals and organizations ranging from non-governmental organizations (NGOs), to independent experts and special rapporteurs elected by UN bodies, to academics and individual activists (Weiss et al., 2009, 2017). Third UN actors work directly with both First and Second UN actors by providing the opportunity for individuals to engage in UN affairs (Weiss et al., 2017). Between 1975 and 1985, the UN made women's issues a top policy priority declaring this the Decade for Women. The shift in focus toward women's issues provided lesbian feminist activists the opportunity to mobilize advocating on behalf of sexual rights at the UN World Conferences on Women held between 1975 and 1995. This early collective action housed the issue of sexual orientation and sexual autonomy under the umbrella of sexual and reproductive rights (Aylward, 2020). While the issue of sexual orientation remained low key during the Mexico (1975) and Copenhagen (1980) conferences, the 1985 Nairobi conference centered the issue during a Lesbian Press Conference where women from multiple geographic locations spoke about their experience to the press (Bunch & Hinojosa, 2000). This public event made it clear that the inclusion of sexual orientation had cross-regional support from Latin America to Asia to Africa (Bunch & Hinojosa, 2000).

Including sexual orientation in forum committee discussions was successful in part because the issue of lesbianism and lesbian rights were discussed in the broader context of feminism (Bunch & Hinojosa, 2000; Çagatay et al., 1986). By the 1995 Beijing World Conference on Women, lesbian feminist organizers rallied around a collective action agenda by naming and publicizing the ill effects of homophobia as "one of the most prevalent and brutal ways by which states, and societies control all women's sexualities: by marginalizing and penalizing dissident forms of sexual expression" (Rothchild, 2005, p. 86). Four references to sexual orientation made it into the Beijing Draft Platform for Action because lesbian participation emerged from transnational organizing at the previous World Conferences on Women and because lesbians participated in preliminary Conferences and NGO forums to ensure that their input was included in the Platform for Action (Radford, 1996; Wilson, 1996). This transnational organizing located within the broader global women's movement led to the creation of a lesbian caucus which, in addition to meeting daily during the Beijing Conference, was granted an NGO slot by the NGO forum to speak at the main plenary (Bunch & Hinojosa, 2000). NGOs forums run parallel to official intergovernmental conferences and are places where civil society actors can give input on conference agenda items. While no mention of sexual orientation, sexual rights, or homophobia made its way into the Beijing Platform for Action, the mere fact that sexual orientation was discussed on the Main Committee floor was considered a success for lesbian feminist organizers (Rothchild, 2005).

A decade after the Beijing Women's Conference, a group of multilateral actors including INGOs, individual activists, United Nations independent experts, and former UN career staff organized to discuss the application of international human rights law in relation to sexual orientation and gender identity. The result was the 2006 Yogyakarta Principles. Although nonbinding, these principles set an international precedent mapping the human rights violations experienced based on one's sexual orientation, gender identity, gender expression, or sex characteristics (SOGIESC); applying international human rights law to said violations; and lastly, delineating states' legal obligations in relation to the violence and discrimination experienced based on SOGIESC (O'Flaherty & Fisher, 2008; The Yogyakarta Principles, 2006, 2017). Of the 29 experts invited to participate, 13 where either "current or former UN human rights special mechanism office holders," including former UN High Commissioner for Human Rights, Mary Robinson (O'Flaherty & Fisher, 2008, p. 233). Updated in 2017, neither the original 2006 version nor 2017 Yogyakarta Principles mention LGBTI identity-based categories (The Yogyakarta Principles, 2006, 2017). Instead, the terms sexual orientation, gender identity, gender expression, and sex characteristics are used throughout the principles.

The creation of the Yogyakarta Principles is a clear example of LGBTI transnational advocacy networks in action. At the time of its conception in 2005, SOGI issues were met with contradictory acceptance among member states at the UN. The 2004 General Assembly resolution on extrajudicial, summary, or arbitrary execution included sexual orientation, while the 2003 Brazilian resolution on SOGI was officially dropped from the former UN Commission on Human Rights agenda in 2005. The international community's inconsistent propensity towards the repression of SOGI within UN policy motivated collective action among Third UN actors to address the issue of international human rights law in relation to SOGI head on. Third UN actors from judges to activists to INGOs like ARC-International, an international LGBTI rights Canadian-based organization, worked alongside former UN career staff to create the principles. When the principles were launched at a Human Rights Council side event in 2007, an array of multilateral actors attended, including member-state delegates. This widespread support reveals two things. First, the omission of identity-based categories suggests an understanding by Third UN actors of their own positionality in the formation of international LGBTI rights. Even if some Third UN actors outwardly identified as LGBTI, omission of the acronym from the Yogyakarta Principles is a testament to the range of individuals who drafted the principles and who represented a diverse range of genders and sexualities from all geographical regions of the world (O'Flaherty & Fisher, 2008). Avoiding western negotiated identity-based categories in an international document speaks to Third UN actors' reflexive capacity to recognize their own positionality in the formation of international LGBTI rights. Second, it suggests that more current expressions, like international LGBTI rights or international LGBTI rights movement, use the acronym as an umbrella placeholder for the vast array of genders and sexualities existing across the globe.

The formation of international LGBTI rights within the Third UN cannot be discussed without addressing one of its key actors: the international non-governmental organization. NGOs and INGOs are particularly important actors within the Third UN because they have the influence to expand or limit the scope of global governance. Their success on the international stage is in part because INGOs have the power to reframe issue discourse, while also seeking to change the policies and behaviors of both government and intergovernmental organizations (Karns & Mignst, 2004). INGOs play a key role in social movements creating coalitions and networks across a vast arrangement of issue areas. The ILGA and ARC-International along with OutRight Action International are three INGOs who advocate on behalf of LGBTI civil society.

Established in 1978, ILGA represents over 1,600 LGBTI organizations. They work directly with the Human Rights Council via human rights mechanisms like the Universal Periodic Review and treaty body committees. The former is a process by which states demonstrate actions taken to improve their human rights commitments and NGOs and INGOS submit shadow reports and oral statements to the Human Rights Council serving as a watchdog over state declarations. Treaty body committees are made up of independent human rights experts who monitor treaty implementation by states. Founded in 1990, OutRight Action International—formerly known as the International Gay and Lesbian Human Rights Commission—advocates on behalf of LGBTI rights at the United Nations headquarters in New York. The organization is part of the UN LGBTI Core Group, an informal cross-regional group of member states, and currently serves as the group's Secretariat. ARC-International, the youngest of the three organizations formed in 2003, is credited with initiating and convening the coalition of NGOs who implemented the Yogyakarta Principles (Arc-International, n.d.).

All three INGOs have consultative status at the UN, which allows them to observe member states' actions at the UN, give statements and reports directly to Second UN actors, and hold member states accountable to their international obligations. Both ILGA and OutRight International work cross regionally and hold conferences that bring civil society members together with other organizations and government officials to discuss contemporary challenges facing LGBTI individuals across the globe. In addition to helping local activists better understand international mechanisms, the above-listed INGOs get called on by Second UN actors and member states as experts in their own field to share information with UN programs and initiatives, like the 2015 UNDP led LGBTI Inclusion Index, which has since stalled due to lack of funding (Trithart, 2021). They also assist with the conception and realization of UN policy on SOGI and played a large role in the development of all three SOGI Human Rights Council resolutions.

Early international LGBTI activism by Third UN actors clearly shows that the formation of international LGBTI rights and subsequent LGBTI mainstreaming across different UN platforms has a rich history going back decades. It also demonstrates how the language used by Third UN actors embraces identity-based categories like LGBTI while simultaneously embracing the wider more neutral language of sexual orientation, gender identity, gender expression, and sex characteristics suggesting that Third UN actors recognize that gender and sexuality are historically and locally constructed.

Conclusion

Using the framework of the First, Second, and Third UNs to structure an analysis of an LGBTI transnational advocacy network, this chapter demonstrates how the formation of international LGBTI rights and subsequent mainstreaming at the UN has a long-nuanced history going back decades prior to the passing of resolution 17/19. Understanding how institutionalized forms of access across the international community of states generates mobilization for policy reform contributes to a wider application of political opportunity theory beyond its regular state-centered focus. At the same time, focusing on the interdependency of the First, Second, and Third UNs illuminates our understanding of transnational advocacy networks' ability to blur the boundary between movement and authority structure while simultaneously advancing our knowledge on the way transnational advocacy networks approach less supported issue areas such as sexual orientation, gender identity, and more recently gender expression and sex characteristics on international agendas.

Conducting a genealogical examination of the formation of international LGBTI rights at the UN challenges the notion that the formation of these rights is solely articulated through western negotiated identity constructs. Instead, it suggests that actors from all three dimensions across the UN strategically use identity-based categories in tandem with more neutral language, such as sexual orientation, gender identity, gender expression, and sex characteristics. This investigation helps to further knowledge on the wider development and implementation of LGBTI politics while simultaneously advancing our awareness on the intricacies of UN advocacy. While the analysis presented here covers only a small portion of international LGBTI activism, it does reveal the need for future investigation as to whether the formation of international LGBTI rights creates varying degrees of institutional oppression through the reinforcement or privileging of certain rights and identities over others as well as the possible negative effects of LGBTI mainstreaming. Additionally, research on LGBTI mainstreaming across other areas of the UN system, including sustainable development and international peace and security, would help advance SOGIESC concerns beyond the realm of human rights. It is therefore necessary to continue questioning the formation of international LGBTI rights and the actors involved in the process.

References

Action Aid. (2009). *Hate crimes: The rise of "corrective rape" in South Africa*. https://shukumisa.org.za/wp-content/uploads/2017/09/hate-crimes-the-rise-of-corrective-rape-report.pdf

ARC-International. (n.d.). *Background*. https://arc-international.net/about/background/

Aylward, E. (2020). Intergovernmental organizations and nongovernmental organizations: The development of an international approach to LGBT issues. In M. J. Bosia, S. M. McEvoy, & M. Rahman (Eds.), *The Oxford handbook of global LGBT and sexual diversity politics* (pp. 103–120). Oxford University Press.

Ayoub, P. M. (2016). *When states come out: Europe's sexual minority and the politics of visibility*. Cambridge University Press.

Barnett, M., & Finnemore, M. (2004). *Rules for the world. International organizations in global politics*. Cornell University Press.

Beetham, G. (2014). Chapter 17: The human rights of gays, lesbians, bisexual, and transgender people. In A. Mihr & M. Gibney (Eds.), *SAGE handbook of human rights* (pp. 284–304). SAGE.

Bunch, C., & Hinojosa, C. (2000). Lesbians travel the roads of feminisms globally. *Rutgers University Center for Women's Global Leadership*, 1–16. www.cwgl.rutgers.edu/docman/coalition-building-publications/378-lesbianstravel-roadfeminisms-pdf-1/file

Çagatay, N., Grown, C., & Santiago, A. (1986). The Nairobi women's conference: Toward a global feminism? *Feminist Studies*, 12(2), 401–412.

Carmona, M. S. (2017). *A contemporary view of "family" in international human rights law and implications for the sustainable development goals (SDGs)*. UN Women. www.unwomen.org/en/digital-library/publications/2017/12/a-contemporary-view-of-family-in-international-human-rights-law

Claude, I. (1956). *Swords into plowshares: The problems and process of international organization*. McGraw Hill.

Cottet, C., & Picq, M. L. (2019). *Sexuality and translation in world politics*. E-International Relations Publishing.

Franke, K. (2012). Dating the state: The moral hazards of winning gay rights. *Columbia Human Rights Law Review*, 44(1), 1–46.

Joint Statement. (2011). *Ending acts of violence and related human rights violations based on sexual orientation and gender identity*. https://arc-international.net/global-advocacy/human-rights-council/hrc16/joint-statement/

Jordaan, E. (2017). South Africa and sexual orientation rights at the United Nations: Batting for both sides. *Politikon*, 44(2), 205–230.

Karns, M., & Mignst, K. (2004). *International organizations: The politics and processes of global governance*. Lynne Rienner.

Kayal, A. Z., Parker, P. L., & Weissbrodt, D. (1993). The forty-fourth session of the UN sub-commission on prevention of discrimination and protection of minorities. *Human Rights Quarterly, 15*, 410–457.

Keck, M. E., & Sikkink, K. (1998). *Activists beyond borders: Advocacy networks in international politics.* Cornell University Press.

Klapeer, C. M. (2017). Queering development in homotransnationalist times: A postcolonial reading of LGBTIQ inclusive development agendas. *Lambda Nordica, 2*(3), 41–67.

McAdam, D. (1996). Conceptual origins, current problems, future directions. In D. McAdam, J. D. McCarthy, & M. N. Zald (Eds.), *Comparative perspectives on social movements* (pp. 23–40). Cambridge University Press.

Mendes, W. G., Furtado, C. M., & da Silva, P. (2020). Homicide of lesbians, gay, bisexuals, travestis, transexuals, and transgender people (LGBT) in Brazil: A spatial analysis. *Scielo Saúde Pública, 25*(5), 1709–1722. www.scielosp.org/article/csc/2020.v25n5/1709-1722/en/

Meyer, D. S., & Minkoff, D. C. (2004). Conceptualizing political opportunity. *Social Forces, 82*(4), 1457–1492.

Office of the High Commissioner for Human Rights (OHCHR). (2012). *Born free and equal: Sexual orientation and gender identity in international human rights law* [Booklet]. www.ohchr.org/Documents/Publications/BornFreeAndEqualLowRes.pdf

Office of the High Commissioner for Human Rights (OHCHR). (2020). *Human rights council* [Booklet]. www.ohchr.org/sites/default/files/Documents/HRBodies/HRCouncil/HRC_booklet_EN.pdf

Office of the High Commissioner for Human Rights (OHCHR) Report. (2011). *Discriminatory laws and practices and acts of violence against individuals based on their sexual orientation and gender identity. A/HRC/19/41.* https://ap.ohchr.org/documents/dpage_e.aspx?si=A/HRC/19/41

Office of the High Commissioner for Human Rights (OHCHR) Report. (2015). *Discrimination and violence against individuals based on their sexual orientation and gender identity. A/HRC/29/23.* https://ap.ohchr.org/documents/dpage_e.aspx?si=A/HRC/29/23

Office of the High Commissioner for Human Rights (OHCHR) Statement. (2008). *Address by Ms. Navanetham Pillay, UN high commissioner for human rights on the theme of gender identity, sexual orientation, and human rights.* http://arc-international.net/ohchr/hc-ga-2008/

O'Flaherty, M., & Fisher, J. (2008). Sexual orientation, gender identity and international human rights law: Contextualizing the Yogyakarta principles. *Human Rights Law Review, 8*(2), 207–248.

Otto, D. (2015). Queering gender [identity] in international law. *Nordic Journal of Human Rights, 33*(4), 299–318.

Radford, J. (1996). Lesbians take on the UN. *Trouble & Strife, 33*, 35–43.

Rahman, M. (2014). Queer rights and the triangulation of western exceptionalism. *Journal of Human Rights, 13*(3), 274–289.

Rittberger, V., Zangl, B., & Staisch, M. (2006). *International organization: Polity, politics and policies.* Palgrave MacMillan.

Rothchild, C. (2005). *Written out: How sexuality is used to attack women's organizing (updated).* International Gay and Lesbian Human Rights Commission (IGLHRC) & Rutgers University Center for Women's Global Leadership (CWGL). https://outrightinternational.org/sites/default/files/16-1.pdf

Sanders, D. (1996). Getting lesbian and gay issues on the international human rights agenda. *Human Rights Quarterly, 18*(1), 67–106.

Secretary-General Statement. (2010). *Message to event on ending violence and criminal sanctions based on sexual orientation and gender identity.* www.ohchr.org/en/statements/2011/04/secretary-general-message-event-ending-violence-and-criminal-sanctions-based

Secretary-General Statement. (2011). *Secretary-General, in message to event on ending sexuality-based violence, bias. SG/SM/14008.* www.un.org/press/en/2011/sgsm14008.doc.htm

Tarrow, S. (1983). *Struggling to reform: Social movements and policy change during cycles of protest.* Cornell University Press.

Tarrow, S. (1996). States and opportunities: The political structuring of social movements. In D. McAdam, J. D. McCarthy, & M. N. Zald (Eds.), *Comparative perspectives on social movements* (pp. 41–61). Cambridge University Press.

Tilly, C. (1978). *From mobilization to revolution.* Addison-Wesley.

Trithart, A. (2021). *A UN for all? UN policy and programming on sexual orientation, gender identity and expression, and sex characteristics.* International Peace Institute. www.ipinst.org/2021/02/un-policy-programming-on-sexual-orientation-gender-identity-expression-and-sex-characteristics

United Nations AIDS (UNAIDS). (1999). *Handbook for legislators on HIV/AIDS, law and human rights: Action to combat HIV/AIDS in view of its devastating human, economic, and social impact.* www.unaids. org/en/resources/documents/1999/19991118_jc259-ipu_en.pdf

United Nations AIDS (UNAIDS). (2002). *A conceptual framework and basis for action: HIV/ AIDS stigma and discrimination.* www.unaids.org/en/resources/documents/2003/20030106_ jc891-wac_framework_en.pdf

United Nations General Assembly (UN GA). (1993). *International year of the family. 47/237* [Resolution]. https://documents-dds-ny.un.org/doc/RESOLUTION/GEN/NR0/018/73/IMG/NR00 1873.pdf?OpenElement

United Nations General Assembly (UN GA). (2003). *Extrajudicial, summary or arbitrary executions. 57/214. Fifty-seventh session* [Resolution]. https://undocs.org/Home/Mobile?FinalSymbol=A%2FRE S%2F57%2F214&Language=E&DeviceType=Desktop&LangRequested=False

United Nations General Assembly (UN GA). (2012). *Extrajudicial, summary or arbitrary executions. 67/168. Sixty-seventh session* [Resolution]. https://undocs.org/Home/Mobile?FinalSymbol=A%2FR ES%2F67%2F168&Language=E&DeviceType=Desktop&LangRequested=False

United Nations Human Rights Council (UN HRC). (2011). *Human rights, sexual orientation and gender identity. A/HRC/RES/17/19* [Resolution]. https://documents-dds ny.un.org/doc/UNDOC/ GEN/G11/148/76/PDF/G1114876.pdf?OpenElement

Vance, K., Mulé, N. J., Kan, M., & Mckenzie, C. (2018). The rise of SOGI: Human rights for LGBTI people at the United Nations. In N. Nicol, A. Jjuuko, R. Lusimbo, N. Mulé, S. Ursel, A. Wahab, & P. Waugh (Eds.), *Envisioning global LGBT human rights: (Neo)colonialism, neoliberalism, resistance and hope* (pp. 223–245). Human Rights Consortium, Institute of Commonwealth Studies.

Voss, M. J. (2017). Contesting sexual orientation and gender identity at the UN human rights council. *Human Rights Review, 19*(1), 1–22.

Waites, M. (2009). Critique of "sexual orientation" and "gender identity" in human rights discourse: Global queer politics beyond the Yogyakarta Principles. *Contemporary Politics, 15*(1), 137–156.

Weiss, T. G., Carayannis, T., & Jolly, R. (2009). The "third" United Nations. *Global Governance, 15,* 123–142.

Weiss, T. G., Forsythe, D. P., Coate, R. A., & Pease, K. K. (2017). *The United Nations and changing world politics.* Westview Press.

Wilson, A. (1996). Lesbian visibility and sexual rights at Beijing. *Signs, 22*(1), 214–218.

World Health Organization. (2015). *HIV and young transgender people.* WHO Document Production Services. https://apps.who.int/iris/handle/10665/179866?search-result=true&query=hiv+transgen der+2015&scope=&rpp=10&sort_by=score&order=desc

The Yogyakarta Principles. (2006). *Principles on the application of international human rights law in relation to sexual orientation and gender identity* [2007 Report]. http://yogyakartaprinciples.org/ wp-content/uploads/2016/08/principles_en.pdf

The Yogyakarta Principles. (2017). *Additional principles and state obligations on the application of international human rights law in relation to sexual orientation, gender identity, gender expression and sex characteristics to compliment the Yogyakarta principles* [Report]. http://yogyakartaprinciples.org/wp-content/uploads/2017/11/A5_yogyakartaWEB-2.pdf

4

UNDERSTANDING HOMOPROFESSIONALISM AND THE POLITICAL CONTEXT

Lesbian and Gay Leaders of International Schools

Robert C. Mizzi

Queer[1] people are living in complex times. On one end of the spectrum, there are now countries, such as Canada, the United States, and the United Kingdom, that provide legal protections against discrimination and create diversity policies and programmes in workplaces, but still struggle with social acceptance of queer people. On the other end, there are approximately 50 countries that impose imprisonment, and there are countries, such as Iran, Saudi Arabia, and Yemen, which use the death penalty just for participating in consensual same-sex sexual acts (Mendos, 2019). A global political context continues to permit trans/homophobic violence. Efforts to respect and protect queer people remain inconsistent and unsteady.

State-sanctioned and socially acceptable trans/homophobia endangers lives (Mizzi et al., 2016) and invisibilizes queer people (deLeon & Brunner, 2009), while cisgender and heterosexual people continue to be the epitome of good citizens and workers. Given this harsh political context, it is no great leap that queer workers will have a different experience than their heterosexual, cisgender counterparts. Queer workers hope for little exposure to dangerous and oppressive encounters and must stealthily navigate their work contexts so that they too flourish in their careers (Mizzi, 2013). Often this is easier said than done. Navigating oppressive work contexts is often rooted in fear, which means being silent, untruthful, secretive, and evasive about personal situations on a daily basis. An erosion of self-worth and participation at work are dire consequences of this navigation.

Typically, organizational leaders are crucial towards creating systems that include sexual and gender diversity. However, any leader who creates anti-trans/homophobic policies or advocates for queer inclusion in general draws immediate attention to their own sexual or gender identity, regardless if they are actually queer or not. Organizational leaders may choose to mask queer-inclusion efforts as "social equity" or "human rights" in order to deflect some of the scrutiny. For queer leaders, like queer followers, any unwanted attention may be too hard to handle and cause them to closely guard their secret identities for the sake of their careers (deLeon & Brunner, 2009).

Queer leaders experience discrimination and prejudice, regardless of their leadership position, which impacts expression of their queer identity. For example, Declan O'Connor, a transgender school principal in Massachusetts, was concerned about how coming out as trans would damage his career. He would therefore be identified as a woman at work, but as a man

DOI: 10.4324/9781003128151-5

42

in his personal life until he felt supported to disclose his gender identity (Schoenberg, 2019). This example emphasizes that organizations need to unequivocally support their queer leaders. Queer leaders, given their unique life experiences, professional role, and leadership skills, can be important players when it comes to creating queer inclusivity throughout the organization.

One emerging complication for queer leaders is that, as Rizvi (2017) suggested, globalization and neoliberalism are changing organizations at a rapid pace, and there are moral, intercultural, and equity concerns underpinning this change. There are more organizations "going global" by expanding operations beyond national borders to maintain a competitive edge and break into new markets. Globalization increases the migration of people and work (Herod, 2000). Although it may be profitable for organizations to globalize their workforces, services, and products, there may be a heavy toll on workers who cross national borders and do not "fit" their new country contexts due to strict and oppressive moral codes and laws (Mizzi et al., 2021). For example, an openly queer leader in Canada may have a very different work experience leading teams and programmes in Egypt, where laws and social attitudes that discriminate against homosexuality are permitted. While calls for greater queer representation in mainly Western countries satisfies equity concerns in the workplace (e.g. Rand, 2013), there can still be organizational expectations that erase queerness in transnational contexts, which diminishes goals for diversity, inclusion, participation, and queer knowledge production. The fact that expatriates are primarily viewed as heterosexual is heteronormativity in action. Work visas, spousal visas, or traditional views towards "family" in official discourse exclude queer leaders as they cross borders (Gedro et al., 2013). This form of gatekeeping may very well expose queerness before queer leaders begin their jobs, depending on what is shared through official documentation.

This chapter builds on the extant scholarship on queer expatriates and offers a queer leader perspective, drawing on literature from business studies, human resource development, and educational administration. The purpose of this chapter is to explore how international queer leaders navigate their work situations and strive to improve the lives of LGBTQ people in their organizations. This chapter also shifts the discourse on queer leadership to consider international educational contexts. This chapter continues with a literature review on queer leaders and professionalism. I then share vignettes of four lesbian and gay leaders of international schools as a case study. I introduce "homoprofessionalism" as a conceptual lens to analyse their stories. I conclude this chapter with recommendations.

Localizing and Globalizing Queer Leaders

Leaders enter a promissory relationship with their staff and clients. Leaders support their employees, lead initiatives that strengthen the organization and its productivity, demonstrate a knowledge and understanding of the organizational and administrative arrangements, maintain budgets and financial stability, communicate and safeguard the rights and responsibilities of workers, and so forth (Bush et al., 2010). Leaders are always on call, are accountable for their organizations, have a higher profile, and are scrutinized based on their behaviours and presentation. Leaders are primarily recognized in their organizations as "boss," and their other roles, such as parent, spouse, or learner, are peripheral. Queer leaders have more challenging work experiences than their cisgender, heterosexual counterparts, and a gender analysis forms a starting point for which these challenges have to be analysed.

Leadership is undoubtedly a gendered profession, marking men as the dominant and natural leaders of organizations. In many countries, a "good" leader is considered white, heterosexual, cisgender, male, and able, which causes others not fitting that archetype to face barriers in obtaining leadership positions (deLeon & Brunner, 2009; Evan, 2019; Gedro, 2010; Muhr & Sullivan, 2013). When women do enter leadership positions, Lugg and Tooms (2010) argued that there are preferences for "womanly women" leaders, which are female leaders who are gender conforming and visually interesting to heterosexual men. They wrote, "Leadership required a particular presentation of self, centred on clothes, hairstyle, weight, race and supposed sexual orientation, to 'pass' as a real educational leader" (p. 79). In addition, Evan (2019) reflected on how masculine-gender expression presents a barrier for female leaders and suggested that the female gender is more of a hindrance to men than a lesbian identity when it comes to leadership roles. Leadership is based on a hierarchical, heterosexual matrix that includes the leaders' biological sex, gender expression, and assumed sexual behaviour (Muhr & Sullivan, 2013). This matrix, by nature of its design, reduces the possibility of queer workers entering leadership positions.

Queer leaders may not be protected in their jobs due to not being a member of a union or granted tenure, and therefore, they are often compliant with upper management (Pryor, 2020). Hiring queer leaders into organizations and *queering* leadership so that any leader can engage various masculine and feminine expressions can be useful steps (Brard, 2020; Courtney, 2014; Muhr & Sullivan, 2013; Rottmann, 2006). Muhr and Sullivan (2013) explained that "queering leadership suggests that *all* managers perform leadership according to certain scripts set by the expectations generated by their gendered bodies, which produces limitations to the way leadership is seen as natural/unnatural for a specific leader's body [original italics]" (p. 418). Openly queer leaders are in a position to connect with other queer persons and unsettle organizational heteronormativity (Courtney, 2014; Tooms, 2009). Courtney wrote, "Campness, however essentially conceived, is queer in disrupting the assumed gender/sexual alignment of 'leader'" (p. 392). Courtney's research pointed to how queer leaders used their authority to target homophobia and not heteronormativity, without consideration that homophobia emerges out of heteronormativity. Leaders of any difference are foremost expected by their superiors to conform to the workplace and reify a certain organizational culture, which, as Evan (2019) argued, has more harmful effects on lesbian or bisexual female leaders who must also confront a deeply entrenched masculinized profession. Queer leaders may not interact with stakeholders as freely as cisgender, heterosexual counterparts as a result (Lee, 2022).

Workplace initiatives that aim to foster a deeper appreciation of sexual and gender diversity can create experiences with blowback and backlash, which further challenge queer workers (Hill, 2009). Hill explained that blowback is "the reaction of individuals or groups to something that has gained, or is growing in popularity, importance, or power" (p. 38). Backlash occurs when there are threats to straight privilege, visibly queer workers, creation of inclusive policies, "special treatment" or equity language, responses to sexism and heterosexism, or action on political anti-queer rhetoric. According to Hill, what results from blowback and backlash is a sense of queer tolerability as long as homosexuality is not flaunted and remains hidden.

The literature is clear in that there is a connection between disclosure of queer identity and discrimination, which impacts the relationship between queer leaders and their followers. "Coming out" is an ongoing process for queer leaders; there are emotional experiences that underpin being a queer leader, and there are valid concerns over organizational support for their queer identities and relationships (Williams, 2018). Typically, queer leaders find themselves being perpetually silenced through heteronormative organizational systems (Brard, 2020; deLeon & Brunner, 2009; Duarte, 2020). Queer leaders may consequently put limitations around their outness or LGBTQ activism so that they can endure oppression and discrimination (Chang & Bowring, 2017), mitigate blowback or backlash (Collins & Callahan, 2012), or sustain perceptions of themselves as leaders and not as "gay activists" (Tooms, 2009). These limitations may result in queer leaders not becoming advocates for social justice or queer inclusion (Brard, 2020; Williams, 2018). However, some queer leaders, such as CEOs Tim Cook (Apple) or Beth Ford (Land O' Lakes), may be shielded from overt oppression due to their positions in leading powerful global enterprises that countries require to fuel their economies.

Since queer leaders are under constant scrutiny of their behaviour and presentation due to professional expectations of their role, queer leaders do not know who is watching and reporting them (Lugg & Tooms, 2010). Lugg and Tooms shared, "*what* we talk about and *how* we talk changes depending on *whom* we are talking [original italics]" (p. 80). There is a question of leadership fit, which is not only about conformity but is also about reproducing norms. Lugg and Tooms suggested that a "Right Kind of Queer," which is a queer leader who is an overachiever and a workaholic, may (not) be closeted, may not be helpful for LGBTQ rights, downplays (their) sexuality and avoid conflict, has a "straightened office" (i.e. contains no sign of queerness), is concerned with presentation, maintains loyalty to the board, and is careful with words (see also Fassinger et al. [2010] and Lee [2022] for further examples of this overcompensation). Because of this concern for scrutiny, choosing not to disclose queer identities can also be a political act just as much as a safety concern (Tooms, 2009). Queer leaders are clearly in a double-bind, which limits their potential to do their jobs and sustains a lavender ceiling (Hill, 2009).

Although the aforementioned challenges can negatively impact queer leaders' relationships and practices, there can be some positive experiences associated with disclosing a queer identity. Queer leaders can build community and promote equity and inclusivity (Brard, 2020; Lee, 2022; Williams, 2018). They can be motivated to do LGBTQ equity work because of their personal backgrounds and to improve the lives of queer stakeholders through advocacy and inclusive policies and programmes (Pryor, 2020). Queer leaders can also frame their work environments to determine how permissible queer people can be out (Fassinger et al., 2010; Lugg & Tooms, 2010). For instance, coming out as transgender can mark a positive change in the way the leader supports difference (Lee, 2022; Muhr & Sullivan, 2013; Schoenberg, 2019; Tooms, 2009). Disclosing a queer identity to staff can impact social perceptions and attitudes towards them and to other queer workers. Queer leaders' work relationships may not be negatively impacted with disclosure when they have built respectful relationships (Chang & Bowring, 2017; Lee, 2022). Leaders can signal non-issue around sexuality and gender during the hiring stage of staff, and then foster supportive relationships in the workplace (Duarte, 2020). For queer followers, the presence of out queer leaders in their organizations functions as safety nets in case of experiences with homo/transphobia in the workplace (Mizzi & Star, 2019). One practical way to foster queer inclusivity is through queer employee resource groups, which can help create policies that support queer leaders, promote social change, and improve organizational effectiveness (Githens & Aragon, 2009).

Overall, while this body of literature is useful at understanding the contexts and issues facing queer leaders, there is a general lack of research on queer leaders in international settings (Gedro, 2010). A minimal attention to globalized work situations for queer leaders is problematic because expatriation presents an opportunity to develop globally skilled leaders. Gedro argued that a "global closet" exists for expatriate lesbian workers, which consists of challenges around invisibility, discrimination, stigmatization, safety, and security. Lesbian workers need to navigate this global closet when working overseas. Gedro called for human resource development practitioners to educate their organizations on the needs facing lesbian workers. These are useful points for queer leaders in international settings, but I am also sensitive to Lugg and Toom's (2010) concern that queer leaders are influenced by the political contexts that surround them. If there are legal issues surrounding queer identities in certain countries, queer leaders may choose to "professionalize" their identities, which means keeping their sexuality and/or gender a closely guarded secret as a protective measure. As I explain in the following, sexuality and professionalism are not mutually exclusive concepts in an organization.

(Hetero)professionalism as Regulatory Discourse

Professionalism relates to the conduct, behaviours, and attitudes considered acceptable in the workplace. When workers are compliant to professional norms, they benefit from job success and rewards, a positive reputation, and broader networks. The global expansion of neoliberalism has caused professionalism to include aspects of accountability, productivity, managerialism, standardization, appearance, and performance (Marom & Ruitenberg, 2018). While these tenets remain constant across disciplines, there are some contextual differences. In the field of educational administration, Hargreaves (2000) suggested that there are four ages of teacher professionalism. There is the *pre-professional age*, which is that teaching adopts principles and parameters of unquestionable common sense and inducts a "good" teacher through trial and error. There is the *professional autonomy age*, which is that teachers have the right to choose the methods that are best for their students. There is the *collegial professional age*, which maintains its focus on teaching methods, with sharp distinctions being drawn between traditional and student-centred methods. Administration as a dominant power becomes further imposed during this age, and, as an adjoining force, there is a strong professional culture of collaboration to cope with change and establish a common purpose. Finally, there is the *post-professional age* or *post-modern professional age*, where globalized and competitive economic forces create policies to strengthen national economies at a loss of autonomy and cultural identity. This age is characterized by the rapidly changing technologies that enable efficient communication systems and global mobility.

These different ages provide some context as to how teacher professionalism has evolved over time. There were occasions where leaders allowed teacher autonomy, and at other times, there was an increased regulation of workers. Critical researchers have suggested that professionalism has been a negative and regulatory influence on workers more broadly, pointing out that it is not gender neutral (Rumens & Kerfoot, 2009; Whitehead, 2003). For example, wearing "acceptable" attire in the workplace has been recognized as expressions of professionalism and conformity and is "symbolic of sexist and heterosexist elite conventions regarding women and educational leadership" (Lugg & Tooms, 2010, p. 78). What interests me is the third age of teacher professionalism—the rise of administrative power—and the fourth age—the encroachment of globalized forces in educational contexts. If administrative power becomes entrenched in school systems, then what does this mean for queer leaders, especially at times when queerness is peripheralized in society? Globalization complicates such matters, as a loss of autonomy means greater struggle to ameliorate equity concerns. What needs further exploration is how queer leaders challenge heteronormative underpinnings of professionalism and panoptic scrutiny (Pryor, 2020).

Heteroprofessionalism, as a theoretical concept, positions professionalism as a regulatory and unmediated discourse to control queer workers and queer knowledge. Although originally situated within a cisgender gay/bisexual male context, I consider the term pertinent to women and nonbinary or trans people. Heteroprofessionalism functions to "reassert heteromasculinist dominance as a normative functioning of an organization," "operate through discourses of professionalism to devalue homosexual histories, identities, and understandings," "silence, undervalue, or marginalize workers who try to address heteronormativity in the workplace," and "create policies and programs that do not take into account homosexuality" (Mizzi, 2013, p. 1618).

While relatively nascent in scope, some researchers are already noticing how heteroprofessionalism negatively affects the lives of queer leaders. Evan (2019) stated that, within the context of executive presence, an outward appearance is linked to professionalism and suggests one's sexual orientation. In her research involving lesbian executives, Evan observed that expression of a lesbian identity was a source of pride in the workplace. However, there was a sense of competition among heterosexual women, who relied on performance impact and outward appearances as being important. These performances and appearances are rooted in professional regulation, often based on unspoken value systems and yet subsumed through organizational culture, norms of interaction, and policy discourse.

In light of our current era of advanced globalization and neoliberalism, a transnational perspective of queer leaders and leadership warrants the development of a broader perspective of leading organizations. When viewing a work environment through a queer leader, transnationalism, and professionalism nexus, what emerges is a realization that queer leaders are caught in a triple-bind through the *globalized political context* (e.g. working in homophobic countries or international organizations with little support systems), the *scrutiny of their leadership* (e.g. dodging questions about their sexual and/or gender identity for safety reasons), and *heteroprofessional regulation* (e.g. downplaying queer identities in policy landscapes). This triple-bind may result in greater secrecy, surveillance and safety concerns, and self-censorship, all of which diminish the rich knowledge and practice contributions of queer leaders.

Lesbian and Gay Leaders of International Schools

In 2019, I led a global study exploring the professional and personal lives of 23 LGBTQ international educators situated within elementary, secondary, and postsecondary education (Mizzi et al., 2021). International education organizations are unique research sites as they represent a workplace where multiple identities from across the globe work together under the same roof. The goal of this study was to acquire an understanding of how queer international teachers shaped their expressions of sexual and gender difference. Four lesbian and gay leaders were interviewed while collecting data for this primary study, and their vignettes are presented in the following. My discussions with these leaders allowed for deeper insights about queer international leader identities, professional relationships and practices, and LGBTQ activism. Names have been changed to protect anonymity.

Louisa's Story

Louisa is an American cisgender lesbian who works in rural China as vice-principal of an international school. She has disclosed her lesbian identity to her school staff and students. Louisa lives with her Canadian cisgender wife, both working at the same international school. What brought both of them to China was the offer of good teaching positions and an excellent salary. Neither are fluent Mandarin language. She described, "I handle a lot of school initiatives. I do a lot with our school improvement plan. I oversee all the heads of department." The political context is that Louisa and her wife are not recognized as spouses by the Chinese government, and so the only way for her wife to stay in the country was to be employed by the school.

Louisa feels that a strong work ethic is important for success as a queer leader. She shared, "the biggest part of my job is to work with the teachers to make sure that they have a systematic approach for the next coming years. I work with them on measurable goals and inventories." Louisa feels that her work ethic and position in the school shield her from experiencing homophobia and provides privileges, such as being able to travel home for personal reasons. The trade-off for these privileges and respect is having to work long hours and on weekends.

Louisa shared how her leadership team "just spent the last four years figuratively and literally tearing that school down and rebuilding it. We even built a new campus. We've had ripped our school apart and rebuilt it." During this rebuilding process, queer-inclusion initiatives were not a part of the new changes taking place. When prompted to explain the exclusion, Louisa described, "I think if that were to happen, I believe that my head of school and our school culture would completely be open to having healthy conversations about that. Even with our students." The route towards queer inclusion, however, has not been taken despite feeling supported to do so.

Because of Louisa's out lesbian identity, she has had experiences with being considered the "gay mascot" among her foreign colleagues. For example, while staff orientation is a part of her job, she is often the de facto contact for newly hired LGBTQ staff. She also networks students who are questioning their sexuality or gender identity to support organizations in the United States, but not to those organizations in China. Despite the tokenism, Louisa feels supported by her school principal. She shared:

> I know my head of school and I trust him, and I think that he would be very open to having a conversation about what it is like for gays and lesbians. I also think that he would immediately come to me and want me to be there. So, if it was a first-grade teacher, for example, and those questions came up, in terms of how that person would be in the community, I think he would immediately ask me to do that.

Obtaining her principals' support for her lesbian identity is important, but she chooses not to be proactive about queer inclusion. Rather, she adopts a reactive and compliant stance to whatever sexual and gender diversity issues surface as a way to set an inclusive tone. Furthermore, Louisa does not know of cases of homophobia in her community, and so she shares with new gay or lesbian teachers that "there is no problem" to express their sexual identities outside the school. There might be a missed opportunity for Louisa to learn more about the struggles facing the LGBTQ community in rural China and further conceptualize possible implications for new LGBTQ expatriates.

Stephen's Story

Stephen is a Canadian cisgender gay man working in an undisclosed South-east Asian country. He is a Vice-Principal of an international school. He lives in the country and works with his cisgender husband, Evan, who is also Canadian. What brought them overseas was the lack of permanent teaching positions in Stephen's home province. They chose their country because, in part, homosexuality is legal. Because his destination country does not recognize same-sex marriage, Evan was not granted a spousal visa. This caused Evan to initially join Stephen as an international graduate student at a local university. When his graduate programme ended, the international school hired Evan so that he can stay in the country. The other option was for Evan to leave and re-enter the country every three months on a holiday visa. Stephen explained that this is a risky choice and would likely set off red flags to immigration officials.

Stephen is "out" as a gay cisgender man to his colleagues but is not as forthcoming with the students as he is afraid of public rebuke. He has observed how the local queer population is treated, such as being refused health care, and does not want to be treated in the same way. Stephen shared:

I'm personally more protective of my sexuality. I am less forthcoming. Not that I am necessarily trying to hide anything. But I don't come out, especially as a teacher. It is not like we are a straight married couple that my partner can just come with me and stay in the apartment. They will not do that here.

Stephen illustrates how heterosexual couples can receive visas for his host country, but gay couples are not allowed that same privilege. Being in the same apartment together can also be treated by landlords, school officials, or customs agents as suspect.

Stephen had a similar experience as Louisa of being a gay mascot and shared that he is a person that staff approach when a student is questioning their sexuality. Stephen discussed this informal role with his Canadian principal, who was sympathetic:

He basically said I don't need to do that, it's not a role I need to take on if I am not ready to do that, which I still don't think I was. Maybe I am still not, but that was the other part: Do I take this opportunity to be the gay mascot at the school? The person for LGBTQ kids who are struggling through identity to come forward?

Over time, to a certain extent, Stephen began opening up to his staff and students, as he gained confidence in his role and the country context. He explained, "in that very first meeting, I talk about how I am with my partner. I put it out there right away. That has taken me some time to get to that point. But I don't actively advertise."

Stephen also described employing a strong work ethic and a high degree of professionalism to shield him against possible encounters with homophobia. He also becomes consumed with his work, especially during times when his partner is away. He stated, "work kept me occupied, which is good. It just kept me focused. It didn't give me time to ruminate or anything like that. It was stressful, but thankfully work was there." Because of his fear over his sexual identity and losing his job, Stephen has not used his position to advance LGBTQ-inclusion in his school. However, he did assist with creating small, informal projects, such as a rainbow-painted "buddy bench" in the schoolyard for students to use if they need immediate assistance. Students do not need to identify queer issues as a reason to use the buddy bench.

Hannah's Story

Hannah is an American cisgender lesbian who works in an undisclosed Western European country as a Principal of an international school. Although Hannah lives in a country that provides work visas for same-sex spouses, Hannah and her partner decided to live in separate, but nearby countries, in order to draw attention away from their personal relationship. Hannah was working in another country that has a long history of homophobia, and, as a result, experienced homophobia in her workplace. She moved because of an urgent need to live in a country that respected LGBTQ rights in case there was any further dangerous incidents.

Hannah is afraid of public backlash for being a lesbian head of school, which she feels would cast a shadow on her leadership capabilities. Hannah hides her sexuality from colleagues, staff, and even lifelong friends. Hannah shared:

When I came out, I was just moving into administration at the time. In my previous country, I'll say in a country that is behind when it comes to LGBT rights, there is a large expatriate Russian community which is especially hostile to those who were out. In addition, one of my first board chairs was a missionary from the US, and he worked actively in the community speaking out against gay people. I learned to be closeted very, very quickly.

Hannah eventually shared her lesbian identity with a few people but explained that "it took me a long time because it was very dangerous for my career and just being in that community." She summarized, "I'm in this fearful position all the time trying to support the kids and trying to support teachers, but not having in my own mind all the courage to be fully out."

Hannah recognizes the importance of being a visible queer leader for political reasons and to build community. She declared, "I've been 10 years in administration now. I have yet to meet some other head of an international school who's gay." Despite Hannah's secrecy over her sexual identity, she is a social justice advocate and uses that lens to create an inclusive space for LGBTQ students. She expressed, "I'm doing exactly what is needed to protect these kids [by advocating for them], because the kids are targeted at school."

Hannah tries to improve school culture through mechanisms like a Diversity Charter and explicitly stating support for LGBTQ causes at school assemblies. She shared, "there's some sort of coded things that you can say and that show your support." When she began publicly announcing support for queer identities, "every single LGBT teacher, during that first week, came and spoke to me" and students also started to confide their sexualities in her. Although Hannah has not disclosed her lesbian identity to her staff, publicly declaring LGBTQ support through diversity discourses initiated supportive conversations with students and staff. She tries to be proactive in her queer inclusivity at the hiring stage. Hannah shared:

> when we get closer to making an offer to the applicants, we want to know if they have a same-sex partner. If so, is that a problem? How can we deal with that? I would say in this region, the heads of schools are very much aware of this as an issue, and many have tried to find work for spouses. But I would guess in other parts of the world that they would feel it's not possible to get your partner into the country.

Despite having an interest into the lives of international LGBTQ teachers, Hannah has placed limitations over what she can provide as a school leader, without drawing attention to her sexual identity. For example, there is no explicit mentorship programme for LGBTQ teachers or a support programme for LGBTQ students.

Katie's Story

Katie is a cisgender Canadian lesbian who works in an undisclosed South-East Asian country as a director of an international programme in higher education. She travels back and forth to Canada to recruit participants and staff for the programme. What drew Katie to this country is the opportunity to advance her intercultural and global leadership skills. She was primarily hired as an international teacher at another school, but she later received her director position. Katie has a long-term partner in Canada, but they decided not to get married out of fear that their marriage will "out" Katie in some government database in her country. She shared, "I just don't want to have problems with borders and visas and those types of things."

When Katie was a teacher at her school, her school principal learned of and subsequently threatened to have her deported due to her lesbian identity. Katie had to lie about her sexuality and pretend to have a boyfriend for months in order to avoid a potentially dangerous situation. Katie vividly remembers this traumatic experience, and in response, when she became a leader, she chose to conceal her sexual identity.

Gendered norms around dress and appearance are a concern for Katie. Katie stated:

> I will say every single time when I go out, I get pulled out of a bathroom or I see people double check the wall marking for women's and men's washrooms. They think they might be walking into the wrong one. The local people typically say it is because I have really short hair, and that men have short hair.

Katie has also experienced being a "gay mascot," but it is mainly through her university in Canada and not when she is in Asia. Katie shared:

> One of my staff members was in a session involving transgender students, and she sort of had this feeling that she was not approaching the situation well. I respected her for the fact she realized that. She came over to me and said, "how do I handle this?" So, we brought in some people who were teaching people on how to use the right vocabulary. I think it was really helpful because nobody expected that in the international community. Just because I am gay, it doesn't mean that I know everything [about being queer].

Similar to Hannah, Katie suggested that one way of navigating this tokenism is by changing countries to allow for a fresh start as a queer leader. When this happens, she shared:

> Nobody knows anything about you from the past. I think that that was part of a way to just start fresh and find out who I really was, not trying to negotiate everybody who knew me before I came out.

Katie engages LGBTQ-inclusion in the Canadian portion of her programme, but not in Asia even though she is in charge of 80–100 facilitators and close to 800 students in Asia. This silence is a result of being traumatized while being a lesbian teacher, as described earlier. She calls for more resources for queer leaders and teachers in order to help them "negotiate culture and politics."

Discussion

These vignettes confirm Williams and Giuffre's (2011) point that sexuality cannot be removed from the workplace. However, there can be a panoptic gaze that shapes public expressions of sexuality, depending on how the leader engages the work and learning environment and builds relationships. Fear underpins the vignettes, with three participants clearly relying on heteronormativity to portray a straight identity for them when they do not mention their sexuality.

When the study participants became a bit more comfortable with disclosure, or in the case of Hannah, who felt competent in raising queer inclusion under the umbrella of school diversity discourses, then they were expected to avail themselves as a resource. Functioning as an organizational resource for queer inclusion can be considered a "minority tax," which is added time and labour placed onto minorities to operationalize diversity in their workplaces in addition to their regular duties (Clarke & Matthews, 2021). This labour is often unrecognized within job evaluations, adds to workload, and tokenizes workers. It also causes non-queer workers to have a new reason to not engage queer inclusivity if they have an out queer staff member to complete the work for them. In addition to navigating a trans/homophobic political context, the new expectation to perform as queer-inclusion resource personnel may also deter queer workers from disclosing their sexual or gender identity. The risky political context and the expectation to be resource personnel may be too much to bear. That said, there is accretion of social, cultural, and political capital through developing new initiatives and networks when queer workers avail themselves as resources (Gedro et al., 2004; Lugg & Tooms, 2010). Those benefits have yet to be actualized in these vignettes.

What needs to happen is a systemic change whereby all school staff feel comfortable and knowledgeable in addressing sexual and gender diversity issues. In light of the research on queering leadership (Courtney, 2014; deLeon & Brunner, 2009; Muhr & Sullivan, 2013; Rottmann, 2006), leaders can enhance masculine and feminine expressions and competencies among all staff so that everyone feels capable in providing effective responses to questions and concerns around gender and sexuality. The vignettes depicted the queer leaders as vulnerable to a system that could legally and socially cast them out, which limits their support of others or ambitions for systemic change. Considering how the leaders in this study created some avenues for inclusion, but still participated in keeping queerness silent in other areas—including their own degree of visibility—suggests that each legal and social situation is unique and that a uniform approach to queer inclusivity is not possible for international queer leaders.

On this point, one cannot evade some element of homonormativity in the vignettes. As Williams and Giuffre (2011) explained:

> Some research suggests that to be successful in gay-friendly workplaces, gays and lesbians must appear "virtually normal", that is, indistinguishable from heterosexuals. A new "homonormativity" may be replacing the old "heteronormativity"—allowing gays and lesbians to succeed but only if they enact a narrowly circumscribed and conventional performance of gender, family, and the politics in the workplaces. It also appears from the limited studies that have been done that gay-friendly does not necessarily mean racially inclusive or welcoming of other kinds of diversity, leading some to wonder what is really new and improved about this organizational form.
>
> *(p. 553)*

Homonormativity is about gay men and lesbians reinforcing heteronormativity and wrapping queerness within cishetero-acceptability. Examples of homonormativity can be gay men and lesbians seeking rights that mirror heterosexual counterparts, such as marriage and reproduction, or upholding white privilege internal or external to the queer community. Gay men and lesbians seek advancement and acceptance through sanctioned institutions, which constrains sexuality to a heteronormative system. It may be that homonormativity occurs in the workplace because queer workers seek affirmation and promotion, do not want to be viewed more as an outcast or disrupt a status quo, or are living in fear of repercussions. Through homonormativity, there is little contestation of heteronormativity and other forms of oppression, which, concomitantly, privatizes and depoliticizes queerness and upholds normatively queer, white, able, middle-class subjects. This results in divisiveness among LGBTQ people as those who do not assimilate into heteronormative systems or cannot challenge oppression may receive fewer rights or privileges (Robinson, 2016; Duggan, 2003).

I propose that these vignettes are demonstrating tenets of an emergent *homoprofessionalism*. Homoprofessionalism draws on the political energies of homonormativity and professionalism and becomes operationalized by LGBTQ people, perhaps unknowingly and in response to working in an uncertain political and social context. There are three tentative principles to homoprofessionalism emerging out of these vignettes, which may be particularly heightened in a neoliberal or global context.

The first principle is that queer workers wrap queer realities within traditional heterosexualizing discourses and consider queer identities outside the heteronorm as being out-of-step with contemporary queer politics. Compelling workers to portray a heteronormative image (e.g. married, monogamous couple, with or without children), at the loss of queer expressions and queer imaginary is an example here. In this study, none of the leaders demonstrated significant evidence of queering curriculum, leadership, pedagogy, or organizational culture. Their presence functioned as reminders to staff of being inclusive, but only to a type of queerness that sustains heteronormativity. Queer-inclusion efforts were superficial, which involved isolated incidents of supporting LGBTQ staff and students or creation of policy artefacts that support LGBTQ identities. The organizational system remains unchanged, and queer identities are expected to fit within the current system, layering a cosmetic queerness onto the organization. For example, Louisa felt that her lesbian presence was enough for the school to be considered "queer-positive," and yet made few attempts to institute change when rebuilding the school. This reluctance may be because China needs to signal greater support for LGBTQ rights in the education field (Zhang, 2020). The only participant who was able to move the discussion further along was Hannah, and she is located in a Western European country that politically and socially supports LGBTQ rights. It may also be because Hannah is a school principal, and therefore, she has more power and authority than the other participants. Notably, however, Hannah decided not to live with her partner out of safety concerns. This part of her vignette contradicts the assumption that Western countries are safe spaces for queer expatriates. While Western countries may be safer, homophobia does not stop at borders, and therefore, fear of experiencing harm may cause expatriate queer leaders to keep their sexual identities a secret despite the location.

The second principle of homoprofessionalism is that there is engagement of professionalism by queer workers to censor expressions of homosexuality or queerness in general. Queer workers may purposefully downplay their appearance so that they do not appear as "gay," "femme," "camp," "butch," or transcend a masculine/feminine binary. In the study, evidence of professional regulation surfaced among all participants, which was often rooted in fear. For example, participants reified a professional self-image as a way to protect them from potentially dangerous situations, citing a high work ethic as capital, conformity to organizational values and administrative control, and adherence to a heteronormative relationship model. While comments about dress and hair were mentioned as causes for backlash, these comments seemed to be more reflective of gendered realities for female leaders.

The third principle of homoprofessionalism draws on queer people to create boundaries, sometimes invisible and unintentional, and these boundaries limit queer knowledge, histories, contributions, or innovation. A queer leader who seeks to professionalize their organizations through appearance, language, or space at the expense of queer expression is a form of boundary-marking. For example, while the vignettes highlighted passive initiatives such as a school diversity statement, a rainbow flag in the classroom, or a buddy bench, there was little engagement of the local LGBTQ community as representative of queer culture. This boundary-making dismisses local queer identities, who are often racialized in non-Western contexts, and how race, ability, gender, class, and religion interact with queerness. There was also demonstrable resistance to "queer" professional organizations or to disrupt the normative values that underpin organizational regimes. This resistance includes minimal engagement with global queer politics as a means to broaden understandings of sexual and gender diversity and confront behaviours that tokenize queer identities. The focus for these participants was maintaining a heteronormative status quo, rather than, as Rofes (2005) argued, a status queer where an environment is created that leaders, teachers, and students would not have to suppress parts of themselves or not feel fearful of being removed from the school.

In summary, homoprofessionalism draws on principles of homonormativity and profession-alism as regulatory discourses. Homoprofessionalism engages queer workers to stifle efforts that go beyond contemporary queer politics, constrain equity and inclusion gains, maintain a gender binary, and adhere to hetero/homo political system, all under professionalism discourses. There is no doubt that the political context that surrounds these study participants negatively affects them; therefore, a homoprofessional analysis includes problematizing workplace politics and their effects on all workers.

Conclusion

This chapter reviewed current research involving queer leaders and considered a transnational perspective that shape their work situations. Through analysing lesbian and gay leaders of inter-national schools, a broader understanding of international queer leadership can be further real-ized. This chapter profiled four queer leaders placed in different globalized work situations and considered how they are navigating their sexuality differences in light of heteronormative and risky work situations.

The fact that queer leaders are choosing to work in restrictive international settings, where there is a limitation to available support and guidance, suggests that queer leaders remain stead-fast in their global ambitions and that their experiences will be different than queer leaders who remain within their home countries or cisgender, heterosexual international leaders. Fear of blowback and backlash may be a common attribute among queer leaders, but based on the vignettes in this study, fear may be felt more deeply when working internationally. Leaders of international organizations need to learn about intersectionality, the politics of professional regulation, and how space produces social identities, and then prepare their workplaces to respect differences in identity and human experience.

More research is necessary to explore queer politics in global organizations and to examine work experiences and negotiation tactics among queer workers. Ensuring everyone's safety and being empathetic to all staff help build an inclusive organization (deLeon & Brunner, 2009). Queer leaders occupy power-filled roles, and the tensions that surface when navigating leader-ship can consume them. Homoprofessionalism may be a result of these tensions. Confronting homoprofessionalism will need a critical and comprehensive effort, whereby professionalism, homonormativity, and heteronormativity are called out for its regulatory and oppressive nature. Queer leaders could build their confidence and strength by connecting to one another, espe-cially in international contexts where supports and resources are not so easily accessible. All leaders, especially those in international spaces, need to work towards supporting queer identi-ties in their organizations.

Note

1 In this chapter, I use "queer" as a global term to include those who may or may not use LGBTQ labels, but they otherwise have sexuality or gender variances that differ from heterosexual and cisgender people.

References

Brard, H. (2020). *A study exploring the narratives of gay and lesbian school principals in Ontario* [Unpub-lished doctoral dissertation, University of Toronto].

Bush, T., Bell, L., & Middlewood, D. (Eds.). (2010). *The principles of educational leadership and manage-ment*. SAGE.

Chang, J., & Bowring, M. A. (2017). The perceived impact of sexual orientation on the ability of queer leaders to relate to followers. *Leadership*, *13*(3), 285–300. https://doi.org/10.1177/1742715015586215

Clarke, C., & Matthews, J. (2021). Advancement and leadership development. In D. Telem & C. Martin (Eds.), *Diversity, equity and inclusion* (pp. 11–21). Springer.

Collins, J. C., & Callahan, J. L. (2012). Risky business: Gay identity disclosure in a masculinized industry. *Human Resource Development International*, *15*(4), 455–470. https://doi-org.uml.idm.oclc.org/10.1080/13678868.2012.706427

Courtney, S. J. (2014). Inadvertently queer school leadership amongst lesbian, gay and bisexual (LGB) school leaders. *Organization*, *21*(3), 383–399. https://doi.org/10.1177/1350508413519762

deLeon, M. J., & Brunner, C. C. (2009). Lesbian and gay public school administrators: Early experiences that shape today. In J. W. Koschoreck & A. K. Tooms (Eds.), *Sexuality matters: Paradigms and policies for educational leaders* (pp. 157–178). Rowman & Littlefield Education.

Duarte, B. J. (2020). Forced back into the closet: A (queer) principal's attempt to maintain queer erasure. *Journal of Cases in Educational Leadership*, *23*(4), 20–34. https://doi.org/10.1177/1555458920956310

Duggan, L. (2003). *The twilight of equality: Neoliberalism, cultural politics and the attack on democracy*. Beacon Press.

Evan, R. J. (2019). Queering executive presence. *Journal of Critical Thought and Practice*, *8*(2), 1–16. https://doi.org/10.31274/jctp.8205

Fassinger, R. E., Shullman, S. L., & Stevenson, M. R. (2010). Toward an affirmative lesbian, gay, bisexual, and transgender leadership paradigm. *American Psychologist*, *65*(3), 201–215. https://doi.org/10.1037/a0018597

Gedro, J. (2010). The lavender ceiling atop the global closet: Human resource development and lesbian expatriates. *Human Resource Development Review*, *9*(4), 385–404. https://doi.org/10.1177/1534484310380242

Gedro, J., Cervero, R., & Johnson-Bailey, J. (2004). How lesbians learn to negotiate the heterosexism of corporate America. *Human Resource Development International*, *7*, 181–195.

Gedro, J., Mizzi, R. C., Rocco, T. S., & van Loo, J. (2013). Going global: Professional mobility and concerns for LGBT workers. *Human Resource Development International*, *16*(3), 282–297. https://doi.org/10.1080/13678868.2013.771869

Githens, R. P., & Aragon, S. R. (2009). LGBT employee groups: Goals and organizational structures. *Advances in Developing Human Resources*, *11*(1), 121–135. https://doi.org/10.1177/1523422308329200

Hargreaves, A. (2000). Four ages of professionalism and professional learning. *Teachers and Teaching: History and Practice*, *6*(20), 151–181.

Herod, A. (2000). Workers and workplace in a neoliberal global economy. *Environment and Planning A: Economy and Space*, *32*(10), 1781–1790. https://doi.org/10.1068/a32222

Hill, R. J. (2009). Incorporating queers: Blowback, backlash, and other forms of resistance to workplace diversity initiatives that support sexual minorities. *Advances in Developing Human Resources*, *11*(1), 37–53. https://doi.org/10.1177/1523422308328128

Lee, C. (2022). How does openness about sexual and gender identities influence self-perceptions of teacher leader authenticity? *Educational Management Administration & Leadership*, *50*(1), 140–162. https://doi.org/10.1177/1741143220929036

Lugg, C. A., & Tooms, A. K. (2010). A shadow of ourselves: Identity erasure and the politics of queer leadership. *School Leadership and Management*, *30*(1), 77–91. https://doi.org/10.1080/13632430903509790

Marom, L., & Ruitenberg, C. W. (2018). Professionalism discourses and neoliberalism in teacher education. *Alberta Journal of Educational Research*, *64*(4), 364–377.

Mendos, L. R. (2019). Author's preface. In L. R. Mendos (Ed.), *State-sponsored homophobia* (13th ed., pp. 13–16). International Lesbian, Gay, Bisexual, Trans and Intersex Association.

Mizzi, R. C. (2013). "There aren't any gays here": Encountering heteroprofessionalism in an international development workplace. *Journal of Homosexuality*, *60*(11), 1602–1624. https://doi.org/10.1080/00918369.2013.824341

Mizzi, R. C., Hill, R., & Vance, K. (2016). Beyond death threats, hard times, and clandestine work: Illuminating sexual and gender-minority resources in a global context. In R. C. Mizzi, T. S. Rocco, & S. Shore (Eds.), *Disrupting adult and community education: Teaching, learning, and working in the periphery* (pp. 101–115). SUNY Press.

Mizzi, R. C., Schmidt, C., & Moura, G. (2021). Complexity amidst diversity: Exploring the lives of LGBTQ international teachers. *Comparative and International Education, 50*(1), 1–17. https://doi.org/10.5206/cieeci.v50i1.11063

Mizzi, R. C., & Star, J. (2019). Queer eye on inclusion: Understanding gay and lesbian student and instructor experiences of continuing education. *Journal of Continuing Higher Education, 67*(2/3), 72–82. https://doi.org/10.1080/07377363.2019.1660844

Muhr, S. L., & Sullivan, K. R. (2013). "None so queer as folk": Gendered expectations and transgressive bodies in leadership. *Leadership, 9*(3), 416–435. https://doi.org/10.1177/1742715013485857

Pryor, J. T. (2020). Queer advocacy leadership: A queer leadership model for higher education. *Journal of Leadership Education, 19*(1), 69–93. https://doi.org/10.12806/V19/I1/R2

Rand, E. J. (2013). An appetite for activism: The Lesbian Avengers and the queer politics of visibility. *Women's Studies in Community, 36*(2), 121–141. https://doi.org/10.1080/07491409.2013.794754

Rizvi, F. (2017). *Globalization and the neoliberal imaginary of educational reform. Educational research and foresight working papers.* UNESCO. http://repositorio.minedu.gob.pe/bitstream/handle/20.500.12799/5283/Globalization%20and%20the%20Neoliberal%20Imaginary%20of%20Educational%20Reform.pdf?sequence=1&isAllowed=y

Robinson, B. A. (2016). Heteronormativity and homonormativity. In N. A. Naples (Ed.), *The Wiley Blackwell encyclopedia of gender and sexuality studies* (pp. 1–3). Wiley.

Rofes, E. (2005). *A radical rethinking of sexuality and schooling: Status quo or status queer?* Rowman & Littlefield Publishers.

Rottmann, C. (2006). Queering educational leadership from the inside out. *International Journal of Leadership in Education, 9*(1), 1–20.

Rumens, N., & Kerfoot, D. (2009). Gay men at work: (Re)constructing the self as professional. *Human Relations, 62*(5), 763–786. https://doi.org/10.1177/0018726709103457

Schoenberg, S. (2019, June 4). "I was living different lives": Springfield middle school principal Declan O'Connor comes out as transgender. *Masslive.* www.masslive.com/news/2019/06/i-was-living-two-different-lives-springfield-middle-school-principal-declan-oconnor-comes-out-as-transgender.html

Tooms, A. (2009). Dancing with the queers: A lesson in D/discourse. In J. W. Koschoreck & A. K. Tooms (Eds.), *Sexuality matters: Paradigms and policies for educational leaders* (pp. 179–204). Rowman & Littlefield Education.

Whitehead, S. (2003). Identifying the professional 'man'ager: Masculinity, professionalism and the search for legitimacy. In J. Barry, M. Dent, & M. O'Neill (Eds.), *Gender and the public sector: Professionals and managerial change* (pp. 85–103). Routledge.

Williams, C., & Giuffre, P. (2011). From organizational sexuality to queer organizations: Research on homosexuality and the workplace. *Sociology Compass, 5*, 551–563. https://doi.org/10.1111/j.1751-9020.2011.00392.x

Williams, I. (2018). *LGBT school leaders: Exploring the experiences and challenges of LGBT school administrators.* AERA Online Paper Repository. www.aera.net/repository

Zhang, P. (2020, May 31). Teacher reveals high price of coming out as gay in China. *South China Morning Post.* www.scmp.com/news/china/society/article/3086491/teacher-reveals-high-price-coming-out-gay-china

5

MOVING BEYOND MYOPIA

Towards a Global Queer Pedagogy in the 21st Century

Robert C. Mizzi and Gerald Walton

Along with feminist pedagogies (Crabtree et al., 2009; Nicholas et al., 2015), critical theory (Giroux, 2011; Wink, 2011), and holistic education (Miller et al., 2014; Ricci & Pritscher, 2015), queer pedagogy has emerged in adult education as a way to deconstruct norms and question the status quo on gender and sexuality. However, queer pedagogy continues to exist mostly on a pedagogical periphery (Allen, 2015; Potvin, 2020), with few scholars advancing the field and demonstrating its relevance to adult education more broadly. We aim to shift the tide here. In light of globalization discourses that are now claiming space in adult education (Alfred, 2015), we aim to "re-view" how queer pedagogy can be useful in globalized adult education beyond the compulsion towards self-serving affirmation. To that end, we offer this chapter in hopes that it (1) provides an overview of queer pedagogy and its relevance in adult education and (2) suggests some potential new directions for queer pedagogy in light of globalization. We draw on queer studies in primary, secondary, and adult education to frame our argument, which expounds and unpacks what it might mean to adopt a pedagogy that is distinctly queer. We then bridge to globalized adult work and learning sites and offer some implications, recommendations, and conclusions.

The Context of Globalization

Globalization can be roughly described as increased patterns of international influence on the corporate marketplace, which continues to expand into every corner of the globe (Davis, 2018; Miki, 2017). Kubow and Fossum (2007) suggest that patterns of globalization operationalize through various domains: sociocultural (i.e. multiculturalism, social movements, and immigration), economic/political (i.e. marketization and economic growth), information and communication technology (i.e. rate and reach of knowledge everywhere), and philosophical/ethical (i.e. outlooks that shape attitudes and behaviours). Haig-Brown (2008) also implicates colonialism, stating that globalization "has almost inevitably ignored persisting colonial relations, imperialism, Indigenous peoples and nations, and, of course, Indigenous thought" (p. 17). In light of the COVID-19 pandemic, we also add health as a pattern of globalization, whereby inadequate work and life conditions exacerbate diseases that rapidly spread across the globe.

 DOI: 10.4324/9781003128151-6

In globalization, goods and services are increasingly offered across borders, shaping the patterns of engaging, manufacturing, importing, and exporting. Egregiously, such "goods" include people, including those ensnared in sex trafficking across national borders. Patterns of globalization might also include entire industries rising or falling, the former infusing communities with prosperity, the latter leaving behind a trail of poverty and crumbling infrastructure (Anderson et al., 2013; Rizvi & Lingard, 2010). The presence of these patterns suggests that globalization fosters interdependence, which especially benefits wealthy nations of the global north, leaving others anchored in a cycle of economic insecurity and exploitation (Kubow & Fossum, 2007). The global vaccine rollout for COVID-19 is an example of this interdependence; wealthy nations were the first to manufacture, purchase, and distribute vaccines to its citizens, while less wealthy nations waited for handouts and leftovers.

Clearly, globalization has its pros and cons but also presents opportunities and conundrums. Through globalization, there are greater opportunities to compare to how "things are run" elsewhere, which, on the one hand, creates possibilities for collaboration, innovation, inquiry, and adaptation. Connections can now be made across the globe and create new forms of engagement. On the other hand, globalization generates vulnerability and competitiveness due to a neoliberal ideology that extolls privatization, managerialism, regulation, accountability, and "diversity" as an entrepreneurial benefit. These practices form the foundations for a version of globalization that ushers in nationalist and corporate violence on a global scale. Even so, new organizational policies may be adopted to enhance a liberal economy and accelerate globalization processes. These policies, in turn, impact work and learning spaces through the proliferation of standardized curricula and teaching for performance measures (Adhikary, 2014). For example, adult education may be delivered in a standardized way in various countries to promote "competences" and "quality education," without much consideration to socioeconomic and cultural differences of adult learners or their political contexts.

The rapid advancement of neoliberalism and globalization in work and learning sites may, with valid reason, raise the ire of equity and social justice advocates (Rezai-Rashti et al., 2017; Rizvi & Lingard, 2010). Emancipatory and anti-oppressive education may be cast as being of meagre quality, lacking fitness for purpose, too slow, or poor value for the money, and therefore subject to minimal or no space in educational processes. Cutbacks to adult education leads to standardization of programmes and fewer opportunities (Drewes & Meredith, 2015), which causes critical thinking and achievement to suffer and equity and social justice matters to fall by the wayside. This deterioration and erasure implicate queers, to name one identity domain, due to their long-standing interest in human and equal rights and social inclusion, dialogue, and justice. Ludwig (2016) wrote, "under neoliberalism rigid heteronormative politics have become flexibilized, same-sex lifestyles [sic] are no longer criminalized and pathologized, and same-sex partnerships have gained legal recognition" (p. 427). We do not agree that such liberal manifestations are evident uniformly across the world. Yet we recognize that within this same context of neoliberalism, as Ludwig explained, homonormativity and homonationalism flourish as shared norms, framed within allowances as "plurality," "tolerance," and "freedom." These allowances privilege White, middle class, cisgender gay, or lesbian identities and results in what Ludwig referred to as "heteronormalization" in a neoliberal state.

Considering these oppressions and privileges, it is becoming increasingly important to leverage globalization and neoliberalism to be a helpful influence on work and learning sites. A positive influence may result in expansive social awareness, activism, and deep inclusion and illuminate what these concepts might mean in various contexts, and how to strengthen them. A global queer pedagogy represents one way to shift the oppressive discourse of globalization and neoliberalism towards an opportunity for queer emancipation.

Queer Theory and Queer Pedagogy

Queer pedagogy, as an educational philosophy and practice, is informed by queer theory (Shlasko, 2005). There are multiple interpretations of queer theory, and we do not cover them all here. For the sake of focus, we draw on Britzman (1995), who suggested that queerness, as an expression of deviance, forms a lens of social analysis that critiques normalization as a process. By decentring that which is taken to be "normal," queer theory gains insights on the processes that construct borders of normalcy and deviance. Britzman wrote, "Queer Theory occupies a difficult space between the signifier and the signified, where something queer happens to the signified – to history and bodies – and something queer happens to the signifier – to language and to representation" (p. 213). In other words, queer theory explains how normalcy is constructed and deconstructed, simultaneously but in different ways, and how bodies, perceptions of history, and representations of identities are shaped accordingly. Britzman further explained that the notion of queer in queer theory is about actions, and not about persons evoking essential queerness. Queer theory, according to Britzman, problematizes gender and sexuality borders and identities that are replicated in everyday social norms and validated through social institutions and policies. This problematization includes disrupting the concept of "identity" in general and inquiring into the borders policing gender and sexuality acceptability. Queer theory has begun to integrate nuances of globalization, such as exploring decolonial queer theory. Decolonial queer theory theorizes the impact of colonialism on sexual and gender minorities (e.g. Dénommé-Welch & Mizzi, 2023).

Like queer theory, there is no unified definition of queer pedagogy (Shlasko, 2005), as one might expect, given that "queer" defies static and stable identity categories (Thiel, 2018). In general, however, we refer to queer pedagogy as philosophies and practices within education that bring sexuality and gender into focus as a way of disrupting and "decentring" them. Outside of queer pedagogy, such norms are taken as givens. Shifting to adult and higher education, recent interpretations of, and applications within, queer pedagogy have been helpful at evolving critical gender and sexuality studies (e.g. Allen, 2015; Seal, 2019). Bryson and de Castell (1993) suggested almost three decades ago that queer pedagogy means "education as carried out *by* lesbian and gay educators, to curricula and environments designed *for* gay and lesbian students, to education for everyone *about* queers, or to something altogether different" (p. 298, italics in original). This earlier work, though dated by its language that was normative at the time, created the foundation to develop queer pedagogy over time not limited to educational spaces that are specific to gender and sexuality education.

Conceptualizations of queer pedagogy involve teaching against heteronormativity (Britzman, 1995) and deconstructing heterosexually oriented educational spaces (Alexander, B., 2005). However, while teaching "against" wields power in the socio-political context in which education is enmeshed, there are limitations of its utility. Bryson and de Castell (1993) explained, for instance, that taking anti-homophobia as an ethical or pedagogical orientation does not necessarily lead to safer spaces for queer students and teachers (see also Potvin, 2021). Being "anti" anything is a position against a social prejudice but it is not explicitly "pro" what might be called deep inclusion. More than merely adding queer identities to the curriculum and then showing examples of homophobia and heterosexism (Allen, 2015), deep inclusion would address straight privilege in pedagogy (and the broad inability and refusal to acknowledge it, much less address it), practices that go unaddressed that support hetero/cisnormativity, and pedagogy that is sex-positive, gender-diverse, and identity-inclusive. Deep inclusion, beyond mere diversity, is assertive, insistent, and even pushy when it needs to be. It means that educators who are marginalized by their sexual or gender identities actualize their agency by taking space and presence in pedagogical contexts that normalize their cisgender heterosexual ("cishet") counterparts (see, for instance, Allen, 2015). Taking a "beyond-anti" approach in pedagogy means that adult educators consider what safer spaces can actually look like and how to enact their potential and possibilities.

Deep inclusion has implications for educational practices. A general pattern of social prejudice is that the targeted group tends to be burdened with educating the group with the lion's share of social power. Racialized people, for instance, tend to bear the weight not only of White supremacy and the effects of racism but also with educating White people about whiteness (DiAngelo, 2012; Johnson, 2020). In a parallel way, Britzman (1995) raised the argument that queer subjects become burdened to "solve" the problem of homophobia for straight people. Britzman added that thinking about pedagogy begins with consideration of how *knowledge* is a problem for leaders and their teachers, especially when particular ways of knowing are steeped in ignorance, entitlement, and bias. In other words, straight privilege underscores how many straight-identified people in the world remain ignorant about how sexual and gender minorities cannot take legal or social rights for granted and, in most places across the globe, must continue to fight for basic human rights and dignity (Brettschneider et al., 2017; Rocco & Gallagher, 2006).

Cishet educators should not passively assume that queer pedagogy is irrelevant to their teaching practice. The social identities of the person at the front of the room matter to queer students, as it does to marginalized students in general. A teacher who is also a person of colour, for instance, would likely resonate stronger with students of colour than most White teachers would (Milton Williams, 2011). Endless and tedious claims among some White people that they "don't see colour" are an attempt to hide from the facts of racism in the daily experiences of people of colour. Similarly, and in the context of queerness, a queer pedagogy, as practiced by queers and cishet people alike, rethinks and moves beyond duplicating knowledge by exploring spaces of marginality and liminality occupied by not only queers but other marginalized subjectivities as well. Luhmann (1998) described a similar premise and suggested that queer pedagogy needs to build upon the mere inclusion of queer content into curricula, which tends to incite worries about student reaction and, instead, promote a pedagogy that facilitates new understandings of relationships that emerge through queer critiques of knowledge. This means that a queer pedagogy, according to Luhmann, explores limitless identifications and examines the conditions that facilitate learning. For example, queer pedagogy may mean "searching out texts to read queerly" and remaining steadfast and unapologetic in doing so (Rumens, 2017, p. 237). What this means is adopting texts that are not necessarily queer-focused but represent queer sexualities and genders as a matter of course. Along a similar vein, Jonathan Alexander (2005) suggested that queer pedagogy become "working queerness in the writing classroom should be an invitation to *all* students—gay *and straight* [sic]—to think about the 'constructedness' of their lives in a heteronormative society" (p. 375, italics in original). Following Alexander, cishet educators can point to themselves as examples of how gender and sexuality norms continue to privilege some but not others.

The practices of queer pedagogy need to be informed from and connected to the complex history of queer studies. For example, in Canada, there are multiple historic homes that are now offered as museums whereby visitors have a glimpse into a colonizer's life at the earlier stages of colonialism. Robert visited one of these sites and noted in one house that there was a book by Oscar Wilde in the library. He immediately suggested to the tour guide that the colonizer could be queer based on his knowledge of Oscar Wilde's writings. The tour guide confirmed the colonizer's known homosexuality, but noticeably, that piece of history would have been absent if a queer reading of the room was not offered by Robert. There was also little discussion into queer settlers and their impact on or engagement with Indigenous peoples. This tension is akin to Halberstam (2003), who commented that queer pedagogy "must also try to break with the oedipal deadlock that creates and sustains intergenerational conflict" (p. 363) between first wave queer theorists and newer generations.

Adult education scholars have also contributed to conceptualizations of queer pedagogy. Earlier work by Brooks and Edwards (1999) focused on heteronormativity in pedagogy and challenged adult educators to defuse masculine/feminine and hetero/homo binaries in the classroom and workplace, disrupt normalizing and marginalizing forms of social regulation, and confront dominant and static constructions of sexuality and gender. Grace and Hill (2001) also explored a radical, emancipatory queer pedagogy to transgress learning spaces, build on queer knowledge, and engage queer political activities for social transformation. Grace (2001) additionally suggested that autobiography can lead to queer knowledge, culture, and identity being visible and present in pedagogy, calling heteronormativity into question and interrogating its status as "normal" and thus, largely invisible in pedagogical discourses. Vicars (2006) stated that describing one's story can be a useful, yet risky, pedagogical tool, adding that educators, in telling their stories of engaging queer pedagogy, engage in a "refusal to be pinioned by the weight of professional roles, one that rigidly delineates student from teacher, private from public" (p. 24). On the point about risk, Allen (2015) described queer pedagogy in higher education as realizing the limits of non-normative sexualities, political disagreements, hostility, and understanding that universities do not want their instructors to "rock the boat" too much, and in fairness, instructors want to keep their jobs. Last, Mizzi (2021) engaged queer pedagogical principles to suggest ways in which online instructors can engage new technologies that proffer queer knowledge and identities.

Some authors have identified tensions inherent to queer pedagogy. Seal (2019) connected Baizerman's work on challenging the status quo in social work education to heteronormativity and wrote, "people often have a powerful belief in normalcy, and in the permanent nature of their personal trouble and problems and constructions such as heteronormativity" (pp. 258–9). Beliefs construct a "hegemony of the normal" (p. 259), whereas through queer pedagogy, normative assumptions need to be viewed as a "failed hypothesis" (p. 259), rather than as a basis for fact. Normalcy therefore becomes an elusive and impossible concept, especially for queers. Similar to earlier work by adult education scholars, Seal suggested that queer pedagogy is about interrupting heteronormativity and perceptions of each other in the classroom, which can lead to power diffusion, equitable treatment, and a realization of the "humanity in all of us" (p. 259). In the next section, we integrate principles of queer pedagogy with critiques of globalization to suggest a global queer pedagogy.

Towards a Global Queer Pedagogy

Shlasko (2005) wrote, "queer is paradoxically not only an identity but also a political opposition to the stability and boundedness of identity" (p. 127). We agree with Shlasko, but add that neither queer theory nor queer pedagogy are an island, yet decades of activism would suggest a pattern of myopic self-interest. In this context, myopia is a tendency for activists to be politically active on matters of self-identity. Humanist ideas expressed as social norms fly in the face of those who radically set themselves apart from the norm, including disavowing the moral guidepost of respectability that pervades LGBT activism. One example would be the battle for marriage equality, where "same as" is the organizing politic of legal rights for queers. Queer activism favours disruption of normative status quos that foster privilege but stop short of calling it out. In other words, gender and sexuality activists might recognize heterosexist privilege but not recognize the significant ways that "same as" shapes the everyday lives of queers.

It is also the tendency of those outside of marginalized groups to do very little for others, thus framing activism as self-serving. Advancing to 2023, we assert that queer pedagogy must shift from a self-focus to a global one. We queers must lift our collective eyes outward, as it were, beyond our own self-regard. This means thinking through how queerness is performed and expressed globally, and not just within the confines of Western theorizing. It is no longer tenable to advance queer self-interest without making clear alignments and coalitions with other marginalized and oppressed people of the world, including but not limited to racialized, Indigenous, religious, class, and disability groups and communities. Doing so would be to actualize the concept and theory of intersectionality, a term coined in 1989 for and by Black women "to deal with the fact that many of our social justice problems like racism and sexism are often overlapping, creating multiple levels of social injustice" (Crenshaw, 2016, para. 11). Simply put, many people are oppressed in multiple ways that queer theory has yet to adequately address. Queer pedagogy within a broader scope would at least attempt to build a coalitional politics with other marginalized groups. We envision more queers advocating for other marginalized people, other marginalized people advocating for queer people, and non-marginalized people advocating for all marginalized groups through a global queer pedagogy. In a similar way, queer pedagogy, with its connection to critical pedagogy, is about troubling fixed and traditional roles in the classrooms, according to Seal (2019). Such roles might include those who are the learners and the learned, pedagogical relationships, and "experts" or "decision-makers." As Seal explained, the instructor should also experience a change of consciousness or transformation along with the students so that learning is a mutual experience. This approach also rethinks pedagogy as looking for new insights, rather than offering simplistic strategies (Allen, 2015; Kumashiro, 2002). For example, Allen positioned safety in the classroom as being a "fantasy" and argued that "a 'truly' queer pedagogy might embrace a lack of 'safety' in the pedagogically productive, dislodging it from its negative connotations for learning" (p. 767).

Queers in wealthy countries have no reason to feel complacent or smug about rights that have been won in western countries like Canada or the United Kingdom, while, concomitantly, queers in more legally and socially restrictive countries fight daily battles for survival let alone rights and recognition. On the one hand, the mobility of queer identities made possible through discourses and conduits of globalization enhances queer presence but action leads to reaction. With enhanced visibility and legal gains comes pushback, sometimes violently so. Anti-queer campaigns are underway, for example, in Chechnya (*Human Rights Watch*, 2019), eastern Europe (Walker et al., 2019), several countries in Africa (GlobePost, 2019; Reid, 2023), and other jurisdictions. Fervent nationalism and motherland Christianity have led to "LGBT-free zones" created across Poland, in addition to violence at Pride marches and festivals (*Canadian Broadcasting Corporation*, 2019). Religious fervency, which also underscores anti-gay/trans rhetoric in Canada and the United States, combined with a disavowal of supposed western influence, fuels much of the hostility, resulting in an influx of queer asylum seekers fleeing their own countries (*Envisioning Global LGBT Human Rights*, 2015). These political campaigns are hell-bent on stigmatizing, torturing, imprisoning, and killing sexual and gender-minority lives across the globe. Meanwhile, progress to transform schools as welcoming places for queer youth is uneven at best, including the United States (Dwedar, 2016) and other locations that purport to be "progressive." Visiting spaces that are queer or non-queer, but socially radical, may be one approach to draw attention to the hostility towards marginalized people and question privilege.

Clearly, the drive to confront and contain such conspicuous and brash queerphobia is not solely on queer shoulders. In light of the contexts of dangerous fervency, we argue that a *global queer pedagogy* is now paramount in adult education classrooms (and other learning spaces as well) not just for the sake of queer students and their instructors but also for bridging and making relevant queer content and perspectives representative of queers in various global spaces. The implications of a queer pedagogy for the development of adult education theory and practice are a proliferation of sexual and gender diversity across mainstream pedagogical practice, including those of cishet educators. In line with scholarship in the study of transnational sexualities and postcolonial queer studies, the underlying foundation is to challenge the stability of identity and interrogate the dominance of "LGBT" identity categories and problematize or affirm newer terminologies (Mizzi & Walton, 2014) and engage larger international bodies that work towards alleviating queer people as objects of scorn and oppression (Hill, 2013). As Brooks and Edwards (1999) pointed out, a queer pedagogy for global awareness opens possibilities for addressing what we refer to as a "conspicuous normalcy" that replicates stasis and stigma. A global queer pedagogy explores the notion that sexual subjects are not a product of or produced only through social movements or local identity politics but emerge from the relationships between globalized organizations and their prescribed work and learning systems. This may mean applying queer critiques of power, history, contact, and belonging to pedagogical practices, in whatever context that explores queer knowledge and experience.

Although not intending to be prescriptive, which would be antithetical to queer theory, an example of a global queer pedagogy is situated within Robert's undergraduate course on sexual and gender diversity in schools and community. The emphasis on "community" is purposive, as it moves past discussions based on what is taking place in school hallways and classrooms and envision community members, movements, and agencies as being influential and important to educational development. The course begins with a global and historical outlook, examining Indigenous sexualities worldwide, and how they are affected by colonialism and globalization (Smith, 2013). It then bridges to Two-Spirit/Indigiqueer experiences and onward into a broader Canadian context. There are critical discussions questioning why, for example, a public same-sex kiss can cause greater fervour than children who are starving on a mass scale (e.g. Creelman, 2007). The course concludes with a discussion of transnational sexualities, such as immigrants, refugees, and international students. Focusing on transnational sexualities allows for discussions on the intersectionality of human rights, sexuality, neoliberalism, colonialism, and mobility. It also attempts to re-shift the dominant Western-oriented discourses around sexuality and gender to consider the influence of non-Western sexualities and genders on Western institutions and people. There is also rich potential for change when exploring the types of discussions among non-Western queers (e.g. how impacts of globalization, neoliberalism, and colonialism can be felt differently for queers across the globe). Globalizing the course content is necessary, given the seemingly unstoppable advance of globalization, where identities and spaces converge through virtual and in-person exchanges.

Global queer pedagogy should also expand beyond "LGBT" categorizations or cisgender/transgender binaries to include various sociocultural understandings of sexual and gender difference. Concomitantly, this view also demonstrates how western understandings of sexual and gender diversity continue to police boundaries that limits inclusion efforts (Mizzi & Walton, 2014). When attention is given to sexual and gender diversity in various cultural spaces, the default response is to imprint a social script that fixes diversity discourses into "LGBT" categorizations. A Muslim woman who wears a hijab at a pride march could find her sexual, gender, and religious identity doubted due to assumptions about what constitutes queer. Conversely, a rainbow flag flying at a protest aimed towards government oppression in Iran creates opportunities to engage intercultural dialogue and shared interests. As Shlasko (2005) wrote, "any teacher can bring multiple, fluid identities and knowledges into the classroom, and that is pretty queer" (p. 131). A global queer pedagogy disrupts the boundaries and privileges set up by Western agencies when it comes to sexuality and gender, challenges their dominance, and centres Indigenous knowledge.

A global queer pedagogy also exposes queerness more broadly, without concentration on sexual or gender diversity, heteronormativity, or sexual regulation that is sometimes necessary. There are conditions in which certain identities and practices are rendered subversive, normative, or illegal, yet there are also underlying tones of resistance, agency, and subjectivity in the movement for acceptance and inclusion of these identities. The social and political positioning of sex workers, refugees, and Indigenous or homeless people as being illegal and unwanted are tropes that queer subjects share with them (Kovacevic & Luka, 2021). The pedagogical focus is to understand the forces that continue to bind certain identities to the periphery, explore how such relegation is sustained, and develop insights and strategies towards social emancipation as deep inclusion (Shore et al., 2016).

Implications, Recommendations, and Conclusions

There are implications of a global queer pedagogy for cishet people. First, there would be fewer restrictions on norms and expectations that are restrictive on everyone. Cishet people who resist social expectations of their own identities and lifepaths, such as being compelled to be married once, have children, own a home, and have a career despite the costs, may find a global queer pedagogy more amenable to their life choices that seem to defy restrictive norms and expectations. A global view allows for a broader understanding of sexuality and relationships. Second, there will be a broadened possibility for gender performativity that would erode violence against gender creativity. Herdt (1997) suggested that sexuality is everywhere and crosses time, and we add that gender too is everywhere and has a long history. A global queer pedagogy allows for exploration of gender diversity that transcends a gender ternary forming in the West (i.e. male, female, and trans). For example, Mizzi (2020) suggested that "a two-spirit person can be a sexual minority . . . or can also be their own gender, which some perceive as trans or genderqueer in a Western context" (p. 39). Understanding the myriad of genders in the world can emancipate narrow views of gender. Third, there will be a diminished shame meant to keep norms and expectations in place. Globalized identities will be able to contribute to a global queer pedagogy and describe their lived realities, regardless of whether there is an apparent connection to gender and sexual diversity or not. Those without as much global experience will learn about differences and expectations that shape lives elsewhere and consider where there are parallels to or divergences from their own lives. In this circumstance, we agree with Landorf et al. (2013) that global learning is more than examining a world map. Instead, there is exploration of relationships with others to help foster self-identity and understandings of equitable treatment and complex problems beyond borders of various kinds. Our contribution is a heightened sense of queer reflexivity, as one cannot fully understand diversity and complexity without unpacking the history and treatment of sexual and gender difference. Showing how oppressive systems have ruled and ruined lives, and still do, may be helpful at shifting attention away from shame.

Last, globalization is recast as a connective tool for everyone to learn and take action against atrocities committed elsewhere. Globalization, despite its disastrous effects for many people around the world and for the environment, may have, to put it cautiously, some benefits for global queer pedagogy. People can now connect with each other through technologies, especially validating for marginalized people to find others with similar experience. Some examples include sharing information and depictions of lives across the globe, questioning restrictive language and assumptions, or inviting guest speakers to provide a different view on curricula, all of which can take place in classrooms, on streets, in community spaces, online, and so forth. In contexts of legal, social, or curricular restrictions, such as those in many Asian and African nations, a global queer pedagogy may unfold in various ways. These might include challenging gender binaries and hierarchies, linking to broader human rights and peace movements, highlighting Indigenous histories of sexual and gender diversity, discussing the impact of systemic and social oppression, or problematizing the West's engagement of declaring sexual and gender identities to stimulate social change (e.g. "coming out" as LGBTQ and using "sexual orientation" and "gender identity" in political discourses).

We recommend that cishet and queer educators adopt a new lens through which they situate themselves and their students, local and global. This means that there is disruption of heteronormativity in classrooms whenever possible, what constitutes as "student" and "teacher," the hegemony of the gender binary or ternary, and sameness and its comforts. This is not an easy process, nor should it be. Ultimately, adult educators need to create conditions for learning that are inclusive and connective, not unintentionally exclusive and narrow. Adult educators can offer a broader view of queer knowledge, identities, expressions, and cultures in the classroom and confront neoliberal tendencies that erode social justice and equity. Adult educators can examine the systems that divide and conquer queers, and probe ways to alleviate these struggles. Raising awareness to the insidious connection between heteronormativity, neoliberalism, and globalization will hopefully produce more critically reflexive, politically astute, and deeply inclusive adult learners.

In summary, we propose a global queer pedagogy that expands beyond myopia to a broader social inquiry. Furthermore, we argue that adult educators, through their initial and ongoing professional development, should be aware of global queer pedagogy. In light of marginalization, torture, and murder of sexual and gender-minority lives across the globe, a global queer pedagogy also positions human rights and global activism as foundational to work and learning and draws linkages to colonialism, racism, and sexism, among other forms of violence. Embedded in this global view are principles of deep inclusion, interrogation of cishet privilege, and applications of queer critiques of power, privilege, history, contact, and belonging. A global queer pedagogy disrupts the boundaries set up by Western agencies around tokenistic "equity," "diversity," or "inclusion" discourses, amplifies differences in identities and contexts, and challenges heterodominance at every step. A global queer pedagogy provides space for non-Western and Western educational spaces to interrogate the construction and positioning of sexual and gender diversity in their own contexts, shed light on queer histories, and discuss the potency of social actions, however different they may be across the globe.

References

Adhikary, R. W. (2014). Relating development to quality of education: A study on the World Bank's neoliberal policy discourse in education. *KEDI Journal of Educational Policy*, *11*(1), 3–25.

Alexander, B. (2005). Embracing the teachable moment: The black gay body in the classroom as embodied text. In E. Johnson & M. Henderson (Eds.), *Black queer studies: A critical anthology* (pp. 249–265). Duke University Press.

Alexander, J. (2005). "Straightboyz4Nsync": Queer theory and the composition of heterosexuality. *JAC: A Journal of Rhetoric, Culture and Politics*, *25*(2), 371–395.

Alfred, M. V. (2015). Diaspora, migration, and globalization: Expanding the discourse of adult education. *New Directions in Adult Education*, *2015*(146), 87–97. https://doi.org/10.1002/ace.20134

Allen, L. (2015). Queer pedagogy and the limits of thought: Teaching sexualities at university. *Higher Education Research & Development, 34*(4), 763–775. https://doi.org/10.1080/07294360.2015. 1051004

Anderson, G., Mungal, A., Pini, M., Scott, J., & Thomson, P. (2013). Policy, equity, and diversity in a global context: Educational leadership after the welfare state. In L. Tillman & J. Scheurich (Eds.), *Handbook of research on educational leadership for equity and diversity* (pp. 43–61). Routledge.

Brettschneider, M., Burgess, S., & Keating, C. (2017). *LGBTQ politics: A critical reader.* New York University Press.

Britzman, D. (1995). Is there a queer pedagogy? Or, stop reading straight. *Educational Theory, 45*(2), 151–165.

Brooks, A., & Edwards, K. (1999). *For adults only: Queer theory meets the self and identity in adult education.* AERC Conference Proceedings. https://pdfs.semanticscholar.org/79ff/09cb4870878ebe018e bf635b4cedcc6cde13.pdf

Bryson, M., & De Castell, S. (1993). Queer pedagogy: Praxis makes im/perfect. *Canadian Journal of Education, 18*(3), 285–305.

Canadian Broadcasting Corporation. (2019, July 27). *Why "LGBT-free zones" are on the rise in Poland.* cbc.ca/radio/day6/britain-s-other-new-leader-impeach-o-meter-mister-rogers-radical-theology-lgbt-free-zones-in-poland-more-1.5224060/why-lgbt-free-zones-are-on-the-rise-in-poland-1.5224067

Crabtree, R., Sapp, D., & Licona, A. (2009). *Feminist pedagogy: Looking back to move forward.* Johns Hopkins University Press.

Creelman, B. (2007, July). Kiss-in against homophobia a success! Queer couple gets apology from Mexicali Rosa's owner. *Xtra Magazine.* https://xtramagazine.com/power/kiss-in-against-homo phobia-a-success-18444

Crenshaw, K. (2016, October). *The urgency of intersectionality.* ted.com/talks/kimberle_crenshaw_the_urgency_of_intersectionality?language=en

Davis, B. P. (2018). Globalization/coloniality: A decolonial definition and diagnosis. *Transmodernity, 8*(4). https://doi.org/10.5070/T484042045

Dénommé-Welch, S., & Mizzi, R. C. (2023). Shifting the gaze: A queer analysis of photographs of the Canadian Indian Residential Schools. In N. Rodriguez, R. C. Mizzi, L. Allen, & R. Cover (Eds.), *Queer studies in education: An international reader* (pp. 138–155). Oxford University Press.

DiAngelo, R. (2012). *What does it mean to be white? Developing white racial literacy.* Peter Lang.

Drewes, T., & Meredith, T. (2015, September 15). *If at first you don't succeed: Toward an adult education and training strategy in Canada.* Institute for Research on Public Policy. https://irpp.org/research-studies/if-at-first-you-dont-succeed/

Dwedar, M. (2016). *"Like walking through a hailstorm": Discrimination against LGBT youth in US schools.* Human Rights Watch. www.hrw.org/report/2016/12/07/walking-through-hailstorm/dis crimination-against-lgbt-youth-us-schools

Envisioning Global LGBT Human Rights. (2015). *Envisioning LGBT refugee rights in Canada: Is Canada a safe haven?* ocasi.org/sites/default/files/lgbt-refugee-rights-canada-safe-haven_0.pdf

Giroux, H. (2011). *On critical pedagogy.* Continuum International Publishing Group.

GlobePost. (2019, February 20). *Anti-gay laws widespread in Africa despite gains.* theglobepost. com/2019/02/20/africa-lgbt-rights/

Grace, A. P. (2001). *Being, becoming, and belonging as a queer citizen educator: The places of queer autobiography, queer culture as community, and fugitive knowledge* (pp. 100–106). Proceedings of the 20th Annual Conference of the Canadian Association for the Study of Adult Education, Laval University, Quebec City, PQ.

Grace, A. P., & Hill, R. (2001). *Using queer knowledges to build inclusionary pedagogy in adult education.* Paper presented at the Annual Meeting of the AERC. www.edst.educ.ubc.aa/aerc

Haig-Brown, C. (2008). Taking Indigenous thought seriously: A rant on globalization with some cautionary notes. *Journal of the Canadian Association for Curriculum Studies, 6*(2), 8–24.

Halberstam, J. (2003). Reflections on queer studies and queer pedagogy. *Journal of Homosexuality, 45*(2–4), 361–364. https://doi.org/10.1300/J082v45n02_22

Herdt, G. (1997). *Same sex, different cultures: Gays and lesbians across cultures.* Westview Press.

Hill, R. (2013). Queering the discourse: International adult learning and education. In P. Mayo (Ed.), *Learning with adults: A reader* (pp. 87–98). Sense.

Human Rights Watch. (2019, February 15). *Russia: New wave of anti-LGBT persecution.* www.hrw.org/news/2019/02/15/russia-new-wave-anti-lgbt-persecution

Johnson, T. (2020, June 11). When black people are in pain, white people just join book clubs. *Washington Post*. www.washingtonpost.com/outlook/white-antiracist-allyship-book-clubs/2020/06/11/9edcc766-abf5-11ea-94d2-d7bc43b26bf9_story.html

Kovacevic, D., & Luka, B. (2021, January 21). Croatia returned 7,000 refugees in 2020, Bosnian minister says. *Balkan Insight*. https://balkaninsight.com/2021/01/15/croatia-returned-7000-refugees-in-2020-bosnian-minister-says/

Kubow, P., & Fossum, P. (2007). *Comparative education: Exploring issues in international context*. Pearson.

Kumashiro, K. (2002). *Troubling education: Queer activism and anti-oppressive pedagogy*. Routledge Falmer.

Landorf, H., Doscher, S., & Hardrick, J. (2013). *Making global learning: Promoting inclusion and success for all students*. Stylus.

Ludwig, G. (2016). Desiring neoliberalism. *Sexuality Research and Social Policy*, *13*(2016), 417–427. https://doi.org/10.1007/s13178-016-0257-6

Luhmann, S. (1998). Queering/querying pedagogy? Or, pedagogy is a pretty queer thing. In W. Pinar (Ed.), *Queer theory in education* (pp. 1–15). Routledge.

Miki, R. (2017). Globalization, (Canadian) culture, and critical pedagogy: A primer. In C. Sugars (Ed.), *Home-work: Postcolonialism, pedagogy, and Canadian literature* (pp. 87–100). Les Presses de l'Université d'Ottawa and University of Ottawa Press.

Miller, J. P., Irwin, M., & Nigh, K. (Eds.). (2014). *Teaching from the thinking heart: The practice of holistic education*. Information Age Publishing, Inc.

Milton Williams, T. (2011). *Black teachers caring for Black students: Intersecting identity, culturally responsive teaching, and life history* [Doctoral dissertation, University of North Carolina].

Mizzi, R. C. (2020). Out of the closet and into the classroom: Exploring sexual and gender diversity in Canadian adult education. In S. Brigham, R. McGray, & K. Jubas (Eds.), *Adult education and lifelong learning in Canada: Advancing a critical literacy* (pp. 37–47). Thompson Educational Publishing.

Mizzi, R. C. (2021). Teaching for LGBTQ-inclusion in online settings. *New Horizons in Adult Education and Human Resource Development*, *33*(3), 70–74. https://doi.org/10.1002/nha3.20339.

Mizzi, R. C., & Walton, G. (2014). Catchalls and conundrums: Theorizing "sexual minority" in social, cultural and political contexts. *Philosophical Inquiry into Education*, *22*(1), 81–90.

Nicholas, J., Penny Light, T., & Bondy, R. (2015). *Feminist pedagogy in higher education: Critical theory and practice*. Wilfrid Laurier University Press.

Potvin, L. (2020). Queer pedagogies. In N. Naples (Ed.), *Companion to sexuality studies* (pp. 122–139). Wiley. https://doi-org.uml.idm.oclc.org/10.1002/9781119315049.ch7

Potvin, L. (2021). It's not all rainbows and unicorns: Straight teacher allies reflect on privilege. *Journal of LGBT Youth*, *18*(3), 273–286. https://doi.org/10.1080/19361653.2020.1719952

Reid, G. (2023, March 22). *It is vital for South Africa to oppose Uganda's dangerous anti-gay bill*. Human Rights Watch. www.hrw.org/news/2023/03/31/it-vital-south-africa-oppose-ugandas-dangerous-anti-gay-bill

Rezai-Rashti, G., Segeren, A., & Martino, W. (2017). The new articulation of equity education in neoliberal times: The changing conception of social justice in Ontario. *Globalisation, Societies and Education*, *15*(2), 160–174.

Ricci, C., & Pritscher, C. P. (2015). *Holistic pedagogy: The self and quality willed learning*. Springer.

Rizvi, F., & Lingard, B. (2010). Education policy and the allocation of values. In F. Rizvi & B. Lingard (Eds.), *Globalizing education policy* (pp. 71–92). Routledge.

Rocco, T. S., & Gallagher, S. J. (2006). Straight privilege and moral/izing: Issues in career development. *New Directions for Adult and Continuing Education*, *2006*(112), 29–39. https://doi.org/10.1002/ace.234

Rumens, N. (2017). Queering lesbian, gay, bisexual and transgender identities in human resource development and management education contexts. *Management Learning*, *48*(2), 227–242. https://doi.org/10.1177/1350507616672737

Seal, M. (2019). *The interruption of heteronormativity in higher education: Critical queer pedagogies*. Palgrave MacMillan.

Shlasko, G. D. (2005). Queer (v.) pedagogy. *Equity & Excellence in Education*, *38*(2), 123–134. https://doi.org/10.1080/10665680590935098

Shore, S., Mizzi, R. C., & Rocco, T. (2016). Teaching, learning, and working in the periphery: Provocations for researchers and practitioners. In R. C. Mizzi, T. S. Rocco, & S. Shore (Eds.), *Disrupting adult and community education: Teaching, learning, and working in the periphery* (pp. 307–318). SUNY Press.

Smith, K. (2013). Decolonizing queer pedagogy. *Journal of Women and Social Work, 28*(4), 468–470. https://doi.org/10.1177/0886109913505814

Thiel, M. (2018). Introducing queer theory in international relations. *E-International Relations.* www.e-ir.info/pdf/72252

Vicars, M. (2006). "Queer goings-on": An autoethnographic account of the experiences and practice of performing a queer pedagogy. *Auto/Biography, 14,* 21–40.

Walker, S., Davies, C., & Tait, R. (2019, October 25). Anti-LGBT rhetoric stokes tensions in eastern Europe. *The Guardian.* www.theguardian.com/world/2019/oct/25/anti-lgbt-rhetoric-stokes-tensions-in-eastern-europe

Wink, J. (2011). *Critical pedagogy: Notes from the real world* (4th ed.). Pearson.

6

WHEN GOD'S NOT ON YOUR SIDE

Toward Religious Institutional Developmental Identity Transformation

Warren J. Blumenfeld

I gave a presentation on the topic of heterosexism and cissexism at Pace University in New York City several years ago. I talked about my own experiences as the target of harassment and abuse growing up gay and non-gender normative, and I addressed my book, *Homophobia: How We All Pay the Price* (1992). In the book, I argue that everyone, regardless of their actual sexuality and gender identity and expression, is hurt by heterosexism and cissexism, and therefore, it is in everyone's self-interest to work to reduce and ultimately eliminate these very real and insidious forms of oppression.

Following my presentation, two students came up to me—one woman and one man—to continue the discussion. The young woman began by telling me:

> I'm really sad to hear about the abuse that you and others have received because you are gay or lesbian.
>
> I am here to tell you that I have a way to prevent that from ever happening to you again. I believe that Jesus Christ can help you. If you ask Jesus and pray hard, Jesus will save you from your homosexual feelings and help you to achieve the life that is meant for you, in his service, as a happy and healthy heterosexual. This will save you from the abuse you have suffered.

My response:

> So, let me see if I understand you: If I accept Jesus in my life and ask him to help me become heterosexual, then I won't suffer from homophobia any longer? So, to be sup-ported in society, I must change who I am and conform to the dominant standards of society? So, for people like yourself to truly support me, I have to become like you? While I understand that you are offering me, in your mind, a gift, do you not see how this itself is a form of homophobia, a form of oppression? Do you not see how this perpetuates oppression?

She responded with surprise and claimed that she knew the "truth" and that if I accepted her truth, Jesus could grant me salvation and happiness. If I rejected this, though, I would remain in earthly and eventual eternal torment.

  DOI: 10.4324/9781003128151-7

We continued our dialogue for more than one hour, and we ended cordially. All the while, the young man had been closely looking on and listening to the young woman and my discussion. Then, the young man spoke to me. He asked: "Professor Blumenfeld, you stated that you are a writer, that you had published a number of articles and books. Is this correct?"

"Yes," I responded.

"Okay, then," he continued. "You know that in the writing process, the first draft is never really complete or isn't any good."

"Yes, that's often the case," I agreed.

> Okay, then after you have had some time for reflection and you write your second draft, this is an improvement over the first draft, but still, it can be improved. So after further reflection and writing, your third version is great. Now you can send it to your publisher.

I said to him, "Oh no, please don't tell me that this is a metaphor for religious texts."
"Yes, indeed," he uttered.

> The first draft is the Hebrew Bible—not so good. The second draft is the Christian scriptures—somewhat better, but not much. But the best version, the third, is the Koran. The real truth. The ultimate truth. The only truth.

My response to this young man:

> As we speak, we are standing a few short blocks from the former World Trade Center towers. Utterances and understandings like yours and like the young woman I just spoke with, and by many people of any faith, that there is one and only one ultimate religious truth results in people taking it upon themselves, for example, to crash airplanes into buildings. Utterances like yours of many people of any faith give people justification to kill in the name of their interpretation of "God."

> "Why," I argued, "cannot the young woman I just spoke with realize that her understanding of God, while valid and reliable for her, may simply not be valid and reliable for me or for you, too? And why cannot you realize that your understanding may be great for you, but not necessarily for me and for the Christian woman? How many deaths must occur before we realize that there are many ways toward the truth, not one way for everyone when it comes to religion and spirituality?"

Recalling my conversations with these young students at Pace University, I wrote a short satirical editorial for a local newspaper in 2006 (Jewish year 5766) related to events occurring in Israel in what could be viewed as extraordinary. There the leaders from three major monotheistic world religions that were often at odds with one another—Judaism, Christianity, and Islam— joined in a united demonstration to protest and to prevent a ten-day international Lesbian, Gay, Bisexual, Transgender, Queer Pride festival planned for Jerusalem in August that summer.

While the Middle East has been a flash point of conflict and warfare for millennia, this coalition between orthodox religious leaders indicated that agreement, at least of sorts, was possible. In bringing these leaders together, I nominated the International LGBTQ Community for the 5766/2006 Nobel Peace Prize, an award well deserved for converting warring parties into allies and for reducing tensions that have traditionally separated them.

My point, though filled with irony, was simple: *the* prime stimulus keeping oppression toward LGBTQ people locked firmly in place and enacted throughout our society—on the personal/interpersonal, institutional, and larger societal levels—are the destructive doctrines and judgments emanating from primarily orthodox and fundamentalist religious communities.

Today, many people continue to cite religious texts that may call into question their support for LGBTQ people. It must be acknowledged, however, that various religious scholars and various faiths, with their many denominations, interpret religious textual passages regarding same-sex sexuality, same-sex relationships, and identities and expressions of gender very differently, for there is no monolithic religious view on these topics.

Though many religious denominations throughout the years have worked vigorously to end oppression toward a number of groups, including LGBTQ people, history also records a number of religious textual passages that individuals and organizations have referenced throughout the ages to justify and rationalize the marginalization, harassment, denial of rights, persecution, and oppression of entire groups of people based on their social identities. At various historical periods, people have applied these texts, sometimes taken in tandem, and at other times used selectively, to establish and maintain hierarchical positions of power, domination, and privilege over individuals and groups targeted by these texts.

For example, individuals, organizations, and entire nations have quoted specific textual passages to justify the construction and maintenance of the institution of slavery, the persecution and murder of Jews, male domination over and denial of rights of women, adult domination and persecution of young people, and demonization, marginalization, denial of rights, and extreme forms of oppression against LGBTQ people, considering them anywhere from being creations of the Devil, to sinners and immoral, to being the embodiment of evil in the world, which, left unchecked, would result in the destruction of peoples and nations.

History has shown a symbiotic relationship between religious and secular teachings on the issue of homosexuality, bisexuality, and gender variance, with one influencing and used to justify the other. Religious, philosophical, social, and political attitudes set the groundwork for restrictive laws enacted toward the latter stages of imperial Roman civilization (Boswell, 1980); Roman law was used as a basis for Medieval Canon Law (the law of the Catholic Church); Canon Law along with Roman law has been used as the cornerstone for punitive civil laws to the present day (Boswell, 1980). Laws doling out punishments ranging from denial of marriage and child custody benefits, to restrictions on engaging in military service, to constraints in gaining employment, housing, insurance, health benefits, public accommodations, and more, all the way to floggings, banishment, bodily mutilation, and incarceration, to death of the accused have existed at various times in many countries.

So, several questions remain:

- Does a society, whether or not it is founded on the guiding principle of the separation of religion from government, have the right to formulate and pass legislation based on religious tenets, which are not accepted by all?
- How can one include LGBTQ people as integral threads in the human tapestry and issues of heterosexism and cissexism in conceptualizations of issues of domination and subordination, even when one struggles with some religious interpretations of same-sex sexuality, same-sex relationships, and identities and expressions of gender diversity?
- Is it possible for one to separate one's specific religious interpretations from overriding religious mandates to treat others with respect, and to work to end oppression toward everyone?

Polytheism and Monotheism

Many ancient and non-Western cultures—including, for example, Hindu, most Native American, Mayan, and Incan cultures—base their religions on polytheism (multiple deities). In general, these religious views seem to attribute similar characteristics to their gods. Particularly significant is the belief that the gods are actually created, and they age, engage in sex, and give birth. The universe is seen as continuous, ever-changing, and fluid (Whiting, 2004). These religious views often lack rigid categories, particularly gender categories, which become mixed and often ambiguous and blurred. For example, some male gods give birth, while some female gods possess considerable power.

The ancient Greek philosopher, Plato, discussed in his *Symposium* (1951 edition) the creation story of the three human sexes and how males descended from the Sun, females from the Earth, and hermaphrodites (known today as intersex) he believed were half male and half female who came from the union of the gods Hermes and Aphrodite. Hermaphrodite was the god/goddess of Love, called Eros by the ancient Greeks and Cupid by the Romans.

Originally to Plato, all people had rounded backs and sides, four arms, four legs, one head on a cylindrical neck, one face on one side of the head, and a second face on the other side of the head. Then Zeus, the King of the gods, wanted to weaken the humans, but not to destroy them. He thus split them into two down their middle. Life for the humans then became a quest to reunite with their missing half to complete the self: man with woman, woman with woman, and man with man. In ancient Greek cosmology, gods were said to have had same-sex sexual relations with human mortals, for example, Zeus and Ganymede, and the Sun god Apollo and Hyacinthus (Nussbaum, 1999).

Some Hindu deities transcend sexuality and gender norms and manifest multiple combinations of sex and gender. On the Indian subcontinent, *hijra* are sexual and gender-diverse and intersex people. They are also known as *aravani*, *aruvani*, and *jagappa*, though the *hijra* community in India prefer to call themselves *kinnar* or *kinner*, referring to the mythological beings that delighted in singing and dancing. They have long performed religious ceremonies celebrating Sri Ardhanarishvara, a composite form of the Hindu deities Shiva and Parvati as half man and half woman.

In addition, indigenous peoples throughout the world viewed their spirituality through the perspectives of their multiple deities who connected them to their natural environments. They appreciated the complexity of gender as constituting a vast and wide continuum rather than the primarily western binary male-/female-only conceptualization.

Within many indigenous communities on what would come to be called the North American continent, the *nadleeh*, sometime referred to with general descriptor of "two spirit," are said to retain a balance of masculine and feminine traits. This was true of the Navajo people, for example, who believed that humans must maintain a balanced interrelationship between the feminine and masculine qualities within the individual, in families, within the culture overall, and in the natural world (Roscoe, 1998). Several tribal communities in pre-Columbian North America valued the presence of their two-spirit people whom they accorded reverence and esteem: *nadleehi* and *dilbaa* (Navajo), *winkte* (Lakota Sioux), *lhamana* (Zuni), *achnucek* (Aleut and Kodiak), and many others (Roscoe, 1998).

In contrast to polytheism, monotheistic Abrahamic (Judaism, Christianity, Islam) religions view the Supreme Being as without origin, for this deity was never born and will never die. This Being, viewed as perfect, exists completely independent from human beings and transcends the natural world. In part, such a Being has no sexual desire, for sexual desire, as a kind of need, is incompatible with this concept of perfection. This accounts for the strict separation between the Creator and the created. Just as the Creator is distinct from *His* creation, so too are divisions between the Earthly sexes in the form of strictly defined sexes, genders, and gender roles. This distinction provides adherents to monotheistic religions a clear sense of their designated *socially constructed* roles: the guidelines they need to follow in connection to their God and to other human beings (Kirsch, 2004).

The verb "to colonize" can be described as the process of appropriating a place or domain to establish political and economic control. Throughout history, nations have invaded not only their neighbors' lands but also territories clear across the globe for their own use. During this practice, the dominant nation attempts to colonize not only indigenous peoples' domains (territorial imperialism) but also their minds, their customs, their language, in fact, their very way of life. In countries with a historical legacy of colonization, and even in those without this history, members of dominant groups have accumulated unearned privileges not accorded to others. Though the official terms "colonization," "colonizer," and "colonized" may have changed somewhat, nowhere in the world have we experienced a truly post-colonial society. The imperialism remains, though at times possibly in less visible forms.

Europeans, when they invaded the North and South American continents and Africa, were surprised and offended when they came into contact with indigenous populations who did not conform to rigidly enforced gender roles including styles of dress, and sexual and gender expression. Missionaries attempted to impose primarily Christian, and in some places, Islamic orthodoxy. For example, they oppressed two-spirit people while killing many and forcing these individuals to go underground. Europeans nearly virtually exterminated two-spirit traditions from throughout North America.

Joel Spring (2004) discusses "cultural genocide" defined as "the attempt to destroy other cultures" (p. 3) through forced acquiescence and assimilation to majority rule and Christian cultural and religious standards. This cultural genocide works through the process of "deculturalization," which Spring describes as "the educational process of destroying a people's culture and replacing it with a new culture" (p. 3). An example of "cultural genocide" and "deculturalization" can be seen in the case of Christian European American domination over Native American Indians, whom European Americans viewed as "uncivilized," "godless heathens," "barbarians," and "devil worshipers" (Takaki, 1993; Zinn, 1980).

White Christian European Americans deculturalized indigenous peoples through many means: confiscation of land, forced relocation, undermining of their languages, cultures, and identities, forced conversion to Christianity, and the establishment of Christian day schools and off-reservation boarding schools far away from their people (Perlmutter, 1992; Spring, 2004), which combined constitute "settler colonialism."

"Civilizing" Indians became a euphemism for Christian conversion. Christian missionaries throughout the United States worked vigorously to convert Indians. A mid-19th-century missionary wrote: "As tribes and nationals the Indians must perish and live only as men, [and should] fall in with Christian civilization that is destined to cover the earth" (quoted in Nasaw, 1979).

Patriarchy

What is patriarchy? A society is patriarchal to the degree that it promotes male privilege by being *male dominated, male identified,* and *male centered.* It is also organized around an obsession with control and involves as one of its aspects the oppression of women.

(Johnson, 1997, p. 5)

Laws are built upon and reflect the society in which they are meant to affect. Patriarchal individualistic societies oppress and inhibit women's reproductive freedoms, encourage the inequities in salaries between men and women, establish and maintain the massive development of wealth for a very few while encouraging the enormous financial disparities between the very rich and everyone else, and many other issues (Johnson, 1997).

If a patriarchal social and economic system of male domination can keep women pregnant and taking care of children following birth, they can restrict their entry, or at least their level and time of entry, into the workplace, and ensure women's dependence upon men economically and emotionally. As women produce more and more children, expanding numbers of little consumers emerge to contribute to the capitalist system ever increasing profits for owners of business and industry. The patriarchal system necessary to control women's bodies amounts to imperatives to control women's minds and life choices.

In addition, the family's incessant reification and promotion of hegemonic binary gender categories are now (partially) what drive families in the United States to ex-communicate their LGBTQ children and provide fuel for the socially conservative capitalist class to spread sexism, cissexism, and heterosexism because of capitalists' direct benefit from traditional gender roles rooted in the family-household system (Collins, 1998). Thus, when a patriarchal family structure converges with a patriarchal religious system, which itself reinforces and intensifies the enforcement of strictly defined gendered hierarchies of male domination by restricting women's reproductive freedoms and decision-making and maintaining requisite sexual and gender matrices, women's oppression and the oppression of those who transgress sexual- and gender-based boundaries became inevitable.

Women's equality, lesbian, gay, and bisexual equality, transgender equality, and equality of people of color all challenge the hierarchal binary structure entrenched within patriarchal and white supremacist and religious systems of domination because when people fight for and achieve the right to control their bodies, this in turn better guarantees them the freedom to control their own minds.

Religion and a Legacy of Oppression

Prior to the concept of a single God and the creation of holy texts, which followers purported were "inspired" or written directly by this God, extreme condemnations against same-sex sexuality were relatively rare. This changed radically with the writing of the Jewish Bible and extended in the Christian gospels, and to an extent later in the Quran.

Such texts related to same-sex sexuality and gender non-conformity include but are certainly not limited to:

- Jewish Bible: Leviticus 18:22: Thou shalt not lie with mankind, as with womankind: it is an abomination (The Jewish Publication Society, 1992).
- In Orthodox Judaism, same-sex sexuality, including male-male anal sex, is in the category of *yehareg ve'al ya'avor*, "die rather than transgress."
- Christian Bible: Romans 1:26: In consequence, God has given them up to shameful passions. Their women have exchanged natural intercourse for unnatural (Holy Bible: King James Version).
- Christian Bible: Romans 1:27: Likewise, the men abandoned natural relations with women and burned with lust for one another. Men committed indecent acts with other men, and received in themselves the due penalty for their error.

- Christian Bible: Timothy 1:10: For whoremonger, for them that defile themselves with mankind, for menstealers, for liars, for perjured persons, and if there be any other thing that is contrary to sound doctrine.
- Christian Bible: 1 Corinthians 6–9: Know ye not that the unrighteous shall not inherit the kingdom of God? Be not deceived; neither fornicators, nor idolaters, nor adulterers, nor effeminate, nor abusers of themselves with mankind.
- Roman Catholic Catechism 2357:

> Basing itself on Sacred Scripture, which presents homosexual acts as acts of grave depravity, tradition has always declared that "homosexual acts are intrinsically disordered." They are contrary to the natural law. They close the sexual act to the gift of life [reproduction]. They do not proceed from a genuine affective and sexual complementarity. Under no circumstances can they be approved.

Pope Francis wrote on the archdiocesan website (Pastoral Guidelines, July 1, 2016) that "Catholic belief, rooted in Scripture, reserves all expressions of sexual intimacy to a man and a woman covenanted to each other in a valid marriage," calling this an "unchangeable" tenet. And he commanded of same-sex sexual attractions:

> "Those with predominant same-sex attractions are therefore called to struggle to live chastely for the kingdom of God," he wrote. "In this endeavor they have need of support, friendship and understanding if they fail. They should be counseled, like everyone else, to have frequent recourse to the Sacrament of Penance, where they should be treated with gentleness and compassion."

The Vatican hierarchy fenced off Alex Salinas, a 21-year-old transman in 2015 from Cadiz, Spain, by informing him that it had denied his request to become the godparent of his nephew because being transgender is incongruent with Catholic teaching. According to the Church's Congregation for the Doctrine of the Faith, its doctrine-enforcing agency:

> [Transgender status] reveals in a public way an attitude opposite to the moral imperative of solving the problem of sexual identity according to the truth of one's own sexuality. Therefore, it is evident that this person does not possess the requirement of leading a life according to the faith and in the position of godfather and is therefore unable to be admitted to the position of godfather or godmother.
>
> *(Catholic News Agency, 2015, n.p.)*

- Quran: 26:161: Your Lord is the Mighty One, the Merciful, Lot's people, too disbelieved their apostles. Their compatriot Lot said to them:

> Will you not have fear of Allah? I am indeed your true apostle. Fear Allah then and follow me. I demand of you no recompense for this; none can reward me except the Lord of the Creation. Will you fornicate with males and leave your wives, whom Allah has created for you? Surely you are great transgressors.

- Quran: 27:54: Lot, when he said unto his people: "Would you commit this abomination with your eyes open (to its being against all nature)?" And remember Lot, when he rebuked the men of his people, "Do you commit that shameful deed while you can see one another?" And Lot, when he said to his people, "How can you commit this indecent act with your eyes wide open?"

"*Hudud*" (literally meaning "limit" or "restriction") is a punishment mandated by God in the Quran, and "*liwat*" is the term for the act of anal sex between males. For ISIS, the *hudud* for *liwat* is death. In addition, in Iran since the Iranian Islamic Revolution of 1979, which replaced the Shah with an orthodox Shiite theocracy, many segments of the population have experienced repression under Iranian Sharia law (*The Telegraph*, 2008). Among the segments include LGBT inhabitants. Since 1979, some human rights activists estimated that between 4,000 and 6,000 LGBT people have been executed in Iran (*The Telegraph*, 2008). Same-sex sexuality between consenting partners in private is defined as a crime. Iranian law condemns males involved in sexual penetrative acts (sodomy or *lavat*) with the possibility of death, and so-called non-penetrative acts with flogging. After the fourth non-penetrative "offense," the penalty is death. Females convicted of engaging in same-sex sexuality (*mosahegheh*) may be made to undergo flogging with 50 lashes. And following the fourth conviction, they too are eligible for the death penalty (Islamic Penal Code of Iran, 1996).

Following the Islamic Revolution, trans identity and expression were also classified as crimes. However, the government reclassified these in 1986 as "heterosexual" if the person under-goes gender-confirmation surgery (formerly known as "sex-reassignment") surgery. Today, Iran stands as the country performing the most gender-confirmation surgeries in the world, second only to Thailand. Iranian trans people, however, still suffer frequent harassment and persecution.

What if Leviticus had not included Leviticus 18 though? Would the Christian gospels and Quran have had nothing on which to pattern their heterosexist discriminations? In this event, would they have invented their own, or would there never have been these "religious" justifications to persecute people for the past several millennia based on same-sex sexuality and gender diversity?

Biblical scholar, Idan Dershowitz, believes that Leviticus 18 did not appear in the original text of Leviticus:

> "Like many ancient texts, Leviticus was created gradually over a long period and includes the words of more than one writer," Dershowitz wrote. "Many scholars believe that the section in which Leviticus 18 appears was added by a comparatively late editor, perhaps one who worked more than a century after the oldest material in the book was composed."
>
> *(Dershowitz, 2018, n.p.)*

Dershowitz continued:

> No text has had a greater influence on attitudes toward gay people than the biblical book of Leviticus, which prohibits sex between men. Before Leviticus was composed, outright prohibitions against homosexual sex—whether between men or women— were practically unheard-of in the ancient world.

Well, maybe God simply had not decided to condemn homosexuality on the first draft, and it took another Earthly century to come to a decision. Much more likely, though, this thing we call "God" is simply a human creation in our often-desperate attempts to make sense of the mysteries of the universe regarding creation and existence.

More ultimate questions need to be raised as the world spins around, as individuals and nations since recorded history have attempted to explain the mysteries of life, as spiritual and religious consciousness was first developed and carried down through the ages, as people have come to believe their spiritual and religious consciousness stood as the right way, the only way, with all others as simple pretenders, which could never achieve THE truth, the certainty, the correct and right connection with the deity or deities, and as individuals and entire nations raped, pillaged, enslaved, and exterminated any "others" acting differently.

In reality, all religious doctrine stems from uncertainty and conjecture, from multiple gods, hybrid gods and humans, from Mount Olympus and before, to Earthly deities and the heavens, to Adam and Eve in the Garden of Eden, to the Burning Bush, to the Covenant and the parting of the Red Sea, to the Immaculate Conception and Resurrection, to Muhammad's rising to Heaven from the Rock, to the Golden Tablets, all beginning with the human *creation* of god(s).

Anyone can believe anything they wish, whether others find those beliefs laudable or offensive. When, however, the *expression* of those beliefs denies other individuals or groups their full human and civil rights, a critical line has been crossed, for their actions have entered the realm of oppression.

Social Construction of Knowledge

"Truth" is what the dominant group declares to be "true." "Knowledge" is anything the dominant group defines as "knowledge," though "knowledge" itself is socially constructed and produced. Dating back to ancient Greek philosopher Thrasymachus (c. 427 B.C.E.; Rauhut, n.d.) the social construction of knowledge theorizes how social phenomena, ideas, concepts, and practices develop in social contexts and are created by a group of people.

> Socially constructed (or produced) knowledge pertains to the everyday understandings that mediate our lives. Much of how we act, our social relationships, and how we perceive different phenomena are tempered by this knowledge. Even though this knowledge is important for living within the social world, it is considered to be taken-for-granted and commonsensical.
>
> *(Riley, 1996, p. 21)*

How many wars are we going to justify in the name of "God," our "God" versus their so-called "false gods"? Someone said to me once that throughout the ages, more people have been killed in the name of religion than all the people who have ever died of all diseases combined. I don't know whether this is actually the case, but I do think it highlights a vital point that we continually kill others and are killed by others over concepts that can never be proven.

Throughout history, the Jews and Muslims have killed each other, the Christians and Muslims have killed each other, the Christians and Jews have killed each other, the Hindus and Muslims have killed each other, the Catholics and Protestants have killed each other, the Sunni Muslims and the Shiite Muslims have killed each other, many faith communities have killed Atheists and Agnostics, and on and on and on. Individuals and entire nations continue to believe that their reality fits all and that it is proper and right to force their beliefs onto others "with God on our side."

Combined with pronouncements opposing women's reproductive freedoms, obstruction to contraception, and antagonism to the ordination and ascension of women in the overall hierarchy of many orthodox denominations, these beliefs correspond perfectly with monotheistic patriarchal *fundamental* attempts to control people's bodies, behaviors, and minds. And when patriarchal social and family structures converge with patriarchal religious systems, which reinforce strictly defined gender hierarchies of male domination, women and girl's oppression and oppression of those who transgress sexual-, sexuality-, and gender binaries and boundaries became inevitable.

When religious leaders preach their negative interpretations of their sacred texts on issues of same-sex relationships or identities and gender diversity within and outside their respective houses of worship, they must be held accountable and responsible for aiding and abetting those who target and harass, bully, physically assault, and murder people perceived as LGBTQ. In addition, they must be held accountable as accomplices in the suicides of those who are the targets of these aggressive actions.

When the religious/theocratic right declares that LGBTQ people are sinners and psychologically ill and that they must not be allowed to promote their so-called "homosexual" or "gay agenda" (Wikipedia, 2020) indeed, as the line between religion and government is increasingly blurred, and when we are taught to hate ourselves, each one of us is demeaned, which denies us all our freedoms. Therefore, we have a right, or rather an obligation, to speak up, to fight back with all the energy, with all the unity, and with all the love and passion with which we are capable.

From our vantage point at the margins, we have a special opportunity, or rather a responsibility, to serve as social commentators, as critics, exposing and highlighting the wide-scale inequities of all kinds that saturate and engulf our environment, and to challenge the culture to move forever forward and to grow.

The Liberation of Identities

"[Identity involves] the organization of the individual's drives, abilities, beliefs, and history into a consistent image of self. It involves deliberate choices and decisions, particularly about work, values, ideology, and commitments to people and ideas" (Woolfolk, 2004, p. 68). Most of us hold intersectional "social identities" (consciously or unconsciously) based on "socially constructed" categories: for example, on our personal and physical characteristics, on our moral beliefs and values, on our ages, abilities, interests, professions, socioeconomic class backgrounds, and on our cultural, racial, ethnic, national, linguistic, sex, gender, sexual and affectional, and religious identifications. Sometimes, these identities are *ascribed* to us by others (sometimes at our birth), and/or sometimes we self-identify, or these identities are *achieved* throughout our lives. Most of these identities are considered *dominant* in any given society, while others are *subordinated*.

Tatum (1999) states that identity is shaped by several factors including individual characteristics, family dynamics, historical factors, and social and political contexts. Everywhere a child is born—for example, Atlanta, New Guinea, Moscow, and Tokyo—all children undergo the process of socialization, which can be defined as the life-long process through which people acquire personality and learn the values, attitudes, norms, and societal expectations of their culture. Though the content varies from one culture to the next, the process of socialization is very similar. Through this process, people come to understand their culture, begin to develop a sense of who they are, and come to know what is expected of them in terms of their social role. While an acorn will inevitably become an oak tree, humans require socialization to realize their humanity. Cooley (1902) talks about the "looking glass self," whereby other people are the mirrors through which we see ourselves. An individual's *positionality* includes the social location that considers all of that individual's multiple social identities.

Erik Erikson (1950/1963), the preeminent developmental psychologist, asserted that individuals possess an innate drive or quest for identity, an inborn lifetime quest to know who they are, which powers their personality development. In a basic sense, then, identity is the detailed and multifaceted answer to the question, "Who am I?" Foundational to Erikson's theory of psychosocial development is that throughout life, individuals progress through a series of eight discrete periods or stages. During each, they confront "identity crises" (or "developmental crises"), which they must successfully negotiate and resolve in order to advance to the next stage. "Healthy development" at any one stage rests on meeting the challenges posed by the crises at previous stages.

In Erikson's "Stage 1" of the first year of life, for example, infants are challenged to develop a primary sense of trust with the world around them. Depending on how they resolve this life stage, they will go on to view the world either as a predictable and manageable place, which they can influence (basic trust), or as an unpredictable and volatile place over which they have little control (mistrust) (Borich & Tombari, 1997). A crisis in the Eriksonian sense, however, need not be considered negative.

Though Erikson's theories apply to human identity and personality development, organizations and institutions can travel a continual and ever-evolving path of identity spurred on by various crises. We can use similar developmental models to chart the development identity trajectory of organizations, social institutions, and entire societies and cultures. Indeed, several theorists have charted these institutional trajectories. Burton Clark (1960, 1973), for example, looked at the character or identity of institutions of higher education. Clark listed as the components of its character or identity a college or university's traditions, values, sources of support, patterns of responses, internal, external, and historical sources of influence, and its systems of organization.

Erikson's work on identity crises and Clark's work on institutional identity provide an important springboard for understanding the potential for both institutional and pedagogical identity and change at social institutions. We can consider the issue of institutional identity by investigating opposing forces which struggle, on the one hand, to maintain and permanently entrench the status quo and, on the other hand, to transform an institution to a new, qualitatively distinct developmental position.

The fifth stage in Erikson's (1950/1963) developmental model relates to "Identity versus Role Confusion." Identity continually evolves and transforms on both the individual as well as the institutional level, and it is dependent on how crises are resolved during this period.

> Power concedes nothing without a demand. It never did and it never will. Find out just what any people will quietly submit to and you have found out the exact measure of injustice and wrong which will be imposed upon them, and these will continue till they are resisted with either words or blows, or with both. The limits of tyrants are prescribed by the endurance of those whom they oppress.
>
> *(Frederick Douglass, 1845, quoted in Counterpunch, 5/29/2018)*

As more formerly marginalized and subordinated individuals are gaining the collective and personal support and strength to claim and assert pride in their sexual and gender variant diversity, they have become a driving oppositional force to many social institutions, including orthodox religious, "to transform an institution to a new, qualitatively distinct developmental position" (Blumenfeld, 1992, p. 22).

A central tenet of liberation is the right and freedom of people to self-define, to maintain their subjectivity and agency over the course of their lives. With their loving allies within some of the more orthodox as well as progressive religious communities in addition to those unaffiliated with religious denominations, they are taking back the discourse and demanding that religious institutions curb their offensive dogma and take their interpretations of scripture off their bodies.

Education for Brazilian philosopher and educator Paulo Reglus Neves Freire (1970) should provide a path toward permanent liberation in which people became aware (*conscientized*) of their multiple positionalities (identity intersectionality) and, through praxis (reflection and action), transform the world.

> [C]onsider a vision for social justice and liberation that values critical consciousness, participation, connectedness, passion, bridge building across divides through dialogue and action, and alliances and coalitions for change, as pathways to individual and collective empowerment, equity, safety, and security for all social groups in society. Such a vision requires an understanding of how various forms of privilege and oppression are connected at the psychological, interpersonal, intergroup, structural/institutional, and global levels.
>
> *(Zuñiga, 2013, p. 590)*

People are no longer accepting the detestable mantra, "We hate the sin but love the sinner." They accept no longer anyone or any denomination telling them why and how we have come to our same-sex attractions and our gender diversity, and that it is a "choice" that we can change. They continue to fight against efforts to legislate them into second-class citizenship and codify religions' so-called "values" into law. They are fighting attempts to restrict them from entering the social institutions of their choice.

Sexual and gender-diverse people throughout the world are taking back their traditions and their intersecting identities on the individual, institutional, and larger societal levels following millennia of colonial domination and authoritarian patriarchal religious and social structural control.

> When we are committed to liberatory praxis, we must engage in a process of *conscientization* that includes deconstructing the multiple layers of colonization in our internal and external spaces and practices in order to chart a new territory for ourselves, our fields of study, and our communities. The process of *concientization* is a group process, a community process, and a political process.
>
> *(Scharrón-Del Río, 2020, p. 301)*

While we had no input in constructing the systems of oppression, by coming to a deeper understanding of ourselves and of these systems, we can function integrally as "liberation workers" by developing with mindful intentionality, in Barbara Love's terms, a "liberatory consciousness" (2013, p. 601) free from the self-guilt one may experience and the blaming of others for its continuance. Love discusses her four elements of liberatory consciousness.

1. Awareness

As the term denotes, "awareness" involves developing the critical facility to perceive fully the depth and substance of our cultural and political environments, to attend to the details, the overt and covert meanings in language, in our and other people's behaviors and thoughts. As Love states, "It means making the decision to live our lives from a waking position" (p. 602).

2. Analysis

With the awareness, the information we gather from our "waking position," we have the means to reflect, examine, and posit what is happening as we make meaning from our perceptions. This analysis will provide us with practical options for actions we may need to take whenever what we perceive stands counter to our values of social justice.

3. Action

Following our awareness and analysis of our perceptions, we can now determine if any action is required, either by us as an individual, collectively by coalescing in unity with others, or by supporting and encouraging others to engage in action. "The action component of a liberatory consciousness includes deciding what needs to be done, and then seeing to it that action is taken" (Love, 2013, p. 603).

4. Accountable/Allyship

While acknowledging and accepting the axiom that it is not the responsibility of minoritized peoples to teach people of dominant groups about systems of oppression and to dismantle social oppression all on their own, Love believes that when members of subordinated and dominant groups join as allies "across and between 'role' groups," a synergism derived from these unions can result in the furtherance of a liberatory consciousness for all involved.

Throughout the past decades, many individual progressive Jewish, Christian, and Muslim congregations on virtually all continents (maybe not many in Antarctica) and some entire denominations have supported and welcomed LGBTQ people as full and essential members. Some of these denominations ordain women and LGBTQ clergy. These institutions understand that they must either change and move forward—to progress along their developmental trajectory as they meet each developmental crisis or task—or stagnate in the past and die.

Once colonial domination and its attendant hegemonic discourses and systems have entrenched into the foundations of indigenous populations, though, these remain difficult to lift and dismantle in the aftermath of colonialism even following easing or retreat of colonial powers. After literally decades and even centuries of domination, political, economic, linguistic, religious, and other systems tend to remain insinuated within the institutional and cultural environments.

Two spirit, hijra, and other sexually diverse and gender-diverse peoples, however, from previous or continuing polytheistic spiritual heritages are reclaiming their cultural traditions and identities in their attempts to raise and dispel the yoke of colonization, which attempted to thoroughly and ultimately commit cultural genocide and render their heritage to the lost list of historical extinction. In the final analysis, challenging oppressive dogma does not fall into the category of "religious intolerance" or "religious bigotry," but rather amounts to standing up to correct a devastating social injustice.

References

Blumenfeld, W. J. (1992). *Homophobia: How we all pay the price*. Beacon Press.

Borich, G., & Tombari, M. (1997). *Educational psychology: A contemporary approach* (2nd ed.). Addison-Wesley.

Boswell, J. (1980). *Christianity, social tolerance, and homosexuality: Gay people in western Europe from the beginning of the Christian era to the fourteenth century*. University of Chicago Press.

Catholic News Agency. (2015, September 2). *Vatican says "no" to transsexual godparents amid Spain controversy*. Retrieved May 20, 2020, from www.catholicnewsagency.com/news/vatican-says-no-to-transsexual-godparents-amid-spain-controversy-54280

Clark, B. R. (1960). The open door college: A case study. *British Journal of Educational Studies, 9*(1), 89–90.

Clark, B. R. (1973). Development of the sociology of higher education. *Sociology of Education, 46*(1), 2–14. https://doi.org/10.2307/2112203

Collins, P. H. (1998). It's all in the family: Intersections of race, gender, and nation. *Hypatia, 13*(3), 62–82.

Cooley, C. H. (1902). *Human nature and the social order*. Charles Scribner's Sons.

Dershowitz, I. (2018, July 18). The secret life of Leviticus. *New York Times*. Retrieved May 24, 2020, from www.nytimes.com/2018/07/21/opinion/sunday/bible-prohibit-gay-sex.html

Douglass, F. (2018, May 29). *Narrative of the life of Frederick Douglass*. The Anti-Slavery Office, quoted in *Counterpunch*. Retrieved November 27, 2020, from www.counterpunch.org/2018/05/29/power-concedes-nothing-without-a-demand-the-new-poor-peoples-campaign/ (Original work published 1845)

Erikson, E. (1963). *Childhood and society*. Norton. (Original work published 1950)

Freire, P. R. N. (1970). *Pedagogy of the oppressed*. Continuum Publishing.

Islamic Penal Code of Iran. (1996). www.refworld.org/cgi-bin/texis/vtx/rwmain/opendocpdf.pdf?reldoc=y&docid=52b812384

James, K. (n.d.). *Holy Bible: King James version*. Christian Art Publishers.

The Jewish Publication Society. (1992). *Torah: The five books of Mose* (3rd ed.). The Jewish Publication Society.

Johnson, A. G. (1997). *The gender knot: Unraveling our patriarchal legacy*. Temple University Press.

Kirsch, J. (2004). *God against the Gods: The history of the war between monotheism and polytheism*. Penguin.

Love, B. J. (2013). Developing a liberatory consciousness. In M. Adams, W. J. Blumenfeld, R. Castañeda, H. Hackman, M. Peters, & X. Zúñiga (Eds.), *Readings for diversity and social justice* (3rd ed., pp. 601–605). Routledge.

Nasaw, D. (1979). *Schooled to order: A social history of public schooling in the United States*. Oxford University Press.

Nussbaum, M. C. (1999). *Sex and social justice*. Oxford University Press.

Pastoral Guidelines for Implementing *Amoris Laetitia*. (2016, July 1). *Archdiocese of Philadelphia*. Retrieved May 24, 2020, from http://archphila.org/wp-content/uploads/2016/06/AOP_AL-guidelines.pdf

Perlmutter, P. (1992). *Divided we fall: A history of ethnic, religious, and racial prejudice in America*. Iowa State University Press.

Plato. (1951). *Symposium: Translation and introduction by Walter Hamilton*. Penguin Classics.

Rauhut, N. (n.d.). Thrasymachus (fl. 427 B.C.E.). In *Internet encyclopedia of philosophy*. https://iep.utm.edu/thrasymachus/

Riley, R. (1996). Revealing socially constructed knowledge through quasi-structured interviews and grounded theory analysis. *Journal of Travel and Tourism Marketing, 5*(2), 21–40.

Roscoe, W. (1998). *Changing ones: Third and fourth genders in native North America*. Palgrave Macmillan.

Scharrón-Del Río, M. R. (2020). Intersectionality is not a choice: Reflections of a queer scholar of color on teaching, writing, and belonging in LGBTQ studies and academia. *Journal of Homosexuality, 67*(3), 294–304.

Spring, J. (2004). *Deculturalization and the struggle for equality: A brief history of the education of dominated cultures in the United States* (4th ed.). McGraw-Hill.

Takaki, R. (1993). *A different mirror: A history of multicultural America*. Little Brown.

Tatum, B. D. (1999). *Why are all the Black kids sitting together in the cafeteria, and other conversations about race*. Basic Books.

The Telegraph. (2008, May 22). *UK grants asylum to victims of Tehran persecution of gays, citing publicity*. Retrieved May 26, 2020, from www.telegraph.co.uk/news/wikileaks-files/london-wikileaks/8305064/IRAN-UK-GRANTS-ASYLUM-TO-VICTIM-OF-TEHRAN-PERSECUTION-OF-GAYS-CITING-PUBLICITY.html

Whiting, A. B. (2004). The expansion of space: Free particle motion and the cosmological redshift. *The Observatory, 124*, 174–189. https://arxiv.org/pdf/astro-ph/0404095.pdf

Wikipedia. (2020, November 27). *Homosexual, gay agenda.* https://en.wikipedia.org/wiki/Homosexual_agenda

Woolfolk, A. (2004). *Educational psychology* (9th ed.). Allyn and Bacon.

Zinn, H. (1980). *A people's history of the United States.* Harper.

Zuñiga, X. (2013). Introduction: Working for social justice. In M. Adams, W. J. Blumenfeld, R. Castañeda, H. Hackman, M. Peters, & X. Zúñiga (Eds.), *Readings for diversity and social justice. An anthology* (3rd ed., p. 590). Routledge.

II

National and Societal Contexts

7

CONTEMPORARY LEGAL AND POLICY PRACTICES ON LGBTQ AND ACTIVIST WORK IN KENYA

Dorothy Owino Rombo and Anne Namatsi Lutomia

Colonial and neocolonial narratives, both cultural and institutional, shape local politics, religious beliefs, and other social trends and construct the social environment within which LGBTQ individuals live. The same narratives become the force that also influences the activists in the LGBTQ community and their allies. Kenyan activists rely on the 1948 UN declaration of Human Rights in 1948 and the 2010 Constitution of Kenya when agitating for LGBTQ rights (Moyosore, 2019). The passing of anti-LGBTQ laws in some African nations such as Nigeria and Uganda in 2014 (Amnesty International UK, 2019) also created a reactionary wave in sub-Sahara Africa (Rombo & Lutomia, 2022). Although Africa is not a federation, the responses to LGBTQ issues in the region bear the ramifications of shared experiences with colonialism and the influence of missionaries (Dugmore, 2015).

According to Bulboz and Sontag (1993), macrosystems are socially constructed norms where society may use stereotypes, biases, and myths to create hierarchies ranging from high to low social status. For example, patriarchy, sexism, and classism favor individuals based on the hierarchies associated with identities while marginalizing others. The status of LGBTQ people and rights in Kenya shows the gap between social acceptance espoused in policy and practice, and how LGBTQ people are actually treated. Although smaller social units, such as families and individual friends and allies, may accept members' LGBTQ self-identification (Rombo & Lutomia, 2022), societal macroforces can and do bear heavily on LGBTQ experiences. For example, Kenya made international news in April 2018 when the Kenyan Film Classification Board (KFCB) director refused the screening of *Rafiki*, a Kenyan-made lesbian-themed film that won an award at the Cannes Film Festival, because it promoted homosexuality, which is still punishable by 14 years in prison in Kenya (BBC, 2018a). In-country screening for at least seven days is required for consideration as a Best Foreign Language Film submission to the Academy Awards. Ultimately, Judge Wilfrida Okwany ruled that Kenyans could handle a gay-themed movie and cleared the way for its screening, albeit only for the seven days to meet the Academy Awards' requirement (BBC, 2018b).

In The Kenya 2010 Constitution, Chapter 4, Articles 21 and 27, clauses 3 and 4 (National Legislative Bodies/National Authorities, 2010) specify protection of rights accorded to all Kenyans. The latter clause promises to uphold the rights of every citizen without explicitly mentioning members of LGBTQ community. Consequently, The Human Rights Watch (2015) reports that the LGBTQ community is subjected to discrimination and violence. Discrimination against

DOI: 10.4324/9781003128151-9

the LGBTQ community is tolerated, as some macrosystems exhibit doublespeak by claiming to offer protection on the one hand while denying it on the other hand. For example, in the same Human Rights Watch report, the executive coordinator of the Gay and Lesbian Coalition of Kenya (GALCK) observed that Kenya rejected a recommendation to decriminalize same-sex conduct between consenting adults by the United Nations Human Rights Council in 2015. The country, however, adopted a comprehensive anti-discrimination position affording protection to all individuals, regardless of sexual orientation or gender identity by the same Council. On February 24, 2023, The High Court of Kenya ruled in favor of the LGBTQ community against the NGO Board that had refused the registration of associations. A ruling that was condemned by many including the president Gathara (2023). Such mixed positions obscure the reality of differential treatment of the LGBTQ community by presenting a myth of equal treatment for all.

Given the fact the LGBTQ communities in Kenya face mixed reactions from policy to practice, this chapter aims to trace the origins in Kenya of othering of the LGBTQ communities beginning with precolonial, colonial, to present day and the impulse of activism. A postcolonial framework affords descriptions of macrosystems precolonial, colonial, and postcolonization. For instance, precolonial cultural expressions of homosexuality and the patterns of colonial condemnation and suppression have been maintained and further normalized during postcolonial Kenya. Questions this chapter addresses include: What macrosystems influenced precolonial, colonial, and postcolonial LGBTQ experiences? How has the continuation of imperialism influenced policy and practice related to the LGBTQ community in Kenya? What is the role of activism as a response to the oppressive macrosystems that have emerged historically?

LGBTQ Lives in Precolonial Kenya—Pre-1895

Scholarly accounts of African culture and traditions during precolonial era, documented by anthropologists and missionaries, reveal the presence of a diverse range of sexualities, gender identities, and expressions within numerous African communities (Evans-Pritchard, 1950; Lewis, 1973). According to Global Rights 1. (2013, October 1), Gitari noted that queer males known as *mugawe* existed among the Meru ethnic community of Kenya. *Mugawe* were simultaneously held in high regard as healers and as herders who stayed away from the community for extended periods. Similarly, the Luo and Luhya of Kenya had queer men called *msumba* who failed to get married at the customarily stipulated time.

Other forms of queerness included both male–male and female–female expression among the Nandi, Kipsigis, Keiyo, Maragoli, Kuria, Akamba, Gikuyu, and Swahili communities, as well as woman–woman marriage and varieties of cross-dressing during initiation rites and annual festivals (Amory, 2019; Gay and Lesbian Coalition of Kenya, 2016). Among the Kalenjin people of Kenya, a woman born to a family with no sons could take a wife to ensure the patrilineal legacy of her father's family continued. She would choose a man to have children with her wife and take up the role of a provider just as expected of a husband. The biological father would have no claim over the children. Privilege allowed Kikuyu women to lead queer lives, while cultural traditions that believed in sustaining family lineage as paramount allowed Kalenjin women to practice queerness. In the aforementioned examples, the specific ethnic groups justified the co-existence of queer members in society. Each ethnic community had customs and traditions that governed the behavior of the members. Retelling stories of LGBTQ lives in precolonial Kenya, however, does not inform us of the unconstricted freedoms these individuals enjoyed, but they confirm the presence of such folk.

LGBTQ Lives in Colonial Kenya 1895–1963

Colonial rule was driven by the agenda of grabbing power—a goal that would be achieved through the subjugation of the Africans by various means, including physical punishment and psychological manipulation (Dei & Imoka, 2018). Upon colonizing Kenya in 1895, the British set up parallel laws to the customary traditions used to govern the diverse ethnic groups that make up Kenya. According to Finerty (2012), in the East Africa Order of 1897, the British imposed the 1860 Indian Penal Code on the East Africa Protectorate, of which Kenya was a part. The customary laws gave way to English laws if they were deemed repugnant to justice or morality or inconsistent with the provisions of any order in council or with any other law in force in the colony. Customary laws gradually became inferior and were replaced by the penal codes. Article 162 of the Penal Code punishes "carnal knowledge against the order of nature" with up to 14 years in prison, while Article 165 makes "indecent practices between males" liable to up to five years in prison (Human Rights Watch, 2019). The missionaries were in lock and step with the colonial government in asserting a binary sexual behavior in which heterosexual sex was acceptable while other forms were not (McClintock, 1995; Young, 1995).

Although British laws informed the laws applied in the British colonies, they were not applied evenly when dealing with the colonized subjects. For one, the customary laws were selectively permissible, and there was evidence of different treatments of the colonialists. Governor Rechenberg of the East Africa Protectorate from 1906 to 1912 was accused of having sexual relations with one of his male servants, and a concerted effort had to be launched by the courts to protect the governor as the face of the colonial government even as rumors circulated among civil servants (Schmidt, 2008). While this scandal exhibited a convergence of class tensions, a crisis of masculinity, and the white supremacy of colonial projects, it also suggests that colonial legal concern about homosexuality has less to do with social production and more to do with condemning and controlling the people colonized.

LGBTQ Lives in Post-Independence Kenya 1963—Present

Independence ushered in new and renewed lenses through which gender and sexuality in Kenya are conceptualized, albeit with continued contestations and negotiations. The relics of colonial laws still underpin how LGBTQ people are treated in Kenya. According to Human Rights Watch (2019), The Kenya High Court in 2019 upheld Articles 162 and 165 of the penal codes. While the Court declined in 2019 to rule these laws unconstitutional, the grandfathering of British colonial legal language into the Kenyan Penal Code demonstrates the afterlife of colonialism in postcolonial Kenya (Han & O'Mahoney, 2018; Kanna, 2020).

Despite the legacy of the penal codes, international, regional, and national policies imply equality for all, including LGBTQ people. Being a signatory to the United Nations, Kenya upholds the 1948 Declaration of Human Rights principles. For example, in 1976, the International Covenant on Civil and Political Rights (ICCPR) declared rights to self-determination, privacy, liberty, and security to all without discrimination. In the same year, the International Covenant on Economic, Social and Cultural Rights (ICESCR) also declared to protect rights to favorable working conditions, education, health, and ability to take part in cultural life. The 1986 African Charter on Human and People's Rights ensured rights in ICCPR and ICESCR, to which Kenya acceded in 1992.

The African Commission on Human and Peoples' Rights included Resolution 275 that protects against violence and other human rights violations against persons based on their actual or imputed sexual orientation or gender identity (Commonwealth Forum of National Human Rights Institutions, 2018). After much lobbying by human rights activists, the Africa Commission addressed abuses of human rights defenders, including those focused on LGBTQ issues (Isaack, 2017). In June 2018, the World Health Organization (WHO) removed all trans-related categories from its chapter on mental health and behavioral disorders (BBC, 2019).

Section 27 item no. 4 of the 2010 Constitution asserts that The State shall not discriminate directly or indirectly against any person on any ground, including race, sex, pregnancy, marital status, health status, ethnic or social origin, color, age, disability, religion, conscience, belief, culture, dress, language, or birth. Although sexual orientation is excluded while sex is not explicitly inclusive of diverse gender identities, Kenya upholds the supremacy of the 2010 Constitution in Article 2. In Item 4, Kenya declared to uphold the constitution when faced with an outdated customary law as the alternative, and in Item 5, the international covenants are incorporated where the general rules of international law form part of the law of Kenya and Item 6, which states that "any treaty or convention ratified by Kenya shall form part of the law of Kenya under this constitution" (Republic of Kenya, 2010, Article 2 section 6).

The political leaders in Kenya do not espouse what is presented in the international, regional, and national policies that protect LGBTQ individuals' rights. They have a great deal of influence over public opinion by making statements that do not support the LGBTQ community. In his anthropological publication of 1938, President Kenyatta denied that homosexuals existed among the Kikuyu and, by extrapolation, in Africa (Kenyatta, 1938). President Daniel Arap Moi once stated, "[H]omosexuality is against African norms and tradition. . . . Kenya has no room for homosexuals and lesbians" (News24, 2006). At a political rally in 2010, Prime Minister Raila quoted the Constitution as clear about punishing homosexuality (Kassim & Leposo, 2010). President Uhuru Kenyatta made a double speak on CNN (2018) that gay rights were not being violated and were not a priority for the Kenyan people.

Present-day political and religious adherents to nation-states across Africa, including Kenya, Ghana, Gambia, Uganda, Nigeria, and Zimbabwe, refer to homosexuality as having no place in their countries, as un-African, or Western (van Klinken, 2019). Kenya has held a record of high moral standing that deemed LGBTQ activities a sin. Mutua, as the chief executive officer of the Kenya Film Association, took it upon himself to be the moral standard keeper of the Kenyans. He used his office to express moral judgment in the country for six years (van Klinken, 2021). The country is deeply religious such that religion permeates every aspect of social life, including politics, attitudes toward public policy, world views, cultural life choices, including dressing codes (Mbote et al., 2018). Fariah (2022) indicates that about 86% are Christians, with 33.4% Protestant, 20.6% Catholic, and 20.4% Evangelical. Only 7% belong to African churches which are led by Africans and have deviated from mainstream churches with colonial roots, and 11% are Muslim.

Mbote et al. (2018) collected quantitative data from religious leaders concerning their views on sexual orientation and gender identity while considering the role of religious doctrine and public policy. They found that the majority of church leaders had negative attitudes towards diversity and plurality in sexual orientation and gender identity especially LGBTQ. In short, these church leaders mainstreamed heteronormativity while spreading homophobic narratives.

However, Mbote et al. (2018) found that religious leaders who had personal knowledge of a member of the LGBTQ community held more positive attitudes towards the group than those who had not. Such leaders were not the majority.

Even though religion seemed closed off to LGBTQ, van Klinken (2021) sought to explore religion, LGBTQ activism, and using art for resistance in Kenya. He used qualitative inquiry, specifically, case-study method with Christian gay participants (van Klinken, 2021). van Klinken

(2021) found out that Kenyan mainstream Christian churches were reluctant to embrace LGBTQ who seek to be embraced but have formed their own church.

Access to mobile phones, television, and the internet has provided space for conversations that engage LGBTQ people and their allies with those who are anti the community. Rombo and Lutomia (2022) analyzed a selected sample of these conversations from YouTube and found that LGBTQ and LGBTQ allies provided educative insights about the experience of the community members. To a community seeking acceptance, these opportunities on television centered their experience for the public's consumption. Not all information on LGBTQ that is presented on various media platforms is positive. For example, a study by Pellot (2020) compared the quality of journalism in terms of professionalism, authenticating LGBTQ voices, and being sensitive when reporting about LGBTQ people. The study aimed at determining if journalists would seek to give voice to the LGBTQ community and ensure that the community was correctly and respectfully reported. The results showed that Kenya and Uganda reported about LGBTQ people in inhumane ways. They did not include their voice and used sensationalized language to report about LGBTQ.

Despite Kenya's anti-gay laws, religious beliefs that view LGBTQ behaviors as sinful, a populace that think LGBTQ people are un-African, Kenya is viewed as relatively LGBTQ-friendly within the southeast region of Africa. Members of the community from neighboring countries seek refuge and asylum in Kenya. For example, at least 400 LGBTQ Ugandans sought safety and asylum in Kenya following the passing on Anti-homosexuality Act in December 2013 (Zomorodi, 2016). Kenya is attractive for two reasons: First, the United Nations' Commission on Refugees regional office is located in Nairobi, Kenya. The Commission facilitates relocation of LGBTQ refugees to other destinations especially in the west. Second, the LGBTQ community and allies agitate through activism and advocacy to create a safe space. Some of these advocates use their privilege to lead resistance and champion LGBTQ rights. For example, the late Binyavanga Wainaina, an LGBTQ activist and writer who supported the LGBTQ movement in Kenya and beyond, was the first Kenyan to come out on Kenyan national television. He acknowledged his privilege as a member of the Kenyan middle class who could leave the country if under attack allowed him to come out (Kopf, 2021; Wainaina, 2011). Markedly, he cautioned others against coming out as he did lest they face attacks by anti-LGBTQ activists, family members, and the public. Some activists are college-educated, which also offers some privileges that protect them from discrimination, especially violence.

Moyosore (2019) observes that Africans are collectivistic which promotes belongingness in family, clan, or ethnic groups. It is not easy to conceptualize individual freedom as separate from the common goal. Additionally, religion and politics influence legislative processes which do not align with the liberty of minorities. Resistance to the human rights approach is also based on pushback against the West's interference in making social policies (Kanna, 2020; Moyosore, 2019).

The United Nations and regional Human Rights bodies have uniformly declared their support for LGBTQ, but Kenya has mixed declarations in policy thereby perpetuating vulnerability of the community. Despite this reality, LGBTQ members have a history of being part of the social fabric of Kenya. In their study, Njambi and O'Brien (2000) interviewed women in woman-to-woman marriages in present-day Kenya as situated in their culture. The practice is customary among the Kikuyu ethnic group of Kenya. In the current form, the women expressed appreciation of the arrangement for it afforded them the flexibility to pursue social, economic, political, and personal interests. Markedly, women with the economic privilege of land and animals could take up wives who bore them children. These women who acted as husbands chose who to father their children. Such may reflect an evolution in making meaning of a customary practice while being evidentiary of diversity in forms of marriage or means of family creation that have existed from precolonial times.

Using Postcolonial Theory to Deconstruct Kenya's LGBTQ History

Postcolonial theory anchors the deconstruction of LGBTQ concepts and rights in Kenya. Mishra and Hodge (2005) pointed out that postcolonialism is not about the aftermath of colonialism but is concerned with the continuities and discontinuities of the new modes and forms of old practices. The theory focuses on the cultural dimension of colonialism as essential in maintaining the relations between the colonists and the colonized. Authors such as Frantz Fanon, Aimé Césaire, Edward Said, Homi K. Bhabha, and Gayatri C. Spivak provided some of the seminal works that informed postcolonialism. Although postcolonialism deals with the effects and consequences of unequal relations of power, the colonized subjects have agency in understanding, reclaiming, and rethinking their experiences in their encounter with the process of colonization (Dei & Imoka, 2018). Postcolonial studies started consolidating themselves at the end of the 1970s and emerged in 1990s academia, where postcolonialism allows theory users to complicate colonial narratives, question national assumptions, and become activists who challenge dominant narratives by questioning what/who is silenced to create the said narrative (Lazarus, 2011; Raja, 2020).

Postcolonialism is in alliance with postmodernity, in solidarity with feminism and critical race theory, because it recognizes the different experiences of minorities and how a ruling majority is instrumental in creating the foundation of hierarchies (Mohanty, 2003). Postcolonial studies identify and explore the consequences of controlling and exploiting colonized people (Cunneen, 2011). Furthermore, postcolonial studies examine the relationship between the culture, history, political economy, literature, and discourse literature produced by a colonizing hegemonic power and the colonized subjects (Elam, 2019). The postcolonial theory posits that imperialism does not end with independence but rather transcends into the future by either holding on to the same models that led to the oppression of the colonized or morphing into new ways that still meet the goals of colonialism, that is, oppression and marginalization. Additionally, the principles of the theory allow for examining the inequalities that existed in precolonial times (Raja, 2020).

Responding to Oppressive Systems: Activism by LGBTQ Community in Kenya

While activism is used interchangeably with advocacy, we differentiated activists from advocates to provide a lens through which to view the role of those stakeholders championing LGBTQ concerns. Collins (2012) differentiates activists from advocates as follows. Activists are tasked with criticizing the state, seeking structural change, and confronting and claiming innocence and rights to justice. At the same time, advocates work with state officials to respond to violence, enable information sharing, establish and maintain trusted relationships, and be present when decisions are made (Collins, 2012). Collins further argued that the roles of activists and advocates converge when they build local, national, and international networks and participate in coalition spaces to reform existing laws influencing the provision of justice and mobilization (Collins, 2012).

Kenyan LGBTQ activism, as in other African countries, includes communication, mobilization, and action in nation-states that oppose LGBTQ people (van Klinken, 2019). Specifically, van Klinken (2019) positions Kenyan activists not as docile, subordinate, or fearful of the sociopolitical context in which they work but rather as explicitly and actively engaged in public forms of resistance that make them feel emboldened and empowered. These forms of resistance do not exist in a vacuum and are often facilitated by transnational, Western LGBTQ actors, human rights organizations, and movements and progressive elements within Kenyan society. Most of these activities happen within the administrative structure of registered non-governmental organizations.

Since the millennium, several Non-Governmental Organizations (NGOs) have been formed to meet the different needs of LGBTQ. The first NGO focused on the LGBTQ in Kenya was registered with the ministry of social services in 1999, focusing on Men who have Sex with Men (MSM) (Amory, 2019). Ishtar MSM was initiated during the height of the HIV/AIDS crisis. Other NGOs that advocate for LGBTQ Rights organizations were formed in the early 2000s. In 2016, a group of NGOs, namely, National Gay and Lesbian Human Rights Commission (NGLHRC), Gay and Lesbian Coalition of Kenya (GALCK), Nyanza, Rift Valley, and Western Kenya Network (NYARWEK), and individuals whose lives have been affected by Kenya's punitive anti-homosexuality laws filed a petition challenging these laws (Human Rights Watch, 2019).

Additionally, LGBTQ NGOs serve as workplaces for some activists who are identified as LGBTQ and spaces for volunteerism, including their allies (Amakobe et al., 2018; Blessol, 2013). Most LGBTQ activists' lives and work intersect; their personal stories traverse from individual to socio-structural domains and policymaking. The use of life experience to demonstrate how societal norms and policies target LGBTQ allows for private affairs to become public. The YouTube posts by Immah Reid (2019) and the A24Media.com (2013) interview with Nzioka exemplify how personal is also public for the LGBTQ community.

For instance, Immah Reid (2019) is a lesbian activist who is part of several LGBTQ groups that use art to promote social justice for the LGBTQ community and Kenyan society. Her approach to seeking acceptance for the community is by fighting for social justice through art disbursed through social media and more. Using her personal life story, she explains how she had to quit college due to gender-based discrimination. When her mother ran out of money to pay for her college, the extended family did not help her mother but chose to help her cousins who were in the same predicament but were male.

Immah Reid evokes intersectionality as a basis for activism in social justice. According to Crenshaw (1991), intersectionality provides a basis in activism for considering multiple identities (some privileged) and distinct experiences within hierarchical structures. Like Crenshaw (1991), different identities may provoke demeaning reactions from society (Reid, 2019). For example, acceptable femininity provides what society values, such as attracting dowry payment in marriage. Women who do not attract dowry payments by staying single or being divorced are less acceptable. Equally, as a lesbian, Reid is positioned as lesser than her cisgender sisters despite her also being a mother. Moreover, Imma Reid (2019) speaks of the disparities in funding for LGBTQ issues where gay issues are prioritized over those of lesbians. As society models marginalization, so does the LGBTQ alliance. To do fair social justice work, one must work on their consciousness and put a concerted effort to network with like-minded people for a common purpose. Immah Reid (2019) believes that through gaining consciousness, one should be able to see through dehumanization and resist.

Activism is a private and public act. For example, though frightening, the act of coming out is one means of activism (van Klinken, 2019). Kenyan LGBTQ activists reported that coming out made them feel free and liberated as they now experienced their identity without hiding it and with no fear of being outed or persecution (Rombo & Lutomia, 2022). In coming out, the LGBTQ community can form communities, recognize, or validate one another's experiences and organize to extend support as they make their presence known to the public. Activities such as gay parades create public awareness. The media have also provided a platform for activism where the community has presented their case for equal treatment and debunked myths and stereotypes associated with the group. With the 21st century signing of punitive LGBTQ laws in some African countries, media houses were prompted to invite members of the LGBTQ community for interviews. These platforms exposed sexuality and gender-based binary assumptions and disclosed to Kenyans that diversity exists both in gender and sexual identities.

Activism on LGBTQ rights is driven by NGOs and civil society. The issues pursued by activists can be permanent, such as organizing for change in the laws or seasonal depending on national, regional, or global events. The activists often rely on funding from private foundations and international trusts in the United States, Germany, the Netherlands, Finland, and the United Kingdom (The Global Resources Report, n.d).

Activists use digital media for instant rebuttals, traditional media to create awareness, and street marching demonstrations to publicize the plight of LGBTQ people individually and as a group. Additionally, they use art to educate while entertaining the masses. Within the movement, they expose the disparate treatment and outcomes for distinct groups within the community. While it is realistic to bundle together to fight for their common cause, it is also paramount to acknowledge and address inequities that emanate from the structural forces of patriarchy, classism, sexism, and rural-urban residency.

Activism work has increased and been facilitated through mobile phones to organize communities. Although Kenyan activists face challenges in accessing and affording technology, the proliferation of mobile phones and the internet has increased the use of social media for activism and led to hashtag activism (Mwaura, 2020; Sanya, 2013). According to Technopedia (2012), hashtag activism, also known as social activism, uses social media platforms such as Twitter, Facebook, WhatsApp, and Google+ to agitate for or support a cause through posting, sharing, and commenting.

A specific example of hashtag activism by the LGBTQ community was #ProtectQueerKenyans, #JusticeForSheila trended on Twitter after the murder of a Kenyan lesbian, Sheila Lumumba. In 2021, the hashtags #JusticeForErica and #JusticeForJoash were trending following the murder of trans-woman activist Erica Chandra and LGBTQ activist Joash Mosoti (Ogola, 2022). In 2023, the hashtag #JusticeforEdwinChiloba trended on Twitter after the murder of Edwin Chiloba a Kenyan gay LGBTQ activist. Castells (2012) suggests that activist hashtags use the Internet and mobile phones to organize social movements. Castells states that hashtags galvanize community creation and form public spaces for engagement, "which ultimately becomes a political space, a space for sovereign assemblies to meet and to recover their rights of representation" (Castells, 2012, p. 11).

Additionally, the mobile phone has offered Kenyans opportunities to participate in national, continental, and international activism and movements such as national #warembo ni yes, #My dress my choice; international #Metoo, #March on Nairobi, #BlackLivesMatter, and #BringBackOurGirls. The experiences of shared cultural change—actions that are international—allow the groups to bond and be encouraged that they are not alone in the fight. Kushner (2019) noticed a shift in discourses around LGBTQ rights in Kenya and other African countries as follows:

> The Kenya petition had been a test case for a new approach. When I began covering LGBTQ rights in Africa, in 2014, those who campaigned against sodomy laws argued that they violated international and national law, or basic human rights and dignity. More recently, I've noticed a different argument take hold: Confronted with the

common refrain that homosexuality is fundamentally un-African, activists have sought to argue the reverse—that *homophobia* is un-African.

(para. 7)

Activism also takes place informally away from non-profits and NGOs when LGBTQ community members organize and informally use social networks to provide services to each other, including providing a space for those who have been chased from home, nursing the assaulted, and providing food. This activism work of care is invisible but counts just as professional activism does (Amakobe et al., 2018).

Social media has also provided space for LGBTQ activists and allies to engage in activism in many ways directly. Anonymous contributors on social media could play devil's advocate or offer actual, real-time rebuttals to bigoted, homophobic, and transphobic statements (Mwangi, 2014). Furthermore, Mwangi (2014) reported that digital media like Facebook, YouTube, blogs, and Twitter contain more homophobia than mainstream media like TV, books, and newspapers, in part because the latter afford platforms for immediate interactions while the former have rules and procedures that would not allow outright homophobic slurs.

Evan Mwangi, Keguro Macharia, Besi Muhonja, and van Klinken are Kenyan and Kenyanist scholars who participate in research, activism, and advocacy for the Kenyan LGBTQ community. Mwangi (2014) has written extensively about social media and queerness, the queer archive, and the law as it relates to LGBTQ people. Macharia (2009) interrogates the claim that homosexuality is un-African. Muhonja (2020) has written on Utu/Ubuntu and queerness and van Klinken (2019) turned to Kenyan queer Christians and LGBTQ activism.

Amory (2019) writes about the use of artivism by Kenyan LGBTQ activists. Artivism uses music, poetry, visual art, and performance art for political change.

While artivism is a term that draws on contemporary global trends, there are also historical precedents in Kenya for the use of poetry, song, and theater in the fight against colonialism and inequality in post-colonial Kenya. Today, savvy young people are leading the struggle for social change through the creative use of social media, film, music videos, and blogs.

(Amory, 2019, p. 2)

Successes and Challenges in Kenyan LGBTQ Activism

Kenyan activism is not neutral but reflects existing social, economic, political, and geographical tensions. Here, we capture the success and challenges faced by LGBTQ activism in Kenya.

Leaders who work with LGBTQ people oppose the introduction of new perspectives even when they come from the constituents they serve. For instance, Amakobe et al. (2018) write that Audrey Mbugua, who was the first Kenyan to organize around trans issues, was received with ambivalence by GALCK:

I remember how Audrey got space at the GALCK center, after she said that she as a trans person wanted to organize around trans issues. Then the whole board of GALCK had to sit down because this was so new for them, and they were against the idea of a "man changing into a woman," as they put it. There were religious reasons, social reasons, just fear in itself. This existed even within the more progressive feminist spaces. It was only in 2014 that the government acknowledged and called for the identification and counting them in the census.

(p. 365)

There are glimpses of policy success and through the judiciary regarding some members of the LGBTQ community. For example, in 2014, a transgender activist won a series of cases in The Kenya High Court (Migiro, 2014). They included a name change on the school certificate, gender identity removal from the certificate, and registration of her trans education and advocacy group by the National Non-Governmental Organization Council. According to Njeru (2021), Kenya Appeals Court ruled that conducting forced anal exams on people accused of same-sex relations is unconstitutional.

Similarly, the government has also taken steps to acknowledge select members of the queer community and extend legal protection to all members. The government authorized the inclusion of intersex as a distinct group of people beginning with the 2019 census. Markedly, the Census registered 1,524, which is 0.003% of the population. The number is lower than expected, likely due to intersex people's discomfort with or uncertainty about the government's handling of the data and fear of the response from the public (Bhalla, 2019). In 2021, the government formed a state agency to investigate human rights violations against LGBTQ people and give regular, timely reports to promote equitable treatment (Njeru, 2021). Again Njeru (2021) observed that the government had merged the agency with a non-profit, The National Gay and Lesbian Human Rights Commission (NGLHRC).

According to Mukami Marete, Deputy Executive Director of the UHAI-East African Sexual Health and Rights Initiative (UHAI EASHRI, based in Nairobi), three challenges face the LGBTQ community: personal security, healthcare, and education (The King Baudouin Foundation United States, n.d.). The report shows that even when LGBTQ-friendly policies are passed, members are still prone to violence and other maltreatment by individuals, groups, and even state-sponsored police raids. van Klinken (2019) wrote that "queer folk live in constant fear of humiliation, pestering, aggression, and violence from fellow citizens, and cannot count on the protection of the law or the police" (p. 116).

The Kenyan LGBTQ community also faces challenges that are two-pronged. Along with LGBTQ activism for rights and at the organizational level, challenges related to LGBTQ rights activism include the Kenyan LGBTQ community which is constitutionally denied the right to marry or adopt children, and security forces routinely harass, demand bribes from, falsify charges against, and even sexually assault the LGBTQ community, especially sex workers (Finerty, 2012; Isaack, 2017). Around healthcare, more health practitioners are not trained to provide LGBTQ-specific services, and the LGBTQ community can often feel traumatized when they seek these services (Okall et al., 2014). For example, trans-activist Audrey Mbugua shared she sought medical help from a healthcare worker, who took her hands and prayed for her to be freed from the devil (Migiro, 2014). Around education, LGBTQ youth in Kenya, similar to others on the continent, are often dismissed from school or chased from their homes, leading to poverty, lower education, and sometimes turning to sex work (The King Baudouin Foundation United States, n.d.).

The role of political leadership in protecting or promoting the rights of LGBTQ people cannot be underestimated. For example, in July 2015, President Barack Obama officially visited Kenya, and during the press conference, the issue of gay rights was raised. Whereas the president of Kenya, Uhuru, was non-committal in defending the rights of LGBTQ people in Kenya, President Obama underscored his belief that the state should not discriminate against people based on their sexual orientation (van Klinken, 2019). The public opinion and media outlets in Kenya follow the pattern set by the head of state. Social structures of patriarchy have also pushed the gay agenda to the back as it is deemed anti-patriarchal. The Kenya penal codes 162 and 165a overly target males. For example, code 165 criminalizes male same-sex relations and 162 criminalizes oral and anal sex.

In 2020 when COVID-19 increased in Kenya, violence increased against the LGBTQ community (Ombuor, 2020). Always vulnerable, restrictions on movement have exacerbated this issue. When otherwise freer to move, the LGBTQ community can interact in spaces more distant from their residences and be safer from the gaze of potentially hostile neighbors. In 2020, the LGBTQ community was being identified and targeted for mob-based violence, with an average of ten attacks per month (Ombuor, 2020). Due to the COVID-19 prevention guidelines, it wasn't easy to do activism that required person-to-person contact; most of the organizing was done online. Combining online and physical activism tends to yield better results.

The organizational and institutional challenges that Kenyan LGBTQ activism register bring to the fore those colonial vestiges that still permeate Kenyan organizations and the donor-driven nature of these organizations. Amakobe et al. (2018) provide a rich description of LGBTQ organizations in Kenya, especially their growth and challenges since the 2000s. As fledgling non-profit organizations, all the LGBTQ organizations relied on donor funding and operated as directed by these funders. Amakobe (2018) adds that these organizations were also not inclusive and primarily worked in Nairobi with a leadership and membership that marginalized those from low-income settings in the city and rural Kenya by using English and not engaging these populations. There has been a change in these organizations through professionalization by creating payable positions with roles and responsibilities and building their capacity through attending workshops and conferences. Kenyan LGBTQ organizations face challenges such as hierarchies that lead to a lack of transparency and poor communication.

Amakobe et al. (2018) remark on the lack of mentoring in Kenyan LGBTIQ organizations by highlighting how learning and advancement possibilities are maintained at the top. An NGO's staff is not mentoring a group of volunteer activists, resulting in a gap in the organization's skills and expertise. As a result, the leaders are highly trained and have access to possibilities often reserved for those at their level. Gathoni Blessol (2013) recounts the origins of several NGOs in Kenya by describing how western liberals who advocate universal principles and oppose oppressive capitalist systems end up forming and directing these organizations. While some have provided the impetus for initiatives that have resulted in specific changes, some donor groups believe they have the ideal solution and operate with a savior mindset. She further writes,

The end-result of this catastrophic ideal, as in most struggles, has been a rise of donor-motivated LGBTIQ activism and organizations that are "visionary" driven, impractical, capitalistic, and commercialized-mostly marginalizing the grassroots (Blessol, 2013, p. 223). As a result, LGBTIQ organizations are focused on meeting donor demands and figuring out how to raise funds rather than cooperating with other organizations that undertake comparable work. According to Blessol (2013), these hand-picked leaders hinder the creation of a powerful LGBTQ movement. She writes:

> As a result, the bourgeois cadre has given birth to a few "liberators" of the LGBTI community, who again are donor chosen. They have become the public face of the struggle and are well-funded gatekeepers. This has led to further divisions around economic status, and class such that one queer person cannot relate to another without considering how well known they are and the depth of their pockets.
>
> *(Blessol, 2013, p. 223)*

Dearham (2013) points out that activists in Kenya have knowledge and sensibilities that can inform new frameworks for activism rather than relying on dominant NGO models. The decolonizing movement has provided an impulse for including indigenous knowledge and giving voice to local activists.

Hierarchies created by class and patriarchy and the competition to access funds have presented divisions within and among LGBTQ organizations. Immah Reid (2019) decried the priority given to men who were gay, especially as it pertains to HIV/AIDS prevention. She, however, points out that through the many organizations she belongs to, they fight for any Kenyan who is subjected to discrimination. Audrey Mbugua, a transgender female, has made a case for her community as separate from gays and lesbians. Despite the difference in acceptance and inclusion, treatment and collaboration, the reality is that in practice, their fate is tied together in the eyes of the public that marginalizes them. Even as they each need to have space to validate their experience as a group with a uniquely shared identity, they do so through respective non-profit organizations though the need to act in solidarity with each other is ideal.

van Klinken (2019) writes that there are narratives of a homophobic and heteronormative Kenyan public and a counter-hegemonic public that supports and protects LGBTQ activists and the community. The divide keeps the progress in achieving equality for LGBTQ people at a crossroads (Rombo & Lutomia, 2022). Although van Klinken (2019) does not account for those who hold neutral views, such individuals still add to the number of those against LGBTQ. Given such an environment, the work of LGBTQ people and allies becomes arduous.

Non-governmental challenges to law and policy that discriminate against the LGBTQ community are successfully mounted where the capacity for advocates can build sustainable organizations as platforms to pursue reform. Shifts in Kenya now allow the registration of LGBTQ-supportive organizations. For instance, a trans organization won a challenge in 2014 and was registered as a non-governmental organization (NGO) by the Non-Governmental Organization Coordination Board (NGOCB), and a year later, an LGBTQ organization—National Gay and Lesbian Human Rights Commission (NGLHRC)—won a decision by the High Court of Kenya to be allowed to register (National Gay and Lesbian Human Rights Commission, 2023). The NGO Coordination Board appealed that NGLHRC continues to await the Court's decision to resolve its registration status (National Gay and Lesbian Human Rights Commission, 2023; van Klinken, 2019). Ironically, Audrey Mbugua Ithibu, executive director of Transgender Education and Advocacy (TEA), sided with NGOCB despite her having faced a registration rejection of her application for registration earlier on (van Klinken, 2019). In relation to TEA, Audrey later successfully petitioned against NGOCB in the High Court of Kenya (van Klinken, 2019).

Mbugua's refusal to support the registration of NGLHRC points in part to the lack of solidarity and the divisions that exist in Kenya's LGBTQ activism. These divisions emanate from competition for funds, hierarchies of non-profits, conflict in interests, and non-aligning missions of NGOs. According to van Klinken (2019), Mbugua argues that transgender community issues and struggles differ from the other groups under the LGBTQ acronym. Mbugua said that "the transgender community can articulate its own issues and did not request this gay and lesbian commission to be our mouthpiece" (p. 63).

Correcting Anti-Gay Colonial Laws

The Kenyan law, as it stands, is borrowed from the law of the British. During colonialism, some of the enacted laws differed from those in the United Kingdom because they were intended to protect British capitalist accumulation (Mamdani, 1996). According to Mamdani (1996), the overarching progress in postcolonial republics like Kenya was deracialization rather than decolonization, ensuring the continuation of existing British laws. Tielman and Hammelburg (1993) observed that the English anti-homosexuality legislation adopted in the colonies had far more severe effects on homosexual men than lesbians. Additionally, the impact of the legislation in the former colonies of the Dutch, French, Spanish, and Portuguese is less severe than in the former British colonies.

In 2018, Prime Minister Theresa May said that the rules made by Britain were incorrect then and now while speaking to a meeting of the Commonwealth, a collection of 53 countries, the majority of which are former British colonies. She also argued that discriminatory laws implemented by the British in its colonies continue to impact the lives of those living in the former colonies, criminalize same-sex relationships, and fail to protect women and girls. Same-sex intimacy is illegal in 35 of the Commonwealth's 54 states. Kenya is one of the 35 countries that make up the group. Theresa May apologized for Britain's part in enacting anti-homosexuality legislation in its former colonies and urged authorities to amend the "outdated" laws (BBC, 2018c).

BBC (2018c) further reports that former British colonies such as Kenya have refused to heed the United Kingdom's request to repeal the colonial period's outmoded oppressive laws. Moreover, such efforts to reconsider laws and practices established by the British have been followed by a rising readiness on Britain's part to admit its role in criminalizing homosexuality around the world.

Future Research Directions

This section offers opportunities for future research such as focusing on inclusivity and the decolonization of LGBTQ activism in Kenya. There are two levels of inclusivity. At the individual level, they seek to be treated like all Kenyans are. Therefore, in the fight for equal protection under the law, the LGBTQ people and their allies are agitating for equal treatment, such as being accorded privacy, and not being subjected to profiling, violence, and marginalization based on their identities. The second level is inclusivity among the LGBTQ community in Kenya. Discussions on inclusivity posit that research and media articulations about issues in the LGBTQ community globally and in Kenya tend to focus on gay men more than other categories (Collins et al., 2015). Therefore, future research can focus on the varied experiences of bisexuals, lesbians, queers, and trans.

Future research can also consider how LGBTQ activists in Kenya anchor decolonization discourses by examining the legal, cultural, and political possibilities associated with LGBTQ activists' framing of law reform as a decolonization project. LGBTQ activists can identify laws governing gender and sexual nonconformity as in particular need of reform. Lastly, future research can seek to understand how class informs participation in LGBTQ activism in Kenya. Mwaura (2020) already found that it affects how social activism participation occurs in the general Kenyan activism milieu.

Conclusion

In this chapter, we traced the history of LGBTQ people in Kenya through postcolonial theory to identify the structural forces that influence the formation of the social environment within which the group lives. These included various policies embedded in colonial legacy, religion, and biological determinism. Anti-LGBTQ people have been countered by activism. We noted the milestones attained and identified contradictions and challenges and extant literature.

Despite the UN and regional human rights bodies such as the African Charter and Human Rights Council making recommendations to protect the rights of LGBTQ, Kenya has chosen to hold to inherited anti-LGBTQ laws. As a result of activism, the community has made inroads to influence the macrosystems that hold the key to ensuring equality as they reduce discrimination. They have used the tools of social creation both in formal and non-formal media settings. They have received financial support and training from the region and even internationally to fight at every level of society: for example, working with the politicians and the church where most negative ideas emanate from.

There are contradictions as Kenya accedes to international and regional charters upholding the rights of LGBTQ people while holding on to the penal codes that criminalize sexual behaviors often associated with LGBTQ people. Subsequently, the LGBTQ community is vulnerable to maltreatment, violence, and murder as evidence of hate crime, including state-sponsored omissions to offer protection. Policy change, for LGBTQ people in Kenya, shifts erratically and is complicated; consequently, activism is a personal and public milieu for those involved. Due to this, activists should build and maintain alliances with scholars, advocates, and other allies to attain cutting-edge knowledge and strategies that can allow them to push for changes both in policy and in the cultural world.

References

A24media.com. (2013, October 13). *Interview with Denis Nzioka: LGBTQ rights activist, 2012*. YouTube. www.youtube.com/watch?v=-24TCYOGCqs

Amakobe, G., Dearham, K., & Likimani, P. (2018). Gender theatre: The politics of exclusion and belonging in Kenya. In N. Nicol, A. Jjuuko, R. Lusimbo, N. J. Mulé, S. Ursel, A. Wahab, & P. Waugh (Eds.), *Envisioning global LGBT human rights: (Neo)colonialism, neoliberalism, resistance and hope* (pp. 347–370). University of London Press. www.jstor.org/stable/j.ctv5132j6.21

Amnesty International UK. (2019). *Mapping anti-gay laws in Africa*. www.amnesty.org.uk/lgbti-lgbt-gay-human-rights-law-africa-uganda-kenya-nigeria-cameroon

Amory, D. P. (2019, May 14). *LGBTQ rights in Kenya: On artivism and social change*. www.georgetownjournalofinternationalaffairs.org/online-edition/2019/5/9/lgbtiq-rights-in-kenya-on-artivism-and-social-change?rq=amory

BBC. (2018a, April 27). *Kenya bans Rafiki ahead of Cannes debut over lesbian scenes*. www.bbc.com/news/world-africa-43922780

BBC. (2018b, September 21). *Kenya briefly lifts ban on lesbian film Rafiki ahead of Oscars*. www.bbc.com/news/world-africa-45605758.

BBC. (2018c, April 17). *Theresa May deeply regrets' UK's colonial anti-gay laws*. www.bbc.com/news/world-africa-43795440

BBC. (2019, May 29). *Transgender no longer recognised as "disorder" by WHO*. www.bbc.com/news/health-48448804

Bhalla, N. (2019, November 4). *Kenyan census results a "big win" for intersex people*. Thomson Reuters Foundation. www.reuters.com/article/us-kenya-lgbt-intersex-trfn/kenyan-census-results-a-big-win-for-intersex-people-idUSKBN1XE1U9

Blessol, G. (2013). LGBTI-queer struggles like other struggles in Africa. In Sokari Ekine & Hakima Abbas (Eds.), *Queer African Reader* (pp. 229–242). Pambazuka Press.

Bulboz, M. M., & Sontag, M. M. S. (1993). Human ecology theory. In P. G. Boss, W. J. Doherty, R. LaROssa, W. R. Schumm, & S. K. Steinmetz (Eds.), *Sourcebook of family theories and methods: A contextual approach* (pp. 419–448). Plenum Press.

Castells, M. (2012). *Networks of outrage and hope: Social movements in the internet age*. John Wiley & Sons.

CNN. (2018, April 20). *President: Gay rights 'of no importance' in Kenya*. [Video]. Youtube. https://youtu.be/lwTgU-RZLHQ?si=nxI14ja6Rl3fr6vU

Collins, J. C. (2012). Identity matters: A critical exploration of lesbian, gay, and bisexual identity and leadership in HRD. *Human Resource Development Review, 11*(3), 349–379.

Collins, J. C., McFadden, C., Rocco, T. S., & Mathis, M. K. (2015). The problem of transgender marginalization and exclusion: Critical actions for human resource development. *Human Resource Development Review, 14*(2), 205–226.

Commonwealth Forum of National Human Rights Institutions. (2018, October 12). *Resolution 275—What it means for the state and nonstate actors in Africa.* https://cfnhri.org/resources/resolution-275-what-it-means-for-the-state-and-non-state-actors-in-africa/

Crenshaw, K. (1991). Mapping the margins: Intersectionality, identity politics and violence against women of color. *Stanford Law Review, 43*(6), 1241–1299.

Cunneen, C. (2011). Postcolonial perspectives for criminology. In M. Bosworth & C. Hoyle (Eds.), *What is criminology* (Online ed.). Oxford Academic. https://doi.org/10.1093/acprof:oso/9780199571826.003.0018

Dearham, K. (2013). *NGOs and Queer women's activism in Nairobi* (S. Ekine & H. Abbas, Eds.). Queer African Reader Pambazuka Press.

Dei, S. G., & Imoka, C. (2018, January 3). *Colonialism: Why write back?* E-International Relations. www.e-ir.info/2018/01/03/colonialism-why-write-back/

Elam, D. J. (2019, January). Post colonial theory. In *Oxford bibliographies.* www.oxfordbibliographies.com/view/document/obo-9780190221911/obo-9780190221911-0069.xml; https://doi.org/10.1093/OBO/9780190221911-0069

Evans-Pritchard, E. E. (1950). Marriage customs of the Luo of Kenya. *Africa, 20*(2), 132–142. https://doi.org/10.2307/3180571

Fariah, J. (2022, March 31). *Distribution of the population of Kenya 2019, by religion.* Retrieved August 25, 2015, from www.statista.com/statistics/1199572/share-of-religious-groups-in-kenya/

Finerty, E. C. (2012). Being gay in Kenya: The implications of Kenya's new constitution for anti sodomy laws. *Cornell International Law Journal, 45*, 431–456.

Gathara, P. (2023, March 19). *How an LGBTQ court ruling sent Kenya into a moral panic.* www.aljazeera.com/opinions/2023/3/15/how-an-lgbtq-court-ruling-sent-kenya-into-a-moral-panic#:~:text=Under%20the%20same%20laws%2C%20for,judges%20equated%20sex%20to%20marriage

Gay and Lesbian Coalition of Kenya. (2016). *Community engagement, health, research. Research on the lived experiences of lesbian, bisexual and queer women in Kenya.* http://icop.or.ke/wp-content/uploads/2016/10/Research-on-the-lived-experiences-of-LBQ-women-in-Kenya.pdf

Global Resources Report. (n.d.). *Funding for LGBTI issues in the global South and ast. Fund for NGOs.* www.fundsforngos.org/foundation-funds-for-ngos/20-foundations-trusts-fund-lgbt-programs/

Global Rights 1. (2013, October 13). *Kenyan LGBT activist speaks with global rights.* [Video]. YouTube. https://youtu.be/JI0bv-SiA74?si=ADaxX12jCMPBeRFm

Han, E., & O'Mahoney, J. (2018). *British colonialism and the criminalization of homosexuality: Queens, crime and empire.* Routledge.

Human Rights Watch. (2015, September 28). *The issue is violence attacks on LGBT people on Kenya's coast.* Human Rights Watch. www.hrw.org/sites/default/files/report_pdf/kenya0915_4upr.pdf

Human Rights Watch. (2019, May 24). *Kenya: Court upholds archaic anti-homosexuality laws.* Human Rights Watch. www.hrw.org/news/2019/05/24/kenya-court-upholds-archaic-anti-homosexuality-laws#

Immah Reid. (2019, March 23). *Gay Kenyans are fighting for all.* YouTube. www.youtube.com/watch?v=hD68gTfOzE4

Isaack, W. (2017, June 1). *African commission tackles sexual orientation, gender identity.* www.hrw.org/news/2017/06/01/african-commission-tackles-sexual-orientation-gender-identity

Kanna, M. (2020). Furthering decolonization: Judicial review of colonial criminal law. *Duke Law Review, 70*, 411–449.

Kassim, A. I., & Leposo, L. (2010, November 30). Gay, lesbian groups criticize Kenyan leader's remarks. *CNN.* http://articles.cnn.com/2010-11-30/world/kenya.gay.reaction_1_lesbian-groups-lesbian-community-gay-rights?_s=PM:WORLD

Kenyatta, J. (1938). *Facing Mount Kenya: The tribal life of the Gikuyu.* Mercury Books.

The King Baudouin Foundation United States. (n.d.). Against all odds -making gains for LGBTI communities across Africa. *Kbfus Insights.* https://kbfus.org/wp-content/uploads/2016/09/Against-All-Odds-Making-Gains-for-LGBTI-Communities-in-Africa.pdf

Kopf, M. (2021). Binyavanga Wainaina's narrative of the IMF-generation as development critique. *Journal of African Cultural Studies,* 1–17. https://doi.org/10.1080/13696815.2021.1976118

Kushner, J. (2019, May 24). The British empire's homophobia lives on in former colonies. *The Atlantic.* www.theatlantic.com/international/archive/2019/05/kenya-supreme-court-lgbtq/590014/

Lazarus, N. (2011). What post-colonial theory doesn't say. *Race & Class, 53*(1), 3–27. https://doi.org/10.1177/0306396811406778

Lewis, D. (1973). Anthropology and colonialism. *Current Anthropology, 14*(5), 581–602.

Macharia, K. (2009). Queering African studies. *Criticism, 51*(1), 157–164.

Mamdani, M. (1996). Indirect rule, civil society, and ethnicity: The African dilemma. *Social Justice, 23*(1/2 (63–64)), 145–150. www.jstor.org/stable/29766931

Mbote, D. K., Sandfort, T. G. M., Waweru, E., & Zapfel, A. (2018). Kenyan religious leaders' views on same-sex sexuality and gender nonconformity: Religious freedom versus constitutional rights. *The Journal of Sex Research, 55*(4–5), 630–641. https://doi.org/10.1080/00224499.2016.125570

McClintock, A. (1995). *Imperial leather: Race, gender, and sexuality in the colonial contest.* Routledge.

Migiro, K. (2014, October 7). *Transgender activist wins landmark case in Kenya court.* Thomson Reuters Foundation. www.reuters.com/article/us-foundation-rights-kenya/transgender-activist-wins-landmark-case-in-kenyan-court-idUSKCN0HW14820141007

Mishra, V., & Hodge, B. (2005). What was postcolonialism? *New Literary History, 36*(3), 375–402. www.jstor.org/stable/20057902

Mohanty, C. T. (2003). "Under Western eyes" revisited: Feminist solidarity through anticapitalist struggles. *Signs, 28*(2), 499–535. https://doi.org/10.1086/342914

Moyosore, L. O. (2019). The African moral perspectives on human rights and their influences on anti-gay laws in Nigeria and Kenya. *International Journal of Legal Studies and Research (IJLSR), 8*(2). https://doi.org/10.2139/ssrn.3454043

Muhonja, B. B. (2020). *Radical Utu: Critical ideas and ideals of Wangari Muta Maathai.* Ohio University Press.

Mwangi, E. (2014). Queer agency in Kenya's digital media. *African Studies Review, 57*(2), 93–113.

Mwaura, J. (2020). Class interplay in social activism in Kenya. In E. Polson, L. S. Clark, & R. Gajjala (Eds.), *The Routledge companion to media and class* (1st ed., pp. 280–292). Routledge Press.

National Gay and Lesbian Human Rights Commission. (2023, February 23). *Supreme court affirms NGLHRC's right to register as an NGO in Kenya.* National Gay and Lesbian Human Rights Commission. https://nglhrc.com/wp-content/uploads/2023/02/SUPREME-COURT-AFFIRMS-NGLHRCS-RIGHT-TO-REGISTER-AS-AN-NGO-IN-KENYA.pdf

National Legislative Bodies/National Authorities. (2010, August 27). *Refworld.* The Constitution of Kenya. www.refworld.org/docid/4c8508822.html

News24. (2006, February 22). Being gay in Kenya. *News24.* www.news24.com

Njambi, W. N., & O'Brien, W. (2000). Revisiting "woman-woman marriage": Notes on Gĩkũyũ women. *NWSA Journal, 12*(1), 1–23. www.jstor.org/stable/4316706

Njeru, G. (2021, July 9). *Despite ongoing homophobia, Kenya forms an LGBTQ+ state agency.* https://xtramagazine.com/power/kenya-lgbtq-state-agency-dispatch-204474

Ogola, E. A. (2022, April 22). #JusticeForSheila: Kenyan anger after lesbian's murder. *BBC.* www.bbc.com/news/world-africa-61192594

Okall, D. O., Ondenge, K., Nyambura, M., Otieno, F. O., Hardnett, F., Turner, K., Mills, L. A., Masinya, K., Chen, R. T., & Gust, D. A. (2014). Men who have sex with men in Kisumu, Kenya: Comfort in accessing health services and willingness to participate in HIV prevention studies. *Journal of Homosexuality, 61*(12), 1712–1726.

Ombuor, R. (2020, November 4). Kenya's LGBTQ community faces increased abuse during the pandemic. *Voice of America.* www.voanews.com/africa/kenyas-lgbtq-community-faces-increased-abuse-during-pandemic

Pellot, B. (2020). *Media representation of LGBTQ people in Africa.* Arcus Foundation. www.arcusfoundation.org/wp-content/uploads/2020/03/Arcus-Media-Representation-of-LGBTQ-People-in-Africa.pdf

Raja, M. (2020, September). *Postcolonialism course (session 1): Edited version/Robert Young on postcolonialism.* www.youtube.com/watch?v=Lj6g8GTmw2c

Rombo, D. O., & Lutomia, A. N. (2022). Still at a crossroad: Theories in activism and fight for rights of the LGBTI community in Kenya. In B. Muhonja & B. Mbaye (Eds.), *Gender and sexuality in Kenyan societies.* Lexington Book.

Sanya, B. N. (2013). Disrupting patriarchy: An examination of the role of e-technologies in rural Kenya. *Feminist Africa 18 E-Spaces: E-Politics,* 12–24.

Schmidt, H. (2008). Colonial intimacy: The Rechenberg scandal and homosexuality in German East Africa. *Journal of History of Sexuality, 17*(1), 25–59. https://doi.org/10.1353/sex.2008.0011

Technopedia. (2012, November 12). Hashtag activism. *Technopedia*. www.techopedia.com/definition/29047/hashtag-activism

Tielman, R., & Hammelburg, H. (1993). World survey on the social and legal position of gays and lesbians. In *The third pink book: A global view of lesbian and gay liberation and oppression* (pp. 250–251). Prometheus Books.

van Klinken, A. (2019). *Kenyan, Christian, Queer. Religion, LGBT activism and arts of resistance in Africa*. The Pennsylvania State University Press.

van Klinken, A. (2021, October 28). *The power of Kenyan, Christian, Queer imagination*. The University of Notre Dame. https://contendingmodernities.nd.edu/theorizing-modernities/kenyan-queer-imagination/

Wainaina, B. (2011). *One day I will write about this place: A memoir*. Graywolf Press.

Young, R. J. C. (1995). *Colonial desire: Hybridity in theory, culture and race*. Routledge.

Zomorodi, G. (2016, May). *Responding to LGBT forced migration in East Africa*. www.fmreview.org/sites/fmr/files/FMRdownloads/en/solutions/zomorodi.pdf

8

LGBTQ RIGHTS IN CANADA

Less Progressive Narrative, More Reparative Morality

Brenda Cossman

Canada is often held up as a model of the power of constitutional rights discourse to advance the equality of LGBTQ rights. The equality protections of the *Canadian Charter of Rights and Freedoms* (1982) were used to prohibit discrimination against gay and lesbian Canadians, strike down opposite-sex definitions of spouse and eventually grant same-sex couples the right to marry. In many ways, the Canadian experience follows the progress narrative of LGBTQ rights: from the decriminalization of homosexuality to anti-discrimination laws to same-sex relationship recognition (e.g. Eskridge, 2000). Homosexuality was (partially) decriminalized in 1969, anti-discrimination laws were passed in the 1980s, and relationship recognition began in the 1990s, culminating in same-sex marriage in 2003. In this chapter, I tell a more complicated narrative, in which the Canadian case study IS a model, but a model for thinking about the potential of LGBTQ equality rights in more complex ways. Much was achieved through the deployment of constitutional equality rights, but much has also been left out. Moreover, the terms of inclusion themselves need to be interrogated. The particular ways in which LGBTQ equality rights discourse are interwoven with other discourses has made some modes of belonging more visible and more possible than others.

There is a well-worn debate within LGBT communities around legal rights and recognition. From the struggle for human rights legislation to same-sex relationship recognition and marriage, LGBT activists have divided in relatively predictable ways along a liberal/critical axis (Cossman, 2020). Along the liberal legal axis, activists have sought rights protections enshrined in law. On same-sex marriage, many argued for the fundamental importance of formal equality for LGBT peoples and their inclusion in the institution of marriage. The failure to recognize same-sex marriage was seen as an exclusion from an important social and legal institution that provided both symbolic and material resources. Moreover, the only reason for the exclusion of LGBT people from marriage was homophobic discrimination. Along the critical left axis, other activists have critiqued a rights strategy as hopelessly naïve, placing faith and power in a capitalist, homo-nationalist, white settler state. On marriage, critics have argued that it represents a heteronormative institution, oppressive and exclusionary, premised on establishing a hierarchy of normatively legitimate relationships. Assimilation within marriage would obscure the diversity of relationships within LGBT communities and undermine the political and subversive nature of LGBT relationships (Warner, 1999, 2000).

I have long argued that these debates force us into an unnecessary either/or position (Cossman, 1994, 2007, 2019). I am hardly alone in this observation. Others, like Carl

DOI: 10.4324/9781003128151-10

Stychin, Jeffrey Weeks and Miriam Smith, have argued that the inclusion of LGBT people within citizenship contains elements of both normalization and subversion (Weeks, 1998; Stychin, 1998, 2001; Smith, 2019). Others have suggested that the fault lines of the debate are themselves foreclosing. Judith Butler, for example, has argued that to be for or against gay marriage, gay rights, or inclusion within citizenship is to engage the framework of normalcy and deviance, of legitimacy and illegitimacy, that forecloses other ways of thinking about the sexual field (2004). In attempting to move beyond the stultifying binaries of the same-sex marriage debate, Butler suggests that there are "middle zones and hybrid formations" between legitimacy and illegitimacy; "nonplaces . . . are not sites of enunciation but shifts in the topography from which a questionably audible claim emerges; the claim of the not-yet-subject and the nearly recognizable" (2004, p. 108). As I have argued, these debates operate to foreclose zones of ambivalence. In such polarized debates, questions cannot be asked because, if one is not for it ("it" being same-sex marriage, legal equality rights and/or a commemorative coin), one is against it (2004). This polarized either/or approach misses many subtleties and complexities that underlie these debates. They repeatedly fail to capture the constitutive and contradictory nature of law. My position has long been that both sides make important contributions to our understanding of LGBT life, struggle and law.

I propose a more reparative reading of the legacy of LGBT equality rights in Canada. Eve Kosofsky Sedgwick argued against that literary criticism needed to loosen its attachment to what she called paranoid readings based on the "hermeneutics of suspicion" (Sedgwick, 2002, p. 124). Paranoid readings provided a set of analytic tools that helped to unveil what lies hidden beneath; in the context of queer theory, for example, the critical tools to reveal the deep structures and discourses of homophobia. But Sedgwick argued that this also led to a kind of reading that was negative and rigid; one that did not like surprises; one that sought to expose deep truths that lay beneath texts. While the paranoid reading was often negative ("X is bad for gays"), it could equally be affirmative ("X is good for gays"). The paranoid element lay in the revealing of deep and unsurprising truths. Sedgwick argued for a different kind of reading; instead of always looking for the hidden truths that lie beneath texts, she argued for embracing uncertainty through a deliberate form of reading that did not already know what it was looking for. In this kind of reparative reading, the reader would be open to surprise, to seeing things differently, so that the "the reader has the room to realize that the future may be different from the present" (146). For Sedgwick, "[T]he desire of a reparative impulse . . . is additive and accretive" (Sedgwick, 1996, p. 5). Reparative reading is about nurture, about "confer[ring] plenitude on an object." Instead of reading beneath, behind or beyond, Sedgewick suggests that we learn to read beside: "Beside is an interesting preposition also because there's nothing very dualistic about it; a number of elements may lie alongside one another, though not an infinity of them" (Sedgwick, 2003, p. 8). Sedgewick's work has generated a multitude of reading strategies, from thinking sideways (McCallum & Bradway, 2019), to reading sideways, to lateral reading (Seitler, 2019). Each is a queer reading strategy that in some ways takes its inspiration from Sedgwick that there are other ways of reading across texts that might better allow us, as Dana Seitler argues "to see in a new light, their connections, challenges, and productive frictions" (Seitler, 2019, p. 2).

With this reparative sensibility in mind, I return to the specific question of the legacy of constitutional equality rights for LGBTQ people in Canada. Almost 20 years ago, I argued:

> The legacy of the first twenty years of the *Charter* for lesbians and gay men is a legacy of victories and defeats, of a transformation in the legal and political landscape, in

which many lesbians and gay men are accorded greater legal protection and in which others are not accorded the protection that they desire.

(Cossman, 2000, p. 246)

As I wrote then, it was a legacy in which formal equality rights were vindicated but sexual freedom rights remain largely unprotected. Twenty years later, not much has changed. Formal equality rights have continued to emerge victorious, epitomized by the recognition of same-sex marriage. But LGBT sexualities continue to be policed through a range of criminal laws that do not formally discriminate on the basis of sexual orientation. From obscenity and sex work laws, to HIV non-disclosure and public sex laws, some LGBT sexualities remain the subject of surveillance. Precisely because these laws do not formally discriminate on the basis of sexual orientation, equality rights have had less traction in challenging them. Interrogating the legacy of constitutional rights for LGBTQ people in Canada must involve not only what has been won but also—equally importantly—what remains hidden from view through a formal equality lens. Moreover, the ins and outs, the victories and defeats, do not, on their own, tell the full story. Legal regulation, in both its inclusionary and exclusionary modes, is constitutive of the very subjects that it regulates, and a deeper interrogation reveals the contradictory nature of these new legal subjects. These debates, around the legacy of LGBT rights in Canada, are better read reparatively, that is, beside rather than against one another.

Equality Rights: What's In

When the equality rights provisions of the *Canadian Charter of Rights and Freedoms* came into effect in 1985, there was little protection of LGBT rights. Quebec had been the first province to prohibit discrimination on the basis of sexual orientation in their human rights code in 1977 (Quebec Charter, 1977). It took Ontario another ten years to include sexual orientation within its *Human Rights Code* (1990). The first 20 years of Charter litigation for LGBT rights saw a series of Supreme Court of Canada decisions inching toward LGBT equality and same-sex relationship recognition (Cossman, 2002b, 2002c). Sexual orientation had not been included within the list of prohibited grounds of discrimination in the *Charter*'s section 15 equality rights. As a result, one of the first obstacles was to have the courts recognize sexual orientation as an analogous ground, which refers to whether a group or personal characteristic is analogous to those enumerated within section 15 and deserving of protection. In *Egan v. Canada* (1995), the first equality challenge on the basis of sexual orientation to reach the Supreme Court of Canada, the court held that, given the significant historical and continuing discrimination faced by gay and lesbian Canadians, sexual orientation should be recognized as a prohibited ground of discrimination. However, *Egan* was at best a partial victory. It involved a challenge to an opposite definition of spouse for the purposes of old-age security benefits. While the majority of the Supreme Court found that the opposite-sex definition was discriminatory, it also found that the discrimination was justifiable within section 1 of the Charter.

In 1998, the Supreme Court heard its second sexual orientation equality rights challenge in *Vriend v. Alberta*. Vriend was a schoolteacher who had been fired from his job for being gay. He wanted to bring a human rights complaint against the school, but Alberta did not include sexual orientation within its human rights code. Vriend challenged that exclusion is violating his section 15 equality rights. The Supreme Court agreed and held that the *Charter* required Alberta to include sexual orientation in its human rights protection, reading the protection into the offending legislation. Formal equality for gay and lesbian Canadians had been vindicated. What remained was whether these formal equality protections extended to same-sex spousal recognition. That question was answered the following year, when the Supreme Court struck down an opposite-sex definition of spouse in *M. v. H* (1999). The case involved a definition of spouse that applied to unmarried opposite-sex couples but not same-sex couples for the purposes of spousal support (s. 29, Ontario *Family Law Act*). On the breakdown of their ten-year relationship, one of the women in a lesbian relationship challenged the constitutionality of the definition of "spouse" in order to obtain spousal support from her former partner. Following its previous decision in *Egan*, the Supreme Court held that the opposite definition of spouse was discrimination on the basis of sexual orientation and that it violated section 15 of the Charter. But, this time, the Court found that the violation was not a reasonable limit within the meaning of section 1. The objectives of the legislation, that is of providing for the equitable resolution of financial disputes that arise when intimate, interdependent relationships break down, and alleviating the "burden on the public purse" by imposing a private obligation for support (shifting away from any public responsibility for dependency), would both be furthered if same-sex couples were included in the definition. On the heels of *Egan*, *Vriend*, and *M. v. H.*, both the federal and provincial governments moved to amend their statutory definitions. Some did so broadly, others more narrowly. But the powerful discourse of formal equality had prevailed, and the opposite-sex definitions of spouse began to tumble.

LGBT equality advocates then turned their sights on marriage equality. In the ensuing years, several challenges were brought to the opposite-sex definition of marriage. All but one of the challenges were successful, with courts in Ontario, Quebec and British Columbia finding that the definition violated formal equality (see *Halpern v. Canada, Hendricks v. Quebec, EGALE v. Canada*). The turning point came with a 2003 decision of the Ontario Court of Appeal in *Halpern v. Canada*, where not only did the Court strike down the opposite-sex definition, and redefine marriage as including same-sex couples, but it also made the decision effective immediately. In an about face, the federal government, which had been defending the opposite-sex definition, decided not to appeal the decision to the Supreme Court. Instead, it introduced new legislation, sent it to the Supreme Court by way of a reference to advise on its constitutionality, and introduced it into Parliament on a free vote. After considerable toing and froing, in 2005, the *Civil Marriage Act* was passed, which redefined marriage as "the lawful union of two persons to the exclusion of all others" (s. 2, *Civil Marriage Act*, 2005).

By 2005, formal equality for gay and lesbian Canadians was more or less complete. Explicit protection for trans and non-binary Canadians would only come later. Initially, human rights tribunals in several provinces found that trans persons were protected by prohibitions on discrimination on the basis of sex (*Montreuil v. National Bank of Canada*, 2004; *Kavanagh v. Canada (Attorney General)*, 2001). Few cases would proceed to court and none would do so on the basis of Charter equality rights. Explicit protection for trans people, by adding discrimination on the basis of gender identity and/or gender expression as prohibited grounds, would begin to be included in provincial and territorial human rights codes, but would take over a decade to come to fruition. The process was largely legislative, rather than litigation driven. The Northwest Territories was the first Canadian jurisdiction to include gender identity as a prohibited ground in their human rights code in 2002 (*Human Rights Act*, 2002). The Federal government would be the last; it was not until June 2017 that the federal government passed an act amending the *Canadian Human Rights Act* to add "gender identity or expression" (*An Act to amend the Canadian Human Rights Act and the Criminal Code*, 2017). The scope and content of these rights continue to be worked out through human rights commissions and tribunals, but judicial comment remains thin.

Much has been written on these equality rights and the judicial and legislative processes that established them, in equal amounts glowing and critical. While some celebrated the inclusion of LGBTQ Canadians, others were more circumspect on their limitations. Critical legal scholars have long pointed out the limitations of formal equality rights more generally, noting that their tendency to individualize the harms of discrimination diminishes their ability to tackle structural forms of oppression (Tushnet, 1994; Gordon, 1998). So too have scholars engaged with LGBTQ rights in particular. Some have argued that the discourses of inclusion have operated to reinforce structural inequalities. LGBTQ people have been recognized as rights-bearing subjects, but they have become so within the privatizing discourses of neo-liberalism (Boyd, 1996, 1999; Cossman, 2002b). In the ground-breaking case of *M. v. H.*, for example, individuals within a same-sex relationship won the right to sue the other for support on the breakdown of their relationship, thereby expanding the scope of spousal support obligations and reducing demands on the state. Indeed, the Court emphasized the importance of "reducing the strain on the public purse" by "shifting the financial burden away from the government on to those partners with the capacity to provide support for dependent spouses" (*M v. H*, 69). As I and others argued at the time, it was a ruling all too consistent with the politics of reprivatization, whereby the costs of social reproduction were shifted from the public to the private spheres, and the family reconstituted as the natural site of economic dependency (Boyd, 1996, 1999; Cossman, 2002b). Legal recognition did nothing to redress underlying structural inequalities; indeed, the processes of neo-liberal privatization did much to reinforce them.

At the same time, however, the legislative reform that followed *M. v. H.* extended formal equality to a broad range of other government rights and responsibilities. While the neo-liberal state offers fewer benefits, those that remained were now fully extended to same-sex couples. Furthermore, while the decision included same-sex couples within the rubric of conjugality, thus reinforcing the discourses of sameness, it could also be read as destabilizing the category of conjugality. The Court endorsed a functional equivalency approach to conjugality, with its "generally accepted characteristics . . . of shared shelter, sexual and personal behavior, services, social activities, economic support and children, as well as the societal perception of the couple" (*M. v. H*, at para. 59), but it also observed that a conjugal relationship could exist even in the absence of a sexual relationship (*M.v. H.* at para 60). It is a comment on the part of the Supreme Court that begins to undermine the very distinction between conjugal and non-conjugal relationships, on which the legislative definitions of spouse rest. Specifically, if a sexual relationship is not a requirement of a conjugal relationship for the purposes of legal rights and responsibilities, then why would only more traditional understandings of "spouses" be included? Why might the rights and responsibilities not be extended to those in so-called "non-conjugal relationships," such as adult sisters? The Law Commission of Canada, in its report titled *Beyond Conjugality: Recognizing and Supporting Close Personal Adult Relationships* (2001), continued this rethinking of the centrality of conjugality in the legal regulation of adult relationships, suggesting instead that emotional and economic interdependencies might be more appropriate criteria (Law Commission of Canada, 2001).

Somewhat paradoxically, Alberta, in seeking to avoid recognizing same-sex relationships as spouses, enacted far-reaching legislative reform that extended rights and responsibilities beyond conjugality. In the *Adult Interdependent Relationships Act* (2002), the province replaced cohabiting spouses living in a conjugal relationship with a "relationship of interdependence." A relationship of interdependence exists where two people "share one another's lives; are emotionally committed to one another; and function as an economic and domestic unit" (*Adult Interdependent Relationships Act*, 2002, 1(1)(f)). While conjugality is a factor that may be considered in determining whether two persons live in an economic and domestic unit, it is not a required criterion. Persons who are in adult personal relationships may gain access to provincial rights and responsibilities, much like married couples. The Alberta legislation represents the first to decentre conjugality—the existence of a sexual relationship—in the extension of legal rights and responsibilities.

While the inclusion of LGBTQ people for the purposes of relationship recognition may have occurred within the terms of sameness and privatization, reconstituting the nature of the legal subjects, it can also be seen to have contributed to a partial reconstitution of the very nature of conjugality. The process of recognition and inclusion through formal equality rights, then, can be seen as an ambivalent and contradictory one. Recognition transforms the subjects who are brought within its folds, but it also has the potential to change the legal relationships and institutions into which they are included (Cossman, 2007).

Here is a final caveat about a narrative of LGBT equality rights that focuses exclusively on the courts: the progress narrative, about the power of constitutional rights discourse to advance the equality of LGBTQ rights, is one that often focuses disproportionately on the role of the courts. While equality rights advocates framed claims in the discourse of constitutional equality rights speaking directly to the courts and their role in constitutional interpretation, an exclusive focus on the judicial role obscures the many other actors and factors that were at play. Even those scholars most committed to the progress narrative, like William Eskridge, have recognized that successful same-sex relationship recognition in the courts was only possible as a result of changing public attitudes, although they also emphasize the role of the constitutional discourse in contributing to that change (Eskridge, 2000, 2013). A broad array of factors contributed to changing public attitudes on LGBT rights and people through the 1990s, including greater visibility in mainstream culture (Cossman, 2007). In Canada, by the time the Supreme Court released its decision in *M. v. H*, there had been a significant change in public opinion on the recognition of same-sex relationships (Bateup, 2007, p. 53). That change continued, and by the time the Ontario Court of Appeal decided *Halpern*, rewriting the legal definition of marriage to include same-sex couples, the majority of Canadians were in favour of same-sex marriage (Bateup, 2007).

There was also an important role for the government in the eventual recognition of full formal equality for LGBT Canadians. Much of the discussion around government and Charter rights in Canada has been framed through the lens of dialogue; of legislatures responding to judicial decisions (Hogg & Bushell, 1997; Roach, 2004). Indeed, much has been written about same-sex marriage through this lens of dialogue (van Kralingen, 2004). The concept of dialogue is contested and controversial; some like Emmett Macfarlane have argued that more complex institutional relationships are "obfuscated by the invocation of the term dialogue" (Macfarlane, 2012, p. 99). Along similar lines, I have argued that the relationship between courts and Parliament in the lead up to the federal recognition of same-sex marriage was far more complex (Cossman, 2019). The federal Liberal government was deeply divided on the question of same-sex marriage recognition. Proponents of same-sex marriage inside government used each subsequent court decision to persuade others and advance their political preferences, amid a highly divided Cabinet, caucus and legislature. The closer the issue came to marriage, the more those inside government needed court decisions to move the needle. The apparent about face that the federal government made on the heels of the Ontario Court of Appeal in Halpern was years in the making; what changed was that the supporters of same-sex marriage within Cabinet and Caucus finally built a majority consensus. And in the strategy that followed—sending the draft law to the Supreme Court by way of the reference—was one last deployment of the courts to persuade wayward liberal Members of Parliament to vote for same-sex marriage. The story of same-sex marriage in Canada is then far more complicated than one of the judiciary vindicating the constitutional equality rights of LGBT Canadians.

Equality Rights: What's Out

There is another line of cases—or perhaps a menagerie of cases, since they follow no clear lines—that tells a different story about the regulation of LGBT sexuality. Constitutional challenges to laws that regulated LGBT sexuality but did not formally or explicitly discriminate on the basis of sexual orientation have fared less well. This section explores some of the Supreme Court cases that have considered obscenity, HIV non-disclosure and sex work laws. While most of these cases did not involve constitutional challenges on the basis of sexual orientation per se (since these laws did not formally discriminate on this basis), the cases nevertheless gesture to the limitations of equality rights for LGBT and other non-normative sexualities.

In *Little Sisters Bookstore and Art Emporium v. Canada* (2000), a gay and lesbian bookstore in Vancouver brought a constitutional challenge against Canada Customs. For 15 years, Canada Customs had been detaining and seizing shipments en route to the bookstore. In a protracted legal battle, Little Sisters argued that Canada Customs was unfairly targeting gay and lesbian materials headed to gay and lesbian bookstores. The bookstore challenged both the administrative practices of Canada Customs, as well as the provisions of the *Tariff Code'* that empower customs officials to detain materials that are obscene within the meaning of section 163(8) of the *Criminal Code*, arguing that the law violated the right to freedom of expression in section 2(b) and the right to equality in section 15 of the *Charter*.

The Supreme Court held that Little Sisters did suffer differential treatment when compared to other bookstores that imported heterosexual, sexually explicit material and that this differential treatment was discriminatory. But the Court concluded that there was nothing on the face of the legislation itself that encouraged this discriminatory treatment; since the discrimination occurred at the administrative level of implementation, the legislation was capable of being implemented in a manner that did not violate *Charter* rights. Despite the finding of administrative discrimination, the Court provided no remedy. The Court noted that Customs had made many changes in the intervening years, and without more evidence, was unwilling to conclude that the changes were inadequate. Rather, the Court opined that Little Sisters could always launch a further action in the future if need be. Little Sisters and some of the intervenors claimed that the ruling was a partial victory—their claim to harassment and discrimination at the hands of Customs was vindicated. But this partial victory was contained within what was otherwise a resounding defeat. The power of Customs to censor sexually explicit materials at the border was upheld, and the test previously established by the Supreme Court for obscenity in *R. v. Butler* (1992) was reaffirmed (Cossman, 2002a; Cossman et al., 1997). Moreover, virtually no remedy was provided for the administrative discrimination.

Unlike the preceding cases, *Little Sisters* was not just about gay and lesbian equality; it was also about sexual freedom and sexual expression. Little Sisters emphasized the importance of sexual freedom and sexually expressive materials for lesbian and gay identity and community. They challenged not only the administrative discrimination of Customs officials but also the very obscenity framework that was being deployed to do so. Little Sisters argued that the *Butler* harms-based test for obscenity was a heteronormative one, predicated on contested assumptions about the harms that heterosexual pornography does to women. They argued that this framework should not be formulaically applied to gay and lesbian representations. Furthermore, they argued that gay and lesbian sexual representations are crucial to gay and lesbian identity, dignity, self-worth and community, and accordingly they should not be dismissed as lower form of speech (*Little Sisters*, 2000, Factum of the Appellant). *Little Sisters* was simultaneously a claim to sameness and difference. As an equality claim, it was about the right to be free from discrimination on the basis of sexual orientation; it was about the right to be treated the same. But, as a sexual freedom and expression claim, *Little Sisters* was an assertion of gay and lesbian sex, the very aspect of gay and lesbian identity that marked difference. And this freedom claim was unsuccessful; the Court insisted that the harm test could be applied equally to LGBT representations, without prejudice. The norms of formal equality effectively trumped the freedom claim.

There are a number of other areas of the criminal law that are similarly formally neutral, yet present disproportionate surveillance of LGBT people. For example, the *Criminal Code* does not specifically address the non-disclosure of HIV-positive status prior to engaging in sexual activity. However, a number of existing criminal offences, most notably aggravated sexual assault, have been used to prosecute individuals who have failed to disclose their HIV status or put others at risk of HIV transmission. In *R v. Cuerrier* (1998), the Supreme Court held that the failure to disclose HIV status before engaging in sexual activity that poses "a significant risk of serious bodily harm" constitutes fraud, thereby vitiates the partner's consent. In the absence of consent, the sexual activity becomes sexual assault, regardless of whether or not the victim contracts HIV (*Cuerrier*, 1998). The question of what constitutes "significant risk of serious bodily harm" has been controversial (Shaffer, 2013; Canadian AIDS Society, 2004). In 2012, the Supreme Court sought to clarify the obligation in *R. v. Mabior* (2012). The Court held that a significant risk of serious bodily harm would be triggered by sexual activity that presented a "realistic possibility of HIV transmission" (2012). Kyle Kirkup has argued that the decision in *Mabior* "warrants criticism for its deep and uncritical heteronormativity" noting that the Court remained silent on the application of the test beyond "heterosexual penile vaginal sex" (Kirkup, 2015, p. 139). In assuming only heterosexual sex, it was silent on the possible risks of anal or oral sex, or otherwise with LGBTQ sexual encounters.

While gay men have been disproportionately impacted by HIV, in the aftermath of *Cuerrier* and *Mabior*, it has been men who engaged in sex with women who represented the majority of those charged (Mykhalovskiy & Betteridge, 2012). However, studies have also demonstrated that certain vulnerable groups are disproportionately targeted by the criminalization of HIV non-disclosure, including, in particular, black people, Indigenous women and LGBTQ people (House of Commons, 2019). Kyle Kirkup demonstrates the ways in which gay men continue to be targeted in unique ways that rely on historical tropes of homophobia—promiscuity, deviance and pathology, for example—in the prosecution of HIV non-disclosure (Kirkup, 2020). He concludes:

> It would be a mistake to conclude, however, that the criminal law has abandoned targeting queer people all together—the criminalization of HIV non-disclosure constitutes but one example of the ways in which queer people, particularly those situated at multiple axes of oppression, continue to find themselves ensnared in the repressive aspects of the criminal legal system.
>
> *(2020)*

It is another example of how formally equal laws continue to target LGBTQ peoples, in ways that have been immune from the challenge of equality rights.

There are a range of other, formally neutral criminal laws that continue to regulate non-normative sexuality and sexual practices. None are specifically directed at LGBT people or sexualities; yet each continues to be deployed in ways that affect members of the LGBT community, particularly, some of the more vulnerable members. Canadian sex work laws prohibit the purchase of sexual services, as well as advertising for sexual services, obtaining material benefits from sexual services, and soliciting in some public areas. The former sex work laws were challenged as unconstitutional in *Canada v. Bedford* (2013). In that case, the Supreme Court held that the laws prohibiting the operation of a bawdy house (s. 210, Criminal Code), living off the avails of prostitution (s. 212(1)(j), Criminal Code), and communication in public for the purposes of prostitution (s. 213(1)(c)) were unconstitutional. Each of the laws was found to violate section 7 of the Charter, in particular, the right to security of the person. The Court held that each law made sex work more dangerous, and thereby violated the security of the person of sex workers. In the aftermath of *Bedford*, however, the Conservative government introduced new, more restrictive sex work laws. Bill C-36, *Protection of Communities and Exploited Persons Act* (2014), adopted a Nordic approach of criminalizing the purchase but not the sale of sex. The new law has been criticized by scholars and activists alike as every bit as dangerous to sex workers as the laws that were struck down by the Supreme Court, noting that the sex work laws will most negatively impact the most marginalized of sex workers (Bruckert, 2015; POWER, date). The laws have in turn been challenged, and an Ontario trial court has held that the laws are unconstitutional, on grounds very similar to the Bedford decision. However, it will be some time before the constitutionality is settled by higher courts.

There is nothing in the law that specifically targets LGBT people. Indeed, much of the public and legal debates surrounding sex work laws are cast in specifically cis heterosexual terms—the risks that women face from male clients and pimps. Yet trans women, particularly trans women of colour, are among the most vulnerable groups at risk under the new sex work laws. As Leon Laidlaw has observed:

> [D]ominant discourse on sex work has largely overlooked marginalized groups who sell sex, such as trans people. In Canada, little research has focused exclusively on the experiences of trans people in sex work. Rather, trans women are most often invisibilized in broader sex work studies.
>
> *(Laidlaw, 2018, p. 357)*

Studies have shown that trans women are disproportionately represented among those who sell sex, often working at the street level, where the risks of both violence and criminal surveillance is higher. Trans women, and particularly trans women of colour, face disproportionate risks of violence, arrest and incarceration (Bauer & Scheim, 2015; Lyons et al., 2017). Moreover, interviews with trans sex workers highlight the extent to which violence was specifically attributable to transphobia (Laidlaw, 2018). It is violence and harassment that are intricately tied to gender expression and gender identity. Yet precisely because the sex work laws are gender and sexuality neutral, challenging them on the basis of gender identity is unlikely to have traction.

These three examples of criminal laws—obscenity, HIV non-disclosure and sex work—demonstrate the ways in which non-normative LGBTQ sexualities continue to be targeted by formally equal laws. LGBT Canadians have crossed the threshold into legality and respectability. They are entitled to the protection of the law and cannot be discriminated against on the basis of their sexual orientation, gender identity and gender expression. But LGBT sexuality, to the extent that it does not accord with the norms of respectability or homonormativity—that is, the privileging of heterosexual norms and practices onto LGBT culture and identity—continues to be at risk of surveillance and punishment. The discourse of equality may have prevailed, but the discourses of sexual liberty have not. Despite the extent to which Canadian equality laws have incorporated standards of substantive equality, interrogating the ways in which laws impact on historically disadvantaged groups, this lens has not been particularly effective in challenging laws that regulate non-normative sexualities. In the equality/liberty axis, equality has not only been more successful, but it has also been arguably operated to trump the very liberty claims.

Conclusion

Constitutional equality rights have been very effective at challenging formal discrimination on the basis of sexual orientation: laws that explicitly excluded benefits or protections to individuals on the basis of their sexual orientation. But this inclusion comes largely in the terms of sameness; that is, assimilation into previously existing categories, relationships and institutions. Those who are most the same are the ones who can most belong. Yet, as I have argued, the process of inclusion is an uneven one. Same-sex couples' recognition and inclusion, first into conjugality then into marriage, bring LGBT people into citizenship on its terms: privatized, familialized and domesticated. At the same time, bringing LGBT people into conjugality and marriage reconstitutes those legal institutions, displacing their heteronormativity. It is a process of mutual reconstitution, creating new subject identities and legal relationships. Furthermore, despite the success of constitutional equality rights in challenging formally unequal laws, as we moved to a post-formal equality world in 2005, equality rights lost their traction in challenging the multiple axes of inequality and oppression that continue to plague LGBTQ communities.

A progress narrative does not do justice to the uneven and contradictory nature of LGBTQ engagement with equality rights. It is, I would suggest, more of a morality tale, though perhaps more of a postmodern one. I use the term "postmodern" here lightly, to gesture towards the partiality of truth claims and the contingency of normative claims. A morality tale is a story from which one can derive a moral of right and wrong. They are stories of good and evil, with heroes and victims on the side of justice and righteousness, villains and oppressors on the side of injustice. Indeed, in the debates within LGBTQ communities, each side claims the side of justice. Liberals are on the side of the historically oppressed LGBTQ victim, delivering them from inequality to constitutional protection. Critics too are on the side of the historically oppressed, but see the state as the continuing oppressor, with liberals at best functioning as its handmaidens. But the story of LGBTQ equality rights is not simply a story of good versus evil, virtue versus vice. It tells neither a linear story of the victory of the oppressed nor an equally linear story of the perils of homonormativity. Rather, the moral of the story is a bumpy one, with no clear heroes or villains. It is a complex narrative of inclusions and exclusions, normalizations and subversions, of steps forward, sideways and backwards.

These debates are best read reparatively. I have recently argued in relation to the feminist debates around the regulation of sexual harm that the contested legal claims beside rather than against each other (Cossman, 2021). In the context of LGBT rights, this would involve reading equality claims *beside* freedom ones; liberal defences of rights strategies *beside* more left critiques of these strategies. We can read these claims not as a dichotomous either/or where one must be right and the other wrong, where there is only one truth beneath the texts. Rather, we should explore what we might be able to see, to understand and to feel, if we instead accept the claims of both sides and hold them in tension, beside each other. Constitutional equality rights have been transformative for LGBT Canadians, but not in ways that are easily grasped by a progress narrative. The discourses of inclusion and exclusion have been partial and contradictory. Liberals and critics are both right, but they are each only partially right. We need to be able to hold those competing claims and their tensions in view to fully appreciate the complicated legacy of constitutional equality rights.

References

An Act to Amend the Canadian Human Rights Act and the Criminal Code, SC 2017, c 13 (Can.).
Adult Interdependent Relationships Act, SA 2002, c A-4.5 (Can.).
Bateup, C. (2007). Expanding the conversation: American and Canadian experiences of constitutional dialogue in comparative perspective. *Temple International & Comparative Law Journal*, 21(1), 1–58.

Bauer, G. R., & Scheim, A. I., for the Trans PULSE Project Team. (2015, June 1). *Transgender people in Ontario, Canada: Statistics to inform human rights policy.*

Bedford v. Canada (Attorney General), 2013 SCC 72 (Can.).

Boyd, S. B. (1996). Best friends of spouses? Privatization and the recognition of lesbian relationships in M v. H. *Canadian Journal of Family Law, 13*(2), 321–342.

Boyd, S. B. (1999). Family, law and sexuality: Feminist engagements. *Social & Legal Studies, 8*(3), 369–390.

Bruckert, C. (2015). Protection of communities and exploited persons act: Misogynistic law making in action. *Canadian Journal of Law and Society, 30*(1), 1–3.

Butler, J. (2004). *Excitable speech: A politics of the performative.* Routledge.

Canadian AIDS Society. (2004). *HIV transmission: Guidelines for assessing risk: A resource for educators, counsellors and healthcare providers.* librarypdf.catie.ca/pdf/p25/22303.pdf

Canadian Charter of Rights and Freedoms, Part I of the *Constitution Act, 1982,* being Schedule B to the Canada Act 1982(UK), 1982, c 11, s 91(24).

Civil Marriage Act, SC 2005, c 33.

Cossman, B. (1994). Family inside/out. *University of Toronto Law Journal, 44*(1), 1–39. https://doi.org/10.2307/825753

Cossman, B. (2000). Canadian same sex relationship recognition struggles and the contradictory nature of legal victories. *Cleveland State Law Journal, 48*(1), 49–59.

Cossman, B. (2002a). Disciplining the unruly: Sexual outlaws, little sisters and the legacy of Butler. *University of British Columbia Law Review, 36,* 77–99.

Cossman, B. (2002b). Family feuds: Neo-liberal and neo-conservative visions of reprivatization project. In B. Cossman & J. Fudge (Eds.), *Privatization, law and the challenge to feminism* (pp. 169–217). University of Toronto Press.

Cossman, B. (2002c). Lesbians, gay men, and the Canadian charter of rights and freedoms. *Osgoode Hall Law Journal, 40*(3), 223–249.

Cossman, B. (2007). *Sexual citizens: The legal and cultural regulation of sex and belonging.* Stanford University Press.

Cossman, B. (2019). Same-sex marriage beyond charter dialogue: Charter cases and contestation within government. *University of Toronto Law Journal, 69*(2), 183–210. https://doi.org/10.3138/utlj.2018-0018

Cossman, B. (2020). The 1969 criminal amendments: Constituting the terms of resistance. *University of Toronto Law Journal, 70*(3), 245–262.

Cossman, B. (2021). *The new sex wars: Sexual harm in the age of #MeToo.* NYU Press.

Cossman, B., Bell, S., Gotell, L., & Ross, B. L. (1997). *Bad attitude/s on trial: Pornography, feminism, and the Butler decision.* University of Toronto Press.

EGALE v. Canada, 2003 BCCA 251 (Can.).

Eskridge, W. (2000). Comparative law and same-sex marriage debate: A step-by-step approach toward state recognition. *McGeorge Law Review, 31,* 647–648.

Eskridge, W. (2013). Backlash politics: How constitutional litigation has advanced marriage equality in the United States. *Boston University Law Review, 93*(2), 275–323.

Family Law Reform Act, ONT 1978, c 2 (Can.).

Gordon, R. (1998). Some critical theories of law and their critics. In D. Kairys (Ed.), *The politics of law* (3rd ed., pp. 621–661). Basic Books.

Hendricks v. Quebec, 2002 RJQ 2506 (Can. Que. CA).

Hogg, P. W., & Bushell, A. A. (1997). The charter dialogue between courts and legislatures. *Osgoode Hall Law Journal, 35*(1), 75–124.

House of Commons. (2019). *The criminalization of HIV non-disclosure in Canada: Report of the standing committee on justice and human rights. (Chair: Anthony housefather).* www.ourcommons.ca/DocumentViewer/en/42-1/JUST/report-28/

Human Rights Act, SNWT 2002, c 18 (Can.).

Kavanagh v. Canada (Attorney General) (2001), 41 CHRR 119 (Can. CHRT).

Kirkup, K. (2015). Releasing stigma: Police, journalists and crimes of HIV non-disclosure. *Ottawa Law Review, 46*(1), 127–160.

Kirkup, K. (2020). The gross indecency of criminalizing HIV non-disclosure. *University of Toronto Law Journal, 70*(3), 263–282. https://doi.org/10.3138/utlj/2019-0054

Laidlaw, L. (2018). Challenging dominant portrayals of the trans sex worker: On gender, violence, and protection. *Manitoba Law Journal, 41*(4), 351–372.

Law Commission of Canada. (2001). *Beyond conjugality: Recognizing and supporting close personal adult relationships.* Law Commission of Canada.

Little Sisters Book & Art Emporium v. Canada (Commissioners of Customers & Revenue Agency), 2007 SCC 2 (Can.).

Lyons, T., Krusi, A., Pierre, L., Small, W., & Shannon, K. (2017). The impact of construction and gentrification on an outdoor trans sex work environment: Violence, displacement and policing. *Sexualities, 20*(8), 881–903.

M. v. H., [1999] 2 SCR 3 (Can.).

Macfarlane, E. (2012). Conceptual precision and parliamentary systems of rights: Disambiguating "dialogue". *Review of Constitutional Studies, 17*(2), 73–100.

McCallum, E. L., & Bradway, T. (2019). Introduction: Thinking sideways, or an untoward genealogy of queer reading. In E. L. McCallum & T. Bradway (Eds.), *After queer studies: Literature, theory, and sexuality in the 21st century* (pp. 1–17). Cambridge University of Press.

Montreuil v. National Bank of Canada, 2004 CHRT 7 (Can.).

Mykhalovskiy, E., & Betteridge, G. (2012). Who? what? when? And with what consequences? An analysis of criminal cases of HIV non-disclosure in Canada. *Canadian Journal of Law and Society, 27*(1), 31–53.

Protection of Communities and Exploited Persons Act, SC 2014, c 25 (Can.).

R v Butler, [1992] 1 SCR 452 (Can.).

R v Mabior, 2012 SCC 47 (Can.).

Roach, K. (2004). Dialogic judicial review and its critics. *Supreme Court Law Review, 23*(2), 49–104.

Sedgwick, E. K. (1996). Introduction: Queerer than fiction. *Studies in the Novel, 28*(3), 277–280.

Sedgwick, E. K. (2002). Paranoid reading and reparative reading; or you're so paranoid you probably think this essay is about you. In *Touching feeling: Affect, pedagogy, performativity* (pp. 123–151). Duke University Press.

Sedgwick, E. K. (2003). Introduction. In *Touching feeling: Affect, pedagogy, performativity* (pp. 1–26). Duke University Press.

Seitler, D. (2019). *Reading sideways: The queer politics of art in modern American fiction.* Fordham University Press.

Shaffer, M. (2013). Sex, lies, and HIV: Mabior and the concept of sexual fraud. *University of Toronto Law Journal, 63*(3), 466–474.

Smith, M. (2019). Homophobia and homonationalism: LGBTQ law reform in Canada. *Social and Legal Studies, 29*(1), 65–84.

Stychin, C. F. (1998). *A nation by rights: National cultures, sexual identity politics, and the discourse of rights.* Temple University Press.

Stychin, C. F. (2001). Sexual citizenship in the European Union. *Citizenship Studies, 5*(3), 285–301. https://doi.org/10.1080/13621020120085252

Tushnet, M. (1994). The critique of rights. *SMU Law Review, 47*(1), 23–26.

Van Kralingen, A. (2004). The dialogic saga of same-sex marriage: EGALE, Halpern and the relationship between suspended declarations and productive political discourse about rights. *University of Toronto Faculty of Law Review, 62*, 149–192.

Vriend v. Alberta, [1998] 1 SCR 493 (Can.).

Warner, M. (1999). Normal and normaller: Beyond same sex marriage. *GLQ: A Journal of Lesbian and Gay Studies, 5*(2), 119–171.

Warner, M. (2000). *The trouble with normal: Sex, politics and the ethics of queer life.* Harvard University Press.

Weeks, J. (1998). The sexual citizen. *Theory, Culture and Society, 15*(3–4), 35–52. https://doi/10.1177/0263276498015003003

9

THE RELEVANCE OF HUMAN RIGHTS AND SOCIAL JUSTICE MINDING INTERSECTIONAL CONTEXT OF AFFIRMATIVE PSYCHOLOGICAL PRACTICE WITH LGBTQ+ PEOPLE— CROATIAN EXPERIENCE

Iva Žegura

Importance of Human Rights in Psychology

Human rights are fundamental rights that protect the basic human freedoms and dignity of all human beings, regardless of their nationality, gender, ethnic background, religion, language and other social statuses (UN General Assembly, 1948). They are inseparable, interdependent, universal and indefeasible in the sense that they cannot be denied and are appointed to individuals as well as to groups (Lassen, 2014). Different psychological associations explicitly identify human rights as a guiding principle. For example, the American Psychological Association (APA, 2009) states that psychologists have a leading role in the promotion of human rights, well-being and health in general. In Europe, the European Federation of Psychologists' Association (EFPA [2015, 2016]) points out an equally important vision and accompanying activities for psychologists which resulted in an edited book (Hagenaars et al., 2020).

The Croatian Psychological Chamber's Ethical Code describes similar values: in their professional work, psychologists should adhere to the acceptance and respect for human rights, dignity and values of all people. They should encourage the development of these values in each individual with whom they work professionally, accepting people's right to privacy and confidentiality and their right to self-determination and self-identification (Croatian Psychological Chamber-CPC, 2004, pp. 1–2).

Socio-Political and Professional Background of LGBTIQ+ Human Rights in Croatia

The Republic of Croatia is a unitary parliamentary constitutional republic located between Central Europe and South-Eastern Europe with a population of 4,047,680 (Croatian Bureau of Statistics, 2021). Croatia declared independence from the Socialist Federative Republic of

DOI: 10.4324/9781003128151-11

Yugoslavia in 1991, resulting in the Croatian war of independence "Homeland war" that lasted until August 1995 (Goldstein, 2013). Croatia has been a member of the United Nations since 1992 and the country joined the Council of Europe in 1996. Since July 1, 2013, Croatia has become a member-state of the European Union.

The contemporary LGBTIQ+ movement in the Balkans region and thus Croatia were a byproduct of the feminist movement (Bilić & Radoman, 2019). The first Pride Parade in Croatia's capital Zagreb (and Southeast Europe) was held in 2002 (Bilić & Kajinić, 2016). Organized by two LGBTIQ+ nongovernmental organizations "Iskorak" and "Kontra", it had coming out as its main theme "Gay Pride Zagreb: Iskorak (engl. 'step forward', AN) and Kontra (engl. 'against', AN) prejudice" (Čemažar & Mikulin, 2017; Herceg Kolman, 2020). More than 30 people were attacked before or after the Pride Parade in 2002, and 27 were arrested (Herceg Kolman, 2020). In 2020, the 19th Pride Parade under the motto "Freedom and equality inside and outside the 4 walls" was held in Zagreb (Pride, n.d.). The first Pride Parade occurred outside of Zagreb in Split in 2011 (Herceg Kolman, 2020). Located in the middle of the Dalmatians coast, Split has a traditional society. The 300 participants that marched through the city were outnumbered by opponents which police did not block adequately. They attacked Pride activists and their allies with stones, teargas, bottles and fire cannons, and many people were injured (All the Pride Parades in Croatia, n.d.). In 2012, Rijeka gave its support to the Split Pride by organizing a similar march, which took place three hours before the start of Split Pride. In September 2014, Osijek was the third city in Croatia to host a Pride Parade. The Pride Parade was not continued in Osijek due to organizational problems (All the Pride Parades in Croatia, n.d.). On March 30, 2019, the first Parade of transgender people was organized in Zagreb (First Transgender March, 2019).

In the decades that preceded, during the former socialistic regime, homosexuality was connected to the decadent bourgeoisie and considered a product of insatiable capitalism (Dota, 2017). It was thought that only those with tendencies of spoiling healthy socialistic youth have homosexual inclinations (Dobrović, 2007; Dota, 2017). Sexual intercourse with people of the same sex was considered a criminal act and known under the term "unnatural impurity" until 1977, when it was decriminalized with the exception of anal intercourse that was still legally prohibited (Dota, 2017; Košiček, 1986). Anyone who was caught in homosexual intercourse could be punished with a prison sentence. In the former Republic of Yugoslavia, in the period from the end of the Second World War until 1977, 1,494 homosexual men were sentenced and imprisoned, and 497 of them were from Croatia (Dota, 2017). Most of these men were prosecuted during the period of 1945–1950 ($N = 602$ in the former Yugoslavia, and $N = 256$ were from Croatia; Dota, 2017). Some archives suggest similar treatment for lesbian women, with fewer victims (Košiček, 1986), even though lesbian relationships and sexual intercourse have been omitted from criminal law since 1951 (Dota, 2017). The law that punishes sex between two men and does not punish sexual practices between two women is based on a binary concept of gender and traditional patriarchal understanding of sexuality and gender roles, where heterosexuality serves as the foundation of biological, economic, political, military and social power (Dota, 2017). The term "unnatural impurity" was excluded from Croatian criminal law in 1977, when criminally prohibited sexual delicts were defined by two categories: (a) "sexual intercourse without mutual consent or other sexual actions that are correspondent to it" or (b) "other lustful acts" (Dota, 2017). Such "lustful acts" in heterosexual couplings are punishable only and exclusively in sexual harassment attacks and abuses of privileged relationships (teachers-pupils). Homosexual lustful acts are forbidden by the law despite being consensual, and for anal sex when a partner is a minor between the ages of 14 and 18 and the other an adult (Dota, 2017), while the law recognizes as pedophilia sex with the child (below the age of 14) and sex with minor person (from the age of 14 until the age of 18). But, if homosexual intercourse is consensual between two adult men, then it is not prohibited (Dota, 2017; Čaušević et al., 2012). Additionally, the law applies to lesbian women. This discriminatory law remained valid for another 20 years, until January 1, 1998, when the new Criminal Law of the Republic of Croatia entered into force (1997).

The existence of long-standing economic problems (unemployment, low gross national income, corruption during the transition period to name some) and the lack of socio-political dialog make it difficult to achieve social and economic rights for all Croatian citizens, especially young people and vulnerable minority groups (Novosel et al., 2018). Conflict between conservative and liberal values within the parliamentary majority causes stagnation of democratic societal processes, and creation and implementation of public policies aimed at the protection and promotion of human rights are de facto paralyzed. The importance of human rights is downplayed. A low level of civil education and lack of enough competences of citizens to participate in contemporary democratic society present a cultural background making a long-term challenge for the sustainable democratic development of Croatian society that has its foundations in the acceptance, promotion and protection of human rights and social justices. This socio-political situation leads to strengthening of those socio-political groups that are calling for a return to traditional values and systematically distort and oppress standards of human rights protection to limit the fundamental rights of everyone who is different (Žegura, 2017b; Žegura & Vrbat, 2017).

The past and present status of LGBTIQ+ issues in the Croatian psychological profession mirrors the invisibility of SGM people in society more generally. Until 2000, topics related to sexual health, gender identity and sexual orientation were almost never mentioned during university education and therapy training (Žegura, 2006). The SGM population began to attract research interest in 2010. There are no specific guidelines aimed toward an affirmative psychological approach from the professional association and professional chamber. The stigma affecting SGM diversity is mentioned in very few (if any) handbooks, reviews, or research papers on the health and mental health in general but also of LGBTIQ+ people in Croatia (Žegura, 2017a).

Human sexuality is one of life's core phenomena, which is expressed in variety of ways in all living beings. It is an inseparable component of the living organism as one of the primary needs. Contemporary society therefore seeks complete and professional answers to issues concerning sexuality. The vacuum that currently exists in the Croatian scientific literature is filled with popular universal answers or plain advice, but more dangerously with quasi-scientific interpretations based on personal prejudice. Examples of these quasi-scientific interpretations include the statements that all gay men are pedophiles or that same-sex orientation is a sign of immaturity and personality disorder; the concerns expressed by "gender ideology" right-wing oriented organizations and their representatives in politics and medicine that implementing sexual education in the school curriculum will force children to change their gender identity; quoting the "Regnerus study" (Regnerus, 2012) in debate aiming to legally prohibit LGBTIQ+ parenting and LGBTIQ+ marriages; proclaiming that interventions aimed to change sexual orientation and gender identity are widely professionally excepted and not harmful; and proposing that gender dysphoria is a psychiatric disorder and that transgender people thus have severe psychological problems. This approach causes great damage to the personality development, health, well-being and general adaptive functioning of people who are affected by these practices (APA, 2005, 2011; American Sociological Association, 2015). The effect is doubled as these quasi-scientific approaches have a deleterious impact on the psychological profession. There is a clear need for more integrative scientific research on human sexuality. Psychologists should be familiar with scientific facts, evidence-based practices and the professional position on sexuality and gender-identity issues. The continuous education of professionals should be ensured so as to provide adequate professional help when clients contact them with issues relating to sexual and/or gender identity (Žegura & Vrbat, 2016). Issues related to sexual orientation and gender diversity still represent a great source of polemics among professionals, although this should not be the case (APA, 2002, 2011, 2012; British Psychological Society-BPS, 2012a, 2012b, 2017; EFPA, 2013, 2015, 2016).

Based on research conducted on a sample of Croatian psychologists, 20.5% said that they did not receive enough knowledge and skills in the area of human rights and their protection during the undergraduate study; 24.5% said the same for the postgraduate study; 19.1% reported that psychotherapy education has not equipped them with necessary knowledge and skills in the field of human rights; and 33.5% declared that they rarely actively participate in the promotion and protection of human rights through their professional work (Žegura & Vrbat, 2017). The lack of education leaves room for unethical actions based on personal beliefs and opens up a possibility for violation of the client's human rights. The awareness of interrelatedness of human rights and psychology in Croatia is only starting to develop. The founding of the Section for Psychology of Human Rights and Social Justice by the Croatian Psychological Association in 2017 made a milestone in present practices.

Mental Health and Human Rights of Sexual Minorities Through the Croatian Cultural Prism

The past 50 years has brought some drastic changes in society regarding de-pathologization, inclusion, visibility and acceptance of LGBTIQ+ people; though significantly different societal conditions exist for LGBTIQ+ people (Beetham, 2014; Bigner & Wetchler, 2012; Dobrović, 2007; Dota, 2017), LGBTIQ+ affirmative societal setting is not yet universal principle. In cultures in which rigid traditionalism and religious fundamentalism are shaping mainstream worldviews (Kashubeck-West & Whitley, 2017; Tremble et al., 2008), as is the case in Croatia, appreciation of human rights of SGM is not a guiding principle (Novosel et al., 2018; Štulhofer & Rimac, 2009; Žegura & Vrbat, 2017). Research with Croatian university students showed that slightly positive attitudes toward LGBTIQ+ people were stable and remained unchanged from 2005 till 2013 (Mušica et al., 2013). Specific attitudes toward human rights of lesbians and gays range from moderately negative to moderately positive (Huić et al., 2015).

Lack of comprehensive sex education denies young persons the right to become a responsible human being in a such a way that they lack knowledge and skills about sex and sexuality they need for their well-being, to accept themselves for who they are and to have good sexuality across the lifespan (Bieschke et al., 2007; Goldfarb & Lieberman, 2020). Sex education provides competencies of how to form healthy relationships, how to make informed decisions about sex and how to prevent sexually transmitted infections and unintended pregnancies. When youth are provided sex education, they can have better critical reflections about the world around them. It helps them to be good allies for minority populations. According to the Goldfarb and Lieberman (2020) the benefits of culturally responsive sex education can be seen in young people capacities for social and emotional skills they need to become responsible and empathic adults. If there is age-appropriate sex education from the early ages, young people appreciate more sexual and gender diversities, they are aware of how to prevent dating and intimate partner violence, they develop healthy relationships, improve social and emotional learning and have increased media literacy, and it also prevents child sexual abuse (Goldfarb & Lieberman, 2020). This is why the lack of sexual education is particularly harmful for LGBTIQ+ youth

(Žegura, 2014). Among heterosexual and cisgender individuals who adopted prejudicial beliefs toward SGM, high rates of heterosexism, homophobia and transphobia can be found (Žegura, 2013, 2014). This leads to different forms of aggressive behavior against LGBTIQ+ people (Bigner & Wetchler, 2012; Herek, 1991; Ritter & Terndrup, 2002). Being an LGBTIQ+ citizen in such societies is hard. In extreme cases, homophobia, transphobia and heterosexism may lead to emotional, physical, sexual and economic (when an LGBTIQ+ person is underage and still financially dependent on a parent or caregiver) violence against LGBTIQ+ people. The prevalence of these forms of violence in Croatia is high. In one of the first studies on this topic, 51.3% of LGB participants reported some kind of violent behavior against them because they were perceived as sexual minority members; 41.7% had experienced psychological violence; 29.9% had experienced sexual violence, 18.1% were exposed to economic violence; and 14.4% were exposed to physical violence (Pikić & Jugović, 2006). In a follow-up study (Bosnić et al., 2013), the results were even more disturbing: 58.3% of LGB participants had experienced some form of violence in their life because of their sexual orientation. Psychological violence was the most frequent. Lesbian and bisexual women had experienced significantly more general violence, economic violence and sexual violence; while gay men and lesbian women did not differ in the frequency of experienced physical and psychological violence (Bosnić et al., 2013). Research has shown that LGBTIQ+ persons who have adequate support from their families, friends and the wider society have far less symptoms of depression and anxiety and report higher levels of life quality (Bieschke et al., 2007; Žegura et al., 2012). The most recent study dealing with problems and challenges of SGM in Croatia showed that stress resilience, social support and inclusion in the LGB society are key determinants of different indicators of mental health in this population (Kamenov et al., 2016). The contemporary research task is to examine the impact of the COVID-19 pandemic on SGM in Croatia, though there are some data based on the cross-sectional online survey in 63 upper-middle-income and high-income countries including Croatian sample (Koehler et al., 2021).

Human Rights in the Context of Health Care of Transgender and Gender-Nonconforming (TGNC) People in Croatia

There are a number of scientific papers about medical care of transexual and transgender persons in the clinical medical centers in Slovenia, Croatia and Serbia that date back in the time of former Republic of Yugoslavia (Buzov, 2016). The first gender-affirming surgery (GAS) in the former Republic of Yugoslavia was done in Belgrade by the Serbian surgeon V. Božinović in 1937 (Marković Žigić et al., 2015). Despite the lack of exact information, the person undergoing the operation most probably had the intersex condition. Within the health care system in Croatia, there is no specific gender clinic for TGNC clients. Hormonal treatment is partially covered by health care insurance, but GAS costs are not covered at all (Novosel et al., 2018; Žegura et al., 2016).

Currently, there is a national team for transgender health care, consisting of educated specialists who are working in different clinical hospitals, mostly in Zagreb, and others in the private sector. The national team that mainly form clinical psychologists, psychiatrists, endocrinologists, one surgeon for top surgery only and one gynecologist is trying to broaden the team by including specialists (e.g., gynecologists, urologists, surgeons, speech therapists, social workers, and nurses) who are all mentioned to be a part of the interdisciplinary teams in trans health care by the World Professional Association for Transgender Health (WPATH). The existing national team of specialists in the field of transgender health care works according to the Standards of Care for the Health of Transgender and Gender Diverse People (Coleman et al., 2022;

WPATH, 2012) in order to provide high quality professional health and mental health care for children, adolescents and adults with gender dysphoria and their families (Žegura & Arbanas, 2016).

Professional societies and chambers should include in their existing professional guidelines and ethical codes, specific paragraphs about comprehensive care of TGNC people based on the Standards of care (Coleman et al., 2022) and human rights principles. The paragraphs should consist of ethical and professional recommendations based on up-to-date scientific knowledge and best practice recommendations, and avoid inclusion of or work to eliminate culturally or religiously colored prejudicial belief systems.

In 2008, Croatian Ministry of Health adopted "The bylaw about appropriate collection of medical documentation, determination of conditions and presumptions for sex change" (2008) that allowed only fully transitioned transsexual people (complete SRS done) the change of gender designation in personal documents (Žegura et al., 2016). Due to the efforts of professionals and LGBTIQ+/TGNC nongovernmental organizations, the Croatian Parliament adopted in 2013 on the behalf of Ministry of Public Administration "The law of national registers" (2013), which defines the process for the change of personal name and surname and change of gender designation in personal documents (Žegura, 2015). On March 27, 2014, the Croatian Ministry of Health adopted the "The bylaw about appropriate collection of medical documentation, determination of conditions and presumptions for sex change and/or life in other gender identity" (2014). For the first time, no surgical intervention in gender-transitioning individuals was needed as a condition for the change of gender mark on personal documents. On April 23, 2014, following a four-year court process, the first transgender F2M adolescent, living completely as a man with fully developed masculine gender identity (he underwent a mastectomy in 2012, but without the bottom surgery), changed the gender designation on his birth certificate and personal documents from woman to man (Žegura, 2015). This was possible due to the verdict of The Constitutional Court in Croatia, which allowed for the change of the gender designation in his personal documents. This has made the 19-year-old young man the first transgender person whose human rights were acknowledged in Croatia, offering him the prospect of better life quality, and freedom from being stigmatized in daily situations such as verification of personal documents.

In the field of medical and mental health care, there are some insurmountable problems related to uncovered costs of the gender transition process, lack of educated professionals and sensibility by the legal system to ensure each transgender client the time-appropriate treatment and legal protection. Although 64.4% of transgender participants are highly informed about the new law, only 24.5% are very satisfied with it (Žegura et al., 2015). The majority of SGM participants from two studies (80% of M2F and F2M participants in Žegura et al., 2015, and 64% of female and 80% of male LGBTIQ+ participants in Bosnić et al., 2013) prefer clinical psychologists to other mental health and medical professionals involved in gender transition process based on their competences. A study by Žegura et al. (2015) revealed that trans-women, in comparison to trans-men, have significantly lower levels of quality of life and experience significantly higher levels of sexual violence victimization.

The clinical psychologist should take into account that there is gender difference in prevalence of psychopathology and that personality traits and personality disorders might be expressed differently in men and women. Because different assessment inventories access a variety of psychological processes, it is necessary to approach the psychological diagnostic procedures using multiple methods. Understanding the sex and gender differences in assessment of personality requires clinicians and researchers to transcend epidemiology and focus on the underlying psychological processes (Mihura & Brabender, 2016). This process differs with respect to sex and gender. Minority stress and trauma in clinical presentation should be differentiated from symptoms of gender dysphoria.

Recent proposals among professionals working with TGNC people aim toward removing the category of gender dysphoria from DSM-5 and ICD-11 as a form of de-pathologization of gender identity (Cabral et al., 2016; Winter et al., 2016a, 2016b) similar to the de-pathologization of sexual identity and sexual orientation (APA, 1973, 1998). Scientifically and ethically based arguments given against the diagnosis are understandable as a way of removing stigmatization of TGNC persons. However, the challenge is to find a balance between concerns related to the stigmatization of mental disorders and the need for diagnostic categories that facilitate access to health care in countries and cultures that do not have high levels of affirmative approach toward supporting TGNC persons. The lack of specific diagnostic categories could lead to a limited provision of health care (Jokić-Begić et al., 2016).

Psychotherapy and Human Rights of LGBTIQ+ People in Croatian Socio-Political Context

Psychotherapists of any specialization and modality have to understand the specific cultural and socio-political history of the region as well as the family dynamics (Waterston, 2009) of their LGBTIQ+ clients, as there is a very strong influence of nationalism and ethnic history on ego identifications and personality development with implications for identity expressions and sexuality. The westernized therapist, with a background of post-industrial, democratic, capitalistic culture, driven toward an individualistic orientation, has to understand the position of clients whose core formative experience is centered on a more collectivistic orientation. After the Croatian Homeland war, the political repression authority of impersonal nationalism, which punishes those who dare to express individuality and different identities, was replaced with strict traditional values based on right-wing politics and religion. Social theory (Elliot, 1992; Totton, 2009) combined with intersectionality (Meyer, 1995; Moradi, 2017; Padilla et al., 2007) and a level of cultural competence of psychologists working with LGBTIQ+ clients (Boroughs, Bedoya et al., 2015) can in detail depict the processes by which the system of power impacts on identity formation (Waterston, 2017), coming out process or fragmentation of self, shame and the mental health of SGM. Intersectionality is a framework for conceptualizing a person, group of people, or social problem either as having privileged position or affected by a number of discriminations and disadvantages (Cameron, 2020; Carastathis, 2016). Intersectionality takes into account people's overlapping identities and experiences in order to understand the complexity of prejudices they face (Brown, 2019; Turner, 2021).

LGBTIQ+ people can be divided into those who are hiding their identity, "live in the shadow" or are "closeted", and those who have self-disclosed, are "out" and open about their minority status concerning sexualities and gender identity (Kort, 2018; Žegura, 2014). The process of coming out includes self-awareness and acceptance of one's sexual orientation and gender identity (Žegura, 2006). Social acceptance or social ostracism influences self-perception, self-confidence and self-esteem (Kort, 2018). The contemporary movement for LGBTIQ+ human rights ("gay is OK") and affirmative psychotherapists provide a healing ground in which GSM find an affirming community instead of a shaming one, which marginalized and oppressed their experience (Singer, 2008). When therapists invite clients to pay attention to their own negative self-evaluation and shame and to consider when and where they introjected those beliefs, they make it possible for clients to differentiate between their own experience and the cultural values. At the same time, they signal their own empathic acceptance of the client's experience, and give support for a new integration of self-experience. This allows promotion of deconstruction and reconstruction of values and beliefs (Huckaby, 2008; Nichols & Shernoff, 2007). Therapists should be careful about implicit shaming of the client for holding negative homophobic and transphobic self-beliefs, which is especially likely to happen in authoritarian cultures such as Croatia.

Here lies the danger of conversion or reparative therapy that refers to sexual orientation and gender-identity change interventions, which include different treatment techniques that are in most cases quasi-scientific (Bieschke et al., 2007). Many mental health professional organizations, including APA (Glassgold et al., 2009), European Association for Psychotherapy (2017) and the British Psychological Society (2012a, 2012b, 2019), have clearly highlighted the official position of the profession on the negative consequences of practicing conversion therapy. In the absence of national professional guidelines, as is the case in Croatia, psychologists should be aware of their personal belief systems and biases toward LGBTIQ+ people (Žegura, 2017b). They can rely on the Ethical Code developed within their professional association if it contains special comments on sexual orientation and gender identity, or they can follow the international guidelines and/or Ethical Codes such as the Meta-Code of Ethics (EFPA, 2013).

In a recent study of 215 Croatian psychologists (91% females, 8% males, 1% gender non-conforming), 91% said that there should be special professional guidelines developed within the Croatian Psychological Association (CPA) for psychologists working with vulnerable and marginalized groups, and 87% thought that these professional guidelines should be developed by the (CPC) (Žegura & Vrbat, 2017).

Conclusion

Significant political and social change for SGM people in Croatia in the last several years has contributed to greater public visibility. Exposure of transgender issues together with those of sexual minorities in public media enabled a greater societal sensitivity for SGM. Those changes happen with cooperation of activist collective identity movements and through great struggle, supported by the interdisciplinary scientific findings and evidence of best practices.

As allies of LGBTIQ+ people, psychologists have the leading role in ensuring that the results of their scientific findings and professional corpus of knowledge have an ethical and practical implementation in society. This begins with anti-oppressive and LGBTIQ+ affirmative practices in order to create safe environments for LGBTIQ+ people and their relationships, securing parenting and adoption rights, educational institutions and curriculum free from heterosexism, genderism, homophobia and transphobia, and a violence-free atmosphere. Equally important are other life span issues with respect to intersectionality: LGBTIQ+ inclusive work politics and job security; services for LGBTIQ+ elderly people; social space for LGBTIQ+ individuals with disabilities, and racial and ethnical minority groups; and informed professional mental health and medical interdisciplinary teams. Lastly, affirmative practices and intersectional issues should be included in academic education for university students and colleagues enrolled in postgraduate programs and training to become counselors and psychotherapists (Dickey et al., 2017).

Psychologists as mental health professionals should recognize that positive cultural changes and development of state and professional legislative for SGM are perceived as much-needed progress. Psychologists should address this process and help overcome negative counter-reactions from those who oppress SGM and deny their human rights (Žegura, 2017b). Another task for psychologists is to be aware of how their own membership in the privileged majority of educated citizens and specific professional groups may shape their contact with LGBTIQ+ people. As practitioners and researchers, psychologists should be mindful of their personal identity struggles and biases, no matter if they belong to SGM or the majority group. Professionals can ethically address the anti-oppressive principles of social justice and human rights in their practice and personal life, only when they are aware of the privileges they enjoy. The very awareness of intersectionality should help end the marginalization of multiple stigmatized identities and their invisibility. All clients will benefit from an increased self-awareness of psychologists and other caregivers.

Healthy development of sexual orientation and gender identity and their integration is one ostensible prerequisite for healthy psychosexual and integrative psychological development of human beings (Coleman & Reece, 1988). The heterosexual and cisgender majority may take their privilege as majority for granted in both professional spheres and wider society. However, the task of developing an integrated and positive sexual orientation and gender identity is a challenging one for many LGBTIQ+ people given the present oppressive social and cultural climate. Affirmation of sexual orientation and gender as a personal construct of each client can lead to better understanding and support of different identities. This can be achieved by (a) systematic and continuous education in the field of sexual health specifically on LGBTIQ+ issues for all health and mental health professionals who provide care of SGM; (b) strengthening communication between LGBTIQ+ affirmative and informed professionals, researchers, policymakers and LGBTIQ+ community; (c) adapting anti-oppressive and affirmative practices with the awareness of intersectionality; (d) initiation of guidelines for psychologists (transparent resume of scientifically based psychological knowledge about sexuality, sexual orientation and gender); and (e) education of general public to stress the issues created by prejudices, homophobia and transphobia (Žegura, 2017a, 2017b; Žegura & Vrbat, 2017).

References

All the Pride Parades in Croatia. (n.d.). *Expat in Croatia: All you need to live and travel like a local in Croatia.* Retrieved February 1, 2020, from www.expatincroatia.com/pride-parade-croatia/

American Psychiatric Association. (1973). Position statement on homosexuality and civil Rights. *American Journal of Psychiatry, 131*(4), 497.

American Psychiatric Association. (1998). Position statement on psychiatric treatment and sexual orientation. *American Journal of Psychiatry, 156,* 1131.

American Psychological Association. (2002). Ethical principles of psychologists and code of conduct. *American Psychologist, 57,* 1060–1073.

American Psychological Association. (2005). *Lesbian and gay parenting.* www.apa.org/pi/lgbt/resources/parenting-full.pdf

American Psychological Association-APA. (2009). *American association strategic plan.* APA. www.apa.org/about/apa/strategic-plan/default.aspx

American Psychological Association-APA. (2011). *Policy statements and resolutions.* The Committee on Lesbian, Gay, Bisexual, and Transgender Concerns; and the Lesbian, Gay, Bisexual, and Transgender Concerns Office, Author. http://www.apa.org/about/policy/booklet.pdf

American Psychological Association-APA: Division 44/Committee on Lesbian, Gay, and Bisexual Concerns Joint Task Force on Guidelines for Psychotherapy with Lesbian, Gay, and Bisexual Clients. (2012). Guidelines for psychological practice with lesbian, gay, and bisexual clients. *American Psychologist, 67*(1), 10–42.

American Sociological Association. (2015). *Brief of Amicus Curiae American sociological association in support of petitioners.* www.asanet.org/sites/default/files/savvy/documents/ASA/pdfs/ASA_March_2015_Supreme_Court_Marriage_Equality_Amicus_Brief.pdf

Beetham, G. (2014). The human rights of gays, lesbians, bisexual and transgender people. In A. Mihir & M. Gibney (Eds.), *The Sage handbook of human rights* (Vol. 1, pp. 284–304). SAGE.

Bieschke, K. J., Perez, R. M., & DeBord, K. A. (Eds.). (2007). *Handbook of counseling and psychotherapy with lesbian, gay, bisexual, and transgender clients* (2nd ed.). American Psychological Association.

Bigner, J. J., & Wetchler, J. L. (Eds.). (2012). *Handbook of LGBT- affirmative couple and family therapy.* Routledge.

Bilić, B., & Kajinić, S. (Eds.). (2016). *Intersectionality and LGBT activist politics: Multiple others in Croatia and Serbia*. Palgrave Macmillan.

Bilić, B., & Radoman, M. (Eds.). (2019). *Lesbian activism in the (post-) Yugoslav space: Sisterhood and unity*. Palgrave Macmillan.

Boroughs, M. S., Bedoya, C. A., O'Cleirigh, C., & Safren, S. (2015). Toward defining, measuring, and evaluating LGBT cultural competence for psychologists. *Clinical Psychologist, 22*(2), 151–171.

Bosnić, L., Žegura, I., & Jelić, M. (2013, March). *Outness about sexual orientation, experienced level of violence and quality of life of LGBT persons*. Oral presentation presented on 21st "Ramiro and Zoran Bujas' Days"—International Biennial Psychological Conference at Faculty of Humanities and Social Sciences, Department of Psychology, University of Zagreb, Zagreb.

British Psychological Society—BPS. (2012a). *Guidelines and literature review for psychologists working therapeutically with sexual and gender minority clients*. www.bps.org.uk/content/ guidelines-and-literature-reviewpsychologists-working-therapeutically-sexual-and-gender-min

British Psychological Society—BPS. (2012b). *Position statement: Therapies attempting to change sexual orientation*. www.bps.org.uk/system/files/images/therapies_attempting_to_change_sexual_orienta tion.pdf

British Psychological Society—BPS. (2017). *Practice guidelines* (3rd ed.). https://rec.chass.ncku.edu.tw/ sites/default/files/page-file/BPS%20Practice%20Guidelines%20%28Third%20Edition%29.pdf

British Psychological Society—BPS. (2019). *Guidelines for psychologists working with gender, sexuality and relationship diversity. For adults and young people (aged 18 and over)*. https://explore.bps. org.uk/binary/bpsworks/986e577a2e5c686b/dd77909e434237fe7bd656c718998a266faa1f-304fa51648cfd96ff20db3cc0d/rep129_2019.pdf

Brown, J. D. (2019). *Reflective practice of counseling and psychotherapy in a diverse society*. Palgrave Macmillan.

Buzov, I. (2016). *Transseksualizam* [Transsexuality]. Medicinska naklada.

Cabral, M., Suess, A., Ehrt, J., Seehole, T. J., & Wong, J. (2016). Removal of gender incongruence of childhood diagnostic category: A human rights perspective. *Lancet Psychiatry, 3*, 405–406.

Cameron, R. (2020). *Working with difference & diversity in counselling & psychotherapy*. SAGE.

Carastathis, A. (2016). *Intersectionality: Origins, contestations, horizons*. University of Nebraska Press.

Čaušević, J., Gavrić, S., Aganović, A., Bavčić, E., Bošnjak, E., Ćuzulan, J., Čaušević, J., Čaušević, J., Dekić, S. B., Dračo, I., Durkalić, M., Đikić, N., Đokanović, B., Gavrić, S., Huremović, L., Jugo, A., Krivokapić, B., Midžić, A., Spahić, A., . . . Ždralović, A. (2012). *Pojmovnik LGBT culture* [Glossary of LGBT culture]. Sarajevski otvoreni centar/Fondacija Heinrich Böll. https://ba.boell.org/sites/ default/files/pojmovnik_lgbt_kulture.pdf

Čemažar, S. A., & Mikulin, T. (2017). Europeizacija kao (ne)prijateljica: Razvoj LGBT pokreta u Hrvatskoj [Europeisation as friend (enemy): Development of LGBT movement in Croatia]. *Mali Levijatan, 4*(1), 29–58.

Coleman, E., Radix, A. E., Bouman, W. P., Brown, G. R., de Vries, A. L. C., Deutsch, M. B., Ettner, R., Fraser, L., Goodman, M., Green, J., Hancock, A. B., Johnson, T. W., Karasic, D. H., Knudson, G. A., Leibowitz, S. F., Meyer-Bahlburg, H. F. L., Monstrey, S. J., Motmans, J., Nahata, L., . . . Arcelus, J. (2022). Standards of care for the health of transgender and gender diverse people, version 8. *International Journal of Transgender Health, 23*(S1), S1–S258. https://doi.org/10.1080/26895269.2022.2100644

Coleman, E., & Reece, R. (1988). Treating low sexual desire among gay men. In S. R. Leiblum & R. C. Rosen (Eds.), *Sexual desire disorders*. The Guilford Press.

Croatian Bureau of Statistics. (2021). *Population estimates of Republic of Croatia, 2020. First release 7.1.3*. https://podaci.dzs.hr/media/pchp4exb/7-1-3_procjena-stanovnistva-rh-u-2020.pdf

Dickey, L. M., Singh, A. A., Chang, S. C., & Rehrig, M. (2017). Advocacy and social justice: The next generation of counseling and psychological practice with transgender and gender nonconforming clients. In A. A. Singh & L. L. Dickey (Eds.), *Affirmative counseling and psychological practice with transgender and gender nonconforming clients* (pp. 247–262). American Psychological Association.

Dobrović, Z. (2007). *Usmena povijest homoseksualnosti u Hrvatskoj: dokumentiranje svjedočanstva o privatnom i javnom djelovanju seksualnih i rodnih manjina- preteča LGBT pokreta u Hrvatskoj* [Oral history of homosexuality in Croatia: Documented witnessing about private and public work of sexual and gender minorities- ancestors of LGBT movement in Croatia]. Domino.

Dota, F. (2017). *Javna i politička povijest muške homoseksualnosti u socijalističkoj Hrvatskoj (1945–1989): doktorski rad* [Public and political history of male homosexuality in socialist Croatia (1945–1989): Doctoral dissertation (Doktorska disertacija), Sveučilište u Zagrebu: Filozofski fakultet].

Elliot, A. (1992). *Social theory and psychoanalysis in transition*. Blackwell.

European Association for Psychotherapy. (2017). *EAP statement on conversion therapy*. www.europsyche.org/quality-standards/eap-guidelines/eap-statement-on-conversion-therapy/

European Federation of Psychological Associations-EFPA. (2013). *Metacode of ethics*. EFPA. http://ethics.efpa.eu/meta-code

European Federation of Psychological Associations-EFPA. (2015). *Psychology matters in human rights – human rights matter in psychology EFPA policy and action in the area of human rights and psychology. Doc 14.3.13 annexe to TF human rights_psychology matters in human rights GA 2015*. file:///C:/Users/iva/Desktop/Annexe%20to%20TF%20Human%20Rights_Psychology%20matters%20in%20Human%20rights%20GA%202015.pdf

European Federation of Psychological Associations-EFPA. (2016). *December 10: International human rights day – psychologists play important role. EFPA statement December 10 2016*. www.bfp-fbp.be/sites/default/files/pdfs/international_human_rights_day_dec_10_2016_efpa_statement_0.pdf

First Transgender March Held in Croatian Capital of Zagreb. (2019, March 31). *Total Croatian News*. www.total-croatia-news.com/lifestyle/35014-zagreb

Glassgold, J. M., Beckstead, L., Drescher, J., Beverly, G., Miller, R. L., Worthington, R. L., & Anderson, C. W. (2009). *Report of the American psychological association task force on appropriate therapeutic responses to sexual orientation*. Lesbian, Gay, Bisexual, and Transgender Concerns Office Public Interest Directorate American Psychological Association. www.apa.org/pi/lgbt/resources/therapeutic-response.pdf

Goldfarb, E. S., & Lieberman, L. D. (2020). Three decades of research: The case for comprehensive sex education. *Journal of Adolescent Health*, *68*(1), 13–27. https://doi.org/10.1016/j.jadohealth.2020.07.036

Goldstein, I. (2013). *Hrvatska povijest* [History of Croatia]. Novi Liber.

Hagenaars, P., Plavšić, M., Sveaass, N., Wagner, U., & Wainwright, T. (Eds.). (2020). *Human rights education for psychologists*. Routledge.

Herceg Kolman, N. (2020). *How Europe works for LGBT* rights: The Croatian story*. Friedrich Naumann Foundation for Freedom.

Herek, G. M. (1991). Stigma, prejudice, and violence against lesbians and gay men. In J. C. Gonsiorek & J. D. Weinrich (Eds.), *Homosexuality: Research implications for public policy* (pp. 60–80). SAGE.

Hrvatska psihološka komora [Croatian Psychological Chamber-CPC]. (2004). *Kodeks etike psihološke djelatnosti* [Ethical code of psychological profession]. Hrvatska psihološka komora.

Huckaby, M. A. (2008). Lesbian identity and the context of shame. In R. G. Lee & G. Wheeler (Eds.), *The voice of shame: Silence and connection in psychotherapy* (pp. 117–201). GestaltPress.

Huić, A., Jugović, I., & Kamenov, Ž. (2015). Stavovi studenata o pravima osoba homoseksualne orijentacije. *Revija za socijalnu politiku*, *22*(2), 219–244.

Jokić-Begić, N., Altabas, V., Antičević, V., Arbanas, G., Begić, D., Budi, S., Dumić, M., Grubić, M., Grujić, J., Jakušić, N., Stipančić, G., & Žegura, I. (2016). Croatia needs a gender incongruence diagnosis for prepubertal children. *Archives of Sexual Behavior*, *45*(8), 1877–1878.

Kamenov, Ž., Jelić, M., & Huić, A. (Eds.). (2016). *Problemi i izazovi seksualnih manjina u Hrvatskoj* [Problems and challenges of sexual minorities in Croatia]. FF Press.

Kashubeck-West, S., & Whitley, A. M. (2017). Conflicting identities: Sexual minority, transgender, and gender nonconforming individuals navigating between religion and gender-sexual orientation identity. In K. A. DeBord, A. R. Fisher, K. J. Bieschke, & R. M. Perez (Eds.), *Handbook of sexual orientation and gender diversity in counseling and psychotherapy* (pp. 213–238). American Psychological Association.

Kazneni zakon [The Criminal Law] (1997). *Narodne novine, 110/97–57/11*. https://narodne-novine.nn.hr/clanci/sluzbeni/1997_10_110_1668.html

Koehler, A., Motmans, J., Mulió Alvarez, L., Azul, D., Badalyan, K., Basar, K., Dhejne, C., Duišin, D., Grabski, B., Dufrasne, A., Jokic-Begic., N., Prunas, A., Richards, C., Sabir, K., Veale, J., & Nieder, T. O. (2021). How the COVID-19 pandemic affects transgender health care – a cross-sectional online survey in 63 upper-middle-income and high-income countries. *International Journal of Transgender Health, AHEAD-OF-PRINT*, 1–14. https://doi.org/10.1080/26895269.2021.1986191

Kort, J. (2018). *LGBTQ clients in therapy: Clinical issues and treatment strategies*. W.W. Norton & Company.

Košiček, M. (1986). *U okviru vlastitog spola* [In the context of same sex]. Mladost.

Lassen, E. M. (2014). Universalism and relativism. In A. Mihir & M. Gibney (Eds.), *The Sage handbook of human rights* (Vol. 1, pp. 39–55). SAGE.

Marković Žigić, D., Zulević, J., & Maksimović, K. (2015). Rad sa transseksualnim klijentima- specifičnosti tranzicije i izazovi nakon nje [Work with transsexual clients- specificities of transition and challenges after the process of transition]. In V. Miletić & A. Milenković (Eds.), *Priručnik za LGBT psihoterapiju* [Handbook for LGBT psychotherapy]. Udruženje za unapređenje mentalnog zdravlja.

Meyer, I. H. (1995). Minority stress and mental health in gay men. *Journal of Health and Social Behavior, 36*(1), 38–56.

Mihura, J. L., & Brabender, V. M. (2016). Sex, gender, and sexuality in psychological assessment: Where do we go from here? In V. M. Brabender & J. L. Mihura (Eds.), *Handbook of gender and sexuality in psychological assessment* (pp. 655–678). Routledge.

Moradi, B. (2017). (Re)focusing intersectionality: From social identities back to systems of oppression and privilege. In K. A. DeBord, A. R. Fisher, K. J. Bieschke, & R. M. Perez (Eds.), *Handbook of sexual orientation and gender diversity in counseling and psychotherapy* (pp. 105–127). American Psychological Association.

Mušica, T., Dumančić, M., Radoš, L., Davidović, N., Parmač Kovačić, M., & Kamenov, Ž. (2013, April). *Jesu li se u posljednjih 10 godina promijenili stavovi hrvatskih studenata o osobama homoseksualne orijentacije?* [Did shift in attitudes of Croatian students take place within last 10 years about people with homosexual orientation?]. Izlaganje održano na 21. Danima Ramira i Zorana Bujasa, Odsjek za psihologiju Filozofskog fakulteta Sveučilišta u Zagrebu.

Nichols, M., & Shernoff, M. (2007). Therapy with sexual minorities: Queering practice. In S. Leiblum (Ed.), *Principles and practice of sex therapy* (4th ed., pp. 379–415). Guilford.

Novosel, I., Sharifi, S., & Vejić, I. (Eds.). (2018). *Ljudska prava u Hrvatskoj: pregled stanja u 2017. godini* [Human rights in Croatia: Review of situation in the year 2017]. Kuća ljudskih prava Zagreb.

Padilla, M. B., del Aguila, E. V., & Parker, R. G. (2007). Globalization, structural violence and LGBT health: A cross-cultural perspective. In I. H. Meyer & M. E. Northridge (Eds.), *The health of sexual minorities: Public health perspectives on lesbian, gay, bisexual and transgender populations* (pp. 209–241). Springer.

Pikić, A., & Jugović, I. (2006). *Nasilje nad lezbijkama, gejevima i biseksualnim osobama u Hrvatskoj: Izvještaj istraživanja* [Violence against lesbians, gays and bisexual persons in Croatia: Research report]. Lezbijska grupa Kontra.

Pravilnik o načinu prikupljanja medicinske dokumentacije o promjeni spola [The Bylaw about Medical Documentation Collection and Sex Change Conditions]. (2008). *Natrona novine, 150/2008, rev. 71/2010, rev. 139/2010, rev. 22/2011 & rev. 84/2011.* https://narodne-novine.nn.hr/clanci/sluzbeni/2011_10_121_2418.html

Pravilnik o načinu prikupljanja medicinske dokumentacije te utvrđivanju uvjeta i pretpostavki za promjenu spola ili o životu u drugom rodnom identitetu [The Bylaw about Medical Documentation Collection and Determination of Conditions and Presumptions for Sex Change and Life in Other Gender Identity]. (2014). *Narodne novine, 123/2014.* https://narodne-novine.nn.hr/clanci/sluzbeni/2014_11_132_2487.html

Pride. (n.d.). *Pride Parade.* Retrieved February 1, 2021, from https://povorka.zagreb-pride.net/

Regnerus, M. (2012). How different are the adult children of parents who have same-sex relationships? Findings from the new family structures study. *Social Science Research, 41*, 752–770. https://doi.org/10.1016/j.ssresearch.2012.03.009

Ritter, K. Y., & Terndrup, A. I. (2002). *Handbook of affirmative psychotherapy with lesbians and gay men.* The Guilford Press.

Singer, A. (2008). Homosexuality and shame: Clinical meditations on the cultural violation of self. In R. G. Lee & G. Wheeler (Eds.), *The voice of shame: Silence and connection in psychotherapy* (pp. 123–142). GestaltPress.

Štulhofer, A., & Rimac, I. (2009). Determinants of homonegativity in Europe. *Journal of Sex Research, 46*, 1–9.

Totton, N. (2009). Body psychotherapy and social theory. *Body, Movement and Dance in Psychotherapy: An International Journal for Theory, Research and Practice, 3*, 187–200. https://doi.org/10.1080/17432970802079018

Tremble, B., Schneider, M., & Appathurai, C. (2008). Growing up gay or lesbian in a multicultural context. *Journal of Homosexuality, 17*(3–4), 253–267.

Turner, D. (2021). *Intersections of privilege and otherness in counselling and psychotherapy.* Routledge.

United Nations (UN) General Assembly. (1948). *Universal declaration of human rights.* www.un.org/en/about-us/universal-declaration-of-human-rights

Waterston, J. (2009). Body psychotherapy, social theory, Marxism and civil war. In L. Hartley (Ed.), *Contemporary body psychotherapy: The Chiron approach* (pp. 228–242). Routledge.

Waterston, J. (2017). The great invention in the history of life. In J. E. Waterston (Ed.), *Someone's done something wrong: Revenge, hatred and humility* (pp. 60–76). CreateSpace Independent Publishing Platform. ISBN-13:978-1533361073

Winter, S., De Cuypere, G., Green, J., Kane, R., & Knudson, G. (2016a). The proposed ICD-11 gender incongruence of childhood diagnosis: A world professional association for transgender health membership survey. *Archives of Sexual Behavior, 45*, 1605–1614.

Winter, S., Ehrensaft, D., Pickstone-Taylor, S., De Cuypere, G., & Tando, D. (2016b). The psycho-medical case against a gender incongruence of childhood diagnosis. *Lancet Psychiatry, 3*, 404–405.

WPATH. (2012). *Standards of care (SOC) for the health of transsexual, transgender, and gender nonconforming people. Version 7.* www.wpath.org/publications/soc

Zakon o državnim maticama [The Law about State Registers]. (2013). *Narodne novine, 96/93, and rev. 76/13.* https://mpu.gov.hr/pristup-informacijama-6341/zakoni-i-ostali-propisi/zakoni-i-propisi-6354/drzavne-matice-24426/zakon-o-drzavnim-maticama/24429

Žegura, I. (2006). *Coming out: Razumjeti vs./feat. Prihvatiti* [Coming out: To understand vs./feat. To accept]. Naklada MD.

Žegura, I. (2013). Transrodnost kod djece i adolescenata. Psihološki aspekti rada s rodno disforičnim osobama. Samopoimanje i coming out vezan za rodnu disforiju/transseksualnost [Transgender children and adolescents. Psychological aspects of working with gender dysphoric persons. Self-concept and coming out concerning gender dysphoria/transsexuality]. In *Transrodnost, Transseksualnost, Rodna nenormativnost- Put u prosTRANStvo* [Transgenderism, transsexuality, gender dysphoria- the path to TRANS] (pp. 20–40). LORI.

Žegura, I. (2014). Drugačiji oblici partnerskih zajednica-psihološki aspekti LGBT partnerstva i roditeljstva. In A. Brajša-Žganec, J. Lopižić, & Z. Penezić (Eds.), *Psihološki aspekti suvremene obitelji, braka i partnerstva* [Psychological aspects of modern family, marriage and partnership] (pp. 297–239). Naklada Slap i Hrvatsko psihološko društvo.

Žegura, I. (2015, May). The greatest first step in acknowledging rights of transgender persons in Croatia-case report. Poster presentation at 17. Congress of the European society for sexual medicine. Copenhagen, Denmark (5–7 February, 2015). Book of abstracts; ESSM. The *Journal of Sexual Medicine Special Issue: Proceedings of the 17th Annual Congress of the European Society for Sexual Medicine, Copenhagen, Denmark, February 5–7, 12*(S3), 188–271. https://doi.org/10.1111/jsm.12872

Žegura, I. (2017a). Rodna disforija [Gender dysphoria]. In N. Mrduljaš-Đujić & I. Žegura (Eds.), *Osnove seksualne medicine* [The principles of sexual medicine] (pp. 41–56). Redak.

Žegura, I. (2017b). Enrolment of psychologists in the protection of human rights in Croatian society, based on examples of sexual and gender minorities. Invited oral presentation at symposium "human rights and applied psychology: Inclusion and development" of EFPA's board for psychology of human rights. In *15th European congress of psychology: "Psychology addressing society's greatest challenges": Book of abstracts* (p. 24). EFPA.

Žegura, I., & Arbanas, G. (2016). Mental health care of transsexual, transgender and gender nonconforming people in Croatian health system. ABSTRACTS. *Klinička psihologija, 9*(1), 23. https://doi.org/10.21465/2016-KP-OP-0012

Žegura, I., Arbanas, G., & Vrbat, I. (2015). Quality of life and other mental health variables of transgender patients from the perspective of the current level of available health and legal care of transgender patients in Croatia. In *Book of abstracts: 1st European biannual conference on transgender health. European professional association for transgender health* (p. 91). Center for Sexology and Gender, Ghent University Hospital.

Žegura, I., Arbanas, G., & Vrbat, I. (2016). Quality of health and mental health care of gender dysphoric persons in Croatia. In *Book of abstracts: 24th scientific symposium WPATH* (p. 53). WPATH.

Žegura, I., Jelić, M., & Bosnić, L. (2012, November). *Partnerski odnosi i kvaliteta života LGBT osoba u Hrvatskoj* [Partnership relations and life quality of LGBT persons in Croatia]. Usmeno izlaganje održano na 20. godišnjoj konferenciji hrvatskih psihologa-"Psihološki aspekti suvremen obitelji, braka i partnerstva". rvatsko psihološko društvo i Društvo psihologa Dubrovnika.

Žegura, I., & Vrbat, I. (2016). Afirmativni dijagnostički i tretmanski rad kliničkih psihologa i psihologinja s osobama različitih seksualnih orijentacija i rodnih identiteta kroz prizmu svjetskih standarda, smjernica i primjera iz prakse [Clinical psychologists affirmative assessment and psychotherapy of persons with different sexual orientations and gender identities through the prism of world standards, guidelines and examples of best practice]. In A. Pokrajac-Bulian, I. Miletić, J. Juretić, & J., Lopižić (Eds.), *Knjiga sažetaka 24. godišnje konferencije hrvatskih psihologa- Znanstveno stručni skup: Psihologija u prevenciji poremećaja i očuvanju zdravlja* [Book of abstracts form the 24th conference of Croatian psychologists-scientific expert meeting] (pp. 379–380). Hrvatsko psihološko društvo.

Žegura, I., & Vrbat, I. (2017, November). Prepoznavanje potrebe i uključenost psihologa u zaštitu ljudskih prava u Hrvatskoj [Identification of a necessity of enrolment of psychologists in the protection of human rights in Croatia]. Usmeno priopćenje na 25. In *Godišnjoj konferenciji hrvatskih psihologa "Psihologija u zaštiti i promociji ljuskih prava i društvene pravednosti"*. Odjel za psihologiju Filozofskog fakulteta Sveučilišta u Zadru & Hrvatsko psihološko društvo.

10

NOW YOU SEE IT, NOW YOU DON'T

Contesting the LGBTQ Politics of (In)Visibility in (Post)Socialist China

Liyun Wendy Choo

Introduction

On June 21, 2016, Wang Xiaoyu's lesbian girlfriend, Ouyang Jean, publicly proposed to her at her graduation ceremony "to express our feelings, and raise awareness of LGBT issues" (BBC News, 2020). Photographs of the marriage proposal went viral on Chinese social media platform, and in response to their visible act of resistance to the heteronormative order, the university threatened the lesbian couple with disciplinary action (BBC News, 2020; China Digital Times, 2016). The university attempted to contain the visibility of the issue. Deputy Secretary Du from the university's Communist Party Committee attempted to persuade the newly engaged woman, Wang Xiaoyu, to reject media interviews and stay quiet. She suggested to Wang Xiaoyu that the university was tolerant of LGBTQ people as long as they managed their sexual identity well, "keep it from impacting others", and "don't cause any harm to others" (China Digital Times, 2016, n.p.). Censors also deleted coverage of the public proposal by some LGBTQ and feminist advocacy groups, such as *Girlfriend* and *Women Awakening* (China Digital Times, 2016).

Same-sex marriage has never been legalized in China despite repeated proposals to the National People's Congress from sociologist Li Yinhe (Bao, 2017). Although her proposals were rejected, they have generated controversy in Chinese media and served to increase the visibility of LGBTQ issues. This chapter examines the LGBTQ politics of (in)visibility in (post) socialist China. In their anthology on queer politics in the post-socialist countries of Europe, Fejes and Balogh (2013) used the hyphenated term "post-socialist" to highlight the cultural legacies of the countries' socialist past on the public sphere. However, in this chapter, I follow Tian (2019) and use the bracketed (post)socialist to signal "not simply as 'beyond/after social- ism' but also as 'as the result of socialism'" (p. 58).

Visibility politics, which can involve collective coming-out in events such as Pride parades, is a crucial aspect of LGBTQ politics in White, Anglo-Saxon countries (Taylor, 1994). This chapter uses Anglo-Saxon countries to refer to the group of English-speaking countries that share common roots in British culture and history, such as the United Kingdom, the United States, Australia, New Zealand and Canada. I also use "Western" to refer to ideas and works that derive from these Anglo-Saxon countries. However, visibility is a double-edged sword

DOI: 10.4324/9781003128151-12

(Brighenti, 2010; Edenborg, 2020), as Wang Xiaoyu's experiences detail. While visibility may help marginalized groups achieve equality and inclusion by raising public awareness of their conditions and their right to be part of the political society, it can also trigger state surveillance and control and expose LGBTQ organizations and activists to state domination and danger (Brighenti, 2010; Edenborg, 2017; Foucault, 1995; Ho et al., 2018; Huang, 2016). Wang Xiaoyu's experiences illustrate the possible repercussion of visibility politics in China and why many Chinese LGBTQ subjects might have chosen to practice a more subtle and indirect reticent politics instead (Bie & Tang, 2016; Huang & Brouwer, 2018; Liu & Ding, 2005; Wang et al., 2009).

This chapter considers the social and cultural configurations of non-normative sexuality and gender in China to critically interrogate dominant, Western representations of LGBTQ politics (Bao, 2010). It argues that LGBTQ identities in contemporary China are as much Chinese as they are transnational (Bao, 2010; Wong, 2011.). Drawing on the range of in/visibility strategies that Chinese LGBTQ subjects deploy to navigate conservative cultural norms and the watchful eye of an authoritarian and repressive (post)socialist state, this chapter highlights the dynamic relationship between visibility and invisibility.

Why Look at LGBTQ Politics in China?

First, in China, Marxist traditions have been co-opted by an authoritarian, (post)socialist state and taught monolithically in school as the official ideology (Huang, 2017). This makes Marxist traditions unavailable for subversive activism, while rights-based LGBTQ politics that incite narratives of discrimination and rights abuse struggle to garner popular support (Huang, 2017). A look at visibility politics in China can provide much-needed insight into the socio-cultural specificity of transnational sexual subjectivities (Hu, 2019).

Additionally, visibility politics in China provides an interesting lens into how local LGBTQ communities in different geographical parts of the world exercise their subjective agency differently (Hu, 2019). In their anthology on LGBTQ politics in the post-socialist countries of Europe, Fejes and Balogh (2013) argue that while non-normative sexualities have grown in visibility in public spaces, LGBTQ people continue to face rampant discrimination and violence. This raises the question of what visibility politics has achieved for LGBTQ people in post-socialist states? Indeed, in (post)socialist China, while raising the visibility of sexual minorities is the goal of many university-based LGBTQ organizations, public advocacy brings higher risks for student activists. They might be outed to their parents by their university, forced to drop out of the university, or subjected to "counselling" by the student affairs administrator (*fudaoyuan*).

This chapter uses the hanyupinyin system of transliteration for Chinese words. It is probably not surprising that Peterson, Wahlstrom and Wennerhag's examination of Pride parades and LGBTQ movements in Europe only included "democratic countries and regions where Pride parades are generally permitted and typically not violently repressed by counter demonstrators" (2018, p. 1).

This is not to say that visibility politics should be categorically rejected as "Western"; rather, we need to explore how visibility politics may be expanded, supplemented and revised by different contexts, such as that of China, where LGBTQ subjects have to negotiate their same-sex orientation alongside familial expectations and a socialist state (Huang & Brouwer, 2018; Liu, 2010; Moreno-Tabarez et al., 2014). An examination of LGBTQ politics in China from the lens of visibility may provide a "productive theoretical tool around which a much-needed study of such contradictions of post-socialist sexual politics can be structured" (Fejes & Balogh, 2013, p. 3).

Although mainland China is the primary geographical location of discussion, I concur with Petrus Liu that the signifier of China can refer to relations other than the nation-state of the People's Republic of China:

> China can be a mode of consciousness and a sense of belonging. It is an institution of citizenship, a cultural identity, a territory, and an ethnic group. It is also a historical division of human birth- accidents and life opportunities along artificially created borders.
>
> *(Liu, 2010, p. 314)*

In using China as a case study, this chapter seeks to contribute to what Liu (2010) describes as the "productive tension between those who insist that sexuality is an acultural or universal phenomenon and those who argue that sexuality is linguistically distinct and nontranslatable" (p. 314). LGBTQ politics in Asian societies can be revealing of nuances in transnational subjectivity formation (Hu, 2019). As Goldberg (2016) rightly points out, East Asian sexuality studies is "not only an empirically rich field . . . but also a source of new theory and innovative approaches for the broader study of sexualities" (p. 349). Additionally, Asia as an analytic concept can challenge the centrality of Western approaches and paradigms in studies on gender and sexual diversities (Hu, 2019). Overall, this chapter contends that an examination of LGBTQ politics in China can exemplify how both Western and non-Western gender and sexual cultures are mutually transformed, as sexual knowledges from different cultures travel across national boundaries and come into encounters with each other (Hu, 2019).

Such critical attention paid to local knowledges and concerns may better support the liberation of LGBTQ subjects in other parts of the world, though there is a danger of reinforcing the historical tendency to regard Asian countries such as China as the paradigmatic "other" (Engebretsen et al., 2015; Huang, 2016; Kong, 2016; Liu, 2010). As Petrus Liu (2010) rightly cautioned, "the very language of difference may naturalize and justify the 'West' as an indispensable and normative point of comparison" (p. 314). Yet such tensions between the universal and the local can be very productive for LGBTQ theory and politics, with bearings on how each is enriched by the other (Bao, 2018; Engebretsen et al., 2015; Liu, 2010).

A Brief History of LGBTQ Sexuality Formation in China: From *Tongxinglian* to *Ku'er*

As Altman (1996) rightly points out, "almost all societies have indigenous ways of conceptualising sexuality and gender" (para. 9), and this is often reflected in the indigenous terms they use to describe, if not label, different homosexual identities. This section provides a brief historical overview of LGBTQ sexuality formation in mainland China, before introducing a non-exhaustive list of common social categories with which LGBTQ Chinese identify. It highlights the historical contingencies behind the different same-sex identities in China and sets the stage for understanding the kinds of politics Chinese LGBTQ subjects practice.

Homoerotic practices were common in pre-modern China, with many literary representations featuring same-sex intimacies among male elites. In that historical period, homoerotic practices were not bound up with a person's identity and existed alongside the gendered hierarchies of the Confucian family and marriage institutions (Bao, 2010; Kong, 2010; Vitiello, 2014). Most erotic fiction featured socially superior, bisexual adult men attracted to boys even as those men had several beautiful wives and concubines (Vitiello, 2014). They also highlighted male homoerotism in the imperial court and suggested that male bisexuality was the default (Vitiello, 2014). For example, *duanxiu* (i.e. cut sleeve) is a term used to refer to the passion that Emperor Ai of the Han dynasty had for a male favourite (Vitiello, 2014). As the story goes, the emperor was resting with the boy when he had to leave for official business. The sleeping boy's head was lying on the sleeve of the emperor's robe, so the loving ruler cut it off to avoid disturbing the boy when he got off from the bed. These erotic fiction and stories suggested that homoerotic practices, while not widely accepted, were tolerated as long as they did not transgress social hierarchies or affected a man's filial duties of getting married and carrying on the family lineage (Bao, 2010).

The republican era (1911–1949) saw the introduction of Western scientific sexology into the new republican state and the end of the pre-modern "cut sleeve" tradition (Vitiello, 2014; Kong, 2010). Western sexology diffused into China through translated works. Havelock Ellis' medical theory of homosexuality, which saw homosexuality as a form of psychological perversion, came to gain hegemonic status in China after the 1920s (Kong, 2010). Vitiello (2014) argues that Westernization and modernization changed Chinese attitudes towards homosexuality:

> The 1920s and 1930s represent indeed a watershed in terms of the understanding of sexuality in China . . . for the first time in Chinese history homoerotic relations are seen as the expression of an exclusive, inborn sexual orientation, and not simply as one option for a man to satisfy his desire; at the same time, female-female eroticism is yoked together with male-male eroticism under the new rubric of "homosexuality".
>
> *(p. 136)*

By the 1930s, a Chinese equivalent of homosexuality, *tongxingai* (i.e. literally same-sex love), came into being (Vitiello, 2014). Sexuality came under increasing regulation and sexual practices such as adultery, masturbation, prostitution and homosexuality were condemned as shameless and abnormal (Kong, 2010).

During the Maoist era (1949–1979), homosexuality was seen as feudal and disappeared from public discourse (Bao, 2010). In 1950, the Maoist state encoded monogamous, heterosexual marriage and outlawed polygamy and arranged marriages. The 1950 Marriage Law left little room for non-normative sexualities (Kong, 2016). Against this background, homosexuality became pathologized, silenced and criminalized. People who engaged in homoerotic practices could be charged for *jijian*[1] (i.e. sodomy) and *liumangzui* (i.e. hooliganism) (Bao, 2010; Kong, 2010).

The reform and opening era (1979 to present) marked the shift from revolutionary class struggle to an emphasis on market reforms, developmentalism, modernization and scientism (Bao, 2010; Kong, 2016). State-led market reforms in the 1970s and 1980s opened China to the global economy and tolerated, if not promoted, neoliberalism and economic individualism through consumption and entrepreneurship. However, other forms of individualism, such as homosexuality, continued to be repressed (Tian, 2019). The opening up of (post)socialist China saw a slight relaxation of state control over its citizens' private lives and the emergence of new social and sexual spaces (Kong, 2016). Although sexual culture in (post)socialist China generally remained conservative, the onset of the HIV/AIDS epidemic meant that gender, sexuality and homosexuality returned to public discourses in the 1980s (Bao, 2010; Kong, 2016). While the HIV/AIDS epidemic provided an avenue for LGBTQ activists to engage with the Chinese Government, homosexuality also came to be associated with promiscuity and AIDS, thus heavily stigmatized (Deklerck, 2017; Wang et al., 2009). Much of the literature in the

1980s focused on "treating" homosexuality, which was seen as a sexual disorder (Kong, 2016). However, by 2001, homosexuality was deleted from the third edition of Chinese Classification of Mental Disorder (CCMD-3). In 1997, *liumangzui* (i.e. hooliganism), which had previously been used to criminalize LGBTQ people, was deleted from China's criminal law. Most scholars saw these two acts as the decriminalization and depathologization of homosexuality[2] (e.g. Bao, 2010; Kong, 2016; Tian, 2019).

Although the growth of the HIV/AIDS epidemic accelerated the growth of international discourses around sexuality and contributed to political organizing in China to prevent AIDS/HIV transmission among gay men, the expansion of global capitalism and consumerism is probably the most significant factor behind the diffusion of homosexual identities (Altman, 1996, 2002). Ho et al. (2018) argue that the opening up of China and the accompanying freedoms contributed to the emergence of LGBTQ communities in major Chinese cities. In the 1990s and 2000s, various LGBTQ consumer markets and communities emerged in China. Many commercial businesses embraced the LGBTQ cause to tap into the lucrative "pink economy" (Deklerck, 2017). Bao (2018) noted how queer commercial venues grew rapidly in Chinese cities, such as Shanghai. Shopping centres, restaurants, cafes and bars became popular "gay spaces" in Shanghai because of their association with cosmopolitanism and a middle-class lifestyle. LGBTQ representations also became increasingly visible in the media and the internet, though these sexual spaces continue to be heavily monitored (Kong, 2016). With the emergence of a middle class, and the rise of youth and urban culture, the stage was set for the construction of contemporary LGBTQ identities in China (Bao, 2010).

In summary, homoerotism in pre-modern China is different from the homosexuality as an identity category as we know today (Ho et al., 2018). LGBTQ sexuality and politics in China are nurtured in the specific social and cultural context of post(socialist) China, and it is best revealed in the terminologies that Chinese LGBTQ people identify with (Kam, 2013; Bao, 2010; Kong, 2016). The later part of this section asks:

> What does it mean if a Chinese man calls himself *tongxinglian* or *tongxingai* ("same-sex love", or homosexual), gay (or *lala* for lesbian), or *tongzhi* (a synonym for lesbian, gay, bisexual, transgendered, or LGBT)?
>
> *(Kong, 2016, p. 496)*

One of the most common terms used to name an LGBTQ person in China is *tongxinglian* (i.e. same-sex love). Rooted in Western biological and psychiatric framework, the term *tongxinglian* (i.e. same-sex love) symbolizes a biological understanding of sexuality and developed into an identity in the late 1970s.

Chinese economic growth in the 1990s set the stage for intra-Asia exchanges of queer knowledge and sexual identities, which gave rise to different kinds of sexual subjects in China (Kong, 2016). In contrast to the pathological and deviant *tongxinglian*, Chinese same-sex subjects such as gay, *lala* and *tongzhi* represented cosmopolitanism, sophistication, modernity, liberty and individuality (Kong, 2016). In the 1990s, Hong Kong and Chinese gay activists appropriated *tongzhi* as a label of self-identification. *Tongzhi* is a term that was used by the Chinese Communist Party to refer to supporters of the revolutionary struggle up to the end of the Maoist era (Bao, 2010; Ho et al., 2018). The emergence of *tongzhi* marked a semantic shift towards a more politicized sexual identity for the Chinese LGBTQ community (Bao, 2010). Scholars such as Wong (2011) and Gao Yanning (2009) argue that *tongzhi*, rather than "gays and lesbians", are the most common same-sex subjects in China.

For some scholars, such as Chou Wah-Shan, the term *tongzhi* reflected a different sexual subject from that of the Western gay or lesbian. In Anglo-Saxon countries such as the United States, "individual frankness, the willingness to verbalize one's feelings, and the determination to defend one's right to speak up are treated as major salient features of the individual's life" (Chou, 2001, p. 33). The Western gay or lesbian is based on the notion of "an individual with unalienable rights" (Chou, 2001, p. 34). In contrast, Chinese *tongzhi* are "first and foremost members of the family and wider society" (Chou, 2001, p. 34). They are simultaneously constituted and oppressed by their familial and social relations, and *xiao* (i.e. filial piety) is central to their social contexts. However, other scholars contend that local and global influences on LGBTQ identities are more entangled and ambiguous than Chou Wah-san might have portrayed (e.g. see Wong, 2011). In her examination of the linguistic appropriation and creation of LGBTQ identity labels in Hong Kong and China, Wong (2011) found that while the label "gay" was transliterated into *gei* in Hong Kong and invested with derogatory meanings, Westernized identities associated with "gay" were readily adopted by young same-sex subjects in China for self-identification and retained its literal meaning of cheer and happiness. She concluded that the production of gay identities is never a straightforward process of replication nor indigenization. Therefore, "the longing for belonging in not only a family but also a gay globality will reconstitute Chinese culture and family as a complex and shifting terrain" (p. 165). Overall, it seems that LGBTQ identities in contemporary China are always shifting and as much Chinese as they are transnational (Wong, 2011; Bao, 2010).

Although *tongzhi* can also be used by lesbians directly or feminized as *nütongzhi* (i.e. female comrades), it is more common for Chinese lesbians to call themselves *lala*. As a new social category that emerged in the 1990s, *lala* is distinct from earlier forms of female same-sex bonds in its simultaneous demand for sex, emotions, exclusivity and long-term relationships (Huang, 2017). Based on the Taiwanese term "*lazi*", a transliteration of "les" from "lesbian", *lala* borrow heavily from Western language about sexual identity and is typically used in informal or lesbian-specific contexts to refer to collective identity for women with non-normative gender and sexual identifications (Huang, 2017; Kam, 2013). At more formal and political occasions, *tongzhi* is usually used to emphasize community solidarity (Kam, 2013). Regardless of *tongzhi* or *lala*, these forms of identification are generally seen as more positive and less stigmatizing than the alternative *tongxinglian*.

In the early 2000s, the globalization of Western queer culture brought a new term to name LGBTQ persons: *ku'er*. Literally translated "cool child", Tian (2019) sees the term as "an innovation that attempts to bring North American queer theory to bear on Chinese linguistic characteristics" (p. 59). In contrast to the English word "queer" which may bear negative connotations, *ku'er* (i.e. cool child) rebranded Chinese sexual minorities with "a positive, different and celebratory cosmopolitanism" (Tian, 2019, p. 59). Tian (2019) argues that the rise of the term *ku'er* marked the Chinese turn from planned economy to participation in global capitalism. However, despite increasing take-up of the term in sexuality studies and social activism, most LGBTQ people in China seem to prefer to call themselves *tongzhi, lala* or *gay* (Bao, 2018; Kong, 2010). Having said that, Elisabeth Engebretsen and William Schroeder (2015) observe that "in everyday uses, *tongzhi* and *ku'er* are not always separate in meaning and are sometimes used interchangeably" (p. 8)

What this section shows is the fact that different transnational cultural flows, from translations of Western academic works and media representations of homosexuality, to the borrowing and appropriation of terms such as *lazi* and *tongzhi*, have resulted in different forms of hybridized Chinese LGBTQ identity (Liu & Ding, 2005; Wong, 2015). Additionally, the different terms used to identity same-sex subjects in China are always multiple, contradictory and contingent (Liu & Ding, 2005; Wong, 2015).

LGBTQ Identity Politics, Not Queer Politics

Having historicized the invention of indigenous sexual identities in China, this section now turns to the kinds of LGBTQ politics practiced in China. It begins with a historical examination of the visibility politics of coming out in Anglo-Saxon countries, before discussing the nature of LGBTQ politics in China. Visibility politics is not only a political project but also a socio-cultural one that grew out of Western experiences of collective struggle against discriminatory exclusion and models of subject formation (Schlossberg, 2001). The closet refers to the social condition where gay individuals feel pressured to project a public heterosexual identity and confine their homosexuality to the private sphere (Seidman, 2001). LGBTQ social movements in the United States and Europe began in the late 1960s with sexual minorities publicly disclosing their sexualities to celebrate their identities and reject the conventional sexual regime (Edenborg, 2017; Whittier, 2017). By the 1970s and 1980s, coming out of the closet came to be seen in the United States as essential and beneficial to self-identity and the collective struggle of gay men (Seidman, 2001; Wang et al., 2009).

As a response to social pressure to keep homosexuality out of public sight, coming out is closely associated with visibility politics, where visibly expressing one's sexuality or gender identity is deemed desirable, perhaps even necessary, in the struggle for marginalized groups to achieve social inclusion and political rights (Edenborg, 2017; Seidman, 2001; Whittier, 2017). Modelled after ethnic minorities' politics of recognition (Taylor, 1994), LGBTQ visibility politics often draw on identity as a resource to extend the rights of gender or sexual minority groups. By organizing around a distinct identity and publicly displaying this collective identity through specific practices, discourses and appearances that are visibly recognizable to others, such as rainbow flags and Pride parades, LGBTQ activists seek to challenge dominant views of sexuality and gender and produce social change.

An example of LGBTQ visibility politics is the Pride Parade, which has taken off internationally. Providing what Peterson et al. (2018) term "the most visible manifestations of lesbian, gay, bisexual, trans, queer and intersex movements and politics" (p. 1), Pride parades exemplify visibility politics in its call to "take to the streets to publically contest stigmatization, manifest identity, and demand equality and change" (Edenborg, 2020, p. 351). For many Pride activists, these coming out performances make visible their previously hidden sexual and gender identities, demonstrate their belonging to a wider community and provide an opportunity for them to challenge dominant heterosexual norms (Erni & Spires, 2001; Peterson et al., 2018).

Seidman (2001) differentiates between identity politics that seek to normalize homosexuality from queer politics, which "aim less to normalize gay identities than to free all sexualities from normalizing regulation" (pp. 321–322). As a response to the social condition of the closet, most LGBTQ identity movements primarily pursue a politics of sexual citizenship aimed at equal rights and symbolic incorporation into the national community (Seidman, 2001). In contrast to LGBTQ politics, queer politics seek to deconstruct the hetero/homo binary by creating new norms of selfhood that challenge the category of the normal and its disciplinary effects (Seidman, 2001; Bernstein, 2005). In queer politics, the norm of heterosexuality is challenged "but in the context of contesting a range of social controls over sexualities" (p. 322). It is thus a more radical form of politics that seeks transformative cultural change that can bring diverse groups of marginalized people together (Bernstein, 2005).

In this chapter, I use LGBTQ politics to denote the reformist nature of LGBTQ activism in China (Huang, 2017). The goal of LGBTQ identity politics is to normalize homosexuality and reduce the significance of the closet (Seidman, 2001). However, in seeking to mainstream same-sex relationships, LGBTQ politics in China sometimes take for granted the desirability of heterosexual institutions and leave unchallenged oppressive social institutions (Huang, 2017). The rights of gay citizens become privileges that they can only claim because other than their non-normative sexuality, they are deserving citizens and "normal" in other aspects of their lives (Huang, 2017; Seidman, 2001). Additionally, the normalization of homosexuality in LGBTQ identity politics tends to render sexual difference to a minor aspect of a person's self and "leaves in place the norm of binary gender identities and the ideal of a heterosexual marriage and family" (Seidman, 2001, p. 324). As a result, while LGBTQ identity politics offers LGBTQ individuals a life beyond the closet, the "legitimation is conditional on the homosexual displaying dominant social conventions" (Seidman, 2001, p. 326) and "recognition only of a minority status, not the contestation of heteronormativity" (Seidman, 2001, p. 326).

As several scholars pointed out, LGBTQ community members and activists generally disapprove of radical queer politics in China and prioritize mainstream acceptance of same-sex orientation (Huang, 2017; Ching, 2010; Bao, 2017). This is not surprising, given that many Chinese LGBTQ subjects desire visibility, but also acceptance and assimilation. Ching (2010) describes the tensions Chinese LGBTQ subjects face as "dreaming of normal while sleeping with impossible" (p. 1). She noted that for many *tongzhi*:

> the moment of being closest to normativity is also the moment of confirming the impossibility of one's desire is also the moment of knowing one's queerness. It is only upon acknowledgement of one's not being straight that one needs to put one's finger on straightness in other ways, including in ways apparently impossible.
>
> *(Ching, 2010, p. 3)*

To address their "not being straight" (Ching, 2010, p. 3), many *tongzhi* cling onto heteronormative ideals of a "good life", characterized by "a lifelong same-sex partner, the blessings of family and friends, in a positive social environment that mimics the LGBTQ-friendly cultures of the perceived West" (Huang, 2017, p. 228).

Responding to a (Post)socialist Authoritarian State and a Heteronormative, Confucian and Family-Centred Social Order

Having established the reformist nature of LGBTQ politics in China, this section briefly describes the socio-cultural and political contexts of LGBTQ activism in China, before using Tian's framework of graduated in/visibility to highlight how different LGBTQ subjects have drawn on different strategies to respond to the demands of a (post)socialist authoritarian state and a heteronormative, Confucian and family-centred social order.

Edenborg (2020) argues that the idea of "coming out" and visibly expressing one's sexuality or gender identity to others as normatively desirable has become an unquestioned assumption in LGBTQ politics and theory. As globalization and the rise of transnational LGBTQ movements in the 1990s facilitated the travelling of Western LGBTQ and identitarian discourses around the world, their particular experiences of LGBTQ politics have gained hegemonic status in contexts with different histories and notions of selfhood (Edenborg, 2020). As a result, Chinese LGBTQ subjects who resist the idea of "coming out" are often criticized for "being closeted, dishonest, and self-denying" (Chou, 2001, p. 28) or deemed to be deferred in their process of becoming modern sexual subjects (Huang, 2016). One LGBTQ activist in Beijing reported her frustration working with European and American funders who pressure Chinese activists to prioritize anti-discrimination and legal advocacy work:

> There is apparently a hierarchy of activism, where pride parades and law reform count as the bravest, most effective methods, and culture and art activism are looked down upon as a compromise by activists who are not brave enough to go public. This is a very warped idea. China doesn't operate under the same political system. LGBT people in China do not face the same kinds of problems and do not need the same set of solutions, carried out in the same order.
>
> *(Moreno-Tabarez et al., 2014, p. 130)*

Huang and Brouwer (2018) caution that the politics of visibility "risks becoming a new hegemony that Chinese LGBTQ subjects might be expected to embrace to become intelligible members in a transnational LGBTI imaginary" (p. 100). A few scholars have paid attention to the fact that visibility politics posit homosexuality and homophobia as universal categories and might have contradictory and differentiated consequences in contexts where other forms of oppression might also be at play (Edenborg, 2020). In these contexts, public visibility may not mean becoming part of the public; rather it may make impossible one's participation in the community (Brighenti, 2010; Edenborg, 2017).

Although a vibrant, young, urban and cosmopolitan LGBTQ culture has emerged in recent years, the (post)socialist state continues to strictly regulate the community (Tian, 2019). The space for activism has contracted even further under President Xi Jinping. Many Chinese LGBTQ organizations have adopted more conservative, *didiao* (i.e. lower key) strategies and less public advocacy activities (Young Activists Alliance, 2020). Recently, the Chinese government tightened its social control and clamped down on social media accounts associated with feminists and China's campus LGBTQ movement (Ni & Davidson, 2021; Yang, 2021). It also banned "sissy men" from television (McDonald, 2021).

Thus, LGBTQ activists in China need different strategies that enable them to reach out to other LGBTQ persons without triggering the state's "fight" mechanism. One LGBTQ activist describes how he navigates the authoritarian, post-socialist state:

> You have to calculate how sensitive it might be and how much of a chance there is that law enforcement authorities will intervene. . . . A big part of LGBTQ activism in China is about playing that game, and balancing this invisible line between what's acceptable and what's not.
>
> *(Moreno-Tabarez et al., 2014, p. 128)*

While the process of global queering has contributed to the increasing visibility of LGBTQ people in public life, such as advertising and mass media, the close association between homosexuality and identity politics in Anglo-Saxon countries has lent credence to claims that homo-erotism is a western and dangerous import to be feared and opposed (Altman, 2002):

> Homosexuals are the enemy of the Chinese socialist state. It is so because to be Ku'er [i.e., queer] is to reject the national heterosexual imaginary. In addition, queerness has a global presence. The possibility of uniting all queers frightens the Chinese state, who

perceives a queer planet as a new possibility of international connections that poses a threat to the stability of the (post)socialist state.

(Tian, 2019, p. 70)

LGBTQ activism is tolerated when it is sporadic, but the state is always wary of LGBTQ organizations' ability to mobilize on a larger scale (Tian, 2019). Therefore, nonconfrontational tactics and strategies with different levels of visibility are crucial to the safety and survival of LGBQT activists in China.

Another important consideration about LGBTQ politics in China is the heteronormative, Confucian and family-centred social order. A 2016 national survey on being LBGTQ in China found that only around 5% of sexual and gender minorities are out (UNDP, 2016). The same survey also revealed family as the primary site of struggle for Chinese LGBTQ subjects. When asked about the attitudes of their family, school, workplace, or religious community towards sexual or gender minorities, more than half of the respondents (57.6%) perceived their families to have "low acceptance" or "complete rejection", while over half of the LGBTQ subjects surveyed (56.1%) reported family to be the most frequent site of discrimination. Instead of highlighting to family members or fellow citizens the injustice of one's exclusion based on gender and/or sexual identity, it appears that making their sexualities visible may provoke public antipathies and result in a denial of belonging (Edenborg, 2017). As a result, 47.6% of the LGBTQ subjects surveyed never came out to their families, while 74.9% chose not to come out at their workplace. Overall, the survey findings seemed to suggest that coming out is a double-edged sword that can lead to alienation, rejection and discrimination and that the family institution is deeply entangled with the LGBTQ politics in China.

In particular, a confrontational and visible coming out for the Chinese LGBTQ subject can be culturally problematic, given the importance of the family-kinship system. Within the family-kinship system, the discourses of *chuanzongjiedai* (i.e. patrilinear continuity) and value of *xiao* (i.e. filial piety) intersect to inform Chinese understandings of sexual deviance (Huang, 2016; Wong, 2015) and the ways Chinese LGBTQ subjects negotiate with their minority sexual identity (Chou, 1997; Hu & Wang, 2013; Huang & Brouwer, 2018; Wong, 2015). The ethics of filial piety is central in framing the experiences of Chinese LGBTQ subjects and their families. It demands that children submit their will to the authority of their parents, especially fathers (Wang et al., 2009). Coming out often means having to violate the ethics of filial piety, which requires one to strive to meet parental expectations and bring honour and prosperity to the family. Openly living as an LGBTQ person can make the family vulnerable to gossips and bring disgrace and stigma to the family name (Hu & Wang, 2013). It may also involve the loss of face for parents, who must deal with accusations of having failed in their parenting duty and the shame of raising a sexually deviant child (Chou, 2001; Huang, 2016).

The sexual division of labour in the Chinese family meant that marriage is seen as a significant family duty (Erni & Spires, 2001). The Book of Filial Piety stated that the foremost misbehaviour against filial piety is not bearing a male heir to continue the family line (Wang et al., 2009). Despite rapid social transformation and economic development, neoliberal (post) socialist China has yet to dismantle the heterosexual marriage imperative (Huang, 2017). Many LGBTQ subjects see social tolerance and same-sex marriage as their ultimate goals, but they are also compelled to accept the imperative of heterosexual marriages as their filial obligations (Engebretsen, 2014; Huang, 2017). A 2013 survey with 149 Chinese LGBTQ subjects found that participants who endorsed the value of filial piety and perceived their parents to hold stronger values towards heterosexual marriages tended to feel more negative about their minority sexual identity (Hu & Wang, 2013). This is not surprising. Contra Anglo-Saxon societies where individuality and self-affirmation constitute the basis of personal and cultural identity, scholars such as Chou (1997) and Hu and Wang (2013) posit that the family-kinship system is the basis of Chinese subject formation. Many *tongzhi* cannot disarticulate their subjectivities from their families, who see heterosexual marriages as their family responsibility, so sexual identities and coming out for *tongzhi* is a highly complex struggle.

The demands of a (post)socialist authoritarian state and a heteronormative, Confucian and family-centred social order set much of the parameters for China's "politics of recognition with Chinese characteristics" (Tian, 2019, p. 60), an identity politics that is largely unconfrontational and depoliticized. For Tian (2019), graduated in/visibility is a "guerrilla war of visibility" (p. 70) critical to the survival of LGBTQ subjects in China. The notion of graduated in/visibility describes how levels of visibility in LGBTQ activism may vary based on local political, economic and cultural conditions, such as state control, financial cost of organizing and local levels of acceptance (Tian, 2019).

The Politics of Recognition With Chinese Characteristics in China: Now You See It, Now You Don't

In this section, I draw on the framework of graduated in/visibility to help readers understand how Chinese LGBTQ subjects navigate the heteronormative, Confucian and family-centred social order as well repressive state policies in China. The framework has five grades of in/visibility, ranging from full invisibility, dislocated visibility, targeted visibility, collective visibility to celebratory visibility. Chinese LGBTQ subjects who adopt tacit accommodationist strategies to compartmentalize their queer life from their familial and social duties tend to be at fully invisible and unseen, while confrontational tactics such as coming out and the rights discourse tend to be highly visible.

An example of a fully invisible form of oppositional politics that many LGBTQ subjects in China practise is *xinghun* (i.e. cooperative marriages). In contrast to Wang Xiaoyu and Ouyang Jean who held their same-sex marriage proposal in public to subvert normative ideas about heterosexual marriages, Chinese LGBTQ subjects tended to deploy a more *hanxu* (i.e. reticent) kind of politics (Liu & Ding, 2005), where the principle of *meiyoujiechuan* (i.e. not laying it bare) is observed with regards to one's LGBTQ sexuality (Huang & Brouwer, 2018). In the familial context, reticent politics require Chinese LGBTQ subjects to communicate their sexuality in indirect and more subtle ways to fulfil their filial duties towards their parents and maintain harmonious relations. Since family members are usually tolerant of homoeroticism if one conforms and fits to societal norm or fulfils his reproductive duty of carrying on the family bloodline, many LGBTQ subjects in China marry so that they can be publicly heterosexual while privately homosexual (Wang, 2019). A 1998 survey claims that an estimated 70–80% of male homosexuals/bisexuals in Chinese cities have married or will marry a woman (Wong, 2015). Chinese gay men often engage in heterosexual marriages, while practising their same-sex desires on the side in private (Goldberg, 2016) or engaging in *xinghun* (i.e. cooperative marriages) with lesbian women to pass as heterosexuals and appease social expectations (Kam, 2013; Engebretsen, 2014; Huang & Brouwer, 2018; Wang, 2019). *Xinghun* (i.e. cooperative marriages) allow Chinese LGBTQ subjects to be "normal", which they define as fulfilling their filial and social obligations, and provide family members with evidence of their commitment to the public performance of heterosexual marriages (Engebretsen, 2014; Huang & Brouwer, 2018). Although their practices of masking their identity by marrying a heterosexual person may not always be seen as morally acceptable, some scholars see this manoeuvring of the heterosexual-familial system as a personal form of oppositional politics that highlights the fragility of normativity (Engebretsen, 2014; Tian, 2019). Tian (2019) sees LGBTQ persons who carry out daily resistance even as they hide their sexuality or gender identities through non-disclosure or heterosexual marriages as practising a fully invisible form of oppositional politics.

Xinghun (i.e. cooperative marriages) take away parental surveillance and interference, allow Chinese LGBTQ subjects to affirm both their sexuality and open up spaces for LGBTQ family structures with same-sex partners (Tian, 2019). However, such reticent politics may also be complicit in the maintenance of the heteronormative order. The queer agency exercised in *xinghun* (i.e. cooperative marriages) leaves unchallenged the idea that homosexuality must remain invisible and never spoken of (Engebretsen, 2014). Liu and Ding (2005) contend that the reticent politics of tolerance is a structuring pressure for many Chinese LGBTQ subjects. By constantly reminding them to toe the line of invisibility, the silent tolerance of LGBTQ sexuality in Chinese societies is in fact, also a reticent, homophobia that represses, disciplines and keeps LGBTQ subjects in their place (Liu & Ding, 2005; Engebretsen, 2014).

Dislocated visibility refers to the use of queer symbols or objects, such as rainbow flags and *zhongxing* (i.e. gender neutral) dressing, to represent queer bodies. Tian (2019) discussed how he and a group of activists used rainbow flags to bring attention to LGBTQ issues in Weihai, China. They knew that the university administrators would reject their application if they had asked to set up a booth in the student residential area. They were also concerned that a public gathering of large groups of students would violate the student code and caused harm to the students involved. Eventually, the group placed rainbow flags around the campus to raise awareness of LGBTQ issues. Although school administrators labelled the flags as "unsolicited advertisements" and removed them, the flags raised the visibility of LGBTQ community on campus and contributed to the formation of the first LGBTQ student group on the university campus. However, the university threatened the student organizers with academic penalties and forced them to dissolve after they called out sexism on campus, again highlighting the limits of visibility politics in China (Tian, 2019).

Another example of dislocated visibility is the use of *zhongxing* (i.e. gender neutral) dressing by lesbian women in Taiwan. Although Chinese women can identify and live semi-openly as lesbians, the space they have to freely express their sexuality is limited (Hu, 2019). Within a conservative cultural environment, some Taiwanese lesbian women draw on different bodily and behavioural signs, including Japanese/Korean beautiful-boy style fashion related to *zhongxing* (i.e. gender neutral) dressing, to inform others about their sexual identification in a *hanxu* (i.e. reticent) manner (Hu, 2019). Sky, a lesbian woman responded to the researcher's question about whether she had come out:

> Come out? You mean telling people that I am a lesbian? They should know when they see me, shouldn't they? I mean, isn't my look obvious enough? Why do I have to go around telling people that I am [a lesbian]? Don't get me wrong. I am very proud of being who I really am, but it is one thing that people think I am [a lesbian], and it is another thing if I say I am. You can never be sure whether some people would stab you in the back.
>
> (Hu, 2019, p. 196)

Sky exemplifies a *hanxu* (i.e. reticent) tacit subject, whose non-normative sexual subjectivity is assumed and understood despite not having spoken about it (Decena, 2008). For Sky, her cross-gender expression in fashion declares her lesbian identity, while allowing her to avoid the unpredictable harm that may accompany a direct coming out. While such reticent politics may not be viewed authentic, *zhongxing* (i.e. gender neutral) performance allowed the lesbian women participants in Hu's study to "identify fellow lesbian women, to form support groups and communities, and to negotiate a social space where they can enact lesbian visibility without breaching without breaching normative social relations" (Hu, 2019, p. 196). Hu's study highlights how resistance and complicity are confounded in these lesbian women's practices.

Targeted visibility is riskier than the previous two levels because it requires LGBTQ subjects to reveal their identities in public, such as what Wang Xiaoyu and Ouyang Jean had done, to highlight LGBTQ rights or to raise public awareness of specific LGBTQ issues. Targeted visibility is a strategy LGBTQ activists in China sometimes utilized for advocacy. Bao (2017) discussed a public gay wedding event that took place in Beijing on Valentine's Day. He noted that the visibility of the same-sex wedding scene provoked public awareness of LGBTQ issues and brought gay identities into existence, whether the spectators like it or not:

> As spectators watch the same-sex wedding scene, they are either surprised, or amused, or curious about the event, thus constructing their subject positions as "straight", "pro-gay", "anti-gay", or even as "gay" in the process of watching. Even when some are deeply convinced of the "absurdity" of the event, they still have to acknowledge the existence of a group of people whose social identities might be different from the majority of people. In this field (*chang* 场) of emotional flows, connections and interactions, gay and lesbian identities became known and visible to the participants of the event.
>
> (Bao, 2017, p. 111)

Additionally, to reduce personal risks for those involved, the organizers deliberately chose gay performers who did not know each other, so that those not yet out to their parents, relatives or colleagues could pass themselves off as mere performers and deny their same-sex identity if asked (Bao, 2017).

Another popular advocacy strategy that utilizes targeted visibility relates to the production of LGBTQ documentary and art works. Cultural activism simultaneously "struggles against and works with government strictures and capitalist institutions that intersect with a conservative moral order" (Deklerck, 2017, p. 234). LGBTQ subjects on public display in documentaries often practise public correctness and meet high standards of normative ideals associated with heteronormative and cisgender norms, such as stable and monogamous relationships, and familial respectability, for their deviant sexualities to be accepted (Deklerck, 2017; Kam, 2013). Queer Comrades is an independent LGBTQ webcast founded in 2007 to document queer culture and raise public awareness of queer issues in China (Deklerck & Wei, 2015). In 2012, Queer Comrades collaborated with Fan Popo, a prolific queer documentary filmmaker, and PFLAG China[3] (Parents, Friends and Family of Lesbians and Gays China) to produce a documentary titled *Mama Rainbow* (2012) (Deklerck, 2017). The 80-minute documentary focused on six mothers who explained how they came to terms with their children's non-normative sexualities. It highlighted the public correctness of their LGBTQ children: they are all successful, highly educated, filial and productive members of society. Many Chinese LGBTQ subjects and organizations use *Mama Rainbow* to prepare parents for their children's coming out and to guide them in the process of acceptance (Deklerck, 2017). However, while the film seeks to destigmatize and claim a more socially acceptable image for LBGTQ subjects, it also reifies dominant heterosexual and cisgender norms, such as mainstream family values, as a universal, desirable standard (Deklerck, 2017). Such documentaries may also marginalize and divide the LGBTQ community into good and bad people (Rofel, 1999). Only those that conform to heteronormative ideals are featured in these documentaries for public consumption, leading to questions about who has visibility in Chinese LGBTQ politics (Deklerck, 2017).

Strategies that rely on collective or celebratory visibility are least common in Chinese LGBTQ politics. Collective visibility refers to a gathering of LGBTQ persons, which is largely visible to insiders but not necessarily the public. Tian (2019) used Shanghai Pride as an example, where only insiders knew about the event. He described this form of visibility as geared towards building supportive LGBTQ communities for the isolated Chinese queer subject (Deklerck, 2017). In contrast, celebratory visibilities are outward-focused. Celebratory visibility characterizes LGBTQ organizing in many Anglo-Saxon countries, such as New Zealand, where Pride parades are held in public to raise public awareness and understanding of LGBTQ issues (Deklerck, 2017; Tian, 2019). These two forms of LGBTQ visibility politics are uncommon in China in part because of the state's three no's policy: no approval, no disapproval and no promotion (Moreno-Tabarez et al., 2014). There is neither an active policy of persecution of LGBTQ subjects (i.e. no disapproval) nor explicit legal recognition or protection of their rights (i.e. no approval). In addition, there are rules to contain the public awareness and visibility of LGBTQ subjects (i.e. no promotion). Because of the lack of explicit support and acknowledgement of LGBTQ subjects, state institutions prefer to err on the side of caution when dealing with LGBTQ activists and organizations, which led to very low visibility for sexual and gender minorities in state-controlled mass media (Tian, 2019; UNDP, 2016). The civil affairs bureaus, which oversee the regulation of NGOs, also generally deny registrations to LGBTQ organizations despite lacking the legal basis to do so (Ho et al., 2018; Moreno-Tabarez et al., 2014).

Conclusion: The Depoliticized Nature of LGBTQ Politics in China

While global queering has helped built an international LGBTQ identity, LGBTQ politics often bear cultural specificities, which takes into consideration the local political contexts and cultural traditions (Bao, 2017). How queer people in different geographical and social locations struggle with visibility depends on how queer marginalization is conceptualized. LGBTQ movements in North America and Europe see coming-out and the avoidance of passing as key to their out and proud gay and lesbian subjectivity (Hu, 2019). However, such conception of LGBTQ visibility marginalizes the importance of an in-between space between being seen and being unseen for Chinese LGBTQ subjects (Hu, 2019). As this chapter shows, the social and cultural configurations of non-normative sexuality and gender in the Chinese context are very different from that of Anglo-Saxon countries (Bao, 2010). In China, it is conservative cultural norms that largely regulate the social and political life of *tongzhi* and informed their emerging political consciousness. There is also the watchful eye of an authoritarian and repressive (post) socialist state to consider. Although the slight relaxation of state control in (post)socialist China in the wake of the HIV/AIDS epidemic created a small opening for LGBTQ social movements and identity politics, in a socio-political context where political expressions of sexuality are not always viable and often dangerous, LGBTQ identity has to co-exist and negotiate with other types of identities, rather than simply constituting a person's core identity (Bao, 2017).

Visibility queer politics come with high political and personal risks and are generally uncommon in the Chinese context. In response, the strategies Chinese LGBTQ subjects deploy to navigate the socio-political contexts they find themselves in are also different. Bao (2017) use two Chinese idioms to describe Chinese LGBTQ politics: *ruoyinruoxian* (i.e. now concealed, now disclosed) and *shiyinshixian* (i.e. at times concealed at times disclosed). Similar to Tian's (2019) notion of graduated in/visibility, the two idioms suggest that the relationship between visibility and invisibility is "multiple, contingent and sometimes fleeting" (Bao, 2017, p. 116).

LGBTQ activism in China is not merely about being seen or not seen, but "about being unseen by the state and seen by other *ku'ers*[queers]" (Tian, 2019, p. 61). The graduated in/visibility model Tian (2019) developed, which takes into consideration political and economic conditions, as well as cultural factors, provides a useful framework to develop mechanisms that support the visibility of LGBTQ subjects.

Notes

1 Homosexuality is officially not illegal in China even though sodomy was only deleted from China's criminal law in 1997 (Bao, 2017).
2 The deletion of hooliganism in China's 1997 Criminal Law was not targeted at decriminalizing homosexuality. Rather, the decriminalization of homosexuality was an unintended effect (Bao, 2017). The 2001 version of the Chinese Classification of Mental Disorder (CCMD-3) required self-discordant (i.e. ziwobuhexie) homosexuals to seek medical treatment, which suggests that the depathologization of homosexuality is still incomplete (Bao, 2017).
3 PFLAG China is an organization that draws on shared family values and supportive parents (mostly mothers of gay sons) to increase the visibility of Chinese LGBTQ subjects and rally public support (Huang, 2017).

References

Altman, D. (1996). On global queering. *Australian Humanities Review*. http://australianhumanitiesreview.org/1996/07/01/on-global-queering/?utm_source=rss&utm_medium=rss&utm_campaign=on-global-queering
Altman, D. (2002). Globalization and the international gay/lesbian movement. In *Handbook of lesbian and gay studies* (pp. 415–426). https://doi.org/10.4135/9781848608269.n25
Bao, H. (2010). "We who feel differently": LGBTQ identity and politics in China. *We Who Feel Differently Journal*. https://wewhofeeldifferently.info/files/WWFD_Hongwei_Bao.pdf
Bao, H. (2017). "Same-Sex Wedding", Queer performance and spatial tactics in Beijing. In Lin, X., Haywood, C., & Mac an Ghaill, M. (Eds.), *East Asian men: Masculinity, sexuality and desire* (pp. 107–121). Palgrave Macmillan.
Bao, H. (2018). *Queer comrades: Gay identity and Tongzhi activism in postsocialist China*. NIAS Press.
BBC News. (2020, July 29). Petition demands apology for Chinese lesbian student denied diploma. *BBC News*. www.bbc.com/news/world-asia-china-36921331
Bernstein, M. (2005). Identity politics. *Annual Review of Sociology, 31*, 47–74. https://doi.org/10.1146/annurev.soc.29.010202.100054
Bie, B., & Tang, L. (2016). Chinese gay men's coming out narratives: Connecting social relationship to co-cultural theory. *Journal of International and Intercultural Communication, 9*(4), 351–367. https://doi.org/10.1080/17513057.2016.1142602
Brighenti, A. M. (2010). *Visibility in social theory and social research*. Palgrave Macmillan UK. https://doi.org/10.1057/9780230282056
China Digital Times. (2016, July 1). *Lesbians' proposal fans fear of "foreign forces"*. https://chinadigitaltimes.net/2016/07/lesbian-couples-public-proposal-stokes-fear-foreign-forces/?__cf_chl_jschl_tk__=599e29335fa6e9aae00ca1laa3a2b4473028ba31-1592351903-0-AVkjNHb5X4xTKe6zohgkXUMFriHz3y7jJfdePU8zZGodxaX576X4PSk8hA8DbPF7dtlu_7-sf63jCd8xhgE
Ching, Y. (2010). Dreaming of normal while sleeping with impossible: Introduction. In *As normal as possible: Negotiating sexuality and gender in mainland China and Hong Kong* (pp. 1–14). Hong Kong University Press. https://doi.org/10.5790/hongkong/9789622099876.003.0001
Chou, W. S. (1997). *Post-colonial Tongzhi*. Hong Kong Queer Press.
Chou, W. S. (2001). Homosexuality and the cultural politics of Tongzhi in Chinese societies. *Journal of Homosexuality, 40*(3–4), 27–46. https://doi.org/10.1300/J082v40n03_03
Decena, C. U. (2008). Tacit subjects. *GLQ: A Journal of Lesbian and Gay Studies, 14*(2–3), 339–359. https://doi.org/10.1215/10642684-2007-036

Deklerck, S. (2017). Bolstering queer desires, reaching activist goals: Practicing queer activist documentary filmmaking in Mainland China. *Studies in Documentary Film*, *11*(3), 232–247. https://doi.org/10.1080/17503280.2017.1335564

Deklerck, S., & Wei, X. (2015). Queer online media and the building of China's LGBT community. In E. L. Engebretsen, W. F. Schroeder, & H. Bao (Eds.), *Queer/Tongzhi China: New perspectives on research, activism and media cultures* (pp. 18–34). NIAS Press.

Edenborg, E. (2017). Politics of belonging from speech to visibility. In *Politics of Visibility and Belonging : From Russia's Homosexual Propaganda Laws to the Ukraine War* (pp. 21–47). Taylor & Francis Group.

Edenborg, E. (2020). Visibility in global queer politics. In M. J. Bosia, S. M. McEvoy, & M. Rahman (Eds.), *The Oxford handbook of global LGBT and sexual diversity politics* (pp. 349–363). Oxford University Press. https://doi.org/10.1093/oxfordhb/9780190673741.013.34

Engebretsen, E. L. (2014). *Queer women in urban China: An ethnography*. Taylor & Francis Group.

Engebretsen, E. L., & Schroeder, W. F. (2015). Introduction: Queer/Tongzhi China. In E. L. Engebretsen, W. F. Schroeder, & H. Bao (Eds.), *Queer/Tongzhi China: New perspectives on research, activism and media cultures* (pp. 1–17). NIAS Press.

Engebretsen, E. L., Schroeder, W. F., & Bao, H. (Eds.). (2015). *Queer/Tongzhi China: New perspectives on research, activism and media cultures*. NIAS Press.

Erni, J. N., & Spires, A. J. (2001). Glossy subjects: G&L magazine and "Tonghzi" cultural visibility in Taiwan. *Sexualities*, *4*(1), 25–49. https://doi.org/10.1177/136346001004001002

Fejes, N., & Balogh, A. P. (2013). Introduction: Post-socialist politics of queer in/visibility. In N. Fejes & A. P. Balogh (Eds.), *Queer visibility in post-socialist cultures* (pp. 1–8). Intellect Books Ltd.

Foucault, M. (1995). *Discipline and punish: The birth of the prison*. Vintage.

Gao, Y. (2009). "Zhongguo you gay ma? tongzhi yu gay/lesbian de kuawenhua bijiao" [Are there gay people in China? A cross- cultural comparison between Tongzhi and gay/lesbian]. In Barry & Martin Prize-Giving Ceremony (Ed.), *Conference proceedings of the national conference on HIV/AIDS prevention and treatment among men who have sex with men/the tenth anniversary celebration of friends project/friends project* (p. 197). Pengyou xiangmuzu.

Goldberg, A. E. (2016). East Asian sexualities. In *The SAGE encyclopedia of LGBTQ studies* (pp. 349–353). SAGE. https://doi.org/10.4135/9781483371283.n131

Ho, P. S. Y., Jackson, S., Cao, S., & Kwok, C. (2018). Sex with Chinese characteristics: Sexuality research in/on 21st-century China. *The Journal of Sex Research*, *55*(4–5), 486–521. https://doi.org/10.1080/00224499.2018.1437593

Hu, X., & Wang, Y. (2013). LGB identity among young Chinese: The influence of traditional culture. *Journal of Homosexuality*, *60*(5), 667–684. https://doi.org/10.1080/00918369.2013.773815

Hu, Y. Y. (2019). Mainstreaming female masculinity, signifying lesbian visibility: The rise of the zhongxing phenomenon in transnational Taiwan. *Sexualities*, *22*(1–2), 182–202. https://doi.org/10.1177/1363460717701690

Huang, A. (2017). Precariousness and the queer politics of imagination in China. *Culture, Theory and Critique*, *58*(2), 226–242. https://doi.org/10.1080/14735784.2017.1287580

Huang, S. (2016). *Post-oppositional queer politics and the non-confrontational negotiation of queer desires in contemporary China*. Arizona State University. https://repository.asu.edu/attachments/170515/content/Huang_asu_0010E_15996.pdf

Huang, S., & Brouwer, D. C. (2018). Coming out, coming home, coming with: Models of queer sexuality in contemporary China. *Journal of International and Intercultural Communication*, *11*(2), 97–116. https://doi.org/10.1080/17513057.2017.1414867

Kam, L. Y. (2013). *Shanghai lalas: Female Tongzhi communities and politics in urban China*. Hong Kong University Press.

Kong, T. S. K. (2010). *Chinese male homosexualities: Memba, tongzhi and golden boy*. Routledge. https://doi.org/10.4324/9780203849200

Kong, T. S. K. (2016). The sexual in Chinese sociology: Homosexuality studies in contemporary China. *The Sociological Review*, *64*(3), 495–514. https://doi.org/10.1111/1467-954X.12372

Liu, J. P., & Ding, N. (2005). Reticent poetics, queer politics. *Inter-Asia Cultural Studies*, *6*(1), 30–55. https://doi.org/10.1080/1462394042000326897

Liu, P. (2010). Why does queer theory need China? *Positions*, *18*(2), 291–320. https://doi.org/10.1215/10679847-2010-002

McDonald, J. (2021, September 3). China bans "sissy men" from TV. *The Diplomat*. https://thediplomat.com/2021/09/china-bans-sissy-men-from-tv/

Moreno-Tabarez, U., Chávez, K. R., Leonelli, S. J., Huang, A., Deklerck, S., & Rother, C. (2014). Queer politics in China: A conversation with "western" activists working in Beijing. *A Journal in GLBTQ Worldmaking*, *1*(3), 109–132. www.jstor.org/stable/10.14321/qed.1.3.0109

Ni, V., & Davidson, H. (2021, July 8). Outrage over shutdown of LGBTQ WeChat accounts in China. *The Guardian*. www.theguardian.com/world/2021/jul/08/outrage-over-crackdown-on-lgbtq-wechat-accounts-in-china

Peterson, A., Wahlström, M., & Wennerhag, M. (2018). *Pride parades and LGBT movements*. Routledge.

Rofel, L. (1999). Qualities of desire: Imagining gay identities in China. *GLQ: A Journal of Lesbian and Gay Studies*, *5*(4), 451–474. https://doi.org/10.1215/10642684-5-4-451

Schlossberg, L. (2001). Rites of passing. In M. Sanchez & L. Schlossberg (Eds.), *Passing: Identity and interpretation in sexuality, race, and religion* (pp. 1–12). NYU Press.

Seidman, S. (2001). From identity to queer politics: Shifts in normative heterosexuality and the meaning of citizenship. *Citizenship Studies*, *5*(3), 321–328. https://doi.org/10.1080/13621020120085270

Taylor, C. (1994). The politics of recognition. In D. T. Goldberg (Ed.), *Multiculturalism: A critical reader* (pp. 75–106). Blackwell.

Tian, I. L. (2019). Graduated in/visibility: Reflections on Ku'er activism in (post)socialist China. *QED: A Journal in GLBTQ Worldmaking*, *6*(3), 56–75. https://doi.org/10.14321/qed.6.3.0056

United Nations Development Programme. (2016). *Being LGBTI in China: A national survey on social attitudes towards sexual orientation, gender identity and gender expression*. www.cn.undp.org/content/china/en/home/library/democratic_governance/being-lgbt-in-china.html

Vitiello, G. (2014). China: Ancient to modern. In E. L. McCallum & M. Tuhkanen (Eds.), *The Cambridge history of gay and lesbian literature* (pp. 125–142). Cambridge University Press. https://doi.org/10.1017/CHO9781139547376.009

Wang, F. T. Y., Bih, H.-D., & Brennan, D. J. (2009). Have they really come out: Gay men and their parents in Taiwan. *Culture, Health & Sexuality*, *11*(3), 285–296. https://doi.org/10.1080/13691050802572711

Wang, S. Y. (2019). When Tongzhi marry: Experiments of cooperative marriage between Lalas and gay men in urban China. *Feminist Studies*, *45*(1), 13–35. https://doi.org/10.15767/feministstudies.45.1.0013

Whittier, N. (2017). Identity politics, consciousness raising, and visibility politics. In H. McCammon, V. Taylor, & J. Reger (Eds.), *The Oxford handbook of U.S. women's social movement activism* (pp. 376–397). Oxford University Press.

Wong, D. (2011). Hybridization and the emergence of "gay" identities in Hong Kong and in China. *Visual Anthropology*, *24*(1–2), 152–170. https://doi.org/10.1080/08949468.2011.527810

Wong, D. (2015). Sexual minorities in China. In *International encyclopedia of social & behavioral sciences* (pp. 734–739). Elsevier Ltd.

Yang, S. (2021, June 8). China is repressing the feminist movement, but women's voices are only getting louder. *ABC News*. www.abc.net.au/news/2021-06-08/feminism-in-china-internet-crackdown-erase-womens-voices/100165360

Young Activists Alliance. (2019). *Annual Report on Chinese Young Activists*. Young Activists Alliance. https://issuu.com/youngactivists2019/docs/annual_report_on_chinese_young_activists__2019_

11

FORGOTTEN DAUGHTERS

Customizing Supports for Black and
Afro-Caribbean Lesbian, Bisexual, Queer,
and Trans Women

Charlene Désir and Kimoré Reid

Black and Afro-Caribbean Lesbian, Bisexual, Queer, and Transgender (B⚥LBQT) women face diverse experiences of discrimination, structural injustice, violence, and murder. The unique constellations of life stressors and resiliency factors are further complexified by the intersection of multiple marginalized identities (i.e., race, culture, sexuality, gender identity/expression, and religion) causing psychological fragmentation which impacts their emotional and academic wellness. To effectively address their psychological and academic needs, B⚥LBQT women require healing and support responses that center their experiences and worldviews. From the outset, this chapter attempts to redefine the sparse understandings of black lesbian, bisexual, queer, and trans womanhood and provide a critical perspective to dismantle Eurocentric, heterosexist points of view. The primary objectives of this chapter include highlighting the socio-cultural barriers facing B⚥LBQT women, examining the psycho-social and emotional trauma resulting from their experiences, and providing culturally relevant interventions for their psychological and educational success.

The path to wellness for B⚥LBQT women is best defined from the perspective of B⚥LBQT practitioners who are committed, personally and professionally, to their individual and communal healing. The authors of this chapter represent the unique cross section of African American socio-racial understanding and Afro-Caribbean ethnic identity and culture. Désir is a Haitian-American school psychologist and educator who was raised in Catholic and Haitian ancestral practices. Reid is a Jamaican mental health counselor raised in the Pentecostal Christian tradition. As black, queer practitioners, we demonstrate the power of the *wounded healer*, whose parallel struggle and survival provide a deeply intuitive understanding of B⚥LBQT women's healing and liberation. We propose and illustrate techniques for customizing therapeutic and educational supports for B⚥LBQT women, employing diasporic African consciousness, spirituality, and community as holistic frameworks for improving their mental wellness and academic success.

King (1997) reminded black women to counter Euro-heterosexist notions that they are "undesirable" by reclaiming African symbols and rituals that honor their divinity. It was imperative in this chapter to reclaim the naming of this group with an empowering African symbol, recognizable across the black diaspora. Renaming is an integral process that allows B⚥LBQT women to redefine their experiences and promote empowering self-narratives. The authors use the *ankh* (⚥) as an inclusive symbol of the Goddess black woman-a balanced, unified, divine,

 DOI: 10.4324/9781003128151-13

androgynous energy within black lesbian, bisexual, queer, and trans women. The ankh is an ancient Egyptian symbol that exemplified spiritual illumination, the continuous life force, and the emblematic image of the spirit, mind, and body in balance (Bailey, 2015). There are various interpretations of the ankh's sacred symbolism-some depict the ankh as a womb and phallus, representing the union of man and woman, bringing forth life, while others view it as a woman's mirror (in the shape of a womb) where she sees herself as a reflection of the divine (Everhart, 2004; Imhotep, 2010). In a public essay, Imhotep (2017) defined the ankh not only as a symbol of life in the physical sense but also as a symbol of service, vitalism, healing, wisdom, infinite love, solidarity, eternal life, power, and authority. We include the ankh to honor the illumination of black lesbian, bisexual, queer, and trans women-B♀LBQT women-as women of perseverance, healing, and sacred worth (Afua, 2001).

Forgotten in the Margins

Black people in the United States represent an incredible array of ethnicities, cultures, traditions, and spiritual practices. The majority of the black populace is made up of African Americans–U.S.-born individuals whose ancestral bloodlines in this country began with the transatlantic slave trade. African Americans possess a "singularly bitter history of coerced importation, enslavement, and discrimination," setting them apart from other racial and ethnic groups whose immigration to the United States was "voluntary" (Rogers, 2006, p. 7). The historic subordination, commodification and dehumanization perpetrated against enslaved Africans set gruesome precedents for the racism, systemic and economic oppression, and brutal violence experienced by black Americans today (Reid-Merritt, 2019b).

Afro-Caribbean-black people from non-Hispanic countries in and around the Caribbean Sea (i.e., Haiti, Jamaica, the Bahamas, Turks and Caicos, the Cayman Islands, Anguilla, Trinidad and Tobago, Guyana, the United States and British Virgin Islands, Montserrat, Dominica, Antigua and Barbuda, Barbados, Guadeloupe, St. Vincent and the Grenadines, St. Kitts and Nevis, St. Lucia, Aruba, and Grenada) also began to immigrate to the United States in the late nineteenth century due to economic and political instability in their home countries (Hamilton, 2020). By 2014, there were over four million Afro-Caribbean living in the United States, making them the largest black immigrant group in the country (Hamilton, 2020; Rogers, 2006). Unlike European, Asian, or Latin immigrants, Afro-Caribbean experience "harsh, systemic forms of discrimination" due to their "common racial classification with African Americans," as well as a "deplorable legacy of enslavement and racial domination by whites" (Rogers, 2006, pp. 8–9). Although Afro-Caribbean and African Americans represent a wealth of social, cultural, and spiritual differences, their shared racial identity and ancestry means that they are "most likely to encounter and experience the same strain of American racism" (Rogers, 2006, p. 9).

The Human Rights Campaign glossary (2021) defines the terms lesbian, bisexual, queer, and transgender as follows:

Lesbian—A woman who is emotionally, romantically, or sexually attracted to other women.
Bisexual—A person emotionally, romantically, or sexually attracted to more than one sex, gender, or gender identity though not necessarily simultaneously, in the same way or to the same degree.
Queer—A term people often use to express a spectrum of identities and orientations that are counter to the mainstream. Queer is often used as a catch-all to include many people, including those who are not identified as exclusively straight and/or folks who have non-binary or gender-expansive identities.

Transgender—An umbrella term for people whose gender identity and/or expression is different from cultural expectations based on the sex they were assigned at birth.

The definitions of these terms do not and *cannot* provide a clear understanding of the socio-
racial and psychological stressors that non-heterosexual people face when they are black and
female/feminine identified. B♀LBQT women face complex discrimination layered with racism,
sexism, cissexism, homophobia, and xenophobia.

Kimberlé Crenshaw (2013) articulated the "Theory of Intersectionality" which emphasizes
the ways that discrimination (e.g., sexism, racism, cissexism, xenophobia, and homophobia) is
targeted *more* profoundly toward black people than toward majoritarianism. Crenshaw' s theory highlights the complex relationship between power and multiple forms of oppression. In an
article on the health outcomes of B♀LBQT women, Peek et al. (2016) specifically interpreted
Crenshaw' s theory as follows:

> "Intersectionality" is the study of how multiple systems of social stratification (e.g.,
> race, ethnicity, gender, sexual orientation) influence an individuals' identity and lived
> experience, recognizing that every person holds a position (privilege or disadvantage)
> in different systems simultaneously, and that such positions can vary in magnitude and
> direction depending on time, place, and circumstance.
>
> *(p. 679)*

B♀LBQT women seamlessly and courageously integrate "multiple systems of social stratification" (blackness, femaleness, queerness, and transness) within the narrow margins of our
social, cultural, political, and economic systems (Peek et al., 2016, p. 679). As individuals and
as a collective, B♀LBQT women represent a specific point of convergence for multiple identities that deviate significantly from the white, heterosexual, cisgendered male "standard." Their
identities, whether visible or not, act as identifiers for discrimination and prejudice. Blackness
and cis-femaleness are genetic identifiers for racially charged misogyny, blatant disregard, violence, and neglect. Queerness and transness are innate and intrinsic (less visible) identifiers for
ridicule, ostracism, spiritual trauma, and physical harm.

B♀LBQT women's survival involves the reconciliation of multiple marginalized identities
within several socio-cultural contexts enmeshed with prejudice and trauma. As black women,
they are the most vulnerable to social abuses, poverty, sexism, marginalization, and intimate
partner violence (Petrosky et al., 2017). Their experiences of sexuality and gender discrimination increases their risk of developing cancer and heart disease (Malta et al., 2019). Their queer
identities are viewed as "abnormal" within African American and Afro-Caribbean cultural communities, which are "often overridden by the disciplinary power of normative categories of
gender and sexuality" (Young, 2016, p. 12). Afro-Caribbean cultural beliefs around sexuality
and gender are often reflective of the "wide-spread discrimination, violence, stigma, and prejudice against [sexual and gender minorities]" in Afro-Caribbean countries (Malta et al., 2019,
p. 5). Many of these countries—including Haiti, Jamaica, Grenada, Dominica, St. Kitts and
Nevis, St. Vincent and the Grenadines, and St. Lucia—maintain laws that target queer and trans
people (Malta et al., 2019). Although these laws are considered "relics of British colonialism,"
most Afro-Caribbean countries have yet to pass laws that explicitly protect the rights of gender
and sexual minorities (Malta et al., 2019, p. 5). Despite federal mandates protecting queer and
trans people from discrimination in the United States, African American cultural communities
tend to view gender and sexuality through the lens of Christian doctrine (Douglas, 2004).
The Christian church is considered the oldest social institution in the black community and

the doctrine taught by clergy is considered the literal words of God (Allen, 2019). The Black church is central to the overall black identity development in the United States and influences the social and ethical behavioral expectations that most often deems homosexuality and trans identity as an abomination cited in the bible—Leviticus 18:21 & 20:13 (Olyan, 1994).

As a result of this social context, B♀LBQT women's queer identities "[disrupt] normalization and [make] room for new norms to take shape" (Young, 2016, p. 98). Although many B♀LBQT women find the process of disrupting and recreating norms to be liberating, rejection from their communities of origin leave them more vulnerable to systemic hardships that affect their social, psychological, economic, and physical well-being (Young, 2016). B♀LBQT women often find themselves living compartmental rather than fully integrated lives, lacking access to work, housing, medical and community supports (Marinucci, 2016). Black lesbian women reject the societal expectation of womanhood that requires romantic alignment with men and embrace women who love women (Rich, 2003). Black bisexual and queer women face distrust from same-sex and different-sex partners and are often sexualized. Black bisexuals, in general, have the highest rates of depression often having to minimalize or hide their same-sex feelings and partners (Ka'ahumanu & Hutchins, 2015). Black trans women reject male privilege, choosing to align with and express their female or feminine identity, and often become targets of vicious hate crimes (Juang, 2013). Black trans women are disproportionately the victims of homicide (Momen & Dilks, 2020). In the summer of 2020 alone, 16 black trans women were killed:

> Cameron Breon, Merci Mack, Brayla Stone, Akhenton Jones, Riah Milton, Dominique Fells, Shakie Peters, Draya McCarty, Tatiana Hall, Monika Diamond, Nina Pop, Dior Ova, Queasha Hardy, Aja Rhone-Spears, Aerrion Burnett, and Bree Black.

As we critically examine the intersectional oppression of B♀LBQT women, it is imperative that we reference the Black Lives Matter Movement (BLM). BLM was created by three black women, Patrisse Cullors, Alicia Garza, and Opal Tometi, two of whom were identified as queer. The overall essence of the BLM movement is to acknowledge and honor the sacredness of *all* black lives that are targeted for socio-economic oppression, abuse, and murder. Despite the heinous murders of black trans women, the overall personification of the BLM movement remains focused on heterosexual black men.

B♀LBQT Women's Survival

Even with the crippling circumstances that continuously undermine their well-being, B♀LBQT women are incredibly resilient. Lewis and Miller (2018) described B♀LBQT women as agents of a transformational and liberatory praxis, whose pursuit of liberation becomes a model for others. A clear understanding of the ways in which B♀LBQT women reconcile their identities and create spaces for their own existence and expansion is integral to any work that attempts to define or support them. Their survival and resilience manifest through several avenues including their ability to code-switch, shape-shift, and self-name: their connection with community and chosen family, and their use of Afro-Indigenous consciousness as a framework for identity integration and emotional healing.

Code-Switching and Shape-Shifting

Code-switching is a process of translation that allows people of color to subvert and adapt to the oppressive (and impossible) standards of white respectability (Apugo, 2019). Though most individuals have had to code-switch at some point in their lives, black and brown people master this survival tool at a young age, through the instruction and modeling of their families and communities, and the negative reinforcement of peers, teachers, institutions, and the media. Code-switching involves changing speech patterns (i.e., verbiage, tone, volume, and accent) and non-verbal facial cues in order to "soften one's authentic racial and ethnic identity" and appear less threatening to white people (Apugo, 2019, p. 54). In the same respect, *shape-shifting* involves a more overt transformation by which marginalized people mask the parts of their identity that are considered unacceptable within their current environment (Foster, 2018). For BꟼLBQT women, shape-shifting is about hiding in plain sight-methodically altering modes of dress, behaviors, mannerisms, postures, and expressions to "perform deference, grace, and respectability lest [they] be subject to a wide range of punishments" (Foster, 2018, p. 1). Used in tandem with code-switching, shape-shifting allows BꟼLBQT women to project carefully curated images of themselves-simultaneously engaging with and undermining the hostile power structures that interpolate their personal and professional lives.

Code-switching and shape-shifting are not simply conditioned habits or strategies for socio-economic advancement these behaviors are integral survival mechanisms—epigenetically encoded trauma responses—that preserve BꟼLBQT women within the racist, misogynist, homophobic, transphobic, xenophobic, and classist systems that make up our society. Apugo (2019) asserts that widespread "strong black woman" stereotypes "give way to 'shifting' . . . code-switching and hypervigilance," in BꟼLBQT women (p. 53). Hypervigilance is a form of increased anxiety and awareness of one's environment as a means of psychological self-protection which often manifests as a response to trauma. The strong black woman stereotype creates a distressing cycle in which BꟼLBQT women must appear strong while constantly assessing their environment for microaggressions, discrimination, or other physical or psychological threats. When systemic oppression, discrimination, or microaggressions do occur, BꟼLBQT women may feel pressured to meet these challenges with a mask of strength which can deepen the psychological, emotional, and even physical impacts these incidents have on them. To protect themselves from future incidents, BꟼLBQT women may become even more hypervigilant of their surroundings, experiencing increased distress and anxiety, and strengthening the traumatic response. To code-switch or shape-shift is a traumatic re-experiencing of BꟼLBQT women's marginalized status, made doubly painful by exhausting and isolating expectations of strength and self-reliance. BꟼLBQT women are constantly being forced to choose between their authentic selves and survival—to split themselves apart in order to "keep it together." This is a deeply wounding process that often leads to identity fragmentation and mental illness.

Self-Naming

Bell (2016) highlighted that oppression is pervasive and manifests in many ways. Bierema (2020) categorized oppression as having restricted opportunities, being devalued, cumulative negative social effects, socially constructed, hegemonic, normalized, intersectional, durable, and mutable. BꟼLBQT women by their sexual identification are targets of oppression. Yet BꟼLBQT women do not allow society's oppressive and limited ideologies of race, sexuality, womanhood, or spirituality to claim their autonomy, but redefine themselves in ways that affirm their unique expressions. This is done through the process of *self-naming* which allows BꟼLBQT women to more authentically own and affirm their sexuality and gender. In many diasporic African communities, BꟼLBQT women reject the dichotomy of using labels like "lesbian" or "bisexual" because these names limit their ability to fully embody culturally black ideologies of sexuality. These words are often used with disdain from a Eurocentric, androcentric lens. As a result, many BᕼLBQT women use the term *women loving women* (Glave, 2008). Other BᕼLBQT women have simply accepted the term *queer*, and in some spaces *androgynous*, to better capture the fluidity, freedom, and unified energy of their sexuality (Carter & Baliko, 2017). BᕼLBQT women in the Haitian Vodou tradition have attached their identity spiritually as daughters of Ezili Dantor, a goddess lwa/orisha that accepts and honors them as sacred (Tinsley, 2018). In these examples, identity is reclaimed by denouncing names historically laced with oppressive intent.

Spirituality, Community, and Chosen Families

Reconciling BᕼLBQT women's identities through healing spiritual practice can promote a liberating praxis for well-being. Means et al. (2018) define *"spirituality* as an internal congruence, a personal relationship with a higher power/spirit, and connectedness with other people" (p. 620). Before many BᕼLBQT women can experience true wellness, they must first come to terms with the spiritual trauma, isolation, and negative sense of self fostered by religious organizations, and construct new spaces of worship (Melton, 2020; Stanford, 2013). Parker (2018) explored the healing components of the tribal collective which manifests as traditional communalism, redemptive self-care, radical subjectivity, and critical engagement. Traditional ideas of spirituality must be reframed and utilized for BᕼLBQT women's upliftment, where their sacredness is embraced and validated. Identity, community, and spirituality reimagined then become conduits for sacred, unconditional self-love (Tinsley, 2018).

Ghisyawan (2016) explained that BᕼLBQT women must create new possibilities of care, family, and passionate friendships where *love* becomes the foundation for resistance and revolution. BᕼLBQT women create and bond with chosen families and communities to combat societal abuse, racism, sexism, cissexism, despair, and self-hatred (Sivanandan, 2019). Many BᕼLBQT women have found safe spaces within Afro-Indigenous spiritual communities. Afro-Indigenous religions such as Yoruba, Ifá, Vodou, Santeria, Obeah, Candomblé, and Shango are often rejected by Western ideology as fantasy, witchcraft, or devil worship. Afro-Indigenous spirituality, practice, and consciousness are all but banished from "traditional" Western spaces of education, healing, and worship, inhabiting a similar space within the social order as BᕼLBQT women themselves. Each tradition is a unique manifestation of Black, Afro-Caribbean, and Afro-Latin survival in the Americas, inextricably tied to one another by Pan-African consciousness and epistemology. Afro-Indigenous spiritual practices subverted and defied the whitewashed, androcentric Christianity of European slave owners, preserved the rich cultural and spiritual practices of the enslaved, and provided a framework for liberation and freedom.

Afro-Indigenous consciousness centers the interconnectedness and interdependence of the individual, the family, the community, ancestry, nature, and the spirit world. It creates a safe space for BᕼLBQT women to feel connected to their genetic ancestry through spiritual and cultural practice and provides an intuitive lens through which these women can view themselves, the traumas they survive, and their unique role within their communities. Although each derivation of Afro-Indigenous consciousness maintains its own set of principles and practices, they all reiterate similar themes: the delicate balance between light and shadow, the interplay of the spiritual and physical worlds, the essential wisdom of the collective, and the importance of learning from the past. These essential tenets align seamlessly with themes often found in clinical trauma recovery which teaches survivors to care for their body and mind (the physical and nonphysical aspects of being), to understand the nature of their trauma while choosing to release toxic cycles (the balance of dark and light, learning from the past), and to create new healthy connections with available supports (the wisdom of the collective). Tinsley (2011) highlights the ways that Pan-African centered frameworks provide diverse and multiple expressions of gender and sexuality, exemplifying earthly manifestations of the magnitude of God/Goddess through the internal, liberated higher self. Through Afro-Indigenous consciousness, B♀LBQT women find deep meaning, direction, and affirmation in their identities, roles, and experiences, laying the groundwork for spiritual and psychological reconciliation and healing.

The Wounded Healer

Both authors identify within the spectrum of B♀LBQT women and recognize the significance of being wounded healers supporting B♀LBQT clients. Gresson (2015) defined the "*wounded healer* as one whose pain, wounds, and endurance have enabled her to be authentic with those receiving counsel" (p. 266). For the women she serves, the B♀LBQT healer becomes a mirrored reflection of resilience, perseverance, and the possibility of integrating self towards healing. The wounded healer must use "Self" to model vulnerability, exude compassion, and co-create hopeful alternatives (Gresson, 2015). The *wound* becomes an empathetic bridge that recognizes and intuitively understands the painful experiences which create the need for mental health intervention (Conchar & Repper, 2014). Duran (2019) further emphasized that bridging the wounded worlds of the healer and client does not make the relationship vulnerable, but rather becomes the primary source of healing. With this awareness, the role of healer-educator is paramount. In this process, the wounded healer helps to re-educate B♀LBQT women, providing a renewed understanding of the root of their emotional wounds. The healer-educator guides B♀LBQT women to uncover mistruths that became conditioned beliefs, such as being "tainted" or "an abomination." In these moments, re-education is essential to formulating healthy self-understanding, and the wounded healer-educator becomes a spiritual conduit to their client's mind, body, and spirit (Chapman et al., 2017).

In recent years, the realms of clinical and counseling psychology have come under increased scrutiny for their lack of cross-cultural application to populations that are not white, Western, heterosexual, male, or rich (Shiraev & Levy, 2020). Though clinical techniques have evolved greatly, traditionally "empirical" interventions may not be inclusive of the experiences of certain racial, cultural, sexual, and gender identities. B♀LBQT women face various challenges in the therapeutic interactions as it relates to a lack of integrating relative culturally sensitive models, not being in a supportive clinical environment that understands and integrates LGBTQ+ history and a lack of awareness of their institutional oppressions due to providers' unconscious racism and heteronormative biases, and denied feelings of homosexual social stigma (Reynolds et al., 2017). Although clinicians working with populations who face continued marginalization have the additional responsibility to create collaborative healing spaces and identify effective coping mechanisms, there is a lack of awareness of how to do so.

In the education and preparation of mental health clinicians, there are very few resources focused on best practices for supporting black clients, and even less for B♀LBQT women. There is a dearth of research and identified modalities that are specifically designed for treating mental illness in B♀LBQT women, causing a limited clinical understanding of the complex healing needs of this community (Russell & Fish, 2016). A lack of clinical understanding and research creates a widening gap in the treatment of B♀LBQT women and perpetuates further stigma against therapeutic care within black populations. In light of this gap, the authors have constructed their own therapeutic and educational techniques, influenced by their personal journeys as B♀LBQT women and healing practitioners.

Customizing Mental Health Supports

B♀LBQT women have developed unique survival adaptations to the systems and circumstances that repeatedly fragment their identities. Despite employing their own unique strategies for coping (i.e., code-switching, shape-shifting, self-naming, and chosen communities), as a way of surviving in the world, these strategies do not address the cumulative trauma and wounds that necessarily result from lifelong oppression. Kelly et al. (2020) explore how B♀LBQT women's experiences result in collective cultural trauma which manifests as the negative effects of "indelible and lasting" memories of "events or occurrences" that "[threaten] the community's existence or otherwise violates fundamental ideals that the community holds (p. 1524)." B♀LBQT women cannot escape the continuously traumatizing realities in which they survive, making standard (cognitive or thought focused) treatments somewhat ineffective for their healing. Any framework that would aim to promote B♀LBQT women's wellness *must* provide a process for acknowledging, soothing, and reconciling the wounded and fragmented parts of their identity. Jantz and Wall (2023) explore *identity reconciliation* as a process of hope and meaning making in the face of devastating circumstances, which is the combined result of navigating uncertainty, recognizing one's brokenness, finding bearings of hope, and managing grief. Identity reconciliation in B♀LBQT women is integral to promoting self-acceptance and balance through the creation of a unified self that is capable of healthy and dynamic personal, interpersonal, societal, and political functioning (Clegg, 2007).

The Intrapersonal Reconciliation Process

The Intrapersonal Reconciliation (IPR) process is an integrative therapeutic framework developed by Kimoré Reid through her work with adult B♀LBQT women. The IPR process engages Afro-Indigenous and queer consciousness as a means for customizing traditional treatment modalities to truly align with B♀LBQT women's healing needs. The IPR process builds on techniques used in Trauma-Informed Cognitive Behavioral Therapy (Goldstein et al., 2020), inner child healing (Capacchione, 1991), Narrative Exposure Therapy (Schauer et al., 2011), and intuitive feedback (Macdonald & Mellor-Clark, 2015) by helping B♀LBQT clients to understand each intervention through the lens of their own cultural values, norms, practices, and worldviews. This process of personal meaning making allows B♀LBQT clients to see the therapeutic process as an extension of their own sacred stories, an essential step in improving their mental health outcomes, emotional wellness, and identity development.

The conditions and environments in which B♀LBQT women are forced to survive often cause emotional disruption, identity fragmentation, and psychological trauma. Although the interventions that make up the foundation of the IPR process are based in white-centered psychological research, they were selected due to their general efficacy in treating trauma. In the same way that early practitioners of Haitian Vodou married Catholic and Afro-Indigenous spiritual practices, the IPR practitioner draws on inherent knowledge of black and queer cultural understandings to re-present clinical techniques in a way that resonates with the client. From the outset, the IPR practitioner understands the deep stigma against mental health treatment that often exists within black and Afro-Caribbean communities. With this understanding in mind, the practitioner will help the B♀LBQT client view their clinical symptoms as conditioned and overused survival tools that were employed by a past self (*inner child*) to become the present adult self. Throughout the process, the practitioner acts as assessor, healer, guide, and re-educator, helping the client to identify parallels between past and present, reconnect with fragmented identities, and take responsibility for their own healing. As treatment continues, the client learns to view their experiences from a space of compassion, embracing favorable and unfavorable parts of themselves equally. The primary focus of treatment is to create a strong sense of self, or *reconciled self*, that is capable of integrating past knowledge to navigate present challenges.

The IPR process progresses in a series of fluid, overlapping phases. The process begins with *assessment*, during which the practitioner gathers information about client needs and goals while building rapport by reinforcing the client's decision to start therapy and establishing a culturally relevant bond. During this phase, the practitioner encourages complete authenticity from the client, affirming the client's innate resilience factors. Thorough assessment will reveal initial issues or conflicts to be addressed. In the *self-care* phase, the practitioner assists the client in creating and practicing coping strategies to address the initial concerns. The practitioner takes on the role of healer-educator, teaching the client essential grounding, soothing, and stabilization skills necessary for later phases of treatment.

As the practitioner continues to reinforce safety, stability, and self-care, she will guide the client into the *psyche exploration* phase. During this phase, the practitioner uses present conflicts to gently probe into the client's history, keeping in mind that B♀LBQT women may naturally feel guarded in clinical settings. The practitioner anchors the client to the present while helping her to identify similar experiences from her past. In this phase, the client's defense mechanisms, or psychological "firewalls," may come up. The practitioner maintains a state of relaxed curiosity and acceptance, encouraging the client to look at her experiences and reactions from a space of neutrality. The *deep dive* phase is a second stage of psyche exploration, during which the practitioner may call out repetitive emotional cycles, behavior patterns, and core fears. Emotional responses brought up during the deep dive are used as an empathetic bridge between the client's past and present selves as the practitioner gently presses the client to compassionately face her subconscious patterns and drives.

Throughout the IPR process, the process of *renaming* will occur. In rural Jamaican communities, it was a traditional practice to rename sick or weak infants to protect them from malevolent spirits that could bring further illness. The process of renaming ties the essence of this tradition with cognitive behavioral and narrative techniques of reframing, as well as B♀LBQT women's liberating use of self-naming. Renaming is a re-education tool that encourages the client to use honest, accurate, helpful, and empowering words to create new meaning for uncomfortable or unfavorable parts of themselves or their experience, thus "protecting" these parts from further fragmentation. For example, defense mechanisms and toxic behavior patterns become "protectors" that deserve to be soothed rather than chastised. In the same vein, the client's experiences of trauma and discrimination become part of her "sacred story" to be revered and shared mindfully rather than hidden in shame.

The practitioner continues to guide the client through cognitive/emotional dissonance and subconscious firewalls until the inner child is identified. The realm of the inner child is the "ground floor" of the psyche, exposing the root circumstances, conditioning, and wounds that manifest as current symptoms. During the *inner child healing* phase, the practitioner and client explore the inner child's behaviors, emotions, fears, desires, and drives. Using specialized guided imagery techniques, the practitioner "introduces" the present adult self to the inner child self, facilitating the adult self's ability to give the inner child the compassion, care, guidance, and affection that she craves. The practitioner assists the client in identifying, unpacking, and renaming faulty thought patterns, beliefs, or defense mechanisms that come from the wounded inner child. During this phase, the practitioner will often assign therapeutic homework to help clients continue interactions with the inner child outside the session.

As the clinical process continues, deeper psychological wounds will present themselves, making it necessary for the practitioner and client to revisit previous phases repeatedly. As the client begins to show marked and consistent improvement, the process moves into its final stages, *reassessment*, and *reconciliation*. During reassessment, the practitioner reviews the client's progress and remaining barriers, while facilitating the development of essential soft skills (i.e., clear communication, appropriate boundaries, and maintaining self-care) with special attention to their unique social, familial, and systemic environments. During reconciliation, the practitioner may see an overall reduction in clinical symptoms as well as increased self-awareness, self-efficacy, and self-compassion. The client may explore new ways of being and living in alignment with her reconciled self, spending more time engaged in life activities and relationships that support her full authenticity. Sessions become less exploratory, and less frequent, and may transition to a coaching and planning format as the client prepares to discharge from care.

The Case of Jessica

Jessica is a black, queer woman from the American Midwest. Though her family was a well-established part of their small community, Jessica found herself extremely isolated from other black and queer identified women due to the largely white, heterosexual demographic of the area. Impacted by chronic illness, trauma, financial disparities, and racism, Jessica's parents were verbally/physically abusive and emotionally neglectful throughout her childhood and adolescence. As a pre-teen, Jessica lost several members of her family in a short period of time. While grieving, Jessica struggled through depression, anxiety, fragmentation, self-hatred, and abuse. Jessica sought solace at church, throwing herself into the Christian faith. At school and church, she was constantly forced to degrade her blackness and hide her queer identity to gain a modicum of acceptance. Despite her efforts Jessica was often singled out and mistreated by her teachers and peers and shamed by her church's doctrine. The compound effects of Jessica's upbringing developed into chronic PTSD, panic attacks, dissociative episodes, and suicidal ideation.

Reid used the IPR process as a new approach to Jessica's case. Though she had received previous trauma therapy, Jessica still experienced frequent dissociative episodes. During the assessment phase, Reid helped Jessica to identify the steps that led to dissociation. These episodes were renamed as a protective impulse, allowing Jessica to become curious about what the episodes were trying to protect her from. As they moved into self-care, Reid took note of Jessica's creative nature and love of the outdoors. Reid encouraged a self-care plan that incorporated creative writing, time in nature, and physical movement to create a stabilizing routine. As they moved into psyche exploration, Reid assisted Jessica in understanding that her dissociative behaviors were learned mechanisms that first appeared in early childhood as she faced continued social and familial abuse and chaos, without any emotional support. In the deep dive phase, the client became increasingly aware of her fear of questioning the imposing, abusive structures that had been there all her life-particularly her parents. Reid used the inner child healing phase to break through to various child-selves and helped Jessica to rename and release burdens of shame and self-blame. As part of a therapeutic assignment, Jessica "took" her child self to the library, one of her favorite places growing up. After the exercise, Jessica reported that she felt buoyant and found herself writing more freely than she had in a long time, as if her writing had suddenly returned to her.

Reid revisited phases throughout the process to assist Jessica in reconciling parts of her that grieved lost family members, struggled with panic and control, and tried desperately to fit into white, heterosexual, Christian standards while hiding who she really was. At each step in the process, Reid focused on the *meaning* that Jessica placed on her experiences, paying close attention to the emotions and beliefs she held about herself and others. As Jessica moved into the reassessment and reconciliation phases, she reported decreased panic attacks, no dissociative symptoms, increased self-care, increased desire to socialize, increased desire to honor her deceased relatives, and increased interest in Yoruba spirituality.

The Case of Marie-Anaïs

Désir utilized Reid's Intrapersonal Reconciliation Process as a framework with clients in her psycho-education spiritual program called the Black Androgynous Genius Project (BAGP) that provide mental health and life coaching services to Afro-Caribbean B♀LBQT women. The following is a case study of Marie-Anaïs (pseudonym), a young, Haitian trans woman who she worked with in reaching her goals of graduating college and adapting to her transition to an independent life in the United States. Marie-Anaïs began her transition in Haiti at the age of 14. Like many Caribbean countries, Haiti maintains a homophobic, heterosexist social culture that utilizes conservative Christian principles as the perceived societal norm. Within most Vodou spiritual communities and ceremonies, however, B♀LBQT women are accepted as part of the sacred space. The spiritual goddess/deity energy Ezili Dantor honors all her children, including her queer followers who honor her in return. Marie-Anaïs and her parents were part of a spiritual Vodou community and accepted her spiritual expression as a non-straight spirit. After her father—who was the primary breadwinner of the family—passed away, her mother became dependent on the support of family members who were not as open to Marie-Anaïs.

Facing this reality, Marie-Anaïs moved out of her family's home in search of a safe and accepting living environment. She continued to worship in the Vodou community and eventually gained support from Kourage (Courage), a Haitian LGBTQ organization that is often a target of violence. In November 2019, Charlot Jeudy, the director of Kourage was assassinated, like many out-queer people in Haiti who are targeted and attacked. Nonetheless, Marie-Anaïs obtained a scholarship for beauty school and was hired as a hairdresser, though she was paid far less than her cisgender colleagues. With this money, she lived in a slum neighborhood and managed to pay her high-school fees.

At the age of 17, Marie-Anaïs migrated to the United States with her mother to live with a maternal aunt. At first her aunt appeared accepting, but soon labeled Marie-Anaïs as a curse and forced her out on the streets. She faced complex layers of social isolation, physical/verbal attacks, racism, and transphobia that were culturally unfamiliar. With these layered complications, she found herself a senior in high school, homeless, and a stranger to the societal norms of this country. She was in survival mode and desperately needed support to achieve her educational goals, meet her psychological needs, and reaffirm her sacred, spiritual worth.

Known for her work as a Haitian Vodou spiritual healer-educator and school psychologist, Désir was contacted by the LGBTQ coordinator in Marie-Anaïs' school district. Désir created the Androgynous Genius Project, which is psycho-spiritual coaching program primarily for B♀LBQT young women of Caribbean descent. When Désir first met Marie-Anaïs she began to speak in Haitian Creole. Immediately feeling a sense of cultural connection, she disclosed her acceptance and connection to Vodou as well as her current feelings of isolation and brokenness. They began a journey together in supporting Marie-Anaïs' academic goals, providing community resources, and establishing a culturally relevant healing relationship.

The IPR process (Reid-Merritt, 2019a) provided a procedure to support Marie-Anaïs' psycho-educational needs. As the framework outlines, the assessment phase established a cultural bond based on their shared Haitian spirituality and worldview which naturally established rapport and trust. Speaking in Haitian Creole allowed Marie-Anaïs to divulge the significance of Vodou as the primary context for her grounded self-understanding and her parents' acceptance of her gender identity and expression. Through the self-care phase, they co-created a self-care process which included maintaining her feminine appearance, creating positive affirmations, and maintaining a daily schedule that included educational responsibilities and self-care practices. During the psyche exploration phase, Marie-Anaïs began to speak about her daily life in Haiti, the death of her father, and her transition to the United States. Through her stories, Désir came to realize Marie-Anaïs' ambition to further her education and live a life of healthy independence. She would say, "I want a life like everyone else, to have a spouse, children, and my own family."

During the deep dive phase, Marie-Anaïs had established housing and began her post high school training at a community college. Désir identified problematic psychological patterns, poor study habits and reactive patterns due to feelings of loneliness, sadness, and shame. When these emotions were overwhelming, Marie-Anaïs could not concentrate on studying. Instead, she focused on the memories of her aunt's verbal abuse, and worried about her mother who remained in that household. Désir helped Marie-Anaïs to recognize, soothe, and shift her thoughts through listening to music, makeup design, cooking, and singing Vodou folklore music.

Although Marie-Anaïs began "adulting" at 14 years old, she believed that her innate intelligence, God, and the Vodou spirits guided her. She still lamented and grieved for the child that her parents accepted, and the loss of her father's protection after he died. Désir used visual journey techniques to help Marie-Anaïs retell and reconstruct her childhood history, telling the story many times, adding different nuances forgotten with each telling. Together they worked on healing, loving, and reparenting this grieving child towards confident adulthood in the United States. The inner child healing phase allowed Marie-Anaïs to identify areas of trauma and endurance in her childhood and reimagine the possibilities for her future.

Legally claiming her feminine name and gender, creating spaces for a chosen family, and shifting her expectations of her biological mother to defend and protect her led Marie-Anaïs naturally to the reassessment phase. In this stage, Marie-Anaïs began to claim her agency. She was able to step out of herself, maintain a sustained awareness of her thought patterns, and continue her progress toward a healthy independent life. The reconciliation phase is still ongoing. After three years of support, Marie-Anaïs continues to work toward her goals, though meetings with Désir have reduced from weekly to monthly. Their work together continues to ground Marie-Anaïs in her strengths and spirituality as essential tools for obtaining her educational and personal life goals.

A New Path

In the United States, clinicians and educators—who play a pivotal role in the well-being and success of people of color—are typically trained in white, Western, middle-class paradigms fraught with stereotypes and prejudice. Culturally relevant worldviews are rarely visible or engaged to understand and heal those who are made vulnerable by inequitable systems, as unconscious/intrinsic bias and systemic oppression abound. This chapter has captured a small facet of B♀LBQT women's experiences of invisibility, trauma, and resiliency, and provided a model of care and a program of advocacy with a psycho-educational lens integrating and Afro-centered approaches to supporting their psychological and educational healing beyond symptom management. The authors invite clinicians and educators to move beyond the exclusive healing of the mind and emotions to include culturally relevant approaches that also heal the spirit.

In the midst of the Haitian revolution, colonizers were losing the liberation war to the enslaved people who sang "nou tout se zanj o, zanj ambarase mwen"—*we are all sacred, sacred angels surround us*. To this day, this chant opens sacred Vodou spiritual ceremonies. It is our sincerest hope this chapter will continue the legacy of acknowledging and building systems in which all people are valued and considered sacred including B♀LBQT women.

The entertainment milieu and social media outlets cannot be the primary sources of support and solutions for B♀LBQT women's healing and wellness needs. There is an immediate need for trained mental health practitioners who understand aspects of their spiritual and socio-political positionalities with the skills to facilitate healing as a process of re-education. The issues of B♀LBQT and solutions need to come from black spaces, practitioners, and black consciousness theories such as the double consciousness theory, standpoint theory, third-world feminist theory, and critical race feminism (Crenshaw et al., 1995), as a foundational stage of learning towards a more culturally sensitive lens in the mental health field. Culturally aware clinicians and educators must act as models for this process of mourning and re-building and provide resources that B♀LBQT women can access to facilitate post-traumatic growth (Blodgett & Dorado, 2016; Gross, 2018). Afro-Indigenous religions can play a central role in this process of reclaiming name, space, and spirit. Both authors claim a level of African diasporic ancestral knowing that is inextricable from their commitment to healing the minds *and* spirits of the populations they serve. The authors acknowledge that there is a certain level of *witch-doctory—vodou magic* in what they do; that their daily work is grounded in their own Afro-indigenous consciousness. It is the marrying of art and science, spirituality, psychology, and education, that will create inclusive institutions and ideologies that hold space for the gifts that B♀LBQT woman have to offer.

Clinicians and educators are in desperate need of professional development opportunities that focus on the dynamics of working with people with extreme intersectionality such as B♀LBQT women. Loewen (2014) expressed:

> [T]he queer black woman stands at the convergence of every aspect of the Euro-centric, heteropatriarchal oppression, so it's her voice that should ring the loudest, her interest that must become central if the oppression to all Blacks, queers, and women shall ever come to an end.
>
> *(p. 163)*

The use of The Reid IPR process for Désir and Reid's work with their clients provided a framework for connection through story-telling rather than traditional clinical assessment. This unique model builds on these frameworks to better understand and support the intersectionality of B♀LBQT women. This healing journey should include black community practitioners and allies that simultaneously play the role of therapist-healer and teacher-coach who have a critical awareness of socio-political and spiritual positionality of B♀LBQT women.

References

Afua, Q. (2001). *Sacred woman: A guide to healing the feminine body, mind, and spirit*. One World/Ballantine.

Allen, S. E. (2019). Doing black Christianity: Reframing black church scholarship. *Sociology Compass*, *13*(10), e12731.

Apugo, D. (2019). A hidden culture of coping: Insights on African American women's existence in predominately white institutions. *Multicultural Perspectives*, *21*(1), 53–62.

Bailey, J. A. (2015). *The Ankh of African tradition*. Retrieved September 13, 2020, from https://theievoice.com/the-ankh-of-african-tradition/

Bell, L. A. (2016). Theoretical foundations for social justice education. In M. Adams, L. A. Bell, D. J. Goodman, & K. Y. Joshi (Eds.), *Teaching for diversity and social justice* (3rd ed., pp. 3–26). Routledge.

Bierema, L. (2020). Ladies and gentlemen, your implicit bias is showing: Gender hegemony and its impact on HRD research and practice. *Human Resource Development International, 23*(5), 473–490. https://doi.org/10.1080/13678868.2020.180925

Blodgett, C., & Dorado, J. (2016). A selected review of trauma-informed school practice and alignment with educational practice. *CLEAR Trauma Center. University of California, 1*, 1–88.

Capacchione, L. (1991). *Recovery of your inner child: The highly acclaimed method for liberating your inner self.* Simon and Schuster.

Carter, C., & Baliko, K. (2017). "These are not my people": Queer sport spaces and the complexities of community. *Leisure Studies, 36*(5), 696–707.

Chapman, D. A., Durban-Albrecht, E. L., & LaMothe, M. (2017). Nou mache ansanm (We walk together): Queer Haitian performance and affiliation. *Women and Performance: A Journal of Feminist Theory, 27*(2), 143–159.

Clegg, C. (2007). Embracing a threatening other: Identity and reconciliation in Northern Ireland. *International Journal of Public Theology, 1*(2), 173–187.

Conchar, C., & Repper, J. (2014). "Walking wounded or wounded healer?" Does personal experience of mental health problems help or hinder mental health practice? A review of the literature. *Mental Health and Social Inclusion, 18*(1), 35–44.

Crenshaw, K. W. (2013). Mapping the margins: Intersectionality, identity politics, and violence against women of color. In *The public nature of private violence* (pp. 93–118). Routledge.

Crenshaw, K. W., Gotanda, N., Peller, G., & Thomas, K. (1995). *Critical race theory. The key writings that formed the movement.* The New Press.

Douglas, K. B. (2004). The black church and the politics of sexuality. In *Loving the body* (pp. 347–362). Palgrave Macmillan.

Duran, E. (2019). *Healing the soul wound: Trauma-informed counseling for Indigenous communities.* Teachers College Press.

Everhart, J. S. (2004). Serving women and their mirrors: A feminist reading of exodus 38: 8b. *The Catholic Biblical Quarterly, 66*(1), 44–54.

Foster, K. (2018). How do black people navigate white worlds? Shape-shifting. *The Guardian*, p. 7.

Ghisyawan, K. (2016). Social erotics: The fluidity of love, desire, and friendship for same-sex loving women in Trinidad. *Journal of International Women's Studies, 17*(3), 17–31.

Glave, T. (Ed.). (2008). *Our Caribbean: A gathering of lesbian and gay writing from the Antilles.* Duke University Press.

Goldstein, E., Benton, S. F., & Barrett, B. (2020). Health risk behaviors and resilience among low-income, black primary care patients: Qualitative findings from a trauma-informed primary care intervention study. *Family & Community Health, 43*(3), 187–199.

Gresson, A. D. (2015). POSTSCRIPT: Relational justice and the pedagogy of the wounded healer. *Counterpoints, 476*, 215–232.

Gross, R. (2018). *The psychology of grief.* Routledge.

Hamilton, T. G. (2020). Black immigrants and the changing portrait of Black America. *Annual Review of Sociology, 46*(4), 295–313. https://doi.org.ezproxy.fiu.edu/10.1146/annurev-soc-121919-054728

Human Rights Campaign. (2021). *Glossary of terms.* www.hrc.org/resources/glossary-of-terms

Imhotep, A. (2010, March). Reinterpretations of the ankh symbol: Emblem of a Master Teacher. *Semantic Scholar.*www.semanticscholar.org/paper/Reinterpretations-of-the-ANKH-symbol

Imhotep, A. (2017, April). Reinterpretations of the ankh symbol part 2. *Yumpu.* www.yumpu.com/en/document/view/7207535/reinterpretations-of-the-ankh-symbol-part-2-asar-imhotep

Jantz, G. L. P., & Wall, K. (2023). *Triumph over trauma: Find healing and wholeness from past pain.* Baker Books.

Juang, R. (2013). Transgendering the politics of recognition. In *The transgender studies reader* (pp. 722–736). Routledge.

Ka'ahumanu, L., & Hutchins, L. (2015). *Bi any other name: Bisexual people speak out.* Riverdale Avenue Books LLC.

Kelly, M., Lubitow, A., Town, M., & Mercier, A. (2020). Collective trauma in queer communities. *Sexuality & Culture*, 1–22.

King, K. L. (Ed.). (1997). *Women and goddess traditions: In antiquity and today* (p. 17). Fortress Press.

Lewis, M. M., & Miller, S. J. (2018). How does it feel to be a problem? A conversation between two feminist black queer femme chairs. *Feminist Formations, 30*(3), 79–90.

Loewen, K. D. (2014). Reframing hate crimes: Identifying and combatting the systems of violent oppression that converge upon queer black women. *Women's Rights Law Reporter, 36*, 137.

Macdonald, J., & Mellor-Clark, J. (2015). Correcting psychotherapists' blind sidedness: Formal feedback as a means of overcoming the natural limitations of therapists. *Clinical Psychology & Psychotherapy, 22*(3), 249–257.

Malta, M., Cardoso, R., Montenegro, L., de Jesus, J. G., Seixas, M., Benevides, B., das Dores Silva, M., LeGrand, S., & Whetten, K. (2019). Sexual and gender minorities rights in Latin America and the Caribbean: A multi-country evaluation. *BMC International Health and Human Rights, 19*(1), 1–16.

Marinucci, M. (2016). *Feminism is queer: The intimate connection between queer and feminist theory.* Zed Books Ltd.

Means, D. R., Collier, J., Bazemore-James, C., Williams, B. M., Coleman, R., & Wadley, B. A. (2018). "Keep your spirit aligned": A case study on black lesbian, gay, bisexual, and queer students defining and practicing spirituality. *Journal of College Student Development, 59*(5), 618–623.

Melton, M. (2020). What god hath put together: Hurston, black queer love, and the act of creation. *The Langston Hughes Review, 26*(1), 1–28.

Momen, R. E., & Dilks, L. M. (2020). Examining case outcomes in US transgender homicides: An exploratory investigation of the intersectionality of victim characteristics. *Sociological Spectrum, 41*(1), 1–27.

Olyan, S. M. (1994). "And with a male you shall not lie the lying down of a woman": On the meaning and significance of Leviticus 18: 22 and 20: 13. *Journal of the History of Sexuality, 5*(2), 179–206.

Parker, A. N. (2018). One womanist's view of racial reconciliation in Galatians. *Journal of Feminist Studies in Religion, 34*(2), 23–40.

Peek, M. E., Lopez, F. Y., Williams, H. S., Xu, L. J., McNulty, M. C., Acree, M. E., & Schneider, J. A. (2016). Development of a conceptual framework for understanding shared decision making among African-American LGBT patients and their clinicians. *Journal of General Internal Medicine, 31*(6), 677–687.

Petrosky, E., Blair, J. M., Betz, C. J., Fowler, K. A., Jack, S. P., & Lyons, B. H. (2017). Racial and ethnic differences in homicides of adult women and the role of intimate partner violence—United States, 2003–2014. *Morbidity and Mortality Weekly Report, 66*(28), 741–746.

Reid-Merritt, P. (2019a). *The intrapersonal reconciliation (IPR) process* [Unpublished manuscript].

Reid-Merritt, P. (2019b). *A state-by-state history of race and racism in the United States* (2 Vols.). Greenwood.

Reynolds, A. L., Singh, A. A., Kopala, M., & Keitel, M. (2017). *Counseling issues for lesbian, bisexual, transgender, and queer women.* SAGE.

Rich, A. C. (2003). Compulsory heterosexuality and lesbian existence (1980). *Journal of Women's History, 15*(3), 11–48.

Rogers, R. R. (2006). *Afro-Caribbean immigrants and the politics of incorporation: Ethnicity, exception, or exit.* Cambridge University Press.

Russell, S. T., & Fish, J. N. (2016). Mental health in lesbian, gay, bisexual, and transgender (LGBT) youth. *Annual Review of Clinical Psychology, 12*, 465–487.

Schauer, M., Schauer, M., Neuner, F., & Elbert, T. (2011). *Narrative exposure therapy: A short-term treatment for traumatic stress disorders.* Hogrefe Publishing.

Shiraev, E. B., & Levy, D. A. (2020). *Cross-cultural psychology: Critical thinking and contemporary applications.* Routledge.

Sivanandan, A. (2019). *Communities of resistance: Writings on black struggles for socialism.* Verso.

Stanford, A. (2013). *Homophobia in the black church: How faith, politics, and fear divide the black community.* ABC-CLIO.

Tinsley, O. E. N. (2011). Songs for Ezili: Vodou epistemologies of (trans) gender. *Feminist Studies, 37*(2), 417–436.

Tinsley, O. E. N. (2018). *Ezili's mirrors: Imagining black queer genders.* Duke University Press.

Young, T. N. (2016). *Black queer ethics, family, and philosophical imagination.* Palgrave Macmillan.

III

Law, Political Structures, and Policy

12

OVERVIEW OF LEGISLATIVE, JUDICIAL, AND EXECUTIVE BRANCH U.S. POLICIES IMPACTING THE RIGHTS AND RISKS OF TRANSGENDER AND NONBINARY PEOPLE IN THE WORKPLACE

Gina R. Rosich

In the United States, a complex evolving history exists over the fight for employment rights among people who are transgender or nonbinary. Between litigation and legislation on local to federal levels, activists have been fighting for trans rights since the emergence of a collective political trans identity (Stryker, 2008a; Taylor et al., 2018). The legal landscape over the last several decades has ranged from one of slow progress and evolving local and judicial support, to one of retraction and outright hostility from the Executive Branch of government under the Trump administration (NCTE, 2020; Taylor et al., 2018). Employment rights are important to all members of the LGBTQ community but trans and nonbinary individuals face unique challenges that require specific legal protections. The purpose of this chapter is to give a brief overview of the history of judicial, legislative, and executive actions, and apply the concepts of cisgender entitlement and transmisogyny to frame the underpinnings of discrimination and rights protections. Readers should be able to gain a sense of why this information is needed as part of ongoing research and advocacy work in pursuit of advancing employment rights for transgender and nonbinary people.

Key Terms and Concepts of Gender That Frame the Legal Context

Sex refers to one's biological sex, which is assigned at birth (sex assigned at birth [SAAB]), and in medical terms, it is based on visible and internal reproductive organs, chromosomes, pheno-type, and hormonal patterns (Greenberg, 2006; Russell & Viggiani, 2018). Biological sex is not an inviolable binary, however. Grabham (2007) cites that between 1 in 1,500 and 1 in 2,000 babies are born with or later discovered to have an intersex condition or traits. Witchel (2018) estimates this to be roughly .02%–.05% of the population.

 DOI: 10.4324/9781003128151-15

Gender is a social construct commonly viewed as a binary, with two socially imposed opposites—male and female. The terms male and female are used to convey two sexes with corresponding genders: male-sexed bodies are masculine *boys* or *men*, and female-sexed bodies are feminine *girls* or *women*. Sex and gender are often conflated. Conflating the words *sex* and *gender* so that they are used interchangeably stems from the unspoken assumption that genitals define gender (Rothenberg, 2017). Viewing gender as a distinct and immutable binary is known as gender essentialism (Stargel & Bell, 2022). Outside of the constraints of a binary system individuals can embrace a multiplicity of genders. Thus, biological sex, internal or *unconscious* gender identity, social gender, and gender presentation need not be inextricably linked. Gender identity is a person's internal, subconscious, deeply felt sense of self as a gendered person whether male, female, neither, or something in between (Serano, 2007). Individuals may have a gender identity or presentation that differs from their biological sex assigned at birth, may have been born with an intersex condition, and/or may make gender expression choices without feeling incongruence between their gender identity and biological sex. Individuals who experience incongruence between their gender identity and sex assigned at birth are commonly referred to under the umbrella term transgender. Those who experience no incongruence between their sex assigned at birth and gender identity are referred to as cisgender (or cis), a linguistic terminological counterpart to transgender (Currah, 2006; Serano, 2007; Stryker, 2008a). As language evolves, those who feel their identities fall outside of the male/female binary have utilized other terms to self-identify including nonbinary, gender nonconforming, gender expansive, two spirit, and genderqueer (Puckett et al., 2020). In this chapter, the term nonbinary will be used to reflect these varied identities. However, the term gender nonconforming (GNC) will be used to mirror the language as specifically used within research cited in this chapter.

All people—cis, trans, and nonbinary—have a gender presentation. Gender presentation can change and is not exclusively tied to trans-identified individuals since anyone can opt to have a more feminine or masculine appearance in hair, clothing, and other grooming choices. Gender presentation is a key component of a trans individual's life and transitioning can be a time of significant vulnerability. Transition includes a number of steps and individuals often endure scrutiny regarding appearance, motives, and medical choices in conversations about their transition process (Kirk & Belovis, 2008; Tobin, 2011). Someone transitioning male-to-female would say she is *presenting as female*. Transition can be social (change of name and/or pronouns, change of legal identifying documents), medical (hormones, gender-confirming surgeries, hair removal), non-medical (clothing, grooming choices), or a combination of all of these. Whether the transition includes social, medical, or non-medical measures depends on individual personal, financial, or health needs and resources (Gehi & Arkles, 2007; Martin & Yonkin, 2006). Government-wide standards for changing one's legal gender are inconsistent. One state (Tennessee) explicitly prohibits gender marker changes on birth certificates (NCTE, 2021). Other states require documented medical and/or mental health treatment to change documentation, creating potentially significant barriers to basic citizenship rights. The right to vote, marry, and travel can become problematic when there is a mismatch between a person's appearance, name, pronoun usage, and the information listed on their documentation (Cray & Harrison, 2012).

Cisgender people maintain their gender identity in social alignment with their sex assigned at birth. Their gender expression does not give cause for concern, scrutiny, or discussion. The unearned advantage of evading scrutiny for their identity is called cisgender (or cis) privilege. Trans people do not evade this scrutiny and historically have had to either prove themselves as acceptable, pass (or blend) so that their trans-ness is invisible, or face treatment that is invalidating of their gender identity. This stems from cisgender entitlement, which is the belief by cis people that they can set standards of acceptability for gender presentation in the workplace. The development and imposition of gender standards, coupled with scrutinizing to determine acceptability, is known as gender gatekeeping (Serano, 2007). This manifests in a variety of ways that make it difficult for trans people to navigate the workplace.

Trans women face a particular and intersectional burden under the scrutiny of cisgender entitlement in that they are simultaneously expected to conform to a heavily scrutinized and narrow definition of femininity while simultaneously having their gender identity questioned and being devalued both for being women and for being trans. This is called transmisogyny (Serano, 2007).

Misgendering is the deliberate and consistent misuse of incorrect pronouns and pre-transition name. It has been found to produce feelings of stigmatization and loss of self-esteem around personal appearance (McLemore, 2018). The use of correct pronouns signals acceptance, affirmation, and conveys value and respect (Dietert & Dentice, 2009; Thoroughgood et al., 2020).

Employment Discrimination: Prevalence and Examples

According to the Movement Advancement Project (2020), approximately 4.5% of the U.S. population are identified as LGBTQ. The Williams Institute estimates that 0.6% or 1.4 million adults are identified specifically as transgender (Flores et al., 2016). Stroumsa (2014) estimates that 1 in 11,900 to 1 in 45,000 U.S. adults are MtF and 1 in 30,400 to 1 in 200,000 are FtM individuals.

Information on employment discrimination against transgender and GNC people comes largely from community-based cross-sectional studies that employ convenience sampling. The National Transgender Discrimination Survey (NTDS), the first national study on transgender discrimination, was sponsored by the National Center for Transgender Equality (NCTE) and the National Gay and Lesbian Task Force (NGLTF) and released in 2011. In their study (n = 6,456), Grant et al. (2011) found 47% of respondents reported facing job discrimination, while 90% reported being mistreated or harassed at work. NCTE followed this with the United States Transgender Survey (USTS) (n = 27,715). In the USTS, 67% of all respondents reported discrimination in relation to hiring, firing, or denial of promotions while 77% of employed respondents reported taking measures to avoid gender identity and expression-related workplace mistreatment (James et al., 2015). Smaller studies corroborate these findings, such as Minter and Daley (2003) (n = 155) who found nearly one of every two respondents in San Francisco had experienced employment discrimination. The Transgender Law Center (TLC) statewide study (n = 646) found about 67% of respondents in the state of California reported experiencing one or more types of mistreatment in the workplace (Hartzell et al., 2009). A study in Virginia (n = 387) found 41% of participants reported transgender-related discrimination, among them 22% specifying the discrimination to be employment related (Bradford et al., 2013). In a Coloradan study (n = 3,838), 50% of transgender participants reported workplace discrimination experiences as compared to 25.1% of their cisgender LGBQ counterparts (Kattari et al., 2016). An average of 40% of respondents in a cross-study analysis faced job discrimination (MAP, 2009).

Trans and GNC people face a broad range of negative workplace experiences, beginning with hiring biases during the interview process. Once employed, workplace harassment can be both aggressive and subtle, explicit, and covert. In numerous studies, trans people repeatedly and consistently reported having experienced the indignities of daily hostile work environments

(Broadus, 2006; Grant et al., 2011; Hartzell et al., 2009; James et al., 2015; MAP, 2013). Hostile work environments involved general harassment, gossiping, deliberate misgendering, threats of or actual workplace violence, being outed as a trans person (among other privacy breaches), scrutiny of dress code adherence and overall appearance, compulsory wearing of uniforms not in line with the person's self-identified gender, plus restrictions on the use of sex segregated bathrooms and changing areas. These incidents can be humiliating, make work life intolerable, and ultimately make work life both traumatic and unsafe for trans employees (MAP, 2013; Sangganjanavanich & Cavazos, 2010). Misgendering and hostilities around bathroom access are the most frequently reported forms of microaggressions (James et al., 2015; Nadal et al., 2016). Safety in the workplace should be guaranteed as a basic human right. Yet, in the USTS study (James et al., 2015), 23% of employed transgender and gender-nonconforming respondents reported experiences of extreme mistreatment that ranged from verbal harassment to physical attack and sexual assault. A staggering range of performance-evaluation-related hostilities have also been documented including demotions, being overly supervised and scrutinized coupled with deliberately negative reviews, and termination for non-performance reasons. A meta-analysis of 50 studies conducted between 1996 and 2006 found that 56% of trans people reported being fired, 13–47% denied employment, 22–31% harassed, and 19% denied a promotion (Badgett et al., 2007). In the NTDS, among the 90% of respondents reported being mistreated or harassed at work, 26% reported losing their jobs, 23% denied a promotion, and 47% denied a job specifically because of being transgender (Grant et al., 2011).

Impact of Workplace Discrimination on Other Areas of Life

Exposure to trans-related stigma and discrimination is known to have negative mental health impacts including anxiety, depression, and attempted suicide (Clements-Nolle, 2006; Bockting et al., 2013; Yang et al., 2015). Stigma and discrimination among transgender and gender-nonconforming individuals produces a near constant expectation of rejection, which induces stress. In the workplace, avoiding situations where rejection is anticipated is not always possible (Rood et al., 2016). This includes bathrooms, which are contested spaces rooted in unsubstantiated transphobic fears of safety and privacy (Hasenbush et al., 2019). The scrutiny and harassment trans people experience around bathroom usage are a systemic microaggression exemplifying cisgender entitlement and institutionalized bullying (Nadal et al., 2016; Serano, 2007; Sudbeck, 2019). In the USTS (James et al., 2015), 59% of respondents reported avoiding the use of public restrooms out of fear of confrontation. A common tactic is to limit the amount of food and drink consumed. Unsurprisingly, 8% of respondents reported restroom avoidance that resulted in kidney infections, urinary tract infections, or other kidney problems.

Regular employment is integral to financial, mental, and overall stability. A sense of well-being in the workplace has positive impact on mental and physical health, social relationships, subjective well-being, and engenders a sense of purpose (Gates, 2010). Conversely, workplace mistreatment and irregular employment impact other areas of life. Depression, anxiety, somatization, substance abuse, and suicide are reported outcomes when trans people experience chronic poor treatment (Clements-Nolle et al., 2006; dickey & Budge, 2020; Tebbe & Moradi, 2016). No less than 40% of trans people have made at least one suicide attempt (dickey & Budge, 2020). Unemployment, gender-based discrimination, and gender-based victimization (both verbal and physical) are among factors associated with attempted suicide (Clements-Nolle et al., 2006).

Unemployment rates are higher among trans people than the general population, and unemployment leads to poverty. Unemployment rates among trans people are three times higher than the national unemployment rate and nearly one-third (29%) of their respondents live in poverty (James et al., 2015). In one study, 60% of respondents reported being unemployed (Badgett et al., 2007) and a later study found 29.4% of trans-identified participants living in poverty (Badgett et al., 2019) with the likelihood of living in poverty higher among people of color, young adults, and people with disabilities. The impact of multiple marginalized identities cannot be underestimated when examining the lives of trans people. Black and brown trans women face greater barriers to healthcare access and housing, and higher rates than their white counterparts in unemployment, poverty, violence (including murder), police harassment, and other experiences of oppression (Chang & Singh, 2016; NCTE, 2019).

Legislative History

Protections against employment discrimination have been a goal for LGBTQ activists in the United States since the pre-Stonewall era when the Mattachine Society and Daughters of Bilitis first marched for employment rights in 1957 (Kohler, 2011). Although not transgender-specific because trans activism was not in the vernacular at the time, it is important to include early lesbian and gay civil rights efforts because of the long history of collective (and sometimes divisive) activism around the longstanding failure to secure protective employment legislation. Post-Stonewall, trans and gender-nonconforming people were subsumed along with gay men, lesbians, and bisexuals under the term "gay" for over a decade (Gan, 2007). Indeed, a collective trans identity as a political force only started gaining real traction in the 1990s when trans activists began to pressure lesbian and gay political advocacy organizations for inclusion (Taylor et al., 2018).

The Employment Non-Discrimination Act (ENDA) has been the primary piece of legislative advocacy, since it was first introduced in 1974 by Bella Abzug and Edward Koch as the Equality Act of 1974. They sought to ban discrimination in housing, employment, and public accommodations based on sexual orientation, gender, and marital status. The bill never made it out of committee until its reintroduction in 1994. First voted in the Senate in 1996, it was narrowly defeated by a vote of 59 to 49 (Althauer & Greenberg, 2011; Button et al., 1997; Gates, 2010; Stryker, 2008).

The 1996 bill did not include gender identity or gender expression provisions as these were emerging concepts, and trans activism was still too early in its development to influence public policy (Mananzala & Spade, 2008). Trans inclusion in the lesbian and gay community has a tumultuous and still-evolving relationship. As the lesbian and gay movement grew more inclusive of trans issues, activists started using the term LGBT (and later LGBTQ) for a more cohesive social movement. LGBTQ organizations started to recognize how gender-normative binary expectations on appearance and behavior negatively affected all members of the community. Organizations such as the National Gay and Lesbian Task Force (NGLTF, now the "Task Force"), Lambda Legal, and PFLAG supported trans inclusion in ENDA (Currah et al., 2008; Stone, 2009). The Human Rights Campaign (HRC) faced criticism for years for failing to support trans inclusion and prioritizing the interests of monied white gay assimilationist constituents (Juro, 2016; Molloy, 2014; Stryker, 2008a). Assimilationist activists favored an image of homonormativity, which is an approach to normalize same-sex relationships by eschewing gay stereotypes and promoting "straight acting" appearances to increase the comfort level of affluent and middle class white straight people. The goal of this approach was to gain social and political inclusion through acceptance (Stryker, 2008b)

ENDA was reintroduced in every Congress between 1994 and 2003 except the 109th Congress. The 2007 reintroduction by Rep. Barney Frank and three other legislators was a litmus test for the transgender rights movement when, for the first time, both sexual orientation and gender-identity protections were included (Althauer & Greenberg, 2011). However, after it failed to pass in 2007, Rep. Barney Frank (D-MA) attempted to split the bill in two in the hopes that protections for lesbians and gays would pass if transgender discrimination was excluded. Excluding provisions designed to protect trans people such as adherence to dress codes and use of restrooms in line with a worker's gender identity created a division among LGBTQ activists. The Human Rights Campaign (HRC) supported Rep. Frank's strategy. Transgender activists felt that they had been sacrificed for the sake of lesbians and gays, marginalizing and displacing trans people and making them second-class citizens within the LGBTQ movement (Molloy, 2014; Vitulli, 2010). This version of ENDA passed the House on November 7, 2007, on a vote of 235 to 184 but was never acted on by the Senate where Democrats had only a very slight majority. HRC now publicly supports inclusion of gender identity and gender expression in ENDA (introduced most recently as The Equality Act in the 117th Congress). This history highlights the tenuous standing trans and GNC people faced in fighting for inclusion. The support for a united ENDA marks a milestone in the LGBTQ rights movement as reflected in the consistent inclusion of trans people within LGBTQ legislative activism since 2007 (Johnson, 2017).

As of November 2020, a total of 22 states plus two territories and the District of Columbia have laws prohibiting employment discrimination based on both sexual orientation and gender identity. Six states interpret their existing nondiscrimination laws to include sexual orientation and/or gender identity, while in 22 states trans people have no laws explicitly protecting their employment rights. MAP (2020) estimates that 33% of LGBTQ adults live in states without employment discrimination law protections.

Title VII of the Civil Rights Act (see Landmark Cases) protects certain classes of workers and applicants from discrimination. It does not cover protections in public accommodations, housing, or healthcare. A number of states have hosted anti-transgender legislative initiatives that threaten the freedom and rights of trans people such as public restroom bills and the exclusion of trans students in school sports via Title IX (Levenson & Vigdor, 2020; Wang et al., 2016). Title IX of the Education Amendments of 1972 prohibits discrimination on the basis of sex in federally funded educational programs and activities (Office for Civil Rights, 2021).

Landmark Cases

In the United States, court decisions are made through the concept of legal precedent. In the absence of precedent, the courts interpret the meaning of a law by considering the language of the statute as understood when the Act was codified into law, the purpose of the law, intent of the legislators, and the circumstances when enacted.

On the Problem of Sex

Employment discrimination protection and redress have rested on Title VII of the Civil Rights Act of 1964, which was enacted to protect job applicants and employees from employment discrimination based on the categories of sex, race, color, religion, and national origin. The Act applies to employers with at least 15 employees (Civil Rights Act, 1964; Reeves & Decker, 2001). The category of sex has been contested since the inception of Title VII. Rep. Howard Smith (D-VA) added sex two days before the vote in Congress. His intentions are still debated. The speculation is he added sex because either he backed women's rights or he opposed protections against racial discrimination and assumed adding sex would be objectionable enough that the bill would fail (Clough, 2000; Freeman, 1991; Lee, 2012). This complicates the ability of judges to base decisions on the original intentions of the law.

To file a claim under Title VII, a plaintiff must demonstrate their case falls under one of the protected categories enumerated in the statute. In the early decades after the initial passing of the law, the courts of the 1970s and 1980s were skeptical that Title VII should cover the rights of trans people (who were referred to as transsexuals at that time). Given the contested nature of sex under Title VII, transgender litigants seeking remedy for sex discrimination faced inconsistent interpretations and judges tended to favor a narrow *plain meaning* of sex based on biology (i.e., visible sex organs). Litigants sought a broader definition of sex that included gender identity, change of sex, gender stereotyping, gender nonconformity, and gender expression (Cail & Wang, 2008; Lee, 2012; Reeves & Decker, 2001; Turner, 2007).

Among the earliest cases tried under Title VII were *Voyles v. Ralph K Davis Medical Center (1975)*, *Grossman v. Bernards Township Board of Education* (1976), and *Holloway v. Arthur Andersen & Co* (1977). In the Voyles case, a hemodialysis technician was terminated after informing her employer of her plan to transition from male to female. The U.S. District Court in California granted the defendant's motion to dismiss the plaintiff's complaint reasoning that "change of sex" or "sexual preference" were not mentioned in the statute of Title VII. Nor, the court reasoned, was there any case law or legislative history indicating any congressional intent to "embrace 'transsexual discrimination' or any permutation or combination thereof" (Broadus, 2006, p. 95).

In *Grossman v. Bernards Township Board of Education* (1976), the plaintiff was a grade school music teacher who was fired after undergoing gender-confirming surgery. The decision rested in part on the belief that the teacher's transition would cause psychological harm to the students, which meant the plaintiff could not properly fulfill her role—thereby establishing her incapacity to teach. Yet she was not stripped of her right to teach elsewhere, presumably where students would not be aware of her sex change (Times, 1974; Weiss, 2009). The U.S. District Court in NJ held that the prohibition on discrimination "because of sex" did not cover dismissal because of a change in sex. The court reasoned that she was fired because she transitioned from male to female, and not because of her status as a female or because of any stereotypical concepts about the ability of females to perform certain tasks (Broadus, 2006; Weiss, 2009). This decision relied on a "plain meaning" doctrine.

In *Holloway v. Arthur Andersen Co* (1977), the court held that the Title VII definition of "sex" did not cover trans discrimination. Ramona Holloway was hired as a man by Arthur Andersen & Co. She informed her employers that she was starting hormone therapy to transition from male to female and wanted to change her documents. Before being terminated, a company official suggested she might be happier finding a job where her transition would be unknown. Holloway argued that being discriminated against for being trans fit the definition of being discriminated against for her sex, which was unlawful under Title VII. She separately argued that excluding transsexuals as a class from Title VII violated the Equal Protection Clause of the Fourteenth Amendment. Lacking a clear definition of "sex" under Title VII, the court cited Webster's Seventh New Collegiate Dictionary entry for the word "sex" to mean biological sex and ruled that this "plain meaning" approach did not extend to transgender discrimination (Kelly, 2010). The Ninth Circuit ruled that transsexuals are not a *suspect class* under the Equal Protection clause because they do not constitute a *discrete and insular minority* and do not, like race or national origin, occur as an immutable characteristic determined by birth alone. The court also reiterated the *Grossman* decision that she was discriminated against because of her decision to change sex, and not her treatment as either a man or as a woman (Clough, 2000; Sherwood, 2015). In a footnote, the court also mentioned *Voyles* and cited the *Grossman* decision's rationale of treatment because of the decision to change her sex and not her treatment as either a man or as a woman (Clough, 2000).

The reasoning applied to *Holloway* was later upheld in the 7th Circuit Court of Appeals case of *Ulane v. Eastern Airlines* (1984). In this case, gender policing through cis gender entitlement is plainly found because the plaintiff was described in essentialist terms as "a biological male who takes female hormones, cross-dresses, and had surgically altered parts of her body to make it appear female" (Pierceson, 2018, p. 148).

Price Waterhouse v. Hopkins (1989) was brought to the Supreme Court not by a transgender plaintiff but by a cisgender woman who did not conform to feminine stereotypes. Despite securing a $25m State Department contract and favorable work reviews, she was denied a partnership for being *insufficiently feminine* in demeanor, appearance, and personality (Broadus, 2006; Kelly, 2010; Sherwood, 2015). The court ruled in favor of Ms. Hopkins; finding discriminatory motives were evidenced as the reason for her lack of consideration for partnership. This case is pivotal because sex stereotyping was recognized as a form of discrimination expanding the interpretation of sex to include conformity to cultural stereotypes of gender, gender roles, and gender expression (Kelly, 2010; Twing & Williams, 2010; Weiss, 2009). The 1989 *Price Waterhouse* decision was followed by several successful cases based on sex stereotyping. However, it did not protect workers whose employers were objecting to the idea of gender transition in and of itself (Levasseur, 2015).

The Equal Employment Opportunity Commission (EEOC) case of *Macy v. Holder* (2012) involved a transgender woman, Mia Macy, who applied for a position with the Walnut Creek Crime Laboratory of the Federal Bureau of Alcohol, Tobacco and Firearms (ATF) while still presenting as male and a police detective in Phoenix, Arizona. She was informed she would have the job if there were no issues with the background check. Having started her transition, Macy informed Aspen (the staffing firm hired to conduct the background check) that she intended to report to the new job as Mia, presenting as female. She received an email five days later that the position was being eliminated due to budget cuts. Macy contacted an EEOC counselor who told her the position was given to someone further along in the background investigation process. Suspicious of this explanation, Macy filed a complaint with the ATF which initially dismissed her claim and referred her to file a complaint with the Dept. of Justice (DOJ). However, DOJ procedures do not offer certain important rights such as the right to request a hearing before an EEOC administrative judge or the right to file an appeal. Macy filed a notice of appeal for dismissal of her claim, and the EEOC accepted. The EEOC found in favor of Macy using reasoning from *Price Waterhouse v. Hopkins*. While EEOC cases are not binding on the judiciary, the *Macy* case was the first time that sex could be interpreted under Title VII to include both sex and gender, and specifically to include gender nonconformity, gender expression, or change of sex as cognizable forms of discrimination (Geidner, 2012; Taylor, 2013). This was pivotal in the fight for trans rights and the ability to file claims of discrimination based on transgender status under Title VII (Taylor, 2013).

On June 15, 2020, the Supreme Court issued a landmark ruling in the case of *Bostock v. Clayton County, Georgia* (2020) which joined two companion cases—*R.G. & G.R. Harris Funeral Homes Inc. v. Equal Employment Opportunity Commission (EEOC)* (2020) and *Altitude Express Inc v. Zarda* (2020). Even though the three cases were consolidated into one opinion, the *R.G. & G.R. Harris Funeral Homes Inc. v. EEOC* case was the first Supreme Court opinion to specifically reference transgender people and directly address whether discrimination protections extended to transgender people. The case involved a transgender woman, Aimee Stephens, fired after revealing in writing her intention to transition and what this entailed (presenting as female in name, attire, personal grooming, and pronoun usage). Her employers dismissed her for gender nonconformity and the owner's personal discomfort stating in court "Well, because he was no longer going to represent himself as a man. He wanted to dress as a woman" and "I'm uncomfortable with the name, because he's a man" (Liptak, 2018, p. 19).

In a 6–3 decision, the Supreme Court acknowledged that the drafters of Title VII may not have anticipated this situation in 1964. The opinion of the court in *Bostock v. Clayton County Georgia* (2020) firmly states that the "limits of the drafters' imagination supply no reason to ignore the law's demands" (p. 2) and that the plain meaning of the statutory phrasing "It shall be an unlawful employment practice for an employer . . . to discriminate against any individual . . . because of such individual's . . . sex" (p. 8) covers gender identity and sexual orientation because an employer who fires someone for being gay, lesbian, bisexual or transgender is firing them at least in part "for traits or actions it would not have questioned in members of a different sex" (p. 2). This "but-for" reasoning holds true even when assuming "sex" refers only to traditional notions of biological maleness or femaleness. The phrase "because of sex" was thus unambiguous. Title VII is triggered when a decision is made "but-for" the employee's sex, meaning that the decision would not have been made absent considerations of the employee's sex.

The journey to the Bostock ruling was 45 years in the making and hinged on how to legally and uniformly define "sex" in sex discrimination cases under Title VII of the Civil Rights Act of 1964. In practical terms, Title VII affords protections in hiring, firing, and compensation (wages, sick leave, insurance, etc.); and trans people cannot be penalized for using workplace restrooms in alignment with their gender identity.

Americans With Disabilities Act Approach

The Americans With Disabilities Act (ADA) (1990) prohibits discrimination against people with disabilities, with Title 1 specifically covering employees and job applicants. In *Jane Doe v. Boeing Company* (1993), Jane Doe (pseudonym) filed an ADA claim seeking protections based on mental impairment. The courts were beginning to explore whether gender dysphoria and transsexualism could be considered cognizable forms of discrimination under the ADA. Doe worked for Boeing as an engineer from 1978 to 1985 when she started transitioning male to female. No issues were documented in her work performance until she began to transition. The transition included mental health counseling and dressing as a woman full-time before beginning hormone therapy, following the Benjamin Standards of Care recommendations of the time (Martin & Yonkin, 2006; Stryker, 2008a). Doe agreed to a gender-neutral dress code wearing clothing perceived to be androgynous, male, or neutral to minimize workplace disruption. When a complaint was made that she used the women's restroom after work hours, daily meetings with her supervisor were required to assess compliance with the dress code. On her final day at Boeing, she wore work appropriate slacks, sweater, and accessorized with a necklace, earrings, and nail polish. The supervisor felt that her pink pearl necklace was not in compliance (Clough, 2000; Myers, 2010). Boeing won the case both initially and on appeal, arguing that they made reasonable accommodations for her gender dysphoria (Bennett & Jasnow, 2012; Clough, 2000; Myers, 2010; Twing & Williams, 2010). This case exemplifies the concept of gender gatekeeping and scrutiny trans people have faced on the job in relation to cis gender entitlement.

Seeking protections under Disability law is a contested idea among members and allies of the trans community. By associating trans people with disability, there is the concern of perpetuating social stigma and the myth that trans identities are inherently abnormal, or that gender diversity itself is a mental illness. The perpetuation of a medical model of transition also disproportionately negatively impacts individuals who cannot access transition-related health-care (Levi & Klein, 2006).

Executive Branch History

Executive orders are Presidential directives setting forth rules for the management of federal agencies and to set specific terms with federal contractors. As Chief Executive of the executive branch of the United States, the President can use the position as a bully pulpit to be heard on important issues. Executive orders cannot surpass legislative and judicial branch roles in setting rules for employers and employees outside of the executive branch, but they can send a message and sway opinion regarding what is acceptable (Jansson, 2018).

Transgender and gender-nonconforming people were not mentioned in presidential executive orders until 2014 when President Obama issued Executive Order 13672 prohibiting discrimination based on sexual orientation and gender identity. This order amended the 1969 federal civilian workforce antidiscrimination order and was the first to expressly protect transgender and gender-nonconforming federal employees and in federal contract employment (E.O. 13672, July 21, 2014; McCandless & Hooker, 2019).

The Trump administration implemented a number of actions resulting in the reversal and/or denial of rights of trans people. Within two hours of being sworn into office, the official White House webpage was stripped of all mentions of LGBTQ issues (HRC, 2019). In October 2017, Attorney General Jeff Sessions ordered the Justice Department to interpret "sex" as biologically male or female in all pending and future workplace discrimination cases (Savage, 2017). The Trump administration took one of two stances—either that transgender identities are unsupported by science and accepting only an essentialist gender binary, or that protective policies place an undue burden on the constitutional right to freedom of religion. Under Trump's narrow approach, the Department of Justice, Department of Education, and its Office for Civil Rights, Health and Human Services, and other agencies revoked all Obama-era policy directives and regulations that previously offered protections by removing LGBTQ nondiscrimination requirements, carving out religious exemptions, and specifically defining gender as a person's biological sex (Ballard Spahr LLP, 2018; NCTE, 2020; U.S. Department of Health and Human Services, 2020). In direct contrast to the *Bostock* decision, the U.S. Department of Education Office for Civil Rights interpreted the Title IX prohibitions on discrimination "on the basis of sex" to "unambiguously refers to biological sex" and disregard gender identity (Battle & Wheeler, 2017, p. 1). A final rule required schools receiving Title IX funds to ban transgender students from participating in sports threatening to withdraw funding to schools in the state of Connecticut (Blanchard, 2020; NCTE, 2020).

While these rule changes are not employment-specific, they have far-reaching ramifications for the lives of transgender and nonbinary people. The anti-trans rhetoric and policies of the Trump administration led to increased feelings of rejection, a heightened sense of anxiety and fear, and vigilance against a perceived lack of safety among members of the trans community (Price et al., 2020). Institutionalized discrimination and historical oppression are negatively associated with mental health outcomes including depression, anxiety, PTSD, and suicidal ideation (David & Derthick, 2017; Mizock & Mueser, 2014). Youth who experience harassment, victimization, and discrimination in adolescence may enter the workforce in adulthood already dealing with depression and PTSD (Mustanski et al., 2016).

Biden began his Presidency thanking his supporters, including transgender people, in his victory speech—the first to mention the transgender community (Johnson, 2020). A series of Executive Orders were issued between January and March directly addressing concerns of the trans community. Executive Order 13985 focuses on racial equity and includes the language of LGBTQ+ persons as "persons otherwise adversity affected by persistent poverty or inequality" (Exec. Order No. 13985, 2021). Executive Order 13988 enforces prohibitions on sex discrimination based on gender identity or sexual orientation (Exec. Order No. 13988, 2021). The U.S. Department of Education issued a notice of interpretation upholding the rights of LGBTQ+ students and protecting them from discrimination in educational settings (U.S. Department of Education, 2021) and Housing and Urban Development (HUD) issued a memorandum applying the *Bostock* decision to the Fair Housing Act (HUD, 2021). Biden established a White House Gender Policy Council (Exec. Order No. 14020, 2021) to advance LGBTQ-inclusive mandates and gender equity in domestic and foreign policy (Exec. Order No. 14020, 2021). On March 31, 2021, he issued a proclamation for Transgender Day of Visibility acknowledging the struggles of LGBTQ+ people and urging the passage of the Equality Act (Proclamation No. 10164, 2021).

The Military

A documented ban on LGBTQ people serving in the military extends as far back as World War I. U.S. military regulations issued in 1943 established an outright ban against lesbians and gays serving in the military. Considerably more scrutiny was placed on military men than on the women who served in the Women's Army Corp. If discovered, gay soldiers and sailors were imprisoned, followed by dishonorable discharge from the military. This ban lasted for over five decades (Berubé, 1990; Rimmerman, 2014).

Unlike changes in military regulations impacting LGB service members, transgender service members were still considered "administratively unfit" to serve per the Department of Defense (DoD) Standards of Medical Fitness Regulation 40–501 (U.S. Department of the Army, 2008). In 2014, a research panel organized by the Palm Center issued a report finding that there was no basis for excluding transgender people from military service (Elders & Steinman, 2014). This report recommended lifting the transgender military service ban, employing fitness testing using standards applied to transgender military personnel in 12 other countries, and the utilization of established medical practices for transgender people (Elders & Steinman, 2014). Of note, in 2013, the DSM-V replaced gender-identity disorder with gender dysphoria, making it a treatable condition comparable with other treatable mental health conditions that did not preclude military service (Crocq, 2021). In February 2015, the Secretary of Defense, Dr. Ash Carter, spoke in favor of allowing transgender troops. Then, in March 2015, the Army, Navy, and Air Force issued directives protecting transgender people from outright dismissal. This led to a RAND National Defense Research Institute study which determined that allowing trans people in the military would have minimal financial and operational impact (Schaefer et al., 2016). On June 30, 2016, Directive-Type Memo 16–005 announced service members who were otherwise qualified could not be discharged or denied reenlistment because of gender identity (Carter, 2016). Training and guidance regarding transgender service members was implemented.

Beginning in July 2017, President Trump issued a series of tweets claiming that he had consulted with experts, Generals, and other members of the military, determined that transgender military service members brought disruption and medical cost burdens to the military, and that transgender individuals would not be accepted or allowed to serve in the U.S. military in any capacity (Wamsley, 2017). This statement was made without evidence of disruption in the military and before the issuance of an executive order vetted by administration lawyers. U.S. District of Columbia Judge Colleen Kollar-Kotelly temporarily blocked action and administration lawyers claimed the order was being reviewed by the Pentagon (Hawkins, 2017). Discussion regarding medical costs took up a significant portion of the debate, with one legislator (Vicky Hartzler, R-MO) asserting $1.3b in costs for 4,500 trans personnel seeking gender-confirming surgeries (Hartzler, 2017). The Palm Center estimated fewer than 2% of transgender service members (approximately 230 individuals) would seek gender-confirming surgeries in a year, with an average cost of $29,929 per person or $6.88m in total (Elders & Steinman, 2014).

In *Karnoski v. Trump* (2019), the United States Supreme Court ruled in favor of the ban on military service for transgender citizens. The 5–4 ruling came down along ideological lines, with no evidence that military effectiveness, readiness, or lethality was affected after transgender military members began serving openly under the Obama administration (Goodwin & Chemerinsky, 2019). Per Directive-type Memorandum 19–004 and later DoD regulation Instruction 1300.28, current-serving transgender troops who were "grandfathered in" were allowed to remain in the military, but beginning April 12, 2019 transgender personnel with a diagnosis of gender dysphoria were not allowed to serve or enlist in the U.S. military unless they served as their sex assigned at birth or were given a (very rare) exemption waiver to serve in their "preferred gender" (Department of Defense, 2021).

This directive was reversed by Executive Order 14004, in which President Biden states, "It is my conviction as Commander in Chief of the Armed Forces that gender identity should not be a bar to military service" (Exec. Order No. 14004, 2021, p. 1). The DoD announced that the revised policies prohibiting discrimination based on gender identity or identification as transgender would go into effect on April 30, 2021. After a review of policies and procedures, DoD also issued Instruction 1300.28 which outlines the process which service members seeking to transition must follow (DoD, 2021).

Relevance for Policy Change

As readers can see, the history of transgender rights in the United States has been uneven and fraught with contention both externally and within the LGBTQ community. The U.S. Constitution and Bill of Rights, however, establishes a vehicle through which trans people can secure antidiscrimination protections using the law. According to Lecours (2005), an institutionalist policy model predicts policy and policy outcomes by centering the government as the vehicle lending legitimacy and universality to policies, while also exercising coercion to ensure compliance with the law. Furthermore, governmental institutions can have a direct impact on social groups, group identities, and the capacity for equity and equal opportunity under the law. While societal attitudes towards trans people may be moving in a more accepting direction generally, there are still significantly powerful groups who continue to use a moral reasoning to wage culture wars in order to sway the public and influence public policy (Haider-Markel et al., 2019). These groups may never respect the rights of trans people without invoking or threatening to invoke the coercive power of the government.

The United States government operates under a federalist system, as established by the U.S. Constitution. So, while the separation of powers creates checks and balances among the three branches of government, the Supreme Court serves as the ultimate arbiter of what can be considered constitutional. Seeking relief via the Supreme Court can thus have a broad and powerful impact across the country. It can also be something of a "high stakes" proposition because losing at the level of the Supreme Court could mean the loss of rights and benefits previously established at lower levels of government. This is because the recognition of powers at the federal level and at state and local levels of government is a key component of federalism. Advocates must decide where to focus efforts for policy change, and whether policies will withstand both public pressure and judicial scrutiny (Dye, 2005; Gerston, 2007). Knowledge of the judicial, legislative, and executive histories surrounding trans rights is important to move forward with advocacy work. For advocacy work to be successful, knowledge of the powers and limits of the government, precedents, and insight into what makes lasting legislation should be considered while developing a strategy. The current 6–3 conservative majority in the Supreme Court supports the stance of judicial "Originalism" and creates the likelihood of retrogressive decisions undoing years of progress for trans people (King & Richardson, 2020).

The Importance and Limitations of Research

Policy advocacy and analysis will benefit from research to illuminate emerging and unaddressed areas and to track the success of policy changes in preventing or ameliorating the conditions that lead to negative outcomes for trans and nonbinary people. For example, community needs assessments inform the direction for policy advocacy efforts, while attitudinal surveys can measure public support or opposition. Policymakers can use survey research in a central or supporting role when considering whether to support or oppose new legislation, begin or end programs, or measure the outcomes of policies after implementation (Mitchell, 2007). The Palm Center Report (Elders & Steinman, 2014) on military inclusion is an example of evidence-based research being used by a Presidential administration to shape and extend policies.

The research on employment discrimination done through community-based convenience samples and cross-sectional studies has been invaluable to the cause of employment rights for transgender and nonbinary people. The concerns of trans people are gaining traction in the larger LGBTQ community, partially because attention has been freed up since the achievement of same-sex marriage on a national level (Haider-Markel et al., 2019). Trans rights advocacy groups such as the National Center for Transgender Equality, GLAD, NCLR, the Transgender Law Center, and the Sylvia Rivera Law Project join the list of organizations and policy institutes such as the Movement Advancement Project, UCLA Williams Institute, HRC, the Center for American Progress and the ACLU, in leading research efforts aimed at securing trans equality before the law. Research from the academe is needed to further support this work. Peer-reviewed research that focuses on health issues such as HIV/AIDS prevention among sex workers, health disparities, mental health, and counseling needs and the studies that conflate gender and sexual orientation (or only focus on LGB people) dominated the field among researchers in academe for years (Currah et al., 2008; Serano, 2007; Tadlock & Taylor, 2017).

Responding to the Shifting Landscape

To move employment rights forward, researchers and advocates should understand all standpoints regarding transgender and nonbinary employees, the history of the interpretation of "sex," and legal precedents on policies. Researchers and advocates should stay current in other areas of policy that directly impact the well-being of trans people. These include local and state laws that oppose transgender rights, limit freedom of participation in public life (such as state anti-trans bathroom bills), state nullification laws that ban jurisdictions from establishing anti-discrimination policies (such as has been proposed in several states including North Carolina and Texas), test cases that seek to reduce the scope of Supreme Court rulings, laws that favor religious liberty, policies that ban gender-confirming medical treatments for trans-identified youth, and interpretations of existing laws that exclude trans people from sex discrimination protections (Murib, 2020; Swan, 2019).

Political partisanship and religious views are likely to continue playing a role in advancing transgender rights. The growing trans rights movement has in part relied on changing public attitudes in support of trans people (Flores et al., 2018). A Pew Research Poll found that 80% of Republicans believe that gender is determined by a person's sex assigned at birth, while 64% of Democrats believe a person's gender can be different than their sex assigned at birth. In terms of societal acceptance, 60% of Democrats felt that society has not gone far enough, while 57% of Republicans feel that acceptance has already gone too far (Brown, 2017). Among religious groups, an overwhelming 61% of White evangelicals reported feeling that society has gone too far in accepting transgender people, while other Christian groups were more evenly divided (Smith, 2017). Campbell et al. (2019) found significant relationships between a strong identification as a religious Christian, religious fundamentalist, and literalism in Bible interpretation with prejudice against transgender people. Think tanks will continue to produce position papers to sway culture and policy, such as the "Parent Resource Guide" produced by the Minnesota Family Council (2019) in collaboration with conservative and radical feminist groups such as The Heritage Foundation and Women's Liberation Front that promote gender essentialism. This new and unlikely partnership between conservative groups and radical feminists represents a shift in political alignment that trans advocacy strategists cannot afford to ignore (Schmidt, 2020).

Conclusion

Policy advocates must always be ready to act, particularly when opportunities arise. The Biden Administration presents possibly the clearest opportunity within a Presidential administration, considering that Biden was the first ever President Elect to mention transgender people in a Presidential victory speech (Johnson, 2020). A coalition of organizations released a preliminary list of immediate and long-term actions for the Biden administration to take upon inauguration. These recommendations inform ways to reverse the damage inflicted by the Trump Administration and support transgender and gender-nonconforming people along with other members of the LGBTQ community (Project et al., 2020). Advancing transgender equality will take continued effort through all three branches of government, with vigilance at all levels in the federalist system.

References

Althauer, S., & Greenberg, S. (2011). *FAQ: The employment non-discrimination act.* American Progress. www.americanprogress.org/issues/lgbtq-rights/news/2011/07/19/9988/faq-the-employment-non-discrimination-act/

Altitude Express v. Zarda, 590 U.S. (2020). www.supremecourt.gov/opinions/19pdf/17-1618_hfci.pdf

Americans With Disabilities Act of 1990, 42 U.S.C. § 12101 *et seq.* (1990). www.ada.gov/pubs/adastatute08.htm

Badgett, M. V., Choi, S. K., & Wilson, B. (2019). *LGBT poverty in the United States: A study of differences between sexual orientation and gender identity groups.* The Williams Institute UCLA School of Law. https://williamsinstitute.law.ucla.edu/wp-content/uploads/National-LGBT-Poverty-Oct-2019.pdf

Badgett, M. V., Lau, H., Sears, B., & Ho, D. (2007). *Bias in the workplace: Consistent evidence of sexual orientation and gender identity discrimination.* The Williams Institute UCLA School of Law. https://williamsinstitute.law.ucla.edu/wp-content/uploads/Bias-Workplace-SOGI-Discrim-Jun-2007.pdf

Ballard Spahr LLP. (2018). *What remedy for transgender students if HHS succeeds in narrowly redefining gender under title IX?* www.jdsupra.com/legalnews/what-remedy-for-transgender-students-if-63995/

Battle, S., & Wheeler, T. E. I. (2017). *Dear colleague letter February 22, 2017.* U.S. Department of Education. https://www2.ed.gov/about/offices/list/ocr/letters/colleague-201702-title-ix.pdf

Bennett, K., & Jasnow, D. (2012). Annual review article: Employment discrimination against LGBTQ persons. *Thirteenth Annual Gender and Sexuality Law: The Georgetown Journal of Gender and the Law, 257*(257), 2–38.

Berubé, A. (1990). *Coming out under fire.* Free Press.

Blanchard, T. C. J. (2020). *Re: Case Nos. 01-19-4025, 01-19-1252, 01-20-1003, 01-20-1004, 01-20-1005, 01-20-1006, and 01-20-1007.* United States Department of Education www.adflegal.org/sites/default/files/2020-05/Soule%20v.%20Connecticut%20Association%20of%20Schools%20-%20U.S.%20DOE%20Office%20for%20Civil%20Rights%2C%20Letter%20of%20Impending%20Action.pdf

Bockting, W. O., Miner, M. H., Swinburne Romine, R. E., Hamilton, A., & Coleman, E. (2013). Stigma, mental health, and resilience in an online sample of the US transgender population. *American Journal of Public Health Research, 103*(5), 943–951. https://doi.org/10.2105/AJPH.2013.301241

Bostock v. Clayton County, Georgia, 590 U.S. (2020). www.supremecourt.gov/opinions/19pdf/17-1618_hfci.pdf

Bradford, J., Reisner, S. L., Honnold, J. A., & Xavier, J. (2013). Experiences of transgender-related discrimination and implications for health: Results from the Virginia transgender health initiative study. *American Journal of Public Health, 103*(10), 1820–1829. https://doi.org/10.2105/ajph.2012.300796

Broadus, K. W. (2006). The evolution of employment discrimination protections for transgender people. In P. Currah, R. M. Juang, & S. P. Minter (Eds.), *Transgender rights* (pp. 93–101). University of Minnesota Press.

Brown, A. (2017). *Republicans, democrats have starkly different views on transgender issues.* http://pewrsr.ch/2iHpwt4

Button, J. W., Rienzo, B. A., & Wald, K. D. (1997). *Private lives, public conflicts.* Congressional Quarterly Press.

Cail, J., & Wang, T. (2008). Sexuality and transgender issues in employment law. *Georgetown Journal of Gender and the Law, 9*(855).

Campbell, M., Hinton, J. D. X., & Anderson, J. R. (2019). A systematic review of the relationship between religion and attitudes toward transgender and gender-variant people. *International Journal of Transgenderism, 20*(1), 21–38. https://doi.org/10.1080/15532739.2018.1545149

Carter, A. (2016). *DTM 16–005 "military service of transgender service members".* Department of Defense. https://dod.defense.gov/Portals/1/features/2016/0616_policy/DTM-16-005.pdf

Chang, S., & Singh, A. (2016). Affirming psychological practice with transgender and gender nonconforming people of color. *Psychology of Sexual Orientation and Gender Diversity, 3*(2), 140–147. https://doi.org/10.1037/sgd0000153

Civil Rights Act of 1964 § 7, 42 U.S.C. § 2000e *et seq.* (1964).

Clements-Nolle, K., Marx, R., & Katz, M. (2006). Attempted suicide among transgender persons: The influence of gender-based discrimination and victimization. *Journal of Homosexuality, 51*(3), 53–69. https://doi.org/10.1300/J082v51n03_04

Clough, A. S. (2000). Illusion of protection: Transsexual employment discrimination. *Georgetown Journal of Gender and the Law, 1,* 849–886.

Cray, A., & Harrison, J. (2012). *ID accurately reflecting one's gender identity is a human right.* www.americanprogress.org/issues/lgbtq-rights/reports/2012/12/18/48367/id-accurately-reflecting-ones-gender-identity-is-a-human-right/

Crocq, M. (2021). How gender dysphoria and incongruence became medical diagnoses—a historical review. *Dialogues in Clinical Neuroscience, 23*(1), 44–51. https://doi.org/10.1080/19585969.2022.2042166

Currah, P. (2006). Gender pluralism under the transgender umbrella. In P. Currah, R. M. Juang, & S. P. Minter (Eds.), *Transgender rights* (pp. 3–32). University of Minnesota Press.

Currah, P., Green, J., & Stryker, S. (2008). *The state of transgender rights in the United States of America.* Paper presented at the National Sexuality Resource Center Annual Meeting, New York City.

David, E. J. R., & Derthick, A. O. (2017). *The psychology of oppression.* Springer Publishing Company.

Department of Defense (DoD). (2021). *DoD instruction 1300.28 military service by transgender persons and persons with gender dysphoria.* Department of Defense. www.esd.whs.mil/Portals/54/Documents/DD/issuances/dodi/130028p.pdf?ver=2020-09-04-115910-477

dickey, l. m., & Budge, S. L. (2020). Suicide and the transgender experience: A public health crisis. *American Psychologist, 75*(3), 380–390. https://doi.org/10.1037/amp0000619

Dietert, M., & Dentice, D. (2009). Gender identity issues and workplace discrimination: The transgender experience *Journal of Workplace Rights, 14*(1), 121–140.

Dye, T. R. (2005). *Understanding public policy* (11th ed.). Pearson Prentice Hall.

Elders, J., & Steinman, A. M. (2014). *Report of the transgender military service commission.* www.palm center.org/wp-content/uploads/2014/03/Transgender-Military-Service-Report_1.pdf

Exec. Order No. 13,672 41 CFR 60 (2014). www.federalregister.gov/documents/2014/12/09/2014-28902/implementation-of-executive-order-13672-prohibiting-discrimination-based-on-sexual-orientation-and

Exec. Order No. 13,985 86 FR 7009 (2021). www.federalregister.gov/documents/2021/01/25/2021-01753/advancing-racial-equity-and-support-for-underserved-communities-through-the-federal-government

Exec. Order No. 13,988 86 FR 7023 (2021). www.federalregister.gov/documents/2021/01/25/2021-01761/preventing-and-combating-discrimination-on-the-basis-of-gender-identity-or-sexual-orientation

Exec. Order No. 14,004 86 R 7471 (2021). www.federalregister.gov/documents/2021/01/28/2021-02034/enabling-all-qualified-americans-to-serve-their-country-in-uniform

Exec. Order No. 14,020 86 FR 13797 (2021). www.federalregister.gov/documents/2021/03/11/2021-05183/establishment-of-the-white-house-gender-policy-council

Flores, A. R., Herman, J. L., Gates, G. J., & Brown, T. N. T. (2016). *How many adults identify as transgender in the United States?* Williams Institute. https://williamsinstitute.law.ucla.edu/wp-content/uploads/Trans-Adults-US-Aug-2016.pdf

Flores, A. R., Miller, P., & Tadlock, B. (2018). Public opinion about transgender people and policies. In J. K. Taylor, D. C. Lewis, & D. P. Haider-Markel (Eds.), *The remarkable rise of transgender rights.* University of Michigan Press.

Freeman, J. (1991). How "sex" got into title VII: Persistent opportunism as a maker of public policy. *Law and Inequality: A Journal of Theory and Practice, 9*(2), 163–184.

Gan, J. (2007). Still at the back of the bus: Sylvia Rivera's struggle. *CENTRO, 19*(1), 125–139.

Gates, T. G. (2010). The problem, policy, and political streams of the employment non-discrimination act of 2009: Implications for social work practice. *Journal of Gay & Lesbian Social Services, 22,* 354–369.

Gehi, P. S., & Arkles, G. (2007). Unraveling injustice: Race and class impact of Medicaid exclusions of transition-related health care for transgender people. *Sexuality Research & Social Policy, 4*(4), 7–35.

Geidner, C. (2012, April 23). Transgender breakthrough. *Metro Weekly,* 7. www.metroweekly.com/2012/04/transgender-breakthrough/

Gerston, L. N. (2007). *American federalism: A concise introduction.* Routledge.

Goodwin, M., & Chemerinsky, E. (2019). The transgender military ban: Preservation of discrimination through transformation. *Northwestern University Law Review, 114*(3), 751–808.

Grabham, E. (2007). Citizen bodies, intersex citizenship. *Sexualities, 10*(1), 29–48.

Grant, J. M., Mottet, L. A., & Tanis, J. (2011). *Injustice at every turn: A report of the national transgender discrimination survey.* National Center for Transgender Equality. https://transequality.org/sites/default/files/docs/resources/NTDS_Report.pdf

Greenberg, J. A. (2006). The roads less traveled: The problem with binary sex categories. In P. Currah, R. M. Juang, & S. Minter (Eds.), *Transgender rights.* The University of Minnesota Press.

Grossman v. Bernards Township Board of Education, 429 U.S. 897 (1976). https://cite.case.law/us/429/897/7871/

Haider-Markel, D., Taylor, J., Flores, A., Lewis, D., Miller, P., & Tadlock, B. (2019). Morality politics and new research on transgender politics and public policy. *Forum (2194–6183), 17*(1), 159–181. https://doi.org/10.1515/for-2019-0004

Hartzell, E., Frazer, M. S., Wertz, K., & Davis, M. (2009). *The state of transgender California: Results from the 2008 California transgender economic health survey.* The Transgender Law Center. https://transgenderlawcenter.org/wp-content/uploads/2012/07/95219573-The-State-of-Transgender-California.pdf

Hartzler, V. (2017). *Hartzler statement on white house decision to repeal Obama transgender military policy* [Press release]. https://hartzler.house.gov/media-center/press-releases/hartzler-statement-white-house-decision-repeal-obama-transgender

Hasenbush, A., Flores, A. R., & Herman, J. L. (2019). Gender identity nondiscrimination laws in public accommodations: A review of evidence regarding safety and privacy in public restrooms, locker rooms, and changing rooms. *Sexuality Research and Social Policy, 16,* 70–83. https://doi.org/10.1007/s13178-018-0335-z

Hawkins, D. (2017). Trump's tweets come back to bite him in court again, this time in transgender military case. *The Washington Post.* www.washingtonpost.com/news/morning-mix/wp/2017/10/31/trumps-tweets-come-back-to-bite-him-in-court-again-this-time-in-transgender-military-case/

Holloway v. Arthur Andersen & Co, 566 F.2d 659 (9th Cir.1977). https://casetext.com/case/holloway-v-arthur-andersen-co

The Human Rights Campaign (HRC). (2019). *Trump's timeline of hate.* www.hrc.org/resources/trumps-timeline-of-hate

James, S. E., Herman, J. L., Rankin, S., Keisling, M., Mottet, L., & Anafi, M. (2015). *The report of the 2015 U.S. transgender survey.* National Center for Transgender Equality. https://transequality.org/sites/default/files/docs/usts/USTS-Full-Report-Dec17.pdf

Jane Doe v. Boeing Company, 121 Wn2d 8 aff'd 846 P2d 531 (1993). https://law.justia.com/cases/washington/supreme-court/1993/59117-2-1.html

Jansson, B. S. (2018). *Becoming an effective policy advocate* (8th ed.). Cengage Learning.

Johnson, C. (2017). 10 years later, firestorm over gay-only ENDA vote still informs movement. *Washington Blade.*

Johnson, C. (2020). Biden name-checks gay and transgender Americans in victory speech. *Washington Blade.* www.washingtonblade.com/2020/11/07/biden-name-checks-gay-and-transgender-americans-in-victory-speech/

Juro, R. (2016, February 2). Even after all these years, HRC still doesn't get it. *Huffpost.* www.huffpost.com/entry/even-after-all-these-years-hrc-still-doesnt-get-it_b_2989826

Karnoski v. Trump, 926 F.3d 1180 (9th Cir.) (2019). www.cwl.org/assets/docs/Karnoski_v._Trump.pdf

Kattari, S., Whitfield, D. L., Walls, N. E., Langenderfer-Magruder, L., & Ramos, D. (2016). Policing gender through housing and employment discrimination: Comparison of discrimination experiences of transgender and cisgender LGBQ individuals. *Journal of the Society for Social Work and Research, 7*(3), 2368–2386.

Kelly, M. K. (2010). (Trans)forming traditional interpretations of title VII. *Duke Journal of Gender Law & Policy, 17*(219), 219–239.

King, A. J., & Richardson, H. C. (2020). Amy Coney Barrett's judicial philosophy doesn't hold up to scrutiny. *The Atlantic.*

Kirk, J., & Belovis, R. (2008). Understanding and counseling transgender clients. *Journal of Employment Counseling, 45*(1), 29–43.

Kohler, W. (2011, April 17). *46 years ago today: First lesbian & gay protest at the white house.* www.bilerico.com/2011/04/46_years_ago_today_1st_lesbian_gay_protest_at_the.php

Lecours, A. (2005). *New institutionalism: Theory and analysis.* University of Toronto Press, Scholarly Publishing Division.

Lee, J. (2012). Lost in transition: The challenges of remedying transgender employment discrimination under title VII. *Harvard Journal of Law & Gender, 35,* 423–461.

Levasseur, M. D. (2015). Gender identity defines sex: Updating the law to reflect modern medical science is key to transgender rights. *Vermont Law Review, 39,* 943–1004.

Levenson, M., & Vigdor, N. (2020). Inclusion of transgender student athletes violates title IX, Trump administration says. *The New York Times.* www.nytimes.com/2020/05/29/us/connecticut-transgender-student-athletes.html

Levi, J. L., & Klein, B. H. (2006). Pursuing protection for transgender people through disability laws. In P. Currah, R. M. Juang, & S. Minter (Eds.), *Transgender rights.* University of Minnesota Press.

Liptak, A. (2018, November 13). Can a fired transgender worker Sue for job discrimination? *The New York Times.* https://nyti.ms/2z6yzgx

Macy v. Holder, EE-CA-0354. (2012). https://harvardlawreview.org/wp-content/uploads/pdfs/vol126_macy_v_holder.pdf

Mananzala, R., & Spade, D. (2008). The nonprofit industrial complex and trans resistance. *Sexuality Research & Social Policy, 5*(1), 53–71.

Martin, J. I., & Yonkin, D. R. (2006). Transgender identity. In D. F. Morrow & L. Messinger (Eds.), *Sexual orientation and gender expression in social work practice.* Columbia University Press.

McCandless, S., & Hooker, J. (2019). Ally training: A model for collaboration. In W. Swan (Ed.), *The Routledge handbook of LGBTQIA administration and policy.* Routledge Taylor Francis Group.

McLemore, K. (2018). A minority stress perspective on transgender individuals' experiences with misgendering. *Stigma and Health, 3*(1), 53–64. https://doi.org/10.1037/sah0000070

Minnesota Family Council. (2019). *Parent resource guide: Responding to the transgender issue.* Author. https://genderresourceguide.com/wp-content/themes/genderresource/library/documents/NPRG_Full_Document_Links_V18.pdf

Minter, S., & Daley, C. (2003). *Trans realities: A legal needs assessment of San Francisco's transgender communities.* National Center for Lesbian Rights and Transgender Law Center. www.nclrights.org/wp-content/uploads/2013/07/transrealities0803.pdf

Mitchell, J. (2007). The use (and misuse) of surveys in policy analysis. In F. Fischer, G. Miller, & M. Sidney (Eds.), *Handbook of public policy analysis: Theory, and methods* (pp. 369–380). Taylor & Francis.

Mizock, L., & Mueser, K. T. (2014). Employment, mental health, internalized stigma, and coping with transphobia among transgender individuals. *Psychology of Sexual Orientation and Gender Diversity, 1*(2), 146–158. https://doi.org/10.1037/sgd0000029

Molloy, P. M. (2014). Op-ed: What Barney Frank still gets wrong on ENDA. *The Advocate.*

Movement Advancement Project (MAP). (2009). *Snapshot: Advancing transgender equality.* https://www.lgbtmap.org/policy-and-issue-analysis/advancing-transgender-equality-snapshot

Movement Advancement Project (MAP). (2013). *A broken bargain for transgender workers.* Author. www.lgbtmap.org/file/a-broken-bargain-for-transgender-workers.pdf

Movement Advancement Project (MAP). (2020). *Equality maps: Employment nondiscrimination laws.* www.lgbtmap.org/equality_maps/employment_non_discrimination_laws

Movement Advancement Project, Center for American Progress, Equality Federation, GLSEN, National Center for Transgender Equality, & SAGE. (2020). *Week #1. 10 ways president Biden can support LGBTQ people.* https://lgbtmap.us14.list-manage.com/track/click?u=dccdb6f1f425fbfc51cf53f41&id=7a3fe3e0a5&e=b890ab33fa

Murib, Z. (2020). A new kind of anti-trans legislation is hitting the red states. *The Washington Post.*

Mustanski, B., Andrews, R., & Puckett, J. A. (2016). The effects of cumulative victimization on mental health among lesbian, gay, bisexual, and transgender adolescents and young adults. *American Journal of Public Health Research, 106*(3), 527–533. https://doi.org/10.2015/AJPH.2015.302976

Myers, P. R. (2010). Jane Doe v. Boeing company: Transsexuality and compulsory gendering in corporate capitalism. *Feminist Studies, 36*(3), 493–517.

Nadal, K. L., Whitman, C. N., Davis, L. S., Erazo, T., & Davidoff, K. C. (2016). Microaggressions toward lesbian, gay, bisexual, transgender, queer, and genderqueer people: A review of the literature. *The Journal of Sex Research, 00*(00), 1–21. https://doi.org/10.1080/00224499.2016.1142495

NCTE. (2019). *Failing to protect and serve executive summary.* Author. https://transequality.org/sites/default/files/docs/resources/FTPS_ES_v3.pdf

NCTE. (2020). *The discrimination administration: Trump's record of action against transgender people.* https://transequality.org/the-discrimination-administration

NCTE. (2021). *ID documents center: Tennessee.* Author. https://transequality.org/documents/state/tennessee

The New York Times. (1974, February 21). Dismissal over sex change upheld, brief. *The New York Times.* https://genderidentitywatch.files.wordpress.com/2013/02/grossman4.pdf

Office for Civil Rights (OCR). (2021, June). *Title IX and sex discrimination.* U.S. Department of Education. https://www2.ed.gov/about/offices/list/ocr/docs/tix_dis.html

Pierceson, J. (2018). Transgender rights and the judiciary. In J. K. Taylor, D. C. Lewis, & D. P. Haider-Markel (Eds.), *The remarkable rise of transgender rights.* University of Michigan Press.

Price, S. F., Puckett, J., & Mocarski, J. (2020). The impact of the 2016 presidential elections on transgender and gender diverse people. *Sexuality Research and Social Policy.* https://doi.org/10.1007/s13178-020-00513-2

Price Waterhouse v. Hopkins, 490 U.S. 228 (1989). https://tile.loc.gov/storage-services/service/ll/usrep/usrep490/usrep490228/usrep490228.pdf

Proclamation No. 10164 86 FR 17495 (2021). *Transgender day of visibility, 2021.* www.federalregister.gov/documents/2021/04/05/2021-07064/transgender-day-of-visibility-2021

Puckett, J. A., Brown, N. C., Dunn, T., Mustanski, B., & Newcomb, M. E. (2020). Perspectives from transgender and gender diverse people on how to ask about gender. *LGBT Health, 7*(6), 1–7. https://doi.org/10.1089/lgbt.2019.0295

Reeves, E. J., & Decker, L. (2001). Before ENDA: Sexual orientation and gender identity protections in the workplace under federal law. *Law & Sexuality, 20*, 61–78.

RG & GR Harris Funeral Homes Inc. v. Equal Employment Opportunity Commission, 590 U.S. (2020). www.supremecourt.gov/opinions/19pdf/17-1618_hfci.pdf

Rimmerman, C. A. (2014). Don't ask, don't tell: Policy perspectives on the military ban. In *The lesbian and gay movements* (2nd ed.). Westview Press.

Rood, B., Reisner, S., Surace, F., Puckett, J., Maroney, M., & Pantalone, D. (2016). Expecting rejection: Understanding the minority stress experiences of transgender and gender-nonconforming individuals. *Transgender Health, 1*(1), 151–164. https://doi.org/10.1089/trgh.2016.0012

Rothenberg, P. (2017). The social construction of difference: Race, class, gender, and sexuality. In *Race, class, and gender in the United States* (7th ed.). Worth Publishers.

Russell, E. R., & Viggiani, P. A. (2018). Understanding differences and definitions. In M. P. Dentato (Ed.), *Social work practice with the LGBTQ community*. Oxford University Press.

Sangganjanavanich, V. F., & Cavazos, J. (2010). Workplace aggression: Toward social justice and advocacy in counseling for transgender individuals. *Journal of LGBT Issues in Counseling, 4*, 187–201.

Savage, C. (2017). Reversal by justice department in transgender protections. *New York Times, 167*(57742), A19.

Schaefer, A. G., Plumb, R. I., Kadiyala, S., Kavanagh, J., Engel, C. C., Williams, K. M., & Kress, A. M. (2016). *Assessing the implications of allowing transgender personnel to serve openly*. www.rand.org/pubs/research_reports/RR1530.html

Schmidt, S. (2020). Conservatives find unlikely ally in fighting transgender rights: Radical feminists. *The Washington Post*. www.washingtonpost.com/dc-md-va/2020/02/07/radical-feminists-conservatives-transgender-rights/

Serano, J. (2007). *Whipping girl*. Seal Press.

Sherwood, M. (2015). *Transgender employees, part one, a history of landmark decisions, cases and laws*. http://amarillo.com/blog-post/mattsherwood/2015-06-12/transgender-employees-part-one-history-landmark-decisions-cases

Smith, G. A. (2017). *Views of transgender issues divide along religious lines*. www.pewresearch.org/fact-tank/2017/11/27/views-of-transgender-issues-divide-along-religious-lines/

Stargel, B., & Bell, A. (2022). Examining relationships between transgender prejudice, gender essentialism, and defining and categorizing transgender people. *Psi Chi Journal of Psychological Research, 27*(4), 276–285. https://doi.org/10.24839/2325-7342.JN27.4.276

Stone, A. L. (2009). More than adding a T: American lesbian and gay activists' attitudes towards transgender inclusion. *Sexualities, 12*(3), 334–354.

Stroumsa, D. (2014). The state of transgender health care: Policy, law, and medical frameworks. *American Journal of Public Health, 104*(3), 31–38.

Stryker, S. (2008a). *Transgender history*. Seal Press.

Stryker, S. (2008b). Transgender history, homonormativity and disciplinarity. *Radical History Review, Winter, 2008*(100), 145–157.

Sudbeck, D. (2019). The current state of transgender America. In W. Swan (Ed.), *The Routledge handbook of LGBTQIA administration and policy*. Routledge Taylor & Francis. https://doi.org/10.4324/9781351258807

Swan, W. (2019). Understanding what is happening to LGBTQIA public policy in the new federal administration. In W. Swan (Ed.), *The Routledge handbook of LGBTQIA administration and policy*. Routledge Taylor & Francis Group.

Tadlock, B. L., & Taylor, J. K. (2017). Where has the field gone? An investigation of LGBTQ political science research. In M. Brettschneider, S. Burgess, & C. Keating (Eds.), *LGBTQ politics: A critical reader*. New York University Press.

Taylor, J. K., Lewis, D. C., & Haider-Markel, D. P. (2018). *The remarkable rise of transgender rights*. University of Michigan Press.

Taylor, L. A. (2013). A win for transgender employees: Chevron deference for the EEOC's decision in Macy v. Holder. *Journal of Law & Family Studies, 15*(4), 181–207.

Tebbe, E. A., & Moradi, B. (2016). Suicide risk in trans populations: An application of minority stress theory. *Journal of Counseling Psychology*, (5), 520.

Thoroughgood, C., Sawyer, K., & Webster, J. (2020, March–April). Trans inclusive workplace: How to make transgender employees feel valued at work. *Harvard Business Review*, 115–123.

Tobin, H. J. (2011). Fair and accurate identification for transgender people. *LGBTQ Policy Journal at the Harvard Kennedy School, 1*, 63–72.

Turner, I. M. (2007). Sex stereotyping Per Se: Transgender employees and title VII. *California Law Review, 95*(561), 561–596.

Twing, S. D., & Williams, T. C. (2010). Title VII's transgender trajectory: An analysis of whether transgender people are a protected class under the term "sex" and practical implications of inclusion. *Texas Journal on Civil Liberties and Civil Rights, 15*(2), 173–203.

Ulane v. Eastern Airlines, Inc., 742 F.2d 1089 (7th Cir.) (1984). https://law.justia.com/cases/federal/appellate-courts/F2/742/1081/213900/

U.S. Department of the Army. (2008). *Army regulation 40–501 standards of medical fitness.* Headquarters Department of the Army. http://arotc.osu.edu/wp-content/uploads/2017/10/AR-40-501-Standards-of-Medical-Fitness.pdf

U.S. Department of Education. (2021, June 16). *U.S. department of education confirms title IX protects students from discrimination based on sexual orientation and gender identity.* www.ed.gov/news/press-releases/us-department-education-confirms-title-ix-protects-students-discrimination-based-sexual-orientation-and-gender-identity

U.S. Department of Health and Human Services. (2020, August 18). *Nondiscrimination in health and health education programs or activities, delegation of authority document number 2020-11758.* https://www.federalregister.gov/documents/2020/06/19/2020-11758/nondiscrimination-in-health-and-health-education-programs-or-activities-delegation-of-authority

U.S. Department of Housing and Urban Development. (2021, February 11). *Implementation of executive order 13988 on the enforcement of the fair housing act.* www.hud.gov/sites/dfiles/PA/documents/HUD_Memo_EO13988.pdf

Vitulli, E. (2010). A defining moment in civil rights history? The employment non-discrimination act, trans-inclusion and homonormativity. *Sex, Research and Social Policy, 7*, 155–167.

Voyles v. Ralph K Davis Medical Center, 403 F. Supp. 456 (1975). https://law.justia.com/cases/federal/district-courts/FSupp/403/456/1560096/

Wamsley, L. (2017). *Trump says transgender people can't serve in military.* NPR. www.npr.org/sections/thetwo-way/2017/07/26/539470211/trump-says-transgender-people-cant-serve-in-military

Wang, T., Solomon, D., Durso, L., McBride, S., & Cahill, S. (2016). *State anti-transgender bathroom bills threaten transgender people's health and participation in public life.* https://fenwayhealth.org/wp-content/uploads/2015/12/COM-2485-Transgender-Bathroom-Bill-Brief_v8-pages.pdf

Weiss, J. T. (2009). Transgender identity, textualism, and the supreme court: What is the "plain meaning" of "sex" in title VII of the civil rights act of 1964? *Temple Political and Civil Rights Law Review, 18*, 573–643.

Witchel, S. F. (2018). Disorders of sex development. *Clinical Obstetrics & Gynaecology, 48*, 90–102. https://doi.org/10.1016/j.bpobgyn.2017.11.005

Yang, M., Manning, D., van den Berg, J., & Operario, D. (2015). Stigmatization and mental health in a diverse sample of transgender women. *LGBT Health, 2*(4), 306–312. https://doi.org/10.1089/lgbt.2014.0106

13

THE INTERSECTION OF LGBTQ INDIVIDUALS AND THE CRIMINAL JUSTICE SYSTEM

Kathleen Trotta

Introduction

Currently in the United States, LGBTQ individuals are a minority population. Actual numbers in the general population are difficult to ascertain, and what data do exist are likely under representative. No matter the percentage of LGBTQ individuals, they are at an increased risk for interacting with the criminal justice system in various ways (Dwyer, 2010; Wolff & Cokely, 2007). Transgender individuals are especially at an increased risk for contact with the police (Mogul et al., 2011; Stotzer, 2014).

There are multiple ways in which LGBTQ individuals are at an increased risk to interact with law enforcement and the possibility of becoming incarcerated (Dwyer, 2010; Wolff & Cokely, 2007). This chapter will examine multiple reasons for increased interaction with law enforcement and the criminal justice system as well as a brief overview of a few challenges for LGBTQ individuals if they do become incarcerated. These risks are not specific to the LGBTQ community but are compounded by the fact that LGBTQ individuals experience these various challenges statistically more often than the general population and therefore face increased risk for law enforcement and criminal justice interaction (Amnesty International, 2005; Hunt & Moodie-Mills, 2012; Stotzer, 2014; Wilber, 2015). This chapter will focus on the complex intersectionality of an LGBTQ identity (or sometimes even the perception that someone is LGBTQ) with these other factors that also increase law enforcement interaction and confrontation. This information is important not only due to the very nature of increasing law enforcement interaction but also because LGBTQ individuals often experience law enforcement differently and often more negatively than their heterosexual and cisgender peers (Dwyer, 2010).

Extent and Nature of Literature

There are several caveats that should be considered when examining this chapter and the literature that is discussed within. It first should be noted that gender identity and sexual orientation identity are vastly different although commonly grouped together in the same "community." The similarities and/or differences between those communities are too broad to discuss in this chapter. It should be stated that there are voices on both sides of the argument that gender identity and sexual orientation should or should not be included in the same community.

 DOI: 10.4324/9781003128151-16

Unfortunately, this discourse is out of context and too intricate to discuss in this chapter. This chapter will attempt to distinguish the literature that is specific to sexual orientation identity and gender identity individually whenever possible but there are times that the literature broadly positions LGBTQ individuals into the same data and research and therefore are unable to specifically state if it pertains to sexual- or gender-minority individuals specifically. If there is a specific group discussed it will be highlighted and labeled as such (gay men, transgender women, etc.). Unfortunately, the data are often broad and general and refer to LGBT or LGB as one group, as if their experience is all the same. Specificity in regard to the particular population being discussed will be used whenever possible and whenever the data are specific. Even within sexual orientation, the challenges discussed may affect gay men differently than lesbian women for one instance, but may affect bisexual men and women differently, etc.

Some of the terminologies used in this chapter may be outdated due to the research being referenced and the terminology that was used at the time. For instance, male-to-female and female-to-male are used and/or referenced in the literature reviewed but are considered outdated terms. These will be defined as they come up in this chapter or are self-explanatory. There will be some international data that will be examined as well although briefly and often terminology differs from country to country, even region to region in some places.

This chapter will focus on the specific issues related to LGBTQ youth and adults and their disproportionate representation and increased scrutiny within the criminal justice. This chapter will examine factors related to LGBTQ individuals, including the impact of family acceptance as an adolescent and across the lifespan, support, and rejection upon mental health and related outcomes. It should be noted that there is an increasing amount of data and research being compiled on LGBTQ youth and the criminal justice system that is often missing when it comes to LGBTQ adults within the same system (Institute of Medicine, 2011). The American criminal justice system has taken notice to the increasing rates of increased criminal justice interactions and incarcerated LGBTQ youth and has started implementing practices and policies to protect LGBTQ youth (Wilber, 2015). Many government agencies, non-profits, non-governmental organizations (NGOs), and private organizations have taken notice and have begun not only examining this trend but have already begun researching solutions as well as implementing them (Amnesty International, 2005; Bassichis, 2007; Institute of Medicine, 2011). As such, research may reference youth or adult populations separately or collectively and will be noted when possible to each population specifically in this chapter.

Finally, the topics and discussion contained in this chapter will be a very brief synopsis of each subject. Some areas are brief due to the limited nature of the available academic literature, and others and limited due to space. Due to the brief nature and limited space available in this chapter, some very important topics, ideas, and expansion of ideas will not be able to be covered. Areas not covered or topics or ideas that are summarized are not meant to diminish the important topics in this chapter, but unfortunately there is so much rich and important data to discuss that much of it must be limited due to the scope and size of this chapter.

Family Acceptance Versus Family Rejection

Family acceptance of LGBTQ individuals has been shown to be a strong protective factor for LGBTQ individuals in many ways, providing protection regarding both physical and mental health effects (Ryan et al., 2010). "Protective factors are characteristics associated with a lower likelihood of negative outcomes or that reduce a risk factor's impact. Protective factors may be seen a positive countering events" (SAMHSA, 2019, p. 1). These effects can be especially powerful surrounding the disclosure or "coming out" experiences (Ryan et al., 2010). It should be noted that family acceptance and rejection are separate constructs and not the converse of each other and both can occur at the same time (Perrin et al., 2004).

Risk factors "are characteristics at the biological, psychological, family, community, or cultural level that precede and are associated with a higher likelihood of negative outcomes" (SAMHSA, 2019, p. 1). Family rejection can lead to increased interaction with law enforcement because family rejection increases the likelihood of many health and social factors that increase interactions with law enforcement including suicide, homelessness, substance abuse, and sex work (Ream & Peters, 2021; Ryan et al., 2009; Ryan et al., 2010). Law enforcement contact itself has been "increasingly recognized as an adverse childhood experience . . . (although) little population-level research has examined police contact disparities by sexual orientation or gender identity" (Schwartz et al., 2022, p. 1). The discussion that follows in subsequent sections will highlight many of the social, health, and mental health effects that LGBTQ individuals experience at higher rates compared to their cisgender and heterosexual peers; family rejection is just one possible risk factor.

Rosario et al. (2009) examined whether the types of family reactions to disclosure of being lesbian, gay, or bisexual were associated with substance use and abuse among LGB youths and young adults (ages 14–21 years). In this study, the authors found that the "number of rejecting reactions to disclosure was associated with current and subsequent alcohol, cigarette, and marijuana use even after controlling for demographic factors, social desirability, and emotional distress" (Rosario et al., 2009, p. 1). Another study analyzed specific family rejecting reactions regarding sexual orientation and/or gender expression and its predictors of current health problems in LGB White and Latino young adults aged 21–25. That study found overall that "higher rates of family rejection were significantly associated with poorer health outcomes" (Ryan et al., 2009, p. 346). These young adults who were rejected by their family in adolescence were

> 8.4 times more likely to report having attempted suicide, 5.9 times more likely to report high levels of depression, 3.4 times more likely to use illegal drugs, and 3.4 times more likely to report having engaged in unprotected sexual intercourse compared with peers from families that reported no or low levels of family rejection.
>
> *(Ryan et al., 2009, p. 346)*

It should be noted that Latino men indicated the highest frequency of negative family reactions to their gender expression or sexual orientation (Ryan et al., 2009).

Ryan et al. (2010) examined family acceptance on self-esteem, social support, and overall health. When examining family acceptance, individuals "who reported high levels of family acceptance scored higher on all three measures of positive adjustment and health: self-esteem, social support, and general health" (Ryan et al., 2010, p. 208). Low levels of family acceptance had worse outcomes for depression, substance abuse, suicidal ideation, as well as suicide attempts. Those in highly accepting families had half as many suicidal thoughts (18.5%), compared to those with low family acceptance (38.3%). This trend was also true with suicide attempts with high levels of family acceptance (30.9%) compared to those with low levels of family acceptance (56.8%) (Ryan et al., 2010). When examining family acceptance on substance abuse specifically, higher levels of accepting reactions were found to protect youth from alcohol use (Rosario et al., 2009).

Family rejection has shown that LGBTQ youth are "8.4 times as likely to have attempted suicide, 5.9 times as likely to experience significant depression, .4 times as likely to use illegal drugs (and) 3.4 times as likely to have engaged in unprotected sexual intercourse" (Wilber,

2015, p. 10). Family rejection is one factor that is "driving disproportionate numbers of LGBT youth into the justice system" (Wilber, 2015, p. 4). This is partially due to family rejection leading to higher levels of homelessness and substance use and abuse which increase interaction with law enforcement (Wilber, 2015) and will be discussed individually later in this chapter.

Mental Illness and Suicidality

LGBTQ individuals experience mental illnesses at higher rates than their cisgender and heterosexual peers. Both LGB youth as well as LGBT adults experience mood disorders at much higher rates compared to their cisgender and heterosexual peers (Institute of Medicine, 2011). These mood disorders are most commonly depression and anxiety. Gay, lesbian, and bisexual adults had higher rates of anxiety and mood disorders compared to their heterosexual peers in one Canadian study (Pakula et al., 2016). Gender and sexual minority homeless youths experience depression, depressive symptoms, posttraumatic stress disorder (PTSD), anxiety, and other internalizing and externalizing behaviors at "much higher rates than their cisgender and heterosexual counterparts" (Rhoads et al., 2018, p. 643).

Prevalence of mood disorders is different between men and women and varies across the lifespan but general statistics place depression in adults at about 7% (American Psychiatric Association, 2013; Reeves et al., 2011). Biological females do tend to have higher rates of depression starting in late adolescence, but these rates typically taper off mid-life when depression in biological males tends to increase (American Psychiatric Association, 2013). One study found that major depression and generalized anxiety in LGB youths were between 1.8 and 2.9 times higher compared to their heterosexual peers (Mustanski et al., 2010). Many studies have found even higher rates of depression in transgender individuals in the general population (Nuttbrock et al., 2010). One study that examined depression in male-to-female (MtF) transgender individuals found a lifetime prevalence rate of 54.7% for those aged 19–29 and 52.4% for those 40–59 years old (Nuttbrock et al., 2010).

Individuals with a mental illness

> are at a significantly greater risk of arrest than the general population. This pattern of arrests has been associated with a phenomenon referred to as the criminalization of mental illness such that people with mental illnesses are inappropriately diverted to the criminal justice system rather than to treatment.
>
> *(Dewa et al., 2018, p. 1)*

The largest providers of mental health care in the United States are jails and prisons (Reingle Gonzalez & Connell, 2014; Torrey et al., 2010). In the 1960s, when there was a mass shutdown of state hospitals, the criminal justice system became a "revolving door" for many individuals with mental illnesses and/or who were homeless (Baillargeon et al., 2009).

In 2004 and 2005, there were three times as many individuals with a mental illness who were in prisons and jails than were in private and state hospitals (Treatment Advocacy Center, 2010). It has been repeatedly demonstrated over the past three decades, and beyond that, incarcerated individuals are found to report higher rates of mental illness compared to national prevalence rates (Bureau of Justice Statistics, 2013; Reingle Gonzalez & Connell, 2014; Wilper et al., 2009). While each individual mental illness affects various populations differently, national rates of diagnosable mental illness are approximately 9% (Reingle Gonzalez & Connell, 2014). For example, the CDC found that depression, one of the most common mental illness diagnoses, was found to be prevalent in 6.8% of adults in the general population from 2005 to 2008

(Reeves et al., 2011). Multiple studies have found that mental illness prevalence rates were approximately 75% for incarcerated females above 50% for incarcerated males (Bureau of Justice Statistics, 2006; Bureau of Justice Statistics, 2013; Reingle Gonzalez & Connell, 2014; Wilper et al., 2009).

While it is true that some individuals may develop a diagnosable mental illness while they are incarcerated (like depression or an adjustment disorder), the majority of those with diagnosable mental illnesses have them before they become incarcerated. Those who have had untreated mental health conditions are at a higher risk to reoffend as well and return to jail or prison (Reingle Gonzalez & Connell, 2014). One study highlighted that those who had received a diagnosis after incarceration were 70% more likely to be arrested after release and return to prison than those without a diagnosis (Baillargeon et al., 2009). The system is set up to create a revolving door for individuals with a mental illness to ping pong back and forth between prison and being homeless (Baillargeon et al., 2009).

Suicidality, although not a specific mental health disorder or illness, is prevalent in many LGBTQ individuals. Eisenberg and Resnick (2006) completed a study of over 2200 LGB high-school students. This study revealed over half had experienced suicidal ideation and 37.4% reported at least one suicide attempt. This study demonstrated that females in the sample who are identified as lesbian or bisexual were especially at risk and reported a 52.4% suicide attempt rate. This rate was almost double what their female heterosexual peers experienced at 24.8% (Eisenberg & Resnick, 2006). "The same dramatic trend was true for gay or bisexual men with a suicide attempt rate of 29% compared to heterosexual males at a rate of 12.6%" (Eisenberg & Resnick, 2006). "Decades of research, as well as recent data, have consistently found that LGBTQ youth are at greater risk of experiencing suicidal ideations and attempts when compared to their heterosexual counterparts" (Hatchel et al., 2019, p. 2443).

One large study of over 11,000 Wisconsin students grades 7–12 found that "LGBTQ-identified students were 3.3 times as likely to think about suicide ($p < .0001$), 3.0 times as likely to attempt suicide ($p = .007$), and 1.4 times as likely to skip school ($p = .047$)" (Robinson & Espelage, 2012, p. 309). Many may think that this level of suicidality may be due to bullying or victimization by peers but this study specifically examined victimization rates and found and "matched" their heterosexual student counterparts and they reported "equivalent levels of peer victimization" (Robinson & Espelage, 2012, p. 309). Not only did they find similar levels of victimization in their heterosexual peers, but they also found "substantial differences in suicidal ideation and suicide attempts at both higher and lower levels of victimization" (Robinson & Espelage, 2012, p. 309).

Transgender individuals may be especially at risk for suicidality. In one study of younger (19–29 years old) male-to-female transgender individuals, lifetime prevalence rates of thinking of suicide were reported at 53%, planning suicide was at 34.9%, and attempting suicide was at 31.2% (Nuttbrock et al., 2010). This same study also examined lifetime prevalence rates in older male-to-female transgender individuals and found similar patterns of suicidal ideation at 53.5%, planning suicide at 34.9%, and 28% suicide attempt rate (Nuttbrock et al., 2010). Unfortunately rates of other mental health disorders (such as schizophrenia, bipolar disorder, ADHD, and OCD) are not easy to ascertain in the LGBTQ population as many researchers have not included gender identity or sexual orientation in their background information data collection.

It is important to note that there are several confounding and intersecting factors with mental illness, as there are with all of the topics being covered in this chapter. For instance, "Rates for injuries, both intentional (e.g., homicide and suicide) and unintentional (e.g., motor vehicle), are 2–6 times higher among persons with a mental illness than in the overall population"

(Reeves et al., 2011, p. 2). Substance abuse and depression are both confounding factors in suicidality for both adolescents and adults (Esposito-Smythers et al., 2011; Fergusson et al., 1999).

Law enforcement is often involved when a person is in crisis, particularly if they are suicidal. Many with more serious mental illnesses like bipolar or schizophrenia are often arrested and incarcerated for petty crimes such as trespassing or stealing small amounts of food or cigarettes. Law enforcement is often called when someone is acting bizarrely or disorganized in public and may not understand what is happening and may resist arrest. Don't mention how often law enforcement is called or is involved when a person is accused of or is using substances. One Canadian study found that "7%–30% of calls for police service involve a person with a mental illness" (Coleman & Cotton, 2010, p. 39).

Mental illness and its etiologies are a complex problem and there is no one reason why someone may have a mental illness. To be clear, having an LGBTQ identity is not a mental illness (although "homosexuality" has a torrid history of being pathologized until 1973) (Drescher, 2015). Being a person who identifies as LGBTQ brings both unique challenges and joys. An increased risk of depression, anxiety, and suicidality is one risk factor that individuals may face.

Substance Use and Abuse

Although research on substance abuse in the LGBTQ community is limited, many studies have found increased levels of use. The minority stress model describes how those in the LGBTQ community are at a much higher risk of substance use and abuse compared to their heterosexual and cisgender peers due to the increased levels of stress that they experience due to their minority status coupled with compounding other identities and other factors (Meyer, 2015). LGBTQ youth and young adults have higher rates of both alcohol and substance use (Felner et al., 2020; Institute of Medicine, 2011; Medina-Martínez et al., 2021). When LGBTQ adults seek individual counseling, substance abuse is one of the most common concerns (Hendricks & Testa, 2012). Another study found that "openly LGBT clients entered treatment with greater frequency of substance use" compared to heterosexual and cisgender individuals (Cochran & Cauce, 2006, p. 143). In that same study, LGBT individuals had more severe substance abuse concerns and used medical services at a much higher level compared to their heterosexual and cisgender peers (Cochran & Cauce, 2006).

Some studies have shown that older gay men (and sometimes lesbian women) may be less likely to abuse substances at higher levels due to concerns about lowered inhibitions and safe sex practices and concerns surrounding sexually transmitted infections (STIs) (Hughes & Eliason, 2002; Cochran & Cauce, 2006). Younger LGBT adults are at an increased risk for substance use and abuse (Hughes & Eliason, 2002). One study of 428 younger (mean age was 25.8) gay and bisexual men found that 13.6% of them were heavy alcohol users and 43% reported poly-drug use (Greenwood et al., 2001).

Although there is a small body of evidence and literature on this subject, the Substance Abuse and Mental Health Services Administration found it necessary to publish a manual titled "A Provider's Introduction to Substance Abuse Treatment for Lesbian, Gay, Bisexual, and Transgender Individuals" (Center for Substance Abuse Treatment [US], 2001). This manual examines some older research from the 1970s to the later 1990s stating that up to 30% of lesbians may have an alcohol problem, 20–25% of gay men and lesbian women are heavy alcohol users, and marijuana and cocaine use is higher in lesbian women than their heterosexual peers (Center for Substance Abuse Treatment [US], 2001). This manual also points to particular drugs that may be more commonly abused in the LGBTQ community at that time. "Gay men and men who have sex with men (MSM) are significantly more likely to have used marijuana, psychedelics, hallucinogens, stimulants, sedatives, cocaine, barbiturates, and MDMA" along with poppers as well as other "party drugs" (Center for Substance Abuse Treatment (US), 2001, p. xiii).

There are many reasons why individuals engage in substance use, but many LGBT individuals face particular challenges compared to their heterosexual and cisgender peers. "Social stigma, family rejection, and discrimination subject LGBT youth to increased risk of substance use" (Wilber, 2015, p. 4). Heterosexism, internalized homophobia, shame, and negative self-concept may lead to increased substance abuse (Center for Substance Abuse Treatment (US), 2001). Many aspects of LGBT social life and gatherings happen at alcohol centric places such as gay bars or drag clubs (Greenwood et al., 2001; Hughes & Eliason, 2002). Greenwood et al. (2001) found that gay and bisexual men who frequented gay bars were at an increased risk for heavy alcohol use. "These disparities have been predominantly explained by minority stress theory, which posits that LGBTQ-related stressors shape negative mental health outcomes and associated coping behaviors, including substance use" (Felner et al., 2020, p. 112).

Interacting with law enforcement when using substances or excessive alcohol is a common occurrence. One study found that 20% of individuals (out of 331) with a severe mental illness has been arrested or picked up by law enforcement in the previous four months (Borum et al., 1997). This study found that the majority of these offenses were related to drugs and alcohol or public disorder such as loitering or trespassing. Many of those individuals are not captured in other data sets since many are not officially arrested or charges are dropped once they become sober. That report stated, "Risk of a police encounter was significantly related to (a) recent use of alcohol or drugs and (b) recent violent behavior" (Borum et al., 1997, p. 236). Interactions with law enforcement are not just simply due to drug offenses (buying, selling, paraphernalia, etc.) but other offenses as well including DUI/DWI, domestic violence, violent offense, property damage, public nuisance, and often times theft/robbery or white collar crimes to obtain money to support their substance abuse habit. In 2004, 17% of state prisoners and 18% of federal prisoners reported that they committed their crime to obtain money for drugs (Bureau of Justice Statistics, 2004). "In 2002, jail inmates convicted of robbery (56%), weapons violations (56%), burglary (55%), or motor vehicle theft (55%) were most likely to have reported to be using drugs at the time of the offense" (Bureau of Justice Statistics, 2002).

Homelessness

Homelessness and housing insecurity is something that affects hundreds of thousands Americans, and many more worldwide. One of the most recent counts of homeless individuals found that 17 out of every 10,000 Americans were experiencing homelessness during the yearly point-in-time count from January 2019 (National Alliance to End Homelessness, 2020). This was a total of 567,715 Americans living without a home. Homelessness affects LGBTQ individuals at a higher proportion (The Williams Institute, 2012; Wilber, 2015). Although rates vary from study to study, one study found that 40% of homeless youth are identified as LGBT (The Williams Institute, 2012). Homelessness for LGBTQ individuals often start when they are adolescents. The top five reasons for homelessness according to one study of almost 400 LGBT youths are as follows: ran away because of family rejection of sexual orientation or gender identity (46%), forced out by parents because of sexual orientation or gender identity (43%), physical, emotional, or sexual abuse at home (32%), aged out of the foster care system (17%), and financial or emotional neglect from family (14%) (Durso & Gates, 2012). Although only 32% of individuals explained that the abuse is why they were homeless, 54% of respondents had been abused at home (Durso & Gates, 2012). When examining the data, more than two or more factors may be present for some individuals given the percentages. One study found that LGBTQ youth comprised 43% of youth in drop in centers, 30% of street outreach program participants, and 30% of housing program participants (Durso & Gates, 2012). Transgender individuals are particularly vulnerable to homelessness and are often large percentages of these populations given their smaller percentage of the national population.

Overall, homeless LGBT youths are also more likely to have contact with law enforcement (Ray, 2006; Wilber, 2015). One study of homeless and law enforcement interactions found that 63% of the police departments that were surveyed (75) had "frequent contacts" with the homeless and 24% had at least one person or a department assigned to "deal with individuals living on the streets" (McNamara et al., 2013, p. 365). Of these departments that were surveyed, 72% reported that their officers were "regularly informed about the availability of shelters" and 47% provided transportation to homeless shelters (McNamara et al., 2013, p. 365). Although many of these departments were dealing with the homeless population, 59% of municipal departments and 72% of sheriff's departments offered no training to their officers in working with those who are homeless (McNamara et al., 2013).

Exploitation, Survival Sex, and Sex Work

Sex work can be a real part of many LGBTQ individuals, experience for a variety of reasons and pathways. Sex work can be forced as a form of exploitation, engaged in willingly, or often used as what is referred to as survival sex (Dank et al., 2015; Lankenau et al., 2005). It is a subsection under homelessness due to the high co-occurrence with homelessness or limited/inadequate housing (Grant et al., 2011). Nationally, 48% of transgender individuals who have reported being engaged in sex work also report being homeless (Grant et al., 2011). This trend has been found consistently across LGBTQ adults and youths in many studies; that many who engage in survival sex, sex work, or become exploited are homeless or housing insecure (Curtis et al., 2008; Lankenau et al., 2005; Wilson et al., 2009).

Unfortunately "LGBT sex trafficking is commonly overlooked and rarely reported by local and national governments" (Martinez & Kelle, 2013) which makes the scope and knowledge in this area difficult to measure and understand. LGBT child trafficking is reported even less often to local authorities (Martinez & Kelle, 2013) which may be due to homelessness, family rejection (child is kicked out and no one knows they are missing or are being exploited) or other factors. A study of 215 homeless adults found that over one-third had been sex trafficked and of those, over half were LGBTQ+ (Hogan & Roe-Sepowitz, 2020). "The odds of being LGBTQ+ and sex trafficked were two times higher compared to being heterosexual" (Hogan & Roe-Sepowitz, 2020, p. 1).

LGBT youths are at an increased risk for interaction with law enforcement due to any type of sex work (whether willingly, for survival sex, or as a result of exploitation (Irvine & Canfield, 2016; Wilber, 2015). Researchers at the Urban Institute have done great work in a first of its kind in-depth study of LGBT youth who have engaged in survival sex. This study found some LGBTQ young people may have started in sex work by someone exploiting them but may eventually engage in survival sex to meet basic needs (Dank et al., 2015). Many of these individuals begin engaging in survival sex because their LGBTQ peers have introduced them into the survival-sex economy. "Many youth engaged in survival sex experience frequent arrest for various 'quality-of-life' and misdemeanor crimes, creating further instability and perpetuating the need to engage in survival sex" (p. 2). Homelessness is one of the top reasons why LGBT youths engage in survival sex, and various studies have placed percentages between 10% and 50%

of homeless youths who engage in survival sex (Dank et al., 2015). Hogan and Roe-Sepowitz (2020) found among LGBTQ+ adults that those who had been exploited were significantly more likely to be engaged in exchanging sex for money. Although survival sex is not a phenomena that is unique to LGBT individuals, LGB youths were seven times more likely to engage in survival sex than their heterosexual peers and transgender youth were eight times more likely to have engaged in the practice than their cisgender peers (Freeman & Hamilton, 2008).

There are also those who willingly engage in sex work. The academic research on this topic is limited, especially in the United States due to very limited sex work laws, but it is happening in places where it is legal and not. There are some individuals and organizations working on decriminalizing sex work since there are many who engage in it willingly (Brooks-Gordon et al., 2021). There are many LGBT individuals who engage in consensual sex work for a variety of reasons, too many to name here. Unfortunately, law enforcement can often become involved in consensual sex work, particularly when LGBTQ individuals are involved since sex work is illegal in most parts of the country. LGBTQ youth are "more likely that their straight and cisgender peers to be arrested and criminally charge with sex offenses for consensual sexual activity" (Wilber, 2015, p. 11). This law enforcement presence is not always welcome, particularly if willingly or when someone is trying to get their basic needs met through their sex work.

Law Enforcement Harassment

"The United States has had a significant history of mistreatment of LGBT people by law enforcement, including profiling, entrapment, discrimination and harassment by officers" (Mallory et al., 2015, p. 1). Profiling and mistreatment by law enforcement can occur to LGBT individuals, or even those perceived as LGBT, just by being in LGBT neighborhoods (Dank et al., 2015; Make The Road New York, 2012). One 2014 report found that 73% of LGBT individuals, and people living with HIV, had face-to-face contact with law enforcement in the past five years (Mallory et al., 2015). Of those reports, 21% reported hostile attitudes from law enforcement, 14% were verbally assaulted by law enforcement, 3% were sexually harassed, and 2% reported physical assaults by law enforcement officers (Mallory et al., 2015). Transgender individuals consistently report higher frequencies of misconduct by law enforcement than their cisgender peers. One 2012 report found that two-thirds of Latina transgender women in Los Angeles reported that they had been verbally harassed by law enforcement, 21% indicated that they had been physically assaulted and 24% reported being sexually assaulted (Mallory et al., 2015). Another report from 2011 of one of the largest surveys of transgender people found the 22% of transgender individuals reported being harassed by law enforcement because of bias and 6% had been physically assaulted by law enforcement (Mallory et al., 2015). Almost half (46%) reported feeling uncomfortable seeking law enforcement assistance for any matter (Mallory et al., 2015).

LGBTQ BIPOC Individuals

Throughout much of the data that are discussed earlier, each of these individual disparities are even further compounded for LGBTQ individuals of color. The more layers of intersectionality that exist, creates a more intricate situation not only for the individual who may be experiencing the complexities of their multiple identities, health disparities, and social and economic constructs but also for the larger systems at play; thus, the solutions are even more complex. This section will highlight only a few of the intersections of the challenges discussed earlier for individuals of color.

Law enforcement harassment and profiling can be particularly challenging for both LGBT youth and adults of color (Dank et al., 2014). "Stop and frisk" policies focused on individuals of color have made headlines in cities across the country. During 2011, in the Jackson Heights Neighborhood in New York, 90–93% of stop and frisk stops were individuals of color (Make the Road New York, 2012). "Data from a wide range of sources show that such harassment and discrimination is greatest for LGBT people of color" (The Williams Institute, 2012, p. 1). LGBT individuals of color are more likely to be incarcerated as well. One survey of incarcerated LGBT youth, found that 85% of them were identified as youths of color (Irvine & Canfield, 2016).

When considering other challenges in the aforementioned sections, multiple studies have shown that the majority of youths in urban environments that engage in survival sex are people of color (Curtis et al., 2008; Dank et al., 2014). This is consistent with research over time that conclude that Black and Latinx youth are more likely to engage in survival sex (Dank et al., 2014; Wilson et al. 2009). Homelessness effects individuals of color at higher percentages. One study of Los Angeles homeless individuals found that 57% were Black and approximately 15% were Latino (SAMHSA, 2011).

BIPOC LGBTQ individuals face some differences while incarcerated as well. "Chi-square testing found no significant differences between racial groups and sexual violence (unwanted touching or sexual assault) from prison staff, but found significant differences between racial groups and sexual violence from other prisoners" (Aftab, 2017, p. 46). This included mostly unwanted touch from other prisoners of all races. This analysis also provided qualitative analysis on LGBTQ BIPOC individuals and found "For Black prisoners, race is more relevant in the experience of sexual violence from prison staff" as "Black respondents were the only ones to mention race when writing about abuse from prison staff" (Aftab, 2017, p. 50).

Challenges While Incarcerated

Although discussing the challenges LGBTQ individuals may experience while incarcerated could be a chapter in itself, it should be briefly explored as many issues are very serious and even life-threatening. LGBTQ individuals are overrepresented in prisons (Drake, 2018; Irvine & Canfield, 2016). All LGBTQ individuals face dangers while incarcerated but transgender individuals are at a particularly high risk within the correctional system and have more nuanced difficulties compared to their LGB peers (Brown & McDuffie, 2009; Irvine & Canfield, 2016).

Although a federal law called the Prison Rape Elimination Act of 2003 (PREA) was enacted in order to protect all prisoners from sexual assault, it assisted in shedding light on the rape of incarcerated LGBTQ individuals. The law requires sexual assault data to be collected and examined in adult and juvenile correctional facilities (Wilber, 2015). The data have consistently shown that LGBTQ individuals are at a greater risk of sexual assault compared to their peers (Wilber, 2015). Once this came to light, the Department of Justice (DOJ) has explicitly instituted protections for LGBTQ individuals in prisons and jails with a particular focus on youth facilities at a federal level; many states have followed suit instituting protections (Wilber, 2015). Although this information has been helpful in many ways, it may also reveal to both staff and peers of someone's LGBTQ identity and put them at increased risk for victimization based on their identity or by being outed. "Before PREA, a LGBT youth's safety was not commonly considered when placing them into a housing unit, or placing an individual" into administrative segregation or protective isolation (Trotta, 2019, p. 49). PREA was passed to protect all incarcerated persons but has played a significant role in considering housing options and safety for LGBTQ youth (Wilber, 2015). Due to the increased risk of self-harm and abuse, solitary confinement and other administrative custody arrangements need to be carefully considered.

These housing arrangements should only be used in the most extreme cases but is still used far more often than clinically indicated.

Individuals who are LGBTQ, or even perceived to be LGBTQ, are more likely to experience abuse while incarcerated, particularly sexual abuse (Simopoulos & Khin, 2014). Transgender inmates are 13 times more likely to be sexually assaulted compared to cisgender individuals (Jenness & Fenstermaker, 2016). Two large-scale studies found that 58.5% and 59% of female transgender (MtF) inmates in California prisons had been sexually assaulted at least once while incarcerated compared to just over 4% of cisgender males (Jenness & Fenstermaker, 2016; Jenness et al., 2007). The Bureau of Justice Statistics also found a high rate of staff to inmate sexual misconduct (Bureau of Justice Statistics, 2013b; Jenness & Fenstermaker, 2016). In 2011 and 2012, staff to transgender inmate sexual assault was 15.2% for prisons and 18.3% for jails compared to 2.1% and 1.7%, respectively, for cisgender individuals (Bureau of Justice Statistics, 2013b; Jenness & Fenstermaker, 2016).

Abuse and sexual assault unfortunately are only two aspects of difficulties LGBTQ individuals face when incarcerated. Difficulties with appropriate and safe placement, the overuse of administrative segregation (solitary confinement), increased risk of suicidality and/or self-harm (particularly genital self-harm for transgender individuals), access to gender-affirming products or clothes, and access to proper competent medical and mental health care and professionals are all problems for this population. This area of study is new (particularly since PREA was passed by Congress in 2003), and data are limited but each of these factors make incarceration more difficult, dangerous, and at times life-threatening to LGBTQ individuals (Jenness et al., 2007; Li, 2021; Simopoulos & Khin, 2014; Wilber, 2015).

What Does It All Mean?

The aforementioned information is a brief illustration of several possible ways that LGBTQ individuals are at an increased risk of interacting with the criminal justice system. These examples are no way causal in nature or something that should be used to stigmatize LGBTQ individuals even further than society already does. Although not a causal relationship, there are serious and often lifelong consequences for even brief interactions with the police and the criminal justice system. The goal of this discussion is merely used as a discourse to highlight difficulties that LGBTQ individuals may face so that society can continue to study and improve conditions for all LGBTQ individuals. Improving conditions and circumstances during criminal justice contact, or reducing or eliminating contact all together, would improve life for not only LGBTQ individuals but also individuals with other minority identities (people of color, homeless individuals, individuals who struggle with substance abuse or mental illness, etc.). These interactions are too prevalent and too common in LGBTQ communities to continue to happen. Real work and change need to be implemented to lessen criminal justice involvement in unnecessary areas where proper social structure and support would be a better solution for all. This important work and change cannot happen without first having a conversation of the difficulties and intersectionality of multiple identities which this chapter just begins to touch the surface of.

References

Aftab, S. J. (2017). *A mixed-method study examining the intersection of race and sexual violence among LGBTQ prisoners* [Master's thesis]. https://scholarworks.smith.edu/theses/1880/

American Psychiatric Association. (2013). *Diagnostic and statistical manual of mental disorders* (5th ed.). American Psychiatric Association.

Amnesty International, USA. (2005). *Stonewalled: Police abuse and misconduct against lesbian, gay, bisexual, and transgender people in the US.* Amnesty International.

Baillargeon, J., Binswanger, I. A., Penn, J. V., Williams, B. A., & Murray, O. J. (2009). Psychiatric disorders and repeat incarcerations: The revolving prison door. *American Journal of Psychiatry: Official Journal of The American Psychiatric Association, 166*(1), 103–109.

Bassichis, D. M. (2007). *It's war in here: A report on the treatment of transgender and intersex people in New York State men's prisons.* Sylvia Rivera Law Project SRLP.

Borum, R., Swanson, J., Swartz, M., & Hiday, V. (1997). Substance abuse, violent behavior, and police encounters among persons with severe mental disorder. *Journal of Contemporary Criminal Justice, 13*(3), 236–250.

Brooks-Gordon, B., Morris, M., & Sanders, T. (2021). Harm reduction and decriminalization of sex work: Introduction to the special section. *Sexuality Research and Social Policy, 18,* 809–818.

Brown, G., & McDuffie, E. (2009). Health care policies addressing transgender inmates in prison systems in the United States. *Journal of Correctional Health Care, 15*(4), 280–291.

Bureau of Justice Statistics. (2002). *Substance dependence, abuse, and treatment of jail inmates, 2002.* U.S. Government Printing Office.

Bureau of Justice Statistics. (2004). *Drug use and dependence, state and federal prisoners, 2004.* U.S. Government Printing Office.

Bureau of Justice Statistics. (2006). *Mental health problems of prison and jail inmates, 2006.* U.S. Government Printing Office.

Bureau of Justice Statistics. (2013). *Correctional populations in the United States, 2012.* U.S. Government Printing Office.

Bureau of Justice Statistics. (2013b). Sexual victimization in prisons and jails reported by inmates, 2011–12. Washington, DC: U.S. Government Printing Office.

Center for Substance Abuse Treatment (US). (2001). *A provider's introduction to substance abuse treatment for lesbian, gay, bisexual, and transgender individuals.* US Dept. of Health and Human Services, Substance Abuse and Mental Health Services Administration, Center for Substance Abuse Treatment.

Cochran, B. N., & Cauce, A. M. (2006). Characteristics of lesbian, gay, bisexual, and transgender individuals entering substance abuse treatment. *Journal of Substance Abuse Treatment, 30*(2), 135–146.

Coleman, T. G., & Cotton, D. H. (2010). Reducing risk and improving outcomes of police interactions with people with mental illness. *Journal of Police Crisis Negotiations, 10*(1–2), 39–57.

Curtis, R., Terry, K., Dank, M., Dombrowski, K., & Khan, B. (2008). *The commercial sexual exploitation of children in New York City.* Center for Court Innovation.

Dank, M., Yahner, J., Madden, K., Bañuelos, I., Yu, L., Ritchie, A., Ritchie, A., Mora, M., & Conner, B. M. (2015). *Surviving the streets of New York: Experiences of LGBTQ youth, YMSM, and YWSW engaged in survival sex.* Urban Institute.

Dewa, C. S., Loong, D., Trujillo, A., & Bonato, S. (2018). Evidence for the effectiveness of police-based pre-booking diversion programs in decriminalizing mental illness: A systematic literature review. *PLoS One, 13*(6), e0199368.

Drake, D. S. (2018). Incarceration of LGBTQ people. In *The Routledge handbook of LGBTQIA administration and policy* (pp. 314–334). Routledge.

Drescher, J. (2015). Out of DSM: Depathologizing homosexuality. *Behavioral Sciences, 5*(4), 565–575.

Durso, L. E., & Gates, G. J. (2012). *Serving our youth: Findings from a national survey of services providers working with lesbian, gay, bisexual and transgender youth who are homeless or at risk of becoming homeless.* The Williams Institute.

Dwyer, A. (2010). Policing lesbian, gay, bisexual and transgender young people: A gap in the research literature. *Current Issues in Criminal Justice, 22*(3), 415–433.

Eisenberg, M. E., & Resnick, M. D. (2006). Suicidality among gay, lesbian and bisexual youth: The role of protective factors. *Journal of Adolescent Health, 39*(5), 662–668.

Esposito-Smythers, C., Spirito, A., Kahler, C. W., Hunt, J., & Monti, P. (2011). Treatment of co-occurring substance abuse and suicidality among adolescents: A randomized trial. *Journal of Consulting and Clinical Psychology, 79*(6), 728.

Felner, J. K., Wisdom, J. P., Williams, T., Katuska, L., Haley, S. J., Jun, H. J., & Corliss, H. L. (2020). Stress, coping, and context: Examining substance use among LGBTQ young adults with probable substance use disorders. *Psychiatric Services, 71*(2), 112–120.

Fergusson, D. M., Horwood, L. J., & Beautrais, A. L. (1999). Is sexual orientation related to mental health problems and suicidality in young people? *Archives of General Psychiatry, 56*(10), 876–880.

Freeman, L., & Hamilton, D. (2008). *A count of homeless youth in New York City.* Empire State Coalition of Youth and Family Services.

Grant, J. M., Mottet, L. A., Tanis, J., Harrison, J., Herman, J. L., & Keisling, M. (2011). *Injustice at every turn: A report of the national transgender discrimination survey.* National Center for Transgender Equality and National Gay and Lesbian Task Force.

Greenwood, G. L., White, E. W., Page-Shafer, K., Bein, E., Osmond, D. H., Paul, J., & Stall, R. D. (2001). Correlates of heavy substance use among young gay and bisexual men: The San Francisco young men's health study. *Drug and Alcohol Dependence, 61*(2), 105–112.

Hatchel, T., Ingram, K. M., Mintz, S., Hartley, C., Valido, A., Espelage, D. L., & Wyman, P. (2019). Predictors of suicidal ideation and attempts among LGBTQ adolescents: The roles of help-seeking beliefs, peer victimization, depressive symptoms, and drug use. *Journal of Child and Family Studies, 28,* 2443–2455.

Hendricks, M. L., & Testa, R. J. (2012). A conceptual framework for clinical work with transgender and gender nonconforming clients: An adaptation of the minority stress model. *Professional Psychology-Research and Practice, 43*(5), 460–467.

Hogan, K. A., & Roe-Sepowitz, D. (2020). LGBTQ+ homeless young adults and sex trafficking vulnerability. *Journal of Human Trafficking,* 1–16.

Hughes, T. L., & Eliason, M. (2002). Substance use and abuse in lesbian, gay, bisexual and transgender populations. *Journal of Primary Prevention, 22*(3), 263–298.

Hunt, J., & Moodie-Mills, A. (2012). *The unfair criminalization of gay and transgender youth.* Center for American Progress. www.americanprogress.org/wpcontent/uploads/issues/2012/06/pdf/juvenile_justice.pdf).

Institute of Medicine. (2011). *The health of lesbian, gay, bisexual, and transgender people: Building a foundation for better understanding.* National Academies Press.

Irvine, A., & Canfield, M. P. P. (2016). The overrepresentation of lesbian, gay, bisexual, questioning, gender nonconforming and transgender youth within the child welfare to juvenile justice crossover population. *Journal of Gender, Social Policy & the Law, 24*(2), 2.

Jenness, V., & Fenstermaker, S. (2016). Forty years after Brownmiller: Prisons for men, transgender inmates, and the rape of the feminine. *Gender & Society, 30*(1), 14–29.

Jenness, V., Maxson, C. L., Matsuda, K. N., & Sumner, J. M. (2007). Violence in California correctional facilities: An empirical examination of sexual assault. *Bulletin, 2*(2), 1–4.

Lankenau, S. E., Clatts, M. C., Welle, D., Goldsamt, L. A., & Gwadz, M. V. (2005). Street careers: Homelessness, drug use, and sex work among young men who have sex with men (YMSM). *International Journal of Drug Policy, 16*(1), 10–18.

Li, A. (2021, December). To what extent does society need to support LGBTQ+ prisoners in American prison housing?. In *2021 4th international conference on humanities education and social sciences (ICHESS 2021)* (pp. 572–575). Atlantis Press.

Make the Road New York. (2012, October). *Transgressive policing: Abuse of LGBTQ communities of color in Jackson Heights.* Make the Road New York.

Mallory, C., Hasenbush, A., & Sears, B. (2015). *Discrimination and harassment by law enforcement officers in the LGBT community.* The Williams Institute.

Martinez, O., & Kelle, G. (2013). Sex trafficking of LGBT individuals: A call for service provision, research, and action. *The International Law News, 42*(4).

McNamara, R. H., Crawford, C., & Burns, R. (2013). Policing the homeless: Policy, practice, and perceptions. *Policing: An International Journal of Police Strategies & Management, 18*(22), 11801.

Medina-Martínez, J., Saus-Ortega, C., Sánchez-Lorente, M. M., Sosa-Palanca, E. M., García-Martínez, P., & Mármol-López, M. I. (2021). Health inequities in LGBT people and nursing interventions to reduce them: A systematic review. *International Journal of Environmental Research and Public Health, 18*(22), 11801.

Meyer, I. H. (2015). Resilience in the study of minority stress and health of sexual and gender minorities. *Psychology of Sexual Orientation and Gender Diversity, 2*(3), 209–213.

Mogul, J. L., Ritchie, A. J., & Whitlock, K. (2011). *Queer (in) justice: The criminalization of LGBT people in the United States* (Vol. 5). Beacon Press.

Mustanski, B. S., Garofalo, R., & Emerson, E. M. (2010). Mental health disorders, psychological distress, and suicidality in a diverse sample of lesbian, gay, bisexual, and transgender youths. *American Journal of Public Health, 100*(12), 2426–2432.

National Alliance to End Homelessness. (2020). *State of homelessness: 2020 edition.* National Alliance to End Homelessness. https://endhomelessness.org/homelessness-in-america/homelessness-statistics/state-of-homelessness-2020/

Nuttbrock, L., Hwahng, S., Bockting, W., Rosenblum, A., Mason, M., Macri, M., & Becker, J. (2010). Psychiatric impact of gender-related abuse across the life course of male-to-female transgender persons. *Journal of Sex Research, 47*(1), 12–23.

Pakula, B., Shoveller, J., Ratner, P. A., & Carpiano, R. (2016). Prevalence and co-occurrence of heavy drinking and anxiety and mood disorders among gay, lesbian, bisexual, and heterosexual Canadians. *American Journal of Public Health, 106*(6), 1042–1048.

Perrin, E. C., Cohen, K., Gold, M., Ryan, C., Savin-Williams, R., & Schorzman, C. (2004). Gay and lesbian issues in pediatric health care. *Current Problems in Pediatric and Adolescent Health Care, 34*(10), 355–398.

Ray, N. (2006). *Lesbian, gay, bisexual and transgender youth: An epidemic of homelessness.* National Gay and Lesbian Task Force Policy Institute and National Coalition for the Homeless.

Ream, G., & Peters, A. (2021). Working with suicidal and homeless LGBTQ+ youth in the context of family rejection. *Journal of Health Service Psychology, 47,* 41–50.

Reeves, W. C., Stine, T., Pratt, L. A., Thompson, W., Ahluwalia, I. B., Dhingra, S. S., McKnight-Eily, L. R., Harrison, L., D'Angelo, D. V., Williams, L., Morrow, B., Gould, D., & Safran, M. A. (2011). *Mental illness surveillance among adults in the United States.* U.S. Department of Health and Human Services Center for Disease Control and Prevention.

Reingle Gonzalez, J. M., & Connell, N. M. (2014). Mental health of prisoners: Identifying barriers to mental health treatment and medication continuity. *American Journal of Public Health, 104*(12), 2328–2333.

Rhoades, H., Rusow, J. A., Bond, D., Lanteigne, A., Fulginiti, A., & Goldbach, J. T. (2018). Homelessness, mental health and suicidality among LGBTQ youth accessing crisis services. *Child Psychiatry & Human Development, 49,* 643–651.

Robinson, J. P., & Espelage, D. L. (2012). Bullying explains only part of LGBTQ–heterosexual risk disparities: Implications for policy and practice. *Educational Researcher, 41*(8), 309–319.

Rosario, M., Schrimshaw, E. W., & Hunter, J. (2009). Disclosure of sexual orientation and subsequent substance use and abuse among lesbian, gay, and bisexual youths: Critical role of disclosure reactions. *Psychology of Addictive Behaviors, 23*(1), 175.

Ryan, C., Huebner, D., Diaz, R. M., & Sanchez, J. (2009). Family rejection as a predictor of negative health outcomes in white and Latino lesbian, gay, and bisexual young adults. *Pediatrics, 123*(1), 346–352.

Ryan, C., Russell, S. T., Huebner, D., Diaz, R., & Sanchez, J. (2010). Family acceptance in adolescence and the health of LGBT young adults. *Journal of Child and Adolescent Psychiatric Nursing, 23*(4), 205–213.

Schwartz, G. L., Jahn, J. L., & Geller, A. (2022). Policing sexuality: Sexual minority youth, police contact, and health inequity. *SSM—Population Health, 20,* 101292. https://doi.org/10.1016/j.ssmph.2022.101292

Simopoulos, E. F., & Khin, E. K. (2014). Fundamental principles inherent in the comprehensive care of transgender inmates. *The Journal of The American Academy of Psychiatry and The Law, 42*(1), 26–36.

Stotzer, R. L. (2014). Law enforcement and criminal justice personnel interactions with transgender people in the United States: A literature review. *Aggression and Violent Behavior, 19*(3), 263–277.

Substance Abuse and Mental Health Services Administration (SAMHSA). (2011). *Current statistics on the prevalence and characteristics of people experiencing homelessness in the United States.* SAMHSA.

Substance Abuse and Mental Health Services Administration (SAMHSA). 2019. *Risk and protective factors* [Infographic]. www.samhsa.gov%2Fsites%2Fdefault%2Ffiles% 2F20190718-samhsa-risk-protective-factors.pdf

Torrey, E. F., Kennard, A. D., Eslinger, D., Lamb, R., & Pavle, J. (2010). More mentally ill persons are in jails and prisons than hospitals: A survey of the states (pp. 1–18). Treatment Advocacy Center.

Trotta, K. A. (2019). *Training staff to serve transgender individuals in correctional settings* [Doctoral dissertation, Regent University].

Wilber, S. (2015). *A guide to juvenile detention reform. Lesbian, gay, bisexual and transgender youth in the juvenile justice system.* The Annie E. Casey Foundation. www.aecf.org/resources/lesbian-gay-bisexual-and-transgender-youth-in-the-juvenilejustice-system/

Wilper, A., Woolhandler, S., Boyd, J., Lasser, K., McCormick, D., Bor, D., & Himmelstein, D. (2009). The health and health care of US prisoners: Results of a nationwide survey. *American Journal of Public Health, 99*(4), 666–672.

Wilson, E. C., Garofalo, R., Harris, R. D., Herrick, A., Martinez, M., Martinez, J., Belzer, M., & Adolescent Medicine Trials Network for HIV/AIDS Interventions. (2009). Transgender female youth and sex work: HIV risk and a comparison of life factors related to engagement in sex work. *AIDS and Behavior, 13*(5), 902–913.

Wolff, K. B., & Cokely, C. L. (2007). "To protect and to serve?": An exploration of police conduct in relation to the gay, lesbian, bisexual, and transgender community. *Sexuality and Culture, 11*(2), 1–23.

14

THE ECONOMICS OF BEING LGBT. A REVIEW

2015–2020

Nick Drydakis

Currently, being gay or lesbian is illegal in approximately 70 countries (Human Rights Watch, 2020). At least nine countries have national laws that criminalize forms of gender expression and target trans people (Human Rights Watch, 2020). Surveys in the EU and OECD regions indicated that LGBT people experience societal biases (European Union Agency for Fundamental Rights, 2020; Valfort, 2017). The surveys found the persistence of discrimination in everyday life, such as at school, work, securing housing, and accessing healthcare or social services (European Union Agency for Fundamental Rights, 2020; Valfort, 2017). In the EU, the proportion of LGBT respondents who felt discriminated against at work in 2019 (21%) was higher than in 2012 (19%) (European Union Agency for Fundamental Rights, 2020). Furthermore, a higher proportion of trans respondents felt discriminated against at work in 2019 (36%) compared to 2012 (22%) (European Union Agency for Fundamental Rights, 2020).

Prior review studies illustrated that LGBT people reported more incidents of harassment and were more likely to report discriminatory treatments in the labor market. Additionally, they experienced a lower life satisfaction level in comparison to heterosexual and cisgender people (Drydakis, 2019a; Valfort, 2017; Ozeren, 2014). Moreover, sexual minorities experienced poorer physical and psychological well-being than their heterosexual peers (Hafeez et al., 2017; Lick et al., 2013; Meads, 2020; Semlyen et al., 2019). Sexual minorities' poor well-being was primarily attributed to the negative consequences of sexual minority stigma (Meyer, 2003). Such stigma complicates sexual minorities' lives. A 2018 national representative study in the United Kingdom found that 70% of respondents avoided being open about their sexual orientation for fear of an adverse reaction, predominantly in the workplace. They scored their life satisfaction on average 6.48 out of 10, compared to 7.66 for the general U.K. population (Office for National Statistics, 2018).

This chapter offers a brief review of the economics of being LGBT based on studies published between 2015 and 2020. The study attempts to translate and synthesize the available findings in a systematic manner (Tranfield et al., 2003), in addition to offering a review of contemporary knowledge of the subject matter. Outcomes are grouped into eight thematics: (a) access to occupations based on sexual orientation and gender identity, (b) poverty rates based on sexual orientation and gender identity, (c) earnings differences based on sexual orientation, (d) earnings differences based on gender identity, (e) job satisfaction differences based on sexual

DOI: 10.4324/9781003128151-17

orientation, (f) job satisfaction and gender identity, (g) family support and long-run outcomes for LGB people, and (h) LGBT inclusivity and outcomes.

Method

A systematic literature review (Ozeren, 2014) is conducted applying a multi-faceted approach including the planning, conducting, reporting, and dissemination of appropriate studies (Tranfield et al., 2003). In the initial stage of planning, the domain of the subject matter, namely, LGBT discrimination in the labor market, and the main data extraction source, Google Scholar, was identified. In the conducting phase of the systematic review, a four-stage approach was utilized. Aligning with Ozeren (2014), this study (a) identified keywords, defined selection criteria, and papers to be extracted, (b) evaluated abstracts to determine the papers' relevance, (c) downloaded the screened papers, and (d) evaluated the downloaded papers. All the selected articles, published between 2015 and 2020, were required to contain at least one of the following keywords in their titles or abstracts: LGBT/sexual orientation/trans identity and workplace discrimination; labor discrimination; wages/income; poverty; unemployment; workplace bullying; workplace inclusivity, or positive actions. The recently reviewed research findings, the application of reproducible methods of selection and evaluation of related literature, and the grouping around the eight thematics represent the methodological strengths of the current study. Little evidence exists of any other recent literature review on being LGBT presenting simultaneous patterns of occupational barriers, income and poverty differences, job satisfaction, family support, and workplace bullying, as well as inclusivity's payoffs.

Occupational Access Constraints Based on Sexual Orientation and Gender Identity

Applicants who were identified as gay men or lesbian women during the initial stage of the hiring process were discriminated against in favor of comparable heterosexual applicants (Drydakis, 2019a). Hiring discrimination potentially leads to increased rates of unemployment and poverty, which can adversely affect mental health and well-being (Drydakis, 2019a; Paul & Moser, 2009). A 2020 meta-analysis of field experiments (correspondence tests) in OECD countries, covering the period between 1981 and 2018, found that gay men experienced 39% lower access to occupations than heterosexual men (Flage, 2020). Additionally, lesbian women were found to face 32% lower access to occupations than heterosexual women (Flage, 2020). The meta-analysis indicated that if only studies that had been carried out in the last decade were considered, the penalties would still be of the same magnitude (Flage, 2020).

Moreover, Drydakis (2019a) conducted a literature review and found that the occupational access barriers varied for gay men between 3% and 40%, while for lesbian women, the figure ranged from 6% to 27%. These patterns were experienced in the United States, the United Kingdom, Cyprus, Austria, Greece, and Sweden (Drydakis, 2019a; Drydakis & Zimmermann, 2020). Biases during the hiring stage against sexual minorities might highlight firms' preferences for sexual majorities and not be a result of uncertainty regarding the vocational behavior of sexual minorities (Drydakis, 2014). In addition, the occupational access constraints against gay men are potentially higher in male-dominated occupations, whereas occupational access constraints against lesbian women might be higher in female-dominated roles (Drydakis, 2015a). The discourse of gender might play critical roles in promoting and sustaining the sexual division of labor, the social definition of tasks as either men's work or women's work, and the exclusions for those who deviate from gender assumptions (Drydakis, 2015a).

In Sweden, Granberg et al. (2020) presented the results of the first field experiment on trans peoples' hiring prospects. A comparison of trans and cisgender people in male- and female-dominated occupations found patterns of discrimination. In Belgium, Van Borm et al. (2020) presented a scenario experiment aiming to evaluate the treatment of trans men during the selection and hiring process. The study uncovered evidence of distaste against trans men among co-employees and customers.

Poverty Rates Based on Sexual Orientation and Gender Identity

In relation to sexual orientation, Schneebaum and Badgett (2019) used data from the American Community Survey from 2010 to 2014. The study found that gay male couples were one percentage point more likely to be in poverty than heterosexual married couples. In addition, the study found that lesbian women were 2.4 percentage points more likely to be in poverty than heterosexual married couples. The study indicated that prejudice against sexual minorities among social workers potentially generates barriers to accessing benefits for sexual minorities with low incomes. Additionally, in the United States, Badgett (2018) used the National Health Interview Survey for the period 2013–2016, which found that bisexual men experienced a higher level of poverty by 5.3 percentage points than heterosexual men. Bisexual women were more likely to be in poverty by 5.4 percentage points than heterosexual women.

Moreover, in the United Kingdom, Uhrig (2015) employed the UK Household Longitudinal Study for the period 2011–2012. The findings show that gay men and bisexual men faced greater poverty compared to heterosexual men. Comparable patterns were found to be held for bisexual women compared to heterosexual women. Drydakis (2012) indicated that bisexuality is punished more than homosexuality. There is a belief that bisexual people are gay people who falsely declare a desire for the opposite sex to 'improve' their position in the society (Drydakis, 2012). It might be the case that bisexual people face two penalties: one penalty for being attracted to same-sex partners and another penalty for being seen as lying about their attraction to the opposite sex (Drydakis, 2012).

In terms of gender identity, in the United States, Ciprikis et al. (2020) used data from 2015's Behavioral Risk Factor Surveillance System. The study found that cis men are 10% more likely than trans women and trans men to annually earn above $50,000. In the same region, Carpenter et al. (2020) utilized the Behavioral Risk Factor Surveillance System from 2014 to 2017. The study found that trans women experienced higher poverty by 6.8% than cis men. Trans people's poverty rates are potentially driven by high levels of unemployment (Leppel, 2020). A review study indicated dramatically higher trans unemployment rates than those for the general population in Australia, the United States, the United Kingdom, and Ireland (Leppel, 2020).

Earnings Differences Based on Sexual Orientation

This section provides information on earnings differences based on sexual orientation in four countries: the United States, Canada, the United Kingdom, and Australia. The section ends with discussion of the 18 studies in terms of time periods.

Earnings Differences Based on Sexual Orientation in the United States

This research identified five U.S. studies on earnings differences based on sexual orientation published between 2015 and 2020, covering the period 1991–2016 (Carpenter & Eppink, 2017; Chai & Maroto, 2020; Jepsen & Jepsen, 2017; Mize, 2016; Sabia, 2015).

Sabia (2015) used the National Longitudinal Study of Adolescent Health Survey covering the period 1994–2005, which found that gay men experienced earnings penalties of 30.6%. For bisexual men, the earnings penalties were 8.5%. Lesbian women faced earnings premiums of 9.9%, while bisexual women faced earnings penalties of 0.9%. Mize (2016) used the General Social Survey between 1991 and 2014. The study found that bisexual men encountered earnings penalties of 12%. Bisexual women were found to face earnings penalties of 7%.

Carpenter and Eppink (2017) used the 2013–2015 National Health Interview Survey. The study estimated that gay men faced higher earnings (earnings premiums) of 9.7% than comparable heterosexual men. Bisexual men experienced lower earnings (earnings penalties) of 2.1% than comparable heterosexual men. Lesbian women were found to experience earnings premiums of 8.6%. Bisexual women experienced earnings penalties of 3.1%. Meanwhile, Jepsen and Jepsen (2017) utilized the American Community Survey from 2007 to 2011. The authors found that gay men faced earnings penalties of 20.4%. Lesbian women experienced earnings premiums of 21.2%. Additionally, Chai and Maroto (2020) utilized the General Social Survey for 1991–2016 and found that gay men faced earnings penalties of 2.8%. Bisexual men faced earnings penalties of 14.9%. Carpenter and Eppink (2017) suggested that gay men's stronger earnings patterns might stem from the improvement in attitudes towards gay men over the past decade. It is indicated that an effective earnings response to legislative and attitude changes for sexual minorities proves more positive than what tends to be realized for the gender pay gap and ethnicity (Aksoy et al., 2018).

Two studies on intersectionality provided additional insights. Douglas and Steinberger (2015) utilized the 2000 U.S. Census. White gay men experienced lower earnings than white heterosexual men, and black gay men experienced lower earnings than black heterosexual men. White lesbian women experienced earnings premiums in comparison to white heterosexual women, and black lesbian women experienced earnings premiums in comparison to black heterosexual women. Comparable patterns were found to be held for Hispanic and Asian population groups. del Rio and Alonso-Villar (2019) utilized the American Community Survey for the period between 2010 and 2014. The study found that the racial penalty is larger for heterosexual men whereas the sexual orientation penalty is greater for white men. The sexual orientation wage premium of lesbian women is quite small for blacks and much higher for Hispanics and Asians than for whites.

Earnings Differences Based on Sexual Orientation in Canada

Four studies were identified from Canada encompassing the period 2001–2017 (Cerf, 2016; Dilmaghani, 2018; Waite, 2015; Waite et al., 2020). Waite (2015) used the 2001 and 2006 Census, as well as the 2011 National Household Survey. It is found that in 2001, gay men experienced earnings penalties of 7.2%; in 2006, the earnings penalty was 6.3%; and in 2011, the earnings penalty was 6.7%. Lesbian women in 2001 experienced earnings premiums of 6.6%; in 2006, the earnings premium was 9.2%; and in 2011, the earnings premium was 6.9%. Cerf (2016) utilized the Canadian Community Health Survey for the period 2003–2009. Gay men experienced an earnings penalty of 9.0%. Lesbian women were found to experience an earnings premium of 2.7%.

Dilmaghani (2018) utilized the Canadian Alcohol and Drug Use Monitoring Survey over the period 2008–2012. Gay men were found to experience earnings premiums of 4.5%. Additionally, lesbian women were found to face earnings premiums of 11.6%. Moreover, Waite et al. (2020) utilized the Canadian Community Health Survey from 2007 to 2017. Gay men experienced earnings penalties of 5.2%. Bisexual men faced earnings penalties of 18.7%. Lesbian women were estimated to experience earnings premiums of 7.7%, while bisexual women faced earnings penalties of 8.2%.

Earnings Differences Based on Sexual Orientation in Europe

Six European studies captured the period 2007–2015 (Aksoy et al., 2018; Bridges & Mann, 2019; Bryson, 2017; Humpert, 2016; Hammarstedt et al., 2015; Wang et al., 2018).

In Sweden, Hammarstedt et al. (2015) used the Longitudinal Integrated Database for Health Insurance and Labour Market Studies data set from 2007. They found that gay men experienced earnings penalties of 18.6%. Lesbian women faced earnings premiums of 0.6%. In Germany, Humpert (2016) utilized the German Mikrozensus data for 2009. The study estimated that gay men experienced earnings penalties of 5.5%, while lesbian women experienced earnings premiums of 9.6%.

In Britain, Bryson (2017) utilized the Workplace Employment Relations Survey covering the period 2011–2012. The study found that gay men experienced earnings penalties of 1%. Bisexual men experienced earnings penalties of 14%. Lesbian women experienced earnings penalties of 5%. Bisexual women were found to experience earnings penalties of 8%. Moreover, Aksoy et al. (2018) utilized the 2012 UK Integrated Household Survey. The study found that gay men experienced earnings penalties of 2.7%, while bisexual men faced earnings penalties of 14.9%. Lesbian women enjoyed earnings premiums of 5.4% and bisexual women faced earnings penalties of 3.6%.

Wang et al. (2018) utilized the British Workplace Employment Relations Study covering the period 2011–2012 and found that gay men faced earnings premiums of 8%. Lesbian women enjoyed earnings premiums of 7%. Furthermore, in Britain, Bridges and Mann (2019) utilized the Labour Force Survey over the period 2010–2015. The study found that gay men faced earnings penalties of 3.8%. Lesbian women experienced earnings premiums of 5.8% compared with heterosexual women.

Earnings Differences Based on Sexual Orientation in Australia

Three studies from Australia covered the period 2001–2017 (Preston et al., 2020; Sabia et al., 2017; La Nauze, 2015).

La Nauze (2015) used the Household Income and Labour Dynamics Survey over the period 2001–2010. The author found that gay men experienced earnings penalties of 13.6%. Lesbian women were found to experience earnings premiums of 12.8%. Sabia et al. (2017) utilized the Household Income and Labour Dynamics Survey in 2012. The study found that gay men experienced earnings that were 8.7% lower than heterosexual men. Lesbian women's earnings were found to be 0.3% higher than heterosexual women. Bisexual men's earnings were 2% lower than heterosexual men, while bisexual women experienced earnings that were 1.3% lower than heterosexual women.

Preston et al. (2020) utilized data from the Household Income and Labour Dynamics Survey in Australia covering the periods 2010–2012 and 2015–2017. The study estimated that in 2010–2012, gay men experienced earnings penalties of 3.4%, and bisexual men experienced earnings premiums of 0.3%. In 2015–2017, gay men experienced earnings penalties of 0.1%, and bisexual men faced earnings penalties of 6.1%.

Average Earnings Differences per Sexual Minority and Period

Based on the presentation in the previous four sections between the period 2015 and 2020, 18 studies were published capturing the period spanning 1991 and 2017. On average, gay men faced earnings penalties of 7.1%, bisexual men experienced earnings penalties of 9.2%, and bisexual women faced earnings penalties of 4.5%. Lesbian women were found to experience earnings premiums of 7.1%. Moreover, splitting the sample into studies utilizing data sets after 2010, revealed that gay men faced earnings penalties of 2.3%, bisexual men experienced earnings penalties of 7.3%, and bisexual women faced earnings penalties of 4.3%. Lesbian women experienced earnings premiums of 5.3%. The patterns from more recent data sets indicate a reduction in earnings penalties for gay men and bisexual people. However, these population groups continue to experience earnings penalties.

Earnings Differences Based on Gender Identity

Only two studies provide information on earnings differences based on gender identity (Carpenter et al., 2020; Geijtenbeek & Plug, 2018).

In the United States, Carpenter et al. (2020) utilized the Behavioral Risk Factor Surveillance System from 2014 to 2017. The authors found that trans women experienced lower earnings of 20.1% than cis men. Trans men faced higher earnings of 4.1% than cis men.

In the Netherlands, Geijtenbeek and Plug (2018) used administrative registers held by Statistics Netherlands between 2003 and 2012. The study found that before transitioning, trans women faced earnings penalties of 4% compared with cis men, and that trans men experienced earning penalties of 53% in comparison to their cis men counterparts. The study indicated that the earnings patterns consistently aligned with a discriminating labor market in which trans people were paid less as both openly LGBT individuals and registered women. In addition, the study found that post-transition, trans women experienced a 20% fall in annual earnings as registered females, whereas trans men faced an 8% rise as registered males. The study found that after transitioning, trans women moved into lower-paid sectors that are more female orientated. The study suggested that the transition penalty offsets the earnings gain of trans men as registered men but amplifies the earnings loss of trans women as registered women.

Job Satisfaction Differences Based on Sexual Orientation

Job satisfaction evaluates employees' self-evaluations in relation to their workplace opportunities, relationships with colleagues and supervisors, salary, progression, and quality of working conditions (Drydakis, 2017a). The first review study on job satisfaction based on sexual orientation found that between 2007 and 2016, gay men and lesbian women in the United States, Canada, and Europe reported lower job satisfaction than their heterosexual counterparts (Drydakis, 2019a). It was found that gay men's job satisfaction was 14.8% lower compared to heterosexual men. Lesbian women, meanwhile, experienced 12.2% lower job satisfaction than heterosexual women. The patterns indicate that the satisfaction sexual minorities derived from their jobs may reflect how they respond to characteristics of their role and workplace. The reason for the average job satisfaction gap against sexual minorities potentially stems from the disadvantaged position of sexual minorities in the labor market (Drydakis, 2019b). Gay and lesbian employees experience high levels of workplace bullying (i.e., unwelcome verbal or physical behavior) and experience inequality in terms of promotions. Such conditions may affect job satisfaction levels (Drydakis, 2019a, 2019b, 2015b).

A study found a negative association between workplace bullying and job satisfaction experienced by sexual minorities (Drydakis, 2019b). If employees, due to their sexual orientation, experience elements such as ostracism by co-employees and supervisors, being humiliated in front of others, or psychological mistreatment, such experiences could negatively impact victims' job satisfaction in relation to self-respect, opportunities for promotion, and managers' perception of them (Drydakis, 2019b).

Bullying might be a chronic problem for gay and bisexual men and lesbian women, which could continue from school to the workplace (Drydakis, 2019b). Analyses found that school-age bullying experienced by both gay/bisexual men and lesbian/bisexual women bore a positive association with workplace bullying, and a negative association with job satisfaction (Drydakis, 2019b). In the United Kingdom, studies found that gay/bisexual men and lesbian/bisexual women who experienced frequent school-age bullying faced a 35% and 29% chance respectively of frequent workplace bullying (Drydakis, 2019a, 2019b). These findings suggest that school-age bullying can extend into the workplace (Drydakis, 2019b). It is indicated that school-age and workplace bullying share common underlying principles: minority population groups attract societal discrimination and harassment (Drydakis, 2019b). Post-school-age bullying victims might exhibit characteristics of vulnerability, which make them attractive targets for unfavorable treatments in the workplace (Drydakis, 2019b).

It is indicated that gay men and lesbian women who disclosed their sexual orientation at the outset demonstrated greater satisfaction with their jobs than gay men and lesbian women who did not disclose their sexual orientation (Drydakis, 2015b). Such findings indicate that gay men and lesbian women who disclosed their sexual orientation to their colleagues could demonstrate positive work attitudes that enable them to foster a happier work environment (Drydakis, 2019a, 2015b). It is found that sexual orientation diversity in the workplace could boost sexual minorities' self-esteem and workplace commitment (Drydakis, 2015b). In the UK, a positive association exists between the existence of an LGBT group in the workplace and job satisfaction (Drydakis, 2019b). Policies that support diversity could result in employees' higher workplace evaluations through the reduction of disturbing and unfavorable experiences (Drydakis, 2015b). Firms with formal written statements barring inequalities based on sexual orientation and gender identity, and inclusive HR practices in relation to recruiting and retaining LGBT people could prompt positive outcomes concerning LGBT employees' job satisfaction (Drydakis, 2015b).

Job Satisfaction and Trans People

A review (Drydakis, 2020) of trans people's workplace outcomes and well-being indicated that transitioning positively created the beneficial ability to cope with stress, self-reported health, social relations, self-esteem, body image, job rewards, and relations with colleagues. The review study found that these relationships were positively affected by gender affirmation surgeries and support from family members, stigma prevention programs, and positive actions (Drydakis, 2017a, 2020). Moreover, trans peoples' well-being bore a positive association with legislation, such as the ability to change one's sex on government identification documents without having to undergo sex-reassignment surgery, high-quality surgical techniques, adequate preparation and mental health support before and during transitioning, accessible and affordable transitioning resources, hormone therapy, surgical treatments, and proper follow-up care (Drydakis, 2020). Equally, societal marginalization, family rejection, violations of human and political rights in health care, employment, housing, legal systems, gendered spaces, and the internalization of stigma negatively affected trans people's well-being and integration in society (Drydakis, 2017a, 2020).

According to Drydakis (2017a), positive relationships between mental health, life satisfaction, and job satisfaction arise from changing one's appearance to match gender identity, as shown through the so-called Trans Curve. This curve was created after evaluating relevant empirical patterns for employed trans people, during and after transitioning, in England, Wales, and Scotland (Drydakis, 2016, 2017b). The results indicate that after transition, employees demonstrated stronger self-perception and could bring much more to their job, due to enhanced psychology, confidence, and emotion, than they did before transitioning (Drydakis, 2016, 2017a). Areas of potential improvement included relationships with colleagues, self-organization, productivity, negotiation, and communication skills (Drydakis, 2016, 2017a, 2017b).

Drydakis (2017b) estimated that after transition, the relationship between job satisfaction and mental health was stronger than before transitioning. Since transitioning could enable individuals to address adverse mental health symptoms and body dysphoria, and as long as strong mental health traits boosted job satisfaction, the relationship between job satisfaction and mental health should be stronger post-transition. Moreover, according to Drydakis (2017b), after transitioning, the relationship between job satisfaction and life satisfaction was stronger than before. The study evaluated that, since transitioning bore a relationship with life satisfaction, a stronger relationship between job satisfaction and life satisfaction could occur after transitioning (Drydakis, 2020, 2017a, 2017b, 2016). The study indicated that increases in happiness and optimism could enable trans people to overcome stressful workplace conditions and become more productive and efficient (Drydakis, 2020). Additionally, as long as transitioning positively affected positive moods and self-esteem-oriented indicators, such changes can result in increased motivation and job satisfaction (Drydakis, 2020). The Trans Curve demonstrates that during and after transitioning, trans people experience better mental health and higher life and job satisfaction than they do before transitioning.

Family Support and Long-Run Outcomes for LGB People

Sidiropoulou et al. (2020) found that supportive family environments surrounding LGB children can reduce bullying at school and in the workplace. The study indicated that warm family environments enabled LGB children to feel accepted and comfortable with their sexual orientation and that having family members support them during challenging times due to their sexuality can positively impact short-term and long-term experiences. The study suggested that if LGB children received effective aid and their parents were proactive in preventing and addressing adverse consequences due to homophobic experiences, a reduction in school bullying incidents can occur. Moreover, the study suggested that an accepting family environment for LBG children might ensure they do not internalize the adverse effect of homophobia, such as pessimism, loneliness, and shame (Sidiropoulou et al., 2020).

Supportive families can enable LGB children to meet developmental demands which can help tackle homophobic demonstrations (Sidiropoulou et al., 2020). If LGB children received support from their families which positively impacted their self-esteem, this feature could influence how adult LGB individuals prevent, avoid, and deal with victimization (Sidiropoulou et al., 2020). Furthermore, LGB individuals with a strong sense of self might reflect a culture of diversity and inclusivity in the workplace that does not allow harassment due to sexuality (Sidiropoulou et al., 2020). In addition, if LGB people were raised in supportive families, they might want to find accepting workplace environments that can, in turn, reduce victimization incidents (Sidiropoulou et al., 2020).

Law and LGBT Inclusivity

In the United States, Delhommer (2020) found that anti-discrimination laws reduced hourly earnings penalties by 11% for gay men relative to heterosexual men. Hossain et al. (2020) found that U.S. anti-discriminatory laws prohibiting discrimination in the workplace based on sexual orientation and gender identity can spur innovation, resulting in improved firm performance.

Badgett et al. (2019) found that the eight-point Global Index on Legal Recognition of Homosexual Orientation scale of legal rights for LGB persons was associated with an increased real Gross Domestic Product per capita of approximately $2,000 for 132 countries between 1966 and 2011. The study found that LGBT inclusion and economic development mutually reinforced one another. The exclusion of LGBT people can harm the economy, while legal rights for LGBT people can result in higher levels of economic development (Badgett et al., 2019).

Workplace Policies and LGBT Inclusivity

Bozani et al. (2020), using UK data, found that trans people's self-esteem and self-respect could be enhanced by policymakers' attempts to promote inclusivity in the workplace through national workplace guidance. Positive workplace behavior can make trans people feel more accepted, valued, and trusted. The study indicated that if a workplace policy recognizes trans people's worth, such perceptions may be internalized and result in positive self-evaluations by trans people (Bozani et al., 2020). If trans people perceived positive workplace actions as an achievement of the trans community, positive self-esteem enhancements can result (Drydakis, 2017a). Positive governmental actions might positively impact trans people's self-assessments because such actions aim to minimize transphobia in society (Bozani et al., 2020).

Moreover, Bozani et al. (2020) found that national workplace guidance for trans people positively affected the creation of a more inclusive workplace. These actions improved the corporate profiles of firms and staff organizational behaviors, such as achieving results, fostering collegiality, and reducing complaints, and addressed LGBT business and trans staff-members' needs. The study found that firms adopting policymakers' positive and inclusive workplace policies can result in positive organizational outcomes (Bozani et al., 2020). Similarly, in Britain, Wang et al. (2018) found that working in a diverse organization with an equitable management policy positively affected the earnings of gay men.

In the United States, Patel and Feng (2021) found that an LGBT workplace equality policy could positively influence customer satisfaction levels. The study also found positive relationships between LGBT workplace equality, firm performance, and marketing capability. Shan et al. (2016) found that U.S. firms with a higher degree of corporate sexual equality experienced higher stock returns and market valuations.

Discussion

The current study offered a literature review of the economics of being LGBT based on studies published between 2015 and 2020. The outcomes of the study indicated that gay men and bisexual men and women experienced greater earnings penalties than comparable heterosexual people. The assigned patterns could be evaluated through theories of distaste against minority population groups (Becker, 1957) and/or uncertainties against the credentials of minority populations (Arrow, 1973). The labor market penalties against LGBT people should bear a direct connection to the strength of firms' antipathy to minority populations (Charles & Guryan, 2008; Drydakis, 2009). The higher the level of bias experienced by LGBT people, the higher the workplace penalties (Charles & Guryan, 2008; Drydakis, 2014; Drydakis, 2009; Pager & Karafin, 2009). In addition, biases could exist if firms use sexual orientation and gender identity to infer job-related characteristics, productivity, and commitment (Arrow, 1973). If LGBT people do not conform to traditional gender roles, they might face negativity in the workplace (Drydakis, 2015a). Deviations from heteronormativity and cisnormativity potentially spur biased evaluations in relation to ones' competitiveness (Drydakis, 2015a).

The review indicated that lesbian women experienced earnings premiums in comparison to heterosexual women. Studies indicated that a combination of factors, such as stereotypes, labor, and household specializations, might positively impact lesbian women's earnings (Drydakis, 2011). Masculine traits, which stereotypically characterize lesbian women, could represent productivity characteristics that can boost lesbian women's remuneration in the workplace (Clain & Leppel, 2001; Drydakis, 2011). Moreover, if lesbian women work longer hours due to household arrangements, they might earn higher incomes (Black et al., 2003; Elmslie & Tebaldi, 2007; Jepsen, 2007). Questions arise over lesbian women's earning premiums. The majority of qualitative studies indicated that lesbian women face prejudices in the labor market (Drydakis, 2011, 2019a). In addition, the field studies on occupational access indicated that lesbian women faced more adverse experiences (Flage, 2020) and lower job satisfaction than heterosexual women (Drydakis, 2019a). Whether biased treatment toward lesbian women at the hiring stage can lead to earnings premiums remains an open question (Drydakis, 2011, 2019a).

The earnings analysis found that although a reduction in earnings penalties for gay men and bisexual people might have occurred after 2010, these groups continue to experience greater earnings penalties than comparable heterosexual people. Additionally, lesbian women have experienced lower earnings premiums since 2010. Although a potential improvement in gay and bisexual men and women's earnings represents a positive outcome, generalized arguments may give erroneous signals in countries where socio-political changes have not yet been realized in favor of sexual minority groups (Drydakis & Zimmermann, 2020).

The evidence presented in recent data sets indicated that gay men and bisexual people continued to experience earnings penalties, provoking a call for law or policy responses. The case becomes more serious, especially when (a) in the EU the proportion of LGBT people who felt discriminated against at work in 2019 was higher than in 2012 (European Union Agency for Fundamental Rights, 2020), (b) LGBT people in recent data sets continued to face occupational access constraints (Drydakis, 2019a; Flage, 2020), and (c) LGBT people continued to experience higher poverty rates than heterosexual and cis people (Badgett, 2018; Schneebaum & Badgett, 2019).

Recent studies attempted to evaluate the reduction in gay men's earnings penalties. For instance, Delhommer (2020), Aksoy et al. (2018), Carpenter and Eppink (2017), and Bryson (2017) indicated that the reduction in gay men's earnings penalties can result from the improvement in public policies and attitudes toward LGBT people over the last decade. Moreover, Delhommer (2020) found that anti-discrimination laws reduced the earning premiums for lesbian women by 16% in relation to heterosexual women. These changes might stem from the fact that lesbian women began to have more children in response to the laws. Thus, a shift to a more heteronormative family structure might characterize contemporary lesbian households (Delhommer, 2020).

The present study indicated that gay and lesbian people experienced more persistent bullying and job dissatisfaction than their heterosexual counterparts (Drydakis, 2019a, 2019b, 2015b; Sidiropoulou et al., 2020). The reason for the average job satisfaction gap against gay men and lesbian women might be the adverse workplace experiences in terms of lower earnings and bullying for gay men and bullying for lesbian women. Evidence suggests that gay men and lesbian women who disclosed their sexual orientation to their colleagues experienced positive work attitudes, and might emphasize inclusivity's positive payoffs (Drydakis, 2015b). The present study indicated that inclusivity and/or positive workplace actions can bring a range of positive outcomes at both micro and macro levels. Policymakers and firms should observe that inclusivity can reduce the earnings penalties for gay men, boost trans people's self-esteem, spur innovation, and enhance firms' performance, marketing capability, corporate profiles, customer satisfaction, and countries' GDP (Badgett et al., 2019; Bozani et al., 2020; Hossain et al., 2020; Patel & Feng, 2021; Shan et al., 2016). In addition, because the majority of studies in the literature indicated that negative attitudes toward LGBT people constituted the source of labor market prejudices, policymakers should try to influence the public's attitudes toward LGBT people and the positive effects of inclusivity (Drydakis & Zimmermann, 2020).

The focus on families indicated the possible developmental benefits of family support that include reducing future workplace bullying for sexual minority children by equipping them with self-confidence, self-esteem, and the ability to navigate their school environments (Sidiropoulou et al., 2020). Given the increasing number of people self-identifying as LGBT, the significant amounts of school and workplace bullying incidents, and the corresponding negative effects on people's lives, examining the benefits of family support can reduce school and workplace victimization (Sidiropoulou et al., 2020).

Research should focus on trans people's unique challenges. Trans people have experienced extremely high levels of bias, violent assault, and even murder, just for being who they are (Drydakis, 2020, 2017a, 2017b). Additionally, trans people faced higher poverty, unemployment, and lower incomes than non-trans people (Carpenter et al., 2020; Leppel, 2020). A vector of factors positively affects trans people's transitioning and smooth progression. Such factors include support from family, peers, schools, and workplaces, socioeconomic conditions, anti-discrimination policies, the ability to change one's sex on government identification documents without having to undergo sex-reassignment surgery, accessible and affordable transitioning resources, adequate preparation and mental health support before and during transitioning, and proper follow-up care (Drydakis, 2020).

It is important to connect future research to questions posed by past research. There exists a need for representative longitudinal data on sexual orientation and gender identity in order to examine the level of earnings differences, poverty, unemployment, and well-being indicators, namely, health and mental health, per sexual orientation, and gender-identity groups. Representative longitudinal data might allow policymakers to evaluate 'what works' in reducing bias in the labor market. Prompt evaluations should determine how supportive families, schools, law, anti-bullying policies, and social and workplace strategies might boost LGBT peoples' progression. Due to limited LGBT data sets, there exists a dearth of studies on the topic. Without data, firm generalizations based on previous studies cannot be made for countries that have not yet been examined (Drydakis, 2019a).

Acknowledgments

I appreciate the time and effort that the Editors Julie A. Gedro and Tonette S. Rocco dedicated to provide feedback on the manuscript.

References

Aksoy, C. G., Carpenter, C. S., & Frank, J. (2018). Sexual orientation and earnings: New evidence from the United Kingdom. *Industrial and Labor Relations Review, 71*(1), 242–272.

Arrow, K. J. (1973). The theory of discrimination. In A. Orleyand & R. Albert (Eds.), *Discrimination in labor markets* (pp. 3–33). Princeton University Press. eISBN: 978-1-4008-6706-6

Badgett, M. V. L. (2018). Left out? Lesbian, gay, and bisexual poverty in the US. *Population Research Policy Review, 37*, 667–702.

Badgett, M. V. L., Waaldijk, K., & van der Meulen Rodgers, Y. (2019, August). The relationship between LGBT inclusion and economic development: Macro-level evidence. *World Development, 120*, 1–14.

Becker, G. S. (1957). *The economics of discrimination.* University of Chicago Press. eISBN: 9780226041049

Black, D. A., Makar, H. R., Sanders, S. G., & Taylor, L. J. (2003). The earnings effects of sexual orientation. *Industrial and Labor Relations Review, 56*(3), 449–469.

Bozani, V., Drydakis, N., Sidiropoulou, K., Harvey, B., & Paraskevopoulou, A. (2020). Workplace positive actions, trans people's self-esteem and human resources' evaluations. *International Journal of Manpower, 41*(6), 809–831.

Bridges, S., & Mann, S. (2019). Sexual orientation, legal partnerships and wages in Britain. *Work, Employment and Society, 33*(6), 1020–1038.

Bryson, A. (2017). Pay equity after the equality act 2010: Does sexual orientation still matter? *Work, Employment and Society, 31*(3), 483–500.

Carpenter, C. S., & Eppink, S. T. (2017). Does it get better? Recent estimates of sexual orientation and earnings in the United States. *Southern Economic Journal, 84*(2), 426–441.

Carpenter, C. S., Eppink, S. T., & Gonzales, G. (2020). Transgender status, gender identity, and socio-economic outcomes in the United States. *Industrial and Labor Relations Review, 73*(3), 573–599.

Cerf, B. (2016). Sexual orientation, earnings, and stress at work. *Industrial Relations, 55*(4), 546–575.

Chai, L., & Maroto, M. (2020). Economic insecurity among gay and bisexual men: Evidence from the 1991–2016 U.S. General Social Survey. *Sociological Perspectives, 63*(1), 50–68.

Charles, K. K., & Guryan, J. (2008). Prejudice and wages: An empirical assessment of Becker's the economics of discrimination. *Journal of Political Economy, 116*(5), 773–809.

Ciprikis, K., Cassells, D., & Berrill, J. (2020). Transgender labour market outcomes: Evidence from the United States. *Gender. Work and Organization, 27*(6), 1378–1401.

Clain, S. H., & Leppel, K. (2001). An investigation into sexual orientation discrimination as an explanation for wage differences. *Applied Economics, 33*(1), 37–47.

del Río, C., & Alonso-Villar, O. (2019). Occupational achievements of same-sex couples in the United States by gender and race. *Industrial Relations, 58*(4), 704–731.

Delhommer, S. (2020, June 16). Effect of state and local sexual orientation anti-discrimination laws on labor market differentials. *Social Science Research Network SSRN.* https://ssrn.com/abstract=3625193 or http://dx.doi.org/10.2139/ssrn.3625193

Dilmaghani, M. (2018). Sexual orientation, labour earnings, and household earnings in Canada. *Journal of Labor Research, 39*(1), 41–55.

Douglas, J. H., & Steinberger, M. D. (2015). The sexual orientation wage gap for racial minorities. *Industrial Relations, 54*(1), 59–108.

Drydakis, N. (2009). Sexual orientation discrimination in the labour market. *Labour Economics, 16*(4), 364–372.

Drydakis, N. (2011). Women's sexual orientation and labor market outcomes in Greece. *Feminist Economics, 11*(1), 89–117.

Drydakis, N. (2012). Sexual orientation and labour relations new evidence from Athens, Greece. *Applied Economics, 44*(20), 2653–2665.

Drydakis, N. (2014). Sexual orientation discrimination in the Cypriot labour market. Distastes or uncertainty? *International Journal of Manpower, 35*(5), 720–744.

Drydakis, N. (2015a). Measuring sexual orientation discrimination in the UK's labour market; a field experiment. *Human Relations, 68*(11), 1769–1796.

Drydakis, N. (2015b). Effect of Sexual Orientation on Job Satisfaction: Evidence from Greece. *Industrial Relations: A Journal of Economy and Society, 54*(1), 162–187.

Drydakis, N. (2016). Transgenderism, sex reassignment surgery and employees' job-satisfaction. In T. Köllen (Ed.), *Sexual orientation and transgender issues in organizations global perspectives on LGBT workforce diversity* (pp. 83–99). Springer Publishing.

Drydakis, N. (2017a). *Trans people, well-being, and labor market outcomes* (No. 386). IZA World of Labor. https://doi.org/10.15185/izawol.386

Drydakis, N. (2017b, February). Trans employees, transitioning, and job satisfaction. *Journal of Vocational Behavior, 98*, 1–16.

Drydakis, N. (2019a). *Sexual orientation and labor market outcomes* (No. 111(v2), pp. 1–10). IZA World of Labor. https://doi.org/10.15185/izawol.111.v2

Drydakis, N. (2019b). School-age bullying, workplace bullying and job satisfaction: Experiences of LGB people in Britain. *Manchester School, 87*(4), 455–488.

Drydakis, N. (2020). Trans people, transitioning, mental health, life, and job satisfaction. In K. F. Zimmermann (Ed.), *Handbook of labor, human resources and population economics: Gender* (pp. 1–22). Springer. https://doi.org/10.1007/978-3-319-57365-6

Drydakis, N., & Zimmermann, K. F. (2020). Sexual orientation, gender identity and labour market outcomes: New patterns and insights. *International Journal of Manpower, 41*(6), 621–628.

Elmslie, B., & Tebaldi, E. (2007). Sexual orientation and labor market discrimination. *Journal of Labor Research, 28*(3), 436–453.

European Union Agency for Fundamental Rights. (2020). *A long way to go for LGBTI equality.* European Union Agency for Fundamental Rights.

Flage, A. (2020). Discrimination against gays and lesbians in hiring decisions: A meta-analysis. *International Journal of Manpower, 41*(6), 671–691.

Geijtenbeek, L., & Plug, E. (2018, October). Is there a penalty for registered women? Is there a premium for registered men? Evidence from a sample of transsexual workers. *European Economic Review, 109,* 334–47.

Granberg, M., Andersson, P. A., & Ahmed, A. (2020, August). Hiring discrimination against transgender people: Evidence from a field experiment. *Labour Economics, 65,* 101860. https://doi.org/10.1016/j.labeco.2020.101860

Hafeez, H., Zeshan, M., Tahir, M. A., Jahan, N., & Naveed, S. (2017). Health care disparities among lesbian, gay, bisexual, and transgender youth: A literature review. *Cureus, 9*(4), e1184. https://doi.org/10.7759/cureus.1184

Hammarstedt, M., Ahmed, A. M., & Andersson, L. (2015). Sexual prejudice and labor market outcomes for gays and lesbians: Evidence from Sweden. *Feminist Economics, 21*(1), 90–109.

Hossain, M., Atif, M., Ahmed, A., & Mia, L. (2020). Do LGBT workplace diversity policies create value for firms? *Journal of Business Ethics, 167,* 775–791.

Human Rights Watch. (2020). *Outlawed: The love that dare not speak its name.* Human Rights Watch.

Humpert, S. (2016). Somewhere over the rainbow: Sexual orientation and earnings in Germany. *International Journal of Manpower, 37*(1), 69–98.

Jepsen, C., & Jepsen, L. (2017, October). Self-employment, earnings, and sexual orientation. *Review of the Economics of the Household, 15,* 287–305.

Jepsen, L. K. (2007). Comparing the earnings of cohabiting lesbians, cohabiting heterosexual women, and married women: Evidence from the 2000 census. *Industrial Relations: A Journal of Economy and Society, 46*(4), 699–727.

La Nauze, A. (2015). Sexual orientation–based wage gaps in Australia: The potential role of discrimination and personality. *The Economic and Labour Relations Review, 26*(1), 60–81.

Leppel, K. (2020). Labor force status of transgender individuals. In N. Drydakis & K. F. Zimmermann (Eds.), *Handbook of labor, human resources and population economics: Gender* (pp. 1–16). Springer.

Lick, D. J., Durso, L. E., & Johnson, K. L. (2013). Minority stress and physical health among sexual minorities. *Perspectives on Psychological Science, 8*(5), 521–548.

Meads, C. (2020). Health and wellbeing among sexual minority people. In K. F. Zimmermann & N. Drydakis (Eds.), *Handbook of labor, human resources and population economics: Gender* (pp. 1–17). Springer.

Meyer, I. H. (2003). Prejudice, social stress, and mental health in lesbian, gay, and bisexual populations: Conceptual issues and research evidence. *Psychological Bulletin, 129*(5), 674–697.

Mize, D. T. (2016). Sexual orientation in the labor market. *American Sociological Review, 81*(6), 1132–1160.

Office for National Statistics. (2018). *National LGBT survey.* Office for National Statistics.

Ozeren, E. (2014). Sexual orientation discrimination in the workplace: A systematic review of literature. *Procedia-Social and Behavioral Sciences, 109*(8), 1203–1215.

Pager, D. D., & Karafin, D. (2009). Bayesian bigot? Statistical discrimination, stereotypes, and employer decision making. *ANNALS of the American Academy of Political and Social Science, 621*(1), 70–93.

Patel, P. C., & Feng, C. (2021). LGBT workplace equality policy and customer satisfaction: The roles of marketing capability and demand instability. *Journal of Public Policy and Marketing, 40*(1), 7–26.

Paul, K. I., & Moser, K. (2009). Unemployment impairs mental health: Meta-analyses. *Journal of Vocational Behavior, 74*(3), 264–282.

Preston, A., Birch, E., & Timming, A. R. (2020). Sexual orientation and wage discrimination: Evidence from Australia. *International Journal of Manpower*, *41*(6), 629–648.

Sabia, J. J. (2015). Fluidity in sexual identity, unmeasured heterogeneity, and the earnings effects of sexual orientation. *Industrial Relations*, *54*(1), 33–58.

Sabia, J. J., Wooden, M., & Nguyen, T. T. (2017). Sexual identity, same-sex relationships, and labour market dynamics: New evidence from longitudinal data in Australia. *Southern Economic Journal*, *83*(4), 903–931.

Schneebaum, A., & Badgett, M. V. L. (2019). Poverty in US lesbian and gay couple households. *Feminist Economics*, *25*(1), 1–30.

Semlyen, J., Curtis, T. J., & Varney, J. (2019). Sexual orientation identity in relation to unhealthy body mass index: Individual participant data meta-analysis of 93.429 individuals from 12 UK health surveys. *Journal of Public Health*, *42*(1), 98–106.

Shan, L., Fu, S., & Zheng, L. (2016). Corporate sexual equality and firm performance. *Strategic Management Journal*, *38*(9), 1812–1826.

Sidiropoulou, K., Drydakis, N., Harvey, B., & Paraskevopoulou, A. (2020). Family support, school-age and workplace bullying for LGB people. *International Journal of Manpower*, *41*(6), 717–730.

Tranfield, D., Denyer, D., & Smart, P. (2003). Towards a methodology for developing evidence-informed management knowledge by means of systematic review. *British Journal of Management*, *14*(3), 207–222.

Uhrig, N. S. C. (2015). Sexual orientation and poverty in the UK: A review and top-line findings from the UK household longitudinal study. *Journal of Research in Gender Studies*, *50*(1), 23–72.

Valfort, M. A. (2017). *LGBTI in OECD countries: A review*. OECD.

Van Borm, H., Baert, S., Dhoop, M., & Van Acker, A. (2020). What does someone's gender identity signal to employers? *International Journal of Manpower*, *41*(6), 753–777.

Waite, S. (2015, November). Does it Get Better? A quasi-cohort analysis of sexual minority wage gaps. *Social Science Research*, *54*, 113–130.

Waite, S., Pajovic, V., & Denier, N. (2020, June). Lesbian, gay and bisexual earnings in the Canadian labor market: New evidence from the Canadian community health survey. *Research in Social Stratification and Mobility*, *67*, 100484.

Wang, J., Gunderson, M., & Wicks, D. (2018). The earnings effect of sexual orientation: British evidence from worker-firm matched data. *British Journal of Industrial Relations*, *56*(4), 744–769.

15

INTERGENERATIONAL JUSTICE

A Concept for Grounding Policy, Including 2SLGBTQ+-Specific Housing Policy

Shawn H. E. Harmon and Jacqueline Gahagan

Introduction

For centuries (and still), non-heterosexuality has been classified as sin (Zachary, 2001), as crime (Kimmel & Robinson, 2001), and, more recently, as pathology (Witten, 2014). Throughout the 20th century, successive Canadian governments have characterized homosexuality as incompatible with discipline, judgement, good character, and bureaucratic authority, and as security threat (Kinsman, 1995), and have viewed homosexuals as a danger to youth, to society, and to national interests. This led to programmes aimed at maintaining heteronormativity in public institutions, and at isolating and obliterating gender difference. In the era prior to the adoption of the *Canadian Charter of Rights and Freedoms* (Charter), actions taken included:

1. a 40+ year campaign through security and policing forces to collect the names of those suspected of being gay, and to purge homosexuals from the civil service, the Canadian Armed Forces, and the Royal Canadian Mounted Police;
2. the imposition of limitations on immigration to prevent homosexuals from entering Canada (a campaign which was also tied to social class); and
3. the expansion of *Criminal Code* provisions relating to 'gross indecency' and 'buggery' to capture 'sexual deviancy' and impose penalties that could include indefinite detention.

A key antagonist was the Canadian Security Panel, which denied or rescinded security clearances and dismissed non-heterosexual individuals from employment in government departments and agencies, including the Canadian Mortgage and Housing Corporation (Wall, 1959; Chair of Security Panel, 1960; Chair of Security Panel, 1961; Kinsman, 1987; Haddad, 1993; Kinsman, 1995; Kinsman & Gentile, 2010).

Canadian policies in healthcare, education, employment, housing, and more have systematically disadvantaged two-spirit, lesbian, gay, bisexual, transgender, and queer (2SLGBTQ+) populations, and have reinforced discrimination and disenfranchisement. There now exists substantial literature around the circumscribed socio-economic opportunities and status of 2SLGBTQ+ individuals, and the added costs they bear in obtaining suitable public services such as healthcare (Mulé et al., 2009; Koch et al., 2020). Predictably, 2SLGBTQ+ communities have resisted, taking the fight for recognition and rights into the courts. Cases such as *Association*

DOI: 10.4324/9781003128151-18

pour les droits des gai(e)s du Québec v. Commission des écoles catholiques de Montréal (1979; access to meeting spaces), *Vriend v. Alberta* (1998; inclusion of sexual orientation in human rights legislation), *M v. H* (1999; definition of spouse in the family law setting), *Reference re Same-Sex Marriage* (2004; expanding access to civil marriage to same-sex partners), and *Canada (Attorney General) v. Hislop* (2007; access to spousal CPP benefits) have been important in advancing the status of 2SLGBTQ+ individuals in society.

Though positive non-heterosexual identities were asserted through these victories (Smith, 1998), there were many defeats, and discrimination based on sexual orientation and gender identity persists in both public and private spheres (Lewis, 2012; Poulin et al., 2018). 2SLGBTQ+ individuals continue to face unique stressors, social challenges, and discrimination in myriad settings throughout their life-course, and this can have cumulative and intergenerational impacts on health and well-being (Gahagan & Colpitts, 2017; Gahagan & Subriana-Malaret, 2018; Gahagan et al., 2018; McKee et al., 2017; Redden et al., 2023). By way of example, despite housing being a core focus of the movement's strategy, appropriate housing remains elusive, and there is insufficient research into 2SLGBTQ+ housing needs (Grenier et al., 2016; Majumder et al., 2017; Weeks et al., 2019). Furthermore, remedies for discrimination in housing have been frustrated by the difficulty of even identifying discrimination in this setting. For example, inquiries relating to rental housing can simply go unanswered, mortgage financing for certain neighbourhoods can be refused on multiple grounds that mask gender as an issue, and purchasers can be steered toward or away from certain neighbourhoods (Ahmed & Hammarstedt, 2009; Bardwell, 2019; Heckman, 1998; Kattari et al., 2016; Lauster & Easterbrook, 2011; Lyons et al., 2016; Ross, 1995).

The 2SLGBTQ+ experience in housing (and other policy settings) makes clear that, for those facing generations-spanning discrimination and intergenerational trauma, human rights have not been a panacea, or even a significant source of effective alleviation. This is due in part to the limits and blinders we have built into the law. To achieve outcomes more supportive of (enduring) human flourishing, law and policy must be reimagined to accommodate notions of 'intergenerational justice' (Wardle, 2012; Vanhuysse, 2013). At present, our laws fail to accommodate the demands of intergenerational justice, in part because the theories that inform our laws hardly contemplate the concept. In this chapter, we argue that intergenerational justice must not only rejuvenate human rights, expanding their scope, but it must also play a more central role in setting objectives, shaping operational mechanisms, and informing assessment tools in specific policy fields.

First, we offer a conception of intergenerational justice outside the sustainability setting where it was first conceived, contending that it can be understood as reflecting—and needs to advance—three interrelated values: relationality; solidarity; and responsibility. We then offer a view as to what intergenerational justice demands in policy formulation. Finally, we turn to housing more specifically, and in doing so, we draw on some of the evidence generated in the 'National LGBT Housing Matters' study, an interdisciplinary qualitative research study funded by a Social Sciences and Humanities Research Council Phase 1 Partnership Grant. It held focus groups with older LGBT individuals and community organizations in Halifax, Ottawa, Winnipeg, Calgary, and Nanaimo (Gahagan & Harmon, 2020). We assess whether the demands imposed by an intergenerational justice lens are acknowledged in the *National Housing Strategy 2018* (Canada, 2018), and what can be done through the NSH 2018 to better realize them.

A General Understanding of Intergenerational Justice

It should be relatively uncontroversial to observe that across our liberal democracies, policy interventions in multiple fields, including housing, have failed to deliver good outcomes.

Stitching these policy fields together is a foundational understanding of both reality and the (legitimate) aims and limits of law that is informed by liberalism, and increasingly economic liberalism (i.e. a deeply conservative, regulation-eschewing, financial disparity-generating strain captured by the term neoliberalism). While a comprehensive analysis of foundational liberal legal theories is beyond the scope of this chapter, we contend—with Dierksmeier (2006)—that they rely on:

- an inaccurate and impoverished account of both human experience and ambition, accepting only that it is driven almost entirely by self-interest;
- an economics-heavy lens for all social issues that renders them mostly incapable of advancing principles more sensitive to values not favoured in economics;
- abstractions that represent an extremely low threshold for human morality, connectivity, and social meaning, and therefore an incredibly narrow justification for legal intervention.

Our ambitions for law, and our interpretations and deployments of law, require a reorientation so that better outcomes can be achieved, especially for equity-seeking groups like the diverse 2SLGBTQ+ communities.

Postmodern theories of law appreciate this need. They have adopted a broader notion of 'justice', and a sensitivity to social context and plurality, moral values and humanity, ethics and the impact of law on our bodies, our systems of control, and our lived spaces (Philippopoulos-Mihalopoulos, 2021). They understand that societies within which law must work are fluid spaces where existing and successive generations are linked together in relationships of interdependence, bequeathing, sharing, and inheriting exhaustible resources, and unified by a shared desire to see humanity continue into the future. In short, they have embraced the need for reorientation, but how might that reorientation look?

We contend that it must begin with a more explicit reliance on the notion of 'intergenerational justice'. But what does this concept demand? In the ecological setting, it is accepted to mean that actors should be prohibited from exhausting the basket of capital and goods— physical, technological, institutional, environmental, cultural, and relational—that might be used by subsequent generations to survive and flourish (Campos, 2018). Generations and individuals are recast as custodians (of planet, diversity, genome, etc.) rather than 'owners' and inherently entitled consumers. It imposes on actors moral duties to pass global inheritances on in no worse shape than they receive them (Barry, 1977; Woodward, 1985; Mulgan, 2006), and it erects legal duties aimed at facilitating those moral duties (Caney, 2019). Some suggest that a failure to attend to the needs of future generations is a 'moral corruption' (Gardiner, 2006) which becomes more egregious as our ability to interfere with more distant futures becomes more pronounced (Birnbacher, 2006).

Our position is that the intergenerational character of discrimination against 2SLGBTQ+ communities—which discrimination has visited intergenerational traumas on communities and individuals—demands an intergenerational justice approach to rights. As a general notion (i.e. one not limited to the sustainability/ecological setting), intergenerational justice can be understood as both grounded in, and advancing, three interrelated and overlapping values: 'relationality'; 'solidarity'; and 'responsibility'. Each one highlights a critical aspect of intergenerational justice and suggests measures for assessing whether a law or policy engages with or advances intergenerational justice. We unpack these values before considering what they might mean for (or impose on) policy generally, and how they might operate in the housing setting more specifically, from the perspective of 2SLGBTQ+ individuals and communities.

Relationality

This centres on the individual, who is well known to liberal theory as an atomistic, autonomous, 'island' existing in isolation from others. Here, it is more realistically understood as a relational being with multiple identities that impose limits on its agency. The social connections we maintain are key to both individual identity and need. This position of the individual is described by MacIntyre (1981) as follows:

> [W]e all approach our own circumstances as bearers of a particular social identity. I am someone's son or daughter, someone else's cousin or uncle; I am a citizen of this or that city. . . . I belong to this clan, that tribe, this nation. Hence what is good for me has to be the good for one who inhabits these roles. As such I inherit from the past of my family, my city, my tribe, my nation, a variety of debts, inheritances, rightful expectations and obligations. These constitute the given of my life, my moral starting point.
> *(p. 220)*

Essentially, the story of one's life is embedded in the story of one's communities. To cut oneself off from that past—in the individualist mode—would skew identity and deform relationships (MacIntyre, 1981, p. 221), as has happened in liberal thought and through liberal policies. Related to this, our agency—and autonomy and rationality—is heavily tempered by relationships, some of which are chosen and some of which are imposed by the nature and structure of society (Eisen et al., 2018). Nedelsky (2011, p. 278) explains:

> When we focus on the relationships that make autonomy possible, we must recognize that we do not choose many of the relationships most central in developing our capacity for autonomy. . . . [W]e are forced to recognize both the interdependence that makes autonomy possible and our lack of control over it.

Relationships can be long and lineal, but they are uneven and multi-threaded. They can empower and enable agency, and they can impose social costs and obligations and restrict agency. And they are not limited to relationships with people. Social structures and material things assume agency that limits our own so we must take into account the social relevance of 'things', from ecologies and their toxins, to economic forces and their protagonists, to institutions and organizations, to built spaces, including housing (Bennett, 2004; Alaimo, 2008). The structures we build—and the physical places where we place people—are also 'relationships' that affect other relationships; they can impose burdens and limit life chances, or they can empower and facilitate well-being.

Ultimately, individuals have multiple complimentary and conflicting relationships. Some we choose, some we cannot choose, nor can we necessarily reject or alter them in substantive ways, and some will not permit positive choice in relation to all manner of activities and decisions. As such, a policy field constructed entirely on autonomy/choice will in fact disempower many. Importantly, the identities that our relationships bequeath need not be accepted as static, or as the correct moral character for the present; transmitted identity—or moral inheritance—may be a valuable tether to the past, but it need to be a manacle. As such, room must be made for identities and relationships that are alternative, liminal, or disempowered.

Solidarity

This takes up the centrality of relationships but broadens it to those with whom we have no direct or personal links (i.e. to the 'polity', which is that society which persists through time and across generations). Thompson (2009, p. 1) argues that the polity is an organized entity capable of acting as an agent and taking responsibility for its actions. One can understand society as an ongoing partnership between those who are dead, those who are living, and those who are not yet born (Thompson, 2002, p. 148).

As a value, solidarity acknowledges that all humans—not just those with whom we have some shared identity—are connected through biology, culture, and communities, and that these connections impose on us obligations to care for one another (Harmon, 2006), and to bear burdens or costs for one another (Prainsack & Buyx, 2012). It has been described as both meaning and demanding that we stand together, especially where people are threatened, that we support each other's interests, and that we have and should pursue shared aims and ideals (Dawson & Verweij, 2012).

To respect and advance the well-being of individuals and society, paying attention to flourishing and the nature of the society that we want, it is critical to meet the general needs of the collective. A solidarity stance, however, helps us appreciate that responsibility does not end with meeting those general or 'common goods', which are often informed by normative bodies (and embodiment). Like relationality, it celebrates the mosaic that is humanity, signaling a broader moral responsibility than typically acknowledged by the imperatives of individualism, self-hood, and bio-privileging.[1] It emphasizes that duties are shaped by circumstances and are owed in myriad directions. A sense of solidarity, therefore, emphasizes that the 'uncommon' needs of groups must also be met.

Attention to the common *and the uncommon* highlights that duties are owed not only to the collective but also to its constituent parts, and in different measures. When this connectivity is considered in combination with relationality, we are reminded that duties are owed horizontally/laterally across existing generations and vertically/prospectively to future generations. With respect to the former, actors are commended to take care of co-existing generations, particularly those groups which have been marginalized by preceding generations and within the existing structures (i.e. to achieve intergenerational equity of those pro tem). With respect to the latter, actors are commended to consider the reasonably anticipatable needs of future generations of these equity-deserving groups and to find ways to meaningfully represent those generations so their interests are better protected.[2]

Responsibility

This emphasizes that there can be no liberty without responsibility, no right without duty, and that everyone bears some responsibility for the world we have and the direction it moves. Solidarity in particular, with its foregrounding of duty, anticipates this value, which is captured by Hough's (2019, p. 845) reflections on her work with the Independent Assessment Process under the Indian Residential Schools Settlement Agreement:

> Because I cherish my joint Anglo-French heritage, I honour my forebears by speaking their languages and maintaining many of their traditions, though some traditions, regular Sunday mass, for example, have fallen away over the years. I have reaped the benefits of existing in a bilingual and multicultural space that was created for me by generations of genealogical and political ancestors. 'Canada' as a polity allows me to unite my Anglo- and Franco-Ontarian halves into a single unit, 'Canadian,' when I might otherwise be required to divide my loyalties. I locate myself not so much in the 'present' but at a point on the continuum my ancestors started and that will continue after I am dead. In this simple, personal way, I have accepted a responsibility

to my two cultures. I also accept, both as a practical reality of modern life, and as a choice I have made, to tie myself to the Canadian polity that, on a larger scale, made commitments to my forebears and to me from which I benefit and intend to defend and carry forward for subsequent generations of Canadians whether they are my direct descendants or members of the polity generally. My identity is tied to my membership in Canadian society. My personal narrative is therefore tied to the intergenerational narrative of my country. Following this concept, as a corollary of the benefits I have received, if my polity has failed to uphold a commitment, or has caused a harm, I live with the consequences. The fact that I played no part in the harmful act is irrelevant, just as I played no role in the good Canada and Canadians had done before I appeared.

In essence, there is a need for a shared sense of responsibility for adjusting structures to help achieve justice (Young, 2011, p. 78). Although present actors and/or temporally bounded communities may not be blameworthy for a particular circumstance or character of the community (i.e. for specific structural or systemic injustices), they nonetheless bear the responsibility of correcting the circumstance or resolving the harms resulting from that character or state. On this issue, Young (2011, pp. 91–92) draws on Arendt's ideas about 'historical continuum' and argues as follows:

> [G]uilt should be attributed to persons who commit crimes or wrongs, or directly contribute by their actions to crimes or wrongs. Being responsible, but not guilty, is a designation that belongs to persons whose active or passive support for governments, institutions, and practices enables culprits to commit crimes and wrongs. As I read it, this distinction is a matter not of degree but of kind.
>
> This responsibility falls on members of a society by virtue of the fact that they are aware moral agents who ought not to be indifferent to the fate of others and the danger that states and other organized institutions often pose to some people. This responsibility is largely unavoidable in the modern world, because we participate in and usually benefit from the operation of these institutions.

Ultimately, liability models are inappropriate, and the language of blame is unhelpful. What is needed is an acknowledgement that our polity, which is an 'intergenerational agent', has historically breached its obligations to some peoples, and must take responsibility to rectify this through actions undertaken, in part, by public bodies.

From Values to Questions

Each of these values—relationality, solidarity, and responsibility—reflects a facet of the complex notion that is intergenerational justice, a core characteristic of which, of course, is longitudinal sensitivity. They highlight the multiple human connections that is suggested by the term, and they make clear that those connections are not just temporal, but structural, imposed, and identity-forming. This means that, regardless of the policy setting, the relationships and identities of those affected must be taken into account in both the interpretive and operational undertakings, *and a much-longer-term view must be applied than currently informs much political and policy thinking.* Furthermore, that accounting must be more than a cursory reference to context and diversity-driven need despite the imposition of standards that may be informed by the dominant (identity, body, perspective, etc.). Finally, the justice element of the term is not just about rights, it is about duties. And it must always be appreciated that duties may be owed horizontally (across co-existing generations) and vertically (to prospective generations), and so may be enduring (generation-spanning), but duty-talk must take its place beside rights-talk.

If one understands intergenerational justice as linked to relationships, complex connectivity, including across generations to those we haven't met, and to solidarity with same, then one can more readily accept the limits on agency (not well recognized in liberalism) and accept duties aimed at more perfectly realizing human dignity and sustainable and equitable human flourishing. Bearing this in mind, the demands of intergenerational justice might be captured by this very general statement:

> There exists a *duty* to promote in an equitable manner the best standard of living of co-existing generations and future generations as far into the future as can reasonably be foreseen so that diversity is respected and healthy and sustainable communities are enabled now and into the future.

This general proposition can be operationalized by posing the following questions of a given intervention (law, regulation, policy, funding scheme, etc.):

1. Is the policy supportive of human flourishing (i.e. improved and sustainable standard of living having regard to the social determinants of health) in an equitable way, having regard to the possible need for corrective measures (i.e. measures to address or reverse historically marginalizing actions)?
2. What actors in this policy setting have *interests and duties* (i.e. governments, non-governmental public institutions, powerful society-shaping private actors, thought-leaders)?
3. What actors in this policy setting have *interests and needs*, taking special notice of equity-seeking groups and intergenerational connections (i.e. does the interventions take sufficient notice of all constituent parts of society (i.e. the old, young, and those whose future existence we can anticipate from all corners of society, especially equity-seeking groups)?
4. Who is owed duties and by whom, and are any of those duties special or uncommon arising from historical context and relational connections?
5. Are duty-holders clearly assigned appropriate responsibilities within their authority and capabilities, or does duty-holder authority or capabilities need to be revised to ensure policy objectives are reached in an equitable manner, vertically and horizontally?
6. Once all duty-holders are assigned responsibilities, are there gaps or barriers to accessing the benefits of the intervention by specific groups, especially equity-seeking groups?
7. How can this intervention's positive impact on equality, solidarity, sustainability, and social justice for equity-seeking groups be described in the short, medium, and long terms?

Every intervention in every policy field should be considered through this intergenerational justice lens. To this end, an 'intergenerational justice-in-all-policies' (IJIAP) approach to policymaking is warranted. Such might reflect the 'health-in-all-policies' approach to policymaking (Ståhl et al., 2006; Kickbusch & Buckett, 2010; Rudolph et al., 2013; Leppo et al., 2013), which recognizes the following propositions: an important aspect of the modern social contract is the improvement of population health; health is largely mediated by determinants of health which fall outside the core medical or healthcare domain; so health considerations must be integrated into all policymaking in all fields. An IJIAP approach would recognize that all present policy decisions will impact on individuals and communities horizontally and vertically, so history and identity, relationships and agency, and responsibility and duties are all critical to understanding the true impact and true potential of the intervention.

The Demands of Intergenerational Justice in Housing From the LGBTQ Perspective

We now turn to intergenerational justice in housing. We outline the rights that are implicated in this setting before considering the nature of this setting generally and the content of the NHS 2018 more specifically. We assess whether there is any evidence in the NHS 2018 itself to suggest that intergenerational justice was a touchstone for the development of the Strategy, and then we consider what such a lens might suggest for outcomes in housing funding.

The Rights Landscape

Article 22 of the Universal Declaration of Human Rights 1948 (UDHR) states that everyone is entitled to the rights necessary for one's dignity and development of personality. Article 29 notes that the free and full development of personality is only possible through communities, to which we all owe duties. These rights are entirely in keeping with the intergenerational justice values enumerated earlier. Housing is also erected as a fundamental human right. Article 25 states that everyone has the right to a standard of living adequate to *sustain their health and well-being*, including access to housing, which right is to be enjoyed without discrimination.

Article 11 of the International Covenant on Economic, Social and Cultural Rights 1966 (ICESCR), which is legally binding on signatories, reaffirms *adequate* housing as a fundamental right. In addition to the ICESCR, Canada has ratified other treaties affirming the right to housing (e.g. the International Convention on the Elimination of All Forms of Racial Discrimination, the Convention on the Elimination of All Forms of Discrimination Against Women, and the Convention on the Rights of the Child).

These rights suggest an entitlement of everyone to housing that equates to something more than simple access to four walls and a roof; it acknowledges that housing has a profound impact on physical, psychological, and emotional well-being, and so must be sufficient, appropriate, safe, and humane. The UN Committee on Economic, Social and Cultural Rights (1991) has interpreted the right to housing as multi-faceted, entailing: freedom to participate in housing policy development; freedom to choose locale and residence; freedom from discrimination in relation to access, eviction, interference, and demolition; entitlements to security of tenure and restitution. Drawing on the constituent values of intergenerational justice, one could go further and argue that the right to housing enables claims and imposes obligations, in support of housing that is affordable, habitable, accessible, and secure in tenure, connected to services and infrastructure, sensitive to culture, and sustainable. All of these elements have been recognized as important to giving life to the right to housing (UNHCHR, 2009).

Unfortunately, neither the right to develop one's identity nor the right to housing is well supported in Canada despite our adoption of these instruments. Under the Charter, rights to security of the person (s 7) and equality (s 15) exist and could be claimed in the housing context. For example, in *Sparks v. Dartmouth/Halifax County Regional Housing Authority* (1993), the Nova Scotia Court of Appeal struck down certain sections of the NS *Residential Tenancies Act* as overbroad and inconsistent with the right of public housing tenants to equal benefit of the law without discrimination. Similarly, the right not to be discriminated against on the basis of gender identity and sexual orientation in housing is contained in human rights legislation throughout Canada. In *McMahon v. Wilkinson* (2015), the Ontario Human Rights Tribunal found discrimination in housing on the basis of gender identity when the landlord refused to rent a unit that he had committed to rent to the claimants prior to learning that one claimant was transgendered.

221

However, a right to adequate housing is not enumerated in the Charter, and rights experiences have been particularly unsatisfying where marginalizing characteristics such as gender identity, race, age, and poverty intersect. For example, in *Tanudjaja v. Attorney General (Canada)* (2013), a claim was advanced on behalf of homeless individuals that the governments infringed ss. 7 and 15 of the Charter by creating and maintaining conditions that enabled and sustained homelessness and/or inadequate housing. The claimants sought a declaration that the Charter (and international law) requires governments to implement effective housing strategies to reduce homelessness and sub-standard living conditions. On motions by the governments of Canada and Ontario, the claim was struck out as disclosing no cause of action, the matter being more in the nature of a policy issue than a justiciable conflict, highlighting the limited possibilities represented by litigation.

Canadian Housing Policy

Beginning in the 1980s, Canada retreated from its historical welfare housing model, neglected new social housing needs, and pursued a profoundly neoliberal, market-driven development model. The market approach to housing became so insular and entrenched that the problems thrown up by neoliberalization were tackled through further neoliberalization, and CMHC's mortgage insurance operations became the new centre for affordable housing action (Walks & Clifford, 2015). As part of this transition, the demands of the financial sector became key determinants in how housing would be structured and accessed, and this both entrenched existing housing inequalities and intensified the need for affordable housing without meeting that need (Zhu et al., 2021). Furthermore, race, immigration status, and gender identity became key characteristics of housing inequity and need (Zhu et al., 2021; Dej & Ecker, 2018).

In 2019, Canada adopted the *Budget Implementation Act 2019, No. 1*, SC 2019, c. 29, s. 313 of which enacted the *National Housing Strategy Act*. Section 4 of the latter articulates Canada's housing policy as follows:

- recognizing adequate housing as a fundamental human right essential to dignity and well-being and to building sustainable and inclusive communities;
- supporting improved housing outcomes for the people of Canada; and
- furthering the progressive realization of the right to adequate housing.

Section 5 requires government to adopt a National Housing Strategy which sets out a long-term vision for housing, establishes goals relating to homelessness, focuses on improving housing outcomes for those in greatest need, and erects participatory processes.

In response, the government adopted the NHS 2018, which reiterates that housing is a human right (p. 8). With respect to vision, the NHS 2018 states that new housing will support Canada's sustainability and climate change goals, housing programmes will recognize the housing barriers faced by vulnerable populations, and that no federally enabled housing programme will negatively impact on the basis of gender (p. 27). It acknowledges (p. 24) the existence of vulnerable groups, particularly women, the pressing nature of their housing needs, and the application of a 'gender-based analysis plus' process to the development of the NHS 2018. It identifies in Chapter 10 a number of vulnerable communities but does not list 2SLGBTQ+ communities.

With respect to operationalization—programmes—the NHS 2018 states that new funding will be made available for housing (p. 10), including co-funding for community housing (p. 13), that federal land will be transferred to housing providers, including private sector actors

(p. 12), that barriers in the housing development process will be removed (p. 14), and that further research on housing needs will be provided (pp. 20–21). At the individual level, a housing benefit will be developed (p. 15), and, in keeping with past approaches, mortgage insurance will be extended to expand access to financing (p. 22–23).

Of course, an emphasis on programmes that rely on and empower private actors represents further reliance on the neoliberal approach that generated Canada's current housing crisis in the first place. The emphasis on simplifying barriers to housing development suggests that programme changes could primarily benefit developers and remediators, who have shown a marked reluctance to get involved in affordable housing construction (Tsenkova & Witwer, 2011). There is little indication as to what 'removal of barriers' means or how it will be achieved; poor zoning and planning choices, the easing of building standards, the urban development of land that is better protected for habitat preservation and sustainability, and inequitable tax incentives/relief could result, none of which will attend to human flourishing or the elements of intergenerational justice. Such will serve commercial developers rather than those facing housing precarity.

In fact, the kind of interventions that are emerging include substantial forgivable loans to developers to encourage them to include some 'affordable' housing units as part of larger for-profit developments. For example, in Halifax, Nova Scotia, one of the largest land developers in the province will get almost $22 million to include 373 affordable units in an 875-unit development (Doucette, 2022). The affordable units will generate rent at 20–40% below the market average, and units will be made available in stages over the course of the development. For those who need further support, the province will provide rent supplements payable to the developer/landlord. Examples abound of projects containing only nominal amounts of affordable housing units in affirmed developments, of those units being delayed to later stages of the development, and of the number of units being reduced as developments unfold, sometimes through the payment of a penalty or buy-out.

Housing and Intergenerational Justice for 2SLGBTQ+ Individuals

Given the intergenerational justice-related questions articulated earlier, it seems clear that an intergenerational justice lens was *not* applied in the development of the Canada NHS 2018. While a range of stakeholders were clearly identified, it seems clear that the full range of those with obvious interests and needs were not consulted in the development of the Strategy. This is suggested by the claim at p. 27 of the NHS 2018 that there is little evidence with respect to 2SLGBTQ+ individuals and their needs, a claim offered, perhaps, as an excuse for the lack of specificity relating to them in the Strategy. However, the accuracy of this claim is questionable. As noted, the history and nature of social inequality of 2SLGBTQ+ communities are well documented, and there exists significant scholarship around 2SLGBTQ+ housing needs in Canada and elsewhere (Grenier et al., 2016; Majumder et al., 2017; Weeks et al., 2019).

Though 2SLGBTQ+ communities are identified as a group to which duties are owed, the NHS 2018 does not clearly identify what those duties are, or who is responsible under the Strategy for ensuring that their housing needs are actually met in a timely and equitable manner. Significant reliance is implicitly placed on private commercial actors, but the NHS 2018 does not articulate for them clear duties for engagement, thresholds for developments which can be viewed as suitable for, or popular with, these communities, or specific conditions applicable to developments aimed at this community (if indeed any developer even bothers to take up the baton and try to develop something for this community).

Questions of corrective measures and critical principles are essentially about clarity of standards of conduct and standards for outcomes. On this, the NHS 2018 is tellingly quiet; it fails to set standards for how the special needs of 2SLGBTQ+ communities and individuals should be met. The National LGBT Housing Matters study issued a national online survey (open for six months and resulting in 970 completed or partially completed responses) and conducted nine focus groups (from 45 to 120 minutes long involving a total of 52 participants from ages 39–94). It found the following:

- Cost: Many respondents experienced housing challenges in recent years. Some 59% experienced rising rent, 30% had to move neighbourhoods due to unaffordability, and 28% have fallen behind on rent or mortgage payments, or had to borrow money for housing costs. Some 93% identified affordable housing policies such as rent control and landlord licensing as being important.
- Safety: A common concern of LGBT individuals revolves around safety in their place of residence relating to their gender identity. Some 40% of respondents indicated that they felt unsafe in their communities, at least sometimes, as a result of their sexual orientation. Similarly, 53% attributed feeling unsafe due to others' perceptions of their gender identity or expression.
- Inclusivity: A lack of inclusivity was a common experience. Some 13% of respondents felt that their *communities* were unsupportive of LGBT people, with 20% uncertain. Some 39% thought that *housing facilities* in Canada were 'somewhat' or 'very' non-inclusive, with 46% uncertain. Some 36% reported having negative housing-related experiences in the past five years. Of these respondents, 48% did not feel comfortable discussing their sexual orientations with housing staff or landlords, and 32% did not feel comfortable discussing their gender identity/expression generally. Some 29% indicated that negative experiences were due to the housing environment being non-inclusive (i.e. intake forms containing heteronormative or cis-normative language, staff or landlords making assumptions about gender identity or expression, and having suffered negative interactions with other residents related to identity).
- Affirmation: Creating affirming and affordable housing was considered important. Almost all respondents (94%) agreed that community acceptance of LGBT people was important. Indeed, 83% indicated that creating intergenerational LGBT housing programmes would be salutary, and 80% indicated that living with other LGBT people was important to them. Over half (57%) reported that having housing staff or landlords who are identified as LGBT is important.
- General Conditions: To improve housing conditions, respondents recommended housing-specific anti-discrimination laws, mandatory diversity training for staff working in the housing sector, including landlords, and the funding of co-op housing and intentional and intergenerational LGBT developments and communities.

This experiential evidence gives some indication as to what structural barriers to safe and affordable housing exist for 2SLGBTQ+ individuals. For example, social and ideological conditions (including prejudice) and economic marginalization converge to generate feelings of insecurity, encourage interactions that are harmful, and erect barriers to adequate housing. This evidence also offers some insight into what 'uncommon' housing conditions might be enabled to furnish 2SLGBTQ+ individuals with equitable and adequate housing. The modifier 'adequate' used in the human rights instruments acknowledges the need for housing that takes into account a group's history, experience, alienation, victimization, needs, desires, etc. Applying an intergenerational justice lens, we contend that housing actors must:

- improve the housing landscape for 2SLGBTQ+ youth and upcoming generations so they can avoid the life-course problems experienced by preceding generations (i.e. recognize in housing policy the unique issues facing 2SLGBTQ+ Canadians across the life-course);
- pay special attention to meeting the aging-related needs of older LGBT individuals to live in safe and affirming housing (which may have eluded them most of their lives) so they can live out their lives in dignity, and potentially 'age in place';
- ensure that the development of built environments, and of housing within them, meet the social and relational needs of multiple 2SLGBTQ+ generations simultaneously (i.e. enable intergenerational housing models, which are found to improve socialization and intergenerational understanding) (Hernandez & Zubiaur Gonzalez, 2008; Knight et al., 2014; Souza, 2003);
- ensure that housing developments are gender-affirming (i.e. attend to diversity, representation in staffing, and rely on sufficiently trained staff aware of 2SLGBTQ+ histories);
- ensure that housing developments meet stringent sustainability standards, including those relating to anticipated geophysical and climate challenges.

Nowhere in the NHS 2018 are such conditions alluded to; in their absence, it is unlikely that cost- and profit-sensitive commercial developers will account for needs relating to, and the design demands of, diversity, relationality, different embodiments, and positive intergenerational living. In other words, developers are unlikely to account for conditions and needs outside of the dominant biopolitics, and they are even less likely to invest in the design demands that can be anticipated for upcoming generations in an increasingly hostile climate. While developers are certainly duty-holders, they have consistently failed to attend to their duties and will continue in this failure without explicit direction.

Conclusion

Given the generally negative experiences of 2SLGBTQ+ communities in relation to the state and public policies and programmes, and the woefully imperfect realization of social standing and dignity, it is incumbent on actors to take proactive steps to vouchsafe the rights of 2SLGBTQ+ individuals (i.e. to acknowledge responsibility and take corrective measures). The concept of intergenerational justice—with its touchstones of relationality, solidarity, and responsibility—offers a lens for thinking about justice between, and ways of respecting, cohorts of people (past, co-existing, and future). It demands that actors acknowledge and understand the past and should be prepared to face the challenges of the future with a value-informed perspective that does not draw on the baser qualities of that past or its ideologies. Unfortunately, successive Canadian governments have eschewed a general policy perspective sensitive to intergenerational justice; there have been very few policies in the last half-century that have applied an intergenerational view to social development (Kershaw, 2018). As one would expect, there is immature policy architecture for considering intergenerational justice and few programmes supportive of intergenerational justice (Torjman, 2018).

For the 'right to housing' to find traction, the NHS 2018, however inadequate it is, must be approached as an intergenerational *investment*, helping different generations horizontally and vertically through the facilitation of housing developments that are equitably accessible, culturally sensitive, and sustainable, and the cost of this should not be placed on individuals or families, but rather on the powerful commercial actors who have designed the (currently unsustainable) built environment. This can be achieved through the support of only *humane housing developments* that pay attention to relationships, solidarity, responsibility, and so to multiple-generations simultaneously. Most programmes, including housing programmes, are not designed to bring generations together for mutual benefit or to encourage and equip existing generations to act on behalf of future generations in a relational and sustainable way. A purely market-based approach will not deliver the justice or health (or housing) that is needed by this community. The prevailing approach is likely to produce cheap, cookie-cutter brutalist, low-rise housing blocks, or the meandering tree-and-branch suburban sprawl-generating developments that it has served up for the last several decades. What we need, however, are property developments that encourage diversity and integrative approaches; balance density with habitability; design in public services utilization; and are mixed-use, energy-efficient, and attractive (because all structures of the built environment are 'public' and contribute to the public environment and vista).

Attention to intergenerational justice in housing offers the possibility of addressing some of the acute imbalances that exist between communities and generations. It can also help ensure that housing does not remain yet another site for the normative individual to be favoured over diverse individuals, and for existing generations to be favoured at the expense of future ones. One solution that becomes apparent is 'co-housing', a form of community living that contains a mix of private and communal spaces, thereby supporting autonomy and privacy, and the sharing of responsibilities within each individual's capability (Wathern & Green, 2017; Reidy et al., 2017; Baldwin et al., 2019). In positive co-housing environments, duties flow to and from the different generations in both directions, providing each other with the necessary materials for the satisfaction of physical needs and comforts, paying attention to residents' wishes and preferences, and behaving in ways that show respect, encourage happiness, and bring honour to the community (Chow, 2006).

Developments with young and older 2SLGBTQ+ individuals living together in bespoke and blended mixed-use structures that are accessible and sustainable would respond to many deficiencies identified earlier. They would encourage 'filial piety' in the context of 'families of choice' rather than normative nuclear families. To achieve this, developers must be given significantly more instruction and stricter standards than are currently provided through the NHS 2018, and community organizations need to be given significantly more funds not only to generate evidence about their specific community but also to commission developments appropriate to the identities and character of their communities. Some of this could be facilitated through the adoption of an intergenerational justice-informed *Canadian Housing Act.*

Notes

1 Foucault's observations around biopower and biopolitics highlight the fact that existing liberal systems of politics, law, and regulation (and their enforcement) are often deployed with an acute sensitivity to the narrowly defined normative body, with the aim of privileging certain ways of being over others, and with marginalizing and destroying those others (Nadeson, 2008). This trend is discernable in the ever-narrowing scope of the diversity that theorists are willing to accommodate in their theories of justice (Muldoon, 2016).

2 The voicelessness of future persons has been an issue of recent but widespread concern: Thompson (2005); Kates (2015); House of Commons Standing Committee of Environmental and Sustainable Development (2016).

References

Ahmed, A., & Hammarstedt, M. (2009). Detecting discrimination against homosexuals: Evidence from a field experiment on the internet. *Economica, 76*, 588–597.

Alaimo, S. (2008). Trans-corporeal feminisms and the ethical space of nature. In J. Alaimo & S. Hekman (Eds.), *Material feminisms* (pp. 137). Indiana University Press.

Association pour les droits des gai(e)s du Québec v. Commission des écoles catholiques de Montréal (1979), 111 DLR (3d) 230 (QSC).

Baldwin, C., Dendle, K., & McKinlay, A. (2019). Initiating senior co-housing: People, place and long-term security. *Journal of Housing for the Elderly, 33*. www.tandfonline.com/doi/full/10.1080/0276 3893.2019.1583152

Bardwell, G. (2019). The impact of risk environments on LGBTQ2S adults experiencing homelessness in a midsized Canadian city. *Journal of Gay & Lesbian Social Services, 31*, 53–64.

Barry, B. (1977). Justice between generations. In B. Barry (Ed.), *Liberty and justice: Essays in political theory* (Vol. 2, pp. 242–258). Clarendon.

Bennett, J. (2004). *Vibrant matter: A political ecology of things.* Duke University Press.

Birnbacher, D. (2006). Responsibility for future generations—scope and limits. In J. Tremmel (Ed.), *Handbook of intergenerational justice* (pp. 23–38). Edward Elgar.

Campos, A. (2018). Intergenerational justice today. *Philosophy Compass, 13*, e12477.

Canada. (2018). *Canada's national housing strategy: A place to call home.* Department of Employment and Social Development. https://assets.cmhc-schl.gc.ca/sites/place-to-call-home/pdfs/canada-national-housing-strategy.pdf?rev=5f39d264-0d43-4da4-a86a-725176ebc7af

Canada *(Attorney General) v. Hislop*, [2007] 1 SCR 429.

Canada (Attorney General) v. Mossop, [1993] 1 SCR 554.

Caney, S. (2019). Justice and posterity. In R. Kanbur & H. Shue (Eds.), *Climate justice: Integrating economics and philosophy* (pp. 157–174). Oxford University Press.

Chair of Security Panel. (1960, December 19). *Memorandum to the Prime Minister and the minister of justice.* Government of Canada.

Chair of Security Panel. (1961, January 26). *Memorandum to the Prime Minister and the minister of justice.* Government of Canada.

Chow, N. (2006). The practice of filial piety and its impact on long-term care policies for elderly people in Asian Chinese communities. *Asian Journal of Gerontology & Geriatrics, 1*, 31–35.

Dawson, A., & Verweij, M. (2012). Solidarity: A moral concept in need of clarification. *Public Health Ethics, 5*, 1–5.

Dej, E., & Ecker, J. (2018). *Homelessness and precarious housing in Canada: Where we have been and where we are going.* Public Sector Digest: The Housing Issue.

Dierksmeier, C. (2006). John Rawls on the rights of future generations. In J. Tremmel (Ed.), *Handbook of intergenerational justice* (pp. 72–85). Edward Elgar.

Doucette, K. (2022, March 28). *Nova Scotia announces $22 million to help build affordable units in Halifax area.* The Canadian Press.

Egan v. Canada, [1995] 2 SCR 513.

Eisen, J., Mykitiuk, R., & Nadine Scott, D. (2018). Constituting bodies into the future: Toward a relational theory of intergenerational justice. *UBC Law Review, 51*, 1–54.

Gahagan, J., & Colpitts, E. (2017). Understanding and measuring LGBTQ pathways to health: A scoping review of strengths-based health promotion approaches in LGBTQ health research. *Journal of Homosexuality, 64*, 95–121.

Gahagan, J., & Harmon, S. (2020). *LGBT housing matters: Results of the Canadian LGBT older adults and housing project.* The Gender and Health Promotion Studies Unit, Dalhousie University. https://bit.ly/LGBTQhousingCanada

Gahagan, J., Humble, A., Gutman, G., & de Vries, B. (2018). Older LGBT adults' end-of-life conversations: Findings from Nova Scotia, Canada. *Atlantis, 39*, 31–40.

Gahagan, J., & Subriana-Malaret, M. (2018). Improving pathways to primary health care among LGBTQ populations and health care providers: Key findings from Nova Scotia, Canada. *International Journal for Equity in Health, 17*, 1–9.

Gardiner, S. (2006). Protecting future generations: Intergenerational buck-passing, theoretical ineptitude and a brief for a global core precautionary principle. In J. Tremmel (Ed.), *Handbook of intergenerational justice* (pp. 148–169). Edward Elgar.

Gay Alliance Toward Equality v. Vancouver Sun, [1979] 2 SCR 435.

Grenier, A., Barken, R., Sussman, T., Rothwell, D., & Bourgeois-Guerin, V. (2016). Homelessness among older people: Assessing strategies and frameworks across Canada. *Canadian Review of Social Policy, 74*, 1–39.

Haddad, T. (Ed.). (1993). *Men and masculinities: A critical anthology*. Canadian Scholars Press.

Harmon, S. (2006). Solidarity: A (new) ethic for global health policy. *Health Care Analysis, 14*, 215–236.

Heckman, J. (1998). Detecting discrimination. *J Economic Perspectives, 12*, 101–116.

Hernandez, C., & Zubiaur Gonzalez, M. (2008). Effects of intergenerational interaction on aging. *Educational Gerontology, 34*, 292–305.

Hough, M. (2019). The harms caused: A narrative of intergenerational responsibility. *Alberta Law Rev, 56*, 841–880.

Kates, M. (2015). Justice, democracy and future generations. *Critical Review of International Social and Political Philosophy, 18*, 508.

Kattari, S., Whitfield, D., Walls, E., Langenderfer-Magruder, L., & Ramos, D. (2016). Policing gender through housing and employment discrimination: Comparison of discrimination experiences of transgender and cisgender LGBQ individuals. *Journal of the Society for Social Work & Research, 7*, 427–447.

Kershaw, P. (2018). *Intergenerational injustice in Canadian public finance*. Generation Squeeze.

Kickbusch, I., & Buckett, K. (2010). *Implementing health in all policies*. HIAP Unit.

Kimmel, D., & Robinson, D. (2001). Sex, crime, pathology: Homosexuality and criminal code reform in Canada, 1949–1969. *Canadian Journal of Law & Society, 16*, 147–165.

Kinsman, G. (1987). *The regulation of desire: Sexuality in Canada*. Black Rose Books.

Kinsman, G. (1995). "Character weakness" and "fruit machines": Towards an analysis of the anti-homosexual security campaign in the Canadian civil service. *Labour/Le Travail, 35*, 133–161.

Kinsman, G., & Gentile, P. (2010). *The Canadian war on queers: National security as sexual regulation*. UBC Press.

Knight, T., Skouteris, H., Townsend, M., & Hooley, M. (2014). The act of giving: A systematic review of nonfamilial intergenerational interaction. *Journal of Intergenerational Relationships, 12*(3), 257–278. https://doi.org/10.1080/15350770.2014.929913

Koch, J., McLachlan, C., Victor, C., Westcott, J., & Yager, C. (2020). The cost of being transgender: Where socio-economic status, global health care systems, and gender identity intersect. *Psychology & Sexuality, 11*, 103–119.

Lauster, N., & Easterbrook, A. (2011). No room for new families? A field experiment measuring rental discrimination against same-sex couples and single parents. *Social Problems, 58*, 389–409.

Leppo, K., Ollila, E., Pena, S., Wismar, M., & Cook, S. (Eds.) (2013). *Health in all policies: Seizing opportunities, implementing policies*. Finnish Government.

Lewis, N. (2012). Gay in a "government town": The settlement and regulation of gay-identified men in Ottawa, Canada. *Gender, Place & Culture, 19*, 291–312.

Lyons, T., Krüsi, A., Pierre, L, Smith, A., Small, W., & Shannon, K. (2016, October). Experiences of trans women and two-spirit persons accessing women-specific health and housing services in a downtown neighborhood of Vancouver, Canada. *LGBT Health, 3*(5), 373–378. doi: 10.1089/lgbt.2016.0060. Epub 2016 Aug 30. PMID: 27575593; PMCID: PMC5073237.

M v. H, [1999] 2 SCR 3.

MacIntyre, A. (1981). *After virtue: A study in moral theory* (2nd ed.). Duckworth.

Majumder, S., Aghayi, E., Noferesti, M., Memarzadeh-Tehran, H., Mondal, T., & Pang, Z., Deen, M. J. (2017, October 31). Smart homes for elderly healthcare-recent advances and research challenges. *Sensors (Basel), 17*(11), 2496. doi: 10.3390/s17112496. PMID: 29088123; PMCID: PMC5712846.

McKee, K., Hoolachan, J., & Moore, T. (2017). The precarity of young people's housing experiences in a rural context. *Scottish Geographical Journal, 130*, 115–129.

McMahon v. Wilkinson (2015), 81 CHRR 265 (HRTO).

Muldoon, R. (2016). *Social contract theory for a diverse world: Beyond tolerance*. Routledge.

Mulé, N., Ross, L., Deeprose, B., Jackson, B., Daley, A., Travers, A., & Moore, D. (2009). Promoting LGBT health and wellbeing through inclusive policy development. *International Journal for Equity in Health, 8*, 1–11.

Mulgan, T. (2006). *Future persons*. Clarendon.

Nadeson, M. (2008). *Governmentality, biopower, and everyday life*. Routledge.

Nedelsky, J. (2011). *Law's relations: A relational theory of self, autonomy and law*. Oxford University Press.

Philippopoulos-Mihalopoulos, A. (2021). Postmodern theory of law. In M. Sellers & S. Kirste (Eds.), *Encyclopedia of the philosophy of law and social philosophy*. Springer.

Poulin, C., Gouliquer, L., & McCutcheon, J. (2018). Violating gender norms in the Canadian Military: The experiences of gay and lesbian soldiers. *Sex Res Social Policy, 15*, 60–73.

Prainsack, B., & Buyx, A. (2012). Solidarity in contemporary bioethics: Towards a new approach. *Bioethics, 26*, 343–350.

Redden, M., Gahagan, J., Kia, J., Humble, A., Stinchcombe, A., Manning, E., Ecker, J., de Vries, B., Gambold, L., Oliver, B., & Thomas, R. (2023). Housing as a determinant of health for older LGBT Canadians: Focus group findings from a national housing study. *Housing and Society, 50*, 113–137.

Reference re Same-Sex Marriage, [2004] 3 SCR 698.

Reidy, C., Wynne, L., Daly, M., & McKenna, K. (2017). *Cohousing for seniors: Literature review*. Prepared for the NSW Department of Family and Community Service and the Office of Environment and Heritage, by the Institute for Sustainable Futures, University of Technology Sydney.

Ross, B. (1995). *The house that Jill Built: A lesbian nation in formation*. University of Toronto Press.

Rudolph, L., Caplan, J., Ben-Moshe, K., & Dillon, L. (2013). *Health in all policies: A guide for state and local governments*. American Public Health Association and Public Health Institute.

Smith, M. (1998). Social Movements and Equality Seeking: The Case of Gay Liberation in Canada. *Canadian Journal of Political Science, 31*, 285–309.

Souza, E. (2003). Intergenerational interaction in health promotion: A qualitative study in Brazil. *Revista de Saúde Pública, 37*, 463–469.

Sparks v. Dartmouth/Halifax County Regional Housing Authority (1993), 119 NSR (2d) 91 (CA).

Ståhl, T., Wismar, M., Ollila, E., Lahtinen, E., & Leppo, K. (2006). *Health in all policies: Prospects and potentials*. Finnish Ministry of Social Affairs and Health.

Tanudjaja v. Attorney General (Canada) (2013), 116 OR (3d) 574 (SC), aff'd (2014), 123 OR (3d) 161 (CA), leave refused 2015 CanLII 36780 (SCC).

Thompson, D. (2005). Democracy in time: Popular sovereignty and temporal representation. *Constellations, 12*, 245.

Thompson, J. (2002). *Taking responsibility for the past: Reparation and historical justice*. Polity Press.

Thompson, J. (2009). *Intergenerational justice: Rights and responsibilities in an intergenerational polity*. Routledge.

Torjman, S. (2018). *Intergenerational policies and programs*. Maytree.

Tsenkova, S., & Witwer, M. (2011). Bridging the gap: Policy instruments to encourage private sector provision of affordable rental housing in Alberta. *Canadian Journal of Urban Research, 20*, 52–80.

UN Committee on Economic, Social and Cultural Right. (1991). *General comment no. 4*. UNCESCR.

UN High Commissioner for Human Rights. (2009). *The right to adequate housing: Fact sheet no. 21* (Rev. 1st ed.). Office of the UNHCHR.

Vanhuysse, P. (2013). *Intergenerational justice in aging societies: A cross-national comparison of 29 OECD countries*. SSRN. https://doi.org/10.2139/ssrn.2309278.

Vriend v. Alberta, [1998] 1 SCR 493.

Walks, A., & Clifford, B. (2015). The political economy of mortgage securitization and the neoliberalization of housing policy in Canada. *Environment & Planning, 47*, 1624–1642.

Wall, D. (1959). Security cases involving character weaknesses, with special reference to the problem of homosexuality. *Memorandum to the Security Panel, 12*, 12–13.

Wardle, L. (2012). Intergenerational justice, extended and redefined families and the challenge of the statist paradigm. *International Journal of the Jurisprudence of the Family, 3*, 167–212.

Wathern, T., & Green, R., (2017). Older LGB&T housing in the UK: Challenges and solutions. *Housing Care & Support, 20*, 128–136.

Weeks, L., Bigonnesse, C., McInnis-Perry, G., & Dupuis-Blanchard, S. (2019). Barriers faced in the establishment of cohousing communities for older adults in Eastern Canada. *Journal of Housing For the Elderly, 34*, 70–85.

Witten, T. (2014). End of life, chronic illness and trans-identities. *Journal of Social Work & Palliative Care, 10*, 34–58.

Woodward, J. (1985). The non-identity problem. *Ethics, 96*, 804–831.

Young, I. (2011). *Responsibility for justice*. Oxford University Press.

Zachary, A. (2001). Uneasy triangles: A brief overview of the history of homosexuality. *British J Psychotherapy, 17*, 489–492.

Zhu, Y., Yuan, Y., Gu, J., & Fu, Q. (2021). Neoliberalization and inequality: Disparities in access to affordable housing in urban Canada 1981–2016. *Housing Studies*, 1–28.

16

ACCOMMODATING DISLOCATED SEXUAL- AND GENDER-MINORITY YOUNG PEOPLE

Intersecting Research, Advocacy, and Action

André P. Grace and Jeffrey R. Hankey

Sexual and gender minorities compose a demographically complex and diverse population, as indicated by the LGBTTIQQ2SA initialism used by WorldPride 2014 organizers in Toronto (Armstrong, 2014). This abbreviation, which stands for "lesbian, gay, bisexual, transgender, transsexual, intersex, questioning, queer, two-spirited and allies" (Armstrong, 2014, p. A1), signifies a spectral list of descriptors—spectral like the rainbow composition of light—used to name sexual and gender identities. These identities have minority status when differences in sexual orientations and/or gender identities and expressions fall outside perceived normative categorizations of sex, sexuality, and gender as well as outside the dichotomies of the male/female and heterosexual/homosexual binaries (Grace, 2015). However, it is no longer sufficient to focus simply on sexual and gender identities in making sense of the intricacies and complexities marking sexual- and gender-minority (SGM) lives. Amid contemporary concerns with diversity, equity, human rights, and inclusion, efforts to recognize and accommodate sexual and gender minorities also require us to work in intersections where their sexual and gender identities are impacted by race, ethnicity, class, age, ability, and other personal identifiers as well as by contextual elements including culture, sociality, economics, history, law, and politics (Grace, 2023). It is within these intersections that an extant hierarchy of queer and trans people, variously privileged and subjugated, has emerged. In recent years, this hierarchy is composed of an array of SGM identity groups, commonly and increasingly oppositional to one another due to their different cultural and political locations. These contemporary dynamics work against possibilities for building community so it is cohesive across sexual and gender differences as modified by other relational differences. Work is needed to advance connection and synergy among these groups to assist the most displaced and disenfranchised SGM persons among them.

Within this hierarchy, those SGM young people living precarious lives are among the most dislocated, subjugated, and peripheralized as they variously navigate out-of-home placements in foster care and group homes, homelessness, street involvement including sex work, and interactions with the justice system. Statistically, they are overrepresented in all of these situations (Abramovich, 2017; Grace, 2015; Office of the Child and Youth Advocate Alberta [OCYA], 2017). Their life histories are commonly marked by experiences of adversity and trauma,

 DOI: 10.4324/9781003128151-19

noticeably physical and sexual abuse and emotional maltreatment, as they attempt to mediate life in the intersections of sexual and gender differences and other relational characteristics while traversing a heteronormative, cisgenderist culture (Gattis & Larson, 2017; Grace, 2015, 2017; Lalonde et al., 2018). They get caught up in dysfunctional social ecologies marked by stressors and risk taking that cause harm and affect their self-concept, behavior, relationships, learning, coping, adaptability, stability, and well-being (Grace, 2015; OCYA, 2017). As a spectral population, SGM young people have an array of individual, social, cultural, economic, legal, and comprehensive health needs intensified by their sexual and gender marginality and exclusion. Accordingly, they constitute a diasporic public whose constituents are likely to migrate to urban settings where they hope their needs will be met and their lives will be better. However, moving to cities usually fails to resolve their issues and concerns because they remain largely unnoticed and unsupported by core social institutions—social services, healthcare, education, and justice—and the general public (McCreary Centre Society, 2017; Miller et al., 2017; OCYA, 2017).

As our impetus and ground zero for our learning about disenfranchised and forgotten SGM young people, we begin this chapter with a synopsis of our inner-city intervention and outreach project that works to meet the individual, social, and comprehensive healthcare needs of those we serve. With this example as a backdrop, we review research literature and other documentation locating these persons and elucidating their life predicaments in social-services and justice-system contexts as well as in street-involved and unhoused or precariously housed contexts in Canada, the United States, and beyond. Then we provide examples of other urban initiatives accommodating diasporic and dislocated SGM young people. We conclude by listing principles to guide frontline work that meets their needs.

The Community ~ Health ~ Empowerment ~ Wellness (Chew) Project

Our work in this chapter is inspired and informed by the Community ~ Health ~ Empowerment ~ Wellness (Chew) Project (https://chewprojecteg.org/), which the first author of this chapter, André P. Grace, established in Edmonton, Canada, in 2014 to help address sexual-health issues affecting highly vulnerable SGM young people (Grace, 2018). Of particular concern, Alberta Health (2013) had reported that provincial age–gender-specific rates of newly diagnosed HIV cases among those aged 15–29 were disturbingly high. Furthermore, consecutive 2010–2012 rates as well as the 2013 annualized rate of HIV in Edmonton were the highest in the province. This and other research indicated that homeless and street-involved sexual-minority young people exhibited significantly higher rates of such sexual risk behaviors as unprotected sexual intercourse, survival sex, and reduced condom use, all of which increased their susceptibility to contracting HIV and other sexually transmitted infections (STIs) including infectious syphilis, gonorrhea, and chlamydia (Chief Public Health Officer, 2011; Saewyc, 2011). In the city, trans-identified females and young men who have sex with men, with some identifying as heterosexual, were two groups particularly affected by the spike in HIV-positive diagnoses. While all these SGM young people certainly needed sexual healthcare services, from the beginning workers found that individuals accessing the Chew Project required services that focused not only on their sexual health but also on their mental health and individual and social needs. Moreover, we learned that some SGM young people may avoid services that target them when there is a heavy focus on sexual health and HIV prevention, which they see as a barrier to addressing their broader stressors and consequential needs associated with such relationalities as being poor, Indigenous, or immigrants, newcomers, and refugees (Grace, 2018; Travers et al., 2010). This awareness compelled us to accommodate marginalized SGM young people as whole persons and to listen to them as experts on their own lives as they live them in gay/ queer/trans/nonbinary, Indigenous, and other racial and ethnocultural intersections. In this regard, the Chew Project has utilized a wraparound approach in providing holistic intervention, outreach, resources, and supports to the SGM young people we serve. Our work usually starts with helping them to take care of their basic needs. As both our data gathering and interactions with our clientele have indicated, most of these individuals are unable to access clean drinking water, take a shower, or do laundry on a regular basis. Most do not eat or sleep for extended periods. They will not go to shelters because they consider them to be unsafe for sexual and gender minorities. Many also require counseling in order to find healing from stressors (notably racism, homo/bi/transphobia, and poverty) and other adversity and trauma (notably physical and sexual assault). Indigenous youth as well as other youth across an array of ethnocultural backgrounds also need help to connect with cultural mentors and supports that assist their healing journeys.

SGM young people accessing the Chew Project disproportionately experience an array of crimes and violence committed against them. For the most part, they do not report their victimization to the police. This lack of reporting is connected to common experiences of police homo/bi/transphobia and their belief that police officers act on the presumption that street-involved and homeless youth compose a high-risk criminal population. Most of these SGM young people have run away from or have been kicked out of their homes, telling us home was a place where they experienced poor and often abusive reactions to disclosing their sexual or gender identities. Most also have a history of involvement with child welfare and family services, but they commonly left the system because they had no access to SGM-affirming resources and supports and often experienced physical, emotional, and sexual abuse while in care. Indeed, out-of-home placements have often brought increased risk of harassment and violence, leading to multiple placements, street involvement, engaging in survival sex, using alcohol and illicit substances (particularly opioids), living with addictions, and ideating about, attempting, or completing suicide (Grace, 2018; OCYA, 2017). As another grave concern, most trans-identified young people utilizing our services have reported using hormones not prescribed by a doctor to help facilitate their transition. Our data gathering has also indicated an upsurge in SGM youth under 18—the age of majority in Alberta—needing our services. These minors are particularly susceptible to recruitment by gangs and other criminal groups because they are hungry, homeless, broke, lonely, and lack a sense of belonging somewhere.

In summary, the Chew Project exists to provide particular accommodation to SGM young people who are street-involved, homeless, or receiving often piecemeal social services and healthcare supports from the provincial government. In assisting them, the project focuses on collective and cohesive problem solving, employing our C3 model: comprehensive health education and outreach, community support services, and compassionate policing (Grace, 2018). The C3 model emerged from principles shaping the resilience typology developed using research elucidated in *Growing Into Resilience: Sexual and Gender Minority Youth in Canada* (Grace, 2015). This model considers individuals' experiences of stressors and risk taking as it emphasizes asset building that supports individuals' survival and their health and wellness. Desired positive outcomes include having SGM young people build a support system and demonstrate indicators of thriving. The model is collaborative, relying on contributions from a team of caring professionals. For example, the project partners include members of Edmonton Police Service who take a compassionate policing approach to addressing survival crimes as we work with displaced SGM young people. We also partner with nurses from Alberta Health Services who work at the inner-city STI Clinic. They come to the project's downtown outreach space on a regular basis to provide SGM young people with testing for HIV, infectious syphilis, and other

STIs. Their work is vital since the majority of these young people are not consistently accessing testing, if they access it at all, due to stigma, fear, and lack of knowledge.

Synchronicity With the Literature

Paralleling the adversity and trauma experienced by Chew Project clientele, a growing body of research literature and other documentation have amply demonstrated the sorry predicaments of dislocated SGM young people in urban and other geographical settings across Canada, the United States, and beyond. Here we review what these diasporic youth have experienced in systems/institutional contexts and in street-involved and homeless contexts.

SGM Young People Involved With the Social-Services and Justice Systems

In Canada and the United States, SGM youths are overrepresented in child welfare and protection within governments' social-services systems (OCYA, 2017; Reitman et al., 2013; Wilson & Kastanis, 2015). Across identities and differences locating young people in these systems, it is important for adults who look after them to treat SGM youth like other youth, establishing rules for behavior that include standards for friendships, dating, and acceptable sexual behavior (Child Welfare League of America [CWLA], 2012; Human Rights Campaign [HRC], n.d.; McCormick et al., 2016). However, this focus on equity in relation to social expectations needs to be tempered by the recognition that youth within the SGM diaspora present unique challenges inextricably linked to their diverse sexual orientations and gender identities. These challenges impact whether SGM youth in care can make connections and become part of some proximal sociality. They may include family rejection that brought them into care as well as other adversity and trauma resulting from experiences of homo/bi/transphobia while in care (Child Welfare Information Gateway [CWIG], 2021; OCYA, 2017). Indeed, "once they enter care, LGBTQ youth often experience harassment, incompetence, stigma, and rejection. These experiences largely contribute to placement instability, running away, social and emotional problems, and limited support networks" (McCormick et al., 2016, p. 69).

Given their predicaments in unsupportive family and social-services contexts, it is important to realize that disoriented SGM youths often experience mental-health issues related to stressors like family rejection and lack of permanency and may need counseling to deal with anxiety, depression, and other problems (CWIG, 2021; HRC, n.d.; Reitman et al., 2013; Wilson & Kastanis, 2015). To help them address their vulnerabilities and factors exacerbating their negative life predicaments, SGM youths need consistent access to readily available resources and programs to counter depression and isolation (Marksamer et al., 2011). In addition to counseling, SGM youth can profit from vehicles for improving their comprehensive health, reducing risk taking, and promoting their individual and social development. For example, SGM youths can benefit from structured group activities (Conn et al., 2014) as well as Internet access to sexual-health services when they need information about engaging in sexual activities, accessing testing for STIs, or navigating life with HIV (DeHaan et al., 2013; Goldbach & Gibbs, 2015).

When SGM youth end up street-involved and homeless, they often experience a revolving door between the streets and the juvenile justice system (Mountz, 2011). Indeed, they face unique challenges when they are put in detention centers: "LGBTQ youth in detention centers that do not have LGBTQ policies tend to travel deeper and deeper into the system. Harassment in detention centers leads to administrative segregation, isolation, or lockdown" (Albracht-Crogan, 2012, p. 3). As well, SGM youths do not fare well in settings like overcrowded youth shelters (Hunter, 2008). Even SGM-specialized agencies for out-of-home care tend to be in restrictive congregate settings (Mountz, 2011). Commonly, these venues do not provide family-like environments and are associated with lower levels of family-of-origin contact and higher levels of homelessness for youth who "age out" within them (Mountz, 2011). When SGM youths experience difficulties or are in danger in these settings, workers should not isolate or segregate them from peers as a first step to protect them, although single occupancy rooms are often appropriate for transgender youth in sex-segregated facilities so they have a living space that accommodates their self-affirmed gender identity (Abramovich, 2013; CWIG, 2021; HRC, n.d.; Marksamer et al., 2011; Orr et al., 2015). Human Rights Campaign (n.d.) has provided this perspective:

> In sex-segregated facilities, don't assign transgender youth to the girls' or boys' units strictly based on their anatomical sex. Instead, make individualized decisions based on the physical and emotional well-being of each youth, considering their level of comfort and safety, the degree of privacy afforded, the types of housing available and the recommendations of qualified mental health professionals.
>
> *(p. 14)*

Negative housing scenarios experienced by SGM youth demonstrate the need for institutional sites to have SGM-inclusive policies that enable accommodation. Without such policies in detention centers, shelters, and group homes, SGM youths tend to be treated unjustly and inappropriately, which deters possibilities for building trust and rapport with workers who should support them to become stronger and more self-sufficient as they grapple with their SGM identities (Albracht-Crogan, 2012). In general, there is a need for clear and well-communicated SGM-specific nondiscrimination policies for those working with displaced SGM youth (Abramovich, 2013; CWLA, 2012; Hunter, 2008; Reitman et al., 2013). To ensure that workers are caring and accountable professionals across institutional settings, these policies need to be implemented in regulations including procedures for addressing threats and harassment, which need to involve an easy reporting process and mechanisms to ensure confidentiality (Grace, 2015; Marksamer et al., 2011).

SGM Young People on the Streets

The problems that SGM youth experience in families, social services, and justice as systems historically grounded in heteronormative and cisgender-normative structures help to explain why many of them are runaways and end up homeless (Abramovich, 2013; Durso & Gates, 2012; HRC, n.d.; McCormick et al., 2016; Reitman et al., 2013). While out-of-home care ought to be a respite from a harmful family and a safe and secure place for SGM youth to develop and function, non-accommodative care often brings increased risk of harassment and violence, leading to multiple placements or youth leaving the system altogether (CWIG, 2021; Hunter, 2008; McCormick et al., 2016; OCYA, 2017). Reitman et al. (2013) spoke further about these consequences:

> Lesbian, gay, bisexual, or transgendered youth may also run away from foster homes and shelters, adding to the disproportionate numbers of homeless LGBT youth. These homeless youth report greater victimization, alcohol abuse, survival sex, and suicidal ideation than their non-LGBT homeless peers.
>
> *(p. 308)*

Approximately half of all people experiencing homelessness in Canada and the United States are 13–25 years old (Barrow, 2018) and 25–40% self-identify as SGM (Durso & Gates, 2012; Lalonde et al., 2018). These troubling statistics are indicative of a longstanding collective failure among those with power and privilege in research, policy, and practice arenas to address the specific vulnerabilities, needs, and circumstances of SGM young people. Indeed, "historically, there has been little political will or action to address this problem" (Barrow, 2018, p. 415). Consequently, countless SGM young people experience chronic transience, with many living in, or taking great pains to avoid, situations they view as toxic and unsafe. Vulnerable SGM young people often choose to live on the streets or exchange sex for shelter rather than continue to face the pervasive anti-SGM bullying and abuse experienced in shared spaces like housing programs and emergency shelters (Abramovich, 2017; Barrow, 2018; Côté & Blais, 2019; Daniel & Cukier, 2015). Still, the streets are typically unsafe for SGM young people who are significantly more likely than their cisgender and heterosexual peers to be physically and sexually victimized by members of the public (Côté & Blais, 2019; Ecker, 2016). They are also more likely to be targeted and harassed by police and security personnel (Barrow, 2018; Daniel & Cukier, 2015), particularly if they are transgender young women of color (Wheeler et al., 2017). Mountz (2011) specified the clear anti-SGM bias at play:

> The conflation of homosexuality and gender nonconformity with social deviance is a contributing factor to the institutional criminalization and community-level profiling of LGBTQ youth—particularly LGBTQ youth of color—that results in their disproportionate representation in the very institutions and child "protective" systems that are the least affirming of their lives and identities.
>
> *(p. 30)*

This calamity is a broad-based reality. For example, more than half of Côté and Blais's (2019) sample of SGM young persons aged 17–25 and experiencing homelessness in Montréal endorsed the strategy of sleeping on the street rather than suffering through homo/bi/transphobic prejudice and violence within homelessness agencies. Nevertheless, approximately one-third of their samples indicated that rather than subsist on the street, they would resign themselves to living with the institutionalized heteronormative and cisgender-normative policies within these agencies, enduring the prejudice and violence experienced "as the price to pay for safety from street violence" (p. 441).

As indicated, homelessness agencies, emergency shelters, and the streets themselves comprise toxic environments for numerous SGM young people, constituting a harmful domino effect following the experience of family as their first toxic environment. Family rejection resulting from disclosure of an SGM identity is often cited as the fundamental narrative associated with homelessness for SGM young people (CWIG, 2021; Lalonde et al., 2018; Wheeler et al., 2017), with trauma, addiction, and mental illness also tightly woven into the causal narrative (Munro et al., 2017). However, while these are crucial variables in the matrix of street-involvement and homelessness, Wheeler et al. (2017) have argued that centralizing the family-rejection narrative, which applies to many but not all SGM young people, distracts from considerations of systemic poverty and racism as root causes of homelessness. The assertion here is that it is "more palatable for the general public to see the cause of a young person's housing insecurity as a single person or family, giving the sense that there is definite cause and effect with an apparent solution" (p. 50). Munro et al. (2017) similarly contended that a preoccupation with "the usual suspects" (p. 139) of addiction, trauma, and mental illness proliferates an individualist ethos that obscures the structural causes of homelessness, thus permitting society to disavow its responsibility to provide human rights and the necessities of life to all citizens. Moreover, as Barrow (2018) maintained, "The normative world is repressive, and it is not enough to suggest that queer youth are disproportionately represented in homeless populations—what matters more are the conditions in our society that caused and perpetuate the issue" (p. 417).

May (2000) has also cautioned against a myopic appraisal of the role of individual vulnerabilities in the homelessness dynamic; even among older adults and those who are not SGM-identified, experiences of homelessness may in large part be explained "by simple reference to a position of multiple structural disadvantage" (p. 615) with respect to labor, housing markets, and legislative frameworks that deny secure housing to those who are already impoverished. Jones and Dugan (2017), reflecting on their experiences with vulnerable young people in New York City, have likewise highlighted the cyclical dynamics of housing instability, as transience and homelessness can make it hard to secure a job due to difficulties in maintaining reliable contact information, barriers in sustaining good personal hygiene and professional attire, and challenges in accessing and safekeeping documentation necessary for employment. On an even more visceral level, the authors suggested that "young people experiencing homelessness may be living in a constant state of distress and fear. This stress affects their ability to put energy toward anything other than searching for housing" (p. 263). Recognizing that housing instability is a pivotal stressor for SGM young people that can impede progress in securing employment, maintaining education, and accessing healthcare (Barrow, 2018; Munro et al., 2017), many youth-serving agencies have adopted what they call housing-first strategies, which entail "removing barriers to housing and recognizing that it is very difficult for anyone to begin to change their life circumstances and respond to suffering, oppression and violence until they have safe housing" (Munro et al., 2017, p. 145). We elaborate on housing-first strategies and some exemplary agencies espousing them in the following.

Multiple structural disadvantage is aggravated for racialized street-involved and homeless SGM young people. For these persons mediating several relational intersections, experiences of discrimination are compounded:

> The burden of navigating workplace discrimination as a person of color who is also LGBTQ2S is further exacerbated by issues of age and class when an employee is also young and has a history of family poverty, which can affect their level of preparedness for the work force and raise the stakes when they do not succeed.
>
> *(Wheeler et al., 2017, pp. 51–52)*

Similarly, in their experience with Black youth in Milwaukee, Wisconsin, Gattis and Larson (2017) asserted that racial minority status can be especially stressful for young SGM persons experiencing homelessness, as sexual and gender identities and homelessness can be strategically concealed more easily than racial location, although attempting to "fly under the radar" comes with its own stressors and vulnerabilities (Côté & Blais, 2019). In the end, power differentials arising from intersecting personal markers such as racial, sexual, and gender identities compose skeins of interlocking and mutually enforcing oppressions that cannot be addressed in isolation (Mountz, 2011; Yeh et al., 2017). Moreover, as Barrow (2018) related, "There is no 'natural' solution to the issue of queer youth homelessness, because the people, events, emotions, worldviews, policies, and economic circumstances that lead to homelessness are too complex to address with one overarching solution" (p. 417).

In what might be construed as a solution-based action, but more often as an immediate survival mechanism problematically wrapped up in substance use, many street-involved and homeless SGM youths engage in sex work (Asakura, 2017; Grace, 2015, 2017; Hankey, 2020).

Certainly, there are significant health and safety risk factors associated with sex work, including increased risk for HIV and other STIs and heightened depressive symptoms and suicidality (Barker et al., 2019; Barreto et al., 2017; Marshall et al., 2010; Patton et al., 2014; Wilson et al., 2009). However, a growing contingent of researchers has begun to interrogate the discursive, cultural, and juridical factors underlying the dangers commonly attributed to sex work, which they have argued overshadow those risks that may be intrinsic to the trade itself. Barker et al. (2019), for instance, contended that increased suicidality experienced by street-involved sex workers is attributable to systematic discrimination, unaddressed trauma, and disengagement from services and supports precipitated by deeply entrenched stigma associated with sex work. Similarly, Bruckert and Hannem (2013) asserted that paternalistic discourses around sex work proliferate victimhood, eliding sex workers' agency and their narratives of resistance: "The deeply embedded stigmatic assumptions of sex workers as at-risk and risky, simultaneously victim and victimizer, exist in tension; discourses that have little basis in fact come to be seen as true" (p. 48). They concluded:

> [This creates a] stigma feedback loop—stigmatic assumptions and ascription of victimhood, inconsistent with sex workers' subject position, are drawn upon to delegitimate and then reproduced in order to rationalize talking over, and for, sex workers, denying their voice and negating their agency.
>
> *(p. 58)*

Lankenau et al. (2005) observed that the troubled experiences that young men in their study had with various institutions—the family, school, foster care, healthcare, drug treatment, and jail—allowed them to build street competencies and capital, which "coalesced into street careers as sex workers that not only made sense to the youth, but also formed the basis for a pragmatic way of surviving on the streets" (p. 17). Meanwhile, Wilson et al. (2009) found a positive association between engagement in sex work and social support in their sample of transgender females, with sex work enabling a sense of community that affirmed participants' gender identity and provided connections with other transgender women. Similarly, van der Heijden and Swartz's (2014) study of transactional sex in South Africa observed that such exchanges are not only common but even considered essential among those who engage in them:

> Young [people] are not always hapless victims in sexual relationships and can make decisions to enter into transactional sex as a creative way to assert themselves and benefit from it materially and socially, while simultaneously protecting themselves within these relationships.
>
> *(p. 60)*

These accounts of asset building and expressions of agency facilitated by sex work unsettle dominant narratives surrounding sex work, which are rooted in specious assumptions that sex work is a threat to public health and the established social order, and that sex workers are intrinsically vulnerable and therefore have a higher risk of suffering violence (Hayes-Smith & Shekarkhar, 2010). As Barreto et al. (2017) have argued, policymakers and legislators should approach sex work from a human-rights standpoint, treating it as a public-health issue, employing empirical evidence in support of decriminalization, and acting to ensure positive social determinants of health, including nutritional requirements and safe housing. In this regard in Edmonton, the Chew Project offers wraparound services embedded in a harm-reduction model, empowering young persons who are engaged in sex work and/or using substances to do so more safely

(Grace, 2018). The following section surveys a number of other agencies in urban centers in North America and Europe that are doing exemplary work to support street-involved and homeless SGM young people.

Engaging in SGM-Accommodative Practices in Urban Contexts

Organizations serving homeless and street-involved SGM young people have success when they employ a holistic philosophy that recognizes how all unmet needs are interrelated, provide SGM-specific cultural diversity training for staff, implement a peer-to-peer model ensuring clients feel accepted, and emphasize mental-health services (Dolamore & Naylor, 2018). What follows are examples of youth-serving agencies in Canada, the United States, and the United Kingdom exemplifying accommodative practices in their approaches to supporting SGM young people.

In Canada, the YMCA of Greater Toronto, based on consultations with vulnerable SGM young people in Ontario, considers affirmation of sexual and gender identities to be paramount when offering services to them (Miller et al., 2017). In February 2016, the organization opened Sprott House, Canada's first and largest SGM-specific transitional housing program for SGM young people aged 16–24 (Miller et al., 2017). A three-story brick building with 25 individual units, Sprott House operates as a one-year transitional housing program geared toward cultivating emotional safety, community, and relationships: "Our belief is that by healing from trauma, experiencing safety and creating relationships, young people will have a firm foundation upon which to build their lives in a way that is true to what they want" (Miller et al., 2017, p. 172). Mentored by a team of case managers and youth workers, residents enjoy structured skill-building exercises, peer support, and recreational programming such as Sunday dinners, workshops, and house meetings (De Liberato, 2017). The house meetings allow youth to provide feedback about the program, which has helped Sprott House adapt to better meet the needs of residents by prioritizing the hiring of SGM staff and educated and conscientious allies and celebrating SGM identity through arts programming. De Liberato (2017) declared, "The importance of youth making long-lasting connections is a key component of the program's focus, and will support their success after they leave Sprott" (¶ 4). In their first year after opening, Sprott House staff recognized the need for more culturally relevant services for Indigenous young people who comprise 20% of their clientele (Miller et al., 2017).

On Canada's west coast, Vancouver's housing organization called RainCity operates British Columbia's first housing program for SGM young people aged 18–24. Like the YMCA, Rain-City is not a specifically queer organization. Rather, it is a housing organization that recognizes an expressed need to take up the work of supporting SGM young people "who are at great risk because structural oppressions they face make their lives precarious" (Munro et al., 2017, p. 135). Indeed, many have a history of housing instability, government care, mental-health challenges, and safety issues, particularly trans youth who access gender-segregated shelters and group homes (McCreary Centre Society, 2017). Compared to 20% at Sprott House in Toronto, 59% of clients using RainCity's SGM housing program are identified as Indigenous, and 69% are identified as trans (and most of them as trans women) (Munro et al., 2017). Since in Canada only 3% of the overall population are Indigenous (Statistics Canada, 2017), and only 1% are trans-identified (Munro et al., 2017), the overrepresentation of these minorities at RainCity says "much about who is left out of the LGBTQ2S movement, who is showing up on our streets, and who is staying outside" (Munro et al., 2017, p. 138). In addition to housing, the RainCity team helps youths connect to healthcare, employment, and community, offering opportunities to build caring social networks (Munro et al., 2017). Establishing permanent connections such as these—with caseworkers, friends, a chosen family, or anyone else who can provide safety and stability—is a crucial first step toward acquiring secure housing (Wheeler et al., 2017). Importantly, RainCity employs a housing-first model, emphasizing choice and self-determination and recognizing that a lack of safe housing can be chronically disempowering as a young person strives to improve their life circumstances and overcome trauma, oppression, and violence. As Munro et al. (2017) affirmed, "We do not view youth as broken or mentally ill and addicted—we understand them as unhoused and oppressed" (p. 145). Unlike other shelter and housing programs that require total discontinuation of substance use and adherence to strictly regimented goal planning, RainCity's housing project does not erect barriers to being housed:

> Housing First allows people to make mistakes. This is an essential part of the program's usefulness. If a young person loses their housing, we have a conversation about what happened and then we house them again. . . . Youth have taught us that in their experiences of prison, and other institutional spaces, they do not learn life skills and autonomy, because their entire life is regimented.
>
> *(Munro et al., 2017, p. 146)*

In the United States, the Home for Little Wanderers in Waltham, Massachusetts, a Boston suburb, opened in 2002 (Home for Little Wanderers, 2019). It is a large, comfortable residential group home, staffed 24/7, that houses up to 12 SGM young people aged 14–18. The first SGM-specific group home in New England, and reportedly only one of two in the country, Waltham House offers a safe living environment and multidisciplinary team approach to help residents prepare for independent living, further their education, and secure future self-sufficiency. Services offered include family outreach and support services, life skills development, peer education and social support groups, mentorship and tutelage with SGM adults, and trauma-focused and cognitive-behavioral therapies emphasizing restorative practice. Waltham House "was founded on the principles of responsibility, respect and pride, with the belief that all youth deserve to live in an environment in which they feel safe, respected, supported and cared for" (Home for Little Wanderers, 2019, p. 2).

Opened in 1969, the iconic Los Angeles LGBT Center employs 800 staff and provides a vast array of services for SGM youths, including temporary housing, STI testing, counseling and addiction recovery services, an employment program, peer mentorship, and counseling support groups (Los Angeles LGBT Center, n.d.). In 2019, the center unveiled a second campus, including a 100-bed transitional residence for homeless SGM youth, in the heart of Hollywood where staff assist youth with their search for employment, school enrollment, and financial management (Sitz, 2019; Los Angeles LGBT Center, n.d.). The center also offers a Host Homes program, matching youth aged 18–24 who are experiencing housing instability with supportive community members for stays of 3–6 months. Hosts work together with the youth and with center staff to establish house rules, boundaries, and expectations; matches are based on shared interests and goals, laying the foundation for lasting, meaningful relationships (Los Angeles LGBT Center, n.d.). With services that encompass social services, housing, culture, education, healthcare, leadership, and advocacy, the Los Angeles LGBT Center also runs a research program focused on the prevention, intervention, and treatment of HIV and other STIs, in partnership with major universities in Southern California (Los Angeles LGBT Center, n.d.).

In the United Kingdom, the Albert Kennedy Trust (akt) was launched in Manchester in 1989 and expanded to London in 1995 (akt, n.d.). The organization celebrates SGM identities as it supports young people aged 16–25, 61% of whom are persons of color and nearly one-third of whom are identified as trans or nonbinary. It helps them find safe and supportive emergency accommodation, access specialized support, and cultivate agency and a sense of identity through life-skills training, social events, and peer mentorship. Purple Door, which akt launched in London in 2012, is the UK's first emergency accommodation for SGM young people. It composes a safe space to secure long-term housing and employment while promoting skill development for independent living (akt, n.d.). In 2018–2019, akt provided 5,976 nights of safe accommodation to vulnerable SGM young people at its sites, and 97% of the young people believed their lives improved after receiving akt services (akt, n.d.). Like the examples of safe and accommodative housing in Canada and the United States, akt constitutes a space to emphasize connection and community in providing wraparound supports to displaced SGM young people.

Guiding Principles for Working With Vulnerable SGM Young People

SGM young people experiencing displacement, disconnection, and dislocation in navigating life need to be listened to and included in problem solving to make their lives better now. Those who work with this vulnerable population need to be educated to employ principles that provide struggling SGM young people with a holistic support system that engenders agency and the asset building needed so they can survive and thrive. Guiding principles emphasizing mentoring and supports fostering connection and community building include (a) engaging in a social ecology of learning whereby SGM young people develop a sense of commitment to self, others, and their living environments; (b) utilizing a team of caring professionals to enhance their comprehensive—physical, mental, emotional, social, sexual, and spiritual—health; and (c) countering a damaging kind of individualism caught up in nihilism (a profound sense of hopelessness and incapacity) and the neoliberal tendency to blame youth rather than the systems and situations that impair their growth and development. In the end, we want SGM young people to be advocates and agents of change in their own lives and, when they are ready, in the lives of their peers. There is still much work to do because SGM young people remain suspect and subject to systemic fracturing in a dominant culture where heterosexism, cisgenderism, and homo/bi/transphobia remain pervasive. Moreover, ignorance and fear of sexual and gender differences in core life spaces provoke structures, strictures, assumptions, prescriptions, and stereotypes that are reinforced to make those spaces unsafe and unsupportive. However, with the help of significant knowledgeable and supportive adults across life spaces, SGM young people can build strengths, accrue protective factors, and hopefully grow into resilience (Grace, 2015).

References

Abramovich, I. A. (2013). No fixed address: Young, queer, and restless. In S. Gaetz, B. O'Grady, K. Buccieri, J. Karabanow, & A. Marsolais (Eds.), *Youth homelessness in Canada: Implications for policy and practice* (pp. 387–403). Canadian Homelessness Research Network Press. https://yorkspace.library.yorku.ca/xmlui/bitstream/handle/10315/29367/YouthHomelessnessweb.pdf?sequence=1&isAllowed=y

Abramovich, I. A. (2017). Understanding how policy and culture create oppressive conditions for LGBTQ2S youth in the shelter system. *Journal of Homosexuality*, 64(11), 1484–1501. http://dx.doi.org/10.1080/00918369.2016.1244449

akt. (n.d.). *Our history.* www.akt.org.uk/our-history

Alberta Health. (2013). *Notifiable sexually transmitted infections and human immunodeficiency virus: 2013 annual report.* Government of Alberta, Surveillance and Assessment Branch. www.canada.ca/en/public-health/services/publications/diseases-conditions/report-sexually-transmitted-infections-canada-2013-14.html

Albracht-Crogan, C. C. (2012). *Children's rights litigation: Recognizing and addressing LGBTQ issues*. American Bar Association. www.americanbar.org/groups/litigation/committees/childrens-rights/articles/2012/recognizing-and-addressing-lgbtq-issues/

Armstrong, L. (2014, June 25). Pride abbreviation covers colours of the rainbow—and then some. *Toronto Star*, A1, A4.

Asakura, K. (2017). Paving pathways through the pain: A grounded theory of resilience among lesbian, gay, bisexual, trans, and queer youth. *Journal of Research on Adolescence, 27*(3), 521–536. https://doi.org/10.1111/jora.12291

Barker, B., Hadland, S. E., Dong, H., Shannon, K., Kerr, T., & DeBeck, K. (2019). Increased burden of suicidality among young street-involved sex workers who use drugs in Vancouver, Canada. *Journal of Public Health, 41*(2), 152–157. https://doi.org/10.1093/pubmed/fdy119

Barreto, D., Shannon, K., Taylor, C., Dobrer, S., St. Jean, J., Goldenberg, S. M., Duff, P., & Deering, K. N. (2017). Food insecurity increases HIV risk among young sex workers in Metro Vancouver, Canada. *AIDS and Behavior, 21*, 734–744. https://doi.org/10.1007/s10461-016-1558-8

Barrow, S. K. (2018). Scholarship review of queer youth homelessness in Canada and the United States. *American Review of Canadian Studies, 48*(4), 415–431. https://doi.org/10.1080/02722011.2018.1531603

Bruckert, C., & Hannem, S. (2013). Rethinking the prostitution debates: Transcending structural stigma in systemic responses to sex work. *Canadian Journal of Law and Society, 28*(1), 43–63. https://doi.org/10.1017/cls.2012.2

Chief Public Health Officer. (2011). *The chief public health officer's report on the state of public health in Canada 2011: Youth and young adults—life in transition*. Office of the CPHO. www.phac-aspc.gc.ca/cphorsphc-respcacsp/2011/index-eng.php

Child Welfare Information Gateway. (2021). *Supporting LGBTQ+ youth: A guide for foster parents*. www.childwelfare.gov/pubs/LGBTQyouth

Child Welfare League of America. (2012). *Recommended practices to promote the safety and well-being of lesbian, gay, bisexual, transgender and questioning (LGBTQ) youth and youth at risk of or living with HIV in child welfare settings*. www.lambdalegal.org/sites/default/files/publications/downloads/recommended-practices-youth.pdf

Conn, A., Calais, C., Szilagyi, M., Baldwin, C., & Jee, S. H. (2014). Youth in out-of-home care: Relation of engagement in structured group activities with social and mental health measures. *Children and Youth Services Review, 36*, 201–205. http://dx.doi.org/10.1016/j.childyouth.2013.11.014

Côté, P., & Blais, M. (2019). Between resignation, resistance and recognition: A qualitative analysis of LGBTQ+ youth profiles of homelessness agencies utilization. *Children and Youth Services Review, 100*, 437–443. https://doi.org/10.1016/j.childyouth.2019.03.024

Daniel, L., & Cukier, W. (2015). *The 360 project—addressing racism in Toronto*. Diversity Institute. www.ryerson.ca/content/dam/diversity/reports/UARR_2015.pdf

De Liberato, J. (2017, February 1). *YMCA sprott house grows into second year of operation*. YMCA Greater Toronto. https://blog.ymcagta.org/blog/2017/02/01/ymca-sprott-house-grows-into-second-year-of-operation/

DeHaan, S., Kuper, L. E., Magee, J. C., Bigelow, L., & Mustanski, B. S. (2013). The interplay between online and offline explorations of identity, relationships, and sex: A mixed-methods study with LGBT youth. *The Journal of Sex Research, 50*(5), 421–434. https://doi.org/10.1080/00224499.2012.661489

Dolamore, S., & Naylor, L. A. (2018). Providing solutions to LGBT homeless youth: Lessons from Baltimore's youth empowered society. *Public Integrity, 20*, 595–610. https://doi.org/10.1080/10999922.2017.1333943

Durso, L. E., & Gates, G. J. (2012). *Serving our youth: Findings from a national survey of service providers working with lesbian, gay, bisexual, and transgender youth who are homeless or at risk of becoming homeless*. The Williams Institute with True Colors Fund and The Palette Fund. www.homelesshub.ca/resource/serving-our-youth-findings-national-survey-service-providers-working-lesbian-gay-bisexual

Ecker, J. (2016). Queer, young, and homeless: A review of the literature. *Child & Youth Services, 37*(4), 325–361. https://doi.org/10.1080/0145935X.2016.1151781

Gattis, M. N., & Larson, A. (2017). Discrimination & mental health outcomes of Black youth experiencing homelessness. In A. Abramovich & J. Shelton (Eds.), *Where am I going to go? Intersectional approaches to ending LGBTQ2S youth homelessness in Canada and the US* (pp. 73–98). Canadian Observatory on Homelessness. https://homelesshub.ca/sites/default/files/Where_Am_I_Going_To_Go.pdf

Goldbach, J. T., & Gibbs, J. (2015). Strategies employed by sexual minority adolescents to cope with minority stress. *Psychology of Sexual Orientation and Gender Diversity, 2*(3), 297–306. https://doi.org/10.1037/sgd0000124

Grace, A. P. (2015). *Growing into resilience: Sexual and gender minority youth in Canada.* Part II with K. Wells. University of Toronto Press.

Grace, A. P. (2017). Difference is: Sexual and gender minority youth and young adults and the challenges to be and belong in Canada. In S. Carpenter & S. Mojab (Eds.), *Youth in/as crisis: Young people, public policy, and the politics of learning* (pp. 95–106). Sense Publishers.

Grace, A. P. (2018). Learning for life, living with hope: The comprehensive health education workers project. In *Proceedings of the 48th annual standing conference on university teaching and research in the education of adults* (pp. 372–379). University of Sheffield. https://drive.google.com/file/d/136b0P iP8jQholEcifq9JBCpDRk13iZmO/view

Grace, A. P. (2023). Accommodating sexual and gender identities in societal, cultural, and lifelong learning contexts. In K. Evans, W. O. Lee, J. Markowitsch, & M. Zukas (Eds.), *Third international handbook of lifelong learning* (pp. 1283–1303). Springer International Handbooks of Education. https://link.springer.com/referenceworkentry/10.1007/978-3-031-19592-1_52

Hankey, J. R. (2020). *The hidden resilience of street-involved and homeless sexual and gender minority young adults who engage in sex work* [Unpublished doctoral dissertation, University of Alberta, Education & Research Archive]. https://doi.org/10.7939/R3-6F0Z-KD60

Hayes-Smith, R., & Shekarkhar, Z. (2010). Why is prostitution criminalized? An alternative viewpoint on the construction of sex work. *Contemporary Justice Review, 13*(1), 43–55. https://doi.org/10.1080/10282580903549201

Home for Little Wanderers. (2019). *Waltham house: A group home for lesbian, gay, bisexual, transgender, and questioning (LGBTQ) youth.* www.thehome.org/images/uploads/files/Waltham_House_2019-F.pdf

Human Rights Campaign. (n.d.) *Caring for LGBTQ children and youth: A guide for child welfare providers.* https://assets2.hrc.org/files/assets/resources/HRC_Caring_For_LGBTQ_Children_Youth. pdf?_ga=2.95304412.1550222723.1568654849-1948708897.1568654849

Hunter, E. (2008). What's good for the gays is good for the gander: Making homeless youth housing safer for lesbian, gay, bisexual, and transgender youth. *Family Court Review, 46*(3), 543–557. https://doi.org/10.1111/j.1744-1617.2008.00220.x

Jones, N., & Dugan, M. (2017). LEAP into action: Preparing LGBTQ2S youth for the workforce. In A. Abramovich & J. Shelton (Eds.), *Where am I going to go? Intersectional approaches to ending LGBTQ2S youth homelessness in Canada and the US* (pp. 263–272). Canadian Observatory on Homelessness. https://homelesshub.ca/sites/default/files/Where_Am_I_Going_To_Go.pdf

Lalonde, D., Abramovich, A., Baker, L., & Tabibi, J. (2018). LGBTQ2S youth, violence, and homelessness. *Learning Network Newsletter, 24.* Centre for Research & Education on Violence Against Women & Children. www.vawlearningnetwork.ca/our-work/issuebased_newsletters/issue-24/index. html

Lankenau, S. E., Clatts, M. C., Welle, D., Goldsamt, L. A., & Gwadz, M. V. (2005). Street careers: Homelessness, drug use, and sex work among young men who have sex with men (YMSM). *International Journal of Drug Policy, 16*(1), 10–18. https://doi.org/10.1016/j.drugpo.2004.07.006

Los Angeles LGBT Center. (n.d.). *About the center.* https://lalgbtcenter.org/about-the-center

Marksamer, J., Spade, D., & Arkles, G. (2011, Spring). *A place of respect: A guide for group care facilities serving transgender and gender non-conforming youth.* National Center for Lesbian Rights and Sylvia Rivera Law Project. www.nclrights.org/wp-content/uploads/2013/07/A_Place_Of_Respect.pdf

Marshall, B. D., Shannon, K., Kerr, T., Zhang, R., & Wood, E. (2010). Survival sex work and increased HIV risk among sexual minority street-involved youth. *Journal of Acquired Immune Deficiency Syndrome, 53*(5), 661–664. https://doi.org/10.1097/QAI.0b013e3181c300d7

May, J. (2000). Housing histories and homeless careers: A biographical approach. *Housing Studies, 15*(4), 613–638. https://doi.org/10.1080/02673030050081131

McCormick, A., Schmidt, K., & Terrazas, S. R. (2016). Foster family acceptance: Understanding the role of foster family acceptance in the lives of LGBTQ youth. *Children and Youth Services Review, 61,* 69–74. https://doi.org/10.1016/j.childyouth.2015.12.005

McCreary Centre Society. (2017). *Final evaluation report: RainCity's LGBTQ2S housing first project.* www.raincityhousing.org/wp-content/uploads/2018/11/McCreary-final-evaluation-report.pdf

Miller, K., Bissoondial, K., & Morgan. (2017). YMCA sprott house: Creating a better space for LGBTQ2S youth in Toronto. In A. Abramovich & J. Shelton (Eds.), *Where am I going to go? Intersectional approaches* to ending LGBTQ2S youth homelessness in Canada and the US (pp. 169–182). Canadian Observatory on Homelessness. https://homelesshub.ca/sites/default/files/Where_Am_I_Going_To_Go.pdf

Mountz, S. (2011). Revolving doors: LGBTQ youth at the interface of the child welfare and juvenile justice systems. *LGBTQ Policy Journal at the Harvard Kennedy School, 1*, 29–45. http://lgbtq.hks publications.org/wp-content/uploads/sites/20/2015/10/LGBT_3-14-11_Final.pdf. (Original work published 2010)

Munro, A., Reynolds, V., & Townsend, M. (2017). Youth wisdom, harm reduction, & housing first: Rain-City housing's queer and trans youth housing project. In A. Abramovich & J. Shelton (Eds.), *Where am I going to go? Intersectional approaches to ending LGBTQ2S youth homelessness in Canada and the U.S.* (pp. 135–154). Canadian Observatory on Homelessness. https://homelesshub.ca/sites/default/files/Where_Am_I_Going_To_Go.pdf

Office of the Child and Youth Advocate Alberta. (2017). *Speaking OUT: A special report on LGBTQ2S+ young people in the child welfare and youth justice systems.* www.ocya.alberta.ca/wp-content/uploads/2014/08/SpRpt_2017November_Speaking-OUT.pdf

Orr, A., Baum, J., Brown, J., Gill, E., Kahn, E., & Salem, A. (2015). *Schools in transition: A guide for supporting transgender students in K-12 schools.* http://hrc-assets.s3-website-us-east-1.amazonaws.com//files/assets/resources/Schools-In-Transition.pdf

Patton, R. A., Cunningham, R. M., Blow, F. C., Zimmerman, M. A., Booth, B. M., & Walton, M. A. (2014). Transactional sex involvement: Exploring risk and promotive factors among substance-using youth in an urban emergency department. *Journal of Studies on Alcohol and Drugs, 75*, 573–579. https://doi.org/10.15288/jsad.2014.75.573

Reitman, D. S., Austin, B., Belkind, U., Chaffee, T., Hoffman, N. D., Moore, E., Morris, R., Olson, J., & Ryan, C. (2013). Recommendations for promoting the health and well-being of lesbian, gay, bisexual, and transgender adolescents: A position paper of the society for adolescent health and medicine. *Journal of Adolescent Health, 52*(4), 506–510. https://doi.org/10.1016/j.jadohealth.2013.01.015

Saewyc, E. (2011). Research on adolescent sexual orientation: Development, health disparities, stigma, and resilience. *Journal of Research on Adolescence, 21*(1), 256–272. https://doi.org/10.1111/j.1532-7795.2010.00727.x

Sitz, M. (2019). Los Angeles LGBT center opens new campus. *Architectural Record, 207*(6), 27–28. www.architecturalrecord.com/articles/14062-los-angeles-lgbt-center-opens-new-campus

Statistics Canada. (2017). *Vancouver, city [census subdivision], British Columbia and Canada [country]* (table). Census Profile. 2016 Census. Statistics Canada Catalogue no. 98–316-X2016001. Retrieved November 29, 2017, from https://www12.statcan.gc.ca/census-recensement/2016/dp-pd/prof/details/page.cfm?Lang=E&Gco1=CSD&Code1=5915022&Geo2=PR&Code2=01&Data=Count&SearchText=vancouver&SearchType=Begins&SearchPR=01&B1=Visible%20minority&TABID=1

Travers, R., Guta, A., Flicker, S., Larkin, J., Lo, C., McCardell, S., & van der Meulin, E. (2010). Service provider views on issues and needs for lesbian, gay, bisexual, and transgender youth. *The Canadian Journal of Human Sexuality, 19*(4), 191–198. https://go.gale.com/ps/anonymous?id=GALE%7CA253926193&sid=googleScholar&v=2.1&it=r&linkaccess=abs&issn=11884517&p=AONE&sw=w

van der Heijden, I., & Swartz, S. (2014). "Something for something": The importance of talking about transactional sex with youth in South Africa using a resilience-based approach. *African Journal of AIDS Research, 13*(1), 53–63. https://doi.org/10.2989/16085906.2014.886602

Wheeler, C., Price, C., & Ellasante, I. (2017). Pathways into and out of homelessness for LGBTQ2S youth. In A. Abramovich & J. Shelton (Eds.), *Where am I going to go? Intersectional approaches to ending LGBTQ2S youth homelessness in Canada and the U.S.* (pp. 49–62). Canadian Observatory on Homelessness. https://homelesshub.ca/sites/default/files/Where_Am_I_Going_To_Go.pdf

Wilson, B., & Kastanis, A. A. (2015). Sexual and gender minority disproportionality and disparities in child welfare: A population-based study. *Children and Youth Services Review, 58*, 11–17. https://doi.org/10.1016/j.childyouth.2015.08.016

Wilson, E. C., Garofalo, R., Harris, R. D., Herrick, A., Martinez, M., Martinez, J., Belzer, M., & the Transgender Advisory Committee and the Adolescent Medicine Trials Network for HIV/AIDS Interventions. (2009). Transgender female youth and sex work: HIV risk and a comparison of life factors related to engagement in sex work. *AIDS Behavior, 13*, 902–913. https://doi.org/10.1007/s10461-008-9508-8

Yeh, D., Elin, L., Miller, L., O'Connell, K., & Sears, R. (2017). Central Toronto youth services. In A. Abramovich & J. Shelton (Eds.), *Where am I going to go? Intersectional approaches to ending LGBTQ2S youth homelessness in Canada and the US* (pp. 99–114). Canadian Observatory on Homelessness. https://homelesshub.ca/sites/default/files/Where_Am_I_Going_To_Go.pdf

IV

Cultural Structures

17

LANGUAGE MATTERS

Gender Pronouns and Identity Terminology for Transgender and Nonbinary People

Douglas Knutson, Chloe Goldbach, Satveer Kler, Itxaso Rodríguez-Ordóñez, Parker McDurmon, and Benton Goff

When a person is misgendered or when they are treated as if they are identified with a gender that is incongruent for them, they may experience negative emotions and distress (McLemore, 2018; World Professional Association for Transgender Health, 2012). Misgendering is most often discussed in research about transgender and nonbinary (TNB) people or individuals who are identified with a gender identity that differs from the sex they were assigned at birth (American Psychological Association, 2015). The negative psychological impact of misgendering adds to the already elevated, sometimes lethal levels of distress experienced by TNB individuals (see James et al., 2016). Furthermore, repeated mischaracterizations of TNB people contributes to compound distress that, in turn, negatively impacts health (e.g., Nadal et al., 2014).

Although attempts to create more inclusive linguistic practices are not new, specifically at the grassroots level, there is much to be gained from taking a global view of recent linguistic advocacy. In an effort to forward the worldwide conversation about linguistic and cultural inclusivity for TNB people, we provide a brief overview of steps toward gender inclusivity in several languages and cultures, current controversies surrounding the establishment of more inclusive language systems, and guidance on how such language impacts the well-being of transgender people. To ground the conversation, we provide case examples of languages and advocacy efforts throughout the globe.

The Current Project

In an effort to be as inclusive and representative as possible, we obtained a list (Ethnologue, 2020) of the six largest language families (Niger-Congo, Austronesian, Trans-New Guinea, Sino-Tibetan, Indo-European, and Afro-Asiatic) and assigned each one to a research assistant in the Diversity and Rural Advocacy Group (DRAG) lab. DRAG is a consortium of scholars at various levels of training in multiple states and countries who share the common goal to increase health and resilience in LGBTQ+ people, particularly people in rural and remote areas. Douglas Knutson and Julie Koch co-founded the DRAG lab which Knutson currently directs at Oklahoma State University as an assistant professor in the counseling and counseling psychology program.

DRAG research collaborators (undergraduate and graduate students from Southern Illinois University) reviewed existing scholarly and popular literature (e.g., blogs, newspapers,

DOI: 10.4324/9781003128151-21

and YouTube videos) being produced in the countries represented in the language family they were assigned. Based on their findings, they selected a focus country and language to further explore current movements of linguistic inclusivity in the selected languages. In addition to the students listed as authors on this chapter, Stephanie Alvarado and Cassandra Scarcinelli helped gather information for this project. The final list of languages included Spanish, Hebrew, Swahili, Tagalog, Burmese, and Turkish.

Before proceeding, it is important to recognize that all of the researchers and authors are currently located in the United States, and the majority of team members speak English and/or Spanish. We instituted several checks and layers of review to ensure that our work was decolonized to the furthest extent possible. The authorship team included Itxaso Rodríguez-Ordóñez, a linguist who focuses on linguistic variation in minoritized language contexts (e.g., 'The role of social meaning in contact-induced variation among new speakers of Basque', 2021). Additionally, the researchers identified and corresponded with scholars with expertise in each of six selected languages throughout the composition of this chapter, including Lourdes Albuixech (Spanish, Southern Illinois University Carbondale), Eyal Rivlin and Lior Gross (Hebrew, co-facilitator of the Nonbinary Hebrew Project), Vicki Carstens (Swahili, University of Connecticut), Marie Aubrey J. Villaceran (Tagalog, Center for Women's and Gender Studies at the University of the Philippines), David Gilbert (Burmese, Australian National University), and Ceylan Engin (Turkish, Boğaziçi University).

Even though we attempted to provide a broad variety of perspectives, we recognize that our overview may not be fully representative of the experiences of transgender and nonbinary people across the globe. Everyone involved in this chapter shared the perspective that it is important to provide affirming spaces for TNB people everywhere in the world. One way to include and support TNB people is to expand and revisit the fundamental assumptions and cultural mores that underlie human speech. To facilitate important dialogue, we divide six globally representative languages into three grammatical language classes and provide an overview of how users of those languages have pushed to both include and/or exclude transgender and nonbinary people. Building on our survey of gender in language, we provide recommendations for continued advocacy and we offer resources for individuals who are interested in continuing the push for equity and inclusion in language.

A Sampling of Global Linguistic Challenges, Adaptations, and Advocacy

All languages are known to make some sort of gender-based distinction, but the way these distinctions are linguistically represented varies tremendously. There are multiple ways in which 'gender' is understood or theorized in linguistics (Corbett, 1991; Dixon, 1982), but languages tend to be classified into three major groups depending on how gender is marked structurally: grammatical gendered language, natural gender language, and genderless language (for further details see Corbett, 1991, 2013a, 2013b).

Grammatical gender is a type of noun class system that categorizes words that may reflect the behavior of associated words (Corbett, 1991). Although some languages may use 'grammatical gender' not to associate it with any relevant gender, but more as a general way to describe noun classes (e.g., Bantu languages), most languages tend to be categorized into three big prototypes. Grammatically gendered languages are often associated with the ways in which morphological information is encoded to mark gender-based distinctions. These languages tend to categorize both animate and non-animate nouns based on gender classifications, usually masculine or feminine such as Spanish, French, Hebrew, Russian, Hindi, or an additional neuter may be added as in Norwegian, Dutch, or German (German: *Karre* (f.) 'car', *Tisch* (m.)

'table', *Haus* (n.) 'house'). Natural gender languages are understood as languages in which a noun's referent sex may determine gender agreement. In most languages classified as 'natural gender' (i.e., English, Swedish, Slavic languages, Marathi), this distinction occurs in personal pronouns as English pronouns s/he, they or Danish *hun* 'she'/*han* 'he'. Genderless languages (also known as gender-neutral language) such as Turkish, Finnish, and Basque are languages where the gender of most nouns and pronouns are unspecified although may make animate/non-animate distinctions (Basque: *bera* 's/he', *hori* 'it/that').

In what follows, we present a short overview on the processes that some of these languages resort to in order to advocate for more inclusive language practices by first briefly exploring the connection between language, culture, and identity.

Grammatically Gendered Language

Even though languages are grouped based on how gender distinctions are grammatically marked, all languages make some sort of sex-based distinctions, usually in terms of kinship terms, also known as lexical gender. For instance, every language has a term for *mother* or *father*, and despite efforts to de-gender mother/father through the choice of 'parent' in non-binary households (Eli, 2015), the existence of lexical gender suggests that language is intrinsically connected to socially constructed gender distinctions. While it is not entirely clear why languages have developed different kinds of grammatical gender distinctions (Foundalis, 2002), these differences have spurred increased interest in psychology and socio-cultural linguistics as a way to understand the relationship between language, thought, and behavior (Gygax et al., 2019; Prewitt-Freilino et al., 2012).

From a sociocultural linguistic perspective, one thing is clear: language matters. The way people speak may index attributes associated with their identities such as nationality, ethnicity, religion, age, gender, and/or sexuality. When people use language to invoke their beliefs (consciously or unconsciously) and to reinforce their position in society, they bring themselves into being in space and time. What this is to mean is that not only do cultural norms exert some influence in how language is used, but language also helps re-define such cultural norms whereby expressions of identity become redefined. For example, McConnell-Ginet (2014, p. 6) questions the 'natural gender' status of English-like languages and instead proposes the 'notional gender' label to explain that 'pronominal usage cannot be understood without considering sociocultural gender and the ideas about sex and sexuality current at a given time'. Expanding such understanding of language to linguistic phenomena beyond pronoun usage, it is clear that hegemonic gender ideologies (usually assumed binary categorizations and/or in favor of male dominance) are still present in influencing individuals' linguistic choices, but more inclusive linguistic practices have become more visible in the recent decades, as a way of re-shaping, re-defining, and re-constituting the existence of non-binary individuals.

Not only is language a matter of identity expression, but it is also a political artifact. Language reflects the way people see the world, and language is one of the means by which such reflections become apparent, making the relationship between language and identity inseparable. When a TNB individual is misgendered, the speaker runs the risk of invalidating the social identities of the TNB person, a process known as *erasure* in the sociocultural literature. Conversely, becoming conscientious about inclusive language and utilizing the appropriate linguistic gender patterns are steps toward supporting TNB people. Research indicates that the amount of support that a TNB individual receives predicts their well-being, demonstrating that language is an important tool by which health risks may be diminished (see James et al., 2016).

In this chapter, we use inclusive language to refer to any linguistic strategies that move away from assumed gender-binary dichotomies and that are sensitive to the differences in various gender-related identities. These include modifications in use of certain lexical items (*parent* instead of mother/father); implicitly gendered words (beautiful vs. handsome); the creation of new uses of pronoun forms (singular 'they'); and/or novel grammatical suffixes for languages that express gender as such (see Zimman, 2017). In what follows, we provide examples of current linguistic movements and issues, led by scholars and activists, that directly and/or indirectly impact TNB people around the world. The examples are intended to ground and explain complex linguistic issues and it is our hope that readers will be inspired to continue to learn about, support, and initiate their own advocacy efforts after reading about global movements toward linguistic inclusion.

Spanish

Spanish is a Romance language within the Indo-European language family. It is the official language of at least 21 countries (Ethnologue, 2020). With around 489 million native speakers, it is currently the second most spoken language in the world, with a total of 585 million (or 7,5% of today's world population) (Cervantes Institute, 2020). As a grammatically gendered language, Spanish pronouns, nouns, formal titles, and adjectives include reference to the gender of the object with which they are associated. Generally, grammatically gendered words end with either an *-a* or an *-o* (feminine/masculine, respectively).[1] Simply put, *Latina* may refer to a woman, whereas *Latino* may refer to a man from Latin America.

In an effort to include TNB people and to resist linguistic structures that privilege men, large movements are springing up throughout the world to push for diverse gender inclusion in the Spanish language. One of the most common efforts, and one that may be most familiar to English-speaking readers, is the addition of an x to Latin (Latinx) that effectively creates a gender-neutral category. However, the 'echs' [eks] sound is not naturally occurring in Spanish, and although it is a well-meaning attempt to be inclusive, it may also reflect colonizing attempts to 'correct' a language by imposing Western linguistic conventions. In fact, gender-neutral derivatives of Latino/a were originally created by English-speaking activist movements in the United States to refer to individuals of Latin American descent, but continues to be a thorny issue in the entire Spanish-speaking world, including the United States (Vidal-Ortiz & Martínez, 2018). The Pew Research Center conducted a recent survey that provides interesting insight into the use of Latinx, including that most self-identified Latino/a adults who completed their survey (76%) had not heard of the term (Noe-Bustamante et al., 2020). In popular use, such as on blogs and in online forums, writers use conventions that are easier for Spanish speakers such as *Latin@*, *Latin Ⓐ*, and *Latine*.

Given that Spanish is a widely spoken language, a number of suggestions and manifestos exist as guides for the development of inclusive language practices. For instance, Rocío Gómez (2016) is a transfeminist translator who presents three important gender-neutral strategies in Spanish, one of which includes the innovative pronoun *elle* (instead of *él* 'he' or ella 'she'). Although the proposal has briefly made its way to the Observatory Word List of the Royal Spanish Academy (RAE), the national authority on prescriptive Spanish usage, its inclusion in the radar of RAE does not mean that it is recognized as a valid 'Spanish' word (La Real Academia Española, 2020). Despite being the preferred pronoun choice among many non-binary Spanish speakers, usage of the modification has received pushback similar to the debate over use of they/them in English. Critics argue that a gender-neutral variant is confusing, creates atypical spellings, is grammatically cumbersome, and is just improper (Bonnin & Coronel, 2021).

Meanwhile, Chilean feminist groups like *Las Tesis* gained tremendous visibility as they called attention to gender-based violence and femicide through protest songs like *Un Violador en tu Camino* (The Rapist is You) that have gained international traction (Soldati, 2019). Although some of the feminist and gender inclusive movements in Spanish-speaking countries are not focused on language usage, they are integral to movements toward the sorts of gender justice that underlies inclusive linguistic change. The song is particularly moving as it includes lexical features (mainly masculine nouns) that are used to contest femicide. Other activists in Spain are pushing for changes to the Spanish constitution aimed at removing gendered language from the document. RAE received a report recommending that the masculine nouns in the Spanish constitution be changed to more gender inclusive forms (Burgen, 2020).

Scholars argue that transgender and nonbinary issues and people are increasingly becoming centralized in feminist activism, including language reform (Bucholtz, 2014). Feminist linguistic movements of the 1970s and onward have laid the foundation for creating linguistic practices that expand beyond binary understandings of sex, gender, and sexuality (Zimman, 2018). Transgender and nonbinary identities challenge binary systems of categorization and many societal systems, including language, need to be reformed in order to challenge transphobia and increase the acceptance of transgender and nonbinary identities and people (Zimman, 2017). The two aforementioned examples of activism related to Spanish language reform demonstrate how grassroots efforts consider language directly or indirectly to push systemic change that could not otherwise be undertaken.

Hebrew

Hebrew is a member of the Afro-Asiatic language family and it is spoken, primarily, in Israel. Like Spanish, Hebrew is also a grammatically gendered language, whereby nouns are assigned either *zachar* (male) or *nekevah* (female). In Hebrew, adjectives and verbs agree with the grammatical gender of the noun. For instance, *talmid tov* 'good male student' is juxtaposed to its feminine counterpart *talmidah tovah* 'good female student' whereby the adjective agrees with the corresponding gender of the noun. In terms of noun–verb agreement, the verb ללמוד *lilmod* 'to learn' agrees with the gender of the subject as in התלמיד לומד *hatalmid lomed* 'the student (masculine) is learning'/לומדת התלמידה *hatalmidah lomedet* 'the student (female) is learning'. At present, there is a convention in Hebrew that, when referencing a group, the speaker should default to using male verb and adjective forms if at least one male is present in the group. The issue of defaulting to male linguistic conventions is starting to be challenged by Hebrew speakers in the United States but it may not be as widespread in other Hebrew-speaking communities (Masad, 2017).

Several foundations like Keshet, Eshel, and Sephardi-Mizrachi Queer Network promote advocacy and inclusion of the LGBTQ+ community. However, linguistic practices have been more explicitly addressed by the *Nonbinary Hebrew Project* that has constructed a comprehensive additional third grammatical gendered system to gender-neutral syntax in the Hebrew language (Rivlin & Gross, n.d.). This third grammatical gender system has been used for ritual, conversation, and prayer by lay leaders and rabbis in many countries to honor the TNB members of their communities. For example, the alternative system offered by the Project allows speakers to use the segol and the letter 'Hei' ה, making an 'eh' sound at the end of the word instead of the conventional male or female ending. For example, תַלְמִידָה is rendered gender expansive for 'student'. Additionally, the *Nonbinary Hebrew Project* has cited previous scholarship that highlights biblical precedent for intersex, transgender and nonbinary textual interpretations.

251

Prior to the *Nonbinary Hebrew Project*, Hebrew speakers were beginning to modify and adapt their language to make it more inclusive. Subversion of the traditional gender markers is how some Hebrew speakers express their gender and/or sexual identities; however, some speakers may use both gender markers in the same word to express themself (Bershtling, 2014). For example, Hebrew speakers modified the word 'you', by combining the male plural form *atem* and the female plural form *aten* to create a gender-neutral word *atemen*. By mixing feminine and masculine grammatical gender systems, speakers were able to create more neutral versions of common words. Some LGBTQ+ communities combine the masculine plural suffix *-im* (*talmid-im* 'male students') along with feminine plural *-ot* (*talmid-ot* 'female students') resulting in inclusive *talmidimot* 'students'. Such a strategy also applies to verbs, whereby *lomdimot* 'they are studying' encompasses different genders collectively.

It is also common for Hebrew LGBTQ+ activists and community members to engage in *gender reversal*, or *lashon m'orevet*, which is the practice of using gendered language that is binary opposite of their identity (e.g., men may use female language to refer to themselves) and others switch back and forth between genders during a conversation. Altogether, *The Nonbinary Hebrew Project* created a parallel system of nonbinary conjugations and declensions, capitalizing on ways that Hebrew grammatical gender already works and broadening the application of preexisting innovations (e.g., combining gendered suffixes and creating new hybrid words altogether).

Please note that work to make Hebrew a more inclusive language is a dynamic process, and many of the ongoing modifications are documented by the *Nonbinary Hebrew Project* (Rivlin & Gross, n.d.). Given the evolving nature of Hebrew and other living languages, we relied on examples and feedback from the experts listed in the introduction to this chapter. In some cases, we generated examples of our own and asked our expert contacts to offer their acceptability judgment. In other words, external experts reviewed our work and confirmed its accuracy because the examples and anecdotes we used were not available elsewhere and had to be created for this chapter.

Swahili

Swahili, known as Kiswahili by its speakers, is a Bantu language from the Niger-Congo language family. Swahili is used as a lingua franca in the Great African Lakes and other Eastern and Southern parts of Africa (e.g., Kenya, Tanzania, and the Democratic Republic of the Congo). Swahili does not have gender-differentiated pronouns analogous to those of Romance languages. Instead, Swahili shows a complex gender system, whereby nouns are classified into 15 noun classes and natural sex does not determine the classification of nouns (including animate ones) (Carstens, 2008). Given its complexity, the term 'noun class' is used instead of gender in this section. Noun classes are sometimes based upon the characteristics of their referents. Among scholars of Bantu languages, there have been debates about whether noun classes in Swahili correspond to terms with similar semantic content. Some scholars have argued against such (see Richardson, 1967), whereas other scholars have attempted to provide evidence for similar semantic content across various Swahili noun classes (see Denny & Creider, 1976; Zawawi, 1979). Although gender noun/class distinctions are purely morphological (adding a morpheme to the beginning of the root), there are gender-neutral options for gender-differentiated pronouns. In terms of pronouns, some individuals have used the word *yeye* in a gender-neutral manner even though its common usage is usually for 'he', 'she', and the third person singular where the gender of an individual is unknown. For example, the sentence *Yeye anaitwa Jeremy* 'They are called Jeremy' would be an example of using the third person singular in a gender-neutral manner (Ojiambo, 2010).

There has been a wide variety of activism and advocacy for intersex, transgender, and gender non-conforming (ITGNC) individuals in Kenya. For example, an activist named Kwaboka Kibagendi pushed for the creation of a safe house for ITGNC individuals in Nairobi, Kenya (Nelson, 2019). Kibagendi further aims to combat stigma and discrimination by advocating for government policies such as recommending to the Bureau of Statistics in Kenya that agencies adopt a third-gender option, ensure intersex options on birth certificates, and improve access to gender-affirmative surgeries. Moreover, Jinsiangu is an organization that was established in 2012 with the goal of advocating for and providing a safe space for ITGNC individuals in Kenya. The name of the organization comes from the Swahili words *jinsia* and *yangu* which together translate to 'my gender'. The organization provides educational access to gender-affirmative medical services, psychosocial support, as well as education for religious leaders, families, and healthcare professionals on ITGNC issues.

Genderless or 'Gender-Neutral' Languages

Given the likely familiarity that readers have with the English language, we do not spend time in this chapter focusing strictly on natural gender languages. Some of the authors of this chapter have written about English language usage elsewhere (Knutson et al., 2019) or may consult transmasculine linguist Zimman (2017). Instead, we examined the way that natural gender languages and colonizing cultures have impacted some genderless or gender-neutral languages. Although the languages we discuss in this section did not fully become natural-gender or grammatical gender languages through these colonial influences, the impact and reactions elicited of such languages (e.g., English and Spanish) shape how TNB people are both understood and referred to linguistically in legal texts today.

Turkish and Lubunca

As part of the Turkic family, Turkish is primarily and widely spoken as a majority language in Turkey and as a minoritized language in the former Ottoman Empire (Iraq, Greece and North Macedonia). Turkish is considered a gender-neutral language, meaning that inanimate objects are not assigned a gender, unlike in Romance languages (e.g., Spanish). Personal pronouns in Turkish also do not show any sex-based distinctions (i.e., the pronoun *o* may refer to 'he', 'she', and demonstrative 'that').

However, gender neutrality in grammar does not preclude the Turkish language from containing an androcentric bias (Braun, 2001; Saraç, 2016). Although Prewitt-Freilino et al. (2012) argue that countries with gender-neutral languages may have a higher degree of gender equality compared to countries with gendered languages, other scholars have argued that androcentric bias is even harder to challenge in gender-neutral languages because the language gender bias is covert (Braun, 2001; Vasvári, 2015). Many Turkish terms still include covert gender (e.g., professions) because they are often assumed to be associated with men (Saraç, 2016). Similar covert gender biases related to professions and other social positions show up in other gender-neutral languages. For example, Vasvári (2015) describes Uralic languages (e.g., Hungarian, Finnish, Estonian) as being rooted in the inclination to view male humans as human prototypes.

Androcentric bias in language, and addressing androcentric bias through feminist linguistic reform, directly connects to reforming language to be more inclusive of transgender and nonbinary identities and individuals. Early feminist language reform in the 1970s sought to challenge the normalization of androcentric bias in language (Zimman, 2018). Challenging androcentric normativity provided a foundation of the emergence of subsequent queer linguistic practices as a way to also address heteronormativity and homophobia prevalent across languages. One such example of queer language reform is the creation of terms that markedly refer to heterosexist practices (i.e., cisgender) as a way to also normalize and naturalize transgender and nonbinary identities. Such reforms stem from the idea of markedness theory (see Eckman et al., 1986), the idea that what becomes 'marked' is not the assumed normed, these practices offer a dual purpose: (1) to call for a 'destabilization' of presumed androcentric biases and (2) to bring visibility to historically marginalized non-binary and TNB individuals. Because language is one of the primary avenues through which gender is conveyed and negotiated, feminist and queer linguistic scholars and TNB people have emphasized the importance of reforming language to be more inclusive of TNB people. In short, while feminist movements lead the way in addressing androcentric biases in language (yet still based in binary terms), current queer movements have expanded such legacy beyond binary oppositions.

Divorced from its androcentric bias, the Turkish language could be considered inclusive because the same gender-neutral pronoun is applied to everyone. Still, the gender-neutral structure of Turkish would not preclude someone from misgendering a TNB person in other ways. For example, a person could be directly labeled as a man (*adam*) or woman (*kadın*), or as male (*erkek*) or female (*dişi*), which may or may not align with an individual's gender identity. Moreover, removing gender bias from language does not eliminate the heteronormative gender and sexual binaries.

The rights, protections, and treatment of TNB people have long lagged in many other Western countries (see Engin, 2015). For example, LGBTQ+ events were banned in Ankara, Turkey's capital, until April 2019 (Reid, 2019). Furthermore, gender-confirmation surgery is often required to legally change documentation, many Turkish leaders believe that transgender identity is immoral, and TNB people are frequently discriminated against in housing, healthcare, employment, and education (Engin, 2015). Additionally, many aspects of Turkish society are gender-segregated between men and women, making things especially complex for nonbinary people (see Cale, 2019; Kameron, 2017). Therefore, a gender-neutral language does not necessarily equate to gender neutrality or gender equality in the society in which that language is spoken.

Many TNB people experience a lack of safety in many parts of Turkey and that lack of safety has increased the push for linguistic change. Toward that end, some LGBTQ+ people in Turkey use Lubunca, a secret or enregistered variety that is derived from numerous languages including Romani, Arabic, French, Greek, Italian, and Russian (Barrett, 2018). Similar to Hijra Farsi in India (Hall, 1997), a secret language spoken by transgender individuals, Lubunca is another language known as a 'queer argot' developed by the community to create safer spaces for LGBTQ+ individuals (Anna, 2014; Bertoša & Pišković, 2018). Lubunca is particularly used when there is fear of being overheard or identified by law enforcement (see Magid, 2017).

Lubunca is used primarily by transgender women involved in unlicensed, criminalized sex work (Magid, 2017). Licensed sex work is legal but is inaccessible for transgender people because the current brothel system in Turkey allows only cisgender women to be registered and licensed as sex workers (Engin, 2018). Although some words and phrases in Lubunca have become more mainstream in recent years, Lubunca is not nearly as popular as some other queer argots (e.g., Polari; Magid, 2017). Therefore, as Lubunca continues to evolve over time, it is safer for transgender women involved in sex work to utilize Lubunca (e.g., using the Romani word for prostitute, *lubni*) rather than speaking only in Turkish to other sex workers and potential clients, but Lubunca's usefulness may decrease if the language gains more popularity in the mainstream and/or as LGBTQ+ experience higher levels of acceptance and safety (see Gratien & Harrington, 2013).

Tagalog

Tagalog is an Austronesian language primarily spoken in the Philippines along with a variety of other indigenous languages. Although typologically a gender-neutral language, the language has maintained some engendering patterns through various waves of colonization (Spanish and then English). For example, 'Filipina/Filipino' may be used to designate the gender of a person from the Philippines. Consistent with Nadal (2019), we use Filipino/Filipina throughout this section, and we encourage readers to refer to Nadal (2004) for a broader discussion of the linguistic and cultural development of Filipino American identities and terminology.

About 24 million people speak Tagalog in the Philippines, and due to colonizing influences, many also speak English (a natural gender language). Similar to efforts to the Latinx movement, some Filipinos in the United States have adopted the term Filipinx. However, some individuals who are identified as Filipino have pushed back, claiming that the term Filipino has always been gender neutral (see Filipinxs in Education Reaffirming Community Empowerment, 2018).

Despite the fact that standard Tagalog does not make gender-based distinctions in pronouns and certain lexical items (*asawa* refers both to husband/wife) on which to base discriminatory policies (e.g., marriage is between a husband and a wife), people in the Philippines have been heavily influenced by Catholicism and other Westernizing influences. As a result, the majority of Tagalog speakers are resistant to codifying LGBTQ+ rights in law. Similar to countries that address sexual orientation first and then progress to TNB issues, the conversation in the Philippines seems to be focused on lesbian, gay, and bisexual issues (Yarica et al., 2019). Several groups such as Metro Manila Pride, Lagablab Network, and Babaylanes Inc. are dedicated to providing support and advocacy for LGBTQ+ people in the Philippines.

Burmese

Burmese is a member of the Sino-Tibetan family spoken by about 22 million people in Myanmar (also known as Burma), where it is official along with other regional languages. Burmese is also widely spoken in Bangladesh, Malaysia, and Thailand. Although Burmese is considered a grammatically genderless language (it does not mark the gender of inanimate objects), suffix particles are used to make gender distinctions of animate objects (especially with animals and plants) (i.e., ကြောင်ထီး *kraung hti* 'male cat' vs. ကြောင်မ *kraung ma* 'female cat').

A variety of terms have been developed by LGBTQ+ communities in Burmese, and most refer to diverse forms of gender expression, including deeply offensive words that refer to third genders and to cross-binary gender expression (Independent Television Service, 2015). As with other marginalized communities around the world, LGBTQ+ terms in Myanmar are both time and context dependent. A word that was once insulting may be re-appropriated by the community. Also, some groups such as transgender and nonbinary people may use terms within the community that would be offensive coming from someone outside of the community. As an example, Aye Min Thant describes how 'အခြောက်။' (/*Achau'*/) is loosely translated to 'gay'. The sociohistoricity behind this word may resonate with the multi-layered meanings behind the word 'queer' in English throughout its history; unlike English 'gay' but similar to 'queer', in Burmese, *Achau'* or 'gay' describes people who transgress gender norms. When used by people outside of the LGBTQ+ community, the term can be offensive. However, Thant explains how the same word can be used positively among LGBTQ+ persons. *Achau'* and variations of this word may can be used as terms of endearment between friends who are LGBTQ+ (2017).

As with many other countries, colonialism exerted a considerable impact on some cultures in Myanmar, particularly in the area of literacy and language development (see Britannica, n.d.).

Within the country, some Buddhist institutions perpetuate LGBTQ+ stereotypes and reinforce gender biases that impact LGBTQ+ people (e.g., Me, 2018). In response to restrictive laws and cultural norms, some advocates in the country are pushing for LGBTQ+ rights. Despite Section 337 of the Penal Code which criminalizes homosexuality, the Myanmar government allowed a public pride party to take place in 2018 on the International Day Against Homophobia, Biphobia and Transphobia. Although the law enforcement rarely enforces Section 337 of the Penal Code, TNB people still experience harassment and sexual assault from police and their gender identities are not formally recognized.

Burmese is tending towards the opposite direction when it comes to unmarking gender-based distinctions. Traditionally, the Burmese did not make gender distinctions in the third person personal pronouns, that is, သူ (*thu*) was used to refer to both 'he' and 'she'. In recent years, the pronoun သူမ (*thu ma*) 'she' has emerged, a usage that has also made its way to print media as well as official documents (Fifty Viss, 2016). The exact origins of this new usage are unknown. The scant evidence suggests that it was introduced in an English-Burmese translation grammar, whereby the he/she distinction in English was demarcated onto Burmese. The process of borrowing pronouns, in this case following a pattern-based distinction known as 'pattern-replication' (Matras & Sakel, 2007), is not only rare cross-linguistically (Thomason, 2001) but it also runs contrary to the other more inclusive movements that are being slowly undertaken in other parts of the world.

Regardless of how they are written, laws and policies can in Myanmar and beyond still be used to maintain restrictions on LGBTQ+ people's lives. For example, laws that criminalize same-sex intimacy and policies that omit transgender and nonbinary identities may be written with gender neutrality, but they are no less gender restrictive. Depending on how they are delivered (e.g., sarcastically, with derision), even inclusive words can be weaponized.

Recommendations/Advocacy

Despite the fact that our overview of languages is far from exhaustive, it may be used as a starting point for discussion about linguistic dynamics that impact TNB people and ways to advance positive change. The recommendations and calls for advocacy that follow are drawn from the evidence we presented earlier in this chapter. In the sections that follow, we attempt to draw connections between linguistic developments around the globe to inform future movements and advocacy initiatives. We offer some general suggestions, followed by resources and reference lists that may be used as guides for further reading. Our suggestions are organized by topic.

Beyond Inclusive Language

Even if a language is genderless or gender neutral, it may not be grounded in an inclusive sociopolitical and/or legal framework. The way words are combined and used to perpetuate sexist and cissexist dynamics may still negatively impact TNB people, even if the language itself is not inherently binary or restrictive. Furthermore, societies that are moving to embrace gender-neutral aspects of their languages (e.g., they, them pronouns) are not necessarily more inclusive just because they change the way they talk. Efforts to alter linguistic conventions to make them more inclusive and/or to embrace gender neutrality in language should also focus on changing the underlying structures and sociopolitical movements that created those components of language in the first place.

Beyond Good Intentions

Just because language is intended to be inclusive does not mean that it is culturally appropriate. Sometimes, in a rush to 'fix' language, we destroy its cultural context and linguistic form. For example, Latinx and Filipinx appear to be good ideas on the surface, but adaptations of those terms may be both culturally incongruent and/or culturally unnecessary. For example, as discussed by Kevin Nadal (Nadal, 2019), terms used to reference Filipino Americans (Filipinx, Filipin@, and so on) all carry cultural limitations, and many are rooted in colonization and the disenfranchisement of Filipino people. Alternatively, while Latinx may also be considered 'colonizing', it has also been argued to act as a new frame of inclusion (e.g., indigeneity and resistance of whiteness) (Vidal-Ortiz & Martínez, 2018). Modifications to language should be made thoughtfully and with an awareness of the cultural resonance of structural reorganizations. This is not to say that progress should be stifled where grammar rules must be altered, or spelling conventions must be realigned. Rather, we recommend making TNB affirmative changes with the least culturally destructive outcomes.

Ask the Community

It is important to resist the impulse to speak for minoritized communities. The easiest linguistic 'fix' may not be the healthiest or most healing wording/grammar/spelling for TNB communities within a given community or cultural context. Changes to linguistic structures and languages should be conducted in a way that empowers TNB voices and that places TNB communities at the center of the decision-making process.

Try Not to Silo Efforts

As has been indicated in this chapter, social movements and human rights efforts may dovetail to produce mutually beneficial change. As is the case in some Spanish-speaking countries, the fight for women's rights is also changing and positively impacting systems that have limited TNB peoples' lives. Likewise, the fight among Hebrew speaking men to alternate between gender conventions in language also queers and depolarizes binary language. This is to say that, when we make language more inclusive, it benefits everyone. The colloquial phrase, 'trans rights are human rights', applies to language.

Remember That Language Impacts Health

At the beginning of this chapter, we provided evidence that restrictive, binary, sexist language, specially misgendering, negatively impacts TNB people. It may be easy to get focused on the fine points of grammar and spelling and to forget the subtle ways in which binary gender ideals are also reinforced in our choice of words. Continual consciousness of the implications of linguistic choices is a vital step toward supporting, affirming, and including TNB people.

Conclusions

By exploring linguistic dynamics around the world, we sought to provide an overview of current trends, advocacy efforts, and challenges that face TNB rights advocates as we fight for more inclusive language and policy for TNB people. Despite the fact that a systematic and comprehensive accounting for all languages was beyond the scope of this chapter, we hope that our overview adds to the challenges and conversations about appropriate ways in altering long-standing and culturally ingrained linguistic practices. We encourage readers of this chapter to dig into the additional resources and references we provided because they include rich sources of further insight, interactive maps, primary texts, and glossaries of new and evolving terms. The conversation about TNB inclusion in language is just beginning, and we hope that the content this chapter provides becomes part of that dialogue. As a reader, you are invited to take the conversation to the next level.

Some Additional Resources

- Rocío Gómez (Spanish) transfeminist translator: https://linguaultrafinitio.wordpress.com/author/rociofgomez/
- The Linguistic Society of America guidelines: www.linguisticsociety.org/resource/guidelines-inclusive-language
- Gender-Inclusive language in France: A manual: www.motscles.net/ecriture-inclusive
- Gender-Inclusive guidelines from University of Pittsburgh: www.gsws.pitt.edu/node/1432
- Gender-inclusive guidelines from University of Maryland: https://lgbt.umd.edu/good-practices-inclusive-language

Note

1 For a more exhaustive treatment of grammatical gender in Spanish, see Harris (1991) and Roca (2005).

References

American Psychological Association. (2015). Guidelines for psychological practice with transgender and gender nonconforming people. *American Psychologist, 70*(9), 832–864. https://doi.org/10.1037/a003996

Anna, T. (2014). The opacity of queer languages. *e-flux Journal, 60*, 5–10.

Barrett, R. (2018). Speech play, gender play, and the verbal artistry of queer argots. *Suvremena Lingvistika, 44*(86), 215–242.

Bershtling, O. (2014). Speech creates a kind of commitment. In *Queer excursions: Retheorizing binaries in language, gender, and sexuality.* Oxford University Press. https://oxford.universitypressscholarship.com/view/10.1093/acprof:oso/9780199937295.001.0001/acprof-9780199937295-chapter-3.

Bertoša, M., & Pišković, T. (2018). Foreword: On gender, language and genderlectology. *Suvremena Lingvistika, 44*(86), IX–XIII.

Bonnin, J. E., & Coronel, A. A. (2021). Attitudes toward gender-neutral Spanish: Acceptability and adoptability. *Frontiers in Sociology, 6*, 629616. https://doi.org/10.3389/fsoc.2021.629616

Braun, F. (2001). Turkish: The communication of gender in Turkish. In M. Hellinger & H. Bußmann (Eds.), *Gender across languages: The linguistic representation of women and men* (Vol. 1, pp. 283–310). John Benjamins.

Britannica. (n.d.). Myanmar. In *Britannica.com.* Retrieved May 23, 2022, from www.britannica.com/place/Myanmar/Cultural-life

Bucholtz, M. (2014). The feminist foundations of language, gender, and sexuality research. In S. Ehrlich, M. Meyerhoff, & J. Holmes (Eds.), *The handbook of language, gender, and sexuality* (2nd ed., pp. 23–47). Wiley Blackwell.

Burgen, S. (2020, January 19). Masculine, feminist or neutral? The language battle that has split Spain. *The Observer.* www.theguardian.com/world/2020/jan/19/gender-neutral-language-battle-spain

Cale, L. (2019). What it's like traveling the world as a gender non-conforming person. *Six-Two.* www.contiki.com/six-two/gender-non-conforming-non-binary-travel/

Carstens, V. (2008). DP in Bantu and romance. In C. De Cat & K. Denmuth (Eds.), *The Bantu-romance connection: A comparative investigation of verbal agreement, DPs and information structure* (pp. 131–166). John Benjamins.

Cervantes Institute. (2020). *El español: una lengua viva—Informe 2020 (report)*. Instituto Cervantes.

Corbett, G. G. (1991). *Gender*. Cambridge University Press.

Corbett, G. G. (2013a). Number of genders. In M. S. Dryer and M. Haspelmath (Eds.), *The world Atlas of language structures online*. Max Planck Institute for Evolutionary Anthropology. https://wals.info/chapter/30

Corbett, G. G. (2013b). Sex-based and non-sex-based gender systems. In M. S. Dryer & M. Haspelmath (Eds.), *The world Atlas of language structures online*. Max Planck Institute for Evolutionary Anthropology. https://wals.info/feature/31A#2/26.7/149.1

Denny, J. P., & Creider, C. (1976). The semantics of noun classes in Proto-Bantu. *Studies in African Linguistics, 7*(1), 1–30. Reprinted in Craig (ed.), pp. 217–239.

Dixon, R. M. W. (1982). *Where have all the adjectives gone?: And other essays in semantics and syntax*. Walter de Gruyter.

Eckman, F. R., Moravcsik, E. A., & Wirth, J. R. (1986). *Markedness*. Springer. https://doi.org/10.1007/978-1-4757-5718-7_1

Eli. (2015). Gender neutral parent titles. In *Adventures in non-binary land*. Retrieved October 21, 2020, from https://drugssexpolitics.wordpress.com/2015/08/19/gender-neutral-parent-titles/.

Engin, C. (2015). LGBT in Turkey: Policies and experiences. *Social Sciences, 4*(3), 838–858.

Engin, C. (2018). Sex work in Turkey: Experiences of transwomen. In L. Nuttbrock (Ed.), *Transgender sex work and society* (pp. 196–213). Harrington Park Press.

Ethnologue. (2020). What are the largest language families? *Author*. www.ethnologue.com/guides/largest-families

Fifty Viss. (2016, February 19). The emergence of gender-specific pronouns in Burmese. *WordPress*. https://viss.wordpress.com/2016/02/19/the-emergence-of-gender-specific-pronouns-in-burmese/

Filipinxs in Education Reaffirming Community Empowerment. (2018). Why we say 'Filipinx.' *Author*. http://kpfierce.weebly.com/blog/why-we-say-filipinx

Foundalis, H. E. (2002). *Evolution of gender in Indo-European languages* [Paper presentation]. Proceedings of the Annual Meeting of the Cognitive Science Society, Sapporo.

Gómez, R. (2016). *Pequeño manifiesto sobre el género neutro en castellano* (1st ed.). https://linguaultrafinitio.wordpress.com/author/rociofgomez/

Gratien, C., & Harrington, L. (2013, December 18). Lubunca and the history of Istanbul slang [audio podcast episode]. In *Ottoman history podcast*. www.ottomanhistorypodcast.com/2013/12/istanbul-slang.html

Gygax, P. M., Elmiger, D., Zufferey, S., Granham, A., Sczesny, von Stockhausen, L., Braun, F., & Oakhill, J. (2019). A language index of grammatical gender dimensions to study the impact of grammatical gender on the way we perceive women and men. *Frontiers in Psychology, 10*, 1604.

Hall, K. (1997). "Go suck your husband's sugarcane!" Hijras and the use of sexual insult. In A. Livia & K. Hall (Eds.), *Queerly phrased: Language gender and sexuality* (pp. 430–460). Oxford University Press.

Harris, J. (1991). The exponence of gender in Spanish. *Linguistic Inquiry, 22*, 27–62.

Independent Television Service. (2015). A map of gender-diverse cultures. *Independent Lens*. www.pbs.org/independentlens/content/two-spirits_map-html/

James, S. E., Herman, J. L., Rankin, S., Keisling, M., Mottet, L., & Anafi, M. (2016). *The report of the 2015 US transgender survey*. National Center for Transgender Equality. www.transequality.org/sites/default/files/docs/USTS-Full-Report-FINAL.PDF

Kameron. (2017). Traveling non-binary: Gender perceptions in two cultures. *Transgender Universe*. http://archive.transgenderuniverse.com/2017/09/08/traveling-non-binary-gender-perceptions-in-two-cultures/

Knutson, D., Koch, J. M., & Goldbach, C. (2019). Recommended terminology, pronouns, and documentation for work with transgender and non-binary populations. *Practice Innovations*. https://doi.org/10.1037pri0000098

La Real Academia española retira el pronombre "elle" de su Observatorio de palabras. (2020, November 3). *La Nación*. www.lanacion.com.ar/sociedad/la-real-academia-espanola-retira-pro nombre-elle-nid2498809/

Magid, P. (2017, September). The changing nature of Lubunca, Turkey's LGBTQ slang. *Atlas Obscura*. www.atlasobscura.com/articles/lubunca-lgbtq-language-slang-turkey

Masad, I. (2017, March 17). On Hebrew and living in gendered language. *The Toast.* https://the-toast.net/2015/03/17/hebrew-living-gendered-language/

Matras, Y., & Sakel, J. (2007). Investigating the mechanisms of pattern replication in language convergence. *Studies in Language, 31*(4), 829–865.

McConnell-Ginet, S. (2014). Gender and its relation to sex: The myth of "natural" gender. In G. G. Corbett (Ed.), *The expression of gender* (Vol. 6, pp. 3–38). DeGryuter.

McLemore, K. A. (2018). A minority stress perspective on transgender individuals' experiences with misgendering. *Stigma and Health, 3*(1), 53–64. https://doi.org/10.1037/sah0000070

Me, N. (2018, May). Not very gay. *Myanmar Times.* www.mmtimes.com/news/not-very-gay.html

Nadal, K. L. (2004). Pilipino American identity development model. *Journal of Multicultural Counseling and Development, 32*, 45–62. https://doi.org/10.1002/j.2161-1912.2004.tb00360.x

Nadal., K. L. (2019). *#DearFilipinoAmericans.* https://twitter.com/kevinnadal/status/1146502379019407363

Nadal, K. L., Davidoff, K. C., Davis, L. S., & Wong, Y. (2014). Emotional, behavioral, and cognitive reactions to microaggressions: Transgender perspectives. *Psychology of Sexual Orientation and Gender Diversity, 1*(1), 72–81. https://doi.org/10.1037sgd0000011

Nelson, K. (2019). *Improving the lives of intersex people in Kenya.* https://theweek.com/articles/864252/improving-lives-intersex-people-kenya

Noe-Bustamante, L., Mora, L., & Lopez, M. H. (2020). About one-in-four U.S. Hispanics have heard of Latinx, but just 3% use it: Young Hispanic women among the most likely to use the term. *Pew Research Center.* www.pewresearch.org/hispanic/2020/08/11/about-one-in-four-u-s-hispanics-have-heard-of-latinx-but-just-3-use-it/

Ojiambo, P. (2010). *Lesson 4: Personal pronouns.* https://www2.ku.edu/~kiswahili/pdfs/lesson_04.pdf

Prewitt-Freilino, J. L., Caswell, T. A., & Laakso, E. K. (2012). The gendering of language: A comparison of gender equality in countries with gendered, natural gender, and genderless languages. *Sex Roles, 66*(3–4), 268–281. https://doi.org/10.1007/s11199-011-0083-5

Reid, G. (2019, April). In Turkey, Ankara wakes up to court lifting LGBTI events ban. *Human Rights Watch.* www.hrw.org/news/2019/04/25/turkey-ankara-wakes-court-lifting-lgbti-events-ban

Richardson, I. (1967). Linguistic evolution and Bantu noun class systems. In *La classification nominale dans les langues N₁gro-Africaines.* CNRS.

Rivlin, E., & Gross, L. (n.d.). Grammar and semantics. *Nonbinary Hebrew Project.* www.nonbinaryhebrew.com/grammar-systematics

Roca, I. M. (2005). La gramática y la biología en el género del español. *Revista Española de Lingüística, 35*(1), 17–44.

Rodríguez-Ordóñez, I. (2021). The role of social meaning in contact-induced variation among new speakers of Basque. *Journal of Sociolinguistics.* https://doi.org/10.1111/josl.12477

Saraç, Ş. (2016). Türkçe ile Rusçada dil bilgisel cinsiyet ve bu dillerdeki cinsiyetçi deyim ve atasözleri. *Türk Dili Araştırmaları Yıllığı—Belleten, 64*(1), 125–137. https://dergipark.org.tr/en/pub/belleten/issue/33858/374884

Soldati, C. (2019, December 17). The rapist is you, the Chilean protest song against gender violence that sparked a global movement. *Lifegate.* www.lifegate.com/the-rapist-is-you-un-violador-en-tu-camino#:~:text=Gender-,The%20rapist%20is%20you%2C%20the%20Chilean%20protest%20song%20against%20gender,that%20sparked%20a%20global%20movement&text=Un%20violador%20en%20tu%20camino%20%E2%80%93%20the%20rapist%20is%20you%20%E2%80%93%20is,impunity%20of%20gender%2Dbased%20violence.

Thant, A. M. (2017). *Choosing to be LGBT: Gender and sexuality activism in contemporary Myanmar* [Master's thesis, Cornell University, Cornell University Library]. https://ecommons.cornell.edu/handle/1813/51587

Thomason, S. G. (2001). *Language contact.* Edinburgh University Press. https://digitallibrary.tsu.ge/book/2022/Jul/books/Thomason_Language_Contact_an_Introduction.pdf

Vasvári, L. O. (2015). Gender trouble in a grammatically genderless language: Hungarian. In M. Hellinger & H. Motschenbacher (Eds.), *Gender across languages: The linguistic representation of women and men* (Vol. 4, pp. 203–225). John Benjamins.

Vidal-Ortiz, S., & Martínez, J. (2018). Latinx thoughts: Latinidad with an X. *Latino Studies, 16*, 384–395.

World Professional Association for Transgender Health. (2012). *Standards of care for the health of transsexual, transgender, and gender nonconforming people [7th Version].* Author. https://www.wpath.org/publications/soc

Yarica, L. E., de Vela, T. C., & Tan, M. L. (2019). Queer identity and gender-related rights in post-colonial Philippines. *Australian Journal of Asian Law, 20*(1), 1–11. https://ssrn.com/abstract=3488543

Zawawi, S. (1979). *Loan words and their effect on the classification of Swahili nominals.* E. J. Brill.

Zimman, L. (2017). Transgender language reform: Some challenges and strategies for promoting trans-affirming, gender-inclusive language. *Journal of Language and Discrimination, 1*(1), 84–105.

Zimman, L. (2018). Transgender voices: Insights on identity, embodiment, and the gender of the voice. *Language and Linguistics Compass, 12*(8), e12284.

18

LGBTQ+ YOUTH AND THE GEOGRAPHIC COMMUNITY

Opportunities for Advancing Research and Understanding

Megan S. Paceley and Jessica N. Fish

Abbreviations

LGBTQ+ lesbian, gay, bisexual, transgender, queer, questioning, and all sexual and gender minority individuals

EST Ecological Systems Theory

LGBTQ+ Youth and the Geographic Community: Opportunities for Advancing Research and Understanding

Lesbian, gay, bisexual, transgender, and queer (LGBTQ+) youths are situated within social contexts that affect their identity, health, and well-being. Anti-LGBTQ+ stigma, marginalization, and victimization are associated with increased rates of depression, anxiety, substance use, stress, self-harm, and suicidality among LGBTQ+ youths (Almeida et al., 2009; Ballard et al., 2017; Burton et al., 2013; Paceley, Fish et al., 2020). Alternatively, environments that are supportive of diverse genders and sexualities are associated with lower substance use, reduced sexual risk-taking, reduced suicidality, and higher self-esteem among LGBTQ+ (Hatzenbuehler et al., 2012). An important takeaway from this research is that LGBTQ+ youths are not inherently more likely to experience mental and behavioral health issues; rather, their health and well-being are altered because of the social contexts in which they are situated. It is essential that we understand and identify factors within LGBTQ+ youth's social contexts that enable negative health outcomes or promote positive identity development and well-being. Doing so will allow us to intervene within social contexts to prevent or reduce disparities and promote health equity for LGBTQ+ youth at a critical time in the life course.

Families and schools are important contexts that have received substantial empirical attention, demonstrating their importance to the identity, health, and well-being of LGBTQ+ youths (see Coulter et al., 2016; Day et al., 2020; Ryan et al., 2009). However, the geographic community (i.e., town, city, and county) in which LGBTQ+ youths live has received less empirical attention than these other social contexts, despite evidence to suggest that these environments exert distinct and multifaceted influence on LGBTQ+ youth's health and well-being (Hatzenbuehler, 2011; Hatzenbuehler et al., 2012; Paceley, Fish et al., 2020; Watson et al., 2020). Additionally, when researched, the community is often examined separate from other important

DOI: 10.4324/9781003128151-22

social contexts, even though families and schools are situated within the broader community (Goffnett et al., 2022). Relatedly, there are methodological and measurement challenges that provide opportunities to understand geographic communities more holistically and their influence and relationship with the embedded contexts that youth traverse (e.g., family, school, faith-communities).

In this chapter, we issue a call to action for LGBTQ+ scholars and professionals working with LGBTQ+ youths to understand the role of community in promoting the support and empowerment of LGBTQ+ youths. We situate our work within two complementary theoretical frameworks, the Strengths Perspective (Saleebey, 1996) and Ecological Systems Theory (Bronfenbrenner, 1979), to emphasize the importance of studying communities as capable, holistic, and integrated social contexts. After a description of these theories, we define and attend to the multi-faceted components of community related to LGBTQ+ youth, specifically community size, community climate, and LGBTQ+ community resources. We review the relationship between these factors and the identity, health, and well-being of LGBTQ+ youth. Building on this literature, we discuss the methodological, theoretical, and measurement opportunities related to LGBTQ+ youth and geographic context using a strengths perspective and Ecological Systems Theory. We end by posing opportunities for research and practice at the nexus of LGBTQ+ youth development, health, and geographic community contexts.

Centering LGBTQ+ Youth and Communities Within a Strengths Perspective and Ecological Systems Theory

We emphasize two important theoretical frameworks to consider when researching LGBTQ+ youths and their communities: the Strengths Perspective (Saleebey, 1996) and Ecological Systems Theory (Bronfenbrenner, 1979). First, the Strengths Perspective emerged within social work practice as a response to a deficit and problem-focused approach to clinical practice. It provides clinicians with tools to center the strengths and resilience of individuals and families, rather than focus solely on their risks and challenges. Importantly, a strengths perspective does not ignore risks and challenges, but frames them within an understanding of how individual- and community-level strengths, resilience, and capabilities can address or reduce these risks. The Strengths Perspective has since been used within community-based practice and research to frame community risks and problems within the ways in which communities can cultivate resilience among individuals (Paceley, 2020; Saleebey, 1996). Saleeby noted that supportive communities provide opportunities for connection and generative impact, nurturing the strengths of individuals within the community.

Historically, LGBTQ+ youth research has focused on the risks and challenges faced by LGBTQ+ youth due to stigma, marginalization, and victimization (Horn et al., 2009). This research has been critically important to understand how youth experiences in context facilitate poor mental, behavioral, and physical health outcomes. For example, this literature established that anti-LGBTQ+ bullying, victimization, and stigma are associated with poor mental health outcomes among LGBTQ+ youths (Almeida et al., 2009; Fish et al., 2019; Mereish & Poteat, 2015); Paceley et al., 2017; Woodford et al., 2015). However, health equity and promotion work must also include acknowledgment and promotion of LGBTQ+ youth strengths and resilience. Positive development and thriving require the elimination of the structural and interpersonal forces that oppress and marginalize LGBTQ+ youth; however, large system change takes time. Because of this, researchers and people who work with youth must both acknowledge the risks that arise as a result of these factors but also LGBTQ+ youth strengths and resilience and identify strategies for cultivating strengths.

LGBTQ+ youth scholars have called for a shift from a risk lens to one of attending to "understanding the ways in which (LGBTQ+) youth negotiate their development within various social contexts" (Horn et al., 2009, p. 863). Although some have made this shift (e.g., Asakura, 2019; Gray, 2009; Paceley et al., 2018), much of the scholarship surrounding LGBTQ+ youth remains risk based. Alternatively, strength-based research on and with LGBTQ+ youth often focus on the factors that promote or support resiliency among LGBTQ+ young people (Paceley, 2020). For example, scholars have examined the impact of strength-based interventions to support the well-being of LGBTQ+ youth (Craig, 2012; Craig & Furman, 2018) and explored components of resilience at individual and community levels (Asakura, 2016; Singh et al., 2014; Zeeman et al., 2017). These studies address the risks LGBTQ+ youth face, such as stigma and victimization, but do so with an understanding that they also have strengths and that these strengths or resilience strategies can mitigate the challenges they face.

The narrative surrounding geographic communities as a social context for LGBTQ+ youth has also been focused on risk. Communities are often described by how they thwart and harm LGBTQ+ youth, the risks LGBTQ+ youth face within them (e.g., victimization and stigma), and the lack of supportive people and resources. Exploring communities from a strengths perspective does not mean we ignore these risks; rather, it situates risks within the context of community strengths, resources, and opportunities for resilience (Paceley, 2020). It begins with a belief that communities are capable—even with their challenges—of supporting LGBTQ+ youth. As discussed later in this chapter, communities may demonstrate their capacity for supporting and caring for LGBTQ+ youth by increasing visibility of LGBTQ+ support, enacting and enforcing policies that affirm LGBTQ+ youth and prohibit discrimination, and providing access to LGBTQ+-supportive resources (e.g., community organizations, gender and sexuality alliances; Paceley, 2016, 2018; Paceley, Fish et al., 2020). These strategies for supporting LGBTQ+ youths at a community level do not remove the risks that LGBTQ+ youths face but provide mechanisms for reducing risk, providing access to support and resources, and promoting resilience. Therefore, we argue for the consideration of geographic communities within this strengths lens, as well as a attention to their multiple, integrated factors that coalesce to make a community that impacts LGBTQ+ youth.

Ecological Systems Theory (EST) identifies how the various social contexts within youth's environments affect their identity, development, and well-being and emphasizes the importance of understanding the ways in which these contexts interact to influence the positive development of an individual (Bronfenbrenner, 1979; Bronfenbrenner & Morris, 2006). In the EST model, the child or youth is situated within a series of nested environments and social systems over time. Youths bring with them their own experiences, strengths, traumas, and values. The innermost circle, the layer of the model directly proximal to the youth, is their microsystem—the individuals and groups with whom they have direct contact (e.g., parents, teachers). The next level out is the mesosystem, which reflects the interactions between two or more microsystems, but separate from youth (e.g., a parent meeting with the school principal). Beyond that is the exosystem, forces that indirectly affect embedded systems and individual youth (e.g., access to LGBTQ+ resources; LGBTQ+ representation in neighborhoods). Macrosystems are the broader ideological and cultural influences within the community and larger society that influence these other systems (e.g., media related to LGBTQ+ people, federal and state policies mandating school rules). Finally, the chronosystem includes individual and societal changes over time (e.g., the passage of civil rights laws).

Importantly, in more recent conceptualizations of the model, Bronfenbrenner and Morris (2006) describe the role of processes and interactions, describing how these nested contexts interact with each other and the youth in complex ways. Recent literature on transgender youth supports this conceptualization as it relates to community (Paceley, Sattler et al., 2020). The varying social contexts interact across levels to affect LGBTQ+ youths' experiences and well-being. Within communities, families and schools are affected by local attitudes, laws, and resources. A proposed policy change at the community level, such as instituting chosen name/pronoun use in schools, sends a positive message to LGBTQ+ youth; however, the backlash to such a policy change may show up at the microsystem level—through negative interactions with peers and policy debates in class or among family (see Hatzenbuehler et al., 2019; Paceley et al., 2023). Therefore, it is essential to consider the community in context of these broader and interlocking systems, their bidirectional influence, and their confluence on LGBTQ+ youth experiences and health.

Geographic Community and LGBTQ+ Youth Identity, Health, and Well-Being

The geographic community in which LGBTQ+ youths live plays an important role in their sense of identity, health, and well-being. The community is a critical social context and is instrumental to LGBTQ+ youth experiences across more proximal microsystems, such as schools (see Goffnett et al., 2022). The three community characteristics most commonly studied in relation to LGBTQ+ youth are community size, community climate, and LGBTQ+ community resources.

Community Size

Community size is generally conceptualized through geographic dispersion and/or population density. Geographic dispersion refers to the physical distance between community members as well social and economic resources within a given area, whereas population density refers to the number of people in an area, city, or county. In the United States, several federal agencies uniquely define communities based on size, providing LGBTQ+ researchers options for distinguishing between specific community characteristics. For example, the U.S. Census Bureau (2020) utilizes population density to categorize geographic areas as urbanized areas (50,000+), urban clusters (2,500–49,999), and rural areas (<2,500). Other agencies use a combination of population density and geographic dispersion, measure counties instead of areas, and include varied distributions of community size that include three (Office of Management and Budget; Health Resources Services Information, 2020), six (Centers for Disease Control, 2013), or nine (United States Department of Agriculture, 2020) category identifiers. The variability with which community size can be captured helps illustrate the complexity of conceptualizing communities in which youth are growing up, particularly with regard to characterizing or quantifying community-level strengths and risks and the intersections across ecological contexts.

Despite this variation in how scholars define community size, studies illustrate important differences in both the lived experiences and well-being of LGBTQ+ youth on the basis of where they live. This comparative research primarily explores the risks and challenges LGBTQ+ youths face in rural communities (i.e., low-density communities) as compared to urban communities or compared with heterosexual and cisgender youth within the same area or region. For example, LGBTQ+ youth in rural areas report greater suicidality and substance use than LGBTQ+ youth in urban areas (i.e., high density) and rural heterosexual and cisgender peers (Ballard et al., 2017; Cohn & Leake, 2012; Poon & Saewyc, 2009). Additionally, LGBTQ+ youths in rural communities report greater anti-LGBTQ+ sentiment, hostility (Kosciw et al., 2018), and victimization (Paceley, Fish et al., 2020) compared with urban LGBTQ+ youths.

These studies help to identify the important differences between LGBTQ+ youth's experiences in rural and urban spaces, specifically in relation to the risks they face and the negative outcomes they experience because of these risks, yet they do not explore the community-level strengths or resilience opportunities for LGBTQ+ youth in smaller communities.

Alternatively, qualitative research expands understanding of the complexity of community size and its relationship to LGBTQ+ youth, recognizing the strengths of youth and communities. For example, research on rural LGBTQ+ youth tends to compare their identity development processes, lived experiences, and well-being with that of urban LGBTQ+ youth; however, Gray (2009) utilized a different approach. Using ethnographic methods and attending to the strengths of LGBTQ+ youth, she immersed herself in rural Appalachian LGBTQ+ youth communities. Her findings countered those of comparative research; she illustrated how LGBTQ+ youths in the rural Southern United States found healthy pathways to identity development and resilience. For example, she described how youth engaged with the internet and social media to create connection and community where there were limited options in their physical communities. In one community, LGBTQ+ youths gathered regularly for an impromptu drag show at a local Walmart. These pathways were different from, but not inferior to, the ways in which urban LGBTQ+ youth formed community and identity—findings that encourage the study of rural communities as a distinct context, rather than in comparison to urban areas. A more recent study, situated in the Strengths Perspective, utilized interviews with LGBTQ+ youth in small towns and rural communities in the Midwest to identify community-level challenges and opportunities for growth, as identified by LGBTQ+ youth (Paceley et al., 2018). These studies challenge the notion of a rural–urban dichotomy that portrays urban, high-density communities as more supportive and rural, and low-density communities as hostile. Rather, communities are complex, providing nuanced and simultaneous strengths and challenges for LGBTQ+ youth to navigate. Additionally, they highlight the need to understand communities of all sizes house and contribute to the culture of other important youth contexts, such as schools and families.

Community Climate

Community climate is often defined by the level of support for and hostility toward LGBTQ+ people in a given community (Oswald et al., 2010) and has been measured via objective indicators of structural stigma and subjective assessments based on individual perceptions. Structural stigma, as a construct, reflects "macro-social forms of stigma" (Hatzenbuehler, 2016) and can be operationalized across multiple ecological systems via the presence or absence of institutional laws and policies, cultural norms, and social attitudes. These objective assessments of community climate demonstrate how the political and cultural milieu surrounding LGBTQ+ youth shape their experiences and subsequently their identity, health, and well-being. Some objective measures assess the presence or absence of a factor, such as LGBTQ+-inclusive policies, while others capture climate through composite indices that include the county proportion of same-sex couples, registered Democrats, the presence of gender-sexuality alliances (GSAs), and enumerated anti-bullying and nondiscrimination policies in schools (Charlton et al., 2019; Hatzenbuehler, 2011). Subjectively, perceived climate has been assessed using quantitative and qualitative methods. For example, a survey question might ask youth to indicate how they perceive their community's climate toward LGBTQ+ people with response options such as "hostile," "tolerant," or "supportive" (Paceley et al., 2017). Alternatively, a qualitative interview could provide prompts for LGBTQ+ youth to describe and identify the factors in their community that feel hostile and supportive (Paceley et al., 2018; Paceley, 2020). Importantly, there is a positive correlation between how a person perceives their community climate and the objective indicators in a community (Oswald et al., 2010). For example, in a sample of LGBTQ+ adults, Oswald and colleagues (2010) validated an objective measure of community climate (that included factors such as voting patterns, presence of same-sex couples, number of open-and-affirming religious congregations, and LGBTQ+-inclusive non-discrimination policies) with a perceived measure of climate, matched at the county level. They found that participants were significantly more likely to perceive their community as supportive, compared to tolerant, when the objective climate measure score was higher (e.g., more supportive).

In all the ways it has been measured, community climate is related to identity, health, and well-being for LGBTQ+ youth. Structural factors in the community are associated with exposure to victimization and bullying (Hatzenbuehler, 2016), suicidal behavior (Hatzenbuehler, 2011; Hatzenbuehler & Keyes, 2013), STI risk (Charlton et al., 2019), and substance use (Pachankis et al., 2014). LGBTQ+ youths who perceive their community as supportive report significantly less anxiety, depression, and victimization than youths who perceive their community as tolerant or hostile (Paceley, Fish et al., 2020). Importantly, experiences of growing up in stigmatizing environments has been shown to be formative for later stress-responses to stigma. In one study, researchers found that LGB young adults who grew up in high-stigma environments had similar stress responses to young adults who grew up with other types of trauma such as child maltreatment and poverty, illustrating the critical role that structural stigma plays across the life course (Hatzenbuehler & McLaughlin, 2014).

Qualitative assessments of climate expand our understanding of how youth perceive and navigate their community, and their identities within them. Via interviews with rural, LGBTQ+ youth, Paceley (2016) described the needs youth had related to their communities. A key finding was a sense of isolation in communities where it felt unsafe to come out or be visible about one's LGBTQ+ identity. Youth described needed support in numerous contexts (schools, with families, etc.), assistance with their LGBTQ+ identity development, and peers with whom they could explore and understand their identity. In another study, LGBTQ+ youth described the aspects of their communities that contributed to a supportive climate, such as supportive people, LGBTQ+ visibility, access to LGBTQ+ resources, and LGBTQ+-inclusive policies (Paceley et al., 2018).

It is important to note the nuances and consistencies across the ways in which community climate has been measured. The influence of policy and rhetoric pertaining to LGBTQ+ people and issues makes an interesting example. In a qualitative study, transgender youth identified aspects of their communities that were supportive and hostile, complicating the ways in which we think of these factors as separate and static (Paceley, Sattler et al., 2020). They reiterated how policies that are trans-inclusive (e.g., school-based policies that allow for chosen name and pronouns; gender-inclusive bathroom policies) are critical to creating a supportive community, but described how the rhetoric surrounding policy implementation (e.g., discussions pertaining to bathroom bills) could create a hostile community through anti-transgender sentiment. In related research, scholars have leveraged natural experiments to identify how the implementation of discriminatory state policies (e.g., state same-sex marriage bans) are related to increases in mood and substance use disorders among lesbian, gay, and bisexual (LGB) adults (Hatzenbuehler et al., 2009), but also how the enactment of protective policies improved well-being (Ogolsky et al., 2019; Riggle et al., 2017). Raifman and colleagues (2017), using repeated cross-sectional data from the Youth Risk Behavioral Survey, found that rates of suicide attempts among LGB students living in states that passed same-sex marriage laws—prior to national rulings—statistically declined relative to LGB youth living in states that did not pass these laws.

Consistent with qualitative studies of transgender youth, public commentaries regarding LGBTQ+ people and rights are also implicated in LGBTQ+ health and well-being. In one study that analyzed repeated cross-section data from California, Hatzenbuehler and colleagues (2019) found that—in the time leading up to the Proposition 8 vote in California—youth reports of homophobic bullying increased and then declined in the years following the vote. Interestingly, no other format of bias-based bullying (e.g., race or disability bias) followed that same trajectory, further strengthening the inference around public discourse and increases in LGBTQ-related stigma. Notably, increases in homophobic bullying were more pronounced in schools without a gender-sexuality alliance, suggesting that these programs have effects on the climate of schools and, more broadly, communities (Hatzenbuehler et al., 2019). Findings suggest that public policy debates regarding LGBTQ people and rights (e.g., marriage equality, employment benefits, bathroom bills) likely have an untoward effect on LGBTQ youth and that school-based programs for LGBTQ youth have a protective function during times of stigmatizing public discourse in communities. Additionally, Hatzenbuehler and colleagues (2022) examined the impact of litigation related to bias-based bullying in California high schools finding that in districts where a student won a case (e.g., received relief in monetary or other ways), there was a 23% reduction in bullying based on sexual orientation).

LGBTQ+ Community Resources

Finally, LGBTQ+ community resources are an important community context for LGBTQ+ youth. Although they are sometimes examined as a characteristic of the geographic community, particularly within the context of community climate, as the presence or absence of LGBTQ+ resources (Eisenberg et al., 2020; Oswald et al., 2010; Watson et al., 2020), LGBTQ+ community resources are also studied outside of climate literature and thus warrant specific attention. LGBTQ+ resources in a community include local LGBTQ+-specific organizations and community centers (see Movement Advance Project [MAP] & Centerlink, 2020; Williams et al., 2019), as well as other informal or formal resources, such as open-and-affirming faith communities, youth programs (e.g., 4-H, Girl Scouts), sports groups, or GSAs. One of the more understudied community resources are LGBTQ+ community centers, which have grown in number in recent years and are increasingly more important as modern cohorts of LGBTQ+ youth "come out" at younger ages and are seeking services and support (Fish, 2020; Floyd & Bakeman, 2006). Estimates suggest that LGBTQ+ centers in the United States serve over 58,000 clients per week, the majority of whom are youth (58%), people of color (56%), and experiencing economic instability (66%) (Fish et al., 2019; MAP & Centerlink, 2020; Williams et al., 2019).

The earliest research on LGBTQ+ community resources sought to establish an understanding of the services they provided, documenting a range of support and educational programming for LGBTQ+ youth, adults, families, and communities (Allen et al., 2011; Williams et al., 2019). This early research suggests that community-based organizations may be more accessible to LGBTQ+ youth of color due to the lack of intersectionality of race/ethnicity in school-based clubs (Blackburn & McCready, 2009). Recent studies provide evidence that youth who participate in these types of programs have better mental health and lower substance use than youth who do not (Fish et al., 2019). LGBTQ+ youths growing up in communities without LGBTQ+ community resources express a need for a place to connect to other LGBTQ+ youth (Paceley, 2016) and often travel to other cities to access these services (Allen et al., 2011). Despite their association with improved health and well-being, these types of services remain limited—particularly in low-population-density areas. Yet given an expanding network of centers, research suggests that these organizations are well positioned to address the mental health needs of LGBTQ+ youth and adults (Pachankis et al., 2021; Williams et al., 2019).

Intersections Between Size, Climate, and Resources

It is important to note that community size, community climate, and LGBTQ+ community resources are related constructs, yet they are often studied independent of one another. Few studies shed light on the intersections between these community characteristics. One study found that both community size and community climate were separately associated with anxiety and depression, but when modeled together, community climate attenuated the effect of community size, suggesting that community climate was a more robust indicator of well-being than community size (Paceley, Fish et al., 2020). Another study using the same data found that community climate was associated with the provision of LGBTQ+ supportive resources, whereas community size was not (Paceley et al., 2017). Importantly, the same study revealed that community size is related to support through perceived climate. Given the interdependent nature of these community characteristics, and the relative dearth of literature attempting to assess the complexity of these constructs, there are many unearthed opportunities for future research and practice.

Research Issues and Opportunities

Despite evidence linking these aspects of the geographic community to LGBTQ+ youth's sense of identity, health, and well-being, the research in this area lags behind other research on relevant social contexts, such as schools and families. For example, we lack important research explicating the ways in which community operates to promote positive identity and well-being and the ways in which this research can be used to intervene within diverse communities to prevent and/or ameliorate stigma, victimization, and along with the related mental health concerns. To advance this field of research, we contend that it is essential for scholars engaged in LGBTQ+ youth research to identify ways to improve and refine our research questions, methodologies, and measures related to the geographic community. Doing so would create innovative opportunities and community-level interventions to promote health equity and resilience among LGBTQ+ youth and across the various contexts that they navigate in their day-to-day lives (see Fish, 2020). In this section, we explore some of these research issues and opportunities within three broad categories: (1) conceptual opportunities, (2) measurement opportunities, and (3) research opportunities.

Conceptual Opportunities

First, we argue that research on LGBTQ+ youth and geographic communities requires several conceptual shifts to better specify and understand the gestalt of the communities in which youth grow up. Given that much of the community-based literature is risk and deficit focused, we contend that research in this area must be intentional about centering strengths and resilience. Utilizing a strength-based perspective does not ignore the challenges LGBTQ+ youth face in their communities; rather, it situates an understanding of these challenges within both the resilience and power that LGBTQ+ youth demonstrate, as well as the capabilities and opportunities within a given community. For example, in the school literature, we recognize that schools are both a space of trauma and support; that LGBTQ+ youth experience harassment in schools, but that schools also offer unique opportunities to seek out supportive peers and mentors (Kosciw et al., 2020; Poteat et al., 2020). By recognizing and embracing the opportunities for change, support, and resources within a community, we can use research to identify interventions that capitalize on the community's strengths in addition to mitigating deficits.

Furthermore, it is time for community context research to advance conceptualizations of geographic community to extend beyond a focus on single characteristics such as size *or* climate *or* resources. To enable a more accurate understanding of community, we must consider and identify how community size, community climate, LGBTQ+ resources, and other factors work in concert to influence the day-to-day experiences of LGBTQ+ youth. The small amount of research that explores these relationships demonstrates logical connections between these factors, yet we need a more critical and nuanced understanding of how they contribute to one another, counteract one another, and how different configurations of community size, climate, and resources may uniquely impact LGBTQ+ youth development and health. For example, there may be instances where size or geographic region and climate are correlated (e.g., rural, conservative areas or Southern states with anti-LGBTQ+ policies), but not for others (e.g., rural, liberal areas or Southern states with LGBTQ+ inclusive cities). It is important that future research consider how these different profiles of community translate to distinct experiences, if at all.

Measurement Opportunities

There are also opportunities for growth and innovation in the measurement of geographic communities. First, it is essential that researchers extend beyond binary measures of community size. Although scholars have identified important differences between rural and urban communities, moving forward, we contend the need for greater variability and heterogeneity of community size through the development of more nuanced assessments and measures. A rural–urban dichotomy tends to categorize all non-rural spaces together; this means that a small town of 60,000, for example, may be categorized as "urban" and grouped with a major metropolitan city, despite very real differences between them (e.g., availability of public transit; youth services). Similarly, a town of 60,000 people is not the same as a town of 200 in a part of a state far from any urban and suburban communities. More nuanced assessments of community size will provide more accurate perspectives on how these contextual characteristics influence LGBTQ+ youth experiences with strengths and risks in their communities.

The field is also in need of measurement work on both objective and subjective measures of community climate. Many objective measures of LGBTQ+ youth climate include tallying the structural factors that examine policies, protections, and resources for LGBTQ people—often at the state level (Hatzenbuehler et al., 2009; MAP et al., 2019; Oswald et al., 2010). Although these measures demonstrated associations with LGBTQ+ health outcomes among youth and adults, there has not been rigorous testing to better assess and refine the properties of these measures and more rigorously test their predictive validity. Such endeavors may also help to define distinct policy patterns that are more or less protective of LGBTQ+ people, and differential protections between LGBTQ+ youth (i.e., school policies) and adults (i.e., employment policies).

More recently, Gower et al. (2018) developed "The LGBTQ Supportive Environments Inventory" as an objective measure of LGBTQ+ community climate. The tool includes measures related to LGBTQ+ youth resources, other community resources, and the socioeconomic and political environment in a community. This measure provides researchers with a tool to assess the climate toward LGBTQ+ people in a community and then attach it to other types of data, such as youth surveys or school climate data, to assess community climate across a multitude of outcomes and other measures. Such innovations in measurement are an important step forward in this research area; however, we lack a comprehensive measure of community climate from the LGBTQ youth's perspective. A subjective measure that includes a variety of factors that influence how LGBTQ+ youth perceive their climate across numerous system levels would provide researchers with more nuanced details about community climate, beyond "hostile, tolerant, or supportive." The development of more subjective indicators of LGBTQ+ community climate, alongside development in objective measures, will also be useful in better understanding and testing the ways in which policy shape youth's perceptions of their communities which is related to their identity, health, and well-being (Paceley, Sattler et al., 2020).

Finally, as we deepen our understanding of the complexity of community, we posit a need for innovative measures and assessments that attempt to capture a multitude of community characteristics and contexts. A measure illustrating the interconnected nature between objective climate, perceived climate, school climate, and family dynamics could provide rich and holistic information for identifying and implementing interventions, policy change, and practical solutions to heterosexism and cissexism at the community level.

Research Opportunities

Finally, we argue that there are opportunities to evolve our perspective of research on LGBTQ+ youth and communities in the hopes of pursuing new and innovative research questions. It is critical that we understand how LGBTQ+ community resources (cf. Williams et al., 2019) impact other dimensions of community across various levels of the ecological systems, such as the sociopolitical climate, family dynamics, school climate, and state-level policies. Like the communities in which they are situated, these resources vary appreciably in terms of funding, staffing, visibility, services, and impact, among other factors. Given the reach of these programs in communities around the United States, it is essential that we develop an understanding of these programs and how they impact LGBTQ+ youth's community experiences. It will be critical for this research to consider how to study these organizations in rural and underserved communities, as well.

Given the relevance of policy and surrounding discourse related to LGBTQ+ populations, future research might consider ways to examine how enacted policies impact changes in population experiences (e.g., victimization, mental health). Although we know LGBTQ+ youth in protective climates are less likely to experience victimization, we are unaware of how long it takes from policy enactment to real-world change in the experiences of LGBTQ+ youth. Additionally, LGBTQ+ youth in more affirming contexts, such as those with LGBTQ+-inclusive policies, still regularly report depression and stress related to LGBTQ+ stigma (Hammack et al., 2022), suggesting a need to understand and identify strategies for shifting contexts in complex and multifaceted ways. With increased availability of large LGBTQ+ inclusive data sources, and a dynamic policy environment, researchers can explore these types of research questions. More importantly may be the degree to which researchers could assess the differences in the enactment of policies at the state or local level. For example, are there ways in which policies and programs can be implemented to more quickly and effectively bring about change in the day-to-day lives of LGBTQ+ young people. Such investigations emphasize not only the importance of community contexts but also the ways in which policymakers and key stakeholders can leverage policy and context changes to bring about the most positive change for LGBTQ+ youth in their communities.

Future research must consider the overlapping nature of different social contexts, frequently studied in isolation but embedded within the broader community. That is, families and schools do not exist in isolation but they are developed and sustained within a community context (Goffnett et al., 2022). Research in this area must consider how and in what ways these contexts intersect and overlap; how the evolution of these embedded systems (e.g., families where a youth "comes out"; or a school that starts a GSA) disrupt and interact with the larger community context. This includes the bidirectional nature of embedded systems across time and the subsequent influence for LGBTQ+ youth. For example, communities of varying sizes have witnessed hostile acts and sentiment toward LGBTQ+ people and yet have also become beacons of equality in other ways. Most notably, the 1969 Stonewall Riots in New York City were a response to police brutality toward LGBTQ+ individuals and represent both a history of struggle and oppression, but also resistance and pride (Aust, 2014). In 1998, the murder of Matthew Shephard in an act of anti-gay violence was a clear indication of the hostility LGBTQ+ people face(d) in Laramie, Wyoming; however, his death was the impetus for a 2009 federal bill to include LGBTQ+ identity in hate crime laws and prompted Laramie to become an LGBTQ+ historical landmark (Aust, 2014; Seckinger, 2019). Relatedly, Topeka, Kansas, the urban capital seat of Kansas, is home to Westboro Baptist Church, which made infamous for their hostile protesting of anything connected to LGBTQ+ people or communities (Murray, 2016). It is also the home of Equality House, a house directly across the street from Westboro Baptist Church and painted in rainbow colors, as well as the house next door painted in transgender pride colors. Their website describes them as "a symbol of peace, compassion, and positive change" (Equality House, n.d.). In 2016, the Pulse Nightclub shooting in Orlando, Florida, resulted in the death of 49 mostly Latinx LGBTQ+ people. Considered the deadliest attack on LGBTQ+ people in U.S. history, research also demonstrates how surviving community members demonstrated resilience and formed strong community connections following this collective trauma (Molina et al., 2019). These examples demonstrate the complexities of the intersections of systems, strengths, and resilience, and even history in our understanding of how communities impact the well-being of LGBTQ+ youth. Research is needed to better understand how communities embrace or challenge anti-LGBTQ+ sentiment and how LGBTQ+ individuals in these communities perceive these events.

In these efforts to address the complexity of youth context and community, we argue for an ongoing and critical examination of *who* is represented in our studies. Scholars and activists have called for a trickle-up approach to justice that centers the most marginalized in our advocacy and research efforts (Mehrotra et al., 2016; Spade, 2009). Contrary to traditional advocacy movements and research with historically marginalized populations, a trickle-up approach centers those with the most marginalization—such as LGBTQ+ youth of color, transgender and immigrant youth, and youth who are homeless—with the idea that if we promote equity and justice for those who experience the largest degree of marginalization, the impacts will also be felt by those who experience less. For example, LGB youths are overrepresented in LGBTQ+ health equity research, particularly regarding community context; there is a great need to better understand how community context, climate, and structural stigma influence the experiences of transgender and gender-diverse youth (Hatzenbuehler, 2017). It is especially important to center transgender and gender-diverse youth in these research explorations given the current policy debates and volatile policy environment that impacts them directly and through rhetoric (Paceley et al., 2021). In 2020 and 2021, policies targeting transgender youth have increased across the United States, primarily in Southern and Midwestern states. These proposed bills and enacted policies aim to limit or restrict transgender-affirming healthcare for transgender youth, restrict transgender youth from participating in sports teams consistent with their gender identity, and restrict the use of bathrooms based on sex assigned at birth (Paceley et al., 2021). In these investigations, it is also critical to understand how LGBTQ+ youths different identities contribute to varied experiences in context. For example, LGBTQ+-disabled youth may lack adequate ADA and support resources in rural communities that uniquely marginalize their experiences. LGBTQ+ youth of color are also often overlooked in the study of context, and LGBTQ+ youth health research more broadly (Toomey et al., 2017)—this is especially true for LGBTQ+ youth of color in rural communities and in southern rural communities, in particular.

Opportunities in Practice With LGBTQ+ Youth

Although there are numerous ways in which to improve the research on LGBTQ+ youth and geographic communities moving forward, the findings thus far have important implications for people who work with or advocate on behalf of LGBTQ+ youth. We call on social workers, therapists, advocates, teachers, activists, and other stakeholders to consider the community and how their work fits, or could fit, into the broader community context. In many communities, there may not be a visible LGBTQ+ community or community resource. In these instances, it may be useful for practitioners to identify ways to elevate visibility and promote or provide a community resource. Even the smallest efforts can have great impact. In smaller communities, in particular, LGBTQ+ youth may benefit from a weekly or bi-weekly youth group meeting in an affirming space or a monthly social outing with other LGBTQ+ people (Paceley, 2016).

Relatedly, practitioners can utilize existing research on community climate to assess the important community-level factors that influences LGBTQ+ perceptions of their community's climate. Doing this type of assessment can help identify the specific areas in which a community may be doing well or need improvement. For example, does your county have a non-discrimination policy that is inclusive of both gender identity and sexual orientation? Is there a visible LGBTQ+ community or community organization? How many open-and-affirming faith communities are there? This type of community-level needs assessment can help determine how to proceed moving forward.

Conclusion

Throughout this chapter, we shared conceptual, empirical, and practical evidence for the relevance and importance of the geographic community context in the identity, health, and well-being of LGBTQ+ youth. Regardless of how practitioners or researchers decide to intervene or engage in scholarship, we suggest that they do so from a strength-based perspective and by directly including and centering LGBTQ+ youth in these efforts. Attending to the strengths of both youth and communities provides opportunities to resist a deficit narrative and embrace the goodness of community, even when challenges exist. Centering youth in these efforts minimizes the likelihood that changes will be misguided by adult-centric leadership in planning and organizing. Bring youth to the table, give them leadership roles, and create change in their communities alongside them.

References

Allen, K. D., Hammack, P. L., & Himes, H. L. (2011). Analysis of GLBTQ youth community-based programs in the United States. *Journal of Homosexuality, 59*(9), 1289–1306. https://doi.org/10.10 80/00918369.2012.720529

Almeida, J., Johnson, R. M., Corliss, H. L., Molnar, B. E., & Azrael, D. (2009). Emotional distress among LGBT youth: The influence of perceived discrimination based on sexual orientation. *Journal of Youth and Adolescence, 38*, 1001–1014. https://doi.org/10.1007/s10964-009-9397-9

Asakura, K. (2016). Paving pathways through the pain: A grounded theory of resilience among lesbian, gay, bisexual, trans, and queer youth. *Journal of Research on Adolescence, 27*, 521–536.

Asakura, K. (2019). Extraordinary acts to "show up": Conceptualizing resilience of LGBTQ youth. *Youth and Society, 51*(2), 268–285. https://doi.org/10.1177/0044118X16671430

Aust, C. (2014). *Be proud: The recognition and preservation of lesbian, gay, bisexual, transgender, and queer cultural heritage in the United States* [thesis]. RUcore: Rutgers University Community Repository.

Ballard, M. E., Jameson, J. P., & Martz, D. M. (2017). Sexual identity and risk behaviors among adolescents in rural Appalachia. *Journal of Rural Mental Health, 41*, 17–29. https://doi.org/10.1037/rmh0000068

Blackburn, M. B., & McCready, L. T. (2009). Voices of queer youth in urban schools: Possibilities and limitations. *Theory into Practice, 48*(3), 222–230. www.jstor.org/stable/40344618

Bronfenbrenner, U. (1979). *The ecology of human development.* Harvard.

Bronfenbrenner, U., & Morris, P. A. (2006). The bioecological model of human development. In R. M. Lerner & W. Damon (Eds.), *Handbook of child psychology: Theoretical models of human development* (pp. 793–828). John Wiley & Sons Inc. University Press.

Burton, C. M., Marshal, M. P., Chisolm, D. J., Sucato, G. S., & Friedman, M. S. (2013). Sexual minority-related victimization as a mediator of mental health disparities in sexual minority youth: A longitudinal analysis. *Journal of Youth and Adolescence, 42*, 394–402. https://doi.org/10.1007/s10964-012-9901-5

Centers for Disease Control. (2013). *National center for health statistics urban-rural classification scheme for counties.* www.cdc.gov/nchs/data_access/urban_rural.htm

Charlton, B. M., Hatzenbuehler, M. L., Jun, H., Sarda, V., Gordon, A. R., Raifman, J. R. G., & Austin, B. S. (2019). Structural stigma and sexual orientation-related reproductive health disparities in a longitudinal cohort study of female adolescents. *Journal of Adolescence, 74*, 183–187. https://doi.org/10.1016/j.adolescence.2019.06.008

Cohn, T. J., & Leake, V. S. (2012). Affective distress among adolescents who endorse same-sex sexual attraction: Urban versus rural differences and the role of protective factors. *Journal of Gay & Lesbian Mental Health, 16*, 291–305. https://doi.org/10.1080/19359705.2012.690931

Coulter, R. W. S., Birkett, M., Corliss, H. L., Hatzenbuehler, M. L., Mustanski, B., & Stall, R. D. (2016). Associations between LGBTQ-affirmative school climate and adolescent drinking behaviors. *Drug & Alcohol Dependence, 161*, 340–347. https://doi.org/10.1016/j.drugalcdep.2016.02.022

Craig, S. L. (2012). Strengths first: An empowering case management model for multiethnic sexual minority youth. *Journal of Gay & Lesbian Social Services, 24*, 274–288.

Craig, S. L., & Furman, E. (2018). Do marginalized youth experience strengths in strengths-based interventions? Unpacking program acceptability through two interventions for sexual and gender minority youth. *Journal of Social Service Research, 44*, 168–179.

Day, J. K., Fish, J, N., Grossman, A. H., & Russell, S. T. (2020). Gay-straight alliances, inclusive policy, and school climate: LGBTQ youths' experiences of social support and bullying. *Journal of Research on Adolescence, 30*, 418–430. https://doi.org/10.1111/jora.12487

Eisenberg, M. E., Erickson, D. J., Gower, A. L., Kne, L., Watson, R. J., Corliss, H. L., & Saewyc, E. M. (2020). Supportive community resources are associated with lower risk of substance use among lesbian, gay, bisexual, and questioning adolescents in Minnesota. *Journal of Youth and Adolescence, 49*(4), 836–848. https://doi.org/10.1007/s10964-019-01100-4

Equality House. (n.d.). *Equality house.* www.plantingpeace.org/campaign/equality-house/#cover

Fish, J. N. (2020). Future directions in understanding and addressing mental health among LGBTQ youth. *Journal of Clinical Child & Adolescent Psychology*, 1–14. https://doi.org/10.1080/15374416.2020.1815207

Fish, J. N., Moody, R. L., Grossman, A. H., & Russell, S. T. (2019). LGBTQ youth-serving community-based organizations: Who participates and what difference does it make? *Journal of Youth and Adolescence, 48*(12), 2418–2431. https://doi.org/10.1007/s10964-019-01129-5

Floyd, F. J., & Bakeman, R. (2006). Coming-out across the life course: Implications of age and historical context. *Archives of Sexual Behavior, 35*(3), 287–296. https://doi.org/10.1007/s10508-006-9022-x

Goffnett, J., Paceley, M. S., Fish, J. N., & Saban, P. (2022). Between cornfields and kinfolk: Identity management among transgender youth in Midwestern families and communities. *Family Process.* Advanced online publication. https://doi.org/10.1111/famp.12759

Gower, A. L., Forster, M. F., Gloppen, K., Johnson, A. Z., Eisenberg, M. E., Connett, J. E., & Borowsky, I. W. (2018). School practices to foster LGBT-supportive climate: Associations with adolescent bullying involvement. *Prevention Science, 19*, 813–821. https://doi:10.1007/s11121-017-0847-4

Gray, M. (2009). *Out in the country: Youth, media, and queer visibility in rural America.* NYU Press.

Hammack, P. L., Pietta, D. R., Hughes, S. D., Atwood, J. M., Cohen, E. M., & Clark, R. C. (2022). Community support for sexual and gender diversity, minority stress, and mental health: A mixed methods study of adolescents with minoritized sexual and gender identities. *Psychology of Sexual Orientation and Gender Diversity.* Advanced online publication. https://doi.org/10.1037/sgd0000591

Hatzenbuehler, M. L. (2011). The social environment and suicide attempts in lesbian, gay, and bisexual youth. *Pediatrics, 127,* 896–903. doi:10.1542/peds.2010-3020

Hatzenbuehler, M. L. (2016). Structural stigma and health inequalities: Research evidence and implications for psychological science. *The American Psychologist, 71*(8), 742–751. https://doi.org/10.1037/amp0000068

Hatzenbuehler, M. L. (2017). Advancing research on structural stigma and sexual orientation disparities in mental health among Youth. *Journal of Clinical Child & Adolescent Psychology, 46*(3), 463–475.

Hatzenbuehler, M. L., & Keyes, K. M. (2013). Inclusive anti-bullying policies and reduced risk of suicide attempts in lesbian and gay youth. *Journal of Adolescent Health, 53*(1), S21–S26. https://doi.org/10.1016/j.jadohealth.2012.08.010

Hatzenbuehler, M. L., Keyes, K. M., & Hasin, D. S. (2009). State-level policies and psychiatric morbidity in lesbian, gay, and bisexual populations. *American Journal of Public Health, 99,* 2275–2281. https://doi.org/10.2105/AJPH.2008.153510

Hatzenbuehler, M. L., McKetta, S., Kim, R., Leung, S., Prins, S. L., & Russell, S. L. (2022). Evaluating litigation as a structural strategy for addressing bias-based bullying among youth. *JAMA Pediatrics, 176*(1), 52–58. https://doi.org/10.1001/jamapediatrics.2021.3660

Hatzenbuehler, M. L., & McLaughlin, K. A. (2014). Structural stigma and hypothalamic–pituitary–adrenocortical axis reactivity in lesbian, gay, and bisexual young adults. *Annals of Behavioral Medicine, 47*(1), 39–47. https://doi.org/10.1007/s12160-013-9556-9

Hatzenbuehler, M. L., Pachankis, J. E., & Wolff, J. (2012). Religious climate and health risk behaviors in sexual minority youths: A population-based study. *American Journal of Public Health, 102*(4), 657–663. https://doi.org/10.2105/AJPH.2011.300517

Hatzenbuehler, M. L., Shen, Y., Vandewater, E. A., & Russell, S. T. (2019). Proposition 8 and homophobic bullying in California. *Pediatrics, 143*(6), e20182116. doi:10.1542/peds,2018-2116

Health Resource and Services Information. (2020). *Defining rural population.* www.hrsa.gov/rural-health/about-us/definition/index.html

Horn, S. S., Kosciw, J. G., & Russell, S. T. (2009). Special issue introduction: New research on lesbian, gay, bisexual, and transgender youth: Studying lives in context. *Journal of Youth and Adolescence, 38*(7), 863–866. https://doi.org/10.1007/s10964-009-9420-1

Kosciw, J. G., Clark, C. M., Truong, N. L., & Zongrone, A. D. (2020). *The 2019 national school climate survey: The experiences of lesbian, gay, bisexual, transgender, and queer youth in our nation's schools.* GLSEN.

Kosciw, J. G., Greytak, E. A., Zongrone, A. D., Clark, C. M., & Truong, N. L. (2018). *The 2017 national school climate survey: The experiences of lesbian, gay, bisexual, transgender, and queer youth in our nation's schools.* GLSEN.

Mehrotra, G. R., Kimball, E., & Wahab, S. (2016). The braid that binds us: The impact of neoliberalism, criminalization, and professionalization on domestic violence work. *Affilia: Journal of Women in Social Work, 31*(2), 153–163. https://doi.org/10.1177/0886109916643871

Mereish, E. H., & Poteat, V. P. (2015). A relational model of sexual minority mental and physical health: The negative effects of shame on relationships, loneliness, and health. *Journal of Counseling Psychology, 62,* 425–437.

Molina, O., Yegidis, B., & Jacinto, G. (2019). The pulse nightclub mass shooting and factors affecting community resilience following the terrorist attack. *Best Practices in Mental Health, 15*(2), 1–14.

Movement Advancement Project, Center for American Progress, GLAAD, & Human Rights Campaign. (2019, June). *Understanding issues facing LGBT people in the US.* www.lgbtmap.org/understanding-issues-facing-lgbt-americans.

Movement Advancement Project, & Centerlink. (2020). *2020 LGBTQ community center survey report.* www.lgbtmap.org/2020-lgbtq-community-center-survey-report

Murray, B. (2016). Words that wound, bodies that shield: Corporeal responses to Westboro Baptist Church's hate speech. *First Amendment Studies, 50*(1), 32–47. https://doi.org/10.1080/21689725.2016.1189345

Ogolsky, B. G., Monk, J. K., Rice, T. M., & Oswald, R. F. (2019). Personal well-being across the transition to marriage equality: A longitudinal analysis. *Journal of Family Psychology, 33*(4), 422–432. https://doi.org/10.1037/fam0000504

Oswald, R. F., Cuthbertson, C., Lazarevic, V., & Goldberg, A. E. (2010). New developments in the field: Measuring community climate. *Journal of GLBT Family Studies, 6,* 214–228. doi:10.1080/15504281003709230

Paceley, M. S. (2016). Gender and sexual minority youth in nonmetropolitan communities: Individual and community-level needs for support. *Families in Society*, *97*(2), 77–85. doi:10.1606/1044-3894.2016.97.11

Paceley, M. S. (2020). Moving away from a risk paradigm to study rural communities among LGBTQ+ youth: Promotion of a strengths perspective in research, practice, and policy. In A. N. Mendenhall & M. M. Carney (Eds.), *Rooted in strengths: 30 years of the strengths perspective in social work*. University of Kansas.

Paceley, M. S., Dikitsas, Z. A., Greenwood, E., McInroy, L. B., Fish, J. N., Williams, N., Riquino, M., Lin, M., Birnel Henderson, S., & Levine, D. (2023). The perceived health implications of policies and rhetoric targeting transgender and gender diverse youth: A community-based qualitative study. *Transgender Health*. Advanced online publication. https://doi.org/10.1089/trgh.2021.0125

Paceley, M. S., Fish, J. N., Thomas, M. M., & Goffnett, J. (2020). The impact of community size, community climate, and victimization on the physical and mental health of SGM youth. *Youth & Society*, *52*(3), 427–448. https://doi.org/1.1177/044118X19856141

Paceley, M. S., Goffnett, J., Diaz, A. L., Kattari, S. K., Navarro, J., & Greenwood, E. (2021). "I didn't come here to make trouble": Resistance strategies utilized by transgender and gender diverse youth in the Midwestern US. *Youth*, *1*(1), 29–46. https://doi.org/10.3390/youth1010005

Paceley, M. S., Okrey-Anderson, S., & Heumann, M. (2017). Transgender youth in small towns: Perceptions of community size, climate, and support. *Journal of Youth Studies*, *7*, 822–840. doi:10.1080/13676261.2016.1273514

Paceley, M. S., Sattler, P., Goffnett, J., & Jen, S. (2020). "It feels like home": Transgender youth in the Midwest and conceptualizations of community climate. *Journal of Community Psychology*. Advanced online publication. https://doi.org/10.1002/jcop.22378

Paceley, M. S., Thomas, M. M. C., Toole, J., & Pavicic, E. (2018). "If rainbows were everywhere": Nonmetropolitan SGM youth identify factors that make communities supportive. *Journal of Community Practice*, *26*, 429–445. doi:10.1080/10705422.2018.1520773

Pachankis, J., Clark, K., Jackson, S. D., Pereira, K, & Levine, D. (2021). Current capacity and future implementation of mental health services in U.S. LGBTQ community centers. *Psychiatric Services*, *72*(6), 1–8. https://doi.org/10.1176/appi.ps.202000575

Pachankis, J. E., Hatzenbuehler, M. L., & Starks, T. J. (2014). The influence of structural stigma and rejection sensitivity on young sexual minority men's daily tobacco and alcohol use. *Social Science & Medicine*, *103*, 67–75. https://doi.org/10.1016/j.socscimed.2013.10.005

Poon, C. S., & Saewyc, E. M. (2009). Out yonder: Sexual-minority adolescents in rural communities in British Columbia. *American Journal of Public Health*, *99*, 118–124. doi:10.2105/AJPH.2007.122945

Poteat, V. P., Marx, R. A., Calzo, J. P., Toomey, R. B., Ryan, C., Clark, C. M., & Gulgoz, S. (2020). *Addressing inequities in education: Considerations for LGBTQ+ children and youth in the era of COVID-19*. Society for Research on Child Development. www.srcd.org/sites/default/files/resources/FINAL_AddressingInequalities-LGBTQ%2B.pdf

Raifman, J., Moscoe, E., Austin, S. B., & McConnell, M. (2017). Difference-in-differences analysis of the association between state same-sex marriage policies and adolescent suicide attempts. *JAMA Pediatrics*, *171*(4), 350. https://doi.org/10.1001/jamapediatrics.2016.4529

Riggle, E. D., Wickham, R. E., Rostosky, S. S., Rothblum, E. D., & Balsam, K. F. (2017). Impact of civil marriage recognition for long-term same-sex couples. *Sexuality Research and Social Policy*, *14*(2), 223–232.

Ryan, C., Huebner, D., Diaz, R. M., & Sanches, J. (2009). Family rejection as a predictor of negative health outcomes in white and Latino lesbian, gay, and bisexual young adults. Pediatrics, *123*(1), 346–352.

Saleebey, D. (1996). The strengths perspective in social work practice: Extensions and cautions. *Social Work*, *41*(3), 296–305. https://doi.org/10.1093/sw/41.3.296

Seckinger, B. (2019). *Laramie inside out: Reflections 20 years later*. Routledge.

Singh, A. A., Meng, S. E., & Hansen, A. W. (2014). "I am my own gender": Resilience strategies of trans youth. *Journal of Counseling & Development*, *92*, 208–218.

Spade, D. (2009). *Trans politics on a neoliberal landscape* [Video file]. http://bcrw.barnard.edu/videos/dean-spade-trickle-up-social-justice-excerpt/

Toomey, R. B., Huynh, V. W., Jones, S. K., Lee, S., & Revels-Macalinao, M. (2017). Sexual minority youth of color: A content analysis and critical review of the literature. *Journal of Gay & Lesbian Mental Health*, *21*(1), 3–31. https://doi.org/10.1080/19359705.2016.1217499

United States Census Bureau. (2020). *Urban and rural.* www.census.gov/programs-surveys/geography/guidance/geo-areas/urban-rural.html

United States Department of Agriculture. (2020). *Rural-urban continuum codes.* www.ers.usda.gov/data-products/rural-urban-continuum-codes.aspx

Watson, R. J., Park, M., Taylor, A. B., Fish, J. N., Corliss, H. L., Eisenberg, M. E., & Saewyc, E. M. (2020). Associations between community-level LGBTQ supportive factors and substance use among sexual minority adolescents. *LGBT Health, 7*(2), 82–89. https://doi.org/10.1089/lgbt.2019.0205

Williams, N. D., Levine, D. S., & Fish, J. N. (2019). *2019 Needs assessment: LGBTQ+ youth centers and programs.* CenterLink.

Woodford, M. R., Paceley, M. S., Kulick, A., & Hong, J. S. (2015). The LGBQ social climate matters: Policies, protests, and placards and psychological well-being among LGBQ emerging adults. *Journal of Gay & Lesbian Social Services, 27,* 116–141.

Zeeman, L., Aranda, K., Sherriff, N., & Cocking, C. (2017). Promoting resilience and emotional wellbeing of transgender young people: Research at the intersections of gender and sexuality. *Journal of Youth Studies, 20,* 382–397.

19

QUEER ARCHITECTURE

Sarah Bonnemaison

Main Body

Queerness and architecture are not obvious bedfellows. To be sure, there is much scholarly writing about "queer space"—that is, how queer people experience, inhabit, and reclaim urban space. But notwithstanding architecture's long history of gendering styles, rooms, and decorative interiors, there is no "queer" architectural style. However, many architects and interior designers think that "queered" space can contribute to queer identity formation. For example, while "a skeleton in the closet" once referred to a dubious family history, for queer people, the "closet" has become an enduring metaphor. Whether one is in the closet or coming out of it, the closet remains a symbol of self. Coming out of the closet is a way to realize one's human potential. As Clare Cooper Marcus argues, "The self signifies the unification of consciousness and unconsciousness in a person, and represents the psyche as a whole, an encompassing whole which acts as a container" (Cooper Marcus, 1974, p. 12).

For many queer people, self-realization begins with the body as a container of the self. From prosthetics and makeup to tattoos and gender-confirmation surgery, the body can be an instrument for exploring and testing one's gender identity and presenting one's sexual preferences. Similarly, the clothes one wears and the room one inhabits can be transformed to express a queer-friendly place to encounter the world and interact with it. Coming out on the dance floor remains one of the most powerful and memorable experiences for many queer youth—a safe public place that is licensed for liminality, a place where one can, in a newly altered body, engage and perform the new self (Urbach, 1996).

Then comes the opportunity to nest and transform one's home. Here, queer people can express their difference, surround themselves with affirming imagery and mementos, and perhaps even design an ideal "container". In his autobiography *Memories, Dreams, Reflections*, Carl Jung describes the gradual evolution of his home on Lake Zurich and how it reflected his state of mind, from ecstasy to deep depression (Jung, 1965). Clare Cooper Marcus builds on Jung to argue how the house is the symbol of self, in its most expressive and enduring form (Cooper Marcus, 1974, p. 12).

For contemporary queer culture, the house expands its visible presence beyond its walls with the aid of digital media. Interactive platforms have expanded the notion of home into a large network of localized memories. For example, the interactive project *Queering the Map* allows

DOI: 10.4324/9781003128151-23

queers to tag a digital map of the world with their lived experience (Echenique & Boone, 2018). The majority are good memories, such as romantic encounters in public places where they felt at home. The memories are described with a short text and pinned anonymously, even in countries where homosexuality is illegal, showing the power of new media to provide visible alternatives and a sense of belonging.

As an architectural historian, I believe queer material culture merits careful study. Fortunately, young scholars are finding support to research queer topics that may be difficult or even impossible to take on in their home country, increasing the geographical reach of queer studies. Deep dives into the archives of queer architects and designers are all contributing to the development of queer architectural history.

Many places resonate in the collective memory of queer people and should be celebrated with monuments, plaques on buildings where a famous queer person lived, and to protect queer-significant urban districts such as the Castro in San Francisco. The first monument dedicated to queer people was Amsterdam's *Homomonument* (1987), described by the artist as a commemoration of the suffering of queer people. Other monuments followed. Pierre Nora calls these *lieux de mémoire* (site of memory), whether they can be a monument, a house, a bar, or a discotheque (Nora, 1989). But unlike monuments to commemorate fallen soldiers, queer places of memory are continually under threat. For this reason, it is important to archive, create exhibitions, and write books about queer material culture.

This chapter reflects on queer material culture from the point of view of both architectural history and architectural practice. I show how architecture in the 20th century has evolved in response to homophobia—from protecting one's house behind high walls and fences, to buildings increasingly more open to the street. In terms of practice, I investigate designers' contributions to queer identity formation in a variety of places: museums, street parades, and vacation houses. But we first need to ask, "what is queer architecture"?

Defining Queer Architecture, an Entangled Debate

Judith Butler argues that "gender is not something that is attributed to an already pre-existing subject because of this subject's biological characteristics, but rather something that is produced through its repetitive enactment in response to discursive forces" (Butler, 2007, p. 34). These "discursive forces" include the built environment. In fact, the discourse of Western architecture is fundamentally gendered, and these gendered associations have been reinforced through education and architectural theory. For example, "the classical 'orders' of Ancient Greece and Rome were gendered—according to Vitruvius, the Doric order was associated with the masculine, Ionic with matronly, and Corinthian with maidenly genders" (Forty, 1996, p. 143). During the 18th and 19th centuries, European architects perfected the art of associating gender to rooms and their proper interior decoration. In the houses of the upper middle class for example, light colors and decorative wallpaper were used in a feminine boudoir and dark colors and leather coverings for a masculine study (Kinchin, 1996).

The massive social change of the *fin de siècle* was expressed in buildings that played with traditional gender associations. Art Nouveau architects began to invert gender associations to create a new architectural language. Charles Rennie Mackintosh for example, designed the boardroom of his extraordinary Glasgow School of Art with large windows flooding the room with sunlight, further brightened by a color scheme of white and apple green. The all-male board members experienced this as a visceral shock—instead of a club-like sanctum of dark wood and leather, here was a light-filled room more fitting for a women's tearoom (Kinchin, 1996).

The early resort hotels in American National Parks present another example of queering gendered architectural norms. While the rhetoric of rustic hunting lodges was well developed by the early hunter/conservationists—such as George Bird Grinnell and Teddy Roosevelt of the Boone and Crockett Club—the first concessionaires in Yellowstone National Park had to appeal to family vacationers and particularly women (Macy & Bonnemaison, 2003). We can see the result of this collaging of masculine and feminine references in the architecture of the Old Faithful Inn, designed by Robert Reamer in 1905. The building can be described as "butch", a combination of a "masculine" hunters' lodge or log cabin, and a "feminine" Arts and Crafts expression of the "simple life"—plainly and gracefully decorated with attention to everyday comforts (Bonnemaison, 2000). Although it featured a massive eight-hearth stone chimney and oversized wood columns expected of "the world's largest log cabin", it also advertised sitting nooks, lace-like balustrades offering intimate areas for the genteel pastimes of card-playing and conversation, and a "honeymoon suite" replete with a fresh cotton counterpane on a four-poster bed and a bay window for gazing out at the scenery.

In short, the Old Faithful Inn was designed to attract women and men, armed not with guns but with cameras (Macy & Bonnemaison, 2003). Such play with gender references was a central feature of *fin de siècle* and early modern architecture, as we will see later in the work of Eileen Gray (Bonnemaison, 2019).

Figure 19.1   Lobby at the Old Faithful Inn, 1904.

Source: Photograph by J. F. Haynes

Figure 19.2   Honeymoon Suite at the Old Faithful Inn, 1904.

Source: Photograph by J. F. Haynes

But it is not until the "gay liberation" of the 1970s that architectural critics finally began to acknowledge the possibility of a queer architecture. Influenced by Linda Nochlin's famous essay of 1971, "Why have there been no great women artists?", Charles Jencks was the first to acknowledge a queer presence in architecture, in his characterization of the "post-modern" style (Jencks, 1977). Robert A. Gorny explains:

> Speaking of the "Gay Eclectic" Jencks identified the uses of irony, parody and travesty. Semantic double coding was part and parcel of his project of abandoning the reductive and universalist claims of modern architecture . . ., while a number of gay architects figured prominently in Jencks' rewriting of architectural history, most notably Philip Johnson and Charles Moore.
>
> *(Gorny & van den Heuvel, 2017, p. 2)*

Beatriz Colomina suggests that queer architects have contributed to the history of architecture for hundreds of years, yet "their stories, their imagination, their aesthetics is left out of architectural history" (as cited in Kotsioris, 2020, p. 19). But Colomina wants to go even further by looking at the canonical works of modern architecture from a different angle. In her book *Privacy and Publicity*, she unpacks the hyper-masculinized dimensions of Le Corbusier's architectural promenade and its over-emphasis on the gaze (Colomina, 1994). Similarly, Alice Friedman probed the tensions between Mies van der Rohe's insistence on transparency in his famous Glass House and the frustration of his prominent client, the Chicago heiress Alice Farnsworth, who—feeling like she was living in a fishbowl—famously slammed him publicly in the pages of *Ladies Home Journal* (Friedman, 2006, p. 152). The Glass House designed by Philip Johnson, however, conceived as an *hommage* to Mies was not so much a house as a setting for a theatrical-ritual-enacting domestic activity. As Arthur Drexler observed in his 1949 review of the building:

> [T]he dignified proportions of the counter effectively transform it from a mere workspace to the scene of pontifical ceremonies. The mixing of a gin and tonic, or the scrambling of eggs, becomes a luxury which is the significant blend of ritual and necessity.
> *(Drexler, 1949, p. 96)*

A review of the literature on queer architecture sheds light on some architects while keeping others under cover. In addition to Johnson's Glass House, both Harwell Hamilton Harris's Weston Havens House (Adams, 2010) and Paul Rudolph's Manhattan apartment (Rohan, 2014) define the contours of a male homosexual residential typology—what George Wagner calls the "bachelor pad" (Wagner, 1996). Rather quickly, a narrative about queer architecture unfolds with key players and key buildings. Yet other queer issues remain unaddressed, such as the periodic transformation of quotidian spaces to support queer gatherings—in the urban alleys of large cities, or in the curling rinks and barns of smaller rural communities, rented for the evening as a place to dance, party and socialize (Metcalfe et al., 1997). Once queer bars became permanent venues, more readily visible and located near heterosexual bars, gay bashing intensified. So when bars became visible on the street, this did not liberate queer people.

To that end, Jasmine Rault reminds us "to interrupt the narrative of progress, from sexual representation to post-Stonewall liberation, which we are encouraged to reiterate and compelled to identify with" (Rault, 2011, p. 3) and instead cautions us to remain aware that queerness is a continual struggle and an evolving discourse. When the debates around queer space elude issues of race and class, a new homonormativity appears, a uniform neoliberal vision of a homosexual community rendered visible by rich white men (Vallerand, 2020). According to Vallerand, homonormativity obscures fundamental issues that are strongly marked by gender, class, and race—such as access to resources and the agency of inhabitants in the design of their homes and places of work.

A good example of this push back, on a homogenous queer architectural discourse, is a recent exhibition on Luis Barragan's well-known home, office, and garden in Mexico City (Moffit, 2019). Evan Moffit showed that this house was designed not for one, but for two people—the other person was not Barragan's lover but his maid, who occupied very small rooms in the back of the house, an enduring tradition from Spanish colonial times (p. 2). Moffitt does not attempt to reduce the aesthetic impact of this iconic architect who was strictly closeted throughout his long career, but he teases out the contradictions that are present in, what at first glance appears to be an integral, complete work of architecture. The hidden dialectic of class required the maid to be invisible at all times, disappearing into hidden staircases and tucked into the deepest recesses of the dwelling. And the class issue is combined with a deeply repressed homosexuality, wrapped in a cloak of intense Catholic spirituality. For Moffit, these divisions are fundamental to the enduring appeal of Barragan's work. He writes:

[F]raccionar, to divide or parcel, gives root to the *fraccionamientos*, or official neighbourhoods, of Mexico City. The verb applied to Barragan's life in many ways: the
modernist play of architectural volumes; the consubstantial power of the holy trinity;
the irreconcilability of queerness and religious conservatism; the design of suburban
housing developments [of gated communities and convents].

(p. 4)

Through this exhibition, one can see the extent to which certain aspects of Barragan's work
have been ignored or even erased, as his work was promoted as emblematic of Mexico's contribution to modernism. As a result, Barragan's contributions as a queer architect have been
marginalized, and the persistence of colonial social patterns expressed in his buildings left
unquestioned.

The Lesbian Feminist Contribution

Most of the history, theory, and criticism of queer architecture focuses on places for gay men
and the work of gay male architects. However, feminist historians have done a great deal of
work over the past 20 years ranging from sexuality to the history of domestic spaces (Heynen,
2005) and are starting to include lesbianism as an aspect of their research, such as Eileen Gray's
active participation in the lesbian networks in Paris of the 1920s (Rault, 2011). As I move forward, I propose to draw on the work of feminist and queer philosopher Rosi Braidotti for her
critique of oppositional identity politics, in which one gender/"race"/religion/sexual orientation is considered to be less than the other (Braidotti, 2013).

[Braidotti's] concept of figurations unpacks the various practices and discourses to
demonstrate that they are situated and take form in specific constructs. Such configurations are materially embodied and embedded, relational and affective.

(Gorny & van den Heuvel, 2017, p. 4)

Architecture is one means through which such configurations are "materially embodied and
embedded". As Michel Foucault has argued, architecture is a "visible statement" of a discursive
formation around power and knowledge (Hirst, 1993, p. 52). Bodies inhabit buildings, and
building designs are imbedded with assumptions about what bodies should and should not do.
Architecture is one of the discursive forces we tangle with in our daily life. If we agree with
Shakespeare who said that the world is a stage, it seems clear that people enact roles with architecture as a stage set. But unlike other discursive forces, architecture is experienced in a state
of distraction (Benjamin, 1968). So the impact of architecture on our lives is strangely more
pervasive but also more unconscious.

For the purpose of this chapter, queer architecture is understood to be buildings created by
queer architects as well as designs aimed at the queer community. As it will soon become evident, many of the examples are in Canada. I am also drawing on queer aspects of my research
and from my own architectural practice, Filum Ltd—shared with Christine Macy, my lifelong
partner. This chapter first explores places of queer memory—from monuments and celebrations
to the growth of entire districts. Then, it looks at modern leisure architecture, such as summer
homes for lesbians on the Côte d'Azur in the 1920s and gay men's beach houses on Fire Island
in the 1960s and 1970s. Finally, this chapter turns to the architectural profession and explores
how queer couples collaborate in an anti-gay environment. To do this, I compare two such

couples active in Canadian post-war modernism: Arthur Erickson and Francisco Kripacz and less flashy but, as it will become apparent, important to lesbian architectural culture, Mary Imrie and Jean Wallbridge.

Places of Memory of Queer Culture

Places of memory in the form of monuments and celebrations are important to queer culture, as they recall the oppression of queer people. Commenting on literature about queers, Heather Love says:

> The embarrassment of owning such feelings, out of place as they are in a movement that takes pride as its watchword, is acute. . . . These texts do have a lot to tell us, though: they describe what it is like to bear a "disqualified" identity, which at times can simply mean living with injury . . . not fixing it.
>
> *(Love, 2007, p. 129)*

Monuments recognizing and commemorating the suffering of queers play an important role in validating queer identity and naturalizing queerness in larger social contexts. These places of memory may have their origins in local histories, but they are today subsumed in a touristic machinery, transforming them into places of pilgrimage for queer visitors from across the world.

Monuments

Karen Daan's *Homomonument* commemorates all gay men and lesbians who have been subjected to persecution because of their sexual orientation (Daan, 1987). It was erected in 1987 in the center of Amsterdam, on the bank of the Keizersgracht. Three large pink triangles of granite are set into the ground to form a larger triangle. The purpose, according to the artist, is "to inspire and support lesbians and gays in their struggle against denial, oppression and discrimination" (Daan, 1987).

Subsequent monuments to persecuted homosexuals have been realized in cities around the world: in Germany, the *Angel of Frankfurt* (1994), the *Rosa Winkel* monument in Cologne (1995), and the *Memorial for Homosexuals Persecuted by the Nazis* in Berlin (2008). This most recent memorial, by artists Michael Elmgreen and Ingar Dragset, is located at the edge of the Tiergarten, across the avenue from the *Memorial to the Murdered Jews of Europe*. It is a tilted cuboid of concrete, with a window embedded on its front; here, visitors can peer at a video of two men kissing. Nearby, a panel explains that "you could be arrested for a kiss during the persecution of homosexuality that began under the Nazis and continued until it was finally voided in 1994" (Wockner, 2008).

Of the placement of this monument, Berliner architect Peter Sassenroth observes:

> It is a very prominent place—just vis-à-vis the very well-known *Memorial to the Murdered Jews of Europe*—it is positioned at a major street leading to the Brandenburg Gate, in the center of the city! We can recognize the Holocaust Memorial by Peter Eisenman in the right edge of the image. The memorial of homosexuals persecuted by the Nazis feels like it is almost a satellite of the big memorial . . . it has the same material, same colour . . . similar proportions. It feels as if one of the big stones (*stelae*) was ejected from the bigger memorial, thrown over—and landed on the other side of the street, somehow tilted . . . you can feel the connection.
>
> *(Sassenroth, personal communication, November 20, 2020)*

Figure 19.3   Memorial to the Murdered Jews of Europe in Berlin 2008.

Source: Photograph by Peter Sassenroth, 2020

Figure 19.4 Detail of the Memorial to the Murdered Jews of Europe in Berlin 2008.

Source: Photograph by Peter Sassenroth, 2020

In the year following its dedication, the monument was frequently vandalized, and its artists endured numerous controversies by Jewish historians (Wockner, 2008)—showing that the persecution of homosexuals during the Nazi regime is still seen by some people as less important than the persecution of the Jews—even if many homosexuals were also Jews.

Festivals and Parades

While architectural historians focusing on queer spaces tend to look at buildings, geographers looking at queer spaces have turned their attention to the streets and square of cities. Yet often ephemeral events that reclaim the city as queer space are also designed and staged—by artists, designers, architects, and performing arts groups. We might imagine that ephemeral events such as demonstrations, parades, performances, and parties leave few traces behind. However, they are often photographed, providing us with documentary records that reveal the development of collective queer identity, the bricolage aesthetic of clubs formed by lighting and dance platforms, and the transformation of urban public space to create a queer city, even if only for a limited time.

For example, the edited book *Queers in Space: Communities, Public Places, Sites of Resistance* maps queer urban domains in several cities (Ingram et al., 1997). It also explores performative happenings and installations by groups such as Act-Up, intended to raise public awareness of the queer experience and mobilize support against discriminatory laws and practices (Ingram et al., 1997). Anthropologist Victor Turner calls such events "liminal"—from the Latin word *limes* for threshold (Turner, 1969). Most cultures sanction liminal events in specified times and places. Historians distinguish between spectacle (which is imposed from above by the state or corporation) and festival (grassroots and liberatory phenomenon). Grassroots carnivalesque festivals like Halloween present images of alterity that, at some level, ultimately empower those who are disenfranchised or oppressed by society. Natalie Zemon Davis argues that some festivals, by presenting images which are multivalent, can put into the public realm potentially liberating representations (Davis, 2006).

One example of a liminal event was Greenwich Village's first Gay Pride parade in 1970. This took place a year after the Stonewall riots and stretched over 57 blocks from Greenwich Village to Central Park. When puppeteer Ralph Lee started the Greenwich Village Halloween Parade three years later, it was quickly adopted by the queer community as an opportunity for the artistic expression of queerness. Unlike most Manhattan parades that proceed up or down the city's major avenues, the Greenwich Village Halloween Parade had a cross-town trajectory, beginning at West Beth Artists Colony and culminating in Washington Square.

The event re-cast the city as a backdrop for the public performance of queerness, feeling like a giant block party (Bonnemaison & Macy, 2002).

Curating and Archiving Queer Culture

Ephemeral events like Pride parades, public actions, and protests all contribute to the identity and development of queer communities, either because they have been directly experienced and remembered, or these experiences are shared as stories, shaping what Maurice Halbwachs calls "collective memory" (Halbwachs, 1992). Other ephemera—the minor mementos of a moment—are rarely catalogued yet offer a glimpse into queer countercultures of the past. Because queer history has been marginalized or excluded from the written record, such ephemera and oral histories are especially important and sometimes the only way into the construction of a collective memory.

Figure 19.5   Cross-Town Route of the Greenwich Halloween Parade, New York City, 1985.
Source: Drawing by Christine Macy

Robin Metcalfe's, 1997 exhibit titled *Queer Looking, Queer Acting (Lesbian and Gay Vernacular)* displayed the ephemera of a quarter century of queer activism in Halifax, Nova Scotia. An activist, art critic, and independent curator, and a native of Cape Breton Island, Metcalfe had experienced firsthand the emergence of queer activism in Atlantic Canada. And he had collected innumerable mementos from these years: posters, placards, t-shirts, performances, and videos. All were created by professional artists and designers, but they also shared a vernacular quality, a home-grown aesthetic, and a love of word play. The exhibition took place in Mount St. Vincent University Art Gallery, a 1970s-era rough concrete container.

Filum, my design partnership with Christine Macy, was commissioned to create an installation that would "queer" this formidable Brutalist space. We attached a series of stretched white lycra screens to the full height of the gallery, shaping the flow of people from one zone into another. The curved fabrics' surfaces also provided support to display small ephemera (pin-back buttons, stickers, and posters) and project films.

By re-presenting queer ephemera in the context of an art gallery, and asserting their cultural value through critical catalogue essays, Metcalfe showed the centrality of these objects in shaping queer culture in Atlantic Canada and asserted their cultural value and significance. According to him, the exhibition and catalogue were a "celebration of the past, an important social and historical documentation, and a passing of the proverbial baton" (Metcalfe et al., 1997, p. 4). Our installation was a metaphor for queer life in Nova Scotia: a small community nourished by creatives for whom living on the margins of power is not a weakness, but a strength.

Homosocial Party Houses

In the 20th century, lesbian and gay professionals—even those living and working in large cities—faced pervasive anti-gay sentiment that required them to keep their private lives securely closeted. But summer offered an opportunity for license, when queers wanting to socialize with like-minded friends sought out secluded coastal settlements with a reputation for a freer, bohemian lifestyle. Such summer houses, designed for socializing as much as for leisure or retreat, often reveal a queer sensibility in their inversion of conventional room types and arrangements,

Figure 19.6   Queer Looking 1997.
Source: Photograph by Robin Metcalfe

and in their complex design strategies to achieve both exposure to and privacy from their natural settings.

Two well-known summer vacation regions are discussed here: for lesbians in early 20th-century France, the rocky escarpments of the Côte d'Azur; and for gay men in New York City of the 1960s, the surf-caressed beaches of Fire Island. The vacation houses in these two locations, designed or adapted for queer lifestyles, provide us with insights into the spatial and architectural expression of an unconstrained queer life.

Sapphic Modernity on the Côte d'Azur

In early 20th century, Paris was a magnet for wealthy lesbian women who wanted to throw off the harness of familial and social restrictions and find an environment that would allow them the latitude to live their life as they chose. Many of these women were artists, writers, performers, designers, or patrons of the arts, and Paris offered them a fruitful context for their creative, professional, and social life.

The writer Natalie Clifford Barney and the painter Romaine Brooks were two such strong-willed heiresses, at the center of an influential circle of friends, lovers, and acquaintances that included most of the creative women living in Paris at that time. Barney's house on the Left Bank of the city was a rarity—a free-standing pavilion surrounded by a large garden, which also contained a small garden folly she dubbed the *Temple de l'Amitié* (temple of friendship). This secluded yet expansive pavilion surrounded by a lush overgrown garden projected a captivating atmosphere of freedom and romantic decay. Barney's salons on rue Jacob were famous for the guests they attracted and the artistic rituals that took place on Friday afternoons.

To paint however, Brooks needed solitude. Traditionally, the French bourgeoisie vacationed on the coasts of Normandy or the Riviera, so it is unsurprising that many wealthy lesbian couples built their summer houses on the Côte d'Azur between Saint Tropez and Monaco. The land was relatively inexpensive, the new "modern style" of architecture offered a different approach to domestic life, and they could socialize with friends and lovers in the public beaches and cafes of Saint Tropez, Cannes, and Menton. Barney and Brooks called their architect-designed modern home the *Villa Trait d'Union* (the Hyphenated Villa). This was a house of two wings—one for each of them—sharing a dining room in the middle. The house was destroyed during the Second World War, and its traces are more literary than visual. Yet the notion of a "hyphenated villa" offers a powerful metaphor for a lesbian lifestyle—two dwellings connected by what they share yet separated, each with their own integrity and autonomy. This is undisputedly an idea of home, but one that has been changed, "queered" in its assertion of independence and togetherness being two compatible states.

In this regard, as Judith Butler says, "the task is not whether to repeat [normative family structures] but how to repeat or, indeed, to repeat and through a radical proliferation of gender, to displace the very gender norms that enable the repetition itself" (as cited in Heynen, 2005, p. 25). In the *Villa Trait d'Union*, the bedroom is duplicated—displacing the singular optics of what happens in these rooms and to propose an alternative. "Such displacement might be enhanced", Hilde Heynen continues, "not only through the queer practices of bodily inscription that Butler takes as her main examples, but also through spatial set-ups that refuse simply to reproduce received patterns. Architecture can contribute to that by mimetically displacing domesticity" (Heynen, 2005, p. 25).

A second significant summer house on the Côte d'Azur is Eileen Gray's *E.1027*, her *maison en bord de mer* (house by the seaside). This Anglo-Irish heiress moved first to London to study art and then to Paris to realize her ambition of becoming an artist. Integrated into Parisian lesbian circles through her long relationship with the singer Damia (Marie-Louise Damien), Eileen Gray was also an aristocrat, and the social equal of other wealthy women—attracting a large clientele for her lacquered furniture and interior designs. In the early 1920s, she expanded into architecture, and *E.1027* was her first realized building. It is a house for two people to live and work, as well as a housekeeper. Gray's oeuvre, as a furniture designer and as an architect, demonstrates with great sophistication the art of "mimetically displacing domesticity" (Heynen, 2005, p. 25)

One way that Gray does this is well, as Jasmine Rault argues, is for Gray to design a sapphic modernity and to cultivate a space of transition where sexuality is deliberately obscured, an impossible object of knowledge and pleasures are sustained in suspense (Rault, 2011, p. 6). Nowhere is this more evident than in Gray's choreography of the path one must take to enter the house. From the *chemins des douaniers* (coastal path), one descends through terraces of lemon trees to arrive at the entry walk which parallels a blank wall.

This ends abruptly at the front door, where one reads the words *entrez lentement* (enter slowly) stenciled above the door. After crossing the threshold and into the foyer, one can glimpse the sea but not the inside of the house. Here, the view is blocked by a solid freestanding wall, which offers up instead a place to hang one's hat and jacket. Gray called this piece of architectural furniture an *épine paravant* (spine-screen)—suggesting that it was an integral feature of the house with a structuring importance. It prevents a visitor from seeing the living space unless they are invited in. The architect Le Corbusier found it intolerable, as it interfered with his expectations of uninterrupted views along an "architectural promenade"—a feature he prized in modern architecture (Bonnemaison, 2019).

Figure 19.7 Entrance to Eileen Gray's House E.1027, 1929.
Source: Photograph by Christine Macy

Further scrutiny of Gray's house reveals that it also toys with Le Corbusier's tenet of the "free plan" which promises complete visual command. To be sure, when one is inside the main living space, the room opens entirely up to a magnificent view of the bay. On the other hand, according to Rault, *E.1027* frustrates the eye of the visitor with hidden corners, dark alcoves, and private spaces.

> These were not simply contraventions of the modernist "free plan" but dishonest visual obstructions that produced deceptively ambiguous bodies and desires. Indeed, breaking up the clarity of communication, designing sensually rich spaces for visual and physical privacy, generated possibilities for bodies and pleasure whose incommunicability or refusal to public intelligibility seemed designed to evade the discursive reach of power-knowledge-pleasure.
>
> *(Rault, 2011, p. 5)*

For example, the windows of the house that open onto public paths are equipped with sophisticated sliding louvers that can be adjusted to admit sunlight or allow views to the desired degree; they can be closed entirely or opened completely. This control over what can be seen by others, and what can be seen from within, reveals Gray's sophisticated negotiation and intentional ambiguity in the spaces of sociability, autonomy, and privacy while providing above all, control and agency over one's "container". "A house", she wrote,

> is not a machine to live in. It is the shell of humans, their extension, their release, their spiritual emanation. Not only its visual harmony but its entire organization, all the terms of the work, comes together to render it human in the most profound sense.
>
> *(as cited in Bonnemaison, 2019, p. 28)*

Fire Island as a Gay Haven

Like the lesbian community on the Côte d'Azur during the 1920s and 1930s, Fire Island near New York City became a summer destination for gay men starting in the 1960s. Located five miles off the southern shore of Long Island, this 30-mile-long spit of sand was dotted with vacation homes. The community of Pines—700 houses tucked into a square mile of dunes and scrub pine—was a place where gay men felt free to express their sexuality at a time when that was not possible elsewhere (Trebay, 2013). Tom Bianchi, photographer and Pines resident, recalls:

> [It is] difficult to remember in an era of marriage equality and widespread social acceptance of gay people, the social and political tenor of those decades. When in many places it remained illegal for two men to dance together in public, when stereotypes of gay men as "sick deviants, weak and ineffectual and involved in sterile, unimportant relationships" still held sway.
>
> *(Trebay, 2013)*

Architect Horace Gifford states:

> [A]n openly gay man, in a time when this made him a true outlier, . . . arrived in The Pines on Fire Island in 1961. Understanding the area's potential—he bought a small plot of land and built himself a beach house. It was not long after that everyone wanted a modern beach house designed by him.
>
> *(Hillier, 2015, p. 5)*

Over the next few decades, Gifford designed more than 70 modern houses that were artfully integrated in the landscape, modestly sized, and communal in their layout.

The walls and floors of Gifford's houses are built from unfinished cedar—which weathers well—with large windows framing the trees against the sky and ocean dunes. Their simple geometric forms and integration in the landscape recall the rustic development of Sea Ranch in California, a 1964 collaboration between landscape architect Lawrence Halprin and architects Joseph Esherick and MLTW—but those houses were designed for individual families with conventional layouts. Gifford's houses, by contrast, were designed to accommodate the social needs of the gay community he knew so well. Each house has a large central social space with built-in furniture and sunken seating "maxi couches" and with "make-out" lofts. The nascent gay community of The Pines became a joyful and hedonistic expression of the gay liberation movement. Gifford's designs reflected and supported this social change. His early houses were more enclosed and discreet, but as visible expressions of a gay lifestyle became more socially acceptable, Gifford began to use larger windows and opened the social spaces to the outside, offering voyeuristic pleasure for the community he helped move into a full uproarious swing (Hillier, 2015).

In these examples, we see that the "beach house" positioned on the margins of society allowed queer people to enjoy the traditional benefits of leisure and health, while redefining the "family vacation" into a sensual homosocial environment.

Queer Couples in the Design Fields

We now turn to the architectural profession, taking a look at homosexual couples who shared both life and work. Women have long found entry into the architectural profession a slow and arduous process, and many could do so only in collaboration with a male partner. Only recently have architectural historians begun to uncover and celebrate women's contributions to architecture—for example in the 2018 exhibition *Couples modernes*, held by the Centre Pompidou-Metz, which focused on the collaborations of couples working in the creative fields from 1900 to 1950.

Gay male architect couples felt obliged to conceal the personal dimensions of their collaborative partnerships, and lesbian couples faced even greater difficulties to obtain large commissions due to their gender and their sexual orientation. To this end, I compare the Vancouver home of Canada's best-known architect Arthur Erickson and his partner Francisco Kripacz, with the home and office of Jean Wallbridge and Marie Imrie, a lesbian couple who shared a professional partnership in Edmonton, Alberta. The comparison shows how gender and sexual orientation in this period figured in the ability of designers to obtain large public commissions. Both couples were quite artful in their relationship to publicity, in the way they always slightly displaced any possible reference to their domestic partnership.

Gay Men as Partners in the Design Fields

Architects have long been assumed to play a stereotypically "feminine" or a "gay" role in the construction industry—as compared to engineers and contractors—by their role in translating a client's desires, and the need to be current with fashion and style. These attributes were recast as other stereotypes: the architect as genius (Frank Lloyd Wright) or as an *enfant terrible* (Le Corbusier). In such mediatized depictions, the architect is loaded with hyper-masculine attributes to draw out big money from the boardrooms and reassure the corporations and institutions they served. Playing the media well became part and parcel of an architect's practice. Queer architects and queer couples had to be even savvier. Arthur Erickson excelled in this—successfully creating a media persona based on rule-breaking, while never revealing his personal relationship to his lifelong collaborator, the interior designer Kripacz.

Erickson was astute in his relations with the media to promote his design philosophy and profile. He is best known for his public buildings—iconic campuses for Simon Fraser and the University of Lethbridge, Roy Thomson Hall in Toronto, the UBC Museum of Anthropology and Robson Square in Vancouver—and many private houses. Erickson's great contribution was his ability to integrate buildings in their natural settings, establishing a dialogue between nature and the artful manipulation of space (Sabatino & Fraser, 2016). Little has been written about Kripacz who designed most of the interiors for Erickson's best-known buildings, adding texture, color, and sensuality to the often puritanical palette of modern architecture. But after Kripacz's untimely death in 2000, Erickson commemorated the professional accomplishments of his lifelong partner in the monograph *Francisco Kripacz Interior Design* (Erickson, 2015). Today, the on-line retailer Amazon promotes this book as a "legacy to the working partnership of a charismatic and passionate artistic duo—a last testament from a remarkable architect to the man who shared in his greatest achievements".

Homosexuality—still implied rather than expressly stated—has now moved from taboo topic to selling point.

Erickson's home in Vancouver offers an intriguing contrast to the luxurious houses he designed for his wealthy clients. In 1957, he bought a 40-year-old garage on a double lot in the wooded neighborhood of Point Grey. He retained this garage-home throughout his career; he called it "a place to camp" as his "real home was in the world" (Gray, 2018, p. 10).

Ultimately, this was the house that meant the most to him. Tinkered with over decades:

> Erickson projected an intricate entanglement of narratives around his home that served varying purposes in sustaining his public persona. Within the center of the narrative swirl, the building remained a touchstone to Erickson who declared in 1992: "The house is very much a part of me. It's one of the constants in my life."
>
> *(Gray, 2018, p. 5)*

For the media, "Erickson was prone to using his curious garage-home as a narrative device that emphasized his visionary rule-breaking persona" (Gray, 2018, p. 3). In a National Film Board documentary by Jack Long, Erickson speaks about his Vancouver home as a renovated garage in a garden. When inside, he says "it is a house with no bedroom"—thereby setting aside his private life as a queer architect—and yet giving a detailed tour for all to see (Long, 1981).

Figure 19.8 Portrait of Francisco Kripacz.

Source: Erickson Family Collection

Figure 19.9 Erickson Kripacz, Point Grey garden.
Source: Photograph by Scott

The interior is precious—walls in gold leaf, settees clad in raw silk, precious woods and custom-designed furniture all testify to Kripacz's assurance in creating a luxurious and comfortable setting. The lot is surrounded by a high fence to protect from intrusions by nosy neighbors, but Erickson speaks about shaping the land to accommodate the house, as opposed to shaping the house to accommodate the land. There are two inversions here: the lack of a "bedroom" and the placement of a small loft accessed with a ladder, and the shaping of the land to adapt to the neighborhood's suburban setting and conservative neighbors. Erickson explains that he excavated a large amount of earth and piled it into a hill to hide the ugly door of the house across the street. The excavated pit became a pond in the center of the garden.

Erickson and Kripacz's non-traditional domestic space provided a setting for their famed parties. One evening, the garden was illuminated with paper lanterns as Rudolf Nureyev danced around the pond, stripping down to very little before he "fell" in the water. Attracting A-list artists, celebrities, and politicians, Erickson's parties impressed future clients and helped him secure large commissions. Although newspapers frequently reported on these star-studded evenings, no photographs depict Erickson and Kripacz in the same frame.

By contrast, at their beach house in Pines on Fire Island, the couple found release from the closet and enjoyed an openly gay relationship in the summer. The weather-beaten cedar siding and lounging couches in the living room were an established vernacular, and Erickson and Kripacz's renovation drew from this architectural language. But with money to spend, they transformed a humble cedar box into a fabulous party house.

The original shack became the chrysalis to an elaborate makeover which the locals christened "The White House". A wide, two-storied porch concealed the front façade of glass. Wide

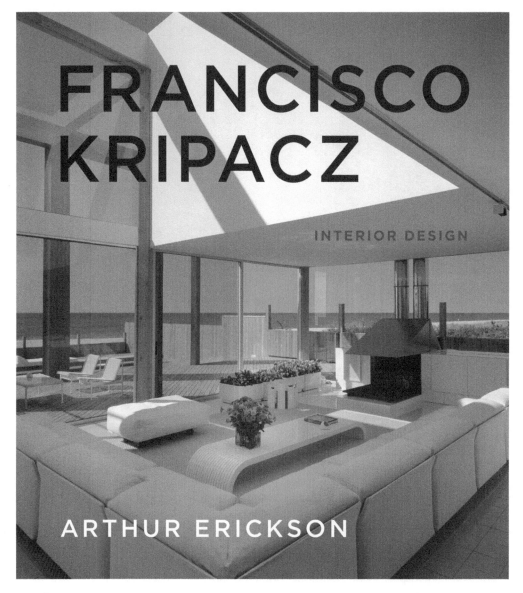

Figure 19.10 Front Cover of the Book *Francisco Kripacz: Interior Design* by Arthur Erickson.

Source: Reproduced with permission from Figure 1 Publishing.

piers, angled to the east view of the beach, supported deep angled beams across the front—a somewhat inconspicuous look of weathered siding instead of limestone that earned the house its name (Erickson, 2015, p. 15).

The subdued and minimalist interior palette allows the house to merge with the grasses, sand, and sea beyond. The floor-to-ceiling glass walls could be entirely opened allowing for a seamless transition to the outdoor deck and pool. Beyond, a slatted fence used as protection from the unwanted glances of people strolling on the beach could be lowered on hinges, once the crowds were gone, to expose a full view of the ocean. Similarly, the living room ceiling was designed to slide open to reveal the sky. Thus, surrounding its inhabitants lounging on low white couches, the "skin" of the house could dilate, opening in all directions, allowing the warmth of a summer night and the sound of the surf to fill the open-air house. The gay community also called it "Lincoln Center", suggesting its fantastic and theatrical qualities in the era of disco and gay liberation.

Lesbian Architectural Partners

Mary Louise Imrie and Jean Wallbridge were among the first women to graduate from schools of architecture in Canada before the Second World War. After working three years in Edmonton's Department of the City Architect, in 1950, they established their own office, the first architectural partnership of women in Canada. They were professional and life partners (Mehmetoglu, 2019, p. 8).

Imrie was on the editorial board of the *RAIC Journal* from 1949 to 1960, at the center of contemporary discussions and concerns in the field of architecture. "They travelled the globe to do research on post-war reconstruction and wrote several articles about their findings . . . [Imrie's position on the editorial board] also led to the publication of at least two of the firm's projects" (Adams & Tancred, 2000, p. 55). Over 30 years, their firm undertook 224 projects. A third of these were private houses, a quarter were apartment buildings, and 10% were commercial projects, including small office buildings, machine shops, stores, a shopping center, and a church (Dominey, 1992, p. 16). Of this project mix, Annmarie Adams remarks:

> Despite the fact that they designed a variety of building types, the projects by the firm published in the [RAIC] Journal were exclusively housing. Imrie commented herself on the assumption made by clients that women architects might excel in domestic design, "People will get us to do their houses, be thrilled with them, and go to larger male firms for their warehouses or office buildings."
>
> *(Adams & Tancred, 2000, p. 55)*

An architectural office with two women in Edmonton raised a few eyebrows.

> Much speculation was given to their free lifestyle. The two unmarried women, living and working together, made an unusual impression in a male dominated profession. Rationalizing their personal decisions for the social structure of the era, Imrie was quoted in 1984 as saying "it was hard work with long hours . . . and the practice could not have supported two families."
>
> *(Conreras, 1993, p. 19)*

In the mid-1950s, Wallbridge and Imrie built their home and office "Six Acres", so named for its generous lot size and bucolic setting. Originally a week-end retreat outside of Edmonton along the North Saskatchewan River, they designed a live-work building that would suit their way of life. Ipek Mehmetoglu suggests that this dual-purpose-built architecture needed careful management.

> Upon entering the house, one is faced first and directly with a sign "Wallbridge & Imrie Architects", obscuring any other functional attribution to the space. . . . Six Acres functioned as a professional mask, it acted as a "double sided" space hiding the

gay relationship from the eyes of the public, this time deliberately arranged and constructed as such by the owners.

(Mehmetoglu, 2019, p. 10)

The floor plans for this home-office, which include its furniture layout, indicate a couple lives and works there. The living quarters on the ground floor provide a large bedroom furnished for a couple. On the lower level, facing a spectacular view of the river gorge, there is a large office and a second bedroom to the side—this corresponds to the traditional "master bedroom" and "guest room" scenario, reinforcing their life as a couple.

Wallbridge and Imrie stood out from the other architectural firms in Edmonton—they were seen as hands-on, "studio" architects. Perhaps one of their distinctive characteristics was their hands-on approach to construction. This began with Six Acres, "they built a large part of it themselves, including window frames, and became, in Mary Imrie's words, 'half-decent carpenters'" (Dominey, 1992, p. 17). In addition, they often helped their cash-short clients by organizing work "bees" to build windows or shingle façades. Drawing on the Prairie tradition of collective barn-raising, they had, according to a tribute published by the Province of Alberta, a "flair for organizing volunteer work parties to reduce construction costs", creating bonds between people through cooperation. As a result, they attracted a large circle of businesses and professionals "who soon became friends and admirers" (Mahaffy, n.d.). Their house plans were compact and efficient and brought scenic views into the working areas of the house, often considered "secondary" spaces by male architects—for example, a long narrow horizontal window over a kitchen counter. This integration of nature into all rooms of the house became a characteristic feature of modern Edmonton architecture in the 1960s and 1970s.

Wallbridge and Imrie loved the Albertan landscape and were avid sportswomen. A photograph of Six Acres shows two pairs of skis leaning on an outside wall.

While "both benefited from privileged upbringing, [they] were equally at home on skates and in canoes on the North Saskatchewan River or kicking back over scotch and cigars" (Mahaffy, n.d.). Outdoor recreation was a source of pleasure, but outdoor camping became a necessity when it came to studying the site of a future project. Unlike many architects who might spend a day to take the lay of the land, they camped out to experience the landscape over time, to be better equipped to design a building that could fit in its surroundings. Imrie's second cousin, Mark Slater, recalls:

> Mary Imrie would come to a town and, if they didn't have a place where they could camp, she would buy up a piece of land and set up camp. Ultimately, she owned pieces of property all over Alberta. When Imrie passed away, one of the provisions of her will was that all these campgrounds belong to the province, so other people could use them.
>
> *(Dominey, 1992, p. 16)*

Well into their 60s, this working couple was referred to as "The Girls". The tributes that accumulated after their passing celebrated their contribution to Edmonton's architectural scene, recognized their influence and their example as an inspiration for future generations.

Conclusion

I now return to the original proposal that through the 20th century, queerness in architecture has become increasingly open to the outside world. In 1994, Mark Robbins curated the

Figure 19.11   Jean Louise Emberly Walbridge (left) Mary Louise Imrie (right) at a Train Station in the United Kingdom, 1947.

Source: Provincial Archives of Alberta PR1988.0290.0853.0001

Figure 19.12   Imrie Walbridge Six Acres Interior.

Source: Provincial Archives of Alberta PR1988.0290.0777

Figure 19.13   Imrie Walbridge Six Acres Exterior.
Source: Provincial Archives of Alberta PR1988.0290.07

exhibition *House Rules*, at Ohio State's Wexner Center for the Arts. Writers were partnered with designers and asked to collaborate on a vision of dwelling for the future. Poet bell hooks collaborated with architect Julie Eizenberg to dream of a "house without boundaries"—of race, class, or gender (hooks et al., 1994, p. 22). The poet began by sending Eizenberg a letter:

> the little house of many rooms that is my
> home holds no secrets—
> like arms it reaches out to embrace
> and hold me close when i leave and when i
> return . . .
> a concern for light and shadows—delicate
> lace curtains everywhere contrast with
> mission oak and soft black leather—
> red is the primary color throughout—
> it is a simple dwelling—little rooms—
> with very little in them—
> just enough to bring grace, elegance, and
> comfort
> to all who enter—i would miss this home

more if i were not making some version of it everywhere in
the world my spirit dwells.

(hooks, quoted in Jones, 1995, p. 53)

Eizenberg's response was to reimagine suburban living, with four dwellings sharing a common yard, kitchens, workspaces and childcare, while keeping spaces for solitude (hooks et al., 1994, p. 22).

What are the qualities of queer-affirming spaces and places? How might they re-define community, family, and self? How have queer designers toyed with critiques of norms as forms felt oppressive or constraining? What new models or proposals are they shaping that will enable people to be themselves at home and with others and to contribute to a more diverse, inclusive, and safer society? In this, bell hooks has the last word:

it is our capacity to imagine that lets us move beyond boundaries
—without imagination we cannot reinvent and recreate the work
—the space we live in so that justice and freedom for all can be realized in our
lives—everyday and always.
in sisterhood,
bell hooks

(Jones, 1995, p. 56)

I would like to thank Christine Macy for her astute editing work on this chapter.

References

Adams, A. (2010). Sex and the single building: The Weston Havens House, 1941–2001. *Buildings and Landscape: Journal of the Vernacular Architecture Forum, 17*(1), 82–97.

Adams, A., & Tancred, P. (2000). *Designing women: Gender and the architectural profession.* University of Toronto Press.

Benjamin, W. (1968). The work of art in the age of mechanical reproduction. In H. Arendt (Ed.), *Illuminations* (pp. 214–218). Fontana.

Bonnemaison, S. (2000). A room of her own at the Old Faithful Inn: Gender and architecture in Yellowstone National Park. In B. Szczygiel, J. Carubia, & L. Dowler (Eds.), *Gendered landscapes: An interdisciplinary exploration of past place and space* (pp. 58–67). The Center for Studies in Landscape History, Pennsylvania State University.

Bonnemaison, S. (2019). A dying moth on a modern window: Eileen gray and Virginia Woolf's tales of nature and life. *Scroope: Cambridge Architectural Journal, 28,* 27–39.

Bonnemaison, S., & Macy, C. (2002). Queering the grid. *Journal of the Society for the Study of Architecture in Canada/Le journal de la Société pour l'étude de l'architecture au Canada (JSSAC/JSEAC), 27*(1–2), 21–26.

Braidotti, R. (2013). *Metamorphoses: Towards a materialist theory of becoming.* Wiley.

Butler, J. (2007). *Gender trouble: Feminism and the subversion of identity.* Routledge.

Colomina, B. (1994). *Privacy and publicity: Modern architecture as mass media.* MIT Press.

Conreras, M., Ferrara, & Karpinski, D. (1993, November). Breaking in: Four early female architects. *Canadian Architect,* 18–20.

Cooper Marcus, C. (1974). *House as a mirror of self: Exploring the deeper meaning of home.* University of California Press.

Daan, K. (1987). *Homoonument Amsterdam.* www.homomonument.nl/

Davis, N. Z. (2006). Women on top. In J. B. Collins & K. L. Taylor (Eds.), *Early modern Europe: Issues and interpretations* (pp. 398–411). Blackwell Publishing.

Dominey, E. (1992). Wallbridge and Imrie: The architectural practice of two Edmonton women, 1950–1979. *Women and Architecture, JSSAC/JSEAC, 17*(1), 12–18.

Drexler, A. (1949, October). Architecture opaque and transparent: Philip Johnson's glass and brick houses in Connecticut. *Interiors + Industrial Design, 109*(3).

Echenique, M., & Boone, A. (2018). Queering the map.com. *CityLab*.

Erickson, A. (2015). *Francisco Kripacz interior design*. Figure 1 Publishing.

Forty, A. (1996). Masculine, feminine or neuter? In K. Rüedi, S. Wigglesworth, & D. McCorquodale (Eds.), *Desiring practices: Architecture, gender, and the interdisciplinary* (pp. 140–145). Black Dog Publishing.

Friedman, A. (2006). *Women and the making of the modern house*. Yale University Press.

Gorny, R. A., & van den Heuvel, D. (Eds.). (2017, December). New figurations in architecture theory: From queer performance to becoming trans. *Footprint 21 (Delft Architectural Journal)*, 1–10.

Gray, C. (2018). Domestic boundaries—Arthur Erickson at home. *JSSAC/JSEAC, 43*(2), 3–14.

Halbwachs, M. (1992). *On collective memory*. University of Chicago Press. (Original work published 1925)

Hirst, P. (1993, Autumn). Foucault and architecture. *AA Files, Architectural Association School of Architecture, 26*, 52–60.

Heynen, H. (Ed.). (2005). *Domesticity negotiating domesticity: Spatial productions of gender in modern architecture*. Routledge.

Hillier, D. C. (2015, July 17). *Horace Gifford: Hedonistically modern*. Retrieved January 8, 2016, from MCMDaily.com.

hooks, b., Eizenberg, J., & Koning, H. (1994, August). House rules. *Assemblage, 24*, 22–29.

Ingram, G. B., Bouthillette, A.-M., & Retter, Y. (Eds.). (1997). *Queers in space. Communities, public places, sites of resistance*. Bay Press.

Jencks, C. (1977). *The language of post-modern architecture*. Academy Editions.

Jones, K. B. (1995, September). Review of *house rules* and *assemblage 24*: Exhibition curated by Mark Robbins, Wexner center for the arts, Ohio State University, 1994. *Journal of Architectural Education, 49*(1), 53–56.

Jung, C. (1965). *Memories, dreams, reflections*. Random House.

Kinchin, J. (1996). Interiors: Nineteenth-century essays on the "masculine" and the "feminine" room. In P. Kirkham (Ed.), *Gendered objects* (pp. 13–29). Manchester University Press.

Kotsioris, E. (2020). The queering of architecture history has yet to happen: The intra-canonical outlook of Beatriz Colomina. *Architectural Histories, 8*(1), 22. http://doi.org/10.5334/ah.547.

Long, J. (1981). *Arthur Erickson*. National Film Board of Canada (Film 28 minutes).

Love, H. (2007). *Feeling backward: Loss and the politics of queer history*. Harvard University Press.

Macy, C., & Bonnemaison, S. (2003). *Architecture and nature: Creating the American landscape*. Routledge.

Mahaffy, C. (n.d.). *Jean Louise Emberly Wallbridge & Mary Louise Imrie*. Women Building Alberta: The Early Female Architects of Alberta. https://womenbuildingalberta.wordpress.com/jean-louise-emberly-wallbridge-mary-louise-imrie/

Mehmetoglu, I. (2019). Les Girls en voyage: Gender and architecture in the travels of Mary Imrie and Jean Wallbridge. *JSSAC/JSEAC, 44*(1), 7–20.

Metcalfe, R., Kansas, J., & MacSwain, J. (1997). *Queer looking, queer acting: Lesbian and gay vernacular*. Mount Saint Vincent University Art Gallery.

Moffit, E. (2019, May 5). *Uncovering the sexuality and solitude of a modern Mexican icon. Essay in catalogue of exhibition "Fraccionar"*. Estancia Femsa, Casa Luis Barragán.

Nora, P. (1989). Between memory and history: Les Lieux de Mémoire. *Memory and Counter-Memory, Representations, 26*, 7–24.

Rault, J. (2011). *Eileen gray and the design of Sapphic modernity: Staying in!* Ashgate.

Rohan, T. M. (2014). *The architecture of Paul Rudolph*. Yale University Press.

Sabatino, M., & Fraser, L. (2016). *Arthur Erickson: Layered landscapes*. Dalhousie Architectural Press.

Sassenroth, P. (2020, November 20). Personal Correspondence.

Trebay, G. (2013, May 22). The architecture of seduction. *New York Times*. www.nytimes.com/2013/05/23/fashion/looking-back-on-fire-island-pines-and-its-importance-to-gay-culture.html

Turner, V. (1969). Liminality and communitas. *The Ritual Process: Structure and Antistructure, 94*(113), 125–130.

Urbach, H. (1996). Closets, clothes, disclosure. In K. Rüedi, S. Wigglesworth, & D. McCorquodale (Eds.), *Desiring practices: Architecture, gender and the interdisciplinary* (pp. 246–263). Black Dog Publishing.

Vallerand, O. (2020). *Unplanned visitors: Queering the ethics and aesthetics of domestic space.* McGill-Queen Press.

Wockner, R. (2008, August 30). Berlin gay holocaust memorial vandalized. *QX.* www.qx.se/english/7858/berlin-gay-holocaust-memorial-vandalized/

Wagner, G. (1996). The lair of the bachelor. In D. Coleman, E. Danze, & C. Henderson (Eds.), *Architecture and feminism* (pp. 183–220). Princeton Architectural Press.

20

AMERICAN MUSICAL THEATER
Queer Representation and Public Pedagogy

Craig M. McGill, Alan Chaffe, and Kyle Ross

In heterocentric societies—characterized by the assumption that all people are heterosexual—how do queer people learn to construct their identities? People are not schooled in queer identity. They do not learn the norms, behaviors, and values of being queer from a teacher in a classroom. They observe, consciously or unconsciously, through cultural spaces what it means to be queer and how to behave. Public pedagogy offers "spaces of learning" in which "our identities are formed. . . . Master narratives of adult identity—who we are with regard to race, class, gender, sexuality, and so on—are portrayed to us and perpetuated through various public pedagogies" (Sandlin et al., 2013, p. 5). Consuming popular culture helps to teach us who we are, what roles we play in society, and how we should behave. We learn "whose cultures and histories are considered 'normal' and 'dominant' through the ways these cultures and identities are portrayed to us and perpetuated through public pedagogies" (Sandlin et al., 2011, p. 7).

Theater is an important site for public pedagogy (Katz-Buonincontro, 2011; Hickey-Moody, 2014). To name one prominent example, Lin-Manuel Miranda's *Hamilton* (2015) has become a cultural phenomenon, a place where people learn about historical events that shaped the American political landscape. Some texts are specifically created using the materials of theater to explore a person's emotional life and serve as sources of healing, understanding, and catharsis. As a form of arts-based research, ethnodrama (Saldaña, 2005) dramatizes a text (e.g., acting or singing) of research transcripts, for example.

The Broadway musical theater, as a genre, has been a significant purveyor of *compulsory heterosexuality* (Rich, 1980). In a heteronormative society, people are assumed to be hetero-sexual, and patriarchal values are implanted into children at birth (Marchia & Sommer, 2019). Our chapter is grounded in the paradox that despite being a refuge for queer people and being largely supported and produced by queer people, Broadway has been a significant site for the unequivocal endorsement of heteronormativity. The dominant narrative of the Broadway musi-cal as a genre is the completion of the heterosexual couple (e.g., Dolly Levi and Horace Van-dergelder in *Hello, Dolly!* [Stewart & Herman, 1964]).

While the Broadway musical has been a site of and a haven for some queer people, particu-larly gay men (Clum, 1999; Miller, 1998), this cannot be directly reflected in the representation of characters (Gelfand, 2018; Lovelock, 2019) or those chosen to work in theater (Broadway By the Numbers, 2019). In our review of the literature, we found only one published (popular press) article (Gelfand, 2018) surveying the number of musicals with queer people since the

DOI: 10.4324/9781003128151-24

first musical in the mid-1800s. Gelfand (2018) suggested that just below 5% of all Broadway musicals portray explicitly queer characters. This is just one example of conflict between how Broadway is a queer cultural space and the direct presentation and representation of queerness in the musical, both on stage and behind the curtain.

Although there is ample work exploring musical theater as a refuge for gay men (Clum, 1999; Miller, 1998) and lesbians (Weinzierl, 2016; Wolf, 2002, 2006), very little has considered it through the lens of public pedagogy: what people are learning *about* their queer identity from these popular culture texts, and what people in majority groups are learning about minoritized and marginalized populations. Additionally, scant academic literature has examined how cultural products are consumed by people in terms of shaping identity for queer people or shifting attitudes *about* queer identity for non-queer people.

The purpose of this chapter is to explore Broadway musical theater as a site of queerness and queer representation through the lens of queer public pedagogy. Examining what draws queer people to American musical theater will illuminate it as a site of queer public pedagogy.

Conceptual Framework

Our framework is informed by three threads: public pedagogy, queer theory and a queer politic, and reception theory. The amalgamation of these theoretical strands provides a theoretical lens through which to examine the Broadway musical as a site of queer public pedagogy.

Public Pedagogy

Although the field of adult education has long been interested in how adults learn outside of the classroom, recent literature has taken up issues with the pedagogy of the public sphere (Charman & Dixon, 2021; O'Malley et al., 2020; Stead & Elliott, 2019). The scholarship of public pedagogy explores "spaces, sites, languages of education and learning that exist outside of the walls of the institution of schools" (Sandlin et al., 2010, p. 1). Through a review of the literature over 116 years, Sandlin et al. (2011) found five different sites of public pedagogy: (a) citizenship within and beyond schools, (b) popular culture and everyday life, (c) informal institutions and public spaces, (d) dominant cultural discourses, and (e) public intellectualism and social activism. One of these, popular culture and everyday life, form the basis of this chapter.

The term *public* has been extensively theorized, famously described "as the sphere of private people [coming] together as a public" (Habermas, 1962, p. 27). In this space, ideas are generated, shared, discussed, debated, and extended. Through this public, a discourse is facilitated, and a knowledge base is formed. Two types of publics are particularly relevant to the Broadway musical: *Popular publics* describes the consumption of popular culture products which "*come into being* through processes of cultural distribution and consumption that often transcend specific geographical or political fields" (Savage, 2014, p. 84; emphasis in original). Popular publics allows for the intrapersonal examination of queerness of the musical: a good example is the long history of obsessively listening to cast albums in the privacy of one's bedroom and imagining a life of free of the constraints of compulsory heterosexuality (Miller, 1998). *Concrete publics* are specific physical institutions of cultural learning (e.g., museums, zoos) or events (e.g., theatrical performances or protest rallies). When musical theater is performed live, people consume it in the physical location of the theater, a concrete public space. Since musical theater is at once a text *and* a cultural experience (i.e., performance), this chapter deals equally with popular and concrete publics.

Queer Theory and a Queer Politic

Queer theory aims to disrupt "hetero-and-homosexual identities, revealing the ways they are disciplinary and normalizing with the hope of creating physical and social spaces that are hospitable to multiple, heterogeneous ways of figuring bodies, desires, social relations, and forms of collective life and politics" (Seidman, 1994, p. 175). The theory attempts to bring sexuality—what is often considered a private matter confined to the bedrooms of individuals—to the forefront of social life (Hall, 2003). Queer theory "offers a postmodern critique of meta-narratives of identity, a critique of universal homogenous and fixed identity gender/sexuality categories, which are deemed essentialist" (Jagose, 2005, p. 162).

Though often thought of as an invention of modern-day society, queer theory has a distinct evolutionary history along the lines of homosexuality and gay and lesbian studies (Salamon, 2021). Queer theory commenced in 1869 with the study of homosexuality (Zimmerman & Haggerty, 2000). Despite the wide suppression that drove homosexuals underground, Kinsey, with his seminal sexology studies in the 1940s, and Foster, with her lesbians in literature study in the 1950s, became "heroic role models" (Zimmerman & Haggerty, 2000, p. xi) for scholarly research related to homosexuality. The study of homosexuality marked a shift in focus from behavior to identity that established the foundation for identity politics (Zimmerman & Haggerty, 2000). Without "a prior identity politics to deconstruct . . . queer theory is unlikely to have emerged" (Allen, 2015, p. 681). Butler's (1990) *Gender Trouble: Feminist and the Subversion of Identity* and Sedgwick's (1990) *Epistemology of the Closet* are considered two founding texts in queer theory (Halperin, 2003). Building on Foucault, who posited that we must liberate ourselves from the binary norms that constitute homo–hetero sexuality, Butler (1990) argued that heterosexuality and gender are imitations produced and performed within a society.

Despite its academic relevance, queer theory is rooted in social activists and organizations, such as ACT UP, Queer Nation, Body Politic, AIDS Action Now, and Pink Triangle, that sought to challenge heterosexism, homophobia, and transphobia (Grace, 2008; Sullivan, 2003). Thus, in its focus on those excluded by heteronormativity and non-straight sexualities, queer theory "contests, interrogates, and disrupts the systematic and structural relationships of power that are historically caught up in heteronormative attitudes, values, and practices as well as heteronormative ideological, linguistic, existential, and strategic conventions and constructs" (Grace, 2008, p. 719). In addition, queer theory resists the limited categories brought about by heteronormativity and "assumes a spectrum of fluid sex, sexual, and gender differences that are always in a state of becoming; being is never fixed and belonging is never a certainty" (Grace, 2008, p. 720).

Reception Theory

Reception theory "refers . . . to a general shift in concern from the author and the work to the text and the reader" (Holub, 1984, p. xii). Reception theory is concerned with how texts are received by a reader. Fundamental to reception theory is that works are received against a *horizon of expectations*, in which meaning is shaped by anything the reader, spectator, or audience member receives, interprets, and evaluates the work (Baldick, 2008; Charles & Townsend, 2011). Jauss (1982) distinguished between three types of expectations: a productive aesthetic praxis, a receptive praxis, and a communicative praxis. Of importance to this project is communicative aesthetic praxis, "the enjoyment of the affects as stirred by speech or poetry which can bring about both a change in belief and the liberation of . . . [the] mind" (p. 92) of the audience member.

Though initially focused on literary works, reception theory extends to other media like film and theater (Bennett, 1997). In the context of the Broadway musical, an audience member's existing horizon of expectation, and thus, their reception to a performance, is constituted by their knowledge of Broadway musicals, their social experiences, the contemporary dominant culture of society, the subculture(s) (e.g., queer culture) to which the individual belongs, the values and beliefs held by the individual and of society at the time of viewing, and the diversity of the audience and other audience members' horizon of expectations (Jauss, 1982). Since queer "describes a horizon of possibility whose precise extent and heterogeneous scope cannot in principle be delimited in advance" and "is at odds with the normal, the legitimate, the dominant" (Halperin, 1995, p. 62), our queer reading of Broadway musicals and queer audiences' receptions will never consist of a fixed horizon of expectations and interpretation of a performance. Importantly, the "horizon of expectation is never fixed" (Bennett, 1997, p. 98), and "multiple horizons of expectations are bound to exist within any culture and these are, always, open to renegotiation" (p. 106).

What is essential is that the text is more than what an author may have intended it to be. Reception theory posits that meaning is a co-construction of the author, performer, and audience. In his famous essay, *La mort de l'auteur* ("Death of the Author"), Barthes (1967) argued that the author's intention for a text does not matter as much as how the receiver of the text interprets it. Drawing from this, queer scholars such as Doty (1993) have argued that queer audiences have a license to read queer aspects into non-explicitly queer texts. Reception theory, therefore, provides a theoretical justification for understanding how queer audiences might be moved in seeing a musical text that, on its surface, seems non-queer/heterosexual.

Queer + Public + Pedagogy

Cultural artifacts pervade every aspect of our lives and shape whom we become as people. Therefore, studying popular culture illuminates who we are and how we construct our identities. Popular culture can be thought of

> as the broad range of texts that constitute the cultural landscape of a particular time and/or place, as well as the ways in which consumers engage with those texts and thus become producers of new negotiated meanings. We view a text as any artifact or experience that we can read to produce meaning.
>
> *(Maudlin & Sandlin, 2015, p. 369)*

In public spaces and through cultural artifacts, people can *experience* their queer identity. Musical theater is also a primary example of a cultural artifact that holds the potential to shape cultural attitudes and provides a space for queer public pedagogy. Queer theory is useful as a critical theoretical lens through which to examine this site of identity and learning for several reasons. First, queer theory acknowledges the multiplicity of participants and that their experiences are "fluid, unstable, and perpetually becoming" (Browne & Nash, 2016, p. 1). Second, queer theory allows for an understanding and juxtaposition of queer lives and experiences with those considered to be "normal" (Dilley, 1999). Through this understanding and juxtaposition, queer theory provides a framework for identifying whether heteronormative discourse is being deconstructed or reproduced in cultural artifacts and spaces like musical theater. Third, queer theory is useful for taking up subjugated and embodied knowledge:

> Queer theory shakes and unsettles sedimented knowledge. . . . It explores how bodies and ideas are constituted and often constrained. The slippages of sensibility often highlighted through the use of queer conceptual tools foregrounds the rigidity of many

social attitudes and practices, thus begging the question of why such tight boundaries are put into place. It also examines the porousness, recrafting and deterritorialization of the rules governing social convention and knowledge. These slippages, fissures, breaks and cracks are highlighted because they cast a spotlight onto the possibility of doing life differently and this is extremely political.

(Gowlett & Rasmussen, 2014, p. 333)

In short, infusing queer theory into public pedagogy "offers an alternative paradigm, a richer possibility of insights into ways to facilitate individual and organizational learning because it questions relations of power, privilege, and identity" (Gedro, 2010, p. 355). Thus, queer knowledge is a site of learning for queer praxis, "a practical, expressive, and reflective encounter with sex, sexual, and gender differences historically considered taboo terrain and relegated to fugitive spaces" (Grace & Hill, 2004, p. 168). Queer praxis destabilizes taken-for-granted (and oftentimes, hierarchical) binaries (e.g., male/female or straight/gay), challenges assumptions like the conflation of sex and gender, and the privileging of "private acts over public ones" (Grace & Hill, 2004, p. 182). It recognizes the complexities of society and challenges adults to think about issues as more than either/or propositions. In this way, queer praxis "opens up the possibility of 'straight queers'" and accepts that some heterosexuals are "on the margins of heteronormativity" (p. 182). By problematizing heteronormative assumptions, queer praxis offers a "site of learning in adulthood, offering [the] potential for personal development" and the possibility "for self-reinforcement and for queer persons to write themselves into an alien (heteronormative) world" (p. 182).

The Broadway Audience

Each Broadway season, the Broadway League produces a study on the demographics of the Broadway audience. In their latest report, The Broadway League (2019) found that 68.3% of Broadway audience members were female, 74% of audience members were identified as white, the average age of the Broadway theatergoer was 42.3 years old, the majority (75.3%) of audience members had a college or graduate degree, and the average annual household income of a Broadway audience member was $261,000 (statistics provided by The Broadway League are for both plays and musicals on Broadway). Given the average reported cost to see a Broadway musical was nearly $144 in 2019, it is not surprising that Broadway audience members tend to be white and affluent—"The Great White Way" (Hoffman, 2020). As has been the case since the inception of the Broadway theater district, the average Broadway audience member is not representative of the American population. For instance, the median household income in the United States was $68,703 in 2019—a far cry from the average Broadway audience member (Semega et al., 2020).

Despite lacking representation from minority communities, there is evidence that the Broadway audience has, albeit slowly, become increasingly diverse over time. For instance, 26% of audience members in the 2018–2019 Broadway season were identified as non-white—a greater proportion than the 20.9% average over the past 20 seasons. In addition, the Broadway musical has long been considered a haven for LGBTQ theatergoers (Clum, 1999; Lovelock, 2019; Miller, 1998; Wolf, 2002). Unfortunately, there has been a dearth of statistical evidence to support this view. Though minimal, the Broadway League does provide some statistics on LGBTQ audience representation. During the 2018–2019 Broadway season, 0.5% of audiences were identified as neither male nor female, and at least 2% of female-identified and 8.1% of male-identified audience members were LGBQ given they attended a Broadway performance with their same-sex partner (The Broadway League, 2019). These statistics underestimate the true extent of LGBTQ theatergoers, as audience members were not asked to identify as LGBTQ. The later statistics provide credence to the stereotype that gay men are attracted to the Broadway musical (Clum, 1999; Halperin, 2012; Miller, 1998). Indeed, a historical code phrase for a homosexual in the 1920s was "He's musical" (Clum, 1999, p. 51). Historically, "musicals were always gay. They always attracted a gay audience, and, at their best, even in times of a policed closet, they were created by gay men" (Clum, 1999, p. 9). In fact,

> gay culture is built in part on musical spectacle: drag shows, pride parades, disco . . . the most fabulous musical production number fifteen years ago was a disco full of queens [i.e., the musical *Priscilla: Queen of the Desert*] dancing to "It's Raining Men".
>
> *(p. 30)*

While the actual Broadway audience (i.e., the audience sitting in Broadway theaters, a concrete public) is largely white, female, and affluent, the Broadway theater has transcended its physical space and has become accessible to audiences across the world (a popular public). Through cast recordings and albums, televised performances, traveling productions, community theater, and other means, the Broadway musical extends beyond the literal space in New York and into the privacy of one's bedroom or at a local karaoke bar (Miller, 1998). Thus, while exploring the Broadway musical through queer public pedagogy, we must also attend to these different spheres of influence for queer audiences.

A "Place for Us": Queer Public Sphere

In considering the Broadway musical as a site of public pedagogy, we consider three broad aspects in which queerness can be understood: the structure of the musical form, character representation and tropes, and queer themes and messages. Through all of these, we acknowledge and examine two parallel tensions: the journey of self-discovery is both uniquely personal and private as well as a social behavior explored within the larger context of a community. So too is the Broadway musical, serving as a private and solitary act of pure ecstasy and fantasy and also a shared public space for the queer community (Clum, 1999; Halperin, 2012; Miller, 1998).

Genre and Structure

Regardless of the actual content of the musical, the musical as a genre is and of itself queer (Clum, 1999; Halperin, 2012; Miller, 1998). The biggest complaint about musicals is that characters break into song for no logical reason. For some audiences, this absurdity is too much to overcome. These objections are not held for opera as a genre: because every word is sung, there is not an oscillation between speech and song. In other words, the structure of the musical is queer because of the mode-shifting that takes place between song and dialogue. Musical theater composers, lyricists, and librettists have grappled with this very issue almost since the beginning of the form in the 1920s (McMillin, 2014). In the early decades, songs in musicals were dispensable and interchangeable: a song could be removed from one show and then inserted into another. As the integrated musical developed beginning in the 1940s, writers like Rodgers and Hammerstein developed characters who sang when their speech alone could not adequately express their emotions. The songs were intricately tied to context and thus could not be easily inserted into other shows at random (Block, 2018).

Lovers of the musical genre embrace this fantastical element of the musical. Scholars (Halperin, 2012; Miller, 1998) have theorized that the speech/song format queers the musical as a genre and that this structure, in and of itself, draws in queer people. These scholars argue that the queerness inherent in the structure transcends the (often heteronormative) substance of the musical. For instance, a love song like "A Man Doesn't Know" (*Damn Yankees*, Adler et al., 1955) with lyrics such as "A man doesn't know what he has until he loses it/When a man has the love of a woman, he abuses it" can still impel the attention of queer people (who may, in turn, insert their preferred gender: i.e., "when a man has the love of a *man*"). Citing a litany of examples, Clum (1999) and Halperin (2012) go so far as to suggest that often musicals with actual gay content are paradoxically less queer than non-gay musicals for the simple reason that the genre's form is so inextricably queer and that gay musicals are often less experimental and more traditional.

Character Representation and Tropes

In this section, we present a brief history of queer representation in musicals and tropes that signify and/or reflect queer men's identification with ostensibly straight female characters due to the similarities of struggle and oppression.

Queer Representation in Musicals

Theater has long served as a space where people could see the lives of characters examined. LGBT legal victories together with the dramatic improvement in social acceptance of the queer community have led to an increase in explicit queer representations in Broadway musicals (Lovelock, 2019).

The Boys in the Band (Crowley, 1968) (not a musical) is usually cited as the pivotal play for queer representation on Broadway. Up to the late 1960s, gay men were not directly represented in Broadway productions (Colleran, 2020). However, queer presentation of characters through innuendo has been documented since the beginning of American musical theater (Colleran, 2020). Early characters were termed "pansies," to which gay audiences related. Pansy characters would come up over time in musicals like *Anything Goes* (Porter et al., 1934) and *Kiss Me, Kate* (Porter et al., 1948) (Colleran, 2020). These characters received mixed responses from queer people. On the one hand, these characters would be received positively because at least there was some level of queer representation at a time in which there could be no explicit queer representation. However, activists criticized the pansy characters because they were playing to stereotypes of gay men, reifying societal oppression (Colleran, 2020).

The majority of gay productions were not represented in mainstream media in the 1970s and 1980s (Kenrick, 2017). In fact, plays were relegated to off-off-Broadway. "Many of these works concentrated on gay self-hatred, the search for sexual fulfillment, and flights of humorous fantasy" (Kenrick, 1996, para. 4). The 1969–1970 Broadway theater season was somewhat of a watershed. Two supporting characters in high-profile musicals were explicitly queered: the first openly gay character was Sebastian Baye in *Coco* (Previn & Lerner, 1969) (Kenrick, 2017). Sebastian was the antagonist and was criticized as a stereotypical, excessively flamboyant caricature (Cantu, 2018). However, the part won René Auberjonois a Tony award for Best Performance by a Featured Actor in a Musical, which at least, partially, demonstrates substance. The first openly gay character that was portrayed in a positive, non-antagonistic, and sympathetic manner in a Broadway musical was Duane in *Applause* (Strouse et al., 1970) (Cantu, 2018; Kenrick, 2017). Both musicals were a commercial success with *Coco* running almost a year (329 performances) and *Applause,* which won four Tony awards including Best Musical, running over two years (896 performances).

Somewhat surprisingly, there have been few explicitly gay characters in the years since. However, contemporary musicals have complicated gay characters. Rather than employing idealistic or stereotypical gay characters, musicals like *Falsettos* (1992) and *Fun Home* (Tesori & Kron, 2013) demonstrated the struggles straight women faced when married to (and divorced) gay men.

> While the stereotypes are still there and have not been excluded entirely from musical theater, LGBTQ+ characters are now being portrayed more realistically and in a way that the community can be proud of instead of finding the characterization offensive.
>
> *(Thompson, 2020, p. 102)*

There have been demonstrably fewer trans characters (Snook, 2018) and lesbians for Broadway productions (Colleran, 2020). At the time of this writing, *Fun Home* (Tesori & Kron, 2013) remains "the only Broadway musical that features a lesbian character where the original source material, the book, and the lyrics are all written by lesbian women" (Lovelock, 2019, p. 199). Additionally, bisexuality is often minimized in mainstream musicals (Whitfield, 2020). While openly bisexual characters do exist in musical theater, these characters often fall into several stereotypes, such as the bisexual character wanting to sleep with anyone or being incapable of monogamist relationships (Whitfield, 2020). For instance, Maureen (*Rent;* Larson, 1996) is a bisexual woman, and her partners complain about her lack of relational fidelity, highlighted in the number "Tango Maureen."

The Drag, Drama, Dancing, and Fabulous Queens

Despite the lack of explicit LGBTQ representation until recently, queer people—and particularly gay men—found a gay subtext that "offered personal, emotional, and cultural validation" (Wolf, 2002, p. 21) in Broadway musicals. As Clum (1999) indicated, "it has usually been the gay audience member, 'out there in the dark,' who queers the musical, who finds or invents a gay reading to the spectacle presented to him" (p. 1). Despite explicit queer characters in the past, it is through three narrative tropes—the drag queen, the drama queen, and the dancing queen—that queer audience members found gay representation in Broadway musicals (Lovelock, 2019). It is still possible, however, to locate most explicit queer characters today within the boundaries of these tropes (Gowland, 2019). Expanding on Lovelock's (2019) tropes, Gowland (2019) proposed the tragic-gay trope instead of the drama queen and an additional trope of the fabulous.

The drag queen character trope challenges hegemonic masculinity and gender stereotypes, as the male performer embodies femininity without necessarily revealing their sexuality (Lovelock, 2016). The archetype of the drama queen describes musical characters who face personal tragedies and are often denied a happy ending. The term tragic-gay may be more suitable than drama queen, as the term tragic-gay acknowledges "the trauma present in these narratives without offering a tacit judgment of them" (Gowland, 2019, p. 46). The dancing queen trope is "a threefold conflation between camp, homosexuality and musical theater, without promoting any alterative representations of queer characters" (Lovelock, 2019, p. 190). The dancing queen is often presented as an "exuberant and frivolous" character (Gowland, 2019, p. 48). Drawing on Kushner (2018) and Moore (2018) who explored what it means to be fabulous, Gowland (2019) proposed the trope of fabulous as a companion to the drag queen and the dancing queen. Fabulous articulates "the visceral nature of spectacular looks" (Moore, 2018, p. 23) and "emerges from black gay culture, and particularly from the social world of voguing" (Moore, 2018, p. 24).

The significance of these tropes is that they simultaneously proclaim a sense of "inclusivity for a heterosexual (male) audience while continuing to display the level of 'camp' traditionally associated with musical theater" and gay men (Lovelock, 2019, p. 187). In fact, "musicals are camp" (Clum, 1999, p. 7). Though camp has taken on many meanings over time, one commonality between the multiple meanings is that camp is a queer sensibility (Harris, 1997; Sontag, 2002; Taylor, 2012; Wolf, 2013). Camp "sees everything in quotation marks" as people are "being-as-playing-a-role" (Sontag, 1978, p. 280). Sontag differentiated between two kinds of camp: "the camp of failed seriousness" (p. 280) (naïve/pure camp) and intentional or deliberate camp in which an artist is aware of what they are doing. In referring to the latter as *high camp*, Isherwood (1956) stresses its "underlying seriousness. You can't camp about something you don't take seriously. You're not making fun *of* it; you're making fun *out* of it" (p. 106; emphasis in original). However, "not all homosexuals have Camp taste. But homosexuals, by and large, constitute the vanguard—and the most articulate audience—of Camp" (Sontag, 2002, p. 64). Camp is also "a queer sense-making practice that subverts dominant gender norms and heteronormative practices and institutions" (Wolf, 2013, p. 284). Camp involves "the total body of performative practices and strategies used to engage queer identity, with enactment defined as the production of social visibility" (Meyer, 2004, p. 139). Thus, the campness of the Broadway character tropes provides a way for queer audiences to insert their queer selves into the heterosexual narratives, resulting in a queer reception of the performances and a resistance to the heterosexual world they are viewing onstage (Barnes, 2015; Gowland, 2019).

Little Shop of Horrors (musical opened in 1982; the following excerpt from Menken et al., 1985) serves as an effective example of camp. *Little Shop of Horrors* is both a stage play and live-action film, its camp qualities give it a cartoon-like, animated feel. In a preface in the published script, Ashman, a gay writer/lyricist, instructed performers:

> *Little Shop of Horrors* satirizes many things: science fiction, "B" movies, musical comedy itself, and even the Faust legend. There will, therefore, be a temptation to play it for camp and low-comedy. This is a great and potentially fatal mistake. The script keeps its tongue firmly in cheek, so the actors should not. Instead, they should play with simplicity, honesty, and sweetness—even when events are at their most outlandish. The show's individual "style" will evolve naturally from the words themselves and an approach to acting and singing them that is almost child-like in its sincerity and intensity.
>
> *(Menken et al., 1985, p. 7)*

Although the actors were encouraged to play the characters with as much earnestness as possible, the performances were deliberately goofy because of the writing.

When gay men lacked representation, they often turned to "strong" female or diva characters like Mama Rose in *Gypsy* (Styne et al., 1959) and Dolly Levi in *Hello, Dolly!* (Stewart & Herman, 1964) (Colleran, 2020). These "strong" female and diva characters dominated the male characters they were connected to in the storylines, and gay male audience members identified with these women more than the male characters. For a gay male viewer, the diva's performance in the Broadway musical can serve as a reference to their backstage performance—a performance of their more authentic gay selves that they typically only put on in private. Thus, a gay male viewer connects with the diva characters in the Broadway musical because the diva performs in ways that a gay male desires to but often cannot in society because their performance in most societal contexts is governed by punitive and regulatory heterosexual and gender social norms (Butler, 1988).

Jordan Roth, the president of a Broadway theater company, discussed his experience with theater as an openly gay man and the ability for the audience to connect with characters and messages that relate to them. He particularly highlighted an example with the message in *Kinky Boots* (Lauper & Fierstein, 2012):

> Just be who you want to be. But I think the message is actually a layer beyond that, because it's not just watching the story. It's also watching the audience react to the story. You watch everybody on that stage have a journey. And at the end, you feel 1,400 people stand up in rapturous applause. And to a young person—any person, frankly—who thinks *I wonder what anybody would say if I ever said, "This is me,"* the answer is 1,400 people are standing up and applauding. The theater is a great way to talk without talking. It's a great way to begin a conversation, because you can just talk about the show.
>
> *(Thomas, 2015, para. 7)*

Themes and Messages

One powerful aspect of musicals is that social and collective learning can serve as a catalyst that empowers audiences to advocate and champion for larger social justice movements. Musicals also can affect public opinion like other popular culture media (Heide et al., 2012). By adding melody to text, dramatic moments become more memorable and may evoke emotional reactions from the audience that can lead to attitudinal shifts over the theme(s) of the musical. These messages do not have to be explicit within the content of the musical itself. It does not matter what the author's intent was in their written content, but rather how the audience constructs the message (Barthes, 1967). For instance, "Somewhere over the Rainbow," bolstered by the "Friends of Dorothy" movement (in which queer people could identify other queers) contains lyrics that suggest a gay utopia of acceptance, a shared cultural message, even if unintended by the author:

> When you're gay, or lesbian, or LGBTQ+ in any way feeling like an outsider, and somebody is singing about "somewhere over the rainbow," where you can be safe, physically and emotionally . . . what does that mean to you? You're getting beat up. You're getting raided. If you're in a gay bar that's off the beaten track and you're dancing with a man or two women are dancing together, you're dancing to "Anything Goes" . . . you're feeling like you're in a place that "Somewhere Over the Rainbow" talks about.
> *(Colleran, 2020, para. 12)*

In the 1980s, musicals with explicitly queer characters also included musical numbers that encouraged community building and belonging, especially during the AIDS crisis. *La Cage Aux Folles* (Herman & Fierstein, 1983) presents an explicitly queer message. The number "I am what I am" is a powerful moment in the show when the drag queen character Albin owns their identity.

I am what I am
I am my own special creation.

So come take a look,
Give me the hook or the ovation.
It's my world that I want to take a little pride in,
My world, and it's not a place I have to hide in.
Life's not worth a damn,
'Til you can say, "Hey world, I am what I am."

Interestingly, while this musical was received positive reviews and garnered nine Tony Award nominations, there was still resistance to the explicit representation of queer characters at the Awards Show, evidenced by the fact that George Hearn (who won the Tony for Outstanding Actor in a Musical) wore a suit while singing this number, even though the character Albin is a drag queen. Despite embracing the musical (awarding the show six Tony awards including Best Musical), the awards committee was concerned about what the provocative performance in costume would do for show ratings. Another number from *La Cage Aux Folles* is "The Best of Times Is Now," which emphasizes living life to the fullest, implicitly an anthem to the surging gay rights movement. With the AIDS crisis looming at the time this musical premiered, it became an anthem of hope for queer people (Kantor & Maslon, 2004).

Other musicals have also incorporated messages to catalyze social activism or to provide explicit social commentary and critique. *Falsettos* (Finn & Lapine, 1992), set during the AIDS crisis, featured several moments in which characters criticized the Reagan administration, linked to their poor handling of the epidemic. At the conclusion of the musical, one character sings, "This is where we take a stand," shortly after a character died from AIDS, and their family is mourning. The lyrics before this moment rally folks from different backgrounds: "Homosexuals, women with children, short insomniacs." And the character calls for people to take action and support those who died in the AIDS epidemic, to be activists.

Regardless of lyricists' intent, queer audiences still built community, fostered a sense of belonging and hope, and called for social activism and change. Queer audiences read and interpret these messages, shaping the Broadway musical as a site of queer public pedagogy, both in the concrete space and in the larger popular public.

Conclusion: The Broadway Musical: A "Safer" Place for Queer Public Pedagogy

In the last decade, public pedagogy scholarship has begun to uncover the wide array of cultural sources, institutions, and spaces through which people learn outside of the classroom. However, despite an ever-growing body of work (Charman & Dixon, 2021; O'Malley et al., 2020; Stead & Elliott, 2019), issues of how public pedagogy is practiced have not received enough research, and the concept itself is still under-theorized (Burdick et al., 2014). Theorizing the concept further is important, given how much of our life's learning occurs outside the classroom and how little scholarship focuses on this type of informal learning. Queer aspects of musicals ought to be explored because public pedagogy scholars are "well situated as specific intellectuals whose writing might aid in the insurrection of subjugated knowledges that have been overlooked, buried, and obscured by established educational discourses and modes of academic inquiry" (Brass, 2014, p. 101).

Musical theater can be a site of acceptance of queer identity and learning to defy toxic heteronormative scripts. Because of societal heteronormativity, much of the learning adults must do to challenge the patriarchy involves "unlearning" societal messages they have internalized over their lifetimes. Grace and Hill (2004) described queering knowledge and understanding the identity politics and power behind knowledge production. Queering knowledge means:

> building adult education as a lived and knowable community that involves deliberate and engagements with queer—a term representing our spectral community that incorporates a diversity of sex, sexual, and gender differences—and queerness—our ways of being, believing, desiring, becoming, belonging, and acting in life-and-learning spaces.
>
> *(Grace & Hill, 2004, p. 168)*

As a location of concrete publics (Savage, 2014), theaters can be viewed as classrooms in which attendees are provided opportunities to "move beyond the boundaries of what they know and are familiar with to take an active part in a learning process that engages multiple 'texts' . . . as a path to understanding" (Mackinlay, 2001, p. 15). The multiple texts consist of the visual, audio, collective dialogue and interaction, embodied, and the performing self. In this way, musicals teach as they entertain and entertain as they teach (Weiner, 2001).

Several scholars have articulated the Broadway musical as a haven for queer people, particularly gay men and lesbians (Barnes, 2015; Clum, 1999; Lovelock, 2019; Miller, 1998; Wolf, 2013). Rather than safe spaces, we argue here that they are "safer," acknowledging that a sense of safety is a personal construct. We also acknowledge that more needs to be done to enhance the sense of safety for trans, queer people of color, and queer people of lower socioeconomic status. While queer people may be significantly underrepresented in one or more of these aspects when examined in isolation, perhaps the interaction between characters, messages, writers, and production elements illuminates why Broadway has become the haven it is for queer people. A sense of safety for queer people in public spaces like theaters has been found to initiate the development of a queer sense of community, encourage queer audience members to perform and embody their vulnerable and authentic queer selves, and promote critical thinking (Chaffe, 2021; Chaffe, 2022). Feeling a sense of safety in public spaces like the Broadway musical is important for queer people, as such spaces can provide audience members with a "refuge against oppression" (Chin, 2017, p. 391).

Theater allows patrons to suspend social norms of the outside world and to "behave with abandonment and freedom away from the constraints of the everyday" (Pielichaty, 2015, p. 235). Behaving with abandonment and freedom provides an opportunity for audiences to embrace their vulnerable and authentic queer selves, experiment with their identities, and openly question their beliefs and identities. Thus, theater can serve as a space to empower queer people to act with agency and fosters identity development. Overcoming queer shame results in improved personal security, sense of worthiness, self-acceptance, self-esteem, happiness, and mental health, causing individuals to embrace their queer selves and live more authentically (Kaufman & Raphael, 1996).

In addition to serving as a site for queer people to explore and experience their own queer identity, musicals also hold the potential to change minds and hearts about queer identity and life. Although under-theorized in the research literature, musicals can serve as a vehicle to transform societal attitudes about queerness. Heide et al. (2012) demonstrated that musicals have the power to change societal perceptions of social issues. This area holds much promise for future researchers.

Finally, the central power of musicals is their ability to cultivate a sense of hope. Hope is a positive feeling and motivational state about the imaginative possibilities of the future and is expressed as a way of feeling, a way of thinking, and a way of behaving that propels people forward (Akinsola, 2001; Bailis & Chipperfield, 2012; Turner, 1995). Feeling hopeful is significant because it increases confidence and provides a sense of agency, which results in and encourages individuals to change their behavior (Lopez, 2013; Yosso, 2005). Musicals can temporarily suspend structures or spaces of society and offered attendees a glimpse of a world that might be—one that is queerer. Connected to a sense of hope are positive emotions: healing, agency, desire, and dreams of a better future (Akinsola, 2001; Bailis & Chipperfield, 2012; Freire, 2006; Jacobs, 2005; Turner, 1995). Collective hope, "a shared desire for a better society" (Braithwaite, 2004, p. 146), can be contagious in community places (Chaffe, 2021). Having hope is significant because it provides physiological and psychological benefits, including increased happiness, reduced stress, positive emotions, and promotes healthy behavior (Lopez, 2013; Groopman, 2005). Hope is also significant because it can function as a source of aspirational capital—a resource for personal and societal change (Yosso, 2005). For hooks (2003), "hopefulness empowers us to continue our work for justice even as the forces of injustice may gain greater power for a time" (p. xiv).

References

Adler, R., Ross, J., Abbott, G., & Wallop, D. (2017). *Damn Yankees [musical score]*. Hal Leonard. (Original work published 1955)

Akinsola, H. A. (2001). Fostering hope in people living with aids in Africa: The role of primary health-care workers. *Australian Journal of Rural Health, 9*(4), 158–165.

Allen, L. (2015). Queering the academy: New directions in LGBT research in higher education. *Higher Education Research & Development, 34*(4), 681–684.

Bailis, D. S., & Chipperfield, J. G. (2012). Hope and optimism. In V. S. Ramachandran (Ed.), *Encyclopedia of human behaviour* (2nd ed., pp. 342–439). Elsevier.

Baldick, C. (2008). *The Oxford dictionary of literary terms* (3rd ed.). Oxford University Press.

Barnes, G. (2015). *Her turn on the stage: The role of women in musical theatre*. McFarland & Company.

Barthes, R. (1967). *The death of the author*. Aspen.

Bennett, S. (1997). *Theatre audiences: A theory of production and reception* (2nd ed.). Routledge.

Block, G. (2018). Integration. In R. Knapp, M. Morris, & S. Wolf (Eds.), *The Oxford handbook of the American musical* (2nd ed., pp. 153–176). Oxford.

Braithwaite, V. (2004). The hope process and social inclusion. *The Annals of the American Academy of Political and Social Science, 592*(1), 128–151.

Brass, J. (2014). Problematizing the public intellectual: Foucault, activism, and critical public pedagogy. In J. Burdick, J. A. Sandlin, & M. P. O'Malley (Eds.), *Problematizing public pedagogy* (pp. 115–128). Routledge.

The Broadway League. (2019). *The demographics of the Broadway audience NYC: 2018–2019*. www.broadwayleague.com/research/research-reports/

Browne, K., & Nash, C. J. (Eds.). (2016). Queer methods and methodologies: An introduction. In *Queer methods and methodologies: Intersecting queer theories and social science research* (pp. 1–23). Routledge.

Burdick, J., Sandlin, J. A., & O'Malley, M. P. (Eds.). (2014). *Problematizing public pedagogy*. Routledge.

Butler, J. (1988). Performative acts and gender constitution: An essay in phenomenology and feminist theory. *Theatre Journal, 40*(4), 519–531. https://doi.org/10.2307/3207893

Butler, J. (1990). *Gender trouble: Feminism and the subversion of identity*. Routledge.

Cantu, M. (2018). "The world belongs to the young?" Age and the golden age diva in *Coco* (1969) and *Applause* (1970). *Studies in Musical Theatre, 12*(1), 25–41.

Chaffe, A. (2021). *More than just theatre: Queer theatre festivals as sites of queer community building, learning, activism, and leadership* [Doctoral dissertation, University of Victoria]. UVicSpace. http://hdl.handle.net/1828/12530

Chaffe, A. (2022). Queer discourse: Queer theatre festivals as pedagogical sites. In R. Hawa (Ed.), *Proceedings of the CASAE/ACÉÉA 2022 annual conference/Conférence Annuelle* (pp. 64–73). www.casae-aceea.ca/conferences/

Charles, M., & Townsend, K. (2011). Full metal jarhead: Shifting the horizon of expectation: Full metal jarhead. *Journal of Popular Culture, 44*(5), 915–933. https://doi.org/10.1111/j.1540-5931.2011.00880.x

Charman, K., & Dixon, M. (2021). *Theory and methods for public pedagogy research*. Routledge.

Chin, M. (2017). Feelings, safe space, and LGBTQ of color community arts organizing. *Journal of Community Practice, 25*(3–4), 391–407. https://doi.org/10.1080/10705422.2017.1347119

Clum, J. M. (1999). *Something for the boys: Musical theater and gay culture*. St. Martin's Press.

Colleran, J. (2020). *Musical theatre and the LGBTQ+ audience: An interview with Patrick Pacheco*. Breaking Character: A Concord Theatricals Publication. www.breakingcharacter.com/home/2019/6/19/musical-theatre-and-the-lgbtq-audience-an-interview-with-patrick-pacheco

Crowley, M. (1968). *The boys in the band*. Samuel French, Inc.

Dilley, P. (1999). Queer theory: Under construction. *International Journal of Qualitative Studies in Education, 12*(5), 457–472.

Doty, A. (1993). *Making things perfectly queer: Interpreting mass culture*. University of Minnesota Press.

Finn, W., & Lapine, J. (1992). *Falsettos [musical score]*. Alfred Publishing. (Original work published 1992)

Freire, P. (2006). *Pedagogy of hope: Reliving pedagogy of the oppressed*. Bloomsbury.

Gedro, J. (2010). Understanding, designing, and teaching LGBT issues. *Advances in Developing Human Resources, 12*(3), 352–366.

Gelfand, R. (2018, March 2). Broadgay?: An examination of queer representation in musicals. *The OSA Telegraph*. www.osatelegraph.org/artmusic/broadgay-an-examination-of-queer-representation-in-musicals

Gowland, G. (2019). *"Standing in the shadows"? Reframing homosexuality in musical theatre* [Doctoral dissertation, University of Wolverhamton]. WIRE. http://hdl.handle.net/2436/623671

Gowlett, C., & Rasmussen, M. L. (2014). The cultural politics of queer theory in education research. *Discourse: Studies in the Cultural Politics of Education, 35*(3), 331–334.

Grace, A. P. (2008). Queer theory. In L. M. Given (Ed.), *The SAGE encyclopedia of qualitative research methods* (pp. 719–723). Sage.

Grace, A. P., & Hill, R. J. (2004). Positioning queer in adult education: Intervening in politics and praxis in North America. *Studies in the Education of Adults, 36*(2), 167–189.

Groopman, J. E. (2005). *The anatomy of hope: How patients prevail in the face of illness*. Random House Trade Paperbacks.

Habermas, J. (1989). Strukturwandel der Öffentlichkeit. In T. Burder & F. Lawrence (Trans.), *The structural transformation of the public sphere: An inquiry into a category of bourgeois society*. Polity Press. (Original work published 1962)

Hall, D. E. (2003). *Queer theories*. Palgrave Macmillan.

Halperin, D. M. (1995). *Saint Foucault: Towards a gay hagiography*. Oxford University Press.

Halperin, D. M. (2003). The normalization of queer theory. *Journal of Homosexuality, 45*(2–4), 339–343.

Halperin, D. M. (2012). *How to be gay*. Harvard University Press.

Harris, D. (1997). *The rise and fall of gay culture*. Hyperion.

Heide, F. J., Porter, N., & Saito, P. K. (2012). Do you hear the people sing? Musical theatre and attitude change. *Psychology of Aesthetics, Creativity, and the Arts, 6*(3), 224.

Herman, J., & Fierstein, H. (1983). *La cage aux folles [musical score]*. Hal Leonard. (Original work published 1983)

Hickey-Moody, A. (2014). Little public spheres. In J. Burdick, J. A. Sandlin, & M. P. O'Malley (Eds.), *Problematizing public pedagogy* (pp. 117–129). Routledge.

Hoffman, W. (2020). *The great white way: Race and the Broadway musical*. Rutgers University Press.

Holub, R. C. (1984). *Reception theory*. Routledge.

hooks, b. (2003). *Teaching community: A pedagogy of hope*. Routledge.

Isherwood, C. (1956). *The world in the evening: A novel*. Macmillan.

Jacobs, D. (2005). What's hope got to do with it? Theorizing hope in education. *JAC: A Journal of Composition Theory, 25*(4), 783–802.

Jagose, S. (2005). Queer theory. In C. Beasley (Ed.), *Gender and sexuality: Critical theories, critical thinkers* (pp. 161–174). Sage.

Jauss, H. R. (1982). *Toward an aesthetic of reception* (T. Bahti, Trans.). University of Minnesota Press.

Kantor, M., & Maslon, L. (2004). *Broadway: The American musical*. Bulfinch Press.

Katz-Buonincontro, J. (2011). Improvisational theatre as public pedagogy: A case study of "aesthetic" pedagogy in leadership development. *Policy Futures in Education, 9*(6), 769–779.

Kaufman, G., & Raphael, L. (1996). *Coming out of shame: Transforming gay and lesbian lives*. Doubleday.

Kenrick, J. (1996). Our love is here to stay VII: Stonewall & after. *Musicals101.com: The Cyber Encyclopedia of Musical Theatre, Film & Television*. www.musicals101.com/gay7.htm

Kenrick, J. (2017). *Musical theatre: A history*. Methuen Drama.

Kushner, T. (2018). Foreword: Notes toward a theater of the fabulous. In J. M. Clum (Ed.), *Staging gay lives: An anthology of contemporary gay theater* (pp. vii–xi). Routledge.

Larson, J. (2005). *Rent [musical score]*. Hal Leonard. (Original work published 1996)

Lauper, C., & Fierstein, H. (2013). *Kinky boots [musical score]*. Alfred Music. (Original work published 2012)

Lopez, S. J. (2013). *Making hope happen: Create the future you want for yourself and others*. Atria Paperback.

Lovelock, J. (2019). "What about love?" Claiming and reclaiming LGBTQ+ spaces in twenty-first century musical theatre. In S. Whitfield (Ed.), *Reframing the musical* (pp. 187–211). Red Globe Press.

Lovelock, J. M. (2016). *"Not just for gays anymore": Men, masculinities and musical theatre* [Doctoral dissertation, University of Brimingham, University of Birmingham Theses Repository]. http://etheses. bham.ac.uk/id/eprint/7533

Mackinlay, E. (2001). Performative pedagogy in teaching and learning Indigenous women's music and dance. *The Australian Journal of Indigenous Education, 29*(1), 12–21.

Marchia, J., & Sommer, J. M. (2019). (Re)defining heteronormativity. *Sexualities, 22*(3), 267–295. https://doi.org/10.1177/1363460717741801

Maudlin, J. G., & Sandlin, J. A. (2015). Pop culture pedagogies: Process and praxis. *Educational Studies, 51*(5), 368–384.

McMillin, S. (2014). *The musical as drama*. Princeton University Press.

Menken, A., Ashman, H., & Corman, R. (1985). *Little shop of horrors*. Samuel French, Inc.

Meyer, (2004). Reclaiming the discourse of camp. In H. Benshoff & S. Griffin (Eds.), *Queer cinema: Film reader* (pp. 137–150). Routledge.

Miller, D. A. (1998). *Place for us: Essay on the Broadway musical*. Harvard University Press.

Miranda, L.-M. (2016). *Hamilton: An American musical [musical score]*. Hal Leonard. (Original work published 2015)

Moore, M. (2018). *Fabulous: The rise of the beautiful eccentric*. Yale University Press.

O'Malley, M. P., Sandlin, J. A., & Burdick, J. (2020). Public pedagogy theories, methodologies, and ethics. In *Oxford research encyclopedia of education* (pp. 1–16). https://doi.org/10.1093/acrefore/9780190264093.013.1131

Pielichaty, H. (2015). Festival space: Gender, liminality and the carnivalesque. *International Journal of Event and Festival Management, 6*(3), 235–250.

Porter, C., Bolton, G., Wodehouse, P. G., & Lindsay, H., & Crouse, R. (1936). *Anything goes [musical score]*. Chappell & Co. (Original work published 1934)

Porter, C., Spewack, B., & Spewack, S. (1981). *Kiss me, Kate [musical score]*. Hal Leonard. (Original work published 1948)

Previn, A., & Lerner, A. J. (1969). *Coco [musical score]*. Unpublished musical score.

Rich, A. (1980). Compulsory heterosexuality and lesbian existence. *Signs: Journal of Women in Culture and Society, 5*(4), 631–660.

Salamon, G. (2021). Queer theory. In K. Q. Hall & Ásta (Eds.), *The Oxford handbook of feminist philosophy* (pp. 506–116). Oxford University Press. doi:10.1093/oxfordhb/9780190628925.013.42

Saldaña, J. (Ed.). (2005). *Ethnodrama: An anthology of reality theatre*. Rowman & Littlefield Publishers.

Sandlin, J. A., O'Malley, M. P., & Burdick, J. (2011). Mapping the complexity of public pedagogy scholarship: 1894–2010. *Review of Educational Research, 81*(3), 338–375.

Sandlin, J. A., Schultz, B. D., & Burdick, J. (Eds.). (2010). *Handbook of public pedagogy: Education and learning beyond schooling*. Routledge.

Sandlin, J. A., Wright, R. R., & Clark, M. C. (2013). Reexamining theories of adult learning and adult development through the lenses of public pedagogy. *Adult Education Quarterly, 63*(1), 2–23. https://doi.org/10.1177/0741713611415836

Savage, G. (2014). Chasing the phantoms of public pedagogy: Political, popular and concrete publics. In J. Burdick, J. A. Sandlin, & M. P. O'Malley (Eds.), *Problematizing public pedagogy* (pp. 79–90). Routledge.

Sedgwick, E. K. (1990). *Epistemology of the closet*. University of California Press.

Seidman, S. (1994). Queer pedagogy/queer-ing sociology. *Critical Sociology, 20*(3), 169–176.

Semega, J., Kollar, M., Shrider, E. A., & Creamer, J. (2020). *Income and poverty in the United States: 2019*. United States Census Bureau. www.census.gov/library/publications/2020/demo/p60-270.html

Snook, R. (2018, June 19). Trans performers are finally making it to Broadway. *TimeOut*. www.timeout. com/newyork/theater/trans-performers-are-finally-making-it-to-broadway

Sontag, S. (1978). *Against interpretation: And other essays*. Macmillan.

Sontag, S. (2002). Notes on "camp". In F. Cleto (Ed.), *Camp: Queer aesthetics and the performing subject: A reader* (pp. 53–65). The University of Michigan Press.

Stead, V., & Elliott, C. (2019). Pedagogies of power: Media artefacts as public pedagogy for women's leadership development. *Management Learning, 50*(2), 171–188.

Stewart, M., & Herman, J. (1982). *Hello, Dolly!* [*musical score*]. Hal Leonard. (Published 1964).

Strouse, C., Adams, L., Comden, B., & Green, A. (1970). *Applause* [*musical score*]. Edwin H. Morris. (Original work published 1970)

Styne, J., Sondheim, S., & Laurents, A. (1959). *Gypsy* [*musical score*]. Hal Leonard. (Original work published 1959)

Sullivan, N. (2003). *A critical introduction to queer theory*. New York University Press.

Taylor, J. (2012). *Playing it queer: Popular music, identity and queer world-making*. Peter Lang.

Tesori, J., & Kron, L. (2017). *Fun home* [*musical score*]. Samuel French, Inc. (Original work published 2013)

Thomas, J. (2015, June 5). Why is the theater so meaningful to gay people? *Slate Magazine*. https://slate.com/human-interest/2015/06/why-is-theater-so-meaningful-to-gay-people-broadway-s-jordan-roth-interviewed.html.

Thompson, C. (2020). LGBTQ+ representation in musical theatre. *Merge, 4*(6), 102–134.

Turner, F. (1995). *The culture of hope: A new birth of the classical spirit*. The Free Press.

Weiner, E. (2001). Making the pedagogical (re)turn: Henry Giroux's insurgent cultural pedagogy. *JAC: A Journal of Composition Theory, 21*(2), 434–451.

Weinzierl, F. (2016). Making a *Fun Home*: The performance of queer families in contemporary musical theater. *Current Objectives of Postgraduate American Studies, 17*(1). https://copas.uni-regensburg.de/article/view/255/335.

Whitfield, S. K. (2020). A space has been made: Bisexual+ stories in musical theatre. *Theatre Topics, 30*(2), E-5–E-12.

Wolf, J. M. (2013). Resurrecting camp: Rethinking the queer sensibility: Resurrecting camp. *Communication, Culture & Critique, 6*(2), 284–297.

Wolf, S. E. (2002). *A problem like Maria: Gender and sexuality in the American musical*. University of Michigan Press.

Wolf, S. E. (2006). "We'll always be bosom buddies": Female duets and the queering of Broadway musical theater. *GLQ: A Journal of Lesbian and Gay Studies, 12*(3), 351–376. doi:10.1215/10642684-2005-002.

Yosso, T. J. (2005). Whose culture has capital? A critical race theory discussion of community cultural wealth. *Race Ethnicity and Education, 8*(1), 69–91.

Zimmerman, B., & Haggerty, E. H. (2000). Introduction. In G. E. Haggerty (Ed.), *Gay histories and cultures: An encyclopedia* (pp. ix–xv). Garland.

21

NEGOTIATING AND COMMUNICATING LGBTQ+ IDENTITIES THROUGH DRESS AND LGBTQ+-FOCUSED FASHION BRANDS IN THE 21ST CENTURY

Kelly L. Reddy-Best, Andrew Reilly, and Kyra G. Streck

Kaiser (1997) described the *self* as "an individual's consciousness of being" (p. 146). In the dramaturgical perspective, the self is formed through the social interactions wherein the individual attempts to manage the impressions they present to society and learns the social mores (Goffman, 1959); therefore, the overarching idea of the self is formed through interactions with others and with society (Cooley, 1902; Mead, 1934). The self is developed throughout one's life; through socialization, the individual creates awareness of the self and one's identities for various social positions. *Identity* refers to the "organized set of characteristics an individual perceives as representing or defining the self in a given social situation" (Kaiser, 1990, p. 186). That is, our multiple and sometimes conflicting identities (e.g., race, gender, sexuality, ability, body size and shape, and/or religion) that make up the self are deeply interconnected to our social contexts (Bourdieu, 1990; Entwistle, 2000; Goffman, 1959). One way we communicate our varying identities is through dress (Davis, 1992; Kaiser, 1997, 2012; Lennon et al., 2017). In this chapter, we review the ways through which dress is used to negotiate identities within the LGBTQ+ community and how entrepreneurs have recently responded by creating numerous LGBTQ+-focused fashion brands and products.

Dress refers to "an assemblage of modifications of the body and/or supplements to the body" (Roach-Higgins & Eicher, 1992, p. 1). The term dress is much more encompassing than clothing or accessories because it includes both body modifications and supplements. *Modifications* refers to changes to hair, skin, or nails, whereas *supplements* can refer to enclosures, attachments to the body, attachments to enclosures, or handheld objects. Although the terms appearance, adornment, apparel, clothing, costume, and fashion may be used interchangeably, they all fall under the comprehensive umbrella term dress, as defined in Roach-Higgins and Eicher's (1992) seminal paper in the fashion studies discipline.

Entwistle (2000) further argued the importance of the body in context with the development of the concept *situated bodily practice*; she proposed "it is through our bodies that we come to see and be seen in the world" and that "the body forms the envelope of our being

DOI: 10.4324/9781003128151-25

in the world, and our selfhood comes from this location in body and our experience of this" (p. 334). She elaborated that the physical body on which dress is enacted is an important aspect of understanding dress and identity negotiations (Entwistle, 2000). The living, fleshy body and the physical actions it engages in interact constantly with the materiality of the dress and the meanings constructed through the dress—all occurring in a way that cannot be disentangled (Entwistle, 2000; Kaiser, 2012).

Within the fashion studies field, much has been written about the ways different individuals or communities negotiate their identities through dress, particularly those in positions of power and privilege (e.g., White, heterosexual, able-bodied individuals). In this chapter, we explore the scholarship examining the intersections of the LGBTQ+ community, identity negotiations, and dress, which is an area that comparatively has received much less attention in the broader fashion studies field. Therefore, the purpose of this chapter is to review past literature in which scholars have examined how dress is used as a communicative tool to negotiate varying identities in the LGBTQ+ community. However, doing so is a tricky process because significant nuance lies in identity and the scholarship is not necessarily provided in clear categories, given identity's fluidity and complexity. Therefore, while we present the work under the different stable headings outlined in the following, we note when tensions arise in the literature. Overall, the plethora of work written on these topics dissolves the stereotype that there is one monolithic aesthetic or style for different LGBTQ+ identities.

Lesbian Identities and Dress

In a survey of mainstream popular press articles in the United States from 1960s to the 2010s, publications featured mostly White, thin, feminine lesbian aesthetics and styles (Reddy-Best & Jones, 2020). These mainstream representations lacked the nuance, tension (Kaiser, 2012), and variety of styles that lesbian-identifying women have embraced over time. Many of these styles are intricately related to gender negotiations; however, lesbian styles expand beyond the stereotypical notion of butch and femme often perpetuated in media.

Early documented evidence of women's styles in same-gender relationships dates to the 18th century. Elanor Butler and Sarah Ponsonby, two Anglo-Irish women aristocrats who were thought to have been in a love relationship, often adopted a masculine style of clothing; more specifically, they routinely adopted riding habits or equestrian outfits comprised of a masculine-style jacket and long skirt, which was considered a subversive act because the outfits they wore for riding were not customarily worn by women at that time (Wilson, 2013). Anne Lister, a wealthy White woman from Yorkshire who died in the late 19th century, wrote in her diaries of her desires and relationships with other "mannish women," and Lister also embraced an eccentric, masculine style of the time (Wilson, 2013, p. 171). In the 1928 novel *The Well of Loneliness*, author Radclyffe Hall crafted a lesbian identity in a masculine aesthetic (Geczy & Karaminas, 2013). Additionally, photographs by Albert Harlingue from the 1920s of women at Le Monocle, a lesbian club in Paris, depicted White-appearing women in the popular *garçonne* look, a fashionable women's style in larger society (Farrell-Beck & Parsons, 2007), "which was characterized by an absence of feminine curves and very short hairstyles" (Steele, 2013, pp. 26–27). Harlingue's images also featured women in highly feminine styles and wearing bias-cut dresses with a formfitting silhouette, longer hair, and makeup. Faderman (1991) discussed lesbian-dress aesthetics in the early part of the 20th century and explored these recognizable masculine and feminine norms, frequently referred to as "butch" and "femme," which she argued emerged in 1940s bar culture, where butch and femme lesbians congregated. The popular novel *Stone Butch Blues* by Leslie Feinberg gave vivid descriptors of the mid-20th century butches and femmes. For example, Jess, the main character, related their experience when first entering a bar in Niagara Falls:

> What I saw there released tears I'd held back for years: strong, burly women wearing ties and suit coats. Their hair was slicked back. They were the handsomest women I'd ever seen. Some of them were wrapped in slow motion dances with women in tight dresses and high heels who touched them tenderly. Just watching made me ache with need.
>
> *(Feinberg, 1993, p. 28)*

Rothblum (1994) argued that lesbian communities have adopted styles and aesthetics that differ from those of mainstream society. One of the ways this has manifested is through embracing and negotiating a masculine aesthetic, sometimes referred to as butch. The butch, masculine-lesbian style is often recognizable within as well as outside the lesbian community (Maltry & Tucker, 2002; Taylor, 2007). A butch aesthetic may include comfortable shoes, little or no makeup, tattoos and piercings, alternative-style haircuts or hair colors, and masculine-leaning garments or accessories (Clarke & Spence, 2013; Clarke & Turner, 2007; Esterberg, 1996; Reddy-Best & Pedersen, 2014, 2015; Rothblum, 1994, 2010). While different lesbian styles, including the butch aesthetic, are often considered uniform, women adopt a masculine style in complex and varied ways (Levitt & Hiestand, 2004; McLean, 2008). For example, in Reddy-Best and Goodin's (2020) research, their participant, Cyndi—a White, lesbian-identifying woman—claimed that her overall style was masculine-leaning but said she felt like a "delicate flower on the inside" and preferred the phrase "soft butch" (p. 125). In Blake's (2019) work, she analyzed Black androgynous lesbians from North Carolina:

> [I am] hesitant to essentialize Black lesbian styles of dress . . . instead of naming these gender presentations Black lesbian style, I call these articulations of Black lesbian androgyny *BlaQueer* Style because they represent—rather than essentialize—the racial and class politics illuminated by their dress.
>
> *(p. 11)*

Blake (2019) outlined the ways these women embraced masculinity and tensions surrounding their multiple subjectivities, with emphasis on their Black identity. Lane-Steele's (2011) work examined studs, or Black lesbians who embrace masculinity; the studs she interviewed relayed that they dressed similar to their Black male peers with "baggy pants and shirts, hats, high top shoes, Timberland boots, and fairly flashy jewelry" (p. 484). Lane-Steele (2011) drew connections between these women's styles and "protest masculinity" (p. 483) which Connell and Messerschmidt (2009) defined as

> [the] pattern of masculinity constructed in local working-class settings, sometimes among ethnically marginalized men, which embodies the claim to power typical of regional hegemonic masculinities in Western countries, but which lacks the economic resources and institutional authority that underpins the regional and global patterns.
>
> *(p. 848)*

One way that protest masculinity surfaces is through a hyper-masculine aesthetic—such as the one these Black lesbian women embraced.

In addition, much research has analyzed feminine-leaning aesthetics, sometimes referred to as femme, high-femme, or lipstick lesbian styles or identities. Feminine-leaning lesbians may adopt long hair, makeup, and feminine-coded clothing such as dresses or high heels (Hemmings, 1999; Levitt et al., 2003; Levitt & Hiestand, 2004; Levitt & Horne, 2002; Maltry & Tucker, 2002). Because of the long-standing association between femininity and heterosexuality, feminine-leaning lesbians are often misread as straight (Huxley et al., 2014; Levitt et al., 2003) and can experience assertions of not being "queer enough" within the LGBTQ+ community (Reddy-Best & Goodin, 2020). They may hide their lesbian identity until they are physically with their masculine-leaning partner (Rossiter, 2016).

While many folks adopt and embrace these stereotypical aesthetics that are thought to have developed out of the mid-20th century, there have been significant critiques and rejections of these styles altogether. As social movements gained traction in the latter part of the 20th century, some criticized these feminine- and masculine-leaning aesthetics for producing a heteronormative performance (Walker, 1993). In Freitas et al.'s (1996) study, participants related that they did not want to limit themselves to one particular type of style. Additionally, Hammidi and Kaiser (1999) theorized that there was no single way to imagine beauty for lesbian women, and these negotiations are intertwined with ambivalence and tensions in everyday life. This notion is evident in a recent *New York Times* article titled "Hipsters Broke My Gaydar," in which Burton (2016) asserted, "You're all lesbians now, America . . . I'm sorry. But mostly for myself. Because it's hard to tell who's queer now" (paras. 23 & 25).

Gay Identities and Dress

Because of the stigmatization and criminalization of homosexual behavior in much of European–American modern history, gay men have frequently adopted coded simulacra to display their gay identity. These symbols have included adorning one's lapel with green carnations and wearing red neckties or suede shoes. As legal progress has been made and the social climate for the LGBTQ+ community improved, the symbols shifted from knowledge among the few to commonplace, as in the case of dress that now includes rainbow flags, the inverted pink triangle, or an earring worn in the right ear (Cole, 2000; Reilly, 2010).

During the early modern gay liberation movement, gay men were mostly divided into two ideologies on how to present themselves through dress: to embrace traditional masculine gender presentation or to subvert it (Edwards, 1994). Cole (2013) noted the Gay Liberation Front of the 1970s employed genderfuck aesthetics, combining stereotypical masculine and feminine clothes, makeup, and styling into one form to subvert Western binary gender expectations in Britain and the United States to combat, question, and highlight gender's artificial nature. These two philosophies and tensions—to embrace traditional Western gender presentation or to disrupt it—continue in contemporary post-postmodern forms of androgyny (Barry & Reilly, 2020).

The conflict over how to present one's self resulted in the "butch shift" where gay men developed dress styles based on masculine archetypes (Humphries, 1985), such as leather men, bears, and Castro clones. Bears, noted for their hirsute, either muscular or husky/large/fat and blue-collar representation of masculinity, became visible in the 1980s during the early AIDS crisis and were eroticized for their perceived health as compared to the emaciated appearance of those suffering in the latter stages of AIDS. Mosher et al. (2006) argued that leather identity is socially constructed and performative and both "bear and leather aesthetics can be understood as expressions of culturally valued traits and as a reconciliation of masculine and gay identities" (pp. 119–120). Cole (2000) noted that the clones style emerged from American cowboy and blue-collar dress (e.g., jeans, plaid shirts, cowboy boots, construction boots, Levi 501 button fly jeans, T-shirts, short hair, and mustaches) and was symbolic of "toughness, virility, aggression, strength, [and] potency" (p. 128), although Levine (1998) argued that the look was parody. Although clone aesthetics were patterned after heterosexual masculine styles, a knowing gay consciousness acknowledged that the outfits were coordinated, perfected, and worn to show off the male physique. Cole (2000) further argued the clone image of masculinity influenced other gay men's styles, including "queer nation" and "act-up" looks (e.g., T-shirts and jeans), gay skinheads, and gay rockabillies. The clone style assisted in redefining gay men as masculine. Other gay subcultures that embrace masculine aesthetics include muscle boys, scallies, and homothugs (Cole, 2008).

In contrast to masculine archetypes, other gay men, such as drag queens and punks, embraced camp, feminine, or androgynous aesthetics, including makeup and jewelry. Contemporarily, a result of the butch shift has been the tendency among some gay men to embrace femininity (Reilly, 2022) and to incorporate apparel items marketed to both men and women into their wardrobe (Barry & Reilly, 2020; Moore [Sic], 2020). Per Barry and Martin (2015), gay men view contemporary aesthetics as more varied than previous generations, and gender identity, sexual orientation, and race intersect not only to express individuality but also to challenge binary gender norms by mixing traditionally feminine and masculine fabrics, textures, products, and other signifiers (Barry & Martin, 2016). Clarke and Turner (2007) similarly argued that clothing is used to negotiate gay identity, but it is also used to express individuality; thus, there may be expectations when one "comes out" to dress a certain way, but enough room exists in the unwritten rules of gay aesthetics to show one's persona in a multitude of ways.

Gay men adopted other items that included a sailor's uniform and sneakers. In England and France between the world wars, gay and bisexual men adopted the sailor's uniform because of the outfit's association with masculinity and voracious sexuality and its figure-revealing fit and silhouette. Use of the style faded when the sailor uniform was adapted into mainstream fashion (Stephenson, 2016). Scott (2011) proposed that sneakers were important to gay men in three ways. First, sneakers can be viewed as feminine and are thus discouraged if one wants to appear masculine (e.g., biker and leather subcultures eschew sneakers and favor boots). Second, sneakers can be viewed as masculine among middle-class gay men and, as part of the butch shift, or as gay men assimilated (e.g., jocks and straight-acting mainstream masculinity). Third, sneakers are considered masculine but fetishized, as in the example of working-class subcultures or gay skinheads.

Much of the research on gay men's dress has been conducted on White men, leaving significant opportunities for future research on other races and ethnicities. However, the research that has been conducted has yielded important findings. Cole's (2019) work on gay Black men in Britain and the United States found that gay Black men note attention to detail as important, considering age, race, class, and how one wanted to present oneself with consideration of time and place: "What constitutes gay men's style and what constitutes *Black* gay men's style raises questions about whether it is possible to identify gay styles broadly and black gay styles specifically at this time" (p. 54). Drummond (2005) argued that gay Asian men have different styles of clothes for home, straight/mainstream, and gay spheres. Tan (2019) documented the dissemination of the bear style from the United States to Japan, through Northeast Asia, and into Taiwan and found bears in Taiwan cultivate their look to achieve sexual capital by using clothes—such as tank tops or bright colors on sleeves and torsos of shirts—to draw attention to their thick or beefy bodies. Finally, Horton's (2020) research on the regulation of flamboyant dress (or fabulousness) in India, from within its own gay communities, argued that dress has become politicized: a matter of respectability politics rather than one of enjoyment of pushing boundaries.

Bisexual Identities and Dress

Some scholars have focused their research specifically on the ways in which bisexual-identifying individuals negotiate their identity through dress. Taub (2003) surveyed mostly White, bisexual-identifying women and reported a variety of ways these women fashioned their bodies; in their responses, there was significant discussion of negotiating societal gender norms and stereotypical lesbian appearance norms. Some of these women rejected dominant culture's norms and created "personalized and affirming beauty ideas and practices" (Taub, 2003, p. 21), whereas others felt pressure to conform to lesbian norms such as the "soft butch" aesthetic (p. 21).

Hartman (2013) conducted interviews with mostly White, bisexual-identifying women. Participants frequently relayed a desire to make themselves visual as bisexual in public settings because of their belief that society often deems them invisible, sometimes referred to as bi-erasure (for discussions of bisexual invisibility, see Bradford, 2004; Firestein, 1996; Fox, 1995; Tabatabai & Linders, 2011). Participants used the terms attitude, androgyny, and a hybrid of heterosexual and homosexual aesthetics to describe a bisexual display, and participants placed significant emphasis on gender negotiations through style. The participants described that their use of overt pride aesthetics, such as pins or slogan T-shirts—particularly those with the bi-pride colors (pink, blue, and purple). Although Hartman's (2013) participants articulated specific aesthetics to highlight their bisexual identity, they also expressed that it was "difficult to pin down such a description" (p. 49). Similarly, other researchers found a lack of distinct dress aesthetics for bisexual individuals (Clarke & Spence, 2013; Clarke & Turner, 2007; Hayfield, 2011; Hayfield et al., 2013; Holliday, 1999; Huxley et al., 2014).

In a follow-up study, Hartman-Linck (2014) discussed the importance of bisexual signifiers in private or intimate spaces such as around close friends or family. Although not on the body directly, her participants related using aesthetics of the home, such as magnets or artwork with lesbian symbols, to signify their identity. Artwork or magnets are arguably not "hand-held objects" (Roach-Higgins & Eicher, 1992, p. 1), yet they are debatably an extension of the body in the context of these private spheres.

In one of the most recent studies, Daly et al. (2018) again examined bisexual women's appearance and dress. Similar to the aforementioned studies, the bisexual participants' appearance markers conformed to stereotypical lesbian aesthetics (or masculine-leaning styles), or they adopted mainstream gender norms by using feminine signifiers. The participant's partner's gender often motivated adoption of various styles. For example, some women in same-gender relationships adopted feminine aesthetics to avoid others assuming that they are identified as lesbian.

Duffin (2016) interviewed African American men who were behaviorally bisexual but chose to identify as straight and described themselves as "on the down low" or "DL" (p. 484). The down low or DL phenomenon is significant in the Black community because of the stigmatization of homosexuality; the phrase emerged in rap music lyrics in the 1990s (Cohen, 1999) and has been discussed in other popular press articles (Denizet-Lewis, 2014). In Duffin's (2016) work, dress was not the research's primary focus, but in one part of the results, he reported that men often associated femininity with being gay. That is, these bisexually behaving men asserted their masculinity by wearing baggy or other stereotypically masculine styles. By contrast, one participant defined being gay as wearing "tight clothes, swish[ing] up and down the street, [and] act[ing] like a girl" (Duffin, 2016, p. 499).

Trans, Genderqueer, and Nonbinary Identities and Dress

Dress of trans and nonbinary (TNB) individuals can conform to cisgender stereotypes in an effort to pass and/or challenge notions of femininity and masculinity to appear visibly TNB. Appearances that challenge binary gender constructions by combining or negating feminine and masculine aesthetics are often interchangeably referred to as genderqueer, genderfuck, genderless, nonbinary, or unisex (Beemyn, 2015). Some people may want to appear more cisgender (or "passing"), and some may want to appear more TNB (Allen, 2010); however, TNB expression is less binary. Furthermore, TNB individuals continually negotiate their gender performance (Butler, 1990) and may engage in "shape shifting" or altering their appearance depending on the situation (McGuire et al., 2016). Numerous factors influence gender presentation. For example, some individuals may wish to appear cisgender because it can lead to correct gender identification by others or avoid dangerous situations (Garfinkel, 1967; Schrock et al., 2009; Snorton, 2009). Being visibly TNB can also allow individuals to promote visibility and challenge cultural assumptions about gender. Dress is additionally used to camouflage body parts individuals may feel do not align with their gender identity or to highlight and reveal body parts that align with their gender identity (Corwin, 2009; McGuire et al., 2016; Reilly et al., 2019).

McGuire and Reilly (2022) developed an "aesthetic identity" framework using a combination of aesthetic, gender, and human development theories to study TNB clothing choices. Their model incorporates performativity and safety aspects of presentation; sensory, cognitive, and emotional aspects of clothing; exploration and commitment; scaffolding and feedback; and role-making and role-taking. McGuire and Reilly (2022) argued:

> As individuals mature in their sense of transforming gender identity, they will consolidate their aesthetic identity and begin to take on gendered social roles (role taking) that they will adapt (role making). The gendered aesthetic identity will be a way of claiming and shaping an individual's placement within a gender role, as well as making meaning of that gender role for themselves and others.
>
> *(n.p.)*

Rahilly (2015) suggested that TNB people are often forced to wear clothing that is physically or psychologically uncomfortable. However, the majority of participants were White (Rahilly, 2015), so these feelings may not be applicable to all racial and cultural backgrounds. Still, apparel designed for cisgender bodies may not fit TNB bodies appropriately. Mass-produced (ready-to-wear) clothing items often do not meet TNB individuals' functional and aesthetic needs. Reilly et al. (2019) identified three themes some TNB people associate with searching for clothing: fit, cut, and sizing issues with mainstream ready-to-wear clothing; desire to hide body parts that reveal a TNB identity with clothing; and desire to reveal body parts "to celebrate or show pride in one's body and a design to highlight bodily changes post gender confirmation treatment" (p. 12). The study's participants were diverse in racial and ethnic identities (Reilly et al., 2019), suggesting that these themes reflect experiences of TNB people regardless of race. With regard to mass-produced apparel, some TNB individuals may employ tailoring services. Additionally, with the growing visibility of TNB individuals, some clothing brands are responding to TNB consumers' needs by offering apparel designed specifically for the TNB market (e.g., FtM Detroit, Official Rebrand, Saint Harridan, and Transguy Supply).

Catalpa and McGuire (2020) found that dress contributes to Serano's (2007) "mirror epiphany" or the first encounter with one's authentic self. "Dress helps transpersons make a conscious connection between how they imagined themselves and the material reality of their physical presence" (Catalpa & McGuire, 2020, p. 57). Moreover, TNB individuals may employ tattoos as a sign of self-acceptance, to connect with their body, to mark their identity, or to celebrate physical changes to the body (McGuire et al., 2016; McGuire & Chrisler, 2016).

LGBTQ+ Activism and Dress

From the middle of the 20th century to the present, dress has been an important component of LGBTQ+ activism in North America. Many of the previously mentioned styles *are* arguably forms of activism. For example, in the 1950s, the butch style subverted the societal expectation that all women had to be gentle, passive, and feminine (Stein, 1998). Although the femme/butch dichotomy had been prominent since the late 19th century (Griffin, 2017), it waned in the 1970s because many feminists argued femme–butch relationships mimicked heterosexual dynamics (Blackman & Perry, 1990). In the 1970s, many lesbian revolutionary feminists encouraged anti-fashion. They associated makeup, high heels, and formfitting dresses with heteropatriarchal femininity and capitalism, from which they wanted to distance themselves visually and ideologically (Clark, 1995; Stein, 1998). More ascetic styles became popular among White lesbian feminists, and lesbian feminists of color incorporated racial or ethnic dress as activist statements (Stein, 1998). Despite ascetic aesthetics being the dominant lesbian feminist rhetoric, butch and femme presentations persisted. Femmes were derided for "passing," but many used their femininity to stay safe and infiltrate traditionally heterosexual geographies (Blackman & Perry, 1990). After women's liberation lost traction, lesbian feminists became less concerned with avoiding consumerism, and their styles became more diverse, further embracing punk, roots, and sadism/masochism (S/M) (Blackman & Perry, 1990; Stein, 1998). Gay men struggled with a similar tension from the 1960s to today, often being labeled as effeminate and inferior to masculine heterosexual men. Some embraced the stereotype, using it to bring attention to problems with gender roles through "genderfuck." However, as the Gay Liberation Front struggled for legitimacy, gay leaders started to denounce drag queens and political drag (Hillman, 2015).

In the 1980s and 1990s, the AIDS crisis triggered a new trend in LGBTQ+ activist dress. In his seminal work, Katz (2013) explored lesbian, gay, and queer activists' fashion through analysis of slogan T-shirts; however, his work lacked an intersectional lens. For example, ACT UP used the slogan T-shirt to identify activists as a collective force. First used in the 1960s to advocate for candidates, the LGBT community quickly adopted the slogan T-shirt. ACT UP activists were outraged by the lack of media attention given to HIV/AIDS, so large protests in which everyone wore slogan T-shirts created a powerful visual message irresistible to news outlets (Katz, 2013). Katz (2013) suggested that this unity represented a fundamental switch from lesbian or gay ideologies to a more universal queer ideology and posited slogan T-shirts as part of the "development of historically queer modes of resistance like camp as self-consciously activist strategies" (p. 227).

On many of the LGBTQ+ slogan T-shirts produced, an upside-down triangle is used as a sign of solidarity. The use of this sign symbolically refers to when the Nazi party came into power in 1933. Almost 100,000 gay men were arrested and sent to concentration camps, where they were forced to wear a pink triangle on their prison uniform (Elman, 1996; Kaiser, 2012). The pink triangle is often used as a sign of activism—for example, on the graduation stoles used for lavender graduation, a ceremony at universities specifically for the LGBTQ+ community (Reddy-Best & Goodin, 2020). A brief survey of Wearing Gay History (n.d.), the "home to the digitized t-shirt collections of numerous lesbian, gay, bisexual, and transgender archives across the United States," revealed the use of the pink triangle on slogan T-shirts has been significant throughout history.

Today, oppression created by neoliberalism and the new Right in the United States heavily influences queer and trans activist dress. Barry and Drak (2019) approached activist fashion through a "hacking" lens (Von Busch, 2009). They created a two-day hacking workshop where queer and trans public high-school students were provided with materials and asked to refashion a garment or accessory to express their identities. All the students considered themselves to have multiple marginalized identities, which many displayed through their garment. For example, one student painted "psycho" on a T-shirt to reclaim the pejorative hurled at her by classmates because she was identified as autistic and lesbian (Barry & Drak, 2019). LGBTQ+ activist clothing is now sold on the Internet. The Asexual Visibility and Education Network, a website fostering community for asexual people, had between 19,000 and 30,000 members as of 2010. The site also hosts a store where people can purchase asexuality-themed novelty items (Cerankowski & Milks, 2010).

LGBTQ+ activists in South Africa have also utilized dress. Milani and Kapa (2015) analyzed how T-shirts from the Transformation and Employment Equity Office at the University of the Witwatersrand (or Wits) evolved between 2011 and 2014. For the annual pride parade, Wits designed T-shirts for students to wear. The T-shirts served to both identify the office's patrons and communicate its mission. Milani and Kapa (2015) argued that the T-shirt graphics have pivoted according to Wits's changing ideologies. They claimed that the T-shirt from 2011 portrayed the ambivalence one may have when reconciling their LGBTQ+ identity; the slogan "It's For All Of Us," printed in white on black, is ambiguous, allowing space for identity ambivalence. However, the 2012 T-shirt design was much more assertive, proclaiming, "STOP SEXUAL APARTHEID." The shirt was dyed pink, possibly alluding to the pink triangle symbol Nazis forced on homosexuals during the Holocaust. In 2013, the shirt read "Being Me," suggesting optimism and individualism. The final T-shirt analyzed was from 2014, and its large multicolored graphic illustrated the multiple identities recognized by its text: "All Oppression Is Connected" (Milani & Kapa, 2015).

The Fashion Industry and LGBTQ+ Identities

In the 2010s, there was a significant emergence of queer-focused brands in the fashion industry selling a variety of different products such as suit and suit coordinates, sportswear, accessories, swimwear, shoes, and undergarments or other objects worn near or against the skin (Reddy-Best et al., 2020; Reddy-Best, 2017, 2020; Reddy-Best & Goodin, 2018). Many of these brands garnered widespread attention in 2016 when HBO released *Suited*, a documentary about Bindle & Keep—a Brooklyn, New York-based company that produces suits and suit coordinates for gender nonconforming people. Many of Bindle & Keep's clients described feeling—for the first time in their life—comfortable in their suit and even liking the way they looked in the mirror (Benjamin, 2016). Because many LGBTQ+ individuals push gender boundaries in their dress, they often have difficulty shopping for clothes that fit their bodies and desired gender and/or sexual presentations (Pierre, 2020; Reddy-Best & Pedersen, 2015); many of these queer-focused fashion brands emerged to address these issues.

Many of the entrepreneurs who started these businesses cited entering the industry because they were unable to find clothing that fit themselves or their partners (Benjamin, 2016; Reddy-Best, 2020; Reddy-Best et al., 2020). For example, Thúy of Thúy Custom Clothier asserted that they could personally empathize with their clients and the inability to find masculine-leaning clothes, and this ability to empathize has created a trusted shopping environment for their customers (Reddy-Best et al., 2020). Bindle & Keep designer Rae Tutera recalled their first suit: "I just never felt so good about myself before. . . . It was just such a powerful experience for me. I couldn't help but want to take it and adapt it to a landscape that welcomed people like me" (Benjamin, 2016, 5:14). Some brand owners may not personally have difficulty finding clothing, but a loved one might. For example, Abby Sugar was inspired to start Play Out because her ex-wife was unable to find masculine-style underwear (Reddy-Best et al., 2020).

The development of the Internet and the increase in LGBT+ rights in the United States were catalysts for the creation of some brands. For example, Saint Harridan, now closed, developed alongside the legalization of same-sex marriage and the need for masculine-leaning wedding attire for gender nonconforming individuals (Reddy-Best, 2020). Additionally, with the changing retail landscape and the boost in e-commerce, designers are no longer required to pitch to wholesale buyers or generate the overhead to build and sustain a storefront (Worsley, 2011). Therefore, these brands can enter the market with little to no capital investment. Social media has also allowed brands to target and attract customers (Reddy-Best et al., 2020). For example, Rebirth Garments—a company that designs garments and accessories that promote queerness, disability, and fat identities—sells products from its Etsy store and accepts orders via direct messages on social media (Reddy-Best & Goodin, 2018). These virtual spaces have also allowed brands to politicize fashion by circulating imagery that challenges larger hegemonic gender norms. For example, Saint Harridan worked with Miki Vargas, a queer-fashion photographer, to capture gender-boundary-pushing aesthetics. As these images circulated on Saint Harridan's social media, discussions often focused on "gender and identity politics," "shifting ideologies surrounding gender," and "signs of solidarity with other groups experiencing oppression," such as people of color (Reddy-Best, 2020, p. 99).

Unfortunately, several brands have since closed (e.g., Saint Harridan stopped operations only four years after its founding in 2012 because of a lack of capital investment; Reddy-Best, 2020). Overall, these brands reflect the numerous ways individuals in the LGBTQ+ community fashion their bodies and will largely have a lasting impact as trailblazers of the queer-fashion brands movement in the early part of the 21st century.

Conclusion

Overall, it is evident from the literature that individuals in the LGBTQ+ community fashion their bodies as well as multiple and shifting identities in unique and varied ways. However, much of the work reviewed highlights that gender presentation and negotiations are often central to LGBTQ+ dress. Although scholars working in the area of dress and the LGBTQ+ community have examined numerous identity intersections, much of the literature focuses on White, able-bodied, and thin individuals and communities highlighting the need for more work on LGBTQ+ communities of color, Indigenous people, fat bodies, and disabled bodies.

References

Allen, M. P. (2010). Connecting body and mind: How transgender people changed their self-image. *Women & Performance, 20*(3), 267–283. https://doi.org/10.1080/0740770X.2010.529248

Barry, B., & Drak, D. (2019). Intersectional interventions into queer and trans liberation: Youth resistance against right-wing populism through fashion hacking. *Fashion Theory, 23*(6), 679–709. https://doi.org/10.1080/1362704x.2019.1657260

Barry, B., & Martin, D. (2015). Dapper dudes: Young men's fashion consumption and expressions of masculinity. *Critical Studies in Men's Fashion, 2*(1), 5–21. https://doi.org/10.1386/csmf.2.1.5_1

Barry, B., & Martin, D. (2016). Gender revels: Inside the wardrobes of young gay men with subversive style. *Fashion, Style & Popular Culture, 3*(2), 225–250. https://doi.org/10.1386/fspc.3.2.225_1

Barry, B., & Reilly, A. (2020). Gender more: An intersectional perspective on men's transgression of the gender dress binary. In A. Reilly & B. Barry (Eds.), *Crossing boundaries: Fashion to deconstruct and reimagine gender* (pp. 122–136). Intellect Books.

Beemyn, B. G. (2015). *Genderqueer. GLBTQ: An encyclopedia of gay, lesbian, bisexual, transgender, and queer culture.* www.glbtqarchive.com/ssh/genderqueer_S.pdf

Benjamin, J. (Director). (2016). *Suited* [Film]. A Casual Romance Productions.

Blackman, I., & Perry, K. (1990). Skirting the issue: Lesbian fashion for the 1990s. *Feminist Review, 34*(1), 67–78. https://doi.org/10.2307/1395306

Blake, D. A. (2019). "It ain't he, it ain't she, it's we." *Dress: The Journal of the Costume Society of America, 45*(1), 1–21. https://doi.org/10.1080/03612112.2019.1559529

Bourdieu, P. (1990). *Distinction: A social critique of the judgment of taste.* Harvard University Press.

Bradford, M. (2004). The bisexual experience: Living in a dichotomous culture. *Journal of Bisexuality, 4*(1–2), 7–23. https://doi.org/10.1300/J159v04n01_02

Burton, K. (2016, December 31). Lesbians invented hipsters. *The New York Times.* www.nytimes.com/2016/12/31/opinion/sunday/hipsters-broke-my-gaydar.html

Butler, J. (1990). *Gender trouble: Feminism and the subversion of identity.* Routledge.

Catalpa, J. M., & McGuire, J. K. (2020). Mirror epiphany: Transpersons' use of dress to create and sustain their affirmed gender identities. In A. Reilly & B. Barry (Eds.), *Crossing boundaries: Fashion to deconstruct and reimagine gender* (pp. 47–59). Intellect Books.

Cerankowski, K. J., & Milks, M. (2010). New orientations: Asexuality and its implications for theory and practice. *Feminist Studies, 36*(3), 650–664. https://doi.org/10.2307/27919126

Clark, D. (1995). Commodity lesbianism. In E. K. Creekmur & A. Doty (Eds.), *Out in culture* (pp. 484–500). Duke University Press. https://doi.org/10.2307/j.ctv1220htt.35

Clarke, V., & Spence, K. (2013). Will the real lesbian please stand up? Constructing and resisting visible non-heterosexual identities through dress and appearance. *Psychology of Sexuality, 4*(1), 25–33. https://doi.org/10.1080/19419899.2013.748240

Clarke, V., & Turner, K. (2007). Clothes maketh the queer? Dress, appearance and the construction of lesbian, gay and bisexual identities. *Feminism & Psychology, 17*(2), 267–276. https://doi.org/10.1177/0959353507076561

Cohen, C. J. (1999). *Boundaries of blackness: AIDS and the breakdown of Black politics.* University of Chicago Press.

Cole, S. (2000). *Don we now our gay apparel: Gay men's dress in the twentieth century.* Berg.

Cole, S. (2008). Butch queens in macho drag: Gay men, dress, and subcultural identity. In A. Reilly & S. Cosbey (Eds.), *Men's fashion reader* (pp. 279–294). Fairchild.

Cole, S. (2013). Queerly visible: Gay men's dress and style 1960–2012. In V. Steele (Ed.), *A queer history of fashion: From the closet to the catwalk* (pp. 135–166). Yale University Press.

Cole, S. (2019). The difference is in the detail: Negotiation black gay male style in the twenty-first century. *Dress: The Journal of the Costume Society of America, 45*(1), 39–54. https://doi.org/10.1080/03612112.2019.1557833

Connell, R. W., & Messerschmidt, J. (2009). Hegemonic masculinity: Rethinking the concept. *Gender & Society, 19*(6), 829–859. https://doi.org/10.1177/0891243205278639

Cooley, C. H. (1902). *Human nature and social order.* Charles Scribner's Sons.

Corwin, A. I. (2009). Language and gender variance: Constructing gender beyond the male/female binary. *Electronic Journal of Human Sexuality, 12.* Retrieved December 7, 2017 from http://mail.ejhs.org/Volume12/Gender.htm

Daly, S. J., King, N., & Yeadon-Lee, T. (2018). "Femme it up or dress it down": Appearance and bisexual women in monogamous relationships. *Journal of Bisexuality, 18*(3), 257–277. https://doi.org/10.1080/15299716.2018.1485071

Davis, F. (1992). *Fashion, culture, and identity.* University of Chicago Press.

Denizet-Lewis, B. (2014, March 20). The scientific quest to prove bisexuality exists. *New York Times.* www.nytimes.com/2014/03/23/magazine/the-scientific-questto-prove-bisexuality-exists.html?_r=0

Drummond, M. J. N. (2005). Asian gay men's bodies. *Journal of Men's Studies, 13*(3), 291–300. https://doi.org/10.3149/jms.1303.291

Duffin, T. P. (2016). The lowdown on the down low: Why some bisexually active men choose to self-identify as straight. *Journal of Bisexuality, 16*(4), 484–506. https://doi.org/10.1080/15299716.2016.1252301

Edwards, T. (1994). *Erotics and politics: Gay male sexuality, masculinity, and feminism*. Routledge.

Elman, R. A. (1996). Triangles and tribulations: The politics of Nazi symbols. *Journal of Homosexuality, 30*(3), 1–11. https://doi.org/10.1300/J082v30n03_01

Entwistle, J. (2000). Fashion and the fleshy body: Dress as embodied practice. *Fashion Theory, 4*(3), 323–348. https://doi.org/10.2752/136270400778995471

Esterberg, K. G. (1996). "A certain swagger when I walk": Performing lesbian identity. In S. Seidman (Ed.), *Queer theory/sociology* (pp. 259–279). Blackwell Publishers Ltd.

Faderman, L. (1991). *Odd girls and twilight lovers: A history of lesbian life in the twentieth century*. Penguin Books.

Farrell-Beck, J., & Parsons, J. (2007). *Twentieth century dress in the United States*. Fairchild.

Feinberg, L. (1993). *Stone butch blues*. Firebrand books.

Firestein, B. A. (1996). Bisexuality as a paradigm shift: Transforming our disciplines. In B. A. Firestein (Ed.), *Bisexuality: The psychology and politics of an invisible minority* (pp. 263–291). Sage.

Fox, R. C. (1995). Bisexual identities. In A. R. D'Augelli & C. J. Patterson (Eds.), *Lesbian, gay, and bisexual identities over the lifespan* (pp. 48–86). Oxford University Press.

Freitas, A., Kaiser, S. B., & Hammidi, T. (1996). Communities, commodities, cultural space, and style. In D. L. Wardlow (Ed.), *Gays, lesbian, and consumer behavior: Theory, practice, and research issues in marketing* (pp. 83–107). The Haworth Press.

Garfinkel, H. (1967). *Studies in ethnomethodology*. Prentice-Hall, Inc.

Geczy, A., & Karaminas, V. (2013). *Queer style*. Bloomsbury.

Goffman, E. (1959). *The presentation of self in everyday life*. Random House, Inc.

Griffin, G. (2017). Butch/femme. In *A dictionary of gender studies*. Oxford University Press. www.oxford reference.com/view/10.1093/acref/9780191834837.001.0001/acref-9780191834837-e-45.

Hammidi, T. N., & Kaiser, S. B. (1999). Doing beauty: Negotiating lesbian looks in everyday life. *Journal of Lesbian Studies, 3*(4), 55–63. https://doi.org/10.1300/J155v03n04_07

Hartman, J. E. (2013). Creating a bisexual display: Making bisexuality visible. *Journal of Bisexuality, 13*(1), 39–62. https://doi.org/10.1080/15299716.2013.755727

Hartman-Linck, J. E. (2014). Keeping bisexuality alive: Maintaining bisexual visibility in monogamous relationships. *Journal of Bisexuality, 14*(2), 177–193. https://doi.org/10.1080/15299716.2014.903220

Hayfield, N. (2011). *Bisexual women's visual identities: A feminist mixed-methods exploration* [Unpublished doctoral dissertation, University of the West of England].

Hayfield, N., Clarke, V., Halliwell, E., & Malson, H. (2013). Visible lesbians and invisible bisexuals: Appearance and visual identities among bisexual women. *Women's Studies International Forum, 40*(8), 172–182. https://doi.org/10.1016/j.wsif.2013.07.015

Hemmings, C. (1999). Out of sight, out of mind? Theorizing femme narrative. *Sexualities, 2*(4), 451–464. https://doi.org/10.1177/136346099002004005

Hillman, B. (2015). *Dressing for the culture wars: Style and the politics of self-presentation in the 1960s and 1970s*. University of Nebraska Press.

Holliday, R. (1999). The comfort of identity. *Sexualities, 2*(4), 475–491. https://doi.org/10.1177/136346099002004007

Horton, B. A. (2020). Fashioning fabulation: Dress, gesture and the queer aesthetics of Mumbai pride. *South Asia: Journal of South Asian Studies, 43*(2), 294–307. https://doi.org/10.1080/00856401.2020.1716288

Humphries, M. (1985). Gay machismo. In A. Metcalf & M. Humphries (Eds.), *The sexuality of men* (pp. 70–85). Pluto.

Huxley, C., Clarke, V., & Halliwell, E. (2014). Resisting and conforming to the 'lesbian look': The importance of appearance norms for lesbian and bisexual women. *Journal of Community & Applied Social Psychology, 24*(3), 205–219. https://doi.org/10.1002/casp.2161

Kaiser, S. B. (1990). *The social psychology of clothing: Symbolic appearances in context* (2nd ed.). Macmillan.

Kaiser, S. B. (1997). *The social psychology of clothing: Symbolic appearances in context*. Macmillan.

Kaiser, S. B. (2012). *Fashion and cultural studies*. Bloomsbury.

Katz, J. D. (2013). Queer activist fashion. In V. Steele (Ed.), *A queer history of fashion: From the closet to the catwalk* (pp. 219–232). Yale University Press.

Lane-Steele, L. (2011). Studs and protest-hypermasculinity: The tomboyism within Black lesbian female masculinity. *Journal of Lesbian Studies, 15*(4), 480–492. https://doi.org/10.1080/10894160.2011.532033

Lennon, S. J., Johnson, K. K. P., & Rudd, N. A. (2017). *Social psychology of dress*. Bloomsbury.

Levine, M. P. (1998). *Gay macho: The life and death of the homosexual clone.* University Press.

Levitt, H. M., Gerrish, E. A., & Hiestand, K. R. (2003). The misunderstood gender: A model of modern femme identity. *Sex Roles, 48*(3–4), 99–113. https://doi.org/10.1023/A:1022453304384

Levitt, H. M., & Hiestand, K. R. (2004). A quest for authenticity: Contemporary butch gender. *Sex Roles, 50*(9–10), 605–621. https://doi.org/10.1023/b:sers.0000027565.59109.80

Levitt, H. M., & Horne, S. G. (2002). Explorations of lesbian-queer genders. *Journal of Lesbian Studies, 6*(2), 25–39. https://doi.org/10.1300/J155v06n02_05

Maltry, M., & Tucker, K. (2002). Female fem(me)ininitics. *Journal of Lesbian Studies, 6*(2), 89–102. https://doi.org/10.1300/J155v06n02_12

McGuire, J. K., & Chrisler, A. (2016). Body art among transgender youth: Marking social support, reclaiming the body, an creating a narrative identity. In Y. Kiuchi & F. A. Villarruel (Eds.), *The young are making their world: Essays on the power of youth culture* (pp. 97–118). McFarland & Company.

McGuire, J. K., Doty, J. L., Catalpla, J. M., & Ola, C. (2016). Body image in transgender young people: Findings from a qualitative, community based study. *Body Image, 18*, 96–107. http://dx.doi.org/10.1016/j.bodyim.2016.06.004

McGuire, J. K., & Reilly, A. (2022). Aesthetic identity development among trans adolescents and young adults. *Clothing and Textiles Research Journal, 40*(3), 235–250. https://doi.org/10.1177/0887302X20975382

McLean, K. (2008). Silences and stereotypes: The impact of (mis)constructions of bisexuality on Australian bisexual men and women. *Gay and Lesbian Issues and Psychology Review, 4*(3), 158–165.

Mead, G. H. (1934). *Mind, self, and society.* University of Chicago Press.

Milani, T. M., & Kapa, K. (2015). Ready-to-wear sexual politics: The semiotics of visibility on Wits pride t-shirts. *Stellenbosch Papers in Linguistics Plus, 46*, 79–103. https://doi.org/10.5842/46-0-671

Moore, M. [sic]. (2020). Critical mascara: On fabulousness, creativity and the end of gender. In A. Reilly & B. Barry (Eds.), *Crossing boundaries: Fashion to deconstruct and reimagine gender* (pp. 192–200). Intellect Books.

Mosher, C. M., Levitt, H. M., & Manley, E. (2006). Layers of leather: The identity formation of leather men as a process of transforming meanings of masculinity. *Journal of Homosexuality, 51*(3), 93–123. https://doi.org/10.1300/J082v51n03_06

Pierre, D. (2020, September 15). New me, new wardrobe: A transformative makeover. *Autostraddle.* www.autostraddle.com/new-me-new-wardrobe-a-transformative-makeover/.

Rahilly, E. P. (2015). The gender binary meets the gender-variant child: Parents' negotiations with childhood gender variance. *Gender & Society, 29*(3), 338–361. https://doi.org/10.1177/08912432145 63069h

Reddy-Best, K. L. (2017). Miki Vargas: Queer fashion photographer and *The Handsome Revolution. Clothing Cultures, 4*(2), 153–170. https://doi.org/10.1386/cc.4.2.153_1

Reddy-Best, K. L. (2020). The politicization of fashion in virtual queer spaces: A case study of Saint Harridan, one of the pioneering queer fashion brands in the twenty-first century. In A. Reilly & B. Barry (Eds.), *Crossing boundaries: Fashion to deconstruct and reimagine gender* (pp. 91–108). Bloomsbury Publishing.

Reddy-Best, K. L., & Baker Jones, K. (2020). Is this what a lesbian looks like? Lesbian fashion and the fashionable lesbian in the United States press, 1960s to 2010s. *Journal of Lesbian Studies, 24*(2), 159–171. https://doi.org/10.1080/10894160.2019.1685816

Reddy-Best, K. L., & Goodin, D. (2018). Queercrip fashion in the 21st century: Sky Cubacub and the queercrip dress reform. *Clothing Cultures, 5*(3), 333–357. https://doi.org/10.1386/cc.5.3.333_1

Reddy-Best, K. L., & Goodin, D. (2020). Queer fashion and style: Stories from the Heartland—Authentic Midwestern queer voices through a museum exhibition. *Dress: The Journal of the Costume Society of America, 46*(2), 115–140. https://doi.org/10.1080/03612112.2019.1686875

Reddy-Best, K. L., Goodin, D., & Streck, K. (2020). *21st century queer fashion brands: Oral history project.* Iowa State University Digital Press. https://iastate.pressbooks.pub/queerfashionbrands/

Reddy-Best, K. L., & Pedersen, E. L. (2014). The relationship of gender expression, sexual identity, distress, appearance, and clothing choices for queer women. *International Journal of Fashion Design, Technology, and Education, 8*(1), 54–65. https://doi.org/10.1080/17543266.2014.958576

Reddy-Best, K. L., & Pedersen, E. L. (2015). Queer women's experiences purchasing clothing and looking for clothing styles. *Clothing & Textile Research Journal, 33*(4), 265–279. https://doi.org/10.1177/0887302X15585165

Reilly, A. (2010). Gay, lesbian, bisexual, and transgendered persons. In J. B. Eicher & P. G. Tortora (Eds.), *Berg encyclopedia of world dress and fashion: The United States and Canada* (pp. 508–513). Berg.

Reilly, A. (2022). The rise of the bottom: Counterdiscourse to challenge heteronormativity within the gay community. In V. Karaminas & A. Geczy (Eds.), *Millennial masculinities: Queers, pimp daddies and lumbersexuals* (112–122). Rutgers University Press.

Reilly, A., Catalpa, J., & McGuire, J. (2019). Clothing fit issues of trans people. *Fashion Studies, 2*(1), n.p. https://doi.org/10.38055/FS010201.

Roach-Higgins, M. E., & Eicher, J. B. (1992). Dress and identity. *Clothing and Textiles Research Journal, 10*(4), 1–8. https://doi.org/10.1177/0887302X9201000401

Rossiter, H. (2016). She's always a woman: Butch lesbian trans women in the lesbian community. *Journal of Lesbian Studies, 20*(1), 87–96. https://doi.org/10.1080/10894160.2015.1076236

Rothblum, E. (1994). Lesbians and physical appearance: Which model applies? In B. Greene & G. M. Herek (Eds.), *Lesbian and gay psychology: Theory, research and clinical applications* (pp. 84–97). Sage.

Rothblum, E. (2010). The complexity of butch and femme among sexual minority women in the 21st century. *Psychology of Sexualities Review, 1*(1), 29–42.

Schrock, D. P., Boyd, E. M., & Leaf, M. (2009). Emotion work in the public performances of male-to-female transsexuals. *Archives of Sexual Behavior, 38*(5), 702–712. https://doi.org/10.1007/s10508-007-9280-2

Scott, D. T. (2011). Contested kicks: Sneakers and gay masculinity, 1964–2008. *Communication and Critical/Cultural Studies, 8*(2), 146–164. https://doi.org/10.1080/14791420.2011.566275

Serano, J. (2007). *Whipping girl: A transsexual woman on sexism and the scapegoating of femininity.* Seal Press.

Snorton, C. R. (2009). "A new hope": The psychic life of passing. *Hypatia, 24*(3), 77–92. www.jstor.org/stable/20618165

Steele, V. (2013). A queer history of fashion: From the closet to the catwalk. In V. Steele (Ed.), *A queer history of fashion: From the closet to the catwalk* (pp. 7–75). Yale University Press.

Stein, A. (1998). All dressed up. But no place to go? The style wars and new lesbianism. In C. K. Creekmur & A. Doty (Eds.), *Out in culture: Gay, lesbian, and queer essays on popular culture* (pp. 476–483). Duke University Press.

Stephenson, A. (2016). "Our jolly *marin* wear": The queer fashionability of the sailor uniform in interwar France and Britain. *Fashion, Style & Popular Culture, 3*(2), 157–172. https://doi.org/10.1386/fspc.3.2.157_1

Tabatabai, A., & Linders, A. (2011). Vanishing act: Non-straight identity narratives of women in relationships with women and men. *Qualitative Sociology, 34*(4), 583–599. https://doi.org/10.1007/s11133-011-9202-4

Tan, C. K. K. (2019). Taipei gay "bear" culture as sexual field, or, why did Nanbu bear fail? *Journal of Contemporary Ethnography, 48*(4), 563–585. https://doi.org/10.1177/0891241617742191

Taub, J. (2003). What should I wear? A qualitative look at the impact of feminism and women's communities on bisexual women's appearance. *Journal of Bisexuality, 3*(1), 9–22. https://doi.org/10.1300/J159v03n01_02

Taylor, Y. (2007). "If your face doesn't fit . . ." The misrecognition of working-class lesbians in scene space. *Leisure Studies, 26*(2), 161–178. https://doi.org/10.1080/02614360600661211

Von Busch, O. (2009). Engaged design and the practice of fashion hacking: The examples of Giana Gonzalez and Dale Sko. *Fashion Practice, 1*(2), 163–185. https://doi.org/10.2752/175693809x469148

Walker, L. M. (1993). How to recognize a lesbian: The cultural politics of looking like what you are. *Signs, 18*(4), 866–890. www.jstor.org/stable/3174910

Wearing Gay History. (n.d.). *About.* https://wearinggayhistory.com/about

Wilson, E. (2013). What does a lesbian look like? In V. Steele (Ed.), *A queer history of fashion: From the closet to the catwalk* (pp. 167–192). Yale University Press.

Worsley, H. (2011). *100 ideas that changed fashion.* Laurence King.

22

CONSUMING HIV

Cause Marketing, the (RED) Brand, and LGBTQ+ Welfare in Modern Times

Tyler M. Argüello

To date, over two-thirds of those living with HIV are in Africa (WHO, 2020). Key populations continue to shoulder the disproportionate burden of HIV, including LGBTQIA+ people, 15- to 49-year-olds, adolescent and young women, and other vulnerable populations. While there have been substantive gains in prevention and treatments, structural factors persist as both increased exposure to risk as well as barriers to effective, quality, and affordable prevention and interventions (WHO, 2020). One structural factor that has begun to be retooled is political economics. In 2006, combating donor fatigue in the West, the singer and activist Bono part- nered with Bobby Schriver (Chairman of DATA, an AIDS advocacy organization) to launch "(RED)" (see www.red.org). This venture sought to engage "consumer power" to deliver AIDS relief in Africa via the Global Fund [(RED), FAQ section, n.d.]. (RED) is *not* a product or charity. It is a brand whose logo is semioticized as two parentheses embracing the word "RED," all bathed in the color of both emergency and HIV/AIDS: red. (RED) signals a shift in the public sphere for how important social issues are communicated, coalescing practices from communications, biomedicine, and business within a patina of social welfare.

The power of semiotics is in play, that is, both the circulation and interpretation of signs and symbols. And, "the systematic act of the manipulation of signs" can be understood as modern-day consumption (Baudrillard, 2001b, p. 25). Objects, like HIV semioticized via the (RED) brand, always "say something" about their users, as the "ideological genesis of needs" precedes the production of goods to meet those needs (Barthes in Baudrillard, 1981). Ostensibly, the needs fulfilled by (RED) appear in service of the social *and* the commercial. Yet how does this occur and what does it say about consumers? This study is a critical analysis of the (RED) brand, troubling the neutrality of branding and cause marketing and employing the prophetic words of Treichler (1999, p. 173), "HIV has become . . . a reality that is too costly to give up." This manuscript begins with a literature review, followed by a review of methodology. Next, a semiological analysis and discussion are presented. Finally, implications are provided related to queer communities.

Literature Review

HIV in the Public Sphere

The public sphere is the normative space for everyday life (Habermas, 1991; Warner, 2002). It is both theory and practice, facilitating the cultural-political-economy, networking people,

DOI: 10.4324/9781003128151-26

and providing a structure for circulating semiotics. HIV entered the public sphere in 1988, when the U.S. government conducted a mass-mailing to every household to, finally, alert the U.S. public to the epidemic, after years of silent presidential administration (Stoddard, 1990). Initially, media coverage proliferated from Western nations, focusing on gay men and those addicted to drugs (Cullen, 2003). During the late 1980s into the 1990s, media attention spiked when HIV affected heterosexuals and mother-to-child transmission. Increasingly, coverage became routinized and encumbered with scientific discourse (Poindexter, 2004), stoking fear, containment, and surveillance (Cullen, 2003). Risk was central to this, focusing on marginalized populations allowing for blame, othering, and hyper-targeted messages. This allowed many to believe themselves not at-risk and disenfranchised people with a paucity of prevention knowledge (Kornblit & Petracci, 2000). Consequently, the general public stayed disengaged from, apathetic towards, and generally unaware of HIV (Dodds, 2002).

HIV's international mediatization initially paralleled the coverage in North America (Bardhan, 2001; Karnik, 2001). By the mid-1990s, U.S. coverage turned to policies and cultural issues; abroad, attention turned to socio-economics, institutional policies, and human rights. Still, the shared global story of HIV was one of poverty and unequal access. Additionally, differential media treatment constructed worthy and unworthy subjects. In the West, mothers and children were pitted against gay man, who then were positioned against the sympathetic yet racialized discourse of AIDS in Africa (Booth, 2000; Cullen, 2003; Emke, 2000).

Parallelly, people living with HIV/AIDS (PLWHA) took media into their own hands, initially through print "zines" (Long, 2000). Activists' strategies reformulated the discourses of AIDS victims, blame, and sexuality, among many (Gillet, 2003). Increasingly, cyberspace provided a place for PLWHA to advocate for recognition and organize for needed resources (Mueller et al., 2004). Similarly, community-based groups engaged advocacy (Callen et al., 1990). A prime example of this is ACT UP, the organization that created the notorious semiotic of Silence = Death. The pink triangle on a black background underscored by two words jostled the public globally, fostering political activism (Watney, 2000). Inevitably, U.S. commercialization also stepped into the fray. The red ribbon emerged in the early 1990s as another way of publicizing HIV/AIDS and acknowledging the ravaging of the those affected, principally LGBTQ+ people. While catchy, the AIDS ribbon seemed to trivialize differences across affected populations as well as the other diseases that appropriated the symbol (Watney, 2000).

Neoliberalism, Post-Fordism

Neoliberalism is "a process and not a thing" (Harvey, 1988, p. 343). It is far from the natural order of things but sells itself as the march of progress for political economies. It argues that human well-being can be advanced through liberating entrepreneurial freedoms, privileging competition, inequality, free markets, public austerity, and law and order (Duggan, 2004). The state serves as the framework to enable such social agendas and practices. Still, neoliberalism is a change from eras past. Today, the New Deal consensus has been dismantled in favor of neoliberalism, and the early industrial "Fordism" labor (i.e., the manufacturing of Ford automobiles) has transformed (Harvey, 1988). As of late, labor is more effectively understood in terms of *flexible accumulation*, or the increasing flexibility in production, workforces, and finance. In this *post-Fordist* era, the economy is based less on materiality and increasingly on the cultivation and consumption of information. It is the *consumption* of discourse that is crucial for understanding social life, and semiotics—inclusive of language and visual communication—are a central organizing force of the social world (Kellner, 1994). The value of semiotics has central importance, as social processes are mediated (e.g., via advertising, fashion, mass media). As commodities become semioticized, discourse becomes commodified (Lyotard, 1986/1987; Fairclough, 1999), or open to economic calculation and designed for market success. In this vein, discourse is an "irreducible element" and "symbolic weapon" of neoliberal flexibility; discourses become *technologized* in service of re-/shaping "institutional cultures" (Fairclough, 1996, 1999). This technologization works to ignore contexts while homogenizing and reducing differences, compromising the democratic potential of the public sphere (Fairclough, 1999).

Branding, Cause Marketing

Branding is not well researched regarding HIV/AIDS. A brand is *not* a logo or corporate identity; it is a "gut feeling," an idea shared with customers to understand a product, service, or company (Neumeier, 2005). Gracefully, it is a "promise" to a consumer (Kotler, 1997). A Western consumer is exposed to over 6,000 marketing messages each day, and each year they are inundated by over 25,000 new products (Wheeler, 2006). A brand helps the consumer negotiate the proliferation of choice. In the mid-20th century, branding functioned more rationally, claiming that a product could logically do a certain thing (e.g., this detergent washes whites whiter). Decades later, branding proved more emotional (e.g., I love this handbag). Contemporarily, a brand works more ethically (e.g., these shoes fit my belief system). Above all, a brand is equity, a return on investment. Positive brand equity increases the average stock return approximately 30%, while a negative equity decreases it by 10% (Wheeler, 2006).

Consequently, the battle for market territory has evolved into a competition for a share of the consumer's mind (Wheeler, 2006). Managing brands is about managing differences; more critically, identity management. In neoliberal times, this proves quite powerful. Olins [who co-founded the branding firm originally used to develop (RED)] speaks to this: "In a world that is bewildering of competitive clamor, in which rational choice has become almost impossible, brands represent clarity, reassurance, consistency, status, membership—everything that enables human beings to help define themselves. Brands represent identity" (Wolff Olins, 2007, p. 5). Equally, a brand needs to be coupled with marketing (Court et al., 1997). Specifically, cause marketing links a brand with a social issue; other corporate giving strategies include strategic philanthropy, sponsorship, and social investments (Marconi, 2002). In the 1980s, American Express conceived cause marketing during its campaign to refurbish the Statue of Liberty (Bloom, 2008), since companies and publics alike have embraced the practice. As of 2004, 72% of consumers believed that companies should impact a cause, and 86% stated that companies should apprise their customers of causes they support (Bloom, 2008). Similarly, 86% of consumers are more likely to buy cause-connected products, 86% positively view companies they believe "make the world a better place," and 64% feel companies should engage cause marketing (Marconi, 2002). For example, the Avon foundation earned $65 million from 1993 through 2004 through its breast cancer initiative, selling lipsticks, mugs, and pins, with an average price-point of $7 (Webster, 2005). Likewise, Avon sold periwinkle bracelets for domestic violence awareness at $3 each, of which the foundation received $2.

Current Study

In all, there is power in brands, and claiming social responsibility is big business. In response, this study interrogates how "HIV" is *commercialized* through the (RED) brand (see www.red. org). The *-ialized* suffix makes consumption and signs a problem, apprehending the interpenetrating technological, semiotic, and economic processes (Schulz, 2004). From this critical perspective, branding and cause marketing make HIV, identities, and knowledge intelligible, stylized, and transmittable. For authorities, that communication duo disseminates goods and prevention strategies; for communities, that process provides the means to advocate, operationalize networks, and consume. For researchers, this critical analytic sets that well-intentioned communication duo against the unequally distributed stakes of political-economic life. This study, then, focuses on semiotic resources, for example, language and signs, used to increase social and financial capital. In post-Fordist economy, social life is reproduced via (social) semiotics, as the public is bathed in media objects that are self-referential. Instead of based on material production, political economy becomes the interplay of images and signs propagating ceaselessly without stable referent or truth, that is simulation or a *hyper-reality* (Baudrillard, 1994). A semioticized world deprives the rational subject of access to truth: "individuals are no longer citizens, eager to maximise their civil rights. . . . They are rather consumers, and hence the prey of objects" (Poster, 2001, p. 7). This is primarily done through marketing, which holds the ability to "induce receptivity (and) mobilize consciousness" (Baudrillard, 2001a, p. 13). Branding and marketing organize a network of commercialized objects that configures a universalizing system of signification. This system classifies and hierarchizes social relationships. Consumption becomes the practice that imbues life with meaning and stands in for human relationships. What is being consumed is the idea of relations, all the while manifested through a calculus of objects (Baudrillard, 2001a); that is, the object is the alibi for the social relation.

HIV made (RED) deserving to be an object of analysis, as it is more than a (new) brand. (RED) is an alibi—but *for what* is not readily apparent (see www.red.org). This study is one of very few efforts to approach HIV as an object (e.g., branded product) versus subject (e.g., person at-risk for infection), focusing on the signs of HIV that are systematically manipulated and consumed. These signs are ideas for HIV and for its identities. Therefore, to get to the truth of "HIV" within hyper-reality, it must be approached semiotically, at the order of signs—or at the logic of the object.

A Social Semiotic Analysis (SSA) was employed to systematically access the dialectic between micro-level communication (e.g., branding) and macro-level social practices (e.g., AIDS relief via cause marketing; Kress & van Leeuwen, 2006; van Leeuwen, 2005). In comparison to other methods under the banner of Discourse Studies, SSA considers semiotic resources beyond language used to make meaning (e.g., visual images). SSA seeks to demystify how certain representations are positioned to be neutral and normal, and, through their repetition over time and texts, how they are naturalized into the assumptions, realities, and social order that are promoted to consumers. In short, this methodology makes professional produced texts accountable for the impact of their ideological work on the consumers who embody the discourses as well as the ideological work on the social systems texts perpetuate.

The design is a case study of the (RED) brand, based on an original archive of empirical data, obtained during summer and fall 2008, just after the brand's full deployment. The dataset includes 81 texts in total: 62 (RED) website pages, 7 Global Fund website texts, one in-depth interview with a branding professional (later to be renamed "Christy"), and one branding agency unpublished annual review. Whereas the entire (RED) website was reviewed at the time of data collection, a select subset of pages (i.e., 62) were included. It is important to note that both the Global Fund and (RED) websites are active; therefore, visual images, marketing materials, and links have been updated since. The reader can go back and view (RED)'s website today to get a general sense of the architecture and claims of the brand (see www.red.org). Quotes and references to the website were not repeatedly cited. The Human Subjects Division at the University of Washington, Seattle, approved this study.

The researcher engaged in an iterative coding of the texts, using a discourse template that facilitated systematic attention to their ideological and material elements, that is, semiotic resources, connotations and myths, participants, difference and intertextuality, visual images, genre, discourses, style, modality, and counter discourses. After, a critical analysis explored how HIV and its contingent identities and disciplines were commercialized (Baudrillard, 1981, 1994, 2001b). Accordingly, this counter-reading showed two primary themes for how the brand comes to commercialize HIV, that is, through two strategies of aestheticization (i.e., the logo and website) and three strategies of recontextualization (i.e., partner brands, language, and the color red).

Aestheticization

How do you sell HIV or prevention? As Christy, the brand strategist from Wolff Olins, explained during the research interview (named changed for confidentiality):

> [The branding team at Wolff Olins] essentially came up with the idea that . . . wasn't a charity . . . wasn't exactly a company. That's somewhere in between.

That somewhere in between is a brand. Globalizing, post-industrial economies are heavily semiotic (Lash & Urry, 1994). There is a "general promiscuity and playful mixing of codes" (Featherstone, 1992, p. 267) in the rapid flow of signs and images, *aestheticizing* daily life. Central to this, cultural specialists harness the power of semiotics, manipulating images, reworking consumption and consumers' desires, blurring cultural boundaries, and collapsing the distinction between art and the everyday. It is the "semioticization of economic life" (Graddol, 2002, in Thurlow & Jaworski, 2006, p. 134). In the case of (RED), HIV is aestheticized anew through the logo and website.

Aestheticization: The Logo

Central to the brand is the logo. Embraced by two parentheses, the word "RED" is saturated in a flat red color, set against a stark white background. This high contrast works to authorize (RED) as a fact of the marketplace, which is only further legitimized by the trademark symbol (i.e., a superscripted "TM"; Grassl, 1999), as well as the logo's extension to their selected, embraced, and elite partners, like Apple, Gap, and Microsoft.

While the logo creates ideological space, the concrete meaning is unstable. Christy, the brand strategist, attempted to define (RED):

> [T]he reason why charities are struggling is that there are just so many demands on people's brains, pockets and wallets. . . . It's about guilting you into doing the right thing. It's pictures of babies in Africa with flies . . . that just make you feel awful and you write a check. So our number one premise was that this had to be something incredibly positive, optimistic, that led with products that you'd want to buy anyway . . . and with the back story of, "Oh and by the way this is also doing something positive for a cause that really matters," creating this scenario where basically everybody wins, right?

(RED) has layers of intention and meaning: (a) pills, (b) products, and (c) partners. First, (RED) is an alibi to provide intervention, or pills, to Africans. (RED), as described in Wolff Olins' annual report, "delivers a source of sustainable income for the global fund (*sic*), provides consumers with a choice that makes giving effortless, and . . . generates profits and a sense of purpose for partner companies." This is described in metaphorical permutations: "raise awareness and money," an "economic initiative to fight the AIDS pandemic in Africa," and, "a chance to stay alive." This discourse is further pronounced when coupled with representations of the African subjects who benefit from (RED). The (RED) website prominently displayed an African woman before and after the (RED)-funded antiretroviral pills, that is, HIV treatment. Like the logo, the woman is tightly framed, demanding an intimate gaze and relation with the consumer viewer. Before, she is somber: something must be done; after, she is jovial: (RED) services are successful.

Second, (RED) means products. (RED) grows choice for consumers, imbuing their consumption with goodness. Across several (RED) website pages, they espouse: "(We) can change the course of life and history on this planet," and "You buy (RED) stuff. We get the money, buy the pills and distribute them." In its self-description for "How RED works," (RED) locates the "smart shopper" in a chain of events, buying (RED) products, in turn helping the Global Fund and African people. In this chain of events, the consumer subject is displayed as a black generic male figure; a red Apple iPod is added, being purchased for $199; $10 is shown going to the Global Fund; then $10 goes to pills; ultimately, Africa is made (RED), and the consumer subject becomes colored as red, wearing their iPod. The consumer, their choice, and consumption are embraced to the power of (RED).

Third, (RED) means partners. Through (RED), businesses can reach new markets and get to feel good about contributing to a cause. As the (RED) website describes its partners:

> We believe that when consumers are offered this choice [(RED)], and the products meet their needs, they will choose (RED) . . . more brands will choose to become (RED) because it will make good business sense to do so. And more lives will be saved.

As well, they espouse: "[(RED) is . . . designed to engage business and consumer power . . . (it) works with the world's best brands."

Just as (RED) does not position itself as a charity, nor do the partners. Christy, the branding professional explained: . . . [(RED) is] *something really positive, inspiring and motivating, not something that's . . . making you feel sorry for people . . . [partners] don't really lead . . . with that message. They make really cool things that work really well, in beautifully designed packages.* These partners get to insert themselves into (RED)'s embrace, enhancing return on investments, harnessing the powerful logo, all the while cloaked in beautiful packaging. Contemporary comparable examples can be found at www.red.org/products.

Given these various meanings, the brand has a virality akin to HIV: (RED) inserts itself into the host's core identity and works to disturb the host on the whole. Indirectly, in her research interview, Christy spoke to this: . . . *you have some really incredible but strong graphic elements that are recognizable even when you disturb them, distort them, stick them on other things.* While the graphics may be strong, (RED)'s virality calls into question its real referent. In late capitalism, financial power is deterritorialized, not connected to one nation, economy, or object (Jameson, 1997). (RED) moves from product-to-product, partner-to-partner through its basking of these objects in red, without any explicit tagging by parentheses or the word "RED." It is everywhere but nowhere; it becomes an image fragment, standing in for the deterritorialized, globalizing power of political economies. (RED) finds life not just from its circulation in the public sphere (albeit on the backs of often elite products), but from its ability to mutate and aestheticize new material touch points, like t-shirts, shoes, and packaging. These fragmented images reduce both (RED)'s and HIV's complex meanings into a stylized semiotic; consuming these products means consuming the neo-narratives (RED) sells.

Aestheticization: The Website

(RED) centralizes itself via its website, extending the minimalist logo; for the current homepage iteration, see www.red.org. The layout provides much value to the displayed information and directs the viewer's attention. Increasing the resonance, each webpage has a white, uncluttered backdrop, providing sharp detail, high contrast, and realistic product representations. The typography is simple, elegant, sans serif. The icons, menu bar, headlines, and link outs are in red. In tandem, across the webpages, variously sized objects are paired with scientific discourses: "[(RED) products] direct up to 50% of their gross profits to the Global Fund," and "Since its launch in March 2006, more than $110 million has been generated." In this, the center menu tab *(You)^RED* centralizes and privileges the consumer and affords minimal distance with the products. The viewer is taken to an "Impact Calculator," allowing them to select (RED) partner products purchased and then chart how much money their purchases have generated as pills for African bodies. This tool brings the consumer into the (RED) network, and the strong web visual overall gives (RED) life, making it a fact in political-economic life (Bourdieu & Wacquant, 1992). But (RED) does not just sell: it can predict how consumption positively benefits people. HIV-made-red aestheticizes the virus—but more the cause—as some-*thing* desirable and consumable, placing the consumer as the principal (social) actor and their consumption as the principal intervention.

There is irony, however. One of the goals of neoliberal capital is to proliferate without restraint (Lefebvre, 1991). (RED) is a brand made by and for money; it relies on the logics of capital and strategic design practices to financialize social life. However, (RED)'s constraints, for example, parentheses, register *less* with the behavior of liberal capital and *more* with an agenda to order consumption. (RED)'s own heavy embrace works against its aim: (RED) seeks to homogenize notions of consumption and power (Baudrillard, 1994). Realistically, its signification is anything but singular. Thus, HIV is no longer simply a non-curable virus that has wreaked havoc on men who have sex with men and poor and marginalized communities; it makes HIV more real than real—a simulacra reproduced over multiple formations. (RED)'s beautiful attempts to control its simulation serves to implode, rather than concretize, its social meaning.

Recontextualization

(RED) also relies on recontextualization. Cultural elements are recontextualized when disembedded from one genre and re-embedded into another, finding new relations to social practices (Fairclough, 2003). Modern life relies on increased consumption and blurred social relationships, for example re-embedding health discourses into ones of market exchange (Gesler & Kearns, 2002). In the case of (RED), recontextualization occurs through the re-embedding of three primary semiotic resources: partner brands, language, and the color red.

Recontextualization: Partner Brands

The thread that ties (RED) partners together is the intention to grow capital and increase brand equity. The (RED) brand recontextualizes partner identities visually. As Wolff Olins explains in their annual report: "we built the brand around the idea that (RED) inspires, connects and gives consumers power, with a visual system that unites participating businesses by literally embracing their logos to the power of (RED)." Visually and at face value, across the (RED) webpages, (RED) places partners into an embrace by their red parentheses, signaling they are enhanced to a (RED) degree. Partner products are distorted, reconfiguring their intentions as socially beneficial and occluding corporate gains into a white background. Partners are not completely passive, however; they do have agency in their (RED)-ification, as explained by Christy, the interviewed branding professional: . . . *each company has their own kinda strategies how and where they launch us. . . . (RED) to be honest doesn't have a huge amount of control over that. . . . Each individual company pays a license fee to (RED) for a set period of years to use the brand and there are very few kinds of limitations beyond that of what they can and can't do.* While they do not have to recolor, they must display the logo, each to some degree of distinction. American Express, for example, re-colored their iconic credit card, with new copy: *This card is designed to help eliminate AIDS in Africa.* Similarly, Gap sells red clothing, with various "badges" of goodwilled consumption: "INSPI(RED)." Microsoft (with Dell) takes this further by reconfiguring their interface, displaying a planet earth embraced by red parentheses, as featured on the (RED) website: "Perhaps more than any previous invention, the PC can help you to change the world. It has fundamentally changed how we connect and communicate with one another, and now it can help eliminate AIDS in Africa."

The narrative sold to consumers is that these products are more than everyday artifacts: They can link individuals to a cause embodied by (RED), made material by the partner product, with their purchasing power to touch the world. This is a tall order for an idea or a t-shirt. Still, the largesse of (RED) and their partners is not wholly illogical. As capital subsumes culture, signs in the public sphere are imbued with structures of value dictated by capital (Baudrillard, 1994). The political economy fomented by (RED) attaches itself onto everyday products to reconfigure their identities to be more in-line with the (RED) world. This world is about Africans with AIDS—and it is surely about the saturation of capital, constantly in-wait of the next thing to recontextualize. It is the reproducing sphere of simulacra (e.g., fashion, media, advertising) that ties capital all together (Baudrillard, 1994).

Recontextualization: Language

Language is a powerful medium for commercial practices, like marketing, to both sell products and to recontextualize meaning. "Each word tastes of the context and contexts in which it has lived its socially charged life; all words and forms are populated by intentions" (Bakhtin, 1981, p. 293). Like the brand's transitive nature, the syntax of (RED) is imprecise. Across the webpages, "(RED)" functions variously, as a:

- noun—"*More about (RED)* ➔"
- adjective—"*But a (RED) product . . .*"
- present perfect verb—"*If you have registe(RED) . . .*"
- compound—"*JOINRED.COM*"

This lexical play is carried across other touch points. For example, Gap and Hallmark place these permutations front and center on their t-shirts and cards, for example, *Inspi(RED), Savo(RED),* as featured across (RED)'s website. Other variations can be found across the website: *assu(RED), sca(RED), (RED)iscover,* and *1hund(RED).* This play signals that (RED)'s virality adheres to the basic language structure of the social order to infect and transform meaning, just as it spins outward on the backs of consumers in the marketplace. (RED) boldly presumes to embed itself *into* the language of everyday life—taking over its host, like HIV, but in this case language that gives it life.

Another way that (RED) plays with language is dialogue. "The (RED) Manifesto" and "Community Toolkit," featured on the top menu bar on (RED)'s website, embody the hybridization that (RED) creates between corporate and social activist language. Despite *not* being a charity, within their Manifesto, (RED)'s central communication is a socio-political declaration demanding: "If they (Africans) don't get the pills, they die," and "Now, you have a choice . . . upgrade your choice." The Manifesto further rationalizes: "We believe that when consumers are offered this choice, and the products meet their needs, they will choose (RED)." Yet this has subtextual levels. It appeals to the viewer's morality: "We don't want them (Africans) to die. We want to give them the pills. And we can. And you can. And it's easy. If you don't consume, you kill African/Black people." Equally, (RED) predicts in their Manifesto: "Buy, get pills, save lives, be happy with yourself and your product."

Both texts dawn stenciled font, suggesting a transgressive quality, affording the appearance these messages were graffitied (Scollon & Scollon, 2003). This dialogue also recontextualizes social activist language into the logic of good business through synthetic personalization (Fairclough, 1989). Consistent with post-Fordist culture, producers manage the relationship with viewers by invoking discourse that appears they are speaking individually to you (the viewer), all the while speaking to all consumers. In the Manifesto on its website, (RED) incorporates the individual viewer through aligning with them: "As first world consumers, we have tremendous power." This is coupled with direct statements: "At no cost to you" and "All you have to do is upgrade your choice." No matter how personalized the discourse and design might be, the dialogue is mediated, and the viewer is passivated through an inability to communicate with the producers. The dialogue occurs *for* the viewer. The public declaration of the Manifesto makes the case for why the viewer(s) should join the mission, thus appropriating them.

However, (RED)'s real power is its reductive solutions. In all, the consumer makes purchases, pills are bought, sent to Africa, sick people are saved, and everyone is happy. This nominalization does a couple of things (Fairclough, 2003). First, it obfuscates HIV/AIDS and its treatments, suppressing the process of commerce, government, and biomedicine. Second, differences are occluded among cultures, populations, and ideologies. Third, the agency of the consumer and Africans are erased, beyond the former being a good consumer and the latter being a good welfare, albeit problematic, recipient (cf. Bell, 2011). And most critically, responsibility for these social problems, information, and proposed solutions is all but erased, in service of making witty ad copy. Effectively, in recontextualizing language, (RED) reduces social divisions and cultural meanings for the prize of profit and pills. This controlled cause marketing and advertising work, or at best seek, to control the meaning of red, HIV, Africa, and doing good out in the cultural public sphere (cf. Fiske, 1989).

Recontextualization: The Color Red

Undoubtedly, red is *the* color to signify HIV/AIDS, and by association LGBTQ+ persons, especially queer men. Many social causes have recognized the power of color. In financial terms, color is big business: 60% of a consumer's decision to buy a product depends exclusively on the color (Wheeler, 2006). It is logical that (RED) use red, though disturbed. Christy, the branding professional explains:

> [I]f you didn't (use red) you'd almost be missing a trick. I think our main concern though was that it didn't feel too kind of too bloody, too angry, too violent . . . the rest of the brand is quite kind of clean and simple and language that pleases, quite positive and optimistic . . . if you had sort of very aggressive almost activist language with it, it would feel you know it would feel "campaigny." It would feel political, it would feel, um, almost like war, which is not again what we were trying to achieve. So it's a fine line.

It is a fine line; (RED) works hard in differentiating itself from the meanings that are associated with red. Across its webpages, it tries variously:

- (RED) is the color of emergency. 4,400 people dying every day and many others fighting for their lives.
- Red is a popular color and word when it comes to charity. It's powerful and it inspires action. But red is not (RED)—helping to eliminate AIDS in Africa—unless it has the embraces around the word (RED) or around the product partner logo.

While (RED) gives a nod to red's historicity, red-to-the-power-of-(RED) has more potential meanings. It becomes some-*thing* productive that can *do* things for society. Red anew has purpose, dis-embedded from lapels and street protests, and re-embedded into marketplaces. It energizes consumers, mobilizes their personalities, and affords they are good people who purchase red/(RED) things. Typically, red is flat suggesting bold and basic: alternatively, (RED) *is* HIV. Yet, with more texture and depth, it is responsive, expressive, and has more naturalistic truth. The red Manifesto and Community Toolkit show that this purposeful maneuver to connect more with the consumer and cultivate an authentic, but realistically synthetic, sense of (social) action.

In design, pure, bright red is associated with modernity (Kress & van Leeuwen, 2006). (RED) capitalizes on this via recontextualizing HIV *ergo* red. The branding professional from Wolff Olins, Christy, explains:

> [S]o it needed to be that simple . . . most of the partners have been really great at using the red color which, um, of course creates that sense of consistency and cohesion . . . it's also been a sorta experiment in how far can something stretch before it breaks . . . and how can you control something like that . . . it's been an interesting ride looking at how each of those brands have made it their own. It's still obviously Gap, but it's still definitely (RED).

And stretch (RED) does. In earlier days, red (AIDS) was about drugs into bodies, in particular the body of the 4 H's: homosexuals, heroin addicts, hemophiliacs, and Haitians (Argüello, 2016); red (RED) now is about specific (African) bodies. (RED) reminds the viewer where exactly their purchased pills will go: "A portion of profits from each (PRODUCT)RED product sold goes directly to the Global Fund to invest in African AIDS programs, with a focus on women and children." This persistent disclaimer detaches (RED) from the narrative of gay men, unworthy HIV-positive individuals, and illicit behaviors that cause AIDS. Whether this maneuver was intentional, it contains the anti-queer stigmas that could arise in consumers that their actions are undesirably gay. Incidentally, this is a strategic maneuver by (RED), as brand equity accrues from cause marketing targeting kids and women (Kingston, 2007). Thus, for business' sake, red/(RED) is still some-*thing* positive, just not gay- or HIV-positive. In this sense, (RED) does stretch red: instead of politics, it is now brand equity.

Finally, (RED) mines red's meaning as blood, or the "fixed capital" of the body (Marx, 1973). (RED) capitalizes on red's productive potential: Blood is everywhere, in every-*body*. It quickly reproduces, offering an efficient opportunity. (RED)'s claims that it can eliminate AIDS in Africa affords the sense of effectiveness: (RED) not only constructs HIV anew, it breathes new life into unproductive blood. (RED) makes both the consumer and worthy receiving subject productive (again). And, every-*body* is a terminal in the red hyperreal, built on design, marketing, and merchandising, rather than violent buying and selling. Red (RED)-contextualized holds promise in infecting the hyperreal, re-/configuring itself, blood, and HIV as capital enterprise. Red is not a risk for (RED): it is its lifeline.

Discussion: Cause Marketing and/as Neo-Colonization

As of late, HIV has become more about "them" over "there" in Africa, occluding structural inequities that perpetuate the epidemic (Patton, 2002). A social distance is afforded to the First World consumer, and (RED) contributes to a commercial process of neo-colonization. Across its webpages, (RED)'s marketing reinforces the *good* works it does for Africans and the epidemic:

- At no cost to you, a (RED) company will give some of its profits to buy and distribute anti-retroviral medicine to our brothers and sisters dying of AIDS in Africa.
- (RED) partners delivered $45m to the global fund (*sic*) in one year, more than was received from the private sector in the last five years. This is enough money to give 290,000 people life-saving drugs for a year.

Images of African subjects buttress this message, grateful all the while to the marketplace. Going beyond supplying pills, (RED) invites Africans to be part of its production, as explained by Christy: . . . *we've spent a lot of time and effort trying to encourage (partners) . . . to manufacture products, make packaging, sourcing materials in Africa . . . almost every single partner . . . has managed to kinda bring Africa "into the fold." And, it's great because it's generating jobs and opportunities for local economies.*

Each (RED) partner variously represents their Third World development, for example, as displayed on (RED)'s webpage American Express' efforts utilizing the spokesperson Elle MacPherson, supermodel. The tag reads:

> (RED) has become a symbol of hope and dignity for many of my brothers and sisters living with HIV/AIDS in Africa. (RED) money has become the lifeline for many people affected by HIV by giving them another chance. (RED) products' increasing popularity is due to the fact that they resonate with our most fundamental nature of making a difference through our choices.

In other related maneuvers across the webpages, Gap visualizes this (RED) lifeline by showcasing workers in Lesotho, manufacturing garments. Hallmark provides an interactive video of a handbag maker, testifying, "This Hallmark project has helped us become specialists in making bogolan product."

These efforts may bring awareness and prosperity, yet they do not account for (RED)'s lack of transparency. It is unclear what the real impact of (RED) is for Africa, beyond smiling faces. On their webpages, (RED) advertises they earned $45 million for the Global Fund, in their first year. They also stated that 99% of the funds go directly to Africans—however, nowhere do they show how monies translate into services. Moreover, (RED) consumers supposedly increased their own charitable giving, but no evidence is provided across the webpages. [Incidentally, at the time of finishing this manuscript, (RED)'s webpage reports having raised $650 million to date; see www.red.org/how-red-works.]

Generally, cause marketing is a $1.4 billion industry in the United States, representing a 23% growth since 2005 (Bennett, 2007). (RED) partners spent over $100 million to advertise, in its early years (Rosenman, 2008). Realistically, (RED)'s initial earnings were less than 2% of the Global Fund's giving (Greenblatt, 2006). So (RED)'s claims appear unsubstantiated. More importantly, while Africans may be gaining treatments and skills, (RED) partners are middlemen, skimming financial and brand equity; and (RED) consumers get bathed in good feelings and beautiful products.

In effect, shopping as a solution for HIV, or (RED)'s "brand aid," appears to do *less* for the recipient and *more* for the First World consumers, who are implicated as "humanitarian fashionistas" (Ray, 2008). (RED) becomes an unnecessary but new barrier for First World consumers simply doing real direct action to affect Africans or HIV. Consumers' action is not measured against social interest, but rather how much they can bargain in compromising their glamorous lifestyle, the lifestyle (RED) wants to beautifully infect. The claims of doing *good* through (RED) are distinct from doing *well* by African recipients. That lack of transparency in (RED) suggests that it may just be an over-produced "patina of philanthropy" (Rosenman, 2008).

In a way, (RED) is like a pair of rose-colored glasses, occluding the structural inequities of HIV and (RED)'s dis/enfranchising effects, which is aptly visualized on the (RED) website by founder rock star Bono wearing a pair of rose-colored shades and then holding two red Motorola cellphones, one over each eye. In post-Fordist culture, imagination is core to modern life and subjectivity. (RED) is part imagination (identity) and part materiality (products). In this, people and places experience modern colonization via material *and* discursive means, including semiotics like brands (Appadurai, 1996; Thurlow & Aiello, 2007). An exemplar of this is displayed on a (RED) webpage, showing a barcoded African woman declaring: "We are the people that we have been waiting for." (RED) facilitates First World consumers to unwittingly become more than a human billboard wearing (RED) goods: they become work horses for neo-colonization on and in the face of African subjects and Africa, both land and ideal. What exactly, then, are "we waiting for." Bono asserts on a (RED) webpage "to lessen the distance between (RED) shoppers around the world and (RED) shareholders in Africa." The First World and Africa have been connected for centuries (O'Manique & Labonte, 2008); more recently during industrialization efforts, the First World has persisted with structural adjustments, government austerity, and financialization efforts that continue to disenfranchise the continent and contribute to social and health inequities, including HIV.

(RED) may send pills to Africa but these pills are a symbol of a "proto-universal culture" (Castree, 2001). (RED)'s seemingly beneficent products symbolize, among other things, an over-simplification of the complex biological, cultural, and media processes that instantiate them as colonizing commodities. Their consumption fosters an imagined closure between the West and Third Worlds; yet the reality is a purposeful keeping distance, believing those worthy subjects desire stylized solutions to the realities of their existence. It is the idea of a relationship that is signified in objects (Baudrillard, 2001a), which grows more real as it circulates in the hyperreal: Africa is more than Africa, HIV is more than HIV, solutions are more than solutions, all made possible by (RED). (RED)'s consumption annuls rather than grounds the relationship. The (RED)der the world grows, the more that its receiving subjects are painted over, eclipsed by the fervent absorption of new products, people, and places to brand as (RED). As Bell (2011, p. 177) aptly critiques: (RED) constructs commodities, celebrities, and consumers as agents of social change and Africans as passive and weak, their only hope another handout. No one wishes to diminish the lives that (RED) money is helping to save. But consumers and citizens must grapple with the reality that consumption is not activism.

Concluding Implications

In finalizing this chapter, this archive and all business practices globally are confronting the crushing effects of COVID-19. Recent modern prevention practices of Pre-Exposure

Prophylaxis (PrEP) and Treatment as Prevention (TasP), along with the sexual ethics of Unde-tectable = Untransmissable (U = U), have held promise to certainly curtail, but drive down, HIV infections amidst investments in increased testing and treatment (CDC, 2019). The effects of COVID-19 on HIV in-/equity are yet to be determined; the power of a brand may be in peril with the onslaught of a global economic recession.

Still, while not statistically generalizable, this study offers analytic generalizability to mod-ern identities, HIV, and the stakes of new business (Polit & Beck, 2010). This study deployed critical theories to intervene at the site of knowledge production to understand how HIV is subjectivated—or obliged to discursively infect consumers through a commercial effort. This was achieved via thinking the logic of the object, that is a "new" brand. It would have increased rigor and trustworthiness to have more access to (RED) producers; still, their products—the objects of HIV—serve as alibis for the certain idea being sold to consumers: the power of the signs rule. Critique therefore proves more worthwhile.

Several conclusions can be had. First, (RED) effectively circumscribes "HIV." The mar-keting collateral centralized this to the general (First World) public, but those who hold the privileged and responsible lifestyle to consume obligated to buy certain stuff in order to be part of a (philanthropic) lifestyle where consumption and self-indulgence equate to cure. Second, (RED) fetishizes all the deserving HIV-affected African subjects with the "face of AIDS" re-/painted as women and children. This renders others as *un*-deserving and cul-pable for having HIV. This directs attention to the anti-queer stigma at the heart of these discourses. Third, what is excluded from the representations of mainstream consumer culture is not just the *un*desired habits of citizens; rather, what is rejected is the possibility that mul-tiplicity exists, for example, bodies, desires, identities, and consumption. To be affected by HIV as a non-cis-heterosexual consumer signals that they have not followed the privileged path in public life. Artificially, (RED) gives preference to women, children, and the consumer subject, while summarily ignoring the empirically validated, persistently overburdened queer person by HIV, but globally. Among other subjectivities, queer people embody that which is expendable to society. In political economic terms, they are bodies full of leisure, not pro-ductive labor. In gender terms, they are penetrable, utilitarian, and expendable. In racialized terms, they are differentiated bodies enslaved to economies. In a word, they are that which you do not want to be, at all cost, lest you become branded with and by HIV. (RED) takes this anti-queer stigma further by eschewing queer sexualities and nonbinary genders from the brand.

This is not to say (RED) must concentrate on queer people; the lack of attention does not make them necessarily anti-queer. Instead, the systematic reproduction of identities and prod-ucts that silence and deny the liberty to experience, advocate for, and find protection for one's sexuality is what is indeed anti-queer. The systematic denial of the lived *experiences* of queerness, in *all* its formations, alongside the HIV pandemic makes these discourses particularly lethal. These discourses contribute to increasing risk for the bodies deemed undisciplined and unre-sponsive to market demands.

Parallel to its limitations, (RED) holds promise for the business of doing good. Disciplines in the health sciences often privilege subjects (e.g., patients, clients), understandably, in the conceptualization and deployment of interventions. It could be more productive for transdis-ciplinary collaborations to—intentionally, strategically, but critically—employ the power of the semiotic. In these post-Fordist times, (RED) shows how publics of people must be thought and experienced semiotically. This shifts attention towards the work that semiotic resources do to provide voice or to silence populations, especially those marginalized and justice-seeking. In the end, objects, as well as subjects, are deserving of social justice.

References

Appadurai, A. (1996). *Modernity at large: Cultural dimensions of globalization*. University of Minnesota Press.

Argüello, T. M. (2016). Fetishizing the health sciences: Queer theory as a social work intervention. *Journal of Gay & Lesbian Social Services, 28*(3), 1–14.

Bakhtin, M. M. (1981). Discourse in the novel. In M. Holquist (Ed.), & C. Emerson & M. Holquist (Trans.), *The dialogic imagination: Four essays by M. M. Bakhtin* (pp. 259–422). University of Texas Press.

Bardhan, N. (2001). Transnational AIDS-HIV news narratives: A critical exploration of overarching frames. *Mass Communication & Society, 4*(3), 283–309.

Baudrillard, J. (1981). *For a critique of the political economy of the sign* (C. D. Levin, Trans.). Telos Press. (Original work published 1972)

Baudrillard, J. (1994). *Simulacra and simulation* (S. F. Glaser, Trans.). The University of Michigan Press. (Original work published 1981)

Baudrillard, J. (2001a). On seduction. In M. Poster (Ed. & Trans.), *Jean Baudrillard: Selected writings* (2nd ed., pp. 152–168). Polity Press.

Baudrillard, J. (2001b). System of objects. In M. Poster (Ed. & Trans.), *Jean Baudrillard: Selected writings* (2nd ed.). Polity Press.

Bell, K. (2011). "A delicious way to help save lives": Race, commodification, and celebrity in Product (RED). *Journal of International and Intercultural Communication, 4*(3), 163–180.

Bennett, J. (2007, August 21). The rage over (RED). *Newsweek*. www.newsweek.com/id/36192

Bloom, P. (2008). Everyone's waxing philanthropic these days, but it pays off—if you do it right. *Cause Marketing, 79*(21), 18–19.

Booth, K. M. (2000). "Just testing": Race, sex, and the media in New York's "baby AIDS" debate. *Gender & Society, 14*(5), 644–661.

Bourdieu, P., & Wacquant, L. (1992). *An invitation to reflexive sociology*. Polity Press.

Callen, M., Grover, J. Z., Maggenti, M., & Contributors (1990). Roundtable: AIDS and democracy, a case study. In B. Wallis (Ed.), *Discussions in Contemporary Culture: Democracy* (Vol. 5, pp. 241–258). Bay Press.

Castree, N. (2001). Commodity fetishism, geographical imaginations and imaginative geographies. *Environment and Planning A, 33*, 1519–1525.

Centers for Disease Control and Prevention. (2019). *PrEP*. www.cdc.gov/hiv/basics/prep.html

Court, D. C., Freeling, A., Leiter, M. G., & Parsons, A. J. (1997, Summer). If Nike can "just do it," why can't we? *The McKinsey Quarterly, 3*, 24–35.

Cullen, T. (2003). HIV/AIDS: 20 years of press coverage. *Australian Studies in Journalism, 12*, 64–82.

Dodds, C. (2002). Messages of responsibility: HIV/AIDS prevention materials in England. *Health: An Interdisciplinary Journal for the Social Study of Health, Illness and Medicine, 6*(2), 139–171.

Duggan, L. (2004). *The twilight of inequality?: Neoliberalism, cultural politics, and the attack on democracy*. Beacon Press.

Emke, I. (2000). Agents and structures: Journalists and the constraints on AIDS coverage. *Canadian Journal of Communication [Online], 25*(3). www.cjc-online.ca/index.php/journal/article/view/1162

Fairclough, N. (1989). *Language and power*. Longman.

Fairclough, N. (1996). *Technologisation of discourse*. In C. R. Caldas-Coulthard & M. Coulthard (Eds.), *Text and practice: Readings in critical discourse analysis*. Routledge.

Fairclough, N. (1999). Global capitalism and critical awareness of language. *Language Awareness, 8*(2), 71–83.

Fairclough, N. (2003). *Analysing discourse: Textual analysis for social research*. Routledge.

Featherstone, M. (1992). Postmodernism and the aestheticization of everyday life. In S. Lash & J. Friedman (Eds.), *Modernity and identity* (pp. 264–290). Blackwell.

Fiske, J. (1989). *Understanding popular culture*. Unwin.

Gillett, J. (2003). Media activism and Internet use by people with HIV/AIDS. *Sociology of Health & Illness, 25*(6), 608–624.

Gesler, W. M., & Kearns, R. A. (2002). *Culture/place/health*. Routledge.

Graddol, D. (2002, July). *The English language and globalization* [Paper presentation]. Language and Global Communication Seminar, Centre for Language and Communication, Cardiff University, UK.

Grassl, W. (1999). The reality of brands: Towards an ontology of marketing. *American Journal of Economics and Sociology, 58*(2), 313–347.

Greenblatt, J. (2006, October 31). Building a better (RED). *WorldChanging: Tools, models and Ideas for Building a Brighter Green Future.* www.worldchanging.com/archives/005150.html

Habermas, J. (1991). *The structural transformation of the public sphere: An inquiry into the category of bourgeois society* (T. Burger, Trans.). MIT Press. (Original work published 1974)

Harvey, D. (1988). *The condition of postmodernity: An enquiry into the origins of cultural change.* Basil Blackwell, Inc.

Jameson, F. (1997). Culture and finance capitalism. *Critical Inquiry, 24,* 246–265.

Karnik, N. S. (2001). Locating HIV/AIDS and India: Cautionary notes on the globalization of categories. *Science, Technology, & Human Values, 26*(3), 322–348.

Kellner, D. (Ed.). (1994). *Baudrillard: A critical reader.* Blackwell.

Kingston, A. (2007). The trouble with buying for a cause. *Maclean's, 120*(11), 40–41.

Kornblit, A. L., & Petracci, M. (2000). Influencias mediáticas y personales sobre la decision de protegerse del VIH/SIDA/Media and personal influence on the decision to protect oneself against HIV/AIDS. *Zer, 8,* 23–40.

Kotler, P. (1997). *Marketing management* (9th ed.). Prentice Hall.

Kress, G., & van Leeuwen, T. (2006). *Reading images: The grammar of visual design* (2nd ed.). Routledge. (Original work published 1996)

Lash, S., & Urry, J. (1994). *Economies of signs and spaces.* Sage.

Lefebvre, H. (1991). *The production of space* (D. Nicholson-Smith, Trans.). Blackwell Publishing. (Original work published 1974)

Long, T. (2000). Plague of pariahs. AIDS 'zines and the rhetoric of transgression. *Journal of Communication Inquiry, 24*(4), 401–411.

Lyotard, J.-F. (1987). Rules and paradoxes and the svelte appendix. *Cultural Critique, 5,* 209–219. (Original work published 1986)

Marconi, J. (2002). *Cause marketing: Build your image and bottom line through socially responsible partnerships, programs, and events.* Dearborn Trade Publishing.

Marx, K. (1973). *Grundrisse: Foundations of the critique of political economy* (M. Nicolaus, Trans.). Random House.

Mueller, M., Kuerbis, B., & Pagé, C. (2004). *Reinventing media activism: Public interest advocacy in the making of U.S. communication-information policy, 1960–2002.* The Convergence Center School of Information Studies.

Neumeier, M. (2005). *The brand gap: How to bridge the distance between business strategy and design* (2nd ed.). Peachpit Press.

O'Manique, C., & Labonte, R. (2008). Rethinking (product) RED. *The Lancet, 371,* 1561–1563.

Patton, C. (2002). *Globalizing AIDS.* University of Minnesota Press.

Poindexter, C. C. (2004). Medical profiling: Narratives of privileging, prejudice, and HIV stigma. *Qualitative Health Research, 14*(4), 496–512.

Polit, D. F., & Beck, C. T. (2010). Generalization in quantitative and qualitative research: Myths and strategies. *International Journal of Nursing Studies, 47*(11), 1451–1458.

Poster, M. (Ed. & Trans.). (2001). *Jean Baudrillard: Selected writings* (2nd ed.). Polity Press.

Ray, C. (2008, February). The dangers of "brand aid". *New African,* 18–19.

(RED). (n.d.). *Frequently asked questions (FAQ & Contact).* www.red.org/faq-contact

Rosenman, M. (2008, no date). The patina of philanthropy. *Stanford Social Innovation Review.* www.ssireview.org/site/printer/the_patina_of_philanthropy/

Schulz, W. (2004). Reconstructing mediatization as an analytical concept. *European Journal of Communication, 19*(1), 87–101.

Scollon, R., & Scollon, S. W. (2003). *Discourses in place: Language in the material world.* Routledge.

Stoddard, T. (1990). Paradox and paralysis: An overview of the American response to AIDS. In B. Wallis (Ed.), *Discussions in contemporary culture: Democracy* (Vol. 5, pp. 259–269). Bay Press.

Thurlow, C., & Aiello, G. (2007). National pride, global capital: A social semiotic analysis of transnational visual branding in the airline industry. *Visual Communication, 6*(3), 305–344.

Thurlow, C., & Jaworski, A. (2006). The alchemy of the upwardly mobile: Symbolic capital and the stylization of elites in frequent-flyer programmes. *Discourse & Society, 17*(1), 131–167.

Treichler, P. (1999). *How to have theory in an epidemic: Cultural chronicles of AIDS.* Duke University Press.

van Leeuwen, T. (2005). *Introducing social semiotics.* Routledge.

Warner, M. (2002). *Publics and counterpublics.* Zone Books.

Watney, S. (2000). *Imagine hope: AIDS and gay identity.* Routledge.

Webster, N. C. (2005). Color coded causes: It's not about slapping on a logo; marketers really connect with passionate consumers. *Cause Marketing, 76*(24), 31–34.

Wheeler, A. (2006). *Designing brand identity: A complete guide to creating, building, and maintaining strong brands* (2nd ed.). John Wiley & Sons, Inc.

WHO (World Health Organization). *HIV/AIDS.* Retrieved October 26, 2020, from www.who.int/news-room/fact-sheets/detail/hiv-aids

Wolff Olins. (2007). *The power (RED).* Retrieved July 9, 2008, from www.wolffolins.com.

23

LESBIANS IN SPORTS MEDIA

From Strategic Distancing to Strategic Acceptance

Katherine Schweighofer

American women like Babe Didrikson Zaharias (golf), Billie Jean King (tennis), Caitlyn Cahow (hockey), Julie Chu (hockey), Sue Wicks (basketball), Layshia Clarendon (basketball), Ali Krieger (soccer), Adrianna Franch (soccer), Melody Maia Monet (softball), Margaret Lu (fencing), and Liz Caramouche (ultimate fighting) fought their way to the most elite levels of their sport despite disapproving public and private messages about their sexual and gender identity.[1] These women and many other lesbian athletes like them have had to contend with a homophobic and sexist sports culture perpetuated by teammates, coaches, league officials, sponsors, fans, reporters, media executives, and the general public (Griffin, 1998; Lenskyj, 2003; Warren, 2006). Gender and sexuality shape sport cultures for all athletes, but for lesbian athletes in the United States, a unique set of pressures has shaped life on the fields, courts, pools, courses, and rinks where they compete (Griffin, 1998). Mainstream messages about women in American culture already conflict with the demands of elite athleticism; queer sexual identity uniquely turns up the intensity of these pressures. This chapter engages in a media analysis of two snapshots in recent sports history as a touchpoint in tracing the ongoing progress—and limitations—faced by lesbian athletes today. While the focus on representation limits this discussion to professional caliber athletes appearing in mainstream media, media scholars have argued that the cultural messages here represent cultural norms that affect everyone (Boutilier & SanGiovanni, 1983). Kane argues that sports media is a key site shaping women's representation:

> The mass media have become one of the most powerful institutional forces for shaping attitudes and values in American culture. . . . How female athletes are viewed in this culture is both reflected in and created by mass media images. Thus, it becomes critical to examine both the extent and the nature of media coverage given to female athletes.
>
> *(Kane, 1988, p. 89)*

Media images are representative of, responsive to, and influence larger cultural norms, and here reveal the often problematic ways that women athletes' sexuality and gender are highly contested sites of meaning (Fink & Kensicki, 2002; Messner, 2002).

This chapter engages several specific representations of lesbian professional athletes in the United States from the early decades of the 2000s to the present time in order to understand the shifting ways lesbians are depicted in sports media. I argue the representations of lesbian

DOI: 10.4324/9781003128151-27

athletes in the early years of the 2000s were marked by ongoing forms of what I define as "strategic distancing," namely the intentional and careful removal of any references to non-normative sexuality and simultaneous emphasis on heteronormative femininity. In strategic distancing, media producers and image shapers (and at times even athletes themselves) carefully avoid cultural discomfort with LGBTQ sexuality by heterosexualizing and feminizing athletes known to be lesbian. However, by the mid-2010s, positive LGBTQ presence in mainstream culture had grown, thanks in part to increasing support for lesbian and gay marriage. As I will show, these trends are evident in media representations of lesbian athletes that unblinkingly celebrate their sexual identity alongside their athletic successes. I will explain how these examples demonstrate a phase of "strategic acceptance" of LGBTQ athletes. Strategic acceptance marks a positive step forward in its openness and inclusivity; however, examples of strategic acceptance are not a sure sign that homophobia and sexism in athletics is over. Homophobia and sexism are intensified or moderated by intersectional factors: an athlete's race, sport, sporting level, and even position on the team, can make or break her ability to be out in sports (Anderson & Bullingham, 2015). Understanding these differences and the ways they are embedded in sporting institutions is critical to the ongoing project of proactively dismantling the dual systems of homophobia and sexism that shape contemporary sporting cultures (Kane, 1988).

From Mannish Lesbians to Homohysteria: Early Representations of Women Athletes

Understanding the problems with changing 21st-century representation of lesbian athletes requires some context, particularly the historical trajectory of changing cultural views on women athletes more broadly during the 20th century. Historian Susan Cahn argues that at the start of the 20th century, sexuality was integral to mainstream press representations that portray female athletes as gender deviant for participating in sports, which were understood as only for men (Cahn, 1993). Women who played sports were dangerous, flirting with immorality, and implied to be (hetero)sexually promiscuous (Cahn, 1993). Athletic phenom and cultural star Babe Didrikson Zaharias, who boasted AAU basketball national titles, Olympic track and field medals, and LPGA victories across the late 1920s and 1930s (Cayleff, 1996), is a prime example of how women's athleticism was tied with sexual and gender deviance at this time. Babe was mocked in the press for her "mannish" features and "tomboyish" behavior until she married pro wrestler George Zaharias (Cahn, 1993, p. 351). Ridiculing female athletes like Babe for being too mannish revealed cultural anxiety that women playing sports would take on other behaviors reserved for men, such as active sexual desire and promiscuous behavior, or no longer be appealing as potential wives. Babe quelled these public fears with her celebrity marriage, though ironically she was already living outside of the heteronormative; scholars agree the marriage was a cover for Babe's lesbianism, as her real relationship was with fellow golfer Betty Dodd, who lived with Babe and George for years (Cayleff, 1996).

By the postwar era in the United States, the representation of female athletes as too "mannish" or as potential heterosexual failures had coalesced into suspicions of lesbianism; now women athletes, physical education teachers, and female coaches were all marked with an uncertain sexuality, one that blended sexual identity with female masculinity (Cahn, 1993). This cultural association between lesbianism and the female athlete remained present from the midcentury through the early 1980s (Cahn), when an increase in homophobia dramatically reshaped American sports cultures (Anderson, 2011). Anderson (2011) has identified how cultural anxieties around homosexuality coalesced into what he calls "homohysteria" during the 1980s and 1990s. Homohysteria is the paranoid fear of being marked as homosexual through association with cross-gendered behavior (Anderson), and results in a variety of homophobic behaviors (including verbal and physical abuse of sexually suspect people) and distancing mechanisms (such as embracing normatively gendered behavior and targeting others to deflect attention from oneself) (Pascoe, 2007). The dominance of homohysteric sports culture in the United States during the 1980s and most of the 1990s meant all female athletes, regardless of sexual identity, experienced some pressure to display heteronormative femininity just as women athletes earlier in the century had done (Cahn, 1993; Griffin, 1998). However, lesbian athletes at a variety of levels of athletic competition experienced shame, fear, and direct abuse should their sexual identities become known (Lenskyj, 2003; Mosbacher and Yacker, 2009). One of the most visible cases of homophobic sports culture surfaced in former player reports and subsequent media attention to the Penn State women's basketball team of the early and mid-1980s, whose coach Rene Portland issued a direct "no lesbians" policy (Figel, 1986; Mosbacher and Yacker, 2009). This homohysteric period in American sports culture lasted throughout the 1980s and 1990s (Anderson). By the 2000s, the homophobia that had shaped sports cultures so vividly began to relax, soon making team cultures like that of Portland's Penn State team obsolete (Anderson, 2011; McCormack & Anderson, 2014).

Thus, the 20th century represented a long history of homophobia and gender-specific scrutiny borne by all women athletes, and specific fears for individual lesbian athletes. As the 21st century began, some of these attitudes began to relax (Anderson, 2011), and lesbian and gay athletes began to come out of the closet, although primarily after retirement (Schweighofer, 2016). However while scholars traced new cultures of openness in men's sport (Anderson & McCormack, 2018), others found women's sport cultures not following the same shift toward inclusivity (Anderson & Bullingham, 2015). Bullingham, Magrath, and Anderson found that the decreases in homohysteria that characterized men's sport cultures in the early 2000s were not universally true for female athletes (2014). Another study pointed to particular factors as key to lesbians thriving in sports, including having an understanding ally, institutional policies supporting LGBTQ athletes, or the presence of a trailblazing out lesbian athlete in on one's team to emulate (Fink et al., 2012). Fink et al further identified that institutional silence and the lack of structural support—for example, domestic partner benefits for professionals, or LGBTQ inclusive language in high school or college settings—continued to be problematic for lesbian athletes at all levels. These studies remind us that specific attention to the experiences of women and girls within homophobic sport cultures is critical to understanding the structures of homophobia in order to dismantle them.

Strategic Distancing: "Little Rascals"

The early years of the 21st century were a time of increasing LGBTQ presence in mainstream America, thanks to a discordant mix of well-received media stars and a slate of regressive state and local laws preventing gay marriage, adoption, and other civil rights. This decade saw the television series *Queer Eye for the Straight Guy* introduce unfashionable middle-aged straight men to skincare products and tailored clothing while Ellen DeGeneres quickly rose to stardom talking openly about being a lesbian on her highly successful talk show (Praderio, 2016). But while Hollywood provided more positive queer representations, political battles produced virulent forms of public homophobia as the debate over same-sex marriage, gay and lesbian military service, and LGBTQ legal protections from discrimination raged (Walters, 2014). California passed citizen ballot initiatives in 2000 and 2008 designed to limit marriage to heterosexual couples (Proposal 8, 2008; Proposal 22, 2000), the Roman Catholic Church explicitly banned gay-identified or gay-supportive priests from joining its ranks (Benedict, 2005), and the governor of Louisiana ended its existing executive order protecting LGBTQ people from employment discrimination (Nanda, 2022). In this rocky period, sports were no safe haven for LGBTQ athletes. While the vitriol and witchhunts of the homohysteric sport cultures of the 1980s and early 1990s seemed to have passed, most women athletes did not feel they would be welcomed should they choose to come out of the closet. The professional and Olympic athletes who made their sexual identity public before 2000, included only a handful of men who came out after retiring (Schweighofer, 2016). Professional tennis player Billie Jean King, however, was forced to come out publicly in 1981 when her personal life was about to hit the tabloids (Kort, 1988). Few other women athletes would publicly disclose their lesbian identities until the early 2000s, when a number of WNBA players shared publicly their lesbian identities that had long been common knowledge within their teams (Schweighofer, 2016).

A particularly revealing artifact from sports media in the first decade of the 21st century is the Nike ad campaign titled "Little Rascals," first released in 2006. Each of the ads features a trio of little girls who approach one of the stars of the WNBA and proceed to harass them about the finer points of their game. Ad #3 of the series features three-time league MVP Houston Comet Sheryl Swoopes (Dante65, 2006b). In Swoopes' ad, the trio of little girls walks up to her at a playground where she is pushing her baby in a swing. The little girls are dressed head to toe in men's basketball gear, with oversized jerseys, high-top shoes, and a basketball held jauntily at the hip. As the girls harass Swoopes about the details of her jump shot and demand to know if the baby has "a jumper" (Dante65, 2006b) it is clear the humor of the ad is derived from their highly competitive, aggressively confident insider knowledge of the game. They embody the masculinized sports expert—the coach, the commentator, the critic, the hardcore fan—a role almost exclusively assigned to men. Meanwhile, Swoopes appears with her hair carefully arranged, a coordinated women's track suit, makeup, and several pieces of jewelry, as a cooing and smiling ideal mother—picture perfect femininity. She deflects the trio's aggressive challenge by asking instead, "where *is* your Momma?" (Dante65, 2006b). The ad uses the age difference between the girls and the professional player not only for humor but also to subtly cover up a more threatening sexuality. Swoopes had just come out of the closet as a lesbian in 2005, publicly claiming her lesbian identity and sharing that she was in a relationship with former coach Alisa Scott (Granderson, 2005). The ad carefully covers her lesbianism with culturally approved motherhood (Messner, 2002). Instead, the specter of the aggressive, mannish lesbian (Cahn, 1993) is offloaded on to a group of 7 year old girls, whose deviant gender display becomes only amusing antics and not threatening resistance. The cultural anxieties produced by masculine women, serious female athletes, and lesbianism are diffused into harmless tomboy bravado. Here female masculinity and it's implied (and real) lesbian connections are carefully erased by a deflection onto childish antics and tomboy braggadocio. This pattern continues with the other ads in the campaign, wherein the same set of girls confront other WNBA stars, each of whom is carefully feminized by wearing dresses and high heels or engaging in culturally feminized activities like shopping or lunching with friends (Dante65, 2006a, 2006b, 2007).

This ad campaign exemplifies the cultural moment for women's basketball and perhaps women's sports more broadly in the first decade of the 21st century, one in which a strategic distancing from the lesbian image characterized most professional and Olympic sport cultures. Strategic distancing allowed league officials and sponsoring corporations like Nike to benefit from the incredible talents of women like Swoopes (Hernandez, 2019) and help build a growing fanbase and cultural demand for women's professional sports, while avoiding the lesbian "elephant in the room." Players were athletes and could be glorified for their accomplishments on the court or the field, but not as whole people with desires, families, and relationships. Swoopes felt differently, however, lauding the ad in interviews because it showed women "you can be great at both [motherhood and career]" (Hernandez, 2019). It did not, however, show lesbianism in such empowering forms. Nevertheless, this strategic distancing characterized women's and girls' sporting cultures during the first decade of the 21st century; the WNBA specifically avoided the lesbian question for years, taking care to downplay any rumors about the sexuality of its athletes, and ignoring the reality that a sizeable chunk of WNBA fans were members of the LGBTQ community (D'Archangelo, 2022).

Twenty years later, the scene at the WNBA has shifted, and league officials and players acknowledge and support LGBTQ identities in very different ways (D'Archangelo, 2022). The number of players who are out about their sexuality to the public continues to grow, and league officials have made important shifts in the ways they market and operate the games (D'Archangelo). The league no longer exclusively focuses on a white, straight, family-friendly client base, but actively engages LGBTQ fans and communities of diverse racial and cultural backgrounds. Now, the LGBTQ fans and families who have been a core set of the league's longtime supporters are acknowledged in Pride events and other marketing strategies (D'Archangelo), including fan apparel for each team printed in rainbow colors and labeled as "Pride" editions available through the WNBA's online store (www.wnbastore.nba.com/pride-collection). This progress appears in the ways individual players are represented as well. New York Liberty guard Layshia Clarendon, who identifies as non-binary, was described with their correct pronouns (they/them) by ESPN play-by-play announcer Ryan Ruocco for the first time in the summer of 2020 (Abrams & Weiner, 2020). Clarendon described the league as the vanguard in progressive sport cultures, "The W[NBA] is the movement. It's where this country is going. It's where progressive and forward-thinking folks are looking to" (Abrams & Weiner, 2020, para. 13). Clarendon's comments are echoed more broadly in sports media about the current players of the WNBA who have embraced their role as leaders and engaged in a wide range of social justice activism on and off the court. The Minnesota Lynx players in particular have been leaders in using their platform to promote change (Reimer, 2020). Black Lives Matter, gun control measures, get out the vote campaigns, LGBTQ rights causes, and even specific political races have benefitted from WNBA players efforts. The league even eventually threw its support behind their work both with media coverage on its webpage (www.wnba.com/socialjustice/) and supporting projects like "Say Her Name" using league platforms (Abrams & Weiner, 2020).

However, even with these recent positive steps, strategic distancing from lesbianism still occasionally resurface in today's WNBA. Players coming out is still considered newsworthy, particularly for star players, and some members of the extended WNBA community publicly express homophobic remarks. In 2017, recently retired player Candice Wiggins made the widely disputed allegation that she was bullied for being straight by other league players who were "98% lesbian" and gave the league a bad name (Leonard, 2017, para. 9). Current and former players quickly jumped to challenge such a statement, but the league made no official comment (Voepel, 2017). Sheryl Swoopes unfortunately contributes to this vein of homophobic commentary in the years following the end of her relationship with Alisa Scott and extended engagement to a long-time male friend (Rupert, 2011; Storm, 2013). Former star Swoopes is now on the coaching staff for the Texas Tech women's collegiate team, and in 2015 made comments to a reporter about the image of the WNBA (Fagan, 2015). She criticized current players, with specific reference to Phoenix Mercury six-time league All-Star Brittney Griner, for reinforcing the stereotype that the WNBA was a league made up of lesbians (Fagan). Griner had a very public relationship with Atlanta Dream forward Glory Johnson in 2014 and 2015 that included domestic violence charges, league suspensions, pregnancy, and a very public break-up, all of which garnered much media attention given Griner's MVP status (Livingston, 2015). Swoopes remarked that Griner's case only confirmed what people thought of the WNBA, implying that it was a league of raucous lesbians (Fagan). Through her press agent, she later clarified that while she believed players should love who they wanted, she was concerned about the reputation of the league. Current player Layshia Clarendon responded by questioning the logic in Swoopes' comments, "if you don't think there's anything wrong with being gay, why is it offensive that everyone thinks the league is gay?" (Fagan, 2015, para. 26) and was quickly echoed by New York Liberty president Kristin Bernert and others. In her comments Swoopes strategically distances from some current players' sexual and gender identities, embodied in the masculine-of-center and more publicly queer Griner. While Swoopes is clearly not the only one to make such comments, her position is one that seems to still hold traction behind closed doors of league officials and sports apparel company management. Strategic distancing might be less necessary in a current moment of increased LGBTQ visibility and acceptance, but it continues to define moments of anxiety over lesbianism in sports cultures.

Strategic Embracing: World Cup Winners

If the first years of the 21st century were defined by strategic distancing, moving forward a decade reveals a shifting picture of lesbian athlete representation. By the early 2010s, top caliber women's sporting events were now a regular part of the sporting landscape. The WNBA celebrate its 25th year anniversary (2013), American women crushed Olympic competitions in tennis, swimming, skiing, basketball, and soccer, and other professional women's sports leagues got their start, including the National Women's Hockey League (2015). Most interesting, however, is a consideration of American women's soccer. The United States Women's National Soccer Team (USWNT) has long been respected as a top women's soccer team in the world (Kann, 2019). Fueled by a pipeline of millions of young girls playing youth soccer across the country and a highly competitive NCAA collegiate program enabled by Title IX of the Education Amendments Act of 1972 (2018), American women have been a powerhouse in women's soccer globally since regular women's international competition was established in the 1980s (Kann). By the 2010s, watching the Women's World Cup tournament every four years had become a mainstream American sporting event. According to the International Federation of Association Football (FIFA) reports, the 2015 Women's World Cup viewership topped 750 million people globally, and the U.S.–Japan final had the highest American soccer match viewership ever (FIFA, 2015). By 2019, this viewership grew to over a billion worldwide viewers, of which over 14 million were American viewers tuned in to the championship between the United States and the Netherlands (FIFA, 2019; Mullin, 2019). In 2015, as the USWNT celebrated its third World Cup title before millions worldwide, cameras were focused on all-time goal scoring champion, international superstar, and publicly out lesbian (Forman, 2013) Abby Wambach. Wambach's incredible career left her atop the all-time scoring charts, driven by her unparalleled ability to send balls tearing into the back of the net with a flick of her head (Graham, 2015). Wambach, finding herself at the pinnacle of soccer success at the end of her career, celebrated her long-awaited World Cup trophy by leaping into the stands to kiss her wife, Sarah Huffman (Greenberg, 2015). Footage of their joyful embrace exploded across the internet and media outlets, in what was dubbed "the kiss heard 'round' the world" (Gambino, 2015, para. 1). The United States was particularly primed for an LGBTQ-themed celebration, as the July 7 soccer championship came just over a week after the U.S. Supreme Court had legalized gay and lesbian marriage nationwide with the *Obergefell vs. Hodges* (2015) decision. Using the #LoveWins hashtag made popular by advocates of same-sex marriage legalization, fans and sports writers alike merged the same-sex marriage legislative victory with the USWNT's soccer success. Media coverage was celebratory, supportive, and thrilled to lavish attention on Wambach; her distinctive blonde, asymmetrical surfer-style undercut hairdo was plastered across advertising, newspapers, and sports media worldwide; as an example, her July 20, 2015 *Sports Illustrated* cover image poses her in a head-down prayer-like position with the trophy, placing her blonde hair front and center in the image (Bruty, 2015). The photo of her celebratory kiss was arguably as momentous as another heavily photographed moment in women's soccer history, the 1999 USWNT World Cup photo of Brandi Chastain celebrating her game-winning penalty kick by tearing off her jersey in traditional soccer victory style (Gambino, 2015). Chastain is not lesbian-identified, but Gambino (2015) pointed to media coverage of the event to argue that if Chastain's celebratory moment marked the shift of the USWNT from "women soccer players" to just "soccer players," that Wambach's kiss marked the moment when "lesbian soccer players" also became simply, "soccer players."

Four years after the 2015 victory, a similar embrace of lesbian footballers occurred as the USWNT repeated their World Cup victory under the leadership of team captain and tournament MVP Megan Rapinoe. Also an out lesbian, Rapinoe was a vocal proponent of LGBTQ rights and other social justice causes on and off the field (Neeley, 2021; O'Dowd & McMahon, 2019; Rivas, 2021). She speaks publicly against homophobia globally, sends messages of support to the closeted gay players in men's professional soccer, and has been adamant about white allies standing with Black Lives Matter protests; Rapinoe was the first white athlete to publicly support Colin Kapernick's kneeling during the national anthem at NFL games by taking a knee at her soccer matches in solidarity despite U.S. Soccer disapproval (Parkinson, 2019; Reimer, 2020). When the 2015 World Cup tournament rolled around, Rapinoe's sense of humor infused her pro-LGBTQ commentary. When asked about the presence of lesbian athletes in professional soccer she quipped, "You can't win a championship without gays on your team—it's never been done before, ever" (Telander, 2019, para. 4). In fact, Rapinoe has been part of a cultural shift that has produced more and more professional athletes—particularly those in the WNBA—speaking out on various social issues, particularly those having to do with racial inequality, gun violence, and LGBTQ rights. Rapinoe is a particularly well-spoken celebrity activist and used her platform to challenge dismissals by President Trump, among others (Neeley, 2021; Parkinson, 2019; Rivas, 2021).

Both Rapinoe's celebrity advocacy and Wambach's victory kiss have been covered in mainstream and LGBTQ media with fanfare and celebration. The presence of these athletes in ad campaigns for various corporate sponsors and in sports media in general have suggested their lesbianism no longer requires a distancing, but rather, that these are moments of strategic acceptance. Here I use "strategic acceptance" to refer to the carefully managed and intentional use of these celebrity lesbian athletes motivated by corporate public relations and profit. Whether or not lesbian athletes are represented in this mode of strategic acceptance depends on three factors. First, the specific position of these players on their teams matter. Rapinoe and Wambach are not bench warmers or listed deep on the roster, they are captains, MVPs, and top goal scorers; without them victory is uncertain. Star status has been identified as a characteristic that positively affects the experiences of LGBTQ athletes at all levels (Anderson & Bullingham, 2015). Second, their successes are World Cup victories, moments of major athletic accomplishment not just on the national stage but in the world's most prestigious international sporting competition. These players have done right by America, and America loves them for it. No longer lesbian pariahs, they are simply exceptional soccer players (Gambino, 2015). Finally, a cultural shift was well underway in 2015, and more fully realized by 2019, in which stylish, successful lesbians like Rapinoe and Wambach were no longer too dangerous for corporate and institutional association, but rather connoted desirable qualities for brands seeking a hip, young, and even "sexy" look (Maheshwari & Friedman, 2021). Wambach and Rapinoe readily fit this desirable category: their whiteness, blonde hair, youth, and even their sport suggest the iconic "girl next door" and invoked the privilege of upper and middle class white suburban life-styles linked with women's soccer in the United States (Allison, 2018). For these reasons, and for others to be discussed shortly, this media and corporate embrace of lesbianism is a strategic one, tailored to fit these athletes during this cultural moment.

On the one hand, strategic acceptance of any lesbian athletes seems like a real victory, and progress has been made when mainstream media celebrates lesbian athletes both for their ath-letic achievements and even for visibly speaking up for LGBTQ rights. Yet at the same time, this is an example of how the experiences of a small minority of American superstar athletes cannot represent the broad diversity of American LGBTQ people. Lesbian strategic acceptance is, by virtue of its specific limits, a rejection and continued homophobic erasure of those who don't qualify. Without careful attention to the unevenness with which strategic acceptance operates, these welcoming moments cannot serve as a foundation for eliminating homophobia in sports culture and American society more broadly.

Strategic Change

The shift from strategic distancing to strategic acceptance for some elite athletes should not be mistaken, however, for evidence of a steadily increasing level of acceptance of LGBTQ identities and communities. Historians agree that a progressivist model of LGBTQ history does not accu-rately encapsulate the periods and places where queer lives flourished long ago (Bronski, 2011; Eaklor, 2008), nor does it address how today's relatively accepting culture still includes targeted forms of violence and discrimination for many queer people (Boykin, 2012). It doesn't always "get better" (Boykin, 2012).[2] At its core, strategic acceptance is uneven and erratic and does not guarantee equal opportunities and supportive sports environments for all LGBTQ athletes.

There are several groups of athletes that seem to be regularly left out of the newfound love mainstream American sports cultures have for some white lesbians. Gay men and boys face cul-tures of homophobic masculinity that keep the number of out gay men in sports artificially low (Dhar, 2019). Transgender athletes face additional barriers including trans-specific discrimina-tion and legislation explicitly barring their participation (Chen, 2022; Dhar, 2019). Junior-level athletes, including collegiate athletes but encompassing players from Little League to adult recreational leagues, may face different challenges than their professional athlete counterparts (Anderson & Bullingham, 2015).

Lesbian athletes of color, however, may also not experience the benefits enjoyed by the stra-tegic acceptance of white lesbian athletes. Feminist scholars have long argued the intersectional impact of racism and homophobia on the lives of queer women of color (Crenshaw, 2017); one oppression cannot be fully understood without simultaneously addressing others. Audre Lorde (1984) famously criticized both white feminists for their inattention to women of color's experience and African-American womanist scholars for their ignoring of lesbian identities. She regularly described herself via a list of intersecting identities that each shaped her experience: "black, lesbian, mother, warrior, poet" (Sehgal, 2020, para. 1). So too will today's lesbian athletes find their experiences shaped by sexuality and gender alongside race, class, and factors like sport and geography. Strategic acceptance operates by producing more favorable media representation for lesbian athletes with certain features, including whiteness, attractiveness, and normative femininity. The intersection of race, sexuality, class, and gender dictates team poli-cies, media responses, endorsement contracts, and even the specific forms of harassment and abuse received by elite Black women athletes (Zenquis & Mwaniki, 2019). In one example of such abuses, radio shock jock Don Imus derided the Rutgers women's basketball team on his radio show after their appearance in the 2007 NCAA women's championship game against Tennessee (Carter & Story, 2007). Imus called the predominantly African-American Rutgers players "rough" and "nappy-headed hoes" (lestarr21, 2007), with coded language critiquing their gender and sexuality. Imus's infamous comments made clear the intersecting ways that racism and sexist and homophobic demands for feminine appearance combine to erase the athletic achievements of African-American women athletes. More recently, the detention of WNBA superstar Brittney Griner by Russian authorities on charges of drug possession and distribution since February 2022 (Ganguli et al., 2022) has offered a less obvious example of the ways that African-American lesbian athletes may receive less institutional support than their white counterparts (Gay, 2022). If one motivation behind Russian detention of Griner is her public lesbian identity which conflicts with the Russian state's anti-gay policy and rhetoric, does she remain imprisoned because the U.S. nation-state's origins have relied upon and continue to dismiss historical and ongoing forms of African-American incarceration? Would Megan Rapinoe have remained in a Russian jail for months on end? National LGBTQ organizations including the National LGBTQ Task Force, GLSEN, Human Rights Campaign, and racial justice organizations including the National Black Justice Coalition have all issued public statements of support for Griner asking similar questions and calling for her release (Belaineh, 2022, para. 2). Clearly lesbian athletes of color are forced to operate within sporting and cultural institutions shaped by norms that dismiss, discriminate, and degrade the black lesbian athlete.

In this analysis, I have described the distancing and acceptance of lesbian athletes as "strategic" to highlight both the unevenness of these practices as well as the intentionality of them. These are strategic responses because media outlets, individual commentators, league officials, corporate sponsors, and other image-shapers always make decisions with the goal of producing economic gains. Within the last decade, corporations have publicly declared support for activist causes; Nike's #BETRUE campaign, begun in 2012, swung into high gear selling rainbow-covered shoes, hats, and clothing in 2015 in perfect coordination with the World Cup win and the *Obergefell* decision (Damante, 2015; Elliot, 2015). Many have argued that these examples of corporate support are actually corporate takeovers of activist movements, "brand activism," or pinkwashing, a term coined to describe the covering up of social and environmental injustices with LGBTQ-friendly policies or marketing, often with the bottom line in mind (Duarte, 2020). That said, lesbian and gay athletes are not simply tools for corporate profits, they too have benefitted from the trendiness of LGBTQ culture via new success in sponsorships and other lucrative endorsement deals (Moreau, 2021; Tumin & Thames, 2022). Occasionally corporations do more than sell merchandise; Nike, for example, also threw its lobbying weight behind legislation designed to protect LGBTQ Americans at work, in schools, and in businesses, along with a handful of other corporate giants, and has at times produced media support and made donations specifically acknowledging the intersectional identities of LGBTQ athletes of color (Elliot, 2015; Ennis, 2020). The results of strategic acceptance of lesbian and other GBTQ athletes have been a complex miasma of profit motives, cultural change, and activist pressure.

Part of the underlying problem behind uneven forms of strategic acceptance for lesbian athletes and LGBTQ people more broadly stems from the assimilationist strategies shaping contemporary LGBTQ politics (Walters, 2014). Assimilation argues that LGBTQ people are "just like" everyone else and therefore deserve acceptance. Duberman challenged the underlying assumptions in the assimilationist position, arguing that LGBTQ people were specifically *not* like everyone else, and in valuable ways.

> [D]espite enormous variations in our individual lifestyles, a distinctive set of perspectives—reflecting our distinct historical experience—exists among gay people

in regard to how they view gender, sexuality, primary relationships, friendships, and family. Gay "differentness" isn't some second-rate variation on first-rate mainstream norms, but rather a decided *advance* over them. Gay sub- cultural values could richly inform conventional life and could open up an unexplored range of human possibilities for *everyone*.

(2013, p. 367)

Duberman points to studies showing LGBTQ people showing higher rates of domestic equity, openness to greater gender individuation beyond binary models, and resistance to essentialist gender expectations, as examples of these advances. He calls for the use of LGBTQ values, experiences, and insights to reshape our relationships, institutions, and culture—including sports—for the benefit of all. Instead of struggling to simply overturn homophobic, and sexist policies and perspectives, lesbian athletes might help drive a reconsideration of sports cultures. How might we enable and celebrate all athletes without regard to sexual orientation, assigned birth sex, gender presentation, race, or socioeconomic background? What structural paradigms perpetuate gender and sexual discrimination, and are there other ways to organize sports outside of those values? By virtue of their experiences with homophobia and sexism, lesbian athletes are positioned to answer these questions and reimagine sport cultures. The queer revolution in sports will not be able to rest solely on individual player personalities or the cultural cache of specific sports but will instead require a broader analysis of the norms and structures that devalue, erase, and attack those athletes with marginalized identities.

Notes

1 A note on inclusion: The athletes in this list have non-heteronormative lived experiences and have identified or been identified publicly at some point as lesbian. Bisexual women, queer women, transwomen, and non-binary athletes experience similar forms of oppression as lesbian athletes, including those shaped by transphobia, biphobia, and bi-erasure, and other intersections of sexism and homophobia. These specific experiences deserve further and careful attention in academic literature as well as mainstream sports coverage.
2 The "It Gets Better" campaign (www.itgetsbetter.org) founded in 2010 by gay columnist Dan Savage and Terry Miller in response to LGBT teen suicide has been critiqued for ignoring the experiences of LGBTQ youth and adults that continue to be shaped by institutional discrimination, exclusion, and violence. See, for example, Keith Boykin (2012), in his introduction to the collection *For Colored Boys Who Have Considered Suicide When the Rainbow Is Still Not Enough*.

References

Abrams, J., & Weiner, N. (2020, October 16). How the most socially progressive pro league got that way. *The New York Times*. www.nytimes.com/2020/10/16/sports/basketball/wnba-loeffler-protest-kneeling.html

Allison, R. (2018). *Kicking center: Gender and the selling of women's professional soccer*. Rutgers.

Anderson, E. (2005). *In the game: Gay athletes and the cult of masculinity*. SUNY Press.

Anderson, E. (2011). The rise and fall of Western homohysteria. *Journal of Feminist Scholarship*, *1*, 80–94.

Anderson, E., & Bullingham, R. (2015). Openly lesbian team sport athletes in an era of decreasing homohysteria. *International Review for the Sociology of Sport*, *50*(6), 647–660.

Anderson, E., & McCormack, M. (2018). Inclusive masculinity theory: Overview, reflection and refinement. *Journal of Gender Studies*, *27*(5), 547–561. https://doi.org/10.1080/09589236. 2016. 1245605

Belaineh, M. (2022, June 27). Brittney Griner is a rallying cry for the LGBTQ+ community to fight for cannabis criminal justice reform. *The Daily Beast*. www.thedaily beast.com/brittney-griner-is-a-rallying-cry-for-the-lgbtq-community-to-fight-for-cannabis-criminal-justice-reform

Benedict XVI. (2005, November). *Instruction concerning the criteria for the discernment of vocations with regard to persons with homosexual tendencies in view of their admission to the seminary and to holy orders.* Congregation for Catholic Education.

Boutilier, M. A., & SanGiovanni, L. (1983). *The sporting woman.* Human Kinetics.

Boykin, Keith. (2012). Introduction. In *Boykin, for colored boys who have considered suicide when the rainbow is still not enough* (pp. xi–xv). Magnus.

Bronski, M. (2011). *A queer history of the United States.* Beacon.

Bruty, S. (2015, July 20). Abby Wambach (image). *Sports Illustrated.* https://sicovers.com/featured/17-us-womens-national-team-2015-fifa-womens-world-cup-champions-july-20-2015-sports-illustrated-cover.html

Bullingham, R., Magrath, R., & Anderson, E. (2014). Changing the game: Sport and a cultural shift away from homohysteria. In J. Hargreaves & E. Anderson (Eds.), *Routledge handbook of sport, gender, and sexuality* (pp. 275–282). Routledge.

Cahn, S. (1993). From the "muscle moll" to the "butch" ballplayers: Mannishness, lesbianism, and homophobia in U.S. women's sport. *Feminist Studies, 19*(2), 343–364.

Carter, B., & Story, S. (2007, April 12). NBC news drops imus show over racial remark. *The New York Times.* www.nytimes.com/2007/04/12/business/media/12dismiss.html

Cayleff, S. E. (1996). *Babe: The life and legend of Babe Didrikson Zaharias.* University of Illinois Press.

Chen, D. (2022, May 24). Transgender athletes face bans from girls' sports in 10 U.S. states. *The New York Times.* www.nytimes.com/article/transgender-athlete-ban.html

Crenshaw, K. (2017). *On intersectionality: Essential writings.* New Press.

Damante, R. (2015, June 4). Nike releases the LGBT-inspired 2015 #BETRUE collection. *GLAAD.org.* www.glaad.org/blog/nike-releases-lgbt-inspired-2015-betrue-collection

Dante65. (2006a, September 7). *Nike WNBA little rascals 1* [Video]. YouTube. www.youtube.com/watch?v=5_DOL061B9c

Dante65. (2006b, September 7). *Nike WNBA little rascals 3* [Video]. YouTube. www.youtube.com/watch?v=WAJfNO3aZGE

Dante65. (2007, June 28). *Nike WNBA little rascals 5* [Video]. YouTube. www.youtube.com/watch?v=I1hn7WHrr50

D'Archangelo, L. (2022, June 15). After years of snubbing LGBTQ+ fans, WNBA is sports' most welcoming league. *The Athletic.com.* https://theathletic.com/3333605/2022/06/15/wnba-lgbtq-fans/

Dhar, P. (2019, November 20). When it comes to being gay friendly, women's sports are ahead of the game. *The Nation.* www.thenation.com/article/archive/women-sports-lgbtq-homophobia/

Duarte, F. (2020, June 12). Big brands have spoken out in support of black communities following George Floyd's killing. How as a consumer do you know which companies genuinely support the cause? *BBC.* www.bbc.com/worklife/article/20200612-black-lives-matter-do-companies-really-support-the-cause

Duberman, M. (2013). Coda: Acceptance at what price? The gay movement reconsidered. In *The Martin Duberman reader: The essential historical, biographical, and autobiographical writings* (pp. 363–371). The New Press.

Eaklor, V. (2008). *Queer America: A people's GLBT history of the 20th century.* New Press.

Education Amendments Act of 1972, 20 U.S.C. §§1681–1688 (2018).

Elliott, P. (2015, July 28). Exclusive: Facebook, corporate giants back new LGBT protections. *Time.* https://time.com/3974267/lgbt-facebook-nike-gay-rights/

Ennis, D. (2020, June 27). Nike's latest BeTrue campaign: "This is our time". *SB Nation—Outsports.* www.outsports.com/2020/6/27/21305415/nike-erica-bougard-adrianna-franch-napoleon-jinnies-quinton-peron-schuyler-bailar-tierna-davidson

Fagan, K. (2015, October 8). What Sheryl Swoopes got wrong about today's WNBA. *ESPN.* www.espn.com/espnw/news-commentary/story/_/id/13835681/what-sheryl-swoopes-got-wrong-today-wnba

FIFA. (2015, December). Record-breaking FIFA women's world cup tops 750 million TV viewers. *FIFA.com.* www.fifa.com/womensworldcup/news/record-breaking-fifa-women-s-world-cup-tops-750-million-tv-viewers-2745963

FIFA. (2019, October 18). FIFA women's world cup 2019 watched by more than 1 billion. *FIFA.com.* www.fifa.com/womensworldcup/news/fifa-women-s-world-cup-2019tm-watched-by-more-than-1-billion

Figel, B. (1986, June 16). Lesbians in world of athletics. *Chicago Sun-Times.* www.yumpu.com/en/document/view/6595473/chicago-sun-times-june-16-1986-lesbians-in-world-of-athletics-

Fink, J. S., Burton, L. J., & Farrell, A. O. (2012). Playing it out: Female intercollegiate athletes' experiences in revealing their sexual identities. *Journal for the Study of Sports and Athletes in Education, 6*(1), 83–106.

Fink, J. S., & Kensicki, L. J. (2002). An imperceptible difference: Visual and textual construction of femininity in sports illustrated and sports illustrated for women. *Mass Communication and Society*, 5(3), 317–339.

Forman, R. (2013, October 9). Soccer superstar Abby Wambach comes out, marries teammate. *Windy City Times*. www.windycitytimes.com/lgbt/Soccer-superstar-Abby-Wambach-comes-out-marries-teammate-/44724.html

Gambino, L. (2015, July 6). Women's world cup joy: Abby Wambach and her wife "just another couple celebrating". *The Guardian*. www.theguardian.com/football/2015/jul/06/womens-world-cup-final-abby-wambach-wife-kiss

Ganguli, T., Abrams, J., & Bubola, E. (2022, July 28). What we know about Brittney Griner's detention in Russia. *The New York Times*. www.nytimes.com/article/brittney-griner-russia.html?name=styln-brittney-griner&region=TOP_BANNER&block=storyline_menu_recirc&action=click&pgtype=Article&variant=show&is_new=false

Gay, R. (2022, July 15). Brittney Griner is trapped and alone. Where's your outrage? *The New York Times*. www.nytimes.com/2022/07/15/opinion/brittney-griner-russia.html

Graham, B. A. (2015, October 27). Abby Wambach, world's all-time leading goalscorer, announces retirement. *The Guardian*. www.theguardian.com/football/2015/oct/27/abby-wambach-worlds-all-time-leading-goalscorer-announces-retirement

Granderson, L. Z. (2005, October 25). Three-time MVP "tired of having to hide my feelings". *ESPN the Magazine*. www.espn.com/wnba/news/story?id=2203853

Greenberg, A. (2015, July 6). Abby Wambach kissing her wife after winning the world cup will warm your heart. *Time*. https://time.com/3946226/abby-wambach-womens-soccer-world-cup-wife-kiss-lgbt-gay-marriage/

Griffin, P. (1998). *Strong women, deep closets: Lesbians and homophobia in sport*. Human Kinetics.

Hernandez, V. (2019, February 14). Sheryl Swoopes, a WNBA superstar, on her big Nike moment: "I still get a little choked up". *Los Angeles Times*. www.latimes.com/fashion/la-ig-sneakers-sheryl-swoopes-nike-womens-sneakers-20190214-story.html

Johnson, P. (2020, May 30). Nike releases "don't do it" video denouncing racism and calling for change. *Hypebeast*. https://hypebeast.com/2020/5/nike-social-justice-dont-do-it-video

Kane, M. J. (1988). Media coverage of the female athlete before, during, and after Title IX: Sports illustrated revisited. *Journal of Sport Management*, 2, 87–99.

Kann, D. (2019, July 5). Yes, the US women's soccer team is dominant. That's because most of the world is playing catch-up. *CNN*. www.cnn.com/2019/06/16/us/uswnt-dominance-womens-soccer-world-cup-history-explained/index.html

Kort, M. (1988, August 18). Billie Jean King—interview. *The Advocate*.

Lenskyj, H. J. (2003). *Out on the field*. Women's Press.

Leonard, T. (2017, February 17). Wiggins: WNBA's "harmful" culture of bullying, jealousy. *San Diego Union-Tribune*. www.sandiegouniontribune.com/sports/sd-sp-wigginsside-20170217-story.html

lestarr21. (2007, April 6). Don Imus calls girls basketball team nappy headed hoes! *YouTube.com*. www.youtube.com/watch?v=ui1jPNDWArM

Livingston, M. (2015, June 10). Brittney Griner, Glory Johnson, the WNBA and domestic violence in LGBT community. *Bleacherreport.com*. https://bleacherreport.com/articles/2479888-brittney-griner-glory-johnson-the-wnba-and-domestic-violence-in-lgbt-community

Lorde, A. (1984). *Sister/outsider: Essays and speeches*. Crossing Press.

Maheshwari, S., & Friedman, V. (2021, June 16). Victoria's secret swaps Angels for "what women want". Will they buy it? *The New York Times*. www.nytimes.com/2021/06/16/business/victorias-secret-collective-megan-rapinoe.html

McCormack, M., & Anderson, E. (2014). The influence of declining homophobia on men's gender in the United States: An argument for the study of homohysteria. *Sex Roles*, 71, 109–120.

Messner, M. (2002). *Taking the field: Women, men, and sports*. University of Minnesota.

Moreau, J. (2021, August 3). From "kiss of death" to competitive edge: out athletes finally score big endorsements. *NBC News*. www.nbcnews.com/nbc-out/out-news/kiss-death-competitive-edge-athletes-finally-score-big-endorsements-rcna1586

Mosbacher, D., & Yacker, F. (2009). *Training rules: No drinking, no drugs, no lesbians* [Film]. WomanVision Productions.

Mullin, B. (2019, July 8). Women's world cup final drew higher U.S. rating than men's final. *The Wall Street Journal*. www.wsj.com/articles/womens-world-cup-final-drew-higher-u-s-ratings-than-mens-final-11562628017

Nanda, S. (2022). *State and federal legal issues: Louisiana executive orders*. LGBT Archives Project. www.lgbtarchiveslouisiana.org/legal-issues.

Neeley, Lyn (2021, April 2). Megan Rapinoe: Soccer star, political activist. *Workers World*. https://www.workers.org/2021/04/55545/

Obergefell v. Hodges, 576 U.S. 644 (2015). www.supremecourt.gov/opinions/14pdf/14556_3204.pdf

O'Dowd, P., & McMahon, S. (2019, December 13). From athlete to activist: Soccer star Megan Rapinoe's "wild" year. *WBUR*. www.wbur.org/hereandnow/2019/12/13/megan-rapinoe-soccer-world-cup-video

Parkinson, H. J. (2019, July 4). Love all: How Megan Rapinoe and other gay players are taking sport to a higher level. *The Guardian*. www.theguardian.com/sport/shortcuts/2019/jul/04/love-all-how-megan-rapinoe-and-other-gay-players-are-taking-sport-to-a-higher-level

Pascoe, C. J. (2007). *Dude, you're a fag: Masculinity and sexuality in high school*. University of California Press.

Praderio, C. (2016, November 29). How Ellen DeGeneres went from unknown comic to talk show superstar. *Insider*. www.insider.com/how-did-ellen-degeneres-become-famous-2016-11

Proposal 8, California. (2008). http://ag.ca.gov/cms_pdfs/initiatives/i737_07-0068_Initiative.pdf

Proposal 22, California. (2000). http://primary2000.ss.ca.gov/VoterGuide/Propositions/22text.htm

Reimer, A. (2020, August 27). How Megan Rapinoe, and other LGBT sports stars, helped set stage for current moment in athlete activism. *SB Nation—Outsports*. www.outsports.com/2020/8/27/21404217/megan-rapinoe-activism

Rivas, M. (2021, March 25). Megan Rapinoe on her allyship, activism, and athleticism. *Shondaland*. www.shondaland.com/act/a35927824/megan-rapinoe-on-allyship-activism-soccer/

Rupert, M. (2011, August 1). What Sheryl Swoopes' engagement means: Understanding the role of identity and combo guards. *HuffPost*. www.huffpost.com/entry/sheryl-swoopes-marriage_b_909288

Schweighofer, K. (2016). LGBTQ sport and leisure history. In *LGBTQ America: A theme study of lesbian, gay, bisexual, transgender, and queer history*. National Park Foundation/National Park Service. www.nps.gov/articles/lgbtqtheme-sport.htm

Sehgal, P. (2020, September 15). A timely collection of vital writing by Audre Lorde. *The New York Times*. www.nytimes.com/2020/09/15/books/review-audre-lorde-selected-works.html

Storm, H. (Director). (2013). *Nine for IX: Swoopes* [Film]. ESPNW.

Telander, R. (2019, July 9). Gay and proud: Megan Rapinoe is the current face of athletic excellence. *Chicago Sun-Times*. https://chicago.suntimes.com/2019/7/9/20688286/gay-megan-rapinoe-uswnt-womens-world-cup-fifa-equality-lesbian-bird-wnba

Tumin, R., & Thames, A. (2022, July 24). Pretty in any color: Women on the court make style rules. *The New York Times*. www.nytimes.com/2022/07/24/sports/basketball/wnba-style-fashion-marketing.html

Voepel, M. (2017, February 21). WNBA has no comment, but many players dispute Candice Wiggins' allegations of bullying culture. *ESPN*. www.espn.com/wnba/story/_/id/18736607/wnba-players-dispute-candice-wiggins-controversial-allegations

Walters, S. D. (2014). *The tolerance trap: How God, genes, and good intentions are sabotaging gay equality*. NYU.

Warren, P. N. (2006). *The lavender locker room*. Wildcat.

Zenquis, M. R., & Mwaniki, M. F. (2019). The intersection of race, gender, and nationality in sport: Media representation of the Ogwumike sisters. *Journal of Sport and Social Issues, 43*(1), 23–43.

V

Social, Psychological, and Research Contexts

24

QUEER IDENTITIES
IN CONTEXTS

Matthew J. Cull

Recent work in analytic feminist metaphysics seeking to engage with queer and especially trans identities has led to the development of contextualist accounts of social identities. These accounts claim that what it is to be a trans woman, or demigender, or gay, is dependent on context. In this chapter, I briefly survey the history of contextualism about gender and sexual identities, looking at gender in Aristotle and Elizabeth Spelman, before looking at recent developments in contextualist approaches to gender, developing work by Jennifer Saul, Talia Mae Bettcher, María Lugones, and Ásta. I suggest that contextually variable accounts of social identities are philosophically robust, but that contextualist and closely related pluralist views still have questions to answer, and room for development.

Aristotle's Proto Pluralism

Aristotle makes two key distinctions as to types of person in his *Politics*: a distinction between men and women, and a distinction between free citizens and slaves. For Aristotle, all things are defined by their function, that is, the purpose that they and their kind were intended to do well. For men, this is the pursuit of the noble life, contemplation, and the pursuit of statecraft as members of the polis. This public sphere in which men can pursue virtue cannot exist in isolation, however. Necessary for the pursuit of virtue is the background condition of the household: the realm of social reproduction. It is in this realm that women find their function, as bearers of children, companions, and preservers of what their husbands acquire (Aristotle, 1905, p. 1277b). Meanwhile, the slave is distinguished from the master by their function as menial labourer under the direction of the master, along with their function of ministering to the needs of others (Aristotle, 1905, p. 1278a). Both distinctions are drawn according to the function that each role is to play in the state. Women and slaves are defined by their respective vital roles as preconditions for the activities of free men in the polis, while those men are themselves defined by the activities that they are to undertake in the public sphere.

Elizabeth Spelman points out that these distinctions cut across one another. The question to ask, she suggests, is what is the status of the slave woman in Aristotle? Spelman suggests that the notion of a slave woman is something of an impossibility in Aristotle's thought, given that women are defined by their functional role as companion to the free man (Spelman, 1988, p. 42). Thus, while there might be slaves with what is often called 'female biology', such slaves

 DOI: 10.4324/9781003128151-29

are not women. On this sort of view, two things become clear. First, that gender is inseparable from a particular political and work context—it is only in virtue of a particular kind of social context (the state as described by Aristotle) that gender can occur. Second, that having a gender is tied to a particular kind of privilege—that of being free. Without the status of being a free person, one cannot have a gender.

This view offers the beginnings of a kind of contextualism about gender. Of course, for Aristotle, the question of whether one is a man, woman, or slave is intended by nature, according to the particular capabilities one has been accorded (see Deslauriers, 2003). However, once we move past this biological essentialism, and regard one's class, slave status, race, and so on as features of social contexts, we might think that a contextualist view is on offer. Spelman, as we will see shortly, offers something like such a view.

Note, however, that even Aristotle recognises that there are occasions upon which slave status is not a result of nature, but instead is the result of human action, as in the case of (Greek) enemies captured in conflict and employed as slaves (Spelman, 1988, p. 41). One way of reading this is precisely to say that Greek gender identity is contextually dependent on whether or not one has been conquered. As such, we might say that Aristotle gave us a contextualist account of gender. Of course, one might argue that things are not so clear, given that Aristotle thinks that 'slave' is an ambiguous term in these contexts (Aristotle, 1905, p. 1255a3–12)—as such one might argue that this sort of slavery (by convention and not by nature) does not have this 'degendering' function. One might think, for instance, that slaves by convention are not slaves proper, but rather 'temporarily embarrassed' free men and women. However, I suggest that even if we buy this sort of argument, and think that Aristotle was not a contextualist himself, he nonetheless provides us with the resources to offer the first contextualist account of gender.

Spelman's Reluctant Pluralism

Spelman herself is largely concerned, in her *Inessential Woman*, to provide arguments against essentialist accounts of women, and arguing forcefully against white feminist overgeneralisation about 'the woman's experience'. One of her more powerful anti-essentialist arguments has become known as the 'inseparability argument'. Spelman suggests that it is impossible to separate her gender from her race—that she cannot imagine her gender independently from her race:

> If it were possible to isolate a woman's 'womanness' from her racial identity, then we should have no trouble imagining that had I been Black I could have had just the same understanding of myself as a woman as I in fact do, and that no matter how differently people would have treated me had I been Black, nevertheless what it would have meant to them would have been just the same. To rehearse this imaginary situation is to expose its utter bizarreness.
>
> *(Spelman, 1988, p. 135)*

What follows from this is, according to Spelman, that there can be no such thing as a social identity considered in isolation from context. What it is to be a woman, suggests Spelman, is constructed differently in different contexts, and differently given different intersecting identities (though Spelman does not use the term 'intersecting' herself, a term we owe especially to Crenshaw (1991)). For Spelman, there is no such thing as a notion of 'womanhood' common to all women and that each woman can isolate from other aspects of her identity. For instance, a lesbian woman's experience of womanhood is going to be different from a straight woman's experience, and the kinds of oppression she will face will often be impacted by her sexuality in ways different to those of straight women. As a side note, not everyone buys the inseparability argument; for instance, the inseparability argument fails qua metaphysical thesis (see Mikkola, 2006).

Spelman explores a number of political consequences of this claim, but most relevantly for us here, she comes to a metaphysical conclusion: that we must be prepared to embrace the claim that different women may '[belong] to different genders' (Spelman, 1988, pp. 174–175). Spelman candidly notes that she is reluctant to draw this conclusion, as she is worried that it may have troubling political consequences for feminist praxis. Indeed, does the claim that women have different gender identities, and face different forms of oppression not undermine a coherent feminist political movement? Moreover, who is feminism for, if not a unified group called 'women'? Spelman ultimately rejects such worries, suggesting that feminism needs to engage with the differences among women, and not silence doubly, or triply marginalised groups. Indeed, she thinks that such conflict may aid feminist movements by better helping feminists to understand the variety of issues that women face (Spelman, 1988, p. 176). (For further argument that pluralism does not undermine feminist praxis, and indeed aids feminist praxis, see Cull, 2020, pp. 150–151.)

Note, however, that if Spelman is correct about the metaphysics of *woman*, two things follow. First, her argument is independent of the worry that this metaphysics undermines feminist praxis. If the metaphysics of woman is context-dependent and that happens to be bad for feminism (though see Cull, 2020 for an argument that it isn't), then so much the worse for feminism. Second, the inseparability argument works *mutatis mutandis* for other social identities. If we are pluralists about *woman* due to inseparability, then we ought to be pluralists about other social identities, including *demiboy*, *lesbian*, *Black*, and *agender*.

Saul's Contextualism, Bettcher's Pluralism

Contemporary discussions of pluralism and contextualism about gender terms arose from the work of three thinkers: María Lugones (2003), Jennifer Saul (2012), and Talia Mae Bettcher (2013). Saul's contextualism, which she puts forward, though does not eventually endorse, holds that the content of the term 'woman' shifts according to the context in which the term is uttered. Saul suggests that we should understand the term 'woman' as follows:

> *X is a woman* is true in a context C iff X is human and relevantly similar (according to the standards at work in C) to most of those possessing all of the biological markers of female sex.
>
> *(Saul, 2012, p. 201)*

A note on terminology: Saul uses the term 'iff'—which indicates a biconditional relation and is generally translated as 'if and only if'.

Saul's account allows us to input different standards according to the context in question. In trans-inclusive contexts, the standards are (generally) based around self-identification, and as such, Saul's definition of 'woman' becomes:

> *X is a woman* is true in C1 iff X is human and relevantly similar (in sincerely self-identifying as a woman) to most of those possessing all of the biological markers of female sex.
>
> *(Saul, 2012, p. 203)*

Meanwhile, in many trans-exclusive contexts (putatively), the standard for whether one counts as a woman is whether one has XX chromosomes. Saul's definition therefore turns into:

> *X is a woman* is true in C3 iff X is human and relevantly similar (in having XX chromosomes) to most of those possessing all of the biological markers of female sex.
>
> *(Saul, 2012, p. 203)*

One issue that should immediately strike the reader is that one might worry that this account is transphobic. The utterance 'trans women are women' comes out true in trans-inclusive contexts, but it is also the case that a lawmaker, who on the floor of legislature that regularly passes transphobic laws, utters the phrase, 'these "trans women" aren't *actually* women' is saying something true. This is doubly troubling—first, the truth or falsity of trans women's claims that they are women seem to be made contingent upon context, and second, that this is a part of the meaning of the term 'woman' on Saul's account seems to lead to political paralysis. The first trouble arises because trans people are misgendered by this account in contexts like C3. The second trouble comes up because it seems that we have no resources to appeal to such that we can claim that the transphobic lawmaker in a context like C3 is *wrong* to misgender trans people. For instance, someone asserting 'trans women are not women', is, in such a context, uttering something true. One might resist this of course: later, we will look at Díaz-León's argument that this is not actually the relevant definition of woman in trans-exclusive contexts, and hence that trans-exclusive statements come out as false (see Díaz-León, 2016).

Note, however, that Saul has a response to the second worry; we can note that the transphobic context is a wrongful context. That is, it is a *morally* vicious context. Recognising the wrongness here gives us the space and opportunity to organise to change the context, such that trans-exclusive utterances are made false. So, instead of political paralysis, the contextualist position actually serves as a call to change the world. How should this be achieved? We might think that in the case of the transphobic legislature, one option might be to elect a number of transfeminist sympathisers. This would change the standards at work in the context and thus the truth conditions for claims about woman.

Bettcher's position differs from Saul's somewhat but maintains the claim that there are different senses of gender terms at work in different contexts. She begins with the claim that we ought to reject the dominant conception of gender in favour of the concept of gender at work in trans communities. Bettcher claims that we should think of trans communities as creating new meanings for gender terms and hence new social realities or spaces. Here, Bettcher draws on the work of Maria Lugones, and especially her work on social worlds (more later).

On this sort of account, trans women, when in mainstream, trans-exclusive contexts, or social worlds, are men, and yet are women in trans-inclusive contexts or social worlds. Importantly for Bettcher, trans women should not feel the need to defer to the meaning of 'woman' in the trans-exclusive social world. Instead, trans women and their allies should embrace the conception of women that is operative in trans-inclusive communities. Bettcher's analysis of 'trans woman' in trans-inclusive worlds here is interesting, suggesting that rather than treating 'trans' as a modifier for the term 'woman', 'trans woman' should be treated as a basic expression that applies to all those who are identified as such and is a sufficient condition for being a woman.

At this point, a challenge that we raised for Saul appears pertinent—aren't we putting forward a transphobic theory in allowing that the truth of the claim that 'trans women are women' is contingent upon social situation, and moreover, false in trans-exclusive social worlds? The response Bettcher offers is virtually the same as the one Saul offered earlier—that this is a political problem to be solved via changing the social world such that trans-exclusive meanings are not operative.

Bettcher's account, just like the one Saul put forward, suggests that the term 'woman' has different senses in different contexts and offers the same response to a challenge that it makes transphobic utterances true. What then is the difference between the two accounts? Here one might sceptically suggest that Bettcher's theory is simply another version of contextualism. This, however, is something that Bettcher is at pains to reject. She suggests that her account actually gives us the potential for a more radical contestation between different conceptions of gender than the contextualist does (Bettcher, 2013, p. 244). However, it seems hard to see what grounds this claim: after all, both Bettcher's and Saul's accounts allow for contestation over the meanings of gender terms and give us the ability to suggest that any given context is a wrongful context. Moreover, whatever tactics are available to change the meaning-making features of contexts we endorse (whether those be filling a legislature with trans-friendly legislators, re-writing a workplace safer spaces policy, or any number of other tactics) both accounts will be able to avail themselves of those resources. If the semantics of terms are therefore up for contestation on both accounts, what is it that Bettcher is pointing to when she claims her account is more radical?

I suggest that there is a difference of some technical importance between these two accounts, *but* that this difference is not of radical import, and that we can think of the Saulian contextualist and the Bettcherian pluralist as offering accounts that are equivalent for political purposes. The difference goes back to a distinction pointed out by David Kaplan, between the *content* and the *character* of a term or sentence (see Kaplan, 1989, pp. 500–507). The content of a term, according to Kaplan, applies only when a term is considered *in a context* and may helpfully be thought of as the meaning of a term in that context. Note that both the account offered by Saul and the account offered by Bettcher suggest that the content of 'woman' changes across contexts. Meanwhile, the character of a term is a function that takes one from a context to a content—it determines the content for any given circumstance. Helpfully, Saul spells out the character of 'woman' on her account:

> *X is a woman* is true in a context C iff X is human and relevantly similar (according to the standards at work in C) to most of those possessing all of the biological markers of female sex.
>
> *(Saul, 2012, p. 201)*

On this account, the character of 'woman' is fixed, and for any given context, tells one what the content of 'woman' is in that context. Contrast this with the account put forward by Bettcher: Bettcher suggests that 'woman' has (at least) two characters—one for trans-exclusive worlds, and one for trans inclusive worlds. Instead of there being a fixed character that tells us the meaning of 'woman' in these worlds, we instead get two wholly different and independent meanings for the term. As such, we see that while both accounts allow that the content of 'woman' varies across circumstances, Bettcher's account also allows for variation in the character of 'woman' whereas Saul's account does not. This, I take it, is the ultimate difference between the accounts, and I suggest that we label accounts that are along these lines in the following way:

Content Varies, Character Fixed: *Semantic Contextualism.*
Content Varies, Character Varies: *Meaning Pluralism.*

Now, is this difference really enough to ground Bettcher's claim that her account offers grounds for a more radical contestation and rejection of transphobic versions of the meaning of 'woman'?

Well, perhaps—after all, meaning pluralists are able to suggest that we can reject the character of the term 'woman' as operative in transphobic contexts, in addition to the content, while semantic contextualists can only reject the content. However, I suggest that this argument is too quick. It is unclear exactly what political gains are made by being able to reject both character and content, and indeed, I suggest that this is a relatively minor difference between the accounts. While Bettcher suggests that on her account 'the shift [across worlds] in usage is *far more radical* than the mere introduction of a new contextually relevant standard" (Bettcher, 2013, p. 244). I struggle to see exactly what this minor difference on the semantics of gender terms amounts to in terms of developing a better world for trans people.

Moreover, recall another problem that faced the account that Saul put forward: that the account made trans women's claims to womanhood contingent on context (call this 'the contingency problem'). While trans women's claims of the form 'I am a woman' are true in trans-inclusive contexts, in trans-exclusive contexts, their claims are rendered false on Saul's account. While we might try to suggest that these trans-exclusive contexts are *bad contexts* which ought to be changed, Saul suggests that this is not satisfactory. She suggests that most trans women want their claims of the form 'I am a woman' to be true regardless of context, and they similarly want the claims of those who deny that they are women to be false, even in the bad contexts. Note that this problem applies equally to Bettcher's account! In transphobic social worlds, Bettcher's account suggests that claims such as 'trans women are men' are true and 'I am a woman' (when uttered by trans women) are false. Bettcher's way of dealing with this problem is to argue that her account is not strictly ameliorative, but rather, is descriptive of a transphobic social reality. Her account, she argues, correctly describes a social reality in which, in trans-exclusive social worlds, trans women do not count as women, and do not count as women precisely because those worlds are oppressive. While I think that this is a rather effective way of dealing with the contingency problem, note that precisely the same response is also available to the defender of a semantic contextualist account like that put forward by Saul. Just as Bettcher could claim that her account is descriptive of a transphobic social reality, so too the contextualist can claim that, in talking about a trans-exclusive context, their theory is descriptive and (accurately) describes an oppressive context in which trans women do not get to count as women.

There is one advantage that I take Bettcher's account to have—over and above the particular contextualist account that Saul puts forward—which is that it does not unnecessarily centre cis women and marginalise trans women. Recall that Saul suggests that the character for the term 'woman' should be understood as being one which is organised around 'most of those possessing all of the biological features of the female sex'. No matter the standard for comparison in any given context, then the group which we measure womanhood by will always be cis women on the account Saul put forward. I suggest that an implicit normative hierarchy is at work here—privileging cis identities over trans identities as the paradigmatic cases of womanhood. Such a normative hierarchy is quite contrary to feminist, queer, and trans concerns, as Heyes (2000) has so forcefully argued from a feminist perspective.

Yet this is not to say that semantic contextualist accounts in general will fall victim to this problem. Bettcher's account gets around this problem by stipulating that (at least for the resistant, trans-inclusive sense of 'woman') trans womanhood forms a fundamental, paradigmatic part of the definition of 'woman'. Moreover, with a small modification, Saul's own account can be updated to avoid this problem. Take the following semantic contextualist character for the term 'woman':

> *X is a woman* is true in a context C iff X is human and is a woman according to the standards at work in C.

This minor adjustment of the account Saul put forward avoids the prioritising of cis over trans women entirely, and we can keep the rest of the account the same. In a trans-inclusive context, where the standards at work for determining whether one is a woman is that one self-identifies as a woman, the aforementioned character spits out the following content:

> *X is a woman* is true in context C1 iff X is human and identifies as a woman.

Meanwhile in a trans-exclusive context where chromosomes are the relevant standard:

> *X is a woman is true* in context C3 iff X is human and has XX chromosomes.

Where does this leave us? Well, semantic contextualist and meaning pluralist accounts both face the same problems and can put forward the same solutions to those problems. There is a technical difference between these accounts that is of some interest to a philosopher of language and those working in linguistics, given their difference over the character of 'woman', but I fail to see any political relevance to this difference. Certainly, it is not enough to sustain Bettcher's claim that her account allows for a more radical rejection of transphobic meanings for 'woman'. The significance of this technical difference in the philosophy of language and linguistics goes beyond the scope of this chapter (see Borg, 2007), Carston, 2013, 2019; Recanati, 2004, 2012). I take it that the queer, trans and feminist activists should happily endorse whichever of pluralism or contextualism eventually wins out in the technical debates taking place in these other fields. If one buys the claim that what being a woman means varies across different contexts, I suggest one can happily endorse either contextualism or pluralism.

What Are These Things We Call Contexts?

At this point, one might be somewhat puzzled. Certainly, if one is a pluralist or contextualist, the meaning of a term varies across contexts. But what are contexts? How should we think about the features of the world that make the content of a term (if one is a contextualist) or the content and character of a term (if one is a pluralist) vary?

One option, put forward by Esa Díaz-León (2016), would be to suggest that it is normative features of the subject of an utterance that are the relevant context and therefore determine the meaning of a term—*subject contextualism*. So, supposing I utter 'Charla is a woman', talking about a trans woman named Charla. For Díaz-León, the content of 'woman' is to be fixed by 'relevant normative considerations having to do with the subject of utterance' (Díaz-León, 2016, p. 252)—in this case, Charla. Díaz-León suggests that it is 'Charla herself, and some relevant features of her context such as the history of oppression of trans women and so on' (Díaz-León, 2016, p. 252) that fixes the meaning of 'woman' in any sentence featuring the word 'woman' about Charla. If the subject of my utterance was a different person, the content of the term may be different, given that it would be normative considerations to do with this new subject that are the relevant context and hence fix the content of my utterance. Importantly, these are ethical and political considerations that give us the meaning of a term.

Díaz-León's subject contextualism is helpfully contrasted with a more traditional position, *attributor contextualism*. According to attributor contextualism, the content of a term is fixed by the context in which some utterance is made. In this case, the context is defined not by normative facts about the subject of an utterance, but rather linguistic facts about acceptable interpretations of the term 'woman' in the place, time, and social situation of the utterer. Thus, when 'Charla is a woman' is uttered in a transphobic community, it is false, but when uttered in a trans inclusive community it is true. Something like this version of contextualism was presupposed in my aforementioned discussion of Saul, and this falsity case is partially Saul's reason for not endorsing the contextualist position she put forward. Note that, by contrast, this utterance about Charla is always true according to the subject contextualist.

Both of these options, subject contextualism and attributor contextualism, provide fairly minimal characterisations of contexts in terms of normative and linguistic facts about the subject or attributor's situation. One might, however, offer a richer account, as María Lugones does. For Lugones, the subject is not unified, but instead is plural (Lugones, 2003, p. 57). Drawing on the experience of bicultural people, she suggests that as such people move between cultural contexts, they experience themselves:

> as more than one: having desires, character and personality traits that are different in one reality than in the other, and acting, enacting, animating their bodies, having thoughts, feeling the emotions, in ways that are different in one reality than another. The practical syllogisms that go through in one reality are not possible in the other, given that they are such different people in the two realities, given that the realities hold such different possibilities for them.
>
> *(Lugones, 2003, p. 57)*

Lugones calls these different realities 'worlds' and, despite some reticence to define them too strictly she suggests that they should be understood as actual (portions of) societies, incorporating all of the social and material norms and practices of that portion of society, along with its power relations and linguistic features. She suggests that these worlds construct individuals in different ways—thus the mainstream white American world constructs Latina women in one way, and Hispano worlds construct them in another. For Lugones, then, there is no one Latina identity. Rather, Latina women must navigate different identities as they move between these worlds (see Lugones, 2003, pp. 87–89).

This notion of navigating worlds is something that has a natural application to queer subjects, who find themselves constructed differently across different environments. Who a gay man is in the world of work where he is not out, who he is in the world of activism where his sexuality is embraced, and who he is in a family context where he is out but treated with suspicion are going to differ, with enormous consequences for what he can say and do.

Politically, Lugones thinks that such 'world travelling' is vital for liberation. Oppressive regimes often portray themselves as inevitable and inescapable, and it is precisely the knowledge that one has seen and existed in another world (no matter how small that world is) that provides the hope that the oppressive world may be changed or overthrown. If a small queer group is able to form relationships and social practices in which queerness and queer identities are welcomed and embraced, then a model of how wider society might be made welcoming to LGBTQIA people is made available to those in that small group. World-travelling, then, provides the means for 'the escape from inescapable oppression' (Lugones, 2003, p. 61).

Ásta's Conferralism

Lugones' account of the construction of contextualist identities was, as we saw, somewhat passive. That is, a background society, despite being constructed by human activity, nonetheless did all the work in constructing social identities. In her recent *Categories We Live By*, Ásta has offered an account of the construction of identities in contexts that involves subjects conferring identities on one another.

For Ásta, having a social identity is a matter of being taken to have some base property in a given context, and being conferred an additional social property by others in that context. The idea is that these various identities are the social significance of base properties. The basic pattern is exemplified by the communal property of being a gender:

Conferred Property: being of gender G, for example, a woman, man, trans*
Who: the subjects with standing in a particular context
What: the perception of the subject S that the person has the base property P
When: in some particular context
Base property: the base property P, for example, the role in biological reproduction; in others it is the person's role in societal organization of various kinds, sexual engagement, bodily presentation, preparation of food at family gatherings, self-identification, and so on.

(Ásta, 2018, pp. 74–75)

According to this model, the gender that is conferred to a person can vary as the base property that is significant varies across contexts and can also vary according to whether that person is taken to have that base property. The base property, and indeed whether a person is taken to have that property, is determined by those in the context with social standing, who themselves will take themselves to be following the social arrangements outside of that context.

In addition to this type of conferred property (which she calls 'communal' properties, as they are conferred by a community negotiating social standing), Ásta thinks that there is an additional type of conferred property—institutional properties. Institutional properties are those that are conferred by a person or group that (in a particular context) stands in a position of institutional authority. Typically, such properties feature explicit rules and rituals for conferral— Ásta's paradigm case is having the property of being President of the United States, which she analyses as follows:

Conferred property: being elected president of the United States
Who: the current US vice president, as president of the US Senate; this is the entity in authority
What: the declaration that someone has received the most electoral college votes for US president
When: on January 6, following a November election, starting at 1 p.m.
Base property: the majority of electoral college votes, that is, 270 or more

(Ásta, 2018, p. 22)

Just like in the case of communal properties, institutional properties are supposed to track a base property, and in the case of the President of the United States, this is the property of actually having won the most electoral college votes. However, unlike communal properties, being conferred the property of being the President of the United States follows a set of fairly strict rules and takes place when a particular authority, the leader of the United States Senate, deems the base property to have been achieved in the right situation.

Are LGBTQ identities communal, or are they institutional? Ásta's position leaves it open that there are both communal and institutional properties of being (say) bisexual. This nicely captures the distinction between institutional (and especially state/legal) recognition of one's bisexual status, and the local recognition of one's bisexual status in particular queer communities. Allowing for such a distinction is important: there are going to be cases of people who have no institutional property of being (say) transgender from the state but do have a communal property of being transgender thanks to local community recognition. Negotiating how to achieve state recognition of one's trans identity, and whether such a recognition is desirable at all forms a key set of questions in contemporary trans (and especially nonbinary) politics.

Moreover, Ásta's account of communal properties nicely captures a number of features of social identities that we might think are worth including. First, it takes into account that many social identities, including (but not limited to) gender, are partly dependent on the background conditions of society. Rather than just being products of particular situations, social identities are conferred, according to Ásta, with reference to broader social norms, social structures, and ideological formations (here Ásta is drawing on Butler, 1990). After all, while it is individuals doing the conferring of identities in particular contexts, those individuals generally take themselves to be following broader rules about how different identities are supposed to work, and which base properties are appropriate grounds for conferring which identities. Second, it captures that fact that these identities get negotiated differently in different local contexts. Some contexts will, for instance, have features that mean that broader rules for how identities should work and which base properties are appropriate will be ignored in favour of locally instituted norms. Moreover, who gets to count as having standing and how their interpretation of broader societal norms will play out in a given context is not wholly determined by society at large, even if the rules themselves are provided by society at large.

In some ways, then, we might think that Ásta's account gives us a nice way of thinking about queer identities. To take an example, think of the social identity *lesbian*. Broad societal norms (generally) suggest that this is an identity that can only be applied to women, and that an appropriate base property for the conferral of this property is a sexual attraction to women to the exclusion of other genders. However, in particular contexts, these norms are sometimes contested and even rejected outright, as lesbian communities negotiate with the complexities posed to lesbian identity by (for instance) members of their communities coming out as trans and the intricacies of butch identity. In such cases, we may find those with social standing in lesbian communities conferring lesbian identity on nonwomen, or those who experience attraction to certain nonwomen (perhaps some of the best explorations of these themes are still to be found in Feinberg, 1993 and Bechdel, 2009).

Furthermore, think of trans identities—we might think that in many contexts, the base property for conferring gender is going to be something like one's role in reproduction, or one's assigned sex at birth. As such, trans people will have (what we would normally consider) the wrong gender property conferred upon them (see Kapusta, 2016). However, in contexts where trans people and their allies are able to achieve social standing, the relevant base property in those contexts can be changed to one which is more trans-inclusive—for instance, self-identification. It therefore becomes a political task to transform various contexts into ones in which trans people and their allies have sufficient social standing, such that trans people are conferred genders which best match up to their sense of self.

However, I want to suggest that this account appears to be somewhat missing an important feature of LGBTQ identities—that one is LGBTQ even when one is in the closet. That is, even if one is taken in a context to not have the relevant base property that would make one a candidate for the conferral of the property *lesbian*, or *transgender*, one is nevertheless still lesbian or transgender. Suppose one is a woman who is happily married to another woman and feels sexual and romantic desire only towards women. In any context where one is not out about this fact, and assumptions of a default heterosexuality are operative, it looks as if Ásta's account will minimally suggest that one is not a lesbian in such contexts, and indeed, perhaps even suggest that one is straight in such contexts. Alternatively, take the case of finally realising that you are nonbinary, having assumed that you were a man up until this point, and everyone around you continuing to assume that you are a man. In any context in which one has not made others aware of one's new self-identification, regardless of the relevant base property, Ásta's position suggests that one is a man in such contexts. It seems as if Ásta's position is missing that queer identities often have a distinctive internal life attached to them, that often precedes any queer social living.

Now perhaps Ásta can bite the bullet here—perhaps passing and closeted LGBTQ people aren't LGBTQ in the kinds of contexts motioned earlier. Indeed, at one point, she seems to suggest that this is the case when she writes that she 'cannot draw a meaningful distinction between passing as a woman in a context and being a woman in a context' (Ásta, 2018, p. 124). So too, we might think *mutatis mutandis* for passing as straight or cisgendered. However, I think the more obvious way of reading the aforementioned challenge is to say that Ásta hasn't given us an account of what gender or sexuality someone is or has in any given context, rather, she has given us an account of what it is for someone to be taken to be, or for someone to be taken to have, a given gender or sexuality in a context. This is not to dismiss the account entirely—the property of *being taken to be gay* is a vitally important one to understand. It is not, however, the property of *being gay*.

Now, Ásta's account might work for other social identities (indeed I think she offers excellent analyses of *cool* and *being president*), but in the case of LGBTQ identities, precisely because these identities so often feature a distinctive interiority or phenomenology, it seems hard to see the attraction of an account that leans so heavily on the beliefs of others about one's identity. For more discussion of Ásta on queer identities, see Andler (2021).

Conclusion

This chapter provided a brief introduction to a rapidly growing field of philosophy that is trying to make sense of the ways in which we might be said to have different identities across different contexts. In terms of future research, I suspect that more focus on identities beyond gender needs to occur, and coming to terms with questions of passing, interiority, and the closet is also a promising area. As more and more philosophers begin to work on this area, such developments are surely just around the corner.

References

Andler, M. (2021). The sexual orientation/identity distinction. *Hypatia, 36*(2), 259–275.

Aristotle. (1905). *Aristotle's politics* (H. Rackham, Trans.). Clarendon Press.

Ásta. (2018). *Categories we live by: The construction of sex, gender, race, and other social categories*. Oxford University Press.

Bechdel, A. (2009). *The essential Dykes to watch out for*. Jonathan Cape.

Bettcher, T. M. (2013). Trans women and the meaning of "woman".

In A. Soble, N. Power, & R. Halwani (Eds.), *Philosophy of sex: Contemporary readings* (6th ed., pp. 233–250). Rowan and Littlefield.

Borg, E. (2007). Minimalism versus contextualism in semantics. In G. Preyer & G. Peter (Eds.), *Context-sensitivity and semantic minimalism: New essays on semantics and pragmatics* (pp. 429–447). Oxford University Press.

Butler, J. (1990). *Gender trouble: Feminism and the subversion of identity*. Routledge.

Carston, R. (2013). Word meaning, what is said and explicature. In C. Penco & F. Domaneschi (Eds.), *What is said and what is not* (pp. 175–204). CSLI Publications.

Carston, R. (2019). Ad Hoc concepts, polysemy and the lexicon. In K. Scott, B. Clark, & R. Carston (Eds.), *Relevance, pragmatics and interpretation* (pp. 150–162). Cambridge University Press.

Crenshaw, K. W. (1991). Mapping the margins: Intersectionality, identity politics, and violence against women of color. *Stanford Law Review, 43*(6), 1241–1299.

Cull, M. J. (2020). *Engineering genders: Pluralism, trans identities, and feminist philosophy* [PhD thesis, University of Sheffield].

Deslauriers, M. (2003). Aristotle on the virtues of slaves and women. *Oxford Studies in Ancient Philosophy*, *25*, 213–231.

Díaz-León, E. (2016). *Woman* as a politically significant term: A solution to the puzzle. *Hypatia*, *31*(2), 245–258.

Feinberg, L. (1993). *Stone butch blues*. Firebrand Books.

Heyes, C. (2000). *Line drawings: Defining women through feminist praxis*. Cornell University Press.

Kaplan, D. (1989). Demonstratives: An essay on the semantics, logic, metaphysics, and epistemology of demonstratives and other indexicals. In J. Almog, J. Perry, & H. Wettstein (Eds.), *Themes from Kaplan* (pp. 481–564). Oxford University Press.

Kapusta, S. (2016). Misgendering and its moral contestability. *Hypatia*, *31*(3), 502–519.

Lugones, M. (2003). *Pilgrimages/Peregrinajes: Theorizing coalition against multiple oppressions*. Rowman and Littlefield.

Mikkola, M. (2006). Elizabeth Spelman, gender realism, and women. *Hypatia*, *21*(4), 77–96.

Recanati, F. (2004). *Literal meaning*. Cambridge University Press.

Recanati, F. (2012). *Mental files*. Oxford University Press.

Saul, J. (2012). Politically significant terms and philosophy of language: Methodological issues. In A. Superson & S. Crasnow (Eds.), *Analytic feminist contributions to traditional philosophy* (pp. 195–214). Oxford University Press.

Spelman, E. (1988). *Inessential woman: Problems of exclusion in feminist thought*. The Women's Press.

25

A SOCIAL IDENTITY PERSPECTIVE OF LGBTQ+ IDENTITY DEVELOPMENT

Implications for Health and Stigma

Jordan D. X. Hinton

The formation of identities has long been thought to play a key role in the psychological development of the self (Erikson, 1968). For some individuals, the development and maintenance of a positive sense of identity can be contingent upon a variety of internal and environmental factors. This process of understanding and forming identities may indeed be challenging, particularly for those with identities that are stigmatized within society. For instance, individuals with sexual minority or gender-diverse identities may often experience confusion or uncertainty about their identities, due to the experience of (cis)heteronormative expectations and values from their environments (Cass, 1979). The maintenance of these identities (i.e. continuing to evaluate the identity as positive), and the impacts associated with belonging to a stigmatized identity group, are fundamental to the health and well-being of the individual. Thus, the primary aim of this chapter is to provide a coherent and critical understanding of how Lesbian, Gay, Bisexual, Transgender, Queer, and other (LGBTQ+) sexual minority and gender-diverse identities are developed, how the processes of forming and maintaining these identities are influenced by negative environmental factors, and how they relate to psychosocial well-being. I first explore and critically analyse the literature on historical LGBTQ+ identity development models, then follow with an overview of *social* identity approaches to understanding LGBTQ+ identity and related health outcomes.

LGBTQ+ Identity Development

LGBTQ+ individuals experience identity processes and developmental milestones that are distinct from cisgender or heterosexual individuals. In this section of this chapter, I present a brief overview of some developmental models that detail the processes involved in forming and accepting LGBTQ+ identities. Specifically, this section reviews and critiques stage models of gay, lesbian, bisexual, and transgender identity development (and notes the scarcity of scholarship on identity development models for other sexual minority and gender-diverse identities). Although detailed overviews and critiques of these developmental models (and their milestones) are already documented elsewhere (e.g. Bilodeau & Renn, 2005; Goodrich & Brammer, 2021; Hall et al., 2021; Kenneady & Oswalt, 2014), less attention has been paid to the *social* aspects of LGBTQ+ identity development. Thus, throughout this section of this chapter,

DOI: 10.4324/9781003128151-30

I centre my discussion of LGBTQ+ identity development through the lens of conceptualizing LGBTQ+ identities as fundamentally *social* identities. This notion is further developed in the latter section of this chapter.

Sexuality Identity Development

Gay and Lesbian Identity Development

The most well-established and prevalent theoretical stage model of gay and lesbian identity development was an early account proposed by Vivienne Cass (1979). Using *Interpersonal Congruency Theory* (Secord & Backman, 1961) as a guiding framework for her model—which broadly states that in order for identity-specific behavioural change to occur and be accepted, one must adopt strategies to help alleviate the incongruency between how they perceive themselves, and how others perceive them—Cass outlines six stages (see Table 25.1) that same-sex attracted individuals progress through in order to develop a positive sense of identity, and to have that identity integrated with their sense of self.

As noted in Table 25.1, Cass's (1979) model posits that gay men and lesbian women begin their identity development by first experiencing initial uncertainty and confusion over who they are. That is, they come to the realization that they might be developing same-sex desires, feelings, attractions, and behaviours. Provided that the individual accepts and begins to normalize these new behaviours and desires, they then start to actively compare themselves (as being 'potentially' gay or lesbian) to their former/once-identified heterosexual identity (i.e. the 'default' of assumed heteronormativity). The individual may then begin to seek out other members of the gay and lesbian community, in order to strengthen their sense of belonging and affirmation. However, in doing so, Cass (1979) notes that this may lead the individual to also experience more salient rejection from the heterosexual community. That is, along the

Table 25.1 Descriptive Outline of Cass's (1979) Stage Model on Gay and Lesbian Identity Development

Stages	Characteristics
Stage 1: Identity Confusion	Initial incongruency between same-sex behaviours, desires, and attractions with self-perception as a 'heterosexual' person.
Stage 2: Identity Comparison	Beginning to see themselves as 'potentially' gay or lesbian and comparing this new self-perception with their prior 'heterosexual' identity.
Stage 3: Identity Tolerance	Starting to seek out similar others within the gay/lesbian community. If positive evaluations and contact are achieved, progression to the next stage occurs.
Stage 4: Identity Acceptance	A greater sense of belonging within the gay/lesbian community and beginning to shift away from heterosexual others. Tension can occur between the new self-perception as gay or lesbian against the perceptions of how others see the individual.
Stage 5: Identity Pride	Salient rejection from the heterosexual society causes the individual to strengthen their belonging to the gay/lesbian community ('us vs. them' dichotomies are established). However, if positive perceptions from others (e.g. heterosexuals) occur, the individual may start to lessen the dichotomy of themselves as a gay or lesbian person against other heterosexuals with regards to values and beliefs.
Stage 6: Identity Synthesis	The gay or lesbian identity is only considered one important aspect of the self (rather than the *most* or *only* important aspect), and the individual begins to assimilate this identity with their other important identities.

developmental journal of achieving pride in one's gay or lesbian identity, a greater sense of community belonging can also bring about increased perceptions of the stigma that is directed towards their identity group. Notably, in the final stage of Cass's (1979) model, she posits that in order for a gay or lesbian identity to be fully developed, the individual will start to see themselves in regard to their other identities that are important to them and thereby assimilate their gay or lesbian identity with their other defining identities.

Although other early models of gay and lesbian identity development exist (see Coleman, 1981; D'Augelli, 1994; Richardson & Hart, 1981; Sophie, 1986; Troiden, 1979; Weinberg & Williams, 1974), Cass's (1979) model is arguably the most well established. This model was revolutionary at the time in which it was developed, as it was one of the first accounts that presented same-sex attracted individuals through a normative (rather than pathological) lens. However, the legacy of this model is not without criticism.

Among the criticisms of Cass's (1979) model, there is the question of whether the developmental stages are necessarily sequential. Although, in some of her later work, the sequential nature of these stages showed some validity (Cass, 1984), some researchers have questioned this (cf. Brown, 1995; Kenneady & Oswalt, 2014; McDonald, 1982; Sophie, 1986; Weinberg, 1984). Both Brown (1995) and Weinberg (1984) asserted that there are multiple ways the individual can reach certain stages, including skipping stages or experiencing aspects of multiple stages simultaneously. In line with this criticism, one can speculate that the nature of gay and lesbian identity development may be largely dependent upon the interpersonal environment. For instance, if the individual receives positive evaluations from heterosexual peers after disclosing their identity (as stated in Stage 4), they might progress onto the identity synthesis stage (Stage 6), rather than pass through the identity pride stage (Stage 5). The identity pride stage (according to Cass, 1979) appears to only be important when the individual experiences rejection from the heterosexual community, so it might also be likely that this stage is repeated *after* the individual has developed identity synthesis, if they receive further rejection from the heterosexual community. This seems to reflect an assumption of Cass's (1979) model that the individual grows up surrounded by pervasive negative attitudes towards homosexuality. Although the prevalence of prejudice towards same-sex attracted individuals was heightened when this model was developed (1970s), there has been a decline in negative attitudes towards homosexuality in the last few decades (Westgate et al., 2015), thus the individual's interpersonal environment is likely significantly different to how it was when Cass's model was developed (affecting the later model stages in particular, see also Kenneady & Oswalt, 2014).

Another criticism of Cass's (1979) model is its applicability to the broad range of sexual minority identities. Sophie (1986) examined this model in a sample of lesbians and found that the sequential nature of the stages was not fully supported and may hold more validity in the earlier stages of development rather than the later stages. She also notes that the interpersonal environment of lesbians might indeed be quite different than for gay men, in that there is more societal acceptance of lesbians over gay men. This different environmental structure provided the lesbians in Sophie's study the ability to form a part of their community prior to self-acceptance (see also Cox & Gallois, 1996). Furthermore, Cass's (1979) model might not be applicable to individuals with non-monosexual identities (e.g. bisexuals). Bisexual identities are briefly discussed in Cass's model, however she describes these in reference to transitioning out of a heterosexual identity towards a gay or lesbian identity, with a bisexual identity being the steppingstone between the two (Cass, 1979). Within the second stage of her model, Cass describes that some individuals might adopt a bisexual label as a coping strategy of maintaining a heterosexual image while transitioning to a gay or lesbian identity. Furthermore, remaining with this bisexual label (according to Cass, 1979) indicated deviation from the developmental pathway (or leading to identity foreclosure). Importantly, and as will be discussed next, a bisexual identity is not just a steppingstone towards a gay or lesbian identity, but rather an identity of its own.

Bisexual Identity Development

Weinberg et al.'s (1994) research provided an early theoretical account of the developmental milestones of bisexual individuals as distinct from gay and lesbian identities. Weinberg and colleagues propose a four-stage model of bisexual identity development (see Table 25.2). Within the first stage, confusion is emphasized in the individual not feeling like they belong in their current environment, given that their environment includes only two (binary) concepts of sexual attraction (same-sex vs. opposite-sex attracted), but not both. Weinberg and colleagues assert that the lack of recognition of a bisexual label also adds to this initial confusion.

With the help of others to navigate what it means to be bisexual, the individual is able to assimilate their sense of self with their new bisexual label. However, Weinberg and colleagues caution that this newly applied label is not always accompanied by positive associations. Some bisexual individuals might still hold confusion of their identity, and even hold negative attitudes towards other bisexual individuals. A greater sense of community belonging, and more positive group associations, is what then leads the individual to further identity development. Through positive evaluations and connections, the individual changes how they perceive their identity against the behaviours associated with it. Weinberg and colleagues note that the individual begins to create a self-perception of themselves as bisexual regardless of their sexual behaviours. For instance, some bisexual individuals in monogamous relationships still perceived themselves as bisexual (as opposed to heterosexual or gay/lesbian, reflecting their partner's gender). The final stage of development is considered a continuous aspect of the model, rather than a fixed end point. Bisexual individuals may experience 'continued uncertainty' over their bisexual identity throughout their lives due to the experiences of societal rejection of bisexuality (from both the heterosexual and gay/lesbian communities) that they may receive (see also Anderson & Maugeri, 2022).

In all, Weinberg et al.'s (1994) model portrays a simplistic approach to developing a bisexual identity. Weinberg and colleagues acknowledge the non-linear nature of this model, indicating the individual can begin the developmental journey at any stage (i.e. the individual does not need to begin at the first stage in order to develop a positive bisexual identity). Since the development of this model, there have been relatively few improvements or adjustments with recent

Table 25.2 Descriptive Outline of Weinberg et al.'s (1994) Stage Model on Bisexual Identity Development

Stages	Characteristics
Stage 1: Initial Confusion	First instances where the individual experiences confusion over their attraction to those of the same and other sex to them.
Stage 2: Finding and Applying the Label	First awareness of the 'bisexual' label. The individual seeks out other bisexual individuals and begins to belong to the bisexual community. Positive or negative evaluations of the bisexual group can occur.
Stage 3: Settling into the Identity	Development of a strong sense of bisexual identity and self-perception, regardless of behaviours that are considered typical of bisexual individuals.
Stage 4: Continued Uncertainty	Continuing to question the bisexual identity throughout the course of their lives due to societal rejection of a bisexual identity (from both the gay/lesbian and heterosexual communities).

literature. Notably, Brown (2002) proposed an extension of Weinberg et al.'s (1994) model in which the final stage (*Continued Uncertainty*) was renamed *Identity Maintenance* to reflect the notation that bisexual individuals continue to accept their self-perception as bisexual, and rather than be uncertain about their identity, they are merely trying to maintain the perception of that identity within certain context in their environment (e.g. concealment/disclosure of that identity in different societal contexts). Brown's (2002) research also demonstrates the unique differences between bisexual women and men in terms of identity development. For instance, Brown proposes that there is conflict between gender roles within one's environment, and their sexuality development (e.g. bisexual men might have conflict between their male gender roles within society, and their bisexuality). However, other research regarding the developmental milestones for bisexual individuals is limited and in need for future exploration.

The Development of Other Sexual Minority Identities

Beyond the historical models of gay, lesbian, and bisexual identity development discussed thus far, recent research has highlighted the diverse experiences and processes involved in the development of other sexual minority identities. Cass (1979) notes that being bisexual, or experiencing no, or little, sexual/romantic attraction towards others (i.e. asexual and aromantic identities), may be indicators of deviating from the path towards successful gay or lesbian identity development. While Weinberg and colleagues (1994) partially address some of these limitations in their model of bisexual identity development, it fails to acknowledge the diverse range of sexual orientations that individuals can identify with.

Guided by the limitations of previous bisexual identity development models, Harper and Swanson (2019) propose a new model of understanding how *all* non-monosexual individuals (e.g. those who are identified as pansexual, polysexual, or queer) develop their identity. In a non-sequential task model, they propose five processes that these individuals may address throughout their developmental journey, and how these processes are influenced by the individual's socio-political and interpersonal environments. These include (1) processes of labelling the identity, (2) managing the impact of oppression and stigma, (3) processes of coming out, (4) engagement with community, and (5) processes of intersectionality among other identities (Harper & Swanson, 2019). Furthermore, research by Foster et al. (2019) exemplifies how asexual individuals develop their identities. Among a sample of asexual women of colour, Foster and colleagues' (2019) research finds several sub-themes associated with asexual identity development, including (1) gradual processes of asexual identification, (2) making sense of identity differences, (3) personal labelling, conceptualizations, and definitions of asexuality, (4) openness to romantic attraction, and (5) acceptance and positive internalization of an asexual identity.

The historical and contemporary sexuality developmental models discussed in this section highlight important milestones and processes that individuals progress through in order to achieve successful identity development. While each model has its own limitations, they all share important elements that centre identity development around the individual's interpersonal and community environments. For instance, navigating oppression and stigma towards the identity group, and processes of positive community belonging are discussed in each model as central environmental factors that may foster (or limit) positive identity development. Nonetheless, future researchers should consider exploring how the processes in these models apply to all sexual minority identities, and also highlight how the nuances and complex dynamics of sexuality (including the fluidity of sexual orientation, e.g. Diamond et al., 2020) can develop and be maintained across time.

Gender-Diverse Identity Development

When discussing LGBTQ+ models of identity development, it is also imperative to highlight the experiences of those with gender-diverse identities. The label of transgender or gender-diverse (TGD) is often considered to be an umbrella term that consists of a wide range of gender identities beyond (or within) the binary of male and female (Diamond et al., 2011). Throughout this section of this chapter, I highlight models of transgender and gender non-binary (or gender queer) identity development. As a caveat, this section will just focus on developmental models from a gender perspective, but I acknowledge that gender-diverse individuals may also hold sexual minority identities which, in turn, may be integrated into their overall sense of identity development (i.e. through a lens of intersectionality in which the development of a gender identity may also involve the simultaneous development of a sexuality identity; see Kassis et al., 2021).

Transgender Identity Development

One of the first developmental models for transgender identities was posited by Devor (2004). Within his model, Devor describes 14 linear stages (which mirror closely to Cass's, 1979 model) in which the individual can progress through in order to develop a sense of identity pride (see Table 25.3). Broadly, this model posits that individuals begin the developmental process by experiencing anxiety and confusion over their gendered behaviours and compares them to others with the same assigned sex. Similar to the previous models discussed, the individual attempts to seek out greater belonging within the transgender community to affirm and accept their identity, however prior to doing this they may wish to make adjustments within their interpersonal environment so that they're surrounded by individuals who are also accepting of a transgender identity (disclosure of identity may also follow from here). The last stages of Devor's model explore the notions of transitioning from one gender to another, and end in pride of identity. That is, in order to re-affirm an individual's identity with their gender, they may seek to transition from one gender to another, in either (or both) a social or physical sense, in order to fully accept and feel pride with their gender identity.

Although Devor's (2004) model posits a comprehensive approach to transgender identity development, he clarifies that there could be multiple pathways within the model that transgender individuals can progress through. Moreover, he notes that this model will not fit every transgender person or other gender-diverse individuals, such as those whose gender identity falls outside of the binary of male and female (for a discussion on other TGD development models, see Diamond et al., 2011). Some aspects of Devor's model might be applicable to these individuals, such as initial confusion and comparison of identity, whereas other stages (such as the transition stages), might be only applicable to the binary concepts of male/female gender-diversity. However, an adaption of these transition stages within this model for gender non-binary individuals might be acceptable (e.g. these individuals might still *transition* from a binary gender identity to a non-binary gender identity from a social and cultural perspective). Given the scarcity of research on the identity development of gender non-binary identities, future researchers should consider how models, such as Devor's (2004), are adaptable to other gender-diverse individuals.

Non-Binary and Gender Queer Identity Development

Although stage models are comprehensive, other researchers have provided more recent thematic overviews on the developmental processes of TGD individuals, particularly for those with

Table 25.3 Descriptive Outline of Devor's (2004) Stage Model on Transgender Identity Development

Stages	Characteristics
Stage 1: Abiding Anxiety *Stage 2:* Identity Confusion Regarding Originally Assigned Gender and Sex *Stage 3:* Identity Comparison of Originally Assigned Gender and Sex *Stage 4:* Discovery of Transgenderism	The first four stages are where the individual begins to exhibit anxiety and confusion over the incompatibility between their gendered behaviours and their assigned sex. The individual may seek to explore how their gendered behaviours compare against others with the same assigned sex, and progress onto the discovery of transgenderism through community connections.
Stage 5: Identity Confusion Regarding Transgenderism *Stage 6:* Identity Comparison of Transgenderism *Stage 7:* Tolerance of Transgender Identity	Once the discovery of transgenderism (and the label of 'Transgender') have been established, the individual might again question and compare their identity as a 'potentially' transgender person against their former gender and sex identities. The individual may seek to strengthen their belonging to the transgender community, which then allows them to begin tolerating and accepting themselves as a transgender person.
Stage 8: Delay Before Acceptance of Transgender Identity *Stage 9:* Acceptance of Transgender Identity	Prior to fully accepting themselves as a transgender person, the individual may delay this process according to how well perceived transgenderism is within their interpersonal and broader environments. The individual might seek to adjust their interpersonal environment to include others who are more accepting of transgenderism, which helps affirm and accept the individual's self-perception as being transgender. Individuals may also begin to start disclosing their transgender identity to others.
Stage 10: Delay Before Transition *Stage 11:* Transition *Stage 12:* Acceptance of Post-Transition Gender and Sex Identities	Once feeling accepted with their transgender identity, the individual may seek to transition their gender in both (or either) a social or physical sense. The individual may first delay this transition by researching and developing strategies to carry out transition goals (e.g. saving money for surgery or researching clothing outlets), but once these goals are achieved, the individual may transition and start to accept themselves as their gender identity (e.g. trans-male).
Stage 13: Integration *Stage 14:* Pride	Finally, now that the individual is accepting of their new gender identity, and they are surrounded by positive affirming evaluations of the identity, they may begin to integrate their gender identity with other important aspect of their self-concept, and thereby experience a sense of identity pride.

non-binary or gender queer identities. For instance, Brumbaugh-Johnson and Hull's (2019) research on the coming out experiences of transgender, gender queer, and other gender-diverse individuals indicate three primary themes of identity development: *navigating the gender expectations of others*, *navigating the reactions of others*, and *navigating the threat of violence*. Each of these themes are likely applicable to all TGD individuals, and, importantly, they reflect environmental and societal obstacles the individual may need to continually overcome. For instance, the individual may seek out how others perceive the concept of gender to affirm whether they might anticipate an adverse reaction from them if they were to disclose their identity. Moreover, a safe and accepting interpersonal environment is paramount to the goal of identity disclosure, as it minimizes the threat of rejection and violence, and in turn promotes more positive well-being for the individual (see also Real-Quintanar et al., 2020).

Summary of LGBTQ+ Identity Development Models

In all, the models discussed in this section provide a framework for understanding LGBTQ+ identity development. Although a review of these models is certainly not new (e.g. Bilodeau & Renn, 2005; Goodrich & Brammer, 2021; Hall et al., 2021; Kenneady & Oswalt, 2014), much less attention has been paid to the *social* aspects the encompass these models. Indeed, there are considerable conceptual similarities between these models that highlight the importance of the individual's social environment. For example, each of the models presented here emphasize how development involves a change in the individual's environment from an initial cis-heteronormative environment to a more positive and safer environment (e.g. through processes of belonging with the LGBTQ+ community), which further supports developmental success (i.e. a positive and integrated sense of self). Although some of the research discussed here expands upon the historical models of gay and lesbian (Cass, 1979), bisexual (Weinberg et al., 1994), and transgender (Devor, 2004) development—such as the insights noted for asexual (Foster et al., 2019), pansexual/polysexual (Harper & Swanson, 2019), and non-binary/gender queer (Brumbaugh-Johnson & Hull, 2019) identity development—further understandings of how, and to what extent, societal factors influence an individual's perception of their LGBTQ+ identity are needed. In light of this, a social group identification perspective on studying identity processes, which emphasizes the individual's social environment and societal factors (e.g. group belonging), may be one important and global approach to understanding the development of *all* LGBTQ+ identities.

A Social Identity Approach

Drawing from social identity theorizing (*Social Identity Theory* and *Self-Categorization Theory*, Tajfel & Turner, 1979; Turner et al., 1987), individuals can perceive their sense of identity through an interpersonal (individual level) or intergroup (social level) lens. There are several documented theoretical processes of evaluating an identity through an intergroup lens (Turner et al., 1987), some of which may provide greater insight into the development of an LGBTQ+ identity (see also Cox & Gallois, 1996). This section of this chapter centres the discussion on two key processes of social identity: group prototypicality, and social identification. Furthermore, I discuss the importance and impact of social identification on the relationships between stigma and health among LGBTQ+ individuals.

Group Prototypicality

As noted earlier, successful LGBTQ+ identity development corresponds with *positive* evaluations of the LGBTQ+ social group. While navigating negative societal rejections, the individual may find it protective to strengthen their belonging to their LGBTQ+ group. In order to do this, especially within the earlier stages of the developmental process where LGBTQ+ community contact is attempted, the individual might seek to adjust their behaviours and beliefs to what is considered typical of their identity group. *Prototypicality* is an identity process defined by how the individual adopts the ideal group and behavioural norms (Turner et al., 1987), and this process may help strengthen group belonging initially. The individual might strive to be an 'ideal' member of their LGBTQ+ group by adopting the behaviours, beliefs, attitudes, and norms of the group to help facilitate group connection. Although a sense of prototypicality might benefit the individual in the initial stages of development, it is important to note that prototypicality is subjective to the individual's own (and society's) perceptions of the group. Indeed, there is incredible variability and diversity *within* LGBTQ+ identity groups, and not all members may strive for the 'ideal' representation of a group member to affirm and validate their identity. This is consistent with the later stages of Weinberg et al.'s (1994) model where bisexual individuals affirm their bisexuality regardless of their typical identity-related behaviours. It is also important to note that among some LGBTQ+ identity groups, high levels of prototypicality (in particular, self-stereotyping) can have negative effects on mental health (Flanders, 2016; Hinton et al., 2019).

The levels in which the individual belongs to their identity group should also be considered. LGBTQ+ individuals may consider the prototypically of their group identity to be that of the superordinate LGBTQ+ group (distinct from the cis-heteronormative community), their ordinate identity group (e.g. gay identity as distinct from bisexual identity), and even their subordinate identity group (e.g. gay 'twink' identity as distinct from a gay 'bear' identity; see Mijas et al., 2020). Put simply, there are several ways in the which the individual can belong with specific LGBTQ+ groups according to how they evaluate the self-perception and behaviours that are associated with their identity. In addition, the availability of resources within the last few decades (e.g. online networking/forums) has made being able to connect with similar LGBTQ+ others more accessible. Thus, the prototypicality and social comparisons of specific LGBTQ+ subcultures and micro-groups is easier to access and explore for individuals who are seeking social group belonging (see Harper et al., 2016; Jenzen, 2017; Webster, 2019).

Social Identification and Psychosocial Outcomes

Recent research indicates that the LGBTQ+ population are still disproportionately at-risk for various well-being and mental health outcomes (Hill et al., 2020). One factor contributing to these negative outcomes is their minority identity status and the prejudice within their environments (Higa et al., 2014; Meyer, 2003; Perales, 2019; Russell & Fish, 2016). Prejudice and discrimination towards LGBTQ+ individuals exist globally (for reviews see Ahmad & Bhugra, 2010; Campbell et al., 2019), but is also essential to understand how LGBTQ+ individuals perceive this discrimination towards their group, and if their sense and strength of group belonging (also referred to as *social identification*) impacts this perception. In this section of this chapter, I present literature on social identification and how this is influenced by negative external societal factors (e.g. prejudice). Furthermore, I discuss the evidence of the relationship between identification and health and well-being outcomes for LGBTQ+ individuals. First, common guiding frameworks on the prejudice-identification-health relationships are discussed, followed by how these models have been applied to LGBTQ+ individuals.

The Prejudice–Identification–Health Relationship

Early research on the relationship between identification with social groups, how members of that social group perceive the prejudice towards their group, and mental health outcomes was conducted by Branscombe et al. (1999). The *Rejection-Identification Model* (RIM; Branscombe et al., 1999) posits that there is an association between experiencing group prejudice and increases in reports of mental health symptomology. Furthermore, the RIM also argues that there is an indirect association between perceived prejudice and mental health via strengthened group belonging. That is, perceived prejudice towards the minority group increases the strength of identification and belonging with that group, which in turn influences *better* mental health and well-being (Branscombe et al., 1999). This proposition corresponds with Cass's (1979) identity pride stage, in that when gay and lesbian individuals' experience rejection from the heterosexual community, their anger towards this community actually strengthens their belonging to the gay/lesbian community, which in turn promotes positive well-being for the individual.

Although some evidence supports the structure of the RIM among LGBTQ+ identities (e.g. Scroggs & Vennum, 2020), other researchers have argued that perceived discrimination *follows* rather than *precedes* greater group belonging (Begeny & Huo, 2017). This lead Begeny and Huo (2017) to develop the *Intragroup Status and Health* (ISAH) model which posits that group identification can increase the perceived prejudice towards one's group, which can lead to *worse* mental health and well-being outcomes. In support of this proposition, they found that gay men's identity centrality (i.e. more frequent thinking about their gay identity, and evaluating their gay identity as an important aspect of one's self-image) leads to increased perceived discrimination about the identity group, and in turn poorer mental health. That is, Begeny and Huo (2017) posit that in this context, gay men with stronger identification towards their identity group were likely to view the world through the lens of their gay identity, thereby being more attentive to, and aware of, the stigma that is directed towards their group. This claim is supported by recent meta-analytic evidence which reveals stronger LGBTQ+ identification is associated with increased perceived discrimination (Hinton et al., 2022). Importantly, the meta-analysis also revealed that stronger LGBTQ+ identification is also related to beneficial outcomes, including increased identity affirmations, pride, and community belonging. Put simply, the more one identifies with their LGBTQ+ identity group, the more they can experience both favourable (e.g. increased belonging) and unfavourable (e.g. increased stigma perceptions) outcomes.

LGBTQ+ Minority Stress

Since prejudice towards LGBTQ+ individuals can play an important role on hindering or slowing the development of this identity (as discussed in the earlier section of this chapter), it is essential to understand the *types* of stigma and stressors LGBTQ+ individuals perceive in their daily lives. Meyer's (2003) minority stress framework describes the type of stressors that some LGBTQ+ individuals experience. As a minority group within society, LGBTQ+ individuals face additional stressors that are considered chronic and uniquely associated with their minority identity. Meyer describes these stressors as falling either distal or proximal to the individual within their environment. Distal environmental stressors include macro-level prejudice events, such as being the victim of systemic societal injustices and blatant discrimination, whereas proximal stressors include negative self-evaluative processes towards the identity (e.g. internalized homophobia, identity concealment, and expectations of rejection; see also Frost, 2011; Meyer & Frost, 2013). This model highlights the importance of various group identification processes that may inhibit or exacerbate the link between these stressors and mental health outcomes. For instance, attributing a strong and positive connection with your identity group can cause the minority stress to be more harmful on one's mental health (Meyer, 2003).

Although Meyer's (2003) model was initially designed in the context of sexual minority identities only, it is unclear whether some elements of the model are applicable to TGD identities. For instance, a recent study by McLemore (2018) found that, among transgender individuals, the relationship between experienced stigma and poorer mental health outcomes was *buffered* when the individual held a strong sense of importance to their transgender identity.

Thus, for transgender individuals, the degree of belonging they have with their transgender identity group may be *protective* of the influence of stigma on health, in contrast to what was proposed by Meyer (2003).

Not only do external environmental factors, such as distal minority stress, affect the individual's well-being, but the importance of internal evaluative processes (e.g. identity concealment), also need to be acknowledged. Unlike other minority social identities (e.g. racial/ethnic identities), LGBTQ+ individuals experience unique proximal stressors, such as concealment and disclosure of identity. The individual may need to maintain this concealment or disclosure over the course of their life in an effort to protect (e.g. concealing the identity for safety, or to avoid rejection and discrimination) or affirm (e.g. disclosing identity to new people to provide authenticity) their identity. The relationship between concealment/disclosure and health outcomes is complex.

Research indicates that the concealment of an LGBTQ+ identity can have both negative and positive consequences for well-being. For instance, Riggle et al. (2017) found that both disclosure *and* concealment of an LGBTQ+ identity can lead to worse mental health outcomes and poorer well-being. Those who disclose their identity may be more at risk of societal rejection (or perceive it as being more pronounced), while those who conceal their identity may feel they decrease their sense of authenticity, also resulting in poorer health (see also Bry et al., 2017; Pachankis et al., 2020). Although some research has suggested that concealing a stigmatized identity may be protective against societal stigma (e.g. Pasek et al., 2017), and indeed some LGBTQ+ individuals might hold this view, other research suggests that regardless of whether the LGBTQ+ individual chooses to conceal or disclose their identity, societal perceptions of them may remain the same (Goh et al., 2019). Given that identity disclosure (or 'coming out') is the ultimate goal of most historical LGBTQ+ identity development models, understanding the health consequences and influences of societal stigma is important to consider. Further development of these existing models should also explore the circumstances under which it may be important for the individual to disclose their identity (and continue to disclose the identity over the course of their lives) because of the benefits disclosure will have to the individual, rather than asserting that disclosure should be the primary goal in developing a positive sense of identity.

Summary and Future Directions

This chapter presented a review of the major theoretical accounts of how LGBTQ+ identities are developed from both a historical and more contemporary perspective. Furthermore, this chapter also discussed current evidence of the health consequences of social identification (and the influences of experienced and perceived stigma) through the lens of social group belonging. As discussed, historical stage models of LGBTQ+ identity development provided an early theoretical account of how an individual can progress through processes of identity confusion, through tolerance and acceptance, to eventually developing a sense of pride of identity. I posed several limitations for these models, including their applicability to the full range of LGBTQ+ identities, and the question of whether the proposed linearity is the only possible pathway for identity development.

Identity development is complex for stigmatized minority groups as several external environmental factors (such as societal prejudice) may influence the process of this development. Thus, understanding this process through a social group lens, specifically emphasizing social group processes of group prototypicality and social identification, may provide better insight in understanding health disparities associated with this development. Furthermore, a social lens shifts attention from development to the *maintenance* of this identity in how it interacts with the individual's interpersonal environment. In light of this, I end this chapter with suggestions and directions for future researchers in the LGBTQ+ identity field.

First, researchers should continue to consider how developmental models can be integrated with social models that emphasize the importance of the individuals external and internal stressors. As Meyer (2003) notes, both proximal and distal stressors can influence health, and the processes in which the individual belongs to their identity group are also able to influence this relationship. Thus, having an integrated approach to LGBTQ+ development including the influences of stressors/prejudice and outcomes of health is also needed. Second, future research should move away from the conceptualization of 'LGBTQ+ identity' as if this were a single homogeneous group. Instead, research should focus on the dynamics of identities at each level of analysis (e.g. 'Trans-masculine' social identity, as belonging within the 'TGD social identity', which further belongs within the larger 'LGBTQ+ social identity'). Each of these subgroup levels may indeed have their own sources of prejudice, identification processes, and proximal stressors, thus future researchers should consider the importance of disaggregating each of these LGBTQ+ identities to provide a better understanding of how they're developed and maintained over time. In line with this, I also encourage future researchers to explore the developmental processes among LGBTQ+ individuals under the assumption that identities can be dynamic and fluid. The research discussed in this chapter assumes that LGBTQ+ identities are often static and unchanging, thus more research exploring the fluidity of these identities over time is needed.

Finally, more attention should be paid to the final stage of Cass's (1979) developmental model. This stage (i.e. identity synthesis) is a unique endpoint and, unlike other models discussed (e.g. Weinberg et al., 1994), it explores how the individual's identity becomes integrated with other identities that are important to them. That is, the individual no longer sees themselves as *just* an LGBTQ+ person, but also in terms of their other identities. This concept is of essential importance, as research on the development and maintenance of LGBTQ+ identity often makes the assumption that this identity is central and unique to the individual's self-concept. However, individuals are more than just one identity. Researchers should consider the health consequences (and influence of prejudice) on what it means to have an important LGBTQ+ identity that is not always central to how the individual defines themselves—What does it mean for the individual's mental health? Do they experience prejudice more heavily than LGBTQ+ individuals with more central and salient identities? Are there differences among the LGBTQ+ subgroups on how central their identity is? These important research questions need to be addressed.

References

Ahmad, S., & Bhugra, D. (2010). Homophobia: An updated review of the literature. *Sexual and Relationship Therapy*, 25(4), 447–455. https://doi.org/10.1080/14681994.2010.515206

Anderson, J., & Maugeri, J. (2022). Correlates of attitudes toward bisexuality: A systematic review and meta-analysis. *Journal of Homosexuality*, 1–34. https://doi.org/10.1080/00918369.2022.2112524

Begeny, C. T., & Huo, Y. J. (2017). When identity hurts: How positive intragroup experiences can yield negative mental health implications for ethnic and sexual minorities. *European Journal of Social Psychology*, 47(7), 803–817. https://doi.org/10.1002/ejsp.2292

Bilodeau, B. L., & Renn, K. A. (2005). Analysis of LGBT identity development models and implications for practice. *New Directions for Student Services*, 2005(111), 25–39. https://doi.org/10.1002/ss.171

Branscombe, N. R., Schmitt, M. T., & Harvey, R. D. (1999). Perceiving pervasive discrimination among African Americans: Implications for group identification and well-being. *Journal of Personality and Social Psychology*, 77(1), 135–149. https://doi.org/10.1037/0022-3514.77.1.135

Brown, L. S. (1995). Lesbian identities: Concepts and issues. In A. R. D'Augelli & C. J. Patterson (Eds.), *Lesbian, gay, and bisexual identities over the lifespan: Psychological perspectives* (pp. 3–23). Oxford University Press. https://doi.org/10.1093/acprof:oso/9780195082319.003.0001

Brown, T. (2002). A proposed model of bisexual identity development that elaborates on experiential differences of women and men. *Journal of Bisexuality, 2*(4), 67–91. https://doi.org/10.1300/J159v02n04_05

Brumbaugh-Johnson, S. M., & Hull, K. E. (2019). Coming out as transgender: Navigating the social implications of a transgender identity. *Journal of Homosexuality, 66*(8), 1148–1177. https://doi.org/10.1080/00918369.2018.1493253

Bry, L. J., Mustanski, B., Garofalo, R., & Burns, M. N. (2017). Management of a concealable stigmatized identity: A qualitative study of concealment, disclosure, and role flexing among young, resilient sexual and gender minority individuals. *Journal of Homosexuality, 64*(6), 745–769. https://doi.org/10.1080/00918369.2016.1236574

Campbell, M., Hinton, J. D. X., & Anderson, J. R. (2019). A systematic review of the relationship between religion and attitudes toward transgender and gender-variant people. *The International Journal of Transgenderism, 20*(1), 21–38. https://doi.org/10.1080/15532739.2018.1545149

Cass, V. C. (1979). Homosexuality identity formation. *Journal of Homosexuality, 4*(3), 219–235. https://doi.org/10.1300/J082v04n03_01

Cass, V. C. (1984). Homosexual identity formation: Testing a theoretical model. *The Journal of Sex Research, 20*(2), 143–167. https://doi.org/10.1080/00224498409551214

Coleman, E. (1981). Developmental stages of the coming out process. *Journal of Homosexuality, 7*(2–3), 31–43. https://doi.org/10.1300/J082v07n02_06

Cox, S., & Gallois, C. (1996). Gay and lesbian identity development: A social identity perspective. *Journal of Homosexuality, 30*(4), 1–30. https://doi.org/10.1300/J082v30n04_01

D'Augelli, A. R. (1994). Identity development and sexual orientation: Toward a model of lesbian, gay, and bisexual development. In E. J. Trickett, R. J. Watts, & D. Birman (Eds.), *The Jossey-Bass social and behavioral science series. Human diversity: Perspectives on people in context* (pp. 312–333). Jossey-Bass, Wiley.

Devor, A. H. (2004). Witnessing and mirroring: A fourteen stage model of transsexual identity formation. *Journal of Gay and Lesbian Psychotherapy, 8*(1–2), 41–67. https://doi.org/10.1300/J236v08n01_05

Diamond, L. M., Alley, J., Dickenson, J., & Blair, K. L. (2020). Who counts as sexually fluid? Comparing four different types of sexual fluidity in women. *Archives of Sexual Behavior, 49*, 2389–2403. https://doi.org/10.1007/s10508-019-01565-1

Diamond, L. M., Pardo, S. T., & Butterworth, M. R. (2011). Transgender experience and identity. In S. Schwartz, K. Luyckx, & V. Vignoles (Eds.), *Handbook of identity theory and research* (pp. 629–647). Springer. https://doi.org/10.1007/978-1-4419-7988-9_26

Erikson, E. H. (1968). *Identity: Youth and crisis.* Norton.

Flanders, C. E. (2016). Bisexuality, social identity, and well-being: An exploratory study. *Sexualities, 19*(5–6), 497–516. https://doi.org/10.1177/1363460715609093

Foster, A. B., Eklund, A., Brewster, M. E., Walker, A. D., & Candon, E. (2019). Personal agency disavowed: Identity construction in asexual women of color. *Psychology of Sexual Orientation and Gender Diversity, 6*(2), 127–137. https://doi.org/10.1037/sgd0000310

Frost, D. M. (2011). Social stigma and its consequences for the socially stigmatized. *Social and Personality Psychology Compass, 5*(11), 824–839. https://doi.org/10.1111/j.1751-9004.2011.00394.x

Goh, J. X., Kort, D. N., Thurston, A. M., Benson, L. R., & Kaiser, C. R. (2019). Does concealing a sexual minority identity prevent exposure to prejudice? *Social Psychological and Personality Science, 10*(8), 1056–1064. https://doi.org/10.1177/1948550619829065

Goodrich, K. M., & Brammer, M. K. (2021). Cass's homosexual identity formation: A critical analysis. *Journal of Multicultural Counseling and Development, 49*(4), 239–253. https://doi.org/10.1002/jmcd.12228

Hall, W. J., Dawes, H. C., & Plocek, N. (2021). Sexual orientation identity development milestones among lesbian, gay, bisexual, and queer people: A systematic review and meta-analysis. *Frontiers in Psychology, 12*, 753954. https://doi.org/10.3389/fpsyg.2021.753954

Harper, A. J., & Swanson, R. (2019). Nonsequential task model of bi/pan/polysexual identity development. *Journal of Bisexuality, 19*(3), 337–360. https://doi.org/10.1080/15299716.2019.1608614

Harper, G. W., Serrano, P. A., Bruce, D., & Bauermeister, J. A. (2016). The internet's multiple roles in facilitating the sexual orientation identity development of gay and bisexual male adolescents. *American Journal of Men's Health, 10*(5), 359–376. https://doi.org/10.1177/1557988314566227

Higa, D., Hoppe, M. J., Lindhorst, T., Mincer, S., Beadnell, B., Morrison, D. M., Wells, E. A., Todd, A., & Mountz, S. (2014). Negative and positive factors associated with the well-being of lesbian, gay, bisexual, transgender, queer, and questioning (LGBTQ) youth. *Youth & Society*, *46*(5), 663–687. https://doi.org/10.1177/0044118X12449630

Hill, A. O., Bourne, A., McNair, R., Carman, M., & Lyons, A. (2020). *Private lives 3: The health and wellbeing of LGBTIQ people in Australia*. ARCSHS Monograph Series No. 122. Australian Research Centre in Sex, Health and Society, La Trobe University.

Hinton, J. D. X., Anderson, J. R., & Koc, Y. (2019). Exploring the relationship between gay men's self- and meta-stereotype endorsement with well-being and self-worth. *Psychology & Sexuality*, *10*(2), 169–182. https://doi.org/10.1080/19419899.2019.1577013

Hinton, J. D. X., de la Piedad Garcia, X., Kaufmann, L. M., Koc, Y., & Anderson, J. R. (2022). A systematic and meta-analytic review of identity centrality among LGBTQ groups: An assessment of psychosocial correlates. *Journal of Sex Research*, *59*(5), 568–586. https://doi.org/10.1080/00224499.2021.1967849

Jenzen, O. (2017). Trans youth and social media: Moving between counterpublics and the wider web. *Gender, Place & Culture*, *24*(11), 1626–1641. https://doi.org/10.1080/0966369X.2017.1396204

Kassis, W., Aksoy, D., Favre, C. A., & Artz, S. T. (2021). Multidimensional and intersectional gender identity and sexual attraction patterns of adolescents for quantitative research. *Frontiers in Psychology*, *12*, 697373. https://doi.org/10.3389/fpsyg.2021.697373

Kenneady, D. A., & Oswalt, S. B. (2014). Is Cass's model of homosexual identity formation relevant to today's society? *American Journal of Sexuality Education*, *9*(2), 229–246. http://dx.doi.org/10.1080/15546128.2014.900465

McDonald, G. J. (1982). Individual differences in the coming out process for gay men: Implications for theoretical models. *Journal of Homosexuality*, *8*(1), 47–60. https://doi.org/10.1300/J082v08n01_05

McLemore, K. A. (2018). A minority stress perspective on transgender individuals' experiences with misgendering. *Stigma and Health*, *3*(1), 53–64. https://doi.org/10.1037/sah0000070

Meyer, I. H. (2003). Prejudice, social stress, and mental health in lesbian, gay, and bisexual populations: Conceptual issues and research evidence. *Psychological Bulletin*, *129*(5), 674–697. https://doi.org/10.1037/0033-2909.129.5.674

Meyer, I. H., & Frost, D. M. (2013). Minority stress and the health of sexual minorities. In C. J. Patterson & A. R. D'Augelli (Eds.), *Handbook of psychology and sexual orientation* (pp. 252–266). Oxford University Press. https://doi.org/10.1093/acprof:oso/9780199765218.001.0001

Mijas, M., Koziara, K., Galbarczyk, A., & Jasienska, G. (2020). Chubby, hairy and fearless. subcultural identities and predictors of self-esteem in a sample of Polish members of bear community. *International Journal of Environmental Research and Public Health*, *17*(12), 4439. https://doi.org/10.3390/ijerph17124439

Pachankis, J. E., Mahon, C. P., Jackson, S. D., Fetzner, B. K., & Bränström, R. (2020). Sexual orientation concealment and mental health: A conceptual and meta-analytic review. *Psychological Bulletin*, *146*(10), 831–871. https://doi.org/10.1037/bul0000271

Pasek, M. H., Filip-Crawford, G., & Cook, J. E. (2017). Identity concealment and social change: Balancing advocacy goals against individual needs. *Journal of Social Issues*, *73*(2), 397–412. https://doi.org/10.1111/josi.12223

Perales, F. (2019). The health and wellbeing of Australian lesbian, gay and bisexual people: A systematic assessment using a longitudinal national sample. *Australian and New Zealand Journal of Public Health*, *43*(3), 281–287. https://doi.org/10.1111/1753-6405.12855

Real-Quintanar, T., Robles-García, R., Medina-Mora, M. E., Vázquez-Pérez, L., & Romero-Mendoza, M. (2020). Qualitative study of the processes of transgender-men identity development. *Archives of Medical Research*, *51*(1), 95–101. https://doi.org/10.1016/j.arcmed.2020.01.003

Richardson, D., & Hart, J. (1981). The development and maintenance of a homosexual identity. In J. Hart & D. Richardson (Eds.), *The theory and practice of homosexuality* (pp. 73–92). Routledge and Kegan Paul.

Riggle, E. D. B., Rostosky, S. S., Black, W. W., & Rosenkrantz, D. E. (2017). Outness, concealment, and authenticity: Associations with LGB individuals' psychological distress and well-being. *Psychology of Sexual Orientation and Gender Diversity*, *4*(1), 54–62. https://doi.org/10.1037/sgd0000202

Russell, S. T., & Fish, J. N. (2016). Mental health in lesbian, gay, bisexual, and transgender (LGBT) youth. *Annual Review of Clinical Psychology*, *12*, 465–487. https://doi.org/10.1146/annurev-clinpsy-021815-093153

Scroggs, B., & Vennum, A. (2020). Gender and sexual minority group identification as a process of identity development during emerging adulthood. *Journal of LGBT Youth, 18.* https://doi.org/10.1080/19361653.2020.1722780

Secord, P. F., & Backman, C. W. (1961). Personality theory and the problem of stability change in individual behavior: An interpersonal approach. *Psychological Review, 68*(1), 21–32. https://doi.org/10.1037/h0045625

Sophie, J. (1986). A critical examination of stage theories of lesbian identity development. *Journal of Homosexuality, 12*(2), 39–51. https://doi.org/10.1300/J082v12n02_03

Tajfel, H., & Turner, J. C. (1979). An integrative theory of intergroup conflict. In W. G. Austin & S. Worchel (Eds.), *The social psychology of intergroup relations* (pp. 33–47). Brooks/Cole.

Troiden, R. R. (1979). Becoming homosexual: A model for gay identity acquisition. *Psychiatry, 42*(4), 362–373. https://doi.org/10.1080/00332747.1979.11024039

Turner, J. C., Hogg, M. A., Oakes, P. J., Reicher, S. D., & Wetherell, M. S. (1987). *Rediscovering the social group: A self-categorization theory.* Blackwell.

Webster, L. (2019). "I am I": Self-constructed transgender identities in internet-mediated forum communication. *International Journal of the Sociology of Language, 2019*(256), 129–146. https://doi.org/10.1515/ijsl-2018-2015

Weinberg, M. S., & Williams, C. J. (1974). *Male homosexuals: Their problems and adaptations.* Harper & Row.

Weinberg, M. S., Williams, C. J., & Pryor, D. W. (1994). *Dual attraction: Understanding bisexuality.* Oxford University Press.

Weinberg, T. S. (1984). Biology, ideology, and the reification of developmental stages in the study of homosexual identities. *Journal of Homosexuality, 10*(3–4), 77–84. https://doi.org/10.1300/J082v10n03_11

Westgate, E. C., Riskind, R. G., & Nosek, B. A. (2015). Implicit preferences for straight people over lesbian women and gay men weakened from 2006 to 2013. *Collabra, 1*(1), 1–10. http://doi.org/10.1525/collabra.18

26

THE CURRENT STATE OF CONVERSION THERAPY IN THE UNITED STATES

Sage A. Mauldin and Lindsey Churchill

Conversion Therapy: An Overview

Conversion therapy is a medically discredited practice that seeks to change a person's sexual orientation or gender identity (American Psychological Association, 2013; Jacob, 2015; Streed et al., 2019). Conversion therapy is a catchall term for gay cure, reparative therapy, reorientation therapy, and reintegrative therapy (Kinitz et al., 2021; Przeworski et al., 2021), all of which are based on the idea that a person's sexual orientation or gender identity can be changed, and that change is necessary for the person, family, community, and state (Alexander, 2017). Studies have shown that conversion therapy leads to "poor psychosocial outcomes" (Kinitz et al., 2021, p. 2). It has been associated with anxiety (Conine et al., 2021; George, 2016), self-hatred (Beckstead & Morrow, 2004; Bradshaw et al., 2015), depression (Salway et al., 2021), internalized homophobia or transphobia (Haldeman, 1994; Veale et al., 2021), poor self-esteem (American Psychiatric Association, 2000), and adaptive substance use (Bancroft, 1974). More generally, it can lead to isolation (Beckstead & Morrow, 2004). Alarmingly, it is estimated that 30% of sexual and gender minorities who undergo conversion therapy attempt suicide (Shidlo & Schroeder, 2002). Adding to this distressing statistic, the percentage does not account for those who have committed suicide as a result of conversion therapy (Green et al., 2020). Due to conversion therapy's harmful effects, 20 professional regulating bodies have condemned the practice (e.g., American Counseling Association, American Psychological Association, and American Psychiatric Association; Human Rights Campaign, n.d.). Despite this, conversion therapy continues to be practiced.

Conversion therapy is not a bygone practice; it is undergone in 100 countries, including the United States (United Nations General Assembly, 2020). Efforts to change a person's sexual orientation or gender identity vary depending on location (Alempijevic et al., 2020). Efforts include behavioral counseling (Armenia, Italy, etc.), isolation (China, Nigeria, etc.), verbal abuse (Uganda, Maurtius, etc.), ritual cleansing (France, Spain, etc.), hypnosis (Russia, Sri Lanka, etc.), hospital confinement (China, Ecuador, etc.), and beatings (Peru, Zimbabwe, etc.), to "corrective" violence, including rape (Barbados, El Salvador, etc.) (Bothe, 2020). In the United States, psychotherapy or talk therapy (Parkinson & Morris, 2021) and the prescription of anxiety medication (Salway et al., 2020) are the most commonly used techniques. Despite these contemporary approaches, the history of conversion therapy in the United States reveals

DOI: 10.4324/9781003128151-31

a darker past involving practices such as electroshock or electroconvulsive therapy (ECT) (Graham, 2018; Mehrotra, 2021), aversion treatments like vomit-inducing drugs (Bracken, 2020), and exorcism (Heinz & Pankow, 2017).

In the United States, approximately 698,000 sexual- and gender-minority adults have undergone conversion therapy (Mallory et al., 2019). Approximately 350,000 of those adults were subjected to conversion therapy when they were youths (Harris, 2018). Estimates show that 16,000 sexual- and gender-minority youths are forced to go through conversion therapy with a health provider before they turn 18 (Mohammadi, 2021). In comparison, approximately 57,000 sexual- and gender-minority youths receive conversion therapy from a religious practitioner or religious leader before they turn 18 (Lapin, 2020). At this time, there are no estimates that indicate how many sexual and gender minorities undergo conversion therapy globally (Adamson et al., 2020).

The practice is not only carried out by health providers, including therapists, medical doctors, and sexologists (Wylie, 2021). It is also carried out by religious practitioners and spiritual leaders, as well as by members of the community and family members, in both private and state settings (Graham, 2018). In private settings, conversion therapy is practiced in homes, religious institutions, at youth camps and retreats (Alempijevic et al., 2020). In state settings, conversion therapy is practiced in hospitals, schools, and juvenile detention facilities (Alempijevic et al., 2020). Sexual- and gender-minority adults and youths undergo conversion therapy due to societal pressure to be heterosexual or cisgender (Kinitz et al., 2021). Others seek out conversion therapy for fear of being kicked out of their religious institution or ostracized by their family if they do not attempt to change (National Association of Social Workers, 2015). Conversion therapy rests on the false premise that same-sex attractions and gender identities that fall outside the gender binary (male/female) are abnormalities because they deviate from societal norms (heterosexuality and cisgender) (Coleman, 1987; Diamond, 2000). Practitioners of conversion therapy tell sexual and gender minorities that their sexual orientation or gender identity is a mental disorder or sin and, therefore, needs to be changed (OutRight Action International, 2019).

19th- and 20th-Century Origins of Conversion Therapy

In 1883, 19-year-old Albert von Schrenck-Notzing started his studies at Munich University with the plan to become a physician (Sommer, 2012). Five years later, after studying hypnotism under Hippolyte Bernheim, Schrenck-Notzing received a Doctor of Medicine degree and focused his attention on hypnotism (Andreas, 2012). Schrenck-Notzing opened a private practice and claimed by the turn of the 20th century, he could divert a gay man's sexual impulses to attraction for women with 45 hypnosis sessions and visits to local sex workers, thus beginning a practice that would evolve and be later known as conversion therapy (Ellis, 1896).

Austrian physiologist Eugen Steinach began his career in the late 19th century by focusing on sex hormones in mammals (Sengoopta, 1998). Initially, Steinach researched hormones and their effects by removing rat testicles and moving them to other places on the rodent's body. He also worked on ovarian extracts and the production of sex hormones for female rodents (Södersten et al., 2014). By the 1910s, Steinach became Director of the Department of Physiology at the Institute for Experimental Biology of the Academy of Sciences in Vienna, Austria. In Vienna, Steinach studied the changes he saw in farm cattle once they had been castrated. He also began to transfer sex organs to the opposite sex in animals such as guinea pigs (Benjamin, 1945).

According to the Embryo Project Encyclopedia housed at Arizona State University, when Steinach "implanted female sex organs onto male guinea pigs, he noted that this impacted behavioral characteristics, including aggression, nurturing, and mating preferences, along with the physical characteristics" (Nunez-Eddy & Turriziani Colonna, 2017, n.p.). Steinach also began discussing these ideas with Sigmund Freud and homed in on his hypothesis that testicular secretions in gay men were abnormal, thus causing their same-sex attractions (Lipschütz, 1917).

In 1918, Steinach worked with a colleague to publish the paper *Conversion of Homosexuality Through Exchange of Puberty Gland* (Benjamin, 1945; Nunez-Eddy & Turriziani Colonna, 2017). This chapter discussed a horrific experiment done with a urologist in Austria, Dr. Lichtenstern, where the testicles of gay men had been replaced by the testicles of ostensibly heterosexual men (Meyerowitz, 2004).

> The testes transplanted from the heterosexual men were undescended third testes that doctors had removed surgically. After the transplantation, Steinach and Lichtenstern observed the homosexual man's sexual tendencies. They concluded that, after implantation, heterosexual tendencies replaced homosexual tendencies.
>
> *(Nunez-Eddy & Colonna, 2017, n.p.)*

It is no surprise that even though Steinach and Lichtenstern claimed these procedures to be a success and offered their services to other men struggling with their sexuality, the experiment did nothing to change sexual orientation.

Torturous and baseless experiments like this, which focused on gay men and their anatomy, no doubt inspired later brutal treatments and punishments for gay men, such as the case of British Mathematician Alan Turing. Despite helping the Allies tremendously during World War II as a code breaker, Turing was convicted of gross indecency with another man. Instead of serving a jail sentence, Turing chose chemical castration. Soon after, Turing committed suicide by ingesting a cyanide doused apple (Bowen, 2016).

Therefore, in the late 19th century and well into the 20th century, the notion of what physiologically creates same-sex attractions and subsequently how to fix this problem became the basis of medicalized homophobia. This approach would be utilized later in the 20th century in religious conversion therapy, which relies heavily on denouncing same-sex attractions as an illness and sin and focuses on cures through painful and often torturous methods (Kunzel, 2020). Ryan (2019) writes:

> medicalized homophobia, which simultaneously taught people that homosexuality existed and that they should despise it . . . [was] so successful in this endeavor that by the time of the Stonewall riots, even though eugenics had long since been discredited, their ideas had become the dominant way of understanding human sexuality.
>
> *(n.p.)*

Indeed, while being gay was considered sinful and deviant by the church, the medical field in the late 19th and early 20th century served to reinforce marginalization of sexual and gender minorities. Because white Western women were believed to be less sexually aggressive than men by the science community, fewer experiments and discussion of same-sex attractions occurred for women (Barron & Hare, 2020; Kauth, 2000). This, however, does not imply they were always exempt from medical judgment and psychoanalysis. At that time, many scientific and medical journals claimed female "self-abuse," or masturbation, caused finger warts, uterine disease, cancer of the womb, sterility, small breasts, and spinal deformities (Oneill, 2016). The very notion of a sexual woman was pathologized by many in the medical field.

Austrian founder of psychoanalysis Sigmund Freud had a complicated and complex relationship regarding his perception and analysis of same-sex attractions. Just a few years after Steinach wrote *Conversion of Homosexuality Through Exchange of Puberty Gland*, Freud (1955) published *Psychogenesis of a Case of Homosexuality in a Woman*, in which he postulated what caused his female patient to have same-sex attractions: an infantile mother-fixation, a strong masculine complex, penis envy, and an aversion to pregnancy. While Freud did not view homosexuality as an illness, he did see it as a developmental arrest, or reduced growth in development (Fisher & Funke, 2019). As early as 1905, Freud fought back against the degeneracy theory of homosexuality, which was a popular theory at the time. Degeneracy theory claimed same-sex attractions was a mental problem caused by a decadent lifestyle. Freud disagreed with the mental disorder caused by decadence theory, and countered it by claiming same-sex attractions occurred

> in people who exhibit no other serious deviations from the normal; in people whose efficiency is unimpaired, and who are indeed distinguished by specially [sic] high intellectual development and ethical culture; among the peoples of antiquity at the height of their civilization; and, finally, as remarkably widespread among many savage and primitive races, whereas the concept of degeneracy is usually restricted to states of high civilization.
>
> *(Freud, 1905, p. 132)*

Fifteen years later, Freud became more negative in his views regarding same-sex attractions, focusing on gay men and their fixations on their mothers (Abelove, 1993). Despite this shift, a letter from 1935 in which Freud wrote to a mother who was concerned about her gay son revealed that he believed same-sex attractions were nothing to be embarrassed about (Sieczkowski, 2015). Freud's views went against most scientific and psychological research at the time which still claimed that same-sex attractions represented a form of deviancy that needed to be cured.

As the 20th century continued, psychiatric interventions included more cruel and vicious methods such as electroshock therapy, lobotomies, and aversion treatments. Dr. Robert Galbraith Heath, who served as Chairman of the Department of Psychiatry and Neurology from 1949 to 1980 at Tulane University, utilized pleasure conditioning techniques that included implanting electrodes on nine separate regions of the brain to attempt to turn gay men heterosexual (O'Neal et al., 2017). From there, gay males would be shown heterosexual pornography and given electroshocks in areas of the brain meant to stimulate pleasure. After days of this conditioning, sometimes sex workers would be brought in to reinforce the work of the conditioning. One analysis of patient B-19 stated about the performance of the sex workers in the pleasure conditioning:

> As the second hour began, she relates that his attitude took an even more positive shift to which she reacted by removing her bra and panties and lying down next to him. Then, in a patient and supportive manner, she encouraged him to spend some time in a manual exploration and examination of her body.
>
> *(Colvile, 2016, n.p.)*

These same techniques were also used on frigid women, or women with a low libido (Philippopoulos, 1967). Frigidity was thought to be caused by several factors, including bisexuality

(Moore, 1961). This demonstrates the extent to which scientists went to preserve cisheteropatriarchy. These experiments lasted well into the 1970s. In 1973, homosexuality was removed from the Diagnostic and Statistical Manual of Mental Disorders (DSM) (Silverstein, 2009). Despite this significant step, in homosexuality's place, sexual orientation disturbance (SOD) became a new diagnosis (Drescher, 2015). SOD considered homosexuality an illness if a person with same-sex attractions found them bothersome and desired to change (Drescher, 2015). Although homosexuality was no longer regarded as a mental illness, SOD legitimized conversion therapy. It was not until 1987 that SOD was removed from the DSM (Daley & Mulé, 2014).

Some may see it as no coincidence then that beginning in the 1980s and 1990s, the Christian Right began focusing their time and money on curing same-sex attractions. In response to the strides made in the 1970s and 1980s for women's and gay rights, the church used the pulpit to preach about the ills of same-sex attractions (Johnston & Jenkins, 2006). This also coincided with the rise of the HIV/AIDS crisis where pastors preached from pulpits that AIDS was the punishment for a society that had become more accepting of same-sex attractions (Conrad & Angell, 2004). By the 1990s, the Christian Right had made conversion therapy a lucrative and increasingly well-known enterprise (Gans, 1998). Christian funders helped bankroll ex-gay ministries like Exodus International, which grew into a coalition of more than 80 ministry partners across 34 states (Jones & Yarhouse, 2011). In 1998, Christian political groups invested a substantial sum of $600,000 in promotional campaigns advocating for conversion therapy. These advertisements were strategically placed in prominent publications such as *The New York Times, USA Today, The Wall Street Journal, Los Angeles Times*, and other publications (Merritt, 2015). Some referred to it as "the Normandy landing in the culture war" (Boxwell, 2000, p. 122).

Even Newsweek, a popular American magazine, wrote a sympathetic article about conversion therapy in the late 1990s (Leland & Miller, 1998). By the 21st century, however, peer-reviewed journals demonstrated conversion therapy was ineffective (Cramer et al., 2008; Haldeman, 2002; Steigerwald & Janson, 2003). In addition, former proponents of conversion therapy began vocally to disavow the practice (Whitley-Berry & McCammon, 2021). Despite this shift in public opinion, conversion therapy did not stop altogether: instead, practitioners had to become more clandestine and insidious with their tactics.

The Legal Landscape of Conversion Therapy in the United States

As of fall 2021, there are no legal prohibitions of conversion therapy at the federal level (Clair, 2013; Movement Advancement Project, n.d.). To fill in the vacuum of legislation left by the federal government, 20 states and Washington D.C. have passed laws prohibiting therapists from practicing conversion therapy on sexual- and gender-minority youths (Mallory et al., 2019). These states are New York, Maryland, New Mexico, Rhode Island, Delaware, New Hampshire, Washington, Nevada, Connecticut, Hawaii, Vermont, Oregon, Illinois, California, New Jersey, Massachusetts, Maine, Colorado, Utah, and Virginia, with more states expected to pass similar laws in the coming years (Higbee et al., 2020; Movement Advancement Project, n.d.).

In many of the 30 states that do not have laws prohibiting therapists from practicing conversion therapy on sexual- and gender-minority youths, cities and counties have passed laws banning the practice (Hampton, 2020). Some of these cities and counties are Norman, Oklahoma, Anchorage, Alaska, Winona, Minnesota, Davenport, Iowa, Berkley, Michigan, St. Louis, Missouri, Pima County, Arizona, and Westchester County, New York (Canady, 2020). As of now, approximately 89 cities and counties have passed laws banning the practice (Lapin, 2020; Movement Advancement Project, n.d.).

For the past ten years, conversion therapy prohibitions have been challenged in courts. In 2012, the American Association of Christian Counselors, the National Association for Research & Therapy of Homosexuality, and several unnamed individuals filed a lawsuit against the State of California (Bracken, 2020). They argued that the ban denied parents their rights to choose how to raise their child(ren). In response, the State of California filed a motion to dismiss the lawsuit, which was upheld by the San Francisco-based Ninth Circuit Court of Appeals (*Pickup v. Brown*, 2014), ruling that the ban was a "permissible regulation of *conduct*" because it only "banned the performance of the therapy" (Bracken, 2020, p. 327). In other words, therapists are allowed to discuss conversion therapy with their patients, but they cannot practice it.

A year later, a lawsuit was filed against the State of New Jersey by therapists Tara King and Ronald Newman, the American Association of Christian Counselors, and the National Association for Research & Therapy of Homosexuality (Bracken, 2020). They argued that the conversion therapy ban on sexual- and gender-minority youths was a violation of privacy and free speech. In response, the State of New Jersey filed a motion to dismiss the lawsuit, which was upheld by the Philadelphia-based Third Circuit Court of Appeals, ruling that the ban was a "permissible regulation of *speech*" (Bracken, 2020, p. 327). The reasoning behind their ruling was that because "conversion therapy constitutes 'professional speech', it receives lesser value protections than other types of speech" (Bracken, 2020, p. 327).

Since 2013, when New Jersey and California passed the first statewide conversion therapy bans, these laws have been subject to legal challenges, which have questioned their constitutionality. In 2019, Liberty Counsel, which represented therapist Dr. Christopher Doyle, filed a lawsuit against the State of Maryland (*Doyle v. Hogan*, 2019). Liberty Counsel argued that the State of Maryland's law violated Dr. Doyle's freedom of speech and free exercise of religion. In response, the State of Maryland filed a motion to dismiss the lawsuit, which was upheld by federal judge Deborah Chasanow, ruling that the law was supported by research that shows conversion therapy is harmful to sexual- and gender-minority youths (Bicovny & Leonard, 2021). Liberty Counsel appealed, which was reviewed by the Richmond-based Fourth Circuit of Appeals. The Fourth Circuit dismissed the appeal, ruling Doyle sued the wrong defendants (*Doyle v. Hogan*, 2021). The Supreme Court of the United States has declined to review the decisions in the Ninth, Third, and Fourth Circuit Courts of Appeals, thus upholding conversion therapy bans, despite being petitioned to do so (Calvert, 2019).

In an outlier decision in 2020, a three-judge panel of the Atlanta-Based Eleventh Circuit of Appeals struck down local ordinances that banned conversion therapy on sexual- and gender-minority youths in Palm Beach County and Boca Raton, Florida, citing the First Amendment (*Otto v. City of Boca Raton, Florida*, 2020). After the ordinances were put into effect in 2017, Liberty Counsel, which represented therapists Robert Otto and Julie Hamilton, sued (*Otto v. City of Boca Raton, Florida*, 2019). A federal judge upheld the laws, but the Eleventh Circuit overturned their ruling, finding that the laws "violate the First Amendment because they are content-based regulations of speech that cannot survive strict scrutiny" (*Otto v. City of Boca Raton, Florida*, 2020, p. 2). With the Eleventh Circuit breaking from the Third and Ninth Circuits, this created what lawyers call a "circuit split" (Vincent, 2004). The conflicting court rulings on conversion therapy prohibitions means it is quite likely that the issue could ascend to the Supreme Court of the United States, which often reviews circuit splits to enforce homogeneity in the application of laws (Knapp, 2002).

Other lawsuits have charged conversion therapy providers with committing consumer fraud for engaging in deceptive business practices such as advertising same-sex attractions as an abnormality that can be cured (Shidlo & Schroeder, 2002). For instance, in 2012, Michael Ferguson, Benjamin Unger, and Chaim Levin, who were represented by the Southern Poverty Law Center, filed a lawsuit against Jews Offering New Alternatives for Homosexuality (JONAH)-which promised that same-sex attractions could be mitigated, if not eradicated completely for fraudulent practices (Dubrowski, 2015).

In their testimonies, Benjamin Unger shared that in a group therapy session, he was given a pillow and then told to imagine it as his mother. He was then forced to beat it, as if he was beating his own mother (Khazan, 2015). Chaim Levin shared that in another group therapy session he was forced to recreate traumatic scenes of sexual abuse from his childhood (Stern, 2015). These techniques reflect conversion therapy's assertions that being too close to one's mother or experiencing sexual abuse during one's childhood plays a major role in one being gay (Rosik, 2001). The plaintiffs alleged that the co-directors of JONAH, Arthur Goldberg and Elaine Berk, and one of the spiritual leaders at JONAH, Alan Downing, violated the New Jersey Consumer Fraud Act (Southern Poverty Law Center, n.d.).

Three years after the lawsuit was filed, it was ruled that the defendants did, in fact, violate the New Jersey Consumer Fraud Act. As a consequence, they were ordered to pay $72,400 to the plaintiffs and permanently close JONAH (Cangany, 2021; Southern Poverty Law Center, n.d.). Despite this, it took an extra ruling in July 2021 to actually force JONAH to stop functioning (Zeitlinger, 2021). This case was the first to use consumer protection laws to challenge the efficaciousness of conversion therapy. In doing so, it set a legal precedent for cases since then (National Center for Lesbian Rights, 2017).

The Legal Landscape of Conversion Therapy Around the World

Conversion therapy is not only a societal problem in the United States; it is a pervasive global issue. Survivors from Australia and Iran, to Ecuador have recounted their harrowing experiences with conversion therapy. For example, Jane, a survivor from Australia, described her experience in the following way:

> with a surgical table, and being restrained . . . having an electrode attached to my labia; and images projected onto the ceiling; [voice breaking] and a lot of pain from the electrodes; and being left there for quite a long time afterwards, exposed and alone.
>
> *(Bothe, 2020, p. 7)*

Another survivor, Jasmine, from Iran shared:

> The pills turned out to be a heavy substance for a teenage body that had never consumed any narcotics or alcohol. They numbed my entire body . . . to the point that I had become incontinent. I burst into tears when I found myself to be wet in the morning. I felt like I had been raped. The notion of rape should not be understood only in relation to sexual relations. I really felt as if this doctor had raped and violated me. This experience made me lose trust in all doctors.
>
> *(Bothe, 2020, p. 8)*

Julio, a survivor from Ecuador, said that he was " exposed to systematic verbal abuse, yelling, humiliation, and rape threats; housed in overcrowded rooms; held in isolation for long periods of time; deprived of food for several days or forced to eat or drink unsanitary food or water" (Bothe, 2020, p. 9).

To address this, support is growing in countries around the world for formal prohibitions of conversion therapy. For instance, in 2018, the European Union (EU) voted, 435 to 109, to pass an amendment that repudiates conversion therapy. The amendment reads:

> [The European Parliament] welcomes initiatives that prohibit LGBTQI conversion therapies and banning the pathologisation of trans identities and urges all Member States to adopt similar measures that respect and uphold the right to gender identity and gender expression.
>
> *(European Union, 2018, para. 65)*

As of now, five countries have prohibited therapists from practicing conversion therapy on sexual- and gender-minority youths. These countries are Taiwan, Brazil, Ecuador, Malta, and Germany (AFP & TOI Staff, 2020; Jones et al., 2021). In Australia, Queensland became the first state to ban conversion therapy (Hislop, 2020; Lee, 2021). Other countries made inroads to ban the practice but faced challenges. Britain and Ireland, for example, drafted legislation but were delayed due to a lack of political support (Savage, 2020; Trispiotis & Purshouse, 2022). In Canada, a bill that would have banned the practice was postponed because more Republican support was needed (Bensadoun, 2020; Salway et al., 2021). In Israel, a bill to ban the practice passed out of parliament, in a 42 to 36 vote (Levy, 2021; Milton, 2020), but must go through two more rounds of votes before it is signed into law (Ilany & Ilany, 2021; Vardi, 2020).

In 2020, 370 religious leaders called for a global ban on conversion therapy (Farley, 2020; Palm & Gaum, 2021). Among the signatories of the declaration are notable figures such as David Rosen, former Chief Rabbi of Ireland; Anglican cleric Desmond Tutu of South Africa; and Mary McAleese, a well-known member of the Roman Catholic Church and the former President of Ireland (Daly, 2021). Mary McAleese signed the declaration to acknowledge the pain and suffering religious teachings have caused sexual and gender minorities and to call on other religious leaders around the world to stand against prejudice towards sexual and gender minorities.

Regardless of geographic location, efforts to ban conversion therapy start with grassroots activism and take years of hard work. This is evidenced in Oklahoma, where efforts to ban conversion therapy are constantly challenged.

Grassroots Activism to Prohibit the Practice of Conversion Therapy in Oklahoma

Efforts to ban conversion therapy, specifically on sexual- and gender-minority youths, in Oklahoma began in October 2017 after Sage A. Mauldin and his friend, both survivors of conversion therapy, broached the issue while they were lamenting the dearth of basic rights afforded to sexual and gender minorities.

After they shared their conversion therapy experiences with each other, for the first time since he experienced this torture when he was 17 years old, Sage felt compelled to act. A couple of months of strategizing later, he knew he needed both local and state platforms in order to effect change in a state where sexual and gender minorities' voices are often silenced. At the local level, Sage did not have to look too far to find the City of Norman's Human Rights Commission (HRC), which has a decades-long history of protecting the civil rights of Norman residents. The HRC is committed to addressing intersectional oppression as experienced by minoritized communities, including the LGBTQIA+ community, and is responsible for recommending proclamations, resolutions, and ordinances to Norman's City Council. This appealed to Sage, so he applied and was appointed to serve a three-year term, starting in January 2018.

At the first meeting he attended, Sage was asked by a fellow Commissioner who also served on the American Civil Liberties Union of Oklahoma (ACLU-OK) Board of Directors if he would be interested in serving a three-year term on the ACLU-OK Board. The ACLU-OK is committed to safeguarding people's civil rights and civil liberties as outlined in the United States Bill of Rights. Known for its advocacy on behalf of minoritized communities, the organization often engages in transformative work within the courts, through campaigns, and in the Oklahoma Legislature (American Civil Liberties Union, n.d.). Sage applied and was appointed to serve a three-year term, starting in April 2018. He now had the two platforms he needed.

In February 2018, Sage petitioned the Oklahoma Legislature to ban conversion therapy on change.org, an online petition website that allows activists to promote causes they care about. Change.org provides signatories with the option to elaborate on why they have chosen to sign a petition, and the comments illustrated a general understanding and recognition that conversion therapy is harmful to the mental health and well-being of its victims. For example, a signatory named Alyssa wrote, "Conversion therapy is bad for a child's mental health. It is unfair to subject a child to this inhumane treatment based only on the opinions of their guardian(s). Being LGBT is not only okay, it is beautiful and is something to celebrate, not repress or be shameful of." Another signatory named Patty wrote, "Conversion therapy is a barbaric pseudoscience that has zero effect on the sexual orientation that a person is born with! It should be banned world-wide." By May 2018, the petition had more than 8,500 signatures.

With the help and guidance of the National Center for Lesbian Rights (NCLR), Sage spent the next four months drafting a piece of legislation to ban conversion therapy on sexual- and gender-minority youths in Oklahoma. NCLR (n.d.) has been the vanguard of the nationwide movement to ban conversion therapy since the launch of their successful #BornPerfect Campaign in 2014 (National Center for Lesbian Rights, n.d.). With their assistance and support confirmed, all Sage needed now was a legislator to sponsor the legislation.

In October 2018, Sage attended a forum on sexuality and spirituality from the Christian perspective at the University of Central Oklahoma in Edmond, Oklahoma. The forum was hosted by the Women's Research Center and BGLTQ+ Student Center, which is directed by Dr. Lindsey Churchill. The forum began with the speakers debating whether the Christian perspective on sexuality is valid and ended with the speakers debating whether a person's sexuality, gender identity, or gender expression can be changed. After the forum, Sage introduced himself to one of the speakers, an Oklahoma City LGBTQIA+ activist named Kris, who made a cogent argument for why therapists should be prohibited from practicing conversion therapy on sexual- and gender-minority youths. Sage told Kris about the legislation he had drafted and asked her which legislator she thought might be interested in sponsoring the legislation. Kris recommended Representative Jason Dunnington, who is a Democrat and represented House District 88, where Oklahoma City's "gayborhood" is located (Slay, 2018).

In December 2018, Sage, Representative Dunnington, Kris, and Elizabeth Horn, Director of Programming at Freedom Oklahoma, met and discussed the legislation. Sage knew that prohibiting therapists from practicing conversion therapy was constitutional and had legal precedence; 14 other states, including California and Nevada, had already passed legislation prohibiting licensed therapists from practicing conversion therapy on sexual- and gender-minority youths. Representative Dunnington agreed to sponsor the bill and explained that to increase the chances of the legislation being successful, it could only prohibit licensed therapists from practicing conversion therapy because places of worship are protected by religious freedom laws.

In January 2019, Representative Dunnington submitted a revised version of Sage's legislation to the House Public Health Committee: House Bill (HB) 2456, "Youth Mental Health Protection Act." In the meantime, Sage used his position on the HRC to recommend Norman's City Council pass a resolution urging the Oklahoma Legislature to ban the practice of conversion therapy on sexual- and gender-minority youths. In February 2019, Norman's City Council passed the resolution. Unfortunately, HB 2456 died in the House Public Health Committee due to insufficient time for discussion. Despite this setback, Sage, Representative Dunnington, and other activists had momentum on their side.

In October 2019, the House Health Services and Long-Term Care Committee conducted a bipartisan interim study, which was co-authored by Representative Dunnington and Republican Representative Randle Randleman, who represents House District 15 and is a licensed psychologist. The purpose of the interim study was to analyze the harmful effects of conversion therapy and educate legislators on what conversion therapy is and urge them to move forward with protecting sexual- and gender-minority youths from its harmful effects.

The interim study was successful. Representative Dunnington made an impassioned plea to his colleagues to support a statewide ban on conversion therapy. The Trevor Project's Senior Fellow for Advocacy and Government Affairs, Casey Pick, and Senior Advocacy Campaign Manager, Troy Stephenson, gave presentations overviewing the harms of conversion therapy. After their presentations, Democrats and Republicans asked questions and expressed their support. The success of the study boosted the pride and optimism of everyone involved.

In January 2020, a year after HB 2456 had died in committee, Representative Dunnington resubmitted the "Youth Mental Health Protection Act"-HB 3872—to the House Children, Youth and Family Services Committee. This time, in a 10–4 vote, HB 3872 passed out of committee. Sage, Representative Dunnington, and the other activists were overjoyed. Yet, when HB 3872 was being discussed, Representative Randleman, who had previously supported it, vociferously withdrew his support. A few days later, Representative Dunnington informed Sage that HB 3872 would not be heard on the House Floor due to a lack of Republican support. Having worked on this legislation for a few years, Sage conceded that there was little to no hope of getting a statewide ban on conversion therapy passed in Oklahoma, at least not anytime soon. Rather than giving up, he redirected his energy and focus on the one place where he knew he could get a ban on conversion therapy passed: Norman, Oklahoma.

In March 2021, Sage became Chair of the HRC. From the start, he made it known that his top priority would be working with local LGBTQIA+ groups to pass an ordinance that would prohibit licensed therapists from practicing conversion therapy on sexual- and gender-minority youths in Norman. To accomplish this, he formed a coalition with the leaders of local LGBTQIA+ nonprofit groups: Norman Pride and Norman PFLAG. Coalition members were responsible for researching the pervasiveness of conversion therapy in Norman. They spent two months gathering and documenting evidence, and in May 2021, they presented their findings to the HRC during a special meeting. The evidence was overwhelming, and the HRC voted unanimously to recommend Norman's City Council pass a law. On June 29, 2021, at the tail-end of Pride Month, Norman's City Council voted unanimously to pass a ban on conversion therapy. Once again, Norman led the way as the first city in Oklahoma in protecting sexual- and gender-minority youths (Wood, 2021).

Sage watched the livestream of the meeting from his hometown as Norman's City Council cast their votes. When the law officially passed, he felt an immediate sense of relief. He knew many sexual- and gender-minority youths in Norman would be spared from the pain and suffering caused by conversion therapy. Following the conclusion of the council meeting ended, he walked to the church where, as a teenager, he voluntarily underwent conversion therapy-a decision that was influenced by societal pressure to conform to heterosexuality. Standing outside the church, memories resurfaced of the bimonthly meetings he attended with a spiritual leader. During these sessions, discussions centered on the perceived sin of same-sex attractions.

For one year, Sage was coerced to read and reread the seven Biblical texts spiritual leaders often use to condemn same-sex attractions: Noah and Ham (Genesis 19:1–11), Sodom and Gomorrah (Genesis 19:1–11), Levitical laws (Leviticus 18:22, 20:13), two words in two Second Testament vice lists (1 Corinthians 6:9–10; 1 Timothy 1:10), and Paul's letter to the Romans (Romans 1:26–27). He was shamed and dehumanized. Though those bimonthly meetings haunt him to this day, he is intent on making sure sexual- and gender-minority youths are protected from conversion therapy not only in Oklahoma, but in the United States and around the world, as well.

He has transformed his suffering into meaningful action.

Conclusion

Though conversion therapy may be a medically discredited practice, it still exists in over 100 countries worldwide. Currently, there are no federal legal prohibitions against conversion therapy in the United States. In the 30 states that have no laws against conversion therapy, many local governments have passed bans. Despite studies showing negative outcomes for those who have experienced conversion therapy, the practice is carried out by health providers, religious practitioners and community and family members. The history of conversion therapy shows the extreme measures so-called "scientists" took in order to preserve heteronormativity.

Work done locally in Oklahoma demonstrates how difficult change can be at a statewide level, particularly in more conservative states. Bans on conversion therapy are necessary, particularly since conversion therapy generally targets LGBTQIA+ youths, who are some of the most vulnerable populations.

References

Abelove, H. (1993). Freud, male homosexuality, and the Americans. In H. Abelove, M. Barale, & D. M. Halperin (Eds.), *The lesbian and gay studies reader* (pp. 381–393). Routledge.

Adamson, T., Wallach, S., Garner, A., Hanley, M., & Howell, S. (2020). *The global state of conversion therapy: A preliminary report and current evidence brief.* O LGBT Foundation. http://osf.io/preprints/socarxiv/9ew78/

AFP & TOI Staff. (2020). Jewish figures join over 300 religious leaders urging "conversion therapy" ban. *The Times of Israel.* www.timesofisrael.com/jewish-figures-join-over-300-religious-leaders-urging-conversion-therapy-ban/

Alempijevic, D., Beriashvili, R., Beynon, J., Birmanns, B., Brasholt, M., Cohen, J., Duque, M., Duterte, P., Es v. A., Fernando, R., Fincanci. K. S., Hamzeh, S., Hansen, H. S., Hardi, L., Heisler, M., Iacopino, V., Leth M. P., Lin, J., Louahlia, S., . . . Viera, D. N. (2020). Statement of the independent forensic expert group on conversion therapy. *Torture Journal, 30*(1), 66–78.

Alexander, M. B. (2017). Autonomy and accountability: Why informed consent, consumer protection, and defunding may beat conversion therapy bans. *University of Louisville Law Review, 55,* 283.

American Civil Liberties Union. (n.d.). *ACLU 100 years.* www.aclu.org

American Psychiatric Association. (2000). Position statement on therapies focused on attempts to change sexual orientation (reparative or conversion therapies). *American Journal of Psychiatry, 157,* 1719–1721.

American Psychological Association. (2013). *Position statement on issues related to homosexuality.* American Psychological Association. www.psychiatry.org/File%20Library/About-APA/Organization-Documents-Policies/Policies/Position-2013-Homosexuality.pdf

Andreas, S. (2012). Policing epistemic deviance: Albert Von Schrenck-Notzing and Albert Moll. *Medical History, 56*(2), 255–276. https://doi.org/10.1017/mdh.2011.36

Bancroft, J. (1974). *Deviant sexual behaviour: Modification and assessment.* Clarendon Press.

Barron, A. B., & Hare, B. (2020). Prosociality and a sociosexual hypothesis for the evolution of same-sex attraction in humans. *Frontiers in Psychology, 10,* 2955. https://doi.org/10.3389/fpsyg.2019.02955

Beckstead, A. L., & Morrow, S. L. (2004). Mormon clients' experiences of conversion therapy: The need for a new treatment approach. *The Counseling Psychologist, 32*(5), 651–690.

Benjamin, H. (1945). Eugen Steinach, 1861–1944: A life of research. *The Scientific Monthly, 61*(6), 427–442.

Bensadoun, E. (2020). Canada just tabled legislation to ban conversion therapy: Why is it necessary in 2020? *Global News.* https://globalnews.ca/news/6649396/canada-conversion-therapy-ban-legislation/

Bicovny, W., & Leonard, A. S. (2021, July). Civil litigation notes. *LGBT Law Notes,* 25–35. www.proquest.com/scholarly-journals/civil-litigation-notes/docview/2581891635/se-2?accountid=10901

Bothe, J. (2020). *It's torture not therapy: A global overview of conversion therapy: Practices, perpetrators, and the role of states: Thematic report.* International Rehabilitation Council for Torture Victims. https://irct.org/uploads/media/IRCT_research_on_conversion_therapy.pdf

Bowen, J. P. (2016). Alan Turing: Founder of computer science. In J. P. Bowen, Z. Liu, & Z. Zhang (Eds.), *School on engineering trustworthy software systems* (pp. 1–15). Springer.

Boxwell, D. A. (2000). Kulturkampf, now and then. *War Literature and the Arts, 12*(1), 122–135.

Bracken, M. D. (2020). Torture is not protected speech: Free speech analysis of bans on gay conversion therapy. *Washington University Journal of Law & Policy, 63,* 325.

Bradshaw, K., Dehlin, J. P., Crowell, K. A., Galliher, R. V., & Bradshaw, W. S. (2015). Sexual orientation change efforts through psychotherapy for LGBQ individuals affiliated with the Church of Jesus Christ of Latter-day Saints. *Journal of Sex & Marital Therapy, 41,* 391–412.

Calvert, C. (2019). Testing the first amendment validity of laws banning sexual orientation change efforts on minors: What level of scrutiny applies after Becerra and does a proportionality approach provide a solution? *Pepperdine Law Review, 47,* 1.

Canady, V. A. (2020). Court ruling on conversion therapy concerning to advocates. *Mental Health Weekly, 30*(46), 6–7.

Cangany, W. (2021). Extending Hoosier hospitality to LGBTQ youth: Why Indiana should pass a conversion therapy ban to protect and promote mental health outcomes for LGBTQ youth. *Indiana Health Law Review, 18,* 155.

Clair, N. (2013). "Gay conversion therapy" ban: Protecting children or infringing rights? *McGeorge Law Review, 44*(3), 550–558.

Coleman, E. (1987). The assessment of sexual orientation. *Journal of Homosexuality, 14*(3), 9–24.

Colvile, R. (2016). *The "gay cure" experiments that were written out of scientific history: Mosaic science.* www.mosaicscience.com

Conine, D. E., Campau, S. C., & Petronelli, A. K. (2021). LGBTQ+ conversion therapy and applied behavior analysis: A call to action. *Journal of Applied Behavior Analysis, 55*(1), 6–18.

Conrad, P., & Angell, A. (2004). Homosexuality and remedicalization. *Society, 41*(5), 32–39.

Cramer, R. J., Golom, F. D., LoPresto, C. T., & Kirkley, S. M. (2008). Weighing the evidence: Empirical assessment and ethical implications of conversion therapy. *Ethics & Behavior, 18*(1), 93–114.

Daley, A., & Mulé, N. J. (2014). LGBTQs and the DSM-5: A critical queer response. *Journal of Homosexuality, 61*(9), 1288–1312.

Daly, G. (2021). Catholicism in modern Ireland-Ellen Coyne's are you there, God? It's me, Ellen. *Studies: An Irish Quarterly Review, 110*(438), 191–200.

Diamond, L. M. (2000). Sexual identity, attractions, and behavior among young sexual-minority women over a two-year period. *Developmental Psychology, 36,* 241–250.

Doyle v. Hogan, 1 F. 4th 249 (4th Cir. 2021).

Doyle v. Hogan, 411 F. Supp. 3d 337 (D. Md. 2019).

Drescher, J. (2015). Out of DSM: Depathologizing Homosexuality. *Behavioral Sciences (Basel, Switzerland), 5*(4), 565–575.

Dubrowski, P. R. (2015). The Ferguson v. Jonah Verdict and a path towards national cessation of gay-to-straight conversion therapy. *Northwestern University Law Review, 110,* 77.

Ellis, H. (1896). A note on the treatment of sexual inversion. *Alienist and Neurologist (1880–1920), 17*(3), 257.

European Union. (2018). *Situation of fundamental rights in the EU in 2016.* European Union Agency for Fundamental Rights. www.europarl.europa.eu/doceo/document/TA-8-2018-0056_EN.html

Farley, H. (2020). Gay conversion therapy: Hundreds of religious leaders call for ban. *BBC News*. www.bbc.com/news/amp/uk-55326461

Fisher, K., & Funke, J. (2019). The age of attraction: Age, gender and the history of modern male homosexuality. *Gender & History, 31*(2), 266.

Freud, S. (1953). Three essays on the theory of sexuality (1905). In *The standard edition of the complete psychological works of Sigmund Freud, vol. VII (1901–1905): A case of hysteria, three essays on sexuality and other works* (pp. 123–246). The Hogarth Press and the Institute of Psycho-Analysis.

Freud, S. (1955). The psychogenesis of a case of homosexuality in a woman. In *The standard edition of the complete psychological works of Sigmund Freud, vol. XVIII (1920–1922): Beyond the pleasure principle, group psychology and other works* (pp. 145–172). The Hogarth Press and the Institute of Psycho-Analysis.

Gans, L. A. (1998). Inverts, perverts, and converts: Sexual orientation conversion therapy and liability. *Boston University Public Interest Law Journal, 8*, 219.

George, M. A. (2016). Expressive ends: Understanding conversion therapy bans. *Alabama Law Review, 68*, 793.

Graham, T. C. (2018). Conversion therapy: A brief reflection on the history of the practice and contemporary regulatory efforts. *Creighton Law Review, 52*, 419.

Green, A. E., Price-Feeney, M., Dorison, S. H., & Pick, C. J. (2020). Self-reported conversion efforts and suicidality among US LGBTQ youths and young adults, 2018. *American Journal of Public Health, 110*(8), 1221–1227.

Haldeman, D. C. (1994). The practice and ethics of sexual orientation conversion therapy. *Journal of Counseling and Clinical Psychology, 62*(2), 221–227.

Haldeman, D. C. (2002). Gay rights, patient rights: The implications of sexual orientation conversion therapy. *Professional Psychology: Research and Practice, 33*(3), 260–264.

Hampton, J. (2020). The first amendment and the future of conversion therapy bans in light of National Institute of Family and Life Advocates v. Harris. *Berkeley Journal of Gender, Law & Justice, 35*, 169.

Harris, B. (2018). Free to be me. *CrossCurrents, 68*(4), 488.

Heinz, A., & Pankow, A. (2017). Return of the religious: Good shamanism and bad exorcism. In H. Basu, R. Littlewood, & A. S. Steinforth (Eds.), *Spirit and mind: Mental health at the intersection of religion and psychiatry* (pp. 57–67). LIT Verlag Münster.

Higbee, M., Wright, E. R., & Roemerman, R. M. (2020). Conversion therapy in the Southern United States: Prevalence and experiences of the survivors. *Journal of Homosexuality, 69*(2), 612–631.

Hislop, M. (2020). *Queensland becomes first state to ban conversion therapy practices.* https://womensagenda.com.au/latest/queensland-becomes-first-state-to-ban-conversion-therapy-practices/

Human Rights Campaign. (n.d.). *Policy and position statements on conversion therapy.* www.hrc.org/resources/policy-and-position-statements-on-conversion-therapy

Ilany, Y., & Ilany, N. (2021). The LGBT community in Israel: Access to the surrogacy procedure and legal right for equality, family life and parenthood. *Ruch Prawniczy, Ekonomiczny i Socjologiczny, 83*(1), 85–97.

Jacob, J. (2015). Conversion therapy ineffective and inappropriate for LGBTQ youth. *JAMA: The Journal of the American Medical Association, 314*(20), 2121.

Johnston, L. B., & Jenkins, D. (2006). Lesbians and gay men embrace their sexual orientation after conversion therapy and ex-gay ministries: A qualitative study. *Social Work in Mental Health, 4*(3), 61–82.

Jones, S. L., & Yarhouse, M. A. (2011). A longitudinal study of attempted religiously mediated sexual orientation change. *Journal of Sex & Marital Therapy, 37*(5), 404–427.

Jones, T., Power, J., Hill, A. O., Despott, N., Carman, M., Jones, T. W., Anderson, J., & Bourne, A. (2021). Religious conversion practices and LGBTQA+ youth. *Sexuality Research and Social Policy*, 1–10. https://doi.org/10.1007/s13178-021-00615-5

Kauth, M. R. (2000). *True nature: A theory of sexual attraction.* Springer.

Khazan, O. (2015, June 4). *When the therapist is a quack.* www.theatlantic.com/health/archive/2015/06/when-your-therapist-is-a-quack/394886/

Kinitz, D., Salway, T., Dromer, E., Giustini, D., Ashley, F., Goodyear, T., Ferlatte, O., Kia, H., & Abramovich, A. (2021). The scope and nature of sexual orientation and gender identity and expression change efforts: A systematic review protocol. *Systematic Reviews, 10*(1), 14. https://doi.org/10.1186/s13643-020-01563-8

Knapp, J. R. (2002). The federal trademark dilution act: The circuit split makes a desperate call to the supreme court for uniformity. *Georgia State University Law Review, 19*, 853.

Kunzel, R. (2020). The "durable homophobia" of psychoanalysis. *Modern Intellectual History*, *17*(1), 215–219.

Lapin, J. J. (2020). The legal status of conversion therapy. *Georgetown Journal of Gender and the Law*, *22*, 251.

Lee, D. (2021). Conversion therapy bans: Enshrining a contested view of human nature in law. *Singapore Academy of Law Journal*, *33*(2), 483–530.

Leland, J., & Miller, M. (1998). Can gays "convert"? *Newsweek*, *132*(7), 46–50.

Levy, B. (2021). *Covenant and the Jewish conversion question: Extending the thought of Rabbi Joseph B. Soloveitchik*. Palgrave Macmillan.

Lipschütz, A. (1917). On the internal secretion of the sexual glands. *The Journal of Physiology*, *51*(4–5), 283.

Mallory, C., Brown, T. N., & Conron, K. J. (2019). *Conversion therapy and LGBT youth-update*. UCLA School of Law Williams Institute. https://escholarship.org/uc/item/0937z8tn

Mehrotra, D. (2021). *The barbaric reality of conversion therapy in India: Why is it vicious?* www.lawctopus.com/academike/conversion-therapy-india/

Merritt, J. (2015). How Christians turned against gay conversion therapy. *The Atlantic*, 15. www.theatlantic.com/politics/archive/2015/04/how-christians-turned-against-gay-conversion-therapy/390570/

Meyerowitz, J. (2004). *How sex changed: A history of transexuality in the United States*. Harvard University Press.

Milton, J. (2020). Israel's parliament just voted for a bill to ban gay conversion therapy: Ultra-orthodox lawmakers aren't best pleased. *Pink News*. www.pinknews.co.uk/2020/07/22/israel-gay-conversion-therapy-ban-parliament-approve-united-torah-judaism-party/

Mohammadi, F. (2021). Protecting the most vulnerable among us. *Criminal Justice*, *35*(4), 27–33.

Moore, B. E. (1961). Frigidity in women. *Journal of the American Psychoanalytic Association*, *9*(3), 571–584.

Movement Advancement Project. (n.d.). *Conversion "therapy" laws*. www.lgbtmap.org/equality-maps/conversion_therapy

National Association of Social Workers. (2015). *Sexual orientation change efforts (SOCE) and conversion therapy with lesbians, gay men, bisexuals, and transgender persons*. www.socialworkers.org/LinkClick.aspx?fileticket=IQYALknHU6s%3D&portalid=0

National Center for Lesbian Rights. (2017). *NCLR files consumer fraud lawsuit against Berkeley therapist for conversion therapy*. www.nclrights.org/about-us/press-release/nclr-files-consumer-fraud-lawsuit-against-berkeley-therapist-for-conversion-therapy/

National Center for Lesbian Rights. (n.d.). *Born perfect*. NCLR. www.nclrights.org/our-work/born-perfect

Nunez-Eddy, C., & Turriziani Colonna, F. (2017). Eugen Steinach (1861–1944). In *Embryo project encyclopedia*. http://hpsrepository.asu.edu/handle/10776/11419

O'Neal, C. M., Baker, C. M., Glenn, C. A., Conner, A. K., & Sughrue, M. E. (2017). Dr. Robert G. Heath: A controversial figure in the history of deep brain stimulation. *Neurosurgical Focus*, *43*(3), E12.

Oneill, T. (2016). *Unmentionable: The Victorian lady's guide to sex, marriage, and manners*. Little, Brown, and Company.

Otto v. City of Boca Raton, Florida, 353F. Supp 3d 1237 (S.D. Fla. 2019).

Otto v. City of Boca Raton, Florida, 981 F.3d 854 (11th Cir. 2020).

OutRight Action International. (2019). *Harmful treatment: The global reach of so-called conversion therapy*. https://outrightinternational.org/sites/default/files/ConversionFINAL_1.pdf

Palm, S., & Gaum, L. (2021). Engaging human sexuality: Creating safe spaces for LGBTIQ+ and straight believers in South Africa. *Theologia in Loco*, *3*(2), 162–182.

Parkinson, A. M. P., & Morris, A. M. P. (2021). Psychiatry, psychotherapy and the criminalisation of "conversion therapy" in Australia. *Australasian Psychiatry*, *29*(4), 409–411.

Philippopoulos, G. S. (1967). The analysis of a case of frigidity (psychopathology—psychodynamics). *Psychotherapy and Psychosomatics*, *15*(2–4), 220–230. www.jstor.org/stable/45112083

Pickup v. Brown, 740 F.3d 1208 (9th Cir. 2014).

Przeworski, A., Peterson, E., & Piedra, A. (2021). A systematic review of the efficacy, harmful effects, and ethical issues related to sexual orientation change efforts. *Clinical Psychology (New York, N.Y.)*, *28*(1), 81–100.

Rosik, C. H. (2001). Conversion therapy revisited: Parameters and rationale for ethical care. *Journal of Pastoral Care, 55*(1), 47–67.

Ryan, H. (2019). *How eugenics gave rise to modern homophobia*. www.hughryan.org/recent-work/2020/1/20/how-eugenics-gave-rise-to-modern-homophobia

Salway, T., Ferlatte, O., Gesink, D., & Lachowsky, N. J. (2020). Prevalence of exposure to sexual orientation change efforts and associated sociodemographic characteristics and psychosocial health outcomes among Canadian sexual minority men. *The Canadian Journal of Psychiatry, 65*(7), 502–509.

Salway, T., Juwono, S., Klassen, B., Ferlatte, O., Ablona, A., Pruden, H., Morgan, J., Kwag, M., Card, K., Knight, R., & Lachowsky, N. (2021). Experiences with sexual orientation and gender identity conversion therapy practices among sexual minority men in Canada, 2019–2020. *PLOS One, 16*(6), E0252539.

Savage, R. (2020). *As survivors speak out, 9 countries seek to ban gay "conversion therapy"*. www.reuters.com/article/us-global-lgbt-health-trfn-idUSKBN20K00T

Sengoopta, C. (1998). Glandular politics: Experimental biology, clinical medicine, and homosexual emancipation in fin-de-siecle Central Europe. *Isis, 89*(3), 445–473.

Shidlo, A., & Schroeder, M. (2002). Changing sexual orientation: A consumers' report. *Professional Psychology: Research and Practice, 33*, 249–259.

Sieczkowski, C. (2015). Unearthed letter from Freud reveals his thoughts on gay people. *Huffpost*. www.huffpost.com/entry/sigmund-freud-gay-cure-letter_n_6706006

Silverstein, C. (2009). The implications of removing homosexuality from the DSM as a mental disorder. *Archives of Sexual Behavior, 38*(2), 161–163.

Slay, E. (2018). *OKC's gayborhood is getting a makeover*. www.gayly.com/okc%E2%80%99s-gayborhood-getting-makeover

Södersten, P., Crews, D., Logan, C., & Soukup, R. W. (2014). Eugen Steinach: The first neuroendocrinologist. *Endocrinology, 155*(3), 688–695.

Sommer, A. (2012). Policing epistemic deviance: Albert von Schrenck-Notzing and Albert Moll. *Medical History, 56*(2), 255–276.

Southern Poverty Law Center. (n.d.). *Michael Ferguson, et al., v. Jonah, et al. SPLC*. www.splcenter.org/seeking-justice/case-docket/michael-ferguson-et-al-v-jonah-et-al

Steigerwald, F., & Janson, G. R. (2003). Conversion therapy: Ethical considerations in family counseling. *The Family Journal, 11*(1), 55–59.

Stern, J. M. (2015). *Unconscionable practice*. https://slate.com/news-and-politics/2015/02/new-jersey-gay-conversion-therapy-case-blocked-expert-testimony-could-be-end-of-abusive-practice.html

Streed, C. G., Jr., Anderson, J. S., Babits, C., & Ferguson, M. A. (2019). Changing medical practice, not patients-putting an end to conversion therapy. *The New England journal of Medicine, 381*(6), 500–502.

Trispiotis, I., & Purshouse, C. (2022). Conversion therapy's degrading treatment. *Oxford Journal of Legal Studies, 42*(1), 104–132.

United Nations General Assembly. (2020). *Practices of so-called conversion "therapy"*. https://undocs.org/A/HRC/44/53

Vardi, A. (2020). *Israel's parliament moves towards ban on gay "conversion therapy"*. www.yahoo.com/now/israels-parliament-moves-towards-ban-gay-conversion-therapy-002738131.html

Veale, J. F., Tan, K. K., & Byrne, J. L. (2021). Gender identity change efforts faced by trans and nonbinary people in New Zealand: Associations with demographics, family rejection, internalized transphobia, and mental health. *Psychology of Sexual Orientation and Gender Diversity, 9*. https://doi.org/10.1037/sgd0000537

Vincent, S. (2004). Unbalanced responses to employers getting even: The circuit split over what constitutes a title VII-prohibited retaliatory adverse employment action. *University of Pennsylvania Journal of Labor and Employment Law, 7*, 991.

Whitley-Berry, V., & McCammon, S. (2021, August 5). *Former "ex-gay" leaders denounce "conversion therapy" in a new documentary* (Morning ed.). NPR. www.npr.org/2021/08/02/1022837295/

Wood, M. (2021). *Norman city council passes conversion therapy ban*. www.normantranscript.com/news/norman-city-council-passes-conversion-therapy-ban/article_c1ce9cc6-d94a-11eb-bc67-eb1d4d823d96.html

Wylie, K. (2021). Masters & Johnson-their unique contribution to sexology. *BJPsych Advances*, 1–3. https://doi.org/10.1192/bja.2021.53

Zeitlinger, R. (2021). *Founders of New Jersey gay conversion therapy practice lose appeal, must pay $3.5 million*. www.nj.com/hudson/2021/08/founders-of-new-jersey-gay-conversion-therapy-practice-lose-appeal-must-pay-35-million.html

27

QUEERING LGBTQ+ PEOPLE IN RESEARCH

Challenges and Opportunities

Bolivar X. Nieto, Geovanna N. Hernandez, Tonette S. Rocco, and Sunny L. Munn

When gathering information on workforce and workplace, political, social and community issues, researchers recognize value in identifying respondents' race, ethnicity, gender, age, and other demographic information but rarely seek demographic information about sexual orientation or gender identity directly. The viewpoint that heteronormativity, homophobia, and heterosexism drive the continued paucity of data on Lesbian, Gay, Bisexual, Transgender, Queer, and other sexual minorities represented by the plus sign (LGBTQ+) in global, social, political, and work contexts is one the authors share. Heteronormativity (posits heterosexuality as the natural/normal state) perhaps plays the largest role by perpetuating beliefs and demeanors that portray LGBTQ+ identities as unimportant or irrelevant (van Loo & Rocco, 2009). While changing, many researchers still believe sexual orientation and gender identity are not relevant demographic details and that heterosexuality is the only sexual orientation that matters. If homosexuality is a sexual orientation, then heterosexuality is as well. Alternatively, homophobia (distaste for LGBTQ+ people and their perceived "lifestyle" or "choice") is a gut reaction based on intolerance and ignorance. Homophobia is pervasive in more workplaces and institutions than most acknowledge. It is an especially dangerous attitude because upon vocalization, its holder can greatly reduce opportunities for common ground, understanding, or learning. Heterosexism (dismissive feelings, statements, or actions directed toward LGBTQ+ people) may be present unintentionally. LGBTQ+ people have had to advocate for their experiences to be considered relevant in workplaces and institutions and in research. Research for and with LGBTQ+ people require challenging and deconstructing heteronormative design practices rooted in privilege (Hall et al., 2022). By queering research, researchers can use queer lenses to be critical of traditional, established, and standardized research approaches to give place to those approaches that center LGBTQ+ lives, their intersectional identities, strengths, and experiences (Hall et al., 2022; Kilgo, 2021; Nadal, 2016).

The focus of this chapter is how research (conceived broadly) can raise the visibility of LGBTQ as a dimension of identity. To do this, we examine challenges and opportunities, research methods and designs, conceptual frameworks common in LGBTQ+ research, review procedural and ethical concerns researchers face, and provide recommendations for lessening these concerns. We share how LGBTQ+ organizations, academic style guides, and publishers address research on or writing about LGBTQ+ people. We hope that this information is helpful

DOI: 10.4324/9781003128151-32

to LGBTQ+ researchers and LGBTQ+-affirming researchers (non-LGBTQ+) with a sincere interest in the strengths of LGBTQ+ individuals and communities.

Challenges and Opportunities in LGBTQ+ Research

There is no doubt that LGBTQ+ research has advanced across many fields (psychology, education, counseling, sociology); nevertheless, challenges around inclusivity, diversity (inclusive of identity), equity, representation, and geography continue to be present in research (Abreu et al., 2022; Guyan, 2022; Nadal, 2016; Salvati & Koc, 2022). The challenges that exist or are simply perceived encompass all types of research, quantitative, qualitative, mixed methods, evaluation studies and historical studies.

- Policymakers are divided on whether the interests of LGBTQ+ people are a legitimate concern since the rhetoric accusing them of requesting special rights or the myth of choice can be confusing to policymakers who are uninformed (Rocco & Gallagher, 2006). Research on LGBTQ+ people is often viewed as illegitimate due to this rhetoric creating barriers to economic research (which examines the monetary costs and benefits of decisions traditionally using quantitative methods) such as (a) discrimination, (b) a lack of interest or knowledge, (c) absence of support, and (d) the scarcity of appropriate data and models (Klawitter & Flatt, 1998). Clark and Serovich (1997) conducted a meta-analysis of over 13,000 articles in family-therapy journals. They found contributing factors to a lack of research on LGBTQ+ people and issues include: authors choosing to publish in LGBTQ+-focused and welcoming journals; heterosexist bias in research design and theory; a concern that investigating LGBTQ+ issues might brand the scholars as LGBTQ+; and an assumption that heterosexual research is applicable to the LGBTQ+ experience. In 2020, these same factors and barriers (Clark & Serovich, 1997; Klawitter & Flatt, 1998), were articulated in a paper published in the field of agriculture education (Murray et al., 2020). While research design and theory might seem neutral and applicable to all groups, traditional research designs and theory development have been based on the experiences of straight, cisgender, white, English speaking, and not disabled (mentally, cognitively, or physically) (often male) people. This view is being challenged by scholars who understand that different identity characteristics produce individual experiences that are varied and unique (Rice et al., 2019).

Stigma and discrimination play a role in gaps in research on sexual minorities. Stigma or the negative beliefs held about LGBTQ+ people provide the justification to discriminate or maintain prejudicial attitudes/bias and exclude LGBTQ+ people from (in this case) research (Goffman, 1963). Stigma is felt by members of the LGBTQ+ community in different ways such as a fear of being outed, experiences being misrepresented, and professional legitimacy being questioned. Stigma around a group affects researchers' beliefs causing them to diminish or dismiss the value of LGBTQ+ people to research questions. An example is in the international leadership literature where Ilac (2021) suggested researcher bias supports the gender binary and not the gender spectrum contributing to a lack of research on sexual identity and gender identity (SOGI). Self-suppression of research participation also affects a lack of research because leaders are afraid to come out or be outed and a lack of trust in the researcher's integrity and ability to portray their identities and experiences appropriately. LGBTQ+ scholars and allies have been deterred from examining questions important to LGBTQ+ people or making explicit reference to LGBTQ+ identities because of the associated stigma known as courtesy stigma (Ragins &

Wiethoff, 2005). The courtesy stigma happens when heterosexuals are afraid of being perceived as LGBTQ+ because they are interested in research about LGBTQ+ people's experiences.

There are also fewer LGBTQ+ scholars and allies available to conduct research on LGBTQ+ people. This is easy to understand when according to a 2023 Gallup poll only 7% of respondents were identified as LGBTQ+ (Wikipedia Contributors, 2023) and the number of people identifying as allies is hard to ascertain because this question is not listed on any survey, we are aware of. LGBTQ+ scholars that do exist may find other questions of interest (as is their right) or may fear discrimination in education and employment. LGBTQ+ scholars and allies who may want to engage in research on LGBTQ+ people might not do so out of fear of discrimination in the tenure and promotion process. Absence of support can be directly linked to the viewpoints of institutions and funding agencies. Funding agencies and other gatekeepers often support research on LGBTQ+ issues related to health but see research on non-health-related issues as too interdisciplinary, political, or nonobjective, especially when it is done by researchers identifying as LGBTQ+. For instance, research on LGBTQ+ issues in education prior to 1990 was dominated by a heteronormative bias which focused on pathology and LGBTQ+ issues such as HIV and mental health (Wimberly, 2015). Institutions may not want to be associated with research about LGBTQ+ people; may be unwilling to count it in tenure decisions, consider LGBTQ+ issues irrelevant to the curriculum, or criminalize LGBTQ+ research as in the case of Florida (Martinez, 2023). Scarcity of appropriate data and models is a barrier to research as it hampers the analysis of LGBTQ+ issues and constrains evidence-based policymaking (Park, 2016).

A prominent challenge in research is when researchers, practitioners, and policymakers make overt decisions to exclude LGBTQ+ people from research because of a fear of offending survey or interview/focus group respondents and by not seeking information about sexual orientation directly (van Loo & Rocco, 2009). Instead, quantitative researchers use multiple variables from within the dataset to create a proxy for sexual orientation such as two same-sex people living in a household (Munn et al., 2011). This practice was exemplified in studies that found gay men earn less than straight men and lesbian women earn more than straight women (Cahill et al., 2002; Leppel, 2009) which used data sets that did not collect demographic information on sexual orientation. These proxies simply increased "the possibility of LGB status" (van Loo & Rocco, 2009, p. 86), but two same-sex people living in the same household could just as easily be siblings or straight roommates rather than romantically involved same-sex partners. Therefore, this was not definitive research because there is no proof those identified are actually sexual minorities.

A step in addressing the challenges to including LGBTQ+ people in research studies and to counter the bias in research on LGBTQ+ issues, The Williams Institute was founded in 2001 (see https://williamsinstitute.law.ucla.edu/about/who-we-are/) to conduct "independent research on sexual orientation and gender identity law and public policy" (n.p.). To counter the use of proxies and exclusionary practices, the Williams Institute commissioned several reports so that there might be a greater possibility of inclusion and diversity in research while decreasing the possibilities of offending the status quo (The Sexual Minority Assessment Research Team, 2009). The "Best Practices for Asking Questions about Sexual Orientation on Surveys" provides recommendations to researchers and policymakers on why, what, how, and where to ask about LGBTQ+ people in survey research. The report also provides insights on other considerations researchers should be aware of such as how a participant's age, racial/ethnic identity, and gender (including transgender and gender non-confirming identity) may impact or intersect with sexual orientation. To further encourage and facilitate research on gender identity, the "Gender-related measures overview" identified large scale federally supported surveys (health, education, employment, justice, and census) that should add gender measures, and gather information on the state of gender and gender expression measures providing insights on 1 and 2 step measures (The Gender Identity in U.S. Surveillance, 2014). The two-step measure, developed in 1997 by the Transgender Health Advocacy Coalition Philadelphia, first asks about the respondent's gender identity (male, female, trans male/trans man, trans female/trans woman, genderqueer/gender non-conforming, and different identity) and second asks about gender assigned at birth. The single item measure, developed in 2007 by the Massachusetts Behavioral Risk Factor Surveillance System, simply asks do you consider yourself to be transgender (Yes, transgender, male to female; Yes, transgender, female to male; Yes, transgender, gender non-conforming; no) (The Gender Identity in U.S. Surveillance, 2014). Another single-item measure for SOGI (straight; gay or lesbian; bisexual; transgender, transsexual, or gender-variant; and not listed above/fill in the blank) was developed in 2008 by the Network for LGBT Tobacco Control. In 2016, "Data Collection Methods for Sexual Orientation and Gender Identity (SOGI)" described SOGI measurements and provided examples for use by non-researchers collecting data globally (Park, 2016).

Another challenge is the continued underrepresentation of bisexual, transgender, gender-neutral, and gender non-conforming people, as well as ethnic and racially diverse communities within the LGBTQ+ research umbrella, which has focused predominantly on white, urban, cisgender gay men (Abreu et al., 2022; Hickner, 2021; Salvati & Koc, 2022). This challenge highlights the limited attention given to understanding and incorporating intersectionality when designing and conducting research for and with LGBTQ+ communities (Cimpian & Herrington, 2017; Hall et al., 2022; Nadal, 2019). There is also the tendency to simplify phenomena that are complex in nature, for example, intersectionality, into orderly categories. This often creates quantifiable data and outcomes that are less insightful and/or appropriate (Hall et al., 2022). This practice may benefit the researcher but is a disservice to the LGBTQ+ community.

Finally, researchers need to pay closer attention to how geography and/or a space's context (countries/states with anti-homosexuality laws, religious institutions, work, and classrooms) can impact recruitment, data collection, and overall research implementation (Gower et al., 2019; Guyan, 2022). Socio-political environments that condemn sexual and gender diversity and other social identities "are not neutral and can foster cultures that police how participants engage" (Guyan, 2022, p. 62). These environments can also impact the safety and confidentiality of participants, an ethical concern that needs the utmost attention to ensure equal and equitable representation (Blackburn & Todd, 2022; Blair, 2016). Blair's article on *Ethical Research With Sexual and Gender Minorities* is a useful resource to help address participants' safety and confidentiality, including recruitment and data collection approaches. Gower et al.'s (2019) work on *LGBT Supportive Environments Inventory (SEI)* is an example of how to ethically and safely engage LGBTQ+ participants in assessing what constitutes a positive environment/space for them, which can be a useful approach to designing participant recruitment and data collection methods with LGBTQ+ people.

Reimagining Research Methods and Design

Many researchers continue to rely on traditional quantitative and qualitative methods, such as Experimental, Correlational, Grounded Theory, and Phenomenology, to support their inquiries about LGBTQ+ individuals (Salvati & Koc, 2022). However, there are innovative practices to engaging participants and using data that are more inclusive. Following are examples of how these practices are included in Consensual Qualitative and Participatory research methods. In quantitative research, reflexibility, borrowed from qualitative research, is being used to address biases in research.

In Consensual Qualitative research, for example, researchers have an opportunity to inductively build and contribute knowledge on the multi-layered inner experiences, beliefs, attitudes, behaviors, interactions, and other phenomena that are particular to LGBTQ+ people (Hill, 2012; Pathak et al., 2013; Pollit et al., 2022; Singh & Shelton, 2011). This is achieved by using data collection methods that will help describe phenomena using words, in which a context's importance is recognized; where there is a consensus among all parties involved on the decisions that are made, and where a system is developed to, using raw data, confirm results (Hill et al., 1997).

Another type of inclusive qualitative research method is Participatory research. This type of design, according to the Institute of Development Studies (see participatorymethods.org), offers a range of methods and an ideology that, by definition, is about representation (engages research subjects as active partners in the inquiry process), equity (disrupts relationships and power dynamics between parties involved), knowledge generation, collective learning, empowerment, and action. Examples of participatory methods used in research with LGBTQ+ people include Duoethnography, Counterstorytelling, Participatory Mapping, Future Workshops (used as part of community-based participatory research), and Participatory Action Research (Freund et al., 2016; Hardy et al., 2022; Wagaman & Sanchez, 2017; Wagaman et al., 2018). Each method centers LGBTQ+ people as drivers of the research process and places the researcher as the facilitator. For example, using Counterstorytelling, Wagaman et al. (2018) had LGBTQ+ youths facing systemic oppression address dominant narratives which facilitated "individual transformation and resistance" (p. 1) in the process. Hardy et al.'s (2022) use of Future Workshops enabled resource-scarce groups and the LGBTQ+ community in a rural area to come together to address the problems they were commonly facing and devise innovative solutions.

In quantitative methods, disruption of the status quo is facilitated through a self-inquiry process throughout the research design process. Researchers can start by assessing and determining who is being excluded, by checking assumptions and biases (reasons for excluding individuals' intersectionalities), and by examining how research participants are or will be categorized (Bussey, 2017; Cimpian & Herrington, 2017). For example, is the demographics section of a survey being designed to include sexuality and gender diversity? Are individuals being instructed to check all that apply? The bimodal analyses in surveys might limit the understanding of results as experienced by LGBTQ+ individuals when broad categories—male and female—are the only ones used (Bussey, 2017; Cimpian & Herrington, 2017).

Recruitment, Sampling, and Data Collection

Engaging LGBTQ+ participants in research requires that all researchers pay attention to key considerations such as where the recruitment is happening (inclusive vs. hostile environments); how it is happening (screening surveys, secondary data); what is being asked from participants, for example, identity disclosure; and who (peer and/or researcher) is doing the recruitment. Potter and Potter (2020) suggest three approaches for the recruitment of LGBTQ people (1) *Active:* the researcher directly interacts and engages with the priority population; (2) *Passive:* recruitment materials publicly distributed are used to engage the intended population; and (3) *Mediated:* gatekeepers (individuals with access or who grant access to the population) are identified and involved in the recruitment process. Regardless of the recruitment approach used, researchers need to build rapport, establish trust, and invest in the community they are looking to engage (Potter & Potter, 2020). Approaching recruitment from this standpoint will help researchers understand how to assure confidentiality and develop strategies to address any safety concerns the population may be worried about.

When it comes to sampling methods, purposeful, convenience and snowball are among the most common in LGBTQ+ research (Pollitt et al., 2023; Potter & Potter, 2020; Walch et al., 2020). It is essential to deconstruct and reimagine inclusive and creative ways to gather LGBTQ+ data. Technology can be used in this process through tools such as online survey research panels, Amazon MTurk, and SurveyMonkey (Chambers et al., 2016; Potter & Potter, 2020). Using social-media networking sites such as Facebook or Instagram as a type of virtual snowball can help open and grow accessibility to sizable LGBTQ+ networks that are otherwise considered hard-to-reach or small (Potter & Potter, 2020).

Similar considerations should be given to the data collection tools used in research for and with LGBTQ+ communities. In queering data collection mechanisms, Guyan (2022) suggests "reimagining identity characteristics" (p. 75) as moving targets. As such, it is recommended that researchers understand social identities as fluid and temporal (including religion, disability, and ethnicity) and consider either a continuous data collection approach or develop methods that allow research participants to make updates (Guyan, 2022). For example, in their screening tool, Wagaman (2015) allowed participants to not choose from a pre-determined list of categorical options and instead had participants describe them themselves. Data collected can then be transformed back into categorical options for quantitative analysis (Teddlie & Tashakkori, 2009). A second example is Gower et al.'s (2019) LGBT Supportive Environments Inventory (SEI), co-created with LGBTQ youths. These two examples demonstrate how researchers can create customized and responsive tools for data collection that center LGBTQ+ people by ensuring LGBTQ+ participants have opportunities to define and describe their lives and identities using qualitative, quantitative, and mixed methods techniques (Wagaman, 2015). This flexible practice should also be used to tailor other frequently used data collection methods such as semi-structured interviews, focus groups, assessments, and surveys (Abreu et al., 2022).

Lastly, qualitative and quantitative researchers are encouraged to implement reflexivity (self-inquiry and openness to assess assumptions when operationalizing and categorizing data) as a practice and methodology during data collection (Cimpian & Herrington, 2017; Wagaman & Sanchez, 2017). Reflexivity demands honesty throughout the process (challenges, work implication, successes) with all parties involved (Goins & Pye, 2013) to make sure LGBTQ+ people participating in research feel recognized, seen, and heard (Guyan, 2022). It also means being aware of biases and emotions that may arise from researching sensitive topics with vulnerable populations (Jamieson et al., 2023). As a methodology, reflexivity can assist in determining how the quantitative and qualitative tools used when conducting research with and for LGBTQ+ individuals are either limiting or supportive/affirming of their identities and experiences (Cimpian & Herrington, 2017; Goins & Pye, 2013). In data collection, reflexivity may also mean asking participants to think about or envision how social change could be impacted by the research outcomes (Wagaman & Sanchez, 2017). Tips for using reflexivity in quantitative research can be found in *Reflexivity in Quantitative Research: A Rationale and Beginner's Guide* (Jamieson et al., 2023). Creating transparency during the research process means practicing reflexivity starting with the research question and throughout research design (sampling, data collection and analysis). An opportunity that reflexivity offers to quantitative and qualitative researchers to "add depth of understanding to the data analysis" is the simple practice of keeping a reflexive journal (Ryan & Golden, 2006, as cited by Jamieson et al., 2023, pp. 2–3).

Conceptual Frameworks in LGBTQ+ Research

Prevalent conceptual frameworks in LGBTQ+ research and literature include intersectionality, resilience, resistance, and empowerment (Chan & Mak, 2021; Colpitts & Gahagan, 2016; Salvati & Koc, 2022; Wagaman, 2015). Though not mutually exclusive, these frameworks help quantitative, qualitative, and mixed-method researchers disrupt the need for heteronormative and heterosexist categorization. These frameworks allow gender and sexual identity to be constructed and exist fluidly, encouraging researchers to be more "critical and expansive" through proactivity and openness in identifying assumptions and in correcting bias-based errors when designing and conducting research (operationalization and categorization of sexual minorities and their experiences) for and with the LGBTQ+ population (Cimpian & Herrington, 2017, p. 496). For example, in health-related research, particularly HIV, Transgender women are often categorized/conflated with Men Who Have Sex with Men (MSM); erasing their identity, experience, and unique social conditions and challenges concerning HIV and other health-related disparities (Poteat et al., 2021). The Center of Excellence for Transgender Health recommends a two-question method to accurately collect data: (1) What is your sex or current gender with a *mark for all that apply* instruction from a list of options, and (2) What sex were you assigned at birth, listing the binary male and female as options (though this does not include intersex). As with the aforementioned example, to assure representation, scholars are urged to recognize intersectionality and its power (Fish & Russell, 2018; Hall et al., 2022; Nadal, 2019; Pollitt et al., 2023) and to "be open to messiness in their research, embrace the precarious, and not approach research presuming linear or static phenomena" (Cimpian & Herrington, 2017, p. 496).

Research on resilience is often focused on coping with stigma and is used to understand and measure the health of the LGBTQ+ population through the implementation of traditional ethnocentric, white models and measures that are non-LGBTQ+ specific (Colpitts & Gahagan, 2016; Salvati & Koc, 2022). Queering resilience allows researchers to re-imagine and contextualize these models and measures from a queer perspective (Colpitts & Gahagan), which is not only about tailoring and/or adapting but deconstructing and rebuilding too. A step further would be to use resistance as both a concept and a type of resilience, particularly in collective action research, to drive changes/improvement of oppressing systems at all levels in the socio-ecological model (Bronfenbrenner, 1979) to positively impact the well-being of LGBTQ+ people (Chan & Mak, 2021; Salvati & Koc, 2022).

Another aspect that needs to be examined in LGBTQ+ research is the use of risk-based frameworks, particularly with youths. The main challenges include the concept of risk being "translated as a status characteristic of the young person rather than a characteristic that describes that person's experiences or context" (Russell, 2005, as cited by Wagaman, 2015, p. 4) and the possible perpetuation of felt stigma (internalized) and enacted stigma (discrimination) this concept may carry within, particularly for the LGBTQ+ population (Wagaman, 2015). Alternatively, empowerment frameworks could help shift the negative framing that risk-based frameworks embody to those that create awareness, help LGBTQ+ people build control and gain power over situations in life, and help drive action to address oppressive systems and issues that contribute to inequalities experienced by LGBTQ+ people across different social sectors such as education, health, employment (Wagaman, 2015).

Ethical Concerns

Biases are an ethical concern in research. Roulston and Shelton's (2015) *Reconceptualizing Bias in Teaching Qualitative Research Methods* explores the concept of bias and its intricate connection to how the quality of research is assessed. Given that biases are both subjective and personal, the recommendation is for researchers to disrupt and deconstruct what is currently known about bias and re-conceptualize it (Roulston & Shelton, 2015). This reconceptualization process, also applicable in quantitative research, requires self-inquiry, self-reflection, and discussions on how biases permeate research at multiple levels, including research topic, population, design, method, implementation, and dissemination of results/knowledge and its potential impact (Roulston & Shelton, 2015). From an ethical standpoint on research with LGBTQ+ people, the reconceptualization of bias may elicit challenging yet important questions that need to be discussed, for example, what assumptions are being made about the population, and bring to light the concerns on how "data is generated and represented" (Roulston & Shelton, 2015, p. 339). Blair's (2016) *Ethical Research With Sexual and Gender Minorities*, part of *The SAGE Encyclopedia of LGBTQ Studies*, provides a comprehensive guide to implementing LGBTQ+ research that is inclusive and ethically sound.

Guidance From Professional and Academic Associations

This section summarizes recommendations shared by national LGBTQ+-focused organizations, style guides, and publishers for conducting research on or writing academically about LGBTQ+ people. Specifically, we draw attention to the existing gap in research guidance for this population.

Organizations

National organizations such as GLAAD (formerly known as Gay and Lesbian Alliance Against Defamation), GLSEN (formerly known as Gay, Lesbian, and Stright Education Network), the Human Rights Campaign (HRC), and the National LGBTQ Task Force provide a host of resources for LGBTQ+ people and community members. GLAAD is an advocacy organization focused on media accountability and LGBTQ storytelling that is accurate and authentic (www.glaad.org). GLAAD's Media Reference Guide (n.d.) is a language resource that can be used by media professionals to describe LGBTQ communities respectfully and fairly. The Media Reference Guide's principal guidance is to ask individuals how they want to be described and to use those names, pronouns, and language when identifying people in media coverage. GLSEN addresses the supports required for creating safe and supportive environments for LGBTQ+ young people in schools (www.glsen.org/our-work). They do this by implementing programming and conducting research on LGBTQ issues in the K-12 education space. HRC works to ensure that all LGBTQ+ people are treated as "full and equal citizens" (www.hrc.org/). The HRC website has a plethora of resources focused on supporting the lives of LGBTQ+ people in areas such as coming out, laws and legislation, health and aging, LGBTQ+ issues in the workplace. Finally, the National LGBTQ Task Force shares samples and templates useful for creating diverse policies on nondiscrimination ordinances, addressing bullying, harassment, and gender identity-based discrimination (www.thetaskforce. org). While these well-known and far-reaching organizations support the many aspects of daily life for LGBTQ+ people, and these guides provide useful information on language, none of them have published guidelines for conducting research on or with LGBTQ+ people. This lack of research guidance could be exacerbating gaps and challenges in LGBTQ+ inclusive research.

Style Guides

Style guides such as the Publication Manual of the American Psychological Association 7th edition (APA, 2020), Chicago Manual of Style 17th edition (CMS, 2017), Modern Language

Association Handbook 9th Edition (MLA, 2021), and American Medical Association Manual of Style 11th edition (AMA, 2020) offer some guidance on how to write academically about LGBTQ+ people. The guidance from each of these style guides is focused on promoting sensitivity and bias-free writing with suggestions for authors to primarily defer to the preferred language used by participants and to only specify sexual orientation when relevant to the research or writing topic (AMA Manual of Style, 2020; Chicago Manual of Style, 2017; MLA Handbook, 2021; Publication Manual of the American Psychological Association, 2020). This suggestion to only mention sexual orientation when relevant to the topic ignores the fact that heterosexual is a sexual orientation, so to pretend this is not relevant perpetuates the lack of research and any topic about human actions, attitudes, or learning should be attentive to identity differences.

Each style guide addresses specific suggestions for writing about LGBTQ+ people in different ways. APA (see 2020, chapter 5, pp. 131–149) and MLA (see 2021, chapter 3, pp. 89–94) have the most guidance to offer, with entire chapters of each style guide dedicated to bias-free and inclusive language which included guidance on LGBTQ+ identity. APA's chapter 5: Bias-free Language Guidelines (subsection 5.8) focused on sexual orientation is the most thorough of all style guides and includes definitions for sexual orientation, suggests terms for describing sexual orientation, and outlines pejorative and inaccurate terms to avoid (2020, pp. 145–147). Some style guides contradict each other (e.g., APA's guidance to avoid using homosexual altogether and AMA's guidance to use homosexual only as an adjective), making the context of each academic field a factor impacting inclusive and bias-free academic writing (AMA, 2020, p. 548; APA, 2020, p. 147).

Publishers

Publishers Emerald, SAGE, Taylor and Francis, and Wiley provide minimal guidance for conducting research on or with LGBTQ+ people. SAGE, Taylor and Francis, and Wiley include some guidelines for writing about sexual minorities within their research ethics policies concerning human subjects. These publishers either referenced American Psychological Association guidelines or in a similar manner to the style guides, these publishers discussed using bias-free language that is non-stigmatizing and non-discriminatory. While each publisher has a posted public statement related to diversity, equity, inclusion, and advancing social justice, there is a gap in practical application especially related to conducting ethical research with LGBTQ+ people.

Conclusion

LGBTQ+ people "experience [a] double jeopardy—diminished voice at work and limited research attention on their voiced experiences" (Bell et al., 2011, p. 132). Insufficient support and an unwelcoming research climate have had important impacts on the design of research on and with LGBTQ+ people. To assess the workforce needs of employees and organizations data must be collected which is representative of all types of workers, organizations, and the workforce as a whole. The workforce data currently available does not usually meet this requirement, as it continues to perpetuate heterocentric views, needs, and values in the workplace. For change to occur, items on sexual orientation and gender identity should be included on surveys and when sampling strategies warrant diversity that an effort be made to ensure LGBTQ+ people are included. Workforce practitioners, policymakers and researchers "should always examine performance with a lens of difference, one that includes sexual orientation" (Hornsby & Munn,

2009, p. 77), making it possible for the needs of LGBTQ+ people to be identified within an organization.

Researchers who wish to investigate the issues affecting LGBTQ+ people will encounter a lack of available secondary data which includes appropriate questions about sexual orientation needed to adequately identify sexual minorities. As an example of this lack of secondary data, consider the U.S. Census Bureau which only began collecting data on sexual orientation and gender identity in 2021 (Anderson et al., 2021). We can institute change in data sets compiled in the future and we should.

To overcome barriers, researchers must challenge heteronormative perspectives and perform adequate data collection, which encourages questions regarding sexual orientation. Self-identification as an LGBTQ+ or heterosexual individual should be an option on surveys and demographic questions should include the possibility of sexual minorities as respondents. All respondents should not be assumed to be cis-gendered and heterosexual. Additionally, funding of research initiatives and policy is directly influenced by laws at the state and federal levels and the degree of recognition and protection afforded to LGBTQ+ people. Overcoming the barriers to including sexual minorities in workforce research will require that researchers and corporate stakeholders press for change to current laws so that protection from employment discrimination is extended to this population.

Minority groups will continue to be under researched if we continue to fear offending the majority allowing for the exclusion of inclusive questions during data collection. Researchers must apply critical perspectives to the application of traditional organizational practices, thus challenging the status quo. As it stands, traditional groups are privileged within the workforce (and in all forms of research), while others continue to be marginalized. In an effort to reform "both workplace organizations and development practices directed towards individuals and groups . . . [which] works towards [aligning the] purposes of justice, equity, and participation" (Fenwick, 2005, p. 228), we ask what rationales are used to exclude LGBTQ+ people from practice, policies, and research? How can these barriers be overcome so that professionals, policymakers, and researchers address and include LGBTQ+ issues in their work? We need to start using the power of queer lenses to design inclusive studies (Hall et al., 2022), disrupting the THEM (LGBTQ+ population)-US (researchers) dichotomy will provide a path to developing, creating, and re-imagining research that is FOR and WITH the LGBTQ+ population.

References

Abreu, R. L., Townsend, D., Mitchell, Y., Ward, J., Audette, L., & Gonzalez, K. A. (2022). LGBTQ qualitative and mixed methods research in counseling psychology: A content analysis. *The Counseling Psychologist, 50*(5), 708–737. https://doi.org/10.1177/00110000221092481

AMA manual of style: A guide for authors and editors (11th ed.). (2020). Oxford University Press.

Anderson, L., File, T., Marshall, J., McElrath, K., & Scherer, Z. (2021, Nov. 4). *New household pulse survey data reveals differences between LGBT and non-LGBT respondents during COVID-19 pandemic*. U.S. Census Bureau. www.census.gov/library/stories/2021/11/census-bureau-survey-explores-sexual-orientation-and-genderidentity.html#:~:text=In%20July%202021%2C%20the%20Census%20Bureau%20began%20collecting,identity%20of%20respondents%20to%20its%20Household%20Pulse%20Survey

Bell, M. P., Özbilgin, M. F., Beauregard, T. A., & Sürgevil, O. (2011). Voice, silence, and diversity in 21st century organizations: Strategies for inclusion of gay, lesbian, bisexual, and transgender employees. *Human Resource Management, 50*(1), 131–146.

Blackburn, A. M., & Todd, N. R. (2022). Pride in our community: Reflecting on LGBTQ publications in the American journal of community psychology. *American Journal of Community Psychology, 71*(1–2), 158–165. https://doi.org/10.1002/ajcp.12618

Blair, K. L. (2016). Ethical research with sexual and gender minorities. *The Sage Encyclopedia of LGBTQ Studies, 3*, 375–380. https://doi.org/10.4135/9781483371283

Bronfenbrenner, U. (1979). *The ecology of human development: Experiments by nature and design*. Harvard University Press.

Bussey, T. (2017, April 18). *Designing your quant course with LGBTQ diversity*. University of Connecticut. https://gcci.uconn.edu/2017/04/18/designing-your-quant-course-with-lgbtq-diversity/

Cahill, S., Ellen, M., & Tobias, S. (2002). *Family policy: Issues affecting gay, lesbian, bisexual and transgender families*. The National Gay and Lesbian Taskforce Policy Institute.

Chambers, S., Nimon, K., & Anthony-McMann, P. (2016). A primer for conducting survey research using MTurk: Tips for the field. *International Journal of Adult Vocational Education and Technology, 7*(5), 54–73.

Chan, R. C. H., & Mak, W. W. S. (2021). Resistance as a form of resilience in sexual and gender minorities: Differential moderating roles of collective action on the discrimination–depression relationship among sexual minority men and women. *Social Science & Medicine, 280*, 114056. https://doi.org/10.1016/j.socscimed.2021.114056

The Chicago manual of style. (17th ed.). (2017). The University of Chicago Press.

Cimpian, J. R., & Herrington, C. D. (2017). Editors' introduction: Introducing a methodological research collection on pressing issues for LGBTQ students. *Educational Researcher, 46*(9), 495–497. https://doi.org/10.3102/0013189X17745500

Clark, W. M., & Serovich, J. M. (1997). Twenty years and still in the dark? Content analysis of articles pertaining to gay, lesbian, and bisexual issues in marriage and family therapy journals. *Journal of Marital and Family Therapy, 23*(3), 239-253.

Colpitts, E., & Gahagan, J. (2016). The utility of resilience as a conceptual framework for understanding and measuring LGBTQ health. *International Journal for Equity in Health, 15*(60), 60. https://doi.org/10.1186/s12939-016-0349-1

Fenwick, T. (2005). Conceptions of critical HRD: Dilemmas for theory and practice. *Human Resource Development International, 8*(2), 225–238.

Fish, J. N., & Russell, S. T. (2018). Queering methodologies to understand queer families. *Family Relations, 67*(1), 12–25. https://doi.org/10.1111/fare.12297

Freund, L., Hawkins, B., & Saewyc, E. (2016). Reflections on the use of participatory mapping to study everyday health information seeking by LGBTQ youth. *Proceedings of the Association for Information Science and Technology, 53*(1), 1–4. https://doi.org/10.1002/pra2.2016.14505301127

Gay and Lesbian Alliance Against Defamation (GLAAD). (n.d.). *GLAAD's media reference guide* (11th ed.). GLAAD. www.glaad.org/reference

The GenIUSS Group. (2014). *Best practices for asking questions to identify transgender and other gender minority respondents on population-based surveys* (J. L. Herman, Ed.). The Williams Institute. https://williamsinstitute.law.ucla.edu/wp-content/uploads/Survey-Measures-Trans-GenIUSS-Sep-2014.pdf

Goffman, E. (1963). *Stigma: Notes on the management of a spoiled identity*. Simon and Schuster.

Goins, E. S., & Pye, D. (2013). Check the box that best describes you: Reflexively managing theory and praxis in LGBTQ health communication research. *Health Communication, 28*(4), 397–407. https://doi.org/10.1080/10410236.2012.690505

Gower, A. L., Saewyc, E. M., Corliss, H. L., Kne, L., Erickson, D. J., & Eisenberg, M. E. (2019). The LGBTQ supportive environments inventory: Methods for quantifying supportive environments for LGBTQ youths. *Journal of Gay & Lesbian Social Services, 31*(3), 314–331. https://doi.org/10.1080/10538720.2019.1616023

Guyan, K. (2022). *Queer data: Using gender, sex and sexuality data for action*. Bloomsbury Academic.

Hall, M., Barbrook-Johnson, P., Bayrakdar, S., & King, A. (2022). Queer(y)ing agent-based modeling for use in LGBTQ studies: An example from workplace inequalities. *Journal of Homosexuality*, 1–27. https://doi.org/10.1080/00918369.2022.2106464

Hardy, J., Geier, C., Vargas, S., Doll, R., & Howard, A. L. (2022). LGBTQ futures and participatory design: Investigating visibility, community, and the future of future workshops. *Proceedings of the ACM on Human-Computer Interaction, 6*(CSCW2), 1–25. https://doi.org/10.1145/3555638

Hickner, A. (2021). LGBTQ health research: Theory, methods, practice [review]. *Journal of the Medical Library Association, 109*(3), 517. Medical Library Association. https://doi.org/10.5195/jmla.2021.1238

Hill, C. E. (Ed.). (2012). *Consensual qualitative research: A practical resource for investigating social science phenomena*. American Psychological Association.

Hill, C. E., Thompson, B. J., & Williams, E. N. (1997). A guide to conducting consensual qualitative research. *The Counseling Psychologist, 25*(4), 517–572. https://doi.org/10.1177/0011000097254001

Hornsby, E. E., & Munn, S. L. (2009). University work-life benefits and same-sex couples. *Advances in Developing Human Resources, 11*(1), 67–81.

Ilac, E. J. D. (2021). Courage required: LGBTQ leadership research in multifaceted realities. In Y. Tolstikov-Mast, F. Bieri, & J. L. Walker (Eds.). *Handbook of international and cross-cultural leadership research processes* (pp. 131–147). Routledge.

Jamieson, M. K., Govaart, G. H., & Pownall, M. (2023). Reflexivity in quantitative research: A rationale and beginner's guide. *Social and Personality Psychology Compass, 17*(4). https://doi.org/10.1111/spc3.12735

Kilgo, C. L. (2021). Queer quantitative research. In K. K. Strunk & S. A. Shelton (Eds.), *Encyclopedia of queer studies in education* (pp. 556–559). Brill. https://doi.org/10.1163/9789004506725_109

Klawitter, M. M., & Flatt, V. (1998). The effects of state and local antidiscrimination policies on earnings for gays and lesbians. *Journal of Policy Analysis and Management, 17*, 658–686.

Leppel, K. (2009). Labour force status and sexual orientation. *Economica, 76*(301), 197–207.

Martinez, A. (2023, March 20). Florida advances a bill censoring university DEI, gender studies, and queer studies. *Prism.* https://prismreports.org/2023/03/20/florida-bill-censor-university-dei-gender-queer-studies/

MLA handbook (9th ed.). (2021). The Modern Language Association of America.

Munn, S. L., Rocco, T. S., Bowman, L., & van Loo, J. (2011). *Work-life research and the representation of sexual minorities.* Critical Management Studies Conference. www.organizzazione.unina.it/cms7/proceedings/proceedings_stream_37/Munn_et_alii.pdf

Murray, K. A., Trexler, C. J., & Cannon, C. E. (2020). Queering agricultural education research: Challenges and strategies for advancing inclusion. *Journal of Agricultural Education, 61*(4), 296–316.

Nadal, K. L. (2016). The intersection of queer theory and empirical methods: Visions for CLAGS, the center for LGBTQ studies. *Women's Studies Quarterly, 44*(3–4), 301–305. https://doi.org/10.1353/wsq.2016.0060

Nadal, K. L. (2019). A decade of microaggression research and LGBTQ communities: An Introduction to the special issue. *Journal of Homosexuality, 66*(10), 1309–1316. https://doi.org/10.1080/00918369.2018.1539582

Park, A. (2016). *Reachable: Data collection methods for sexual orientation and gender identity.* The Williams Institute. https://williamsinstitute.law.ucla.edu/publications/data-collection-sogi/

Pathak, V., Jena, B., & Kalra, S. (2013). Qualitative research. *Perspectives in Clinical Research, 4*(3), 192. https://doi.org/10.4103/2229-3485.115389

Pollitt, A. M., Blair, K. L., & Lannutti, P. J. (2023). A review of two decades of LGBTQ-inclusive research in JSPR and PR. *Personal Relationships, 30.* https://doi.org/10.1111/pere.12432

Poteat, T. C., van der Merwe, L. L. A., Sevelius, J., & Keatley, J. (2021). Inclusion as illusion: Erasing transgender women in research with MSM. *Journal of the International AIDS Society, 24*(1), e25661. https://doi.org/10.1002/jia2.25661

Potter, E. C., & Potter, D. J. (2020). Methods, recruitment, and sampling in research with LGBTQ-parent families. In A. E. Goldberg & K. R. Allen (Eds.), *LGBTQ-parent families.* Springer. https://doi.org/10.1007/978-3-030-35610-1_30

Publication manual of the American psychological association: The official guide to APA style (7th ed.). (2020). American Psychological Association.

Ragins, B. R., & Wiethoff, C. (2005). Understanding heterosexism at work: The straight problem. In R. L. Dipboye & A. Colello (Eds.), *Discrimination at work* (pp. 177–201). Erlbaum.

Rice, C., Harrison, E., & Friedman, M. (2019). Doing justice to intersectionality in research. *Cultural Studies ↔ Critical Methodologies, 19*(6), 409–420.

Rocco, T. S., & Gallagher, S. (2006). Straight privilege and moral/izing: Issues in career development. *New Directions in Adult and Continuing Education, 2006*(112), 29–40. https://doi.org/10.1002/ace.234

Roulston, K., & Shelton, S. A. (2015). Reconceptualizing bias in teaching qualitative research methods. *Qualitative Inquiry, 21*(4), 332–342. https://doi.org/10.1177/1077800414563803

Russell, S. T. (2005). Beyond risk: Resilience in the lives of sexual minority youth. *Journal of Gay and Lesbian Issues in Education, 2*(3), 5–18.

Ryan, L., & Golden, A. (2006). 'Tick the box please': A reflexive approach to doing quantitative *social research. Sociology, 40*(6), 1191–1200. https://doi.org/10.1177/0038038506072287

Salvati, M., & Koc, Y. (2022). Advancing research into the social psychology of sexual orientations and gender identities: Current research and future directions. *European Journal of Social Psychology, 52*(2), 225–232. https://doi.org/10.1002/ejsp.2875

The Sexual Minority Assessment Research Team. (2009). *Best practices for asking questions about sexual orientation on surveys.* Williams Institute. https://williamsinstitute.law.ucla.edu/wp-content/uploads/Best-Practices-SO-Surveys-Nov-2009.pdf

Singh, A. A., & Shelton, K. (2011). A content analysis of LGBTQ qualitative research in counseling: A ten-year review. *Journal of Counseling and Development, 89*(2), 217–226. https://doi.org/10.1002/j.1556-6678.2011.tb00080.x

Teddlie, C., & Tashakkori, A. (2009). *Foundations of mixed methods research: Integrating quantitative and qualitative approaches in the social and behavioral sciences.* Sage.

van Loo, J., & Rocco, T. S. (2009). Sexual minorities, earnings, and career development: Insights from economics. In T. S. Rocco, J. Gedro, & M. Kormanik (Eds.), *Sexual minority issues in HRD: Raising awareness* [Special issue]. *Advances in Developing Human Resources, 11*(1), 82–94.

Wagaman, M. A. (2015). Changing ourselves, changing the world: Assessing the value of participatory action research as an empowerment-based research and service approach with LGBTQ young people. *Child & Youth Services, 36*(2), 124–149. https://doi.org/10.1080/0145935X.2014.1001064

Wagaman, M. A., Obejero, R. C., & Gregory, J. S. (2018). Countering the norm, (re)authoring our lives: The promise counterstorytelling holds as a research methodology with LGBTQ youth and beyond. *International Journal of Qualitative Methods, 17*(1). https://doi.org/10.1177/1609406918800646

Wagaman, M. A., & Sanchez, I. (2017). Looking through the magnifying glass: A duoethnographic approach to understanding the value and process of participatory action research with LGBTQ youth. *Qualitative Social Work: QSW: Research and Practice, 16*(1), 78–95. https://doi.org/10.1177/1473325015595855

Walch, S. E., Bernal, D. R., Gibson, L., Murray, L., Thien, S., & Steinnecker, K. (2020). Systematic review of the content and methods of empirical psychological research on LGBTQ and SGM populations in the new millennium. *Psychology of Sexual Orientation and Gender Diversity, 7*(4), 433–454. https://doi.org/10.1037/sgd0000364

Wikipedia Contributors. (2023, July 3). LGBT demographics of the United States. In *Wikipedia, the free encyclopedia.* Retrieved July 12, 2023, from https://en.wikipedia.org/w/index.php?title=LGBT_demographics_of_the_United_States&oldid=1163152615

Wimberly, G. (2015). *LGBTQ issues in education: Advancing a research agenda.* American Educational Research Association.

VI

Organizational Contexts

28

THEORISING LGBT+ IDENTITIES IN ORGANISATIONS QUEERLY

Nick Rumens

One of queer theory's most influential contributions to gender and sexuality studies has been theorising lesbian, gay, bisexual, queer, trans + (LGBT+) identities not as essential and stabilised properties of the individual, but as fluid, discursively constructed, and contextually contingent (Butler, 1990; de Lauretis, 1991; Edelman, 2004; Halberstam, 1998; Pérez & Radi, 2020; Reed, 2006). The appeal of this approach can be traced to the emergence of queer theory in the early 1990s and thereafter by its scholarly appropriations in new disciplinary terrains and venues. While queer theory may demonstrate a remarkable capacity to mutate and migrate, it remains clear that queer theorists, wherever they are situated, regard identity categories with suspicion, not least because they are frequently organised into binaries (e.g. heterosexual/homosexual, male/female, masculine/feminine) that can constrain how LGBT+ people can live meaningful lives. In particular, hetero- and cisnormative conceptions of sexual and gendered life have been vehemently opposed for regulating identities since they prioritise those identities that reproduce normative heterosexuality (Butler, 1990, 2004). Responding to this, scholars associated with queer theory have sought to destabilise LGBT+ identities. In the seminal text *Gender Trouble*, Judith Butler (1990) proposes that identities are effects of discourse, not easily unified through categorisation and should be permanently open to contestation so it is unclear what they mean. Taking a different tack, Muñoz (1999) advances the concept of "disidentification" as a strategy of resistance and survival for LGBT+ subjects living in hetero- and cisnormative cultures. Researching the rejection of queer identities within highly regulated hetero- and cisnormative cultural contexts, Chéry (2017) explores the provisional and fragile qualities of queer identities in Uganda, arguing that queer Ugandans operate as "identity fugitives", a term that refers to the ways gay and lesbian Ugandans are unable or severely constrained in how they can express their sexuality in public and private spheres. These interventions and the many others that constitute queer discourses on identity represent a radical corrective against hetero- and cisnormative regulation of LGBT+ identities. As such, it is intriguing why queer theory is not widely popular among organisational scholars interested in LGBT+ identities. After all, work organisations have long been identified and problematised as domains of hetero- and cisnormativity that can negatively impact on the identities, lives, and careers of LGBT+ employees (Köllen, 2016; Levine, 1979; Ragins et al., 2007; Rumens & Ozturk, 2019; Woods & Lucas, 1993). So why aren't more organisation studies scholars researching LGBT+ identities engaging with queer theories?

423   DOI: 10.4324/9781003128151-34

There are different ways to respond to this question. Parker (2016) notes that business schools, wherein organisation studies research is largely funded and developed, have never been charmed by queer theory, probably because queer theory has little or no interest in helping organisations to be more profitable or productive. Of course, not all business schools support and produce organisational research driven by this aim, but queer theory's principal concerns reside elsewhere, critiquing what is normative. This may entail destabilising the ontology of organisation and modes of organising that are currently normative and desirable (Parker, 2002), perhaps a stretch too far for some organisation studies scholars? It would be wrong to suggest that queer has not been commandeered by work organisations and capitalism, as accounts of "global queering" show (Jackson, 2009), but queer critiques of capitalism have taken great strides to undermine and transcend its norms (Drucker, 2015). One consequence of this might be undermining capitalistic norms and business schools (Parker, 2002), which might not be a palatable outcome for those employed and studying in these institutions. Additionally, queer theory has been dogged by criticism that it is elite, overly abstract and belongs to its "true" home, the realm of literary theory and the arts, not the world of business and organisations. Furthermore, as Sullivan (2003) observes, queer theory has been admonished for being anti-identity, for wanting to vaporise identity categories altogether. If this is the case, the loss of stable identity categories might impair how LGBT+ employees can represent themselves and organise at work in order to secure employment rights and equalities. Relatedly and under debate is that individuals require a relatively stable identity in order to work effectively (Petriglieri, 2011, p. 644), and although some "identities are more stable than others" (Brown, 2020, p. 6), queer theory's destabilisation of identity categories may be viewed by some organisation scholars as unhelpful or irrational, a point I address later in this chapter. Finally, there is no reason to assume that organisation scholars who identity as LGBT+ must have a natural affinity with or interest in queer theory, not least for any of the reasons mentioned earlier. In summary, it might be said that queer theory is not for the faint hearted; exciting, then, is its capacity to be performative, confrontational, transformative and startling.

It is undeniable that queer theory has journeyed into organisation and management studies over the last few decades or so, where scholarly interest in queer theory appears to be growing (Burchiellaro, 2020; Parker, 2002; Pullen et al., 2016; Rumens, 2018). While it has not lost its central concern with questioning and rupturing normativity (Halperin, 1995; Warner, 1993), queer theory has acquired new life and been put to different uses by organisational scholars, from questioning the normative effects of hetero- and cisnormativity on LGBT+ sexualities and genders (Bendl et al., 2009; Courtney, 2014; Rumens, 2017) to rupturing the norms that constitute management and leadership (Lee et al., 2008; Parker, 2002; Harding et al., 2011). Despite these differences, a common thread running through this body of research is how queer theory is situated at the site of ontology, which provides a compelling reason for why LGBT+ identities and queer theory need to be examined by organisational scholars. In other words, organisational scholarship that engages with queer theory has taken important strides in scrutinising normative accounts of what forms of gender, sexuality, management, and organisation are considered "real". Queer theorising puts normative ontologies into crisis, enabling scholars to ask pertinent questions about what modes of organisation and management, gender and sexuality, too, can exist and which cannot. To underpin these interventions, organisation studies scholars have often borrowed concepts and theories from Judith Butler's oeuvre, in particular her theory of performativity.

Butler's theory of performativity has enabled organisational scholars to critically analyse how ontologies of gender are implicated in the (re)production of gender norms that are "regulatory fictions" (1999, p. 141). This literature underscores the performative constitution and consequences of restrictively normative concepts of gender in organisations (Kelan, 2010; McDonald, 2013; Tyler & Cohen, 2010). In regard to the organisational literature on LGBT+ sexualities and genders, Butler's (1990, 1999, 2004) work has been valuable for theorising gender and sexuality as performative (Benozzo et al., 2015; Gedro & Mizzi, 2014; Riach et al., 2014), underscoring the complexity in how LGBT+ subjects are constituted as organisationally viable. In the rich, long seam of organisational research on LGBT+ identities, Butler's ideas appear less well deployed than concepts and models drawn from sociology and (social) psychology. For instance, there is a well-established track into the field of identity stigma theory with a commanding literature behind it (Clair et al., 2005; Ragins et al., 2007; Stenger & Roulet, 2018; Tilcsik et al., 2015). One reason Butler's (1990, 1993, 1999, 2004) scholarship might be unattractive to researchers of LGBT+ identities is its opposition to the stability of identity and its focus on what it might mean to "undo restrictively normative" LGBT+ identity categories (Butler, 2004, p. 1). Another reason relates to the style of Butler's work, which has been criticised as difficult to understand and mobilise (Kelan, 2009), a criticism that Butler has reflected upon (1999, pp. xviii–xix). Yet a significant strand of organisational research has emerged that dialogues that draws on Butler's writing to theorise LGBT+ identities queerly (Gedro & Mizzi, 2014; Rumens, 2017; Ward & Winstanley, 2005). In other words, this research has not sought to identify specific "types" of LGBT+ identity, but to interrogate how these identity categories are discursively and performatively constituted, regulatory, and rendered (un)intelligible within organisational forms of hetero- and cisnormativity. Aligned with this segment of literature, this chapter enlists Butler's ideas and theories to outline how LGBT+ identities can be understood as performative, explore the subversive possibilities of LGBT+ identity politics and activism, and examine how LGBT+ identities intermingle with identities associated with other aspects of human difference. As this chapter hopes to show, a Butlerian conception of LGBT+ identities represents a fruitful intervention in theorising organisational life queerly.

In terms of organisation, this chapter sets the scene by outlining how queer theory is frequently understood in terms of anti-normativity, its origins and relationship with gay and lesbian studies, and its theorisation of LGBT+ identities. Next, the relationship between Judith Butler's work and queer theory is discussed briefly before delineating the principal components of her theory of performativity. Following this, this chapter discusses some of the implications of Butler's writing on identity for organisational scholars interested in LGBT+ identities.

Queer Theory and LGBT+ Identities

Defining queer theory is difficult or best avoided, not least because, as David Halperin (2003) points out, some queer theorists fret that it will be divested of its magical power to interrogate what is normative and cultivate non-normative ways of living and identifying. We might be more than a little uncomfortable with this proposition, but it delivers a way of thinking about queer theory that avoids fixing it as a set of characteristics or precepts that then become foundational and universalistic. Holding open the definition of queer theory allows us to understand it as a fluid constellation of theoretical resources, or theories, that can generate a critique of normativity, said by Wiegman and Wilson (2015, p. 1) to "mark the spot where queer and theory meet". Indeed, it is fairly safe to state that queer theory's ongoing critical engagement with normativity, which has produced an imposing literature (Edelman, 2004; Halberstam, 2011; Warner, 1993), has furnished queer theory with a bibliographical shape that reveals more about what it can do than what it is. Acknowledging this, some scholars have insisted that queer studies is not the new shorthand for gay and lesbian studies (Piontek, 2006), neither is it anti-heterosexuality theory nor a theory made by queers for queers (Giffney & O'Rourke, 2009;

Hall & Jagose, 2012; Halperin, 1995, 2003; Warner, 1993). By taking normativity as a critical object of analysis, queer theorists in the humanities and social sciences have interrogated an array of normativities (e.g. institutional, cultural, organisational, racial, religious, and theoretical), although much queer theory scholarship, particularly its early seminal works, is centrally concerned with the study of sexual and gender normativities (Butler, 1990; Sedgwick, 1990). A theoretical commitment to anti-normativity beats strong in queer theory, which has been transplanted into the political activism of groups such as Queer Nation (Rand, 2004) that have sought to unhook LGBT+ lives from the barbs of normative regimes that, for example, fasten them to identity categories organised as restrictive binaries (e.g. homosexual/heterosexual, male/female and masculine/feminine). Queer theory's allegiance to anti-normativity is intellectual and political, problematising strategies to assimilate LGBT+ people within hetero- and cisnormativity and campaigning for the transformation of these harmful regimes.

The genesis of queer theory can be traced to the early 1990s, specifically to an academic conference on gay and lesbian studies held in the US where feminist Teresa de Lauretis coined the term as a way of re-theorising gay and lesbian sexualities. As Halperin (2003) explains, de Lauretis had heard "queer" being used in a self-affirming way by "street kids", "activists" and members of the art world in New York in the late 1980s. Whereas "queer" had traditionally been used pejoratively, as a cruel reference to an individual's sexual difference, it was increasingly being used by LGBT+ people as a politically edged identity to signify their sexual and gender non-normativity. Inspired by this, de Lauretis galvanised it as a way of writing about sexuality and gender that did not rely upon heterosexuality, or heteronormative sexual and gender binaries, as a starting point. Indeed, following the conference, De Lauretis's (1991) ideas were published in an essay that outlined her frustration about this and her concerns regarding normative forms of theorising gay and lesbian identities, lives, and cultures. Opening up opportunities for theorising LGBT+ sexualities and genders, de Lauretis (1991) activated "queer" as a mode of critical intervention. Here, queer theory was proposed by de Lauretis (1991) as a more fluid way of thinking about sexuality. This early mobilisation of queer theory aimed to destabilise gay and lesbian studies, which at the time was an important body of theory and knowledge on LGBT+ people but tended to place excessive emphasis on the idea of a common and shared "gay" identity (Seidman, 1997). Arguably, this notion had some virtue in connecting LGBT+ people as a minority group in the aftermath of the 1969 Stonewall Riots in New York, enabling them to mobilise politically against police brutality towards LGBT+ people and for campaigning for LGBT+ equalities. Indeed, one advantage of identity based LGBT+ politics has been the ability to identify what is "normal" and normative, against which LGBT+ sexualities and genders have been cast as "abnormal". However, the idea that a stable gay and lesbian identity could unite people across differences in race, ethnicity, gender, class, age, and (dis)ability was flawed and roundly criticised by, among others, feminists, disability, and race studies scholars. Furthermore, as Piontek (2006) avers, gay and lesbian studies treated LGBT+ groups as minorities on the basis that sexual orientation could constitute a minority. In contrast, queer theory challenged this minoritising perspective, opting instead for a wider social, cultural and political focus on the constitution and operation of sexual and gender normativities within specific contexts. One arm of theorising LGBT+ identities queerly focused on how minority groups are discursively constituted as such to render them visible as an oppressed Other.

Notably, the birth of queer theory represents another turning point in how the meanings and uses ascribed to the term queer have been flexed and reshaped. The etymology of queer is worth discussing briefly for the indications it provides of how queer has come to be understood and deployed, perhaps problematically, as an identity category. Queer theorist Eve Kosofsky Sedgwick has noted the following:

Queer is a continuing moment, movement, and motive—recurrent, eddying, and troublant. The word "queer" itself means across—it comes from the Indo-European root—twerkw, which also yields the German quer (traverse), Latin torquere (to twist), English athwart (1993, p. xii, emphasis in original).

In her reading of queer, Sedgwick places emphasis on how the term refers to a sense of movement, as an adjective that can, as Sedgwick goes on to write, traverse different disciplines and bodies of knowledge. Some of the earliest documented uses of queer in the 1600s suggest that it meant something or someone perverse, but it could also refer to something at a slant or oblique (Sayers, 2005). An old English saying, "There's nowt so queer as folk", can be used as a rather polite way of describing people who are slightly odd, strange, or eccentric. As a noun, queer has been used to describe people thought to be strange, suspicious or of questionable moral character (Sayers, 2005). The expression "in Queer Street" is another instance of how queer has been used, this time in the nineteenth century to describe someone in financial trouble. In regard to LGBT+ people, queer has often been applied as an insult. As mentioned earlier, "queer" has been, and still is, a derogatory act of naming that taps into and redirects queer's association with strangeness and oddity toward LGBT+ sexualities, circulated in discourses that connect LGBT+ sexualities and genders with perversion (Lewis, 2015). Functioning thus, the derogatory use of queer reproduces heteronormativity as it privileges heterosexuality as natural and normal through its positioning of queer as unnatural and abnormal. Notably, LGBT+ people have tried to reverse the negativity associated with queer, transforming it into a form of LGBT+ politics: "if queer is a politically potent term, which it is, that's because, far from being detached from the childhood source of shame, it cleaves to that scene as a near inexhaustible source of transformational energy" (Jagose, 1996, p. 106). Notably, during the late 1980s, in the US and UK, queer political groups such as Queer Nation appropriated queer as a mode of hate speech to oppress LGBT+ people and refashioned it as an identity to draw LGBT+ people together against their oppressors and develop communities of difference.

While the political efforts of Queer Nation to conceptualise queer identities against the discursive pull exerted by normative identity categories appeared to fail in practice, largely because a critique of essentialist identity categories required Queer Nation to articulate that critique from recognisable, stable gay and lesbian identity categories (Gray, 2009), queer identities remain important. Research shows that queer identities can describe and shape variations in non-normative patterns of life and intimate relations (Nash & Bain, 2007; Robertson, 2018). Questions about what kind of people identify as queer and why continue to be debated by scholars, while the ongoing relevance of queer as a positive identity category can be evidenced in a variety of ways, from studies on "queer youth" (Cover, 2016), representations of "queer identity" in U.S. television programmes such as *Glee* (Meyer & Wood, 2013) to "queer Latinidad" identities (Rodríguez, 2003). Nonetheless, queer identities also remain problematic. Queer identities that congeal and are easily defined can present a conundrum for queer theorists who think they should be understood, as Halperin (1995, p. 113; see also Fuss, 1991) intones, as "empty placeholder[s] for an identity that is still in progress and has as yet to be fully realized". In this formulation, theorising queer identities as empty signifiers has implications for how other identities are understood, for if there is no essential truth or meaning held within queer then it follows that identities such as "woman", "man", "heterosexual", "homosexual", "gay", and "lesbian" might also refer to nothing in particular. This is where critiques of queer theory as anti-identity have been sited. Jeffrey's (2002) is one such example, which reasons that lesbians have over decades fought to establish a "lesbian" identity category to be recognised as such, only for queer theory to liquidate its foundations, one outcome of which may be the "disappearance" of lesbian women. Another reading, offered in the following in conjunction with

Butler's (1990, 1999, 2004) writing on performativity and identity, is that theorising identities as a state of becoming does not drain them of meaning or political agency.

Identities as Discursive Effects: Judith Butler's Performative Ontology

Judith Butler occupies an honorific position in the pantheon of queer theory, even though her most influential text *Gender Trouble* (1990) made no mention of it. It is useful to see Butler's *Gender Trouble* as "a moment of queer theory" (Butler, 2004, p. 210) that was the launch pad for developing a Butlerian approach for theorising gender, sexuality, and identity queerly. Queer theorists appropriated Butler's work largely because it provided a radical anti-essentialist theorisation of gender, sexuality, and sex. Countering a view of gender and sexuality as a fixed property or attribute of the individual, Butler conceptualises them both as performative. Drawing on French feminist theory, Jacques Derrida, Michel Foucault, J. L. Austin, among others, Butler's performative approach holds that performativity produces a series of effects, such as when a subject walks, acts, and behaves in ways to consolidate the impression they are male or female. While performing gender can be discussed in terms of acting on an internal state of already being gendered, Butler's claim is that gender, like sexuality, is culturally informed, a phenomenon that is (re)produced through "the gendered stylization of the body" (1999, p. xv). Indeed, Butler asserts that there is no gender at the start of our lives. Said differently, Butler argues that we become gendered subjects at birth when we are interpellated as such through performative speech acts uttered by those around us (e.g. a doctor or nurse who names us at birth as a "boy" or "girl"). Therefore, performativity is about speech acts, but also bodily acts that produce the ontological effects of being gendered, or, for that matter, of being recognised as an intelligible sexual subject. Hence, Butler advances the view that gender is a copy that has no original where "the effect of gender is produced through the stylization of the body and, hence, must be understood as the mundane way in which bodily gestures, movements, and styles of various kinds constitute the illusion of an abiding gendered self" (1999, p. 179). By calling into question what is "real" about gender, Butler raises important questions about what is gender, how it is produced and what are its possibilities for rethinking gender beyond gender norms that have punishing effects on those subjects who cannot approximate its heteronormative ideals.

The role of gender norms in producing the effect of gender is pivotal to understanding how subjects must live with the "constitutive possibility of becoming otherwise" (Butler, 2004, p. 217). Here, Butler assigns norms a constitutive value in how they must be cited in order for the subject to be recognisable as a viable gendered subject; for example, as a "woman" or "man". Nevertheless, Butler argues that gender norms can have deleterious effects if subjects cannot or do not cite those gender norms that constitute the subject as intelligible within the confines of normative heterosexuality. In hetero- and cisnormative contexts, or in Butler's (1990) terms the heterosexual matrix (later re-termed as normative heterosexuality), lines of connection are drawn that maintain gender ensues from sex, and desire follows from gender. Thus, asymmetrical oppositions between feminine and masculine are instituted and understood as the expressive attributes of being male and female (1990, p. 23). In this cultural matrix, intelligible genders are those which maintain relations of coherence with sex, sexual practice, and desire, whereas genders that deviate and disrupt these relations of coherence and continuity are rendered unintelligible. This can be seen in how gay men have been castigated for not being "real men", how women who perform masculinity may be denigrated for expressing "improper" femininity (see also Halberstam, 1998), and how trans persons have been persecuted for blurring the relation between sex and gender. As such, Butler's writing anticipates scholarly debate from which cisnormativity emerges as a term to describe and critique the normative alignment of gender with sex, such that an individual born with male anatomy, for example, is therefore in possession of a "proper" masculinity (Butler, 1990, 2004). The violence associated with the normative operation of gender and sexual norms can be such that subjects are excluded, denied recognition, or have their lives taken from them (Butler, 2004). At the same time, there are benefits for some subjects of "remaining less than intelligible", particularly if the subject's survival depends on "escaping the clutch of those norms by which recognition is conferred" (2004, p. 3). In this sense, subjects can become undone, both positively and negatively, by restrictive gender and sexual norms. In the subject's struggles to become or resist becoming undone by social norms, Butler submits that while the subject is compelled to cite norms that already exist, the citation of norms can destabilise them. In this regard, the subject can exert influence but not unfettered agency or "free play" (1993, p. 95) over what and how gender norms are cited, which can expose gender norms as "nonnatural and nonnecessary" (2004, p. 218). Hence, a locus of agency is located not in the subject but in the citational practices of performativity, with implications, discussed later, for how LGBT+ identity politics can be theorised in organisations.

Following Butler's gender performativity, identity is conceptualised as "an effect, that is, as produced or generated" (1999, p. 187). In other words, identity is an effect of discourses that govern how identities are produced and understood as (un)intelligible. At this junction it is worth stating that, although we can say individuals perform identities repeatedly, Butler's perspective on identity as performative is markedly different to dramaturgical approaches, which cast people as actors who play out their roles in settings with audiences. While Goffman's (1959) dramaturgical analysis enabled an understanding of identity as something that is performed, as individuals occupy roles and interact with others, with consequences for how some identities can be stigmatised, Butler's approach dispenses with the idea of a ready-made identity that exists before the subject is able to act upon it. Indeed, identity is a performative accomplishment and not seamless and coherent always and at all times, although pressure is brought to bear on subjects in numerous contexts, such as places of work, to demonstrate a seamless and coherent gender and sexuality. While Butler asserts that "an identity [is] tenuously created in time, instituted in an exterior space through a stylized repetition of acts" (1999, p. 179), it is also an illusion, which is to say that the performative constitution of identity creates the illusion of an enduring identity that is stable and fixed.

Butler has been associated with what Žižek (2000, p. 132) calls the "anti-identarian turn", but this does not mean Butler abhors identity or advocates the destruction of identity categories. Rather, Butler emphasises the importance of interrogating the limits of identity categories, in particular their "inclusivity and translatability, the presuppositions they include, the ways in which they must be expanded, destroyed, or reworked" (2004, p. 38). Whether this constitutes an anti-identity position has been hotly debated (Nussbaum, 1999), but embarking on research that traces the limits of identity has to understand the regulatory effects of identity categories, whether as the "normalising categories of oppressive structures, or as the rallying points for a liberatory contestation of that very oppression" (Butler, 1991, p. 14). Exploring how identities can function as normative ideals with regulatory effects, it is useful to recap Butler's ideas on the constitutive effect of gender norms. As Butler contends, gender norms are a "form of social power that produces the intelligible field of subjects, and an apparatus by which the gender binary is instituted" (2004, p. 48). Gender and sexual binaries organise and institute gender and sexuality as culturally intelligible notions of identity, whereby coherence and continuity between sex, gender, sexual practice and desire is sustained. It is a point of concern for Butler that gender and sexual binaries appear to exhaust the normative field of meanings that can be assigned to gender and sexuality, but the meanings that fall outside these binaries are also part of gender and sexuality.

Taking into account the identities that are anti-normative or unintelligible can help us to understand identity categories as definitionally incomplete, held permanently open to contestation and alteration. As such, one might, as Butler (1990, 2004) suggests, never completely know what it is to be a "woman", "man", "lesbian", or "gay man". While Butler points out the limits of identities as platforms for political action, principally because they can become instruments of regulation, "that is no reason not to use, and be used, by identity" (1999, p. xxvi). Indeed, in specific contexts and at moments in time, identity categories may have to be deployed strategically to secure rights and equalities within normative discourses of politics, law, medicine, and language. One response to this might be, in what contexts and moments in time exactly can identity categories be mobilised politically, but Butler has always been reluctant to specify this in case a set of universal principles are established, favouring instead context specific analysis. While this may provoke frustration among her critics, for her supporters this counters an overly narrow reading of Butler's work that suggests her theory of performativity and identity cannot function as the basis for political action. The implications of this and other aspects of Butler's writing discussed earlier for theorising LGBT+ identities are elaborated in the next part of this chapter.

Implications for Organisational Scholars Committed to Theorising LGBT+ Identities Queerly

Butler's theory of performativity and her writing on identity have often been critically discussed in terms of its potential for political action (Lloyd, 2007; Nussbaum, 1999; Tyler, 2019). As such, one significant implication concerns how Butler's writing on identity elaborates a non-foundationalist approach to LGBT+ identity politics in the workplace. Research shows that LGBT+ mobilising in organisational and work contexts frequently relies upon LGBT+ subjects articulating their interests and goals from stable LGBT+ identity categories (Raeburn, 2004). This form of identity politics has been hugely beneficial for advancing LGBT+ rights and equalities, but it is positioned within a foundationalist frame wherein identities are assumed to exist before political action can be taken. As such, we might reason that LGBT+ subjects always need to identify as such in order to express political interest and take action to secure various types of equalities. As discussed earlier, Butler is sensitive to how LGBT+ identities must be identified and articulated in order to advocate LGBT+ equality and inclusivity in and outside the workplace. Crucially, Butler does not provide an either/or approach to how LGBT+ identity politics is understood. Although some LGBT+ activists may worry that the Butler's writing constitutes an effort to displace LGBT+ identity politics based on notions of shared commonality, it is, as Butler reasons, "imperative to assert identities at the same time that it is crucial to interrogate the exclusionary operations by which they are constituted" (Butler et al., 1992, p. 108). In other words, Butler is open to the use of "strategic essentialism", whereby, for instance, a group of LGBT+ people with a shared commonality (e.g. employment discrimination based on sexual orientation) assemble and unify because of that commonality. For Butler, this is not a matter of "offering an adequate representation in language of a preconstituted group; in a sense, it is the performative invocation of an identity for the purposes of political resistance to a hegemonic threat of erasure or marginalization" (Butler et al., 1992, p. 109). Put differently, the act of coming together under an "LGBT+" identity is read as a performative act, which allows us to remain sensitive to LGBT+ people's differences in position.

Furthermore, it enables organisational scholars to understand and critique how identifying as a member of an LGBT+ minority group can have regulatory and disciplinary effects, in the sense that the demands and interests of LGBT+ minorities can be controlled by work organisations, and the constitution of sexual orientation and gender diversity as "minorities" renders minority subjects visible and recognisable as the Other to a majority that is constituted as "natural". In this relation of power asymmetry, LGBT+ subjects are heavily dependent on employers and organisations for protection from exclusion, discrimination, and harassment. One might argue this is a good thing, that employers and organisations should shoulder the responsibility of conferring such protections upon LGBT+ subjects, but these safeguards are themselves contingent on there being "norms of recognition that produce and sustain [the] viability" of LGBT+ employees as organisational subjects (Butler, 2004, p. 33). Viewed in this way, while forms of workplace hetero- and cisnormativity may be renegotiated to accommodate and protect LGBT+ subjects, the normative foundations of these regimes remain intact. For organisation studies scholars, questions about whose norms and what conditions govern the recognition of LGBT+ as viable subjects deserving of protection and inclusion may be overlooked, or not asked at all.

Specifically, Butler's identity politics fosters political action in the variation that is possible in citing norms of gender and sexuality repeatedly, for "it is only within the practices of repetitive signifying that a subversion of identity becomes possible" (1999, p. 185). Here, then, opportunities might exist for "a repetition that is not fully constrained by the injunction to reconsolidate naturalised identities" (1999, p. 186). Locating political agency in the performative process of constituting LGBT+ identities rather than in the subject opens up productive avenues for researching those LGBT+ identities that are unintelligible, constituted outside the norms of hetero- and cisnormativity. Hence, one challenge facing organisational researchers is locating "strategies of subversive repetition" (1999, p. 188) enabled by the performativity of LGBT+ identities. This represents an exciting focal point of scholarly inquiry because LGBT+ identities and lives that are constituted perpetually against the regimes of hetero- and cisnormative norms may represent some of the most imaginative, non-normative ways of living and identifying in and outside places of work. Thus LGBT+ identities may be ascribed a political value that exceeds their political capacity as minority identities, for unintelligible LGBT+ identities may exhibit traces of how they have been re-worked from different directions, and it may be the case that, as Butler (2004) submits, these identities have no prior enabling norms or conventions.

Another implication of theorising LGBT identities as performative is the direction it provides for researchers to problematise the norms of gender and sexuality that sustain hetero- and cisnormative LGBT+ identities. One compelling line of inquiry is the critique and destabilisation of gender and sexual binaries that regulate LGBT+ identities. Any effort in this regard must examine how gender and sexual norms operate as a condition of cultural intelligibility, which may produce normative accounts of "which expressions of gender are acceptable, and which are not" (1999, p. xxi). For example, David (2015) examined how female transgender call centre workers in the Philippines struggled to achieve recognition as intelligible subjects in an organisation that besieged them with interrogations about whether and how they were behaving and living as "proper transgender subjects" (2015, p. 188). The gender norms that conferred intelligibility on these trans workers were rigidly anchored in normative discourses of femininity, which circulated organisational injunctions to live "wholesome lives", unconnected to sexual promiscuity and tethered to traditional norms of feminine appearance and a requirement to speak English fluently. Here, trans identities are already presupposed and defined. The ability of David's female trans study subjects to embody these gender norms varied, with consequences for those trans subjects at the limits of intelligibility (e.g. precarious job tenure). Residing at the outer limits of intelligibility may afford the subject an opportunity to supply critical perspectives on how gender norms circumscribe intelligibility (2004), but in David's (2015) study, the need for income and employment benefits appeared to deter female trans subjects from articulating such perspectives to their employers. In another example, Rumens and Ozturk (2019) explored that gay male entrepreneurial identities formed in entrepreneurial work contexts in the UK. They found that gay male entrepreneurial identities were conferred intelligibility when they were constituted through norms of normative masculinity and masculine entrepreneurship that valorised competitiveness, risk taking, and control. Conversely, femininity was repudiated in the accounts gay male entrepreneurs gave of themselves as entrepreneurs, chiefly due to its heteronormative associations with excessive emotionality, irrationality, and softness. One striking element of this study is the desire for recognition and its attachments to identity. This was expressed pointedly by some gay male subjects when they discussed how gay men could be negatively inscribed by norms, which they apprehended in the meanings attached to gay men as "unreal men", unable to inhabit the masculine norms of entrepreneurial discourses.

What these two examples of academic research show is that LGBT+ subjects have to be able to live with identities that are the production of repeated practices of citation, and for some LGBT+ subjects this may be challenging if those identities are increasingly less of their own choosing and fail to approximate the realities of their lives. In regard to organisational research on LGBT+ subjects and identities, Riach et al. (2014) point out, engaging with Butler's (1990, 1999, 2004) theory of performativity and concept of undoing, the lived experiences of how organisational contexts can condition the normative constitution of cultural intelligibility, whereby recognition is attributed to certain forms of subjectivity while disavowing others constitutes a significant, but often overlooked, process of organisation in itself. For Butler, subjectivity in this respect is always a process of undoing through which, as she puts it, "the subject produces its coherence at the cost of its own complexity" (1993, p. 115). For LGBT+ subjects, viable subjectivity and the identities that are accomplished to sustain that subjectivity requires, evident in the work contexts of David (2015) and Rumens and Ozturk (2019), occupying and embodying the norms of hetero- and cisnormativity. Yet, as Riach et al. (2014) aver, the role played by organisations in compelling or constraining seamless and coherent performances of gender and sexuality among LGBT+ employees remains under-researched. Here, then, opportunities exist for researchers to explore how LGBT+ identities are implicated in and constituted by organisational norms that regulate gender and sexuality, particularly where the complexity of the subject is subdued, concealed or forfeit. In turn, one challenge for organisation studies researchers is to mobilise Butler's work methodologically to gain empirical insights into how LGBT+ subjects can produce, in Butler's terms, coherence at the cost of complexity. Riach et al. (2014) offer help here, developing an anti-narrative interviewing method and, from a Butlerian perspective, a reflexive, methodological "undoing" not of organisational subjects but of organisational subjectivities and the normative conditions upon which they depend. Hence, this methodological undoing has potential to reflexively reveal the processes and governmental norms by which workplace subjectivities and identities are shaped, enabling organisational researchers to understand more about the identity work LGBT+ subjects undertake in the process of seeking recognition as intelligible subjects in the workplace.

Conclusion

This chapter has set out to explore the potential of theorising LGBT+ identities in organisations queerly. In doing so, this chapter provided a theoretical underpinning for conversing with queer theory to this end, focusing on the work of Judith Butler, in particular her theory of performativity. It is important to recite an earlier point, that Butler's work is a moment in queer theory, and other strands of queer theorising on identity exist and, importantly, have yet to be woven into research on LGBT+ identities in organisations. As such, there is plenty of scope to advance this field queerly. What Butler brings to the table is a radical theory of identity, and gender and sexuality, which opens the door for theorising LGBT+ identities as performative. One advantage of this is that organisation studies researchers can examine the moments where the binary system of gender and sexuality is ruptured, where the lines of connection between sex, gender, desire, and sexual practice are disputed, and the possibilities to constitute unintelligible or non-normative genders and sexualities. The implications of this for theorising LGBT+ identities have been discussed, where emphasis has been placed on understanding LGBT+ identity politics as performative and based on performative practices of resignification, the regulatory effects of norms and identities and how the constitution of seemingly coherent LGBT+ identities can be at the expense of the subject's complexity. Moving forward, perhaps one of the most valuable insights derived from Butler's writing on identity is the importance of keeping identities open to future re-articulations. As this chapter has demonstrated, the salience of this point is apparent in how LGBT+ identities can be presupposed, defined in advance and in terms not always of their choosing. The consequences of this can be grave. Organisation studies scholars interested in LGBT+ identities might structure their identity research around these concerns, since identities are not just descriptors of the self but, in Butler's terms, modes of becoming that are related to questions about what is a liveable life. Thus, this chapter's engagement with Butler offers a productive and hopeful way of thinking about and theorising LGBT+ identities queerly.

References

Bendl, R., Fleischmann, A., & Hofmann, R. (2009). Queer theory and diversity management: Reading codes of conduct from a queer perspective. *Journal of Management & Organization, 15*(5), 625–638. https://doi.org/10.5172/jmo.15.5.625

Benozzo, A., Pizzorno, M. C., Bell, H., & Koro-Ljungberg, M. (2015). Coming out, but into what? Problematizing discursive variations of revealing the gay self in the workplace. *Gender, Work & Organization, 22*(3), 292–306. https://doi.org/10.1111/gwao.12081

Brown, A. D. (2020). Identities in organizations. In A. D. Brown (Ed.), *The Oxford handbook of identities in organizations* (pp. 1–31). Oxford University Press.

Burchiellaro, O. (2020). Queering control and inclusion in the contemporary organization: On "LGBT-friendly control" and the reproduction of (queer) value. *Organization Studies, 42*(5), 761–785. https://doi.org/10.1177/0170840620944557

Butler, J. (1990). *Gender trouble and the subversion of identity*. Routledge.

Butler, J. (1991). Imitation and gender insubordination. In D. Fuss (Ed.), *Inside/out: Lesbian theory/gay theories* (pp. 13–31). Routledge.

Butler, J. (1993). *Bodies that matter: On the discursive limits of sex*. Routledge.

Butler, J. (1999). *Gender trouble and the subversion of identity* (10th Anniversary ed.). Routledge.

Butler, J. (2004). *Undoing gender*. Routledge.

Butler, J., Aronowitz, S., Laclau, E., Scott, J., Mouffe, C., & West, C. (1992). Discussion. *October, 61*, 108–120. https://doi.org/10.2307/778790

Chéry, T. M. (2017). "No one shakes me": Rejected queer identities and the creation of sacred Ugandan spaces in honor of the Orlando Massacre. *Qualitative Inquiry, 23*(7), 550–556. https://doi.org/10.1177/1077800417718302

Clair, J. A., Beatty, J. E., & Maclean, T. L. (2005). Out of sight but not out of mind: Managing invisible social identities in the workplace. *Academy of Management Review, 30*(1), 78–95. https://doi.org/10.5465/amr.2005.15281431

Courtney, S. J. (2014). Inadvertently queer school leadership amongst lesbian, gay and bisexual (LGB) school leaders. *Organization, 21*(3), 383–399. https://doi.org/10.1177/1350508413519762

Cover, R. (2016). *Queer youth suicide, culture and identity: Unliveable lives?* Routledge.

David, E. (2015). Purple-collar labor: Transgender workers and queer value at global call centers in the Philippines. *Gender & Society, 29*(2), 169–194. https://doi.org/10.1177/0891243214558868

de Lauretis, T. (1991). Queer theory: Lesbian and gay sexualities. *Differences: A Journal of Feminist Cultural Studies, 3*(2), iii–xviii.

Drucker, P. (2015). *Warped: Gay normality and queer anti-capitalism.* Brill.

Edelman, L. (2004). *No future: Queer theory and the death drive.* Duke University Press.

Fuss, D. (Ed.). (1991). *Inside/out: Lesbian theory/gay theories.* Routledge.

Gedro, J., & Mizzi, R. C. (2014). Feminist theory and queer theory: Implications for HRD research and practice. *Advances in Developing Human Resources, 16*(4), 445–456. https://doi.org/10.1177/1523422314543820

Giffney, N., & O'Rourke, M. (Eds.). (2009). *The Ashgate research companion to queer theory.* Routledge.

Goffman, E. (1990). *The presentation of self in everyday life.* Penguin Books. (Original work published 1959)

Gray, M. L. (2009). "Queer nation is dead/long live queer nation": The politics and poetics of social movement and media representation. *Critical Studies in Media Communication, 26*(3), 212–236. https://doi.org/10.1080/15295030903015062

Halberstam, J. (1998). *Female masculinity.* Duke University Press.

Halberstam, J. (2011). *The queer art of failure.* Duke University Press.

Hall, D. E., & Jagose, A. (Eds.). (2012). *The Routledge queer studies reader.* Routledge.

Halperin, D. M. (1995). *Saint Foucault: Towards a gay hagiography.* Oxford University Press.

Halperin, D. M. (2003). The normalization of queer theory. *Journal of Homosexuality, 45*(2–4), 339–343. https://doi.org/10.1300/J082v45n02_17

Harding, N., Lee, H., Ford, J., & Learmonth, M. (2011). Leadership and charisma: A desire that cannot speak its name? *Human Relations, 64*(7), 927–949. https://doi.org/10.1177/0018726710393367

Jackson, P. A. (2009). Capitalism and global queering: National markets, parallels among sexual cultures, and multiple queer modernities. *GLQ: A Journal of Lesbian and Gay Studies, 15*(3), 357–395. https://doi.org/10.1215/10642684-2008-029

Jagose, A. (1996). *Queer theory: An introduction.* New York University Press.

Jeffreys, S. (2002). *Unpacking queer politics.* Polity Press.

Kelan, E. (2009). *Performing gender at work.* Palgrave Macmillan.

Kelan, E. K. (2010). Gender logic and (un) doing gender at work. *Gender, Work & Organization, 17*(2), 174–194. https://doi.org/10.1111/j.1468-0432.2009.00459.x

Lee, H., Learmonth, M., & Harding, N. (2008). Queer(y)ing public administration. *Public Administration, 86*(1), 149–167. https://doi.org/10.1111/j.1467-9299.2007.00707.x

Levine, M. P. (1979). Employment discrimination against gay men. *International Review of Modern Sociology, 9*(2), 151–163.

Lewis, B. (Ed.). (2015). *British queer history: New approaches and perspectives.* Manchester University Press.

Lloyd, M. (2007). *Judith Butler: From norms to politics.* Polity Press.

McDonald, J. (2013). Conforming to and resisting dominant gender norms: How male and female nursing students do and undo gender. *Gender, Work & Organization, 20*(5), 561–579. https://doi.org/10.1111/j.1468-0432.2012.00604.x

Meyer, M. D., & Wood, M. M. (2013). Sexuality and teen television: Emerging adults respond to representations of queer identity on Glee. *Sexuality & Culture, 17*(3), 434–448. https://doi.org/10.1007/s12119-013-9185-2

Muñoz, J. E. (1999). *Disidentifications: Queers of color and the performance of politics* (Vol. 2). University of Minnesota Press.

Nash, C. J., & Bain, A. (2007). "Reclaiming raunch"? Spatializing queer identities at Toronto women's bathhouse events. *Social & Cultural Geography, 8*(1), 47–62. https://doi.org/10.1080/14649360701251809

Nussbaum, M. (1999, February). The hip defeatism of Judith Butler: The professor of parody. *The New Republic, 22,* 37–45.

Parker, M. (2002). Queering management and organization. *Gender, Work & Organization, 9*(2), 146–166. https://doi.org/10.1111/1468-0432.00153

Parker, M. (2016). Queering queer. *Gender Work & Organization, 23*(1), 71–73. https://doi.org/10.1111/gwao.12106

Petriglieri, J. L. (2011). Under threat: Responses to and the consequences of threats to individuals' identities. *Academy of Management Review, 36*(4), 641–662. https://doi.org/10.5465/amr.2009.0087

Pérez, M., & Radi, B. (2020). Gender punitivism: Queer perspectives on identity politics in criminal justice. *Criminology & Criminal Justice, 20*(5), 523–536. https://doi.org/10.1177/1748895820941561

Piontek, T. (2006). *Queering gay and lesbian studies.* University of Illinois Press.

Pullen, A., Thanem, T., Tyler, M., & Wallenberg, L. (2016). Sexual politics, organizational practices: Interrogating queer theory, work and organization. *Gender, Work and Organization, 23*(1), 1–6. https://doi.org/10.1111/gwao.12123

Raeburn, N. C. (2004). *Changing corporate America from inside out: Lesbian and gay workplace rights.* University of Minnesota Press.

Ragins, B. R., Singh, R., & Cornwell, J. M. (2007). Making the invisible visible: Fear and disclosure of sexual orientation at work. *Journal of Applied Psychology, 92*(4), 1103–1118. https://doi.org/10.1037/0021-9010.92.4.1103

Rand, E. J. (2004). A disunited nation and a legacy of contradiction: Queer nation's construction of identity. *Journal of Communication Inquiry, 28*(4), 288–306. https://doi.org/10.1177/0196859904267232

Reed, C. (2006). Design for (Queer) living: Sexual identity, performance, and décor in British Vogue, 1922–1926. *GLQ: A Journal of Lesbian and Gay Studies, 12*(3), 377–403. https://doi.org/10.1215/10642684-2005-003

Riach, K., Rumens, N., & Tyler, M. (2014). Un/doing chrononormativity: Negotiating ageing, gender and sexuality in organizational life. *Organization Studies, 35*(11), 1677–1698. https://doi.org/10.1177/0170840614550731

Robertson, M. (2018). *Growing up queer: Kids and the remaking of LGBTQ identity.* New York University Press.

Rodríguez, J. M. (2003). *Queer Latinidad: Identity practices, discursive spaces.* New York University Press.

Rumens, N. (2017). Queering lesbian, gay, bisexual and transgender identities in human resource development and management education contexts. *Management Learning, 48*(2), 227–242. https://doi.org/10.1177/1350507616672737

Rumens, N. (2018). *Queer business: Queering organization sexualities.* Routledge.

Rumens, N., & Ozturk, M. B. (2019). Heteronormativity and the (re)construction of gay male entrepreneurial identities. *International Small Business Journal, 37*(7), 671–688. https://doi.org/10.1177/0266242619846609

Sayers, W. (2005). The etymology of queer. *ANQ: A Quarterly Journal of Short Articles, Notes and Reviews, 18*(2), 17–19. https://doi.org/10.3200/ANQQ.18.2.17-19

Sedgwick, E. K. (1990). *Epistemology of the closet.* University of California Press.

Sedgwick, E. K. (1993). *Tendencies.* Duke University Press.

Seidman, S. (1997). *Difference troubles: Queering social theory and sexual politics.* Cambridge University Press.

Stenger, S., & Roulet, T. J. (2018). Pride against prejudice? The stakes of concealment and disclosure of a stigmatized identity for gay and lesbian auditors. *Work, Employment and Society, 32*(2), 257–273. https://doi.org/10.1177/0950017016682459

Sullivan, N. (2003). *A critical introduction to queer theory.* New York University Press.

Tilcsik, A., Anteby, M., & Knight, C. R. (2015). Concealable stigma and occupational segregation: Toward a theory of gay and lesbian occupations. *Administrative Science Quarterly, 60*(3), 446–481. https://doi.org/10.1177/0001839215576401

Tyler, J. (2019). *Judith Butler and organization theory.* Routledge.

Tyler, M., & Cohen, L. (2010). Spaces that matter: Gender performativity and organizational space. *Organization Studies, 31*(2), 175–198. https://doi.org/10.1177/0170840609357381

Ward, J., & Winstanley, D. (2005). Coming out at work: Performativity and the recognition and renegotiation of identity. *The Sociological Review, 53*(3), 447–475. https://doi.org/10.1111/j.1467-954X.2005.00561.x

Warner, M. (Ed.). (1993). *Fear of a queer planet: Queer politics and social theory* (Vol. 6). University of Minnesota Press.

Wiegman, R., & Wilson, E. A. (2015). Introduction: Antinormativity's queer conventions. *Differences, 26*(1), 1–25. https://doi.org/10.1215/10407391-2880582

Woods, J. D., & Lucas, J. H. (1993). *The corporate closet: The professional lives of gay men in America.* The Free Press.

Žižek, S. (2000). *The ticklish subject: The absent centre of political ontology.* Verso.

29

ALLYSHIP FOR LGBTQ INDIVIDUALS IN WORK CONTEXTS

Larry R. Martinez and Liana Bernard

There is an increased emphasis on managing diversity and inclusion in workplace contexts, as evidenced by the resources devoted to diversity trainings, discrimination lawsuits, and financial resources lost in productivity due to distractions, turnover, and other negative psychological consequences of experiencing discrimination at work (Goldman et al., 2006). Fostering climates of inclusion for employees who have minority sexual orientation and gender identities (i.e., LGBTQ employees) is often an important component to these efforts (Mor Barak et al., 2016; Shore et al., 2018). The most common strategy organizations utilize is providing diversity training interventions, which usually focus on increasing employees' knowledge about implicit bias (Forscher et al., 2019). Unfortunately, the consensus in the organizational diversity training literature is that these types of interventions are not effective (Forscher et al., 2019; Noon, 2018; Paluck & Green, 2009) or are counterproductive (Dover et al., 2016).

There is still an absence of federal protection from employment discrimination in the United States for LGBTQ populations (King & Cortina, 2010; Martinez et al., 2013), though the recent *Bostock v. Clayton County, Georgia* case established a precedent for sexual orientation being covered under regulations related to discrimination on the basis of sex in the U.S. Protection from discrimination in workplace contexts on the basis of sexual orientation and gender identity is also inconsistent across national borders, with many, but not all, countries instituting various levels of protection at federal and local levels. For example, protections against sexual-orientation discrimination are included in the constitutions for only 5% of United Nations member states, including South Africa and Mexico. Countries spread across Europe, North America, South America, and Africa have protective measures for sexual orientation discrimination in employment; however, the United States does not. Additionally, although the majority of Western countries have legalized same-sex marriage and allow same-sex couples to adopt children, Italy, Switzerland, Poland, and Greece are among a handful of Western countries that only acknowledge civil unions. Israel does allow same-sex couples to adopt, though they do not allow same-sex marriage (Gal & Collman, 2020).

In light of LGBTQ employees' lack of protection from discrimination at the federal level and the extent of the negative repercussions surrounding workplace discrimination, it is important to develop and implement effective strategies for facilitating inclusion and diversity management for sexual and gender minorities. In the following sections, we will provide a brief overview of past and contemporary efforts to improve the working experiences of LGBTQ employees

DOI: 10.4324/9781003128151-35

from both research and practical standpoints. Our discussion will highlight how and why many efforts have been relatively lackluster in achieving positive results and conclude by introducing a new perspective in improving LGBTQ work lives: educating and empowering coworkers to be effective allies for their LGBTQ counterparts. In this chapter, we use the terminology used in each article we reference when appropriate (i.e., if prior research focused on experiences of gay and lesbian people but not bisexual, transgender, or queer we use "gay and lesbian"), but recommend the use of the acronym "LGBTQ" when broadly referencing this population.

Past Research Focused on LGBTQ-Specific Training Interventions

Empirical literature has examined the efficacy of interventions designed specifically to improve organizational climates and cultures for LGBTQ people by reducing anti-gay and anti-lesbian perceptions through increased awareness, education, and empathy (Lindsey et al., 2015; Madera et al., 2013; Pichler et al., 2010). For instance, Madera et al. (2013) examined the impact of setting goals in a gay and lesbian supportive training context with college students. During the annual diversity training, incoming undergraduate students listened to senior students share personal experiences in which they experienced a challenge related to a stigmatized identity, including gay and lesbian identities. The authors randomly assigned students to conditions such that some students set their own goals related to engaging in diversity behaviors (e.g., making friends people who are gay or lesbian), some students were given goals set by senior-student mentors, and other students did not set goals at all. Students making self-set goals were provided guidance so that goals were specific, challenging, attainable, and personal in order to facilitate feasibility. Data collected three months and eight months after the training demonstrated that participants who set their own goals were more likely to have engaged in gay and lesbian supportive behaviors and reported more positive attitudes toward gays and lesbians than those who were given goals by a mentor or who did not set goals at all were asked to generate and document gay and lesbian supportive goals at the beginning of their college careers later reported more supportive attitudes toward gay and lesbian individuals at the end of their first year than those who did not set these goals (Madera et al., 2013).

In a study with a similar focus and design, Lindsey et al. (2015) also provided an experimental intervention with incoming undergraduate students. These students were randomly assigned to training conditions in which they were instructed to (a) set their own goals related to LGB supportive behaviors (as in Madera et al., 2013), (b) engaged in a perspective-taking exercise in which they imagined a day in the life of an LGB person, or (c) responded to a prompt designed to discredit common negative LGB stereotypes. Data collected eight months following training demonstrated that students who engaged in the perspective-taking intervention reported more LGB supportive behaviors than students in either of the two intervention conditions.

Pichler et al. (2010) examined heterosexism in hiring decisions among undergraduate raters. Specifically, they considered the impact of applicant gender, applicant sexual orientation, rater gender, and the masculinity/femininity of the job in question on hireability ratings. Importantly, they also considered the impact of having participated in a diversity training in the past (of any kind, at any time). They found that men rated the candidate to be less hirable in counterstereotypical situations (e.g., straight male or lesbian applicants applying for feminine jobs) when they had not participated in a diversity training in the past—those who had participated in a diversity training did not rate candidates differently on hireability as a function of sexual orientation, gender, or job fit. This study offers weak evidence related to the impact of diversity training on attitudes toward gays and lesbians since no information about the diversity training was obtained.

To evaluate the effectiveness of the Safe Zone project, a free online resource that provides curricula and activities for educators facilitating LGBT-affirming Safe Zone trainings, Finkel et al. (2003) implemented a diversity training program aimed at increasing psychologists' and graduate students' knowledge of lesbian, gay, bisexual, and trans issues, sensitivity, and advocacy behaviors in an exploratory study. The training was mandatory for incoming graduate students and included two training sessions six months apart. At the end of the second session, participants completed the Riddle Homophobia Scale (Wall, 1995) to self-rate their level of homophobia before and after. Training activities rated as beneficial included an "I imagine" exercise in which participants cognitively took the perspective of gay and lesbian people by imagining a world in which heterosexuals were marginalized in society and labeled "breeders," playing a spin-off bingo game ("bingay") in which participants had to fill in bingo squares by obtaining answers to LGBT trivia questions from other participants (e.g., "name an LGBT athlete"), and a role-playing exercise. Forty percent of trainees who attended both the first and second sessions ($N = 48$) self-reported a positive change in attitudes (i.e., support, admiration, appreciation, nurturance) following the training and approximately two-thirds of trainees reported that the training stimulated their interest in learning about LGBT issues and becoming an advocate. The authors concluded that results from this exploratory study were encouraging but that more rigorous empirical research was needed.

The effects of diversity training related to LGBTQ populations have also been examined in non-university settings. Holman et al. (2020) examined the effects of a lesbian, gay, bisexual, and trans-specific diversity training on senior living facility staff's perceived preparedness in working with LGBT older adult residents. The primary aims of the training were to ensure that senior services staff could meet the needs of LGBT residents, and to ensure residents felt accepted by educating staff about LGBT-related culture and concerns. Data were collected before and after the intervention and indicated a significant effect of training on perceived preparedness to meet the needs of an LGBT resident.

Similarly, in a qualitative thematic analysis study, Israel et al. (2017) conducted a training intervention on LGBTQ diversity with law enforcement from a single police department and analyzed law enforcement personnel's reactions to the training (specifically resistance and receptiveness). Participants consisted of mostly heterosexual individuals (90%) and eight participants who did not report their sexual orientation. The purpose of the study was to examine law enforcement reactions to an LGBTQ diversity training program. This research was necessary because law enforcement has often been seen to express hostility toward LGBTQ people (Jones & Williams, 2015). In the training, officers were trained in appropriate ways to address LGBTQ issues including terminology (e.g., which terms should be avoided or preferred), sexuality, gender, LGBTQ experiences, and safety concerns with law enforcement. Additionally, trainees were provided with recommendations for interacting with LGBTQ citizens. Researchers qualitatively observed and coded trainees' behaviors during training as "resistant" or "receptive." Resistance behaviors among police officers included defensiveness about their work and assertions that they were doing a good job, beliefs that LGBTQ community members were too sensitive or were seeking special treatment, an unwillingness to intervene to assist LGBTQ people, and nonverbal dismissive behaviors (e.g., low engagement, joking, and discomfort). Receptive behaviors included requests for elaboration, seeking insight on helping strategies, sharing an awareness of and motivation to address LGBTQ needs, and verbal appreciation for the training, all of which the authors indicated helped make the training successful.

Although these efforts represent important first steps in attempting to improve the working conditions for LGBTQ employees, there are many opportunities to build upon this work. For instance, several of these studies examine the effectiveness of LGBTQ interventions among college students, few collected behavioral field or longitudinal data, and few provide concrete strategies to improve workplaces for LGBTQ employees. Most importantly, there is a tendency in the diversity training literature to focus on building knowledge, or changing attitudes, and hoping that knowledge translates to behavioral changes in the form of reduced discrimination— a challenge that allyship-based interventions can overcome.

A Novel Approach to Improving LGBTQ Work Lives: Empowering Allies

The term "ally" stems from research focused on heterosexual people who try to end the oppression of sexual orientation minorities (Washington & Evans, 1991). Research examining allyship in workplace contexts commonly focuses on allyship for LGBTQ populations (Martinez, Sawyer et al., 2017; Sabat et al., 2013). Empowering workplace allies to aid in improving the working lives of LGBTQ employees is likely to be an effective method of reducing workplace discrimination toward LGBTQ employees (Webster et al., 2018; Ji, 2007). In the following section, we define allyship and provide a general overview of the workplace allyship literature.

Allies and Allyship Behavior

An ally has been defined as "a person who is a member of the 'dominant' or 'majority' group who works to end oppression in his or her personal and professional life through support of, and as an advocate with and for, the oppressed population" (Washington & Evans, 1991, p. 215). Allies are typically majority and non-targeted employees—that is, people who are not experiencing discrimination personally in a specific instance—who use their privilege and power to increase inclusion and opportunities for targeted non-majority colleagues (i.e., people who experience discrimination based on a marginalized identity, Sabat et al., 2013). For example, heterosexual people who support and advocate for LGBTQ people may be considered allies. While ally refers to an individual, allyship refers to the behaviors that non-targeted allies engage in to support marginalized populations. Individuals with other stigmatized identities (i.e., women, racial minorities) are also likely to be allies for LGBTQ employees. Although each person with one or more stigmatized identities has unique experiences that do not generalize to the experiences of other stigmatized groups, many understand the negative consequences related to experiencing prejudice. Allyship behaviors can have positive benefits for stigmatized employees (Griffith & Hebl, 2002; Law et al., 2011), for fostering a positive work environment (Martinez & Hebl, 2010; Priola et al., 2014), and for organizations (Martinez & Hebl, 2010). Because of an appreciation for the positive benefits of allyship, non-LGBTQ employees who have a different stigmatized identity are likely to experience empathetic responses to witnessing discriminatory behavior (Walters et al., 2020) and are also likely to intervene (Jenkins & Nickerson, 2019; Menolascino & Jenkins, 2018). Finally, transgender people have increased empathy for sexual orientation minorities and vice versa (Riggle et al., 2011), and, as previously noted, empathy is a predictor for bystander intervention (Jenkins & Nickerson, 2019; Menolascino & Jenkins, 2018).

The allyship literature has delineated allyship behavior into two major categories, supportive behaviors and advocacy behaviors (Sabat et al., 2013; Washington & Evans, 1991). Supportive behaviors "provide comfort and tangible resources for individuals dealing with their stigmatized identities" (Sabat et al., 2013, p. 483). Support is interpersonal, typically involving an interaction between an ally and an LGBTQ employee. Examples of supportive behaviors include actively listening to LGBTQ employees describe their experiences (Washington & Evans, 1991), supporting other LGBTQ allies to aid in ally development (Ji, 2007), and responding with acceptance and positivity to LGBTQ disclosures (DiStefano et al., 2000; Ruggs et al., 2011). Advocacy behaviors "typically involve outward demonstrations of public support for individual, organizational, or societal level issues pertaining to these stigmatized individuals" (Sabat et al., 2013, p. 483). Examples of advocacy behaviors include challenging discriminatory policies or scenarios with human resources personnel or with one's supervisor (Brooks & Edwards, 2009); using flags, stickers, or other signals that demonstrate support for LGBTQ employees (Evans, 2002); attending diversity training seminars (Ballard et al., 2008); and confronting prejudice (Rattan & Dweck, 2018), a commonly examined advocacy behavior in the social psychology literature (Lindsey et al., 2013).

Literature Examining the Impacts of Allies

In recognition of the potential power that allies have to create an inclusive environment and the lackluster results of traditional LGBTQ diversity training interventions, several scholars have begun to examine how allies can be utilized to improve diversity and inclusion efforts. For instance, Martinez, Sawyer et al. (2017) conducted two complementary (mixed methods) studies to understand allyship behaviors in workplace organizational contexts. Specifically, in Study 1, they conducted focus groups with both lesbian, gay, and bisexual employees (N = 14) and heterosexual employees who self-identified as allies (N = 18) in separate groups and identified how allyship manifests in organizational contexts. These discussions included a particular emphasis on confronting anti-LGB prejudice. Thus, in Study 2, they conducted an experimental study to investigate how best to confront anti-LGB prejudice in which participants watched various video recorded confrontation scenarios. Findings indicated that participants rated confrontations enacted in a direct and calm manner as eliciting the least backlash against confronters and the most perceived blame placed on perpetrators.

Ryan and Wessel (2012) examined sexual orientation harassment in the workplace, drawing on participants' actual experiences observing sexual orientation harassment to determine what hinders or motivates observer intervention (i.e., allyship behavior) upon witnessing sexual orientation-based harassment. Observers—people who watch interactions but may or may not intervene or identify as or be perceived as allies—were most likely to intervene when they perceived that the perpetrator intended to harm the target, when discriminatory comments were directed at a target (compared to indirect or ambient discriminatory comments), and when the target's sexual orientation was known. Ryan and Wessel (2012) concluded that observers likely lack skills when attempting to intervene and that "organizational training that does not only promote intervening but also provides individuals with examples on how to intervene may be particularly effective" (p. 505).

Allyship-Based Interventions Address Problems With Diversity Training

Although several training interventions focus specifically on the inclusion of LGBTQ individuals (Agovino & Corbisiero, 2020; Alhejji et al., 2016; Gedro & Baillie, 2009; Holman et al., 2020), diversity trainings tend to focus on marginalized populations generally rather than on specific groups (e.g., LGBTQ employees in particular; Alhejji et al., 2016; Hussain et al., 2020). Although some research has found decreased discrimination following education related to biases, prejudice, and stereotypes (Morris et al., 2019; Fiske, 1998), other research has found no support for the efficacy of diversity trainings focused on reducing bias (Noon, 2018; Paluck & Green, 2009). Some research has even found an increase in discrimination following diversity training, which may be due to strengthening of stereotypical beliefs or as a form of backlash resulting from highlighting majority group employee privilege (Anand & Winters, 2008; Dover et al., 2016). As a result, organizations are likely to question the efficacy of diversity training strategies for fear of increasing discrimination (Anand & Winters, 2008; Dover et al., 2016), incurring legal ramifications (Von Bergen et al., 2002), or negatively impacting their bottom lines (Dover et al., 2016; Von Bergen et al., 2002).

The disappointing effects and unfavorable outcomes of diversity trainings may be due to their content, strategies, and how they frame discrimination (Anand & Winters, 2008). Anti-bias trainings are increasingly popular in organizational settings (including LGBTQ-specific trainings; Anand & Winters, 2008). Of anti-bias training, implicit bias trainings have grown in popularity (Forscher et al., 2019), because they aim to increase majority group members' knowledge of their own unconscious prejudice and subtle acts of discrimination. Specifically, these trainings rest on the assumption that with increased knowledge, awareness, and internal reflection, majority group members will engage in conscious self-monitoring to decrease discriminatory behaviors (Hahn et al., 2019). There are several problems with this approach, however. In the following section, we discuss common general problems with diversity training interventions.

Beyond Increasing Knowledge

First, increased awareness of biases may actually lead to heightened concern over appearing biased, resulting in increased instances of discrimination. Specifically, awareness of one's bias as a majority group member may induce stereotype threat—a fear of confirming a negative stereotype about oneself (Aronson et al., 1999; Dover et al., 2016)—which may deplete cognitive resources and result (ironically) in increased discriminatory behaviors (Duguid & Thomas-Hunt, 2015; Goff et al., 2008). Worse, majority group members may actively avoid minority group members for fear of appearing biased (Godsil & Richardson, 2017). For instance, the threat of appearing racist has been found to increase White men's distancing between themselves and Black people (Goff et al., 2008). Additionally, during the "#metoo" movement, several men expressed fear of interacting with women at work for fear of appearing sexist (Mahdawi, 2019). As such, merely increasing employees' knowledge of implicit biases toward minority group members without providing concrete behaviors or actions that these employees can engage in is not likely to result in beneficial outcomes.

Allyship-based interventions can address these concerns by teaching trainees how to effectively behave as allies through learning and practice. We believe that allyship is a skill that employees can develop. Allyship training can focus specifically on how employees can serve as allies to their LGBTQ coworkers through support and advocacy. Given that previous literature on LGBTQ employees indicates the importance of these employees feeling comfortable in disclosing their identities (Ng & Rumens, 2017; Webster et al., 2018), LGBTQ-oriented allyship trainings should focus on building trainees' support skills so that they are prepared to listen actively and respond to LGBTQ employees who disclose their identities in compassionate, accepting, and affirming ways (Sabat et al., 2013). Trainees can also learn how to support LGBTQ employees by learning about and practicing advocacy, with a particular emphasis on how to confront prejudice. Prejudicial comments are pervasive in organizational contexts today (Dionisi & Barling, 2018; *Rosalie v. Supreme Glass Co.*, 2020), and may be tolerated under the guise that they are only "jokes" or because the perpetrator is not being serious. However, prejudicial comments create and perpetuate a hostile and threatening environment (Holman et al., 2018; Velez et al., 2013), and signal to LGBTQ employees that they are unwelcome as their authentic selves (Bendl et al., 2009; Martinez, Sawyer, et al., 2017). With more employees willing and able to confront prejudice, organizations will foster cultures that eliminate the ability for individuals to make these types of comments without fear of interpersonal consequences (Bandura et al., 1963), thus reducing the likelihood that these comments will be made in the first place (Czopp et al., 2006; Hyers, 2010; Martinez, Hebl, et al., 2017). Indeed, people learn from the behaviors enacted and consequences experienced by themselves and others and alter their future behavior with this knowledge in mind (Bandura et al., 1963; Skinner, 1963).

Employees can be motivated to confront prejudice when they understand how to eliminate cognitive barriers—thoughts that prevent behavioral action—that they are likely to face to taking action. Specifically, people frequently recognize the importance of being an ally and express desires to behave in ways that align with their ally identity but experience hesitancy when situations arise that would warrant allyship behavior (Martinez, Hebl et al., 2017). This desire to confront prejudice coupled with a lack of behavioral action can be understood within the bystander intervention theoretical framework (Darley & Latané, 1968). Bystander intervention strategies focus on engaging surrounding observers to efficiently and effectively help those experiencing an emergency. Although bystander intervention often focuses on physical emergencies, similar principles can be applied to interpersonal emergencies. Ashburn-Nardo et al. (2008) adapted Darley and Latané's (1968) well-known bystander intervention model for workplace contexts with their Confronting Prejudiced Responses (CPR) model. According to the CPR model, bystanders face five hurdles in intervening on behalf of a coworker who has faced discrimination: interpreting the event as discrimination, deciding whether it is severe enough to warrant one's intervention, taking responsibility for intervening, knowing how to confront (i.e., having confrontation skills) and taking action to confront (Ashburn-Nardo et al., 2008). Implicit in the model is the assumption that failing to respond affirmatively in response to each hurdle will prevent confrontation behaviors. However, it is our stance that efforts to confront prejudice in general are better than a lack of action, and it is possible to learn how to confront prejudice in effective and beneficial ways. As such, teaching ally employees about these cognitive barriers that they are likely to encounter and how to overcome them may promote allyship behaviors.

Eliciting Positive Reactions to Training

Second, individuals who belong to majority groups can have negative, defensive reactions to participating in diversity trainings (Dover et al., 2016; Kulik et al., 2007). Specifically, if an organization has initiated a diversity training, majority group members may assume that the diversity training has been implemented because they individually have been discriminatory or are in some way at fault. Feeling like one is being targeted by diversity training may elicit discrimination concerns and cardiovascular threat responses (Dover et al., 2016), frustration associated with the training (Dobbin et al., 2007), frustration with the organization (Jansen et al., 2015; Thomas & Plaut, 2008), or even negative affective reactions directed at minority group members blaming them for the need to complete a diversity training (Sanchez et al., 2004). These types of reactions are likely to hinder one's ability to reflect on their biases and behaviors. Indeed, marginalized employees have reported experiencing worse interpersonal behaviors from their coworkers after those coworkers participated in a diversity training focused on reducing implicit biases (Sanchez et al., 2004). Allyship-based interventions can decrease the likelihood of threat responses or negative reactions to diversity trainings from majority group members because allyship-based interventions rest on the implicit assumption that these employees want to help LGBTQ employees or at least have positive intentions, rather than that majority group members are being discriminatory.

Hiring Expert Learning and Development Practitioners

Third, most diversity trainings are developed and conducted by human resource professionals (Kirton et al., 2016; Kulik, 2014) who may or may not have expertise in the psychological mechanisms related to prejudice, discrimination, and allyship. Diversity trainings implemented by human resource professionals focus on organizational policies and may underestimate the motivational mechanisms underlying an individual's desires to actually abide by organizational policies (D'Netto et al., 2013; Shen et al., 2009). Trainees can be emotionally sensitive to this topic, and inducing threat has the potential for this resource expenditure to backfire. As such, those conducting diversity training should be highly attuned to the literature on this topic. We recommend hiring consultants who are experts in conducting diversity trainings to implement allyship interventions (Kirton et al., 2019; Mease, 2015).

Infancy of the Literature and Issues Requiring Additional Research

Finally, this work on harnessing allyship in organizational diversity training is very much in its infancy and will require sustained scholarship in the future due to the pernicious and evolving nature of discrimination. For instance, there has been an increase in explicit or overt discriminatory behaviors in recent years (Stein & Allcorn, 2018; U.S. Equal Employment Opportunity Commission, 2020). As such, diversity training may need to focus on changing attitudes and behaviors among those who are high in prejudice and likely to engage in discriminatory behaviors, as opposed to focusing on implicit bias among those low in explicit prejudice. For instance, employees who are overtly discriminatory and participate in implicit bias trainings may learn about the unconscious and inherent nature of implicit bias and perceive this psychological mechanism as a justification for discriminatory behavior. In other words, overtly prejudiced individuals may see the fact that much discriminatory behavior is presumed to be unconscious as an opportunity or excuse for perpetrating intentional discriminatory behavior in subtle ways. Overall, more research is needed to determine the best approaches to diversity training interventions.

Future Research and Practical Considerations

A promising area of scholarship involves leveraging knowledge about allyship behaviors (and the barriers to engaging in these behaviors in work contexts) to educate and empower individuals to engage in allyship. Our lab has developed such an intervention, and we are in the process of validating its efficacy. The training is grounded in the classic bystander intervention literature (Darley & Latané, 1968) and draws from best practices in organizational and cognitive psychology. The allyship skill-building workshop developed with four organizational partners has demonstrated significant increases in knowledge about allyship and intentions to engage in allyship behaviors at work following the training (Hamilton & Martinez, 2019). We have used data from initial trainings to improve and streamline the intervention and are in the process of developing a completely remote (i.e., online) training option.

Future Research

Although we believe that LGBTQ anti-bias training is better framed as an allyship skill-building workshop, this area of research is still relatively nascent. We recognize that allyship—as a behavior and as a personal identity—can be controversial among those who are a part of marginalized groups. First, it is unclear how individual employees come to adopt identities as allies and engage in allyship behaviors over time. Although some work has examined ally identity development processes (Brooks & Edwards, 2009; Collins & Chlup, 2014; Hardiman & Dewing, 2019), this work is limited in its ability to transfer to workplace contexts without consideration of the unique aspects associated with workplace contexts (e.g., power differentials, different expectations for behaviors). As such, future work should attempt to understand how allyship develops over time to identify individual and environmental influences that may foster allyship behaviors. Second, it is vitally important to assess the efficacy of allyship interventions in workplace contexts using the most rigorous methods available. In our own work, we are often constrained to assessments immediately before and immediately after the workshop. Although initial results have been promising, they cannot demonstrate the long-term impact of allyship for LGBTQ employees. As such, future research should utilize randomized controlled trials with longitudinal assessments that include important behavioral and organizational outcomes (e.g., reduced instances of discrimination, improved perceptions of diversity climate, improved work engagement). Without this rigorous, data-driven evidence, interventions to reduce LGBTQ discrimination can be unnecessarily wasteful (e.g., lost investment of time, energy, and financial resources) and potentially introduce new problems, such as backlash among non-LGBTQ employees, which is counterproductive to organizational goals.

Practical Considerations

There are several practical considerations in implementing allyship for LGBTQ individuals in workplace contexts. First, although allyship is often promoted for its prosocial consequences, it is easy for allies to overstep their bounds, acting as "saviors" for LGBTQ people. It is important to ensure that allies do not take power and agency away from LGBTQ employees, thereby (ironically) legitimizing the very power differentials that allies should be attempting to dismantle. Second, allyship for LGBTQ employees can be mentally, emotionally, and physically taxing. It is important for employees engaging in allyship to do so in ways that do not produce unreasonable burdens, which can be detrimental to both the ally and their attempts to provide support to others. Third, it will be important to develop interventions that are fully accessible (and valid) in remote online environments. The COVID-19 pandemic has pushed a large portion of the workforce to remote working environments, so developing interventions that do not require in-person interactions will be paramount as the future related to how work is completed remains uncertain.

References

Agovino, M., & Corbisiero, F. (2020). Diversity management policies for the inclusion of LGBT people into the labour market: The case of Naples. *Papers in Applied Geography*, 6(4), 1–17. https://doi.org/10.1080/23754931.2020.1815236

Alhejji, H., Garavan, T., Carbery, R., O'Brien, F., & McGuire, D. (2016). Diversity training programme outcomes: A systematic review. *Human Resource Development Quarterly*, 27(1), 95–149. https://doi.org/10.1002/hrdq.21221

Anand, R., & Winters, M.-F. (2008). A retrospective view of corporate diversity training from 1964 to the present. *Academy of Management Learning & Education*, 7(3), 356–372. https://doi.org/10.5465/amle.2008.34251673

Aronson, J., Lustina, M. J., Good, C., Keough, K., Steele, C. M., & Brown, J. (1999). When White men can't do math: Necessary and sufficient factors in stereotype threat. *Journal of Experimental Social Psychology*, 35(1), 29–46. https://doi.org/10.1006/jesp.1998.1371

Ashburn-Nardo, L., Morris, K. A., & Goodwin, S. A. (2008). The confronting prejudiced responses (CPR) model: Applying CPR in organizations. *Academy of Management Learning & Education*, 7(3), 332–342. https://doi.org/10.5465/amle.2008.34251671

Ballard, S., Bartle, E., & Masequesmay, G. (2008). *Finding queer allies: The impact of ally training and safe zone stickers on campus climate.* https://files.eric.ed.gov/fulltext/ED517219.pdf

Bandura, A., Ross, D., & Ross, S. A. (1963). Vicarious reinforcement and imitative learning. *The Journal of Abnormal and Social Psychology, 67*(6), 601–607. https://doi.org/10.1037/h0045550

Bendl, R., Fleischmann, A., & Hofmann, R. (2009). Queer theory and diversity management: Reading codes of conduct from a queer perspective. *Journal of Management & Organization, 15*(5), 625–638. https://doi.org/10.5172/jmo.15.5.625

Brooks, A. K., & Edwards, K. (2009). Allies in the workplace: Including LGBT in HRD. *Advances in Developing Human Resources, 11*(1), 136–149. https://doi.org/10.1177/1523422308328500

Collins, J. C., & Chlup, D. T. (2014). Criticality in practice. *Advances in Developing Human Resources, 16*(4), 481–498. https://doi.org/10.1177/1523422314544295

Czopp, A. M., Monteith, M. J., & Mark, A. Y. (2006). Standing up for a change: Reducing bias through interpersonal confrontation. *Journal of Personality and Social Psychology, 90*(5), 784–803. https://doi.org/10.1037/0022-3514.90.5.784

Darley, J., & Latané, B. (1968). Bystander intervention in emergencies: Diffusion of responsibility. *Journal of Personality and Social Psychology, 8*(4), 377–383. https://doi.org/10.1037/H0025589

Dionisi, A. M., & Barling, J. (2018). It hurts me too: Examining the relationship between male gender harassment and observers' well-being, attitudes, and behaviors. *Journal of Occupational Health Psychology, 23*(3), 303–319. https://doi.org/10.1037/ocp0000124

DiStefano, T. M., Croteau, J. M., Anderson, M. Z., Kampa, K. S., & Bullard, M. A. (2000). Experiences of being heterosexual allies to lesbian, gay, and bisexual people: A qualitative exploration. *Journal of College Counseling, 3*(2), 131–141. https://doi.org/10.1002/j.2161-1882.2000.tb00173.x

D'Netto, B., Shen, J., Chelliah, J., & Monga, M. (2013). Human resource diversity management practices in the Australian manufacturing sector. *International Journal of Human Resource Management, 25*(9), 1243–1266. https://doi.org/10.1080/09585192.2013.826714

Dobbin, F., Kalev, A., & Kelly, E. (2007). Diversity management in corporate America. *Contexts, 6*(4), 21–27. https://doi.org/10.1525/ctx.2007.6.4.21

Dover, T. L., Major, B., & Kaiser, C. R. (2016). Members of high-status groups are threatened by pro-diversity organizational messages. *Journal of Experimental Social Psychology, 62*(1), 58–67. https://doi.org/10.1016/j.jesp.2015.10.006

Duguid, M. M., & Thomas-Hunt, M. C. (2015). Condoning stereotyping? How awareness of stereotyping prevalence impacts expression of stereotypes. *Journal of Applied Psychology, 100*(2), 343–359. https://doi.org/10.1037/a0037908

Evans, N. J. (2002). The impact of an LGBT safe zone project on campus climate. *Journal of College Student Development, 43*(4), 522–539. https://eric.ed.gov/?id=EJ650166

Finkel, M., Storaasli, R., Bandele, A., & Schaefer, V. (2003). Diversity training in graduate school: An exploratory evaluation of the safe zone project. *Professional Psychology: Research and Practice, 34*(5), 555–561. https://doi.org/10.1037/0735-7028.34.5.555

Fiske, S. T. (1998). Stereotyping, prejudice, and discrimination. In D. T. Gilbert, S. T. Fiske, & G. Lindzey (Eds.), *The handbook of social psychology* (pp. 357–411). McGraw-Hill.

Forscher, P. S., Lai, C. K., Axt, J. R., Ebersole, C. R., Herman, M., Devine, P. G., & Nosek, B. A. (2019). A meta-analysis of procedures to change implicit measures. *Journal of Personality and Social Psychology, 117*(3), 522–559. https://doi.org/10.1037/pspa0000160

Gal, S., & Collman, A. (2020, May 17). 10 maps showing how different LGBTQ rights are around the world. *Business Insider.* www.businessinsider.com/lgbtq-rights-around-the-world-maps-2018-10

Gedro, J., & Baillie, P. (2009). Perspective on out & equal workplace advocates building bridges model: A retrospect of the past, present, and future of training impacting lesbian, gay, bisexual, and transgender employees in the workplace. *New Horizons in Adult Education & Human Resource Development, 23*(2), 39–46. https://doi.org/10.1002/nha3.10338

Godsil, R. D., & Richardson, L. S. (2017). Racial anxiety. *Iowa Law Review, 102*(5), 2235–2264. https://ilr.law.uiowa.edu/print/volume-102-issue-5/racial-anxiety/

Goff, P. A., Steele, C. M., & Davies, P. G. (2008). The space between us: Stereotype threat and distance in interracial contexts. *Journal of Personality and Social Psychology, 94*(1), 91–107. https://doi.org/10.1037/0022-3514.94.1.91

Goldman, B. M., Gutek, B. A., Stein, J. H., & Lewis, K. (2006). Employment discrimination in organizations: Antecedents and consequences. *Journal of Management, 32*(6), 786–830. https://doi.org/10.1177/0149206306293544

Griffith, K. H., & Hebl, M. R. (2002). The disclosure dilemma for gay men and lesbians: "Coming out" at work. *Journal of Applied Psychology, 87*(6), 1191–1199. https://doi.org/10.1037//0021-9010.87.6.1191

Hahn, A., & Gawronski, B. (2019). Facing one's implicit biases: From awareness to acknowledgment. *Journal of Personality and Social Psychology, 116*(5), 769–794. http://dx.doi.org.proxy.lib.pdx.edu/10.1037/pspi0000155

Hamilton, K. M., & Martinez, L. R. (2019, April). A training to empower allies to reduce workplace discrimination. In S.-N. C. Liu, K. K. Dray, & I. E. Sabat (Chairs). *Building better workplace allies: Where are we lacking and how can we get there?* Symposium presented at the 34th Annual Conference for the Society of Industrial & Organizational Psychology, National Harbor, MD.

Hardiman, M., & Dewing, J. (2019). Using two models of workplace facilitation to create conditions for development of a person-centered culture: A participatory action research study. *Journal of Clinical Nursing, 28*(15–16), 2769–2781. https://doi.org/10.1111/jocn.14897

Holman, E., Fish, J., Oswald, R., & Goldberg, A. (2018). Reconsidering the LGBT climate inventory: Understanding support and hostility for LGBTQ employees in the workplace. *Journal of Career Assessment, 27*(3), 544–559. https://doi.org/10.1177/1069072718788324

Holman, E., Landry-Meyer, L., & Fish, J. N. (2020). Creating supportive environments for LGBT older adults: An efficacy evaluation of staff training in a senior living facility. *Journal of Gerontological Social Work, 63*(5), 464–477. https://doi.org/10.1080/01634372.2020.1767254

Hussain, B., Sheikh, A., Timmons, S., Stickley, T., & Repper, J. (2020). Workforce diversity, diversity training and ethnic minorities: The case of the UK national health service. *International Journal of Cross Cultural Management, 20*(2), 201–221. https://doi.org/10.1177/1470595820938412

Hyers, L. L. (2010). Alternatives to silence in face-to-face encounters with everyday heterosexism: Activism on the interpersonal front. *Journal of Homosexuality, 57*(4), 539–565. https://doi.org/10.1080/00918361003608749

Israel, T., Bettergarcia, J. N., Delucio, K., Avellar, T. R., Harkness, A., & Goodman, J. A. (2017). Reactions of law enforcement to LGBTQ diversity training. *Human Resource Development Quarterly, 28*(2), 197–226. https://doi.org/10.1002/hrdq.21281

Jansen, W. S., Otten, S., & van der Zee, K. I. (2015). Being part of diversity: The effects of an all-inclusive multicultural diversity approach on majority members' perceived inclusion and support for organizational diversity efforts. *Group Processes & Intergroup Relations, 18*(6), 817–832. https://doi.org/10.1177/1368430214566892

Jenkins, L. N., & Nickerson, A. B. (2019). Bystander intervention in bullying: Role of social skills and gender. *The Journal of Early Adolescence, 39*(2), 141–166. https://doi.org/10.1177/0272431617735652

Ji, P. (2007). Being a heterosexual ally to the lesbian, gay, bisexual, and transgendered community: Reflections and development. *Journal of Gay & Lesbian Mental Health, 11*(3), 173–185. https://doi.org/10.1080/19359705.2007.9962489

Jones, M., & Williams, M. (2015). Twenty years on: Lesbian, gay and bisexual police officers' experiences of workplace discrimination in England and Wales. *Policing and Society, 25*(2), 188–211. https://doi.org/10.1080/10439463.2013.817998

King, E. B., & Cortina, J. M. (2010). The social and economic imperative of lesbian, gay, bisexual, and transgendered supportive organizational policies. *Industrial and Organizational Psychology, 3*(1), 69–78. https://doi.org/10.1111/j.1754-9434.2009.01201.x

Kirton, G., & Greene, A. M. (2019). Telling and selling the value of diversity and inclusion—external consultants' discursive strategies and practices. *Human Resource Management Journal, 29*(4), 676–691. https://doi.org/10.1111/1748-8583.12253

Kirton, G., Robertson, M., & Avdelidou, F. N. (2016). Valuing and value in diversity: The policy/implementation gap in an IT firm. *Human Resource Management Journal, 26*(3), 321–336. https://doi.org/10.1111/1748-8583.12110

Kulik, C. T. (2014). Working below and above the line: The research-practice gap in diversity management. *Human Resource Management Journal, 24*(2), 129–144. https://doi.org/10.1111/1748-8583.12038

Kulik, C. T., Robertson, L., & Perry, E. (2007). The multiple category problem: Category activation and inhibition in the hiring process. *The Academy of Management Review, 32*(2), 529–548. https://doi.org/10.2307/20159314

Law, C., Martinez, L., Ruggs, E., Hebl, M., & Akers, E. (2011). Trans-parency in the workplace: How the experiences of transsexual employees can be improved. *Journal of Vocational Behavior, 79*(3), 710–723. https://doi.org/10.1016/j.jvb.2011.03.018

Lindsey, A., King, E., Hebl, M., & Levine, N. (2015). The impact of method, motivation, and empathy on diversity training effectiveness. *Journal of Business and Psychology*, *30*(3), 605–617. https://doi.org/10.1007/s10869-014-9384-3

Lindsey, A., King, E., McCausland, T., Jones, K., & Dunleavy, E. (2013). What we know and don't: Eradicating employment discrimination 50 years after the civil rights act. *Industrial and Organizational Psychology*, *6*(4), 391–413. https://doi.org/10.1111/iops.12075

Madera, J. M., King, E. B., & Hebl, M. R. (2013). Enhancing the effects of sexual orientation diversity training: The effects of setting goals and training mentors on attitudes and behaviors. *Journal of Business and Psychology*, *28*(1), 79–91. https://doi.org/10.1007/s10869-012-9264-7

Mahdawi, A. (2019, August 29). Men now avoid women at work—another sign we're being punished for #MeToo. *The Guardian*. www.theguardian.com/lifeandstyle/2019/aug/29/men-women-work place-study-harassment-harvard-metoo

Martinez, L. R., & Hebl, M. R. (2010). Additional agents of change in promoting lesbian, gay, bisexual, and transgendered inclusiveness in organizations. *Industrial and Organizational Psychology*, *3*(1), 82–85. https://doi.org/10.1111/j.1754-9434.2009.01203.x

Martinez, L. R., Hebl, M. R., Smith, N. A., & Sabat, I. E. (2017). Standing up and speaking out against prejudice toward gay men in the workplace. *Journal of Vocational Behavior*, *103*, 71–85. https://doi.org/10.1016/j.jvb.2017.08.001

Martinez, L. R., Ruggs, E. N., Sabat, I. E., Hebl, M. R., & Binggeli, S. (2013). The role of organizational leaders in sexual orientation equality at organizational and federal levels. *Journal of Business and Psychology*, *28*(4), 455–466. https://doi.org/10.1007/s10869-013-9293-x

Martinez, L. R., Sawyer, K. B., Thoroughgood, C. N., Ruggs, E. N., & Smith, N. A. (2017). The importance of being "me": The relation between authentic identity expression and transgender employees' work-related attitudes and experiences. *Journal of Applied Psychology*, *102*(2), 215–226. https://doi.org/10.1037/apl0000168

Mease, J. (2015). Embracing discursive paradox: Consultants navigating the constitutive tensions of diversity work. *Management Communication Quarterly*, *30*(1), 59–83. https://doi.org/10.1177/0893318915604239

Menolascino, N., & Jenkins, L. N. (2018). Predicting bystander intervention among middle school students. *School Psychology Quarterly*, *33*(2), 305–313. https://doi.org/10.1037/spq0000262

Mor Barak, M. E., Lizano, E. L., Kim, A., Duan, L., Rhee, M. K., Hsiao, H. Y., & Brimhall, K. C. (2016). The promise of diversity management for climate of inclusion: A state-of-the-art review and meta-analysis. *Human Service Organizations: Management, Leadership & Governance*, *40*(4), 305–333. https://doi.org/10.1080/23303131.2016.1138915

Morris, M., Cooper, R. L., Ramesh, A., Tabatabai, M., Arcury, T. A., Shinn, M., Im, W., Juarez, P., & Matthews-Juarez, P. (2019). Training to reduce LGBTQ-related bias among medical, nursing, and dental students and providers: A systematic review. *BMC Medical Education*, *19*(1). https://doi.org/10.1186/s12909-019-1727-3

Ng, E. S., & Rumens, N. (2017). Diversity and inclusion for LGBT workers: Current issues and new horizons for research. *Canadian Journal of Administrative Sciences*, *34*(2), 109–120. https://doi.org/10.1002/CJAS.1443

Noon, M. (2018). Pointless diversity training: Unconscious bias, new racism and agency. *Work, Employment and Society*, *32*(1), 198–209. https://doi.org/10.1177/0950017017719841

Paluck, E. L., & Green, D. P. (2009). Prejudice reduction: What works? A review and assessment of research and practice. *Annual Review of Psychology*, *60*(1), 339–367. https://doi.org/10.1146/annurev.psych.60.110707.163607

Pichler, S., Varma, A., & Bruce, T. (2010). Heterosexism in employment decisions: The role of job misfits. *Journal of Applied Social Psychology*, *40*(10), 2527–2555. https://doi.org/10.1111/j.1559-1816.2010.00669.x

Priola, V., Lasio, D., Simone, S. D., & Serri, F. (2014). The sound of silence: Lesbian, gay, bisexual and transgender discrimination in "inclusive organizations". *British Journal of Management*, *25*(3), 488–502. https://doi.org/10.1111/1467-8551.12043

Rattan, A., & Dweck, C. S. (2018). What happens after prejudice is confronted in the workplace? How mindsets affect minorities' and women's outlook on future social relations. *Journal of Applied Psychology*, *103*(6), 676–687. http://dx.doi.org.proxy.lib.pdx.edu/10.1037/apl0000287

Riggle, E. D. B., Rostosky, S. S., McCants, L. E., & Pascale-Hague, D. (2011). The positive aspects of a transgender self-identification. *Psychology & Sexuality*, *2*(2), 147–158. https://doi.org/10.1080/19419899.2010.534490

Rosalie v. Supreme Glass Co. 18-CV-02064. (2020). United States District Court, Eastern District of New York. https://casetext.com/case/rosalie-v-supreme-glass-co

Ruggs, E. N., Martinez, L. R., & Hebl, M. R. (2011). How individuals and organizations can reduce interpersonal discrimination: Reduce interpersonal discrimination. *Social and Personality Psychology Compass, 5*(1), 29–42. https://doi.org/10.1111/j.1751-9004.2010.00332.x

Ryan, A. M., & Wessel, J. L. (2012). Sexual orientation harassment in the workplace: When do observers intervene? *Journal of Organizational Behavior, 33*(4), 488–509. https://doi.org/10.1002/job.765

Sabat, I. E., Martinez, L. R., & Wessel, J. L. (2013). Neo-activism: Engaging allies in modern workplace discrimination reduction. *Industrial and Organizational Psychology, 6*(4), 480–485. https://doi.org/10.1111/iops.12089

Sanchez, J., & Medkik, N. (2004). The effects of diversity awareness training on differential treatment. *Group & Organization Management, 29*(4). 517–536. https://doi.org/10.1177/1059601103257426

Shen, J., Chanda, A., D'Netto, B., & Monga, M. (2009). Managing diversity through human resource management: An international perspective and conceptual framework. *International Journal of Human Resource Management, 20*(2), 235–251. https://doi.org/10.1080/09585190802670516

Shore, L. M., Cleveland, J. N., & Sanchez, D. (2018). Inclusive workplaces: A review and model. *Human Resource Management Review, 28*(2), 176–189. https://doi.org/10.1016/j.hrmr.2017.07.003

Skinner, B. F. (1963). Operant behavior. *American Psychologist, 18*(8), 503–515. https://doi.org/10.1037/h0045185

Stein, H. F., & Allcorn, S. (2018). A fateful convergence: Animosity toward Obamacare, hatred of Obama, the rise of Donald Trump, and overt racism in America. *The Journal of Psychohistory, 45*(4), 234–243. www.academia.edu/39634960/A_Fateful_Convergence_Stein_and_Allcorn_Journal_PH_Spring

Thomas, K. M., & Plaut, V. C. (2008). The many faces of diversity resistance in the workplace. In K. M. Thomas (Ed.), *Series in applied psychology: Diversity resistance in organizations* (pp. 1–22). Taylor & Francis Group, Lawrence Erlbaum Associates.

U.S. Equal Employment Opportunity Commission. (2020). *EEOC releases fiscal year 2019 enforcement and litigation data.* www.eeoc.gov/newsroom/eeoc-releases-fiscal-year-2019-enforcement-and-litigation-data

Velez, B. L., Moradi, B., & Brewster, M. E. (2013). Testing the tenets of minority stress theory in workplace contexts. *Journal of Counseling Psychology, 60*(4), 532–542. https://doi.org/10.1037/a0033346

Von Bergen, C. W., Soper, B., & Foster, T. (2002). Unintended negative effects of diversity management. *Public Personnel Management, 31*(2), 239–251. https://doi.org/10.1177/009102600203100209

Wall, V. (1995). Beyond tolerance: Gays, lesbians and bisexuals on campus. In *A handbook of structured experiences and exercises for training and development.* American College Personnel Association.

Walters, M. A., Paterson, J. L., McDonnell, L., & Brown, R. (2020). Group identity, empathy and shared suffering: Understanding the "community" impacts of anti-LGBT and Islamophobic hate crimes. *International Review of Victimology, 26*(2), 143–162. https://doi.org/10.1177/0269758019833284

Washington, J., & Evans, N. J. (1991). Becoming an ally. In N. J. Evans & V. A. Wall (Eds.), *Beyond tolerance: Gays, lesbians and bisexuals on campus* (pp. 195–204). American Association for Counseling and Development. https://files.eric.ed.gov/fulltext/ED336682.pdf

Webster, J. R., Adams, G. A., Maranto, C. L., Sawyer, K., & Thoroughgood, C. (2018). Workplace contextual supports for LGBT employees: A review, meta-analysis, and agenda for future research. *Human Resource Management, 57*(1), 193–210. https://doi.org/10.1002/hrm.21873

30

IDENTITY MANAGEMENT OF, AND ORGANIZATIONAL SUPPORT FOR, LGB EXPATRIATES

Challenges and Recommendations

Julian M. Rengers

Expatriates may encounter several issues related to their relocation, such as having trouble adjusting to living in a foreign environment (e.g., Abdul Malek et al., 2015; Filipič Sterle et al., 2018; Takeuchi, 2010). Because of their sexual identity or gender identity and expression, expatriates who are also LGBTQ*, that is, Lesbian, Gay, Bisexual, Transgender, Queer, or in other ways not heterosexual and/or cisgender, face additional challenges (McPhail et al., 2016). These for example relate to personal safety and security, discrimination, prejudice, limited legal recognition and protection, and the management of their identity (the 'global closet'; Gedro, 2010; see also Gedro et al., 2013). Relatedly, employers also encounter additional challenges in supporting, developing, and managing LGBTQ* expatriates. For example, the transferal and applicability of benefits, policies, and rights from the home country to a host country can be a complicated process (Mizzi, 2014).

In this chapter, I discuss several challenges related to the lived experiences of LGB expatriates, or 'legally working [LGB] individuals who reside temporarily in a country of which they are not a citizen in order to accomplish a career-related goal' (McNulty & Brewster, 2017, p. 70)—specifically those who are sent on international assignment by their employer (rather than through self-initiation). As my point of departure, I take the overview of challenges that both LGBT employees and their employers face when considering international assignments by Gedro and colleagues (2013, p. 294). After introducing these, I discuss two more in-depth: first, I describe the complex, ongoing process of LGB expatriates' identity management, and present key challenges therein at three stages: pre-departure, during expatriation, and post-return. Second, I propose how employers, by reviewing their formal organizational policies and practices, can better prepare and support LGB expatriates for and during expatriation. To conclude this chapter, I consider some obstacles that may hinder employers from becoming more LGBTQ*-inclusive.

Most of the identity management and expatriation literature predominantly focuses on LG—and, to a somewhat lesser extent, B—identities (Croteau et al., 2008; McPhail et al., 2016). Since sexual identity and gender identity and expression are separate concepts, I do not feel comfortable making claims about Trans identities in this chapter based on the existing

 DOI: 10.4324/9781003128151-36

literature. Moreover, I cannot unequivocally make inferences about people with other sexual (e.g., asexuality, pansexuality) or gender identities (e.g., non-binary, genderqueer), who may face similar, as well as distinct, challenges in the context of expatriation. Hence, although I wish to be inclusive in my approach, this chapter will predominantly focus on LGB expatriates. Simultaneously, I will stay as close as possible to the cited sources, which means that I will alternate between the terms LG, LGB, LGBT, and LGBTQ* in this chapter.

Challenges in the Context of LGBT Expatriation

Gedro and colleagues (2013, p. 294) first presented a rubric of six challenges commonly encountered in the context of LGBT expatriation (see also McPhail and McNulty (2015) and McPhail et al. (2016)). These relate to (1) the legal status of and (2) social climate toward LGB individuals in the host country, (3) the organizational climate in the host country, (4) the degree to which LGBT expatriates have disclosed their identity, and (5) whether they are relocating with (a) partner and/or (b) child(ren). Besides specifying these problem areas, they also listed possible employer and employee actions that could facilitate navigating each challenge. I will first briefly outline the role of the legal and social climate, as well as of partner/children considerations, before describing in-depth both identity management and organizational support in the context of LGB expatriation, in line with this chapter's focus.

Legal Status

In recent decades, the legal position of LGBTQ* individuals has generally improved across various—mostly Western—countries. For example, since the Netherlands first legalized same-sex marriage in 2001, 28 countries have followed suit as of January 1, 2020 (Business Insider US, 2020). Additionally, 78 countries offer some form of employment protection against sexuality-based discrimination, compared to a mere 19 in 2000 (ILGA, 2019a, 2019b). Progress in the domains of gender identity and expression tends to be slower. Nevertheless, an increasing number of countries worldwide continue to adopt some form of gender identity law (Chiam et al., 2020). That being said: LGBTQ* rights vary widely worldwide, and continue to be heavily debated, denied, and even revoked (Lester Feder, 2019). For example, at the time of writing, 70 countries criminalize same-sex sexual acts between consenting adults (ILGA, 2019a) and LGBTQ* individuals frequently endure faulty or non-existent legal protection—to the point that discrimination and violence against them may even be legalized (Gedro et al., 2013). Because of this 'complex legal landscape' (Gedro et al., 2013, p. 293), LGBTQ* expatriates and their employers would do well to familiarize themselves with the host country's laws when considering international assignment.

Social Climate

The social climate toward LGBTQ* individuals, that is, the extent to which a country's inhabitants demonstrate acceptance and hold positive attitudes, has generally also improved in recent years. For example, a survey by Pew Research Center (2020), making use of nationally representative samples across 34 countries, demonstrated a steady increase between 2002 and 2019 in the percentage of people who said homosexuality should be accepted by society, with some countries (e.g., India, Mexico, and South Africa) even realizing a double-digit increase. However, differences across and within countries persist: the report shows that many countries in Western Europe and the Americas generally demonstrate higher acceptance levels than countries in Eastern Europe, the Middle East, and sub-Saharan Africa. Simultaneously, opinions tend to be more polarized in the Asia-Pacific region. Altogether, there is still a strong global divide on the acceptance of homosexuality, which is predominantly driven by differences in economic development, as well as religious and political attitudes (Pew Research Center, 2020).

In gauging the respective importance of both, McPhail and colleagues (2016) concluded that the local *social* climate towards LGBT individuals is a more significant determinant of how comfortable LG workers felt during expatriation than the local *legal* status. For example, even in countries where LGBT legislation is relatively advanced, there is still considerable risk of being discriminated against based on one's gender/sexuality (Schuler et al., 2011). Contrastingly, oppressive anti-LGBT legislation may not always be enforced. For example, LG expatriates' foreigner status may make their sexual identity of secondary importance, and they are in a sense 'excused' from behaving differently—since they are outsiders anyway (McPhail et al., 2016). Taken together, the social climate, rather than the legal situation, may present a more accurate depiction of the level of threat to LGBT expatriates' safety and security (see also McPhail & McNulty, 2015). LGBTQ* expatriates and their employers would therefore do well to monitor the local social climate, for example by getting in contact with local support networks or fellow expatriates who have been to the region, or by visiting the location before expatriation (McPhail et al., 2016).

Partner/Child(ren) Considerations

LGBTQ* expatriates likely face special considerations in relation to their family life, which tends to differ from that of heterosexual/cisgender expatriates. For example, they need to decide whether traveling with their partner would be safe and appropriate (Gedro, 2010). Additionally, parentage issues may arise, since both partners may not be recognized as legal parents of the child(ren) (McPhail & McNulty, 2015). To deal with such issues, it is important to receive adequate family support from employers (Cole & Nesbeth, 2014). However, since the concept of 'family' is still firmly rooted in a heteronormative framework, expatriate pre-departure orientations are oftentimes tailored to the situation of heterosexual/cisgender expatriates (McNulty, 2014), thereby ignoring the particular needs, questions, and considerations of LGBT expatriate families (Mizzi, 2014). This perpetuates the invisibility of LGBT familial arrangements, and may stifle progress on these matters. LGBTQ* expatriate families would therefore do well to design a 'family plan' before relocation—ideally with their employer's help. For example, they might consider what to do when they are 'outed' (i.e., when their gender/sexuality is (in)advertently revealed to a third party without their consent), prepare an exit strategy in case they need to evacuate, and keep detailed documentation demonstrating the legal validity of their relationship (McPhail et al., 2016).

Identity Management of LGB Expatriates

Workplace sexual identity management, or the various strategies that can be adopted to navigate one's sexual identity at work (Croteau et al., 2008), is a key consideration for LGB employees (Clair et al., 2005). Since their sexual identity may form the basis of discrimination, LGB workers carefully manage whether, and if so when, how, and to whom they disclose their identity (Goffman, 1963; Ragins & Cornwell, 2001). Early qualitative research found that lesbian and gay workers engage in a variety of behavioral strategies (Griffin, 1992; Woods, 1993), ranging from more protective, concealment-oriented (see also Herek, 1996) to more risky, disclosure-oriented behaviors.

To better understand how LGB workers manage their sexual identity at work, two theoretical models were introduced by Clair and colleagues (2005) and Ragins (2008; see also Ragins, 2004). Key assumptions underpinning these models are that (1) sexual identity is an example of an invisible (or concealable) social identity (see Einarsdóttir et al. [2016] for a critical reflection of how concealable sexuality is) and (2) LGB workers' sexual identity can be a source of stigmatization. In addition, they acknowledge that identity management is an ongoing process, rather than a one-time occurrence (King et al., 2017). The core of both models lies in delineating individual *and* contextual antecedents that shape individuals' assessment of the perceived costs, benefits, and anticipated consequences of adopting a certain strategy, within a particular social context. Taken together, these determine how LGB workers manage their identity.

Individual antecedents that may affect LGB workers' identity management, as distinguished by Clair et al. (2005), are individuals' propensity to take risks, their tendency to engage in self-monitoring, their level of self-assuredness, and several personal motives (e.g., their motivation to generate social change). Ragins's (2008) model adds self-verification processes and the centrality of sexual identity to one's self-concept as influential individual antecedents. Both models, however, assign a central role to contextual factors (Croteau et al., 2008). Herein, Clair and colleagues (2005) suggest that an organizational diversity climate, professional and industry norms, legal protections, and LGB workers' relationships with potential disclosure targets—as well as targets' personal characteristics—may play a role. Ragins (2008) introduces the presence of similar others, the existence of supportive relationships, and institutional support as important elements. Altogether, these factors may facilitate disclosure, as well as provide a buffer against the potentially deleterious effects of being stigmatized (Webster et al., 2018).

The central role assigned to contextual factors in understanding identity management processes follows from both models' roots in stigma theory, a commonly adopted perspective to understand LGB workers' experiences (Webster et al., 2018). In his seminal work on stigma theory, sociologist Erving Goffman (1963; see also Crocker et al., 1998) proposes that a stigma is a personal attribute that, within a specific social context, is seen as a personal flaw. Such attributes are socially discrediting, since they convey a negatively evaluated social identity, such that sharing it with others may be costly. A key proposition is that, since stigma is socially constructed, the degree to which disclosure may be costly—as well as beneficial—is contextually dependent.

Examples of such social costs include being discriminated against, stereotyped, ostracized, excluded, or suffering status loss (e.g., Croteau et al., 2008; Link & Phelan, 2001). In an effort to protect oneself against these costs, one may choose to conceal an identity (Ragins, 2008), which may, however, incur other costs. For example, concealment has been related to increased vigilance, guilt, anxiety, and stress, as well as reduced feelings of belonging in social interactions (Newheiser & Barreto, 2014; Pachankis, 2007). Opting for a concealing strategy is therefore generally thought to reduce well-being (Meyer, 2003; Newheiser & Barreto, 2014) and is mostly considered useful when anticipated costs of disclosure are so considerable that it is necessary to protect oneself (Ragins, 2008). Some of these costs can be alleviated by adopting a disclosing strategy. Disclosure, for example, allows LGB workers to devote cognitive resources to their job—rather than to concealment (Pachankis, 2007)—and has been related to higher subjective well-being, affirmation, and self-esteem, as well as strengthened feelings of personal authenticity (Wax et al., 2018). Disclosure offers the possibility of receiving social and institutional support (Ragins, 2008) and allows LGB workers to build authentic, strong relationships with co-workers (Meyer, 2003). Finally, disclosure allows for community building with similar others, and may even lead to organizational and institutional change (Creed & Scully, 2000).

Altogether, identity management is a highly complex, continuous process, involving ongoing cognitive processing, decision-making, and resulting behavior (Pachankis, 2007). Additionally, it is strongly context-dependent, since LGB workers may choose to manage their identity differently as a function of different social contexts (Jones & King, 2014). Therefore, identity management can best be conceptualized on a multidimensional continuum (Berkley et al., 2019), allowing for between-person (i.e., how LGB workers will behave on average) and within-person differences (i.e., how they will behave differently in accordance with varying situational characteristics) (Jones & King, 2014).

Since attitudes towards LGBTQ* individuals vary widely across the globe, LGB expatriates are likely to encounter a multitude of social contexts in which their sexual identity may be the basis of different forms and degrees of social stigma. This means that the costs, benefits, and consequences of identity management likely vary as well. Based on this assumption, I will now explore several common identity management challenges for LGB expatriates.

Pre-Departure

A key pre-departure consideration is that LGB workers may need to disclose their identity vis-à-vis their employer (Gedro, 2010). For example, their HR manager may need to know about their LGB status, in order to arrange specific support (e.g., traveling with their partner). However, not everyone is willing to disclose at work—a recent study even estimated that 83% of LGB individuals worldwide conceal their sexual identity from all or most people in their lives (Pachankis & Bränström, 2019). This consideration is embedded in the 'global closet' (Gedro, 2010), which concerns the complex web of decisions and considerations that L (as well as GBT; McPhail & McNulty, 2015) workers encounter when contemplating international assignments, and includes issues such as personal safety and security, (in)visibility, discrimination, and stigmatization. To help navigate the global closet, LGBT workers may identify at least one trusted 'safe boss' to whom they can safely disclose (McPhail & McNulty, 2015) and who can support them.

In general, LGB workers give considerable thought to how open they can and want to be about their sexual identity in the host country (McPhail & McNulty, 2015; McPhail et al., 2016; Rengers et al., 2019). Since their safety and security during expatriation are vital to them (Gedro, 2010), LGB expatriates express a thorough awareness and understanding that there are contextual differences between countries, for example in the extent to which they may need to engage in different identity management strategies. A warning herein, however, comes from our own work (Rengers et al., 2019): one participant warned that openly 'out' younger LGB expatriates may be insufficiently aware about potentially having to conceal their identity during expatriation. Since their employer did not explicitly warn them about this, they assumed that they had nothing to fear, and could therefore safely be 'out' during expatriation as well. In such cases, they may not have fully assessed the potential risks, benefits, and consequences of adopting a certain strategy, which may be troublesome. Therefore, not only outbound LGB workers themselves, but also their employers carry a certain responsibility herein, by ensuring that LGB employees have an understanding of the potential challenges that their sexual identity may pose in the sociocultural context to which they expatriate.

During Expatriation

A central challenge during expatriation is knowing how openly LGB expatriates can express their sexual identity, if they wish to do so at all. Understanding and identifying in which moments and social interactions disclosure would be met with acceptance, and when it would be met with rejection, it can be lifesaving in certain instances. McPhail and McNulty (2015) refer to this as being able to provide a personal duty of care, consisting of an awareness of local attitudes towards LGB issues combined with a sensitivity to social cues, which is a critical skill for LGB expatriates. Indeed, LGB workers are generally thought to be attuned to cues in their social environment, for example by monitoring their interaction partners for cues that convey how disclosure would be received (King et al., 2008; see also King et al., 2017). The literature on what such cues exactly look like, and how they may affect identity management, is relatively sparse, however. Moreover, since specific social cues could be interpreted differently in distinct sociocultural environments, adopting a cross-cultural perspective may be especially relevant for LGB expatriates: they regularly enter contexts that are new or unfamiliar, and may therefore need to constantly re-attune to these social cues.

Nonetheless, several elements that may help understand when disclosure may be met positively have been put forward. A central element herein could be the degree of anticipated acceptance, or the extent to which an interaction partner is anticipated to be accepting of disclosure (Jones & King, 2014). A general hypothesis is that, to the extent that an interaction partner seems more accepting, a disclosing strategy will be more likely; contrastingly, to the extent that they seem more rejecting, a concealing strategy will be more likely (King et al., 2017). In cases of high ambiguity about the degree of anticipated acceptance, a signaling strategy may be more effective; that is, the LGB expatriate then chooses to drop hints or provide clues about their sexual identity, to gauge the interaction partner's reaction (Clair et al., 2005), based on which they may adopt a certain strategy. Other important mechanisms that may determine which identity management strategies to adopt in social interactions with others are the interaction partners' perceived level of knowledge about, sympathy towards, and similarity to the stigmatized identity (Clair et al., 2005), as well as interpersonal trust (Ragins, 2008) and reciprocated openness (e.g., Rengers et al., 2021).

A related consideration is the general imperative to disclose personal information in order to foster interpersonal relationships (King et al., 2008). Especially in the context of expatriation, building relationships with co-workers on the basis of openness and mutual trust may be very important, for example in order to be able to work well together (Rengers et al., 2019). A common way of building trust in relationships is by disclosing personal information, for example about one's family life, hobbies, and past life experiences. Besides having a relationship-building function, self-disclosure may also contribute to establishing an individual's credibility. Individuals who do not tell a lot about themselves, and who conceal their identity, may be seen as disingenuous and suspicious, and are on average liked less (Chrobot-Mason et al., 2001).

Making sure not to disclose their sexual identity to the 'wrong' person holds special importance for LGB expatriates, since being outed may have disastrous consequences. For example, should this occur in a country where homosexuality is illegal and punishable, being outed may have far-reaching implications for LGB expatriates, who may even have to be evacuated. Moreover, as we found in our own work with LG humanitarian aid workers (Rengers et al., 2019), should this information be shared with the 'wrong' people, either within or outside of the organization, this may endanger the whole team, and potentially the legitimacy of the organization at large. Expatriates who were outed felt vulnerable, experienced a breach of trust with their colleagues, and became even more vigilant of concealing their sexual identity for the remainder of their time abroad. In another study, LG expatriates experienced a lack of employer support when they were outed (McPhail & McNulty, 2015).

Finally, a different range of issues may be at play for LGB workers who are living a completely 'out' life in their home country, and who may now need to adopt concealing strategies. This implies they would have to alter, for example, their behaviors, mannerisms, speech, and general way of presenting themselves. This preoccupation of being found out and the suppression of certain behaviors can be highly stressful and energy-draining (Pachankis, 2007) and may take away cognitive resources from being able to do their job well.

Post-Return

Upon return, LGB expatriates should participate in a debriefing procedure, as is common practice. Topics that could be discussed therein include common repatriation difficulties that expatriate families encounter (e.g., readjusting to the home country's culture) and a 'lessons learned' segment to inform both employer and future expatriates. Moreover, LGB expatriates may need professional care and counseling, in order to discuss and reflect upon their experiences. Especially in the case of forced repatriation (e.g., because of a threatening situation), receiving adequate care would be essential. To illustrate: a participant in our study (Rengers et al., 2019) had been outed by a co-worker, creating a situation that their employer deemed dangerous, which then prompted their evacuation from the mission. Being forced to repatriate by their employer left the participant in a state of distress, for which they did not receive appropriate care upon return. Even if this may be an extreme example, post-return care may be essential for LGB workers, and therefore needs to be provided adequately.

Conclusion: LGB expatriates may carefully manage their sexual identity throughout different stages of the expatriation process, assessing several potential costs, benefits, and consequences of adopting specific identity management strategies. Employers can facilitate this process, for example by offering appropriate forms of support for LGB expatriates. In the following section, I will turn my attention to these matters.

Organizational Support for LGB Expatriates

Receiving adequate and sufficient organizational support ranks among the most important factors contributing to successful expatriation, in general (Cole & Nesbeth, 2014). However, there is little understanding of how this translates to LGBT expatriates, in specific. Given the particular challenges they face, standard measures of organizational support are likely to inadequately and insufficiently accommodate their different situation (McNulty & Hutchings, 2016). A complicating factor is that the specific needs and experiences of LGBT expatriates are understudied, in both HR practice and policy (Gedro et al., 2013) and scientific research (McPhail & McNulty, 2015). Therefore, many organizations currently have little to no experience with and expertise on what it means to provide the necessary support to safeguard LGBT expatriates' performance, safety, and ultimately well-being (McPhail et al., 2016).

Building on the small, but steadily growing scholarly literature focusing specifically on LGBT expatriates (e.g., Gedro, 2010; Gedro et al., 2013; McPhail & McNulty, 2015; McPhail et al., 2016; McNulty et al., 2018; Rengers et al., 2019), I will now discuss some of the challenges employers may encounter in the context of LGBTQ* expatriation, as well as ways in which these might be alleviated. I specifically focus on formal organizational policies and practices, as one of three key forms of contextual support affecting workplace experiences of stigmatized, including, LGBT, workers—the other two being an LGBT-supportive workplace climate and supportive workplace relationships (Webster et al., 2018; following Clair et al., 2005; Ragins, 2008). Within the domain of formal policies, a careful selection procedure and effective pre-departure training are critical for expatriate success (Yeaton & Hall, 2008). Moreover, LGB expatriates commonly perceive limited organizational support during expatriation (McPhail et al., 2016; Rengers et al., 2019). Therefore, this section will discuss several policies that apply to these aspects of LGBT expatriation.

In general, formal organizational policies and practices aim to improve organizational and employee performance by positively influencing employees' attitudes and behaviors (e.g., Kehoe & Wright, 2013) and can be interpreted as a manifestation of an organization's values and beliefs (Schein, 1992). Therefore, adopting supportive policies and practices for LGBT expatriates demonstrates a commitment to their equal treatment. More specifically, it signals to everyone within the organization that LGBT-targeted discrimination and harassment are unacceptable (e.g., Ragins & Cornwell, 2001) and sets behavioral precedents regarding what is expected. In doing so, LGBT expatriates are informed that they should be treated equitably and fairly and that those who discriminate will be held accountable. Simultaneously, such policies set expectations towards non-LGBT workers about how to treat their LGBT colleagues in an inclusive and non-discriminatory fashion (Webster et al., 2018).

Selection

Aspiring LGBTQ* expatriates may already experience discrimination in the selection phase. For example, they may be restricted by a 'lavender ceiling', which systematically prevents LGBTQ* workers from entering positions of power and authority within organizations (Hill, 2009; see also Gedro, 2010). Similarly, LGBTQ* workers may experience a 'lavender border' (Gedro, 2010), wherein they are bypassed for going on international assignment for their non-LGBTQ* counterparts, for example because employers perceive that going on expatriation inherently poses a threat to LGBTQ* workers (Gedro, 2010; McPhail & McNulty, 2015). However, personal safety and security in the host country are a special consideration among LGBT expatriates in determining whether they will go on international assignment (Gedro, 2010; see also Gedro et al., 2013), and they are therefore not likely to make such decisions lightly. Moreover, LGB workers have successfully completed expatriate assignments in some of the most dangerous and oppressive countries (McPhail et al., 2016; Rengers et al., 2019) and should therefore not be prematurely dismissed for consideration on international assignment (Gedro et al., 2013).

Illustration: McNulty and colleagues (2016) found that LG expatriates considered their sexual identity to be both a disabler and an enabler. Indeed, they experienced the lavender ceiling and lavender border, encountered ample instances of discrimination and stigmatization, and experienced little perceived organizational support, in both home and host country. However, their sexual identity also enabled them to contribute meaningfully to debates on inclusivity and policy development. Moreover, most participants in their study opted to expatriate together but independently (i.e., by applying for expatriation as individuals, rather than as a couple). In this setup, both partners work as expatriates, and the trailing partner does not depend on the other for support—which is more common among heterosexual expatriate couples. As a result, LG expatriate couples may experience a larger degree of legal (e.g., both can apply for a work permit) and financial (e.g., both partners receive their own income) independence, which may subsequently contribute to a higher degree of mobility than their heterosexual peers. Altogether, employers would benefit from evaluating their selection criteria and procedures: rather than preventing LGBTQ* workers from engaging in international assignments by only considering safety concerns, employers could take measures to safeguard their safety during expatriation. This could for example be done by reviewing existing pre-departure arrangements.

Pre-Departure Support

Prior to their relocation, outgoing expatriates tend to engage in pre-departure preparations, which commonly cover topics such as cultural sensitivity, language training, and country briefings (e.g., Puck et al., 2008; Yeaton & Hall, 2008) and generally offer relocation assistance (Gedro et al., 2013). Such orientations are oftentimes not inclusive in their approach toward LGB expatriates (Gedro et al., 2013). For example, they may not be offered to accompanying family members—which is also a problem for heterosexual trailing spouses (McNulty, 2012)—and topics particularly important to them may be insufficiently included, or absent altogether. Herein, one can think about including information concerning dual-career support for same-sex partners or the legal status of same-sex marriage in the host country, and how to apply for a spousal visa. Additionally, as is the case for heterosexual/cisgender expatriate families, employers would do well to also provide relocation assistance for LGBT expatriate families and to offer health care benefits to same-sex partners as well (Gedro et al., 2013).

Another central element of pre-departure orientations is a thorough review and briefing of the host country, including identification of potential risks for outbound workers (McPhail & McNulty, 2015). This is even more important for LGBTQ* expatriates, as they are prone to experiencing discrimination and stigmatization (Gedro, 2010). Unfortunately, pre-departure briefings oftentimes provide insufficient information about the sociocultural or legal status of LGBTQ* individuals in the host country (Mizzi, 2014). It is illustrated that in our own work (Rengers et al., 2019), we found that humanitarian aid workers at Doctors without Borders (Médecins Sans Frontières; MSF) received ample pre-departure briefings about country profiles, prevailing social norms, and the organization's security framework, detailing how the employer aims to safeguard staff safety and well-being. Marginalized populations (e.g., women, certain ethnicities) are especially highlighted in that framework, such that every outbound expatriate was made aware of the particular challenges that members of these groups may face. However, specific information for LGB expatriates on how to navigate their sexual identity was not provided anywhere—even if their situation may have especially demanded it. These orientations could hence be adapted to better fit their reality, for example by detailing employment laws, the sociocultural climate, as well as gender/sexuality HR policies and practices in the host country (Friedman, 2007). Importantly, not only LGBTQ* expatriates and their families, but also their colleagues and line managers could be instructed about the challenges that may arise during expatriation, as they play an important role in safeguarding LGBTQ* expatriates' well-being and safety (McPhail & McNulty, 2015).

Support During Expatriation

LGB expatriates oftentimes perceive limited organizational support during expatriation (McPhail et al., 2016; Rengers et al., 2019). Instructing and training local co-workers in the host country—especially line managers—about LGBTQ* issues and acceptable behavior among colleagues may therefore be very important for LGB expatriates to feel supported (Gedro et al., 2013; Rengers et al., 2019). However, starting such conversations may be tricky, especially in countries with an oppressive legal or sociocultural climate towards LGBTQ* individuals. To accommodate this, reaching out to local LGBTQ* individuals and groups, and setting up an employee resource group (ERG) within the host country may be a fruitful endeavor (McPhail et al., 2016). Besides being a source of social support and providing a sense of belonging and community for LGBTQ* expatriates (see Rengers et al., 2019), ERGs may also offer policy advice and provide voice opportunities (McNulty et al., 2018). Relatedly, actively identifying allies can be worthwhile. Allies are heterosexual/cisgender staff who work together with the LGBTQ* community in putting topics on the agenda, thereby striving for organizational change (Brooks & Edwards, 2009). HR professionals are in an excellent position to act as allies and to 'advocate, educate, research, and act as change agents for issues related to LGBT minorities in international contexts' (Brooks & Edwards, 2009, p. 146; see also Gedro [2007] and McPhail and McNulty [2015]). In this regard, establishing a direct and stable line of communication between HR departments in home and host country would be helpful, since 'with sufficient information and communication LGBT expatriates can feel safer about the support that is available to them from their employers' (McPhail & McNulty, 2015, p. 759).

Since acceptance of LGBTQ* individuals varies widely across the globe (Pew Research Center, 2020), employers would do well to accumulate knowledge about local LGBTQ* laws and social customs and to monitor developments as they occur (McPhail & McNulty, 2015). This will help promote insights and awareness of countries that may be safer for LGBTQ* expatriation (Gedro, 2010). Moreover, collecting such information allows for the (further) development of trainings and policies, two essential ingredients to guarantee LGBTQ* workers' safety during expatriation (Gedro et al., 2013). Accumulating such knowledge has another benefit: it raises awareness about topics that have, until recently, been 'undiscussable' (Gedro, 2010, p. 399), ensuring that LGBTQ* expatriates no longer have to carry the responsibility of educating their employer on these issues (Gedro, 2010).

Conclusion: formal organizational policies accommodating for the realities of LGBTQ* expatriates currently range from offering the exact same as to their heterosexual/cisgender counterparts, to providing equivalent policies (i.e., adapted to their situation), to being virtually non-existent in many cases (McPhail et al., 2016). Employers need to be aiming for *equitable* treatment of LGBTQ* expatriates (Gedro, 2010): they should receive the same support provided to their heterosexual/cisgender counterparts, adapted to their particular situation (Gedro et al., 2013; McPhail et al., 2016). Offering such tailor-made policies is especially crucial in the context of LGBTQ* expatriation; the social contexts wherein international assignments take place are dynamic, as are the expatriates living in and moving between these spaces.

Potential Barriers to Becoming LGBTQ*-Inclusive

Organizations might face challenges on their journey toward becoming LGBTQ*-inclusive. For example, they may believe that no action is needed, as all employees are already treated equally, or they may anticipate backlash from stakeholders (e.g., employees) who hold negative attitudes towards LGBTQ* workers (Hill, 2009; Metcalf & Rolfe, 2011). To conclude this chapter, I discuss these potential barriers to becoming LGBTQ*-inclusive for organizations working internationally.

Badgett and colleagues (2013) found that implementing formal organizational policies for LGBT expatriates, such as extending health insurance coverage to same-sex partners, may come at initial costs, but that this effect would be rather small (see also Ash & Badgett, 2006). In fact, adopting such policies can actually provide a substantive return on investment, for three main reasons. First, LGBT-supportive policies do not need to be made from scratch; rather, employers can review their existing policies and ensure that these are extended in such a way that they also cover the specific needs of LGBT expatriates, thereby working towards equitable treatment. Moeller and Maley (2018), for example, offer a six-step process that employers can follow to create a formal support system for LGB expatriate families, by adjusting existing policies and practices to fit their experiences. Second, Badgett and colleagues (2013) also found that implementing LGBT-supportive policies will simultaneously reduce costs in other domains (e.g., lower health insurance costs). Moreover, they demonstrate that LGBT workers are more likely to adopt disclosing strategies in supportive environments (see also Webster et al., 2018), which generally increases their well-being and organizational commitment (Jones & King, 2014). This, in turn, is likely to positively affect their performance. Third, expanding existing formal policies may improve LGBTQ* expatriates' performance, which in turn may increase the likelihood of expatriation success. Obviously, many factors play a role herein, but one especially important determinant of expatriation success is the extent to which expatriates receive adequate organizational support (Cole & Nesbeth, 2014). Since expatriation failure may lead to considerable financial costs (e.g., Lee, 2007), as well as reputational damage vis-à-vis local governments, suppliers, and customers (Harcar & Harcar, 2004), employers may find the adoption of LGBTQ*-supportive policies altogether a worthy investment.

To somewhat offset initial costs of implementing such policies, it might be fruitful to join forces with other organizations working with LGBTQ* expatriates, such that sector-wide equitable treatment programs can be generated. As there are few HR-specific resources about the international status of what it means to be LGBT (Gedro, 2010), widely sharing all available knowledge and expertise would be of benefit, and may prevent committing the mistakes that others have already made. This information sharing could for example take the form of a database containing 'best practices' in the context of LGBTQ* expatriation. Herein, employers can keep an overview of how certain issues (e.g., same-sex partner visa) have been dealt with previously, and how successful this was. Such documentation can then always be used as a guideline for future international assignments. Importantly, such a database needs to be updated regularly; returning LGBTQ* expatriates have gained a ton of valuable experience that could be fed back into the organization, thereby making valuable contributions to further policy development. Relatedly, more systematic research on the effectiveness, adequacy, and sustainability of specific organizational policies related to LGBT expatriation is needed (Gedro et al., 2013).

Another argument that organizations may use to defend their reluctance to implement LGBTQ*-supportive policies hinges on the general assumption that host country locals will not respond well to LGBTQ* expatriates (Gedro et al., 2013). This may be framed as not wishing to impose 'Westernized' norms and values such as homosexuality on locals, who 'may not be ready for these issues' (Rengers et al., 2019). However, low acceptance levels are not always an issue among (solely) the local population; LGBTQ* issues may also be under-discussed because of the presence of homophobic expatriates who are hesitant to discuss these topics. For example, Mizzi (2014) showed that conservative Western expatriates had trouble with their LGBT co-workers—more so than the local (Kosovar) population did. Merely ascribing non-action to 'protecting the locals' is rather condescending, as well as troublesome for LGBTQ* expatriates, as progress around these topics is stifled. Even if it will be difficult, such conversations need to take place if employers truly strive to be fair and equitable to all workers.

In a similar vein, co-workers with negative attitudes towards LGBTQ* workers may also make employers hesitant to adopt supportive policies. Pichler et al. (2017) propose, however, that not only LGBT workers, but also their heterosexual/cisgender colleagues may benefit from LGBT-supportive policies. They assert that implementing such policies will positively affect perceived levels of organizational support among both groups, both directly and indirectly through improving the organizational diversity climate, as well as through enhanced perceptions of organizational justice. That is, even those employees who are not directly affected by these policies will appreciate the fact that their employer offers them, since it shows concern for fair and equal treatment of all. Obviously, there will be boundary conditions to the ideas proposed by Pichler and colleagues (2017), and such initiatives may possibly cause backlash.

Therefore, employers may wish to explore how best to implement such policies, since there are strong incentives to work towards nurturing an LGBTQ*-inclusive work environment.

Conclusion

LGBTQ* expatriates face particular challenges due to their gender/sexuality, for example related to their safety and security, discrimination, and harassment. The creation and maintenance of adequate supportive policies for LGBTQ* expatriates is not a priority for most organizations that work cross-nationally, which reinforces these workers' invisibility and stigmatization (Gedro, 2010). LGBTQ* expatriates require a supportive employer who works in their best interests, towards creating and safeguarding an inclusive environment wherein they can be themselves.

Relatedly, the lavender ceiling may prevent LGBTQ* expatriates from entering positions of power and formal responsibility (Gedro, 2010; Hill, 2009), which may include being overlooked in consideration for international assignment, for example because their employer fears that they will be stigmatized (Moeller & Maley, 2018). Even so, LGBTQ* expatriates have been to some of the most dangerous countries in the world (McNulty et al., 2016; Rengers et al., 2019), demonstrating that successful expatriation as an LGBTQ* individual or family is possible. I therefore invite employers to have an open dialogue with LGBTQ* expatriates, allowing them to partake in the decision-making process and encouraging them to share their own perceptions, for example with regard to how comfortable they would feel going to a specific country. This would allow them to let their own voices be heard, as these decisions would be made *with* them, rather than for them.

Further and more systematic research into the topics discussed here is needed. This could serve as a catalyst for HR professionals to start addressing these issues systematically in policies and practices. By accumulating a body of knowledge, expertise, and experience around the particular challenges of LGBTQ* expatriation, we can create awareness and inform employers, and contribute to more inclusive, equitable, and welcoming workplaces for all (Gedro, 2010). I hope that organizations, HR practitioners, managers, and co-workers will take heed of the challenges and recommendations I have discussed here, and that this will help create more optimal working and living circumstances, wherein LGBTQ* expatriates are able to both perform at their highest level as well as live their best lives.

References

Abdul Malek, M., Budhwar, P., & Reiche, B. S. (2015). Sources of support and expatriation: A multiple stakeholder perspective of expatriate adjustment and performance in Malaysia. *The International Journal of Human Resource Management, 26*(2), 258–276.

Ash, M. A., & Badgett, M. V. L. (2006). Separate and unequal: The effect of unequal access to employment-based health insurance on same-sex and unmarried different-sex couples. *Contemporary Economic Policy, 24*, 582–599.

Badgett, M. V., Durso, L. E., Mallory, C., & Kastanis, A. (2013). *The business impact of LGBT-supportive workplace policies.* The Williams Institute. https://escholarship.org/content/qt3vt6t9zx/qt3vt6t9zx.pdf

Berkley, R. A., Beard, R., & Daus, C. S. (2019). The emotional context of disclosing a concealable stigmatized identity: A conceptual model. *Human Resource Management Review, 29*(3), 428–445.

Brooks, A. K., & Edwards, K. (2009). Allies in the workplace: Including LGBT in HRD. *Advances in Developing Human Resources, 11*(1), 136–149.

Business Insider US. (2020, May 28). The 29 countries around the world where same-sex marriage is legal. *Business Insider.* www.businessinsider.nl/where-is-same-sex-marriage-legal-world-2017-11?international=true&r=US

Chiam, Z., Duffy, S., González Gil, M., Goodwin, L., & Mpemba Patel, N. T. (2020). *Trans legal mapping report 2019: Recognition before the law*. ILGA, International Lesbian, Gay, Bisexual, Trans and Intersex Association. https://ilga.org/downloads/ILGA_World_Trans_Legal_Mapping_Report_2019_EN.pdf

Chrobot-Mason, D., Button, S. B., & DiClementi, J. D. (2001). Sexual identity management strategies: An exploration of antecedents and consequences. *Sex Roles, 45*, 321–336.

Clair, J. A., Beatty, J. E., & MacLean, T. L. (2005). Out of sight but not out of mind: Managing invisible social identities in the workplace. *Academy of Management Review, 30*(1), 78–95.

Cole, N., & Nesbeth, K. (2014). Why do international assignments fail? Expatriate families speak. *International Studies of Management & Organization, 44*(3), 66–79.

Creed, W. E. D., & Scully, M. A. (2000). Songs of ourselves: Employees' deployment of social identity in workplace encounters. *Journal of Management Inquiry, 9*(4), 391–412.

Crocker, J., Major, B., & Steele, C. (1998). Social stigma. In D. T. Gilbert, S. T. Fiske, & G. Lindzey (Eds.), *The handbook of social psychology* (pp. 504–553). McGraw Hill.

Croteau, J. M., Anderson, M. Z., & VanderWal, B. L. (2008). Models of workplace sexual identity disclosure and management: Reviewing and extending concepts. *Group & Organization Management, 33*(5), 532–565.

Einarsdóttir, A., Hoel, H., & Lewis, D. (2016). Fitting the bill? (Dis)embodied disclosure of sexual identities in the workplace. *Work, Employment and Society, 30*(3), 489–505.

Filipič Sterle, M., Fontaine, J. R. J., De Mol, J., & Verhofstadt, L. L. (2018). Expatriate family adjustment: An overview of empirical evidence on challenges and resources. *Frontiers in Psychology, 9*, 1207.

Friedman, B. A. (2007). Globalization implications for human resource management roles. *Employee Responsibilities and Rights Journal, 19*(3), 157–171.

Gedro, J. (2007). Conducting research on LGBT issues: Leading the field all over again! *Human Resource Development Quarterly, 18*(2), 153–158.

Gedro, J. (2010). The lavender ceiling atop the global closet: Human resource development and lesbian expatriates. *Human Resource Development Review, 9*(4), 385–404.

Gedro, J., Mizzi, R. C., Rocco, T. S., & van Loo, J. (2013). Going global: Professional mobility and concerns for LGBT workers. *Human Resource Development International, 16*(3), 282–297.

Goffman, E. (1963). *Stigma: Notes on the management of spoiled identity*. Prentice Hall.

Griffin, P. (1992). From hiding out to coming out: Empowering lesbian and gay educators. *Journal of Homosexuality, 22*(3–4), 167–196.

Harcar, T., & Harcar, T. (2004). Expatriate women's success in international assignments: Exploring the relationship between family issues and human resource policies. *Journal of Transnational Management Development, 8*(4), 19–35.

Herek, G. M. (1996). Why tell if you are not asked? Self-disclosure, intergroup contact, and heterosexuals' attitudes toward lesbians and gay men. In G. M. Herek, J. B. Jobe, & R. M. Carney (Eds.), *Out in force: Sexual orientation and the military* (pp. 197–225). University of Chicago Press.

Hill, R. J. (2009). Incorporating queers: Blowback, backlash, and other forms of resistance to workplace diversity initiatives that support sexual minorities. *Advances in Developing Human Resources, 11*(1), 37–53.

ILGA, International Lesbian, Gay, Bisexual, Trans and Intersex Association. (2019a). *Sexual Orientation Laws in the World*. https://ilga.org/sites/default/files/ENG_ILGA_World_map_sexual_orientation_laws_dec2019_update.png

ILGA, International Lesbian, Gay, Bisexual, Trans and Intersex Association. (2019b). *State-sponsored homophobia. Global legislation overview update*. https://ilga.org/downloads/ILGA_World_State_Sponsored_Homophobia_report_global_legislation_overview_update_December_2019.pdf

Jones, K. P., & King, E. B. (2014). Managing concealable stigmas at work: A review and multilevel model. *Journal of Management, 40*(5), 1466–1494.

Kehoe, R. R., & Wright, P. M. (2013). The impact of high-performance human resource practices on employees' attitudes and behaviors. *Journal of Management, 39*(2), 366–391.

King, E. B., Mohr, J. J., Peddie, C. I., Jones, K. P., & Kendra, M. (2017). Predictors of identity management: An exploratory experience-sampling study of lesbian, gay, and bisexual workers. *Journal of Management, 43*(2), 476–502.

King, E. B., Reilly, C., & Hebl, M. (2008). The best of times, the worst of times: Exploring dual perspectives of "coming out" in the workplace. *Group & Organization Management, 33*(5), 566–601.

Lee, H.-W. (2007). Factors that influence expatriate failure: An interview study. *International Journal of Management, 24*(3), 403–413.

Lester Feder, J. (2019, June 23). Struggle among progress as countries restrict LGBTQ rights. *The New York Times.* www.nytimes.com

Link, B. G., & Phelan, J. C. (2001). Conceptualizing stigma. *Annual Review of Sociology, 27*(1), 363–385.

McNulty, Y. (2012). "Being dumped in to sink or swim": An empirical study of organizational support for the trailing spouse. *Human Resource Development International, 15*(4), 417–434.

McNulty, Y. (2014). Women as female breadwinners in non-traditional expatriate families as a source of global talent: Status-reversal marriages, single parents, split families, and lesbian partnerships. In K. Hutchings & S. Michailova (Eds.), *Research handbook on women in international management* (pp. 332–366). Edward Elgar Publishing.

McNulty, Y., & Brewster, C. (2017). The concept of business expatriates. In Y. McNulty & J. Selmer (Eds.), *Research handbook of expatriates* (pp. 21–60). Edward Elgar Publishing.

McNulty, Y., & Hutchings, K. (2016). Looking for global talent in all the right places: A critical literature review of non-traditional expatriates. *The International Journal of Human Resource Management, 27*(7), 699–728.

McNulty, Y., McPhail, R., Inversi, C., Dundon, T., & Nechanska, E. (2018). Employee voice mechanisms for lesbian, gay, bisexual and transgender expatriation: The role of employee-resource groups (ERGs) and allies. *The International Journal of Human Resource Management, 29*(5), 829–856.

McPhail, R., & McNulty, Y. (2015). "Oh, the places you won't go as an LGBT expat!" A study of HRM's duty of care to lesbian, gay, bisexual and transgender expatriates in dangerous locations. *European Journal of International Management, 9*(6), 737–765.

McPhail, R., McNulty, Y., & Hutchings, K. (2016). Lesbian and gay expatriation: Opportunities, barriers and challenges for global mobility. *The International Journal of Human Resource Management, 27*(3), 382–406.

Metcalf, H., & Rolfe, H. (2011). *Barriers to employers in developing lesbian, gay, bisexual and transgender-friendly workplaces.* National Institute of Economic and Social Research. https://assets.publishing.service.gov.uk/government/uploads/system/uploads/attachment_data/file/85515/LGBT-equality-workplace.pdf

Meyer, I. H. (2003). Prejudice, social stress, and mental health in lesbian, gay, and bisexual populations: Conceptual issues and research evidence. *Psychological Bulletin, 129*(5), 674–697.

Mizzi, R. C. (2014). Troubling preparedness: Investigating the (in) visibility of LGBT concerns within pre-departure orientations. *Development in Practice, 24*(2), 286–297.

Moeller, M., & Maley, J. F. (2018). MNC considerations in identifying and managing LGB expatriate stigmatization. *International Journal of Management Reviews, 20*, 325–3482.

Newheiser, A.-K., & Barreto, M. (2014). Hidden costs of hiding stigma: Ironic interpersonal consequences of concealing a stigmatized identity in social interactions. *Journal of Experimental Social Psychology, 52*, 58–70.

Pachankis, J. E. (2007). The psychological implications of concealing a stigma: A cognitive-affective-behavioral model. *Psychological Bulletin, 133*(2), 328–345.

Pachankis, J. E., & Bränström, R. (2019). How many sexual minorities are hidden? Projecting the size of the global closet with implications for policy and public health. *PLOS One, 14*(6), e0218084.

Pew Research Center. (2020). *The global divide on homosexuality persists.* www.pewresearch.org/global/2020/06/25/global-divide-on-homosexuality-persists

Pichler, S., Ruggs, E., & Trau, R. (2017). Worker outcomes of LGBT-supportive policies: A cross-level model. *Equality, Diversity and Inclusion: An International Journal, 36*(1), 17–32.

Puck, J. F., Kittler, M. G., & Wright, C. (2008). Does it really work? Re-assessing the impact of pre-departure cross-cultural training on expatriate adjustment. *The International Journal of Human Resource Management, 19*(12), 2182–2197.

Ragins, B. R. (2004). Sexual orientation in the workplace: The unique work and career experiences of gay, lesbian and bisexual workers. *Research in Personnel and Human Resource Management, 23*, 37–122.

Ragins, B. R. (2008). Disclosure disconnects: Antecedents and consequences of disclosing invisible stigmas across life domains. *Academy of Management Review, 33*(1), 194–215.

Ragins, B. R., & Cornwell, J. M. (2001). Pink triangles: Antecedents and consequences of perceived workplace discrimination against gay and lesbian employees. *Journal of Applied Psychology, 86*(6), 1244.

Rengers, J. M., Heyse, L., Otten, S., & Wittek, R. P. M. (2019). "It's not always possible to live your life openly or honestly in the same way"—workplace inclusion of lesbian and gay humanitarian aid workers in doctors without borders. *Frontiers in Psychology, 10*, 320.

Rengers, J. M., Heyse, L., Wittek, R. P. M., & Otten, S. (2021). Interpersonal antecedents to selective disclosure of lesbian and gay identities at work. *Social Inclusion, 9*(4), 388–398.

Schein, E. H. (1992). *Organizational culture and leadership* (2nd ed.). Jossey-Bass.

Schuler, R. S., Jackson, S. E., & Tarique, I. (2011). Global talent management and global talent challenges: Strategic opportunities for IHRM. *Journal of World Business, 46*(4), 506–516.

Takeuchi, R. (2010). A critical review of expatriate adjustment research through a multiple stakeholder view: Progress, emerging trends, and prospects. *Journal of Management, 36*(4), 1040–1064.

Wax, A., Coletti, K. K., & Ogaz, J. W. (2018). The benefit of full disclosure: A meta-analysis of the implications of coming out at work. *Organizational Psychology Review, 8*(1), 3–30.

Webster, J. R., Adams, G. A., Maranto, C. L., Sawyer, K., & Thoroughgood, C. (2018). Workplace contextual supports for LGBT employees: A review, meta-analysis, and agenda for future research. *Human Resource Management, 57*(1), 193–210.

Woods, J. D. (1993). *The corporate closet: The professional lives of gay men in America.* Free Press.

Yeaton, K., & Hall, N. (2008). Expatriates: Reducing failure rates. *Journal of Corporate Accounting & Finance, 19*(3), 75–78.

31

LGBTQ ENTREPRENEURSHIP

Balancing the Tension Between Emancipation and Counter-Participation

Renaud Redien-Collot

Introduction

Entrepreneurship studies only address gay and lesbian populations and very marginally bisexual and trans groups (Redien-Collot & Mokkadem, 2021). Moreover, this literature barely addresses queering, which it does not refer to as 'entrepreneurial queering', which will be done in this chapter. Considering this, this text uses the terms homosexual entrepreneurs and entrepreneurship developed by homosexual populations. This chapter seeks to break away from the existing entrepreneurial literature, reporting on the important gaps it reveals.

In this text, the notions of politics or political dimension are used to refer, in the Western world, to the public management of sexual identities and behaviors through legislation, social norms, and prohibitions to control any type of transgression of heterosexual practices. In any society, this double construct of repression aims to maintain social order (Kelan, 2010). In post-capitalist societies, it also aims to exploit sexual minorities that may contravene patriarchal and heterosexual norms (Butler, 1997). Following the feminist and homosexual struggles of the 1970s, the emergence of the inclusive agenda has generated a legislative apparatus and relative tolerance for any kind of assertion of sexual differences, in the public space that will be referred to as sexual difference marking (de Souza, 2017; Naze, 2017).

However, post-capitalist society deploys many stratagems to control the expression of gendered and sexual production of the self both in professional settings (Priola et al., 2018) and in the private domain (Bourcier, 2012). The queering perspective examines behaviors that whistle-blow post-capitalist control of the experience of production of one's sexual identity and practices (Bourcier, 2012). In organizational contexts today, queer populations face the dual challenge of (re)producing themselves professionally by living out their differences without necessarily seeking to assert them and preserving a space of their own within an eminently heteronormative capitalist culture that aims to exploit even the production of their identity (Priola et al., 2018; Wesling, 2012).

By focusing on a population that is highly stigmatized for its sexual practices, this chapter aims to clarify the role of sexual identity work in entrepreneurship by seeking to clearly articulate its political and economic dimensions. Moreover, while the concept of entrepreneurial policy is quite widely studied, the notion of political entrepreneurship, in particular, in the case of minorities, is overlooked (O'Shea et al., 2021).

DOI: 10.4324/9781003128151-37

The understanding of the homosexual entrepreneurial phenomenon is restricted to a logic of emancipation, where it is a matter of marking one's sexual differences, in the political and economic space, by a posture of escape (Galloway, 2007, 2011). This approach obscures the historical consideration of a homosexual activism carried by the entrepreneurial community that allowed the emergence of the inclusive agenda. The latter has legitimized the economic and political participation of homosexual entrepreneurs. This participation still has certain limitations today. Moreover, the inclusive agenda and diversity policies have allowed for the implementation of post-capitalist control mechanisms of self-production. Therefore, we will analyze how, through queering, homosexual entrepreneurs put in place counter-participation strategies to the inclusive agenda, targeting both the capitalist entrepreneurial logic and certain homosexual entrepreneurial models that are now normalized.

First, we examine queer entrepreneurial identity as a marker of difference, in order to understand how the participation of community entrepreneurs seems to be legitimate to a certain extent today. In a second part, we will analyze the tactics of counter-attack or counter-participation of these entrepreneurs through their queering practices. Our conclusion will clarify the nature of the contribution of the study of homosexual entrepreneurs to the field as a whole and will propose a research agenda, knowing that studies in this field are still very incomplete.

Homosexual Entrepreneurial Identity as a Marker of Difference

Regarding the homosexual population, entrepreneurial studies to date propose an essentially methodological debate, based on the treatment of two variables, sexual orientation and perceived discrimination behavior. Fear of discrimination is said to lead to the creation of a business considered as a refuge. This approach values the withdrawal into a sexual difference. Because it ignores the political, this literature does little to address the access of affected populations to resources. Moreover, it does not discuss the negative consequences for the community contained in the figure of entrepreneurship as a refuge. In contrast, related fields of research have taken up the theme to highlight how the entrepreneurial energy of homosexual entrepreneurs has fed the political enterprise of the community as a whole.

A Difference to Be Protected

In entrepreneurship, where value creation is central, the economic segment of businesses created by homosexual people may seem limited. In this regard, researchers cite discrimination and stereotypes that force them to choose a limited number of professional orientations and therefore sectors to undertake (Marlow et al., 2018). However, while this economic segment is in decline (Redien-Collot & Mokkadem, 2021), homosexual entrepreneurs have long proposed original business models in the areas of entertainment, tourism, and consumption of services associated with sexual liberation (Nash, 2014). In this regard, no work examines how AIDS created a broad momentum of social entrepreneurship within the community that persists to this day with the Prep protocol.[1]

In light of this debate, two major quantitative studies (Marlow et al., 2018; Schindehutte et al., 2005), which frame current academic production, aim to identify the specific situations and needs of the community and the subgroups that constitute it. Both rely on an obvious marker of difference, namely the stated variable of sexual orientation. The recent study by Marlow and colleagues (2018), while relying on an intersectional methodology, finds little difference between heterosexual and homosexual entrepreneurial populations. Because it does not pose the question politically, this type of research results in almost no questioning of the means available to these populations to start or take over a business.

Still echoing the debate on the economic value of homosexual entrepreneurship, Galloway (2007) sought to validate the scientific legitimacy of the study of this population. Her approach obscures the political dimension of this type of entrepreneurship. She pointed out that this population is difficult to identify because it is often missing from statistical databases and that it is distinguished on the basis of a random variable, namely the declaration of its sexual orientation. She then wondered what the two fields of homosexual studies and entrepreneurship could contribute to each other. An understanding of homosexuals' entrepreneurial practices would contribute to an understanding of the entrepreneurial context and, from a gendered perspective, challenge the patriarchal heteronormative models that are omnipresent in entrepreneurial studies. Conversely, the analysis of gay and lesbian entrepreneurial initiatives would allow for the valorization of their contributions to the economy in order to gain legitimacy. In 2011, Galloway takes up this argument by exploring the hypothesis of entrepreneurship as a refuge for all gay and lesbian populations, examining the trajectories of entrepreneurs who had benefited from neither a high level of education nor a significant professional network. She bases her study on a large body of work in the human resources field that decries how gay people in the workplace either feel forced to hide or are often harassed if they reveal their sexual orientation (Colgan et al., 2009). In analyzing her results, Galloway (2011) points out that respondents experience less discrimination in their entrepreneurial status than in their employee status. The variable based on perceived discrimination is thus chosen to study the entrepreneurial phenomenon in the lesbian and gay context. The thesis of entrepreneurship as a refuge is echoed in recent reviews of the literature on the subject (Marlow et al., 2018).

This type of research based on a variable does not even have a utilitarian aim for homosexual entrepreneurial populations since it does not lead to any questioning of the means available to them to create or take over a business. Finally, it can be assumed that this type of variable-based approach is above all a ruse of the post-capitalist discourse to make people forget that it tolerates deviations from the gendered norm (and is even interested in them!) on condition that it controls the coexistence of a plurality of sexual practices in the best interests of the system, that is, the reproduction of the system and the maintenance of heteronormative domination (Halperin, 2002).

As a counterpoint, Rumens and Ozturk (2019) identify the harmful political consequences of representing entrepreneurship as a refuge from discrimination. They explore how entrepreneurship can nowadays constitute a lever of exclusive inclusiveness that leads a sample of gay respondents to produce discourses where they affirm themselves as entrepreneurs by censoring in their attitude and that of the members of their community anything that is not heteronormative. This type of attitude jeopardizes the internal functioning of the homosexual entrepreneurial community that was presented, following the AIDS years, as a social rallying surface for the homosexual population. In fact, in these few cases studied by Rumens and Ozturk (2019), it could be that inclusion functions as a Faustian pact that closes in on the one who exchanges his or her economic commitment for the right to non-discrimination, which can turn into an imperative of post-capitalist internalization of the heteronormative model.

Finally, it is worth mentioning that a gap had been opened to address the political dimension of entrepreneurship among gay populations, but it was immediately closed. The quantitative study by Schindehutte and colleagues (2005) pointed out that there was a clear distinction between gay entrepreneurs who did not target the gay market and those who did. Apparently, only the latter group would make a strong connection between the economic and political realms. The authors consider this to be a very small group, suggesting that it is not useful to study it in order to understand the average behavior of the gay entrepreneur! It can be argued that the dichotomy operated by the authors is not factually so clear-cut if one looks at the different operations supporting the LGBTQ cause. According to Taylor (2014) and Olson (2017) many members of the community in key positions in large corporations or even business leaders who did not target the gay market early on subsidized LGBTQ events of both a festive and political nature. Whether or not the boss's activity targets the gay market does not determine his or her ability to make a strong connection between the political and economic dimensions.

A Difference to Be Negotiated

Another literature has established a clear link between the political and economic fields, showing how homosexual entrepreneurship has historically supported the political enterprise of the community. In this view, entrepreneurship is no longer a refuge for differences but a site for political action and negotiation. This approach emanating diffusely from a range of disciplines deserves to be presented and then modeled to enrich current entrepreneurship research.

Entrepreneurs Supporting a Political Enterprise

Entrepreneurship-related disciplines have multiplied studies to suggest that it has asserted itself as a surface of exchange between the community and repressive heteronormative capitalist power. Although there have been deep disagreements between gay political and economic representatives, these two factions have come together in major crises. While looking out for their economic interests, the actions of the entrepreneurs contributed to the struggle for rights as well as to the exposure of the different components of the community.

Like other minority communities, gay entrepreneurs have participated in the development and international opening of American urban centers following the Second World War (Bell & Binnie, 2004). In Europe and North America, gay entrepreneurs have enabled the gentrification of many run-down neighborhoods (Giraud, 2009). Since the interwar period in Europe, lesbian and gay ghettos have attracted a population of fairly well-to-do tourists, which continued to grow after 1960. Bell and Binnie (2004) show that lesbian and gay entrepreneurs exercised real local political power to negotiate with the municipality and the federal government a number of exemptions from penalties and economic privileges for their activities.

In her book *Selling Out*, Chasin (2000) highlights how the homosexual entrepreneurs of the 1980s allowed the emergence of the LG segment targeted by the big corporate groups. Moreover, she shows how the real or imagined consumer power of the members of this community constitutes a lever of pressure against the homophobic positions of the big brands. This lever of economic pressure also constitutes a warning to Western politicians concerned with economic peace.[2]

Within the community itself, after being despised by gay activist circles, commercial venues became rallying points. The police raid of the Barracks Bathhouse sauna in Toronto in 1978 brought together activists and businessmen who had long been at odds (Nash, 2014). Activists publicly and regularly denounced that the gay village businesses locked lesbians and gays into a ghetto and a life of petty pleasure preventing them from asserting their social and political identity by joining advocacy groups. In return, on many occasions, during the debates launched by the associations about pederasty or S&M practices, the gay businesses that wanted to keep their reputation openly took a stand against the associations and temporarily banned the circulation of their magazines. In uniting to condemn the Barracks bathhouse raid, merchants and activists defended the right of gay businesses to sell sexual freedom on behalf of the LG community's rights to be fully recognized politically (Nash, 2014). In addition, they defended the legitimacy of saunas as a place of expression for a third minority, bisexuals who had no place of privacy to live out their sexuality. This event allowed for a rearticulation of the connections between LG[3] identity, LG commercial spaces, and internal community struggles.

In North America and Western Europe, the AIDS crisis has further enhanced the link between the market and politics. In Europe, even though the state has strongly funded the creation of AIDS awareness and prevention associations, nothing could have been done without the constant cooperation between activists and businesses (Dodier, 2003). In France, the gay entrepreneurs' union (SNEG) obtained the right to distribute condoms and prevention materials in commercial spaces in 1992. In addition, the SNEG has evolved AIDS campaigns to include transgender populations.[4]

Over the course of two decades of AIDS struggles, the constant cooperation of the activist and business communities has resulted in the promotion of an inclusive agenda that calls for a right to indifference for LGBTQ populations (Naze, 2017). This right to indifference guarantees the safety of business people, the rights of employees, and the right to medical care without discrimination for anyone in the community.

The Power of Participation of Homosexual Entrepreneurs

Homosexual entrepreneurs therefore do not mark their difference only by flight but also by commitment. Rather than focusing solely on the economic value to be attributed to LGBTQ entrepreneurship, it seems important to better link this phenomenon to the political issues that have shaped it in order to understand how, for these populations, the value created is both economic and political.

In her theory of public space in the West, Nancy Fraser emphasizes how the concept of emancipation contributes to locking subalterns into a limited mode of participation (Fraser, 1998, Fraser et al., 2004). While the dominant class has access to all forms of political participation and can discuss its modalities, the subalterns only have the right to emancipation. Fraser and colleagues (2004) define social justice as the possibility of granting all citizens parity of means through redistribution and parity of participation through recognition. Entrepreneurs and political representatives of the LGBTQ community have acquired political rights that are reflected in the inclusive agenda, more or less extensively, depending on the Western country. However, if we intend to analyze how the political and the economic overlap, it would be important to observe what the inclusive agenda brings to gay economic actors, more specifically, to entrepreneurs.

In terms of recognition, the contributions are notorious. Homosexual entrepreneurs today enjoy a triple recognition, in economic terms. The homosexual consumer segment is recognized and coveted (Chasin, 2000), giving entrepreneurs the legitimacy to obtain financial support if they want to launch their business on this market segment. However, they must have acquired a form of political confidence in their entrepreneurial project in order to share it with bankers and investors (Redien-Collot, 2012). LGBTQ business unions have given entrepreneurs a second type of economic and political recognition. The phenomenon is much more marked in Great Britain and the United States than in France (Pulcher et al., 2020). Finally, the figure of great openly LGBTQ entrepreneurs has progressively asserted itself in Western urban environments, certainly in a limited number of sectors in which, however, they have left their signature. In the 1960s, Jack Campbell opened a sauna with partners in Cleveland that aimed to provide a quality service to gay customers. Twenty years later, he is the head of Campbell's Club Baths, a chain of some 40 saunas in the United States and Canada. Based in Florida, Campbell fought against Anita Bryant's Save Our Children movement in that state, which sought to overturn a gay-friendly regulation. Campbell has also financially supported numerous American LGBT organizations, such as the Gay Games and the National Gay and Lesbian Task Force. After having been, in the 1960s, the editor of The Ladder, the magazine published by the Daughters of Bilitis, the first lesbian group founded in the United States. Barbara Grier created in 1973 with several associates, Naiad Press, one of the first lesbian publishing houses in the United States. She organized the book sector dedicated to lesbian literature, relying on successful novels but also publishing classics. She has been very active in cataloguing and indexing major works of lesbian literature in universities. More recently, the presence of LGBT entrepreneurs is asserting itself in sectors that do not only target their market. This is the case of Vivienne Ming, who created a Think Tank SOCOS that aims to reform education by relying on artificial intelligence and neuroscience. As a researcher, she is very concerned by the failure of educational and professional exclusion and has carried out multiple studies to highlight how the variables used to recruit professional elites have little impact on the success of organizations. She created the machine learning Muse to help parents with learning disabled children. In another field, Martine Rothblatt is the 1996 founder of United Therapeutics, an NASDAQ-listed U.S. biotech company that, by manufacturing organs, extends the lives of patients with lung disease. Married as a man in 1982 to Bina Aspen Prator and they have two children. Martine decided to have a sex change in 1994 and created United Therapeutics two years later to save their second child, who had a rare disease. In 2004, she launched the movement of transhumanist thought Terasem,[5] using her rich experience which crosses technology and life sciences (Vita-More, 2019). Terasem Movement Inc., created by Martine and Bina Rothblatt in 2002, is a foundation that seeks to develop technologies that respect the integrity of nature and humanity.

In the Western world, the power and influence of Campbell, Grier or Rothblatt has allowed the recognition of the role played by the entrepreneurial homosexual population within the community and beyond. However, this recognition is rarely accompanied by a redistribution of resources that would support the efforts of nascent gay entrepreneurs today. While Anglo-Saxon countries are the only ones where many initiatives in favor of the community's creators can be observed, they come from dedicated employer unions or individual initiatives that are not publicly funded (Pulcher et al., 2020). Founded in San Francisco in 2009, StartOut is a non-profit organization that aims to create an LGBT entrepreneurial and professional network. This entity fights against discrimination, offers training, connects entrepreneurs with mentors, and above all promotes access to capital. However, concerning the economic future of the LGBT entrepreneurial community today, actions are still sporadic. The public authorities, so concerned about the future of entrepreneurs in certain sectors, seem to be very little involved in debates on the evolution of the homosexual economic segment, even though it faces many challenges (Redien-Collot & Mokkadem, 2021). In particular, large groups are making an industrial exploitation of the LGBTQ marketing segment. Their brands occupy the most strategic locations in gay neighborhoods where platformization ruins small businesses and applications ruin physical and social interactions in meeting places (Redien-Collot & Mokkadem, 2021). Through this undermining of the small business developed by gay bosses, one may wonder if there is not a loss of the original entrepreneurial spirit. Should this be blamed on an entrepreneurial dynamic that is overly driven by the inscription of differences and the struggle for acceptance of those differences, via the inclusive agenda? Do the guarantees of the inclusive agenda mark the end of the link between political struggles and queer entrepreneurial creativity (Naze, 2017)? A counter-participatory movement, queering, has already emerged, in the 1990s, that supported the idea that it was not enough to gain recognition for one's difference, but that the experience of queer differences must also be preserved, in a capitalist culture that seeks to instrumentalize them, and, ultimately, perhaps, empty them of meaning (De Lauretis, 1991).

The Counter-Participation of Homosexual Entrepreneurs

Counter-participation stems from a lucidity of minority populations towards a dominant culture that seeks to control them in order to better exploit them (Fraisse, 2005). In the context of the waning entrepreneurial spirit of homosexual populations and their ability to renew themselves, the queering perspective offers many advantages. We will examine it here from the point of view of both entrepreneurial practices and the few academic attempts that have emerged. We will highlight how entrepreneurial queering is defensive in order to preserve the (unique) experience of professional production of oneself as a queer entrepreneur, whether this covers the individual's self-perception or their practices and initiatives. Entrepreneurial queering is also proactive bringing out new business models and give legitimacy to certain types of activity, as in the case of the SOS group,[6] in social entrepreneurship (Borello, 2011).

Defensive Entrepreneurial Queering

At odds with the inclusive agenda that dilutes queer identities in the demand for rights, entrepreneurial queering stimulates the heightened expression of differences by promoting the proliferation of queer postures and identities. It promotes a plurality of homophilic, homoerotic, 'homo-political' and homo-economic experiences, particularly in the professional field (Bourcier, 2012). As Burchiellaro (2021) shows, diversity policies seek to control the opening of such a space of possibility, imposing rather quickly reifying categories and subcategories on individuals and their economic propositions. While giving some publicity to their queer entrepreneurial initiatives, the protagonists (entrepreneurs or not) thus seek to preserve collective and/or anonymous, semi-clandestine, and above all open character of their project to the unexpected, improvisation, indeterminacy, everything that goes against an orthodox approach to management (de Souza, 2017). Since the end of the 1990s, we have thus observed the emergence of collective entrepreneurial experiments based on several assumptions that do not exclude the search for improvement of the business model without making it a priority. It would be difficult to classify these initiatives in the categories of social or political entrepreneurship. They unfold in parallel with the LGBT associative movement. Two examples can be cited that trace the evolution of queer entrepreneurial experiments in Paris between 1997 and today. Following the unfortunate conclusion of the first initiative, the second has partially erased the exclusive character of the initial project. However, in both cases, there is a concern to explore the opportunity offered by the 'queer unwanted' of the festive offer, breaking with the aesthetic and political clichés of the gay discotheques.[7]

Created by Michelle Cassaro surrounded by a very active collective, Le Pulp, a lesbian nightclub located on the Boulevard Poissonnière in Paris has, from 1997 to 2007, targeted women, gay or not, who wanted to have fun without being harassed by men. Trans people and drag queens were admitted. The place crosses the festive and political dimensions and the aesthetic engagement. It is the triumph of the electroclash within the French Touch trend represented by DJ Sextoy, Chloé or Arnaud Rebotini. It is a place of artistic and political production: the label Kill the DJ is created there and Housewife is published, one of the most popular fanzines of the time, where it is about, among other things, gay rights, and in particular the PACS[8] (Stamatopoulou, 2018). Unfortunately, the purist nature of this queer experiment, which aimed to avoid any recuperation by the political and economic circles of the establishment, came at a cost. As a result, Le Pulp nightclub did not seek enough support from its stakeholders as the city of Paris acquired the building in 2007 to turn it into a low-rent housing.

In reaction to the unfortunate end of Le Pulp, also in Paris, in 2008, several LGBTQ collectives and local associations launched under the label Rosa Bonheur original projects in the fields of sports, gastronomy, viticulture, festive projects for seniors (the Bal Extravadanse Senior), and a festival of traveling women and electronic music nights (Pulp Is Back). The project Rosa Bonheur plays with its references to and distances itself from heterosexual family party culture and homosexual clichés inherited from the 1970s (Bonheur, 2019). It is also about targeting forgotten homosexual audiences, not locking itself into one place. Through this constant game of demarcation, the organizers seek to maintain the creative power of the project. The Pulp experience having served as a lesson, however, this multiform project maintains a clear interaction with local and public interlocutors. Today, Rosa Bonheur has four locations in Paris. For the founders, the idea was to create daytime entertainment for populations less attracted to the nightlife of nightclubs and saunas. These current successful LGBTQ projects, unlike the small businesses that are failing, draw their entrepreneurial character from a counter-ideology or counter-practices that explore new systems and/or challenge old ones.

Proactive Entrepreneurial Queering

The mix of efforts to preserve the entrepreneurial experience in all its duration and originality is not the only issue that characterizes the queer approach. Entrepreneurs may seek not to create a sustainable creative space that must be protected, but a confrontation or a bias that challenges the dominant heteronormative and homosexual models that infuse managerial practices and economic and social models.

Muhr and Sullivan (2013) seek to clarify the understanding of how queer bosses operate in the workplace by engaging their teams in counter-participatory dynamics that challenge managerial ideology. These authors examine, for example, the way in which Claire, a trans boss, after having overvalued her feminine appearance by guaranteeing the success of her company, decides to show herself sometimes under feminine and sometimes under masculine outward appearances, at a time when feminine leadership is on the rise. This ambivalence destabilizes Claire's employees who wanted to see the essence of her leadership reside in a solely feminine appearance. Perhaps to engage his company in a decisive turning point of its development, this boss considers that sharing his ambivalence and involving his employees in a counter-participation to the masculine versus feminine binary codes of entrepreneurial leadership allows access to another level of exchange in the company in order to learn to think and manage it differently.

Founded in 1987, the SOS Group today includes 650 associations, social enterprises and medico-social establishments and employs 22,000 people with a turnover of 700 Million Euros. Harvard University conducted a case study on the SOS group, considered one of the most original social enterprises in Europe (Battilana et al., 2016). Borello, the founder of SOS, originally created this entity to help AIDS patients and addiction victims, two still very important pillars of the structure. Today, the group asserts a mission of general interest by covering 8 areas, such as solidarity, health, seniors, employment, youth, international action, culture and ecological transition. Proud of its origins, however, in 2020, the group became a shareholder in two gay magazines LGBT+ and Têtu. Borello acknowledges that the group's entrepreneurial momentum stems from its initial desire to target doubly excluded individuals, sick and addicted gays. At the time, he targeted the queer unwanted, that is, homosexuals who did not fit the petty bourgeois image of the well-to-do gays, who alone deserved to be treated. Today, its revenge lies in the capacity of this entity to have transferred to the whole of the social economy a know-how coming from the homosexual milieu in crisis (Borello, 2011). There is a provocative signal here to remind the actors of French social policies conceived in an eminently heterosexual and patriarchal framework that they can learn from the homosexual milieu. Its entrepreneurial energy feeds on this form of queer revenge (Bourcier, 2012).

However, the status of queering as a counter-participation is debated. Indeed, it may have provided an antidote to the disciplinary society of the nineteenth century by encouraging individuals to pluralize their identities as well as discourses about themselves to limit the impact of control devices. But, as Mc Worther (2012) notes, the seemingly transgressive pluralism to which queering invites everyone can seem, in many circumstances of business life, to converge with the entrepreneurialism that claims to transcend individual differences to celebrate the postmodern myth of the all-powerful and supremely agile heterosexual white male entrepreneur. It is therefore important to handle queering with great care by carefully elaborating the counter-participation strategies to which it gives rise. In this context, Mc Worther (2012) encourages defining queering as a focus on self-talk, especially in the business world, so as not to describe oneself as a permanent performance instance. She also recommends making room for desires that are not attempts at self-enhancement and promotion. In another vein, Bourcier (2012) emphasizes the importance of self-deprecation, in queering to avoid playing the pitiful role of the all-powerful freedman (de Souza, 2017)

Conclusion

The counter-participation, whether it takes the form of queering or not, questions in turn the claims that aim at emancipation and participation when they tend to reify themselves, in the Western context. Concerning the understanding that queer entrepreneurs have of their business as a community of intelligibility, that is, a community interacting with other dominant or minority interlocutors, it seems important to examine how they articulate or not the political, the sexual and the economic in the exploitation of their business opportunities, the development and the resale of their structure as well as the networks they frequent (Redien-Collot, 2012). Furthermore, in order to better accompany these populations, it would be interesting to examine any external (controlling) and internal (regulating) discourses to the field of LGBTQ entrepreneurship that may inhibit their entrepreneurial initiatives.

In this context, it would be useful to promote a research agenda on LGBTQ entrepreneurship that would not only contextualize entrepreneurship by exploring the difficulties faced by one minority among many. This agenda must highlight how knowledge of the entrepreneurial phenomenon as a whole requires a better understanding of activism as a form of political entrepreneurship, as well as the politics of controlling desire and sexualities in the post-capitalist economy.

This agenda could include four steps: a genealogy of queer entrepreneurial practice as a surface of exchange; a clarification of the limits of the use of the notion of emancipation, so often used in the literature, to explain the entrepreneurship of these populations; a clarification of the meaning of struggles for redistribution and participation; and a systematic analysis of the various forms of counter-participation.

It would be interesting first to analyze how, in the aftermath of World War II, homosexual entrepreneurial practice has taken on a contractual character that commits its actors to deliver an economic contribution in return for non-discrimination rights. The aim is to assess historically the originality of the economic contributions of homosexual entrepreneurs and to examine how they have been alternately stimulated and constrained by the demands of the inclusive agenda. This economic history marked by shame, repression, and often suppressed protest presents incomplete or contradictory documentation and testimony. As Foucault noted about the social history of madness (Foucault, 1976), it is an economic history that has no history. As such, it would be appropriate to develop a genealogical approach that seeks not so much to reconstruct the facts as to understand the ideological trajectory that has shaped the current conception of LGBT entrepreneurship in the West. Moreover, a sectoral overview would be useful in order not to confine queer entrepreneurship to a few fields of activity. The distinction between gay and lesbian entrepreneurs (Schindehutte et al., 2005) is worth discussing.

It is through the academic literature that the emancipation construct must be challenged as the main explanatory spring of the entrepreneurial approach of (sexual) minorities. Based on studies on gay entrepreneurship, it would be appropriate to show how the emancipatory approach overvalues the economic action of minorities as a form of identity inscription, revealing, in many cases, a submission to the heterosexual order (Rumen & Ozturk, 2019). Indeed, the concept of emancipation leaves in the shadow all the efforts of these communities to preserve the breath of their entrepreneurial experience, through different forms of contestation or transgression whether or not it takes the form of queering (de Souza, 2017).

In order to understand the mechanisms of participation of LGBTQ entrepreneurs and their limits, which explain the current lack of access to resources, it would also be interesting to build a history of the interactions between the economic and political institutions of the community (unions, associations, collectives) and the dominant institutions.

The final set of work to emerge concerns the figures of counter-participation through LGBTQ entrepreneurship. It is important to map how the social science and organizational theory literature positions defensive and proactive entrepreneurial queering, as well as the protective and negotiating (provocative) postures that are unique to it. Mc Worther's (2012) warning about the recuperation of queering as an agent of entrepreneurialism should alert us to the mobilization purposes of such a concept.

Notes

1 Prep is an innovative HIV prevention strategy. It stands for *pre-exposure prophylaxis.d*.
2 In the 1990s, marketing and entrepreneurship studies focused on lesbian and gay populations, hence the acronym LG.
3 With the acronym LG, Nash captures the viewpoint of the 1970s where only the demands of the lesbian and gay populations are considered.
4 It became ENIPSE in 2013.
5 Terasem Movement Inc, created by Martine and Bina Rothblatt in 2002, is a foundation that seeks to develop technologies that respect the integrity of nature and humanity.
6 Created in 1987, the SOS Group is a French social enterprise that initially targeted people with AIDS who were addicted to drugs. With several branches, SOS has become one of the most important medical and social companies in Europe today.
7 The Queer unwanted protest denounces the obsession of the traditional gay culture that values youth, whiteness and good health, rejecting any other form of representation of homosexuality.
8 In France, since 1999, the civil solidarity pact (PACS in French) is, along with marriage, one of the two forms of civil union. It organizes the common life of two adults of different sex or of the same sex.

References

Battilana, J., Dessain, V., & Lenhardt, J. (2016). *SOS group: Scaling a social enterprise conglomerate*. Harvard Business Publishing.

Bell, D., & Binnie, J. (2004). Authenticating queer space: Citizenship, urbanism and governance. *Urban Studies, 41*, 1807–1820.

Bonheur, C. R. (2019). Comptes Rendus Collectif Rosa Bonheur, La ville vue d'en bas: Travail et produc-tion de l'espace populaire. *Géographie, Économie, Société, 21*, 371–377.

Borello, J. M. (2011). Les entreprises sociales: L'exemple du Groupe SOS. *Le journal de l'Ecole de Paris du Management, 1*, 23–29.

Bourcier, M. H. (2012). *Queer zones 3: Identités, cultures et politiques.* Editions Amsterdam.

Burchiellaro, O. (2021). Queering control and inclusion in the contemporary organization: On "LGBT-friendly control" and the reproduction of (queer) value. *Organization Studies, 42*(5), 761–785.

Butler, J. (1997). Merely cultural. *Social Text*, 52–53, 265–277.

Chasin, A. (2000). *Selling out: The gay and lesbian movement goes to market.* St. Martin's Press.

Colgan, F., Wright, T., Creggan, C., & Mc Kearney, A. (2009). Equality and diversity in the public ser-vices: Moving forward on lesbian, gay and bisexual equality. *Human Resource Management Journal, 19*(3), 280–310.

De Lauretis, T. (1991). Queer theory: Lesbian and gay sexualities. *Differences: A Journal of Feminist Cul-tural Studies, 3*(2), iii–xviii.

De Souza, E. M. (2017). Where is queer theory in organizational studies. *Sociology International Journal, 1*(4), 127–134.

Dodier, N. (2003). Les premières années de l'épidémie et la conversion politique du mouvement homo-sexuel. In A. Broqua (Ed.), *Dans Homosexualités au temps du sida. Tensions sociales et identitaires.* ANRS.

Foucault, M. (1976). *Histoire de la folie à l'âge classique.* Gallimard.

Fraisse, G. (2005). Le devenir sujet et la permanence de l'objet. *Nouvelles Questions Féministes, 24*(1), 14–23.

Fraser, N. (1998). From redistribution to recognition? Dilemmas of justice in a post-socialist age. In C. Willett (Ed.), *Theorizing multiculturalism: A guide to the current debate* (pp. 19–49). Wiley & Sons.

Fraser, N., Dahl, H. M., Stoltz, P., & Willig, R. (2004). Recognition, redistribution and representation in capitalist global society: An interview with Nancy Fraser. *Acta Sociologica, 47*(4), 374–382.

Galloway, L. (2007). Entrepreneurship and the gay minority: Why the silence? *International Journal of Entrepreneurship and Innovation, 8*(4), 271–280.

Galloway, L. (2011). The experiences of the male gay business owners in the UK. *International Small Business Journal, 30*(8), 890–906.

Giraud, C. (2009). Les commerces gays et le processus de gentrification. *Varia, 5*, 79–115.

Halperin, D. (2002). *How to do the history of homosexuality.* Chicago University Press.

Kelan, E. K. (2010). Gender logic and (un) doing gender at work. *Gender, Work & Organization, 17*(2), 174–194.

Marlow, S., Greene, F. J., & Coad, A. (2018). Advancing gendered analyses of entrepreneurship: A critical exploration of entrepreneurial activity among gay men and lesbian women. *British Journal of Manage-ment, 29*(1), 118–135.

Mc Worther, L. (2012). Queer economy. *Foucault Studies, 14*, 61–78.

Muhr, S. L., & Sullivan, K. R. (2013). None so queer as folk: Gendered expectations and transgressive bodies in leadership. *Leadership, 9*(3), 416–435.

Naze, A. (2017). *Manifeste contre la normalisation gay.* La Fabrique.

Nash, C. J. (2014). Consuming sexual liberation: Gay business, politics, and Toronto's Barracks bathhouse raids. *Journal of Canadian Studies, 48*(1), 82–105.

Olson, E. D. (2017). An exploration of lesbian, gay, bisexual, and transgender pride festival sponsors. *Journal of Convention & Event Tourism, 18*(1), 60–73.

O'Shea, N., Redien-Collot, R., & Nelson, T. (2021). Adopting an inclusive gender lens as an emancipa-tory practice for entrepreneurship. *Entreprendre Innover, 49–50*(2), 5–10.

Priola, V., Lasio, D., Serri, F., & de Simone, S. (2018). The organisation of sexuality and the sexuality of organisation: A genealogical analysis of sexual "inclusive exclusion" at work. *Organization, 25*(6), 732–754.

Pulcher, S., Guerci, M., & Köllen, T. (2020). Unions as institutional entrepreneurs: The contribution of unions to the diffusion and adaptation of LGBT diversity initiatives. *Journal of Organizational Change Management, 33*, 477–490.

Redien-Collot, R. (2012). Motivations of gay entrepreneurs: A focus on the construct of appropriateness. *International Journal of Entrepreneurship and Innovation, 13*(2), 89–100.

Redien-Collot, R., & Mokkadem, O. (2021). The entrepreneurial contribution of French LGBT popula-tions. *Entreprendre Innover, 49–50*(2), 51–59.

Rumens, N., & Ozturk, M. B. (2019). Heteronormativity and the (re)construction of gay male entrepreneurial identities. *International Small Business Journal, 37*(7), 671–688.

Schindehutte, M., Morris, M. H., & Allen, J. (2005). Homosexuality and entrepreneurship: Implications of gay identity for the venture-creation experience. *International Journal of Entrepreneurship and Innovation, 6,* 27–40.

Stamatopoulou, K. (2018). Girls wanna have more than fun: The alternative geography of lesbian gathering in Paris. *Revista Latino-Americana de Geografia e Género, 9*(2), 7–43.

Taylor, J. (2014). Festivalizing sexualities: Discourses of "pride"; counter-discourses of shame. In A. Bennett, J. Taylor, & I. Woodward (Eds.), *The festivalisation of culture* (pp. 27–48). Routledge.

Vita-More, N. (2019). History of transhumanism. In N. Lee (Ed.), *The transhumanism handbook* (pp. 49–61). Springer.

Wesling, M. (2012). Queer value. *GLQ: A Journal of Lesbian and Gay Studies, 18,* 107–125.

32

CONSIDERING THE RELATIONSHIP BETWEEN LGBTQ ALCOHOLISM, ADDICTION AND RECOVERY, AND CAREER DEVELOPMENT

Julie A. Gedro

Background and Purpose

This chapter examines career development considerations for LGBTQ recovering alcoholics and addicts. LGBTQ people who are recovering from alcoholism and/or addiction face two types of stigma and discrimination. First, they face workplace contexts that continue to be pervaded by assumptions of heteronormativity. Thus, they experience stigmatization based upon sexual minority identity. Research and scholarship in fields of management, human resource development, psychology, and related fields provides career development insights for LGBTQ people (Gedro, 2009; McFadden, 2015; Velez et al., 2021). This research into the issues related to stigma and marginalization contextualizes career considerations for LGBTQ people. For example, McFadden determined that career and identity overlap, "characterized by articles that focused on the interplay of an established LGBT identity with one's vocational aspirations, career decisions, and development" (p. 136) was a prevalent theme and that issues of discrimination and identity management were "key issues" (p. 136). Velez et al. observed career development topics that included "aspirations, interest, self-efficacy . . . barriers, and supports" (p. 356) were a "substantial minority" (p. 356) in the empirical research on the vocational psychology of sexual minorities. Velez et al. noted in the research the prevalence of organizational heterosexism, and "a slight majority addressed the topic domain workplace sexual orientation identity management" (p. 355). In short, these insights revolve around the necessity of developing self-awareness and making connections between self-awareness and vocational (career) decision-making. Even though there has been progress made in terms of workplace LGBTQ equality and inclusion, LGBTQ people continue to face challenges with respect to career development because of the entrenched nature of homophobia and heteronormativity as the default assumption in organizational contexts. Second, LGBTQ people in recovery face stigma related to alcoholism, addiction, and recovery. Being a recovered addict or alcoholic can represent an enduring type of workplace stigmas. Therefore, this chapter draws together two stigmatized, marginalized identities: status as a sexual minority and as a recovered alcoholic and/or addict and interrogates these identities through two selected career development models.

DOI: 10.4324/9781003128151-38   476

This chapter weaves together subjects (LGBTQ career development for LGBTQ persons in recovery) that have been independently examined. The goal is to offer some education, awareness, and sensitivity for those with formal or informal organizational influence and decision-making as well as human resource professionals and LGBTQ recovered alcoholics and addicts. The organization of this chapter is as follows: it examines career and work challenges for LGBTQ people, then the risks for alcohol and other drug (AOD) issues faced by LGBTQ people. Next, it examines career development issues and challenges for LGBTQ people in recovery. These considerations lay the groundwork for discussions of career development, which will utilize two models: the Employability Link Model (Thijssen et al., 2008), and the Psychology of Working Theory (Duffy et al., 2016). Each of these models offers a way to consider both the challenges, as well as the opportunities, for LGBTQ people in recovery to navigate their career journeys and to optimize their well-being as a result. These models were selected based upon the way that they "speak" to the issues of marginalization, stigma, and identity. They problematize assumptions regarding access to resources and access to career development opportunities.

LGBTQ Career and Work Challenges

LGBTQ workplace issues include discrimination and marginalization due to organizational heteronormativity. McFadden's (2015) systematic literature review of LGBTQ career development in HRD, and Velez et al.'s (2021) literature review of empirical studies of LGBTQ workplace issues offer scaffolding and substantive insights into these issues. Velez et al.'s (2021) content analysis of LGBTQ research in the field of psychology focused on vocationally focused, empirical studies. Velez et al. (2021) noted that the majority of the 184 of articles identified through their review focused on heterosexism in the workplace and that a "slight majority addressed the topic domain workplace sexual orientation identity management" (p. 355). Organizational factors included perceived organizational support for LGBTQ people, and the "presence or absence of LGBTQ-supportive workplace policies" (p. 356). Velez et al. (2021) noted that because of the pervasiveness of heterosexism in the workplace, policies that are LGBTQ supportive are crucial for "positive vocational functioning" (p. 356). Velez et al. (2021) observed nearly one half of the studies addressed the domain of career functioning which they described as well-being and "the interface of career with family" (p. 356).

McFadden (2015) notes that literature on LGBT workplace issues has evolved from "only a few articles in the 1980s, to more than 25 per year in recent years" (p. 135) and suggests the increase of research on the subject maps to the increase of the wider social and organizational milieu in which LGBT issues are increasingly and more broadly considered part of the composite of organizational diversity. McFadden's analysis identified literature from fields such as "human resource development, human resource management, gender and sexuality, sociology, and psychology" (p. 127). The major themes that emerged from the analysis were career or identity overlap, organizational and human resources perspectives, discrimination, identity, and social issues and experiences. For purposes of concision, two of the most relevant themes bear explanation. First, the most prevalent theme was that of career/identity overlap. By "career/identity overlap" (p. 136), McFadden explains that one's sexual and gender identity is important throughout the course of a career. Sexual and gender minorities have lower job satisfaction in heterosexist workplaces, and sexual and gender minority status can have an impact on occupational selection. Second, the theme of "identity" (p. 143) presents the decisions that LGBTQ people make about disclosing their identity.

Unspoken and often subtle standards and expectations of heteronormativity and cis-normativity combine with ableism to create workplace cultures that present challenges to those who are sexual minorities and in programs of recovery. Ability and disability status is a social construction (Procknow & Rocco, 2016), and it is deeply embedded as a facet of organizational life. Thriving within workplace contexts permeated by cis-gendered, heteronormative assumptions necessitates the skill and ability to negotiate one's identity (Dispenza et al., 2019; Gedro & Mizzi, 2014). As employers make strides toward LGBTQ inclusion, one dimension of the career development challenges of LGBTQ people in recovery is addressed. The extent to which employers have focused on LGBTQ inclusion in all aspects of human resource development and human resource management (such as recruitment and selection, onboarding, compensation and benefits, career ladders, employee relations), varies. This variety correlates to the historically complex array of employment laws regarding prohibitions against discrimination based upon sexual orientation, gender identity and gender expression. The business case for workplace LGBTQ inclusion has been quantified, see Human Rights Campaign Corporate Equality Index (CEI), and presented as a rationale for corporations to champion LGBTQ people. The CEI provides a framework for corporations to assess and report on their demonstrated commitment to LGBGTQ workplace equality and inclusion (HRC, 2022). In brief, the CEI categories include non-discrimination policies, LGBTQ equitable benefits, and support for an inclusive culture and corporate social responsibility (HRC, 2022).

Despite the inroads toward visibility and inclusion, having an identity as an LGBTQ person continues to present career development challenges. Ng and Rumens (2017) explored and interrogated the research on LGBT workers, and comment upon the "persistence and pervasiveness of hetero- and cis- normativity in the workplace" (p. 2). Ng and Rumens refer to Warner's (1993) articulation of heteronormativity and its requirement that "individuals inscribe themselves into a hierarchical sexual order" (p. 2) and its ever-present deployment as a framework for the establishment and maintenance of what is considered normal versus what is non-normal. Furthermore, Ng and Rumens refer to Schilt and Westbrook (2009) to offer a definition of cisnormativity which refers to the expectation that the sex to which an individual is assigned at birth, aligns with the individual's internal sense of gender identity (p. 3). Dispenza et al. (2019, p. 99), argue that sexual and gender minorities and people with disabilities represent culturally oppressed groups who face stigma, injustice, and prejudice with respect to career development.

LGBTQ Alcoholism, Addiction, and Recovery

Sexual minorities may experience disproportionately high rates of alcohol and other drug (AOD) issues. LGBTQ people are at an elevated risk of addiction compared to the general U.S. population because of the stigma and discrimination faced daily which increases stress and the likelihood of AOD use (McCabe et al., 2010; Ruppert et al., 2020; Ruppert et al., 2021).

Alcoholism and Addiction

Adams et al. (2021) posit that "alcohol use is a significant global public health issue" (p. 1) and that its deleterious effects are not evenly experienced. In specific, they note that heavy use of alcohol results in disparate health outcomes between those who are sexual minorities, and those who are heterosexual and cisgender. Adams et al. (2021, p. 10) state, "Alcohol is a part of the lives of most gender and sexually diverse people, and for some, the amount and pattern of drinking alcohol is heavier than for cisgender and heterosexual people." According to the Substance Abuse and Mentor Health Services Administration (SAMHSA):

Studies indicate that, when compared with the general population, LGBT people are more likely to use alcohol and drugs, have higher rates of substance abuse, are less likely to abstain from use, and are more likely to continue heavy drinking into later life.

(2012, p. xiii)

SAMHSA notes too, that there are drugs that tend to be more popular among LGBTQ people than in the majoritarian community; these drugs include barbiturates, stimulants, sedatives, cocaine, and "party drugs" such as ecstasy.

LGBTQ people in recovery from alcoholism and/or addiction are a marginalized population (Fish & Pasley, 2015; Ruppert et al., 2020; Ruppert et al., 2021). They face a multi-layered, multi-faceted set of challenges and opportunities to strive toward, establish, and maintain meaningful careers. In addition to the stigma and discrimination experienced due to LGBTQ identity, AOD use, addiction, and recovery carry additional burdens of stigma and discrimination and face additional marginalization as a recovering addict. Link et al. (2004, in Becton et al., 2017, p. 12) note that "Negative stereotypes and biases towards individuals in recovery lead to unfavorable employment decisions by employers. These negative opinions and thoughts generate expectancies and anticipatory beliefs based on group stigma about individuals in recovery." The disproportionate rates of alcohol and/or drugs in the LGBTQ community, the stigma attached to substance abuse and recovery, and the resultant personal, economic and community issues add to the significance of examining and giving voice to this population.

Recovery

Given the significance of the construct of "recovery" to this chapter, it is important to offer explicit articulation of its meaning. Haik et al. (2022) offer a way to consider recovery as a "problem resolution pathway" (p. 3) in which there are "assisted" ways of resolving alcoholism or addiction such as outpatient or inpatient treatment, medication that treats cravings, peer support groups such as Alcoholics Anonymous, or community-based types of support groups; and an "unassisted" resolution pathway which means that the person did not use these resources (p. 3). SAMHSA has developed its working definition of recovery: "a process of change through which individuals improve their health and wellness, live a self-directed life, and strive to reach their full potential" (n.d., p. 3). The framework of recovery set forth by SAMHSA consists of four dimensions and ten principles. The four dimensions are health, home, purpose, and community. The ten guiding principles are hope, person-driven, many pathways, holistic, peer support, relational, culture, addresses trauma, strengths/responsibility, and respect. These dimensions and principles are resonant with some of the precepts of critical Human Resource Development, in which patriarchal, cis-normative, and heteronormative assumptions and the dominance of masculine rationality (Bierema & Callahan, 2014, p. 435) are disrupted and in which technical rationality and hierarchy (Bierema & Callahan, 2014) are replaced with democratic, human-centered, equitable models of organizations. The orientation towards workplaces and job contexts that are relational and equitable, foreshadows one of the two selected career development models which will be presented later in this chapter.

Stigma

A person with a stigmatized identity has a characteristic that is discrediting (Goffman (1963). Goffman posits there are three types of stigma which include "abominations of the body, . . . blemishes of individual character, . . . and . . . tribal stigma of race, nation and religion" (p. 4).

Goffman includes addiction, alcoholism, and homosexuality as examples of the second type of stigma. With respect to workplace stigma, Romo et al. (2016, p. 336) indicate that "alcohol represents a pervasive component of U.S. social life and increasingly, the workplace." They note that in light of this pervasiveness, when one does not engage in drinking, they can be stigmatized (even if there are reasons for abstention that do not have to do with alcoholism, addiction and recovery). The ILO (2022) explains that because LGBTQ people are subjected to stigma and discrimination, they are prevented from "fully engaging in the world of work" (p. 27) and that stigma and devaluation can result in the denial of access to opportunities.

Vilsaint et al. (2020) indicate that alcohol and other drug (AOD) disorders present public health concerns and that those concerns affect other people and society to a greater extent than other public health issues such as chronic disease (high blood pressure for example). Therefore, the public health concerns related to AOD contribute to the perpetuation of stigma for people who have AOD problems (Vilsaint et al., 2020). Vilsaint et al. (2020) determined that even for those who are in recovery from AOD problems, there is stigmatization and discrimination. They observed that people in recovery are "held to a higher standard . . . treated less favorably, and being avoided by other people" (p. 9). Hatzenbuehler et al. (2013) observe that stigma "is significant source of stress and social disadvantage" (p. 813) that has deleterious effects on public health. Compound stigma, according to Rojas et al. (2019, p. 447), is "the additive and cumulative impact of being a member of one, or several, marginalized groups . . . and suffering from addiction, mental illness, and/or trauma, each of which carriers its own stigma."

Some of the factors contributing to the stigma of alcoholism and addiction include the assumption of hedonism and selfishness, and the intentional pursuit of a loss of control (Roche, 2019). Room (2005) notes the "heavy moralization and stigmatization of substance use which is defined as problematic" (p. 149). LGBTQ identity remains stigmatized, as does identity as a person in recovery. A linking thread between these two dimensions of stigma includes the ascription of causality to each. The moral implications and judgments regarding sexual minority identity, and identity as a recovering alcoholic/addict, coalesce because of a tendency or a possibility for both to be judged as personal flaws or failings.

Career Development Issues and Challenges for LGBTQ People in Recovery

The relationship between recovery and career remains unchartered terrain in several respects. Perhaps of primary consideration is the risk involved of disclosing an identity as a person in recovery (Roche et al., 2019; Van Laar et al., 2019) and the possible ramifications of explicitly acknowledging this information, particularly to those in an organization who are lacking in skill, context, or knowledge about the boundaries and the protections against employment discrimination of those in recovery. There are career development challenges for LGBTQ recovered addicts and/or alcoholics, and given the dearth of research on the subject, career development is mostly an individual proposition. Human resource development scholars including Bierema and Callahan (2014) have commented on increasing necessity for workers to "self-regulate" (p. 431) in an era in which they are "expected to manage their career development, embrace self-directed learning, and be subject to organization surveillance of their activities" (p. 431). For good or for bad, it is up to the individual to assemble the resources, skills, and competencies related to negotiating their identity in the career marketplace to successfully manage the considerations related to being a sober and clean sexual minority. Career development considerations for LGBTQ recovered alcoholics and addicts necessitate a form of development (the ability to negotiate the job markets and workplaces pervaded by heteronormative, ableist assumptions) *within* development (job-related knowledge, skills, competencies).

Training and development resources for managers and supervisors that relate to addiction and alcoholism have an understandable focus on recognizing problems that result from abuse (see Gedro et al., 2012). These resources include instructions and guides for recognizing signs of alcohol and drug abuse, and the risks associated with alcohol and drug abuse. The *prevalence* of information regarding identifying warning signs and understanding and assessing risks, and the comparative *absence* of information that de-stigmatizes alcohol and drug abuse recovery, reinforces the assumptions regarding people who suffer (and hopefully recover) from alcohol and drug abuse. For example, the Office of Personnel Management (OPM) handbook for supervisors on alcoholism in the workplace discusses considerations such as the need for the employee to attend AA meetings, have counseling, and other actions. It also discusses relapse, characterizing it as important, and as frustrating (n.d.).

The Human Resource Management lens of alcohol and drug use (AOD), addiction and recovery, tends to have a focus on surveillance, productivity, and risk management. Guidance regarding how to identify, confront and "manage" an employee who has disclosed they are a person in recovery from AOD abuse faces a shroud of stigma regarding the specter of relapse (see Becton et al., 2017) and an employee who is suspected of AOD abuse is a problem to be managed. The Office of Personnel Management (OPM) highlights that the costs of alcoholism and abuse are significant (n.d.); there is an absentee rate four to eight times higher for those who are alcoholic or abuse alcohol, that their family members are absent at greater rates than those who do not have alcoholics or alcohol abusers in their families, and that alcoholics and alcohol abusers suffer (or perhaps cause, as implied) more workplace accidents and injuries than those who are not alcoholic or abuse alcohol. Moreover, OPM highlights the issue that alcoholism and alcohol abuse are a public concern because the costs related to these issues of absenteeism, accidents and injury in the federal workplace, "are passed along directly to the taxpayer, and to each and every one of us" (n.d., para. 3).

Because negotiating the workplace as a sexual minority, combined with the identity of a person in recovery, is a subject that is thinly researched in human resources, management, leadership, or related literature, those in positions of career-related decision-making in organizations have few resources upon which to draw to create career development initiatives that take into account the considerations of this population. Gedro (2009) noted that when practitioners of human resource development have knowledge regarding LGBT career considerations including occupation and organizational selection and career management, they are in a stronger position to facilitate choice making and in helping clients understand how to negotiate the heterosexism (whether episodic or systemic) of workplace contexts. This knowledge can also provide a human resource development practitioner with deeper and more sophisticated insights regarding the challenges that may be underneath the surface of what is easily recognized about an employee or prospective employee (or manager, or leader). Career development is a concern for all in positions of decision-making in organizations, not just those who are in formal roles of human resource management or development.

The multiple types of stressors bear highlighting. Foundational to a discussion of stress for LGBTQ people is Meyer's (2003) model of minority stress which "explains the higher prevalence of mental disorders as caused by excess in social stressors related to stigma and prejudice" (p. 691). Minority stress (Velez et al., 2021) has been a consistently discussed explanation (to varying degrees) of the higher rates of alcoholism and addiction in the LGBTQ community. Being a sexual minority in organizational contexts that are heteronormative is stressful. Navigating the workplace as a person in recovery is stressful because of the ongoing challenges associated with decisions around disclosure. Stress has a longitudinal component to it as well. The more junior and novice one is in their career, the riskier it could be to disclose status as a person in recovery. For mid-career or senior career professionals, there might be stress around concealment due to the sense of lost opportunities to disrupt assumptions around alcohol. On the one hand, the higher up the career ladder one goes, the more there could be to lose by disclosing identity as a person in recovery. The calculus of this decision is personal, individual, and difficult.

Recovered LGBTQ Alcoholics and/or Addicts and Career Development: Selected Career Development Models

As Gedro (2009) observed, career development "theories use different lenses through which to understand career development, and include such dimensions as time, age, life stage, interests and aptitudes" (p. 56). Dispenza et al. (2019) noted that "foundational career theories were not explicitly constructed for sexual and gender minority persons, potentially limiting their usefulness" (p. 101). There is a paucity of models and theories that exclusively focus on sexual and gender minorities. However, there are those that problematize the heteronormative, ableist assumptions embedded in traditional, legacy career development models, and with some conceptual adaptation are helpful ways to think about this population and two are identified as relevant foundations.

The Employability-Link Model

The employability-link model (Thijssen et al., 2008) draws together the concepts of employability and employability strategies. Employability represents the "possibility to survive in the internal or external labor market" (p. 167) through different levels of analysis which have changed over time. Those levels are the societal, company, and individual perspectives. According to Thijssen et al., the important measures for employment shifted from an emphasis on government programmatic support for employers to develop the necessary qualifications for people (in the 1970s) to an emphasis on the ability for an employer to be flexible through contingent and core workers (in the 1980s) to an emphasis on the individual's ability to self-manage their career (in the 1990s). In the 1990s and beyond, the responsibility of the individual to self-manage to establish and maintain employability has become a norm and "employees . . . are expected to be ready and capable . . . to take responsibility for career choices and efforts" (p. 171). The individual's employability is comprised of the employability *radius* which represents one's ability to perform a job. According to Thijssen et al., an individual's employability *competencies* (skills) establish the extent to which the individual can apply their job skills "beyond their employability radius" (p. 173). There is also the context of the individual's employability, which means the employer, and the labor market. Thijssen et al. present three employability strategies (broadening, selling, and consuming) which can be considered at both the organizational and the individual level. Thijssen et al. note that a broadening strategy refers to providing (at the organizational level) and heavily using (at the individual level) education and training opportunities. A selling strategy refers to helping employees "find other paid jobs inside or outside the organization" (p. 175) at the organizational level; it refers to "moving themselves easily within the labor market when they are looking for another job" (p. 176) at the individual level. A consuming strategy is, at the organizational level, an exploitative use of employee talents and competencies without regard to planning for future development; at the individual level, it refers to the lack of planning and proactivity on the part of career development and is a risky strategy due to is passivity. Employability and the multi-level dimensions of society, organization, and individual analysis presents a pertinent career development framework because of the significance of the role that work plays in virtually any discussion of recovery (whether for sexual minorities or for majoritarians). Because work (employment) is one of the best predictors of positives outcomes for individuals with substance abuse disorders (SAMSA, 2021), the ability for someone to obtain and sustain employment (employability) is a pertinent lens.

How the Employability Model Informs LGBTQ Recovery and Career Development

The construct of employability aptly considers the extent to which a recovered LGBTQ alcoholic or addict has the capability to self-manage their career through the development and application of individual skills and competencies, and to market them in the job market to obtain and sustain meaningful work. Those who are employed, according to SAMSA, are likelier than those who are unemployed, to have higher rates of abstinence and to experience improvements in their quality of life. In addition to addressing economic necessity, career and work can give meaning and purpose to life. Laudet et al. (2006, in Becton et al., 2017, p. 7) "suggested employment is a key component for individuals in recovery and found a negative association between employment and relapse rates for individuals in recovery."

One's employability radius (Thijssen et al., 2008) can be affected by a myriad of factors which could include organization changes in the use of technology; leadership changes that result in the shifting of organizational strategy; the efficiency and effectiveness of the organization; and the list can go on. In summary, any external shift in a position description or set of qualifications has the potential to affect an employee's employability radius. With respect to the career development of an LGBTQ person in recovery, all of the factors that can affect one's employability radius are relevant for them as they would be for anyone and added to those factors, are considerations regarding the impact of one's recovery status. For example, for an LGBTQ person who is early in recovery, it may be more challenging to resume an occupation or profession they once held and they may have to re-enter their career at a skill or experience level lower than they held before they began recovery. Conversely, they may change careers entirely (see Gedro et al., 2012) and "eliminate their former careers as future options" (Gedro et al., 2012, p. 132). What further complicates these considerations regarding LGBTQ recovery status, and employability radius is the possibility that one might be negotiating one's emerging awareness as an LGBTQ person concurrently with their acknowledgment and acceptance that they have an issue with alcohol and/or drugs and decide to embark on a path of recovery.

This model is particularly relevant for this population. By developing one's employability radius and employability competencies, and by understanding and intentionally implementing employability strategies of broadening and selling, an LGBTQ person in recovery is arguably in a stronger position to navigate employment contexts and workplaces with more self-agency and choice whether or not they disclose either aspect of their identity and no matter how that disclosure is received. Put another way, by having a strong, current and strategic employability radius and by understanding and deploying employability strategies, one's career development is strengthened and empowered because one has the ability to be more selective.

The Psychology of Working Theory

A second career development model that is a helpful lens through which to examine LGBTQ recovered alcoholics and/or addicts and their career development is Duffy et al.'s (2016)

Psychology of Working Theory (PWT) which builds upon the Psychology of Working Framework (PWF). This model problematizes the privileged assumptions embedded in traditional career theories. "In effect, the PWF began initially as a critique of traditional career choice and development discourse, which blended with other social justice-oriented critiques that were advanced by counseling psychology scholars and practitioners" (Duffy et al., p. 128). The PWF is grounded upon principles and assumptions regarding the essential role that work plays in life, and in mental health. It rejects the notion that there is one epistemology to explain the psychological aspects of work and instead, holds up the importance of inclusivity for all who work, and for all who want to work. It suggests that work is important because it fulfills human needs for survival, connection, and self-determination (Duffy et al., 2016). The PWF privileges the position of sociocultural factors as the primary lens through which career and work considerations are to be understood no matter what one's socioeconomic status. It is a model that has a social justice emphasis. It takes into account intersectionality, privilege, and identity (Duffy et al., 2016). For these reasons, it is a useful way to draw together the intertwined, marginalized dimensions of identity for LGBTQ recovered alcoholics and addicts as they navigate their work lives. Given its emphasis on social justice, marginalization, and intersectionality (see Crenshaw, 1989), this model "sees" this population and it speaks to it.

How the PWT Informs LGBTQ Recovery and Career Development

Duffy et al. (2016) offer a framework that seeks to "explain the work-based experiences of people on the 'lower rungs of the social position ladder'" (p. 127) and that presents the predictors, moderators, and outcomes of "decent work" (p. 129). Duffy et al. posit that decent work is an "important component of well-being and access to opportunity" (p. 130) and that those who are marginalized due to their race, class, ethnicity, and sexual orientation face a set of career development considerations that are contextual. Duffy et al. indicate that "sociocultural factors must be treated as primary in understanding the career decisions and work experiences of all people" (p. 127). Predictors of securing decent work include marginalization and economic constraints which "limit the ability to secure decent work" (p. 135). According to PWT, there are moderators for these constraints: a proactive personality, critical consciousness, social support, and economic conditions. The outcomes of decent work are that needs for survival, social connection, and self-determination are met, as well as work fulfillment and well-being. The PWT sheds light on the reality of context and identity for LGBTQ people in recovery; their career experiences are situated within particular challenges (most notably, marginalization) and the model also contains insights for navigating one's career. In specific, it suggests that having a proactive personality (in short, being resilient and having "interpersonal likeability," p. 136) can facilitate career success (Duffy et al., 2016). Duffy et al. (p. 137) observe that a "proactive personality is something that propels an individual forward to change his or her environment." Critical consciousness (Duffy et al., 2016) represents one's ability to critically reflect on social and structural conditions that contribute to inequities, combined with "political efficacy" (p. 137) which means the perception that one can affect change, and finally, "critical action" (p. 137) which refers to action to address inequities. Social support (p. 137) refers to "the degree to which individuals feel supported from their family, friends, significant others . . . for coping with . . . stress and adversity" (Cohen & Willis, 1985, referenced in Duffy et al., p. 137).

LGBTQ people in recovery face a continual series of negotiations of these intertwining aspects of identity and as such, the PWT (Duffy et al., 2016) which addresses concepts such as decent work, social justice, and "real world" issues in relation to career is an important model or lens through which to consider all of the issues related therein. This model is particularly relevant for LGBTQ people in recovery, because of the centrality of the concept of decent work and the role that work plays in one's quality of life (no matter what identity). In particular, decent work plays a role in one's recovery because of the positive relationship between employment and recovery (SAMSA, 2021).

Someone newly in recovery, or who newly realized an LGBTQ identity, has at a minimum two layers of identity negotiation (sexual minority identity and identity as a person in recovery) that impact their career development. Negotiating identity in relation to career development is an ongoing iterative process. Part of the employability (Thijssen et al., 2008) proposition is one's ability to either compartmentalize or de-couple the challenges associated with being a sexual minority and being a person in recovery, so that one traverses through a career journey that is unfettered by stigma, discrimination, and other factors that impact employability. However, it is difficult to imagine a completely fixed and impermeable boundary between identity and career, because of the interpersonal interactions that are part of a workplace context as well as the other ways in which identity and disclosure are relevant aspects of one's career.

Identity Negotiation in the Workplace

Because of the confluence of discrimination and marginalization based upon intersecting identities of sexual minority status, and as a person in recovery, career development is a continual process of negotiating job markets and workplace contexts. Decisions about disclosure represent opportunities and risks, arguably in roughly equal measure. Gedro et al. (2004) discussed how lesbians negotiate workplace environments, and they presented three dimensions of negotiation: pre-screening a work context for receptivity (for LGBTQ people), coming out, and educating others. These are iterative decisions, and they are laden with communication and interpersonal strategies and skills. In addition to Gedro et al.'s work, researchers such as Clair et al. (2005), Romo et al. (2016), and Burns (2021) have investigated similar types of identity negotiations. Clair et al. note that people who have "invisible differences" (p. 79) struggle with the tensions between the decision to conceal or disclose those differences. Clair et al. explain the different types of strategies such as passing which includes the tactics that Herek (1996) described which include fabrication, concealment, and discretion. Fabrication represents the presentation of inaccurate information; concealment means hiding information, and discretion means avoidance. Conversely, revealing represents the disclosure of an invisible identity, and it is also known as coming out.

Coming out is a personal, individual decision that is made iteratively over the course of a career. Clair et al. (2005) note that there are individual and organizational antecedents that influence these decisions. Individual factors include the person's propensity toward risk taking, their self-monitoring behavior, their developmental stage, and their motives. If a person is risk averse, the tendency to not come out is higher than for a person who has an appetite for risk. Those who are high self-monitors take care to behave in ways that signal that they "fit in" in an organizational context. Those who are far along a development stage, who have become comfortable and confident with their identities, are more likely to come out. Clair explains four motives for coming out which are "maintaining self-esteem and coping, building or preserving relationships, arranging accommodations, and creating social change" (p. 88). Burns (2021) explored her journey of disclosing her identity as a person in recovery, as she traversed the tenure track in academia. Burns indicated her awareness of the risks of disclosure as a pre-tenure faculty and reflected on the journey of decision-making about coming out about her recovery.

Implications and Conclusions

Rather than waiting for the organizational conditions to be ideal, or for (well-intentioned but resource-constrained) managers, supervisors, human resource professionals, and others in decision-making positions to have an understanding and awareness of the issues, it might be a worthwhile proposition to suggest that LGBTQ people in recovery empower themselves by implementing the strategies articulated in the selected career development models.

An underlying premise of this chapter is that no one intentionally creates a work environment or situation in which someone's health or career could be compromised. However, LGBTQ people who are in recovery can experience risky situations in the job market and in the workplace. Risky situations include situational, episodic moments in which one is offered a drink at a work-related social event. They can also include broader contexts in which a person in recovery may have to explain gaps in a resume, or career changes involving recovery, or other situations that must be negotiated. In order for the stigma and marginalization of these intersecting identities to be addressed, reduced, or eliminated, there are ways to intervene at multiple levels. The cumulative effects of these episodic moments, combined with the more structural impacts to one's career, create a need to frame the intersectional status of an LGBTQ person who is a person in recovery, through a lens of career development. Otherwise, and at least in concept, all of those who fall under this umbrella remain unseen, unrecognized, and potentially underemployed or unemployed.

At an individual level, LGBTQ people in recovery could consider ways to "own" their identities in explicit ways (e.g., Burns, 2021) that disrupt tacit assumptions of heteronormality and of the invisibility of recovery. It must be acknowledged and affirmed that coming out whether it be as an LGBTQ person, a person in recovery, or both, is a personal choice. However, coming out and putting a "face" on the issues, is a way to disrupt invisibility and stigma, because hiding or concealing these identities can serve as a reinforcing loop. There are individual, micro-level ways that the stigma of being an LGBTQ person are disrupted. Flores et al. (2020) note the "contact effect" that can occur as a result of "the experience of interpersonal contact corresponds with greater support for LGBTQ rights" (p. 7). In a similar vein, disclosing one's identity as a person in recovery can disrupt negative stereotypes associated with these identities. Coming out and claiming one's identity can be a freeing and healthy way to dismantle stigma and stereotypes.

Clair et al. (2005) describe personal motives for disclosing stigmatized identities which are to maintain self-esteem, to build or preserve relationships, to arrange accommodation, and to create social change. With respect to the fourth motive—to create social change—Clair et al. indicate that "revealing can be motivated by a desire to educate others and to change social conditions at work" (p. 88) which "allows individuals to assert their identity and to challenge social norms that lead to discrimination" (p. 89). In their study of successful lesbian managers and executives, Gedro et al. (2004) determined that these "women learned they had a commitment to serving as change agents by educating others about the unique issues that corporate lesbians face" (p. 188). Sometimes, those who are members of a marginalized population take the risk of not only disclosing their identity—whether it be as a person in recovery, or an LGBTQ person, or an LGBTQ person in recovery—not only to demonstrate a sense of individual agency but also, to disrupt social stigma and quite literally put a "face" on the issue. The risks involved in doing so directly relate to career development because of the possibility that one's employability and employment contextual factors (Thijssen et al., 2008) devolve and that one's ability to obtain and secure "decent work" (see Duffy et al., 2016) becomes jeopardized.

If in a workplace or related organizational context, assumptions are allowed to go unchecked (by default, people in the organization are cis-gendered, heterosexual, and non-alcoholics or addicts), the cloak of stigmatization and marginalization likely continues. If, however, there are those who either overtly disrupt both sets of normative assumptions by demonstrating understanding and sensitivity and explicitly using LGBTQ affirming language and other markers of LGBTQ inclusion, and who create work environments (social events) that are not focused on alcohol, these assumptions can be upended.

Certainly, the response to the problem of stigma, discrimination, and prejudice cannot be reduced to a single prescription, such as having a friendly relationship with an LGBTQ person or by extension, an LGBTQ person in recovery. Van Laar et al. (2019) posit that in work settings, "identity safety can be effectively created through contextual identity affirmations, signaling that a social group is valued within this organization" (p. 9). Van Laar et al. suggest that support from an organization, for a stigmatized group, can come from those in the majority high-status group, which can signal acceptance and value and can "create new norms throughout an organization" (p. 9).

By piercing through the invisible layer of heteronormativity and lack of awareness and sensitivity toward work-related drinking, a workplace can become a more inclusive environment in which LGBTQ people in recovery do not have to negotiate their identity because these assumptions are interrupted. LGBTQ people have particular career development considerations such as occupational selection, entrance, and negotiation of the workplace as an LGBTQ person (Gedro, 2009). LGBTQ people who are in recovery, have a double stigma that they must negotiate (Brooks, 2012). As one navigates their identity development as an LGBTQ person, that trajectory may or may not coincide with the onset and development of a drinking or drug abuse problem. These two aspects of identity have the potential to complicate one's career development. One may be, for example, entirely comfortable and established in their identity as an LGBTQ person. As has been indicated previously, coming out is an iterative process, rather than a discrete event. However, what if that person's alcoholism or drug addiction reaches a peak (or perhaps better characterized, bottom), while they have already selected and begun a career? There are two tracks of identity at play, both of which can have significant implications for career development. Therefore, this chapter has presented the considerations related to being an LGBTQ person in recovery, and choices regarding career development through two selected career development models.

The Employability Model of career development describes the employability radius, employability competencies, contextual conditions, and the employability strategies (Thijssen et al., 2008). It presents important ways for LGBTQ people in recovery to approach their career development: to intentionally consider their employability radius and to develop career competencies as well as the ability to "sell" themselves in the job market. The Psychology of Working Theory suggests that a proactive personality, critical consciousness, social support, and economic conditions "moderate the paths from economic constraints and marginalization" (Duffy et al., 2016, p. 129). A fundamental linking thread in both models is the implication of intentionality, self-knowledge and awareness, proactivity, interpersonal skills, and relationships as vital to positive career and employment outcomes.

This chapter intends to move career development research into terrain that has been only thinly explored and illustrates what is missing—a shift of focus from addiction and alcoholism as a risk and a problem to be confronted (with overtones of prejudice and antipathy) and instead, to a humanistic and hopeful response to a dimension of diversity within organizations. Alcohol and substance abuse present challenges, suffering, and impediments to possibilities and productive outcomes on multiple levels.

The context of their career development decisions and negotiations for LGBTQ people in recovery includes issues that are complex and fluid. There are persistent questions that shroud decision-making for this population. For example, to what extent does an LGBTQ person in recovery have the ability to remain in a profession or occupation through the span of a career? Does someone have the ability to remain with an employer during and after "hitting bottom" and beginning a journey of recovery? Alternatively, should a person "reset" their career, and re-skill for a new career? Wherever a person is on their journey of LGBTQ identity and recovery, there are decisions to be made, and negotiations to be done. No matter what the employment context the implications for being LGBTQ and in recovery are salient. If there are gaps in a resume, or if someone has lost the ability to practice a profession and then changes professions, what type of guidance exists in career development research and practice, to help inform the person?

By having awareness that there are employees in an organization who may have aspects of their identity that may or may not be visible or discernible, there are intersections between those identities and the workplace. For LGBTQ people, there are issues of disclosure in the recruitment and selection phase, in the onboarding phase, and then in career development within the organization phase. An employee may or may not feel comfortable disclosing their family configuration, and they may or may not "fit" with respect to gender norms. This could affect career prospects. With respect to being a person in recovery, there are decisions to be made around disclosure there too. The workplace can be a location of varying degrees of heteronormativity, and it can be a location of implicit pressure to drink. Cocktail hours, welcome receptions, retirement parties, and other occasions that might call for a decision about how to turn down a drink, or for those in early stages of recovery, may present peril to even attend. There is a potential risk for not attending work-related functions, because one might miss opportunities to network or further one's professional reputation. There might be career limiting (career inhibiting) effects of coming out as LGBTQ, and/or coming out as a person in recovery. There is a level of self-acceptance, confidence, and then skill building that serve an LGBTQ person in recovery well, to be able to have a sense of internal guidance around such decisions and strategies.

References

Adams, J., Asiasiga, L., & Neville, S. (2021). Justifications for heavy alcohol use among gender and sexually diverse people. *Global Public Health*, *17*(9), 2018–2033. https://doi.org/10.1080/17441692.2021.1957492

Becton, A. B., Chenc, R. K., & Paul, T. M. (2017). A second chance: Employers' perspectives in hiring individuals in addiction recovery. *Journal of Applied Rehabilitation Counseling*, *48*(1), 6–15.

Bierema, L. L., & Callahan, J. L. (2014). Transforming HRD: A framework for critical HRD practice. *Advances in Developing Human Resources*, *16*(4), 429–444. https://doi.org/10.1177/1523422314543818

Brooks, M. K. (2012). *Legal issues for programs treating LGBT clients: In substance abuse and mental health services administration center for substance abuse treatment*. A Provider's Introduction to Substance Abuse Treatment for Lesbian, Gay, Bisexual, and Transgender Individuals. https://store.samhsa.gov/sites/default/files/SAMHSA_Digital_Download/sma12-4104.pdf

Burns, V. F. (2021). The sober professor: Reflections on the sober paradox, sober phobia, and disclosing an alcohol recovery identity in academia. *Contemporary Drug Problems*, *48*(3), 223–240.

Clair, J. A., Beatty, J. E., & Maclean, T. L. (2005). Out of sight by not out of mind: Managing invisible social identities in the workplace. *The Academy of Management Review*, *30*(1), 78–95.

Cohen, S., & Wills, T. A. (1985). Stress, social support, and the buffering hypothesis. *Psychological Bulletin*, *98*, 310–357. http://dx.doi.org/10.1037/0033-2909.98.2.310

Crenshaw, K. (1989). Demarginalizing the Intersection of Race and Sex: A Black Feminist Critique of Antidiscrimination Doctrine, Feminist Theory and Antiracist Politics. *University of Chicago Legal Forum*, *1989*(1), 139–167.

Dispenza, F., Brennaman, C., Harper, L. S., Harrigan, M. A., Chastain, T. E., & Procter, J. E. (2019). Career development of sexual and gender minority persons living with disabilities. *The Counseling Psychologist*, *47*(1), 98–128. https://doi.org/10.1177/0011000018819425

Duffy, R. D., Blustein, D. L., Diemer, M. A., & Autin, K. L. (2016). The psychology of working theory. *Journal of Counseling Psychology, 63*(2), 127–148. https://doi.org/10.1037/cou0000140

Fish, J. N., & Pasley, K. (2015). Sexual (minority) trajectories, mental health, and alcohol use: A longitudinal study of youth as they transition to adulthood. *Journal of Youth and Adolescence, 44*, 1508–1527. https://doi.org/10.1007/s10964-015-0280-6

Flores, A. R., Mallory, C., & Conron, K. J. (2020). Public attitudes about emergent issues in LGBTQ rights: Conversion therapy and religious refusals. *Research and Politics, 7*(4), 1–9. https://doi.org/10.1177/2053168020966874

Gedro, J. (2009). LGBT career development. *Advances in Developing Human Resources, 11*(1), 54–66.

Gedro, J., Cervero, R., & Johnson-Bailey, J. (2004). How lesbians learn to negotiate the heterosexism of corporate America. *Human Resource Development International, 7*(2), 181–195. https://doi.org/10.1080/1367886042000243790

Gedro, J., Mercer, F., & Iodice, J. D. (2012). Recovered alcoholics and career development: Implications for human resource development. *Human Resource Development Quarterly, 23*, 129–132.

Gedro, J., & Mizzi, R. C. (2014). Feminist theory and queer theory: Implications for HRD research and practice. *Advances in Developing Human Resources, 16*(4), 445–456.

Goffman, E. (1963). *Stigma: Notes on the management of a spoiled identity.* Simon and Schuster.

Haik, A. K., Greene, M. C., Bergman, B. G., Abry, A. W., & Kelly, J. F. (2022). Recovery among sexual minorities in the United States population: Prevalence, characteristics, quality of life and functioning compared with heterosexual majority. *Drug and Alcohol Dependence, 232*, 1–9. https://doi.org/10.1016/j.drugalcdep.2022.109290.d

Hatzenbuehler, M. L., Phelan, J. C., & Link, B. G. (2013). Stigma as a fundamental cause of population health inequalities. *American Journal of Public Health, 103*(5), 813–821. https://doi.org/10.2105/AJPH.2012.301069

Herek, G. M. (1996). Why tell if you are not asked? Self-disclosure, intergroup contact, and heterosexuals' attitudes toward lesbians and gay men. In G. M. Herek, J. B. Jobe, & R. M. Carney (Eds.), *Out in force: Sexual orientation and the military* (pp. 197–225). University of Chicago Press.

Human Rights Campaign. (2022). *Corporate equality index.* https://reports.hrc.org/corporate-equality-index-2022?_ga=2.237565632.1755204291.1662496524-968465314.1651598690#rating-system-methodology

International Labour Organization. (2022). *Inclusion of lesbian, gay, bisexual, transgender, intersex and queer (LGBTIQ+) persons in the world: A learning guide.* www.ilo.org/global/WCMS_846108/lang-en/index.htm

Laudet, A. B., Morgen, K., & White, W. L. (2006). The role of social supports, spirituality, religiousness, life meaning and affiliation with 12-step fellowships in quality of life satisfaction among individuals in recovery from alcohol and drug problems. *Alcoholism Treatment Quarterly, 24*, 33–73.

Link, B. G., Yang, L. H., Phelan, J. C., & Collins, P. Y. (2004). Measuring mental illness stigma. *Schizophrenia Bulletin, 30*, 511–541.

McCabe, S. E., Bostwick, W. B., Hughes, T. L., West, B. T., & Boyd, C. J. (2010). The relationship between discrimination and substance use disorders among lesbian, gay, and bisexual adults in the United States. *American Journal of Public Health, 100*(1), 1946–1952.

McFadden, C. (2015). Lesbian, gay, bisexual, and transgender careers and human resource development: A systematic literature review. *Human Resource Development Review, 14*(2), 125–162. https://doi.org/10.1177/1534484314549456

Meyer, I. H. (2003). Prejudice, social stress, and mental health in lesbian, gay, and bisexual populations: Conceptual issues and research evidence. *Psychological Bulletin, 129*(5), 674–697. https://doi.org/10.1037/0033-2909.129.5.674

Ng, E. S., & Rumens, N. (2017). Diversity and inclusion for LGBT workers: Current issues and new horizons for research. *Canadian Journal of Administrative Sciences, 34*(2), 109–120. https://doi.org/10.1002/cjas.1443

Office of Personnel Management. (n.d.). *Alcoholism in the workplace: A handbook for supervisors.* www.opm.gov/policy-data-oversight/worklife/reference-materials/alcoholism-in-the-workplace-a-handbook-for-supervisors/#Alcoholism

Procknow, G., & Rocco, T. S. (2016). The unheard, unseen, and often forgotten: An examination of disability in the human resource development literature. *Human Resource Development Review, 15*(4), 379–403. https://doi.org/10.1177/1534484316671194

Roche, A., Kostandinov, V., & Pidd, K. (2019). The stigma of addiction in the workplace. In J. D. Avery & J. J. Avery (Eds.), *The stigma of addiction: An essential guide.* Springer International Publishing AG.

Rojas, J. I., Leckie, R., Hawks, E. M., Holster, J., Del Carmen Trapp, M., & Ostermeyer, B. K. (2019). Compounded stigma in LGBTQ+ people: A framework for understanding the relationship between substance use disorders, mental illness, trauma, and sexual minority status. *Psychiatric Annals, 49*(10), 446–452.

Romo, L. K., Dinsmore, D. R. & Watterson, T. C. (2016) "Coming out" as an alcoholic: how former problem drinkers negotiate disclosure of their nondrinking identity, *Health Communication, 31*:3, 336-345, DOI: 10.1080/10410236.2014.954090

Room, R. (2005). Stigma, social inequality, and alcohol and drug use. *Drug and Alcohol Review, 24*, 143–155.

Ruppert, R., Kattari, S. K., & Sussman, S. (2021). Review: Prevalence of addictions among transgender and gender diverse subgroups. *International Journal of Environmental Research and Public Health, 18*(8843). https://doi.org/10.3390/ijerph18168843

Ruppert, R., Sussman, S., & Kattari, S. K. (2020). Prevalence and co-occurrence of addictions among sexual minority subgroups. *Annals of LGBTQ Public and Population Health, 1*, 210–248.

Schilt, K., & Westbrook, L. (2009). Doing gender, doing heteronormativity: "Gender normals," transgender people, and the social maintenance of heterosexuality. *Gender & Society, 23*(4), 440–464.

Substance abuse and mental health services administration: Substance use disorders recovery with a focus on employment and education. (2021). HHS Publication No. PEP21-PL-Guide-6. National Mental Health and Substance Use Policy Laboratory. https://store.samhsa.gov/sites/default/files/SAMHSA_Digital_Download/pep21-pl-guide-6.pdf

Substance Abuse and Mental Health Services Administration (SAMHSA). (n.d.). *SAMHSA's working definition of recovery*. https://store.samhsa.gov/sites/default/files/d7/priv/pep12-recdef.pdf

Thijssen, J. L., Van Der Heijden, B. I. J. M., & Rocco, T. S. (2008). Toward the employability-link model: Current employment transition to future employment perspectives. *Human Resource Development Review, 7*(2), 165–183. https://doi.org/10.1177/1534484308314955

U.S. Department of Health and Human Services. Substance Abuse and Mental Health Services Administration Center for Substance Abuse Treatment. (2012). *A provider's introduction to substance abuse treatment for lesbian, gay, bisexual and transgender individuals*. Publication ID SMA12-4104. https://store.samhsa.gov/product/Providers-Introduction-Substance-Abuse-Treatment-Lesbian-Gay-Bisexual-Transgender/SMA12-4104

Van Laar, C., Meeussen, L., Veldman, J., Van Grootel, S., Sterk, N., & Jacobs, C. (2019). Coping with stigma in the workplace: Understanding the role of threat regulation, supportive factors, and potential hidden costs. *Frontiers in Psychology, 10*(1879), 1–21. https://doi.org/10.3389/fpsyg.2019.01879

Velez, B. L., Adames, C. N., Lei, N., & Kerman, M. E. (2021). A content analysis of psychological research on vocational issue among sexual minority people. *Psychology of Sexual Orientation and Gender Diversity, 8*(3), 344–364. https://doi.org/10.1037/sgd0000496

Vilsaint, C. L., Hoffman, L. A., & Kelly, J. F. (2020). Perceived discrimination in addiction recovery: Assessing the prevalence, nature, and correlates using a novel measure in a U.S. national sample. *Drug Alcohol Depend, 206*, 1–19. https://doi.org/10.1016/j.drugalcdep.2019.107667

Warner, M. (Ed.). (1993). *Fear of a queer planet: Queer politics and social theory*. University of Minnesota Press.

33

BREAKING THE MOLD OR MAKING THE MOLD? LGBTQ EMPLOYEE NETWORKS AND THE MANAGERIALIST AGENDA

Ciarán McFadden

LGBTQ networks or employee resource groups (ERGs) have become a common feature within many organizations. As acceptance and inclusion of LGBTQ people grows, so too do the efforts of organizations to better promote LGBTQ diversity in their workplaces. LGBTQ employees routinely benefit from a range of initiatives aimed at improving workplace inclusion (McFadden, 2015) and legislative protections in many countries. In the last decade, many medium to large organizations in the West have introduced LGBTQ employee networks, including government organizations (e.g., Irish Civil Service, Dept. of Energy GLOBE ERG, Scottish Parliament, Welsh Government); broadcasters (e.g., OUT@NBCUniversal, Channel 4's 4Pride); major tech companies (e.g., Microsoft's GLEAM, LinkedIn's out@in); management consulting firms (e.g., McKinsey's GLAM, EY's Unity); and financial services companies (e.g., Deutsche Bank's dbPride; Citi Pride), among others.

The employee network plays a variety of roles within the organization, and it is thus unsurprising that they have become a common tool in attempts to promote a more inclusive and welcoming environment for LGBTQ employees. Their benefits have been promoted by LGBTQ rights charities and advocacy groups like Stonewall (UK) and Human Rights Campaign (USA): their *Workplace Equality Index* and *Corporate Equality Index*, respectively, both include an employee network as a criterion. The functions of LGBTQ employee networks can vary, but usually coalesce around providing a social outlet (Githens & Aragon, 2009; McFadden & Crowley-Henry, 2018), visibility for LGBTQ employees (Colgan & McKearney, 2012), a formal or informal development and inclusion tool (Githens, 2009), and a voice mechanism (Colgan & McKearney, 2012; McFadden & Crowley-Henry, 2018; McNulty et al., 2018).

However, despite their ubiquity within Western organizations, these groups remain underresearched, as noted by Welbourne et al. (2017). As a recognizable 'unit' within the corporate landscape, with the aforementioned power to act as a social outlet, voice mechanism and inclusion tool, it is therefore surprising that they have escaped full scrutiny within the business and management literature. As Githens and Aragon (2009) and Raeburn (2004) highlight, these networks once provided a variety of purposes, were often employee-created and led, and could have overtly political or radical objectives. However, more and more organizations, in fulfilling their diversity and inclusion aims, and perhaps in response to guidance from groups like HRC and Stonewall, appear to be implementing the creation and governance of these networks

 DOI: 10.4324/9781003128151-39

themselves (Foldy, 2019; Welbourne et al., 2017). In many cases, organizational resources and branding are used, and a senior manager acts as a champion for the network and its aims (Foldy, 2019). The potential for these networks to provide a critical, objective and independent voice in the workplace, which may at times run counter to the aims and views of management, could therefore be diminishing. In addition, the network's heavy involvement—and in many cases sponsorship—from their host organization may lead to a corporate normalization of LGBTQ issues in these spaces.

A recurring debate within discussions of diversity and inclusion, both in research and in practice, is the relative importance and merits of the 'business case for diversity' compared to the social, moral and ethical imperative to ensure inclusivity in organizations (Robinson & Dechant, 1997; Tomlinson & Schwabenland, 2010). Financial rationalizations for inclusion efforts can often instrumentalize these practices, while rendering minority employees as a tokenistic means to pursue a normative agenda (Noon, 2007). However, one might argue that, despite the often market-driven incentivization for inclusion practices, the benefits they provide for minority employees, such as visibility and voice (Colgan & McKearney, 2012; McFadden & Crowley-Henry, 2018) justify their current approach and manifestation, regardless of the primary underlying motivation (Lloren & Parini, 2017).

The theoretical underpinning of this chapter is queer theory, which is used to examine the power distribution involved in the introduction and maintenance of LGBTQ networks in organizations, as well as its surrounding discourse. As de Sousa (2017) highlights, queer theory combats the essentializing formation and perception of gender and sexuality and instead positions identities as unstable categories. Queer theory also questions the binarization of gender and sexuality identities (e.g., hetero/homosexual) and regards the identities as a site of potential social and political organization (de Sousa, 2017). Rumens et al. (2018) outline how queer theory 'is widely regarded as a resolutely anti-normative mode of politics because it interrogates and seeks to transform social norms and relations of power' (p. 594). Queer theory, therefore, rejects and problematizes universalist identity categories (de Sousa, 2017; Gedro & Mizzi, 2014) and focuses upon the power relations (through a Foucauldian lens) inherent in the construction and maintenance of these categories (Seidman, 2006). It is thus an appropriate lens through which to examine LGBTQ networks, which bring together a group of people under an umbrella categorization. In using a queer theoretical lens, one is prompted to question the true objectives of such networks, to interrogate the prevailing, taken-for-granted logic behind their development and popularity, and to problematize issues concerning their construction and structuring.

This chapter will first explore employee networks, their current forms, objectives and goals. Then, the potential of these groups and their members to impartially critique their host organizations' plans and policies will be discussed. Queer theory will be used as a lens though which to explore the corporate discourse surrounding LGBTQ networks, and how these networks may contribute to a normative reconstruction of LGBTQ issues in the workplace. Lastly, recommendations will be given for the networks themselves.

LGBTQ Networks—Forms and Functions

Colgan and McKearney (2012) point out that LGBTQ activists led the formation of informal 'company networks' and union groups from the 1980s onwards in the UK; these were informal, employee-constructed and led, with a focus on the rights and concerns of the employees. In contrast, Raeburn (2004) outlines the rise of the employee network/employee resource group in the USA—formal, management or HR-constructed and led, with an ostensible dual-focus on the concerns of employees and goals of the organization. This shift reflects the similar transformation of the typical 'equal-opportunities' approach, with the equality of employee rights as its main concern, to the now ubiquitous 'diversity management' approach, concerned with utilizing individual difference to help meet organizational objectives (McDougall, 1996; Tatli, 2010). The LGBTQ network has been increasingly co-opted as a tool for organizations to improve their diversity management efforts, and this has no doubt been spurred by advocacy groups and charities such as Stonewall and Human Rights Campaign, who include employee networks in their criteria for their employer ranking lists. While union groups continue to focus on social change (Colgan & McKearney, 2012), the persistent decline in unionization over the past four decades in the UK (Department for Business, Energy & Industrial Strategy, 2018), in the USA (Wright, 2016) and in many other countries around the world (Visser, 2006) renders these groups potentially less influential in comparison to their organization-backed counterparts.

The Human Rights Campaign (2020) discusses a number of potential functions for LGBTQ employee networks, including lobbying for improved LGBTQ-related policies within the organization, evaluating diversity training programs with regards to LGBTQ-inclusiveness, improving outreach to potential LGBTQ employees and leadership opportunities for younger LGBTQ employees, and encouraging the organization to take part in pro-LGBTQ political action. HRC's UK counterpart, Stonewall (2020), promotes similar goals: employee networks can offer peer-to-peer support by reducing feelings of loneliness and providing a social outlet; raise awareness by promoting better understanding and visibility of LGBTQ issues; and scrutinize the organization's policies and processes with regards to LGBTQ inclusion.

The small amount of academic literature regarding LGBTQ employee networks reflects these functions, adds a few more, and mainly represent a more nuanced and detailed exploration of their actual efficacy and usage. The particular objectives and goals of an LGBTQ network would most likely be a reflection of how and why it was set up in the first place, and its overall approach and stance towards management. Githens and Aragon (2009) provide a comprehensive overview of differing approaches to network formation and style, with some emphasizing social change (through either subversive action or through official channels) and others emphasizing organizational effectiveness (informal, unofficial groups of LGBT employees, and conventional LGBT employee resource groups).

A number of papers exploring LGBTQ employee networks explore the concept of employee voice. McFadden and Crowley-Henry (2018) discuss how employee networks can work to prevent feelings of isolation that LGBTQ employees can face in the organization, and act as a voice mechanism through which LGBTQ employees can report incidents of discrimination or comment on the organization's commitment to LGBTQ inclusion. However, the network's potential as a voice mechanism may not be realized in an environment where employees distrust management, and the voice function may not be used by LGBTQ employees who take a different approach to their identity management (McFadden & Crowley-Henry, 2018). Colgan and McKearney (2012) retrace the history of both LGBT trade union groups and LGBT employee networks, and also look at the voice capabilities of LGBTQ networks. They find that employee networks represent a mechanism for community and visibility, signaling the organization's commitment to inclusion. Finally, in a more specific context, McNulty et al. (2018) discuss how LGBTQ ERGs act as a voice mechanism in relation to LGBTQ expatriates (or potential expatriates) and their international career assignments. The authors also consider silence, and find that LGBTQ employees may not join ERGs as result of stereotypes and mixed opinions about the efficacy of the network as a mechanism for voice, and instead engage in silence (Donaghey et al., 2011).

Discussion

In utilizing a queer lens in a discussion of LGBTQ networks, a number of sites of investigation and pertinent questions arise. First, do the networks, in bringing together employees of varying (non-heterosexual and/or non-cisgender) identities, conflate the manifold challenges and issues that face the respective groups? Next, do the power relations inherent in the creation of a network have the potential to silence, rather than amplify, the voices of LGBTQ employees? Lastly, one must question to what end the creation of an LGBTQ network serves—are they an extension of a managerialist agenda, or is their creation prompted solely to benefit the respective members? These questions are explored in the following.

Silencing Voice?

Central to queer theory, as discussed earlier, is the examination of power relations, particularly in considering identity categorization. The gathering of employees together into one group does, naturally, form a potential voice mechanism, through which grievances specific to that group can be heard (McFadden & Crowley-Henry, 2018). While this is a discussion of voice, similar to those found in industrial relations literature (e.g., Hirschman, 1970), this discussion also concerns power. A queer theoretical lens prompts us to consider about how power is used (and perhaps *misused*) within this context.

As mentioned earlier, a number of authors have discussed how LGBTQ employee networks can act as voice mechanisms (McFadden & Crowley-Henry, 2018; McNulty et al., 2018), however, in contrast to groups like Stonewall and HRC, have added caveats related to its effectiveness. In examining power relations, therefore, one can argue that the degree of freedom that an LGBTQ network has to use collective voice is surely dependent upon the degree of separation that exists between the network and the organization. In their study of how LGBTQ employee resource groups can act as a voice mechanism for LGBTQ expatriates, McNulty et al. (2018, p. 840) highlight that 'It appears management have a direct controlling relationship over the functioning of ERG as a voice mechanism', with some employees feeling that they cannot use the network's voice function if it is run by or heavily linked to management. Likewise, Githens and Aragon (2009) report that some employee networks are explicitly forbidden by their organization to engage in any lobbying of executives. With this in mind, the use of an employee network as a reliable and helpful voice mechanism for LGBTQ employees may be diminishing (or may not have been that effective in the first place); instead of representing a trusted band of like-minded employees to which one can turn, the employee network may risk being seen as an extension of management power. Indeed, Colgan and McKearney's (2012) discussion of networks compares and contrasts them to LGBT union groups, and highlights the distrust that the latter have with regard to the former. While union LGBT groups were built on the social justice case for diversity, networks were suspected of delivering only commercial objectives and a managerial agenda.

As more and more organizations decide to set up and/or sponsor a new LGBTQ network, following best practice and advice from the Human Rights Campaign or similar advocacy groups, there lies a danger that they will use their power (whether unknowingly or deliberately) to construct a group that will solely serve business needs, rather than the inherent (and potentially disruptive) needs of the employees themselves. Stonewall's Diversity Champions program (offering 'best-practice' advice to member organizations on LGBTQ issues) has been criticized for not taking a pluralist approach, instead focusing on the business case (Colgan & McKearney, 2012). The amalgamation of diverse identities under one uniform category may lead to a normalization of the range of topics that such a group may approach, with an over-focus on issues that involve all (or the majority of) members, regardless of relative urgency and/or importance—potentially leading to the reduction or silencing of voices belonging to those in statistically smaller subgroups (e.g., trans, non-binary). If employees mistrust the network regarding its ability as a genuine voice mechanism, the issues that are brought up may be limited to certain 'acceptable' topics (i.e., those which center around management/organizational objectives) or be presented in a more hesitant, muted manner.

Normalization of Issues

As Colgan (2016, p. 525) points out, 'LGBT people are not a "unified" social group', and instead of viewing LGBTQ employees as a homogenous cohort, we must appreciate the differences in ethnicity, class, culture, occupation, religion, etc. This heterogeneity extends to the subgroups within the LGBTQ umbrella grouping. While there is a social and historical association between the individual groups (McFadden, 2015), there are certain differences that may make the operationalization of LGBTQ employee groups, and the focus of their activities, difficult to refine. For example, trans employees face differing forms, and in many cases increased levels, of discrimination in the workplace than their lesbian and gay peers, and may face the additional issue of transitioning in the workplace (Collins et al., 2015; McFadden, 2020), as well as increasingly hostile media representations in the USA (Dhanani & Totton, 2023) and UK (Montiel-McCann, 2022) in particular. There is evidence to suggest that, while gay men face salary discrimination compared to heterosexual men (Badgett et al., 2009), lesbian women incur a salary premium in comparison to heterosexual women (Blandford, 2003) but still suffer from the gender pay gap and other gender-based discrimination, although these findings are influenced by other factors such as relationship status and age (Allegretto & Arthur, 2001; Daneshvary et al., 2009; Gedro et al., 2007; Martell, 2019). Bisexual employees face specific forms of stigmatization, such as biphobia, bierasure and other harmful stereotyping (Israel, 2018; Köllen, 2013; Monro, 2015) while trans employees face specific forms of both formal and informal discrimination that lesbians, bisexuals and gay men do not (McFadden, 2020). Depending on the type of industry and the gender-related stereotypes that exist therein, the respective groups may face differing challenges from one another (e.g., Collins, 2013; Tilcsik et al., 2015; Wright, 2008) and within each group itself, when one considers intersectional identities. In addition, little research has been conducted on the specific workplace and career challenges facing other queer identities, such as pansexual, asexual, and agender (McFadden & Crowley-Henry, 2016).

Therefore, a multitude of complex and differing issues face each group under the LGBTQ umbrella term. One may thus question how, and if, LGBTQ employee networks can accurately represent its intended membership without introducing an element of normalization—what Foucault (1975) describes as the process through which behaviors, concepts and actions become taken-for-granted. A danger arises, in the construction of an 'LGBTQ' employee group, which suggests a clarity of purpose and a singularity of focus that may not be, in actuality, achievable or effective. These groups may therefore only have the remit to address issues that affect every group, if indeed they are tasked with addressing these issues at all. What is seen as appropriate to devote effort to becomes defined by the resources (time, money, etc.) allocated to the group, which in many cases are, of course, determined by the organization. In such cases, one may suspect that the deeper issues affecting the employees will continue to be unaddressed, while organizational issues, which by definition affect everyone in the network and are the main focus of management, become the main focus (Calvard et al., 2020). Spurred by both the narrowing down of the 'appropriate' range of issues and increasing control from management, the process of normalization of LGBTQ networks may be underway.

Recommendations

A Room of One's Own

The aforementioned discussion suggested that employee networks, in including every non-heterosexual and non-cisgender or gender non-conforming employee in their proposed group membership, may risk being stretched in too many directions and therefore less able to meaningfully address issues and challenges affecting each of the subgroups that make up the LGBTQ umbrella category. This is compounded by a potential increase in the amount of focus given to organizational goals, to the detriment of employee concerns.

On the other hand, a splintering of the LGBTQ employee network into component networks (e.g., a trans employee network, a lesbian employee network, and a gay male network) is evidently unwieldy, and would no doubt suffer from a lack of resources, membership, and momentum. There must exist, therefore, a middle ground wherein employee concerns can be addressed while still retaining the support of the organization (or at least, not seek management backlash). To achieve this, it may be worthwhile to explore alternative ways of organizing employee groups—such as those described by Githens and Aragon (2009). While the taken-for-granted logic for anyone seeking to form a group in an organization may be to form an 'official' employee network, alternative forms, like informal unofficial groups or even subversive radical groups may suit better, depending on the context. With an unofficial group, the organization and its priorities does not have to be the main focus, if at all. Instead, the focus of the network can shift and evolve, as befits the circumstances facing the members themselves, who are not beholden to address the business case. Of course, not all employees may feel comfortable doing this—as Bierema (2005) finds in her study of a women's employee network that eventually failed, members often did not raise their voices because of fear, denial, exhaustion, or frustration.

Alternatively, a structure representing a compromise between management goals and employee goals (which indeed may not always be at odds) could be a feasible, yet unorthodox middle-ground. Management could, perhaps, take a 'hands-off' approach to the goals and daily running of a network, while still being able to call upon the network for relevant advice, input, and representation with EDI-related policies, practices, and events. This allows greater self-determination and independence for the network yet enables them to 'earn their keep' with respect to getting a workload allocation and resources from the organization. Such an arrangement would no doubt be experimental, contentious, and would require careful set-up and ongoing monitoring, but may represent an option that can ultimately suit the interests of both parties.

A Voice of One's Own

As mentioned earlier, the closeness with which LGBTQ networks exist in relation to the human resource department and senior management may compromise the network's ability to act as a genuine voice mechanism for its employees, if the subject matter is a critique of the organization/management or is deemed to run counter to the aims of the organization.

However, it is likely that there would not be quite so many LGBTQ networks in the first place, if it were not for the resources (and, perhaps, validity and recognition) that are afforded to them from the organization. In addition, employees may not want to act entirely outside of the organization's sphere of influence, and set up groups like those suggested earlier. In cases like this, a challenge arises—to create an LGBTQ network that nevertheless exists and works outside of organizational control, and in doing so retains its ability to act as an independent and if necessary critical entity.

How does one go about doing this? Buy-in, if not input, from senior management is most likely important; the onus is on whoever is facilitating the network's creation or separation from management control (be that the HR department or the employees themselves) to stress the importance of this self-determination. While surely an ethical motive in itself, the justification can, if necessary, be espoused in financial and productivity-related terms also—having voice within organizations is linked to employees being more engaged (Rees et al., 2013) and committed (Farndale et al., 2011). At the employee end, a certain amount of self-direction is perhaps needed, with manager not (or no longer) 'calling the shots', as in other organizations.

Conclusion

This chapter has explored, using queer theory as a guide, how power may influence the construction, operation and functionality of LGBTQ networks in contemporary organizations. From organically growing a result of employee organizing in an attempt to improve their workplace conditions, employee networks are in danger of becoming a managerialist tool that is used only to further the organization's aims. While LGBTQ charities and groups advocate the introduction and championing of employee networks as a way of positively influencing the work lives of LGBTQ employees, there is a risk that the business case upon which most of their recommendations are built is pulling focus from the moral, ethical and social obligations that an organization has to its employees. To combat this, an LGBTQ network must try to keep organizational interference, in whatever form that comes, at bay, and strive to best fulfill its duty to its members.

References

Allegretto, S. A., & Arthur, M. M. (2001). An empirical analysis of homosexual/heterosexual male earnings differentials: Unmarried and unequal? *ILR Review, 54*(3), 631–646.

Badgett, M. V. L., Sears, B., Lau, H. S., & Ho, D. (2009). Bias in the workplace: Consistent evidence of sexual orientation and gender identity discrimination 1998–2008. *Chicago-Kent Law Review, 84*(2), 559–595.

Bierema, L. L. (2005). Women's networks: A career development intervention or impediment? *Human Resource Development International, 8*(2), 207–224.

Blandford, J. M. (2003). The nexus of sexual orientation and gender in the determination of earnings. *ILR Review, 56*(4), 622–642.

Calvard, T., O'Toole, M., & Hardwick, H. (2020). Rainbow lanyards: Bisexuality, queering and the corporatisation of LGBT inclusion. *Work, Employment and Society, 34*(2), 356–368.

Colgan, F. (2016). LGBT company network groups in the UK: Tackling opportunities and complexities in the workplace. In T. Köllen (Ed.), *Sexual orientation and transgender issues in organizations* (pp. 525–538). Springer.

Colgan, F., & McKearney, A. (2012). Visibility and voice in organisations: Lesbian, gay, bisexual and transgendered employee networks. *Equality, Diversity and Inclusion: An International Journal, 31*(4), 359–378.

Collins, J. C. (2013). Stress and safety for gay men at work within masculinized industries. *Journal of Gay & Lesbian Social Services, 25*(3), 245–268.

Collins, J. C., McFadden, C., Rocco, T. S., & Mathis, M. K. (2015). The problem of transgender marginalization and exclusion: Critical actions for human resource development. *Human Resource Development Review, 14*(2), 205–226.

Daneshvary, N., Waddoups, C. J., & Wimmer, B. S. (2009). Previous marriage and the lesbian wage premium. *Industrial Relations, a Journal of Economy and Society, 48*(3), 432–453.

Department for Business, Energy & Industrial Strategy. (2018). *Trade union membership: Statistical bulletin.* Department for Business, Energy & Industrial Strategy.

de Sousa, E. M. (2017). Where is queer theory in organizational studies? *Sociology International Journal, 1*(4), 127–134.

Dhanani, L. Y., & Totton, R. R. (2023). Have you heard the news? The effects of exposure to news about recent transgender legislation on transgender youth and young adults. *Sexuality Research and Social Policy,* 1–15. https://doi.org/10.1007/s13178-023-00810-6

Donaghey, J., Cullinane, N., Dundon, T., & Wilkinson, A. (2011). Reconceptualising employee silence: Problems and prognosis. *Work, Employment and Society, 25*(1), 51–67.

Farndale, E., Van Ruiten, J., Kelliher, C., & Hope-Hailey, V. (2011). The influence of perceived employee voice on organizational commitment: An exchange perspective. *Human Resource Management, 50*(1), 113–129.

Foldy, E. G. (2019). Employee resource groups: What we know about their impact on individuals and organizations. *Academy of Management Proceedings, 2019.* https://doi.org/10.5465/AMBPP.2019.10633abstract

Foucault, M. (1975). *Discipline and punish.* Vintage Books.

Gedro, J. A., Cervero, R. M., & Johnson-Bailey, J. (2007). How lesbians learn to negotiate the heterosexism of corporate America. *Human Resource Development International, 7*(2), 181–195.

Gedro, J. A., & Mizzi, R. C. (2014). Feminist theory and queer theory: Implications for HRD research and practice. *Advances in Developing Human Resources, 16*(4), 445–456.

Githens, R. P. (2009). Capitalism, identity politics, and queerness converge: LGBT employee resource groups. *New Horizons in Adult Education and Human Resource Development, 23*(3), 18–31.

Githens, R. P., & Aragon, S. R. (2009). LGBT employee groups: Goals and organizational structures. *Advances in Developing Human Resources, 11*(1), 121–135.

Hirschman, A. O. (1970). *Exit, voice, and loyalty: Responses to decline in firms, organizations, and states.* Harvard University Press.

Human Rights Campaign. (2020). *Establishing an employee resource group.* Retrieved November 14, 2020, from www.hrc.org/resources/establishing-an-employee-resource-group

Israel, T. (2018). Bisexuality: From margin to center. *Psychology of Sexual Orientation and Gender Diversity, 5*(2), 233–242.

Köllen, T. (2013). Bisexuality and diversity management—addressing the *B* in LGBT as a relevant "sexual orientation" in the workplace. *Journal of Bisexuality, 13*(1), 122–137.

Lloren, A., & Parini, L. (2017). How LGBT-supportive workplace policies shape the experience of lesbian, gay men, and bisexual employees. *Sexuality Research and Social Policy, 14,* 289–299.

Martell, M. E. (2019). Age and the new lesbian earnings penalty. *International Journal of Manpower, 41*(6), 649–670.

McDougall, M. (1996). Equal opportunities versus managing diversity: Another challenge for public sector management? *International Journal of Public Sector Management, 9*(5–6), 62–72.

McFadden, C. (2015). Lesbian, gay, bisexual and transgender careers and human resource development: A systematic literature review. *Human Resource Development Review, 14*(2), 125–162.

McFadden, C. (2020). Discrimination against transgender employees and jobseekers. In K. F. Zimmerman (Ed.), *The handbook of labor, human resources and population economics* (pp. 1–14). Springer.

McFadden, C., & Crowley-Henry, M. (2016). A systematic literature review on trans* careers and workplace experiences. In T. Köllen (Ed.), *Sexual orientation and transgender issues in organizations* (pp. 63–81). Springer.

McFadden, C., & Crowley-Henry, M. (2018). "My people": The potential of LGBT employee networks in reducing stigmatization and providing voice. *The International Journal of Human Resource Management, 29*(5), 1056–1081.

McNulty, Y., McPhail, R., Inversi, C., Dundon, T., & Nechanska, E. (2018). Employee voice mechanisms for lesbian, gay, bisexual and transgender expatriation: The role of employee-resource groups (ERGs) and allies. *The International Journal of Human Resource Management, 29*(5), 829–856.

Monro, S. (2015). Bisexuality, organisations, and capitalism. In S. Monro (Ed.), *Bisexuality. identities, politics, and theories* (pp. 109–132). Palgrave Macmillan.

Montiel-McCann, C. S. (2022). "It's like we are not human": Discourses of humanisation and otherness in the representation of trans identity in British broadsheet newspapers. *Feminist Media Studies, 23.* https://doi.org/10.1080/14680777.2022.2097727

Noon, M. (2007). The fatal flaws of diversity and the business case for ethnic minorities. *Work, Employment and Society, 21*(4), 773–784.

Raeburn, N. C. (2004). *Changing corporate America from inside out: Lesbian and gay workplace rights.* University of Minnesota Press.

Rees, C., Alfes, K., & Gatenby, M. (2013). Employee voice and engagement: Connections and consequences. *The International Journal of Human Resource Management, 24*(14), 2780–2798.

Robinson, G., & Dechant, K. (1997). Building a business case for diversity. *Academy of Management Perspectives, 11*(3), 21–31.

Rumens, N., de Souza, E. M., & Brewis, J. (2018). Queering queer theory in management and organization studies: Notes toward queering heterosexuality. *Organization Studies, 40*(4), 593–612.

Seidman, S. (2006). Theoretical perspectives. In S. Seidman, N. Fischer, & C. Meeks (Eds.), *Handbook of the new sexuality studies* (pp. 19–20). Routledge.

Stonewall. (2020). *Setting up an LGBT employee network group.* Stonewall.

Tatli, A. (2010). A multi-layered exploration of the diversity management field: Diversity discourse, practices and practitioners in the UK. *British Journal of Management, 22*(2), 238–253.

Tilcsik, A., Anteby, M., & Knight, C. R. (2015). Concealable stigma and occupation segregation: Toward a theory of gay and lesbian occupations. *Administrative Science Quarterly, 60*(3), 446–481.

Tomlinson, F., & Schwabenland, C. (2010). Reconciling competing discourses of diversity? The UK non-profit sector between social justice and the business case. *Organization, 17*(1), 101–121.

Visser, J. (2006). Union membership statistics in 24 countries. *Monthly Labor Review, 129*(1), 38–49.

Welbourne, T. M., Rolf, S., & Schlachter, S. (2017). The case for employee resource groups: A review and social identity theory-based research agenda. *Personnel Review, 46*(8), 1816–1834.

Wright, M. J. (2016). The decline of American Unions is a threat to public health. *American Journal of Public Health, 106*(6), 968–969.

Wright, T. (2008). Lesbian firefighters: Shifting the boundaries between "masculinity" and "Femininity". *Journal of Lesbian Studies, 12*(1), 103–114.

34

KEEP YOUR HEAD DOWN

Dysfunctional Leadership and Its Impact on LGTBQ+ Employees

Kevin J. Rose

Dysfunctional Leadership and Its Impact on LGTBQ+ Employees

Leader–follower relationships, even highly productive and positive ones, inherently include issues of power (French & Raven, 1959; Tarakci et al., 2016). And where power dynamics exist, the potential for suppression, oppression, and marginalization exist. Some of the most influential aspects of workplace dynamics are the interactions between leaders and followers in an organization. In fact, anecdotal evidence abounds that suggests that employees leave bad bosses, not bad organizations (Lipman, 2015). While this claim is debatable and the decision to leave an organization is predicated on much more complexity (Hom et al., 2017), the fact remains that the relationship between a leader and follower is highly impactful and meaningful, regardless of the style of leadership utilized.

This dynamic and the potential for harm is concerning enough, of course, but I wish to high-light a significant aspect of this dynamic—that LGBTQ+ individuals occupy places of increased vulnerability in the leader–follower relationship. This unfortunate state of affairs is due, at least in part, to continued misunderstanding and discriminatory attitudes against these individuals and, as this book underscores, the idea of *heteromasculinity* (Anderson, 2009) and the systems of oppression in society and organizations. As Gedro and Mizzi (2014) have pointed out, when we begin deeply and critically examining organizational social environments, we find "powerful and power-filled work structures largely based on heteromasculinist values" (p. 446). Heteromasculinity is the idea that those with the most power and influence are those that are outwardly seen as both heterosexual and masculine (Anderson, 2009). In other words, it is not enough that societal power structures favor men; it is the heterosexual men who enjoy the greatest privilege. In organizations, hierarchical structures give varying amounts of power to those in positions of leadership, and, as I shall discuss later, other individuals not in formal positions of leadership with different kinds of power sources. Thus, it is both the individual leader and the heteromasculinist value structure that work to oppress LGBTQ+ individuals, both overtly and inadvertently. While others have addressed the issue of institutional power structures and organizations as oppressive instruments (see, e.g., Morgan's (2012) classical metaphors of organizations as "psychic prisons" and "instruments of domination" [p. 463]), I wish here to emphasize the role of leadership and power, as they are issues of concern shared

DOI: 10.4324/9781003128151-40

by human resource development scholars (Bierema & Callahan, 2014; O'Donnell et al., 2006; Wright et al., 2018). In this chapter, I wish to shine a brighter spotlight on the leader–follower relationship (cf. Collins, 2012) and, specifically, the phenomenon of *dysfunctional leadership* (Rose et al., 2015).

In addition to dysfunctional leadership, I suggest that understanding the experiences of LGBTQ+ individuals in the leader–follower relationship should also be viewed through the lens of *intersectionality* (Crenshaw, 1991). This view suggests that a person can be oppressed in multiple ways based on various aspects of their identity. The intersection of these identities can create *compounded* oppression, which is an important consideration. That is, we must take into account that individuals may hold multiple identities that can be *simultaneously* privileged or oppressed. This presents unique challenges for LGTBQ+ individuals, and, in particular, LGTBQ+ individuals of color, in navigating these various interpersonal and organizational dynamics. This view also urges us to consider that there is more to understand about a group and their varied experiences than a monolithic outlook would imply. One issue that presents difficulty for understanding the impact of dysfunctional leadership on an individual is perception (Schyns & Schilling, 2013). That is to say, not all employees view all dysfunctional leader behaviors equally. The idea of differing perceptions highlights the importance of not viewing the LGBTQ+ community as holding uniform experiences and responses to dysfunctional leadership. Thus, I bring attention to the need to focus on intersectionality and its role in understanding oppression of individuals of historically marginalized groups. The ideas of dysfunctional leadership and intersectionality are connected, conceptually, by the power wielded by leaders in organizations.

The aim of this chapter is to highlight the distinct concerns of LGTBQ+ individuals in dealing with dysfunctional leadership situations. I argue that while poor leadership negatively impacts all employees, LGTBQ+ employees have various and intersecting identities that may be acutely harmed by bad leaders. In this chapter, I will cover areas of dysfunctional leadership using a broad definition of the concept (Schyns & Schilling, 2013; Tepper, 2000) and its impact on employees in general, not just LGBTQ+ folks. I will also include discussion of intersectionality and argue for the need to see the LGBTQ+ community as non-monolithic, which is particularly important when considering the impact bad leadership can have on individuals given their multiple identities. First, I provide an overview of how dysfunctional leadership is a persistent concern in organizations that affects *all* employees. Second, I describe the classical bases of power (French & Raven, 1959) and argue that these power dynamics create situations ripe for the development of dysfunctional leaders. Third, I provide an argument for considering the multiple identities of LGBTQ+ employees through the lens of intersectionality and how these identities contribute to differential impact of bad bosses (e.g., a Black, trans*, lesbian woman does not experience the same oppression as a White, cisgender, gay man although both experience marginalization). Throughout this chapter, I used the term LGBTQ+ as short-hand for a community of people who share the commonality of an oppressed and marginalized sexual orientation and/or gender identity or expression. It is meant to be inclusive of those who identify as lesbian, gay, bisexual, trans*, queer, questioning, intersex, asexual, gender-fluid, gender non-conforming, genderqueer, non-binary, and pansexual (Human Rights Campaign, 2021). I am acutely aware that categorical labels like this can be simultaneously inclusive, and they can be a form of unintentional erasure (Namaste, 2000) of those who experience the most marginalization and oppression. It is my intent that readers of this chapter would see this work as potentially applying to all of those who claim an LGBTQ+ identity and interpret it thusly.

Dysfunctional Leadership

Hierarchical organizational structures and imbalances of expertise and influence give rise to differential power dynamics in the workplace. These power dynamics create situations ripe for abuse and dysfunction. Prolific scholarship has been dedicated to the theory and practice of leadership and, largely, this scholarship has focused on the *who* and the *how* of leadership (Northouse, 2018). That is, leadership over the past century has been dedicated to uncovering who makes good leaders and how leadership is enacted. Largely, this research could be described as focusing on the *positive consideration* of leadership: training better leaders, understanding good leader behaviors, determining causal and correlational chains of leadership impact (Lee et al., 2020). But, in the past several years, attention has turned to negative considerations of leadership: potential for leadership abuses, toxic leadership, dysfunctional behaviors, and other negative behaviors (Mackey et al., 2021). In short, research has begun looking at bad bosses.

This is an important shift if our collective understanding of leadership impact and its function (and dysfunction) is seen as an organizational process (Northouse, 2018). Anecdotally, most readers can probably recount a time spent working for a bad boss or manager. Cross words, withheld information, demotions, undue pressures and stress, feelings of worthlessness, tears, and anxiety are just some of the negative repercussions of having a dysfunctional or abusive manager. Just like good leadership can have extraordinarily positive impacts on an organization and its members, bad leadership can have a deleterious impact on the same. Likewise, just like good leadership comes in different types and styles (e.g., situational leadership, authentic leadership, transformational leadership), researchers are beginning to understand that poor leadership has its own patterns of enactment and impact. For example, there is an obvious difference between negative leader behaviors like sexual harassment and physical abuse, and negative leader behaviors like withholding information and using foul language in an angry tone. These differences have been showing up in the scholarship of bad leadership. While definitive and empirically tested typologies are, as yet, somewhat lacking, we do have some language to help describe these differences: abusive supervision (Ghosh et al., 2011; Tepper, 2000), toxic leadership (Reed, 2004), dysfunctional leadership (Rose et al., 2015), Machiavellianism (Drory & Gluskinos, 1980), narcissistic leadership (Rosenthal & Pittinsky, 2006), incivility (Reio & Ghosh, 2009), and others.

Over the past several years, some of my own scholarship has examined the idea of dysfunctional leadership. In one of the first works on this subject, my research team and I defined dysfunctional leadership as "a person in a position of influence, status, and resource differential overtly exhibiting verbal and nonverbal behavior that impairs operational function of individuals, teams, and organizations" (Rose et al., 2015, p. 67). We saw dysfunctional leadership as separate and distinct from other kinds of bad leadership in not only the kinds of behaviors that were displayed by leaders, but also in the impact on employees. (I now see this as an entirely more complex and problematic issue. More on this later.) In short, dysfunctional leadership can be thought of as perhaps slightly less recognizable and slightly less overt than leadership behaviors as egregious as pressuring an employee to abuse drugs or alcohol, for example. The dysfunctional leader might be more apt to use a veiled threat than outright retribution. Their aggression might be more passive than direct.

Our research on dysfunctional leadership looked at the myriad negative behaviors exhibited by managers and leaders (Shuck et al., 2015). We conceptualized these behaviors as ranging from annoying to traumatic on one axis and less dysfunctional to more dysfunctional on another axis. As an example, we categorized "taking undue credit for work" as an annoying, low dysfunction behavior; we categorized "bribery" as traumatic, highly dysfunctional behavior (Rose et al., 2015). We recognized, however, that although we examined copious research on negative leadership behavior, our taxonomy did not necessarily capture all available dysfunctional behaviors. Similarly, it is difficult to come to a conclusive answer on the impact of these behaviors on those who experience them from their leader or supervisor.

The reason for this is that, to borrow from an idiomatic expression, dysfunction is in the eye of the beholder. That is, everyone will experience dysfunctional and other negative leader behaviors differently. For some, using profanity in the workplace is a non-issue (and maybe even welcomed). For others, the same behavior can be off-putting, tasteless, and even offensive. These differences in perception arise from our varied histories, psychologies, backgrounds, beliefs, and values. There is an intersection of all of these issues that make us who we are and how we see the world. This very idea of diverse experience is at the core of my present argument: dysfunctional leadership behaviors can have a compounding effect on employees from underrepresented and *minoritized* communities. This idea will be explored later in this chapter.

The consequences of dysfunctional leadership and its impact on employees can be profound. Research shows that employees' reactions to dysfunctional behaviors can range from aggressiveness to avoidance to acquiescence (Boddy et al., 2010). Counterproductive workplace behaviors like social loafing, subversion, and even petty theft (Wei & Si, 2011) occur more often under a dysfunctional leader. More alarmingly, it has been observed that dysfunctional behaviors can cascade through an organization through employees mimicking these behaviors with coworkers and subordinates (Mawritz et al., 2012). From this perspective, it can be hard to both identify the source of dysfunctional leadership as well as address it. Although not the focus of this chapter, organizational remedies to dysfunctional leadership do exist and are multi-faceted: organizational culture studies and interventions; leadership training; prevention of placement practices; robust stances on ethics, antiracism, diversity, equity, and inclusion (Bassman & London, 1993; Decoster et al., 2013; Henle & Gross, 2013).

Other impacts of dysfunctional leaders, which are perhaps more germane to the current chapter, include the deleterious effects on an employee's psychological well-being and the downstream effects on the organization. For many who serve under a dysfunctional leader, their self-esteem can suffer (Burton & Hoobler, 2006). They may lessen their commitment to the organization (Demir & Rodwell, 2012). They may experience emotional exhaustion (Wu & Hu, 2009). Some employees act out towards their family and friends because of the stress they are under at work (Restubog et al., 2011). Moreover, organizational citizenship behaviors, an important component of the organization's social system, can be negatively impacted by dysfunctional leadership (Rose, 2016; Rose et al., 2016). Employees begin withholding these important behaviors in response to the perceived imbalance at work and a broken psychological contract. Ultimately, all of this can lead to increased turnover and decreased organizational reputation (Mehdi et al., 2012).

Underlying these dysfunctional behaviors and consequences for employees is the balance and imbalance of power that exists in organizations. In the following section, I will explore the idea of power in organizations further using a classic conceptualization of how power is amassed and utilized. This discussion is an important factor in understanding the processes of dysfunctional leadership and how they interact with the idea of intersectionality and oppression in the wider sociocultural environment. It is also important to note that the very conceptualization of power in organizations seems to uphold, support, and justify a heteromasculine hegemony.

Power

Power differentials are a hallmark of human social systems; the modern organization does not escape this inevitable reality. Indeed, the very domain of leadership implies that there are those with more power and those with less, and that those with more power exert their influence to elicit behavior from those with less power. The seminal work on power dynamics in the workplace is French and Raven's (1959) conceptualization of "bases of power." In their view, power comes in several types: reward power, coercive power, legitimate power, referent power, and expert power. This understanding of power in organizations has formed the theoretical framework of much of the empirical work on power dynamics in organizations over the past seven decades (Lunenburg, 2012). In this section, I will give some attention to the various bases of power as they are generally understood. This is important as, in my view, it is power differential that enables and sustains discrimination and oppression in the workplace. Power dynamics in the workplace do not operate in a vacuum, of course. Organizations exist in societies, cultures, and systems that legitimize these power differentials and the resulting marginalization of LGBTQ+ individuals.

I suggest that the power imbalance that exists between a dysfunctional leader and their subordinates can be exacerbated by overarching sociocultural and economic issues facing LGBTQ+ people. For example, the idea of implicit bias (Gawronski, 2019) might mean that LGBTQ+ folks are not initially considered for leadership roles or promotions by their superiors. Implicit bias, by itself, is a societal-level phenomenon that finds its way into the leader–follower relationship and can exacerbate an already dysfunctional situation. In the following sections, I provide brief discussions of power imbalances at play with regard to dysfunctional leadership and the experiences of LGBTQ+ individuals. I organize these according to French and Raven's (1959) power framework, recognizing, however, that there are multiple avenues by which these imbalances could be examined.

I should note an important caveat around the idea of dysfunctional leadership and its impact on LGBTQ+ employees: dysfunctional behavior versus outright discrimination. Day et al.'s (2022) recent study highlighted this important distinction. They found that a survey commonly used to measure workplace mistreatment (the Negative Acts Questionnaire-Revised [Einarsen et al., 2009]) may yield different results than scales used to measure mistreatment as a result of being gay, lesbian, or bisexual. In part, they found that "the scales are measuring subtly different types of bullying, one based on general workplace bullying, and another based on being targeted due to sexual minority status" (Day et al., 2022, p. 1177). I believe that this points to an issue that researchers must grapple with, namely the motivation behind dysfunctional leader behaviors. And this underlies some of the discussions that follow: are these dysfunctional behaviors or are these discriminatory behaviors? At the same time, I recognize that, on some level, this does not matter. To the employee experiencing the dysfunction, knowing the motivations behind such behaviors is of little comfort.

Reward Power

Managers can reward employees in various ways including with favorable work assignments, time off, and entrée into informal social networks in the organization by introducing employees to powerful people (Molm, 1988). Depending on the geographic location and organization, a dysfunctional leader may or may not be able to use salaries, benefits, time off, and similar "standardized" rewards as tools of control. I would argue, however, that in the absence of publicly provided and legally protected benefits (or rewards), some LGBTQ+ workers may be forced to tolerate dysfunctional leaders out of a need for access. For example, before the U.S. Supreme Court in the *Obergefell v. Hodges* (2015) case made same-sex marriage a constitutional right, same-sex partners were not guaranteed the same rights and access to benefits as opposite-sex married couples. In some cases, employers voluntarily provided equal or similar benefits to married couples and non-married couples as a tool to attract and retain talent. Consider, though, that this benefit offering tethered LGBTQ+ partnered individuals to a specific organization or workplace. Leaving an organization because of a dysfunctional boss would have had major consequences for benefits otherwise afforded to same-sex couples regardless of employer (Pizer et al., 2012). However, one aspect I would like to highlight is how dysfunctional leaders can use informal work networks to their advantage, or rather how dysfunctional leaders can limit access to workplace social networks. Researchers have long known that informal social networks at work are important conduits for career advancement and job satisfaction (Markiewicz et al., 2000; Podolny & Baron, 1997). More often than not, entry into these powerful social networks is provided by an employee's leader or manager (Ibarra et al., 2010). Thus, a dysfunctional leader can withhold access to these networks. The critical factor for LGBTQ+ employees is that, because of their socially marginalized status(es), they may have even fewer opportunities to go around a dysfunctional boss to build these important relationships.

Coercive Power

A favorite tool of the dysfunctional leader is their use of coercive behavior (Xu et al., 2012). This can take many forms, but often manifests as an attitude of hostility, intimidation, and threats (Bassman & London, 1993; Tepper, 2000; Tepper et al., 2006). I would propose that, similar to withholding rewards, LGBTQ+ employees often have to "put up" with a coercive boss because of the need for access to non-protected benefits and because of lack of access to workplace power networks (Ragins et al., 2017). Dysfunctional leaders could legitimately use their coercive power of threat of termination against LGBTQ+ employees, simply for being gay, lesbian, bisexual, or trans*, until the U.S. Supreme Court expanded non-discrimination protections in employment to LGBTQ+ individuals in 2020 (*Bostock v. Clayton County*, 2020). It is important to note that this only applies to employers with 15 or more employees and, in some cases, non-religious organizations. Therefore, some LGBTQ+ employees in certain organizations still face the real prospect of being fired simply for being gay or trans*. Additionally, this very recent change to law does not simply halt the momentum of discrimination where it was present—cultural changes take far longer.

Legitimate Power

Legitimate power is derived from formal position of authority. This is a direct reflection of the power imbalances inherent in most modern organizations. In most every organization with sufficient numbers of personnel, lines of authority (power) are constructed to direct resources, effort, and hold people accountable (Greenberg, 2011). However, a recent analysis indicated that LGBTQ+ individuals are disproportionately *underrepresented* in formal positions of power in organizations (Ellsworth et al., 2020). Despite aspirations to the contrary, less than 2% of managerial positions in the United States are held by LGBTQ+ women and less than 3% are held by LGBTQ+ men. This startling reminder of the lack of representation in places of positional authority has at least two important implications with regard to dysfunctional leadership. First, LGBTQ+ employees lack powerful workplace advocates who fully understand and can empathize with their unique challenges. These are advocates who could otherwise help cope with a dysfunctional leader. Second, dysfunctional bosses necessarily perpetuate this lavender ceiling (Gedro, 2010; Hill, 2006), failing to promote and cultivate talented LGBTQ+ workers.

Referent Power

There is power in positive relationships. When employees respond positively to leaders because they like them or respect them, this is a manifestation of referent power. The unfortunate reality for many LGBTQ+ people living today is that sexual orientation and trans* status are still identities that are stigmatized in broader society. Herek (2007) put it well:

> Regardless of their own sexual orientation or personal attitudes, people in the United States and many other societies know that homosexual desires and behaviors are widely regarded in negative terms relative to heterosexuality. They are aware of the malevolent stereotypes routinely attached to individuals whose personal identities are based on same-sex attractions, behaviors, relationships, or membership in a sexual minority community.
>
> *(p. 907)*

This idea gets at the heart of discrimination and bias in the workplace, but I wish to underscore that this also perpetuates a power imbalance between leaders and followers, creating fertile ground for dysfunctional behaviors. In essence, these "malevolent stereotypes" (Herek, 2007, p. 907) may actually induce implicit and explicit dysfunctional leader behaviors against LGBTQ+ employees.

Expert Power

This form of power is based on an individual's expertise and skills and is granted to others through demonstrable acts of credibility as well as educational attainment (Luthans et al., 2015). To undermine expert power, dysfunctional leaders utilize tactics like taking credit for the work of others (Wu, 2008), demeaning a person's capabilities (Hu, 2012), and public denigration (Tepper et al., 2011). While these kinds of behaviors may be exhibited towards employees from all demographic groups, consider that lesbian women and gay men have greater levels of educational attainment as compared to heterosexual individuals (Mittleman, 2022). Moreover, related to the stigmatization of LGBTQ+ individuals discussed previously, there are prevailing "assumptions of sexual minorities as less competent and less able than heterosexual men and women" (Mize, 2016, p. 1134). Thus, a situation arises where (1) LGBTQ+ individuals are, on average, more highly educated, yet (2) are thought of a less competent, resulting in (3) fewer LGBTQ+ folks in positions of organizational power. This is due, in part, to dysfunctional leaders making ill-informed and prejudicial hiring and promotion decisions (Correll et al., 2007).

As previously noted, discussions of organizational power are predicated on structural and systemic power imbalances. That is, these power imbalances exist *de facto* and *by design*. While, ostensibly, these serve the organization's needs (to direct effort and set priorities), there is undoubtedly the risk of abuse of power in both minor and major ways. Power imbalances in organizations mirrors that of power imbalances in our social systems in a critical way: often, those with the power fail to protect, nurture, and develop those without power. Let me put a finer point on this, by way of example. In recent years, state governments in the United States have moved to disenfranchise trans* individuals by stripping them of access to healthcare, banning them from full access to public services, and even requiring public servants (teachers) to "out" trans* students to parents (Krishnakumar, 2021). In summary, those with power (legislators) are actively harming those without power (trans* folks). In organizations, employees often face the same power dynamic. Those with power (managers and leaders) either actively harm employees or fail to nurture and develop employees. While many organizations are at the forefront of inclusive practices, many individual leaders still engage in behaviors that "serve to maintain heterosexist and cissexist norms and marginalize LGBT people" (Resnick & Galupo, 2019, p. 1380).

Intersectionality

Over 30 years ago, Kimberlé Crenshaw introduced the idea of intersectionality to describe the ways in which Black women are oppressed in multiple and various ways. Crenshaw (1991) described her field studies with abused women of color who faced various obstacles accessing resources and navigating the legal justice system. These experiences were far from uniform. For some, lack of familial support was a major obstacle in obtaining childcare and basic needs. For others, language barriers precluded full access to, and understanding of, the resources available to them. And for yet more of them, lack of education and skills training meant they would not have access to reliable, good paying jobs to support themselves and their families. Crenshaw noted that the few resources or policies adopted to try to help this community treated them as though their experiences were similar, if not identical. What should work for one person, should work for the next. Reality, however, suggested that these varied experiences, based on variously oppressed identities, was not the same for everyone.

The original conceptualization of intersectionality was used to describe the multiple experiences of oppression faced by women of color because of two marginalized identities: gender and race. Since then, the idea has been expanded to a more holistic view of identity by including facets of a person like sexual orientation, trans* identification, socioeconomic status, and educational attainment (Gopaldas, 2013). Clearly, there are an innumerable set of identity categories that might describe an individual. Yet the lens of intersectionality calls on us to focus on those aspects of identity that lead to oppression and marginalization in many contexts, but for organizational scholars the emphasis should be on the workplace and in leader–follower relationships.

There is an inherent "murkiness" (Nash, 2008, p. 1) that comes with an intersectional approach. Understanding someone's reality of oppression and the sources of that oppression can be an infinitely difficult task because of the different ways each facet of one's identity intersect and how each identity can be differently oppressed. As an example, a gay, White man will face oppression and marginalization for his gay identity in many, but not all, social spaces. His racial identity will privilege him in many of those same spaces. A Black, straight man will face oppression because of his racial identity; his sexual orientation will be privileged (Anderson & McCormack, 2010). The degree to which oppression is faced, how each identity is interactive and interlocked, and which identities are oppressed more or less and when and how are complex issues with complex answers, or sometimes no answers.

As I have described before, dysfunctional leadership can have serious negative impacts on all employees, *regardless* of race, gender, sexual orientation, and other facets of identity. When added to the multiple oppressions that multiple identities garners, negative impacts for those with marginalized identities can be *compounded* on top of experiences faced in the employment landscape (Cho et al., 2013; Crenshaw, 1991). For example, research shows that discrimination against LGBTQ+ individuals exists in the hiring process (Ahmed et al., 2013), in pay differentials (Bryson, 2016), in access to benefits (Hornsby & Munn, 2009), and in many other ways (Brooks & Edwards, 2009; Mara et al., 2020). The issue here is that each of these problems are also true for women and racial minorities in the United States, *writ large*, and these various forms of discrimination and oppression are exponentially traumatic.

However, much of the research around discrimination, adverse impact, and other negative workplace consequences for LGBTQ+ individuals presents findings as though they apply equally across all of these identity categories. Statistical analyses, for example, rely on larger sample sizes for greater power and significance. So, in many studies (even some of my own), sexual orientation is "lumped in" with trans* identity as if these identities were "similar enough" to analyze together (Glick et al., 2018). Yet both intuition and empirical evidence point to the fact that, for example, trans* individuals experience *even more* stress, anxiety, and other negative consequences as a result of workplace issues (Collins et al., 2015; Mizock, 2014). This is at the very heart of my present argument: intersecting identities can induce compounded negative impacts of dysfunctional leadership. This spotlights just one aspect faced by LGTBQ+ individuals in the workplace, namely a dysfunctional leader. There are others as noted previously.

I would like to illustrate some of these conceptual connections with an example. Imagine a dysfunctional leader practicing one of the most common forms of dysfunctional behavior, withholding information (Xu et al., 2012). This is an exploitation of the power imbalance discussed previously and is used as a control mechanism. This person keeps important information to themselves and only releases information (e.g., budget) when it benefits them personally or allows them to gain even more control of subordinates. Let us imagine that this deleterious behavior is practiced equally with all subordinates of this dysfunctional leader. Let us also imagine that this particular dysfunctional leader uses organizational policy as a weapon, rather than as tool for equity (Rose et al., 2015). In other words, policies are stringently enforced to the detriment of the employees. In this case, the dysfunctional leader enforces strict adherence to policies concerning advance notice for medical and personal leave and requires doctor's notes for any and all medical leave taken. Again, in this scenario, this is enforced "equally" for all employees as a tactic of fear and control.

The employees who work for this individual all experience stress and emotional trauma as a result of these behaviors. It would be tempting to stop the analysis there, and, assuming an intervention is warranted, and shy away from a deeper look into how these employees have fared under this dysfunctional and despotic boss. Unfortunately, the analysis of the situation often *does* stop with a surface understanding of the situation and only minimal interventions are thought necessary. Those in positions of higher leadership may not be able to adequately empathize (Clark et al., 2018) with members of this team, particularly if they do not share many identity characteristics with these employees.

Many of the employees on this work group cope with the issue of their leader withholding information by turning to their informal social networks inside the organization. This is a common practice of employees facing stressors at work (Shuck et al., 2015). Imagine now, though, that some employees identify as men and some as women. Research suggests that the female employees will receive "less informal help than white [sic] men" (McGuire, 2002, p. 316) when they reach out to their support networks at work. This creates a situation where, on the surface, employees are treated equally badly. But their experiences of bad treatment vary because of their identities. Now imagine that one of the female employees identifies as trans* and requires frequent and ongoing access to healthcare. An assumption might be made that there is no issue with treating all employees equally in this regard and requiring this employee to request time off in advance and document all medical meetings with doctors' notes. But this can be a burden on this employee and, coupled with a boss who is inflexible and recalcitrant in their use of organizational policy, this allows for further oppression of this individual. In summary, their identity as a woman disenfranchises them; their identity as a trans* individual disenfranchises them. The analogy could go on and on and include aspects of race, religion, sexual orientation, and the like. In summary, employees of a bad boss do not experience poor leadership equally.

First, perception plays a role in how dysfunctional behaviors are interpreted. Second, the intersection of various identities can work to oppress or disenfranchise employees in multiple and compounding ways.

In the following section, I offer some recommendations for research and practice based on the conceptual connections between dysfunctional leadership, power, and intersectionality. These are aimed primarily at managers and researchers. I believe it is incumbent upon those who have more privilege to do the hardest work of inclusion: to question their assumptions, to challenge their own hegemonic positions, to listen, empathize, and understand, and to do the most advocacy for the most vulnerable.

Recommendations

In my original conceptualization of dysfunctional leadership, I defined these leaders as having at least some intent to harm or obstruct. On further reflection, though, it is likely difficult or impossible for an employee to know what the intent of a leader is, unless that intent is made clear and explicit. This is related to the idea that dysfunction is experienced differently by different people. There is a sense of subjectivity in the interpretation of some behaviors and the employee's response is potentially moderated by such interpretations (Schyns & Schilling, 2013; Tepper, 2000). What that means in practice is that someone outside of the leader–follower dyad might interpret poor leadership behaviors much differently that the individual *in* the dyad. Intersectionality tells us that there is a high potential for employees even within the same workgroup to interpret and experience their boss's actions much differently. For these reasons, it is imperative that upper management truly listen to employees who voice concerns and complaints about a potentially bad boss. Upper management has to realize, however, that these experiences are subjective. Thus, the starting point of such conversations should always be one of belief rather than skepticism. An empathetic approach is warranted in this situation (Clark et al., 2018).

Be Intolerant of Purposefully Bad Leadership

Unfortunately, I have had the bad fortune of working for my share of dysfunctional bosses. The behaviors I endured ranged from veiled threats to withholding information to the weaponization of organizational policy. I know I am not alone in this experience. What I craved from top management was for someone with greater power than me to do something, anything to help. What I got was avoidance of the issues, chalking up dysfunctional behavior as "learning," and advice to keep my head down and stay out of the way. My current plea is that organizations do anything but ignore dysfunctional leaders. Rather, address these behaviors head-on and in a way that protects the most vulnerable—those without power. Dysfunctional leaders can and do improve their leadership skills. An organization, however, should be absolutely intolerant of the behaviors that actively destroy employee satisfaction, decimate engagement, and lead to a spiral of doubt, stress, and anxiety (Shuck et al., 2015).

Change the Leadership Narrative

Organizations and managers should be lauded for doing the difficult work of actively dismantling heteromasculine structures and narratives around what it means to have an effective organization and what it means to be an effective leader. The case of an employee's annual leave time, for example, presents an opportunity to reconsider the values that have been used to construct such a policy. In most organizations, leave time (medical, personal, and family) is finite and accrued at a set rate. To use such time, employees are required to request use of this time from their managers, and these requests can be denied. As I illustrated previously, these kinds of policies and practices seem, at face value, fair and just and utilized to prevent abuse. However, they can be used in nefarious ways to control, cajole, and coerce. Instead, organizations and leaders might consider implementing generous and flexible leave policies that give agency to the employee to make the best decisions for their own families, health, and well-being. Recent research suggests that policies like unlimited leave time accrue positive results to employees in increased motivation and satisfaction and positive results to organizations in increased productivity and reduced turnover (Bao, 2020). Yet this very same research describes these kinds of progressive policies as "*risky* perk[s] for firms due to the possibility of abuse" [emphasis mine] (para. 1). What if, instead, we changed the narrative to suggest that *finite* leave policies were the riskier endeavor because of the possibility of abuse and oppression of the organization's valuable human resources?

Seek Out the Voices of the "Multiple-Marginalized" Folks

There are excellent examples of scholarship with individuals who have intersecting identities that may face oppression in a heteromasculine work environment. For example, Reddy-Best (2018) looked at the experiences of LGBTQ women in the workforce and their experiences with appearance management. Using an intersectional lens, Allen and Leslie (2018) explored the confluence of immigration status and race for LGBT individuals and its influence on mental health. Amponsah (2020) recounted his experiences as a gay, Black man and how those experiences shaped his view of leadership and authority. Rather than, or perhaps alongside, research that looks at the broad category of LGBTQ+ employees, let us consider research that honors and highlights the experiences of intersecting identities (McCall, 2005). The workplace experiences of older, trans*, Black, married people is likely different from young, gay, Native American, single people. Celebrating these different experiences is a step in the right direction as well as uncovering the various ways in which oppression occurs for them.

Conclusion

My aim in this chapter was to shine a brighter spotlight on the idea that dysfunctional leadership impacts LGBTQ+ employees in a much greater way than our straight, cisgender coworkers through classical and enduring power structures in organizations. This is not to diminish the impact a dysfunctional leader can have on a straight, cisgender individual, but to note that people in the LGBTQ+ community carry this weight along with all the other social baggage of discrimination, hatred, systemic exclusion, bullying, and vilification. Mirroring the broader social, political, cultural, and economic systems, dysfunctional leadership exists, and sometimes thrives, in organizations because of the disparate power structures that provide more power to some and less to others.

I also suggest that we need to take into consideration that folks in the LGBTQ+ community are subject to multiple and compounding forms of oppression based on other factors (like race, disability status). In other words, oppression is not felt equally in the community. This leads us to consider individualized approaches to leadership and development of employees (Schmidt et al., 2012). It should also serve as a call to think about both our research and our practice with a greater level of granularity. Have we done the hard work to include marginalized voices? Have we considered how identity influences perception? Identity work can be extraordinarily complex, frustrating, and limiting and, for that reason, it can be tempting to either ignore this work altogether or to leave it to the "critical scholars" and "diversity experts." But it can also help to de-marginalize people who often get overlooked, excluded, and ignored. Indeed, I believe it is a moral imperative for all of us to do this work.

References

Ahmed, A. M., Andersson, L., & Hammarstedt, M. (2013). Are gay men and lesbians discriminated against in the hiring process? *Southern Economic Journal, 79*(3), 565–585. https://doi.org/10.4284/0038-4038-2011.317

Allen, S. H., & Leslie, L. A. (2018). Considering the role of nativity in the health and psychological well-being of Black LGBT adults. *Journal of Homosexuality, 66*(13), 1769–1796. https://doi.org/10.1080/00918369.2018.1511134

Amponsah, B. (2020). The role of leadership for gay black practitioners: How do we craft authority from micro-aggressions and multiple identities? A personal story. In M. McIntosh, H. Nicholas, & A. H. Huq (Eds.), *Leadership and diversity in psychology: Moving beyond the limits* (pp. 22–30). Routledge.

Anderson, E. (2009). *Inclusive masculinity: The changing nature of masculinities.* Routledge.

Anderson, E., & McCormack, M. (2010). Intersectionality, critical race theory, and American sporting oppression: Examining Black and gay male athletes. *Journal of Homosexuality, 57*(8), 949–967. https://doi.org/10.1080/00918369.2010.503502

Bao, J. (2020). *(How) do risky perks benefit firms? The case of unlimited vacation.* Academy of Management Conference, Virtual. https://wpa.wharton.upenn.edu/wp-content/uploads/2020/04/Jiay-iBao_RESEARCHPAPERcompetition_letterhead_v1_04022020.pdf

Bassman, E., & London, M. (1993). Abusive managerial behavior. *Leadership & Organization Development Journal, 14*(2), 18–24. https://doi.org/10.1108/01437739310032683

Bierema, L., & Callahan, J. L. (2014). Transforming HRD: A framework for critical HRD practice. *Advances in Developing Human Resources, 16*(4), 429–444. https://doi.org/10.1177/1523422314543818

Boddy, C. R., Ladyshewsky, R. K., & Galvin, P. (2010). The influence of corporate psychopaths on corporate social responsibility and organizational commitment to employees. *Journal of Business Ethics, 97*, 1–19. https://doi.org/10.1007/s10551-010-0492-3

Bostock v. Clayton County, 590 U.S. ___ (2020). www.oyez.org/cases/2019/17-1618

Brooks, A. K., & Edwards, K. (2009). Allies in the workplace: Including LGBT in HRD. *Advances in Developing Human Resources, 11*(1), 136–149. https://doi.org/10.1177/1523422308328500

Bryson, A. (2016). Pay equity after the equality act 2010: Does sexual orientation still matter? *Work, Employment and Society, 31*(3), 483–500. https://doi.org/10.1177/0950017016664678

Burton, J. P., & Hoobler, J. M. (2006). Subordinate self-esteem and abusive supervision. *Journal of Managerial Issues, 18*(3), 340–355.

Cho, S., Crenshaw, K. W., & McCall, L. (2013). Toward a field of intersectionality studies: Theory, applications, and praxis. *Signs: Journal of Women in Culture and Society, 38*(4), 785–810. https://doi.org/10.1086/669608

Clark, M. A., Robertson, M. M., & Young, S. (2018). "I feel your pain": A critical review of organizational research on empathy. *Journal of Organizational Behavior, 40*(2), 166–192. https://doi.org/10.1002/job.2348

Collins, J. C. (2012). Identity matters: A critical explorations of lesbian, gay, and bisexual identity and leadership in HRD. *Human Resource Development Review, 11*(3), 349–379. https://doi.org/10.1177/1534484312446810

Collins, J. C., McFadden, C., Rocco, T. S., & Mathis, M. K. (2015). The problem of transgender marginalization and exclusion: Critical actions for human resource development. *Human Resource Development Review, 14*(2), 205–226. https://doi.org/10.1177/1534484315581755

Correll, S. J., Benard, S., & Paik, I. (2007). Getting a job: Is there a motherhood penalty? *American Journal of Sociology, 112*(5), 1297–1338. https://doi.org/10.1086/511799

Crenshaw, K. (1991). Mapping the margins: Intersectionality, identity politics, and violence against women of color. *Stanford Law Review, 43*(6), 1241–1299. https://doi.org/10.2307/1229039

Day, N., Meglich, P., & Porter, T. H. (2022). Measuring bullying in sexual minorities: Testing two bullying scales in an LGB sample. *Journal of Homosexuality, 69*(7), 1160–1184. https://doi.org/10.1080/00918369.2021.1909393

Decoster, S., Camps, J., Stouten, J., Vandevyvere, L., & Tripp, T. M. (2013). Standing by your organization: The impact of organizational identification and abusive supervision on followers' perceived cohesion and tendency to gossip. *Journal of Business Ethics, 118*, 623–634. https://doi.org/10.1007/s10551-012-1612-z

Demir, D., & Rodwell, J. (2012). Psychosocial antecedents and consequences of workplace aggression for hospital nurses. *Journal of Nursing Scholarship, 44*(4), 376–384. https://doi.org/10.1111/j.1547-5069.2012.01472.x

Drory, A., & Gluskinos, U. M. (1980). Machiavellianism and leadership. *Journal of Applied Psychology, 65*(1), 81–86. https://doi.org/10.1037/0021-9010.65.1.81

Einarsen, S., Hoel, H., & Notelaers, G. (2009). Measuring exposure to bullying and harassment at work: Validity, factor structure and psychometric properties of the negative acts questionnaire-revised. *Work & Stress, 23*(1), 24–44. https://doi.org/10.1080/02678370902815673

Ellsworth, D., Mendy, A., & Sullivan, G. (2020). *How the LGBTQ+ community fares in the workplace.* www.mckinsey.com/featured-insights/diversity-and-inclusion/how-the-lgbtq-plus-community-fares-in-the-workplace

French, J. R. P., & Raven, B. (1959). The bases of social power. In D. Cartwright (Ed.), *Studies in social power* (pp. 150–167). University of Michigan, Institute for Social Research.

Gawronski, B. (2019). Six lessons for a cogent science of implicit bias and Its criticism. *Perspectives on Psychological Science, 14*(4), 574–595. https://doi.org/10.1177/1745691619826015

Gedro, J. (2010). The lavender ceiling atop the global closet: Human resource development and lesbian expatriates. *Human Resource Development Review, 9*(4), 385–404. https://doi.org/10.1177/1534484310380242

Gedro, J., & Mizzi, R. C. (2014). Feminist theory and queer theory: Implications for HRD research and practice. *Advances in Developing Human Resources, 16*(4), 445–456. https://doi.org/10.1177/1523422314543820

Ghosh, R., Jacobs, J. L., & Reio, T. G. (2011). The toxic continuum from incivility to violence: What can HRD do? *Advances in Developing Human Resources, 13*(1), 3–9. https://doi.org/10.1177/1523422311410641

Glick, J. L., Theall, K., Andrinopoulos, K., & Kendall, C. (2018). For data's sake: Dilemmas in the measurement of gender minorities. *Culture Health and Sexuality, 20*(12), 1362–1377. https://doi.org/10.1080/13691058.2018.1437220

Gopaldas, A. (2013). Intersectionality 101. *Journal of Public Policy & Marketing, 32*(1), 90–94. https://doi.org/10.1509/jppm.12.044

Greenberg, J. (2011). *Behavior in organizations* (10th ed.). Pearson.

Henle, C. A., & Gross, M. A. (2013). What have I done to deserve this? Effects of employee personality and emotion on abusive supervison. *Journal of Business Ethics, 122*(3), 461–474. https://doi.org/10.1007/s10551-013-1771-6

Herek, G. M. (2007). Confronting sexual stigma and prejudice: Theory and practice. *Journal of Social Issues, 63*(4), 905–925. https://doi.org/10.1111/j.1540-4560.2007.00544.x

Hill, R. J. (2006). Queer challenges in organizational settings: Complexity, paradox, and contradiction. *New Directions for Adult and Continuing Education, 2006*(112), 97–102.

Hom, P. W., Lee, T. W., Shaw, J. D., & Hauskoecht, J. P. (2017). One hundred years of employee turnover theory and research. *Journal of Applied Psychology, 102*(3), 530–545. https://doi.org/10.1037/apl0000103

Hornsby, E. E., & Munn, S. L. (2009). University work-life benefits and same-sex couples. *Advances in Developing Human Resources, 11*(1), 67–81. https://doi.org/10.1177/1523422308329199

Hu, H.-H. (2012). The influence of employee emotional intelligence on coping with supervisor abuse in a banking context. *Social Behavior and Personality: An International Journal, 40*, 863–874. https://doi.org/10.2224/sbp.2012.40.5.863

Human Rights Campaign. (2021). *Glossary of terms.* Retrieved April 13, 2021, from www.hrc.org/resources/glossary-of-terms?utm_source=GS&utm_medium=AD&utm_campaign=BPI-HRC-Grant&utm_content=454854043857&utm_term=trans%20terms&gclid=Cj0KCQjwgtWDBhDZARIsADEKwgPGYzmNRIGUyPCfZl14h7rPphATVeLRJplQEWDPUsBq3fsAQaRk-GJEaAvnNEALw_wcB

Ibarra, H., Carter, N. M., & Silva, C. (2010). Why men still get more promotions than women [Article]. *Harvard Business Review, 88*(9), 80–85. https://hbr.org/2010/09/why-men-still-get-more-promotions-than-women

Krishnakumar, P. (2021). This record-breaking year for anti-transgender legislation would affect minors the most. *CNN*. Retrieved April 15, 2021, from www.cnn.com/2021/04/15/politics/anti-trans gender-legislation-2021/index.html

Lee, Y.-D., Chen, P.-C., & Su, C.-L. (2020). The evolution of the leadership theories and the analysis of new research trends. *International Journal of Organizational Innovation, 12*(3), 88–104.

Lipman, V. (2015). People leave managers, not companies. *Forbes*. Retrieved April 1, 2021, from www.forbes. com/sites/victorlipman/2015/08/04/people-leave-managers-not-companies/?sh=3382706747a9

Lunenburg, F. C. (2012). Power and leadership: An influence process. *International Journal of Management, Business, and Administration, 15*(1), 1–9.

Luthans, F., Luthans, B. C., & Luthans, K. W. (2015). *Organizational behavior: An evidence based approach* (13th ed.). Information Age Publishing.

Mackey, J. D., Parker Ellen, B., McAllister, C. P., & Alexander, K. C. (2021). The dark side of leadership: A systematic literature review and meta-analysis of destructive leadership research. *Journal of Business Research, 132*, 705–718. https://doi.org/10.1016/j.jbusres.2020.10.037

Mara, L.-C., Ginieis, M., & Brunet-Icart, I. (2020). Strategies for coping with LGBT discrimination at work: A systematic literature review. *Sexuality Research and Social Policy, 18*. https://doi.org/10.1007/s13178-020-00462-w

Markiewicz, D., Devine, I., & Kausilas, D. (2000). Friendships of women and men at work. *Journal of Managerial Psychology, 15*(2), 161–184. https://doi.org/10.1108/02683940010310346

Mawritz, M. B., Mayer, D. M., Hoobler, J. M., Wayne, S. J., & Marinova, S. V. (2012). A trickle-down model of abusive supervision. *Personnel Psychology, 65*(2), 325–357. https://doi.org/10.1111/j.1744-6570.2012.01246.x

McCall, L. (2005). The complexity of intersectionality. *Signs: Journal of Women in Culture and Society, 30*(3), 1771–1800. https://doi.org/10.1086/426800

McGuire, G. M. (2002). Gender, race, and the shadow structure: A study of informal networks and inequality in a work organization. *Gender and Society, 16*(3), 303–322. https://doi.org/10.1177/0891243202016003003

Mehdi, A., Raju, R. M., & Mukherji, A. (2012). Abusive supervision and employee attrition: A study of executives in the Indian high technology sector. *Competition Forum, 10*(2), 42–48.

Mittleman, J. (2022). Intersecting the academic gender gap: The education of lesbian, gay, and bisexual America. *American Sociological Review, 87*(2), 303–335. https://doi.org/10.1177/00031224221075776

Mize, T. D. (2016). Sexual orientation in the labor market. *American Sociological Review, 81*(6), 1132–1160. https://doi.org/10.1177/0003122416674025

Mizock, L. (2014). Employment, mental health, internalized stigma, and coping with transphobia among transgender individuals. *Psychology of Sexual Orientation and Gender Diversity, 1*(2), 146–158. https://doi.org/10.1037/sgd0000029

Molm, L. D. (1988). The structure and use of power: A comparison of reward and punishment power. *Social Psychology Quarterly, 51*(2), 108–122. https://doi.org/10.2307/2786834

Morgan, G. (2012). Reflections on Images of Organization and its implications for organization and environment. *Organization & Environment, 24*(4), 459–478. https://doi.org/10.1177/1086026611434274

Namaste, V. (2000). *Invisible lives: The erasure of transsexual and transgender people*. University of Chicago Press.

Nash, J. C. (2008). Re-thinking intersectionality. *Feminist Review, 89*(1), 1–15. https://doi.org/10.1057/fr.2008.4

Northouse, P. G. (2018). *Leadership: Theory and practice* (8th ed.). Sage Publications.

O'Donnell, D., McGuire, D., & Cross, C. (2006). Critically challenging some assumptions in HRD. *International Journal of Training and Development, 10*(1), 4–16. https://doi.org/10.1111/j.1468-2419.2006.00243.x

Obergefell v. Hodges, 576 U.S. ___ (2015). www.oyez.org/cases/2014/14-556

Pizer, J. C., Sears, B., Mallory, C., & Hunter, N. D. (2012). Evidence of persistent and pervasive workplace discrimination against LGBT people: The need for federal legislation prohibiting discrimination and providing for equal employment benefits. *Loyola of Los Angeles Law Review, 45*(3), 715–780.

Podolny, J. M., & Baron, J. N. (1997). Resources and relationships: Social networks and mobility in the workplace. *American Sociological Review, 62*(5), 673–693. https://doi.org/10.2307/2657354

Ragins, B. R., Ehrhardt, K., Lyness, K. S., Murphy, D. D., & Capman, J. F. (2017). Anchoring relationships at work: High-quality mentors and other supportive work relationships as buffers to ambient racial discrimination. *Personnel Psychology, 70*, 211–256. https://doi.org/10.1111/peps.12144

Reddy-Best, K. L. (2018). LGBTQ women, appearance negotiations, and workplace dress codes. *Journal of Homosexuality, 65*(5), 615–639. https://doi.org/10.1080/00918369.2017.1328225

Reed, G. E. (2004). Toxic leadership. *Military Review, 84*(4), 67–71.

Reio, T. G., & Ghosh, R. (2009). Antecedents and outcomes of workplace incivility: Implications for human resource development research and practice. *Human Resource Development Quarterly, 20*(3), 237–264. https://doi.org/10.1002/hrdq.20020

Resnick, C. A., & Galupo, M. P. (2019). Assessing experiences with LGBT microaggressions in the workplace: Development and validation of the microaggression experiences at work scale. *Journal of Homosexuality, 66*(10), 1380–1403. https://doi.org/10.1080/00918369.2018.1542207

Restubog, S. L. D., Scott, K. L., & Zagenczyk, T. J. (2011). When distress hits home: The role of contextual factors and psychological distress in predicting employees' responses to abusive supervision. *Applied Psychology, 96*(4), 713–729. https://doi.org/10.1037/a0021593

Rose, K. J. (2016). Examining organizational citizenship behavior in the context of human resource development: An integrative review of the literature. *Human Resource Development Review, 15*(3), 295–316. https://doi.org/10.1177/1534484316655668

Rose, K. J., Miller, M. T., & Kacirek, K. (2016). Organizational citizenship behavior in higher education: Examining the relationships between behaviors and institutional performance. *Journal of Higher Education Management, 31*(1), 14–27.

Rose, K. J., Shuck, M. B., Twyford, D., & Bergman, M. J. (2015). Skunked: An integrative review exploring the consequences of the dysfunctional leader and implications for those employees who work for them. *Human Resource Development Review, 14*(1), 64–90. https://doi.org/10.1177/1534484314552437

Rosenthal, S. A., & Pittinsky, T. L. (2006). Narcissistic leadership. *The Leadership Quarterly, 17*(6), 617–633. https://doi.org/10.1016/j.leaqua.2006.10.005

Schmidt, S. W., Githens, R. P., Rocco, T. S., & Kormanik, M. B. (2012). Lesbians, gays, bisexuals, and transgendered people and human resource development: An examination of the literature in adult education and human resource development. *Human Resource Development Review, 11*(3), 326–348. https://doi.org/10.1177/1534484312447193

Schyns, B., & Schilling, J. (2013). How bad are the effects of bad leaders? A meta-analysis of destructive leadership and its outcomes. *The Leadership Quarterly, 24*(1), 138–158. https://doi.org/10.1016/j.leaqua.2012.09.001

Shuck, M. B., Rose, K., & Bergman, M. J. (2015). Inside the spiral of dysfunction: The personal consequences of working for a dysfunctional leader. *New Horizons in Adult Education & Human Resource Development, 27*(4), 51–58. https://doi.org/10.1002/nha3.20122

Tarakci, M., Greer, L. L., & Groenen, P. J. F. (2016). When does power disparity help or hurt group performance? *Journal of Applied Psychology, 101*(3), 415–429. https://doi.org/10.1037/apl0000056

Tepper, B. J. (2000). Consequences of abusive supervision. *Academy of Management Journal, 43*(2), 178–190. https://doi.org/10.5465/1556375

Tepper, B. J., Duffy, M. K., Henle, C. A., & Lambert, L. S. (2006). Procedural injustice, victim precipitation, and abusive supervision. *Personnel Psychology, 59*, 101–123. https://doi.org/10.1111/j.1744-6570.2006.00725.x

Tepper, B. J., Moss, S. E., & Duffy, M. K. (2011). Predictors of abusive supervision: Supervisor perceptions of deep-level dissimilarity, relationship conflict, and subordinate performance. *Academy of Management Journal, 54*, 279–294. https://doi.org/10.5465/AMJ.2011.60263085

Wei, F., & Si, S. (2011). Tit for tat? Abusive supervision and counterproductive work behaviors: The moderating effects of locus of control and perceived mobility. *Asia Pacific Journal of Management, 30*, 281–296. https://doi.org/10.1007/s10490-011-9251-y

Wright, U. T., Rocco, T. S., & McGill, C. M. (2018). Exposing oppressive systems: Institutional ethnography as a research method in adult and workforce education. In V. X. Wang & T. G. Reio (Eds.), *Handbook of research on innovative techniques, trends, and analysis for optimized research methods* (pp. 115–131). IGI Global. https://doi.org/10.4018/978-1-5225-5164-5.ch008

Wu, T.-Y. (2008). Abusive supervision and emotional exhaustion: The mediating effects of subordinate justice perception and emotional labor. *Chinese Journal of Psychology, 50*, 201–221.

Wu, T.-Y., & Hu, C. (2009). Abusive supervision and employee emotional exhaustion: Dispositional antecedents and boundaries. *Group & Organization Management, 34*(2), 143–169. https://doi.org/10.1177/1059601108331217

Xu, E., Huang, X., Lam, C. K., & Miao, Q. (2012). Abusive supervision and work behaviors: The mediating role of LMX. *Journal of Organizational Behavior, 33*(4), 531–543. https://doi.org/10.1002/job.768

35

BULLYING OF LBGTQ FACULTY IN ACADEMIA

A Real-Life Challenge Informed by the Literature

Saul Carliner

On the one hand, bullying is a common experience for workers in general and an even more common experience for LGBTQ workers in particular. For example, according to a survey for CareerBuilder by Harris Poll, nearly 40% of all LGBTQ workers have experienced workplace bullying compared to 29% of the general population (Picchi, 2017). A more recent survey of workers in the UK by the Chartered Institute for Personnel and Development (CIPD) also found that nearly 40% of all LGBTQ workers have experienced workplace bullying compared to 29% of the general population (Niewiarowski, 2023). Similarly, according to a 2017 survey of TechLeavers (people who voluntary choose to leave jobs in the high tech industry), LGBTQ workers were more likely to experience bullying and public humiliation than their heterosexual counterparts and, 64% of LGBTQ workers leaving tech jobs did so because of the bullying (Scott et al., 2016). In other words, LGBTQ workers face hostile work environments in many countries and industries. That includes higher education (Hollis, 2017).

On the other hand, when the co-editors of this volume asked me to write a chapter on bullying of LGBTQ people in academia, I had no idea why they asked me. Yes, I am a gay man and yes, I am a faculty member at a university. But my research primarily focuses on providing workers with the information and training they need to perform their jobs. In the field of Human Resources, this is known as Learning (Training) and Development. Although it also falls in the field of Human Resources, workplace civility and, more specifically, bullying, fall into different areas of study. Although I am aware of them, I am not a scholar of them.

At this point, you might be asking: Why, then, would I read a chapter from an author who starts by raising questions about their own credibility on the subject? That's where my current situation (as of the writing of this chapter) comes in. Unbeknown to the co-editors, their request came at a time when I happened to be experiencing severe bullying on the job. The ostensible reason for the bullying was my role as a brand-new chair of a department that had been in academic receivership—led by an external chair for a year to address workplace climate issues—and I began my term by announcing a reorganization of the faculty that was planned without any participation by the majority of the department members. Not announced at that time was a subsequent reorganization of the staff, a reorganization that was also started during the receivership but not ready to announce at the beginning of my term. Because it only involved staff, this reorganization would only be handled by the dean's office and Human

 DOI: 10.4324/9781003128151-41

Resources with no participation of the department. I thought I knew what I was walking into when I accepted the position and was prepared for pushback, but not for pushback that the attorney leading our Rights and Responsibilities office said met the legal standard for harassment. Although I do believe that much of the bullying behavior emerges from my role as Chair, some of my colleagues believe that my LGBTQ status and serving as the first LGBTQ chair of the department might also factor into my experience.

Perhaps as a result of feeling besieged in my work, I often felt deficient to both of the tasks to which I had committed myself—chairing my department and writing this chapter—I persisted in both all the same. A quick search of the literature showed a number of studies and essays and that the subject of bullying LGBTQ faculty in academia has been studied widely. But I further delved into the literature, the more I found that it provided perspective on my own situation, and it is from this first-person perspective of someone grappling with bullying and related behaviors that I approach the topic.

I found that reading the research on bullying actually provided further insights into what I was facing, and I use this chapter to share what I learned. In it, I report on the research, focusing on its application to the real world in real situations. Specifically, this chapter focuses on answering questions that an LGBTQ person who believes they might be bullied might ask: How do I know if I am being bullied? Why me? How is the bullying affecting me? Is the bullying affecting me because I am an LGBTQ person or just because I am me? And what can be done to address the situation?

Although much of the research applies generally to the workplace, specific issues related to academic workplaces are addressed. This chapter tries to raise issues specific to LGBTQ faculty and staff as it relates to the larger literature and to link the larger literature on bullying to the more specific situation of bullying LGBTQ workers in academia.

How Do I Know If I Am Being Bullied?

When one is going through a challenging situation, is bullying the correct term to characterize what is happening? Is this behavior normal? Appropriate? To start to address the issue of bullying in the workplace, one has to figure out whether or not they are being bullied. In some instances, workers are in fields that are adversarial and competitive by nature—academia being one of them (more on that later in this section). This is known as the workplace climate: "the formal and informal characteristics of an employment setting affecting employees' experience and effectiveness" (Bilimoria & Stewart, 2009, p. 87). Not that this is acceptable, but uncooperative and uncivil behavior has been characteristic of many work environments and, as a result, workers in such environments might not want the behavior but might assume that it is simply typical of the work environment. In other instances, the behavior might be immediately recognized as offensive and inappropriate, but it might not be bullying.

A spectrum of offensive behaviors exists in the workplace, ranging from the rude but unintentional to the systemic and targeted towards harming one or more individuals. Along this spectrum are types of named and formally defined behaviors. Individual researchers propose a variety of schemas to differentiate these behaviors, in Figure 35.1, I synthesize their work in a continuum of offensive behaviors in the workplace. The more serious behaviors are characterized not only by their potential harm but also by the underlying intentionality. That is, as one moves from incivility to bullying to harassment to violence, the likelihood that one person is targeting another increases (Baron & Neuman, 1996; Cortina et al., 2001).

Workplace incivilities	Bullying (including cyberbullying and mobbing)	Harassment (psychological and physical)	Violence
Rude but unintentional	Behavior targeted at harming one or more individuals in the behavior but that is not necessarily deemed to be systemic and, therefore, cannot be addressed legally	Systemic and targeted at harming one or more individuals and that can be addressed legally	Threats and actual acts of physical violence, including harassment, intimidation, and similarly threatening behaviors
Least serious		Most serious	
Generally ineligible for formal legal remedies but can be addressed by internal policies and procedures.		Generally eligible for formal legal remedies but should also be addressed by internal policies and procedures to prevent the need for such action.	

Figure 35.1   A Continuum of Offensive Behaviors in the Workplace.

The rest of this section explores these classes of offensive behaviors: workplace incivilities, bullying, harassment, and violence; and closes by explaining why universities can be prone to such behaviors.

Workplace Incivilities

At one end of the spectrum are behaviors labeled as workplace incivility. According to Andersson and Pearson (1999), workplace incivility refers to "low-intensity deviant behavior with ambiguous intent to harm the target. Uncivil behaviors are characteristically rude and discourteous, displaying a lack of regard for others" (p. 457). Workplace incivility may or may not mean anything more than that. In some instances, the behavior might not be linked to a formal intention to harm someone despite the insensitivity and disrespectfulness. In other instances, the incivilities can also be a precursor to the more serious and sustained behaviors that characterize bullying and harassment (Knepp, 2012). Examples of uncivil behavior include someone regularly interrupting meetings between two queer colleagues without excusing themselves and a professor never thanking a trans administrative assistant for providing assistance with difficult or time-sensitive situations. Although some workplace incivility might appear to result from isolated incidents, Faucher et al. (2015) warn that this type of behavior can potentially escalate into one of the more serious forms of behavior, such as bullying, harassment, or violence.

One particular type of incivility is microaggression. The term microaggression refers to everyday slights in speech, behavior, and the environment that may or may not be consciously intentional, but that ultimately convey a hostile or negative attitude towards a stigmatized population (Sue et al., 2007). In some instances, the microaggressions can come from straight people who make slurs or assumptions about LGBTQ people. Research suggests that, to avoid such situations, LGBTQ faculty in some departments either minimize their sexuality by not talking about it (but not denying it, either) or by staying closeted altogether. But sometimes, the microaggressions come from other LGBTQ people. One common microaggression within the LGBTQ community is when bisexual people face comments from other LGBTQ people for not being lesbian, gay, or straight (Bostwick & Hequembourg, 2014). In such instances, LGBTQ people feel further stigmatized by what they believed to be their own community.

Bullying

More serious is bullying which appears closer to the midpoint of the spectrum, which the American Psychological Association defines as

> a form of aggressive behavior in which someone intentionally and repeatedly causes another person injury or discomfort. Bullying can take the form of physical contact, words, or more subtle actions. The bullied individual typically has trouble defending him or herself and does nothing to "cause" the bullying.
>
> *(APA, 2022, paras. 1 and 2)*

Namie (2003) adds that bullying includes not only verbal behavior but also "strategic moves to render the target unproductive and unsuccessful—as it is the aggressor's desire to control the target that motivates the action" (Namie, 2003, p. 2). Namie (2003) adds that the bullying intensifies over time and lasts an average of 22 months.

One significant difference between workplace incivilities and bullying is that the latter has the express aim of intentionally harming the other party, also known as the target. The harms manifest themselves in a number of tangible ways: physical harm including beatings and physical intimidation (such as gay bashings); emotional harm such as threatening to reveal private and potentially damaging information to a target's close contacts (such as outing someone who is not yet ready to come out); and reputational harm (preventing someone from advancing in their work or sabotaging them once they do) (Cortina et al., 2001; Kennedy & Reio, 2024; Lim & Cortina, 2005; Lim et al., 2008).

In higher education, bullying around work often occurs under the guise of promoting quality (Praslova et al., 2022). For example, in a review of someone's work, the bully might make extensive comments on the target's written and oral work, sometimes noting minor or medium issues of logic and reasoning and citation, but just as likely to note issues of style, and use these to conclude that the target's work does not "meet standards." Similarly, the bully might use a minor point in an application for a promotion or award of a word to disqualify the target. Rather than constructive, such carping criticism usually achieves the opposite: causing distress among workers (White, 2023).

Several forms of bullying can occur. Two of the most common in academia including cyberbullying and mobbing. Cyberbullying is a form of bullying that occurs online and perhaps anonymously or by someone using a false identity to harm a target. Examples of cyberbullying often experienced by academic faculty and staff include repeated email messages sent by a bully to a target and that are copied to many other people, and derogatory posts to social media sites or threatening direct messages (DMs). The former often seem to come from colleagues and the latter often seem to come from students (Hollis, 2017; Faucher et al., 2015). A second form of bullying that is prevalent in academia is mobbing, which refers to coordinated efforts at bullying by a group of people (Duffy & Sperry, 2007). Duffy and Sperry (2014) more specifically note that mobbing is "a destructive social process in which individuals, groups, or organizations target a person for ridicule, humiliation, and removal from the workplace" (p. 1). Examples of mobbing include several people sending nearly identical and threatening or otherwise caustic email messages to intimidate a target and several people coordinating their behavior in a public meeting to publicly undermine the target. Mobbing is especially common in higher education, in which a group of faculty work together to thwart a target.

Harassment

A more serious—and more actionable—behavior is harassment. The term harassment has a legal definition: "unwanted behavior intended to annoy, threaten, or intimidate another in settings like workplaces or public places. Harassment might be based on factors like race, gender, religion, sexual orientation" (International Monetary Fund, n.d., point 3). The Canadian Human Rights Commission defines harassment as a "legally defined category of unwanted physical or verbal behaviour that offends or humiliates" (Canadian Human Rights Commission, 2013, cited in Faucher et al., 2015). Many of the same behaviors that characterize bullying characterize harassment too. The primary difference is that harassment is considered an illegal behavior and can be acted upon.

Two types of harassment can occur, and, in many instances, targets might experience both from the same perpetrator. The first type of harassment is psychological. Psychological harassment is defined as

> any vexatious behavior, in the form of repeated and hostile or unwanted conduct, verbal comments, actions or gestures that affect an employee's dignity or psychological or physical integrity, and that result in a harmful work environment for the employee. A single serious incidence of such behavior that has a lasting harmful effect on an employee may also constitute psychological harassment.
>
> *(Lawsider, 2023, para. 1)*

Some jurisdictions recognize psychological harassment, such as the Canadian provinces of Quebec and Ontario (Educaloi, 2023; Government of Ontario, 2019). The second type of harassment is physical harassment, which can involve harassment not only to the victim personally, but also to their property.

Although this chapter primarily focuses on bullying, the overlap in behaviors between bullying and harassment (which is actionable from a legal perspective) suggests that a strong relationship exists between the two. A relationship also exists between harassment and the next category, violence, because harassment often precedes violence (Faucher et al., 2015; Kennedy & Reio, 2024).

Violence

Violence is the most serious form of offensive behaviors in the workplace and refers to threats and actual acts of physical violence, as well as intimidation and threat of violence (Government of Ontario, 2019; U.S. Centers for Disease Control, 2020). The behavior meets and exceeds criminal standards and requires the intervention of law enforcement to ideally prevent but often to prosecute.

According to the US Centers for Disease Control, several groups of people are prone to violent behavior. The first group is people who have criminal intent with no "legitimate relationship to the business or employees" (para. 1). The murder of a store owner in Cedar Glen, California over her Pride flag in the summer of 2023—an attack that followed repeated removals and defacing of earlier Pride flags—is an example of such violence.

A second source of violence in the workplace results from a personal relationship outside of work that spills into the work environment. Consider, for example, the case of a professor who has a sexual relationship with a student. The student terminates the relationship, and the jilted professor begins stalking the student in other classes and at their home. When the student continues to avoid the professor, the professor confronts the student on campus with a gun.

The third source of violence in the workplace is with customers or clients. In the context of academia, this would be students and their parents as well as community members who receive services. An example of such violence is a professor who speaks out about a proposed policy requiring trans athletes to compete in the gender category of their birth. As the faculty member leaves the meeting, they are swarmed by a group of anti-trans activists and blocked from leaving the building while they threaten to follow the faculty member to their home.

A fourth source of violence in the workplace is between co-workers. In the context of academia, this would involve conflicts among students, between faculty and staff, staff and other staff, and among faculty. An extreme example of bias-prompted violence (though not an LGBTQ example) was the murder of 14 female engineering students at Polytechnique, an engineering university in Montreal, by a male student because of their gender amid his concerns about feminism (Dalton et al., n.d.).

Why Offensive Behavior Is a Particular Problem in Universities?

Offensive behavior is a particular problem in universities for several reasons. First is the openness of the institution. Even when privately owned, universities are public places at which all are welcome (West, 2022). For example, even if a student aggressively challenges a professor's stance on privilege in class and the student ends the exchange with "you're a f****ing idiot," that professor is not likely to have grounds for action against the student because of laws and other regulations that ensure all students have fair access to education. Although protective measures can be taken when students threaten faculty, they receive due process before serious action like an academic dismissal would result and the process could take a year or longer (Hollis, 2021; Praslova et al., 2022).

The peer-review process also creates challenges. The double-blind nature of the process means that neither the reviewers nor the recipients of the feedback know who one another are. That, in turn, encourages reviewers to be more blunt in their feedback often bordering on offensive, a characteristic that decade-old research has noted occurs in anonymous communication (Sproull & Kiesler, 1991). Because the peer review is central to the research process that is central to universities, that bluntness often transfers into faculty interactions with others even when the interaction is not blind. For example, doctoral students reported receiving comments such as "bring that back to me when you have something real to say" as feedback on their draft work rather than constructive criticism (Goodarzi, 2019). In meetings, one faculty member might say "You're patently wrong" in response to an observation by a colleague rather than a more neutral "I disagree or Why do you feel this way?" (White, 2023).

Third universities are political institutions by design. With most universities following a bicameral governance model in which faculty have final say over all academic decisions, people often engage in activities to ensure their desired outcome in political processes. At its most positive, this process involves coalition building. But at its most negative, political processes can be divisive and turn on targets, such as several bullies raising points of carping criticism on minor issues in a proposal for a new program presented a targeted faculty member with the intention of delaying or failing the proposal.

Fourth, although most universities promote inclusion of all members of their communities, these individuals are not immune to the biases of the larger societies in which universities operate and from which community members arrive. So even though university policy might actively promote equality for LGBTQ people, if the local community actively discriminates, that behavior could appear on campus, even in the presence of strong local non-discrimination laws and institutional non-discrimination policies.

Fifth is the tenure system. Although meant to protect academic freedom, it also means that peer faculty grant tenure. Many junior faculty worry that challenging tenured faculty in any way could result in a refusal of tenure. Although the tenure process involves a series of reviews (the exact nature varies by institution but usually involves an approval by a college or faculty and, later the Board of Trustees or Directors, the recommendation of the faculty in the department, usually the first in the process, plays a pivotal role in the decisions of later reviews in the tenure process. In other cases, senior faculty might actively block junior faculty from tenure if they feel challenged by their approaches. Indeed, this is at the heart of a storyline running through the Netflix series *The Chair*, in which a promising junior African American faculty member who actively connects with students is undermined in her tenure bid by a senior faculty member who does not agree with her approach to teaching literature and is jealous of her connection with students, one that he seriously lacks. Although the example in that series focuses on teaching and research usually plays the larger role in the tenure decision, the same situations and challenges arise in research. For example, some researchers have objected to queer studies overall or particular aspects of it (like studies of pronoun usage) and might use their objections to vote against tenure.

Perhaps one of the most challenging and perhaps underlying all of these reasons is the intensely personal nature of academic work, especially the long period of time for preparation (at least three years beyond a bachelor's degree and often longer), research, and the tenure process, all of which require great investments of time and funds, and to which personal reputations are closely aligned. A critique of one's work can sometimes feel like a critique of one's person. As David C. Yamada notes:

> Academicians are adept at intellectual analysis, manipulation, and argumentation. When applied to the tasks of teaching, scholarship, and service, these skills reinforce the most socially useful aspects of the academy. But many of us who have worked in academe have seen what happens when they are applied in hurtful or even malicious ways.
> *(2021, p. xiii)*

Why Me?

After classifying the type of behavior one is experiencing and determining that one is, indeed, on the receiving end of bullying behaviors, one of the next that might occur is: Why me? That the definition of bullying specifically notes that the target did nothing to cause the bullying is often of scant consolation at a time like this. So perhaps it's helpful to understand who typically is a target and who is a bully. Although anyone can assume either role, people in these roles tend to have certain characteristics and those, in turn, increase the likelihood that someone will find themselves in one role or the other.

Bullies tend to focus on two general categories of targets. One group of targets lives with characteristics over which they have no control: their gender, race, religion, or ethnic background, or sexuality and, in many cases, combinations of those (also known as intersectionality). As noted at the beginning of this chapter, in the workplace, such targets are more likely to experience bullying more frequently than other parties and this is especially true of LGBTQ workers.

But the other category of targets is less obvious. Although instinct might suggest that bullies target the weak, the research on workplace bullying suggests the opposite: targets tend to be more accomplished workers who have a strong commitment to the organization (Praslova et al., 2022).

That's because the bullies themselves are often "mediocre" performers who fancy themselves as stars. Bullies are often envious of the targets and jealous of the attention targets receive and, at the same time, perceive targets as threats to their careers (Praslova et al., 2022). Although bullying in the workplace can come from customers (or, in the case of universities, students, their parents, and the community), the most immediate bullying often comes from supervisors and other superiors (in universities, chairs and more senior colleagues), and peers (colleagues).

These issues are not unique to LGBTQ people; but because LGBTQ workers often feel as if they have to perform to a higher standard and, therefore, appear to be more competent and accomplished, this tendency actually increases the likelihood of bullies targeting them because they fall into both categories of targets. LGBTQ people would face targeting both for their sexuality as well as their competence (Misawa, 2015).

Given its competitive nature and peer-managed processes like tenure, working in academia provides an environment that lets bullies target LGBTQ colleagues. In addition, departmental and organizational climates can also affect the extent of bullying within universities. Researchers have found that, even in institutions that ostensibly support diversity, faculty feel more comfortable disclosing their sexuality in some departments rather than others because of the political climates (Hollis, 2021; Patridge et al., 2014). Some disciplines, such as some engineering and science-related disciplines—tend to be more conservative than some humanities and social science disciplines (Zipp & Fenwick, 2006). The research emphasizes, however, that every department and institution is unique, and their levels of inclusivity might differ from the general tendency reported in the literature.

How Might the Bullying Affect Me?

After realizing why you might be targeted, another likely question might pertain to its effect on you. The research clearly states that bullying and harassment affect targets physically, psychologically, and socially (Kennedy & Reio, 2024; Misawa, 2015). Because it places the body on alert for danger, bullying and harassment can manifest themselves with physical affects. In some instances, the body puts up the same defenses as if it were facing an imminent physical attack even though most bullying occurs on a psychological level and that can cause heightened levels of adrenaline (Mayo Clinic Staff, 2023). That, in turn, leads to increases in blood pressure, and heart rates (Mayo Clinic Staff, 2023). According to Tsuno et al. (2022), prolonged bullying can lead to respiratory illnesses and other illness-related absences from the workplace. Sleeping and eating are among daily activities that bullying can affect. As bullying and harassment are primarily psychological phenomena, the most significant effects are psychological and emotional (Tsuno et al., 2022). Anxiety is certainly one outcome. So are depression and related mental health challenges. Liang (2021) reports that prolonged bullying can lead to mental exhaustion. If the target remains in the workplace, the target can lose their motivation to succeed, reduce their engagement with their work and these, in turn, affect work performance (Misawa, 2015; Praslova et al., 2022). Economically, the health impacts lead to increased medical expenses and medical leave—sometimes extended leaves (Cullinan et al., 2020).

Why Does Bullying Affect LGBTQ People in Particular?

Although not the exclusive targets of bullying and related behaviors in the workplace, LGBTQ people are frequent targets. For many years, homosexual behavior was illegal and, therefore, homosexuals lived a clandestine life. The threat of exposure often carried with it the loss of status and perhaps a criminal conviction, but also the possibility of blackmail (Levine, 1979). These laws remain on the books in some countries and some countries in Africa, have even strengthened them (Rainbow Railroad, 2023).

Even when the laws were rescinded, social attitudes have been slow to change and have involved a series of two-steps-forward, one-step-backs. For example, only about a decade before the U.S. Supreme Court ruling affirmed gay marriage, many states passed ballot measures affirming marriage as between a man and a woman. Similarly, although some cities and states have passed human rights protections for LGBTQ people, some initially omitted transgendered people and other jurisdictions have not passed such legislation, including the U.S. federal government. Similarly, some companies have established policies that protect LGBTQ people but, in the early 2020s, some states like Florida actually rolled back diversity efforts. Simultaneous with such efforts, trans people—especially trans teenagers—find their rights under fire with some U.S. and Canadian legislators passing legislation that affects their treatment in schools (including how teachers may address them), sports, and restrooms. As a result, many LGBTQ people lack legal protections or face hostile circumstances.

The legal landscape (faced at the time of writing this chapter) results from over a half century of increased and increasing visibility of LGBTQ people that followed the Stonewall riots in 1969 that is beyond the scope of this chapter. But, as one visible lesbian activist once observed to me, the increased visibility of LGBTQ people was likely to spark a backlash. That is actually a sign of general social progress through the individuals on the receiving end of the bullying and harassment in the workplace, that progress seems more of a theoretical construct than a lived reality.

More immediately, a 2023 U.S. Supreme Court ruling gave a business a right to refuse to serve LGBTQ customers if it infringed on their religious freedoms, creating further legally sanctioned harassment in the workplace. Less well known is the case of the Saskatchewan legislature, which used a special legal move called the No Withstanding clause of the Canadian Charter of Rights and Freedoms to require that schools notify parents of children 16 and under when their children wanted to change their names and pronouns. The Not Withstanding Clause lets a legislative body override a court ruling on a temporary basis for five years and can renew the override each five years. In this case, the legislature invoked the Not Withstanding Clause after the courts put the notification law on hold because it was found to violate the Charter.

What Can I Do About Bullying?

Given its serious impact on workers in general and on LGBTQ workers in particular, remedies are needed to address workplace bullying. At one end of the spectrum are efforts to prevent bullying, harassment, violence, and other uncivil behaviors. These efforts start with carrots: legislation and policies that prevent workplace bullying and harassment in general and human rights legislation to provide further protection for marginalized groups (Praslova et al., 2022).

Some jurisdictions, like the Canadian provinces of Quebec and Ontario, have legislation that requires employers to provide a psychologically safe work environment and provides mechanisms for workers to file complaints within the employing organization and with the government if those rights are not fulfilled (Educaloi, 2023). The standard of proof differs between the two provinces: only Quebec views bullying and harassment solely from the perspective of the target. That is, if the target perceives they are being bullied or harassed and can provide evidence, that is sufficient proof. Workplace policies operate similarly to such legislation but within the context of the employing organization. But given the preference of corporations today to use arbitration to resolve disputes and the settlement of many harassment claims out-of-court and with nondisclosure agreements—meaning participants in the case cannot talk about it—the extent of bullying and harassment is often masked (Carliner et al., 2021).

Other proactive efforts to limit bullying and harassment include workplace training programs that build sensitivity towards LGBTQ people. Nonprofit LGBTQ rights organizations like the Human Rights Campaign, OutFront Minnesota, and Egale Canada, as well as specialists provide such training. Some organizations also recognize employers for creating LGBTQ-affirming workplaces through mechanisms like the Human Right Campaign's Equality Index and Newsweek's America's Greatest Workplaces for LGBTQ+.

But prevention often does not work. Most employers have complaint mechanisms for raising concerns about harassment and bullying. In private employers, Human Resources often administers these programs (Carliner et al., 2021). Although Human Resources can often do so in universities, many universities have a separate complaint mechanism through the offices administering their academic code, because bullying and harassment violate most academic codes of conduct as surely as plagiarism does (Hollis, 2021, 2017).

Filing complaints requires that the target make a case against the bully, a task that involves collecting proof of the bullying, documenting incidents, collecting email messages, and other evidence. This is often cited as one of the reasons that many targets avoid reporting bullying and harassment. If the situation were not already stressful, the responsibility for documenting it only adds to the burden (Prasolova et al., 2022). Furthermore, concerns about how the complaint will be received, the length of time involved in processing complaints, and mixed outcomes of such complaints further deter targets from reporting the situation (Liang, 2021; Praslova et al., 2022). In addition, much bullying of LGBTQ workers is implicit. It might occur because of the target's LGBTQ status but that status is not explicitly stated in the bullying. Proving bias becomes more challenging. In addition, the same complaint mechanisms meant to protect workers from bullying can be used by the bullies themselves to further harass their targets. Against these odds, however, Liang (2021) found that, for some targets, prolonged bullying helps them to find their voice and report what is happening to them.

Rooting out incivilities, bullying, harassment, and violence becomes more challenging if these behaviors are systemic. Prasolova et al. (2022) point out that bullying could result from systemically sanctioned behavior, even if the behavior is only tacitly sanctioned. Kennedy and Reio (2024) add that the reason such behaviors could occur is that they are built into the system. They note examples such as having just one accessible bathroom inconveniently located for many workers and reward systems that place meeting sale quotas over other considerations. Any solution must address the systemic issues that encourage and reward incivilities, bullying, and harassment.

So How Does This Inform My Situation?

Consulting the literature on bullying in general and bullying of LGBTQ people and LGBTQ people in academia in particular, has helped me gain perspective on my own situation.

Several questions struck me after reading the literature. Some of the bullies claimed that I had bullied them. I felt like I was bullied but the literature (especially Liang, 2021) suggested that the target can internalize the behavior and become a bully themselves. I sincerely did not want to perpetuate that behavior but was in no position to assess my own behavior.

The second question that arose was whether I was targeted because I am gay. Concerns that diversity and equity issues would arise in conversations: not necessarily supportive of the efforts and in a way that I perceived as derogatory. But explicit evidence that I was targeted for being gay was lacking. This is important because, although LGBTQ people are more often than not targeted because of our identity, we often lack the evidence to demonstrate that.

The fourth question that arose was probably the most basic: why me? Some of my colleagues who observed the situation suggested that some of the bullying was personal; jealousy over perceived advantages and success I had and that, at this point in time, they didn't. But the colleagues who observed the situation believed that more of the bullying was positional: that is, resulting from my role and, in this case, presiding over a reorganization of the department. These colleagues suggested that the bullies probably benefitted from the previous structure of the department and anticipated losing status and other advantages under the new structure. The longer the new structure persisted without alteration, the less likely they were to be restored to their former position and advantage. It seemed to me that I fit the definition of the competent target whose work was somehow threatening.

My husband is very concerned for me and wishes I would resign as chair. In some ways, going through bullying is an experiential learning experience. Some of the personal learning is hard: not just the experience of bullying but wondering what I am doing to encourage it or prolong it. As these supportive colleagues have noted, my visible reactions and tendency to overexplain probably do not aid the situation. That's on me.

But as Liang suggested, the situation has also helped me to find my voice. My impatience can also be an asset; I have asked for support, loudly and persistently enough that I have received it. The support certainly benefits me but more importantly benefits the larger group, the majority of whom want to do their job, do not want to be co-opted into tensions between co-workers, and have a right to a work environment that is free of such avoidable friction.

References

Andersson, L. M., & Pearson, C. M. (1999). Tit for tat? The spiraling effect of incivility in the workplace. *Academy of Management Review, 24*(3), 452–471.

APA. (2022). *Definition of bullying*. American Psychological Association Website. Retrieved October 4, 2023, from www.apa.org/topics/bullying#:~:text=Bullying%20is%20a%20form%20of,words%2C%20 or%20more%20subtle%20actions

Baron, R. A., & Neuman, J. H. (1996). Workplace violence and workplace aggression: Evidence on their relative frequency and potential causes. *Aggressive Behavior, 22*(3), 161–173. https://doi. org/10.1002/(SICI)1098-2337(1996)22:3 < 161::AID-AB1 > 3.0.CO;2-Q

Bilimoria, D., & Stewart, A. J. (2009). "Don't ask, don't tell": The academic climate for lesbian, gay, bisexual, and transgender faculty in science and engineering. *NWSA Journal, 21*(2), 85–103.

Bostwick, W., & Hequembourg, A. (2014). "Just a little hint": Bisexual-specific microaggressions and their connection to epistemic injustices, *Culture, Health & Sexuality, 16*(5), 488–503. https://doi.org /10.1080/13691058.2014.889754

Carliner, S., Driscoll, M., & Thayer, Y. (2021). *Career anxiety: Guidance through tough times*. International Career Press.

Cortina, L. M., Magley, V. J., Williams, J. H., & Langhout, R. D. (2001). Incivility in the workplace: Incidence and impact. *Journal of Occupational Health Psychology, 6*(1), 64–80.

Cullinan, J., Hodgins, M., Hogan, V., & Pursell, L. (2020). The value of lost productivity from workplace bullying in Ireland. *Occupational Medicine, 70*(4), 251–258.

Dalton, M., Klang, A., Grasley, R., & Leschart, M. (n.d.). Remember the 14. *CBC.ca*. Retrieved October 29, 2023, from www.cbc.ca/montreal/features/remember-14/

Duffy, M., & Sperry, L. (2007). Workplace mobbing: Individual and family health consequences. *The Family Journal, 15*(4), 398–404.

Duffy, M. P., & Sperry, L. (2014). *Overcoming mobbing: A recovery guide for workplace aggression and bullying*. Oxford University Press, USA.

EducaLoi. (2023). Psychological harassment at work. *Educa: The Law by Topic*. Retrieved October 29, 2023, from https://educaloi.qc.ca/en/capsules/psychological-harassment-in-the-workplace/

Faucher, C., Cassidy, W., & Jackson, M. (2015). From the sandbox to the inbox: Comparing the acts, impacts, and solutions of bullying in K-12, higher education, and the workplace. *Journal of Education and Training Studies, 3*(6), 111–125.

Goodarzi, Z. (2019, June 2). *Talking around texts in research writing: Bhaktian approach to graduate writing.* Presented at the 2019 Canadian Association for the Study of Discourse and Writing Conference, Vancouver, BC.

Government of Ontario. (2019). *Part III.0.I: Workplace violence and workplace harassment, government of Ontario->jobs and employment->workplace safety and health->occupational health and safety compliance->guide to occupational safety and health act.* Retrieved October 29, 2023, from www.ontario.ca/document/guide-occupational-health-and-safety-act/part-iii0i-workplace-violence-and-workplace-harassment

Hollis, L. P. (2017). Higher education henchmen: Vicarious bullying and underrepresented populations. *Advances in Social Sciences Research Journal, 4*(12), 64–73.

Hollis, L. P. (2021). *Human resource perspectives on workplace bullying in higher education: Understanding vulnerable employees' experiences.* Routledge.

International Monetary Fund. (n.d.) Harassment: Policy on harassment. *UNWomen.org.* Retrieved October 29, 2023, from www.un.org/womenwatch/osagi/pdf/IMFpolicysh3.pdf

Kennedy, C., & Reio, T. G., Jr. (2024). Preventing workplace mistreatment and injury: Incivility, bullying, and violence. In T. S. Rocco, M. L. Morris, & R. Poell (Eds.), *Handbook of human resource development.* Sage Publications.

Knepp, K. A. F. (2012). Understanding student and faculty incivility in higher education. *Journal of Effective Teaching, 12*(1), 33–46.

Lawsider.com. (2023). *Definition of psychological harassment.* Retrieved October 4, 2023, from www.lawinsider.com/dictionary/psychological-harassment#:~:text=Psychological%20harassment%20means%20any%20vexatious%20behaviour%20in%20the%20form%20of,learning%20environment%20for%20the%20individual

Levine, M. P. (1979). Employment discrimination against gay men. *International Review of Modern Sociology, 9*(2), 151–163.

Liang, H. L. (2021). Does workplace bullying produce employee voice and physical health issues? Testing the mediating role of emotional exhaustion. *Frontiers in Psychology, 12*, 610944.

Lim, S., & Cortina, L. M. (2005). Interpersonal mistreatment in the workplace: the interface and impact of general incivility and sexual harassment. *Journal of applied psychology, 90*(3), 483.

Lim, S., Cortina, L. M., & Magley, V. J. (2008). Personal and workgroup incivility: impact on work and health outcomes. *Journal of applied psychology, 93*(1), 95.

Mayo Clinic Staff. (2023). Stress management. *Mayo Clinic Healthy Lifestyle.* Retrieved October 29, 2023, from www.mayoclinic.org/healthy-lifestyle/stress-management/in-depth/stress/art-20046037

Misawa, M. (2015). Cuts and bruises caused by arrows, sticks, and stones in academia: Theorizing three types of racist and homophobic bullying in adult and higher education. *Adult Learning, 26*(1), 6–13.

Namie, G. (2003). Workplace bullying: Escalated incivility. *Ivey Business Journal: Improving the Practice of Management, 68*(2), 1–6.

Niewiarowski, E. (2023, April 10). Dealing with anti-LGBTQ+ bullying at work? Here's what to do. *Pink News.* Retrieved October 3, 2023, from www.thepinknews.com/2023/04/10/homophobic-transphobic-bullying-work-employee-advice/

Patridge, E. V., Barthelemy, R., & Rankin, S. R. (2014). Factors impacting the academic climate for LGBQ STEM faculty. *Journal of Women and Minorities in Science and Engineering, 20*(1), 75–78.

Picchi, A. (2017, October 19). A workplace epidemic of bullying LGBT employees. *CBS News.* Retrieved August 19, 2023, from www.cbsnews.com/news/bullying-lgbt-employees-workplace-epidemic/

Prasolova, L., Carucci, R., & Stokes, C. (2022, November 4). How bullying manifests at work—and how to stop it. *Harvard Business Review.* Retrieved October 4, 2023, from https://hbr.org/2022/11/how-bullying-manifests-at-work-and-how-to-stop-it

Rainbow Railroad. (2023). Issues archives. *Rainbow Railroad.* Retrieved October 29, 2023, from www.rainbowrailroad.org/stories/issues

Scott, A., Klein, F., & Onovakpuri, U. (2016). *Tech-leavers study.* Kapor Center. Retrieved October 3, 2023, from www.kaporcenter.org/wp-content/uploads/2017/04/KAPOR_Tech-Leavers-Final.pdf

Sproull, L., & Kiesler, S. B. (1991). *Connections: New ways of working in the networked organization.* MIT Press.

Sue, D. W., Capodilupo, C. M., Torino, G. C., Bucceri, J. M., Holder, A., Nadal, K. L., & Esquilin, M. (2007). Racial microaggressions in everyday life: Implications for clinical practice. *American Psychologist, 62*(4), 271.

Tsuno, K., Kawakami, N., Tsutsumi, A., Shimazu, A., Inoue, A., Odagiri, Y., & Shimomitsu, T. (2022). Victimization and witnessing of workplace bullying and physician-diagnosed physical and mental health and organizational outcomes: A cross-sectional study. *PLOS One, 17*(10), e0265863.

U.S. Centers for Disease Control. (2020). *Types of workplace violence.* National Institute for Occupational Safety and Health. Retrieved October 29, 2023, from https://wwwn.cdc.gov/WPVHC/Nurses/Course/Slide/Unit1_5

West, J. (2022, April 28). Belonging: Why it is the next step on the equity, diversity and inclusion ladder. *Times Higher Education.* Retrieved October 29, 2023, from www.timeshighereducation.com/campus/belonging-why-it-next-step-equity-diversity-and-inclusion-ladder

White, L. (2023, August 29). *Cultivating collegial spaces workshop.* Concordia University.

Yamada, D. (2021). Foreword. In L. P. Hollis (Ed.), *Human resource perspectives on workplace bullying in higher education understanding vulnerable employees' experiences* (pp. xii–xiv). Routledge.

Zipp, J. F., & Fenwick, R. (2006). Is the academy a liberal hegemony? The political orientations and educational values of professors. *International Journal of Public Opinion Quarterly, 70*(3), 304–326.

36

WALKING A QUEER LIFE

Perspectives on Fear, Hope, and Resistance

Tonette S. Rocco, Debaro Huyler, Bolivar X. Nieto, Geovanna N. Hernandez, Joel Anderson, Warren J. Blumenfeld, Charlene Désir, André P. Grace, Jordan D. X. Hinton, Robert C. Mizzi, Nick Rumens, and Iva Žegura

> I walk a queer life every day, shifting expressions of my identity to the contexts that surround me.
> *(Robert C. Mizzi, chapter author and survey respondent)*

The 2020s have had an alarming surge of anti-LGBTQ+ laws enacted worldwide. Headlines like those announcing Poland or Italy's ban on same-sex partners adopting children (Armellini & Piscioneri, 2023), the British Government blocking a Scottish law that allows individuals to self-declare their gender legally (Associated Press, 2023), or Uganda imposing the death penalty for "aggravated homosexuality" (Sands & Ombour, 2023) have permeated the news cycle. During the first four months of 2023, 417 anti-LGBTQ+ bills were introduced at the state level in the United States. As exemplified by Florida's "Parental Rights in Education" law (Florida Legislature, 2022), which targets free speech in education by prohibiting discussions of sexual orientation and gender identity (SOGI) in schools, as well as any text that discusses SOGI or has a character who might be a sexual minority, these bills impede the rights of many in LGBTQ+ communities. Meanwhile, Tennessee was the first state to enact a law explicitly criminalizing drag shows (Choi, 2023), with over 30 similar bills being debated across 17 states as of 2023 (Nossel, 2023). Worldwide, 67 countries have national LGB criminal laws, and nine countries criminalize transgender and gender nonconformance (Human Rights Watch, n.d). Nonetheless, amidst such a disturbing state of affairs, there is some cause for optimism. For instance, a Japanese court ruled that its ban on same-sex marriage was unconstitutional (Lies, 2023). The Japanese ruling and other developments, like the U.S. Supreme Court's ruling in *Bostock v. Clayton County* ratifying protection for LGBTQ+ employees under Title VII of the Civil Rights Act of 1964, may pave the way for future legal protection internationally.

The purpose of this concluding chapter is to reflect on the current and future realities of LGBTQ+ communities and allies globally. To begin, a Qualtrics survey was sent to the authors involved in this collection, as well as those who intended to contribute but ultimately were not able to do so. We took this approach because we believe the individuals who participated or intended to participate in this project are at the forefront of research and policy considerations for LGBTQ+ people globally. Six questions were posed, and while only nine authors responded to all six, we believe the perspectives shared are important and representative of the issues facing the

DOI: 10.4324/9781003128151-42

LGBTQ+ communities. All responses are organized by question, except for questions two and three, which are merged. Questions two and three were similar in asking about the top priorities for the LGBTQ+ community in terms of policy initiatives and agendas (question 2) and professional practice (question 3). To remain authentic to the respondents' sentiments, we gathered and organized statements into narratives for reader understandability without coding and analysis. We believe these narratives provide insights into the lived experiences of individuals within LGBTQ+ communities. By creating such narratives, we hope to spark ideas for future research. The exact words of the respondents are used with minor editing for readability. The survey communication indicated that responses would be used with author identifying information. For context, the statements are in quotation marks with the respondent's name and country of residence identified.

Question 1: How Does the Current State of Affairs (Regarding LGBTQ+ Identity) Affect You Personally and Individually?

The state of affairs for individuals who identify as a part of the LGBTQ+ community elicits hurt, fear, and feelings of being in dangerous times. André P. Grace (Canada) summed up the situation stating:

> When gay marriage was legalized in Canada in 2005, sexual minorities celebrated this significant move in our quest for full citizenship. Nearly twenty years later, we find ourselves navigating dangerous times for sexual and gender minorities. While we have significant protections in legislation and law, with the federal Canadian Charter of Rights and Freedoms protecting our individual rights with regard to our sexual and gender identities, there is a surge in rightist efforts to harm us in terms of our accommodation in education and other social institutions and society at large. Thus, our fight to sustain human and civil rights continues.

Robert C. Mizzi (Canada) worries "about LGBTQ people when this pushback goes viral." Mizzi believes, "Not all LGBTQ people can weather the storm as well as others." Jordan Hinton (Australia) "a cisgender gay man" notes the struggle of consistently being "on the receiving end of intolerance and prejudice." Hinton additionally underscores how a "lack of acceptance and tolerance is especially prevalent for some LGBTQ+ group members, particularly Trans and gender-diverse individuals who have been the subject and target of pervasive hate-speech, discrimination, and societal mistreatment and inequality." Hinton states the LGBTQ+ community is "hurting" as "we are tired of continually trying to justify our existence, fight for our basic rights, and being constantly reminded of society's misguided and negative views towards us."

These sentiments were echoed by four respondents who reflected on their identities as queer and agender, Black, Latinx, and lesbian (the lesbian respondent is from Croatia), each commenting on their experience while sharing concerns about the threats faced by other sexual minorities. Warren J. Blumenfeld (USA) addressed the "political backlash against discussion of sexuality, race, and gender in the schools and the assault on members of the Trans community regarding the increasing bans on gender-affirming care, participation in sports teams, and use of public facilities." Bolivar X. Nieto and Charlene Désir who both live in Florida, a state in the United States, discussed similar worries about political persecution. Charlene laments "those of African descent (Black) and/or LGBTQ are under attack. Books are banned, and discussions on these two groups in the school settings can be punished and/or charges can be placed against them." Bolivar X. Nieto observes, "It is scary not to know what could happen to one's rights as these are slowly being impacted by policies perpetuating stigma and discrimination. It is not only about being LGBTQ, but also about being Latinx. Though this will not be an issue in my current place of employment, it may not be the case if I decide to change career, for example, academia, where my LGBTQ identity may, in a not-so-distant future, be considered 'undesirable'." Nieto also fears that the wave of anti-LGBTQ+ "policies could lead to challenges in accessing health-care and other needed services, as is already happening with our Trans community."

Iva Žegura (Croatia), a clinical psychologist and pioneer of LGBTQ+ affirmative psycho-logical practices in the Balkan region, reflects on her identity being weaponized to denigrate LBGTQ+ issues. Žegura recounts how she was "the first clinical psychologist that came out as a woman lesbian in Croatian professional society and the general public at the beginning of 2000," successfully supporting "the implementation of new legislation regarding legal gender recognition and implementing [The World Professional Association for Transgender Health's Standard of Care] . . . within the Croatian health system between 2010 and 2015." Yet, due to the rising global anti-LGBTQ+ rhetoric, Žegura highlights derision from "right-wing oriented politicians who are also medical doctors and psychiatrists" that use her identity to "derogate [her] professionalism," labeling her work as pure "activism." Žegura observes "that being an ally of transgender people is claimed to make me non-objective for professional work with Trans and/or LGBIQ people in general." Žegura illustrates her point by noting,

> when a few Trans activists wanted to initiate a Trans-NGO in Croatia, they did not have enough participants that will sign and initiate the NGO because they were afraid to disclose their gender identity in this way, so [Žegura and her colleague] . . . signed as initiators so that the NGO can be established.

Žegura found that her colleague, a "white cisgender heterosexual man is never considered to be an activist because of this, but it's automatically a presumption regarding [her] because of [her] sexual orientation identity."

Most of the respondents expressed significant concern about the backlash against people who identify as Trans and gender diverse. Five respondents noted their privilege as white, male, and cisgender, acknowledging that this protects them to some extent, making their gayness less "prob-lematic" and normalized. As Nick Rumens (UK) put it, "I feel my identity as a cis white gay man is being normalised in ways that entrench heteronormativity, which I feel very uncomfortable with."

Questions 2 and 3: What Do You Think the Top Priorities Should Be for the LGBTQ+ Community in Terms of Policy Initiatives and Agendas and Professional Practice?

Joel Anderson (Australia) states:

> Around the globe, there are continued efforts to encourage LGBTQ individuals to change or suppress their sexuality or gender identity. While there have been rapid changes in laws in certain jurisdictions to limit or forbid this, these laws are often sub-par. There needs to be continued pressure on policymakers to ensure that these anti-conversion laws are nuanced to local needs, cover change or suppression pressures from secular sources (not just religious sources) and apply to gender identity-based conversion pressures as well as those targeting sexuality.

Charlene Désir (USA) suggests that global policy initiatives must include "Continued basic human rights and the respect of LGBTQ folks to live a life of freedom and the pursuit of happiness and more legal scrutiny for abuse against trans folks." Iva Žegura (Croatia) emphasizes, "All efforts that aim to change sexual orientation and gender identity should be legally banned" and proposes "The development of professional Guidelines and Standards" at the "national level." Žegura promotes the idea that "LGBTIQ+ and intersectional identities should be implemented as obligatory in the curriculum for all medical and mental health professionals." Furthermore, Žegura expresses the belief that "Ethical codes should include LGBTIQ+ issues . . . [and that] during the regular psychotherapy and counseling training, participants should develop specific competencies in working with LGBTIQ+ people."

Warren J. Blumenfeld (USA) also emphasizes the need for action on a national level. Blumenfeld promotes the need for

> [p]olitical guarantees on the right to make choices regarding our own bodies, with whom we engage in consensual sexuality, the studying of our stories in curricular materials, guarantees against our books being banned in schools and libraries, speaking up against political and social leaders who oppose our rights, and challenges to religious denominations who marginalize and stereotypes us.

Jordan Hinton (Australia) goes on to describe groups and actions that are important in consideration of the priorities of LGTBQ+ communities. Hinton states:

> There certainly needs to be more of a push from legislators, community members (LGBTQ+ or otherwise), local governments, and healthcare professionals (among others) to establish or enhance protections towards sexual minority and trans/gender-diverse individuals. This includes more policy initiatives to protect LGBTQ+ workers (e.g., working in religious institutions), ensure safe and affirming healthcare and housing are available, and establish curriculum and education initiatives that help ensure the LGBTQ+ community is included, and their voices are heard.

Similarly, Nick Rumens (UK) champions the need for

> [l]egislation that protects all LGBTQI + people in all areas of life, including work, immigration, education, access to human services, healthcare, housing and so on. Overturning recent laws and policies that ban LGBTQ+ literature in schools. Strengthening rights and policies around gender diverse people.

For Robert C. Mizzi (Canada), there is a greater need to expand on how LGBTQ+ people are included in workplaces and organizations. Mizzi notes:

> One priority for the LGBTQ community and allies should be fostering deep inclusion in organizations so tokenism or cosmetic diversity isn't the new benchmark for inclusivity. Deep inclusion means fostering a personal and professional transformation towards LGBTQ inclusion, amplifying LGBTQ voices, and analyzing systems for their impact on LGBTQ communities.

To foster transformation and increase visibility, André P. Grace (Canada) postulates:

> Sexual and gender minorities [need] to be visible and vocal in their professional practices. They need to organize and be a group force in their organizations. They have to

develop policies implemented in procedures that drive recognition and accommodation of sexual and gender minorities in both worker and client roles in their professional practices.

Many of the respondents seem to believe, as Jordon Hinton (Australia) states:

> Top priorities in professional settings (e.g., workplaces, education, healthcare) should include affirmative care, non-discriminatory policies, and developing educational resources that allow for the voices of the LGBTQ+ community to be heard (alongside non-LGBTQ+ folks)—this includes resources that are applicable to all, not just resources that are tailored towards (cis)heteronormative belief systems and ideals.

André P. Grace (Canada) cautions the LGBTQ community of potential divisiveness that hurts the community. Grace posits:

> These days, sexual and gender minorities constitute discrete populations, commonly with their own agendas. They do not compose a community. With some of these populations disrupting Pride parades and other events in recent years, problems have arisen internally, adding to rightist attempts to harm us. Before sexual and gender minorities can impact policy, they need to come together to have strength in unity across differences. They also need to work to sustain gains in law and legislation since this foundation is essential to effective institutional policy making in education and other domains.

Bolivar X. Nieto (USA) insists there is a need for "Community mobilization efforts to help increase civil engagement and advocacy efforts." While Warren J. Blumenfeld (USA) furthers the community mobilization idea through intersectional lenses (intersectional identities-intersectional challenges), Blumenfeld suggests LGBTQ+ groups make "Connections with other movement struggles that are fighting all the various forms of oppression."

Connecting to other movements is

> to foster LGBTQ awareness and inclusion. Offering an "LGBTQ 101 awareness workshop" every few years and then expecting everyone to come on board is a myth. We need new approaches, such as visualizing queer history, exploring spatial justice for LGBTQ communities, and developing new employee engagement methods. Ongoing discussions are paramount in making an impact.
>
> *(Robert C. Mizzi, Canada)*

In addition to ongoing discussions, Bolivar X. Nieto (USA) states:

> Visibility is key. I think a priority is to engage private practices/corporations to be more vocal in support of the LGBTQ+ community and in denouncing these rights violations. There seems to be a societal-level dissonance; on one end, there are active efforts toward cultural responsiveness and appropriateness with no tolerance for discrimination, yet we are seeing how the opposite is happening across the nation through new policies. There is push back, but there is a numbness and a lack of care/concern.

Question 4: What Do You Think the Top Priorities Should Be for the LGBTQ+ Community in Terms of Research Initiatives and Agendas?

Research, policy making, and professional practice are inextricably linked in the most effective educational and other social institutional organizations. Sexual and gender minorities and allies must be more consistent and effective in engaging in quantitative research since social institutions and governments commonly demand statistics if they are to support programming in institutional and other societal contexts. Qualitative research is necessary to create awareness and impact regarding individuals' experiences, with quantitative research demonstrating the ubiquity of such experiences as common concerns.

(André P. Grace, Canada)

Iva Žegura (Croatia) believes that it is imperative for researchers to understand "the plethora and intersections of identities, and adopting the awareness of the usage of appropriate terms." Moreover, Žegura asserts that there is a need for "more research from smaller and less represented communities and nations." Said differently, top priorities for research initiatives and agendas should also explore "gender diversity, such as Trans, non-binary, agender, Two Spirit, and genderqueer identities, and learning what unique perspectives they contribute and how we can ameliorate their hardship" (Robert C. Mizzi, Canada). Nick Rumens (UK), on the other hand, suggests research on the "Normalisation of some but not [all] LGBTQ identities and implications for queer and other non-normative identities." Rumens stresses the need to understand what "inclusion mean[s] for LGBTQ people . . . how it is experienced in various social contexts [and] the lived realities of marginal identities such as non-binary, intersex, pansexual, Demi sexual, hetero flexible, etc."

As suggested by Joel Anderson (Australia), "continued research that is community driven and applies an intersectional lens must become a priority for researchers working in this space." Researchers of the LGBTQ+ community need a greater understanding of "the minority voices within this community (including intersex individuals), the perspectives of intersectionality within this community, and ways to continue to promote (and achieve) real and large-scale social change" (Jordan Hinton, Australia). Additionally,

> It's imperative that we prioritize research that will inform and support professional service providers and practitioners as they support LGBTQA+ community members in their recovery from maltreatment in society—ranging from living with constant minority stressors through to recovery from experiences with conversion practices and hate crimes.
>
> *(Joel Anderson, Australia)*

"Research priorities/initiatives should focus on how new policies impact the wellbeing (physical, mental) of the LGBTQ+ community," according to Bolivar X. Nieto (USA). "Particularly trans and youth; coming-out process in times of cruel policies and attacks on rights; stigma in school settings and its impact on socialization, education outcomes; institutionalized homophobia and transphobia and the community's resilience and [em]power[ment]" are all topics ripe for further exploration (Bolivar X. Nieto, USA). Additional research topics that should be priorities should include "LGBTQ+ topics in world history and connections with current events so that we understand from where we are coming to place current events into context and as a way to plan ahead" (Warren J. Blumenfeld, USA) and "daily life practices, discriminations faced, and solutions to resist disrespect and bad treatment" (Charlene Désir, USA).

Question 5: What Do You Think the Top Priorities Should Be for the LGBTQ+ Community in Terms of Teaching and Learning?

Respondents answered this question in terms of the formal education system from K-12 to graduate education. Nick Rumen's (UK) response that "Eradicating Hetero and cisnormativity in the curriculum," is arguably summative of most responses. Some respondents suggested strategies for accomplishing this eradication, which involved ideas like

> Students from kindergarten to graduate studies need[ing] to see themselves represented in curriculum and instruction. LGBTQ topics abetting inclusion and accommodation cannot be added on. They need to be included as a matter of fact in core curriculum and instruction.
>
> *(André P. Grace, Canada)*

Two respondents who reside in Florida, USA, where the state government is actively trying to eradicate all mention of LGBTQ+ in schools and curriculum, felt certain activities should be continued, such as creating safe spaces and inclusive curriculum. Bolivar X. Nieto (USA) argues for a continued need to

> create a safe and supportive learning space for LGBTQ+ students [as well as] teachers trained and open to supporting LGBTQ+ students in a responsive way, for they could be seen as the only allies. Teachers and students [must] learn to push back and raise awareness. Teachers, [must] be advocates, have resources.

Likewise, Charlene Désir (USA) makes a case to "Continue to have an inclusive curriculum, [and] have teaching staff reflect the population." Meanwhile, two other respondents had specific curriculum suggestions of "Decolonisation" (Joel Anderson, Australia) and "Increased discussions and research on LGBTQ+ topics in world history and connections with current events so that we understand from where we are coming to place current events into context and as a way to plan ahead. Also, [the need to] include the study of social movements" (Warren J. Blumenfeld, USA) as a common part of formal education.

Consistently, it is suggested that the LGBTQ+ social movement (represented by many organizations) focus advocacy and education efforts on several issues around health and wellness.

> This can include (among others) adequate healthcare and support education (e.g., some LGBTQ+ individuals, especially youth, may not be aware of the support networks available to them), more general education for allies (by allies, or LGBTQ+ community members) where they will be able to learn about the LGBTQ+ community in a non-judgmental format, with the intentions on learning to understand and better inform their perspectives (this includes more information for parents/guardians who may have LGBTQ+ children), better sex education and safety education for LGBTQ+ individuals (e.g., STD/HIV risks, education on PreP use, education on safety when it comes to gender affirmation experiences [e.g., trans-men using chest binders], etc.), and more holistic styles of general education that allows room for LGBTQ+ to share their experiences and guidance to better inform the public.
>
> *(Jordon Hinton, Australia)*

Robert C. Mizzi (Canada) ruminates on the learning styles and differences, if any, between LGBTQ community members and the heterosexual community, "How do LGBTQ community members learn? We have developed various approaches to queer pedagogy, which have been very useful. However, we do not know as much about how queer learners learn differently than cishet learners."

Iva Žegura (Croatia) maintains that stigma, critical thinking, autonomy, and scientific literacy are important aspects of a lifelong and global network of formal and informal education priorities. "Destigmatisation of LGBTIQ+ identities, prevention of homophobia, biphobia, transphobia, and discrimination based on sexual orientations and gender identity, education regarding sexuality and sexual well-being in general, respecting rights of autonomy and self-determination. Developing critical thinking skills and how to consume information from the internet, media literacy, and basic scientific literacy- to be able to understand methodological pitfalls from a scientifically sound and strong methodology that allows some generalizations, or to be able to detect the misuse or distortion of scientific facts" should all be top priorities in terms of teaching and learning according to Iva Žegura (Croatia).

Question 6: What Do You Expect to Be the State of Affairs for the LGBTQ+ Community in the Next Five Years?

Responses to this final question were mixed. Some respondents shared optimism and hope for the future state of affairs of the LGBTQ community, while others were unsure if any positive change was possible. Here are the respondents' exact words:

> With hope, I want there to be more protections, legal rights, and acceptance of LGBTQ+ individuals in all societies (not just western societies). With the recent events in Australia (e.g., anti-transgender rallies and increased hate speech and intolerance towards transgender individuals, and drag queens, etc.), it is difficult to see attitudes changing in a more positive light in the next 5 years, however I do hope this to be the case. We are a resilient community, but we shouldn't have to be resilient all the time (i.e., to be resilient, we have to have experienced this negativity). Instead, we would just like to get on with our lives.
>
> *(Jordan Hinton, Australia)*

> For LGBTQ communities in certain parts of the world, things will continue to progress in terms of improved social attitudes and parity in terms of legal issues and treatment. However, it's important to keep salient in our minds that this is not a given—for many communities (or members from our sub communities) in certain jurisdictions this will not be true. For those of us working in the field, we must not forget our peers trying to work in these areas—they will benefit from our support and collaboration in acquiring funding, receiving training, and continuing to conduct the urgent research needed in these spaces.
>
> *(Joel Anderson, Australia)*

> The next five years will see some greater polarization and hardship for LGBTQ communities, I fear. Education will be pivotal in confronting hate and exclusion and fostering resistance. We should put more energy into exploring education for/about LGBTQ people in various settings over the next five years.
>
> *(Robert C. Mizzi, Canada)*

"Conditions will most certainly get worse before they get better, but the movement for LGBTQ+ lives and rights will also continue to grow and expand intersectionally with other movement struggles" (Warren J. Blumenfeld, USA).

535

"Florida is really scary—we are going backward for Black people, LGBTQ, and women—it would be great if these communities would ally together to protest and resist unlawful and inhumane treatment" (Charlene Désir, USA).

> Many states are proposing and passing harsh laws diminishing and devaluing LGBTQ+ lives. As they continue to be approved, I fear these policies will validate/support discrimination across all levels (education, work settings, entertainment settings) and in its different forms (denial of services, harassment, physical violence). I do not see changes happening unless there is action through civil engagement and advocacy.
>
> *(Bolivar X. Nieto, USA)*

We need

> better legislation that ensures equal rights, de-pathologization, and de-criminalization of LGBTIQ+ identities and people. Equal access to health care, social services, social benefits, education, and work. Health care and legislation that is based on scientific facts, not on personal beliefs, and dependent on political orientation.
>
> *(Iva Žegura, Croatia)*

"Not much improvement to be honest. The resurgence in right wing anti LGBTQ politics is frightening, and I do not anticipate any sea change in this anytime soon" (Nick Rumens, UK).

> We are at a watershed moment for sexual and gender minorities across social democracies where the level of rightist threats and harm to our health and well-being compose a contemporary phenomenon of grave concern. We cannot be pushed back. We have to move forward. It always seems to get worse before it gets better in this world. Thus, sexual and gender minority persons have to be visible, vocal, strong, brave, political, and persistent as we work to be recognized as persons and human beings who deserve the human and civil rights associated with full citizenship in social democracies.
>
> *(André P. Grace, Canada)*

Final Thoughts

The current and future realities of LGBTQ+ communities and allies globally appear grim. It seems like the common thread across the various responses is *stigma* operationalized in its multiple forms: internalized, external, public, and institutionalized. Globally, there is an ongoing stigma-based movement (aimed at ostracizing and oppressing people for their identity), perpetuating an atmosphere of divisiveness within and across communities, including LGBTQ+. This movement and its ensuing rhetoric attempt to normalize some identities, while actively invalidating others through legislation, education, and even violence. Being Black, Latinx, woman, immigrant, LGBTQA+, Trans, Gender Non-Conforming (GNC), Non-Binary (NOBI) in any combination of these intersections is essentially depicted as a problem in and for society. The LGBTQ+ community, which has traditionally been active and vociferous in pursuing rights, is being hindered by this oppressive veil of stigma and complacency. Fortunately, there remains a glimmer of hope with some progress accompanying the recent wave of despair. As André P. Grace (Canada) exclaimed, "We HAVE TO move forward." Moving forward can be achieved with a combination of actions that include but are not limited to community mobilization that impacts policy, increasing research by, with, and for LGBTQ+ people, and deconstructing and re-imagining educational approaches tailored for LGBTQ+ communities. It is imperative that we fight for the decriminalization and de-pathologizing of LGBTQ+ people's intersectional identities. Though a few setbacks have rocked the momentum toward equity and equality, LGBTQ+ communities and allies must use these moments of setbacks as the fuel needed to resist and persevere. Our intention for this handbook has been to provide a reference that interrogates LGBTQ identity in organizations and in society. In the early phases of the handbook's development, we had a sense of the timeliness of such a project. After asking these questions and receiving these reflective, sobering, concerning responses, we realized quite clearly how important (and urgent) it is to continue to research, theorize, and write about LGBTQ identity. The work on this is far from complete. For now, we have offered this handbook as a contribution to what we see as a human rights movement.

References

Armellini, A., & Piscioneri, F. (2023). Italy's crackdown on same-sex parenting leaves children bemused. *Reuters*. www.reuters.com/world/europe/italys-crackdown-same-sex-parenting-leaves-children-bemused-2023-04-06/

Associated Press. (2023, January 17). U.K. government to veto Scotland's gender self-recognition law. *NBCNEWS*. www.nbcnews.com/news/world/uk-government-veto-scotlands-gender-self-recognition-law-rcna66044

Choi, A. (2023, April 6). Record number of anti-LGBTQ bills have been introduced this year. *CNN*. www.cnn.com/2023/04/06/politics/anti-lgbtq-plus-state-bill-rights-dg/index.html

Florida Legislature. (2022). *CS/CS/HB 1557: Parental rights in education*. www.flsenate.gov/Session/Bill/2022/1557

Human Rights Watch. (n.d.). *LGBT rights: #Outlawed "the love that dare not speak its name". Maps of anti-LGBT laws country by country*. Human Rights Watch. www.hrw.org

Lies, E. (2023, May 30). Japan court rules that a bar on same-sex marriage is unconstitutional. *Reuters*. www.msn.com/en-us/news/world/japan-court-rules-that-a-bar-on-same-sex-marriage-is-unconstitutional/ar-AA1bSdpg?OCID=ansmsnnews11

Nossel, S. (2023, March 10). The drag show bans sweeping the US are a chilling attack on free speech. *The Guardian*. www.theguardian.com/culture/commentisfree/2023/mar/10/drag-show-bans-tennessee-lgbtq-rights

Sands, L., & Ombour, R. (2023, May 29). Uganda imposes death penalty for "aggravated homosexuality". *The Washington Post*. www.msn.com

INDEX

Note: Page numbers in *italic* indicate a figure and page numbers in **bold** indicate a table on the corresponding page.